Sponsoring Editor: Lauren Silverman
Project Editor: Eric Leonidas
Art Direction/Cover Coordinator: Mary Archondes
Cover Design: Wanda Lubelska Design
Production: Willie Lane
Production Assistant: Sunaina Sehwani
Compositor: David E. Seham Associates, Inc.
Printer and Binder: R. R. Donnelley & Sons Company

Constitutional Law: Cases and Essays, Second Edition

of Congress Cataloging-in-Publication Data

Sheldon.
tutional law : cases and essays / Sheldon Goldman.—2nd

cm.
index.
-042396-X
tates—Constitutional law—Cases.   I. Title.
1991

90-38494
CIP

C- 01 00 99 98

CONSTITUTIONAL LAW

A
this
writ
critic
Publis

Library
Goldman,
Const
ed.

p.
Includes
ISBN 0-0
1. United
KF4549.G65
342.73—dc20
[347.302]

6 7 8 9 10 11 12

Contents

Part Two   The Workings of Government and of the Economy   157

THE CASES

11   The Contract Clause   357

12   Due Process: Economic Rights   378

Part Three   Civil Liberties   409

15   The Religion Guarantees   511

16   Fourth and Fifth Amendment Issues   569

17   Sixth and Eighth Amendment Issues   633

The Conservative Era: 1873–1908

The Conservative Era: 1909–1936

The Constitutional Revolution of 1937 and the Roosevelt Court Aftermath

Preface to the Second Edition

In the preface to the first edition of this book, I noted that it incorporated much that appeared in my *Constitutional Law and Supreme Court Decision-Making: Cases and Essays,* published by Harper & Row in 1982. The first and now second edition of *Constitutional Law: Cases and Essays* differ from my earlier book in several important ways, not only because they include more recent cases as well as case law and statistical and political analyses updated through four years of the Rehnquist Court. Both editions are fundamentally different from the 1982 book in that materials are organized topically to accommodate the majority of teachers of constitutional law who use this approach to teach the subject.

This book, however, has a close affinity with the 1982 publication not only in its use of substantial amounts of text from that book but also in its objective and in its synthesis of a variety of perspectives, with an emphasis on the historical and the political. The objective is to provide the student with a broad survey of the development of constitutional law and the exercise of power by the United States Supreme Court. The different perspectives employed are the historical, political, public policy, institutional, quantitative, and behavioral.

The first part of the book provides the *historical* setting and configuration of events that provide the backdrop for decision making. The topical chapter essays and case introductions also have a historical orientation. The *political* and *public policy* contexts of the major cases are provided, and particular attention is given to the policies that have emerged

from Court decisions and their political, social, and economic impacts. Because the Supreme Court, whatever else it may be, is a court of law, we also consider the *institutional* aspects that make the Court a legal institution and the distinctive characteristics of the Court's work.

By focusing on leading cases and the development of case law, however, we can lose sight of the actual business of the Court and the overall voting statistics, based on large numbers of cases and not just those chosen for inclusion here. Therefore, we offer a simple *quantitative* overview in chapters 4 and 5 making it easier to place the leading cases in the perspective of the totality of the Court's work. Finally, a *behavioral* orientation allows us to consider the voting behavior of justices in terms of their individual attitudes and values, as well as their behavior within the small group context of the Court. Even though the rule of law is the ultimate guiding ideal of our legal system, it is rule by judges that is in large measure our operating reality—although it is a very special kind of rule as we shall see.

Part One provides the basic introductory materials that, in my view, can best enable the student to understand and appreciate the development of case law. Chapters 2 and 3 are organized by historical period, containing an overview of the political setting within which the cases arose and the major public policy issues occupying the attention of the nation during each era. Chapters 4 and 5, also organized historically, recount the politics behind the appointment of each of the justices and contain analyses of their backgrounds. The voting patterns of the justices and the nature of group interaction, particlarly the role played by the Chief Justice, are also explored.

The bulk of the book is contained in Parts Two, Three, and Four, which are arranged by constitutional topics typically of special interest to political scientists. Each of the 15 chapters contains an essay in which decisional trends are traced within the historical framework. The development of case law is emphasized and the cases that are reprinted in each chapter are placed in their doctrinal contexts. Each essay concludes with a table summarizing the impact, insofar as can be determined, of most of the decisions included in that particular chapter. Each reprinted case is preceded by a short introduction. Some significant cases decided in 1990 are appended at the end of the book. Although they were decided after the book was in production and therefore could not be placed within the appropriate chapters, most are mentioned in the relevant essays, as are other decisions from the 1989 Term. The statistics in Part One are also up-to-date through the 1989 Term.

Among the cases chosen for inclusion are, of course, the "landmark" cases. In addition, some cases were selected because they illustrate certain decisional trends or illuminate points made in the essays. As might be expected, considering the focus on developing case law, there are a large number of decisions from the Burger and Rehnquist Courts. Although some of these cases may not be landmarks, they do represent the range of constitutional decision making of recent years. Concurrences and dissents are generally included if the points made demonstrate important differences among the justices or are representative of the constitutional approach of a particular justice.

A NOTE TO TEACHERS

This text can be used in either a one- or two-semester course. For a two-semester se-

quence, I suggest that chapters 6 through 12 be covered in the first semester. These chapters focus on judicial, presidential, and congressional powers, as well as issues of federalism. Chapters 13 through 20, with their focus on civil liberties issues, can serve as the basis for a second-semester course. Whether the text is used in a one- or two-semester mode, I suggest that chapters 1 through 5 be assigned at the beginning as required background reading.

For instructors who prefer to teach constitutional law by historical era, as I do, an Alternate Table of Contents by Historical Era is offered. My suggestion for using this book with the historical format is to assign the relevant portions from chapters 2 through 5 by historical era, corresponding with the Court era cases being discussed in class. The headings in these chapters facilitate such assignment. The headnotes for each reprinted case should allow most cases to stand on their own, facilitating flexibility in case assignment. For a two-semester sequence, such as we have at the University of Massachusetts at Amherst, the instructor could, during the first semester, follow the Alternate Table of Contents through "The Constitutional Revolution of 1937 and the Roosevelt Court Aftermath," with the addition of non-civil liberties cases through the Burger and Rehnquist Courts. During the second semester, the balance of the Alternate Table of Contents could be followed, thereby dividing the number of cases in this book approximately in half for each semester.

ACKNOWLEDGMENTS

As I did in the earlier books, I must express my intellectual debt to four leading students of constitutional law and the Supreme Court: Professors Robert G. McCloskey, Arthur Sutherland, C. Herman Pritchett, and Glendon Schubert. My approach to constitutional law was shaped profoundly by the teaching and writings of the late Robert McCloskey.

He introduced me to the political and historical approaches to the subject, and this book would be very different had I not had the privilege of being his student. So too with the late Arthur Sutherland, who also taught with an eye to the broader political context and consequences of Court decisions and yet instilled in his students an appreciation of legal reasoning and the unique qualities of legal institutions. Herman Pritchett and Glen Schubert have also played an important part in my intellectual development through their writings. I need only mention Professor Pritchett's books *The Roosevelt Court* and *Civil Liberties and the Vinson Court,* and Professor Schubert's books *Quantitative Analysis of Judical Behavior* and *The Judicial Mind*—landmark works that had a profound impact on my graduate education and that of my generation of scholars.

I am deeply indebted to Professors John W. Hopkirk and Richard Cortner for calling to my attention some errors in the earlier book. Professor Cortner's works, including *The Supreme Court and the Second Bill of Rights* (University of Wisconsin Press, 1981), were particularly helpful for the impact tables. So, too, was the work of Dean Jesse H. Choper in his comprehensive study "Consequences of Supreme Court Decisions Upholding Individual Constitutional Rights," which appeared in the October 1984 issue of the *Michigan Law Review* (vol. 83).

I would also like to thank the readers of this edition for their aid, in particular Alan Bigel, James Bolner, Sr., Christine Harrington, Thomas R. Hensley, Lois M. Pelekoudas, Helen S. Ridley, C. K. Rowland and John A. Ziegler. Readers of the first edition, whose comments and suggestions were also most helpful, included Professors Steve Arianas, Loren Beth, George Cole, James Foster, Christine Harrington, Robert Hayes, David Manwaring, Pete Rowland, Freda Solomon, G. Alan Tarr, and Robert Welsh. Readers of the 1982 book whose assistance was invaluable include Professors Roscoe Adkins, Dean Alfange, Loren Beth, John Brigham, Jon Gottschall, Charles Lamb, James Magee, John Schmidhauser, Elliot Slotnick, and Harold Stanley. Surely this book is a better one for my having had the benefit of the reactions of all those named above. Of course, I am responsible for all errors of fact and interpretation. I would also like to express my gratitude to Jennifer Kates for her outstanding help in the preparation of the manuscript, proofreading, and constructing the Index of Cases. and to the staff of Harper & Row for all their help. In particular, I am deeply appreciative of Marianne Russell and Lauren Silverman's encouragement to do this book and Eric Leonidas' expert and careful preparation of the manuscript through the production stage, and outstanding proofreading and editorial suggestions. Finally, I would like to thank my family for all their assistance over the years. I lovingly dedicate this book to them.

Sheldon Goldman

PART
ONE

THE SETTING AND THE JUSTICES

Chapter

1

Constitutional Law and the Supreme Court

If there is one theme that dominates the telling of the story of constitutional law in this book, it is that the United States Supreme Court, *throughout its history,* has been *both* a *political* and *judicial* institution. At various times over the years, the Court has been accused of usurping power, being an "Imperial Judiciary," and of subverting what is supposed to be a democratic form of government to government by judiciary or judicial dictatorship. These criticisms have recently been once again aimed at the judiciary.[1] The implication of these criticisms seems to be that the contemporary judiciary has gone *too far.* And certainly when one sees the wide range of issues handled by today's courts, there is a certain surface plausibility to such charges. In fact, however, the judiciary and the Supreme Court in particular have only kept pace with the expansion of other institutions of American government. The Court throughout its history, as shall be demonstrated, has rarely taken a back seat to governance. Thus, as America's national government has taken on new tasks, so has America's national Supreme Court. This, of course, does not resolve the fundamental question of whether the Court early in its history did in fact usurp power. We shall have more to say about this shortly.

The Court is *political* in the sense that in the course of interpreting the American Constitution policy choices are made within a social, economic, partisan, and bureaucratic context and, to some extent, reflect conditions as they currently exist. The Court is also political in the sense that its decisions are group products and are the result of bargaining and

[1]See, for example, Nathan Glazer, "Toward an Imperial Judiciary?" *The Public Interest,* 41 (1975), pp. 104–123; Raoul Berger, *Government by Judiciary* (Cambridge, Mass.: Harvard University Press, 1977); Lino A. Graglia, *Disaster by Decree: The Supreme Court Decisions on Race and the Schools* (Ithaca, N.Y.: Cornell University Press, 1976); John Hart Ely, *Democracy and Distrust* (Cambridge, Mass.: Harvard University Press, 1980). Also see the account of Attorney General Edwin Meese's critique of the Supreme Court in, for example, the *New York Times,* October 17, 1985, p. B-10. President Ronald Reagan also joined the attack on the federal courts. See the story of his address to a group of United States Attorneys in the *New York Times,* October 22, 1985, p. 1.

negotiating over the result, the precedents relied upon, the wording of opinions, the doctrines that emerge, and the implications that can be read into the decisions. The Court is political in still another context in that most justices before coming to the Court were heavily involved in public life, including partisan politics, and bring with them attitudes and values that influence their approach to many of the "legal" issues before them. Finally, the Court is political in that the "legal" issues brought to the Court are generated by the major political issues of the day. Alexis de Tocqueville was surely right on target when he observed in his masterpiece, *Democracy in America,* that "Scarcely any political question arises in the United States that is not resolved, sooner or later, into a judicial question."[2]

Yet the Court is a *judicial* institution in terms of its forms, procedures, and in terms of the style and even to an extent the substance of judicial decision making. The forms and procedures include such matters as jurisdiction and standing to sue, the requirements that both sides file the proper writs or other formal motions as well as offer legal briefs and participate in oral argument if asked to do so by the Court. The style and substance of decision making include following accepted patterns of legal reasoning and legal justification and, particularly, relying on precedent and opting for results that are reasonable and not patently contrary to law and tradition. Also included are fair-mindedness and neutrality toward the parties that appear before the Court. Matters of form, procedure, and style are important for preserving the mythology surrounding judges that, in the words of Chief Justice John Marshall, "Courts are the mere instruments of the law, and can will nothing."[3]

Before we turn further attention to the Court and its role in the development of con-

stitutional law, we should examine, if only briefly, the roots and shape of American constitutionalism.

CONSTITUTIONALISM

Constitutionalism—What It Means to Have a Written Constitution

A major characteristic of the modern nation-state is the rule of law. That law may be democratically *or* autocratically created and imposed. That law may be written *or* unwritten. It may be subject to the interpretation of the head of state, the bureaucracy, *or* the courts of law. That law may be readily changed and subject to no higher standard *or* it may be of two kinds—ordinary law and the "higher" or fundamental law of the nation, which is difficult to alter and to which ordinary legislation must conform.

The United States, of course, is a representative democracy in which written law is created and, although the law is subject to interpretation by the chief executive and the bureaucracy, the courts of law have the final say as to its validity. And the United States has both "ordinary" law and a written constitution that serves as our "higher" law against which ordinary law is judged. Thus United States government is characterized by constitutionalism—a commitment to be governed by a written constitution, a commitment that has been honored, at least in theory, during the more than 200 years in which the United States has operated under the Constitution.

American constitutionalism has its origins in English history and natural law theory. Although the development of the concept of constitutionalism is a fascinating and somewhat lengthy chapter in the history of ideas, we can nevertheless touch on some of the highlights of that history. Although the concept of a written constitution was not unknown in the ancient world, it was the Magna Carta, stemming from that historic meeting in Runnymede

[2]Phillips Bradley, ed. (New York: Vintage Books, 1954), vol. 1, chap. 16, p. 290.

[3]Osborn v. The Bank, 9 Wheaton 738 (1824), at 866.

in 1215 with the barons and King John, that provided the first precedent of a higher law governing the exercise of sovereignty. The English have never adopted a written constitution along the lines that we have, but they have developed over the centuries what they consider to be an unwritten one. American colonists, in contrast, developed a tradition of written constitutions starting with the Mayflower Compact (1620) and most importantly the Connecticut Constitution of 1639. However, these early constitutions did not embody the higher law–ordinary law distinction. By the time of the American Revolution, however, the rebelling colonists understood the concept of a law higher than ordinary law and they were thoroughly familiar with the development of English history and the growth of certain limits on the exercise of sovereign power. The American colonists felt that they were not treated on an equal footing with their fellow English citizens in the mother country and that their rights as English citizens were not respected by the crown, and this was a source of profound resentment that helped foment the revolutionary movement.

The American revolutionaries were also cognizant of certain ideas about law. Their notions of the nature of rights and the concept of liberty were heavily influenced by English theorists, notably John Locke. They were also affected by the natural law theorists who wrote of a higher moral law that transcends ordinary law. They believed that there were certain immutable principles of right and justice that stood above the laws of legislatures and monarchs. The distinction between ordinary law and a higher law was thus deeply ingrained in the thinking of the Founding Fathers.

Interestingly, the distinction between ordinary and higher law had its beginnings early in the colonial experience. The royal charters given to various colonies provided in one sense the higher law that established the framework for governing and the principles by which the colonies were to be governed. The colonial legislatures enacted ordinary law, but it was reviewed in England by the Board of Trade that reported to the Privy Council. The legislation was "disallowed" if it was found to usurp the royal prerogative, or was seen as incompatible with the basic tenets of English law and justice, or was determined to be inconsistent with England's commercial policy, or was simply considered bad or misguided. Between 1696 and 1775 about 400 pieces of colonial legislation were struck down (disallowed) by the Council.[4] Appeals from colonial courts went to the Committee on Appeals of the Privy Council. Between 1680 and 1780 some 265 appeals were taken.[5] After the colonies declared their independence, they each adopted their own constitutions to establish *their* higher law. And at the national level, the first constitution of the United States, the Articles of Confederation, was written and adopted. The Articles, of course, proved unsatisfactory and ultimately the Constitution of the United States was written in 1787 and ratified by the necessary number of states the following year.

In sum, it should be clear that constitutionalism had its roots in English history and the ideas of certain political thinkers. The end results were the embodiment of the "higher law" in written state constitutions and the United States Constitution.

Constitutionalism—Living Under a Written Constitution

What does it mean for Americans to live *under* a written constitution? It means at the very least that the polity recognizes or is assumed to recognize certain basic assumptions about

[4]Alfred H. Kelly and Winfred A. Harbison, *The American Constitution: Its Origins and Development,* 5th ed. (New York: Norton, 1976), p. 50.

[5]Arthur M. Schlesinger, Sr., "Colonial Appeals to the Privy Council," *Political Science Quarterly,* 28 (1913), pp. 279–297, 433–450.

the nature of political power in the United States, its distribution, its exercise, and most importantly its limitations. A constitutional government is one in which government has certain powers that are set within more or less well-defined boundaries. To exceed those boundaries is to violate *the Constitution,* to betray the basic societal consensus that is presumed to have been institutionalized in the Constitution, and to betray the contractual nature of the Constitution as a pact between government and its people.

But who is to decide when the Constitution has been violated? Who determines the boundaries wherein government may act constitutionally? These questions provoked controversy early in the life of the United States. Although it does not necessarily follow that only courts are equipped to resolve matters of constitutionality, there is evidence that even before the Constitution of the United States came into being some state courts may have been hinting that they had the definitive say in interpreting their state constitutions.[6] Certainly the United States Constitution that establishes the framework for the national government and the nature of its powers, the relationship of the co-equal branches with each other, and the relationship of the national government to the states has a built-in logic calling for one institution to resolve authoritatively disputes for the nation. John Marshall, of course, elaborated upon this point in **Marbury** v. **Madison.*** And in the highest state courts between 1787 and 1803, there were at least 20 cases in which state laws were struck down as being contrary to the state constitutions.[7] Suffice it to note that the United States Supreme Court asserted itself as being *the* in-

stitution that logically must be the ultimate authority in interpreting the federal Constitution. Thus constitutionalism suggests that one of the main branches of government—executive, legislative, or judicial—will fill the role of ultimate constitution interpreter. That the United States, for a variety of reasons, has the judicial branch fulfilling this role has had major consequences for the nation.

THE WORKINGS OF THE SUPREME COURT

The Supreme Court of the United States stands at the head of America's legal system. That legal system, like American government, is a federal one. Each state has its own set of courts from the trial level through the highest state court (usually called the Supreme Court). Decisions from the highest state courts that involve claims based on federal law or the United States Constitution can be appealed to the United States Supreme Court. The federal court system also has its own set of courts—trial courts (federal district courts),* intermediate appellate courts (United States courts of appeals),† specialized federal courts,‡ and at the formal apex of the system, the Supreme Court.

The Constitution provides the basic framework for the federal court system. In Article 3, Section 2, the basis for the Supreme Court's powers is given. The Constitution confers *original jurisdiction* on the Supreme Court in

---

*Cases that appear in **boldface** are reprinted in this book.

[6]See Raoul Berger, *Congress v. The Supreme Court* (Cambridge, Mass.: Harvard University Press, 1969). But also see the conflicting interpretation of the evidence in Louis B. Boudin, *Government by Judiciary,* vol. 1 (New York: William Godwin, 1932), particularly chap. 4.

[7]Kelly and Harbison, op. cit., p. 94.

---

*Today, each state, the Commonwealth of Puerto Rico, the District of Columbia, Guam, the Northern Mariana Islands, and the Virgin Islands have at least one district court. In total there are now 94 federal district courts.

†There are 11 courts of appeals with a geographic span from 3 states (the Second, Fifth, and Eleventh Circuits) to 9 states (Ninth Circuit). There is a twelfth appeals court for the District of Columbia.

‡The specialized federal courts include the United States Claims Court, the Court of International Trade, the Tax Court, the United States Court of Appeals for the Federal Circuit, and the Court of Military Appeals. There are also federal courts with local jurisdiction in the District of Columbia and in the territories.

a narrow class of cases in which foreign ambassadors and public ministers are involved or in which a state is a party to the suit. This means that in these cases the Supreme Court can be the first (and only) court to hear the dispute. In practice, the Court's original jurisdiction has never amounted to more than a few cases each term. Over the history of the Supreme Court, cases taken under the Court's original jurisdiction have averaged less than one case each year.[8] In all other cases the Supreme Court has *appellate jurisdiction;* that is, it hears cases on appeal from another court. The Constitution gives Congress the power to regulate the Court's appellate jurisdiction.

Two principal types of cases are heard by the Supreme Court under its appellate jurisdiction: *federal cases* and *diversity cases.* A federal case is one that concerns either federal statutory law, a provision of the federal Constitution, a federal treaty, or disputes arising under admiralty (occurring on the high seas) or maritime (shipping, rivers, harbors) laws. A diversity case (technically, diversity of citizenship jurisdiction) concerns suits between or among persons from different states. Since 1988 only diversity cases in which at least $50,000 is at issue can be heard in the federal courts. Below that amount the case must go to a state court.

When a state law is challenged as being in conflict with either a federal statute, constitutional law, or a federal treaty, the case may be taken either to the federal district court or to a state court. If the case goes through the state court system, the losing party may appeal to the Supreme Court. Cases that concern only federal law or invoke the federal courts' diversity of citizenship jurisdiction ordinarily go through the federal district and appeals courts before coming to the Supreme Court.

The Judiciary Act of 1789 created the federal judicial system. It provided for federal trial courts and the Supreme Court of the United States with a membership of one chief justice and five associate justices. The act specified the powers and jurisdiction of the federal courts and other matters relating to the operations of the federal courts. Since then, the structure of the lower courts, the number of positions on the Supreme Court, the federal courts' jurisdiction, the use of certain writs, and other aspects of federal court procedure have changed. A new set of intermediate appellate courts was introduced by the Circuit Court of Appeals Act of 1891.

The amount of business coming to the Supreme Court over the years has changed dramatically. During the first three years of the Supreme Court's existence, *no* cases were decided by it. The justices spent their time organizing the Court and also serving in their capacity as circuit judges. Between 1793 and 1796 the Court decided only 7 cases,[9] but by 1830 the number of cases decided that year had grown to 57.[10] By 1845 the Court had 173 cases pending.[11] Forty-five years later, in 1890, some 1816 cases were brought to the Court.[12] Although the Court has always had the technical means to delay or avoid deciding a case, it was formally obliged to take all appeals that came through the federal court system or that concerned a federal question and were appealed from the highest state courts. Judicial reformers thought that the 1891 act establishing the circuit courts of appeals would permanently relieve the Supreme Court, but they were wrong. Finally, in 1925, a Judiciary Act was enacted that for most purposes did

[8]Henry J. Abraham, *The Judicial Process,* 5th ed. (New York: Oxford University Press, 1986), p. 178.

[9]Julius Goebel, Jr., *Antecedents and Beginnings to 1801,* vol. 1, *History of the Supreme Court of the United States* (New York: Macmillan, 1971), p. 801.

[10]Donald G. Morgan, *Justice William Johnson: The First Dissenter* (Columbia, S.C.: University of South Carolina Press, 1954), p. 307.

[11]Felix Frankfurter and James M. Landis, *The Business of the Supreme Court* (New York: Macmillan, 1928), p. 51.

[12]Ibid., p. 60.

away with the writ of error, which was the principal way that cases had come to the Court (asserting legal error committed by the court below), and instead gave the Court wide discretion in broad classes of cases to determine its docket through granting or denying the writ of certiorari.

Currently, the major way by which cases come before the Supreme Court is by the granting of the writ of certiorari. The *writ of certiorari* is an order to the court whose decision is being challenged to send up the records of the case so that the Supreme Court can review the lower court decision. Litigants petition the Court to issue the writ, and that petition is granted if four justices agree that the writ should be issued. In practice, only a small portion of the petitions are granted. In the years soon after passage of the Judiciary Act of 1925, the proportion of certiorari petitions granted never went above 22 percent.[13] By the 1950s the proportion dropped to an average per term of about 15 percent of the Appellate Docket petitions (petitions drafted by a lawyer) and 4 percent of the Miscellaneous Docket petitions (mostly petitions drafted by prisoners).[14] By the late 1960s, however, as the number of petitions continued to burgeon, these proportions dropped to about 8 percent of the Appellate Docket petitions and 3 percent of the Miscellaneous Docket petitions.[15] During the final terms of the Burger Court and the first three terms of the Rehnquist Court,

there was a drop in the percent of Miscellaneous Docket petitions granted to about 1 percent.

Before October 1988 the second principal route to Supreme Court review was by the legal right to *appeal,* whereby the Court had no discretion to refuse to consider the appeal in certain instances such as when the highest state court upheld a state law challenged as conflicting with federal law. However, in 1988 Congress enacted legislation removing the Court's mandatory jurisdiction and making those cases subject to the writ of certiorari. The Supreme Court now has almost complete discretion to choose its cases under its appellate jurisdiction.

There are two other routes to the Court—certification and the extraordinary writ. *Certification* cases arise when the judges of a lower court certify certain questions of law that they are unable to answer satisfactorily in cases pending in their courts. The Supreme Court is then asked to answer those questions. In *extraordinary writ* cases, the Court intervenes directly into the activities of a trial judge by either ordering the judge to do something (mandamus), or not to do something (prohibition), or to issue a writ of habeas corpus. Certification and extraordinary writ cases occur infrequently.[16]

Before 1925 the writ of error was the primary vehicle for cases coming to the Court. Litigants who wished to appeal filed the writ of error, asserting that the court below made an incorrect determination of law. The Court was obliged to act on the writ and could not simply decide not to decide. With the Act of 1925, many of the cases previously subject to

[13]William O. Douglas, "The Supreme Court and its Caseload," *Cornell Law Quarterly,* 45 (1960), p. 410. Also see Paul M. Bator, Paul J. Mishkin, David L. Shapiro, and Herbert Wechsler, *Hart and Wechsler's The Federal Courts and the Federal System,* 2d ed. (Mineola, N.Y.: Foundation Press, 1973), p. 44, n. 58.

[14]Joseph Tanenhaus, Marvin Schick, Matthew Muraskin, and Daniel Rosen, "The Supreme Court's Certiorari Jurisdiction: Cue Theory," in Glendon Schubert (ed.), *Judicial Decision-Making* (New York: Free Press, 1963), p. 113.

[15]Sheldon Goldman and Thomas P. Jahnige, *The Federal Courts as a Political System,* 3d ed. (New York: Harper & Row, 1985), pp. 24, 90–91.

[16]From 1937 to 1946 only 20 cases were certified to the Supreme Court. From 1946 to 1972 only one case was accepted by the Supreme Court on certification. Bator, Mishkin, Shapiro, and Wechsler, op. cit., p. 1586. The extraordinary writ that is most used is habeas corpus. In the 1988 Term of the Supreme Court, some 10 decisions out of the 143 that were decided with full opinion concerned habeas corpus. *Harvard Law Review,* 103 (November 1989), p. 400.

the writ of error were made subject to the writ of certiorari to be granted at the Court's discretion.

Essential to the understanding of how a case comes to the Supreme Court are the concepts of jurisdiction, standing to sue, and justiciability. *Jurisdiction* of a court, as will be recalled from our earlier discussion, refers to whether the court has the authority to hear the dispute between the parties. A court must have jurisdiction over the parties to the case, the subject matter of the dispute, and the geographical area in which the court is asked to hear the dispute. Jurisdiction may be original—that is, the court is the first court to hear the case—or appellate—that is, the court hears an appeal from a decision of another court.

Standing to sue consists of several criteria used to determine under what circumstances a litigant can invoke the court's jurisdiction. First, there must be a real case or controversy in which injury has occurred or is immediately threatened. The Burger Court was liberal with the definition of injury so that it meant not only bodily harm or loss of freedom or economic injury but also aesthetic, conservational, or recreational injury.[17] Second, the right involved must be a personal one. Under most circumstances one cannot sue on behalf of someone else's rights and not one's own. In some situations one can sue on one's own behalf and on behalf of all others similarly situated. This is known as a "class action." Third, if it is the action of some government official or government agency that is being challenged, the complainant must ordinarily exhaust available administrative remedies within the offending agency or the agency of the offending government official. Since the 1960s, however, the Supreme Court has relaxed this requirement, primarily in civil rights cases.

Justiciability usually refers less to the legal domain of jurisdiction or rules of litigant standing than to certain rather pragmatic considerations. Is there something that a court can do for a plaintiff assuming that the plaintiff is in the legal right? Is the dispute moot (no longer a dispute)? Is the subject matter of the dispute one that is essentially a political question best resolved by the political branches of government? Is the subject amenable to judicial resolution? In practice, it has been the Supreme Court itself that has determined justiciability, including what issue is a political question and what is not.

The ways in which the justices go about their work have evolved from the earliest days of the Court's existence. Until the chief justiceship of John Marshall, it was common in the major cases for each justice to write a separate opinion. There was no official "Opinion of the Court." When a decision was to be announced, each justice gave his own opinion *seriatim* (one after the other). John Marshall changed that practice so that the Court would speak with one voice. Of course, justices were and are free to write concurrences and dissents. But the majority view, if there is one, is contained within the Court's official pronouncement—the Opinion of the Court.

What is the process by which a case becomes a Court decision? At the outset, the justices must first decide to take the case. If the Court decides that the case is to go to oral argument, one-half hour is scheduled for each side on a specified date. In the earlier years of the Court, the pace was more leisurely and several days or even longer were occasionally devoted to oral argument in major cases. Printed briefs are provided the justices before oral argument begins, and the tradition is for justices to interrupt the argument with questions and otherwise enter into a dialogue with

---

[17]For a general discussion see Karen Orren, "Standing to Sue: Interest Group Influence in the Federal Courts," *American Political Science Review,* 70 (1976), p. 723. Also see Bator, Mishkin, Shapiro, and Wechsler, op. cit., pp. 150–214. Two of the landmark cases on standing are Association of Data Processing Service Organizations, Inc. v. Camp, 397 U.S. 150 (1970), and Sierra Club v. Morton, 405 U.S. 727 (1972).

counsel. After oral argument, the case is considered by the justices in conference.

The Supreme Court is a collegial body and decisions are reached collectively. Conferences are held in which the justices discuss and decide which of the many certiorari cases to accept. They also discuss the cases in which they have heard oral argument. Currently the practice is to hold conferences on Wednesday afternoons and all day Friday. When the justices enter the conference room, they shake hands with each other. This practice originated during the chief justiceship of Melville Fuller, whose tenure ran from 1888 to 1910. Another tradition is that only the justices themselves are present in the conference room. The justice with the least seniority is given the task of carrying or receiving messages to or from the conference chamber door.

During the conference each case that has been orally argued is discussed, with the Chief Justice speaking first and usually indicating how he will vote. The discussion then proceeds around the table in order of seniority, with the most junior justice speaking last. After each justice has had a chance to talk, a general discussion may take place. In recent years, however, there has been little group discussion.[18] The Chief Justice, when voting with the majority, assigns the task of writing the Opinion of the Court. When the Chief Justice is in the minority, the senior justice in the majority makes the assignment for writing the Opinion of the Court.

The majority that emerges from the conference room is necessarily a tentative one because the draft of the Opinion of the Court may not be as persuasive as a dissenting opinion, and one or more justices may switch sides. Even the reasoning of the majority may

undergo some change as a result of the interchange among the justices.[19] When an Opinion of the Court along with any concurrences and dissents are ready, they are printed in the Court's basement print shop and the decision is subsequently announced in court. A Court decision is the result of the mix of each justice's attitudes and values as to the issues, litigants, and precedents, as well as the collegial nature of the decision-making enterprise.

The Supreme Court first met on February 1, 1790, in the Royal Exchange Building in New York City. When the nation's capital moved to Philadelphia, the Court also moved and met in Independence Hall and then in Philadelphia City Hall. When the federal government was established in 1800 in the District of Columbia, the Supreme Court again resettled and its new quarters were in various rooms in the Capitol Building. From 1860 until 1935 the Court sat in what is known as the "old Senate chamber." In 1929 Congress authorized the construction of a building to house the Court. In 1935, the justices moved into their new quarters across the street from the Capitol Building. The Supreme Court building is an imposing marble structure about four stories tall at its highest. Each justice has a suite of offices.

Until about the mid-nineteenth century, the Supreme Court met for relatively short sessions of approximately two months twice a year. This meant that most justices did not move their families to the District of Columbia but instead went to Washington for the duration of each session and lived in a boardinghouse. During Chief Justice Marshall's tenure,

---

[18]See the observations of Chief Justice Rehnquist and Justice Scalia as reported in *The New York Times*, February 22, 1988, p. A-16. Also see William Rehnquist, *The Supreme Court: How It Was, How It Is* (New York: Morrow, 1987), pp. 289–296.

[19]The classic study of intracourt relationships and their effect on the decisional process is Walter F. Murphy, *Elements of Judicial Strategy* (Chicago: University of Chicago Press, 1964). A journalistic account of these phenomena in the Burger Court can be found in Bob Woodward and Scott Armstrong, *The Brethren* (New York: Simon & Schuster, 1979). Also see the examples offered in Justice William O. Douglas' autobiography, *The Court Years: 1939–1975* (New York: Random House, 1980). Other studies are cited in chaps. 4 and 5.

the practice arose for the justices to live in the same boardinghouse. This meant that off the bench there was constant interchange among the justices and that they not only had institutional ties with each other but also social ties. As the years progressed and the business of the Supreme Court grew, the position of Supreme Court Justice became a full-time job and the Court was in session for most of the year. Then justices began to resettle their families and thus some of the intimacy of the earlier years stimulated by common living arrangements ended. Today the justices live in apartments or homes in the District of Columbia area.

The Supreme Court opens its term on the first Monday in October. Since 1873 the practice has been for the Court to hold one term that is roughly the length of the academic year, usually ending in June or, as has occurred in more recent years, in early July. The designation of the year of the term is the year when the term begins; thus, for example, the 1988 Term began on October 3, 1988, and ended on July 3, 1989.

Cases are reported and cited as follows. The federal government publishes a complete record of Supreme Court actions, and in the years before 1875 the published volumes bore the name of the Court reporter and were cited accordingly. The Court reporters and their dates of service were the following:

Dallas (1790–1800)

Cranch (1801–1815)

Wheaton (1816–1827)

Peters (1828–1842)

Howard (1843–1860)

Black (1861–1863)

Wallace (1864–1875)

Starting with 1875 the volumes were no longer named after the reporter and were entitled *U.S. Reports*. The citation format is given in the following two examples:

2 Dallas 419 (1793), which means the second volume of the reports edited by Dallas, page 419, case decided in 1793.

410 U.S. 113 (1973), which means volume 410 of the *U.S. Reports*, page 113, case decided in 1973.

There are also commercial publishers of Court decisions. The West Publishing Company publishes the *Supreme Court Reporter*. There is also the Lawyer's Edition of the United States Supreme Court Reports that includes portions of the briefs. Frequently these two reporters are cited along with the citation for the *U.S. Reports*. In this book, however, only the *U.S. Reports* citations will be given unless not available. Still another source of published Court decisions is *U.S. Law Week,* which prints Court decisions within one or two weeks after they are handed down.

POWERS OF THE SUPREME COURT

Without question the principal power of the Supreme Court is the power of judicial review—the power to review legislative enactments and executive branch actions to determine their constitutionality and, if the judges believe it necessary, to declare them unconstitutional. Other courts also exercise this power, but when it concerns interpretation of the federal Constitution, the Supreme Court has the final say. The development of American constitutional law is therefore the development of judicial review by the Supreme Court. Judicial review evolved over a long period of time and was not firmly established in principle until about 30 years after the Supreme Court was created. Chapter 6 is devoted to the issue of judicial review and to some prominent examples of the exercise of that power.

Although the development of judicial review into a broad-based power is a result of a long series of judicial decisions, the power of statutory interpretation is a traditional legal power. Much of the work done by the Court has involved statutory interpretation rather than constitutional adjudication. Along with this traditional power are the technical instruments of judicial power such as being able to issue injunctions or declaratory judgments to private persons or public officials and to issue writs of habeas corpus to custodians of prisoners or decrees ordering a change in the status, operations, or relationships of the parties including a state or federal official acting in the name of that official's government.

The Supreme Court has the power to control virtually its docket and to delay making a decision. No one—neither the President nor Congress nor any other person or institution—can force the Court to take a dispute *and* to decide it on the merits.

Some have argued that the Court's ability to legitimize controversial acts of government is a source of power. The fact that the Court is needed to give its constitutional blessing is thought to make the Court politically valuable to the "political" branches of government. However, although the Court does confer legitimacy in the technical sense when it rules a disputed act to be constitutional, there is considerable doubt according to public opinion research that this has an effect on or matters much to the general public.[20] Nevertheless, when the Court declares a controversial act to be constitutional, it is performing a positive function for the polity. The Court is telling the American people that we are living under the law, that we are a nation of law and not of arbitrarily acting power-holders. The power to say *yes* may be as important as the power to say *no*. The Court has the power to reassure us that the Constitution is still our governing charter.

LIMITS ON JUDICIAL POWER

When one reads the vast literature on judicial review and the current examples of the genre attacking judicial power, it is hard to remem-

ber that there are formidable limits to the Supreme Court's power.

A number of limitations are inherent in the Court as a legal and judicial institution. At the outset it must be kept in mind that unlike a legislature that can enact legislation on whatever subject matter the majority wishes, a court of law cannot initiate action. A court must wait for the dispute to be brought to it. A majority of the justices may be ready to move in a certain policy direction, but the Supreme Court must first wait for the appropriate case to come before it. Furthermore, there is a long judicial tradition that a court will only consider the issues briefed and argued by the litigants. There are, to be sure, exceptions to this rule such as **Mapp** v. **Ohio** in 1961, which the Court decided on Fourth Amendment grounds although it had been argued as a First Amendment case. Yet, for the most part, the justices are limited by the issues that are brought before them.

A Supreme Court decision is, after all, a decision on the merits of a dispute between the parties. That decision may be the vehicle for a broad policy declaration or one in a series of small incremental steps that may lead to a major policy change. However, the fact that a real controversy is involved means that legally the decision binds only the parties to the particular case. It is true, however, that when government officials are parties, their successors in office are also bound by the decision. This technical limit to the immediate legal reach of a Court decision is one of the reasons why it took so many decades before the school desegregation policy of **Brown** v. **Board of Education** (1954) was implemented. Legally, only the five school boards involved in the 1954 decisions were obliged to obey. Although in the broader sense of the term all of the over 2200 school boards that maintained racially segregated school systems were not complying with the Court's decision and The Law of the Land, in the narrow sense of compliance they were under no legal obligation

[20]See David Adamany, "Legitimacy, Realigning Elections, and the Supreme Court," *Wisconsin Law Review* (1973), pp. 790–846. In general, see Thomas R. Marshall, *Public Opinion and the Supreme Court* (Boston: Unwin Hyman, 1989).

until each one was sued and ordered by a court to desegregate.

A further limit on the Supreme Court's powers is its jurisdiction. Congress, *not* the Court, determines the Court's appellate jurisdiction, which is the source of almost all of its business. The Constitution limits the federal courts to federal and diversity cases. The Court's own rules of standing to sue provide still other limits on what cases and litigants can come to the Court.

Stare decisis, or the rule of precedent, can be considered a limit on the exercise of judicial power. Stare decisis means that a decision is based on previous rulings of the Court. Although there may be many precedents from which to choose, and they may also be interpreted or applied in different ways, the rule of precedent symbolizes that we are dealing with a court of law as distinguished from a legislative body—although at times throughout the Court's history some critics have argued that in practice this distinction is blurred.

If the legal-technical aspects of being a court of law provide limits on the exercise of power, the special institutional character of the U.S. Supreme Court provides additional constraints. The Court's decisions, the briefs filed in the cases, the lower court decisions that were reviewed are all matters of public record. The Opinion of the Court along with concurrences and dissents are published by the federal government as well as by several privately owned publishing companies. If the justices are to maintain the respect of the legal profession and other knowledgeable persons, they must, at least on the surface of their opinions, adhere to legal forms and legal reasoning and their arguments must at least be plausible if not persuasive.[21] Of course, because the Court is a collegial body, any decision requires the votes of at least five of the nine justices so that within the Court as well legal arguments, legal reasoning, and the precedents relied upon must win approval of a majority. It is therefore difficult and unusual for any one justice to be able to impose on the other justices his or her own individual prejudices and judicial philosophy or attitudes and hierarchy of values—although there have at various times been great intellectual leaders on the Court.

Another feature inherent in the institutional position of the Supreme Court is that the Court typically cannot and does not enforce its own decisions. Rather, it relies on the lower courts both to implement the specific decision and to apply the Court's policy to similar cases. This means that the Court is at the head of a court bureaucracy and faces the problems of all bureaucracies—the communication of policy and the oversight of bureaucratic implementation. Unlike other bureaucracies, the Court has no responsibility for the financing of its subordinate agencies (i.e., the lower courts), nor does it supervise the selection of their personnel, or the disciplining of judges who ignore or deliberately misrepresent Court policy. The Supreme Court decides only a minute fraction of all cases that are decided by American courts each year. The chances of any one decision being reviewed by the Supreme Court are statistically exceedingly small. This means that determined and clever lower court judges—not only on the federal bench but state benches as well—can frustrate Court policy. If the Court's policy is unclear, even well-meaning lower court judges can inadvertently misconstrue the Court's intent. Thus the fact that implementation of Court decisions is generally accomplished through the lower courts provides a built-in limit on what the Court can realistically accomplish.

When we move to the "political" branches of the federal government, we find impressive

---

[21]They must make legal sense, that is, fall within the accepted bounds of legal language and concepts. See the discussion in John Brigham, *Constitutional Language: An Interpretation of Judicial Decision* (Westport, Conn.: Greenwood, 1978). Also see his *The Cult of the Court* (Philadelphia: Temple University Press, 1987).

weapons that Congress and the President have at their disposal to use against the Court should they be sufficiently provoked. Some of their weapons, in fact, have been used at one time or another during the Court's existence. Congress can:

1. Impeach and remove a justice;
2. Withdraw the Court's appellate jurisdiction in one or more legal areas;
3. Increase or decrease the number of justices on the Court;
4. Regulate court procedure;
5. Refuse to appropriate the funds needed to run the Court (but the Constitution forbids any reduction in the justices' salaries);
6. Refuse to appropriate funds necessary to carry out Court decisions;
7. Abolish any of the lower federal courts;
8. Enact legislation reversing a Court decision that interprets a congressional statute;
9. Propose a constitutional amendment to reverse a constitutional ruling by the Court;
10. (The Senate) Refuse to give its advice and consent to any judicial nomination, including one to the Supreme Court; the Senate can also use the confirmation process to voice displeasure with a particular decision or trend of decisions.

The President can:

1. Determine how and to what extent executive branch officials enforce Supreme Court decisions;
2. Pardon persons convicted of criminal contempt of court for defying Court decisions as well as pardon any prisoner convicted of violating federal law;
3. Use the prestige of office and media attention to criticize the Court's work publicly;
4. Exercise presidential leadership and send to Congress measures that will check the Court's exercise of power.

These powers and actions that can potentially limit the Supreme Court have not been frequently used, but the threat of their use or their actual use has occurred at various times. For example:

- Supreme Court Justice Samuel Chase was impeached by the House of Representatives in 1804, but his trial in the Senate early the next year resulted in his acquittal;
- The threat of impeachment proceedings against Justice Fortas is thought to have been a major factor in his decision to resign from the Court in the spring of 1969 rather than fight the campaign being waged against him by the Nixon Administration;
- The withdrawal of the Court's appellate jurisdiction has been threatened on a number of occasions and in 1868 it actually happened in the pending suit of **Ex Parte McCardle;**
- The manipulation of the number of justices on the Court was an occasionally used political device during about the first half of the nineteenth century, and the number fluctuated to as many as ten before the present nine positions were established in 1869;
- A serious attempt at altering the number of justices was made by President Franklin Roosevelt in early 1937 when he introduced a court reform plan after the Court had struck down New Deal legislation;
- Court procedure has been regulated by Congress in the Judiciary Acts of 1802 and 1925. The 1802 Circuit Court Act manipulated the sessions of the Court in order to postpone the hearing in **Marbury** v. **Madison.** The 1925 act gave the Court much more flexibility in determining its docket by limiting the Court's obligatory jurisdiction and expanding the Court's discretionary use of the writ of certiorari;
- An entire set of lower courts was abolished by Congress in the Circuit Court Act of 1802. These courts had been established just the year before by the outgoing Federalist Administration;
- On some occasions, Congress has enacted legislation to reverse Court deci-

sions concerning statutory interpretation (one counting has 63 congressional actions in economic matters overturning 89 Supreme Court rulings between 1944 and 1984);[22]

- Congress has introduced amendments to the Constitution in order to overturn constitutional rulings by the Supreme Court. The Eleventh, Fourteenth, Sixteenth, and Twenty-Sixth Amendments, in fact, reversed Court decisions;
- The Senate has used its confirmation power to prevent certain nominees from serving on the Court. In the nineteenth century close to one in three nominees failed to receive Senate approval, but in the twentieth century the failure rate has been considerably less. Only six nominations have failed in the twentieth century, with four of them in the 1968–1970 period.

When we consider the President, we find instances of presidential displeasure with Court decisions. President Nixon successfully forced Justice Fortas off the bench to make room for a considerably more conservative justice. And as previously mentioned, President Roosevelt attempted to "reform" the Court by packing it. President Reagan and President Bush indicated antipathy to **Roe** v. **Wade** and supported a constitutional amendment to overturn the Court's abortion decision. They also promised to continue to use the appointment power to name those opposed to liberal judicial activism.[23] Bush also pushed for a constitutional amendment to overturn the Court's flag-burning decisions in **Texas** v. **Johnson** and **U.S.** v. **Eichman.**

This by no means exhausts the list of public officials whose words and actions have the po-

tential to limit the Court's powers. But suffice it to note that the constitutionally derived powers of Congress and the President, as well as the behavior of state and local officials, can potentially be used to bring the Court to its knees. That this has rarely happened is as much a testament to the sense of self-restraint on the part of the political branches of government as it is to the Court as national symbol of law and constitutionalism.

Ultimately, then, it is public opinion that effectively limits what the Court can do. If there is widespread opposition to a Court decision and policy, it is likely that there will be defiance and consequent noncompliance. If the Court persists in shocking the conscience of vast numbers of Americans, the Court's prestige will plummet and its authority will be eroded. In fact, this happened to the Court with the **Dred Scott** decision of 1857. For close to a decade after that ruling, the Court was at the nadir of its influence and authority. In the confrontation between the New Deal Administration and the Court, President Roosevelt and Congress were prepared to defy the Court had the Court not backed down. More recently the liberal decisions of the Warren Court, particularly in the criminal procedure field and in racial equality decisions, along with other areas of civil liberties, fomented considerable conservative opposition—so much so that the approval ratings of the Court dramatically fell in the 1960s and widespread evasion of some of the Court's civil liberties policies occurred.[24] The Court, then, must walk a thin line between the constitutional vision of the Court majority and the political reality of the here and now. Statesmanship, diplomacy, knowing when to retreat and when to move forward are the arts, not the science, that a judiciary, to be successful, must master.

---

[22]Abraham, op. cit., p. 351. Also see the discussion in Charles A. Johnson and Bradley C. Canon, *Judicial Policies: Implementation and Impact* (Washington, D.C.: CQ Press, 1984), pp. 142–144.

[23]See, for example, the account of President Ronald Reagan's speech on judicial appointments in the *New York Times*, October 22, 1985, p. 1 ff.

[24]See Goldman and Jahnige, op. cit., and Johnson and Canon, op. cit. In general, see Lawrence Baum, *The Supreme Court,* 3d ed. (Washington, D.C.: CQ Press, 1989), chap. 6.

BRIEFING CASES

Students may find briefing cases an aid to their understanding and mastery of constitutional law. Although there is no universally accepted standard format for a brief, a reasonably comprehensive brief will contain the following points:

1. *The facts of the case.* This section should contain a short summary of the events that shaped the dispute in the case.
2. *The statute or governmental action at issue.* What action of a governmental official or agency has triggered the dispute or what federal or state statute is in controversy?
3. *The provision of the Constitution involved.* The specific part of the federal Constitution should be indicated.

4. *The outcome of the case.* Here students should specify the immediate result of the Court's decision. Who wins, who loses, and what the Court has ruled vis-à-vis the parties to the case should be noted.
5. *The legal reasoning of the majority.* Placed in this section should be a condensation of the legal reasoning and the legal basis used by the majority to arrive at their conclusions.
6. *The doctrine or policy announced in the case.* Here should be a succinct statement of the doctrine or doctrines or policy that emerges from the Court's decision.
7. *Alternative ways of handling the issues.* Concurrences and dissents can be surveyed to point up alternative ways of approaching the issues in the case.

Chapter

2

The Political and Historical Setting of the Development of Constitutional Law, 1789–1937

Before examining in somewhat greater detail the political and historical setting of the cases reprinted in this book, it is useful to have a broad overview of the two main historical periods discussed in this chapter—the period before the Civil War and that between the Civil War and the Great Depression of the 1930s. In order to understand much of the development of American politics and constitutional law during the first period—from the time the Constitution was put into operation in 1789 until the time of the Civil War—it is necessary to appreciate the one overriding issue of that 71-year period, the nature of the American union. The issue was whether the Constitution created a truly national government, supreme over the states in the exercise of its powers, or whether the United States was to be little more than a United Nations, a collection of separate, sovereign states cooperating with each other in limited spheres for mutual bene-

fit. Of course, the Constitutional Convention was convened for the express purpose of replacing the unsatisfactory Articles of Confederation that *had* established such a collection of separate, sovereign states. However, the final document that emerged from the Convention was a compromise between the ardent nationalists and those who wished to protect state sovereignty. Nevertheless, the new Constitution did, in fact, create a national government, although during the ratification controversy the states were assured that the national government was limited to the powers expressly granted it and that all else remained with the states.

It was in the controversy over ratification that the major division arose that in one form or another would emerge and reemerge in American politics until the Civil War would definitively resolve the nation–state issue by the bloodiest and costliest war (in terms of lives and property) in United States history. The supporters of the Constitution and a strong national government were the Federalists (not to be confused with the Federalist Party that was organized in the early 1790s). They included James Madison, one of the principal architects of the Constitution, as well as Alexander Hamilton and in addition such future members of the Supreme Court as John Jay, James Wilson, and John Marshall. Most of the middle and upper classes had a sound economic basis for supporting a Constitution that would end interstate tariffs and bring order to the commercial and financial affairs of the country, although support for the new Constitution cut across class and economic lines.[1] The Anti-Federalists saw little to be gained and more to be lost by the principles implanted in the Constitution. They distrusted this new document, saw defects in the system of government thereby created, predicted that the Constitution would force the states into an inferior position, and feared that they consequently would lose their political influence over policies that vitally affected them. Once the new Constitution and government were launched, political lines shifted somewhat but the nation–state issue continued unabated and overshadowed in one form or another the major political controversies, including that over slavery. The political temperature of the nation rose in the 1830s through the 1850s, eventually reaching combustible levels.

The Civil War marked a major turning point for the nation in many ways. Not only was federal supremacy over the states at last established, but the war and the Civil War Amendments changed the legal relationship of the federal government to the individual citizen. Certain civil rights and civil liberties were now thought to be protected by the federal government against encroachment by the

states. In social terms, the Civil War, by abolishing slavery and by financially devastating the South, set the stage for the emergence of a new social order, but it was one, like the old, that kept black people on the bottom. Politically, the Civil War established the Republican party as the dominant national political party. From 1860 until the election of 1932, the Republican party captured the White House in 14 out of 18 presidential elections. With only a few exceptions, the Republican party was the usual majority party in the states of the Northeast, Middle West, and the West. Only in the South were there solid and consistent Democratic party majorities, although for a time in the 1880s the Populist party seemed to be making advances.

In economic terms, too, there were profound changes from the time of the Civil War. The country entered the Industrial Revolution and the national economy took off. For example, in 1860 there were 30,000 miles of railroad track; by 1900 there were 200,000 miles. In 1860, the value of manufactured goods produced in the country was under $2 billion; by 1900 it was over $11 billion. In 1860, there were 31 million people living in the nation, of whom 16 percent resided in urban areas. By 1900 the population had grown to over 70 million, and half were city dwellers. In 1860, the number of industrial workers was about 1.3 million, but by 1900 that number grew to 5.5 million. By the turn of the century, the United States had become the greatest industrial nation in the world, producing, for example, more iron and steel than the combined total output of Great Britain and Germany.[2]

The overriding questions of public policy during the post–Civil War period were centered around the nature and extensiveness of the states' and the federal government's authority to regulate private enterprise in this

---

[1]See, in general, Forrest McDonald, *We The People: The Economic Origins of the Constitution* (Chicago: University of Chicago Press, 1958).

[2]The statistics in this paragraph are cited in Alfred H. Kelly and Winfred A. Harbison, *The American Constitution: Its Origins and Development,* 5th ed. (New York: Norton, 1976), pp. 468–469.

age of massive economic development and growth. Also at issue, particularly during the last two decades of the nineteenth century, were the nature and extensiveness of the federal government's power in defending civil rights and liberties and the substantive change in those individual rights as a result of the Fourteenth Amendment.

During the last decades of the nineteenth century, the dominant political forces in the country were increasingly in favor of economic laissez-faire (that government should not interfere with the free market economy) and increasingly strident in their attacks on perceived threats to laissez-faire policy. Most Republican and Democratic party leaders were, in general, big business oriented—and were against unions, government regulation, and social legislation. There were, of course, both Republican and Democratic factions that were socially enlightened, and there were occasions when populist or progressive forces won temporary control of states or were successful in Congress in enacting reform legislation. Theodore Roosevelt, to be sure, was reformist in his outlook, but he attained the presidency by accident. Nevertheless, the dominating spirit of the era and the undeniable thrust of Supreme Court decision making was clearly and increasingly conservative, reaching a high point by the late 1890s.

The relationship between business and government dominated political controversy. For a brief period before World War I, progressive politics, thanks to the presidencies of Theodore Roosevelt, Woodrow Wilson, and to some extent William Howard Taft, set the agenda of national politics. The federal government began to assume the role of regulator of business practices and to a very limited extent regulator of the economy. World War I, however, brought about an unprecedented exercise of federal power and control of the economy—but after the war the country by and large returned to a "normalcy" that was, in effect, a reactionary movement to pre-1900 policies concerning government's economic role. The Great Depression, of course, brought about a radical change in thinking about the proper role and scope of governmental responsibilities and activities. It also brought about a transformation of American politics.

This sketchy outline of almost 150 years of American history and politics needs to be filled in with more detail. It is also helpful to place the cases reprinted in this book within this historical and political context. We start with the Administration of our first President.

THE WASHINGTON ADMINISTRATION, 1789–1797

When the New Hampshire ratifying convention voted on June 21, 1788, to approve the Constitution, it became the ninth state required to bring the Constitution into being. After George Washington was elected President and congressional elections were held, the first Congress met and set out to organize the national government. Most of those elected to Congress and those in the executive branch had been supporters of the Constitution. One of the early legislative actions was the Judiciary Act of September 24, 1789, which implemented the constitutional provision relating to the Supreme Court. The legislation called for one chief justice and five associate justiceships.[3] The jurisdiction and powers of the Court were also specified. In Section 25, the act provided for Supreme Court review of state court decisions in which a federal claim based on federal law, the Constitution, or a treaty was rejected. Section 25 was to be a source of controversy over the next several decades as the continuing nation versus state controversy enveloped the federal courts. During the Marshall Court years, matters came to a head in **Martin** v. **Hunter's Lessee.**

[3]In general, see Julius Goebel, Jr., *Antecedents and Beginnings to 1801,* vol. 1, *History of the Supreme Court of the United States* (New York: Macmillan, 1971), chap. 11, "The Judiciary Act of 1789," pp. 457–508.

The Judiciary Act contained Section 13, which gave the Court the power to issue certain writs including the writ of mandamus. Also created were the trial courts—13 federal District Courts and 3 federal Circuit Courts—and their jurisdiction and powers were fixed. Each United States Circuit Court was to be one of general original jurisdiction with some appellate powers and was to consist of two Supreme Court justices and one district judge. (Legislation in 1793 reduced the number of Supreme Court justices to one justice required to sit on each Circuit Court.) Supreme Court justices were thus required to do double duty, first as Supreme Court justices and second as circuit judges. This meant that they were obliged to do much traveling, for each circuit covered a number of states. Evidently the members of the first Congress were untroubled by the possibility that Supreme Court justices might be placed in the position of reviewing cases in which they had participated as circuit judges.

Another major action of the first Congress was to pass a Bill of Rights and send the proposed constitutional amendments to the states for ratification. It took two years to secure the necessary number of states (11) to ratify.

Once the new government was under way, those who supported the concept of a strong national government and, not incidentally, were concerned with federal protection of property rights coalesced into what became known as the Federalist party. Alexander Hamilton was the principal molder of the party. Those suspicious of an expansive national government and who advocated states' rights as the bulwark of genuine democracy soon rallied around Thomas Jefferson, who by the mid-1790s had begun to build America's first opposition party.

At the very beginning of President Washington's Administration, both Hamilton and Jefferson were in the cabinet, with Hamilton as Secretary of the Treasury and Jefferson as Secretary of State. There were many matters of urgent public policy facing the new national government, and aside from important questions of foreign policy, most controversies raised the issue of nation versus state in one form or another.

Of even greater import domestically was the settlement of the nation's tangled financial affairs, including the debts remaining from the Articles of Confederation government and the war bond debts of the states from the Revolution. Hamilton, in particular, wanted to set the national government on a sound financial footing. To win support for his program, he included in the package of proposals to Congress the federal government's assumption of the war bond debt—but this did little for merchants like the South Carolinian in **Chisholm** v. **Georgia** who sold goods to the state of Georgia on credit and was never paid. Hamilton's economic program included institution of a number of taxes including the (horse-drawn) carriage tax whose constitutionality was challenged but nevertheless upheld by the Court in **Hylton** v. **United States.** Hamilton also proposed enacting a protective tariff law and the creation of a national bank.

It was the issue of the bank that brought on a major confrontation in the Washington Cabinet between Hamilton and Jefferson. After some controversy in Congress, the bill to charter a national bank passed in February 1791. Before signing it, President Washington wanted to be sure of its constitutionality and therefore asked his Cabinet for advice. Jefferson and Hamilton responded strongly on opposite sides of the issue. At stake was the interpretation of the federal government's powers as provided for in the Constitution. Hamilton advocated an expansive reading of the powers of Congress. A broad construction of the Constitution, particularly in light of the supremacy clause of the Constitution, would in Jefferson's view spell the end of the federal system and states' rights. This debate was to reemerge some 27 years later in the landmark case of **McCulloch** v. **Maryland.**

The Supreme Court got off to a less than spectacular start. President Washington named only Federalists to the Court. His first six nominees were confirmed, but one, Robert H. Harrison, decided that he preferred to assume a state post offered him after his Senate confirmation. In total, Washington placed ten men on the Supreme Court.

The Court met in early February 1790 with only four justices present and proceeded to establish rules and procedures for its operation. With no cases on its docket, it adjourned on February 10. Indeed, the Court decided no cases during its first three years!

By 1793 three events of some importance concerning the judiciary had occurred. First, Secretary of State Thomas Jefferson, at the direction of the President, asked the Court for its views on some 29 questions relating to international law and American neutrality. This was done in light of the European wars that were threatening to involve the United States because of widespread violations of the Neutrality Proclamation of 1793. But the justices refused to give advisory opinions, citing the independence of the judicial branch of government and its job of deciding actual cases or controversies.

A second event was an outgrowth of the position some of the justices sitting as circuit judges took concerning a 1792 act of Congress that gave the United States Circuit Courts the task of determining the pension claims of disabled war veterans. Under the legislation, the circuit court's determination would be reviewed and subject to revision by the Secretary of War and by Congress. William Hayburn had gone to the United States Circuit Court for the District of Pennsylvania to settle his pension claim, but the court refused to process his claim on the ground that the statute conferred an extrajudicial duty on the federal judiciary in violation of the Constitution. This case, *Hayburn's Case,* was taken to the Supreme Court and in August 1792 the Attorney General of the United States asked that a writ of mandamus be issued directing the circuit court to act on Hayburn's pension claim. The Supreme Court said it would consider the motion and dispose of the matter during the following February term, but it never did, because on February 28, 1793, Congress changed the law, which thus relieved judges of the duty of acting as pension commissioners. Interestingly, in an 1852 case there is a footnote reference to an unpublished Supreme Court decision, *United States v. Yale Todd,* in which the Court without directly saying so suggested that the congressional act involved in both *Hayburn's Case* and the *Yale Todd* case was unconstitutional. The Court apparently did so by simply ruling that the decisions of judges who acted as pension commissioners were without legal force because the act could not give the justices the authority to act as commissioners.

The third event was the famous case of *Chisholm* v. *Georgia.* The Court, contrary to the intent of the Constitutional Convention and contrary to the assurances given in Federalist Paper #81 and to the ratifying conventions, ruled that a state may be sued *against its will* in federal court by a citizen of another state. Soon after the decision was handed down, other suits were filed against four states. This struck at the heart of state sovereignty and was vehemently denounced by Georgia state officials. Although nationwide public sentiment may not have been as vehement as that demonstrated in Georgia, there was the widespread view that the Court had ruled wrongly. A constitutional amendment in effect reversing *Chisholm* was introduced and passed both houses of Congress. Five years later the Eleventh Amendment became part of the Constitution.

The federal courts even in the early years of the Republic were, as we have seen, drawn into the major national controversies. The federal judiciary may not have been the powerful institution that we think of today. But neither was the presidency nor the Congress. The judiciary, like the other branches of government, was establishing *its* power base and its decisions helped to establish the national government as supreme within its sphere.

THE ADAMS PRESIDENCY AND THE "REVOLUTION" OF 1800

The presidential election of 1796 occurred in the context of a severe economic recession (or "panic," as major economic downturns were once called). The panic had severe financial consequences for some Federalist politicians and also for Supreme Court Justice James Wilson. The nation did not have a bankruptcy law, although Congress was empowered in Article 1 to create one, and the issue of whether or not to enact one emerged during Adams' presidency. The Supreme Court's decision in **Calder** v. **Bull,** limiting the guarantee against ex post facto laws to criminal law, was to have implications for the decision to enact a national bankruptcy law with retroactive effect.

During the Adams Administration, one of the overriding issues of public policy was how the government should deal with the political opposition, particularly the Jeffersonian political organization, that was making electoral gains and becoming increasingly critical of Federalist control of the government. The Adams Administration responded by enacting in 1798 a package of the most severe restrictions on civil liberties ever perpetrated by the federal government on the people of the United States. The infamous Alien and Sedition Acts were meant to stifle political criticism and curb Jefferson's growing political strength. The Sedition Act in particular, although it had little more than a two-year time limit that was designed to allow President Adams to run for reelection in 1800 without severe political criticism, was especially repugnant to Jeffersonians because it served as the basis for severe legal harassment. The response of the Jeffersonians came in the states of Virginia and Kentucky, both Jeffersonian strongholds,

with the enactment there of the Virginia and Kentucky Resolutions, which claimed that the states had the power to reject congressional legislation so clearly repugnant to the First Amendment of the Constitution. The Resolutions claimed the right of states to nullify acts of Congress. This development, of course, was welcomed by supporters of states' rights as well as, in this case, supporters of First Amendment rights. But the long-run implications added fuel to the continuing nation versus state conflict.

The political climax was reached with the election of 1800. Jefferson and his followers were triumphant at the polls. The Federalists, crushed by their defeat, were determined to secure for themselves the one branch of national government not immediately touched by the Jeffersonian sweep. The Federalist-controlled lame duck Congress enacted the Judiciary Act of 1801, which created new and separate circuit courts and circuit court judgeships. No longer would Supreme Court justices be obliged to ride the circuit, enduring not only the physical hardship of primitive travel and road conditions but also the lengthy separation from home and family. And of course all these new judgeships would be filled by worthy Federalists.

Among other provisions of the act was one reducing the number of positions on the Supreme Court from six to five; that is, the act specified that the next vacancy on the Court would not be filled and the position would thus be eliminated. This was an obvious ploy to prevent Jefferson from naming a supporter to the Court—in other words, to buy time until the Federalists would regain power. The same Congress also enacted an organic law for the District of Columbia that, among other provisions, created new local justice of the peace positions. These minor District of Columbia judgeships, each with a five-year tenure, were to figure prominently in **Marbury** v. **Madison.**

The clash between the Federalists and Jeffersonians, as previously noted, culminated in the passage of the Alien and Sedition Acts. The federal circuit courts were the site of the trials of Jeffersonian newspaper editors accused of violating the Sedition Act. These trials were presided over by Supreme Court justices, and whenever the defendants sought to challenge the constitutionality of the Sedition Act as violating the First Amendment, the justices refused to consider the issue. Again, as in the carriage tax case, Supreme Court justices (although serving in their capacity as circuit judges) were being asked to strike down an act of Congress as unconstitutional—thereby acknowledging that the federal judiciary has the power of judicial review.

Justice Samuel Chase, in particular, behaved in such a biased, crude, and cruel manner that he earned not only the enmity but also the hatred of the Jeffersonians. During the presidential election of 1800, Chase campaigned vigorously for Adams in Chase's home state of Maryland. When Jefferson became President, Chase continued to provoke the Jeffersonians. They were determined to remove Chase from the bench, and they succeeded in impeaching him in the House of Representatives and fell only four votes short of finding him guilty in the Senate trial held in 1805.

JEFFERSON VERSUS THE COURT

When Thomas Jefferson delivered his inaugural address on March 4, 1801, he magnanimously noted, ''We are all Republicans—we are all Federalists.'' He even went as far as to deliver some of the minor judicial commissions for justice of the peace positions that the outgoing Adams Administration, particularly acting Secretary of State John Marshall, had failed to deliver. But Jefferson, to demonstrate displeasure in principle with the lame duck Federalists' creation of judicial positions for patronage purposes, refused to transmit all the undelivered commissions. Furthermore, the Jeffersonians were determined to undo the

mischief they thought the Federalists had done in the Judiciary Act of 1801, and took steps to repeal that act and replace it with Jeffersonian legislation. Meanwhile, William Marbury and three others who were deprived of the duly signed and sealed justice of the peace commissions decided, apparently after some months of hesitation, to go directly to the Supreme Court. On December 16, 1801, they asked the Court to issue a writ of mandamus to Secretary of State James Madison, ordering him to deliver the commissions. Two days later, on December 18, Chief Justice Marshall, speaking for the Court, directed Madison to appear in Court at the next term (the following June) and show cause why mandamus should not be issued. (The Judiciary Act of 1801 had changed the dates of the terms of the Court to December and June.)

This bold action of the Federalist-dominated Court was seen as a direct challenge to the Jeffersonian-controlled executive branch of the government. Here was a clash of political parties, a clash of branches of the national government, and (not the least) a family feud between the distant cousins Marshall and Jefferson, who also had an apparent personality conflict. Jefferson interpreted the action of the Court as a personal affront to the integrity of the political movement he fathered and suggested in a letter he wrote the day after Madison was ordered to appear:

> The Federalists . . . have retired into the judiciary as a stronghold . . . and from that battery all the works of Republicanism are to be beaten down and erased.[4]

Whereas Marshall himself may not have been itching for a fight, the Jeffersonian Republicans in Congress, already planning legislation to repeal the Judiciary Act of 1801, pulled out the stops and added another provi-

[4]As quoted in Benjamin F. Wright, *The Growth of American Constitutional Law* (Chicago: University of Chicago Press, Phoenix Books edition, 1967), p. 31.

sion to the pending legislation. This new provision canceled the June and December terms of the Court and provided for one annual February term to start in 1803. This meant that more than a year would pass before the Court could consider the *Marbury* case. The repeal legislation was enacted in March 1802 and its principal provision eliminated the newly created circuit judgeships. The justices were obliged to return to their circuit riding responsibilities.

The Court, after being closed down by Congress for over a year, heard argument in the *Marbury* case on February 9 and 10, 1803, with Attorney General Levi Lincoln arguing the government's position. The Court was silent for two weeks and then on February 24 Marshall revealed its decision. From the standpoint of the administration, the decision signaled a major retreat by the Court. Jefferson and Marshall had been eyeball to eyeball, so to speak, and Marshall blinked first. But Marshall, of course, did no about-face. He severely criticized the Jefferson Administration, was most sympathetic to Marbury and his colleagues, and took the opportunity to stake a giant claim for the judiciary. *Marbury* v. *Madison* is rightfully remembered as the classic justification for judicial review, although in the context of 1803 the decision was seen as the judicial branch backing away from a confrontation with the executive branch. Also, in practice, the assertion of the power of judicial review over acts of Congress (with the implication that the Court would strike down what it considered to be violations of the Constitution) did not amount to much, because the fate of the Court was intimately tied to the fate of the national government, and anything that would weaken the latter would weaken the former. For a period of 54 years after *Marbury* the Court upheld every act of Congress challenged before it. Further signaling the Court's retreat from confrontation with the Jeffersonians, barely a week after the *Marbury* decision, the Court in *Stuart* v. *Laird,* 1 Cranch

299, upheld the repeal of the 1801 Judiciary Act.

Marshall and Jefferson were to clash again during Jefferson's presidency, but, despite Jefferson's espousal of a limited national government and of states' rights, his *actions* as President strengthened the presidency and the national government.

NATIONAL POLITICS AND THE JUDICIARY, 1809–1835

The demise of the Federalist party, particularly after the War of 1812, and the repeated success of the Jeffersonian Republicans in presidential elections served to mute somewhat the nation versus state struggle. President James Madison (1809–1817) and a Republican Congress, for example, rechartered the national bank in 1816 for a 20-year period. What earlier had been an issue of great moment pitting a narrow construction versus a broad construction of the Constitution was now a less controversial economic program that was considered well within the powers of Congress. It was only after charges of corruption and mismanagement and when the bank was accused of responsibility for the economic panic of 1819 that the Second Bank of the United States had its constitutionality questioned. Then the nation versus state issue was raised once again. *McCulloch* v. *Maryland* brought these issues before the Court.

The nation versus state issue emerged most clearly, aside from the bank controversy, in two other areas of public controversy—the exercise of judicial review over the states and the commercial warfare among the states. As for the judicial review area, John Marshall and his colleagues made the most of Section 25 of the Judiciary Act of 1789. By meeting the challenge to Section 25 that came, in particular, from the state of Virginia, the Court defended as well the concept of federal supremacy. Virginia, the home of Jefferson and the center of the Jeffersonian Republican party, remained one of the major strongholds of states' rights. The Chief Judge of Virginia's highest court, Spencer Roane, was an ardent Jeffersonian and states' rights theoretician as well as the boss of the Jeffersonian party apparatus. The *Hunter's Lessee* litigation brought matters to a head. Although the Marshall Court sought to meet the challenge to Section 25 in the *Martin* v. *Hunter's Lessee* case, the Court clearly would have to assert itself continually. Another Virginia case came to the Court, **Cohens** v. **Virginia,** and here, too, the Court reminded the Virginians of the validity of Section 25 and the supremacy of the federal judiciary in interpreting federal law. Interestingly, when Maryland state officials were challenging the Baltimore branch of the Second Bank of the United States, they willingly came before the Supreme Court in *McCulloch* v. *Maryland* and not only conceded Supreme Court jurisdiction under Section 25 but also the power of judicial review over acts of Congress by asking the Court to strike down the congressional legislation rechartering the bank. By upholding the constitutionality of the bank and interpreting Congress' power in the broad manner that it did, the Court defended and promoted federal supremacy at a time when it was by no means certain that the national government was or could be supreme.

The continuing difficulty of having a weak national government was most apparent with the commercial warfare among the states that intensified in the early 1820s. The granting of state monopolies, as in New York's grant of a steamboat monopoly to Livingston and Fulton, provoked retaliatory legislation by other states. The Supreme Court's decision in **Gibbons** v. **Ogden,** like *McCulloch,* promoted federal supremacy; in this case Congress' commerce powers were interpreted broadly, so that the destructive commercial antagonisms among the states could be resolved by federal commercial regulation. But the Marshall Court, consisting of five Republicans and one

other Federalist (Justice Washington) besides Marshall himself, was sensitive to at least some of the claims of the states, as is seen in the case of **Willson** v. **Blackbird Creek Marsh Company.**

A continuing undercurrent in politics is seen in the efforts of those who have wealth to keep it, as well as in the efforts of those who enter into commercial transactions to protect themselves from undue governmental intrusions. Indeed, the basis for certain constitutional guarantees was the protection of property rights. The guarantee against states impairing the obligation of contracts was meant to prevent the states from passing legislation favoring debtors, such as granting debtors postponements beyond the contract date for payment of debts or changing the terms of the contract by allowing the payment of debts in installments or in commodities. The contract clause was also meant to apply only to contracts between private parties; but the Marshall Court in **Fletcher** v. **Peck, New Jersey** v. **Wilson,** and in the **Dartmouth College** case used it to create new doctrines with which to protect the rights of corporations and the propertied class. These developing doctrines, however, occurred against the backdrop of growing social unrest.

By the mid-1820s the class divisions in the country had produced a new party system, and Andrew Jackson and the new Democratic party captured the White House in 1828. They were avowed enemies of privilege and wealth and champions of democracy for the lower classes. Jackson was to oppose the Second Bank of the United States not only on constitutional but also on socioeconomic and political grounds. A property-oriented and federal supremacy-minded Court was thus inconsistent, if not with Jackson's policies as President, certainly with the spirit of Jacksonian Democracy's unmistakable states' rights aura. In some respects, however, both the *Willson* and **Barron** v. **Baltimore** cases can be seen as decisions that took Jacksonian values into account. Both were conciliatory to the states at the expense of the assertion of federal power. Of course, no matter how much Marshall might have wished to protect property rights, the constitutional implications of deciding in favor of Barron were too formidable, and Marshall himself would not have wished the legal fallout on the Court that would have inevitably occurred. The political fallout had the Court ruled for Barron would have been equally great. But it was not until Marshall's successor, Roger B. Taney, assumed the Court's helm in 1836 that the Court shifted to reflect more accurately the prevailing political, social, and economic reality.

The Marshall Court clashed indirectly with President Jackson and directly with the state of Georgia over the rights of the Cherokee Indians to their land. One of the great moral blots on the Constitution, aside from its failure to condemn slavery, was its failure to recognize the rights of native Americans. Denied citizenship and unprotected in terms of rights by either the state or federal constitutions, the Indians through a pattern of warfare and treaties saw their land diminished and taken as they were pushed westward. When the Cherokee Indians in Georgia declared themselves an "independent nation," the Georgia legislature authorized the annexation of Cherokee land and the end of Indian self-rule. In the first case to reach the Court, *Cherokee Nation* v. *Georgia,* 5 Peters 1 (1831), the Court ruled that it had no jurisdiction in the case because the Cherokees were neither a state nor a foreign nation. However, the Court suggested that the Indians had a right to their land.

The second case, *Worcester* v. *Georgia,* 6 Peters 515 (1832), also resulted from Georgia's actions and concerned Samuel A. Worcester, a Congregational minister from Vermont, residing on the Cherokees' land and doing missionary work, who was convicted in the Georgia courts of violating a state law requiring white people who wished to live on Cherokee land to obtain a state license. The Court ruled

that the land belonged to the Cherokees, that they formed a distinct political community, and that within the land "the laws of Georgia can have no force, and . . . the citizens of Georgia have no right to enter but with the assent of the Cherokees themselves or in conformity with treaties and with acts of Congress." Worcester was ordered released. It was this decision about which President Jackson, himself a famed Indian fighter, reportedly stated that "John Marshall has made his decision and now let him enforce it." Whether Jackson actually said this is irrelevant, because the fact remains that he made no effort whatsoever to back up the Court's decision and Georgia state officials contemptuously defied the Court by refusing to release Worcester (he was pardoned by the Governor of Georgia one year later) and by maintaining Georgia's hold on Cherokee land.

JACKSONIAN DEMOCRATIC POLITICS AND THE NEW PARTY SYSTEM, 1836–1852

Chief Justice Taney assumed the leadership of the Court at the end of President Jackson's second and final term as President—the year that Jackson's vice-president and chosen successor Martin Van Buren was elected to the presidency. With Taney's and Justice Barbour's appointments in 1836 and with President Van Buren's appointments of Justices Catron and McKinley to two new justiceships generously created by a Jacksonian Congress in 1837, the Court, which was enlarged from seven to nine justices, now had seven Jacksonian Democrats. Only Justices Story and Thompson remained from the Marshall Court, and Justice Story reportedly lamented to his good friend Senator Daniel Webster that "the Supreme Court is gone." Although it is true in a literal sense that the Marshall Court was gone and that the Jacksonian Taney Court reflected the nuances of a new party system, the fundamental constitutional doctrines developed in the first third of the nineteenth century were to remain virtually untouched by Taney and his colleagues.

The Jacksonian Democratic party was characterized by a commitment to democracy, which included the extension of the franchise at least to all adult white males, the breakdown of class distinctions, opposition to monopoly and special privilege, social legislation to improve the lot of debtors, and the defense of state sovereignty. Jackson and his followers had built a grass-roots party organization, and this in turn stimulated the creation of the opposition Whig party. This party system endured for close to three decades.

The year Martin Van Buren became President, the nation experienced a severe economic recession, the panic of 1837. The federal government, unlike today, had few means at its disposal with which to influence the economy. Indeed, one of the potential mechanisms, the national bank, had gone out of existence because of Jackson's fierce opposition to it. This meant that the individual states had to cope with the harsh effects of a major national economic crisis. The Taney Court, dominated by Jacksonian justices, was markedly sympathetic to the states in the trilogy of 1837 decisions: **Mayor of New York** v. **Miln, Charles River Bridge** v. **Warren Bridge,** and *Briscoe* v. *The Bank of Kentucky,* 11 Peters 257 (1837). Although all three cases had their genesis years before the panic and although the decisions were handed down before the full impact of the panic was felt nationally, these decisions nevertheless served as signals to the states to take whatever appropriate actions they could on their citizens' behalf. The *Miln* case, skirting the important commerce clause issues raised, emphasized the state's police powers. The *Charles River Bridge* decision, in tune with Jacksonian Democracy, was hostile to special interests and special privilege, and sought to protect the public interest by strictly construing corporate charters. The *Briscoe* decision saw the Court uphold the issuance of state bank notes and rule that they were not bills of credit

forbidden by the Constitution. With the *Briscoe* decision, the Court for most intents and purposes gave its approval for the states to regulate their currency and banking as they saw fit. The states did so until the Civil War required the federal government to assume control of the nation's monetary system. Interestingly, once the 1837 recession ended, the Court was less sympathetic to state regulation.

The Van Buren Administration was blamed for the panic of 1837 and the country's financial problems, and Van Buren lost his bid for reelection in 1840 to the Whig party's Harrison-Tyler ticket. President William Henry Harrison died barely a month after his inauguration and John Tyler, a states' rights former Democrat, served out the term. The Jacksonian party reclaimed the White House in 1844 with another Tennessean, James K. Polk, winning an electoral victory; but Polk's refusal to run for reelection led to the Whig party's success at the polls in 1848 with Taylor-Fillmore. President Zachary Taylor, like his Whig predecessor, died in office early in his term. This was to be the last national victory for the Whig party because the slavery issue and the economic cleavages between North and South were to result in the breakup of the party by the mid-1850s.

Congress' commerce powers were at issue in a number of cases before the Taney Court, and these cases continually raised the nation versus state controversy. The Court itself was badly divided. Finally, a doctrinal resolution was achieved in **Cooley** v. **Board of Wardens,** thanks to the brilliant compromise devised by Justice Benjamin Curtis of Massachusetts, who was newly appointed by President Millard Fillmore in 1851.

The Taney Court initially had startled the business community in 1837 with the *Charles River Bridge* decision. However, the *Bank of Augusta* v. *Earle,* 13 Peters 519 (1839), and *Bronson* v. *Kinzie,* 1 Howard 311 (1843), decisions, among others, made it clear that the contract clause doctrines developed by the Marshall Court would be honored by the Taney Court. Indeed, *Piqua Branch of the State Bank* v. *Knoop,* 16 Howard 369 (1854), made it unquestionably clear that, as the Marshall Court had held earlier in *New Jersey* v. *Wilson,* the Taney Court would also hold a state to the terms of the corporate charter even when that meant impinging upon the taxing ability of the state.

PRELUDE TO THE CIVIL WAR

Although the Compromise of 1850 seemed for a time to diminish some of the nationwide tension over slavery, the abolition movement continued unabated. In 1854 Congress, in the Kansas-Nebraska Act, repealed the Missouri Compromise of 1820 and adopted the formula of popular sovereignty to determine whether a territory would allow slavery and be admitted to the Union as a slave state. This reopened the issue of slavery in the territories, an issue about which there was increasing intensity of feeling by those on both sides. One direct result of these events was the formation of the Republican party and the virtual dissolution of the Whig party. The Republican party attracted antislavery Whigs and Democrats. Although the Democrats had won the presidency in 1852 (Franklin Pierce) and 1856 (James Buchanan), the two Presidents, both northerners, faced the impossible task of reconciling the irreconcilable. They were men in the middle, and Buchanan was especially distrusted in the North—further accelerating the exodus of antislavery Democrats to the Republican party.

In November 1853, before the Kansas-Nebraska Act debate in Congress had begun, two slaves, Dred Scott and his wife, with the help of abolitionist lawyers, sued for their freedom in the United States Circuit Court in Missouri.[5] The **Dred Scott** v. **Sandford** case made its way to the Supreme Court in February 1856 and raised major legal issues surrounding slavery.

The case was ordered for reargument in the fall of 1856. Initially the justices were inclined to avoid the controversial issues and simply fall back on the 1851 precedent of *Strader* v. *Graham,* 10 Howard 82, whereby the status of Scott would be determined by the state wherein he resided. Since Missouri considered him a slave, that would end the matter. But antislavery Justices McLean and Curtis made it clear that they would write dissents touching on all the controversial issues, and Chief Justice Taney and the other justices, particularly after it was clear that there was a proslavery majority, decided to grapple fully with the issues.

Democrat James Buchanan was elected President in November 1856, and Justices Catron and Grier privately disclosed to the President-elect the status of the Court's decision making in *Dred Scott.* With advance knowledge of how the Court would decide, President Buchanan in his inaugural address of March 4, 1857, inserted the gist of a statement that Justice Catron had previously prepared for him, noting that the question of slavery in the territories "is a judicial question, which legitimately belongs to the Supreme Court of the United States, before whom it is now pending, and will, it is understood, be speedily and finally settled. To this decision [*Dred Scott*], in common with all good citizens, I shall cheerfully submit. . . ."[6] Two days later the *Dred Scott* decision was announced.

Far from resolving the emotionally charged issues surrounding slavery, the *Dred Scott* decision served only to inflame the North and heighten the sectional polarization. The Court's prestige plummeted in the North, and

---

[5]For the definitive account of the Dred Scott case, see Don E. Fehrenbacher, *The Dred Scott Case: Its Significance in American Law and Politics* (New York: Oxford University Press, 1978).

[6]*Messages and Papers of the Presidents,* vol. 5, p. 431, as cited by Carl B. Swisher in *The Taney Period 1836–64,* vol. 5, *History of the Supreme Court of the United States* (New York: Macmillan, 1974), p. 621.

Chief Justice Taney and his colleagues in the majority were vilified. As a contemporary New York newspaper observed, "If epithets and denunciation could sink a judicial body, the Supreme Court of the United States would never be heard of again."[7] Taney, 80 years old and in poor health, was particularly despondent. In a major lapse of good judgment, he refused to send Justice Curtis a copy of his Opinion of the Court, and relations between the two rapidly deteriorated. Curtis, who also had family and financial reasons for dissatisfaction with his Court service, decided that it was now time to leave the Court; he resigned on September 1, 1857. His resignation appeared to the North to be a protest against the *Dred Scott* decision—further lowering the Court's prestige.

As events proceeded, the Republican party gained strength in the North and as a consequence the South became more isolated. With the election of Lincoln in 1860, secession and Civil War seemed inevitable. South Carolina seceded from the Union on December 20, 1860, and several weeks later, joined by six other slave states, formed the Confederacy and drafted the Confederate Constitution. With the Confederate attack on Fort Sumter in South Carolina on April 12, 1861, the four remaining states of the upper South joined the Confederacy and the Civil War began.

THE CIVIL WAR, RECONSTRUCTION, AND THE FRAMING OF THE FOURTEENTH AMENDMENT

The Civil War resolved the most basic aspects of the nation versus state issue. National supremacy over the states, the Union over the Confederacy, was determined on the battlefields of the bloodiest war in our history. President Lincoln exercised unprecedented presidential power; and with Congress cooperating, Lincoln took various actions for the

[7]*New York Tribune*, March 7, 1857, as cited by Swisher, op. cit., p. 633.

conduct of the war that vastly strengthened and enhanced federal power. By the end of the Civil War and with the subsequent adoption of the Civil War Amendments, particularly the Fourteenth Amendment, the actual and constitutional nature of American government had been radically altered. The Civil War had the effect of centralizing and nationalizing power.

At the beginning of the war, Lincoln on his own authority suspended the use of the writ of habeas corpus and authorized military detention of citizens engaged in or suspected of disloyal or treasonous acts. Eventually, Congress in March of 1863 approved these actions with the passage of the Habeas Corpus Act.

Of even greater seriousness was the practice of military commissions trying civilians. During the war the Court was faced with such an instance involving a former Democratic U.S. Senator, Clement Vallandigham. The case, *Ex Parte Vallandigham*, 1 Wallace 243 (1864), resulted in the Court shying away from the certain confrontation that would have occurred had the Court struck down both Lincoln's proclamation of 1862 and the congressional legislation of 1863, which in effect approved Lincoln's actions. But after the war was over, the Court, under the leadership of a new chief justice, struck down the use of military commissions trying civilians in the landmark case of **Ex Parte Milligan.** A civil libertarian principle was proclaimed—but not at the expense of hampering the conduct of the war.

During the war, President Lincoln took numerous unprecedented actions based on the inherent powers of the presidency. He acted first, and Congress eventually upheld his actions. Congress, too, stretched the necessary and proper clause to limits heretofore unreached. As for the President, the Court in a 5–4 decision upheld the broad exercise of presidential power in ordering a blockade of Confederate ports in a series of cases known as **The Prize Cases.** The majority recognized the existence of inherent powers of the President as Commander-in-Chief. Congress had later enacted legislation authorizing the blockade, and, interestingly, when cases came to the Court that had their genesis *after* Congress had acted, the Court *unanimously* upheld enforcement of the blockade.

Chief Justice Taney died on October 12, 1864, at the age of 87, a disheartened old man convinced that the nation was forever torn asunder and that the Supreme Court would never regain the prestige and power it had under Marshall and the first 20 years of his own chief justiceship. President Lincoln named his former Secretary of the Treasury, Salmon P. Chase, to the chief justiceship. Chase had been a Democratic senator from Ohio, but was staunchly opposed to slavery and became a Republican in the 1850s. He was an ambitious man with presidential aspirations and was known to have plotted to take the 1864 Republican presidential nomination away from Lincoln. The chief justiceship was perhaps Lincoln's way of kicking a troublemaker upstairs.

As the war progressed, the Republicans in control of Congress were determined to punish the South and to protect the newly freed slaves (the Emancipation Proclamation was issued on January 1, 1863). They were known as the Radical Republicans, and as the war was drawing to a close they disagreed with President Lincoln as to how to deal with the South. Lincoln was assassinated on April 15, 1865, before he had the opportunity of guiding the rapprochement he sought between North and South. Andrew Johnson took over the presidency, only to be overshadowed by a stern Radical Republican Congress that passed wide-sweeping civil rights laws and the important Thirteenth, Fourteenth, and Fifteenth Amendments. Congress provided for military reconstruction, which meant that the South was to be militarily occupied by the Union Army, and military tribunals were authorized to try civilians who interfered with the military and their operations. Under the watchful eye of the military authorities, elections were to be held, with the newly freed slaves voting and running for office. The civil courts were to be open and functioning, but to ensure that local authorities would in no way hamper federal officials in carrying out their duties or interfere with the rights of blacks, Congress enacted the Habeas Corpus Act of 1867. The new legislation authorized federal courts to issue writs of habeas corpus and provided for appeals from the federal circuit courts to the Supreme Court in habeas corpus cases in ''all cases where any person may be restrained of his or her liberty, in violation of the Constitution or of any treaty or law of the United States.''

The Supreme Court was seemingly headed for a collision with Congress after the Court's decision in *Ex Parte Milligan* to strike down the use of military commissions in trying civilians when the civil courts were open and functioning. One of the cornerstones of military reconstruction was the authority given military commissions to try civilians obstructing reconstruction or the military authorities. The Reconstruction Acts passed Congress, but President Johnson vetoed them. The acts were passed over his veto and the state of Mississippi went directly to the Supreme Court, asking the Court to enjoin the President from enforcing the acts on the grounds that they were unconstitutional. The Court, in **Mississippi** v. **Johnson,** took no notice of the fact that President Johnson would have welcomed and honored any injunction issued by the Court. Instead, the Court examined the nature of presidential powers and came to the conclusion that the Court had no power to force the President himself to do or not to do something.

Although the Court seemed to be off the hook in terms of having to rule on the constitutionality of reconstruction, events were conspiring to bring the issue again before the Court. William H. McCardle, a Mississippi newspaper editor, was arrested by the military authorities for having written and published newspaper editorials severely critical of the reconstruction government. He went to the federal circuit court for a writ of habeas corpus, which was granted; but McCardle was then remanded to the military's custody and he therefore took his appeal to the Supreme Court.

Radical Republicans in Congress did not want the Court to rule on the constitutionality of military reconstruction and so they enacted the Habeas Corpus Act of 1868 withdrawing Supreme Court jurisdiction in habeas corpus appeals. This legislation passed Congress shortly after the House of Representatives had voted to impeach President Johnson and before the beginning of trial proceedings by the Senate. The trial on the impeachment charges started on March 30, 1868, with Chief Justice Chase presiding. The President was eventually acquitted, but only by one vote short of the two-thirds majority necessary for conviction (seven Republican senators had voted for acquittal). However, a two-thirds majority was mustered to override Johnson's veto of the Habeas Corpus Act of 1868, thus conveying a clear message to the Court that it would be asking for trouble to decide McCardle's appeal. The justices, mindful of President Johnson's trauma, sat on the appeal for a year and then issued its ruling in **Ex Parte McCardle,** disengaging itself from the potential confrontation.

In 1868 Republican Ulysses S. Grant was elected President and he was reelected in 1872. From 1864 to 1877 the Radical Republicans were in firm control of Congress. The Joint Committee (of both houses of Congress) on Reconstruction framed legislation and proposed constitutional amendments to protect the newly freed slaves. This was needed because the southern states had in 1865 and 1866 enacted the so-called black codes, which reduced black people to noncitizen or semislave status. The Thirteenth, Fourteenth, and Fifteenth Amendments passed Congress along with other pieces of legislation including the Civil Rights Act of 1866 and the military Re-

construction Acts of 1867. We have already seen how the Court avoided passing on the constitutionality of reconstruction. In 1873, however, the Court decided **The Slaughterhouse Cases** and for the first time considered the meaning and scope of the Fourteenth Amendment, which had become part of the Constitution just five years earlier.

Justice Miller, speaking for the Court majority in *The Slaughterhouse Cases* and in **Bradwell** v. **State of Illinois,** took an exceedingly narrow view of the Fourteenth Amendment's guarantees and in both cases favored the states' exercise of their police powers. Before we proceed further, it is useful to backtrack briefly to the framing of the Fourteenth Amendment. Although motivation and intent are difficult to ascertain, and although different people had conflicting views about what the Fourteenth Amendment was meant to encompass, certain facts do emerge. The Radical Republicans, firmly in control of Congress, sought to extend and protect rights of people who were long denied them, particularly black people. Congress aimed to remove constitutional barriers, either in the form of past Court decisions (namely *Dred Scott*) or the tenets of federalism, by allowing the federal government to take direct action in the states to enforce civil rights. This was to be accomplished both through statutory legislation such as the Civil Rights Act of 1866 and by constitutional amendment. The Joint Committee on Reconstruction began drafting the Fourteenth Amendment in January of 1866 and by mid-June the final version was approved by both houses of Congress.[8]

[8]For the details see William W. Crosskey, *Politics and the Constitution in the History of the United States,* vol. 2 (Chicago: University of Chicago Press, 1953), pp. 1083–1119; Raoul Berger *Government by Judiciary* (Cambridge, Mass.: Harvard University Press, 1977); Charles Fairman and Stanley Morrison, "Does the Fourteenth Amendment Incorporate the Bill of Rights?" *Stanford Law Review,* 2 (1949), pp. 5–139; Joseph B. James, *The Framing of the Fourteenth Amendment* (Urbana, Ill.: University of Illinois Press, 1956); Jacobus Ten Broek, *The Anti-Slavery Origins of the Fourteenth Amendment* (Berkeley, Calif.: University of California Press, 1951).

Against this historical backdrop, the decisions of the Court in *The Slaughterhouse Cases* and the *Bradwell* case (both decided in 1873), the **Civil Rights Cases of 1883,** and **Plessy** v. **Ferguson,** as well as some others, must be seen as contrary to the basic intent of the Fourteenth Amendment and the nation's promise to black Americans. Ironically, the 1873 decisions did not concern black people claiming their rights, but rather involved southern whites and a midwestern white woman. By ruling as it did in *The Slaughterhouse Cases* and upholding the actions of a Republican-controlled state legislature, the Court, although limiting the scope of the Fourteenth Amendment, did not appear to be challenging the Radical Republicans. Indeed, Justice Miller for the Court majority made it clear that the Fourteenth Amendment was to further the rights of blacks and not whites. The decision, coming as it did during the economic panic of 1873 and upholding the exercise of the state police power by a Republican legislature, did not appear to be what it actually was. As for the *Bradwell* case, it presented the novel claims of a woman. As radical as the congressional Republicans may have been, their ideology did not extend to women and women's rights. When later cases that did directly concern black civil rights were decided by the Court in such a way as to strip the Fourteenth Amendment of any meaningful protection for blacks, the Court could act as it did with impunity because the day of the Radical Republicans had long since gone and white America had grown indifferent to black rights.

With the 1874 congressional elections, the Republicans lost control of the House of Representatives. The lame duck Republican Congress passed the Civil Rights Act of 1875, which outlawed racial discrimination in public accommodations. This was to be the last congressional civil rights act for over 80 years. The act was not enforced, and in the 1883 *Civil Rights Cases* the Court ruled the public accommodations provisions unconstitutional.

The presidential election of 1876 was one of the most controversial in United States history. During Grant's second term, his administration had received widespread publicity concerning the corruption of cabinet officers and other administration officials. The Democrats by the mid-1870s had recovered their prestige, adopted conservative economic positions, and like most of the rest of white America preferred to forget about the blacks and the Civil War. The Democratic presidential candidate, New York Governor Samuel J. Tilden, won a majority of the popular vote, and it seemed of the electoral college as well. However, there was a dispute in three southern states over the vote between rival slates of Democratic and Republican electors. There was also a disputed Republican elector in Oregon. If all the disputed electoral votes went to the Republican candidate, Rutherford B. Hayes, he would win by one vote. To end the impasse Congress established a 15-man commission to determine the merits of the dispute. Five members of the Court served on the commission. The Supreme Court justices, it was thought (hoped), would be impartial and see that justice was done. As it turned out there were eight Republicans and seven Democrats on the commission, and *they all* voted in favor of their own party. Congress, after some wheeling and dealing, accepted this finding, and Republican Rutherford B. Hayes won the presidency by one electoral vote. Hayes, as part of the understanding with the Democrats in Congress, withdrew the remaining federal troops from the South, and reconstruction came to an end. In 1884 the Court could and did take the broad position in **Hurtado** v. **California** that the due process clause of the Fourteenth Amendment did not oblige the states to honor *any* of the rights singled out in the Bill of Rights. Hardly anyone objected to this further gutting of the civil liberties content of the amendment.

Morrison R. Waite, named to the chief justiceship by President Grant in 1874, was sympathetic to property rights, unsympathetic to black rights, and sympathetic to states' rights (at least in terms of exercising police powers). He and a majority of his colleagues through the early 1880s were not as fanatic as was Justice Field, who vigorously espoused economic laissez-faire. One of the main instances of the Waite Court's sympathy for states' rights was in **Munn** v. **Illinois.** The Court, by upholding in 1877 the disputed Illinois and similar small farmer (the National Grange) lobby-sponsored legislation, struck an important blow for exercising state police power. But gradually the consensus on the Court shifted as new men came to the Court more in tune with the values of laissez-faire. The presidential election of 1880 resulted in another Republican victory with James Garfield, but even when Democrat Grover Cleveland won the White House in 1884, the men appointed to the Court were sympathetic to the gospel of laissez-faire.

ECONOMIC EXPANSION AND THE POPULIST-PROGRESSIVE CHALLENGE TO LAISSEZ-FAIRE

The 1880s were years of tremendous economic expansion. They were also times of growing economic concentration. The movement was toward monopoly capitalism with the trusts swallowing smaller businesses. Unscrupulous business and consumer practices produced increased resentment and opposition. The railroads, too, were guilty of practices that were detrimental to small farmers and small businesses. Both the railroads and the trusts were eventually the subject of national regulatory legislation. Indeed the Court in 1886 in *The Wabash Case,* 118 U.S. 557, seemed to invite Congress to regulate interstate railroad rates, and Congress obliged by enacting the Interstate Commerce Act of 1887. In 1890, as part of a legislative deal that permitted passage of the highest protective tariff in the history of the country, Congress also enacted the Sherman Anti-Trust Act. Both

pieces of legislation, at best modest starts at regulation, were nevertheless to be weakened considerably by the court in *The ICC Case,* 162 U.S. 184 (1896), and *United States* v. *E.C. Knight Co.,* 156 U.S. 1 (1895).

National politics in the 1880s and through the mid-1890s was fought closely between the two major parties. The Democrats in their bid for respectability, broad appeal, and electoral success in 1884 nominated Grover Cleveland, the Governor of New York, and in a closely contested election he won the presidency. Although Cleveland was no social reformer, he was honest and he was not as probusiness as was the Republican national leadership. Cleveland thought the protective tariff was too high, and he also favored passage of the Interstate Commerce Act of 1887. For these and other "offenses," the large trusts, manufacturers, and utilities vigorously backed and financed Cleveland's Republican opponent, Benjamin Harrison, in the 1888 election. Although Cleveland received more votes than did Harrison, the Republican won the electoral college vote and the presidency. The Republicans then proceeded to enact the highest protective tariff ever. They flouted civil service reform and passed pork barrel legislation in abundance. Corrupt Republican party bosses were seen as running the country. As a result, in the congressional elections of 1890 the Republican majority suffered substantial losses. In the 1892 rematch between Harrison and Cleveland, Cleveland won and the Democrats for the first time since before the Civil War also won control of both houses of Congress. Unfortunately for Cleveland and the Democratic party—as well as for the rest of the country—the nation's economy sank into the recession or panic of 1893 for which the Democrats were blamed. Cleveland's antiorganized labor actions, his hard currency progold anti-silver policies, and his generally conservative stands alienated many potential Democrats and led to the loss of party control by the Cleveland wing of the party in the tumultuous Democratic nominating convention of 1896.

This period, however, was marked by organization. In the economy, the trusts and the railroads organized their industries, thus reducing competition, setting prices, and standardizing trade practices. They not only organized economically but politically as well by sponsoring candidates for public office. Likewise, labor organized into unions, and the nation soon experienced large and sometimes violent strikes. The unions were just beginning in their attempt to exert political influence. Also, the nation's farmers were well organized through the state Granges and other farm organizations. Eventually, the more radical farmers found a receptive outlet in the Populist party.

Most midwestern state legislatures had been responsive to the complaints and needs of farmers and had enacted legislation regulating the prices the railroads could charge farmers for shipping their products. One such piece of legislation was in 1890 struck down by the Court in the **Minnesota Rate Case,** which used the due process clause as a legal formula to hamper government regulation. Significantly, between 1877 and 1890 seven justices who had been on the Court when *Munn* v. *Illinois* was decided were no longer serving. On the whole their replacements were more business and economic laissez-faire oriented.

The panic of 1893 had wide-ranging consequences. Immediately at hand was the fact that the federal treasury had a deficit. This, in turn, led to the enactment in 1894 of an income tax law that levied a flat 2 percent tax on all forms of income over $4000 per year. It was this exceedingly modest tax measure that led to the litigation that resulted in the Court declaring the tax unconstitutional in **Pollock** v. **Farmers' Loan and Trust Co.**

Another repercussion of the panic was the Cleveland Administration's effort to break up the sugar trust, using the Sherman Anti-Trust Act. But the Court frustrated the government's antitrust policies in *United States* v. *E.C. Knight Co.* The Interstate Commerce Commission (ICC) also became more activist during the second Cleveland Administration, but here too the Court displayed its antiregulation bias in the *ICC Case.*

The depression, of course, produced large numbers of unemployed. When these people staged a march on Washington, the federal authorities overreacted by making mass arrests (for walking on the grass). Perhaps it was the vision of hordes of the unemployed descending on Washington, the portrait of labor violence presented daily in the newspapers, the increasing attractiveness of socialism within certain intellectual and political circles (such as the Populist party), and finally, the passage of the "soak-the-rich" income tax that together pushed the conservative majority on the Court to its extreme negative stance in several significant decisions in the mid- and late 1890s.

The presidential election of 1896 was remarkable in many respects. First, it represented a sharp break in the pattern that had prevailed since the end of the Civil War of closely contested presidential elections with Democratic and Republican candidates espousing similar positions. In contrast, in 1896 the Democratic and Populist parties joined forces in nominating William Jennings Bryan, a fiery orator, friend of the farmer and "common man," advocate of unlimited coinage of silver, and enemy of the gold standard and big business. His opponent was the Republican protégé of big business, William McKinley. The election was also remarkable in that it clearly pitted rural America against the urban centers, as well as the South and to some extent the Midwest and the West against the Northeast. Bryan restored the Democratic party to its Jacksonian heritage, but failed to convince the urban underclass that the Democratic party could best advance their interests. The campaign was also unique in the unprecedented amounts of money spent (mostly by the Republicans). Sectional and class cleavages were clearly at a peak. And the election reshaped the structure of America's party system until the Great Depression of the 1930s.

These momentous political events no doubt reinforced the views of the conservative majority on the Court that their stands against threatening social forces and "radical" notions of public policy were appropriate positions to take. The Court continued the path it was on. Between 1897 and 1905 the Court decided 15 cases involving attempted regulation by the ICC and in all 15 cases the ICC lost. The Court was also bolder in its creation of constitutional law doctrines with which to protect business enterprise. (See, e.g., **Allgeyer** v. **Louisiana.**) And, of course, the Court in *Plessy* v. *Ferguson* rewrote the equal protection clause so that it became meaningless as a protector of the rights of blacks. **Lochner** v. **New York** and **Adair** v. **United States** also reflected deep-seated distrust of government regulation and the willingness of the Court majority to be creative constitutional interpreters on behalf of free enterprise.

The presidential election of 1900 was a rematch between McKinley and Bryan, with the Republican McKinley once again successful at the polls; only this time he had a new running mate, Theodore Roosevelt, the progressive-oriented Governor of New York. Roosevelt had been put on the ticket largely because as Governor he was a major nuisance to the New York bosses with his anticorruption activism and his reformist policies. To their horror, and to the initial shock of corporate America, Theodore Roosevelt became President in September 1901 following President McKinley's death by assassination. Roosevelt became President in an America of massive urban slums and sweatshops and widespread poverty. The United States at the turn of the cen-

tury was a nation in which a small fraction of the population owned the large majority of the nation's wealth. Although the idea that the federal government has the responsibility to finance and administer massive social programs was alien to most Americans, the concept of government economic regulation was not. Roosevelt, elected to a full presidential term in 1904, was the spokesman for government regulation, although his accomplishments in office were relatively modest when compared to his rhetoric. Yet there was great sentiment to correct the most glaring evils, and during the Roosevelt years dramatic prosecutions of some of the largest trusts began and several major pieces of reform legislation were enacted. The ICC was given new power with the passage of the Hepburn Act in 1906, and the Roosevelt Administration sponsored and saw enacted in that same year the Pure Food and Drug Act. Other progressive legislation was enacted during the Roosevelt years. The Progressive movement was also pleased with Roosevelt's activities in the area of conservation and his settlement of the mine workers' strike in 1902. For the first time, organized labor did not have an enemy in the White House.

The Supreme Court during the Roosevelt years moderated to some extent its laissez-faire activism, particularly when it came to antitrust prosecutions and railroad regulation. The Court, for example, in **Swift** v. **United States,** upheld the prosecution of the meat trust. The court upheld the Hepburn Act and now permitted railroad rate-fixing and other regulation. In 1904, in **McCray** v. **United States,** the Court was also most permissive in allowing Congress to use its taxing power to regulate. In general, the Court during the Roosevelt years and particularly his second term seemed to be more tolerant of the efforts of federal government regulation, although the Court made it clear in *Adair* v. *United States* that it was not prepared to abandon its antiunion bias. As for state regulation this was, of course, the period of the antilabor *Lochner* decision. But just three years later the Court, in effect, ignored *Lochner* and upheld Oregon's hours legislation in **Muller** v. **Oregon.**

PROGRESSIVE POLITICS THROUGH WORLD WAR I

The Progressive Era saw a number of reforms being promoted at the municipal, state, and federal levels. At the municipal and state levels, Progressives focused much of their attention on reforming the political process itself, making it, or so they thought, more responsive to the will of the majority and more representative of majority sentiments. Progressives devoted much of their energies to breaking the power of the urban political "machines" by promoting such devices as the direct primary and recall of public officials. Policymaking was to be democratized by reforms such as the initiative and the referendum. Progressives also turned their attention to substantive social and economic policy. Minimum wages and maximum hours legislation, the regulation of child labor, the right of workers to form labor organizations, and workmen's compensation were among the major social reforms advocated. Regulation of railroad rates, monopolies, and business practices affecting consumers were among other matters of concern.

The Court's record with regard to the states was mixed. The Court held firm in following the reasoning offered in *Adair* v. *United States*, striking down a state law prohibiting the use of the so-called yellow-dog contract (*Coppage* v. *Kansas*, 236 U.S. 1 [1915]). But in the 1917 case of **Bunting** v. **Oregon,** the Court ignored the *Lochner* precedent and upheld an Oregon wages and hours statute that applied to men and women and included bakers among the protected occupations! Overall, the Court in the decade beginning in 1910 invalidated more state legislation than in any previous decade in the Court's history.

In the federal sphere Progressives vigorously advocated the use of a federal police power to attack the social and economic problems that could best be dealt with nationally. Progressives urged Congress to use its commerce and taxing powers for these purposes, and the Court in *Champion* v. *Ames,* 188 U.S. 321 (1903), and *McCray* v. *United States* had, in effect, seemingly given its approval.

During the Roosevelt, Taft, and Wilson administrations, progressive federal legislation was enacted, and much of it was upheld by the Court. The Roosevelt Administration was responsible for the Food and Drug Act of 1906 upheld in 1911 in *Hipolite Egg Co.* v. *United States,* 220 U.S. 45; the Meat Inspection Acts of 1906 and 1907 upheld in *Pittsburgh Melting Co.* v. *Totten,* 248 U.S. 1 (1918); and the 1906 Hepburn Act rejuvenating the ICC upheld in 1910 in *ICC* v. *Chicago, Rock Island, and Pacific Railway Co.,* 218 U.S. 88. But the antitrust prosecution of Standard Oil, although upheld by the Court, was done on the Court's own terms; that is, the Court declared that it would determine whether or not a trust was reasonable. Only trusts or monopolies "unreasonable" in the eyes of the Court could be prosecuted.

In 1908 Theodore Roosevelt handpicked William Howard Taft to be the Republican party presidential nominee. Taft, who had been Roosevelt's Secretary of War, was victorious over Democrat William Jennings Bryan, who made his third and final try for the presidency. Taft's presidency was moderately progressive, but Taft lacked the dynamism and charisma of Roosevelt. During his term, Congress enacted the White Slave Traffic Act of 1910 (also known as the Mann Act, aimed at interstate prostitution rings), which the Court later upheld. Also under Taft's presidency the Congress in 1910 enacted the Mann-Elkins Act that conferred upon the ICC original rate-setting powers that the Court also upheld.

Taft did not live up to what the Progressives expected of him, and Theodore Roosevelt therefore decided to attempt to wrest the Republican presidential nomination from him in 1912. When Taft won renomination, Roosevelt and his followers bolted the convention and formed a new political party, the Progressive party. The Democrats nominated New Jersey Governor Woodrow Wilson. The deep cleavage within the Republican ranks resulted in Wilson's victory with a plurality of the vote. Taft came in an embarrassing third.

Woodrow Wilson's presidency was marked not only by a progressive outlook, particularly in terms of regulation of the economy, but also by a presidential activism virtually unprecedented. Wilson formulated his program, the executive branch drafted legislation, and the President took an active role in persuading key congressmen to support administration bills. Enacted during Wilson's presidency were the Harrison Anti-Narcotics Act of 1914, the Child Labor Acts of 1916 and 1919, a federal income tax law, the Federal Reserve Act creating the Federal Reserve Board, the Clayton Anti-Trust Act (that exempted labor from antitrust law), the Federal Trade Commission Act, legislation creating five other important commissions, and the Adamson Act of 1916, providing for an eight-hour day for railroad workers. In addition, much wartime legislation bestowed on the federal government vast powers, including the right to take over industries and to nationalize the railroads.

Woodrow Wilson ran for reelection in 1916; his opponent was Charles Evans Hughes, who resigned a seat on the Supreme Court to accept the Republican party presidential nomination—the only justice in American history to resign from the Court for such a reason. Wilson won a narrow electoral victory, and barely 30 days after his second inauguration he was leading a nation at war.

World War I was a totally new experience for the nation. The country was mobilized, the federal government assumed vast new powers, and for the first time since the Sedition Act of 1798, Congress enacted repressive leg-

islation stifling freedom of expression. The Espionage Act of 1917 was tested and upheld in 1919 by the Court in **Schenck** v. **United States** and the Sedition Act of 1918 met with Court approval the following year in **Abrams** v. **United States.** Although Justice Holmes' opinion for the Court in *Schenck* was based on the new standard of "clear and present danger," that *only* speech that is a clear-and-present danger to society can be prohibited, the majority quickly abandoned that standard, and the lower courts ignored it in the over 1500 prosecutions under the Espionage and Sedition Acts.[9] Civil liberties were to fare even worse after the end of the war as the Attorney General, A. Mitchell Palmer, conducted a campaign first against the labor movement and then against domestic radicals, which resulted in mass arrests on New Year's Day of 1920. Palmer disregarded habeas corpus and eventually saw to it that 556 aliens who were communists or who otherwise held radical political views were deported. Palmer was able to whip up national support for his travesty of the Bill of Rights by virtue of his demagogic skills and the fact that President Wilson was gravely ill and for the last two years of his presidency was not in full control.

During the war, Congress enacted sweeping legislation giving the executive branch of government unprecedented power over the economy. In 1917 the Court upheld the Adamson Act in *Wilson* v. *New,* 243 U.S. 332, and in 1924 indicated its approval of the way the railroads were treated by the government in *Dayton–Goose Creek Railway Co.* v. *United States,* 263 U.S. 456. The Court upheld the military draft, and the prohibition statute enacted before the Eighteenth Amendment became part of the Constitution. However, a bare majority rejected the Child Labor Act of 1916 passed under Congress' commerce

[9]Richard Hofstadter, William Miller, and Daniel Aaron, *The United States: The History of a Republic* (Englewood Cliffs, N.J.: Prentice Hall, 1957), p. 618.

power. The 1918 decision in **Hammer** v. **Dagenhart** is in many ways shocking. The five-man majority, using the theory of dual federalism, took a narrow view of Congress' commerce powers and argued that allowing Congress to regulate child labor would mark the end of our federal system of government. All this was in the service of an institution that, in Justice Holmes' words, led to the "ruined lives" of children. Yet the majority was undoubtedly reacting to what must have appeared to be a host of frightening national events, with the federal government taking over the railroads and being armed with the power under 1917 legislation to take over other industries as well. During the war the federal government dominated nearly every facet of the national economy. The decision in *Hammer* v. *Dagenhart* should probably be considered within this context. Ironically, if President Wilson had picked a true progressive for the filling of his first Court vacancy instead of James C. McReynolds, who turned out to be reactionary in his social and economic views, there would have been a majority for upholding the Child Labor Act. However, it should be pointed out that progressives had achieved some success at the state level, so that by 1914 most states had established a minimum age for employing children, with 14 as the usual age set by the northern states and 12 in the southern states. By 1930 some 41 states had enacted legislation restricting the use of child labor. The problem of child labor was nevertheless a serious one that was not to be solved until the late 1930s.

Other momentous constitutional events stemming from the Progressive Era were (1) the adoption of the Sixteenth Amendment that reversed the *Income Tax Decision,* thereby permitting a federal income tax directed at individuals and businesses; (2) the Seventeenth Amendment providing for the direct election of U.S. senators; (3) the Eighteenth Amendment prohibiting the manufacture, sale, or transportation of intoxicating liquors; and (4)

the Nineteenth Amendment giving women the right to vote. The adoption of these four amendments in less than a decade represented successful constitutional amendment activity surpassed only by the 1790s, when the Bill of Rights became part of the Constitution.

RETURN TO NORMALCY

By 1920 most Americans appeared exhausted by progressive politics, World War I, and the hysteria produced by the Red scare initiated by Attorney General Palmer. In the 1920 presidential election the electorate was presented with the Harding-Coolidge Republican ticket, offering what Harding called a return to "normalcy," less government activity and hoopla, less government regulation of business, and more reliance on the forces of capitalism to bring about a better life for all. The Democrats ran a progressive ticket headed by Ohio Governor James Cox and former Assistant Secretary of the Navy Franklin D. Roosevelt. Normalcy prevailed.

Early in his administration Harding had the opportunity to fill four vacancies on the Court, and all four positions were filled by more conservative men than those they replaced. National politics, and the Court even more, took a sharp turn to the right.

Harding died in office in 1923 and Vice-President Calvin Coolidge assumed the presidency. Although the widespread corruption of the Harding Administration burst open during Coolidge's first months in office, he managed to contain the political damage enough to be elected President in 1924. Coolidge declined the opportunity to be renominated in 1928, and the Republican nomination went to Herbert Hoover. The Democrats chose the Governor of New York, Al Smith, who was also the first Roman Catholic to receive a major party presidential nomination. Once again the Republicans captured the White House and Congress. But before his first year in office was completed, Hoover was faced with the greatest economic depression the country had ever experienced.

The 1920s was a decade of impressive material advance. National income, which in 1915 was approximately $35 billion, reached over $80 billion by 1929. Production of durable consumer goods rose by 72 percent over the seven-year period ending in 1929.[10] The 1920s was also the decade of the nation's experiment with Prohibition and the resultant rash of bootlegging operations and flouting of the law.

In the early 1920s the newly reconstituted Supreme Court gave short shrift to social legislation stemming from the Progressive Era. In **Adkins** v. **Children's Hospital,** the majority revived the *Lochner* precedent that had been ignored previously in *Bunting,* and substantive due process was used to stifle wages and hours legislation. In **Bailey** v. **Drexel Furniture Company,** the Court invalidated 1919 legislation that attempted to regulate child labor along the same lines as the 1916 act but utilizing the Congress' taxing powers. The *McCray* precedent was not followed, and the federal government was stripped of its police power in this major problem area. Stolen automobiles, however, seemed a more serious problem to the justices than child labor, and the Court in *Brooks* v. *United States,* 267 U.S. 432 (1925), upheld the National Motor Vehicle Theft Act as a valid exercise of Congress' commerce powers. In a series of cases involving state regulation of business practices, the Court struck down state legislation on due process grounds in over 80 decisions.[11]

The Court's record in civil liberties during the 1920s, although decidedly mixed, was more liberal than its record vis-à-vis government economic regulation and social legislation. The Court in *Meyer* v. *Nebraska,* 262 U.S. 390 (1923), scored a minor breakthrough

in supporting First Amendment freedoms under the due process clause of the Fourteenth Amendment. Here, substantive due process was placed in the service of civil liberties. The "liberty" of the due process clause was not strictly confined to the economic liberty of businessmen. In **Gitlow** v. **New York** the Court, although upholding Gitlow's conviction of criminal anarchy under a New York statute, nevertheless made a major concession to civil libertarians by assuming that First Amendment freedoms of speech and press were among those liberties protected by the Fourteenth Amendment's due process clause. Substantive due process was now being offered, at least in theory, as a vehicle to protect civil liberties. In fact, the Court, two years after *Gitlow,* in *Fiske* v. *Kansas,* 274 U.S. 380 (1927), overturned a state criminal anarchy conviction seemingly on substantive due process grounds. Justice Brandeis, in his famous concurring opinion in **Whitney** v. **California,** sought to revive the clear-and-present danger standard as a potential means by which to protect political speech. The Court turned its attention further to criminal procedures; in *Moore* v. *Dempsey,* 261 U.S. 86 (1923), for the first time it reversed a state conviction on the ground that a fair trial was not provided, contrary to the requirements of the Fourteenth Amendment.

THE GREAT DEPRESSION AND AMERICAN POLITICS

Herbert Hoover, elected President in 1928, came to office with a sterling reputation. He had been well known for his relief work during and after World War I, and he was known during his tenure as Coolidge's Secretary of Commerce as a man of outstanding administrative ability. Hoover was identified with the more progressive wing of the Republican Party, although he was fundamentally business oriented. When the nation slid into the Depression, Hoover, although he tried, was unable to

---

[10]These figures are cited in Kelly and Harbison, op. cit., p. 646.

[11]Wright, op. cit., p. 113.

cope adequately with what became the greatest economic crisis ever faced by the nation. In 1932 Hoover ran for reelection, but he was faced by a Democratic party led by New York Governor Franklin D. Roosevelt. The Democrats blamed the Depression on Hoover and the Republicans. The electorate seemed to agree, in not only electing Roosevelt by an electoral college landslide, but electing an overwhelmingly Democratic Congress (Democrats outnumbered Republicans in the House by 310 to 117 and in the Senate by 60 to 36).

President Roosevelt promised the nation a "new deal," and the first 100 days of his administration saw unprecedented action and legislation to cope with the crisis and to lessen its impact on people and the different segments of the economy.

In the early days of the Depression, some of the states sought to deal with their people's severe problems, and at first the Supreme Court was sympathetic. The Court in 1934, at the high point of its permissiveness toward the states, approved a Minnesota mortgage moratorium statute in which foreclosures on farms and houses were forbidden for a period of up to three years. The case was **Home Building and Loan Association** v. **Blaisdell,** and in it the Court ruled the Minnesota law a valid exercise of the state's police power in order to protect the public welfare during the period of extreme economic emergency. Also in 1934 the Court sustained the New York Milk Price Control Act in *Nebbia* v. *New York,* 291 U.S. 502.

The congressional election of 1934 proved to be a tremendous vote of confidence for the New Deal and the Roosevelt Administration. Democratic majorities in the House and Senate increased (including a gain of ten seats in the Senate). Although the New Deal programs took the sharp edge from the Depression, the country still faced serious economic difficulties. During early 1935 there was much labor unrest, and many Americans began demanding more fundamental reform of American in-

stitutions. It was then that the New Deal took a sharp turn to the left and the Roosevelt Administration sponsored such measures as a Wealth Tax, the Social Security Act, the Works Progress Administration (WPA) program, legislation ending holding companies, and the National Labor Relations Act recognizing and protecting labor's right to organize. At this time the Supreme Court began invalidating New Deal programs in suits before the Court.

In the 16 months starting in January 1935, the Supreme Court heard cases involving ten major New Deal measures or actions; eight of them were declared unconstitutional by the Court. Struck down as unconstitutional were (1) the New Deal code of fair practices for the oil industry in *Panama Refining Company* v. *Ryan,* 293 U.S. 388 (1935); (2) the National Industrial Recovery Act itself in **Schechter Poultry Corp.** v. **United States;** (3) the Railroad Retirement Act of 1934 that provided for pensions for older railway employees forced to retire under the terms of the act in *Railroad Retirement Board* v. *Alton Railroad Company,* 295 U.S. 330 (1935); (4) the Farm Mortgage Law providing for a moratorium on mortgage payments (patterned after the previously upheld Minnesota statute) in *Louisville Bank* v. *Radford,* 295 U.S. 555 (1935); (5) President Roosevelt's removal of an obstructionist on a regulatory commission in **Humphrey's Executor** v. **United States,** which contradicted a broad presidential removal power recognized by the Court only nine years earlier (when a conservative Republican was President) in **Myers** v. **United States;** (6) the Agricultural Adjustment Act of 1933 in **United States** v. **Butler;** (7) the Bituminous Coal Act in **Carter** v. **Carter Coal Company;** and (8) the Municipal Bankruptcy Act of 1934 in *Ashton* v. *Cameron County District,* 298 U.S. 513 (1936). In 1935 the Court, however, upheld the emergency monetary enactments of 1933, particularly Congress' nullification of gold clauses in public and private contracts, in *The Gold*

Clause Cases, 294 U.S. 240. Justice McReynolds was so angry with this decision of his colleagues in the majority that he announced in open court that "this is Nero at his worst—the Constitution is gone." The Court also approved the Tennessee Valley Authority legislation in *Ashwander* v. *TVA,* 297 U.S. 288 (1936), and presidential control over foreign policy in **United States** v. **Curtiss-Wright Export Corporation.**

In economic matters the states also encountered resistance from the Court. One major case from New York in 1936 that caused an uproar was **Morehead** v. **Tipaldo,** in which the state's minimum wage legislation was struck down.

The 1930s were years of grave economic deprivation for many Americans. In terms of civil rights and civil liberties, there were also some hardships imposed on minority groups and political nonconformists as a result of racial prejudice and demagoguery at the state or local levels. The Court during the early to mid-1930s was, however, more sympathetic to civil liberties claims than it had been before 1930. In **Near** v. **Minnesota** the majority delivered a landmark defense of freedom of the press that firmly established that First Amendment liberty as one not to be denied by the states. In **Powell** v. **Alabama,** the first of the so-called Scottsboro cases, the Court established certain criminal procedural rights as part of Fourteenth Amendment due process: the right of all persons to employ counsel *and* the right of poor people to court-appointed counsel in capital cases. In the second Scottsboro case, *Norris* v. *Alabama,* 294 U.S. 587 (1935), the exclusion of blacks from Alabama trial juries was held to violate the Fourteenth Amendment. And in *Brown* v. *Mississippi,* 297 U.S. 278 (1936), the Court overturned convictions based on confessions obtained from black defendants through the use of torture.

Chapter

3

The Political and Historical Setting of the Development of Constitutional Law, 1937–1991

CONFRONTATION WITH ROOSEVELT

As will be recalled from our discussion in the previous chapter, in 1935 and 1936 the Supreme Court struck down as unconstitutional legislation regulating the oil industry, agriculture, and other segments of the national economy. The Railroad Retirement Act of 1934 was invalidated and so was national mortgage moratorium legislation. Progressive state laws such as New York's minimum wage act were attacked by the Court. Undoubtedly, if the Court had had its way, the New Deal would have been dismantled. The national election in November 1936, however, indicated that Americans vigorously supported President Roosevelt and the direction the New Deal had taken. Shortly thereafter, Roosevelt formulated his strategy for removing what he saw as the main obstacle to national recovery.

On February 5, 1937, President Roosevelt

unveiled a proposal for court reform. Under the terms of the proposed legislation, the President would be able to appoint as many as six new justices. Each justice who had served ten years or more on the Court would, upon reaching the age of 70, be expected to retire within six months. If the justice chose not to retire, the President would have the authority to make a new appointment to the Court, thereby increasing its membership to a maximum size of 15 justices. Initially, Roosevelt blandly asserted as the rationale for his plan that the elderly justices were unable to keep up with the Court's work—a falsehood that was eventually to undermine the President's credibility.

About as soon as the plan was announced it generated controversy and was quickly dubbed the "Court-packing" plan. Even some Roosevelt supporters in Congress were profoundly disturbed at the thought of tampering with the Supreme Court. President Roosevelt, in an address to the nation on March 9, 1937, was more forthright than he had been earlier about the real reasons for his Court plan. He told the American people, "We have . . . reached the point as a nation where we must take action to save the Constitution from the Court and the Court from itself."[1]

One of the leading opponents of the Court bill was the Democratic New Deal senator from Montana, Burton K. Wheeler. Justice Brandeis' wife was an old friend of the Wheeler family, and in mid-March 1937 she paid a social call on Senator Wheeler's daughter, who lived outside Washington in Alexandria, Virginia. At the end of the visit, as Mrs. Brandeis was half out the door, she remarked, "You tell your obstinate father we think he is making a courageous fight."[2] Senator Wheeler quickly got the message and made immediate contact with Justice Brandeis. The two men met on Friday afternoon, March 19. Justice Brandeis suggested that Senator Wheeler meet with Chief Justice Hughes, to which Wheeler responded, "I don't know the Chief Justice!" Justice Brandeis snapped back, "But the Chief Justice knows you and what you're doing."[3] The meeting with the Chief Justice occurred the next morning and the two men agreed that Chief Justice Hughes would prepare a letter for Senator Wheeler that would present in detail the evidence demonstrating that the President's original charges of court inefficiency and backlogs were false. On Sunday afternoon, March 21, the Chief Justice hand-delivered the letter to the Senator, and the next day Senator Wheeler made it public. One week later, on March 29, the constitutional revolution of 1937 began as the Court

handed down the **West Coast Hotel** v. **Parrish** decision upholding a state minimum wage law and in the process overturning **Morehead** v. **Tipaldo, Adkins** v. **Children's Hospital,** and **Lochner** v. **New York.** That same day the Court also upheld the national farm mortgage moratorium act of 1935 and the amended Railway Labor Act of 1934. Some weeks later, the Court upheld both the National Labor Relations Act in **National Labor Relations Board** v. **Jones & Laughlin Steel Corp.** and various provisions of the Social Security Act including the unemployment compensation program in **Steward Machine Company** v. **Davis.**

On May 18, Justice Van Devanter announced his intention of retiring at the end of the term; thus President Roosevelt would have his first opportunity to name a New Deal supporter to the Court. The shift of the Court itself, Chief Justice Hughes' letter to Senator Wheeler, and the Van Devanter retirement took the urgency from the President's Court-packing plan. In addition, the death of the leading senatorial supporter of the bill, Senator Robinson of Arkansas, hampered Roosevelt's efforts in the Senate. In the end the bill was unfavorably reported out of committee on June 14 by a vote of 10 opposed to 8 for the bill. Finally, on July 22, the Senate voted, 70 to 20, to return the bill to the Senate Judiciary Committee, thus effectively killing the legislation. As has often been said, however, the President lost the battle but won the war.

By the end of 1939, Roosevelt had appointed a majority of the justices on the Court. The newly constituted Court had no trouble legitimating major congressional regulatory legislation. Congress in 1938 enacted the Fair Labor Standards Act that utilized Congress' commerce powers as the basis for mandating minimum wages, maximum hours, and the regulation of child labor. The Agricultural Adjustment Act (AAA) of 1938 also was based on Congress' commerce powers and resulted in the virtually complete control of agricultural production and marketing. In subsequent

[1]President Roosevelt's address is reprinted in part in Thomas P. Jahnige and Sheldon Goldman (eds.), *The Federal Judicial System* (New York: Holt, Rinehart and Winston, 1968), pp. 341–342.

[2]As quoted in Alpheus T. Mason, *Brandeis: A Free Man's Life* (New York: Viking, 1946), p. 626.

[3]Ibid.

amendments to the AAA, even crops grown solely for on-the-farm use were subject to government control. In a series of decisions in the late 1930s and early 1940s, the Court accepted even the most extreme congressional legislation and in so doing overturned the old negative doctrines. In particular, the Court in *Mulford* v. *Smith,* 307 U.S. 38 (1939), and **Wickard** v. **Filburn** upheld the AAA of 1938 and its 1941 amendments. In **United States** v. **Darby,** the Fair Labor Standards Act of 1938 was upheld.

THE YEARS BEFORE THE WAR

Events in Europe and the Far East during the 1930s grew increasingly ominous. Fascism in all its totalitarian and militaristic glory was on the march. Premier Mussolini of Italy invaded and conquered Ethiopia in October 1935. In 1936, Spanish fascists initiated a Civil War in Spain and, with the help of Nazi Germany and Italy, ultimately overthrew the Republican government in March 1939. In 1937, Japan invaded northern China. In August 1939, Nazi Germany and the Soviet Union signed a non-aggression pact. Within two weeks Hitler's Germany invaded and overran Poland and World War II began.

Against this turbulent world backdrop, the presidential election of 1940 was held, and Franklin Roosevelt was elected to an unprecedented third term. The United States, however, stayed out of the war until the Japanese attack on Pearl Harbor on December 7, 1941.

The Supreme Court during these prewar years became increasingly concerned with questions of civil liberties. The brutal suppression of basic freedoms by the totalitarian regimes, particularly in the Soviet Union and Nazi Germany, undoubtedly made many Americans more self-conscious of the basic rights guaranteed by the Constitution. The hideous racism of the Nazis in all likelihood sensitized the justices and others to the need to improve America's treatment of its racial minorities. A number of Supreme Court decisions during this period recognized these newly salient issues. The Court early on signaled its new constitutional priorities in a footnote—footnote 4 of an economic decision in 1938, *United States* v. *Carolene Products Co.,* 304 U.S. 144.

The *Carolene Products* case concerned an act of Congress that prohibited from interstate commerce the shipment of filled milk (milk with skimmed milk and vegetable fat added). The Court upheld the legislation and Justice Stone for the majority made clear what had been apparent during the preceding year. Stone's opinion reflected the fact that a new constitutional order had arrived whereby the new majority would take a liberal reading of Congress' powers and would no longer substitute its views for Congress' views of social and economic policy. Economic regulation was to be given the presumption of constitutionality. At this point, footnote 4 occurred:

There may be narrower scope for operation of the presumption of constitutionality when legislation appears on its face to be within a specific prohibition of the Constitution, such as those of the first ten amendments, which are deemed equally specific when held to be embraced within the Fourteenth.

It is unnecessary to consider now whether legislation which restricts those political processes which can ordinarily be expected to bring about repeal of undesirable legislation, is to be subjected to more exacting judicial scrutiny under the general prohibitions of the Fourteenth Amendment than are most other types of legislation. . . .

Nor need we enquire whether similar considerations enter into the review of statutes directed at particular religious or national or racial minorities. . . . whether prejudice against discrete and insular minorities may be a special condition, which tends seriously to curtail the operation of those political processes ordinarily to be relied upon to protect minorities, and which may call for a correspondingly more searching judicial inquiry.[4]

Admittedly, the new approach to civil liberties was cautiously and tentatively presented. By 1939, however, what had lurked in the footnotes leaped to the main text and became the doctrine of several cases. The Court now acknowledged that freedom of speech and press are "rights so vital to the maintenance of democratic institutions" that "the courts should be astute to examine the effect of the challenged legislation."[5] No presumption of constitutionality was to be given to statutes that on their face impinged upon these basic rights. Indeed, the Court was to develop this argument into what became known as the "preferred position" doctrine. According to this doctrine, First Amendment freedoms are the most important of our civil liberties, for they are essential to maintain our democratic system of government. Consequently, they must be tenaciously defended by the Court against governmental encroachment. As the Court was to say in the wartime decision of *Murdock* v. *Pennsylvania,* 319 U.S. 105 (1943), "Freedom of press, freedom of speech, freedom of religion are in a preferred [constitutional] position."

Although organized labor had a firm ally in the Roosevelt Administration and received important legislative protection by way of the National Labor Relations Act, some states nevertheless remained hotbeds of antiunion sentiment. The state of Alabama, for example, made picketing a criminal offense. The Court in the 1940 case of **Thornhill** v. **Alabama** struck down the Alabama law and extended First Amendment protection to peaceful picketing. Once again the Supreme Court was emphasizing the distinctiveness of America's heritage of democracy and personal freedoms

[4]United States v. Carolene Products Co., 304 U.S. 144 (1938), at pp. 152–154.

[5]Schneider v. State, 308 U.S. 147 (1939), at p. 161.

that stood in marked contrast to the brutal dictatorships of the 1930s. The right to travel to look for work or for any other reason was furthered in **Edwards** v. **California** in 1941.

In the realm of the rights of the accused, the Court took a liberal view when it came to the federal criminal process. For example, in *Johnson* v. *Zerbst,* 304 U.S. 458 (1938), the Court ruled that the Sixth Amendment requires that in the federal courts any criminal defendant too poor to hire a lawyer has the right to a court-appointed lawyer. Federal law until then had required the appointment of counsel only in capital cases. When it came to state criminal procedures, however, the Court was more cautious, but even so, in **Palko** v. **Connecticut** the Court asserted that fundamental rights, implicit in the concept of ordered liberty, were to be honored by the states.

In a decade in which the world saw the horrible implementation of racism in Nazi Germany, the Supreme Court began to turn its attention to America's principal racial minority—black Americans. In several cases the Court ruled that separate must also be truly equal. These rulings, although welcomed, did not begin to touch the fundamental problem of American racism. America entered World War II fighting for democracy with a segregated army and with separate-but-equal still comfortably enshrined in American constitutional law.

AMERICA AND WORLD WAR II

With the Japanese surprise attack on Pearl Harbor on December 7, 1941, the United States entered the war. War places a great strain on the fabric of society. In a time of total war, extraordinary measures are taken in terms of governmental control of the economy and governmental regulation of civil liberties. The Court had no trouble in finding constitutional the vast assertion of governmental economic regulation, but, when it came to civil liberties, the Court was more sensitive to claims of personal freedoms than it ever had been during earlier wartime periods. The Jehovah's Witnesses were involved in a series of cases decided during the war and, for the most part, the Court supported their civil liberty claims against the exercise of police powers by states and municipalities.

The Court in 1940, as Europe was being overrun by the fascists, decided the first flag-salute case, **Minersville** v. **Gobitis,** involving the freedom of religion claims of Jehovah's Witnesses. The Court upheld the compulsory flag salute, reasoning that it furthered the overriding value of national unity because ''national unity is the basis of national security.'' But just two years later in another Jehovah's Witnesses case, three justices who had been in the *Gobitis* majority announced that their views had changed and that they would now vote to overturn *Gobitis*. Two new justices came to the Court, Jackson and Rutledge, and the Court in 1943 took another flag-salute case. In **West Virginia State Board of Education** v. **Barnette,** a new Court majority reversed the *Gobitis* decision and ruled that the compulsory flag salute violated First Amendment freedoms.

Unfortunately, and quite tragically for the nation, the attack on Pearl Harbor by Japan unleashed a wave of hysteria and racial prejudice aimed at Japanese Americans and Japanese resident aliens. The end results were drastic governmental measures applied to 70,000 American citizens of Japanese descent and 42,000 Japanese resident aliens residing on the West Coast and in part of Arizona. These measures included a curfew and subsequently the forcible removal of these people to ten ''relocation centers'' in seven western states. There was great suffering, psychological and emotional trauma, and the loss of millions of dollars worth of property and personal belongings. American citizens, none of whom was ever convicted of espionage or sabotage and many of whose relatives were fighting in the American army, were shipped off to the camps, placed behind barbed wire, and forced to live in primitive facilities. The inevitable constitutional tests followed in **Hirabayashi** v. **United States** and **Korematsu** v. **United States.** In those cases the Court upheld the federal government, but in *Ex Parte Endo*, 323 U.S. 283, decided the same day in 1944 as *Korematsu*, the Court ruled that once the loyalty of a detainee had been established, that person could no longer be interned. This was important because the War Relocation Authority had formulated regulations governing the release of camp inmates. Release of those whose loyalty had been determined was permitted only if they had the assurance of a job *and* a place to live in a community approved by the War Relocation Authority. The authority, in most instances, did not approve of the Japanese returning to their homes. But the Court forcefully invalidated these restrictions.

The Court also had occasion to consider the issue of military commissions trying civilians. In *Duncan* v. *Kahanamoku*, 327 U.S. 304 (1946), the Court without explicitly restating **Ex Parte Milligan,** nevertheless came to essentially the same result. Civilians were to be tried by the civil courts when those courts were open and functioning.

POSTWAR AND COLD WAR POLITICS

When Chief Justice Vinson took office in 1946, the country had just concluded its total involvement in World War II. The economy had been subjected to massive controls and with the end of the war most of these were lifted. The immediate result was a dramatic rise in the rate of monetary inflation. Organized labor conducted a series of strikes in 1946; the particularly damaging ones in the mines and railroads, which threatened economically to paralyze the country, were dealt with by federal governmental seizure ordered by President Truman. Such presidential actions helped stimulate labor and management to reach settlements. Nevertheless, inflation, strikes, and even occasional food shortages provided issues that politically damaged the Democratic party in the 1946 congressional elections. The Republicans gained control of both houses of Congress for the first time since 1930, and the Republicans won impressive gubernatorial and other local victories throughout much of the country. President Truman's popularity seemed to be at a low ebb, and Republicans eagerly anticipated recapturing the White House in the 1948 presidential election.

The constitutionality of the power of government, both federal and state, to enact social welfare legislation was once again affirmed by the Court, but this time in the controversial area of aiding parochial schools. The 1947 decision of **Everson** v. **Board of Education** can be seen as a strong statement on behalf of the welfare state despite the most disturbing questions of separation of church and state raised by the case.

Two major public policy issue areas emerged in the postwar period. The first concerned the Cold War and domestic subversives and the second, the civil rights of black Americans.

Republican politicians harshly accused the Truman Administration of harboring Soviet sympathizers and employing communists in sensitive government positions. The soft-on-communists charge stung Truman, and the charges seemed to have credibility since Truman's Secretary of Commerce, Henry A. Wallace, was known to be sympathetic to the Soviet Union. When Wallace left his Cabinet post and eventually formed the extreme left Progressive party to challenge Truman's reelection campaign in 1948, the worst earlier fears appeared confirmed. Furthermore, disturbing instances of spying were coming to public attention. When the Soviet Union developed the atom bomb, it was considered a foregone conclusion that the secrets of nuclear power were stolen from the United States through the work of communist spies in and out of government. Against this back-

drop, President Truman ordered the institution of a loyalty program to screen out communist sympathizers from the employ of the federal government. In addition, the President ordered the Justice Department to look into the activities of the American Communist party for possible prosecution. In the 1948 presidential election year, the Justice Department launched a prosecution of the 11 top Communist party leaders whose eventual convictions were upheld by the Supreme Court in **Dennis** v. **United States.**

Not only did President Truman face the Cold War–domestic subversives issue, but he also confronted the long-festering problem of the denial of basic civil rights to black Americans. On February 2, 1948, President Truman presented to Congress a comprehensive civil rights program—that promptly died in a Congress dominated by segregationists. Five months later, when the Democratic National Convention adopted a strong civil rights plank for the party platform, most of the southern delegates walked out of the convention. The rebellious southern Democrats formed the new States' Rights party and nominated then South Carolina Governor Strom Thurmond as its presidential candidate.

President Truman entered the presidential election campaign in 1948 with both the extreme left and right wings of the Democratic party having abandoned him, forming third parties and running their own presidential candidates. The Republicans fielded New York Governor Thomas E. Dewey and his running mate California Governor Earl Warren. Dewey conducted an overconfident and bland campaign buoyed by public opinion polls predicting a Republican landslide. Harry Truman refused to concede defeat; instead, he waged a vigorous, aggressive campaign. In the end, Truman pulled off the most stunning upset in American political history, winning both the electoral and popular votes by a comfortable margin. Furthermore, he brought with him dramatic Democratic congressional victories that resulted in the Democrats regaining control of both houses of Congress.

The subversives-in-government issue gained new life when the civil war in China was won by the communists at the end of 1949 and when Wisconsin Republican Senator Joseph McCarthy in a speech on February 11, 1950, charged that 57 communists were working in the State Department. The intense media interest in McCarthy's charges was maintained as McCarthy made more and more charges of communists and communist sympathizers in government. In the context of increasing anticommunist hysteria, the invasion of South Korea on June 25, 1950, by communist North Korea and the ensuing Korean War involvement of the United States enhanced the McCarthy movement. The war was technically a United Nations peacekeeping operation or "police action" and President Truman did not seek a formal congressional declaration of war. Yet a wartime economy was necessary, and when in the spring of 1952 the steelworkers were about to go on strike, the President ordered the Secretary of Commerce to take over the steel mills. This immediately produced litigation that was expedited through the courts and decided by the Supreme Court in the **Youngstown Sheet and Tube Co.** v. **Sawyer** case.

Although civil rights legislation occupied a prominent place within the Truman Fair Deal and Truman himself unilaterally desegregated the armed forces, no civil rights legislation was forthcoming from Congress. Various northern states enacted legislation prohibiting racial discrimination by employers in their hiring practices and outlawing discrimination in the sale or rental of housing, but there was little enforcement and, of course, in many states there was not even the symbolic significance of having an antidiscrimination law on the statute books. The Supreme Court supported antidiscrimination state activity in the case of *Bob-Lo Excursion Co.* v. *Michigan,* 333 U.S. 28 (1948), and in the case of *Shelley* v.

Kraemer, 334 U.S. 1 (1948), it ruled that racially restrictive covenants (agreements not to sell one's home to a black) were unenforceable in a court of law. In **Sweatt** v. **Painter** and a companion case, the Court struck at racial discrimination in professional education. But in other areas of civil liberties the Court more generally reflected the moderate conservatism of the country.

The 1950 congressional elections saw the issues of inflation, the Korean War, and communists-in-government being emphasized by Republicans, who made major congressional gains. They increased their House membership by 28 seats and came within 2 seats of controlling the Senate. The country was moving further to the right and the Republicans once again sensed victory. But unlike 1948, this time (1952) they won with General Dwight D. Eisenhower as the standard bearer and California Senator Richard M. Nixon as his running mate.

THE AGE OF EISENHOWER AND THE GROWING CIVIL RIGHTS REVOLUTION

The Eisenhower victory in 1952 was a landslide and the Republicans managed to pick up enough seats so that they were able to control, narrowly, both houses of Congress. Senator Joseph McCarthy, by virtue of the Republican majority in the Senate, became Chairman of the Senate Government Operations Committee; using that position he embarked upon a series of investigations of communists in government departments and agencies. The climax of this crusade occurred in the spring of 1954 with the televised hearings of McCarthy's investigation of the army, which had the unintended effect of dramatizing McCarthy's demagoguery and the fraudulent nature of his accusations and probes. McCarthy was censured by the Senate the following December and McCarthyism—as his tactics of smear and innuendo became known—gradually waned.

It was in the context of the receding domestic subversives issue that the Supreme Court decided the **Yates** v. **United States** case that made it more difficult to secure criminal convictions against American communists who committed no overt acts of espionage or sabotage. The Court expressed a more liberal view in several other cases involving alleged domestic subversives, but then, from 1958 through 1961, the Court switched sides again in various "subversives" cases and in those concerning "disloyal" public employees. It should be stressed that in 1957 and 1958 the Court's decisions, in several areas of civil liberties, had come under attack in Congress; some anti-Court bills that would have reversed Court rulings and withdrawn its jurisdiction were only narrowly defeated in the Senate. Furthermore, in August 1958, the Conference of State Chief Justices issued a report highly critical of the Supreme Court. The report attacked the trend of Court decisions since 1937 and specifically condemned the Warren Court.

Earl Warren was named to the chief justiceship by President Eisenhower barely nine months after Eisenhower assumed the presidency. Warren led the Court to a unanimous decision in **Brown** v. **Board of Education** that ushered in the civil rights revolution. Civil rights moved from a muted issue of public policy to one that was trumpeted on the front pages of newspapers and over the broadcast media. Litigation mounted, southern states were defiant, controversy ensued, and more and more demands were made by those seeking an end to all forms of racial discrimination as well as the redress of historic wrongs.

Although the Democrats had recaptured control of Congress in the congressional elections of 1954, this had no effect on President Eisenhower's reelection bid two years later. The country liked Ike, giving him a landslide reelection victory at the same time it sent to Washington a Democratic Congress. But the Democrats had only a 2-vote margin in the Senate and a 33-vote majority in the House.

As a practical matter, this meant that conservative Republicans and conservative southern Democrats still controlled a majority in Congress—a fact that was reflected in the anti-Court activity during 1957 and 1958 in which southern congressmen, angered by the Court's civil rights rulings, joined forces with other conservatives upset with the Court's decisions involving alleged subversives. However, the summer of 1958 was the high point of congressional anti-Court activity as the country, hit by a severe recession, turned out at the polls in November 1958 and elected 49 additional Democratic members of the House and 17 additional Democratic senators, most of whom were liberal. This new liberal strength enabled passage of the Civil Rights Act of 1960, which strengthened the powers of the Civil Rights Commission created three years earlier and also the role of the Attorney General in instances where there was deprivation of the right to vote. Although the Democrats sensed they could regain the White House in 1960, the actual campaign between John F. Kennedy and Richard M. Nixon resulted in one of the closest elections in American political history. Kennedy won by a mere 112,803 votes (but his electoral college margin was 34 above the minimum needed for victory). While Democrats retained control of Congress, they actually lost seats in both houses, making the new Congress more conservative than the previous one.

THE TURBULENT SIXTIES

The Cold War and foreign policy remained major issues of public policy during the 1960s, particularly the 1962 Cuban Missile Crisis and American involvement in the Vietnam civil war. But no longer were domestic subversives or communists-in-government political issues. The liberal activist Warren Court struck down the imposition of certain kinds of loyalty oaths on college teachers in **Keyishian** v. **Board of Regents,** and negative public reaction was minimal. The Court also ruled liberally in some other cases involving the rights of alleged subversives. By 1969 the Court considered political free speech so well established that in a brief *per curiam* opinion (**Brandenburg** v. **Ohio**) the Court overturned **Whitney** v. **California,** a remnant from an earlier era of repression of radicals. But issues ranging over many other areas of civil rights and civil liberties dominated the domestic public policy debate and the Supreme Court increasingly became involved. Soon the Court itself became the focus of public controversy.

Civil rights for black Americans continued to remain an important public policy area in the 1960s and one that continued in the public eye. Sit-ins, civil disobedience, freedom marches, mass demonstrations, and boycotts kept the civil rights struggle well publicized. So did massive resistance by segregationist forces, particularly to *Brown* v. *Board of Education,* as well as shocking violence toward civil rights workers by some southern law enforcement officials and individual racists.

In 1963 President Kennedy submitted to Congress new civil rights legislation including a section prohibiting racial discrimination in public accommodations. On August 28, 1963, at the end of a series of nationwide protests, the civil rights forces assembled in Washington with more than 200,000 participants peacefully meeting to urge an end to racism in all areas of life, particularly employment, public accommodations, and housing. On November 22, 1963, President Kennedy was assassinated and Lyndon B. Johnson became President. In an atmosphere of grief, shock, and sober reflection, Johnson vigorously pushed for the passage of the Civil Rights Act as the right thing to do morally and also as a fitting legislative memorial to the slain President. The Civil Rights Act of 1964 passed Congress and was signed into law on July 2. The act was the strongest and most sweeping piece of civil rights legislation since the Civil Rights Act of 1875 that it resembled in part. Title 2 con-

tained the public accommodations provisions—which the Court later declared to be constitutional in the **Heart of Atlanta Motel** v. **United States** and **Katzenbach** v. **McClung** cases. Other titles strengthened the authority of the Attorney General to file suits for the desegregation of public schools and other public facilities; prohibited discrimination in federally assisted programs; created the Equal Employment Opportunity Commission with powers to enforce the ban on discrimination on the basis of race, color, religion, national origin, *or* sex in employment by employers, labor unions, and employment agencies; empowered the Civil Rights Commission to investigate deprivations of the equal protection of the law on account of race, color, religion, or national origin; and provided measures to protect the right to vote from the racially discriminatory actions of local officials.

The reports of the Civil Rights Commission sharply illustrated the fact that blacks, especially in rural parts of the South, were still being denied the right to vote. The Reverend Martin Luther King, Jr., led a series of marches during the first part of 1965 to dramatize the need for strong legislation to protect the right to vote. The march on Selma, Alabama, attracted nationwide attention as did the murders of white civil rights workers from the North who had joined Dr. King's campaign. President Johnson built on the momentum of the demonstrations and the outrage at the murders. The Voting Rights Act of 1965 was soon enacted and provided for federal supervision of elections in states violating the Fifteenth Amendment and the elimination of literacy or other educational tests used to discriminate on the basis of race. The Supreme Court upheld the law's constitutionality in **South Carolina** v. **Katzenbach** and the Court in another case struck down the poll tax imposed on voters in state elections. Congress and the states earlier had approved the Twenty-Fourth Amendment banning the poll tax in federal elections.

The Johnson Administration also lobbied hard for a national fair housing law to prohibit racial and religious discrimination in the sale and rental of housing. Finally, the Civil Rights Act of 1968 was enacted with Title VIII containing the fair housing provisions. Tragically, it took the assassination of another national leader, Martin Luther King, Jr., to provide the final push through Congress. The Court, independently, furthered the cause of fair housing in its decision in *Jones* v. *Mayer Co.*, 392 U.S. 409 (1968), in which it ruled that a portion of the Civil Rights Act of 1866 prohibited all public and private racial discrimination in the sale or rental of property.

The Warren Court in the 1960s played an important part in one of the more significant public policy issues by its rulings in **Baker** v. **Carr, Reynolds** v. **Sims,** and other reapportionment cases. The implementation of the Court's one-person-one-vote policy had a major impact on state and congressional politics as the more populous cities and especially the suburbs gained representation while the more sparsely populated rural areas lost.

The Warren Court also took the initiative in liberalizing the rights of criminal defendants, particularly at the state level. In such decisions as **Mapp** v. **Ohio, Gideon** v. **Wainwright,** and **Miranda** v. **Arizona,** the Court brought state criminal procedures in line with federal standards. In the **Gault** decision, the Court extended basic rights to juvenile defendants. There were many other decisions affecting state criminal procedures and the Court extended almost all of the basic criminal procedural guarantees of the Bill of Rights to the states via the Fourteenth Amendment due process clause. The standards of *federal* criminal justice were also raised in such cases as **Katz** v. **United States.** All this occurred as the nation was becoming more and more concerned with crime, rising crime rates, and what was being seen as the breakdown of law and order. In the summers of 1964 and 1965, there were urban riots in many of the black ghettos. As the Vietnam War intensified, opponents conducted marches and engaged in civil disobedience. Coming on top of the civil rights activism, the threat of lawlessness seemed to overhang the United States. The increase of black militancy, the spread of the drug culture and drug-related crimes, the sharp rise in violent crime, the spread of the hippie and counter-culture movements and their contempt for private property and traditional values created a public opinion that became increasingly amenable to the appeals of conservative politicians. Soon the Warren Court and its criminal procedural rulings became the scapegoat.

The Warren Court established new precedents in many areas of civil liberties involving First Amendment and other personal freedoms. Some of the Court's decisions proved to be highly controversial and provoked public policy discussion through much of the country. For example, the Court in **Abington School District** v. **Schempp** ruled unconstitutional Bible reading and reciting the Lord's Prayer as part of public school devotional exercises. But for the school committees of the nation this raised troublesome issues of compliance. In Congress the ruling also provoked the introduction of constitutional amendments to overturn the decisions. The Court also changed the legal definition of obscenity, redefining **Roth** v. **United States** and applying it in such a generous fashion, for example, in **Memoirs** v. **Massachusetts,** that a revolution in artistic free speech was stimulated that permitted frank and explicit representations of sex and virtually no inhibitions as to the use of language.

The Warren Court during the 1960s was clearly activist. It expanded the concept of standing to sue, for example, in **Flast** v. **Cohen.** It rarely took a back seat in matters of politics before the Court, as was seen in the reapportionment cases. It gave greater protection to the nation's press from harassment in **New York Times** v. **Sullivan.** The Warren

Court's activism was on behalf of civil libertarian values and its rulings in different areas nearly always provoked intense controversy. The Court in many instances helped set the public policy agenda for the nation.

THE NIXON PRESIDENCY AND FORD INTERLUDE

In the 1968 presidential election campaign, the Supreme Court figured prominently as a campaign issue. Richard Nixon, the Republican Party candidate, made "law and order" one of his main campaign themes. He attacked the Warren Court's judicial activism along with its liberal rights-of-the-accused decisions. He promised to name "strict constructionists" to the Supreme Court. Alabama Governor George Wallace was the American Independent party candidate for President and he, too, attacked the Court. Wallace not only attacked the Court's criminal procedures decisions but also its civil rights, obscenity, and other civil liberties decisions. Only Democratic presidential candidate Hubert Humphrey refrained from attacking the Warren Court. But he did not go out of his way to defend it either. Humphrey, saddled with Johnson's unpopular war policies and the aftermath of the Chicago riot in conjunction with the Democratic party convention, waged an uphill battle and came close to winning. Nixon won with 43 percent of the vote and a plurality of about 500,000 votes. Nixon's first Supreme Court appointment came in 1969 when he named Warren Burger to the chief justiceship.

Although Nixon had won the 1968 election, he did not bring a Republican Congress with him. The Democrats were in firm control with only four fewer House seats and five fewer Senate seats. President Nixon made a strenuous effort in the 1970 off-year elections, but the results were marginal (and only for the Senate, where the Republicans had a net gain of three seats; in the House, they suffered a

net loss of 12 seats). As 1971 progressed with the Vietnam War continuing and the controversy about the war heated up by the publication of the Pentagon Papers (facilitated by the Supreme Court decision in **New York Times Co.** v. **United States**), the public opinion polls showed a sharp drop in the popularity of President Nixon. By the end of 1971, most polls indicated that Maine Senator Edmund Muskie, the front runner for the Democratic party's presidential nomination, would defeat Nixon in the 1972 presidential election. It was then that the Nixon operatives formulated their strategies and plans designed to reelect Nixon. It is likely that these plans included surveillance activities, perhaps even the infamous break-in at Democratic party headquarters at the Watergate complex in Washington, D.C. Other activities included the harassment of the Muskie campaign that eventually led to the end of Muskie's candidacy.

The Watergate break-in occurred on June 17, 1972. President Nixon and his close aides, along with various other officials, engaged in a coverup so that the political and legal damage stemming from the arrests of the Watergate burglars would be held to a minimum. And so it was at first, although many Democrats were skeptical and suspicious. Liberal antiwar South Dakota Senator George McGovern won the Democratic nomination, and the Democratic party platform was more liberal than it had ever been. Despite continuing revelations in the newspapers that raised doubts about the truthfulness of the Nixon Administration's disavowal of any ties to the Watergate burglars, the Nixon reelection campaign gained momentum and the Democratic party was pictured as having been captured by extremists on the left. The law-and-order issue was exploited by the Republicans. The end result was the reelection of President Nixon and Vice-President Spiro Agnew by a landslide of 61 percent of the popular vote and with 521 electoral college votes. Interestingly, this stunning electoral victory did not result in the election of a Republican Congress, although the Republicans had a net gain of 13 seats in the House. In the Senate, however, there was a net loss of 2 seats.

President Nixon's great electoral triumph turned out to be a pyrrhic victory. Federal District Judge John J. Sirica, presiding at the trial of the Watergate burglars, actively sought the truth. Under his prodding, James W. McCord, Jr., the security coordinator for the Committee to Reelect the President, revealed all he knew; in so doing he implicated the White House. The growing public clamor resulting from the revelations from the trial as well as from the investigatory reporting published in the *Washington Post,* the *New York Times,* and some other newspapers resulted in the establishment in February 1973 of the Senate Select Committee on Watergate chaired by North Carolina Senator Sam Ervin.

As the Senate committee's public hearings during the summer of 1973 captured the nation's attention, another scandal, this one involving the Vice-President, was brewing in the Justice Department. The scandal became public in September and involved political payoffs to Vice-President Agnew while he was Governor of Maryland *and* Vice-President of the United States. Attorney General Elliot Richardson plea-bargained with the Vice-President and the end result was the resignation of Agnew, his plea of no contest to one count of income tax evasion in 1967 (i.e., failure to pay the tax on the payoffs he received in 1967 while he was Governor), a suspended sentence, and the placing in the court record of all the incriminating evidence gathered by the Justice Department.

More significant, from the standpoint of Nixon's ability to survive in the White House, was the dramatic revelation before the Senate committee that the Oval Office was bugged, that is, all conversations were tape-recorded. It thus became evident that if indeed an illegal

coverup had occurred involving the Nixon White House, the tapes would then provide incontrovertible evidence. The focus of attention thus turned to the tapes.

Special Watergate Prosecutor Archibald Cox began legal proceedings to obtain from the President certain of the tapes that were thought likely to contain evidence important for the prosecution of the suspected Watergate coverup conspirators. A crisis occurred in October 1973 when President Nixon demanded that Special Prosecutor Cox drop his quest for the tapes. When he refused to do so, Attorney General Richardson was ordered to fire Cox. First Richardson and then his Deputy Attorney General refused to execute that order and both resigned. The firing of Cox by Solicitor General Robert Bork, the resignations of the Attorney General and Deputy Attorney General, and the abolition of the Special Prosecutor's office became know as "the Saturday Night Massacre." In the wake of the severe national criticism, Nixon was forced to relent. He announced that he would turn over nine of the tapes to Judge Sirica. He appointed a new Special Prosecutor, Leon Jawarski, who continued on the course his predecessor had set. The climax, of course, was the Supreme Court decision in **United States** v. **Nixon** in which a unanimous Court upheld the position of the Special Prosecutor. Two weeks after the Court's decision and after the House Judiciary Committee voted unfavorably to the President on various articles of impeachment, President Nixon resigned from office, the first President ever to do so.

President Nixon's apparent malfeasance in office (the Watergate Grand Jury named him an unindicted coconspirator) in connection with the Watergate coverup was not the only action of his that raised serious legal questions. For example, the President on numerous occasions refused to spend the funds on programs for which money had been appropriated by Congress. In 1975, the Supreme

Court disapproved of the administration's impoundment practices in *Train* v. *City of New York,* 420 U.S. 35. To give another example, the administration claimed the right to wiretap alleged domestic subversives without a warrant. Eventually, a unanimous Court struck down this practice in **United States** v. **United States District Court.**

Vice-President Gerald Ford (who had been appointed to that position by Nixon under the terms of the Twenty-Fifth Amendment following the resignation of Vice-President Agnew) assumed the presidency when Nixon resigned. Barely a month passed before Ford extended a blanket pardon to Mr. Nixon, forgiving him in advance for any crimes for which he might otherwise have been convicted. Public reaction against the pardon worked to undercut the widely favorable view the public had of the new President. The November 1974 congressional elections saw major Democratic victories in the wake of the Nixon scandal. Democrats had a net gain of 4 seats in the Senate and 43 seats in the House. Although the trials of the accused criminals from the Nixon Administration proceeded and convictions were obtained, "Watergate" and the imperial presidency assumed less importance as an issue of public policy. By the time of the 1976 presidential election, Ford was being judged on the basis of his record and demonstrated ability—and measured against his Democratic party opponent, Jimmy Carter. The Democratic victory in November 1976 was modest, with Carter winning 51 percent of the popular vote and 297 electoral college votes.

The cultural-sexual revolution of the 1960s continued into the 1970s, and one of the big issues confronted by the Court was that of obscenity. The Court in a series of decisions sought to grant control over standards to local communities and yet retain a core of constitutionally protected sexual expression (see **Miller** v. **California, Paris Adult Theatre** v.

Slaton). The women's rights movement gained some of its momentum from the cultural-sexual revolution as well as the civil rights movement and saw its first successes in the Supreme Court of the 1970s. **Roe** v. **Wade,** although raising several controversial issues (e.g., the rights of the fetus, the right of physicians to administer therapeutic abortions to their patients), was nevertheless a major women's rights decision. However, the Court's decision in *Roe* v. *Wade* was the most controversial decision of this period. Public agencies at the state and federal levels were obliged to respond to the decision and to formulate public policies in this sensitive area.

Two issues of civil rights tended to occupy major political and legal attention. The desegregation of the public schools in both the North and the South stimulated controversy, particularly over court-ordered busing. The Court in **Swann** v. **Charlotte-Mecklenburg Board of Education** unanimously approved the use of busing as a device to implement desegregation. This decision was all the more significant because President Nixon publicly opposed such busing. The Court in **Keyes** v. **School District No. 1, Denver** explicitly brought the North under its school desegregation policies, although **Milliken** v. **Bradley** limited the scope of those policies.

The issues surrounding criminal law and the rights of defendants continually surfaced before the Court. The anti-*Miranda* views of the Nixon Administration were mirrored by Court decisions such as in **Harris** v. **New York.** The right of poor people to court-appointed counsel, however, was generously extended by the Court in **Argersinger** v. **Hamlin,** but then effectively limited to one appeal in *Ross* v. *Moffitt,* 417 U.S. 600 (1974). Perhaps the most publicized public policy issue of criminal law is the appropriateness and constitutionality of the death penalty. The Court in a series of decisions, the **Death Penalty Cases of 1976,** opened the constitutional door to the imposition of the death penalty that seemed to have been shut just four years earlier in *Furman* v. *Georgia,* 408 U.S. 238.

THE CARTER PRESIDENCY AND THE END OF NEW DEAL POLITICS

During the Nixon-Ford presidencies, the nation wrestled not only with the Vietnam War, the vicissitudes of a war-heated economy, and the major social issues that had come to center stage in the 1960s, but also with the deeply disturbing issues of corruption and misuse of power at the highest levels of government. Jimmy Carter's presidential campaign successfully mined the deep discontent and disillusionment of millions of Americans. Carter's election in November 1976 was accompanied by a nationwide desire for competent, honest, and humane national leadership. But Carter's inexperience with government and national politics produced gaffes and misjudgments that began a downward slide in his popularity. Although most of his appointees and programs were liberal, and his civil rights-affirmative action commitment was strong and genuine, liberal (and other) Democrats became disaffected with Carter's pace in developing programs and his difficulty in seeing them through Congress. They saw a lack of leadership ability in his handling of both domestic and foreign affairs, notwithstanding a number of major achievements including the Camp David accords that brought peace between Egypt and Israel. By mid-1979, Carter's political fortunes had sunk so low that some had questioned whether he would be able to reclaim the presidential nomination of the 1980 Democratic National Convention and whether, if renominated, he would be able to win reelection. By the fall of 1979, Senator Edward Kennedy indicated that he would fight for the nomination, but for a variety of reasons was unable to win much success in the party primaries and caucuses. However,

Carter's nomination victory was a hollow one as he lost the 1980 election to Ronald Reagan.

Some issues of national public policy during 1977–1981 were simply not suitable for Court action. For example, the conduct of foreign policy was (as usual) off-limits to judicial intervention. The Panama Canal Treaty, the strategic arms limitation treaty with the Soviet Union (SALT II), middle-eastern policy, the crisis with Iran over the taking of American hostages at the U.S. Embassy there, all raised controversial public policy issues that did not involve the Court (although the financial aspects of the settlement with Iran of the hostage crisis came to the Court and were upheld in *Dames & Moore* v. *Regan,* 453 U.S. 654 [1981]). Similarly, the energy crisis and inflation, both tied to the actions of the international oil cartel, were not the subjects of judicial decisions. But the Court continued to decide cases in many of the controversial areas in which it had ruled earlier in the 1970s. And new issues, as well, developed—in part because of Court decisions.

The issue of women's rights, particularly in the abortion area, raised a host of questions, some of which were dealt with by the Court in **Maher** v. **Roe** and **Harris** v. **McRae.** The civil rights movement and the Carter Administration emphasized affirmative action—but affirmative action was challenged in higher education in **Regents of the University of California** v. **Bakke,** in industry in **United Steelworkers** v. **Weber,** and the awarding of government contracts in **Fullilove** v. **Klutznick.** The death penalty continued to remain an issue as litigation sought to clarify what statutory procedures and standards must be provided before the death penalty could be used—as well as for what crimes that penalty could be imposed. The decision in **Coker** v. **Georgia** dealt with these considerations. The reach of the cruel and unusual punishment guarantee was considered by the Court in **Rummel** v. **Estelle.** The admissibility of confessions and illegally obtained evidence commanded the attention of the Court in **Rhode Island** v. **Innis.** The conflict between freedom of the press and the integrity of the criminal justice system were issues raised in **Richmond Newspapers, Inc.** v. **Virginia.** Freedom of political expression was once again considered by the Court in **Prune-Yard Shopping Center** v. **Robins.** Political free speech was the basis for invalidating portions of a federal campaign financing law in **Buckley** v. **Valeo.** And then, as if to demonstrate its constitutional muscle, the Court decided a commerce clause case such as **National League of Cities** v. **Usery** as well as a major contract clause case, **Allied Structural Steel Co.** v. **Spannaus.**

THE REAGAN–BUSH ERA

It can be argued that the party system that had come into being with the New Deal had run its course by the election of 1968. Public opinion had become more conservative, particularly on the law-and-order issue, while political opponents of the liberal activism and social engineering of the federal government *and* the Supreme Court gained not only credibility but also electoral strength. The time appeared ripe for a new party alignment, and Richard Nixon seemed poised to take advantage of the historic opportunity. Indeed, one can take the position that had the Watergate scandal and the 1974–1975 severe economic recession not occurred, the Republicans would have retained control of the White House in 1976 and been on the road to establishing their party as the new majority party. In this perspective, the Carter presidency was an accident and Ronald Reagan can be seen as picking up where Nixon left off and seizing the historic moment. The elections of 1980 and 1984 can then be seen as realigning elections.

Whether the Reagan presidency was inevitable or whether it was essentially a result of luck and timing (e.g., Carter's political mistakes, the Iranian hostage crisis that further

weakened Carter's political standing at home), Ronald Reagan made the most of his opportunity. Ronald Reagan sought not only to turn the Republican party into the new majority party, he sought to change the shape of American government. He had a social agenda which he pursued and that put him on a collision course with liberal civil liberties precedents of the federal courts.

Ronald Reagan was elected in 1980 with a narrow majority of the popular vote. For the first time since the Eisenhower Administration, Republicans took control of the Senate although the House remained in Democratic party hands. During his first term, President Reagan sought to revive the economy and reverse the high inflation that had plagued the United States for a decade and was considered by a majority of Americans as the country's major economic problem. The President promised to solve the economic problems by applying his economic theories, but he warned the nation that the medicine would hurt and that things would worsen before they improved. He was right. In 1981 and 1982 the country experienced the worst recession-depression since the Great Depression with unemployment rates in some states matching those of the 1930s. There were major pockets of hardship, and the many personal tragedies captured the attention of the mass media. But high inflation was broken, the nation seemed to be unwilling to repudiate Reaganomics in the off-year congressional elections of 1982, and by 1983 the economy was on a marked upswing. Indeed, by election day in 1984, the rate of monetary inflation continued low, the unemployment rate had dropped, the economy was booming, real income was rising, the dollar was exceptionally strong in world currency markets, and a majority of Americans credited the Reagan Administration's economic policies with bringing this about. Americans were less concerned with unprecedented high deficits (after all, Keynesian economics with its emphasis on deficit spending had helped bring about an end to the Great Depression) and the imbalance in world trade that made the United States technically a debtor nation. Ronald Reagan's personal popularity also contributed to his reelection victory with 59 percent of the popular vote.

During his first and second presidential campaigns and administrations, President Reagan emphasized his commitment to economic deregulation, scaling back the scope of the federal government, and strengthening the states by giving them some of the responsibilities that the federal government had assumed. He also articulated a commitment to appointing federal judges who shared his vision of a limited role for the judiciary and his antipathy to liberal activism, which produced civil libertarian policies that extended the rights of criminal defendants, that mandated affirmative action policies, that forbade devotional exercises in the public schools, and that prevented the states from outlawing abortions.

In the off-year election of 1986, Republicans lost control of the Senate and as a result Democratic senators became more aggressive in challenging Reagan nominations to the federal courts. The high point was reached when Robert Bork was nominated to the Supreme Court in 1987 and civil rights and civil liberties groups mounted a successful campaign against him. But this did not augur a change in the nation's preference for Republican presidents. George Bush, a loyal vice-president to Ronald Reagan, was elected to the presidency in 1988 after cultivating the Reagan constituency, although Democrats retained control of both houses of Congress. Bush as vice-president had publicly endorsed the Reagan agenda. He maintained that posture as a presidential candidate and also as President.

The Burger and Rehnquist Courts, during these years, were sympathetic to much of the social agenda although it rarely directly overturned major Warren Court civil libertarian precedents. In the criminal procedures sphere, the Court accelerated the trend of its decision making evident in the 1970s of eroding (at least by comparison with the Warren Court) Fourth and Fifth Amendment guarantees in such cases as **United States** v. **Leon, New Jersey** v. **T.L.O., California** v. **Greenwood, National Treasury Employees Union** v. **Von Raab,** and **New York** v. **Quarles.** Concerning the cruel and unusual punishment guarantee, the Court was also conservative (see, e.g., **McCleskey** v. **Kemp**) with the one major exception of the closely divided decision in **Solem** v. **Helm.**

In the First Amendment sphere, the Court was responsive to several of the conservative positions of the Reagan–Bush administrations. The Court upheld the Park Service's ban on the sleep-in demonstration by the homeless in **Clark** v. **Community for Creative Non-Violence.** The kiddie-porn law of New York was upheld in **New York** v. **Ferber** and the FCC ban on obscene dial-a-porn (but not dial-a-porn that was only "indecent") was upheld in **Sable Communications of California, Inc.** v. **FCC.** Censorship of a high school newspaper was upheld in **Hazelwood School District** v. **Kuhlmeier.** However, the Court upheld the rights of public employees to political free expression in **Rankin** v. **McPherson,** the right to demonstrate by foreign embassies in **Boos** v. **Barry,** and the right to burn the American flag as part of a political protest in **Texas** v. **Johnson.** This latter decision, in particular, earned the displeasure of President Bush, who urged the adoption of a constitutional amendment to overturn it. The Court also reaffirmed **New York Times** v. **Sullivan** in **Hustler Magazine** v. **Falwell** and ruled that public broadcasting stations had a First Amendment right to broadcast political editorials (**FCC** v. **League of Women Voters of California**).

The Court approved state tax credits for parents of parochial school students (**Mueller** v. **Allen**), denied the free exercise of religion claims of Native Americans and gave the go-ahead to the Park Service's plans to build a road through a sacred area (**Lyng** v. **Northwest**

Indian Cemetery Protective Ass'n), rejected another free exercise claim in **Goldman** v. **Weinberger,** and approved the municipal sponsoring of a Christmas display on public property that included a creche (**Lynch** v. **Donnelly),** although it rejected a display of a creche standing by itself (**County of Allegheny** v. **American Civil Liberties Union).** The Court struck down Alabama's moment-of-silent-meditation law because it was tied to religious observance (**Wallace** v. **Jaffree)** and Louisiana's law that mandated that the biblical version of creation be taught whenever evolution was (**Edwards** v. **Aguillard).**

The Reagan Administration claimed a major victory when the Court ruled that affirmative action must take a back seat to seniority when it comes to layoffs of public employees. But the Court drew a distinction between affirmative action in hiring (which is permissible) and in layoffs (which is not). Affirmative action in promotions was acceptable (**United States** v. **Paradise** and **Johnson** v. **Transportation Agency of Santa Clara),** but white workers not a party to a consent decree that affects their promotions can litigate their constitutional claims (**Martin** v. **Wilks).** The Bush Administration seemed to accept if not welcome the series of Court decisions in 1989 (including *Martin* v. *Wilks*) that considerably narrowed the scope of affirmative action in employment and also government contracts (**City of Richmond** v. **J. A. Croson Co.).**

The abortion issue was a top item in the Reagan social agenda. But the Court through the 1985 Term reaffirmed *Roe* v. *Wade* in such decisions as **Thornburgh** v. **American College of Obstetricians.** But on June 17, 1986, in a move coordinated with the Reagan Administration, Chief Justice Burger announced his intention of retiring from the Court and Presi-

dent Reagan elevated William Rehnquist to the chief justiceship and conservative Appeals Court Judge Antonin Scalia to the associate justice position. The following year Lewis Powell retired and eventually that position was filled by another conservative appeals court judge, Anthony Kennedy. In 1989, with the two new justices in place, the Court decided **Webster** v. **Reproductive Health Services,** and it was clear that *Roe* v. *Wade* no longer had the support of a majority.

In 1989 in criminal procedures, affirmative action, and abortion, the Court appeared to be taking a sharply conservative turn. The view by the beginning of 1990 was that President Bush was likely to have the opportunity to replace at least one of the more moderate or liberal justices and were that to happen, it would be inevitable that many of the civil liberties landmarks inconsistent with the Reagan–Bush agenda would fall. With Bush's replacement of Justice Brennan, that outcome now seems possible. With the election of George Bush, it can be argued that we are now well into a new electoral era of conservative Republican domination of the presidency and that the conservative social agenda will sooner or later be realized by the Supreme Court much like the about-face of the Court in 1937 in the economic and social welfare realm. If this analysis is correct, only a major economic recession-depression, a major scandal, or involvement in an unpopular war can stop the Republicans from continued electoral success at winning the presidency; and that means that Republican presidents will continue to fill vacancies on the Court with like-minded conservatives. It is not an exaggeration to suggest that liberal justices are an endangered species. The impact on the development and shape of constitutional law will be seen and felt in the years to come.

Chapter

4

The Justices—Their Appointments, Backgrounds, Voting Patterns, and Patterns of Group Interaction, 1789–1937

The 103 men and one woman who served on the Supreme Court through mid-1990 were appointed for a variety of reasons. For all, the end product—their appointments—was a result of transactions, some rather complex, among key officials in the executive branch and other governmental branches, private persons, and on occasion even private groups. Unlike appointments to the lower courts, senators have little influence at the nomination stage, although they may play an active role in confirmation. Nominees to the Supreme Court are the personal choices of presidents, that is, the President makes a selection after considering the recommendations of his staff and Attorney General. Selection is a winnowing-down process. As will be seen in this chapter and the next, certain key considerations seem

to come into play, including politics, ideology, friendship, geography, religious-ethnic-gender, and competence.

Special note should be taken of the Senate's role in the process. In the nineteenth century, close to one out of three nominations to the Court failed in the Senate. In the twentieth century, however, the rate has been about one out of nine, with four of the six rejections occurring in the 1968–1970 period. The nineteenth-century nominees who failed to receive Senate confirmation were either poorly qualified politicians or were rejected because of partisan and ideological reasons.

The leading study of the backgrounds of Supreme Court justices reveals that close to nine out of ten justices have come from well-to-do families and the remainder from humble backgrounds.[1] Before the Civil War, the justices came primarily from the landed gentry. Since then and until recently they came predominantly from the upper middle class, with their fathers tending to be in one of the professions. This pattern appears to have at least temporarily ended when the Supreme Court of 1968–1969 contained the largest number of justices from humble beginnings ever to sit on the Court at one time. On the Court, then, were the great grandson of a slave (and son of a country club steward), the son of a railroad worker, the son of poor Irish immigrants, the son of an impoverished minister who died when his son was five, and the son of a poor peddler.

Close to nine out of ten justices attended the "best" law schools or, as was the standard legal education in the nineteenth century, served apprenticeships with prominent lawyers or judges. Close to nine out of ten justices have been affiliated with a Protestant denomination and, of these, eight out of ten have been members of what sociologists consider to be high-status Protestant denominations. Low-status Protestants as well as the Catholic and Jewish appointees have typically been Democrats. Previous political activism is also common in the backgrounds of justices. At the time of their nominations, a substantial proportion of justices held high political or legal office or were prominent lawyers or law professors.

The voting patterns and patterns of group interaction are discussed in this and the next chapter. The mix of issues and personalities including the nature of leadership on the Court will be seen in selected examples to have shaped the development of constitutional law.

We begin our systematic overview of the appointments, backgrounds, voting patterns, and patterns of group interaction with the Supreme Court from the 1790s through the Marshall Court, and examine three subsequent eras taking us up to the 1937 period.

[1]John R. Schmidhauser, *Judges and Justices: The Federal Appellate Judiciary* (Boston: Little, Brown, 1979), pp. 49–53.

FROM THE 1790s THROUGH THE MARSHALL COURT

Twenty-two men served on the Supreme Court from the 1790 through the 1834–1835 terms; 1835 was the year of John Marshall's death. Thirteen individuals were appointed by the nation's first two Presidents, both Federalists, and all of their appointees were Federalists. The next four Presidents, Jeffersonian Republicans, accounted for seven Court appointments, all of them Republicans (or, as they were sometimes called, Democratic-Republicans). The final two appointments were Democratic appointments by Democratic President Andrew Jackson during his first term. Let us look a bit closer at those selected to serve on the nation's highest tribunal.

The Washington and Adams Appointees, 1789–1801

President Washington successfully persuaded the distinguished lawyer, diplomat, and loyal Federalist *John Jay* to serve as the nation's first Chief Justice. Jay, a New Yorker, did not think the Court was a very important institution, and when the President asked him to travel to England to negotiate a new treaty he did so. He also harbored political ambitions. While serving as Chief Justice, he ran twice for Governor of New York and when he won in 1795 he resigned from the Court.

John Rutledge, another original appointee, failed to attend any session of the Court during its first two years (although he served as circuit judge) and then resigned to become Chief Justice of the South Carolina Supreme Court. When Jay left the Court, Washington offered Rutledge the Chief Justice position and Rutledge accepted a recess appointment. Unknown to Washington and the Federalist-dominated Congress, Rutledge earlier in the year had made an intemperate attack on the Jay Treaty at a public meeting in Charleston, South Carolina. When word of this became known to the administration and the Senate, there was extreme embarrassment to the former and a refusal to confirm the appointment by the latter—the first instance of the Senate turning down a Court nominee and in this instance one who had been serving as Chief Justice for about four months. Washington then nominated *Oliver Ellsworth,* an eminent Connecticut Federalist, who had formerly served as Chief Justice of the Connecticut Supreme Court and also had been a United States Senator (he was the main drafter of the Judiciary Act of 1789). Ellsworth was confirmed in 1796 and served until his resignation in 1800.

Other Washington appointees included *James Wilson,* one of the Founding Fathers and generally acknowledged to be one of the leading legal minds of the day, whose financial ruin in 1796 led him eventually to flee his creditors and die in disgrace in 1798. *William Cushing* of Massachusetts had been Chief Justice of his state's highest court and had campaigned for ratification of the Constitution. *John Blair* of Virginia had also served his state as its Chief Justice, and like Wilson, Rutledge, Ellsworth, and other justices serving in the 1790s, he had been a delegate to the Constitutional Convention. *James Iredell* had been Attorney General of North Carolina and leader of the ratification forces in his state. At 38 years of age, he was the youngest justice appointed by Washington. *Thomas Johnson,* a former Governor of Maryland, replaced Rutledge when he resigned his associate justiceship in 1791. Johnson, too, had been a member of the Constitutional Convention. Johnson disliked his circuit duties and resigned two years later to be replaced by *William Paterson,* former United States Senator and Chancellor (Governor) of New Jersey. Paterson was an influential framer of the Constitution and while in the Senate helped draft the Judiciary Act of 1789. *Samuel Chase* was an extremely partisan Maryland Federalist. He had been one of the signers of the Declaration of Independence. Chase's partisanship and obvious lack of judicial temperament when presiding over circuit court trials of violators of the

Sedition Act got him into serious trouble with the Jeffersonians and later almost cost him his job.

President Adams named three men to the Court. By far the most important appointment of his entire administration was that of *John Marshall* to the chief justiceship. Marshall was Adams' Secretary of State. Although he was confirmed as Chief Justice on January 27, 1801, he continued to act as Secretary of State until the Adams Administration ended on March 4. (He received, however, only one salary.) John Marshall, born in 1755 in a Virginia frontier farm cabin, was the eldest of 15 children. His formal law training consisted of six weeks of law lectures at the College of William and Mary. He fought in the Revolutionary War and afterward began both the practice of law and a political career. He served in the state legislature and then the U.S. House of Representatives. In 1800 he joined Adams' cabinet. When Marshall came to the Court, he was recognized as a brilliant politician. At the time of his death and through the years he has been considered the greatest of American judicial statesmen. Although the Court he led had a nominal Jeffersonian majority by the end of 1811, it was nevertheless a Court in Marshall's image, emphasizing national supremacy over states' rights as well as judicial supremacy and the protection of property rights.

Adams' two other Court appointees were *Bushrod Washington* and *Alfred Moore.* Thirty-six-year-old Bushrod Washington was the nephew of George Washington, a staunch Federalist, and a former member of the Virginia legislature. Alfred Moore was a former North Carolina Superior Court judge and Attorney General of his state.

Appointees from 1801–1830

President Thomas Jefferson named three men to the Court. *William Johnson,* his first appointee, was a dedicated Jeffersonian Republican from South Carolina who came to the Court at the age of 32 and remained for three decades. Johnson had served on the South Carolina Supreme Court. Although Jefferson expected Johnson to stand up to Marshall and defend Republican principles, in practice Johnson dissented infrequently and generally shared the national and judicial supremacy values as well as the property rights values of the Marshall Court. The same was even more true of Jefferson appointees *H. Brockholst Livingston* of New York and *Thomas Todd* of Kentucky. Livingston's brother-in-law was former Chief Justice John Jay, but they were personally and politically incompatible. Livingston's pre-Court career included service in the New York legislature and the state's judiciary. He helped swing New York to the Jeffersonians in the 1800 election. Whereas Livingston replaced William Paterson on the Court, Todd filled a new position created by the Jeffersonian-dominated Congress in 1807 to hasten the day when the Court would have a Jeffersonian majority. Todd had been Chief Justice of Kentucky's highest court.

The Court from 1811 until the late 1820s enjoyed a large measure of stability in its membership, thereby enabling John Marshall to maximize his personal influence on his colleagues and to exercise intellectual leadership. In 1811 President James Madison named Jeffersonian Republicans *Gabriel Duvall* from Maryland and *Joseph Story* from Massachusetts to the Court. Duvall had served on Maryland's highest state court and was Comptroller of the Treasury in both the Jefferson and the Madison administrations. Story was appointed at the age of 32, but despite his relative youth he was widely recognized as a brilliant legal scholar. Although Story was nominally a Jeffersonian, he was also a friend of John Marshall, which provoked the anger of Thomas Jefferson, who considered Story to be a closet Federalist.

Until Jackson's presidency only two other men came to the Court. President James Monroe (1817–1825) named *Smith Thompson*, a Democratic-Republican from New York and related by marriage to Livingston, the man he replaced. Thompson was serving in the Monroe administration as Secretary of the Navy. Previously he had been a state legislator, a state judge, and a prominent attorney. *While on the Court* he ran for Governor of New York (in 1828) but lost to Martin Van Buren. President John Quincy Adams named *Robert Trimble,* who was serving as a federal district judge at the time of his nomination. This was the first time that a sitting *federal* judge was promoted to the Supreme Court. Trimble served on the Court for less than two years.

Although Andrew Jackson named six men to the Court, the only two who served for any meaningful amount of time with Marshall were *John McLean* and *Henry Baldwin.* McLean was an Ohio Democrat and Jackson's Postmaster General (having also served in that capacity in the previous decade during the Monroe and Adams administrations). He had also served on the Ohio Supreme Court. McLean was a man of great political principle (he turned out to be a federal supremacist and opposed to slavery) as well as ambition and had the reputation of being a schemer. His appointment to the Court is the first known instance of a President kicking a troublemaker upstairs! However, service on the Court did not still McLean's presidential ambitions, and on several occasions over the years McLean tried (but in vain) to win the presidential nomination of whatever political party he thought might have him. Henry Baldwin, on the other hand, was more in the Court tradition, although he, too, had a politically active pre-Court career. Baldwin had served in Congress and he helped deliver Pennsylvania to the Jackson column in the 1828 election.

Background Characteristics of the Justices

Table 4.1 presents some prominent background characteristics or attributes of the justices who served on the Court from the 1790s through the Marshall Court. Collectively, these

22 justices, although from different political parties, were remarkably similar in their background profiles. Whether Federalist or Democratic-Republican, few of the justices were from truly modest beginnings. Most began life with advantages, and certainly at the time of their appointment were among the legal and political elite of the nation. What is truly remarkable about the appointments of the 1790s was that President Washington, in particular, was able to persuade so many eminent men to take positions on the Supreme Court—clearly an institution of modest proportions in those early years. Table 4.1 also reveals that only 5 of the 22 justices failed to have at least some judicial experience before going on the Court. The table also suggests a geographical balance being observed in the appointments.

About 9 out of 10 justices had their ethnic origins in what was then Great Britain (including Ireland). All 22 justices were affiliated with Protestant religious denominations and about 9 out of 10 justices were affiliated with high social status denominations (Episcopalian, Congregational, Presbyterian, and Unitarian). One study of the backgrounds of the justices found that over half had a high-quality undergraduate education.[2] All had been politically involved in the party of the President who appointed them.

Voting Patterns of the Justices

Although there were, to be sure, some individual variations, for the most part Supreme Court justices from 1790 through the end of the Marshall Court displayed a remarkable degree of consensus on the most important constitutional issues of the day. Whether Federalist or Jeffersonian or even Jacksonian, they by and large supported the values of national supremacy, federal judicial supremacy, and the protection of property rights. National supremacy and judicial supremacy were, of course, closely linked. To strengthen the national government was to strengthen the federal judiciary. Only one justice made a distinction between the two; this was William Johnson, the first Jeffersonian appointee, who, while advocating congressional supremacy, nevertheless on several occasions (particularly in the 1820s) took a judicial restraint position when the Court was exercising judicial review over the states.[3]

It should perhaps be no surprise that no matter what party or President the appointees were loyal to before their Court appointments, once on the Court they came to the view that they and the Court had an important place in the system of American government and it simply would not do for them to take positions to weaken their own authority by weakening the power of the Court. It is a rare government official who willingly weakens his own power. One of the major changes initiated by John Marshall was the introduction of one opinion of the Court to replace the practice in major cases of each justice delivering an opinion *seriatim* (one after the other). Table 4.2 reveals that during the 1790s only a minority of cases actually had seriatim opinions. After Marshall assumed the chief justiceship, the practice all but disappeared. The table also shows that the chief justices in the 1790s were responsible for writing only a minority of majority opinions, but, in contrast, John Marshall wrote close to half the opinions of the Court.

There was little open dissension on the Marshall Court, particularly before 1827. John Marshall sought to convince his colleagues that dissent undermined the Court's authority and that it was of the utmost importance for the justices to settle their differences privately and then present a united front to the nation. This pressure was intense, as the first Jeffersonian appointee, William Johnson, indicated

---

[2]Schmidhauser, op. cit., p. 74.

[3]Donald G. Morgan, *Justice William Johnson: The First Dissenter* (Columbia, S.C.: University of South Carolina Press, 1954), pp. 230–253.

Table 4.1 SELECTED CHARACTERISTICS OF JUSTICES APPOINTED BY PRESIDENTS WASHINGTON THROUGH JACKSON (FIRST TERM)

Seat and Justice	Party	Home State	Years on Court	Father's Occupation	Occupation at Time of Nomination	Age at Nomination	Previous Judicial Experience
Washington appointees:							
1 John Jay*	Federalist	New York	1789–1795	Merchant	Secretary for Foreign Affairs, Articles of Confederation	44	State
2 John Rutledge	Federalist	South Carolina	1789–1791	Physician, plantation owner	Chief Judge, South Carolina Court of Chancery	50	State
3 William Cushing	Federalist	Massachusetts	1789–1810	Judge	Chief Justice, Massachusetts Supreme Judicial Court	57	State
4 James Wilson	Federalist	Pennsylvania	1789–1798	Farmer (Scotland)	Private practice of law	47	None
5 John Blair, Jr.	Federalist	Virginia	1789–1796	Landowner, member of Governor's Council	Justice, Virginia Supreme Court of Appeals	57	State
6 James Iredell	Federalist	North Carolina	1790–1799	Merchant (England)	Private practice of law	38	State
2 Thomas Johnson	Federalist	Maryland	1791–1793	Landowner	Chief Judge, Maryland General Court	59	State
2 William Paterson	Federalist	New Jersey	1793–1806	Manufacturer	Governor of New Jersey	47	None
1 John Rutledge*	Federalist	South Carolina	1795	Physician, plantation owner	Chief Justice, South Carolina Supreme Court	55	State, federal

*Note: Seat number 1 is always held by the Chief Justice.

5 Samuel Chase	Federalist	Maryland	1796–1811	Episcopal minister	Chief Judge, Maryland General Court	55	State
Adams appointees:							
1 Oliver Ellsworth	Federalist	Connecticut	1796–1800	Farmer	U.S. senator	51	State
4 Bushrod Washington	Federalist	Virginia	1798–1829	Plantation owner	Private practice of law	36	None
6 Alfred Moore	Federalist	North Carolina	1799–1804	Judge, plantation owner	Judge, North Carolina Superior Court	44	State
1 John Marshall	Federalist	Virginia	1801–1835	Frontier farmer	U.S. Secretary of State	45	State
Jefferson appointees:							
6 William Johnson	Jeffersonian	South Carolina	1804–1834	State legislator, plantation owner	Judge, South Carolina Court of Common Pleas	32	State
2 H. Brockholst Livingston	Jeffersonian	New York	1806–1823	Governor of New Jersey	Judge, New York Supreme Court	49	State
7 Thomas Todd	Jeffersonian	Kentucky	1807–1826	Frontier farmer	Chief Justice, Kentucky Supreme Court	42	State
Madison appointees:							
5 Gabriel Duvall	Jeffersonian	Maryland	1811–1835	Plantation owner	Comptroller, U.S. Treasury	58	State
3 Joseph Story	Jeffersonian	Massachusetts	1811–1845	Physician	Speaker of the House, Mass. lower house	32	None

(continued)

Table 4.1 *(continued)*

Seat and Justice	Party	Home State	Years on Court	Father's Occupation	Occupation at Time of Nomination	Age at Nomination	Previous Judicial Experience
Monroe appointee:							
2 Smith Thompson	Jeffersonian	New York	1823–1843	Landowner	U.S. Secretary of the Navy	55	State
Adams appointee:							
7 Robert Trimble	Jeffersonian	Kentucky	1826–1828	Frontier farmer	U.S. District Judge	49	State, federal
Jackson appointees (first term):							
7 John McLean	Democrat	Ohio	1829–1861	Frontier farmer	U.S. Postmaster General	44	State
4 Henry Baldwin	Democrat	Pennsylvania	1830–1844	Blacksmith, farmer	Lawyer, mill owner	50	None

Sources: Leon Friedman & Fred Israel (eds.), *The Justices of the United States Supreme Court 1789–1969* (New York: Bowker, 1969); Julius Goebel. Jr.. *Antecedents and Beginnings to 1801*, vol. 1. *History of the Supreme Court of the United States* (New York: Macmillan, 1971); selected judicial biographies.

Table 4.2 SERIATIM OPINIONS AND MAJORITY OPINION-WRITING BY CHIEF JUSTICE, 1790–1835

Period and Chief Justice	Total No. of Decided Cases	Cases in Which There Were Seriatim Opinions		Majority Opinions by Chief Justice	
		N	%	N	%
1790–1795: Jay & Rutledge	17	5	29.4	2	11.7
1796–1800: Ellsworth	46	7	15.2	12	26.1
1801–1835: Marshall	1127	5	0.5	547	48.5

Sources: Donald G. Morgan, *Justice William Johnson: The First Dissenter* (Columbia, S.C.: University of South Carolina Press, 1954), pp. 46, 189, 306–307; Charles Warren, *The Supreme Court in United States History*, vol. 1 (Boston: Little, Brown, 1926), p. 813, n. 2; Robert G. Seddig, "John Marshall and Supreme Court Leadership," *University of Pittsburgh Law Review*, 36 (1975), p. 800.

in a letter to Thomas Jefferson recounting his early experience on the Court:

> Some case soon occurred in which I differed from my brethren, and I thought it a thing of course to deliver my opinion. But, during the rest of the session I heard nothing but lectures on the indecency of judges cutting at each other, and the loss of reputation which the Virginia appellate court had sustained by pursuing such a course. At length I found that I must either submit to circumstances or become such a cypher in our consultations as to effect no good at all. I therefore bent to the current, and persevered until I got them to adopt the course they now pursue, which is to appoint someone to deliver the opinion of the majority, but leave it to the discretion of the rest of the judges to record their opinion or not ad libitum.[4]

Johnson, whose biography was entitled *The First Dissenter*, had an overall dissent rate throughout his career on the Marshall Court of slightly over 3 percent of all cases in which he participated. About 7 percent of all cases decided by the Marshall Court over the 34 years of its existence were decided with dis-

sent. Marshall himself dissented in seven cases.[5]

But dissent rates can be misleading. The Court from the 1790s through the Marshall Court decided relatively few cases that raised constitutional questions. Not more than 15 percent of all cases in the 1790s raised constitutional issues and the figure for the Marshall Court is only about 5 percent. Significantly, however, of the relatively small number of constitutional law cases decided by the Marshall Court (62 cases), in some 63 percent (39) there was dissent.[6] In 19 cases, state laws were declared unconstitutional and in 7 of these there was dissent (indeed, a total of 15 dissents were filed in these cases).[7] Clearly, the constitutional law cases raised policy questions of great importance and under the

[5]S. Sidney Ulmer, "Exploring the Dissent Patterns of the Chief Justices: John Marshall to Warren Burger," in Sheldon Goldman and Charles M. Lamb (eds.), *Judicial Conflict and Consensus: Behavioral Studies of American Appellate Courts* (Lexington, Ky.: The University Press of Kentucky, 1986), p. 53.

[6]Charles Warren, *The Supreme Court in United States History*, vol. 1 (Boston: Little, Brown, 1926), p. 813, n. 2.

[7]Richard E. Johnston, "Some Comparative Statistics on U.S. Chief Justice Courts," *Rocky Mountain Social Science Journal*, 9 (1972), p. 90.

[4]As quoted in Morgan, op. cit., p. 182.

circumstances some justices, most prominently William Johnson, felt compelled to dissent. Although Johnson's overall dissent rate, as mentioned earlier, was quite low by today's standards, it was the highest on the Court for the first 40 years of its existence and was responsible for much of the lack of unanimity that existed on the Marshall Court. In contrast to the disagreements between Johnson and Marshall during the 29 years they served together, which found them on opposite sides in over 30 cases,[8] Bushrod Washington, who also served 29 years with Marshall, disagreed with him in only 3 cases.[9]

Patterns of Group Interaction

John Marshall has been described by students of the chief justiceship as a man of great persuasive powers, powerful intellect, and charming personality. Clearly, he was able to win over Jeffersonian appointments to his judicial philosophy of national as well as judicial supremacy and the protection of property rights. He was also able to persuade his colleagues that the way for the Court to maximize its power and influence was for the justices to consider their views of the cases before them privately and to reach a consensus so that the Court would speak with one voice. Justice Johnson observed in a personal letter to Thomas Jefferson that when he came to the Court he was "surprised to find our Chief Justice [Marshall] . . . delivering all the opinions in cases in which he sat, even in some instances when contrary to his own judgment and vote."[10] The view to the outside world was ordinarily one of unanimity.

Aiding the close-knit nature of the group

workings of the Court and providing a suitable environment for John Marshall to exercise leadership were the residential arrangements of the justices. Since the Court met for only about two months a year, the justices did not move their families to the District of Columbia. Instead they all lived at the same boardinghouse on Capitol Hill. They took all their meals at the same table. Justice Story observed: "The Judges here live with perfect harmony . . . in the most frank and unaffected intimacy. . . . We are all united as one. . . . We moot every question as we proceed, and . . . conferences at our lodgings often come to a very quick, and, I trust, a very accurate opinion, in a few hours."[11] Although in 1829 newly appointed Justice McLean preferred to lodge by himself and in 1831 Justice Johnson began to look for new lodgings, the judicial fraternity for the most part stayed together until 1845, when four justices decided to reside in one house and the remaining justices lodged elsewhere.[12]

A leading historian of the Jeffersonian era noted that "in the sociological sense the justices were barely members of the Washington community. . . . The unanimity of their case decisions . . . their singlemindedness on policy questions conformed to the fraternal character of their life style; and the justices were too secretive about their activities in their boardinghouse to afford insights about the group *in camera*. Moreover, they lived . . . a reclusive existence. . . . They rarely received guests and they rarely ventured out of their lodgings after hours except to make obligatory appearances at official functions and to pay an annual courtesy call, en bloc, at the executive mansion."[13] Justice Story wrote of his and his colleagues' monastic-type existence: "I

---

[8]Morgan, op. cit., p. 179.

[9]Albert P. Blaustein and Roy M. Mersky, "Bushrod Washington," in Leon Friedman and Fred L. Israel (eds.), *The Justices of the United States Supreme Court 1789–1969*, vol. 1 (New York: Bowker, 1969), p. 251.

[10]As quoted in Morgan, op. cit., p. 182.

[11]As quoted in James Sterling Young, *The Washington Community: 1800–1828* (New York: Harcourt Brace Jovanovich, 1966), pp. 76–77.

[12]Ibid., p. 77.

[13]This and the following quote are from ibid.

scarcely go to any places of pleasure or fashion . . . [and] have separated myself from all political meetings and associations . . . since I am no longer a political man.''

THE TANEY AND CIVIL WAR COURTS

Twenty new justices came to the Supreme Court from the advent of the Taney Court through the Civil War and the Reconstruction Court headed by Chief Justice Chase. When the Taney Court began in 1836, only two justices remained from the pre-Jacksonian era (Justices Story and Thompson) and by the mid-1840s they had been replaced. The greatest impact on Court membership was made by the Jackson and Van Buren administrations and those of Lincoln and Grant. Together they were responsible for 14 of the 20 new justices appointed during the 38-year period from 1835 through 1873. The Democratic administrations named only Democrats (ten in all). Two additional Democrats came to the Court via one appointment by Whig President Tyler and one by President Lincoln. Republicans Lincoln and Grant (through his first term) named seven Republicans, and Whig President Fillmore picked the only member of the Whig Party ever to serve on the Court. A closer look at those appointed follows.

The Jackson–Van Buren Appointees

Jackson's three second-term appointees and Van Buren's three appointees (including two men to newly created positions) went to slaveholding southerners. *James M. Wayne,* a Georgia Jacksonian Democrat and a member of the House of Representatives, was given the seat that William Johnson of South Carolina had held for 30 years. Angered at South Carolina's politicians over provoking the nullification crisis, Jackson deliberately chose not to fill the vacancy with a South Carolinian. Wayne was an ideal choice, for he was not only a loyal follower of Jackson but also a leading unionist Democrat. Although a slave owner and in favor of the hideous institution of slavery, he was a firm supporter of federal supremacy. When the Civil War broke out, he remained on the Court, loyal to the Union despite his son's high position in the Confederacy.

The single most important judicial appointment President Jackson made was that of *Roger B. Taney* to the chief justiceship. At 59, Taney came to the Court at a relatively advanced age for justices at that time. No older justice was appointed before or during his tenure on the Court. Taney remained on the Court until his death at the age of 87. He was less than two weeks short of 80 when he delivered his **Dred Scott** opinion.

Taney came from a well-to-do Maryland political family. He was a Roman Catholic, the first to sit on the Court, and a strong and active Jackson supporter. Joining Jackson's cabinet in 1831 as Attorney General, he actively backed Jackson's positions on nullification and the Bank of the United States. He became acting Secretary of the Treasury in 1834, but the Senate voted not to confirm him. The next year Jackson nominated him to replace Justice Gabriel Duvall, but the Senate (with the Whigs smarting from the Bank controversy) managed to postpone consideration of the nomination. Then the chief justiceship became vacant with John Marshall's death and Jackson nominated Taney to that post and nominated *Philip Barbour* to fill the vacancy created by Justice Duvall. Barbour had been a Jacksonian congressman from Virginia who had served as Speaker of the House from 1821–1823. In 1830 he was named to the United States District Court for the Eastern District of Virginia. Both Taney and Barbour were confirmed on March 16, 1836. Each was a slaveowner, but Taney held title only to two elderly slaves who had long served his family because, according to Taney, ''they were too old when they became my property to provide for themselves. These two I supported in comfort as long as they lived.''[14] All other slaves that he inherited he set free, but despite this Taney in his personal correspondence was ''almost passionately dedicated to the defense of slavery.''[15]

President Martin Van Buren was responsible for three Court appointments. He agreed to the nomination of *John Catron* by Jackson, which was sent to the Senate on Jackson's last day in office to fill a newly created Court position. Catron had just recently managed Van Buren's presidential campaign in Tennessee and before that had been Chief Justice of Tennessee's highest court. Although a slaveholder and sympathetic to the South, he was also a unionist who remained on the Court during the war—at great financial cost (his Tennessee property was seized by the Confederate government). *John McKinley*, a U.S. Senator from Alabama, received the second newly created Court position. He actively supported Van Buren in 1836. He took a states' rights position on most issues before the Court. Van Buren's final appointment was Virginian *Peter V. Daniel*, a close friend and political ally of Van Buren, who had a long career in Virginia state politics before going on the federal district court in 1836. Daniel was perhaps the most extreme states' rights justice on the Court. Himself a slaveowner, he vigorously supported slavery. Because of his extreme views, he often dissented from his colleagues. He died before the election of Lincoln, but it is likely that had he lived he would have left the Court to join the Confederate cause.

Appointments from 1841–1860

Whig President John Tyler was unable to place any of his first five nominees on the Court (all were rejected by the Senate) to fill

---

[14]As quoted in Frank Otto Gatell, ''Roger B. Taney,'' in Friedman and Israel, op cit., vol 1, p. 652.

[15]Alfred H. Kelly and Winfred A. Harbison, *The American Constitution: Its Origins and Development,* 5th ed. (New York: Norton, 1976), p. 356.

two vacancies, but finally was successful in filling one vacancy with the nomination of Democrat *Samuel Nelson,* a highly respected jurist (Chief Justice of the New York State Supreme Court). The second vacancy, created by the death of Justice Henry Baldwin, was eventually filled by another Pennsylvanian, Pittsburgh state district court Judge *Robert C. Grier.* President James K. Polk was responsible for Grier's appointment as well as the appointment of New Hampshire's Democratic U.S. Senator *Levi Woodbury,* who years earlier had been Governor of New Hampshire and later had served in Jackson's cabinet.

President Fillmore appointed *Benjamin R. Curtis,* the only member of the Whig Party ever to serve on the Court. Curtis, a Massachusetts lawyer, replaced Woodbury, who died after less than six years on the Court. Although abolitionists in the Senate were critical of Curtis because he held to the opinion that the Fugitive Slave Law was constitutional, Curtis was nevertheless confirmed. After the *Dred Scott* decision, in which he wrote a dissent that endeared him to abolitionists (although his own views were not so ''extreme''), personal relations with Chief Justice Taney deteriorated and Curtis, increasingly uncomfortable on the Court, resigned on September 1, 1857.

John A. Campbell, a brilliant Alabama lawyer and Democratic party activist, was President Franklin Pierce's appointee to the Court. Campbell was a states' rights Democrat who was less in favor of corporate enterprise (which often meant the rights of northern corporations) than were most of his colleagues. Although Campbell freed his own slaves the same year he joined the Court and advocated the reform (but not the abolition) of slavery, his first loyalty was to the South. He resigned from the Court shortly after the Civil War began.

When Benjamin Curtis resigned, President James Buchanan decided to fill the vacancy with another New Englander, *Nathan Clifford* of Maine. Years earlier in the Polk Administration, Buchanan and Clifford had served in the cabinet. Buchanan had been Secretary of State while Clifford was Attorney General and the two knew each other well. Clifford was an active Jacksonian Democrat who had served in several capacities in Maine state government as well as having been in the U.S. House of Representatives before joining the Polk cabinet. After his stint as Attorney General, he served for a year as American Minister to Mexico and then returned to private law practice until his nomination. Confirmation was difficult, for Clifford was considered to be too sympathetic to the South. He won confirmation by a mere three votes.

The Lincoln and Grant (First Term) Appointees

President Lincoln placed five men on the Court—four Republicans and one western Democrat who supported the President's war policies. The Democrat was named to a position newly created in 1863 by the Republican Congress to assure a unionist majority on the Court. This meant that the Court now had ten members.

Lincoln's first two appointments went to *Noah H. Swayne,* a former U.S. Attorney and active Republican, and to *Samuel F. Miller,* one of the great nineteenth-century justices and the only physician (he practiced medicine for 12 years before turning to law) to have served on the Court. Miller at the time of his nomination was a noted lawyer, an active party leader, and a strong Lincoln man. He served on the Court for 28 years and wrote 616 opinions.

David Davis, a close friend and adviser, and an Illinois state judge, was Lincoln's third Court appointment. Davis remained on the Court for 15 years and then resigned when elected to the U.S. Senate.

Lincoln was responsible for appointing another major nineteenth-century Court figure, *Stephen J. Field,* a California Democrat who was serving on the California Supreme Court

when appointed. Field became the principal defender of economic laissez-faire, and he vigorously opposed encroachments on the rights of business enterprise. He played an instrumental part in transforming the due process clause of the Fourteenth Amendment from the protection of civil rights to the protection of property rights.

Lincoln also named the third Chief Justice to be appointed in the nineteenth century, *Salmon P. Chase.* Chase had a major political career as senator from and Governor of Ohio. He was one of the founders of the Republican party and a vigorous opponent of slavery. Lincoln chose Chase to serve in his cabinet as Secretary of the Treasury. Although Chase was exceedingly capable, he also lusted for the presidency and achieved the reputation of a schemer. He resigned from the cabinet in 1864, and although his backstage maneuverings to wrest the Republican presidential nomination from Lincoln were unsuccessful (and Lincoln was not appreciative of these moves), Lincoln nevertheless named Chase to the chief justiceship after Taney's death in October 1864. Chase's tenure on the Court was relatively brief; in fact, it was the shortest tenure of any chief justice in the nineteenth century. However, the nine years of his chief justiceship saw the Court cautiously and successfully maneuver around the explosive feud between the Congress and the President. Furthermore, his Court was to start once again to exercise judicial review vigorously.

During his first term as President, Grant appointed three men, all Republicans, to the Court: *William Strong,* a former Pennsylvania Supreme Court justice and a staunch unionist; *Joseph Bradley,* a noted railroad lawyer possessed of one of the best legal minds of the day; and *Ward Hunt,* an organizer of the Republican party and Chief Justice of the New York Court of Appeals. Hunt's active tenure on the Court was only a brief six years before he suffered a paralytic stroke. Strong and Bradley, particularly the latter, were forceful individuals who, along with Miller and Field, dominated the Court in the 1870s and into the 1880s.

Background Characteristics of the Justices

Table 4.3 gives a discription of the 20 justices who came to the Court between 1835 and 1873. Until the Lincoln Administration, with only one exception, politically active Democrats were appointed to the Court.

The traditions of geographic balance established in the earlier period of the Court continued and certain seats even seemed slated for certain states. For example, Virginia had at least one of its sons on the Court for all but two years between 1789 and 1860. New York was "represented" on the Court for all but ten years between 1789 and 1916 and since 1925 through the present has had one of its own on the Court.

Most justices continued to come from comfortable family circumstances, but the Civil War period suggests a break in the occupational backgrounds of the justices' families. From 1835 until 1860, following the pattern of the previous era, about two-thirds of the justices came from agrarian backgrounds. Starting with the Lincoln appointees and continuing through Grant's first term, only one-third came from farm families. The national trend away from an agrarian United States was beginning to be demonstrated in the backgrounds of the justices.

In terms of occupation at the time of nomination, from 1835 until 1850 the appointees tended to hold political or judicial office (7 out of 9), whereas after 1850 the tendency was for the nominees to have been in private law practice when called to the bench (8 out of 11). A similar change is evident with regard to previous judicial experience. Between 1835 and 1850 only 2 out of 9 appointees failed to have previous court experience, whereas after 1850 and until 1873, 7 out of 11 had no previous experience.

All the justices, with the exception of Chief Justice Taney (a Roman Catholic), were affili-

ated with primarily high social status Protestant denominations. Only two justices (John Catron and Samuel Miller) had ethnic origins outside the British Isles. The majority of the justices had high-quality undergraduate training, and of those who went to law school the large majority attended high-quality institutions.[16] Only 2 out of the 20 justices, Grier and Bradley, had not held political office or been extensively involved in party activities (although both had friends in "high places"). With the exception of Nelson and Field, the justices were members of the political party of the President who appointed them.

Voting Patterns of the Justices

There is no question but that the advent of the Taney Court brought with it a noticeable break with the voting patterns of the Marshall Court and its predecessor courts. The Taney Court from the outset experienced division, with Justice Story bitterly resenting what he saw as major doctrinal departures from the jurisprudence of John Marshall. At the time of Taney's nomination to the chief justiceship, Senator Daniel Webster, a close friend of Story's, wrote in a letter, "Judge Story . . . thinks the Supreme Court is *gone*. . . ."[17] As Table 4.4 suggests, in the major cases Story felt free to dissent, although his overall dissent rate was one of the lowest on the Court.

Table 4.4 presents the dissent rate for the justices of the Taney Court in all cases with opinion and in the major divisive cases concerned with slavery, the commerce clause, and the status (and rights) of corporations. Both sets of dissent rates suggest considerably more dissent than that found in the Marshall Court. The highest dissent rate during the course of almost the entire Marshall Court was 3 percent (Justice Johnson) and was never

[16]Schmidhauser, op. cit., pp. 74, 77.

[17]Daniel Webster to Mrs. Webster, January 10, 1836, as quoted in Gerald T. Dunne, *Justice Joseph Story and the Rise of the Supreme Court* (New York: Simon & Schuster, 1970), p. 351.

greater than 6 percent (Justice Baldwin's record during his first four years on the Court beginning in 1830). The overall dissent rates on the Taney Court, however, although higher than those of predecessor courts, were not as high as those of subsequent courts, particularly in the most recent half century.

In considering the dissent rate in all cases with opinion, the two justices who served the longest with John Marshall had two of the lowest three dissent rates on thc Taney Court. The highest dissent rate, close to 12 percent, was that of Justice Daniel, whose biographer chose as the title of his book *Justice Daniel Dissenting,* in recognition of Daniel's reputation. Dissent over the life of the Taney Court was 15 percent.[18]

Observe also that in the major divisive cases, Chief Justice Taney was rarely on the losing side, whereas Justices Story, Daniel, Campbell, McLean, and Catron frequently were. These justices, especially, took extreme positions in these cases as indicated by Table 4.5. In this table, consisting of a group of controversial cases decided with dissent that pitted the North against the South, Daniel is found to have been the most extreme pro-South justice. He vigorously supported slavery and states' rights and was against the rights of primarily northern corporations. Justices Campbell and Catron ranked second and third in pro-South voting. At the other extreme were Justices Story, Clifford, McLean, and Curtis, all northerners (and with the exception of Ohio's McLean, New Englanders) who rarely supported the southern position. Chief Justice Taney supported the South in 51.7 percent of his votes in this group of cases, thereby ranking in the top third of the justices in terms of pro-South support. Close to half of these decisions were decided pro-South by the Court.[19]

An analysis based on all dissents during the Taney Court shows that Justices Daniel, Campbell, Catron, Barbour, Taney, and Nelson tended to agree with each other more than with other justices, whereas Justices Wayne, McLean, Story, Curtis, Woodbury, McKinley, Thompson, Baldwin, Clifford, and Grier tended to be more alike in their overall voting patterns.[20] Of course, these generalities mask differences; for example, Justice Wayne, although a strong proponent of national supremacy, was also a southerner who favored slavery. Chief Justice Taney, to give another example, was generally more moderate than the other southern justices in his wing of the Court.

Without a doubt the 1850s proved to be a particularly divisive time for the court. One study suggested that the 1850s was likely the peak decade of dissent on the Court during the nineteenth century.[21] Another found that in the 1854–1855 Term of the Court one-quarter of the Court's decisions were decided with dissent.[22] In the following term, over one-fifth of its decisions had dissents.[23] In general, it might be noted that of the 20 cases over the life of the Taney Court in which state laws were declared unconstitutional, 55 percent had dissenting votes (in contrast to 37 percent for the Marshall Court and under a third for the Chase Court).[24]

Note also that despite some very real differences among the justices during the Taney Court, there was never a majority that renounced the major constitutional milestones of John Marshall and his Court. The majority

[18]Ulmer, op. cit., p. 53.

[19]See the complete study by John R. Schmidhauser, "Judicial Behavior and the Sectional Crisis of 1837–1860," *Journal of Politics,* 23 (1961), pp. 615–640.

[20]This analysis is based on data presented in John P. Frank, *Justice Daniel Dissenting* (Cambridge, Mass.: Harvard University Press, 1964), p. 237.

[21]Stephen C. Halpern and Kenneth N. Vines, "Institutional Disunity, the Judges' Bill and the Role of the U.S. Supreme Court," *Western Political Quarterly,* 30 (1977), p. 478.

[22]Percival E. Jackson, *Dissent in the Supreme Court: A Chronology* (Norman, Okla.: University of Oklahoma Press, 1969), p. 41.

[23]Ibid.

[24]Johnston, op. cit., p. 90.

Table 4.3 SELECTED CHARACTERISTICS OF JUSTICES APPOINTED BY PRESIDENTS JACKSON (SECOND TERM) THROUGH GRANT (FIRST TERM)

Seat and Justice	Party	Home State	Years on Court	Father's Occupation	Occupation at Time of Nomination	Age at Nomination	Previous Judicial Experience
Jackson appointees (second term):							
6 James Wayne	Democrat	Georgia	1835–1867	Plantation owner	Congressman, U.S. House of Reps.	45	State
1 Roger B. Taney	Democrat	Maryland	1836–1864	Plantation owner	Private law practice	59	None
5 Philip P. Barbour	Democrat	Virginia	1836–1841	Plantation owner	U.S. District Judge	52	State, federal
Van Buren appointees:							
8 John Catron	Democrat	Tennessee	1837–1865	Frontier farmer	Private law practice	51	State
9 John McKinley	Democrat	Alabama	1837–1852	Physician	U.S. senator	57	None
5 Peter V. Daniel	Democrat	Virginia	1841–1860	Plantation owner	U.S. District Judge	57	Federal
Tyler appointee:							
2 Samuel Nelson	Democrat	New York	1845–1872	Farmer	Chief Justice, New York Supreme Court	52	State
Polk appointees:							
3 Levi Woodbury	Democrat	New Hampshire	1845–1851	Farmer, merchant	U.S. senator	55	State
4 Robert C. Grier	Democrat	Pennsylvania	1846–1870	Minister	State district court judge	52	State
Fillmore appointee:							
3 Benjamin R. Curtis	Whig	Massachusetts	1851–1857	Ship captain	Private law practice	41	None
Pierce appointee:							
9 John A. Campbell	Democrat	Alabama	1853–1861	Lawyer	Private law practice	41	None

Buchanan appointee:

3 Nathan Clifford	Democrat	Maine	1858–1881	Farmer	Private law practice	54	None

Lincoln appointees:

7 Noah H. Swayne	Republican	Ohio	1862–1881	Farmer	Private law practice	57	None
5 Samuel F. Miller	Republican	Iowa	1862–1890	Farmer	Private law practice	46	None
9 David Davis	Republican	Illinois	1862–1877	Physician	State judge	47	State
10 Stephen J. Field	Democrat	California	1863–1897	Minister	Judge, California Supreme Court	46	State
1 Salmon P. Chase	Republican	Ohio	1864–1873	Small factory owner	Lawyer	56	None

Grant appointees (first term):

4 William Strong	Republican	Pennsylvania	1870–1880	Minister	Private law practice	61	State
6 Joseph P. Bradley	Republican	New Jersey	1870–1892	Farmer	Private law practice	56	None
2 Ward Hunt	Republican	New York	1873–1882	Bank cashier	Chief Justice, New York Court of Appeals	62	State

Table 4.4   DISSENT RATES, TANEY COURT, 1836–1864

Justice	Dissent Rate (All Cases with opinion)* (%)	Dissent Rate, Major 1837–1860 Cases (Slavery, Commerce Clause, and Status of Corporations)† (%)
Taney	4.6	10.3
Story	2.6	50.0
Thompson	1.9	0.0
McLean	6.9	34.5
Baldwin	4.6	16.7
Wayne	4.6	13.8
Barbour	1.7	0.0
Catron	5.5	30.8
McKinley	3.0	20.0
Daniel	11.8	56.5
Nelson	5.0	21.7
Woodbury	7.8	25.0
Grier	7.1	4.3
Curtis	7.2	23.1
Campbell	8.8	50.0
Clifford	4.7	0.0
Swayne	4.2	Not on Court
Miller	9.2	Not on Court
Davis	2.5	Not on Court

*Dissent rate determined by number of times each justice joined in dissent with every other justice as well as number of lone dissents divided by all cases decided with opinion in which each justice participated. Number of times each justice joined in dissent with every other justice and lone dissents taken from John P. Frank, *Justice Daniel Dissenting* (Cambridge, Mass.: Harvard University Press, 1964), p. 237. Approximations of total number of case participations by justice derived from Richard E. Johnston, "Some Comparative Statistics on U.S. Chief Justice Courts," *Rocky Mountain Social Science Journal*, 9 (1972), p. 93.

†Derived from data presented in John R. Schmidhauser, "Judicial Behavior and the Sectional Crisis of 1837–1860," *Journal of Politics*, 23 (1961), pp. 622–623.

was as devoted to federal supremacy, the exercise of federal judicial power, and the rights of private property as was the Marshall Court. And in the overriding nation versus state controversy, there was always a strong majority favoring the nation. Even when the Civil War broke out, only John Campbell from Alabama resigned from the Court to join the Confederacy. The others, including Georgia's Justice Wayne, Tennessee's John Catron, and, of course, Maryland's Chief Justice Taney, remained loyal to the Union.

The Chase Court had less dissent than did the Taney Court; for example, in 1870, dissent stood under 10 percent of the Court's decisions[25] and was roughly half that of the Taney Court in 1850. By the time Chase assumed the chief justiceship, the most extreme states' righters were no longer on the Court. However, new issues were coming to the Court, issues that had their genesis in the war and Reconstruction. By Chase's last term, the 1872–1873 Term, 11 percent of the Court's decisions were decided with dissents of two or more justices.[26] The combinations of dissenters varied,

[25]Halpern and Vines, op. cit., p. 478.

[26]Charles Fairman, *Reconstruction and Reunion, 1864–1888*, part 1, *History of the Supreme Court of the United States*, vol. 6 (New York: Macmillan, 1971), p. 1451.

Table 4.5   **PRO-SOUTH VOTING ON THE TANEY COURT ON SELECTED NONUNANIMOUS MAJOR CASES (SLAVERY, COMMERCE CLAUSE, STATUS OF CORPORATIONS) DECIDED BETWEEN 1837–1860**

Justice	Rank	Proportion of Votes Pro-South %
Daniel	1	95.7
Campbell	2	80.0
Catron	3	76.9
Barbour	4	66.7
Taney	5	51.7
The Court		48.3% of decisions pro-South
Grier	6	47.8
Nelson	7	39.1
Thompson	8	33.3
Baldwin	8	33.3
Woodbury	9	25.0
Wayne	10	20.7
McKinley	11	20.0
Curtis	12	7.7
McLean	13	3.5
Clifford	14	0.0
Story	14	0.0

Source: Derived from data presented in John R. Schmidhauser, "Judicial Behavior and the Sectional Crisis of 1837–1860," *Journal of Politics,* 23 (1961), pp. 622–623.

although on some issues, such as the constitutionality of the Legal Tender Acts, there was a virtual party cleavage on the Court. The overall dissent rate of the Chase Court years was under 13 percent.[27]

The Chase Court in nine years struck down considerably greater numbers of acts of Congress and state statutes than did the Taney Court during 28 years. The Chase Court invalidated acts of Congress in 8 cases (in 4 cases there was dissent) and state statutes in 33 cases (in 10 cases there was dissent).[28] The Court had to face a number of controversial issues stemming from war and Reconstruction, including the use of military commissions to try civilians, the constitutionality of test oaths, the validity of the Reconstruction Acts,

the constitutionality of the Legal Tender Acts passed during the war, and ultimately the interpretation of the Fourteenth Amendment.

Patterns of Group Interaction

It would have been difficult for any person to follow John Marshall into the chief justiceship. His reputation within the legal community and through most of the country was great and, even among those who disagreed with his decisions, there was great affection, even reverence, displayed toward Marshall. By successfully exercising leadership, both intellectual and social, he shaped the Court into an effective institution of government, achieving a large measure of consensus among the justices. To Roger Taney's credit, despite sharper political divisions on the Court and increasingly tumultuous times, he managed, for the most part, to keep dissension at a rela-

[27]Ulmer, op. cit., p. 53.

[28]Johnston, op. cit., p. 90.

tively low level and the Court functioning smoothly. Indeed, Taney built on Marshall's legacy and raised the reputation of the Supreme Court to such a high level that by 1857 it was being told that *it* was the only institution of government that could resolve the slavery issues that were tearing the nation apart.

Once on the beach, Taney apparently went out of his way to maintain the tradition of cordiality among the justices and the close-knit relationship built so carefully by Marshall. Justice Story, who was so apprehensive about Taney becoming Chief Justice, wrote in a personal letter after Taney joined the Court: "The Judges go on quite harmoniously. The new Chief Justice conducts himself with great urbanity and propriety."[29]

Complicating matters for Taney was the fact that Congress had enlarged the membership of the Court from seven to nine. Justice Story observed in a letter:

> You may ask how the Judges got along together? We made very slow progress, and did less in the same time than I ever knew. The addition to our numbers has most sensibly affected our facility as well as the rapidity of doing business. 'Many men of many minds' require a great deal of discussion to compel them to come to definite results; and we found ourselves often involved in long and very tedious debates. I verily believe, if there were twelve judges, we should do no business at all, or at least very little. So far as my personal comfort and personal intercourse were concerned, everything went well.[30]

Another Justice, John Campbell, described the internal operations of the Court:

> [Our] most arduous and responsible duty [was] in the conference. . . . The Chief Justice presided, the deliberations were usually frank and candid. . . .
>
> In these conferences, the Chief Justice usually called the case. He stated the pleadings and facts that they presented, the arguments and his conclusions in regard to them, and invited discussion. The discussion was free and open among the justices till all were satisfied.
>
> The question was put, whether judgment, or decree should be reversed, and each justice, commencing with the junior judge, was required to give his judgment and the reasons for his conclusion. The concurring opinions of the majority decided the cause and signified the matter of the opinion to be given. The Chief Justice designated the judge to prepare it.[31]

Although by the mid-1840s the justices no longer lived in the same boardinghouse (McLean had been the first to leave the fold), they nevertheless dined together frequently and continued their deliberations informally at or after supper just as in Marshall's day. The fundamental ideological differences among the justices, particularly over the slavery issues, eventually tore the Court apart in the *Dred Scott* case, just as those differences were splitting the nation. Taney, by then 80 years old, clashed with Justice Curtis, which led to Curtis' resignation. But despite this Taney managed to hold the Court together.

In 1863, Congress created a tenth position on the Court to ensure a Republican majority. The next year Salmon Chase assumed the chief justiceship. Chase's nine-year tenure was marked by a dramatic increase in the striking down of acts of Congress (8 cases) and of the states (33 cases). In these cases, however, the rate of dissent (some 30 percent of the state cases and 50 percent of those involving federal actions) was lower than that of the Taney Court—which says as much for

[29]As quoted in Schmidhauser, *Judges and Justices*, op. cit., p. 118.

[30]William Story (ed.), *The Life and Letters of Joseph Story*, vol. 2 (Boston: Charles C. Little and James Brown, 1851), p. 296, as quoted in Schmidhauser, *Judges and Justices*, op. cit., p. 118.

[31]Remarks of John Campbell at a ceremony honoring the then recently deceased Benjamin Curtis, as quoted and cited by Schmidhauser, *Judges and Justices*, op. cit., p. 117.

Chase's leadership as it does for a Court dominated by Republican appointees. Although by Chase's last term about 11 percent of the Court's decisions were decided with two or more justices dissenting, it should be kept in mind that Chase was presiding over a Court that contained some of the strongest individualists ever to sit on the Court (including Justices Miller, Field, and Bradley). Furthermore, Chase's own personality may have prevented him from exercising the sort of leadership that Marshall and Taney had provided. As one friendly observer, historian Henry Adams, noted:

> Like all strong-willed and self-asserting men, Mr. Chase had the faults of his qualities. He was never easy to drive in harness, or light in hand. He saw vividly what was wrong, and did not always allow for what was relatively right. He loved power as though he were still a senator.[32]

THE CONSERVATIVE ERA—THE WAITE AND FULLER COURTS

Eighteen new justices came to the Court from 1874, when Morrison R. Waite became Chief Justice, through the end of the Theodore Roosevelt Administration. The turnover was such that by the late 1890s, perhaps a high point of laissez-faire Court decisions, only two justices (Harlan and Gray) remained from the Waite Court (1874–1888). Three Presidents—Cleveland, Harrison, and Theodore Roosevelt—had a great impact on Court membership. They were responsible for the appointment of 11 of the 18 new justices (the other five Presidents were responsible for only 7). Cleveland, the only Democratic President, appointed four Democrats during his two separate terms of office. One additional Democrat was appointed by Republican President Harrison,

but his other three appointments, and those of the other Republican Presidents, all went to Republicans.

Republican Appointees from Grant (Second Term) Through Arthur

President Grant in his second term had only one appointment to make, and that was the chief justiceship. Grant first offered the job to Senator Roscoe Conkling of New York, but Conkling, who had the reputation of being a wheeling and dealing politician, turned it down. Grant made two other controversial nominations that he soon withdrew, and he toyed with the prospect of nominating a total of three other persons. Finally, *Morrison R. Waite* was nominated and confirmed within two days. Waite, like Salmon P. Chase, the man he replaced, was from Ohio and had helped to organize the Republican party there in 1856. Although not generally well known outside Ohio before his nomination, Waite had been acquainted with President Grant when serving as counsel for the federal government before the General Arbitration Commission in 1871. At the time of his nomination, Waite had been president of the Ohio Constitutional Convention, an indication of the esteem in which his fellow Ohioans held him. Waite, although sympathetic to the rights of private property, was even more sympathetic to the rights of states to exercise their police powers in the public interest. He was to become one of the most prominent supporters of state regulation of utilities, railroads, and grain elevators.

President Hayes was responsible for the appointment of one of the greatest justices ever to serve on the Supreme Court and the greatest supporter of civil rights and civil liberties on the Court during the nineteenth century—*John Marshall Harlan*. Harlan, named by his parents after Chief Justice John Marshall, was born in Kentucky. His family and he were slaveholders, but when the Civil War came he

---

[32]*The Education of Henry Adams*, p. 250, as quoted and cited in Carl B. Swisher, *Stephen J. Field: Craftsman of the Law* (Chicago: University of Chicago Press, Phoenix Books edition, 1969), p. 187, n. 35.

sided with the Union and helped keep Kentucky out of the Confederacy; soon after, he freed his slaves. Harlan had been very active politically, having run for office several times and having been elected attorney general of Kentucky. He became a Republican and a Grant supporter in 1868, and at the 1876 Republican nominating convention he threw crucial support to Hayes that helped clinch the nomination. Harlan was also on the 1877 Louisiana election commission that favored Hayes. Harlan's 34-year service on the Court has been matched by few others, and few others have matched his reputation as a great civil libertarian. Hayes' other appointment went to *William B. Woods*, a transplanted northern politician (from Ohio) who settled in Alabama after the war and was appointed by Grant to the newly created Fifth Circuit judgeship in 1869. Woods, who moved to Atlanta, Georgia, in 1877, was considered to be the first deep South justice to be appointed to the Court since Alabama's John Campbell in 1853. Although Woods was not a native southerner, his antiblack views mirrored the sentiments of much of the white South.

At the end of his term, Hayes nominated his lifelong friend from college days, *Stanley Matthews*, a noted railroad lawyer and counsel to "robber baron" Jay Gould. The Senate Judiciary Committee killed the nomination, but incoming President James A. Garfield resubmitted the name of his fellow Ohioan and, after a struggle, Matthews was approved by one vote. Matthews had served as a state judge in Ohio before and during the Civil War and before the war had also served as U.S. Attorney in Ohio. In that latter post, despite his antislavery views, he nevertheless prosecuted persons working on the underground railroad for violations of the federal Fugitive Slave Law. Matthews became a Republican, fought in the Civil War, and after the war was a successful lawyer and active in Republican politics. When the fate of Hayes' election was left to the electoral commission in 1877, Hayes chose Matthews to

argue his case before the commission. After this successful undertaking, Matthews was elected to the U.S. Senate to fill out a term of office. Once on the Court, Matthews was more moderate in his defense of laissez-faire than had been anticipated by his former senatorial opponents. He is perhaps best known for his Opinion of the Court in **Hurtado** v. **California,** in which he read civil liberties out of the due process clause of the Fourteenth Amendment.

Chester A. Arthur assumed the presidency after Garfield's assassination and named two men to the Court, *Horace Gray* and *Samuel Blatchford,* both northeastern legal establishment Republicans. Gray, whose brother was the great law professor and legal scholar John Chipman Gray, was the youngest appointee ever to sit on the Massachusetts Supreme Judicial Court. At the time he was picked by President Arthur, he was Chief Justice of the Massachusetts court. On the bench Gray was a close friend of Justice Matthews. After Matthews' death Gray married Matthews' daughter. Blatchford was the first appointee to the Supreme Court to have served on the two lower federal court levels. He was appointed a federal district court judge in 1867 and promoted to a Second Circuit judgeship in 1872.

Cleveland–Harrison–Cleveland Appointees

Grover Cleveland, the first Democratic President in 28 years, made two appointments in each of his separate terms. He named *Lucius Q. C. Lamar,* the first southern Democrat and former Confederate official to sit on the Court. Lamar, from Mississippi, had been one of the leaders of secession in his state. After Reconstruction ended, he resumed his political career first as congressman and then as senator. He preached reconciliation between the North and the South. When Cleveland was elected President, Lamar joined the cabinet and became close to Cleveland. Three years later when the "southern seat" held by Justice Woods became vacant, Cleveland turned to Lamar. The nomination was controversial, but he was confirmed by a four-vote margin.

Cleveland was also faced with choosing a Chief Justice after Waite died in office, and he chose *Melville W. Fuller.* Fuller came to the Court with no previous judicial experience. He was a prominent Chicago attorney who was very active in Democratic party politics. Although opposed to secession, Fuller during the Civil War was a caustic critic of the Lincoln Administration's policies and conduct of the war. After the war he continued to be politically active and to build a successful law practice. He was known to be a sound economic conservative.

Cleveland's second term gave him the opportunity to make two more appointments. When Justice Samuel Blatchford, a New Yorker, died in 1893, Cleveland decided to place another New Yorker on the Court, but ran into difficulty with the U.S. senators from New York with whom he was feuding. Cleveland named one and then another New Yorker to the vacancy, but both were defeated on confirmation votes because of the opposition of the New York senators. Cleveland then decided to look for a southerner who could win quick confirmation (the South, of course, being the political base of the national Democratic Party, was a logical place to turn). He chose U.S. Senator *Edward Douglas White* of Louisiana, a former Confederate soldier and a Roman Catholic. White was rapidly confirmed and took his place on the bench at the comparatively young age of 48. In 1910 White was elevated to the chief justiceship by President Taft and presided over the Court until 1921. Cleveland's fourth appointment went finally to a New Yorker, *Rufus W. Peckham,* a former political ally from New York days and once a successful railroad and corporation lawyer who was serving on New York's highest state court at the time of his nomination. This nomination came about after Cleveland mended his fences with the senators from New York.

Benjamin Harrison, who defeated Cleve-

land in his bid for reelection in 1888, named four men to the Court. *David J. Brewer,* nephew of Justice Stephen Field with whom he was to serve jointly for eight years, came to the Court in 1889 from the federal Eighth Circuit Court, where he had served since 1883. Before that he had been on the Kansas Supreme Court for over 13 years. On the Court, Brewer became a leader of the laissez-faire forces. *Henry B. Brown,* a college classmate and friend of Justice Brewer, had been active in Michigan Republican politics before his appointment by Grant to the federal district court in 1875. Brown is perhaps best known for his racist opinion for the majority in **Plessy** v. **Ferguson.** *George Shiras, Jr.,* was named in 1892 to the Court. He was a well-to-do and well-respected railroad and corporation lawyer and was supported for the Court vacancy by his cousin, the important Republican politician and Harrison's Secretary of State, James G. Blaine. Shiras' powerful clients, among them Andrew Carnegie, also used their influence with the President to support Shiras' nomination. President Harrison had his last opportunity to fill a Court vacancy after his defeat by Cleveland for reelection. The vacancy occurred with the death of Justice Lamar, and Harrison looked for a southerner who would be acceptable to the Democrats in the Senate. *Howell E. Jackson,* a former Democratic senator from Tennessee and a good friend of Harrison's, who was serving on the United States Sixth Circuit Court, was the logical choice and he was quickly confirmed. Jackson's tenure was brief, for he became seriously ill shortly after joining the Court.

McKinley–Roosevelt Appointees

One of the handful of Supreme Court justices from a humble background was *Joseph McKenna,* President McKinley's only appointment. McKenna had led a rich political life, serving in local offices before moving to Congress, where he developed a close friendship with then fellow Republican Congressman William McKinley. In 1892 McKenna was named to the Ninth Circuit Court of Appeals by President Harrison. But when McKinley became President, he made McKenna Attorney General; less than a year later he named McKenna to the Supreme Court. McKenna turned out to be one of the more progressive justices, although his voting behavior was sometimes erratic.

President Theodore Roosevelt was determined to place progressives on the Court in an attempt to turn the Court around on the major social and economic issues. To some limited extent he was successful with the three appointments that he made. Of course, Roosevelt's greatest judicial gift to the nation was the appointment of *Oliver Wendell Holmes.* Holmes came to the Court at the age of 61 from the chief justiceship of the Massachusetts Supreme Judicial Court, where he had served for 20 years (although only the last three as Chief Justice). Holmes before that had distinguished himself as a leading lawyer and legal scholar. Although not a progressive in the partisan or ideological sense, his judicial philosophy was such that he, in effect, became the most articulate spokesman of the Court's progressive or liberal wing and one of the most brilliant of America's jurists.

William R. Day had been a close Ohio friend of President McKinley's and had answered the call of his friend when McKinley was elected President. Day served as First Assistant Secretary of State and then Secretary of State before being appointed by McKinley in 1899 to the Sixth Circuit Court of Appeals. On the Supreme Court, Day initially pleased Roosevelt with his votes supporting government trust-busting and by his dissent in the **Lochner** case. But years later Day was to write the opinion of the Court in **Hammer** v. **Dagenhart** striking down congressional legislation curbing child labor.

Roosevelt's last appointee, *William H.*

Moody, was clearly a Roosevelt progressive. Moody was personally and professionally close to Roosevelt, having left his safe seat in Congress to become Roosevelt's Secretary of the Navy and two years after that Attorney General. On the Court, Moody demonstrated great promise as a progressive-minded jurist before being struck by crippling rheumatism within two years of his appointment. Ill health forced his retirement from the Court after barely four years of service.

Background Characteristics of the Justices

Some key background characteristics of the justices who came to the Supreme Court between 1873 and 1909 are presented in Table 4.6 on pages 84–85.

As can be seen from the table and from previous Tables 4.1 and 4.3, the tradition of geographical balance—linked as it was to the circuit duties of the justices—continued in force with one exception. The South and border states had no representation on the Court from the time of the death of Georgia's Justice Wayne in 1867 until the appointment of Kentucky's John Marshall Harlan in 1877. The deep South nominally received an appointment in 1880 when William Woods, who resided in Georgia, came to the Court. But Woods, a Republican and native of the North, had moved south only after the Civil War. The sectional divisions produced by the war were so deep and the partisan nature of the selection process so ingrained that no deep South Democrat had any chance of receiving a nomination from a Republican President, or confirmation from a Republican Senate, in the two decades following the war. It was not until Grover Cleveland's presidency and the return of the Democratic party to national power that a native southerner with a Confederate past was appointed. Cleveland's appointment of Mississippian Lucius Q. C. Lamar returned representation to the deep South. Since then, until 1987, there has always been at least one justice on the Court from the former states of the Confederacy.

As before, almost all of the justices (the exception was Joseph McKenna) came from middle- or upper-class families, and the trend beginning with the Lincoln Administration's appointees away from agrarian backgrounds accelerated. In fact, of the 18 justices appointed during this period, only one had a father whose principal occupation was farming. Two-thirds of the justices' fathers were either lawyers (8 out of 18) or engaged in other professions (4 out of 18). The fact that close to half the justices came from legal backgrounds represented a sharp break from the past. Although the effect such a background may have had in the development of attitudes and values is difficult to document, it may be that it contributed to a sympathetic view toward the protection of property rights and a conservative cast of mind. Both Chief Justices, Waite and Fuller, and Justices White (a future Chief Justice), Blatchford, Lamar, Peckham, Day, but also Harlan, had fathers who were lawyers.

From 1850 to 1873, as noted earlier, the tendency had been for nominees to have been in private law practice at the time of their nominations, and for about two-thirds of them *not* to have had judicial experience. During the 1874–1909 period this trend was reversed: Only 4 of the 18 were in private practice, and just 5 had no previous judicial experience. Fourteen of the 18 justices held political or judicial office at the time they were nominated, and 13 had previous judicial experience. Perhaps it was their judicial experience that taught the justices that they had a wide range of judicial discretion, particularly in constitutional matters, and that they could use this discretion for the protection and promotion of cherished values.

During this period 16 of the 18 justices were affiliated with primarily high-social-status Protestant denominations. Justices Edward White and Joseph McKenna were Roman Catholics. All the justices except Lucius Q. C.

Lamar (of French descent) had their ethnic origins in the British Isles. The study of the backgrounds of justices conducted by John Schmidhauser noted that a majority of the justices, as in the earlier periods, had a high-quality undergraduate education and that after 1889 over 90 percent had attended law school. About half the justices appointed after 1889 attended high-quality law schools.[33] Only Justices George Shiras, Jr., and Oliver Wendell Holmes had not held political office or been extensively involved in party affairs or campaigns (although both had high-placed political contacts). Of the 18 justices only one, Howell Jackson, was not a member of the political party of the President who appointed him.

Voting Patterns of the Justices

The Waite Court did *not* present a sharp break with the Chase Court. The large majority of the justices, although sympathetic to the rights of private property, were not promoters of laissez-faire; they upheld the constitutionality of state and federal legislation in over 75 percent of the cases in which the actions of government were challenged on federal constitutional grounds.[34] In some 61 cases the Court invalidated either state constitutional provisions, state laws, or municipal ordinances. In terms of the Court's total business, only 1.6 percent of its decisions struck down state or municipal law. In these decisions, just as with the Chase Court previously, the proportion decided nonunanimously was relatively low. In fact, the Waite Court's percentage (28 percent) is the lowest dissent rate in such cases of any Court in the nation's history since (and including) the Marshall Court.

On the whole, there was a consensus on the

---

[33]Schmidhauser, *Judges and Justices,* op. cit., pp. 74–76.

[34]This figure is derived from data contained in Charles Fairman, *Mr. Justice Miller and the Supreme Court: 1862–1890* (New York: Russell & Russell, 1966 reissue of 1939 publication), p. 62, and Johnston, op. cit., p. 89.

Table 4.6 SELECTED CHARACTERISTICS OF JUSTICES APPOINTED BY PRESIDENT GRANT (SECOND TERM) THROUGH PRESIDENT THEODORE ROOSEVELT

Seat and Justice	Party	Home State	Years on Court	Father's Occupation	Occupation at Time of Nomination	Age at Nomination	Previous Judicial Experience
Grant appointee (second term):							
1 Morrison R. Waite	Republican	Ohio	1874–1888	Chief Justice, Connecticut Supreme Court	President, Ohio Constitutional Convention	57	None
Hayes appointees:							
9 John M. Harlan	Republican	Kentucky	1877–1911	Lawyer	Private law practice	44	State
4 William B. Woods	Republican	Georgia	1880–1887	Merchant	U.S. Circuit Court Judge	56	State, federal
Garfield appointee:							
7 Stanley Matthews	Republican	Ohio	1881–1889	Educator	Private law practice	56	State
Arthur appointees:							
3 Horace Gray	Republican	Massachusetts	1881–1902	Iron manufacturer	Chief Justice, Mass. Supreme Judicial Court	53	State
2 Samuel Blatchford	Republican	New York	1882–1893	Lawyer	U.S. Circuit Court Judge	62	Federal
Cleveland appointees (first term):							
4 Lucius Q.C. Lamar	Democrat	Mississippi	1888–1893	Lawyer	U.S. Secretary of the Interior	62	None
1 Melville W. Fuller	Democrat	Illinois	1888–1910	Lawyer	Private law practice	55	None
Harrison appointees:							
7 David J. Brewer	Republican	Kansas	1889–1910	Minister	U.S. Circuit Court Judge	52	State, federal
5 Henry B. Brown	Republican	Michigan	1891–1906	Manufacturer	U.S. District Court Judge	54	State, federal

	Name	Party	State	Term	Occupation	Prior Position	Age	Judicial Experience
6	George Shiras, Jr.	Republican	Pennsylvania	1892–1903	Brewery owner, farmer	Private law practice	60	none
4	Howell E. Jackson	Democrat	Tennessee	1893–1895	Physician	U.S. Circuit Court Judge	60	Federal
Cleveland appointees (second term):								
2	Edward D. White	Democrat	Louisiana	1894–1910	Lawyer	U.S. senator	48	State
4	Rufus W. Peckham	Democrat	New York	1895–1909	Lawyer, judge	Judge, New York Court of Appeals	57	State
McKinley appointee:								
8	Joseph McKenna	Republican	California	1898–1925	Baker	U.S. Attorney General	54	Federal
Theodore Roosevelt appointees:								
3	Oliver W. Holmes	Republican	Massachusetts	1902–1932	Physician, author	Chief Justice, Mass. Supreme Judicial Court	61	State
6	William R. Day	Republican	Ohio	1903–1922	Lawyer, judge	U.S. Circuit Court Judge	53	State, federal
5	William H. Moody	Republican	Massachusetts	1906–1910	Farmer	U.S. Attorney General	52	None

Waite Court concerning the balance between private economic rights and the rights of the public. There was also a consensus on the Court to limit the effect of the Fourteenth Amendment and, in particular, the rights of blacks under it. In terms of the power of the federal government, the Waite Court was even more sympathetic to the government than was the Chase Court. Only six acts of Congress were struck down during Waite's tenure (the lowest number of such invalidations since the Taney Court and until the Stone Court in the 1940s).[35]

Dissent on the Waite Court was generally low, about 11 percent of all decisions with full opinion.[36] The individual dissent rates ranged from Justice Blatchford's 0.5 percent to Justice Bradley's 3.4 percent. Two of the "giants" of the Court, Field and Harlan, had identical dissent rates of 2.6 percent, and Justice Miller, another heavyweight, had a dissent rate of 2.3 percent. Justice Gray's dissent rate was 1.8 percent.[37]

The advent of the Fuller Court was perhaps not a turning point to a militant laissez-faire Court, as is usually assumed, but rather a transition. To be sure, there were several famous closely decided decisions that gave laissez-faire a significant constitutional boost. But overall the proportion of state acts struck down by the Court (1.6 percent) was precisely the same as that of the Waite Court. Dissent, however, increased on the Fuller Court because some of the new justices were more sympathetic to economic laissez-faire. In the cases in which state laws were struck down by the Court, 43 percent were decided with dissent (a marked increase from the Waite Court's 28 percent). Overall the Fuller Court's rate of dissent was over 15 percent.[38]

The individual dissent rates are presented in Table 4.7. As is indicated there, the rate of dissent varied from Justice Blatchford's record of no dissents to Justice Harlan's record of 6 percent (close to three times his dissent rate on the Waite Court). Justice Holmes, known as a great dissenter, had one of the lowest dissent rates during the years he served with Fuller (Holmes' first eight years on the Court). Table 4.8 presents the proportion of each justice's agreement with Chief Justice Fuller in cases that were decided nonunanimously. We find that the three justices most in agreement with Fuller were Lamar, Blatchford, and Holmes. The three justices most in disagreement with Fuller were White, Harlan, and Miller.

Unlike the Waite Court, the Fuller Court used the Fourteenth Amendment primarily to invalidate state economic regulation. There were, in total (including noneconomic cases), some 35 state or municipal regulatory actions overturned by the Fuller Court on the basis of the Fourteenth Amendment.[39] When only the economic cases are considered in which the Court used the Fourteenth Amendment to invalidate regulation, we find 29 such cases. The voting of the Fuller Court justices in these cases is presented in Table 4.9. Surprisingly (because of his reputation as a laissez-faire justice), Chief Justice Fuller had the second highest rate of support for state regulation. The most antistate justices were Brewer, White, Field, Brown, Peckham, and Lurton. These findings are for the most part consistent with the more extensive analysis by Donald Leavitt of the Fuller Court, with the exception that Leavitt found Justice Harlan to have been the most liberal justice on all the economic issues (not just those involving the Fourteenth

---

[35]See Johnston, op. cit., pp. 90, 91.

[36]Ulmer, op. cit.

[37]Dissent rates were derived from figures compiled by Justice Blatchford as reported in Fairman, *Mr. Justice Miller*, op. cit., p. 387.

[38]Ulmer, op. cit.

[39]For a listing of cases, see Felix Frankfurter, *Mr. Justice Holmes and the Supreme Court* (Cambridge, Mass.: Harvard University Press, 1938), App. I, in particular, pp. 97–104. Cf. Walter F. Pratt, "Rhetorical Styles on the Fuller Court," *American Journal of Legal History*, 24 (1980), p.193, n. 7.

Table 4.7 DISSENT RATES, FULLER COURT, 1888–1910

Justice	Dissent Rate (All cases with opinion)* (%)	Justice	Dissent Rate (All cases with opinion)* (%)
Blatchford	0.0	Fuller	2.9
Lurton	0.6	Miller	2.9
Bradley	1.0	Field	3.3
Lamar	1.0	Brown	3.8
Gray	1.7	White	4.7
Holmes	2.3	Brewer	4.8
Day	2.4	Peckham	4.9
Jackson	2.5	McKenna	5.0
Shiras	2.6	Harlan	6.0
Moody	2.8		

*The dissent rate is determined by the number of times each justice joined in dissent with every other justice as well as the number of lone dissents divided by all cases decided with opinion in which the justice participated.

Source: The percentages are derived from data presented in Willard L. King, *Melville Weston Fuller: Chief Justice of the United States 1888–1910* (Chicago: University of Chicago Press, 1967), App. I, pp. 339–341.

Amendment).[40] But a broader quantitative perspective on the Fuller Court is also needed. Of the total number of cases involving actions of the states being challenged as violating federal statutes or the federal Constitution, in only 12 percent were state or local laws struck down as unconstitutional.[41]

Patterns of Group Interaction

Morrison Waite became Chief Justice under less than favorable circumstances. President Grant had offered the chief justiceship to five

[40]Donald Leavitt, "Changing Issues, Ideological and Political Influences on the U.S. Supreme Court, 1893–1945," paper presented at the 1974 Annual Meeting of the American Political Science Association, pp. 5–9.

[41]This figure is derived from John D. Sprague, *Voting Patterns of the United States Supreme Court: Cases in Federalism 1889–1959* (Indianapolis: Bobbs-Merrill, 1968), p. 62, and Johnston, op. cit., p. 91. Ulmer reports that, in civil liberties cases during the latter part of the Fuller Court (1903 to 1910), only about 3 percent of the actions of the states or municipalities were successfully challenged. See S. Sidney Ulmer, "Governmental Litigants, Underdogs, and Civil Liberties in the Supreme Court: 1903–1968 Terms," *Journal of Politics,* 47 (1985), p. 907.

men before offering it to Waite. To add fuel to the fire, some of the associate justices believed that they deserved to be promoted to the chief justiceship. Justice Miller, one of the giants on the Court—both physically and intellectually—was unhappy both with being passed over and with the selection of Waite, the little-known small town Ohio lawyer. About a year after Waite assumed the chief justiceship, Justice Miller wrote to his brother-in-law:

I can't make a great Chief Justice out of a small man. I can't make Clifford and Swayne, who are too old, resign, nor keep the Chief Justice from giving them cases to write opinions in which their garrulity is often mixed with mischief. I can't hinder Davis from governing every act of his life by his hope of the Presidency, though I admit him to be as honest a man as I ever knew. But the best of us cannot prevent ardent wishes from coloring and warping our inner judgment.

It is vain to contend with judges who have been at the bar the advocates for forty years of railroad companies, and all the forms of associated capital, when they are called upon to decide cases

Table 4.8   AGREEMENT WITH CHIEF JUSTICE FULLER IN NONUNANIMOUSLY
DECIDED CASES (FROM HIGHEST TO LOWEST AGREEMENT RATE)

Justices	Number of Joint Participations in Nonunanimously Decided Cases	Agreement Rate* (%)
Fuller-Lamar	107	86.9
Fuller-Blatchford	116	84.5
Fuller-Holmes	304	76.3
Fuller-Gray	441	74.4
Fuller-Bradley	75	72.0
Fuller-Jackson	75	72.0
Fuller-Day	282	71.6
Fuller-Shiras	379	71.5
Fuller-Lurton	20	70.0
Fuller-Moody	91	68.1
Fuller-Field	263	67.6
Fuller-Peckham	533	65.9
Fuller-Brown	579	64.9
Fuller-Brewer	732	63.9
Fuller-McKenna	482	62.4
Fuller-White	624	59.9
Fuller-Harlan	747	57.0
Fuller-Miller	38	44.7

*The agreement rate is calculated by dividing the number of agreements of each pair of justices by the number of joint participations in nonunanimously decided cases.

Source: Willard L. King, *Melville Weston Fuller: Chief Justice of the United States 1888–1910* (Chicago: University of Chicago Press, 1967), App. 2, p. 342.

where such interests are in contest. All their training, all their feelings are from the start in favor of those who need no such influence.

I am losing interest in these matters. I will do my duty but will *fight* no more. . . . [42]

Miller's letter reveals some of the problems Waite faced upon assuming leadership of the Court, although Miller distorted the Court's record. Waite, it is true, did not possess a flashy brilliance nor was he loud and forceful. There *was* a problem with Justices Clifford and Swayne who became increasingly enfeebled, and Justice Hunt who became seriously ill, ceasing his Court work in the beginning of January 1879; however, he did not resign from office until three years later, after Congress

[42]Letter dated December 5, 1875, as quoted in Fairman, *Mr. Justice Miller*, op. cit., pp. 373–374.

passed legislation giving him a pension. Justice David Davis was indeed a man of great political ambition, and within about a year after Miller wrote the preceding letter he was elected by the Illinois legislature to the U.S. Senate and consequently resigned his Court seat. Finally, although the justices on the Waite Court with only a few exceptions supported state economic regulation, the majority nevertheless enforced the payment of municipal bonds that were issued to finance railroad construction. The problem here was that some railroad promoters induced municipalities to issue bonds by making false statements and by outright fraud. When the agricultural depression of the early 1870s hit these mostly rural-agricultural communities, many municipalities defaulted or sought other ways to avoid paying the bonds. Justice Miller was strongly op-

Table 4.9 PRO-STATE VOTING OF THE JUSTICES ON THE FULLER COURT IN ECONOMIC REGULATION DECISIONS STRIKING DOWN STATES OR MUNICIPALITIES UNDER THE FOURTEENTH AMENDMENT

Justice	Number of Cases in Which Justice Participated	Number of Pro-State Votes	Proportion of Pro-State Votes (%)
Gray	11	4	36.4
Fuller	29	9	31.0
Holmes	18	5	27.8
McKenna	23	6	26.1
Shiras	11	2	18.2
Day	17	3	17.6
Moody	7	1	14.3
Harlan	29	4	13.8
Brewer	29	3	10.3
White	28	2	7.1
Field	6	—	0.0
Brown	18	—	0.0
Peckham	23	—	0.0
Lurton	4	—	0.0

Source: The list of the 29 cases from which voting behavior was abstracted can be found in Felix Frankfurter, *Mr. Justice Holmes and the Supreme Court* (Cambridge, Mass.: Harvard University Press, 1938), App. I, pp. 97–104. Note that of the 29 cases, 16 were decided nonunanimously (55 percent). Also note that justices who participated in only one case were excluded from the table.

posed to the railroads and in favor of these communities, but his colleagues considered these bonds to be contracts and generally supported the position of the bondholders. This so upset Justice Miller that in another letter to his brother-in-law dated February 3, 1878, he wrote:

> Our court or a majority of it are, if not monomaniacs, as much bigots and fanatics on that subject as is the most unhesitating Mahemodan [sic] in regard to his religion. In four cases out of five the case is decided when it is seen by the pleadings that it is a suit to enforce a contract against a city, or town, or a county. If there is a written instrument its validity is a foregone conclusion.[43]

But keep in mind that Justice Miller himself wrote the opinion of the Court in *The Wabash*

Case striking down state railroad regulation on commerce clause grounds; and in 1890 he joined the majority in **The Minnesota Rate Case,** which used the due process clause to invalidate railroad rate regulation.

It is to Chief Justice Waite's credit that despite the obstacles of strong and sometimes clashing personalities on the bench, senility or disabling illness among some colleagues, *and* some serious policy disagreements, he won the respect and affection of his colleagues and kept the Court on an even keel. As his biographer has reported about Waite, "While he could be firm, he was by temperament a conciliator, an amiable, easygoing person who liked people and enjoyed their company."[44] Chief Justice Waite went out of his way to welcome new justices to the Court. He skill-

[43]As quoted in Fairman, *Mr. Justice Miller,* op. cit., p. 232.

[44]C. Peter Magrath, *Morrison R. Waite: The Triumph of Character* (New York: Macmillan, 1963), p. 252.

fully handled such prima donnas as Field and Miller. He was diplomatic and also generous with praise. He organized whist and bourbon parties in which all the justices participated, and for most of Waite's tenure there were harmonious personal relationships among the justices.[45] Waite, at the very least, was the social leader of the Court and he worked closely with Justice Bradley, who possessed one of the strongest intellects to be found on the bench.[46] There appear to have been similarities between the Waite-Bradley relationship and the Taft-Van Devanter duo (as we shall see shortly) in terms of the sharing of leadership. Unlike the Fuller Court, where the Court, when it divided, was closely split (in 1900 some 13 percent of the cases with written opinions had three or four dissenting votes), the Waite Court had fewer than 3 percent of its decisions with three or four dissents.[47]

When Melville Fuller assumed the chief justiceship in 1888, he had a decided advantage over his predecessor. Fuller was a well-known (within the legal profession) big city (Chicago) lawyer. He was an experienced political infighter, having been active in Democratic Party politics in Illinois. He was furthermore a razor-sharp lawyer. Fuller, however, was also blessed with conciliatory and diplomatic traits that he put to good use. It was Fuller who introduced the custom, which has remained through the present time, of the justices shaking hands with each other before commencing their judicial conferences.[48] Fuller had the knack of making friends and on the bench he developed close personal friendships with Justices Harlan and Holmes. When he came to the Court, he was at once aware of the strong-minded colleagues with whom he would be working including Justices Field, Miller, Bradley, and Harlan. In a letter written soon after becoming Chief Justice, he referred to this by noting: "I think you will understand—No rising sun for me with these old luminaries blazing away with all their ancient fires."[49] Nevertheless, Fuller quickly established himself on the Court and exercised social if not task leadership. Justice Holmes was to write of Fuller: "I think he was extraordinary. He had the business of the Court at his fingers' ends; he was perfectly courageous, prompt, decided. He turned off the matters that daily called for action easily, swiftly with the least possible friction, with imperturbable good humor, and with a humor that relieved any tension with a laugh."[50]

An example of Fuller's social leadership ability to defuse the tension that sometimes occurred during the conferences was recalled by Justice Holmes. He reported that during one conference Justice Harlan was giving his view of the case that was being discussed; but Harlan's remarks so agitated Holmes that he, violating conference etiquette, interrupted Harlan by interjecting, "But that just won't wash." Harlan apparently was incensed at the interruption and immediately tensed up in preparation for a volcanic outburst when the Chief Justice, fully grasping the situation, smiled and began making motions with his hands as if he had a washboard before him, all the while saying, "But I keep scrubbing away, scrubbing away." The electrical charge in the room was defused as the justices laughed uproariously.[51] Years later, after having served under four chief justices, Holmes was to say, "Fuller was the greatest Chief Justice I have ever known."[52]

[45]Ibid., p. 300.

[46]Ibid., p. 299.

[47]Halpern and Vines, op. cit., p. 480.

[48]Willard L. King, *Melville Weston Fuller: Chief Justice of the United States 1888–1910* (Chicago: University of Chicago Press, 1967), p. 134.

[49]Letter from Fuller to Bancroft Davis, January 18, 1890, as quoted in King, op. cit., p. 127.

[50]As quoted by Irving Schiffman, "Melville W. Fuller," in Leon Friedman and Fred L. Israel, op. cit., vol. 2, p. 1480.

[51]King, op. cit., p. 290.

[52]Ibid.

Although the individual dissent rates were relatively low, during the Fuller Court years dissent increased. By 1900, cases decided with dissent exceeded those of the peak years of dissent during the Taney Court era. The Court was divided particularly over the issues surrounding state economic regulation. The number of cases in which state or local laws were challenged on constitutional grounds grew during the Fuller Court years. During the last ten years of the Fuller Court (1900–1910), close to 20 percent of the Court's business included such cases.[53] The Court was divided in 27 percent of these cases. Interestingly, in light of the Fuller Court's reputation as a laissez-faire Court, in the large majority of the cases the Court sustained the constitutionality of the challenged laws; although when it did not (as in the notorious *Lochner* decision) or when it occasionally struck down federal law (as in the **Income Tax** case or in the **Adair** case), its actions deservedly attracted wide attention.

THE CONSERVATIVE ERA—THE WHITE, TAFT, AND HUGHES (TO 1937) COURTS

Between 1909 and 1936 there were a total of 17 appointments to the Court including one elevation of an associate justice to chief justice and a later appointment to the chief justiceship of a former associate justice. As President, William Howard Taft had the greatest impact on judicial selection, accounting for 6 of the 17 appointments. Taft in his one term of office named twice as many persons as did Wilson in his two. President Franklin D. Roosevelt had *no* opportunity to fill a Court position during *his* first term. Democratic President Wilson named two Democrats and one nominal Republican, Taft named conservative southern Democrats to three of the six positions, and Harding and Hoover each included one Democrat among their appointees. Coo-

lidge named only one person to the Court, a Republican. Seven of the 17 appointments thus went to Democrats.

Taft Remakes the Court

Barely two months after becoming President in 1909, Taft wrote about his view of the Supreme Court to his close friend Circuit Judge Horace Lurton:

> The condition of the Supreme Court is pitiable, and yet those old fools hold on with a tenacity that is most discouraging. Really the Chief Justice [Fuller] is almost senile; Harlan does no work; Brewer is so deaf that he cannot hear and has got beyond the point of the commonest accuracy in writing his opinions; Brewer and Harlan sleep almost through all the arguments. I don't know what can be done. It is most discouraging to the active men on the bench.[54]

Taft soon had the opportunity to reconstitute the Court, although as fate would have it only one of his appointees would be alive and serve with him on the Court during the 1920s when Taft himself was Chief Justice. President Taft named to the first vacancy his confidant and former colleague on the Sixth Circuit, *Horace H. Lurton,* a conservative Tennessee Democrat who had fought in the Confederate army. Lurton was almost 66 years old when appointed, and clearly he received his appointment despite his advanced age because of his closeness to Taft. *Charles Evans Hughes,* on the other hand, was, at 48, the youngest man to be named to the Court during the first three and a half decades of the twentieth century. Hughes was the progressive Governor of the state of New York and clearly a major Republican party figure. Taft perhaps saw him as a potential challenger for the leadership of the party.

When Taft heard that Hughes might be in-

---

[53]This figure is derived from Sprague, op. cit., p. 62.

[54]As quoted in Leonard Dinnerstein, "Joseph Rucker Lamar," in Leon Friedman and Fred L. Israel, op. cit., vol. 3, p. 1980.

terested in the vacancy, he sent a letter to
Governor Hughes dangling the prospect of being promoted to the chief justiceship were
Hughes to accept an associate justiceship.
Taft bluntly stated that ''if that office [chief
justiceship] were now open, I should offer it to
you and it is probable that if it were to become
vacant during my term, I should promote you
to it.''[55] Hughes accepted the associate justiceship, and about two months after Hughes'
confirmation Chief Justice Fuller died. Taft,
whose greatest ambition was to become chief
justice, hesitated over a period of months
about whether to keep his implied promise to
Hughes and promote him. Finally he decided
not to. It is likely that he bypassed the 48-
year-old Hughes and instead promoted elderly
Justice *Edward D. White* primarily because he
was well thought of by his Court colleagues
and others as a jurist *and* was over 65 years
old. White would not likely remain on the
Court much beyond a decade and that would
leave open the possibility that some future
President, Republican or even Democratic,
would appoint Taft to the chief justiceship.
White was a southern Democrat and a Catholic. By elevating White, Taft at once provided
a precedent for elevating an associate justice
and one who was not a member of the President's party. This was certainly a shrewd
move on Taft's part, for indeed White's tenure
as Chief Justice was about a decade, and Taft
himself succeeded White to the chief justiceship. Had Taft appointed Hughes, Taft would
never have realized his life's ambition.
Hughes, in a stroke of historical irony, was to
succeed Taft as Chief Justice.

Taft filled the vacancy created by White's
elevation with *Willis Van Devanter,* a relatively young (51 years old) Wyoming Republican who had been appointed by Theodore
Roosevelt to the Circuit Court of Appeals for
the Eighth Circuit in 1903. Van Devanter was

to remain on the Court for 27 years and to
work closely with Taft when Taft served as
Chief Justice. During the 1930s Van Devanter
was one of the leading conservative opponents
of the New Deal. *Joseph R. Lamar,* another
southern Democrat of moderate conservative
views akin to his appointer, came to the Court
in 1910 at the age of 53. Although sympathetic
to property rights, Lamar was also, along with
most of his colleagues during the period before
World War I, sympathetic to state economic
regulation under the state's police powers. Lamar died after six years of service on the
Court. Taft's last appointment went to *Mah-
lon Pitney,* who came to the Court after more
than a decade as a New Jersey jurist, and who
before that had been a rising Republican figure
in the state. He had been a congressman and
then a member of the New Jersey Senate. Pitney had a reputation of being antilabor; thus
his nomination was controversial, with progressive senators opposing him. Pitney was
confirmed and went on to become as antilabor
on the Court as his critics claimed he would
be. He served on the Court for a decade.

Although Taft was able to reconstitute the
Court with these six appointments, all but one
of his appointees had a truncated judicial lon-
gevity. Death claimed Lurton and Lamar after
six years or less on the bench. White (as Chief
Justice) and Pitney each served about a decade. Hughes served six years before resigning to run as the Republican presidential candidate. Only Van Devanter had a relatively
long tenure on the bench, serving until his retirement in June of 1937.

Wilson's Appointees

President Wilson has the distinction of having
named to the Court one of the greatest justices
(Brandeis) and probably the worst justice
(McReynolds) ever to sit on the Court. *James
C. McReynolds* was a Tennessee Democrat
who earned a reputation in the Justice Department during Theodore Roosevelt's Adminis-

---

[55]As quoted in Merlo J. Pusey, *Charles Evans Hughes,*
vol. I (New York: Macmillan, 1951), p. 272.

tration of being an effective trustbuster and a progressive. He supported Woodrow Wilson during the 1912 campaign and became Wilson's Attorney General. In 1914, with the death of Justice Lurton, also a Tennessean, President Wilson nominated McReynolds. Wilson apparently wanted to appoint a southerner; he believed McReynolds to be at heart a progressive, and he also wanted McReynolds out of the cabinet because he was difficult to get along with. McReynolds was rapidly confirmed; he embarked upon a 27-year career on the Court unmatched, insofar as it can be determined, by any other justice before or since in terms of his crude, rude, and mean-spirited behavior toward his colleagues and his racist, sexist, and anti-Semitic views and actions.[56] He was one of the most reactionary justices ever to sit on the Court and his opinions were often badly flawed.

Louis D. Brandeis was the polar opposite of McReynolds. Brandeis' well-deserved reputation as the people's attorney, the nation's first public interest lawyer, earned him great opposition when he was nominated by Wilson in January 1916. Brandeis had been an active progressive. Although he supported progressives of both political parties, until Wilson ran in 1912 Brandeis had worked primarily within the Massachusetts Republican party and was a registered Republican. Brandeis supported Wilson in 1912, actively campaigned for him, and became a close presidential advisor. It is not known whether Brandeis had bothered to change his formal party registration by the time he was nominated to the Court. Nevertheless, because of his previous activity within progressive Republican circles and in light of his formal Republican party registration at least through 1912, he is usually classified as a nominal Re-

publican. When Wilson nominated Brandeis, who was also the first person of Jewish background to be nominated, the conservative bar and bench as well as representatives of industry and banking actively opposed him. They tried to portray Brandeis as a radical, impugned his morals and character, and subtly conducted an anti-Semitic campaign. But after four months of intensive hearings and behind-the-scenes activity, the Senate confirmed Brandeis, voting largely along party lines. Brandeis was to become one of the most eloquent and respected justices of all time.

Wilson's third and final appointment went to *John H. Clarke,* an active Ohio Democrat who had previously been appointed by Wilson in 1914 to the federal district bench. Clarke was an unmistakable progressive and despite his authorship of the majority opinion in **Abrams** v. **United States,** a rare departure for him, he was one of the most liberal justices ever to sit on the Court. But he was also a gentle soul, and McReynolds' incessant badgering, as well as Clarke's frustration with the conservatism of the majority, led to his resignation after only six years of service on the Court. Had he remained on the Court until Franklin Roosevelt was elected, it is possible that the confrontation between the Court and the New Deal would never have occurred.

Harding–Coolidge–Hoover Appointees

In his two and a half years as President, Harding named four men to the Court including a new Chief Justice. Harding's first appointment went to former President *William Howard Taft* to fill the chief justiceship. Taft had long awaited this moment, for it was the climax of his life's ambition. Taft lobbied very strenuously to secure the nomination and once nominated was rapidly although not unanimously confirmed. Never before nor after was the nation to have as Chief Justice a man who had held as many major public offices. On the Court Taft was to be an effective

---

[56]See, for example, David Burner, ''James C. McReynolds,'' in Leon Friedman and Fred L. Israel, op. cit., vol. 3, pp. 2023–2033; Walter F. Murphy, *Elements of Judicial Strategy* (Chicago: University of Chicago Press, 1964), pp. 52–56; Alpheus T. Mason, *Harlan Fiske Stone: Pillar of the Law* (New York: Viking, 1956), p. 220.

administrator, a vigorous lobbyist for court reform, and a generally effective leader of his
colleagues. He was also to be highly conservative, even at times reactionary, in his views of
social and economic policy.

Harding's subsequent three appointments
went to *George Sutherland,* Harding's former
senatorial colleague and close and trusted advisor; *Pierce Butler,* a conservative Minnesota
Democrat who was a leading corporation lawyer and the fourth Roman Catholic to win appointment to a Court seat; and *Edward T.
Sanford,* a Tennessee Republican who had
been appointed to the federal district court by
Theodore Roosevelt in 1908. All proved to be
business-oriented conservatives, and Sutherland emerged in the 1930s as the intellectual
leader of the opponents of the New Deal.

When Coolidge became President at the
death of Warren Harding and the scandals
from the Harding Administration began to surface, Coolidge turned to someone he had
known since they were students together at
Amherst College several decades earlier, *Harlan Fiske Stone.* Coolidge asked Stone (who
was then Dean of the Columbia Law School)
to become Attorney General and clean up the
corruption in Washington. Stone accepted and
also worked hard for Coolidge's election in
1924. When Justice McKenna retired in January 1925, Coolidge elevated Attorney General
Stone who, within a short period, shocked
most observers by falling within the Holmes-
Brandeis orbit. Stone was to become a leading
liberal and supporter of New Deal measures.

Chief Justice Taft became gravely ill and
most reluctantly resigned from the Court on
February 3, 1930. President Hoover then
quickly named *Charles Evans Hughes* to the
highest judicial position in the land. After his
departure from the Court in 1916 and his unsuccessful run for the presidency that year,
Hughes had gone on to a successful law practice until the Republicans regained the White
House in 1920 and Harding appointed him
Secretary of State. Hughes served in that office for four years and then resumed his law

practice. He also served as a Judge on the Permanent Court of International Justice. Hughes
was 67 when he received the nomination to be
Chief Justice. Confirmation was not easy.
Hughes served for 11 years before retiring at
the age of 79.

Shortly after Hughes' confirmation, Justice
Sanford died. President Hoover nominated
another southerner, John J. Parker, to replace
the deceased Tennessee jurist. Parker was a
judge on the Fourth Circuit Court of Appeals.
In 1920 he had been the Republican candidate
for Governor of North Carolina, but during his
campaign, he had issued a racist statement.
As a judge he participated in antiunion court
decisions. As might be expected, both the
NAACP and organized labor actively opposed
Parker's nomination, and it went down to defeat in the Senate. Hoover then named Republican *Owen J. Roberts,* a prominent Philadelphia lawyer, who was promptly confirmed.
Roberts' judicial career was to be erratic,
shifting inconsistently between liberal and
conservative positions.

In mid-January 1932, Justice Oliver Wendell Holmes, then 91 and still productive, retired from the Court. A widespread campaign
was waged to select one of the greatest state
judges in the nation, New York's *Benjamin N.
Cardozo.* Hoover at first resisted because Cardozo was a Jewish liberal Democrat from a
state that already had two of its sons on the
Court. However, powerful Republican senators, among others, pushed for Cardozo, and
Hoover made the nomination, which was
quickly and unanimously confirmed.

Background Characteristics of the Justices

The key background characteristics of the 16
appointees to Court positions during the presidencies of Taft through Hoover are presented
in Table 4.10. As a rule, politically active men
in the President's party received appointments, but there were exceptions; indeed,
there were an unprecedented number of cross-
party appointments. Three Democrats ap-

pointed by Republican Presidents had not been politically active, although they had important political connections. Taft appointed conservative Democrat Lurton, Harding appointed conservative Democrat Butler, and Hoover appointed liberal Democrat Cardozo. Democrat Wilson appointed politically active Republican Louis Brandeis, but Brandeis had actively campaigned for Wilson in 1912 and for most intents and purposes had become a Democrat.

The table suggests that geographic considerations played some part in Court appointments, but apparently at times not a very important one. Harding appointed Edward Sanford, a Tennessean, even though another son of Tennessee, James McReynolds, was on the bench. Hoover, although he first hesitated, nevertheless named Benjamin Cardozo who became the third New Yorker on the Court. Seats were on longer confined to one state or even one region. Seat number five swung from Georgia to Massachusetts; seat number seven went from New York to Ohio to Utah. However, a rough geographical balance was likely to have been a consideration in appointments.

The occupations of the justices' fathers during this period continued the trend from the previous period of about two-thirds of the fathers being in the professions. These justices receiving appointments had fathers who either were doctors (2), lawyers (7), or clergymen (2). Three fathers were businessmen and just two were farmers. Only one justice during this period, Democrat Pierce Butler, came from truly humble beginnings; the rest were from solid middle- or upper-class families.

Almost all the justices had undergraduate education and well over half attended high-quality colleges. About nine out of ten went to law school; of these about half went to high-quality institutions.[57] Two-thirds of Taft's appointees were judges at the time of their

nominations, but only one out of three of the appointees of Presidents Wilson and Hoover and one out of the four Harding appointees were on the federal or state bench when elevated to the Supreme Court. Most of the other appointees had been in private law practice when selected. However, both Wilson and Coolidge chose their Attorney Generals, a practice carried on by Franklin Roosevelt and Harry Truman. Of the 17 appointments, only 7 went to those with no previous judicial experience.

There was an unprecedented number of appointees with minority religious affiliations. Three Roman Catholics served on the Court (White, McKenna, and Butler), and two of the Jewish faith were also chosen (Brandeis and Cardozo). Four of the 16 justices had ethnic origins outside the British Isles. Lamar was of French descent, Van Devanter of Dutch, Brandeis of Austrian, and Cardozo of Iberian ancestry.

Voting Patterns of the Justices

With the advent of the chief justiceship of Edward White, the Court entered a period of markedly less dissension than it had experienced during the chief justiceship of Melville Fuller. In part this was due to the appointments by President Taft of justices in much the same moderate-conservative mold. Dissent was slightly over 12 percent of all decisions,[58] although during the last half of White's tenure dissension climbed, particularly in cases from the states raising constitutional issues (in these, dissent was 25 percent).[59] During the entire White Court period, in cases in which the Court stuck down state statutes, there was dissent in 29 percent.[60] The Taft Court's overall record of dissension was less than that for the White Court—it was, in

[57]Schmidhauser, *Judges and Justices,* op. cit., pp. 74 (undergraduate education) and 77 (law school).

[58]Ulmer, "Exploring the Dissent Patterns," op. cit.

[59]Sprague, op cit., p. 64.

[60]Johnston, op. cit., p. 91.

Table 4.10 SELECTED CHARACTERISTICS OF JUSTICES APPOINTED BY PRESIDENTS TAFT THROUGH HOOVER

Seat and Justice	Party	Home State	Years on Court	Father's Occupation	Occupation at Time of Nomination	Age at Nomination	Previous Judicial Experience
Taft appointees:							
4 Horace H. Lurton	Democrat	Tennessee	1909–1914	Physician	U.S. Circuit Court Judge	65	State, federal
7 Charles E. Hughes	Republican	New York	1910–1916	Minister	Governor of New York	48	None
1 Edward D. White	Democrat	Louisiana	1910–1921	Lawyer	Associate Justice, U.S. Supreme Court	65	State, federal
2 Willis Van Devanter	Republican	Wyoming	1910–1937	Lawyer	U.S. Circuit Court Judge	51	State, federal
5 Joseph R. Lamar	Democrat	Georgia	1910–1916	Minister	Private law practice	53	State
9 Mahlon Pitney	Republican	New Jersey	1912–1922	Lawyer	Chancellor, New Jersey Appellate Court	54	State
Wilson appointees:							
4 James C. McReynolds	Democrat	Tennessee	1914–1941	Physician	U.S. Attorney General	52	None
5 Louis D. Brandeis	Republican	Massachusetts	1916–1939	Grain merchant	Private law practice	59	None
7 John H. Clarke	Democrat	Ohio	1916–1922	Lawyer	U.S. District Court Judge	59	Federal
Harding appointees:							
1 William H. Taft	Republican	Ohio	1921–1930	Lawyer	Lawyer, law professor	63	State, federal

	Party	State	Years	Occupation	Position before appointment	Age	Prior judicial experience
7 George Sutherland	Republican	Utah	1922–1938	Postman, lawyer	Private law practice	60	None
6 Pierce Butler	Democrat	Minnesota	1923–1939	Farmer	Private law practice	56	None
9 Edward T. Sanford	Republican	Tennessee	1923–1930	Lumber, construction business	U.S. District Court Judge	57	Federal
Coolidge appointee:							
8 Harlan F. Stone	Republican	New York	1925–1941	Farmer	U.S. Attorney General	52	None
Hoover appointees:							
1 Charles E. Hughes	Republican	New York	1930–1941	Minister	Private law practice; Judge, Permanent Court of International Justice	67	Federal
9 Owen J. Roberts	Republican	Pennsylvania	1930–1945	Businessman	Private law practice	55	None
3 Benjamin N. Cardozo	Democrat	New York	1932–1938	Judge	Chief Judge, New York Court of Appeals	61	State

Table 4.11   DISSENT RATES, WHITE COURT, 1916–1920 TERMS

Justice	Dissent Rate (%)	Justice	Dissent Rate (%)
Clarke	8.1	Van Devanter	4.8
McReynolds	5.7	White	3.9
Brandeis	5.6	Holmes	3.8
McKenna	5.6	Day	3.7
Pitney	4.8		

Source: The percentages are derived from data presented in Roger Handberg, Jr., "Decision-Making in a Natural Court, 1916–1921," *American Politics Quarterly,* 4 (1976), p. 364 (Table 1), p. 367 (Table 3).

fact, the lowest since the Marshall Court, about 10.5 percent.[61] In cases involving constitutional challenges to state or municipal laws, the Taft Court's dissent rate, however, was higher but still less than that for the White Court.[62] Only in cases in which the Court struck down state statutes as unconstitutional was there less unanimity than on the White Court.[63] In general, Chief Justice Taft was very concerned that the Court not divide and that justices not dissent unless the issue was a momentous one. For most of the Taft Court period this norm prevailed; for example, only the more significant issues, in which the Court struck down state statutes, provoked what for much of the rest of the time was latent dissent. During the first six years of the Hughes Court dissension began to rise, although it remained slightly less than that in the last half of the White Court.

Individual dissent rates during the last half of the White Court ranged from 3.7 percent of all decisions by the Court with opinions (Justice Day) to 8.1 percent (Justice Clarke) as shown in Table 4.11. Justice Holmes, whose reputation was that of the "Great Dissenter," had the second *lowest* dissent rate (3.8 per-

cent) and Justice Brandeis, also known as a dissenter, actually dissented in only 5.6 percent of the Court's decisions.

In Table 4.12, we see the range of voting behavior in the White Court's nonunanimous decisions in both the economic and civil liberties spheres. On the economic issues, Justice McReynolds was the least liberal. He supported the economic position of the government in only about one out of four cases that divided the Court. At the other extreme, Justice Clarke was the most liberal. He supported the economically liberal position about nine out of ten times. Justices Brandeis, Holmes, and Pitney were the second, third, and fourth most liberal. In the civil liberties area, Justices Brandeis, Holmes, and Clarke were the most liberal and Justices Pitney, Van Devanter, and McReynolds the least liberal. Overall Brandeis and Holmes formed the core of the liberal bloc and they were joined by Clarke. Justice Van Devanter and Chief Justice White formed the core of the conservative bloc, with Justice Pitney having the loosest ties with the bloc.[64] Pitney was conservative on civil liberties as well as labor issues, but on economic matters not involving labor he was generally liberal.

One study of the Taft Court found that in

[61]Ulmer, "Exploring the Dissent Patterns," op. cit.

[62]Sprague, op. cit., p. 64.

[63]Johnston, op. cit., p. 91.

[64]Bloc analysis was based on the data presented in Roger Handberg, Jr., "Decision-Making in a Natural Court, 1916–1921," *American Politics Quarterly,* 4 (1976), p. 367.

Table 4.12 PRO-ECONOMIC LIBERALISM AND PRO-CIVIL LIBERTIES
VOTING OF THE JUSTICES ON THE WHITE COURT,
1916–1920 TERMS, IN NONUNANIMOUSLY DECIDED
CASES

Justice	Economic Liberalism (% of votes in favor)	Civil Liberties (% of votes in favor)
Clarke	89.2	51.9
Brandeis	80.8	60.7
Holmes	66.0	53.6
Pitney	61.0	0.0
Day	53.3	14.8
White	44.4	37.0
McKenna	43.3	32.1
Van Devanter	36.8	14.3
McReynolds	27.3	16.0

Source: The percentages are derived from data presented in Roger Handberg, Jr.,
"Decision Making in a Natural Court, 1916–1921," *American Politics Quarterly,* 4 (1976),
p. 365 (Table 2).

economic liberalism cases Justice Brandeis was the most liberal (note that Justice Clarke resigned from the Court in 1922) with Holmes and then Harlan Fiske Stone close behind. Justice Sanford was in the middle. Taft, McKenna, and Van Devanter were conservative, with Butler, Sutherland, and McReynolds being the most extreme antigovernment justices.[65] Although there were relatively few civil liberties decisions, it was found, not unexpectedly, that Holmes and Brandeis supported civil liberties the most and McReynolds, Sutherland, and Van Devanter the least. Butler, however, was surpassed only by Holmes and Brandeis in favoring the civil liberties position in the criminal due process cases, and the same was true for Justice Sanford with First Amendment cases.[66] Stone generally was the fourth most favorable to civil liberties claims.

As mentioned earlier, the norm on the Taft Court was not to dissent unless the issue was of major importance. Suppression of dissent was common.[67] With the passage of the Judiciary Act of 1925, the Court gained control over its docket through the discretionary use of the writ of certiorari for large categories of cases that previously were obligatory for the Court to review. This meant that the Court could and would screen out the unimportant or frivolous cases, leaving essentially the most important or controversial cases for its decisions. Dissent on the Taft Court could be expected to increase after 1925, as the norm of stifling dissent did not apply to the truly momentous cases. Table 4.13 supports this view. In the 1922–1924 Terms, dissent ranged from no dissent (Stone—but note that he came to the Court during the middle of the 1924 Term) to 4.3 percent for McReynolds, the right-wing extremist who marched to the sound of his own drummer. In the 1927–1929 Term period, after the reforms legislated in the Judiciary Act of 1925 took effect, dissent increased on

[65]Leavitt, op. cit., p. 11 and App. III.

[66]Ibid., App. III.

[67]See, for example, Alexander M. Bickel, *The Unpublished Opinions of Mr. Justice Brandeis* (Cambridge, Mass.: Harvard University Press, 1957).

Table 4.13   DISSENT RATES, TAFT COURT, BEFORE AND AFTER PASSAGE OF
THE JUDICIARY ACT OF 1925

Justice	Dissent Rate Before Passage (1922–1924 Terms) (%)	Dissent Rate After Passage (1927–1929 Terms) (%)
McReynolds	4.3	4.9
Brandeis	3.6	7.3
Sutherland	2.9	3.0
Holmes	2.1	7.3
Taft	1.4	0.5
Van Devanter	0.9	0.8
Butler	0.8	3.0
Sanford	0.7	2.4
Stone	0.0	5.6

Source: Dissent rates from Stephen C. Halpern and Kenneth N. Vines, "Institutional Disunity, the Judges' Bill and the Role of the U.S. Supreme Court," *Western Political Quarterly,* 30 (1977), p. 477.

the part of the three liberals (Holmes, Brandeis, and Stone) as well as for the moderate conservative Sanford. For Taft, leader of the conservative majority, and for Sutherland, Van Devanter, and McReynolds, dissent either increased only slightly or even decreased. Only Pierce Butler, with his idiosyncratic criminal-procedures views, markedly increased his dissent rate (which nevertheless was less than half that of Holmes and Brandeis).

During the first seven years of the Hughes Court (through the 1936 Term), the Court was dominated by issues associated with economic liberalism.[68] Stone, although a liberal during the Taft Court, became even more liberal, as Table 4.14 suggests, slightly surpassing Brandeis. During the 1935–1936 Terms, McReynolds, as one might expect, was the most laissez-faire oriented justice, followed closely by Butler and then Sutherland and Van Devanter; these four formed the conservative bloc. Roberts was clearly the "swing man," with Hughes joining the laissez-faire majority in one out of three cases. Brandeis, Stone, and

Cardozo constituted the economically liberal (anti-laissez-faire) core.

The Supreme Court from the time of the Fuller Court through the first half of the Hughes Court established or used a variety of doctrines. These included substantive due process along with commerce and taxing clause doctrines that were employed, when a majority was so moved, to attack the actions of government in defense of laissez-faire. If the majority wished to uphold governmental activity, there were doctrines available for that purpose too. Insofar as economic policy was concerned, the justices could pick and choose among different, even contradictory, doctrines to justify whatever a majority happened to agree upon. By the mid-1930s the conservative bloc, joined by Justice Roberts and sometimes by Chief Justice Hughes, brought the country to the brink of a major constitutional crisis.

Patterns of Group Interaction

Personal relations among the justices and the nature and quality of leadership exercised by the Chief Justice varied during the White, Taft, and early Hughes Courts. When Associ-

[68]Leavitt, op. cit., p. 13.

Table 4.14 LAISSEZ-FAIRE VOTING ON THE SUPREME COURT, 1935–1936 TERMS, NONUNANIMOUS DECISIONS

Justice	Proportion of Pro-Laissez-Faire Antigovernment Votes (%)
McReynolds	89.6
Butler	87.5
Sutherland	79.2
Van Devanter	74.5
Roberts	50.0
Hughes	33.3
Brandeis	4.2
Stone	2.3
Cardozo	2.1

Source: The percentages are derived from David J. Danelski, "Values as Variables in Judicial Decision-Making: Notes Toward a Theory," *Vanderbilt Law Review,* 19 (1966), pp. 734–735 (Figure 4). A laissez-faire case was defined as any case involving governmental activity in economic matters.

ate Justice White was promoted to Chief Justice, the Court was faced with several personality conflicts. Justice Harlan did not like either White or Holmes, and the feelings were mutual.[69] Justice Hughes in the early years of the White Court was "tense and highstrung,"[70] although by his own account his demeanor changed after he gave up smoking.[71] Justice McKenna was unsure of himself and "was hesitant to express a definite view";[72] by the end of White's tenure McKenna began slipping into senility. But by 1912 Harlan had died, the Taft appointees were all in place on the Court, and according to Justice Hughes "the atmosphere of the Court changed and we became a reasonably happy family."[73] White,

happy with his position, "was no longer distant or difficult."[74] Several of the justices formed close friendships with one another: Hughes and Holmes, Chief Justice White and Van Devanter, Brandeis and Clarke. After Clarke was appointed, he had written to Brandeis, "I am looking forward with unusual confidence to pleasant association with you because of what I suppose is something of a community [common] point of view between us."[75] Brandeis and Holmes also developed a close professional association that hit its stride during the Taft Court.

It appears on the basis of available evidence that Chief Justice White was able to exercise successful social leadership on the Court. He maintained good relationships with his colleagues, and according to Justice Hughes, White "was most considerate and gracious in his dealings with every member of the Court, plainly anxious to create an atmo-

[69] *The Autobiographical Notes of Charles Evans Hughes,* David J. Danelski and Joseph S. Tulchin (eds.) (Cambridge, Mass.: Harvard University Press, 1973), p. 168.

[70] Ibid., p. 176.

[71] Ibid.

[72] Ibid., p. 170.

[73] Ibid., p. 169.

[74] Ibid.

[75] As quoted in Alpheus T. Mason, *Brandeis: A Free Man's Life* (New York: Viking, 1946), p. 513.

sphere of friendliness and to promote agreement in the disposition of cases,"[76] White, whose eyesight was failing, came to rely on Van Devanter, Hughes, Holmes, and Brandeis, the strongest intellects on the Court.

White, apparently, was not an effective task leader. In comparing the experience of the judicial conferences under Taft as Chief Justice to those of White at the helm, Justice Brandeis observed that "the judges go home less tired emotionally and less weary physically than in White's day. When we differ we agree to differ without any ill feeling. It's all very friendly."[77] The problem with Chief Justice White, it seems, was not that he lacked the intellectual prerequisites for effective task leadership, but that he lacked the personal skills necessary to be an effective conference leader. White was often indecisive and his conference presentations of cases were models of long-windedness and ambiguity. He allowed his colleagues to be similarly diffuse in their remarks, thus unnecessarily prolonging the conferences.[78]

As Chief Justice, William Howard Taft stood in marked contrast to his predecessor in appearance, health, personality, and especially administrative and conference skills. Taft ran a tight ship. Like his predecessor, Taft effectively exercised social leadership, but, unlike White, Taft recognized his own limitations. As a consequence Taft deferred to Justice Van Devanter, who during much of Taft's tenure was the actual task leader of the conference. This was all the more remarkable because Van Devanter throughout his career suffered from "pen paralysis" and was unable to write more than a handful of opinions for the Court each term, far below his fair share

of the workload. Yet, he was an intellectually gifted and articulate jurist who was capable during the conference of going to the heart of legal problems and drawing upon precedents appropriate for the resolution of the cases. As Taft observed to a friend about Van Devanter, "his power of statement and his immense memory make him an antagonist in conference who generally wins against all opposition."[79] Chief Justice Hughes observed in his autobiographical notes that Van Devanter's "careful and elaborate statements in conference, with his accurate review of authorities were of the greatest value. If these statements had been taken down stenographically they would have served with but little editing as excellent opinions."[80]

Taft, however, had his problems as Chief Justice. When he assumed office, he found McReynolds "always trying to escape work,"[81] and, in addition, McReynolds was a highly disagreeable individual whom Taft privately described as "selfish to the last degree . . . fuller of prejudice than any man I have ever known . . . one who delights in making others uncomfortable . . . a continual grouch . . . [who] really seems to have less of a loyal spirit to the Court than anybody."[82] Added to the McReynolds problem was Justice Van Devanter's difficulty in putting pen to paper, which meant that Taft shouldered much more than his fair share of opinion writing.

During his first several years as Chief Justice, Taft found that Justice McKenna, who was in his late seventies, was for all intents and purposes senile. Taft wrote in a letter to

[76]*The Autobiographical Notes of Charles Evans Hughes,* op. cit., p. 169.

[77]As quoted in Alpheus T. Mason, *William Howard Taft: Chief Justice* (New York: Simon & Schuster, 1965), p. 200.

[78]Pusey, op. cit., pp. 282–283.

[79]As quoted in David J. Danelski, "The Influence of the Chief Justice in the Decisional Process of the Supreme Court," in Thomas P. Jahnige and Sheldon Goldman (eds.), *The Federal Judicial System* (New York: Holt, Rinehart and Winston, 1968), p. 152.

[80]*The Autobiographical Notes of Charles Evans Hughes,* op. cit., p. 171.

[81]As quoted in Mason, *William Howard Taft,* op. cit., p. 195.

[82]Ibid., pp. 215–216.

his brother about McKenna, "In case after case he will write an opinion and bring it into conference, and it will meet objection because he has missed a point in one case, or, as in one instance, he wrote an opinion deciding the case one way when there had been a unanimous vote the other, including his own."[83] McKenna's opinions became garbled and nonsensical. Complained Taft, "He does not know what he means himself. . . . I try to give him the easiest cases but nothing is too easy for him."[84] McKenna, with increasing frequency, disrupted the conferences with senile outbursts. Finally, in November 1924, McKenna's colleagues met at Taft's home, and a consensus was reached that no case would be decided by the Court if the outcome were dependent on McKenna's vote. Soon thereafter Taft met with McKenna and somehow persuaded him to resign.

Further plaguing Chief Justice Taft was the liberal wing of the Court, which was, in Taft's eyes, instigated by Brandeis; it included Holmes, Clarke, and later Stone. Taft sought to minimize the damage to the conservative jurisprudence he espoused by having informal Sunday afternoon conferences quietly held at his home. Van Devanter, Sutherland, Sanford, and Butler were invited (Stone also came until he moved to the Brandeis-Holmes wing of the Court).[85]

One final difficulty Taft faced was the state of his health after he suffered a heart attack in April 1924. Although he sought to cut back on his work and activities, he was soon back at close to full swing. However, during the last two years of his tenure his health declined, he became more irritable as Chief Justice, and dissension on the Court increased.[86]

During most of his tenure as Chief Justice,

Taft clearly exercised social leadership. He was the only member of the Court with a good personal relationship with every other member of the Court. During the summer vacations Taft had a cordial correspondence with all his colleagues.[87] Over the years, Taft went out of his way to be kind and considerate. For example, when Justice Sutherland suffered a nervous breakdown in 1927, Taft wrote to him, "We all love you, George, and we would all regard it as the greatest loss to the country to have you become discouraged over your work, and we realize of what great importance it is to the country that you should be restored to your working capacity."[88] Holmes wrote of Taft's conduct of the conference, "He is good-humored, laughs readily . . . keeping things moving pleasantly." And, on a later occasion, Holmes wrote that "never before . . . have we gotten along with so little jangling and dissension."[89]

Of course, Taft's principal objective was to "mass the Court," that is, have the Court speak with one voice and not with concurrences, or worse, dissent. To achieve this desired teamwork, Taft "exploited personal courtesy and charm, maximized the assignment and reassignment powers, relied on the expertise of his associates."[90] Taft saw to it that his disapproving view of dissent became part of the Code of Judicial Ethics. Canon 19, adopted in 1925, states that "It is of high importance that judges constituting a court of last resort should use effort and self-restraint to promote solidarity of conclusion and the consequent influence of judicial decision. . . . Except in case of conscientious difference of opinion on fundamental principle, dissenting opinions should be discouraged in courts of

[83]Ibid., p. 213.

[84]Ibid., p. 214.

[85]Mason, *Brandeis,* op. cit., p. 606.

[86]Sprague, op. cit., p. 64.

[87]Danelski, "The Influence of the Chief Justice," op. cit., p. 153, n. 33.

[88]As quoted in Mason, *William Howard Taft,* op. cit., p. 205.

[89]Ibid., p. 199.

[90]Ibid., p. 198.

last resort."[91] Of the 1596 decisions handed down by the Taft Court, Taft dissented in 17 (writing dissenting opinions in three of these).[92] Taft suppressed at least 200 of his dissenting votes,[93] and Justice Brandeis suppressed large numbers of his concurrences and dissents.[94] Brandeis admitted to his close friend, Felix Frankfurter, "I can't always dissent, I sometimes endorse an opinion with which I do not agree. I acquiesce."[95] How else does one explain, for example, Brandeis' and Holmes' votes in the child labor tax case (**Bailey** v. **Drexel Furniture Company**)? Justice Butler expressed the antidissent credo of the Taft Court on the back of a draft of an opinion prepared by Justice Stone:

> I voted to reverse. While this sustains your conclusion to affirm, I still think reversal would be better. But I shall in silence acquiesce. Dissents seldom aid in the right development or statement of the law. They often do harm. For myself I say: 'Lead us not into temptation.'[96]

Charles Evans Hughes became Chief Justice in early 1930 and soon demonstrated effective conference leadership. He came to the conference well prepared, and his high-order intellect served him well in channeling conference discussion. As Hughes observed in his autobiographical notes, "I conceived it to be my duty as Chief Justice to make an independent study of each case and to present to the conference accurately and comprehensively, but succinctly, the questions presented and then to state my own views, seeking thus to afford a basis for the discussion of essential points."[97] When the Chief Justice was finished and if the justices wished to discuss the case under consideration, each justice gave his views in order of seniority, indicating whether he agreed or disagreed with the Chief Justice's analysis. Once the colleagues were through, Hughes would recapitulate the discussion, highlighting the points of agreement and of conflict. He then took a vote and the case was dispatched.

Hughes was clearly an efficient conference leader. Justice Roberts noted of Hughes: "The Chief Justice was an intense man. When he had serious business to transact he allowed no consideration to interfere with his operations. He was so engrossed in the vital issue that he had not time for lightness and pleasantry."[98] However, Justice Roberts observed that Hughes had a good personal relationship with the associates and that he was seen by them as being "considerate, sympathetic, and responsive." One student of twentieth-century chief justices ranks Hughes as perhaps the most effective, successfully combining task and social leadership with the end result that "conference production reached the highest point in the Court's history under Hughes and has never been equalled."[99] Although there was division in the Court on constitutional matters, the justices apparently retained a strong sense of institutional loyalty and cordiality.

[91]Ibid., p. 219.

[92]Ibid., pp. 223, 231.

[93]David J. Danelski, "The Influence of the Chief Justice in the Decisional Process of the Supreme Court," paper presented at the 1960 Annual Meeting of the American Political Science Association, p. 20, n. 122, as cited by Mason, *William Howard Taft,* op. cit., p. 223.

[94]See Bickel, op. cit.

[95]As quoted in Mason, *William Howard Taft,* op. cit., p. 201.

[96]Danelski, "The Influence of the Chief Justice," in Jahnige and Goldman, *The Federal Judicial System,* op. cit., p. 159.

[97]*The Autobiographical Notes of Charles Evans Hughes,* op. cit., p. 301.

[98]Danelski, "The Influence of the Chief Justice," op. cit., p. 154.

[99]Ibid.

Chapter

5

The Justices—Their Appointments, Backgrounds, Voting Patterns, and Patterns of Group Interaction, 1937–1991

We continue our consideration of the selection and backgrounds of Supreme Court justices and their patterns of voting and group interaction from 1937 to the present. President Franklin D. Roosevelt, elected in 1932, had no opportunity to name a justice to the Supreme Court during his first term. The confrontation between the Court and the Roosevelt Administration over the constitutionality of the New Deal was recounted in Chapter 3. We pick up the story with Roosevelt's second term.

THE CONSTITUTIONAL REVOLUTION OF 1937 AND THE ROOSEVELT COURT AFTERMATH

President Franklin D. Roosevelt named nine men to Supreme Court positions—appointing eight new justices and elevating one associate justice to the rank of chief justice—a record surpassed only by George Washington. Seven were registered Democrats, one a Roosevelt Independent, and one a Republican (Harlan Fiske Stone, chosen for elevation to the chief justiceship). The first five appointments came before the year in which America entered World War II.

Roosevelt Remakes the Court

When Roosevelt finally had an opportunity to name his first appointee, he chose the ardent New Deal Senator from Alabama, *Hugo L. Black*. At the time of his nomination, Black was not highly regarded by legal scholars, and his chief attribute appeared to be that he was a hell-raising Roosevelt supporter. Black graduated from the University of Alabama Law School and then for 19 years practiced law in various capacities, including that of local police court judge, county prosecuting attorney, and lawyer specializing in personal injury suits (he was hardly one of the leading lawyers in Alabama). He ran for and was twice elected to the U.S. Senate. In the 1920s when he had set his sights on a political career, Black joined the Ku Klux Klan. He left the Klan before taking his seat in the Senate although he was given a life membership in that racist organization. In the interval between confirmation and his taking his seat, newspaper stories widely publicized his membership in the Klan. To stop the damaging publicity and false rumors of continuing Klan membership, Black addressed the nation over the radio. Black assured the public that he had long since severed his ties with the Klan and that he was deeply committed to fighting for the "civil, economic and religious rights of all Americans without regard to race or creed." Black's subsequent 34 years on the Court dramatically demonstrated how wrong his opponents were about his legal ability and how sincere and deep was his liberalism. Black was one of the greatest justices ever to serve on the Court. His intellectual contributions were formidable and over the span of his tenure on the Court his influence was considerable.

Roosevelt's second appointment went to *Stanley F. Reed,* who was serving the administration as Solicitor General. Although Reed, as expected, was to support Roosevelt's economic policies when they were challenged before the Court, he was to be considerably more conservative on matters of civil liberties.

Felix Frankfurter, the brilliant Harvard Law School professor and close advisor to Roosevelt, was the third appointee. Frankfurter came to the Court with the reputation of being a leading civil libertarian and having one of the best legal minds in the nation. He was named to the seat previously occupied by

Justice Cardozo and earlier by Justice Holmes. Once on the bench Frankfurter demonstrated a commitment to upholding the New Deal and the constitutionality of government regulation of the economy. He evolved a philosophy of judicial restraint that he applied to both economic regulation *and* civil liberties. He was an important intellectual force on the Court during his 23 years of service. Frankfurter and Black frequently took opposing sides on civil liberties issues, raising the level and at times the intensity of debate to heights rarely equaled during the Court's history.

William O. Douglas, another brilliant lawyer, was named at the age of 40 to fill the vacancy created by the retirement of Justice Brandeis. Douglas was a strong New Deal supporter and was serving the administration in the capacity of Chairman of the Securities and Exchange Commission when appointed. Douglas had come from a poverty-stricken family (his father had died when Douglas was 5) and childhood of poor health (he had polio). After military service during World War I, Douglas moved East, graduated second in his class at Columbia Law School, and eventually taught at Yale Law School. Douglas was to have a lengthy career on the Court, serving longer than any other justice in the Court's history. Of course, he strongly supported the New Deal. In matters of civil liberties, he sided with Justice Black and their voting records on the Court for about a quarter of a century were similar. In the 1960s, as Justice Black began taking more conservative positions on some civil liberties issues, Justice Douglas moved even further to the left, and his record on the Court during his last decade of service marked him as likely the most liberal—even radical—justice ever to sit on the Court. His legal brilliance matched that of Black and Frankfurter.

Frank Murphy was Attorney General when he was nominated in early January 1940. He had a rich political background, having served previously as mayor of Detroit, Governor

General of the Philippines, and Governor of Michigan. He was a strong New Dealer and committed civil libertarian. His record on the Court during the relatively brief period he served during the 1940s demonstrated an even greater support for civil liberties than that displayed by Black and Douglas.

These five appointments demonstrated Roosevelt's deliberate selection of unquestioned New Deal supporters and those he considered to have a liberal perspective. Domestic New Deal considerations were paramount in the selection process. It was important to Roosevelt that a solid New Deal majority be placed on the Court. As the year 1941 unfolded, it was increasingly apparent to perceptive observers that sooner or later the United States would be drawn into the war against fascism. Certainly, President Roosevelt was anticipating this. Of Roosevelt's four appointments between 1941 and 1943 only one, to the chief justiceship, reflected a broader concern with national unity during wartime. Wartime necessity, however, seemed to have been responsible for a vacancy filled in 1943.

In early 1941 Justice McReynolds announced he would retire from the Court at the end of the term. Roosevelt then turned to one of his leading supporters in the Senate, South Carolinian *James F. Byrnes*. Although Byrnes was much more conservative on matters of civil liberties than any of the other previous Roosevelt appointees, he was closely associated with Roosevelt and the New Deal. Byrnes was to serve, however, for only one term of the Court. Byrnes, apparently uncomfortable as a justice, responded favorably when Roosevelt asked him in the fall of 1942 to leave the Court to become Assistant President for Economic Affairs. Roosevelt wanted to devote his main attention to the war and foreign policy and he trusted Byrnes' administrative and political talents as equal to the job of virtually running the American domestic economy.

When Chief Justice Hughes announced that he would retire on July 1, 1941, Roosevelt was placed in a dilemma. He wanted to name his Attorney General, Robert Jackson, to the chief justiceship. Roosevelt had even talked with Jackson about this possibility and Jackson was eager for the post. However, Associate Justice Harlan Fiske Stone was a logical candidate for the job. Stone was highly regarded as a jurist and many believed that he had earned the promotion to Chief Justice. He certainly had seemed sympathetic to the New Deal. In a quandary, Roosevelt turned to Justice Frankfurter and asked him whom he would choose. Frankfurter replied:

> [O]n personal grounds I'd prefer Bob [Jackson]. . . . But from the national interest I am bound to say there is no reason for preferring Bob to Stone—quite the contrary. Stone is senior and qualified professionally to be C. J. But for me the decisive consideration, considering the fact that Stone is qualified, is that Bob is of your political and personal family, as it were, while Stone is a Republican. Now it doesn't require prophetic powers to be sure that we shall, sooner or later, be in war—I think sooner. It is most important that when war does come, the country should feel that you are a national, the Nation's, President, and not a partisan President. Few things would contribute as much to confidence in you as a national and not a partisan President than for you to name a Republican, who has the profession's confidence, as Chief Justice.[1]

That reasoning must have been persuasive, for Roosevelt then nominated *Harlan Fiske Stone* to be Chief Justice.

To fill the associate justiceship vacated by Stone, Roosevelt nominated *Robert H. Jackson*. Jackson, widely regarded as a brilliant lawyer, had been very active in New York Democratic party politics and had worked closely with Roosevelt from the time Roosevelt was Governor of New York. He served the New Deal in various positions before set-

---

[1]As quoted in Alpheus T. Mason, *Harlan Fiske Stone: Pillar of the Law* (New York: Viking, 1956), pp. 566–567.

tling into the Department of Justice, where he served first as Assistant Attorney General, then Solicitor General, and finally Attorney General. His tenure on the Court was marked by two dramatic episodes. First, he was asked by President Truman to serve as Chief Prosecutor for the United States in the Nuremberg trials of Nazi war criminals. This meant that Jackson had to take a leave of absence from the Court and as a consequence Jackson missed an entire term, thus leaving the Court understaffed. Jackson's experience at Nuremberg apparently shook him profoundly, and after his return he seemed less liberal than before his prosecution of the Nazis. A second dramatic event was the public feud in 1946 between Jackson and Justice Black after Chief Justice Stone's death when Jackson was in Nuremberg.*

Roosevelt's last Court appointment went to *Wiley B. Rutledge,* a liberal federal appeals court judge and former Dean of the University of Iowa Law School. Rutledge was considerably more civil liberties oriented than the man he replaced, James Byrnes.

Background Characteristics of the Justices

Table 5.1 offers the principal background characteristics of Roosevelt's nine appointees. All nine were known New Deal supporters and only one, Harlan Fiske Stone, was a Republican. With the exception of Stone and Rutledge, the appointees were personal friends of Roosevelt and politically close to him. All the justices had a background of political activism, although Frankfurter's activism before his close association with Roosevelt had been on behalf of liberal causes.

Geographic considerations played only a limited role in the selection process, continuing the trends evident in the first three de-

cades of the century. No state or region, with the seeming but unlikely exception of New York, had a claim on a seat. The replacement of one New Yorker (Hughes) by another (Stone) in the chief justiceship slot and the appointment of yet another New Yorker (Jackson) to replace the elevated Stone were, by all accounts, entirely unrelated to geographic considerations. A southerner, Black, replaced a westerner, Van Devanter. A Kentuckian, Reed, replaced a son of Utah, Sutherland. On the other hand, with the exception of midwesterner Rutledge, who replaced southerner Byrnes, the remaining four appointments went to people from the same region (Northeast or Southeast) as the men they replaced.

It has been reported that President Roosevelt wanted to appoint someone from the West and was finally persuaded that Douglas, who grew up in the state of Washington, qualified as a westerner despite his long East Coast residency. Wiley Rutledge, too, may have had the decisive edge in the selection process because he was not another easterner. Also Roosevelt may have been more sensitive during the war to considerations of geographic balance as a means of stimulating national unity. Nevertheless, the Roosevelt Court was a geographically unbalanced Court. In 1943 there were four northeasterners (two New Yorkers and one each from Massachusetts and Pennsylvania), two southerners (Alabama and Kentucky), two midwesterners (Michigan and Iowa), and Justice Douglas who had spent his youth in the West but his adulthood in the East.

The occupations of the justices' fathers departed from what had been the trend since the Civil War. Only one-fourth of the justices had fathers in medicine or law. One-third were farmers. An unprecedented number of appointees had humble origins or were raised in genteel poverty. Two of the justices (Douglas and Byrnes) had no father to raise them. None was from the upper class.

All but Justices Jackson and Byrnes (who studied law as apprentices) were law school

---

*The details of the Jackson-Black feud are recounted in the text in "Patterns of Group Interaction," following the next two sections.

Table 5.1 SELECTED CHARACTERISTICS OF JUSTICES APPOINTED BY PRESIDENT FRANKLIN D. ROOSEVELT

Seat and Justice	Party	Home State	Years on Court	Father's Occupation	Occupation at Time of Nomination	Age at Nomination	Previous Judicial Experience
2 Hugo L. Black	Democrat	Alabama	1937–1971	Farmer, storekeeper	U.S. Senator	51	Local
7 Stanley F. Reed	Democrat	Kentucky	1938–1957	Physician	U.S. Solicitor General	53	None
3 Felix Frankfurter	Independent	Massachusetts	1939–1962	Merchant	Law professor	56	None
5 William O. Douglas	Democrat	Connecticut	1939–1975	Missionary, minister	Chairman, Securities & Exchange Commission	40	None
6 Frank Murphy	Democrat	Michigan	1940–1949	Lawyer	U.S. Attorney General	49	State
4 James F. Byrnes	Democrat	South Carolina	1941–1942	Father died before Byrnes was born	U.S. senator	62	None
1 Harlan Fiske Stone	Republican	New York	1941–1946	Farmer	Associate Justice, U.S. Supreme Court	68	Federal
8 Robert H. Jackson	Democrat	New York	1941–1954	Farmer, storekeeper	U.S. Attorney General	49	None
4 Wiley B. Rutledge	Democrat	Iowa	1943–1949	Minister	U.S. Circuit Court Judge	48	Federal

graduates and the quality of their legal education varied. Stone, Reed, and Douglas earned Columbia law degrees, Frankfurter a Harvard degree, Murphy a degree from the University of Michigan Law School, Black a University of Alabama Law School degree, and Rutledge a degree from the University of Colorado Law School.

Only two of the justices (Stone and Rutledge) were judges at the time of their nomination. However, with the exception of Harvard Law Professor Frankfurter, every Roosevelt appointee held public office at the time of appointment: two Attorney Generals (Murphy and Jackson), two senators (Black and Byrnes), and two high government officials (Reed and Douglas). No Roosevelt appointee was in private practice at the time of appointment—which was a sharp departure from the past. A majority of the appointees (five) had no previous judicial experience and this, too, was in contrast to previous trends.

In terms of minority religion appointments, Roosevelt replaced one Roman Catholic (Butler) with another (Murphy) and one Jew (Cardozo) with another (Frankfurter). It is not known if other Roman Catholics and Jews were simply not considered for other vacancies because of their religions being already "represented." Needless to say, given the pervasive problems of racial and sexual discrimination, no blacks or women were seriously considered for Supreme Court positions. Only one justice, Frankfurter, had ethnic origins outside the British Isles.[2] Frankfurter, born in Vienna, had come to the United States when he was a lad of 12.

Voting Patterns of the Justices

The decade beginning with the 1936 Term of the Court and ending with the 1945 Term was revolutionary in many respects. Not only did

the Court do an about-face by withdrawing constitutional restraints on government economic and social welfare policymaking, but the Court also began to be activist on behalf of civil liberties and, in particular, First Amendment freedoms. Furthermore, the old norm of not dissenting unless absolutely necessary was cast aside as the Court reached unprecedented levels of dissent. Bloc behavior became more frequent and pronounced. During the chief justiceship of Harlan Fiske Stone, several of the justices were not only ideologically but even personally antagonistic toward one another. Just as the nation experienced turbulent times first with the Great Depression and then with World War II, so did the Court experience its own form of turbulence.

The change in the overall dissent rate on the Court was dramatic. During the first six years of Chief Justice Hughes' tenure, from the 1930 through the 1935 Terms, dissent ranged from 11 to 16 percent of the full opinions of the Court. Beginning with the 1936 Term, when the Court did its constitutional about-face, through the end of Hughes' tenure (the 1940 Term), dissent increased markedly and varied from 19 (the 1936 Term) to 34 percent (the 1938 Term), with the 1937 Term at 27 percent, the 1939 Term at 30 percent, and the 1940 Term at 28 percent. The rate of dissent during the five terms in which Stone was Chief Justice grew to unprecedented heights (an overall rate of 48.6 percent) and ranged from 36 (the 1941 Term) to 58 percent (the 1943 and 1944 Terms), with the 1942 Term at 44 percent and the 1945 Term at 56 percent dissent.[3]

With the 1943 Term, the Court for the first

[2]John R. Schmidhauser, *Judges and Justices: The Federal Appellate Judiciary* (Boston: Little, Brown, 1979), pp. 60–61.

[3]These figures on dissent rates are taken from C. Herman Pritchett, *The Roosevelt Court* (Chicago: Quadrangle paperback edition, 1969), p. 25, and S. Sidney Ulmer, "Exploring the Dissent Patterns of the Chief Justices: John Marshall to Warren Burger," in Sheldon Goldman and Charles M. Lamb (eds.), *Judicial Conflict and Consensus: Behavioral Studies of American Appellate Courts* (Lexington, Ky.: The University Press of Kentucky, 1986), p. 53.

time in its history had one or more dissents in a majority of its decisions with full opinion. This became the typical pattern on the Court continuing through the present. The Stone Court had the highest dissent rate up to that time in history (62 percent) in those decisions that struck down state or municipal laws as unconstitutional.[4]

The last five years of the Hughes Court and the five years of the Stone Court saw unprecedented high rates of dissension in cases from the states that raised constitutional issues (56 percent with dissent in the 1939 Term, 68 percent dissent in the 1944 Term).[5] The increased dissension was at first a reflection of the clash between the new liberal majority and the old guard on the Court over economic issues. Then, as the Roosevelt appointees came to dominate the Court, they found themselves divided particularly on the new civil liberties issues. Ideological and even, to some extent, personal antagonisms help to explain what C. Herman Pritchett called "the multiplication of division" on the Court. As we shall see in the next section, Chief Justice Stone's leadership style may also have contributed to the galloping dissensus.

Individual dissent rates during the five terms before and after the constitutional revolution of 1937 and during the Stone Court are presented in Table 5.2. Stone, Cardozo, and Brandeis had the highest dissent rates during the early Hughes Court before the momentous 1936 Term. But both overall dissent and individual dissent rates were low compared to the two later periods. Once the constitutional revolution was underway and Roosevelt appointees took their places on the bench, the dissent rates of Hughes and Roberts shot up. Indeed, Roberts moved from the justice with

the lowest dissent rate (1.8 percent, a rate shared with Hughes) to the justice with the highest dissent rate on the Stone Court (23.1 percent). Van Devanter, Sutherland, Butler, and McReynolds markedly increased their rates of dissent between the first and second half of the Hughes Court. By contrast, the dissent rates of Stone, Cardozo, and Brandeis declined sharply during the second part of the Hughes Court and the Roosevelt appointees' dissent rates were lower than they would be during the Stone Court. During his chief justiceship, Harlan Fiske Stone achieved the highest dissent rate of his entire career on the Court. The average dissent rate of the Roosevelt appointees during the Stone Court years was 12.4 percent as compared to their average dissent rate of 4.3 percent during the last term of the Hughes Court.

Analysis of judicial voting behavior in the nonunanimous decisions of the Court reveals the existence of voting blocs with a high level of cohesion during the Hughes Court and with somewhat lower levels of cohesion during the Stone Court. The findings are presented in Table 5.3. During the 1931–1935 Terms, Chief Justice Hughes and Justice Roberts joined with the four staunch conservatives Van Devanter, Sutherland, McReynolds, and Butler to form a conservative bloc. But the voting behavior of Hughes and Roberts suggests that their allegiance to the Court's right wing was not as strong as that of their more conservative colleagues. Although the dissent rate for Hughes and Roberts was the lowest on the Court, when they dissented their pattern of dissents differed from one another and from that of the four conservatives. When Hughes dissented, he dissented with the liberals. When Roberts dissented, he distributed his dissents between the left and right wings of the Court.[6] Glendon Schubert analyzed the voting behavior of Hughes and Roberts and designated their behavior as the Hughberts

[4]Richard E. Johnston, "Some Comparative Statistics on U.S. Chief Justice Courts," *Rocky Mountain Social Science Journal*, 9 (1972), p. 91.

[5]John D. Sprague, *Voting Patterns of the United States Supreme Court: Cases in Federalism 1889–1959* (Indianapolis: Bobbs-Merrill, 1968), p. 64.

[6]Pritchett, op. cit., p. 32.

Table 5.2   DISSENT RATES, HUGHES AND STONE COURTS

	Dissent Rates		
Justice	1931–1935 Terms (%)	1936–1940 Terms (%)	1941–1945 Terms (%)
Stone	8.2	2.9	12.9
Cardozo	6.7	3.3†	*
Brandeis	7.0	1.8†	*
Hughes	1.8	5.7	*
Roberts	1.8	9.2	23.1
Van Devanter	2.1	6.8†	*
Sutherland	2.8	6.9†	*
Butler	4.4	14.6†	*
McReynolds	4.0	18.1†	*
Black	*	8.1†	14.5
Reed	*	3.3†	10.5
Frankfurter	*	1.5†	14.7
Douglas	*	6.1†	15.3
Murphy	*	2.3†	13.0
Byrnes	*	*	7.4†
Jackson	*	*	10.4†
Rutledge	*	*	12.9†
The Court	15.7	27.3	48.6

*Not on Court.

†Based on actual number of terms served.

Source: The table is derived from data presented in Tables 1 through 12 in C. Herman Pritchett, *The Roosevelt Court* (Chicago: Quadrangle paperback edition, 1969), pp. 25, 32, 34–39, 41–43. Dissent rate for the Court between the 1941 and 1945 Terms is from S. Sidney Ulmer, "Exploring the Dissent Patterns of the Chief Justices," in Sheldon Goldman and Charles M. Lamb (eds.), *Judicial Conflict and Consensus* (Lexington, Ky.: The University Press of Kentucky, 1986), p. 53.

Game.[7] Hughes, and to a somewhat lesser extent Roberts, voted as if his principal concern was participation in the majority. Of course, during the 1936 Term Hughes and Roberts switched sides, joined the three liberals, and formed a new strongly cohesive liberal bloc. Before 1936 Hughes had agreed with Stone in 54 percent of the nonunanimous decisions. During the 1936 Term, Hughes agreed with Stone in 91 percent of the nonunanimous decisions.[8] Roberts had agreed with Stone before 1936 in 43 percent of the cases, but during the 1936 Term he agreed with him in 78 percent of

the nonunanimous decisions. Similar increases occurred with Hughes and Roberts and the other liberals, as did corresponding decreases in their rates of agreement with the conservatives.

As Table 5.3 suggests, the bloc configuration on the Court became more complex as the Roosevelt appointees assumed their posts. By the 1939 Term Hughes and Roberts along with McReynolds comprised the conservative wing of the Court. However, by the 1941 Term there was a new conservative majority on the Court, but it was conservative only in comparison with the liberalism of Black, Douglas, Murphy, and Rutledge.

The dispositional tendencies of the justices are presented in Table 5.4. By the 1941 Term the Court was no longer using the Constitution to strike down federal government economic

[7]Glendon Schubert, *Quantitative Analysis of Judicial Behavior* (Glencoe, Ill.: Free Press, 1959), chap. 4; Glendon Schubert, *Constitutional Politics* (New York: Holt, Rinehart and Winston, 1960), pp. 165–168.

[8]Pritchett, op. cit., p. 242.

Table 5.3 VOTING BLOCS ON THE SUPREME COURT IN NONUNANIMOUS DECISIONS, 1931–1945 TERMS

Term	Bloc Membership	Average Agreement of Justices in Bloc	Type of Bloc
1931–1935	Van Devanter, Sutherland, McReynolds, Butler, Hughes, Roberts	75%	Conservative
	Cardozo, Stone, Brandeis	84	Liberal
1936	Cardozo, Stone, Brandeis, Hughes, Roberts	85	Liberal
	Van Devanter, Sutherland, Butler, McReynolds	84	Conservative
1937	Cardozo, Stone, Black	85	Liberal
	Brandeis, Hughes, Roberts	95	Liberal
	Sutherland, McReynolds, Butler	88	Conservative
1938	Black, Douglas, Frankfurter, Reed	91	Liberal
	Stone, Hughes, Roberts	75	Liberal
	Butler, McReynolds	94	Conservative
1939	Black, Douglas, Murphy, Frankfurter, Reed, Stone	90	Liberal
	Hughes, Roberts, McReynolds	65	Conservative
1940	Black, Douglas	100	Liberal
	Murphy, Frankfurter, Reed, Stone	77	Liberal
	Hughes, Roberts, McReynolds	72	Conservative
1941	Black, Douglas, Murphy	82	Liberal
	Reed, Roberts, Frankfurter, Stone, Byrnes, Jackson	61	Conservative
1942	Black, Douglas, Murphy, Rutledge	82	Liberal
	Stone, Reed, Frankfurter, Jackson, Roberts	66	Conservative
1943	Black, Douglas	86	Liberal
	Murphy, Rutledge	81	Liberal
	Stone, Reed, Frankfurter, Jackson, Roberts	62	Conservative
1944	Black, Douglas	79	Liberal
	Murphy, Rutledge	79	Liberal
	Stone, Reed, Frankfurter, Jackson, Roberts	63	Conservative
1945	Black, Douglas	71	Liberal
	Murphy, Rutledge	73	Liberal
	Stone, Reed, Frankfurter, Burton	68	Conservative

Source: Blocs and average agreements were calculated using data contained in C. Herman Pritchett, *The Roosevelt Court* (Chicago: Quadrangle paperback edition, 1969), pp. 242–247. Blocs were determined using the McQuitty method. See Louis L. McQuitty, "Elementary Factor Analysis," *Psychological Reports*, 9 (1961), p. 71.

regulation. However, there were many economic issues that came to the Court involving statutory interpretation concerning administrative agencies and various federal boards or offices. There were also constitutional challenges to state economic activity. The four most liberal justices on the economic issues (*for* government regulation, *for* workers and organized labor, and *anti* monopoly) were Black, Douglas, Murphy, and Rutledge. The

least liberal justices were Roberts, Stone, Jackson, and Frankfurter in that order. Justice Reed was more moderate but closer to the conservatives than to the liberals. As the bloc analysis reported in Table 5.3 suggested, Justice Reed formed a conservative bloc with Stone, Frankfurter, Jackson, and Roberts.

The voting for the civil liberties issues shows that the four economic liberals were also the most supportive of civil liberties

Table 5.4   PRO-ECONOMIC LIBERALISM AND PRO-CIVIL LIBERTIES VOTING OF THE JUSTICES DURING THE 1941–1946 TERMS IN NONUNANIMOUSLY DECIDED CASES

Justice	Economic Liberalism (% of votes in favor)	Rank	Civil Liberties (% of votes in favor)	Rank
Black	88	1	66	3
Douglas	82	2	63	4
Murphy	82	2	94	1
Rutledge	75	3	83	2
Reed	52	4	28	9
Frankfurter	39	5	34	6
Jackson	38	6	30	7
Stone	34	7	43	5
Roberts	12	8	29	8
The Court	58		49	

Source: C. Herman Pritchett, *The Roosevelt Court* (Chicago: Quadrangle paperback edition, 1969), Tables 23 and 24, pp. 254, 257.

claims. Here, Justice Murphy emerged as the most civil liberties oriented justice on the Court with a 94 percent support level followed by Rutledge's 83 percent support. Black and Douglas were less supportive overall, although their 66 percent and 63 percent support levels set them apart from the more conservative wing of the Court. Black and Douglas in their earlier years on the Court were apparently more reluctant to strike down federal encroachments of civil liberties than they were to strike down alleged state violations. Black and Douglas no doubt identified with the New Deal Administration and simply may have had more confidence in the actions of federal officials. In the civil liberties cases (excluding criminal cases) that involved the *federal* government, Black supported the claims in 47 percent of the cases, and Douglas in 33 percent. However, in civil liberties cases involving the *states*, Black supported the claims in 87 percent of the cases and Douglas in 94 percent.[9] Similarly in *federal* criminal cases, both Black and Douglas supported the claims of criminal defendants in 55 percent of the cases; when

the *state* criminal process was involved, Black supported the claims of state criminal defendants in 83 percent of the cases and Douglas in 78 percent. For Justice Murphy and to a lesser extent for Justice Rutledge, little distinction was made between federal and state treatment of civil liberties.

On the conservative side of the Court, there were also justices who made distinctions between federal and state cases in the civil liberties area. When the federal government was involved, Justice Roberts supported the civil liberties claim in 47 percent of the criminal cases and 67 percent of all other civil liberties cases. But when the states were involved, in no nonunanimously decided criminal or civil liberties case did he support the civil liberties claim. Justice Frankfurter, who developed a judicial theory of federalism, held the federal government to stricter standards than he held the states in the criminal process. Frankfurter voted for the federal criminal defendant in 55 percent of the cases, but for the state criminal defendant in only 11 percent of the cases. This pattern, as we have seen, was also true for Roberts. It also held for Jackson and Reed, but much less so for Stone. In other areas of civil liberties, however, Frankfurter, Reed,

[9]Pritchett, op. cit., p. 254. The figures cited in this paragraph and the next are also from p. 254.

and Stone, but not Jackson or Roberts, followed Black and Douglas by holding the states to strict standards and finding for the civil liberties claimant more frequently than they did when the federal government was involved. Jackson and Roberts did just the reverse.

The Court during the 1937–1946 period underwent profound changes in personnel and constitutional doctrine. The negative commerce clause and tax clause doctrines along with the doctrine of substantive due process as applied to economic policy were discarded and replaced by a generous interpretation of the Constitution, thus permitting widespread governmental regulation of economic and social welfare matters. At the same time, the Court began grappling with and formulating constitutional doctrines in the various areas of civil liberties. Economic policy issues continued to come before the Court, generally not as constitutional questions, but rather as questions of statutory interpretation. The Roosevelt appointees dominating the Court by the 1939 Term were well prepared to administer the coup de grace to the old constitutional order, but were of remarkably different minds as to what should constitute the new. As we have seen, by the beginning of the 1940s there were deep cleavages among the justices. In part, this was due to the leadership style of Chief Justice Stone, the interpersonal relations among the justices, and the novel claims made before the Court that in some instances produced behind-the-scenes shifting back and forth of positions. To these considerations we turn our attention.

Patterns of Group Interaction

The constitutional revolution of 1937 occurred in the middle of Chief Justice Hughes' seventh term as Chief Justice. He served four more complete terms before retiring on July 1, 1941. Although Hughes and Roberts were responsible for the shifts in 1937 and 1938, the subsequent Roosevelt appointees carried the ball even further. Nevertheless, Hughes, even during his last years on the Court, conducted the Court's business efficiently and with firm control of the judicial conferences. Within ten days of Hughes' announced retirement, President Roosevelt named Associate Justice Harlan Fiske Stone to the chief justiceship, a post Stone held until his death in April 1946.

The contrast between the leadership styles of Hughes and Stone could not have been more dramatic. Hughes was clearly the task and social leader of the conference. He set the pace of discussion for each case. He began by giving his views in a forceful, confident manner and then each justice according to seniority had a turn to speak. No one was permitted to talk out of turn, ramblings on subjects not directly related to the case at hand were not tolerated, and matters were typically brought to a quick vote without prolonged debate. He typically adjourned the Saturday conference promptly at 4:30 P.M. with the conference business completed. Hughes was a superb administrator who kept on top of all the minutiae and fully utilized the prerogatives of office including the opinion assignment power to achieve his objectives by employing, in the words of one scholar, "the methods of a military commander."[10] Despite the extraordinary events of the 1930s, Hughes exercised personal leadership and, to a remarkable extent given the circumstances, kept the Court united.

Stone, on the other hand, had a vastly different personality and temperament. In the words of his biographer, "Stone was not born to command equals."[11] His was not a dominating personality. He was unwilling and proba-

---

[10]Mason, *Stone*, op. cit., p. 789.

[11]Ibid., p. 796. Stone's leadership style can be seen as reshaping norms of behavior concerning concurring and dissenting that continue to the present. See Thomas G. Walker, Lee Epstein, and William J. Dixon, "On the Mysterious Demise of Consensual Norms in the United States Supreme Court," *Journal of Politics*, 50 (1988), pp. 361–389.

bly temperamentally incapable of imposing discipline on his colleagues in the conference room. He was unwilling, if not unable, to pull rank and exert authority, and he did not use his opinion-assigning power to achieve an objective such as a united Court. Stone had a poor sense of personal diplomacy and made blunders that had the unintended effect of deepening rifts rather than mending them. On top of all this, he was a poor administrator.

Stone had his own notions of how the Court's conferences should be run. He believed that Hughes had stifled debate and that cases had been inadequately considered. Instead, he undertook to treat each case as worthy of full discussion and to transform the ambience of the conference room from what he saw as sterile formalism under Hughes to that of a lively and intellectually stimulating university-style seminar such as he might have conducted when he was teaching at Columbia. Stone set the pace in the conferences by first presenting his views of a case, usually in a tentative, thinking-out-loud manner. He did not hesitate to interrupt another justice's presentation of views and to engage in give-and-take. Other justices followed suit and "debate was free and easy," indeed, uninhibited.[12] Discussion at times got far afield from the case at hand, but Stone was slow to limit discussion. Conferences dragged on and spilled over into the following week. Although the Stone Court decided as many cases as did the Hughes Court, it took twice the conference time to accomplish this.[13]

As an administrator, according to Stone's biographer, Stone was "a bit neglectful" of his duties and "he frequently misplaced or lost" important papers.[14] The Clerk's office learned it had to make two copies of everything—"one to keep and the other for the Chief to lose."[15] Stone, aware of his failings, joked that he could never find a document but that he never lost one.[16]

Where Hughes was businesslike and formal, Stone was warm and informal. Stone had a special affection for his former law student, Justice Douglas, an affection that was returned. Stone also had a close relationship with Justice Frankfurter, one that had begun in the 1920s when Frankfurter was a law professor. In general, Stone was well liked by his colleagues, but that did not lessen his relative ineffectiveness. However, in fairness to Stone, his chief justiceship was faced with a unique complex of special problems that his predecessors did not have to confront.

First, Stone presided over a Court consisting primarily of new, inexperienced justices. Aside from Justice Roberts, the sole associate justice holdover from before 1937, all the other associate justices were Roosevelt appointees who lacked substantial judicial experience (even Wiley Rutledge had all of four years' experience on the Court of Appeals for the District of Columbia). As a consequence, these new justices were not well grounded in the mores of the Court, nor were there a majority of more experienced brethren present to teach them by example. Furthermore, the new Roosevelt appointees were relatively young (after Byrnes was replaced by Rutledge, the average age of these Roosevelt appointees in 1943 was 53 years) and they shared the impatience and activism associated with the New Deal Administration from whose political soil they sprouted. After the vivid example of the conservative Court superlegislating its own values, several of these new appointees were seemingly eager both to extinguish the constitutional judicial veto power in the economic sphere and yet to exercise it in the civil liber-

[12]Mason, *Stone*, op. cit., pp. 790–791.

[13]David J. Danelski, "The Influence of the Chief Justice in the Decisional Process of the Supreme Court," in Thomas P. Jahnige and Sheldon Goldman (eds.), *The Federal Judicial System* (New York: Holt, Rinehart and Winston, 1968), p. 156.

[14]Mason, *Stone*, op. cit., p. 788.

[15]Ibid.

[16]Ibid.

ties area. This set them on a collision course with Stone, who had a more across-the-board judicial restraint orientation. The subtle and sometimes devious arts of judicial reasoning and incrementalism seemed to be lost or deliberately ignored by some of the newer justices. Apparently, one or more of the justices even leaked confidential information to members of the press on matters such as the voting lineup and conference deliberations in certain controversial cases. This, of course, much distressed the Chief Justice.[17]

Another problem Stone faced was the unique group of personalities on his bench and the personality clashes that followed. Justice Frankfurter was in part responsible for the prolonged conferences and the difficulties Stone had as Chief Justice. Alpheus Mason noted that "Insatiable curiosity and philosophical bent led the former law teacher to explore byways far removed from the issues to be decided, with the result that arguments were impeded, conferences prolonged, and opinions delayed."[18] Frankfurter himself had a tendency to put off writing his opinions until the deadline approached. Because the conferences were so freewheeling, the justice assigned to write the opinion of the Court would on occasion leave the conference room uncertain as to precisely what the majority had agreed to be the grounds and reasoning of the decision. Justice Hugo Black also sought to dominate the conference. He held strong views frequently at odds with those of Frankfurter and was a tenacious infighter. John P. Frank, who once served as Black's law clerk, described him as "a very, very tough man.

When he is convinced, he is cool hard steel . . . his words may occasionally have a terrible edge. He can be a rough man in an argument."[19] Black and Frankfurter frequently clashed and eventually led opposing wings of the Court: Black, the civil libertarian activists, and Frankfurter the judicial conservatives or restraint wing.

Justice Robert Jackson, another forceful individual, also clashed repeatedly with Justice Black and had a particularly dramatic run-in with him during a series of conferences in June 1945. What had happened was that in a controversial labor case, Justice Black had provided the fifth and decisive vote in a five-to-four decision in which the winning side's lawyer was a former law partner of Black's from some 20 years earlier. The losing side petitioned for a rehearing on the ground that Justice Black should have disqualified himself. The normal practice would have been for the Court to have denied the rehearing without comment. But Stone, unable to foresee the consequences of his actions, argued that the denial of the rehearing petition should contain something to the effect that since no rules of the Court govern the practice, each justice determines for himself the propriety of participation in each case. Black strenuously objected to this and, according to Justice Jackson, "said that any opinion which discussed the subject at all would mean a declaration of war."[20] Stone backed down, but Jackson decided (in his words) "that I would not stand for any more of his [Black's] bullying,"[21] and Jackson, with Frankfurter joining him, wrote a brief statement along the lines originally proposed by Stone. The next year, Jackson, who was in Germany, where he was serving as Chief Prosecutor at the Nuremberg Nazi war criminal trials, publicly attacked Black and

[17]Ibid., p. 625.

[18]Ibid., p. 603. For a penetrating analysis of Frankfurter, see H. N. Hirsch, *The Enigma of Felix Frankfurter* (New York: Basic Books, 1981). Also see the description of Frankfurter in James F. Simon, *Independent Journey: The life of William O. Douglas* (New York: Harper & Row, 1980), pp. 8–9, 11–13, 217–222, 245–246; and James F. Simon, *The Antagonists: Hugo Black, Felix Frankfurter and Civil Liberties in Modern America* (New York: Simon & Schuster, 1989).

[19]John P. Frank, *Mr. Justice Black: The Man and His Opinions* (New York: 1949), pp. 134–135, as quoted in Danelski, op. cit., p. 155.

[20]Mason, *Stone,* op. cit., p. 644.

[21]Ibid.

brought the ugly feud onto the front pages of the nation's newspapers. This occurred after Chief Justice Stone's death and after Fred Vinson had been named to replace him. What precipitated Jackson's public airing of the feud was his belief that he was denied the chief justiceship because of Black's opposition. Undoubtedly it was the fact that Jackson was both physically and emotionally exhausted from the Nuremberg war crimes trials that contributed to his extraordinary breach of decorum.

The constant bickering during Stone's chief justiceship involved nearly everyone. For example, Murphy and Roberts squabbled with each other[22] and both Murphy and Douglas took Black's side in the feud with Jackson. Stone at one point lamented in a letter to a friend: "I have had much difficulty in herding my collection of fleas and they have been so busy disagreeing with each other that I have found it necessary to take [on the writing of] more opinions than I really should."[23] Even what should have been a simple, routine courtesy, that of a farewell letter from the justices to Justice Roberts, who retired at the end of June 1945, turned into a confrontation. Justice Black objected to a few lines of praise in the letter written by Chief Justice Stone and Stone, for the sake of harmony, acquiesced to Black's rewriting the letter. But Stone made the mistake of telling Frankfurter, who then nagged him until he agreed to send copies of his *original* letter to the other justices. Both Frankfurter and Jackson refused to sign Black's rewrite. Black himself withdrew his signature from *his own* letter, and the justices had to have a conference on the matter. They could not agree; thus no formal letter was sent to Roberts. Were Stone the leader Hughes had been, Stone would have, initially, insisted that

Black sign the original letter or pass it on unsigned to the next justice. The difficulty with Stone, according to Justice Jackson, was that "Stone dreaded conflict and his dread was so strong that it seemed to me that he feared taking action which would bring it about."[24] The irony was that Stone's inaction or his actions taken to avoid conflict often produced more disharmony than would have occurred with firm, decisive leadership at the outset.

Some of the conflict and disagreements during Stone's chief justiceship should be attributed to the fact that the Court was deciding many cases that raised novel and complex issues. To be sure, the lengthy conference deliberations, then, may have been necessary in order to come to grips adequately with those issues. Even after the conference there was some give-and-take and some shifting of positions.[25] Even in some economic cases it was not easy for some justices to arrive at their final positions. For example, with the case of **Wickard** v. **Filburn,** Justice Jackson had serious doubts about Congress' powers to tell Roscoe Filburn how much wheat he could harvest for strictly on-the-farm use.[26] Farmer Filburn's personal freedom clashed with Congress' regulation of the economy through the use of its commerce powers. But Jackson resolved his doubts and wrote the opinion of the Court, giving no hint of the difficulties Jackson first encountered with the issues.

Ultimately, the constitutional revolution of 1937 produced a revolution on the Court itself. The inhibitions concerning concurrences and dissents disappeared, the sense of institutional loyalty and camaraderie seemingly lessened as did the expectation and practice of the Chief Justice exercising strong leadership. The

[22]J. Woodford Howard, Jr., *Mr. Justice Murphy* (Princeton, N.J.: Princeton University Press, 1968), p. 297.

[23]Mason, *Stone,* op. cit., p. 605.

[24]Ibid., p. 769.

[25]Examples may be found in J. Woodford Howard, Jr., "On the Fluidity of Judicial Choice," *American Political Science Review,* 62 (1968), pp. 43–56, and in his *Murphy,* op. cit.

[26]Mason, *Stone,* op. cit., p. 594.

Court was now widely viewed as a political institution making political choices. The justices themselves, perhaps more than ever before, were more self-conscious of the political nature of their decision making and the political role their decisions played for the country.

THE VINSON AND WARREN COURTS

From 1945 until 1969 four Presidents served the nation and each had the opportunity to name two or more justices to the Supreme Court. Democratic President Truman named one Republican and three Democrats to the Court including Fred Vinson as Chief Justice to replace Harlan Fiske Stone, who suddenly died. Republican President Eisenhower also had the opportunity to name a Chief Justice when Fred Vinson also unexpectedly died in office. Eisenhower named four Republicans and one Democrat. Democratic President John F. Kennedy selected two Democrats, as did his successor in office, Lyndon Johnson. In all, 13 men came to the Court over a 24-year period.

The Truman Appointees

When Justice Owen Roberts retired from the Court in July 1945, President Truman turned to an old senatorial friend and colleague, Republican *Harold H. Burton*. Burton's selection was probably a result of a number of considerations. Burton was a Republican and he would replace a departing Republican justice, thus preserving some semblance of bipartisanship on the Court (two of the nine justices would be Republicans). Truman, having taken office just three months earlier after President Roosevelt's sudden death, could well have looked at a Republican appointment as a gesture of national unity and a signal to Republicans that in the remaining months of the war with Japan a blunting of sharp partisanship would be appropriate. Moreover, by the naming of Ohio Senator Burton to the Court, his

Senate seat would become vacant, and the Democratic Governor of Ohio would likely (and, in fact, did) fill it with a Democrat. Another major consideration was that Harold Burton had been a close personal friend since the days of their joint service in the Senate on the special wartime investigatory committee chaired by Truman. Also, Burton was from a midwestern state and not from the northeast (before Justice Roberts' retirement, five justices were northeasterners). Finally, Burton's legal credentials were impressive. He was a graduate of Harvard Law School, he had had an active and varied legal career, and he was seen as possessing the proper judicial temperament. Burton was unanimously confirmed by his senatorial colleagues, and he was to serve on the Court for 13 years until his bout with Parkinson's disease became too much for him and he retired for health reasons. Burton's judicial service is generally not considered to have been distinguished. He joined the conservative wing of the Court and took a judicial restraint position on most matters of civil liberties. Perhaps his greatest legacy was the unusually complete diary of Court proceedings, conferences, votes, and accounts of personal relationships that he kept and that is now housed in the Library of Congress. Burton's record of conference votes on certiorari petitions and his record of the tentative votes and conference deliberations concerning the major cases before the Court have been a gold mine of data for scholars.

When Chief Justice Stone died in April 1946, President Truman had to decide whether to promote an associate justice—and Justice Robert Jackson had first claim on such a promotion, having accepted Truman's call to duty by serving as Chief Prosecutor at the Nuremberg war criminal trials—or to go outside the Court. Word of personal antagonisms on the Court came to Truman's attention and after consultations with members and former members of the Court he reached into his Cabinet and took his friend and Secretary of the Treasury *Fred M. Vinson* and nominated him to be Chief Justice. Vinson was quickly confirmed. Vinson's pre-Court career included service as a congressman who helped shape the New Deal, as a federal appeals judge on the District of Columbia circuit from 1938 to 1943, and important service in the executive branch. Vinson was considered to possess considerable talents as a conciliator and compromiser. On the bench he was apparently able to improve the atmosphere somewhat, but the Court was as divided as ever over the major policy questions. Vinson was not a particularly talented jurist and he relied heavily on his law clerks to draft his opinions.[27] Vinson joined the conservative wing of the Court.

President Truman's last two appointments came close together because both Justices Murphy and Rutledge died in the summer of 1949. Truman named his Attorney General, *Tom C. Clark,* to one vacancy and his old friend and former senatorial colleague, *Sherman Minton,* to the other. Clark was a Texan who came to Washington to work in the Department of Justice. He worked his way up, serving as Assistant Attorney General in charge of the Antitrust Division and then of the Criminal Division before being elevated in 1945 to the post of Attorney General by his friend President Truman. On the bench Clark generally voted with the conservative wing although on some important occasions he joined the liberals. When President Johnson named Clark's son Ramsey to the post of Attorney General in 1967, Justice Clark retired to avoid any conflict or embarrassment.

Sherman Minton came to the Court with excellent political and legal credentials. He had been a strong New Deal senator and also a very good friend of Harry Truman. When Minton was defeated for reelection in 1940, he

went to the White House to work for President Roosevelt. Minton was instrumental in obtaining White House support for Senator Truman to assume the chairmanship of the special Senate committee investigating the defense industry.[28] It was the chairmanship of this committee that gave Truman national exposure and lcd to his being selected Roosevelt's running mate in 1944. Minton's professional credentials were impeccable. He graduated first in his class (and summa cum laude) from Indiana University and then received his law degree from Yale Law School. Minton did advanced academic work in law before starting to practice. In 1941 President Roosevelt appointed him to the United States Court of Appeals for the Seventh Circuit, where he performed ably. Once on the Supreme Court, Minton tended to support the position of the government in both economic policy (that made him a liberal on those issues) and civil liberties (that made him part of the conservative wing of the Court).

The Eisenhower Appointees

If President Eisenhower were to be remembered for only one accomplishment, it would have to be the appointment of *Earl Warren* to the chief justiceship. Warren, in the view of some students of the Court, was probably the greatest chief justice since John Marshall. The Warren Court had a revolutionary impact on the law of civil rights and civil liberties. Shepherding the justices along that revolutionary path was the soft-spoken, grandfatherly man with a humane and liberal vision of what America stands for.

Warren's pre-Court career was spent in his native California, where he was born in Los Angeles in 1891. He received his legal training at the University of California at Berkeley and

---

[27]Richard Kirkendall, "Fred M. Vinson," in Leon Friedman and Fred L. Israel (eds.), *The Justices of the United States Supreme Court 1789–1969,* vol. 4 (New York: Bowker, 1969), p. 2643.

[28]David N. Atkinson, *Mr. Justice Minton and the Supreme Court, 1949–1956,* Ph.D. dissertation, University of Iowa, 1969, pp. 63–65.

practiced law for three years. He served in the military during World War I. After the war he undertook a career as a prosecutor and for 14 years beginning in 1925 served as district attorney for Alameda County. In 1938 Warren was elected state Attorney General. In 1942, Warren was elected Governor of California and was reelected in 1946 and 1950. Warren was the Republican party's vice presidential candidate in 1948. He was a progressive and diplomatic politician and also an effective administrator. He was considered so nonpartisan a politician that in 1950 he not only won the Republican gubernatorial nomination for reelection but he received 1 million votes in the Democratic primary.[29]

Eisenhower's selection of Earl Warren to be Chief Justice was logical on both political and professional grounds. Warren had been on the national ticket in 1948. He campaigned actively for Eisenhower in the 1952 presidential campaign. He was immensely popular and widely respected. His appointment to the Court would also be effective in removing Warren from California Republican party politics, leaving Vice-President Nixon and Republican Senator William Knowland (who was also the Senate majority leader) the dominant figures in the state party. Eisenhower had been impressed with Warren and thought that they shared a similar perspective. Furthermore, Warren's administrative and diplomatic skills were such that he seemed to be the best possible person to bring harmony to the still contentious Court. For some or all of these reasons, Attorney General Herbert Brownell strongly backed the Warren appointment.[30] Warren received a temporary recess appointment because the Senate was not in session.

Warren served in this capacity while the Court was considering the school desegregation suits. He was finally unanimously confirmed on March 1, 1954. Just a little more than two months later, the Court handed down **Brown v. Board of Education.** Subsequently, some would charge that Warren delayed a Court ruling in *Brown* until he was confirmed. The evidence, however, suggests otherwise, as we shall see later in this chapter. During his tenure Warren provided the badly needed leadership for the Court's liberal wing and, indeed, he seemed to have fully utilized the potential leadership inherent in his position as Chief Justice.

John Marshall Harlan was Eisenhower's second appointee. Harlan replaced Justice Robert Jackson, who died suddenly in October 1954. Harlan's roots were solidly Republican, although he was not particularly active. Harlan was named after his grandfather, the first Justice Harlan, whose distinguished career on the Court spanned over three decades from 1877 to 1911. The younger Harlan distinguished himself academically (e.g., he was a Rhodes scholar) and spent most of his legal career in a prestigious Wall Street firm. Earlier in 1954 President Eisenhower had appointed Harlan to the United States Court of Appeals for the Second Circuit. When the Court vacancy occurred, Eisenhower's close advisors, former Governor Thomas Dewey and Attorney General Herbert Brownell, both New Yorkers, recommended the appointment of New Yorker Harlan to replace the deceased Justice Jackson who also was from New York. On the bench, Harlan joined the Frankfurter wing of the Court and was an intellectual heavyweight during his 16 years of Court service. Unlike his civil libertarian activist grandfather, Harlan tended to be a conservative supporter of the judicial restraint position. After 1962, when the libertarian activists on the Warren Court commanded a clear majority, Harlan became a frequent dissenter, thus sharing at least one of his grandfather's traits.

[29]See the account by Earl Warren in *The Memoirs of Earl Warren* (Garden City, N.Y.: Doubleday, 1977), p. 248.

[30]Henry Abraham, *Justices and Presidents,* 2d ed. (New York: Oxford University Press, 1985), pp. 251–254. For Earl Warren's account see his *Memoirs,* op. cit., pp. 260–261, 268–271.

Just one month before the presidential election of 1956, Justice Sherman Minton retired from the Court. Minton had previously let the administration know his intentions and Attorney General Brownell and Deputy Attorney General William Rogers focused their attention on *William Brennan*. Brennan was a justice on the New Jersey Supreme Court and was particularly close to his Chief Justice, Arthur T. Vanderbilt, who was also a Republican and friend of Attorney General Brownell. The previous May there had been a conference on judicial administration held in Washington. Justice Vanderbilt, who had been scheduled to attend, became ill and sent his colleague and protégé William Brennan in his stead. Brennan apparently made a very favorable impression on Brownell and Rogers. The facts that Democrat Brennan was highly regarded by Republican Vanderbilt and that Brennan was also a Catholic (the Court had no one of the Catholic faith since Justice Murphy's death in 1949) were not lost on Brownell. The vacancy on the Court occurred during the campaign and it seemed good politics for Eisenhower, who projected an above-politics image, to appoint Brennan, a relatively young man, who in the eyes of Vanderbilt and others possessed outstanding judicial qualities. As Deputy Attorney General Rogers remarked, "We were glad that he was both a Democrat and a Catholic."[31] Brennan joined the liberal wing, and he is widely considered to be one of the all-time great liberal justices.

Eisenhower's next appointment went to *Charles Whittaker,* who had been in private practice before becoming a federal district court judge in 1954. In 1956 he was elevated to the Court of Appeals for the Eighth Circuit and some ten months later was named to the Court. Whittaker was a conservative Republican with ties to the Republican establishment in Kansas City, Missouri. Furthermore, he

was a close friend of one of President Eisenhower's brothers. As it turned out, Whittaker spent only five years on the Court; apparently he did not feel comfortable being a justice,[32] and he left the Court in 1962. He voted with the conservative wing. Eisenhower's last appointee was his youngest; *Potter Stewart* was 43 when he came to the Court in 1958. Stewart came from a prominent Cincinnati family. His father was mayor of Cincinnati and later a justice on the Ohio Supreme Court. Potter Stewart served on the City Council and was also vice-mayor. In the 1952 presidential election he actively campaigned for Eisenhower. In 1954 he was appointed to the Court of Appeals for the Sixth Circuit. In 1958 he replaced fellow Ohioan Harold Burton, thereby becoming the ninth man from Ohio to serve on the Court since 1829. As a justice Stewart was identified with the conservative wing, but he also demonstrated some moderate tendencies.

The Kennedy–Johnson Appointees

In 1962 President Kennedy was given two opportunities to name Supreme Court justices. To the first vacancy, created by Justice Whittaker's departure, he named *Byron R. White* and to the second, occasioned by Justice Frankfurter's retirement, he picked *Arthur J. Goldberg*. White is a member of the Football Hall of Fame and is the only professional football player ever to become a justice. His academic accomplishments were equally impressive, for he was elected to Phi Beta Kappa in his junior year at the University of Colorado and was a Rhodes scholar. While in England he became acquainted with John F. Kennedy and thus began a 25-year association with the man who would name him to the Supreme Court. White had a successful law practice in

---

[31]John P. Frank, *The Warren Court* (New York: Macmillan, 1964), p. 121.

[32]According to Justice Douglas, Whittaker suffered a nervous breakdown. See *The Court Years 1939–1975: The Autobiography of William O. Douglas* (New York: Random House, 1980), p. 173.

Denver. In 1960 he joined the Kennedy campaign for the Democratic party nomination. After election, President Kennedy named White to the position of Deputy Attorney General, which he held at the time of his Court appointment. On the bench White has generally been conservative.

In marked contrast was the performance of Arthur Goldberg, who was a member of the liberal wing of the Court during his three-year tenure. Goldberg was a member of Kennedy's cabinet (Secretary of Labor) at the time of his appointment. In the summer of 1965, President Johnson persuaded Justice Goldberg to leave the Court to become Ambassador to the United Nations. Johnson apparently convinced Goldberg that his unique talents as a mediator and negotiator could best be put to use in the service of his country at a time of great international tension. To fill the vacancy caused by Goldberg's departure, President Johnson named, indeed forced, the nomination on his long-time close friend and advisor *Abe Fortas*. Fortas, who had the reputation of being a brilliant lawyer, reluctantly gave up his lucrative partnership in a prestigious Washington, D.C., law firm. Fortas was to spend four years on the bench as one of the leading Court liberals. In 1968 President Johnson nominated Fortas to the chief justiceship, but the nomination failed as Senate Republicans, sensing a 1968 Republican presidential victory, wanted a Republican President to be able to name the new Chief Justice. Not only did Fortas not receive what would have been a precedent-breaking promotion (he would have been the first Jewish Chief Justice), but within eight months of his Senate defeat Fortas was pressured into resigning as a result of charges and innuendoes of improprieties stemming from his association with a financier who ran into trouble with the law.[33]

President Johnson was able to make one

[33]For details, see Bruce Allen Murphy, *Fortas* (New York: Morrow, 1988), pp. 545–590.

precedent-setting appointment—that of the first black American to serve on the Court. *Thurgood Marshall* came to the Court with a wealth of varied legal experience. Marshall had served as counsel for the NAACP and had argued 32 cases before the Supreme Court (winning in 29). President Kennedy had then named Marshall to the United States Court of Appeals for the Second Circuit, and President Johnson subsequently picked him to be Solicitor General, the post he held at the time of his appointment. Marshall has been a leading liberal on the Court.

Background Characteristics of the Justices

Thirteen justices appointed by four Presidents came to the bench between 1945 and 1969. Their major backgrounds are summarized in Table 5.5. The three Democratic Presidents named men who were personal friends or with whom they were politically close. All these justices had a background of political activism. The one Republican President during this period, Eisenhower, by contrast did not name any close friends or associates. Only one of his five appointees had an extensive background of political activism (Warren), although another demonstrated pronounced activism at the local governmental level (Stewart).

Geography continued to play some part in the selection of justices. Truman did not name anyone from the Northeast, which was overrepresented on the Court. In 1949 he chose a southerner and midwesterner to seats that in the twentieth century had been held by either southerners or easterners. Eisenhower, in 1953, named Californian Earl Warren, who became the first person from (and at the time of appointment residing in) the West to serve on the Court since Justice Sutherland was appointed in 1922. For 15 years after Sutherland left the bench in 1938, the West had not been represented on the Court. Justice Harlan, a New Yorker, replaced another New Yorker,

Table 5.5 SELECTED CHARACTERISTICS OF JUSTICES APPOINTED BY PRESIDENTS TRUMAN THROUGH JOHNSON

Seat and Justice	Party	Home State	Years on Court	Father's Occupation	Occupation at Time of Nomination	Age at Nomination	Previous Judicial Experience
Truman appointees:							
9 Harold H. Burton	Republican	Ohio	1945–1958	Faculty member and Dean, M.I.T.	U.S. senator	57	None
1 Fred M. Vinson	Democrat	Kentucky	1946–1953	Jailer, county courthouse	U.S. Secretary of the Treasury	56	Federal
6 Tom C. Clark	Democrat	Texas	1949–1967	Lawyer	U.S. Attorney General	49	None
4 Sherman Minton	Democrat	Indiana	1949–1956	Farmer	U.S. Circuit Court Judge	58	Federal
Eisenhower appointees:							
1 Earl Warren	Republican	California	1953–1969	Railroad repairman	Governor of California	62	None
8 John M. Harlan	Republican	New York	1955–1971	Lawyer; mayor of Chicago	U.S. Circuit Court Judge	55	Federal
4 William J. Brennan	Democrat	New Jersey	1956–1990	Labor leader; Commissioner of Public Safety	Associate Justice, New Jersey Supreme Court	50	State
7 Charles E. Whittaker	Republican	Missouri	1957–1962	Farmer	U.S. Circuit Court Judge	56	Federal

	Party	State	Term	Occupation	Position	Age	Judicial experience
9 Potter Stewart	Republican	Ohio	1958–1981	Lawyer; Associate Justice, Ohio Supreme Court	U.S. Circuit Court Judge	43	Federal
Kennedy appointees:							
7 Byron R. White	Democrat	Colorado	1962–	Branch manager, lumber supply company	U.S. Deputy Attorney General	44	None
3 Arthur J. Goldberg	Democrat	Illinois	1962–1965	Fruit peddler	U.S. Secretary of Labor	54	None
Johnson appointees:							
3 Abe Fortas	Democrat	Tennessee	1965–1969	Cabinetmaker	Private law practice	55	None
6 Thurgood Marshall	Democrat	New York	1967–	Chief Steward at a country club	U.S. Solicitor General	59	Federal

Jackson. Harlan was the thirteenth man from New York to serve on the Court. From 1789 to the present, there were only four short intervals totaling 22 years in which a New Yorker was not on the bench. Also, Eisenhower replaced one Ohioan (Burton) with another Ohio native (Stewart). Moreover, geographic considerations were likely taken into account in the two remaining Eisenhower appointments in the sense that both Brennan and Whittaker came from regions whose support was important to the fortunes of the Republican Party. By 1960 the Court consisted of four northeasterners, one westerner (the Chief Justice), two southerners, and two midwesterners. The appointments of President Kennedy managed to retain midwestern, add to western, and decrease northeastern representation. From what is known of Johnson's selection process, it is unlikely that geography was taken into account.

Continuing the trend begun with the Roosevelt appointees, there were few justices whose fathers were lawyers and none had a physician father. Only 2 of the 13 justices came from a farming background. A majority of the justices came from humble or working-class backgrounds. Chief Justice Vinson's father was the jailer at the county courthouse (Vinson was born there) and died not long after his son was born. Chief Justice Warren's father was a railroad mechanic. Justice Minton was born in a log cabin on his father's small farm. Although Justice Brennan's father eventually made his mark as a New Jersey labor leader, the family was poor when the justice was a youngster. Justice Goldberg's father was a fruit peddler, Justice Fortas' father was a cabinetmaker, Justice White's father worked for a lumber company, and Justice Marshall's father was chief steward at a country club. Of the 13 justices, only 4 were from a relatively high-status background—and 3 of the 4 were Republicans. Justice Burton's father was a professor and Dean at the Massachusetts Institute of Technology, and Justices Clark, Harlan, and Stewart had fathers who were

lawyers (Stewart's father served as a justice on the Ohio Supreme Court).

The quality of legal education of the 13 justices was impressive. Four were graduates of Yale Law School (Minton, Stewart, White, and Fortas), two had Harvard law degrees (Burton and Brennan), and one each received a legal education at Berkeley (Warren), Northwestern (Goldberg), Texas (Clark), Howard (Marshall), Centre College (Vinson), New York Law School (Harlan), and University of Kansas City Law School (Whittaker).

With the exception of Abe Fortas, every justice had held public office at the time of his nomination. However, only one of the four Truman appointees had held a judicial office and none of the Kennedy and Johnson appointees held such office when appointed. After appointing Earl Warren, President Eisenhower insisted that his future appointees be judges, and thus the four subsequent Eisenhower appointees were all members of the judiciary when nominated. The majority of the justices appointed during the 1945–1969 period (seven) had judicial experience, which was a throwback to the pre-1937 pattern.

Religion played no role in the Truman appointments; for example, a Catholic was replaced by a non-Catholic. But Eisenhower appointed a Catholic (and a Democrat as well) before the 1956 presidential election. President Kennedy appointed a member of the Jewish religion (Goldberg) to replace another Jew (Frankfurter) and when Justice Goldberg was persuaded to step down, President Johnson replaced him with his close friend and advisor, Abe Fortas, also Jewish. The ethnic origins of a large majority of the justices serving during 1945–1969 were, as in earlier periods, in the British Isles.

Voting Patterns of the Justices

The Vinson and Warren Courts, although quite different Courts in their policymaking emphases, were similiar in that no matter how conservative a justice's voting patterns were, there was complete consensus as to the legitimacy of the constitutional doctrines that characterized the constitutional revolution of the 1930s. Indeed, the most dogmatic conservatives of the Vinson Court were all known and proven supporters of the New Deal when appointed. This points up the fact that the terms *liberal* and *conservative* as used here and elsewhere to describe judicial voting patterns are relative terms. Compared to the pre-1937 conservative justices, almost all the postwar justices were liberals. But compared to each other and in the context of the new issues before the Court, there were marked differences not only in their views of statutory interpretation involving economic policy, but also constitutional questions in the several areas of civil liberties.

Dissent was typical on the Vinson and Warren Courts in cases decided with full opinion. Chief Justice Vinson's first term was marked by a dissent rate of 64 percent. This was to be the second lowest during his tenure (the lowest was 63 percent during the 1950 Term). The highest dissent rate came during Vinson's last term, the 1952 Term, and was 81 percent.[34] Chief Justice Warren's first term saw a reduction in dissent to a still impressively high 72 percent. But by the following term dissent was down to the 60 percent level and for the remainder of the Warren Court generally fluctuated between the 60 and 70 percent range.[35]

In decisions in which the Court *overturned* a state or municipal law, the Vinson Court had great dissension (67 percent), exceeding that of the Warren Court.[36] Yet, it was the Warren Court that overturned the most state or municipal laws of any Court until that time, although with less dissent than characterized the Vinson Court. The Vinson Court overturned only one act of Congress; the Warren Court in 21 decisions overturned provisions of federal law, and the dissent rate in those cases was about 80 percent.

The Vinson Court had high rates of dissension in cases from the states that raised constitutional issues. Dissension in those cases reached 70 percent in the latter terms under Vinson's leadership. In contrast, during the first two terms of Warren's chief justiceship, the dissent rate in these cases dropped to 34 percent. During the 1957 Term it rose to 67 percent, but by the 1959 Term dropped to 52 percent.[37] The evidence suggests, and this will be pursued in the next section discussing the leadership styles of the two chief justices, that Chief Justice Vinson was unable to smooth over the deep ruptures that had emerged during the Stone Court. The discarding of the tradition of not dissenting unless it is absolutely necessary, combined with the sharp personality and policy conflicts on the bench, ultimately made the Vinson Court even more contentious than its predecessor. Earl Warren, on the other hand, had somewhat better success in promoting harmony on the Court and lowering the overall dissent rate.

Table 5.6 offers the individual dissent rates in decisions with full opinion. The first three terms of the Vinson Court saw unprecedented numbers of justices with high dissent rates. Fully two-thirds of the justices had individual dissent rates over 20 percent. The average dissent rate was 21.5 percent and ranged from the low of 12.9 percent for Vinson to 26.8 percent for both Douglas and Rutledge. In 1949 Rutledge and Murphy were replaced by Minton and Clark, both of whom had lower dissent rates than did their predecessors. Consequently, the number of justices with dissent rates over 20 percent dropped from six to four during the last four terms of the Vinson Court. Dissent rates ranged from 3.8 percent for Clark to 37.2 percent for Black, and the aver-

---

[34]C. Herman Pritchett, *Civil Liberties and the Vinson Court* (Chicago: University of Chicago Press, second impression, 1966), p. 21.

[35]The figures for the Warren Court are taken from the annual November issues of the *Harvard Law Review,* 1954–1969.

[36]Johnston, op. cit., p. 91.

[37]Sprague, op. cit., p. 64.

Table 5.6   DISSENT RATES, VINSON AND WARREN COURTS

	Dissent Rates			
	Vinson Court		Warren Court	
Justice	1946–1948 Terms (%)	1949–1952 Terms (%)	1953–1961 Terms (%)	1962–1968 Terms (%)
Douglas	26.8	32.7	31.2	19.9
Rutledge	26.8	*	*	*
Murphy	23.9	*	*	*
Black	22.1	37.2	23.3	21.5
Reed	13.5	14.8	21.7†	*
Vinson	12.9	10.0	*	*
Burton	17.9	11.1	21.3†	*
Jackson	24.7	20.1	16.7†	*
Frankfurter	24.9	25.4	20.2	*
Minton	*	11.8	17.7†	*
Clark	*	3.8	12.4	14.0†
Brennan	*	*	12.8†	3.8
Harlan	*	*	22.0†	30.6
Stewart	*	*	15.1†	21.9
Whittaker	*	*	23.8†	*
Warren	*	*	16.1	6.6
White	*	*	*	12.8
Goldberg	*	*	*	10.7
Fortas	*	*	*	10.9†
Marshall	*	*	*	3.2†
The Court	68.8	70.6	67.8	61.5

*Not on Court.

†Based on actual number of terms served.

Source: Dissent rates for the Vinson Court justices are derived from data presented in Tables 1, 4, 6 in C. Herman Pritchett, *Civil Liberties and the Vinson Court* (Chicago: University of Chicago Press, 1954), pp. 21, 181, 183. Dissent rates for the Warren Court are derived from data presented in the November issues of the *Harvard Law Review,* 1954–1969. These statistics are for full opinions issued by the Court.

age dissent rate was 18.5 percent. The average dissent rate during the first nine terms of the Warren Court was slightly higher—at 19.6 percent—and 7 of the 13 justices serving during this period had dissent rates over 20 percent. Dissent rates ranged from 12.4 percent for Clark to 31.2 percent for Douglas. It was only during the 1962–1968 Terms, the last seven terms of the Warren Court, that we see a significant drop in dissent rates. Only 4 of the 11 justices serving during this period (36.4 percent) had dissent rates of approximately 20 percent or over, and the average dissent rate fell to 14.2 percent, the lowest since the Stone Court.

In Table 5.6 we can compare individual dissent rates of certain justices over time. For example, Justice Douglas' dissent rate was the highest during the second part of the Vinson Court when the liberal wing of the Court was reduced to two justices and lowest during the second part of the Warren Court when the liberals for the first and only time during the entire period commanded a majority. The same was true for fellow liberal Justice Black. Between the first and second Warren Court periods, the dissent rate also decreased for liberals Warren and Brennan but *increased* for conservatives Clark, Harlan, and Stewart. The first part of the Warren Court had more liberal strength than the last part of the Vinson Court. Conservatives Reed, Burton, Minton, and Clark all increased their dissent rates. Jackson and Frankfurter, however, reduced theirs.

During the Vinson Court, the Chief Justice along with Justices Burton and Reed formed the heart of the conservative bloc on the Court, as suggested by Table 5.7. When Minton and Clark joined the Court in 1949, they too joined that wing. Although both Frankfurter and Jackson also frequently joined the conservatives, their brand of conservatism was different. They tended to be the most conservative justices on the Court in matters of economic policy, but considerably more liberal than the conservative wing on matters of civil liberties. As Table 5.8 shows, during the 1949–1952 Terms Justice Frankfurter had the third highest record of support for civil liberties *and* the lowest support level for economic liberalism. Were only civil liberty cases used as the basis for analyzing bloc patterns, Frankfurter would be classified with liberals Black and Douglas. Justice Jackson joined Frankfurter in the economic cases and with lesser frequency in the civil liberties cases. The main conservative bloc was cohesive and tended to vote together in about three out of four cases decided nonunanimously. The liberals were somewhat less cohesive, particularly during the second part of the Vinson Court.

Table 5.7 also charts the formation of liberal and conservative blocks over the course of the Warren Court. During the first three terms under the leadership of Earl Warren, the bloc configuration was in flux. In his first two terms, Warren cautiously retreated from the more conservative voting stance he first took. Even so, as reported in Table 5.9, his support of civil liberty claims in nonunanimous decisions was a relatively low 38 percent. But over the subsequent seven terms his support jumped to 84 percent. During those early Warren Court terms, Black and Douglas remained at the core of the liberal wing. Jackson joined Frankfurter in over three out of

four nonunanimously decided cases during the one full term Jackson served under Warren. Jackson's replacement, Harlan, joined Frankfurter and, in fact, for the remainder of their joint service they formed the core of the Court's conservative wing, agreeing with one another more than with any other justice. Justice Clark was at first closest to Warren, agreeing with him in about nine out of ten nonunanimously decided cases during the 1953 and 1954 Terms. Clark began decreasing his agreement with Warren in the 1955 Term, although the agreement level rarely went below 50 percent.

Frankfurter also had relatively high levels of agreement with Warren during Warren's first two terms, but starting in the 1955 Term he began disagreeing more markedly with the Chief Justice. On the other hand, Warren agreed with Douglas in only 42 percent of the nonunanimous cases in the 1953 Term, but their agreement rose to 63 percent in the next term and 82 percent in the following term. With Black, the figures were 53 percent agreement with Warren in the 1953 Term, 74 percent agreement in the 1954 Term, and 95 percent agreement in 1955. By the 1956 Term, the bloc pattern was set for the remainder of the Warren Court. New justices came on the bench, but rather quickly they began voting in such a way that they were identified with one of the two major wings of the Court. This was especially so for civil liberties. Only Justice Black in the mid-1960s left the liberals to assume an idiosyncratic position. Justices Warren, Douglas, and Brennan were the mainstays of the liberal wing along with Justice Black from the mid-1950s to the mid-1960s. They were joined by Justice Goldberg, who came to the Court in 1962, and by Goldberg's replacement Abe Fortas in 1965. Justice Thurgood Marshall came to the Court for the 1967 Term and provided the reliable fifth vote for the liberal majority because Justice Black had become less dependable. Justices Harlan, Frankfurter, Clark, Burton, and Whittaker

Table 5.7 VOTING BLOCS ON THE SUPREME COURT IN NONUNANIMOUS DECISIONS, 1946–1968 TERMS

Term	Bloc Membership	Average Agreement of Justices in Bloc	Type of Bloc
1946–1948	Rutledge, Murphy, Black, Douglas	74%	Liberal
	Vinson, Burton, Reed	76	Conservative
	Frankfurter, Jackson	74	Conservative
1949–1952	Vinson, Clark, Reed, Minton, Burton	77	Conservative
	Frankfurter, Jackson	69	Conservative
	Black, Douglas	61	Liberal
1953	Warren, Clark	88	Conservative
	Frankfurter, Jackson	77	Conservative
	Black, Douglas	77	Liberal
	Burton, Minton, Reed	67	Conservative
1954	Harlan, Frankfurter, Burton	72	Conservative
	Black, Douglas, Warren, Clark	71	Liberal
	Minton, Reed	68	Conservative
1955	Warren, Black, Douglas	87	Liberal
	Burton, Minton, Reed, Clark	73	Conservative
	Harlan, Frankfurter	73	Conservative
1956	Black, Douglas, Warren, Brennan	78	Liberal
	Burton, Whittaker, Harlan, Frankfurter, Clark	66	Conservative
1957	Black, Douglas, Warren, Brennan	79	Liberal
	Burton, Whittaker, Harlan, Frankfurter, Clark	69	Conservative
1958	Black, Douglas, Warren, Brennan	76	Liberal
	Whittaker, Harlan, Frankfurter, Clark, Stewart	74	Conservative
1959	Black, Douglas, Warren, Brennan	77	Liberal
	Whittaker, Harlan, Frankfurter, Clark, Stewart	69	Conservative
1960	Black, Douglas, Warren, Brennan	75	Liberal
	Whittaker, Harlan, Frankfurter, Clark, Stewart	73	Conservative
1961	Black, Douglas, Warren, Brennan	80	Liberal
	Whittaker, Harlan, Frankfurter, Clark, Stewart	67	Conservative
1962	Black, Douglas, Warren, Brennan, Goldberg	90	Liberal
	Clark, Harlan	87	Conservative
	Stewart, White	84	Moderate
1966	Douglas, Warren, Brennan, Fortas	85	Liberal
	Harlan, Clark, Stewart, White, Black	67	Conservative
1968	Douglas, Warren, Brennan, Fortas, Marshall, Black	69	Liberal
	White, Stewart, Harlan	60	Conservative

Source: The Vinson Court blocs were determined by the McQuitty technique applied to percentage agreement data presented in C. Herman Pritchett, *Civil Liberties and the Vinson Court* (Chicago: University of Chicago Press, 1954), Tables 5, 7, pp. 182, 184. The Warren Court blocs from the 1953–1961 Terms were derived from phi coefficient matrices presented in Glendon Schubert, *The Judicial Mind* (Evanston, Ill.: Northwestern University Press, 1965), pp. 57–65. The 1962, 1966, and 1968 blocs were derived from an analysis of only the nonunanimous civil liberties decisions. The McQuitty method for determining bloc membership is presented in McQuitty's article, "Elementary Factor Analysis," *Psychological Reports,* 9 (1961), p. 71.

Table 5.8   PRO-ECONOMIC LIBERALISM AND PRO-CIVIL LIBERTIES VOTING OF THE JUSTICES ON THE VINSON COURT IN NONUNANIMOUSLY DECIDED CASES

Justice	Economic Liberalism (% of votes in favor)		Civil Liberties (% of votes in favor)	
	1946–1948 Terms	1949–1952 Terms	1946–1948 Terms	1949–1952 Terms
Murphy	95	—	95	—
Rutledge	92	—	89	—
Black	95	90	68	93
Douglas	86	82	78	85
Frankfurter	17	13	39	74
Jackson	10	17	28	38
Burton	16	37	11	29
Vinson	30	44	10	20
Reed	38	44	10	13
Minton	—	49	—	13
Clark	—	41	—	24
The Court	47	42	35	29

Source: Percentages are derived from E and C scales presented in Glendon Schubert, *The Judicial Mind* (Evanston, Ill.: Northwestern University Press, 1965), pp. 104–107, 130–133.

were generally a less cohesive voting group than the liberals, but they achieved the same sort of stability. Justice Stewart joined the conservatives in 1958, replacing Burton. Justice White also aligned himself somewhat tenuously when he came on the Court. As Table 5.9 shows, White was the most moderate of the Warren Court conservatives, with Stewart close behind.

The dispositional tendencies of the Vinson Court justices in the economic and civil liberties policy areas are presented in Table 5.8. In the economic cases involving primarily statutory interpretation in the federal cases and often constitutional questions in the state cases, the most liberal Vinson Court justices were Murphy and Black, followed closely by Rutledge and then Douglas. Frankfurter and Jackson were the most conservative justices with Burton next. Reed, Vinson, Minton, and Clark were more moderate but still essentially conservative. Even so, the Vinson Court was

more liberal on matters of economic policy than on matters of civil liberties.

The voting on the civil liberties cases shows that the four Vinson Court economic liberals were also the most supportive of civil liberty claims. With the replacement of liberals Murphy and Rutledge with conservatives Minton and Clark, the Court shifted even more to the right. Only 29 percent of the nonunanimous decisions of the Court favored the civil liberties claims. The Court majority's sometimes cavalier disregard of criminal due process and free speech claims rankled Justice Frankfurter, who dramatically improved his civil liberties support during the second part of the Vinson Court.

Frankfurter, consistent with his voting behavior since coming to the Court, gave considerably more support to civil liberty claims vis-à-vis the federal government than he did to civil liberty claims involving state or local government. During the Vinson Court, Frankfurter supported 40 percent of the civil liber-

Table 5.9   PRO-ECONOMIC LIBERALISM AND PRO-CIVIL LIBERTIES VOTING OF THE JUSTICES ON THE
WARREN COURT IN NONUNANIMOUSLY DECIDED CASES

Justice	Economic Liberalism (% of votes in favor)			Civil Liberties (% of votes in favor)		
	1953–1954 Terms	1955–1961 Terms	1962, 1968 Terms	1953–1954 Terms	1955–1961 Terms	1962, 1966–1968 Terms
Black	98	92	88	93	92	58
Douglas	82	96	70	95	98	97
Warren	66	88	81	38	84	79
Clark	45	63	81	38	12	18
Minton	46	49	—	16	5	—
Reed	32	50	—	8	6	—
Frankfurter	29	19	—	63	34	—
Jackson	10	—	—	40	—	—
Burton	12	37	—	23	18	—
Harlan	—	21	22	—	26	24
Whittaker	—	10	—	—	26	—
Brennan	—	64	77	—	77	82
Stewart	—	34	30	—	40	43
White	—	—	62	—	—	46
Goldberg	—	—	53	—	—	87
Fortas	—	—	77	—	—	80
Marshall	—	—	75	—	—	82
The Court	44	68	70	50	50	75

Source: Percentages for the 1953–1962 Terms are derived from E and C scales presented in Glendon Schubert, *The Judicial Mind* (Evanston, Ill.: Northwestern University Press, 1965), pp. 107–112, 133–138.

tarian claims in state cases but 83 percent of the claims in federal cases.[38] Justice Jackson's voting behavior demonstrated a similar trend. Jackson's civil liberty support was 11 percent in state cases but 54 percent in federal cases. But Douglas and Black, who in earlier years supported the claims in state cases at a much higher level than in federal cases, showed much less tendency to make such distinctions during the Vinson Court years. In fact, only in criminal cases did their voting behavior reveal any kind of distinction between federal and state cases. Douglas supported the claims of criminal defendants in 97 percent of the state cases but in "only" 84 percent of the federal cases, whereas Black's figures were 86 percent support in state cases and 62 percent support in federal.

[38]Pritchett, *Civil Liberties and the Vinson Court,* op. cit., p. 225.

Table 5.9 presents the voting records of the justices during the Warren Court. In nonunanimous cases, the proportion of liberal economic and civil liberties decisions made by a Court majority increased sharply. From the Vinson Court's low point of 42 percent support for economic liberal claims, the Warren Court gradually increased its support to 70 percent. From the Vinson Court's low point of 29 percent support for civil liberty claims, the Warren Court quickly increased its support to 50 percent. Then, beginning in 1962, with Goldberg replacing Frankfurter, the liberal majority raised Court support to about 75 percent. During the last term of the Warren Court, about four out of five nonunanimously rendered civil liberties cases were decided in favor of civil liberty claims.

The voting record of individual justices shows some interesting patterns. During the first two terms, the Warren Court was clearly in a transitional stage. Chief Justice Warren was at first conservative on civil liberties and moderate-liberal on economic matters. Then he moved into the distinctive liberal mold with which he became widely identified. Justice Clark moved from a conservative record in civil liberties to a more extreme conservative position. However, in economic policy he became increasingly more liberal. Justice Frankfurter's voting record shifted from a moderate one on civil liberties to a conservative one. Justice Douglas became the most extreme liberal on civil liberties but less liberal on economic policy issues. Justice Black remained liberal on economic issues, but reduced his support of civil liberty claims toward the end of the Warren Court.

The Vinson and Warren Courts, unlike their predecessor Courts, focused their constitutional attention largely on matters of civil liberties including civil rights for black Americans. In the past, in economic matters and social legislation, a justice would be considered liberal if he were to uphold the government. But in the modern era, with civil rights and liberties, upholding the actions of government was and is decidedly *not* the liberal position. The modern liberals consider the Constitution as embodying certain moral values about the rights of individuals, and these include not only the explicitly provided-for freedoms but also such implicit liberties as the right to privacy. The modern Court conservatives have not necessarily rejected those moral values. Rather, for the most part, they have felt that the Court ought not to promote actively those values in the absence of clear-cut constitutional violations. Conservatives look to the democratic process to work its will as to what constitutes just and needed public policy. One of the major differences between Chief Justices Vinson and Warren was that Vinson was more than willing to defer to government in the regulation of civil liberties except when it was absolutely clear that the Constitution was

violated. Benefits of any constitutional doubt were given to the government. Vinson had a limited vision as to the scope of the Constitution, the proper restraints that should be placed on government, and the moral values contained within the Constitution. In contrast, Earl Warren was one of the greatest of chief justices in part because he had a firm constitutional vision that, unlike Vinson's, was positive and expansive in terms of human freedom and dignity. A strong sense of justice and a respect for persons characterized his jurisprudence and that of the liberal majority during his last seven terms. There were additional differences in leadership style between Vinson and Warren. And the two courts differed in terms of the nature of interpersonal relationships on the bench. Our attention turns to these considerations.

Patterns of Group Interaction

When Vinson became Chief Justice, he faced a Supreme Court that was in disarray on every conceivable front. Administratively, ideologically, doctrinally, and interpersonally the Court was in the worst shambles it had ever been in the twentieth century. Justice Jackson believed that Justice Black was responsible for Jackson's having lost out on the chief justiceship, and Justice Frankfurter sided with Jackson. Black and Frankfurter were continually arguing. Frankfurter and Douglas got on each other's nerves. Murphy, Rutledge, and, to a lesser extent, Reed and Burton were drawn into the squabbling. Into this scene came Fred Vinson whose political skills and ingratiating personality were supposed to calm the Court's troubled waters. But although he tried, Vinson was not up to the job.

Justice Frankfurter recorded in his diary his impression of Vinson's conduct of the first conference over which he presided in which argued cases were discussed. Frankfurter observed:

The way Vinson dealt with them [the cases for

which there already had been oral argument] gives further evidence that he is likely to deal with complicated matters on a surface basis. He is confident and easy-going and sure and shallow. Of course it is a heavy burden that he is taking on and one must give him ample time to show his qualities, but he seems to me to have the confident air of a man who does not see the complexities of problems and blithely hits the obvious points. He does it all in good temper and with dispatch.[39]

At a following conference, Frankfurter noted:

Vinson conducts the Conference with ease and good humor, disposing of each case rather briefly by choosing, as it were, to float merely on the surface of the problems raised by the cases. Black, who, since Court opened, has appeared to be all sweetness, let loose for the first time . . . in Black's irascible and snarling tone of voice.[40]

Already the honeymoon was over and Black and Frankfurter resumed their clashes. It soon followed that the conferences became more heated, and, inevitably, they became longer and less productive. Whereas the Court in the 1940 Term had decided 165 cases with signed full opinions, by the 1947 Term that number dropped to 110 decisions and by the 1951 Term the low point for the Vinson Court had been reached—only 83 cases were decided with signed full opinion by the Court.[41] The proportion of nonunanimously decided cases rose as did the individual dissent rates of the holdover justices on the Vinson Court. Indeed, one might question whether it is justifiable, aside from convention, to call the Court the "Vinson" Court. However, it should be

noted that Vinson voted with the majority in about nine out of ten cases.

Vinson lacked the intellectual equipment to be an effective task leader and this was apparent to his colleagues. In fact, according to a former law clerk to Justice Minton, several of Vinson's colleagues "would discuss in his presence the view that the Chief's job should rotate annually and . . . made no bones about regarding him—correctly—as their intellectual inferior."[42] Social leadership as well was difficult for Vinson to exercise as the intrigues on the Court continued unabated. Consider, for example, this entry from Frankfurter's diary for November 20, 1947:

Apropos of nothing in particular, as is the case in so many of his remarks to me on the bench, Murphy said,"I think you ought to know that there are people on the Court who are in a quiet, subtle way, trying to poison the Chief against you. They"— that is the way he always refers to Douglas and Black—"are doing things that I wouldn't approve of and that I don't do, for I don't ever want to be a party to a feud on the Court. But I thought you ought to know it." I made no comment.[43]

After Minton and Clark came to the Court, social leadership was somewhat easier for Vinson to exercise because the new justices were more congenial persons who also happened to share Vinson's judicial outlook. Vinson, Reed, Clark, Burton, and Minton lunched together regularly and more often than not their conversation strayed far from the business of the Court. According to one observer, "Frankfurter considered the conversation somewhat beneath him and a bore and did not join them."[44] Black frequently lunched with his law clerks and often Douglas

---

[39]Entry for October 19, 1946. Joseph P. Lash (ed.), *From the Diaries of Felix Frankfurter,* (New York: Norton, 1975), p. 274.

[40]Entry for October 27, 1946, ibid., p. 283.

[41]Gerhard Casper and Richard A. Posner, *The Workload of the Supreme Court* (Chicago: American Bar Foundation, 1976), p. 76. Cf. Pritchett, *Civil Liberties,* op. cit., p. 21.

[42]As quoted in Richard Kluger, *Simple Justice,* vol. II (New York: Knopf, 1975), p. 740.

[43]Lash, op. cit., pp. 329–330. Note that Frankfurter himself was a master manipulator. See, in general, Hirsch, *Enigma of Felix Frankfurter,* op. cit.

[44]As quoted in Atkinson, op. cit., p. 101.

and Jackson would each lunch separately. In fairness to Vinson, there was probably little he could do with those four strong individualists. Perhaps it is significant that at least Vinson tried to provide some cohesion for the other four justices.

One incident that reflects on Vinson's leadership occurred in December 1947. The previous year the law clerks and the secretaries had hosted a Christmas party for the justices. Now plans were being made for another Christmas party, but this time the law clerks also wanted the black employees of the Court to be invited. The District of Columbia at that time was still a citadel of racial segregation, and most of the white women employees objected to the idea of socializing with blacks. The Marshal of the Court said he could not authorize use of a room in the Court building if blacks were to be invited unless the Chief Justice instructed him otherwise. Instead of giving approval for the party, Chief Justice Vinson decided he needed "a mandate" from the Court and called a conference to consider the matter. The justices spent close to one hour debating the issue and ultimately voted six to two to permit the party as proposed by the law clerks. Frankfurter and Jackson voted in the negative, arguing that no social function initiated by anyone other than a justice should be allowed. After the vote Justice Reed told his colleagues that he would not attend the party and when challenged by Frankfurter replied (according to Frankfurter) that "this is purely a private matter and he can do what he pleases in regard to private parties."[45] Presumably, a strong chief justice would have acted decisively in the first place and would neither have felt the need for "a mandate" (Vinson's words) nor permitted the discussion to get out of hand as it did.

Despite the difficulties on the Court—with Black and Frankfurter competing to exercise task leadership—the justices behaved as justices have traditionally behaved in terms of trying to persuade each other and negotiating over votes and opinions. There was a certain amount of fluidity in voting as the issues before the Court were often novel and complex. For example, **Everson** v. **Board of Education** raised both church-state and social welfare issues and stimulated a great deal of intracourt activity that ultimately resulted in the rather atypical voting lineup of Black, Douglas, Murphy, Reed, and Vinson in the majority with Rutledge, Frankfurter, Jackson, and Burton in dissent.[46] But it was **Brown** v. **Board of Education** that presented the Court with its greatest challenge and where the difference in leadership qualities between Vinson and Warren can be most dramatically contrasted.

The five school segregation cases—the four from the states that were decided together under the title *Brown v. Board of Education* and the fifth case, **Bolling** v. **Sharpe** from the District of Columbia—began coming to the Vinson Court during the 1951 Term. The Court announced probable jurisdiction in two cases on June 9, 1952, and the conference vote taken two days earlier had been seven justices in favor of taking the cases, one justice (Jackson) in favor of delaying Court consideration, and Chief Justice Vinson *not voting*.[47] Later that summer and early fall, the additional school segregation cases came to the Court and were consolidated with the first two cases. Argument was scheduled for December 9, 1952. As Justice Clark was to recollect to writer Richard Kluger, "We felt it was much better to have representative cases from different parts of the country and so we consolidated them and made *Brown* [a Kansas case] the first so that the whole question would not smack of being a purely Southern one."[48]

[45]Lash, op. cit., pp. 335–336.

[46]See Howard, "On the Fluidity of Judicial Choice," op. cit., p. 54, and Howard, *Murphy*, op. cit., pp. 448–450.

[47]Kluger, op. cit., pp. 681–682.

[48]Ibid., p. 683.

Two days after the end of oral argument, the Vinson Court had its first conference discussion of the *Brown* cases. Chief Justice Vinson, speaking first, observed, among other things, that Justice Harlan's dissent in **Plessy** v. **Ferguson** had carefully avoided any mention of public schools. He noted the long-standing precedent of the separate-but-equal doctrine and he noted the grave consequences that would likely arise if the Court struck down segregation. According to the conference notes taken by Justice Burton, Vinson's position was less than clear-cut, but Vinson had said enough so that Burton recorded in his diary that Vinson would probably vote to uphold segregation. Other evidence also supports this view of Vinson's inclinations.[49] Justices Black,[50] Douglas, Burton, and Minton opposed segregation in the public schools. Reed, Clark, Frankfurter, and Jackson were deeply troubled by the cases, but were not then ready to act against segregation. Reed, the southern justice who refused to attend the integrated Christmas party in 1947, indicated that he had some qualms about the desirability of the mixing of the races.[51] Clark, another southerner, was all too aware of the social upheaval a desegregation decision would bring and said he was "inclined to go along with delay."[52]

The evidence suggests that Frankfurter was probably weighing the institutional harm that might befall the Court from a desegregation decision particularly if it were not unanimous. Frankfurter had earlier remarked during oral argument, "I think that nothing would be worse . . . than for this Court to make an ab-

stract declaration that segregation is bad and then have it evaded by tricks."[53] Frankfurter apparently had the greatest qualms about the states and the least about the District of Columbia. He was prepared to vote for an end to segregation in the nation's capital.[54] As a former law clerk of Frankfurter's recalled, Frankfurter "personally was deeply against it [segregation], but his first concern was the Court, and he had a fear that the whole thing was moving along too fast."[55] Frankfurter urged that all the cases be reargued and that the incoming Eisenhower Administration, which would have the responsibility for enforcing court orders, be asked to participate in the reargument and offer its ideas on how desegregation should proceed.[56] Jackson suggested at the conference that it would be better for no formal vote to be taken (this was readily accepted by Chief Justice Vinson) and that the colleagues recognize that these issues would take time to be thrashed over.[57] Jackson saw no *judicial* basis for striking down segregation. He felt that any decision to do so would have to be politically framed and that he would likely go along with it if the offending states had "reasonable time" with which to comply. But if the decision took the position that the South had all along violated the Constitution, he would have difficulty joining it.[58]

As the 1952 Term was drawing to a close, the Court was badly divided over how to resolve *Brown*. Chief Justice Vinson was not capable of providing the necessary leadership. Finally, Frankfurter suggested that the case be reargued the following term and that certain questions relating to historical evidence

[49]See ibid., pp. 746–748. For an analysis based on the Burton papers, see S. Sidney Ulmer, "Earl Warren and the Brown Decision," *Journal of Politics*, 33 (1971), p. 691.

[50]Kluger, op. cit., pp. 748–753.

[51]Ibid., pp. 754–755.

[52]As quoted by Justice Burton and reported in ibid., p. 774.

[53]Ibid., p. 723.

[54]Ibid., p. 761.

[55]Ibid., p. 760.

[56]Ibid., p. 762.

[57]Ibid., p. 769.

[58]Ibid., pp. 770–771.

as well as the process of implementation be the focus of reargument. The Court agreed at its June 8, 1953, conference and reargument was scheduled for the following fall. Then, on September 8, Chief Justice Vinson unexpectedly died. In light of Vinson's failure of leadership and particularly his support for segregation, Justice Frankfurter was heard to have reacted to Vinson's death by saying, "This is the first indication I have ever had that there is a God."[59]

President Eisenhower named Earl Warren to the vacant chief justiceship, which was to have major consequences for the segregation cases. Warren began his tenure by developing a rapport with his new colleagues. He met frequently with Frankfurter at the latter's apartment where he allowed the former law professor to play a favored role, that of learned teacher tutoring Warren on the complexities of *Brown*.[60] Warren also developed personal relationships with his other colleagues and even had success in luring the loner Douglas to frequent luncheons with a group of colleagues. For three days beginning on December 7, 1953, the Court heard the rearguments. The conference was held the following Saturday. Chief Justice Warren in the course of his remarks opening the discussion observed that the Court was obliged to consider the allowability of segregation in the public schools. Further, the more thought he gave the matter, the more he was convinced that racial segregation was based on the premise of the inferiority of the Negro race. Warren continued that he had come to the conclusion that segregation of Negro schoolchildren must be ended and that the law "cannot in this day and age set them apart."[61] To practice racial segregation, stressed Warren, would violate the Thirteenth, Fourteenth, and Fifteenth Amendments, whose objective was to raise the former slaves to a level of equality with all others. Warren emphasized his sensitivity to the difficulty of implementing such a momentous decision and the necessity to recognize diverse conditions in the different states in order to minimize upheaval and strife. The Court would have to be wise and tolerant in the way it proceeded to end segregation in the public schools.[62]

Professor S. Sidney Ulmer perceptively analyzed Warren's opening statement as follows:

> Upon reflection, Warren's opening statement was a masterly one. It condemned no one; it was unemotional; it recognized differences among the states and in conditions relevant to the problem; it suggested tolerance in disposing of the matter; it referred humbly to the need for wisdom. Thus it projected a reasonable and concerned man with malice toward none—a judge faced with a case to decide whatever the impediments. At the same time one must be struck by the firmness with which Warren asserted at the outset that he was prepared and that the Court was obliged to bar consciously segregated public schools. Given the uncertainties with which some of the other justices were plagued at this time, strong leadership on the question was undoubtedly a key factor in the ultimate solution.[63]

After Warren's presentation, the discussion moved around the conference table. At Warren's request it was agreed that no formal vote would be taken; instead, the justices would discuss various facets of the issues at this and at subsequent conferences. After the conference Warren lunched with Burton, Reed, Douglas, Clark, and Minton, and they continued to lunch frequently between that day and

[59]Ibid., p. 829.

[60]Lash, op. cit., p. 84.

[61]Kluger, op. cit., p. 858.

[62]See the detailed statement of Warren's remarks as recorded by Justice Burton and discussed by Ulmer in "Earl Warren," op. cit., pp. 692–693.

[63]Ibid., p. 693.

the time that *Brown* was decided.[64] Over the months Warren met individually with each justice in an effort to secure unanimity not only on the vote but also on the opinion of the Court. One Saturday conference in March 1954, the justices voted 8 to 1 to strike down segregation with the possibility that Jackson and/or Frankfurter would write separate concurrences.[65] Reed was the sole dissenter. Warren assigned himself the task of writing the opinion of the Court and it was understood that no enforcement decree would be issued until the next term, after reargument, and after the South would have a year to get accustomed to the idea of the end of segregated schools.[66]

Warren did not circulate the draft of his *Brown* and *Bolling* opinions until Friday, May 7. Warren and his law clerks hand-delivered the copies of the drafts with a cover memo stating that they were to provide ''a basis for discussion'' and ''were prepared on the theory that the opinion should be short, readable by the lay public, non-rhetorical, unemotional, and, above all, non-accusatory.''[67] Justice Jackson had suffered a serious heart attack the previous March 30. Warren himself brought his draft opinions to Jackson's bedside and secured his consent. Jackson then insisted that he would be present in Court for the reading of the decisions. Warren, who had been lunching regularly with Reed during this period, finally put the question to Reed. He said: ''Stan, you're all by yourself in this now. You've got to decide whether it's really the best thing for the country.''[68] Warren went on and emphasized how important it was that the Court be unanimous on such an important and sensitive issue. After Warren left, according

to Reed's law clerk at the time, Reed decided that his lone dissent might stir up so much trouble that ''for the good of the country'' he would not dissent. He did, however, obtain Warren's assurance that implementation would be gradual instead of immediate. The Warren opinion was formally approved at the May 15 conference. On May 17, 1954, the Court unanimously handed down the *Brown* and *Bolling* decisions. The Court spoke with one voice. Earl Warren exercised the same sort of leadership in securing a unanimous Court for the enforcement decree, *Brown II,* handed down on May 31, 1955.[69]

Earl Warren in his memoirs commented about the *Brown* opinion:

> It was not a long opinion, for I had written it so it could be published in the daily press throughout the nation without taking too much space. This enabled the public to have our entire reasoning instead of a few excerpts from a lengthier document.[70]

Earl Warren's social and to some extent task leadership had its effect on the workings of the Court. The number of cases decided with full opinion rose from the low point of the Vinson Court. There was some lowering of the proportion of nonunanimous decisions and some lowering of individual dissent rates. But the Court nonetheless was divided over controversial issues and spoke infrequently with one voice. Personal tensions, to some extent, still remained on the Court. For example, at the Court conference less than two weeks after the first *Brown* decision was announced, Justices Frankfurter and Douglas clashed. Although Chief Justice Warren prevented a disruption at the conference, Justice Douglas immediately sent a memo to Frankfurter as follows:

[64]Ibid., p. 698, n. 17

[65]Kluger, op. cit., p. 877.

[66]Ibid., p. 878.

[67]As quoted in ibid., p. 879.

[68]Ibid., p. 882.

[69]Ibid., pp. 932–939.

[70]*The Memoirs of Earl Warren,* op. cit., p. 3.

Today at Conference I asked you a question concerning your memorandum opinion in Nos. 480 and 481. The question was not answered. An answer was refused, rather insolently. This was so far as I recall the first time one member of the Conference refused to answer another member on a matter of Court business. We all know what a great burden your long discourses are. So I am not complaining. But I do register a protest at your degradation of the Conference and its deliberations.[71]

Frankfurter's response was to send a copy of Douglas' memo to the other justices with the following cover note:

Since the enclosed memorandum addressed to me purports to deal with a matter of Court concern, it seems appropriate that all the other members of the Court should see it.[72]

Douglas thought little of Minton. On one occasion, Douglas, in a memo circulated to the justices, accused Minton of being "Felix's Charlie McCarthy";[73] that is, Douglas asserted that Frankfurter could manipulate Minton and put words in his mouth as if Frankfurter were the ventriloquist and Minton the dummy. Minton passed a note to Frankfurter during one conference after Black made an impassioned presentation, saying: "He [Black] is a demagogue."[74] After his retirement from the Court, Minton was to write to Frankfurter: "My stay here has been crappy in my relations to all the brethren, but I shall always remember your kindness to me. . . ."[75]

No doubt Earl Warren had a steadying hand at the helm of the Court. There is no question but that he was well liked and that he

kept a lid on the cauldron of conflicting personalities. It is also evident that he had a clear view of where the Court ought to be going. Unlike Vinson, Warren was a man with vision, indeed, a judicial statesman. He had firm ideas about the freedom and dignity of individuals and as such was a committed civil libertarian. Although not a great legal scholar, he was a lucid judicial thinker and writer. His chief justiceship saw the Court becoming more and more embroiled in highly controversial civil liberties issues, and the Warren Court and its policies became the grist for the mill of political campaigns. During the 1960s, polls registered a significant drop in public support for the Court. But when all is said and done, Earl Warren was unquestionably one of the great chief justices in terms of his impact on constitutional law.

THE BURGER AND REHNQUIST COURTS

From 1969 through the 1989–1990 Term, only eight new justices, all appointed by Republican Presidents, came to the Court. Four, including one Democrat, were appointed by Richard Nixon. The fifth, a Republican, was appointed by Gerald Ford, and the remaining three justices, also Republicans, were named by Ronald Reagan, whose appointment of Sandra Day O'Connor sexually integrated the Court. All these new appointees tipped the partisan and ideological balance to the conservative Republican side. Reagan's appointments of Antonin Scalia and Anthony Kennedy resulted in an even more conservative Court.

Nixon Remakes the Court

President Nixon had a unique opportunity in his first year as President to fill both the chief justice slot and an associate justiceship. For the former, Nixon picked as the man to turn around the Warren Court a United States appeals court judge whose first and middle

---

[71]William O. Douglas to Felix Frankfurter, May 29, 1954, in the Felix Frankfurter Papers in the Library of Congress as reproduced in Atkinson, op. cit., p. 105.

[72]Memorandum from Felix Frankfurter to the Court, June 1, 1954, ibid.

[73]Ibid., p. 361, n. 7.

[74]Ibid., p. 106.

[75]Ibid., p. 104.

names turned around Earl Warren's name. *Warren Earl Burger,* a noted conservative jurist, had once been active in Minnesota Republican politics. At the 1952 Republican presidential nominating convention, he helped swing the Minnesota delegation to Eisenhower, which was particularly helpful in Eisenhower's successful capture of the Republican presidential nomination. Once in office, the Eisenhower Administration found a place for Burger in the Justice Department as an Assistant Attorney General in charge of the Civil Division. In 1956 Burger was named to the United States Court of Appeals for the District of Columbia. On and off the bench, he was an outspoken critic of the Warren Court's criminal procedure decisions and his speeches and writings were brought to President Nixon's attention. Attorney General John Mitchell was reported to have strongly backed Burger for the position.[76] On the Court, Chief Justice Burger was a strong law-and-order judge and with the aid of other conservatives he chipped away, although he rarely explicitly reversed, the liberal Warren Court precedents in the criminal and many other areas of civil liberties. He was also an activist judicial administrator, advocating and implementing reform in the operating ways of the judicial system. President Nixon nominated Burger just days after Justice Fortas resigned from the Court, and confirmation came rapidly.

Harry A. Blackmun, a conservative midwestern judge, was nominated in April 1970 to the seat vacated by Justice Fortas that Nixon had difficulty filling. Nixon had first named Fourth Circuit Judge Clement Haynsworth from South Carolina to the vacancy, but Haynsworth was opposed by civil rights and labor organizations and there were questions raised about possible conflict of interest in some of his decisions. Haynsworth was defeated on the Senate floor and Nixon then named another southern judge, Fifth Circuit Judge G. Harrold Carswell. With Carswell

there was not only ideological opposition but serious questions regarding his intellectual ability, judicial integrity, and whether he was a racist. He, too, went down to defeat on a Senate vote. It was then that Nixon turned to Eighth Circuit Judge Harry Blackmun. Blackmun, with impeccable legal credentials, was unanimously confirmed by the Senate on May 12, 1970. Blackmun graduated from Harvard College and Harvard Law School. He has been a lifelong friend of Warren Burger, whom he first met when both attended the same kindergarten class in St. Paul, Minnesota. Blackmun was best man at Burger's wedding. It is reasonable to assume that Burger had recommended his friend for the court of appeals position to which Blackmun was appointed in 1959. Blackmun's name as a possible Court appointee was in all likelihood given by Burger to Attorney General Mitchell and the President. Because both Blackmun and Burger are from Minnesota and their voting records during their first years together on the Court were almost identical, they were dubbed by journalists "the Minnesota Twins." In subsequent years they were not as close in their voting records, Blackmun frequently taking more moderate-to-liberal positions than the Chief Justice (by the time of the Rehnquist Court, Blackmun was clearly a member of the liberal bloc). It has also been reported that they are not as close personally as they once were.

In September 1971 Justices Black and Harlan, both in poor health, retired from the Court. The names of some leading contenders for the vacancies surfaced in the press and provoked severe criticism. President Nixon then moved quickly, and in a nationwide television address unexpectedly named *Lewis F. Powell, Jr.* and *William H. Rehnquist* to fill the vacancies. Powell, a native of Virginia and a former president of the American Bar Association, was a well-known conservative lawyer. Rehnquist, serving as Assistant Attorney General in the Office of Legal Counsel, had the reputation of being extremely conserva-

[76]*New York Times,* July 28, 1969, p. 21.

tive as well as brilliant. Both Powell and Rehnquist had graduated first in their law school classes—Powell at Washington and Lee Law School and Rehnquist at Stanford Law School. Neither had judicial experience. Powell was a nominal Democrat and had ties to the conservative wing of the Virginia Democratic party. Rehnquist had been active in Republican politics in Arizona and an active campaigner for Barry Goldwater in the 1964 presidential election. Although there was some opposition to the Rehnquist nomination, both men were confirmed by the Senate in December 1971. Rehnquist proved to be the most conservative justice on the Burger Court. Powell was more moderate than Rehnquist, but he was generally allied with the conservative wing.

President Nixon made a public issue of redirecting the Court by the use of his appointment power. All four of the Nixon appointees were known conservatives at the time of their appointments, particularly on issues concerning the rights of criminal defendants. In a very real sense, on the law-and-order issue, Nixon remade the Supreme Court.

Ford's Appointment

In the fall of 1975, Justice Douglas, who had been in poor health, retired. This must have been a particularly difficult action to take as Douglas, the most liberal justice on the Court, well knew that his replacement would most assuredly be less liberal, thereby pushing the ideological balance on the Court even further to the right. Moreover, by retiring, Douglas was handing a Court appointment to his long-time political foe, Gerald Ford, who had headed the efforts to impeach Justice Douglas in 1969. But the Ford Administration handled the opportunity to make a Court appointment in a pointedly professional manner. Attorney General Edward Levi, the former president of the University of Chicago, assembled a list of names of leading jurists that was given to the American Bar Association Standing Committee on Fed-

eral Judiciary for examination and rating purposes. Attorney General Levi was personally acquainted with and backed fellow Chicagoan *John Paul Stevens,* a distinguished judge on the United States Court of Appeals for the Seventh Circuit, who was considered by the American Bar Association as one of the best persons available. Stevens, a Republican, received the nomination. As expected, Stevens has been less liberal than the man he replaced. But he has gravitated toward the liberal wing, particularly in the civil liberties area, was the third most liberal justice on the Burger Court, and has continued that record on the Rehnquist Court.

Reagan and the Court

President Carter was the only President serving a full term who did not have the opportunity to name someone to the Court. President Ronald Reagan, in contrast, was handed a vacancy to fill early in his first term with the retirement of Justice Potter Stewart. (Had Stewart not retired, his death in 1985 would still have provided Reagan with his first opportunity for an appointment.) He selected the first woman ever to be chosen for the Court, *Sandra D. O'Connor,* an Arizona state court judge with impressive legal and political credentials. O'Connor graduated third in her Stanford Law School class (and was a classmate of William Rehnquist). She had experience in private practice and as Assistant (state) Attorney General. She served in the state Senate and was elected Republican majority leader. In 1972 she was state co-chair of the Nixon presidential reelection campaign.

During the second term, the Reagan administration made it clear that the President would use his appointment power to appoint judges at all court levels who shared his vision of judicial restraint in the realm of civil rights and civil liberties claims.[77] The administration named several prominent law professors to the courts of appeals, and it appeared that

[77]*New York Times,* October 22, 1985, p. 1.

they were being groomed as possible Supreme Court appointments. Included among them were Robert Bork, Richard Posner, and Antonin Scalia. Then on June 17, 1986, Chief Justice Burger announced his retirement and President Reagan named Associate Justice William Rehnquist to replace Burger. To fill Rehnquist's seat, Reagan named Antonin Scalia. After a bitter fight, including charges by Senate liberals of extreme ideological partisanship and lapses of judicial ethics, Rehnquist was confirmed on September 17, 1986 by a vote of 65 to 33. Scalia's nomination had smoother sailing and the vote to confirm was unanimous.

Antonin Scalia had been a well-known conservative law professor at the University of Chicago Law School when he was named by Ronald Reagan to the Court of Appeals for the District of Columbia Circuit. Although he did not have as high a profile on the appeals court as did his colleague Robert Bork, Scalia was highly regarded by Justice Department officials. The facts that he would be the first Italian-American and a Catholic to serve on the Supreme Court were not lost on an administration that was politically courting these groups.

The Reagan Administration had another opportunity to name a justice to the Court when Lewis Powell announced in mid-June 1987 his intention to retire. President Reagan nominated Robert Bork to fill Powell's seat. Bork had been a well-known Yale Law School professor, had served as Solicitor General from 1973 to 1977, and had been serving on the Court of Appeals for the District of Columbia Circuit, a post to which he had been appointed by Ronald Reagan. He had the reputation of being an intellectually forceful conservative judge and he was highly visible as he gave numerous public speeches and interviews. But civil rights and civil liberties groups mounted a successful campaign against his nomination, which subsequently went down to defeat on the Senate floor by a vote

of 42 in favor and 58 against confirmation. The President than announced his intention to nominate Douglas Ginsburg, who was, like Bork, a former law professor and a Reagan appointee serving with Bork on the same circuit court. But revelations concerning Ginsburg's use of marijuana years earlier when he was a young faculty member at Harvard Law School resulted in such an outcry from conservatives that the nomination was never formally submitted to the Senate. Finally, Reagan was successful with the nomination of conservative Ninth Circuit Judge *Anthony M. Kennedy,* who was unanimously confirmed, and who took his seat on the Court on February 18, 1988. Kennedy had been appointed to the circuit bench by President Ford in 1975. He had maintained a low profile on the bench but had known Attorney General Meese from an earlier era in California politics when Kennedy had been a lawyer practicing at the state capital. Kennedy, a devout Roman Catholic, was expected by the administration to vote "right" on abortion, and his replacing Lewis Powell, who had supported **Roe** v. **Wade,** provided the crucial vote in the **Webster** v. **Reproductive Health Services** decision.

Background Characteristics of the Justices

The key background characteristics of the justices coming to the Court between 1969 and 1990 are presented in Table 5.10. In contrast to previous eras, but similar to the pattern of Republican Eisenhower, Republicans Nixon, Ford, and Reagan did not name any close friends or associates (with the possible exception of Rehnquist, who was a member of the Nixon administration at the time of appointment). Three had extensive backgrounds of political activism (Burger, Rehnquist, and O'Connor), and one (Powell) had a background of some activism.

Geography seemed to have played some role, particularly with one of the nine appointments. President Nixon was determined to re-

Table 5.10 SELECTED CHARACTERISTICS OF JUSTICES APPOINTED BY PRESIDENTS NIXON, FORD, AND REAGAN AND NOMINATED BY BUSH

Seat and Justice	Party	Home State	Years on Court	Father's Occupation	Occupation at Time of Nomination	Age at Nomination	Previous Judicial Experience
Nixon appointees:							
1 Warren E. Burger	Republican	Minnesota	1969–1986	Rail cargo inspector	U.S. Circuit Court Judge	61	Federal
3 Harry A. Blackmun	Republican	Minnesota	1970–	Bank official	U.S. Circuit Court Judge	61	Federal
2 Lewis F. Powell, Jr.	Democrat	Virginia	1971–1987	Businessman (manufacturing)	Private law practice	64	None
8 William H. Rehnquist	Republican	Arizona	1971–1986	Salesman	Assistant Attorney General	47	None
Ford appointee:							
5 John Paul Stevens	Republican	Illinois	1976–	Businessman, investor	U.S. Circuit Court Judge	55	Federal
Reagan appointees:							
9 Sandra Day O'Connor	Republican	Arizona	1981–	Rancher	State Court Judge	51	State
1 William H. Rehnquist	Republican	Arizona	1986–	Salesman	Associate Justice, U.S. Supreme Court	61	Federal
8 Antonin Scalia	Republican	Illinois (New Jersey)	1986–	College professor	U.S. Circuit Court Judge	50	Federal
2 Anthony M. Kennedy	Republican	California	1988–	Lawyer	U.S. Circuit Court Judge	51	Federal
Bush nominee:							
4 David H. Souter	Republican	New Hampshire	1990 nominated	Bank official	U.S. Circuit Court Judge	50	Federal, State

place Fortas, a native of Tennessee, with another southerner. His nomination of southerners Haynsworth and Carswell, however, failed and Nixon finally named Harry Blackmun who, like Warren Burger, came from Minnesota. For the first time in the history of the Court, two justices from Minnesota were serving simultaneously. Nixon was eventually successful in appointing southerner Lewis Powell, who was the sixth Virginia native to serve on the Court and the first Virginian to sit since 1860. Also, it might be observed that Rehnquist's attractiveness to Nixon may have been enhanced by the fact that in addition to the obvious professional, ideological, and political considerations, Rehnquist was a westerner from a state that never had one of its own on the Court. However, there is no evidence, nor is it likely, that geographic considerations governed either the Burger, Stevens, O'Connor, Rehnquist (to Chief Justice), Scalia, or Kennedy appointments. By 1990 the Court consisted of three midwesterners, two northeasterners, and four westerners.

In continuing the historical trends in terms of family background, farming was not the main occupation of the justices' fathers. The justices tended to come from middle-class families. Two of the fathers were in the professions (Scalia's father was a college professor and Kennedy's was a lawyer). Chief Justices Burger and Rehnquist, like the three chief justices before them, came from modest family backgrounds. The fathers of both Burger and Warren were railroad men. Chief Justice Rehnquist's father was a salesman.

The quality of legal education of the appointees varied. Chief Justice Burger was a graduate of a night law school (St. Paul College of Law). Harry Blackmun graduated from Harvard Law School and had been a student of then Professor Felix Frankfurter. Lewis Powell graduated first in his class at Washington and Lee Law School and then spent a year at Harvard Law School where he, too, studied under Frankfurter. William Rehnquist graduated from Stanford Law School and also spent a year at Harvard. John Paul Stevens graduated at the head of his law school class at Northwestern University Law School. Sandra O'Connor graduated from Stanford Law School. Antonin Scalia graduated from Harvard Law School, as did Anthony Kennedy.

Seven justices were in public office at the time of appointment and six had judicial experience. All but Roman Catholics Scalia and Kennedy have religious origins in Protestant denominations. There is no evidence that religion was a consideration in the judicial selection process of these justices, although Scalia's Italian-American heritage may have added to his attractiveness to the Reagan administration, Scalia being the first member of his ethnic group to be appointed to the Court. The ethnic origins of the large majority of justices were in the British Isles, thus continuing the long-standing trend.

Voting Patterns of the Justices

The advent of the Burger Court marked a new departure for the Court. No longer were liberal judicial activists in the majority. As President Nixon made good his promise to appoint conservatives, the Court veered sharply to the right, particularly in the criminal law field. The only major exception was in the area of sexual equality, in which the Court moved in a liberal direction. The first decade of the Burger Court saw dissent on the Court reach historic high levels. During Chief Justice Warren's last term, the dissent rate in cases decided with full opinion was 66 percent. During Chief Justice Burger's first term, the dissent rate rose to 71 percent and during his second term (the 1970 Term) it surpassed 81 percent. During the 1971 Term, dissent remained high at 78 percent and continued at similar high rates until a dip in the 1976 Term to 66 percent dissent. The 1977 Term saw a rise to 73 percent, but the 1978 Term rate was 64 percent, the lowest for the Burger Court during its first decade. Although the 1979 Term rate rose to 75 percent, the subsequent five terms all registered dissent rates below 70 percent, with the dissent rates for the 1983 and 1984 Terms at record lows for the Burger Court—60 percent.[78] The 1985 Term, Burger's last, showed a rise to 69 percent, however. Clearly in terms of overall dissent, the Burger Court in its first decade was a highly contentious Court, equaling if not surpassing the Vinson Court, but into the second decade the level of dissension was reduced. In 31 cases (through the 1985 Term), the Burger Court overturned provisions of federal law and there was dissent in 65 percent of these cases. The comparable figure for the Warren Court was about 80 percent.

Table 5.11 shows the individual dissent rates in decisions with full opinion. During the first two terms of the Burger Court, four justices including Burger himself had dissent rates over 20 percent. The average dissent rate was 19.3 percent, which was only slightly below the high point reached during the Vinson Court; it ranged from a low of about 14 percent for White to over 29 percent for Douglas.

With the 1971 Term, Justices Powell and Rehnquist joined the Court, replacing Black and Harlan. The advent of a solid conservative majority pushed the three remaining liberals to surpass their previous dissent levels. Douglas dissented in about 44 percent of the fully decided cases. Brennan dissented in about 30 percent of those cases, and Marshall was not far behind with close to a 28 percent dissent rate. The average dissent rate rose to

20.3 percent and ranged from Douglas' high to Powell's 10.3 percent dissent rate. In the early part of the 1975 Term, Justice Douglas retired from the Court and was replaced by Justice Stevens. The new Justice quickly established his independence and with Rehnquist, another dissenter, the Court again had four justices with dissent rates above 20 percent. For the 1975 through 1977 Terms, the average dissent rate was again 20.3 percent, with Justice Brennan having the highest dissent rate (35.2 percent) and Justice Powell again having the lowest dissent rate (9.7 percent). For the 1978 through 1980 Terms, the average dissent rate rose to 21.4 percent and for the first time on the Burger Court five justices had dissent rates over 20 percent. Justices Brennan and Marshall were virtually tied with the highest dissent rates (about 33 percent) and Chief Justice Burger was second only to Justice White for the lowest dissent rates (close to 15 percent). Justice Powell increased his dissent rate but still had one of the lowest dissent rates on the Court. Before the 1981 Term began, Justice Stewart retired and was replaced by Justice O'Connor. The average dissent rate for the remainder of the Burger Court dropped slightly to 20.3 percent, with Justice O'Connor dissenting less than the justice she replaced, which meant that now only four justices had dissent rates at about or exceeding 20 percent. The lowest dissent rates were those of Powell, White, and the Chief Justice. The highest rates were again those of Brennan and Marshall. Justice Stevens' dissent rate increased markedly from the previous period and Justice Rehnquist's rate decreased. During Chief Justice Burger's last term, however, Justice Blackmun's dissent rate increased dramatically to 28 percent.

If we compare the Burger and Warren Courts, we find that the Burger Court's average dissent rate was over 20 percent as compared to the 14 percent average dissent rate on the Warren Court during the 1962–1968 Terms. During the 17 terms of the Burger

[78]The figures for dissent were taken from the *Harvard Law Review*, November issues, 1970 through 1985. The 1985 Term dissent rates were calculated by the author. For an illuminating overview of dissent and other voting behavior of the justices with a historical focus, see David M. O'Brien, " 'The Imperial Judiciary': of Paper Tigers and Socio-Legal Indicators," *Journal of Law and Politics*, 2 (1985), pp. 1–56, and his book *Storm Center: The Supreme Court in American Politics*, 2nd ed. (New York: W. W. Norton, 1990).

Table 5.11   DISSENT RATES, BURGER COURT

	Dissent Rates				
Justice	1969–1970 Terms (%)	1971–1974 Terms (%)	1975–1977 Terms (%)	1978–1980 Terms (%)	1981–1985 Terms (%)
Black	23.9	—	—	—	—
Blackmun	15.0	10.9	13.7	15.6	18.3
Brennan	21.6	29.8	35.2	32.5	32.4
Burger	20.2	14.1	15.7	14.7	12.7
Douglas	29.4	43.9	—	—	—
Harlan	16.9	—	—	—	—
Marshall	16.8	27.7	32.6	34.5	34.0
O'Connor	—	—	—	—	13.8
Powell	—	10.3	9.7	14.9	11.5
Rehnquist	—	18.7	22.8	24.8	19.9
Stevens	—	—	21.9	22.0	28.4
Stewart	15.4	16.1	15.9	20.7	—
White	14.1	10.9	15.2	13.3	12.4
The Court	76.9	77.7	72.1	69.4	64.3

Court, 13 justices served during part or all of the period and 9 (69.2 percent) had dissent rates over 20 percent during part or all of this era. By comparison, only 4 (36.4 percent) of the 11 justices serving during the latter Warren Court period had dissent rates over 20 percent. The evidence hints that Chief Justice Burger was significantly less successful in leading his colleagues than was his predecessor.

If the individual dissent rates of justices serving during the latter Warren Court (see Table 5.6) are compared to their dissent rates during the first two terms of the Burger Court as shown in Table 5.11, we find that liberals Douglas, Brennan, and Marshall dramatically increased their dissent rates. Conservatives Harlan and Stewart reduced theirs, whereas the rates for Justices Black and White were only marginally affected. As the conservative Burger Court took shape with increased conservative strength, the dissent rates of the liberals continued their sharp climb, whereas the conservatives for the most part either remained roughly the same or decreased their dissent rates. Justice Blackmun was the only

exception during the latter part of the Burger Court due to his shift away from the core conservative bloc.

The Rehnquist Court is still in its early years, yet a pattern is starting to emerge. Table 5.12 shows the individual dissent rates for the first four terms. During Rehnquist's first term as Chief Justice, the average dissent rate shot up to 27.1 percent and seven justices had dissent rates over 20 percent. There was dissent in three out of four decisions and dissent rates ranged from about 11 percent for Powell to over 40 percent for Marshall. It is a reasonable inference that Rehnquist had not yet adjusted to the leadership role of Chief Justice. Indeed, his own dissent rate was over 26 percent. But the following term saw a dramatic change. Rehnquist's own dissent rate dropped to about 17 percent, the average dissent rate was 18 percent, and dissent rates ranged from about 9 percent for Justice Kennedy (who joined the Court in midterm and whose participation was limited) to about 26 percent for Marshall. Four justices, however, dissented at the rate of 20 percent or more. This was true also for the 1988 Term but the dissent rates for

Table 5.12   DISSENT RATES, REHNQUIST COURT

| | Dissent Rates | | | |
Justice	1986 Term (%)	1987 Term (%)	1988 Term (%)	1989 Term (%)
Blackmun	26.2	20.0	27.3	24.8
Brennan	38.8	23.0	38.3	35.0
Kennedy	—	9.2	7.7	13.2
Marshall	40.1	26.4	39.7	37.9
O'Connor	25.2	20.9	11.5	13.9
Powell	11.3	—	—	—
Rehnquist	26.3	17.3	11.9	17.5
Scalia	20.9	16.7	11.2	18.2
Stevens	36.4	16.4	27.5	31.4
White	18.5	12.1	9.0	10.9
The Court	74.3	56.3	60.0	66.4

the most conservative justices fell, with Rehnquist's own rate achieving his lowest yet on the Court. The 1989 Term revealed a somewhat similar pattern. These figures suggest that Rehnquist has adjusted to the role of Chief Justice, although sharp ideological divisions remain on the Court as Tables 5.13, 5.15, and 5.17 also suggest.

If we compare individual dissent rates during the latter Burger Court to those during the first terms of the Rehnquist Court, we find that by the 1987 Term Justices Brennan, Marshall, and Blackmun had higher dissent rates and Justices Rehnquist, White, and O'Connor had lower rates.

Table 5.13 presents the bloc structure for the Burger and Rehnquist Courts. Douglas, Brennan, and Marshall formed the core of the liberal bloc. Their cohesion was high. When Powell and Rehnquist joined the Court, the bloc structure changed as Justice Stewart gravitated toward the liberals, although, as it turned out, that was only temporary. Later Justice Stevens would be loosely linked with the truncated liberal bloc. As Table 5.14 indicates, Justices Rehnquist, Burger, and Blackmun (in that order) were the most conservative justices on civil liberties matters and were at the heart of the conservative bloc until the

1977 Term. Justices Burger and Blackmun agreed with each other the most during the first five terms of their joint service. In about 90 percent of the nonunanimously decided civil liberties cases, Burger and Blackmun voted together. In subsequent terms they were less cohesive. In the 1976 Term, Burger and Blackmun agreed with each other in 76 percent of the cases. In the 1977 Term, for the first time, Blackmun and Powell formed a separate bloc, agreeing with each other in 75 percent of the cases. However, in the 1977, 1978, and 1979 Terms, Blackmun agreed with Burger in about 70 percent of the nonunanimously decided civil liberties cases. Blackmun's agreement with Burger fell to 46 percent in 1981, rose to 64 percent in 1984, but reached its lowest level during Burger's last term, only 40 percent. Since joining the Court, only in the 1981, 1982, and 1985 Terms did Blackmun agree more with Brennan and Marshall than with Burger. As Table 5.13 indicates, those were the only three terms during the Burger Court in which Blackmun was not allied with the conservative wing. In recent years Blackmun has been considerably more in agreement with Brennan and Marshall than during his first five terms on the Court. Blackmun has clearly shifted from core membership

Table 5.13 VOTING BLOCS ON THE SUPREME COURT IN NONUNANIMOUS CIVIL LIBERTIES DECISIONS, 1969–1989 TERMS

Term	Bloc Membership	Average Agreement of Justices in Bloc	Type of Bloc
1969	Douglas, Brennan, Marshall	79%	Liberal
	White, Harlan	86	Conservative
	Stewart, Burger, Black	62	Conservative
1970	Douglas, Brennan, Marshall	83	Liberal
	Burger, Blackmun, Harlan, Stewart, White, Black	68	Conservative
1971	Douglas, Brennan, Marshall, Stewart	74	Liberal
	Burger, Blackmun, Rehnquist, Powell, White	81	Conservative
1972	Douglas, Brennan, Marshall	86	Liberal
	Burger, Blackmun, Rehnquist, Powell, White, Stewart	73	Conservative
1973	Douglas, Brennan, Marshall	85	Liberal
	Stewart, Powell, White	77	Conservative
	Burger, Blackmun, Rehnquist	83	Conservative
1974	Douglas, Brennan, Marshall	79	Liberal
	Burger, Blackmun, Rehnquist, Powell, White, Stewart	74	Conservative
1975	Marshall, Brennan	97	Liberal
	Burger, Blackmun, Rehnquist, Powell, White, Stewart, Stevens	72	Conservative
1976	Brennan, Marshall, Stevens	75	Conservative
	Burger, Rehnquist, White, Blackmun, Powell, Stewart	73	Conservative
1977	Brennan, Marshall	90	Liberal
	Powell, Blackmun	75	Conservative
	White, Burger, Stewart, Rehnquist, Stevens	61	Conservative
1978	Brennan, Marshall, Stevens	75	Liberal
	White, Blackmun	80	Conservative
	Burger, Stewart, Rehnquist, Powell	76	Conservative
1979	Brennan, Marshall, Stevens	82	Liberal
	Powell, Stewart	78	Conservative
	Burger, White, Blackmun, Rehnquist	64	Conservative
1980	Brennan, Marshall	89	Liberal
	Burger, White, Blackmun, Rehnquist, Powell, Stewart, Stevens	65	Conservative
1981	Brennan, Marshall	91	Liberal
	Stevens, Blackmun	67	Moderate
	Burger, Rehnquist, Powell, White, O'Connor	75	Conservative
1982	Brennan, Marshall, Stevens, Blackmun	70	Liberal
	Burger, Powell, White, Rehnquist, O'Connor	79	Conservative
1983	Brennan, Marshall, Stevens	72	Liberal
	Burger, Powell, White, Rehnquist, O'Connor, Blackmun	78	Conservative
1984	Brennan, Marshall, Stevens	77	Liberal
	Burger, White, Rehnquist, Powell, O'Connor, Blackmun	75	Conservative
1985	Brennan, Marshall, Stevens, Blackmun	70	Liberal
	Burger, Rehnquist, O'Connor, White, Powell	79	Conservative
1986	Brennan, Marshall, Stevens, Blackmun	74	Liberal
	Rehnquist, White, Scalia, Powell, O'Connor	76	Conservative
1987	Brennan, Marshall, Stevens, Blackmun	71	Liberal
	Scalia, Kennedy, White, O'Connor, Rehnquist	78	Conservative
1988	Brennan, Marshall, Stevens, Blackmun	70	Liberal
	Scalia, Kennedy, Rehnquist, White, O'Connor	83	Conservative
1989	Brennan, Marshall, Stevens, Blackmun	74	Liberal
	Kennedy, O'Connor, Scalia, Rehnquist, White	83	Conservative

Table 5.14   PRO-CIVIL LIBERTIES VOTING OF THE JUSTICES ON THE BURGER COURT IN ALL DECISIONS WITH FULL OPINION

Justice	Civil Liberties (% of votes in favor)				
	1969–1970 Terms (%)	1971–1974 Terms (%)	1975–1977 Terms (%)	1978–1980 Terms (%)	1981–1985 Terms (%)
Black	54	—	—	—	—
Blackmun	35	38	33	44	54
Brennan	75	83	77	81	80
Burger	36	31	23	25	23
Douglas	89	93	—	—	—
Harlan	47	—	—	—	—
Marshall	76	85	78	82	83
O'Connor	—	—	—	—	28
Powell	—	39	34	36	31
Rehnquist	—	22	13	13	17
Stevens	—	—	53	59	61
Stewart	46	59	42	41	—
White	50	44	37	43	33
The Court	55	46	37	41	38

in the conservative wing, and as Tables 5.14 and 5.15 suggest, has become a moderate liberal. Blackmun joined the Court as a hard-core conservative but became more moderate or middle-of-the-road and by the time of the Rehnquist Court was a member of the liberal wing.

In the 1975, 1976, and 1977 Terms, Burger was closest to Rehnquist, agreeing with him in 90 percent and more of the nonunanimously decided civil liberties decisions. In the 1978 Term they agreed in 83 percent and in 1979 in 70 percent of such decisions. Burger was closest to Powell in the 1980 and 1982 Terms, closest to Rehnquist in the 1981 and 1985 Terms, closest to O'Connor in the 1983 and 1984 Terms (92 percent agreement in 1983 and 85 percent in 1984). In the 1984 Term, Burger also had the same high agreement with White.

Rehnquist was continually closely allied with Burger. In the 1980 Term they agreed in 84 percent of the nonunanimously decided civil liberties cases. In the 1983 Term the figure was 88 percent agreement. In the 1984 Term Rehnquist's highest agreement was with

both Burger and O'Connor, and in the 1985 Term Rehnquist's highest agreement was 90 percent with Burger followed by 79 percent with O'Connor.

Justice O'Connor's highest agreement in the nonunanimously decided civil liberties decisions in her first three terms on the Court was with Rehnquist, and in her fourth term, the 1984 Term, her highest agreement was with Burger (85 percent agreement) followed by Powell (83 percent) and Rehnquist (81 percent). By contrast, in the 1984 Term O'Connor agreed with Brennan and Marshall in little more than one out of four decisions. In the 1985 Term, O'Connor's highest agreement was with White (84 percent) and Burger (83 percent).

The bloc structure for the conservatives is seen as somewhat unstable. Justice Stevens appears to have fluctuated between the conservatives and the liberals during his first seven years on the Court. Only in the last four terms of the Burger Court did it appear that Stevens severed his links with the conservative fold. As Table 5.14 suggests, Stevens was

Table 5.15   PRO-CIVIL LIBERTIES VOTING OF THE JUSTICES ON THE REHNQUIST COURT
IN ALL DECISIONS WITH FULL OPINION

| Justice | Civil Liberties (% votes in favor) | | | |
	1986 Term (%)	1987 Term (%)	1988 Term (%)	1989 Term (%)
Blackmun	70	69	65	64
Brennan	95	88	86	88
Kennedy	—	47*	31	31
Marshall	95	87	86	92
O'Connor	28	37	37	27
Powell	36	—	—	—
Rehnquist	14	30	26	20
Scalia	27	40	36	28
Stevens	72	70	64	73
White	28	43	34	32
The Court	43	52	38	41

*Limited participation.

a middle-of-the-road, leaning-liberal Justice voting in favor of the civil liberties claim in about three-fifths the cases decided fully on the merits. Justice Stewart, too, but to a lesser extent, had tendencies toward the middle, and earlier in the Burger Court this had seemed true for White as well, who now must be classified generally as a core conservative.

Table 5.14 shows, among other findings, that as the Nixon appointees came to dominate the Court, there was a significant drop in the proportion of decisions decided in favor of civil liberties claims. The table also suggests that Chief Justice Burger, unlike Warren during his last seven terms, was somewhat out of step with the thrust of the Court's decisional trends. Burger was consistently less civil liberties oriented than the overall record of the Court even as the proportion of cases decided by the Court in favor of civil liberties dropped markedly. During the last term of Chief Justice Warren's tenure, some 75 percent of all civil liberties decisions decided with full opinion favored the civil liberties claim. During Burger's first two terms, that proportion dropped to 55 percent. During the subsequent seven terms, the proportion fell to 37 percent.

Although there was some slight fluctuation upward, during the last term of the Burger Court the proportion returned to 37 percent.

Chief Justice Burger's proportion dropped from 36 to 23 percent of his votes favoring civil liberties claims. During the 1981 through 1985 Terms, the Court's proportion was at 38 percent, but Burger's civil liberties support continued low.

Table 5.14 also hints at what most observers acknowledge—that Justice Douglas' departure resulted in the Court losing its most vigorous civil libertarian. Justices Brennan and Marshall did not equal Douglas' extremely high level of civil liberties support until the Rehnquist Court. At the other extreme is Justice Rehnquist with the lowest civil liberties support on the Court. Justice White is seen as becoming more conservative, and in the 1981–1985 Term period he was the fifth most conservative justice, with only one out of three of his votes supporting the civil liberties position.

Table 5.13 contains the bloc structure for the Rehnquist Court which suggests that the Court, particularly in civil liberties cases, is more sharply polarized than during most of the Burger Court era. With the addition of Scalia and Kennedy, the conservative bloc has become the most cohesive that it has been in half a century. As Table 5.15 shows, Chief Justice Rehnquist continues to be the most conservative justice on civil liberties issues followed by Kennedy, White, Scalia, and O'Connor. In the 1988 Term, Justices Scalia and Kennedy agreed with each other the most (90 percent agreement in nonunanimous civil liberties decisions) and Chief Justice Rehnquist agreed with Kennedy and White in 88 percent of the cases. Justice O'Connor agreed with White in 84 percent and with Rehnquist in 82 percent of the decisions.

The bloc structure for the liberals during the Rehnquist Court is not as firm as that for the conservatives. Justices Brennan and Marshall form the core of the liberal bloc, agreeing with each other in about 95 percent of the nonunanimously decided civil liberties decisions. But the agreement between these justices and Blackmun and Stevens has been in the 60 to 70 percent range, as has the agreement rate between Blackmun and Stevens.

Table 5.15 reveals that although Rehnquist continues to have the least support for civil liberties claims, his support after his first term as Chief Justice has been the highest since he has been on the Court. This suggests somewhat of a moderating trend on his part as he attempts to exercise leadership. The table also shows that quantitatively the proportion of decisions favoring civil liberties is similar to that for the Burger Court.

In comparing civil liberties support on the part of individual justices during the Rehnquist Court to that of the Burger Court, we find that Blackmun's civil liberty support increased as did Brennan's, Marshall's, Stevens', Rehnquist's, and O'Connor's. White's support remained about the same.

Table 5.16 records the economic liberalism voting of the Burger Court. The Court, as a whole, moved from the 70 percent record of support of the Warren Court to about a 50 per-

cent support level during the 1969–1970 and 1975–1977 Terms but a low point in the 40 percent range during the 1971–1974 Terms and the 1978–1980 Terms. However, in the 1981–1985 Term period, the Court's support rose to a record high for the Burger Court of 60 percent. The individual voting records show Justices Brennan and Marshall becoming even more liberal and assuming the position of the most liberal justices on the economic issues. Justice White is considerably more liberal on the economic issues than he is on civil liberties. Interestingly, three of the four most economically liberal justices are Democrats, whereas the three most conservative justices on these issues are Republicans. Justice Rehnquist was least sympathetic to the economic underdog or to government regulation of business, and he was followed by the end of the Burger Court by O'Connor, Burger, and Powell. In the more recent period, Justice Blackmun appears to be emerging as considerably more moderate, even liberal, on these issues. Justice Black's last two terms saw him reduce his economic liberalism support so that at the end of his career on the Court Black had become—at least in a statistical sense—a centrist on both the economic liberalism and civil liberties dimensions.

Table 5.17 displays the economic liberalism voting on the Rehnquist Court. On the whole (with the exception of the 1989 Term) it appears that the Rehnquist Court has become more conservative than the latter Burger Court. The most liberal justices on this measure were Brennan, Marshall, Stevens, and Blackmun. The most conservative justices were Rehnquist, Kennedy, White, Scalia, and O'Connor. The biggest change from the Burger Court is the voting of Justice White.

The Burger Court ended on July 7, 1986, and the overall trends were reasonably clear. These trends and the trends for the Rehnquist Court were discovered by an analysis of the justices' public voting records. When we turn

Table 5.16   **PRO-ECONOMIC LIBERALISM VOTING OF THE JUSTICES ON THE BURGER COURT IN NONUNANIMOUS DECISIONS WITH FULL OPINION**

	Economic Liberalism (% of votes in favor)				
Justice	1969–1970 Terms %	1971–1974 Terms %	1975–1977 Terms %	1978–1980 Terms %	1981–1985 Terms %
Black	58	—	—	—	—
Blackmun	27	38	50	61	76
Brennan	78	85	92	80	87
Burger	16	19	30	33	33
Douglas	78	78	—	—	—
Harlan	31	—	—	—	—
Marshall	61	73	86	85	91
O'Connor	—	—	—	—	31
Powell	—	29	41	37	33
Rehnquist	—	21	28	13	24
Stevens	—	—	53	40	52
Stewart	33	40	39	36	—
White	68	53	67	61	64
The Court	52	42	51	46	60

Table 5.17   **PRO-ECONOMIC LIBERALISM VOTING OF THE JUSTICES ON THE REHNQUIST COURT IN NONUNANIMOUS DECISIONS WITH FULL OPINION**

	Economic Liberalism (% votes in favor)			
Justice	1985 Term (%)	1987 Term (%)	1988 Term (%)	1989 Term (%)
Blackmun	80	71	56	67
Brennan	91	83	69	89
Kennedy	—	50*	19	50
Marshall	95	88	69	89
O'Connor	24	21	31	44
Powell	35	—	—	—
Rehnquist	19	30	13	33
Scalia	29	36	19	33
Stevens	57	57	69	56
White	39	38	19	67
The Court	57	50	25	67

*Limited participation.

our attention to patterns of group interaction, we find that the traditional sources of data, the private papers and diaries of the justices, are generally not available to scholars for the Burger and Rehnquist Court period. The book *The Brethren* by Bob Woodward and Scott Armstrong,[79] however, purported to provide an inside account of the Burger Court during its first seven terms, relying heavily on interviews with former law clerks to the justices and also memoranda from the justices to each other, and even the diary of one of the justices. Although the book was criticized as being misleading and unscholarly (no sources were provided), it, along with some other fragments of evidence, shed some light on the group interaction process that occurred within the Burger Court. For the Rehnquist Court, however, there is little hard evidence, although some justices have given interviews to members of the news media.

Patterns of Group Interaction

When Warren Burger came to the Court, there was none of the intense rivalry and personal feuding that had characterized the Court during the Stone and Vinson periods. Justice Black had mellowed over the years and was well past his eightieth birthday at the onset of Burger's chief justiceship. Justice Douglas continued to hold the most liberal views of any justice on the Court, but there were no personality clashes at the intense level that there had been with Justice Frankfurter in years past. The other justices, as best as can be determined, maintained friendly personal relations despite their ideological differences. The Warren legacy was a Court that was relatively harmonious in personal terms and one that dispatched its ever-increasing business in a reasonably efficient way.

Warren Burger added his imprint to the chief justiceship and sought to improve the efficiency of the Court by introducing modern management techniques and by creating the permanent post of Administrative Assistant to the Chief Justice, staffed by an experienced professional administrator. Burger took an active interest in the workings of the entire judicial system and advocated a variety of reforms. As for the extent of personal harmonious relationships on the Court, the evidence is fragmentary, at best, upon which to make an assessment. There was a news report that once Rehnquist and Powell joined the Court some justices were upset with the speed and glee with which the new right-wing majority began flexing its muscles[80]—and we know from Table 5.13 that for that term Justice Stewart voted most with the liberal bloc. There was also a news report that the Justices on the two different extremes—Douglas and Rehnquist—personally got along so well that they and their families vacationed together one summer.[81] And, of course, as noted earlier, Blackmun and Burger have been lifelong friends although *The Brethren* suggests that their relationship suffered to some extent from tensions on the Court. The extent of or even existence of personal harmonious relationships on the Burger Court will have to be determined when more definitive evidence becomes available.

There is some evidence that suggests that Chief Justice Burger had some difficulty exercising task leadership. For example, it was reported that during the initial conference deliberations in the fall of 1971 on the *Roe* v. *Wade* case, Chief Justice Burger strenuously argued that there was no constitutional bar to state statutes forbidding abortions. Nevertheless, a majority of the justices took the opposite view

---

[79]Bob Woodward and Scott Armstrong, *The Brethren* (New York: Simon & Schuster, 1979). Subsequently, Justice Brennan deposited some of his papers with the Library of Congress.

[80]*Newsweek,* February 28, 1972, p. 9. Interestingly, no mention of this is made by Woodward and Armstrong, op. cit.

[81]*Newsweek,* October 15, 1973, p. 27.

and, in apparent defiance of tradition, Chief Justice Burger made the assignment of the writing of the opinion of the Court (to Justice Blackmun). The case was reargued the following term to permit the newcomers, Justices Powell and Rehnquist, the opportunity to participate and, again, there was a majority in favor of striking down the criminal abortion statutes. At that point, according to the report, Chief Justice Burger switched his vote and joined the majority.[82] In a meeting with political scientists, Chief Justice Burger denied this and maintained that the tradition still holds that the Chief Justice makes opinion assignments only when he votes with the majority. He strongly implied that there was no violation of that tradition with *Roe* v. *Wade*.[83]

Another example was reported concerning the Nixon tapes case, **United States** v. **Nixon.** According to the account published by the *New York Times*,[84] when the tapes case initially came to the Court, the question was whether the Court should expedite the appellate process and immediately hear the case. According to this account, Justice Stewart vigorously urged that the Court take the case and was joined by Powell, Douglas, Marshall, and Brennan. Justice Rehnquist recused himself, undoubtedly because of his previous close association with the parties in the case, but Burger, Blackmun, and White disagreed with the majority. Once the case was accepted and argued, the justices unanimously agreed about how the basic issues were to be decided

and Chief Justice Burger assigned himself the task of writing the opinion of the Court. According to the report published by the *Times*, Burger's first draft of the opinion was completely rejected and Justices Stewart and Powell redrafted it. However, the Chief Justice was able to persuade his colleagues to retain that portion of the opinion of the Court that conceded that the Constitution contains a presumption of executive privilege. Woodward and Armstrong in *The Brethren* offer a somewhat different version; they report that most of the associate justices had a hand in the piecemeal redrafting of the opinion, "forcing" the Chief to accept their views. In this account, Justice Brennan played a key role in the behind-the-scenes process. David O'Brien's account, which relies on the Brennan papers, confirms this.

Chief Justice Burger's task leadership abilities seemed to be called into question over the controversy that emerged concerning the Court's decision in *Gannett Co., Inc.* v. *De-Pasquale,* 443 U.S. 368 (1979). The five-to-four decision, in which Chief Justice Burger was in the majority and Justice Stewart wrote the opinion of the Court, concerned pretrial judicial proceedings and the right of the trial judge, when both prosecution and defense agree, to close the proceedings to the press and public. However, Justice Stewart's language was so sweeping that within a month the decision had been used in at least 18 cases across the country as the basis for closing the trials themselves.[85] Shortly thereafter, Chief Justice Burger was interviewed by reporters and observed that judges who were barring the press and public from trials may have misread the Court's decision.[86] But Justice Blackmun, who dissented in the *Gannett* case, publicly contradicted the Chief Justice and asserted that the majority opinion *does* authorize not only the closing of pretrial proceed-

[82]Nina Totenberg, "Behind the Marble, Beneath the Robes," *New York Times Magazine,* March 16, 1975, pp. 64–65. Also see Woodward and Armstrong, op. cit., pp. 169–170, 174, 236; Simon, op. cit., pp. 438–442; and O'Brien, *Storm Center,* op. cit., pp. 23–41.

[83]Meeting with political scientists in connection with the Short Course on the Supreme Court sponsored by the American Political Science Association, August 30, 1979. My thanks to Professors Lawrence Baum and Elliot Slotnick for providing me with a summary of the Chief Justice's remarks.

[84]Totenberg, op. cit., pp. 58 ff. Cf. Woodward and Armstrong, op. cit., pp. 292–293, 310–347 and O'Brien, *Storm Center,* op. cit., pp. 263–266.

[85]*New York Times,* August 4, 1979, p. 1.

[86]Ibid., August 9, 1979, p. A-17.

ings but the trials as well. Justice Stevens, a member of the *Gannett* majority, in a public address agreed with Blackmun's view of what was decided, but Justice Powell, another majority member, speaking at the annual meeting of the American Bar Association opined that judges would be "a bit premature" if they took the *Gannett* decision as the basis for closing trials to the press.[87] The point is that it would appear that effective task leadership might well have prevented such ambiguity from emerging in a closely decided case that the Chief Justice surely must have known would provoke intense interest by the press. The next year, however, the Court, with only Rehnquist dissenting, made amends with the **Richmond Newspapers, Inc.** v. **Virginia** decision. But in a highly personal concurrence, Justice Blackmun scolded the Chief for his bungled leadership.

Implicit criticism of Chief Justice Burger's task leadership can be found as well, for example, in a concurring opinion of Harry Blackmun that charged that the opinion of the Court authored by Burger "perpetuates confusion in an area where clarification and uniformity are urgently needed."[88] University of Chicago law professor and noted scholar Philip Kurland observed that "the Burger Court lacks intellectual leadership."[89] Former law clerks of Chief Justice Burger were purportedly quoted deprecating the Chief Justice's legal ability in a scathing published attack on Burger.[90] However, it may be premature to make a definitive assessment of Burger's task leadership.

It is not yet possible to determine the extent to which there was social leadership on the Burger Court or the social interactions of the justices. It was reported that after Powell and Rehnquist joined the Court there was increased tension and that one of the liberal justices referred to the Nixon appointees as "Nixon's guerrillas."[91] Justice Marshall bitterly criticized Court decisions in a public address.[92] On the other hand, Justice Powell noted in an interview in 1976 that there was an esprit de corps among the justices and he implied that there were good personal relationships among them.[93] There is no evidence to suggest that this did not hold true well into the 1980s. Despite some fundamental disagreements, there was perhaps at work some push for producing a more harmonious working relationship as evidenced by the 60 percent dissent rate for the Court during the 1983 and 1984 Terms, considerably lower than dissent rates earlier in the Burger Court. Even during Burger's last term, in which dissent rose to 69 percent, the rate was below the levels of the earlier years of his Court. But Justice Blackmun told lower court judges at a conference that the term was "the most difficult" in the 16 years he had served and that in Court conferences justices displayed "impatience" and "short temper."[94]

As already suggested there is little other than the statistical record reviewed earlier on which to base informed speculation about patterns of group interaction on the Rehnquist Court. It appears that after his first term as Chief Justice, Rehnquist has settled into a leadership role that has seen dissent rates generally lower than those for the Burger Court, despite the more marked ideological division of the Rehnquist Court. What this suggests is that Rehnquist may be trying to achieve con-

[87]Ibid., September 9, 1979, p. 41.

[88]Michigan v. Doran, 439 U.S. 282 (1978) at 292.

[89]As quoted in Steven Brill, "Is Burger a Weak Chief Justice?" *Boston Globe*, September 27, 1978, p. 19.

[90]Ibid. The thrust of much of Woodward and Armstrong's account in *The Brethren*, op. cit., can be considered an attack on the Chief Justice. The authors claim that they interviewed many former law clerks.

[91]*Newsweek*, February 28, 1972, p. 9.

[92]*New York Times*, May 28, 1979, p. 1.

[93]*New York Times*, August 11, 1976, p. 1.

[94]As quoted in *The National Journal*, August 11, 1986, p. S-3. In general, see the essays and analyses in Charles Lamb and Stephen Halpern, eds., *The Burger Court* (Champaign, Ill.: University of Illinois Press, 1990).

sensus on those cases and issues in which it may be possible to do so. The statistics also suggest that Rehnquist has somewhat moderated his voting behavior. Sharp words have nevertheless appeared in the context of written concurrences and dissents, as will be seen in some of the cases reprinted in this book, for example the attack by Scalia on O'Connor in **Webster** v. **Reproductive Health Services.** Yet there are also reports that Rehnquist himself is well-liked and that, in Justice Kennedy's view, "personal relations here are good."[95] More evidence is needed before we can form a firm judgment about Rehnquist's exercise of task and social leadership. However, with the departure of Justice Brennan from the Court and his replacement by a conservative, Rehnquist is in a stronger position to exercise task leadership.

[95]See the article by Associated Press Writer Richard Carelli, appearing nationally on February 18, 1990.

PART
TWO

THE WORKINGS OF GOVERNMENT AND OF THE ECONOMY

Chapter

6

Judicial Review and the Exercise of Judicial Power

JUDICIAL REVIEW

The power of judicial review is nowhere mentioned in the Constitution, although one can make, as John Marshall did in **Marbury** v. **Madison,** the plausible argument that the supremacy clause of the Constitution (''This Constitution, and the Laws of the United States which shall be made in Pursuance thereof; . . . shall be the supreme Law of the Land'') along with Article 3 (establishing the power of the Supreme Court to decide cases) justifies the exercise of judicial review. Scholars have energetically debated whether the intent of the framers of the Constitution was to give the Court such a power. Three schools of thought can be identified. One position is that the framers intended no such thing, that judicial review was virtually unheard of and had only a few inconclusive precedents, and that if the framers had intended the Supreme Court to have such an awesome power, surely they

would have spelled out their intent.[1] This argument sometimes has a variation along the lines that even if a very limited form of judicial review is implied in the Constitution (i.e., a *clear* conflict between an act of Congress and the letter of a constitutional provision must result in the Court's refusal to enforce the unconstitutional legislation), there is no justification for the broadly conceived power of judicial review exercised by the judiciary. That is, that there is no constitutional basis for the view that when there is *no* clear conflict between an act of Congress and an explicit provision of the Constitution the justices may substitute their views for the views of the democratically elected representatives of the people. Thus, although it may be reasonable to infer a narrow exercise of judicial review (in clear-cut violations of the Constitution)

[1]See Louis B. Boudin, *Government by Judiciary*, vol. 1 (New York: William Godwin, 1932).

158

from the nature of divided powers and our federal system of government as institutionalized in the Constitution, it is nothing but an abuse of power for the Court to strike down legislative acts that violate only a judicial doctrine interpreting a vaguely worded constitutional provision. According to this school of thought, such a broad exercise of judicial review means that we ultimately do not have a democratic form of government, but rather we have government by judiciary[2] or an "Imperial Judiciary" as some modern-day expositors of this viewpoint proclaim.

A second school of thought argues that the concept of judicial review was for the framers inherent in the concept of constitutionalism. According to this view, the framers expected the Court to exercise this power in the rare event that Congress would overstep its constitutional bounds. The reason that no explicit mention of judicial review is made in the Constitution is simply that there was a presumption of congressional competence and that members of Congress would be law-abiding. Furthermore, it is reasonable to assume that the framers believed that the division of the legislative power between the House and the Senate would ensure that no legislation in obvious violation of the Constitution would pass both houses of Congress and that, if by chance it did, surely the President would veto it. The bottom line to preserve the supremacy of the Constitution, of course, would be the Court. Certainly during the ratification controversy, Federalist Paper #78 made it clear that this was the intent of the framers. Furthermore, the first Congress, consisting of many of the framers of the Constitution, enacted Section 25 of the Judiciary Act of 1789 that gave the Court the power of judicial review over *state* court decisions that involved claims based on the federal Constitution, federal laws, or federal treaties.[3] The Constitution, it is argued, was explicit and detailed on matters that the framers felt strongly about but was purposely vague and general in areas in which they realized that experience and societal development must be taken into account to enable the Constitution to be adaptable to new situations and times.

A third school of thought[4] is that most framers did not do much thinking about judicial review of acts of Congress and that the concept was at best in its formative stages. To be sure, some of the framers had strong views on both sides of the question, with the supporters numbered by different sources as varying from 7 to 17 out of the 55 who attended the constitutional convention.[5] But most of the framers did not seriously consider the possibility that both the Congress and the President would knowingly violate the highest law of the land, and thus judicial review was simply not an issue for these framers. The tentative nature of the concept of judicial review over congressional enactments in these early years is demonstrated by the cautious statements of the justices in the first major case in which they ruled on the constitutionality of an act of Congress (**Hylton** v. **United States,** the carriage tax case, reprinted in chap. 9). But the proof of the pudding for those taking this position is the simple fact that during the first 75 years

---

[2]See Raoul Berger, *Government by Judiciary* (Cambridge, Mass.: Harvard University Press, 1977).

[3]See, in general, Charles Warren, *The Supreme Court in United States History,* vol. 1 (Boston: Little, Brown, 1926). Also see Raoul Berger, *Congress v. The Supreme Court* (Cambridge, Mass.: Harvard University Press, 1969).

[4]See, for example, Edward S. Corwin, *The Doctrine of Judicial Review* (Princeton, N.J.: Princeton University Press, 1914); Benjamin F. Wright, *The Growth of American Constitutional Law* (New York: Holt, Rinehart and Winston, 1942), chap. 2; Robert G. McCloskey, *The American Supreme Court* (Chicago: University of Chicago Press, 1960).

[5]Alfred H. Kelly and Winfred A. Harbison, *The American Constitution: Its Origins and Development,* 5th ed. (New York: Norton, 1976), p. 108; Wright, op. cit., p. 16.

of the Court's existence there were only two recorded instances of the Court actually striking down congressional enactments as unconstitutional, although there were more instances in which it was asked to do so but did not. Since then, there have been about 130 decisions that have invalidated congressional enactments, with the large majority of them occurring in the twentieth century. Parenthetically it should be noted that over 1000 provisions of state or municipal law have also been invalidated, again with most such cases decided in the twentieth century.

The issues surrounding judicial review, then, raise two different sets of distinctions. First, there is the distinction between judicial review over acts of Congress and judicial review over state enactments. Here the historical evidence as to the intent of the framers is mixed regarding Congress but reasonably clear regarding state enactments. Section 25 of the Judiciary Act of 1789 gave the Court the power of judicial review of state court decisions that concern state acts or actions in which a federal claim is raised. Second, there is the distinction between judicial review of a limited sort whereby only clear-cut violations of the Constitution are deemed unconstitutional by the Court, and a broadly construed power of judicial review whereby the Court feels free to place its own interpretation of the Constitution above that of the legislature. Here the historical evidence as to the intent of the framers suggests that insofar as the framers gave the matter thought, it was the narrow form of judicial review that they envisioned and not the wide-gauged power we know today. But, in a very real sense, the exercise of a broad concept of judicial review over the acts of Congress and the states as well has been accepted for well over a century and is functionally a part of the Constitution. In part, the framers and ratifiers of the Constitution and subsequent constitutional amendments, particularly the Fourteenth Amendment, invited the development of such a broad concept of judicial review because of the vague, open-ended phrases they inserted such as "due process of law," "privileges or immunities," and "equal protection of the laws."

It is the exercise of a broad concept of judicial review that has stimulated ongoing controversy among scholars and the justices themselves. Sometimes the debate is framed in terms of activism as opposed to restraint or a broad construction of the Constitution as opposed to a strict, narrow construction. This debate surfaced more recently in the mid-1980s in terms of a right-wing critique of the twentieth-century Supreme Court for interpreting the Fourteenth Amendment so as to make applicable certain guarantees of the Bill of Rights against their violation by the states. Attorney General Edwin Meese led the charge against the Supreme Court and argued that the Court exceeded the intent of the framers.[6] In separate public addresses, two Supreme Court justices, Brennan and Stevens, challenged the Attorney General's position and found his grasp of history and constitutional law to be inadequate.[7]

The cases reprinted in this chapter deal with matters of the Court's power to decide a specific dispute or class of disputes as well as some notable landmark examples of the exercise of judicial power. The first category of cases includes **Chisholm** v. **Georgia,** in which the Court's decision to decide a suit against a state led to the adoption of the Eleventh Amendment, which was designed to overturn *Chisholm; Marbury* v. *Madison,* the landmark justification of the power of judicial review

[6]See the account of the Attorney General's speech in the *New York Times,* November 16, 1985, p. 11. Meese's address is reprinted in Sheldon Goldman and Austin Sarat, eds., *American Court Systems,* 2d ed. (New York: Longman, 1989), pp. 584–587.

[7]See the *New York Times,* October 13, 1985, p. 1, for an account of Justice Brennan's speech, and the *New York Times,* October 26, 1985, p. 1, for an account of Justice Stevens' rebuttal of the Attorney General's position. Justice Brennan's rebuttal is reprinted in Goldman and Sarat, op. cit., pp. 588–592.

over acts of Congress; **Martin** v. **Hunter's Lessee,** the classic defense of the Supreme Court's power of judicial review over the decisions of state courts in which federal law is involved; **Barron** v. **Baltimore,** in which the Court declined jurisdiction based on its reading of the Constitution and its understanding of the intent of the framers; **Luther** v. **Borden,** in which the Court declined jurisdiction based on the determination that the issue raised a political question that was unsuitable for the judiciary to resolve because it was best resolved by the political branches of government. The political questions doctrine was considered by the Court in **Baker** v. **Carr,** in which the Court decided it *did* have the power to decide the issue.

The Civil War era case **Ex Parte McCardle,** is an example of the Court declining jurisdiction and, as Chapter 2 suggested, there were potent political reasons for so ruling aside from the legal justification offered in the decision. This case involved standing to sue, that is, whether McCardle had a legal basis for coming before the Supreme Court. Similarly in **Dred Scott** v. **Sandford,** the Court made a decision on Dred Scott's standing to sue and ruled against him. After so doing, the Court also invalidated an act of Congress, resulting in even greater tension between the free and slave states. In **Flast** v. **Cohen,** the Warren Court broadened the concept of standing to sue.

Of course, the cases reprinted in subsequent chapters offer important examples of the exercise of judicial power. Yet six cases are presented in this chapter not only because they are good examples of the exercise of judicial discretion, but also because each has been considered of particular political and legal significance. **Calder** v. **Bull's** historical context was discussed in Chapter 2. The Court's decision interpreting ex post facto as being applicable only to criminal law paved the way for the enactment of bankruptcy laws. **The Slaughterhouse Cases** interpreting the Four-

teenth Amendment showed the Court making choices and at least for the moment choosing not to be (in the words of Justice Miller) "a perpetual censor" on the actions of the states. This decision vitally affected the interpretation of key provisions of the Fourteenth Amendment, particularly the "privileges or immunities" guarantee. **Griswold** v. **Connecticut** was a landmark decision that established a constitutional right to sexual privacy. This decision provided a foundation for yet another privacy landmark, the **Roe** v. **Wade** decision legalizing abortion. *Roe* v. *Wade's* supporters consider the decision to have been a major victory for women and their right to autonomy over their bodies. *Roe's* opponents consider the decision to be a moral disaster on the order of *Dred Scott.* In **Bowers** v. **Hardwick** the Court refused to extend the right of privacy to consenting adult homosexuals. This is an example of the conservative majority on the Court bowing to its perception of the will of the majority of Americans during the Reagan era. The **INS** v. **Chadha** decision is a contemporary example of the Court invalidating an action of Congress and, by implication, similar legislative provisions in numerous statutes. By invalidating the legislative veto, the Court potentially reshaped the relationship between Congress and the executive branch of the national government.

Separation of Powers

Another facet of judicial review is that of the Supreme Court acting as an umpire in disputes that raise questions of the permissible limits of the exercise of power of one branch of the federal government and the point at which it invades the powers of another branch. Cases that raise such questions are raising the issue of separation of powers.

Although there have been relatively few separation of powers cases, they are usually of some importance. *INS* v. *Chadha* is one such separation of powers decision. Though not a dispute between Congress and the President, the decision nevertheless seeks to specify the powers of each branch in the process of enacting laws as specified in the Constitution and to judge the legislative veto in that context of separation of powers. So, too, with the decision in **Bowsher** v. **Synar** (chap. 7). The Court determined the permissible limits of Congress' legislative power and its ability to authorize how the President exercises executive power. In **Morrison** v. **Olson** (chap. 7), the Court examined whether the appointment of special prosecutors requires the advice and consent of the Senate, that is, whether the selection process specified in the legislation unconstitutionally infringed upon the powers of Congress. Other separation of powers cases involving the powers of the President and Congress are discussed in Chapters 7 and 8.

Three topics—political questions, standing to sue, and the right of sexual privacy—raised in several of the cases in this chapter deserve some elaboration.

Political Questions

Although there were some Marshall Court decisions that suggested the political questions doctrine, it was *Luther* v. *Borden,* decided by the Taney Court, that launched the doctrine. The essence of the doctrine is that there are some issues that are not suitable for adjudication because the need for action is great, the competence of the judiciary to solve the dispute is questionable, and the responsibility for resolution lies within the recognized duties of another branch of government. The Supreme Court has considered foreign affairs and national defense policy to be political questions. The terms of ratification of constitutional amendments have been considered to raise political questions (see *Coleman* v. *Miller,* 307 U.S. 433 [1939]). In *Colegrove* v. *Green,* 328 U.S. 549 (1946), the Court, by a plurality vote, refused to interfere with the electoral process

in the face of a challenge that the congressional districts of the state of Illinois were malapportioned as to population. Justice Frankfurter's opinion emphasized the political questions doctrine and was considered as precedent until *Baker* v. *Carr,* decided some 16 years later, reversed it. The issue of malapportioned legislative districts was no longer a political question but one that the judiciary could consider (it was now "justiciable"). Justice Brennan's opinion sought to clarify the political questions doctrine, but in practice a political question is whatever a Court majority happens to think is one. *Powell* v. *McCormack,* 395 U.S. 486 (1969), went so far as to *reject* the argument that Congress' determination to exclude a member of Congress for misconduct is within Congress' political domain and should be considered a political question.

Although the political questions doctrine appears to have fallen into disuse, it has never been repudiated and thus can potentially be revived when it suits the Court's purposes. It can be a useful doctrine if a majority wishes to avoid deciding an issue and wishes to fully articulate its reasons for denying itself judicial power. When the Court wishes to decide *not* to hear a particular dispute or line of disputes, it more typically finds that Congress has not granted it jurisdiction. An example of this occurred in *Heckler* v. *Chaney,* 470 U.S. 821 (1985), when the Court interpreted the Administrative Procedures Act to mean that an agency's decision not to take enforcement action is immune from judicial review unless Congress explicitly indicates to the contrary.

Standing to Sue

As discussed in Chapter 1, there are a variety of criteria that determine whether a case will be heard by the Supreme Court. Not only must the Court have subject-matter jurisdiction over the issue, not only must the issue be deemed justiciable (i.e., not moot, not one where there is no judicial remedy, and not a political question), but the disputants must have standing to sue. There must be a real case or controversy in which injury has occurred or is immediately threatened, the right claimed must be a personal one, and if governmental action is challenged the disputant must have exhausted all administrative remedies.

One of the leading early cases on standing was *Frothingham* v. *Mellon,* 262 U.S. 447 (1923), which concerned a suit by Mrs. Frothingham to prevent the expenditure of federal funds on a congressionally approved health program for mothers and infants that involved grants to states. Frothingham sued as a taxpayer claiming that expenditure of tax revenues for an allegedly unconstitutional purpose was a taking of her property without due process. In the *Frothingham* decision the Court ruled that a taxpayer has no standing to challenge federal government expenditures because there is no direct injury other than a minute financial one. Unless the litigant can show some direct injury as the result of the enforcement of a federal statute, standing will not be granted. Not until *Flast* v. *Cohen* did the Court permit taxpayer suits. In the *Flast* case, unlike *Frothingham,* the taxpayer alleged a violation of a specific constitutional limitation, the establishment of religion guarantee of the First Amendment.

The Burger Court subsequently narrowed the *Flast* ruling in *Valley Forge Christian College* v. *Americans United for Separation of Church and State,* 454 U.S. 464 (1982) by ruling that unlike *Flast* the government's spending power was not involved, only its power to dispose of tangible property. In this case amilitary hospital was given by the government to Valley Forge Christian College, a religious institution. The Court ruled that Americans United for Separation of Church and State had no standing to sue because the government's spending power was not involved and no direct injury was suffered. This

was so, even though, as in *Flast,* the establishment clause of the First Amendment was at issue.

Some other recent Court decisions concerning standing to sue include: *City of Los Angeles* v. *Lyons,* 461 U.S. 95 (1983), which involved a plaintiff who had challenged the Los Angeles police's practice of using choke holds in nonthreatening situations. The Court ruled that even though Lyons had been subjected to a choke hold, he had no real immediate injury or threat of injury to justify issuing an injunction against the use of the choke hold by the Los Angeles Police Department. Lyons, therefore, had no standing and the federal courts had no jurisdiction. The Court in *Diamond* v. *Charles,* 476 U.S. 54 (1986) ruled that a physician did not have standing to sue when he asked the Supreme Court to review an appeals court decision invalidating portions of an Illinois abortion statute. The state was not an appellant, and the Court held that there was no case or controversy because only the state had an interest recognizable by the courts in defending its criminal statutes. In *Karcher* v. *May,* 484 U.S. 72 (1987), to give yet another example, the Court ruled that the appellants, former New Jersey legislators, had no standing to sue before the Supreme Court because their successors in office had declined to pursue the appeal.

The Court, however, expanded the concept of injury that a disputant must suffer before having standing to sue. The Court recognized not only the traditional "injuries" such as bodily harm, loss of freedom, and economic damage but also aesthetic, conservational, and recreational injury. Interest groups have been permitted to sue to protect the rights of their members. Two of the leading cases are *Association of Data Processing Service Organizations, Inc.* v. *Camp,* 397 U.S. 150 (1970) and *Sierra Club* v. *Morton,* 405 U.S. 727 (1972).

There is some play in the Court's determination of standing to sue as well as other jurisdictional issues. Perhaps it is an overstatement and a cynical one at that to claim that when a majority of justices wish to decide a case they will find a way around jurisdictional including standing problems. Only a clear-cut, obvious jurisdictional defect, such as in *Barron* v. *Baltimore*, can stop a determined majority. But it should also be kept in mind that technical considerations of jurisdiction, justiciability, and standing can rescue a majority from having to deal with the merits of a case the majority really does not wish to decide.

The Exercise of Power: An Example with the Right to Sexual Privacy

As noted earlier, every case in this book reflects an exercise of power such as whether or not to decide the main issue and, if so, how to decide the dispute and justify its resolution. The choice points are many and in the realm of constitutional law there are opportunities for creativity. One of the best contemporary examples of such judicial creativity is in the realm of sexual privacy.

The words *privacy* and *sexual privacy* do not appear in the Constitution. Yet there are implied privacy rights in several of the first ten amendments to the Constitution, as Justice Douglas pointed out in *Griswold* v. *Connecticut*. It is the *Griswold* decision that stands as a major turning point in the development of sexual privacy law. With *Griswold*, the right of privacy became a constitutional guarantee.

The *Griswold* decision itself concerned the sexual privacy of married couples. In 1972 the Court in *Eisenstadt* v. *Baird*, 405 U.S. 438 (1972), extended *Griswold* to unmarried persons. The Court, in striking down a Massachusetts law prohibiting single but not married persons from obtaining birth control drugs or devices, noted, "If the right of privacy means anything, it is the right of the *individual*, married or single, to be free from unwanted gov-

ernmental intrusion into matters so fundamentally affecting a person as the decision whether to bear or beget a child."[8]

One year after *Eisenstadt*, the Court handed down its landmark abortion decision in *Roe* v. *Wade* and companion case *Doe* v. *Bolton*. Justice Blackmun, in his opinion of the Court, noted that the right of privacy was "broad enough to encompass a woman's decision whether or not to terminate her pregnancy" during the first two trimesters when the fetus cannot live outside the womb. In subsequent decisions the Court rejected laws giving husbands and parents of unmarried pregnant minors a veto over the abortion decision (*Planned Parenthood of Central Missouri* v. *Danforth*, 428 U.S. 52 [1976] and *Bellotti* v. *Baird*, 443 U.S. 662 [1979]), although unemancipated pregnant minors (that is, those living at home and financially dependent upon their parents) have less privacy protection (a parental notification statute was upheld in *H.L.* v. *Matheson*, 450 U.S. 398 [1981]). State restrictions on access to contraceptives even by minors were struck down (*Carey* v. *Population Services*, 431 U.S. 678 [1977]). *Roe* v. *Wade* was reaffirmed in a series of cases in 1983, the lead case being *Akron* v. *Akron Center for Reproductive Health*, 462 U.S. 416 (1983), and again in 1986 in **Thornburgh** v. **American College of Obstetricians** (chap. 19). **Webster** v. **Reproductive Health Services** (chap. 19) was the first decision to undermine *Roe*, but it still left standing the woman's right to abort a nonviable fetus.

The right of sexual privacy, however, has been limited to heterosexual relationships. In 1976, the Court affirmed without opinion a lower court decision upholding a state law making sodomy between consenting adults of the same sex a criminal act.[9]

In the 1986 decision of **Bowers** v. **Hardwick,** the Court gave a full dress hearing and deci-

---

[8]Eisenstadt v. Baird, 405 U.S. 438 at 453 (1972).

[9]Doe v. Commonwealth's Attorney for City of Richmond, 425 U.S. 901 (1976).

sion concerning a Georgia law making it a state crime to ''perform or submit to any sexual act involving the sex organs of one person and the mouth or anus of another. . . .'' The law, applicable to heterosexuals as well as homosexuals, specified that punishment upon conviction was imprisonment for ''not less than one nor more than 20 years.'' In this decision, the majority did not recognize a right of sexual privacy for homosexuals. In *Webster* v. *Doe,* 486 U.S. 592 (1988), however, the Court ruled that an employee of the Central Intelligence Agency who was fired because of his homosexuality had a constitutional claim that was judicially reviewable. But in *Carlucci* v. *Doe,* 109 S.Ct. 407 (1988), a unanimous Court ruled that the Secretary of Defense had the authority to fire an employee of the National Security Agency who admitted having homosexual relations with foreign nationals.

Conclusion

The cases in this chapter touch on whether the Court has the authority to hear the dispute brought before it and how power is exercised once the Court decides to hear a case. The justices have some flexibility in both the threshold decision to decide or not to decide as well as the judgment on the merits of the dispute. As suggested in Chapters 2 through 5, the Court's decisions must be seen in a broader political, historical, and behavioral context.

THE IMPACT OF THE COURT'S DECISIONS

Supreme Court decisions have at least three kinds of impact. First, there is the immediate impact of the decision on the parties to the case. Second, there is the short-run political or societal impact. Third, of course, is the long-run impact of a decision. As one moves from the first set of impacts to the third, the evidence becomes less clearly tied directly to the decision itself, although a plausible argument can still be made. Information about the first level of impact is often hard to come by and for many cases simply does not currently exist. At the second level, if there are no broader political events that seem to have been immediately precipitated by the decision, it may still be correct to view certain political events as being linked with the trend of decisions of which the particular case was a part. Evaluations of the third level of impact tend somewhat toward the speculative, but here, too, broader trends can be noted. Even if it is impossible to prove a cause-effect relationship between the decision and long-run trends, it is nevertheless possible to offer a plausible argument that suggests at the least some long-run influence of the Court's decision. Table 6.1 summarizes these three kinds of impact for most of the reprinted cases that follow, insofar as the information is available and/or it is plausible to make the claims made in the table.

Table 6.1   THE IMPACT OF SELECTED COURT DECISIONS REPRINTED IN THIS CHAPTER

Case	Year	Impact on Parties	Short-Run Impact	Long-Run Impact
Chisholm v. Georgia	1793	Court's ruling not enforced; Chisholm never recovered on behalf of estate.	Increase in suits against states; Eleventh Amendment adopted, 1798.	Case promoted judicial and national supremacy, but also provoked prolonged hostility and distrust by states' rights forces.
Calder v. Bull	1798	Mr. and Mrs. Bull ultimately successful.	Signal to advocates of national bankruptcy law that ex post facto would not apply to such a law.	Ex post facto unavailable to Marshall Court to protect rights of private property. Ex post facto has remained exclusively a criminal law concept.
Marbury v. Madison	1803	Marbury and associates never received their commissions.	Jefferson Administration sees Court back down from confrontation with executive branch.	Court establishes justification for judicial review over acts of Congress.
Martin v. Hunter's Lessee	1816	It is believed that the Virginia District Court of Shenandoah County enforced ruling favoring Martin.	Court answers challenge to its powers under Sec. 25 of Judiciary Act of 1789.	Judicial supremacy promoted and judicial review defended.
Barron v. Baltimore	1833	Barron out of business.	Court reveals limits to its protection of private property. By deferring to state police powers, Court wins approval of Jacksonians.	States are free to experiment with the civil liberties of Americans because they are not obliged to follow the federal Bill of Rights. Fourteenth Amendment was written in part to correct this situation.
Luther v. Borden	1849	No impact on parties, because issue resolved politically years earlier.	Court at height of its prestige; decision well received.	Political questions doctrine proves useful to Court on several later occasions.

Case	Year		
Ex Parte McCardle	1869	McCardle already free on bail, remained free after the decision and was never tried.	Little long-run impact. Court eventually recoups and expands its powers. Congress later restores habeas corpus jurisdiction.
Dred Scott v. Sandford	1857	Scott and family freed by owner, thus decision had no impact on Scott.	Fourteenth Amendment reverses Dred Scott ruling. But decision nevertheless has negative impact on racial attitudes and helps to entrench racism in U.S. during nineteenth century.
Slaughterhouse Cases	1873	Monopoly victorious but success short-lived. When Reconstruction ended, a new constitution was adopted in Louisiana resulting in the end of the monopoly and renewed competition among slaughterhouses in New Orleans. The monopoly protested, but the Court in an 1883 case upheld the end of the monopoly.	Negative impact on the development of civil liberties particularly by narrow reading of "privileges or immunities."
Baker v. Carr	1962	Tennessee's state legislative districts were reapportioned blunting the sharp inequities of the old system.	Changes in the makeup of state legislatures and the U.S. House of Representatives. Urban and suburban areas gained strength and clout at expense of rural areas.

Led to much litigation in federal courts and heavy involvement of judiciary in drawing legislative districts. Decision unpopular with many legislators and members of Congress. Newspapers generally favorable, public indifferent.

Court withdraws from confrontation with Congress; Reconstruction continues and blacks gain political power.

Further polarized the nation and contributed to the onset of the Civil War. Court's prestige plummets in North.

Discouraged the bringing of Fourteenth Amendment cases to the Court.

(continued)

Table 6.1 *(continued)*

Case	Year	Impact on Parties	Short-Run Impact	Long-Run Impact
Griswold v. Connecticut	1965	Griswold and Buxton did not have to pay $100 fines.	Connecticut repealed its birth control statute. Thirteen states eliminated or curtailed anti-birth control statutes. Numbers of women who gained access to birth control increased substantially.	Decision established concept of rights protected by Court because they fall within penumbras of specific guarantees of Bill of Rights. Landmark defense of right to privacy in sexual matters that, in part, aided the sexual revolution of the 1960s.
Flast v. Cohen	1968	No immediate personal impact on parties. Victory for civil liberties groups challenging governmental aid to religion.	Broadens access to judicial process; encourages constitutional litigation.	Court becomes involved in controversies it otherwise might have completely avoided.
Roe v. Wade	1973	Roe gave birth long before case was decided.	State reaction varies. States defying ruling brought to federal court. Women in major metropolitan areas gain access to abortion facilities. Estimates of number of abortions performed range up to one and a half million each year. Issues of government funding of abortions for poor women and parental consent for minors to have abortion come to Court.	Detrimental effect on the adoption agencies and prospective adoptive parents as supply of infants is drastically reduced. Decision source of intense controversy as pro- and antiabortion forces enter political arena. Decision provides precedent for rights of women and the right to privacy.
INS v. Chadha	1983	Minimal impact on Chadha because at time of decision Chadha had new grounds for citizenship claim (marriage to an American).	Brings into question hundreds of legislative acts that used legislative veto.	Much less of an impact than originally feared by critics of decision. Modified legislative veto continues to be used.

CHISHOLM v. GEORGIA,
2 DALLAS 419 (1793)

During the Revolutionary War, the Executive Council of Georgia authorized the purchase of supplies for the troops based there. Arrangements were made with a South Carolinian merchant that resulted in the sale of provisions to Georgia on credit. The state of Georgia did not pay its debt to the merchant despite repeated requests to do so. When the merchant died, the executor of his estate, Alexander Chisholm, resumed the quest for payment and after continued frustration went to the United States Circuit Court for the District of Georgia to press the claim of the estate. Georgia officials, however, argued that the federal court had no jurisdiction over the suit, for the state of Georgia is a sovereign state and the common law rule is that a sovereign may not be sued without its consent. The state officials argued that the provision in Article 3, Section 2 that "The judicial power shall extend to all cases . . . between a State and citizens of another State" was limited only to suits in which the state was a plaintiff or otherwise agreed to be sued. The circuit court agreed with Georgia and Chisholm went to the United States Supreme Court. The Court accepted the case, but Georgia refused to send anyone to argue Georgia's side. After a year, the justices handed down their opinions and the majority disagreed with the circuit court.

Majority Votes: 4
Dissenting Votes: 1

MR. JUSTICE WILSON:

This is a case of uncommon magnitude. One of the parties to it is a state; certainly respectable, claiming to be sovereign. The question to be determined, is, whether this state, so respectable, and whose claim soars so high, is amenable to the jurisdiction of the supreme court of the United States? This question, important in itself, will depend on others, more important still; and, may, perhaps, be ultimately resolved into one, no less radical than this—"do the people of the United States form a nation?"

To the Constitution of the United States the term sovereign, is totally unknown. There is but one place where it could have been used with propriety. But, even in that place it would not, perhaps, have comported with the delicacy of those, who ordained and established that constitution. They might have announced themselves "sovereign" people of the United States: But serenely conscious of the fact, they avoided the ostentatious declaration. . . .

Let a state be considered as subordinate to the people: But let everything else be subordinate to the state. . . . By a state I mean, a complete body of free persons united together for their common benefit, to enjoy peaceably what is their own, and to do justice to others. It is an artificial person. It has its affairs and its interests: It has its rules: It has its rights: And it has its obligations. It may acquire property distinct from that of its members. It may incur debts to be discharged out of the public stock, not out of the private fortunes of individuals. It may be bound by contracts; and for damages arising from the breach of those contracts. In all our contemplations, however, concerning this feigned and artificial person, we should never forget, that, in truth and nature, those who think and speak and act, are men. . . .

A state, like a merchant, makes a contract: A dishonest state, like a dishonest merchant, willfully refuses to discharge it: The latter is amenable to a court of justice: Upon general principles of right shall the former when summoned to answer the fair demands of its creditor, be permitted, proteus-like, to assume a new appearance, and to insult him and justice, by declaring, I am a sovereign state? Surely not. . . . Who, or what, is a sovereignty? What is his or its sovereignty? On this subject, the errors and the mazes are endless and inexplicable. To enumerate all, therefore, will not be expected: To take notice of some will be necessary to the full illustration of the present important cause: In one sense, the term sovereign, has for its correlative, subject. In this sense, the term can receive no application; for it has no object in the Constitution of the United States. Under that constitution there are citizens, but no subjects. "Citizens of the United States." "Citizens of another state." "Citizens of different states." "A state or citizen thereof." The term, subject, occurs, indeed, once in the instrument; but to mark the contrast strongly, the epithet "foreign" is prefixed. In this sense, I presume the state of Georgia has no claim upon her own citizens: In this sense, I am certain, she can have no claim upon the citizens of another state. . . .

As a judge of this court, I know, and can decide upon the knowledge, that the citizens of Georgia, when they acted upon the large scale of the union, as a part of the "People of the United States," did not surrender the supreme or sovereign power to that state; but, as to the purposes of the union, retained it to themselves. As to the purposes of the union, therefore, Georgia is not a sovereign state. . . .

In order, ultimately, to discover, whether the people of the United States intended to bind those states by the judicial power vested by the national constitution, a previous enquiry will naturally be: Did those people intend to bind those states by the legislative power vested by that constitution? The articles of confederation, it is well known, did not operate upon individual citizens; but operated only upon states. This defect was remedied by the national constitution, which, as all allow, has an operation on individual citizens. But if an opinion, which some seem to entertain, be just; the defect remedied, on one side, was balanced by a defect introduced on the other. For they seem to think, that the present constitution operates only on individual citizens, and not on states. This opinion, however, appears to be altogether unfounded. When certain laws of the states are declared to be "subject to the revision and control of the Congress," it cannot surely, be contended that the legislative power of the national government was meant to have no operation on the several states. The fact, uncontrovertibly established in one instance, proves the principle in all other instances, to which the facts will be found to apply. We may then infer, that the people of the United States intended to bind the several states, by the legislative power of the national government.

In order to make the discovery, at which we ultimately aim, a second previous enquiry will naturally be—Did the people of the United States intend to bind the several states by the executive power of the national government? The affirmative answer to the former question directs, unavoidably, an affirmative answer to this. Ever since the time of Bracton, his maxim, I believe, has been deemed a good one—"It would be superfluous to make laws, unless those laws, when made, were to be enforced." When the laws are plain and the application of them is uncontroverted, they are enforced immediately by the executive authority of government. When the application of them is doubtful or intricate, the interposition of the judicial authority becomes necessary. The same principle, therefore, which directed us from the first to the second step will direct us from the second to the third and last step of our deduction. Fair and conclusive deduction, then, evinces that the people of the United States did vest this court with jurisdiction over the state of Georgia. The same truth may be deducted from the declared objects, and the general texture of the Constitution of the United States. One of its declared objects is, to form a union more perfect than before that time, had been formed. Before that time, the union possessed legislative, but unenforced legislative power over the states. Nothing could be more natural than to intend that this legis-

lative power should be enforced by powers executive and judicial. Another declared object is "to establish justice." This points, in a particular manner, to the judicial authority. And when we review this object in conjunction with the declaration, "that no state shall pass a law impairing the obligation of contracts;" we shall probably think, that this object points, in a particular manner, to the jurisdiction of the court over the several states. What good purpose could this constitutional provision secure, if a state might pass a law impairing the obligation of its own contracts; and be amenable, for such a violation of right, to no controlling judiciary power? We have seen, that on the principles of general jurisprudence, a state, for the breach of a contract, may be liable for damages. A third declared object is—"to ensure domestic tranquillity." This tranquillity is most likely to be disturbed by controversies between states. These consequences will be most peaceably and effectually decided by the establishment and by the exercise of a superintending judicial authority. By such exercise and establishment, the law of nations; the rule between contending states; will be enforced among the several states, in the same manner as municipal law.

Whoever considers, in a combined and comprehensive view, the general texture of the constitution, will be satisfied, that the people of the United States intended to form themselves into a nation for national purposes. They instituted for such purposes, a national government, complete in all its parts, with powers legislative, executive, and judiciary; and in all those powers extending over the whole nation. Is it congruous, that, with regard to such purposes, any man, or body of men, any person, natural or artificial, should be permitted to claim successfully an entire exemption from the jurisdiction of the national government? Would not such claims, crowned with success, be repugnant to our very existence as a nation? When so many trains of deduction coming from different quarters, converge and unite, at last, in the same point; we may safely conclude, as the legitimate result of this Constitution, that the state of Georgia is amenable to the jurisdiction of this court.

But, in my opinion, this doctrine rests not upon the legitimate result of fair and conclusive deduction from the Constitution: It is confirmed beyond all doubt, by the direct and explicit declaration of the Constitution itself. "The judicial power of the United States shall extend, to controversies between two states." Two states are supposed to have a controversy between them: This controversy is supposed to be brought before those vested with the judicial power of the United States: Can

the most consummate degree of professional ingenuity devise a mode by which this "controversy between two states" can be brought before a court of
law; and yet neither of those states be a defendant?
"The judicial power of the United States shall extend to controversies, between a state and citizens
of another state." Could the strictest legal language; could even that language, which is peculiarly appropriated to an art, deemed, by a great
master, to be one of the most honorable, laudable,
and profitable things in our law; could this strict
and appropriated language, describe, with more
precise accuracy, the cause, now depending before
the tribunal? Causes and not parties to causes, are
weighed by justice in her equal scales: On the former solely, her attention is fixed: To the latter, she
is as she is painted, blind. . . .

MR. CHIEF JUSTICE JAY:. . . .

Let us . . . proceed to enquire whether Georgia
has not, by being a party to the national compact,
consented to be suable by individual citizens of another state. This enquiry naturally leads our attention. 1st. To the design of the constitution. 2d. To
the letter and express declaration in it. . . .

It is politic, wise, and good, that, not only the
controversies, in which a state is plaintiff, but also
those in which a state is defendant, should be settled, both cases, therefore, are within the reason of
the remedy; and ought to be so adjudged, unless
the obvious, plain, and literal sense of the words
forbid it. If we attend to the words, we find them
to be express, positive, free from ambiguity, and
without room for such implied expressions: "The
judicial power of the United States shall extend to
controversies between a state and citizens of another state." If the Constitution really meant to extend these powers only to those controversies in
which a state might be plaintiff, to the exclusion of
those in which citizens had demands against a state,
it is inconceivable that it should have attempted to
convey that meaning in words, not only so incompetent, but also repugnant to it; if it meant to exclude a certain class of these controversies, why
were they not expressly excepted, on the contrary,
not even an intimation of such intention appears in
any part of the Constitution. It cannot be pretended
that where citizens urge and insist upon demands
against a state, which the state refuses to admit and
comply with, that there is no controversy between
them. If it is a controversy between them, then it
clearly falls not only within the spirit, but the very
words of the Constitution. What is it to the cause
of justice, and how can it affect the definition of
the word controversy, whether the demands which
cause the dispute, are made by a state against citi-

zens of another state, or by the latter against the
former? When power is thus extended to a controversy, it necessarily, as to all judicial purposes,
is also extended to those, between whom it sub-
sists. . . .

For my own part, I am convinced that the sense
in which I understand the words "controversies between states and citizens of another state," is the
true sense. The extension of the judiciary power of
the United States to such controversies, appears to
me to be wise, because it is honest, and because it
is useful. It is honest, because it provides for doing
justice without respect of persons, and by securing
individual citizens as well as states, in their respective rights, performs the promise which every free
government makes to every free citizen, of equal
justice and protection. It is useful, because it is
honest, because it leaves not even the most obscure
and friendless citizen without means of obtaining
justice from a neighboring state; because it obviates
occasions of quarrels between states on account of
the claims of their respective citizens; because it
recognizes and strongly rests on this great moral
truth, that justice is the same whether due from one
man or a million, or from a million to one man; because it teaches and greatly appreciates the value of
our free republican national government, which
places all our citizens on an equal footing, and enables each and every one of them to obtain justice
without any danger of being overborne by the weight
and number of their opponents; and, because it
brings into action, and enforces this great and glorious principle, that the people are the sovereign of
this country, and consequently that fellow citizens
and joint sovereigns cannot be degraded by appearing with each other in their own courts to have their
controversies determined. The people have reason
to prize and rejoice in such valuable privileges; and
they ought not to forget, that nothing but the free
course of constitutional law and government can insure the continuance and enjoyment of them.

For the reasons before given, I am clearly of
opinion, that a state is suable by citizens of another
state. . . .

MR. JUSTICE BLAIR: [omitted]

MR. JUSTICE CUSHING: [omitted]

MR. JUSTICE IREDELL:. . . .

I have . . . established the following particulars.—1st. That the constitution so far as it respects
the judicial authority, can only be carried into effect
by acts of the legislature appointing courts, and prescribing their methods of proceeding. 2d. That Congress has provided no new law in regard to this
case, but expressly referred us to the old. 3d. That
there are no principles of the old law, to which we

must have recourse, that in any manner authorize the present suit, either by precedent or by analogy. The consequence of which, in my opinion, clearly is, that the suit in question cannot be maintained, nor, of course, the motion made upon it be complied with. . . .

So much . . . has been said on the constitution, that it may not be improper to intimate that my present opinion is strongly against any construction of it, which will admit, under any circumstances, a compulsive suit against a state for the recovery of money. I think every word in the constitution may have its full effect without involving this consequence, and that nothing but express words, or an insurmountable implication (neither of which I consider, can be found in this case) would authorize the deduction of so high a power. . . .

MARBURY v. MADISON,
1 CRANCH 137 (1803)

The national elections of 1800 resulted in the dramatic defeat of the incumbent Federalists. President John Adams lost to Thomas Jefferson, and the Congress that had been dominated by the Federalist Party was replaced by a Congress dominated by Jeffersonian supporters. In the remaining days of their control of government, the Federalists passed legislation creating new judgeships that the fuming Jeffersonians saw as a refuge for Federalist partisans. One act of Congress, the Organic Act for the District of Columbia, authorized the appointment of justice of the peace positions with the term of office to be for five years. President Adams nominated 42 persons for the justice of the peace positions, including William Marbury. The Senate quickly confirmed and the judicial commissions were signed and affixed with the official seal. All that remained was for the Secretary of State to deliver the commissions. In the last-minute rush, John Marshall, who was still acting as Secretary of State although he had already been confirmed as Chief Justice of the United States Supreme Court, failed to deliver many of the commissions. When Thomas Jefferson became President, he made a conciliatory gesture by allowing some of the commissions to be delivered. However, he ordered his Secretary of State, James Madison, not to deliver the remaining commissions, including that designated for William Marbury. Marbury and three others then went directly to the Supreme Court, asking the Court to assume original jurisdiction and to issue a writ of mandamus directed to Secretary of State Madison that ordered him to deliver the commissions. The writ was one of several legal tools for enforcing Court decisions given by Con- *gress in Section 13 of the Judiciary Act of 1789. In the 1790s the Court had exercised original jurisdiction and had assumed it had the power to issue writs of mandamus. This time, however, the Court was pitted against the executive branch and it was clear that the Jefferson Administration, with the support of the Jeffersonian Congress, was prepared to defy the Supreme Court.*

Votes: Unanimous

MR. CHIEF JUSTICE MARSHALL delivered the opinion of the Court:. . . .

In the order in which the court has viewed this subject, the following questions have been considered and decided: 1st. Has the applicant a right to the commission he demands? 2d. If he has a right, and that right has been violated, do the laws of his country afford him a remedy? 3d. If they do afford him a remedy, is it a mandamus *issuing from this court?*. . .

It is . . . decidedly the opinion of the court, that when a commission has been signed by the president, the appointment is made; and that the commission is complete, when the seal of the United States has been affixed to it by the secretary of state. . . .

Mr. Marbury, then, since his commission was signed by the president, and sealed by the secretary of state, was appointed; and as the law creating the office, gave the officer a right to hold for five years, independent of the executive, the appointment was not revocable, but vested in the officer legal rights, which are protected by the laws of his country. To withhold his commission, therefore, is an act deemed by the court not warranted by law, but violative of a vested legal right.

This brings us to the second inquiry; which is: If he has a right, and that right has been violated, do the laws of his country afford him a remedy?

The very essence of civil liberty certainly consists in the right of every individual to claim the protection of the laws, whenever he receives an injury. One of the first duties of government is to afford that protection. . . . The government of the United States has been emphatically termed a government of laws, and not of men. It will certainly cease to deserve this high appellation, if the laws furnish no remedy for the violation of a vested legal right. If this obloquy is to be cast on the jurisprudence of our country, it must arise from the peculiar character of the case. . . .

By the constitution of the United States, the president is invested with certain important political powers, in the exercise of which he is to use his own discretion, and is accountable only to his country in his political character, and to his own conscience. To aid him in the performance of these duties, he is authorized to appoint certain officers, who act by his authority, and in conformity with his orders. In such cases, their acts are his acts; and whatever opinion may be entertained of the manner in which executive discretion may be used, still there exists, and can exist, no power to control that discretion. The subjects are political: they respect the nation, not individual rights, and being entrusted to the executive, the decision of the executive is conclusive. The application of this remark will be perceived, by adverting to the act of congress for establishing the department of foreign affairs. This officer, as his duties were prescribed by that act, is to conform precisely to the will of the president: he is the mere organ by whom that will is communicated. The acts of such an officer, as an officer, can never be examinable by the courts. But when the legislature proceeds to impose on that officer other duties; when he is directed peremptorily to perform certain acts; when the rights of individuals are dependent on the performance of those acts; he is so far the officer of the law; is amendable to the laws for his conduct; and cannot, at his discretion, sport away the vested rights of others.

The conclusion from this reasoning is, that where the heads of departments are the political or confidential agents of the executive, merely to execute the will of the president, or rather to act in cases in which the executive possesses a constitutional or legal discretion, nothing can be more perfectly clear, than that their acts are only politically examinable. But where a specific duty is assigned by law, and individual rights depend upon the performance of that duty, it seems equally clear, that the individual who considers himself injured, has a right to resort to the laws of his country for a remedy. . . .

The question whether a right has vested or not, is in its nature, judicial, and must be tried by the judicial authority. If, for example, Mr. Marbury had taken the oaths of a magistrate, and proceeded to act as one; in consequence of which, a suit has been instituted against him, in which his defence had depended on his being a magistrate, the validity of his appointment must have been determined by judicial authority. So, if he conceives that, by virtue of his appointment, he has a legal right either to the commission which has been made out for him, or to a copy of that commission, it is equally a question examinable in a court, and the decision of the court upon it must depend on the opinion entertained of his appointment. . . .

It is, then, the opinion of the Court: 1st. That by signing the commission of Mr. Marbury, the President of the United States appointed him a justice of [the] peace for the county of Washington, in the district of Columbia; and that the seal of the United States, affixed thereto by the secretary of state, is conclusive testimony of the verity of the signature, and of the completion of the appointment; and that the appointment conferred on him a legal right to the office for the space of five years. 2d. That, having this legal title to the office, he has a consequent right to the commission; a refusal to deliver which is a plain violation of that right, for which the laws of his country afford him a remedy.

It remains to be inquired whether he is entitled to the remedy for which he applies? [The writ of mandamus] This depends on—1st. The nature of the writ applied for; and 2d. The power of this court. . . .

This writ, if awarded, would be directed to an officer of government, and its mandate to him would be, to use the words of Blackstone, "to do a particular thing therein specified, which appertains to his office and duty, and which the court has previously determined, or at least supposes, to be consonant to right and justice." . . .

This . . . is a plain case for a *mandamus,* either to deliver the commission, or a copy of it from the record; and it only remains to be inquired, whether it can issue from this court?

The act to establish the judicial courts of the United States authorizes the supreme court, "to issue writs of *mandamus,* in cases warranted by the principles and usages of law, to any courts appointed or persons holding office, under the authority of the United States." The secretary of state, being a person holding an office under the authority of the United States, is precisely within the letter of this description; and if this court is not authorized to issue a writ of *mandamus* to such an officer, it must be because the law is unconstitutional, and therefore, absolutely incapable of conferring the authority, and assigning the duties which its words purport to confer and assign.

The constitution vests the whole judicial power of the United States in one supreme court, and such inferior courts as congress shall, from time to time, ordain and establish. This power is expressly extended to all cases arising under the laws of the United States; and consequently, in some form, may be exercised over the present case; because the right claimed is given by a law of the United States.

In the distribution of this power, it is declared, that "the supreme court shall have original jurisdiction, in all cases affecting ambassadors, other public ministers and consuls, and those in which a state be a party. In all other cases, the supreme court shall have appellate jurisdiction." It has been insisted, at the bar, that as the original grant of jurisdiction to the supreme and inferior courts, is general, and the clause, assigning original jurisdiction to the supreme court, contains no negative or restrictive words, the power remains to the legislature, to assign original jurisdiction to that court, in other cases than those specified in the article which has been recited; provided those cases belong to the judicial power of the United States.

If it had been intended to leave it in the discretion of the legislature, to apportion the judicial power between the supreme and inferior courts, according to the will of that body, it would certainly have been useless to have proceeded further than to have defined the judicial power, and the tribunals in which it should be vested. The subsequent part of the section is mere surplusage—is entirely without meaning, if such is to be the construction. If congress remains at liberty to give this court appellate jurisdiction, where the constitution has declared their jurisdiction shall be original; and original jurisdiction where the constitution has declared it shall be appellate; the distribution of jurisdiction, made in the constitution, is form without substance. Affirmative words are often, in their operation, negative of other objects than those affirmed; and in this case, a negative or exclusive sense must be given to them, or they have no operation at all.

It cannot be presumed, that any clause in the constitution is intended to be without effect; and therefore, such a construction is inadmissible, unless the words require it. If the solicitude of the convention, respecting our peace with foreign powers, induced a provision that the supreme court should take original jurisdiction in cases which might be supposed to affect them; yet the clause would have proceeded no further than to provide for such cases, if no further restriction on the powers of congress had been intended. That they should have appellate jurisdiction in all other cases, with such exceptions as congress might make, is no restriction; unless the words be deemed exclusive of original jurisdiction.

When an instrument organizing, fundamentally, a judicial system, divides it into one supreme, and so many inferior courts as the legislature may ordain and establish; then enumerates its powers, and proceeds so far to distribute them, as to define the jurisdiction of the supreme court, by declaring the cases in which it shall take original jurisdiction, and that in others it shall take appellate jurisdiction, the

plain import of the words seems to be, that in one class of cases, its jurisdiction is original, and not appellate; in the other, it is appellate, and not original. If any other construction would render the clause inoperative, that is an additional reason for rejecting such other construction, and for adhering to their obvious meaning. To enable this court, then, to issue a *mandamus,* it must be shown to be an exercise of appellate jurisdiction, or to be necessary to enable them to exercise appellate jurisdiction.

It has been stated at the bar, that the appellate jurisdiction may be exercised in a variety of forms, and that if it be the will of the legislature that a *mandamus* should be used for that purpose, that will must be obeyed. This is true, yet the jurisdiction must be appellate, nor original. It is the essential criterion of appellate jurisdiction, that it revises and corrects the proceedings in a cause already instituted, and does not create that cause. Although, therefore, a *mandamus* may be directed to courts, yet to issue such a writ to an officer, for the delivery of a paper, is, in effect, the same as to sustain an original action for that paper, and therefore, seems not to belong to appellate, but to original jurisdiction. Neither is it necessary in such a case as this, to enable the court to exercise its appellate jurisdiction. The authority, therefore, given to the supreme court by the act establishing the judicial courts of the United States, to issue writs of *mandamus* to public officers, appears not to be warranted by the constitution; and it becomes necessary to inquire, whether a jurisdiction so conferred can be exercised.

The question, whether an act, repugnant to the constitution, can become the law of the land, is a question deeply interesting to the United States; but, happily, not of an intricacy proportioned to its interest. It seems only necessary to recognize certain principles, supposed to have been long and well established, to decide it. That the people have an original right to establish, for their future government, such principles as, in their opinion, shall most conduce to their own happiness, is the basis on which the whole American fabric has been erected. The exercise of this original right is a very great exertion; nor can it, nor ought it, to be frequently repeated. The principles, therefore, so established, are deemed fundamental; and as the authority from which they proceed is supreme, and can seldom act, they are designed to be permanent.

This original and supreme will organizes the government, and assigns to different departments their respective powers. It may either stop here, or establish certain limits not to be transcended by those departments. The government of the United States is of the latter description. The powers of the legislature are defined and limited; and that those limits may not be mistaken or forgotten, the constitution is written. To what purpose are powers limited, and to what purpose is that limitation committed to writing, if these limits may, at any time, be passed by those intended to be restrained? The distinction between a government with limited and unlimited powers is abolished, if those limits do not confine the persons on whom they are imposed, and if acts prohibited and acts allowed, are of equal obligation. It is a proposition too plain to be contested, that the constitution controls any legislative act repugnant to it; or that the legislature may alter the constitution by an ordinary act.

Between these alternatives, there is no middle ground. The constitution is either a superior paramount law, unchangeable by ordinary means, or it is on a level with ordinary legislative acts, and, like other acts, is alterable when the legislature shall please to alter it. If the former part of the alternative be true, then a legislative act, contrary to the constitution, is not law; if the latter part be true, then written constitutions are absurd attempts, on the part of the people, to limit a power, in its own nature, illimitable.

Certainly, all those who have framed written constitutions contemplate them as forming the fundamental and paramount law of the nation, and consequently, the theory of every such government must be, that an act of the legislature, repugnant to the constitution, is void. This theory is essentially attached to a written constitution, and is, consequently, to be considered, by this court, as one of the fundamental principles of our society. It is not, therefore, to be lost sight of, in the further consideration of this subject.

If an act of the legislature, repugnant to the constitution, is void, does it, notwithstanding its invalidity, bind the courts, and oblige them to give it effect? Or, in other words, though it be not law, does it constitute a rule as operative as if it was a law? This would be to overthrow, in fact, what was established in theory; and would seem, at first view, an absurdity too gross to be insisted on. It shall, however, receive a more attentive consideration.

It is, emphatically, the province and duty of the judicial department, to say what the law is. Those who apply the rule to particular cases, must of necessity expound and interpret that rule. If two laws conflict with each other, the courts must decide on the operation of each. So, if a law be in opposition to the constitution; if both the law and the constitution apply to a particular case, so that the court

must either decide the case, conformable to the law, disregarding the constitution; or conformable to the constitution, disregarding the law; the court must determine which of these conflicting rules governs the case: this is of the very essence of judicial duty. If then, the courts are to regard the constitution, and the constitution is superior to any ordinary act of the legislature, the constitution, and not such ordinary act, must govern the case to which they both apply.

Those, then, who controvert the principle, that the constitution is to be considered, in court, as a paramount law, are reduced to the necessity of maintaining that courts must close their eyes on the constitution, and see only the law. This doctrine would subvert the very foundation of all written constitutions. It would declare that an act which, according to the principles and theory of our government, is entirely void, is yet, in practice, completely obligatory. It would declare, that if the legislature shall do what is expressly forbidden, such act, notwithstanding the express prohibition, is in reality effectual. It would be giving to the legislature a practical and real omnipotence, with the same breath which professes to restrict their powers within narrow limits. It is prescribing limits, and declaring that those limits may be passed at pleasure. That it thus reduces to nothing, what we have deemed the greatest improvement on political institutions, a written constitution, would, of itself, be sufficient, in America, where written constitutions have been viewed with so much reverence, for rejecting the construction. But the peculiar expressions of the constitution of the United States furnish additional arguments in favor of its rejection. The judicial power of the United States is extended to all cases arising under the constitution. Could it be the intention of those who gave this power, to say, that in using it, the constitution should not be looked into? That a case arising under the constitution should be decided, without examining the instrument under which it arises? This is too extravagant to be maintained. In some cases, then, the constitution must be looked into by the judges. And if they can open it at all, what part of it are they forbidden to read or to obey?

There are many other parts of the constitution which serve to illustrate this subject. It is declared, that "no tax or duty shall be laid on articles exported from any state." Suppose, a duty on the export of cotton, of tobacco or of flour; and a suit instituted to recover it. Ought judgment to be rendered in such a case? Ought the judges to close their eyes on the constitution, and only see the law?

The constitution declares "that no bill of attainder or *ex post facto* law shall be passed." If, however, such a bill should be passed, and a person should be prosecuted under it; must the court condemn to death those victims whom the constitution endeavors to preserve?

"No person," says the constitution, "shall be convicted of treason, unless on the testimony of two witnesses to the same *overt* act, or on confession in open court." Here, the language of the constitution is addressed especially to the courts. It prescribes, directly for them, a rule of evidence not to be departed from. If the legislature should change that rule, and declare one witness, or a confession out of court, sufficient for conviction, must the constitutional principle yield to the legislative act?

From these, and many other selections which might be made, it is apparent, that the framers of the constitution contemplated that instrument as a rule for the government of courts, as well as of the legislature. Why otherwise does it direct the judges to take an oath to support it? This oath certainly applies in an especial manner, to their conduct in their official character. How immoral to impose it on them, if they were to be used as the instruments, and the knowing instruments, for violating what they swear to support!

The oath of office, too, imposed by the legislature, is completely demonstrative of the legislative opinion on this subject. It is in these words: "I do solemnly swear, that I will administer justice, without respect to persons, and do equal right to the poor and to the rich; and that I will faithfully and impartially discharge all the duties incumbent on me as——, according to the best of my abilities and understanding, agreeably to the constitution and laws of the United States." Why does a judge swear to discharge his duties agreeably to the constitution of the United States, if that constitution forms no rule for his government? if it is closed upon him, and cannot be inspected by him? If such be the real state of things, this is worse than solemn mockery. To prescribe, or to take this oath, becomes equally a crime.

It is also not entirely unworthy of observation, that in declaring what shall be the supreme law of the land, the constitution itself is first mentioned; and not the laws of the United States, generally, but those only which shall be made in pursuance of the constitution, have that rank.

Thus, the particular phraseology of the constitution of the United States confirms and strengthens the principle, supposed to be essential to all written constitutions, that a law repugnant to the constitution is void; and that courts, as well as other departments, are bound by that instrument.

The rule must be discharged.

MARTIN v. HUNTER'S LESSEE, 1 WHEATON 304 (1816)

Lord Fairfax was the owner of some 300,000 acres of prime timber and tobacco land in the northern part of Virginia. That land was confiscated by Virginia during the Revolution and in 1789 a portion was sold to David Hunter. Meanwhile Lord Fairfax's heirs challenged the actions of the state. The land was eventually willed to an American citizen of Virginia, Philip Martin, who went to court to establish his right to the ownership of the land. The Virginia courts ruled against Martin and he appealed to the United States Supreme Court. In Fairfax's Devisee *v.* Hunter's Lessee, *7 Cranch 603 (1813), the Supreme Court ruled in favor of Philip Martin, finding that the actions of the state were in violation of the federal treaty of 1794. The Court sent its ruling back to the Virginia Court of Appeals (the highest court in the state). The Virginia Court, headed by Spencer Roane, a staunch Jeffersonian and political enemy of John Marshall, refused to enforce the Supreme Court's decision and instead issued an opinion asserting that the United States Supreme Court did not have jurisdiction to hear Martin's appeal because Section 25 of the Judiciary Act of 1789 did not conform to Article 3 of the Constitution and was therefore unconstitutional. The Supreme Court, it was argued, is not authorized by Article 3 to hear appeals from the state courts. The Virginia Court of Appeals insisted that when determining the validity of Virginia law, its interpretation of the federal Constitution, laws, and treaties could not be reviewed by the United States Supreme Court because the states were co-equal sovereignties with the federal government. The Supreme Court answered this challenge, although John Marshall himself did not participate because of his previous involvement and the involvement of his brother in the litigation.*

Votes: Unanimous

MR. JUSTICE STORY delivered the opinion of the Court:. . . .

Before proceeding to the principal question, it may not be unfit to dispose of some preliminary considerations which have grown out of the arguments at the bar.

The constitution of the United States was ordained and established, not by the states in their sovereign capacities, but emphatically, as the preamble of the constitution declares, by "the people of the United States." There can be no doubt that it was competent to the people to invest the general government with all the powers which they might deem proper and necessary; to extend or restrain these powers according to their own good pleasure, and to give them a paramount and supreme authority. As little doubt can there be that the people had a right to prohibit to the states the exercise of any powers which were, in their judgment, incompatible with the objects of the general compact; to make the powers of the state governments, in given cases, subordinate to those of the nation, or to reserve to themselves those sovereign authorities which they might not choose to delegate to either. The constitution was not, therefore, necessarily carved out of existing state sovereignties, nor a surrender of powers already existing in state institutions, for the powers of the states depend upon their own constitutions; and the people of every state had the right to modify and restrain them, according to their own views of policy or principle. On the other hand, it is perfectly clear that the sovereign powers vested in the state governments, by their respective constitutions, remained unaltered and unimpaired, except so far as they were granted to the government of the United States. . . .

The third article of the constitution is that which must principally attract our attention. . . . It is the voice of the whole American people solemnly declared, in establishing one great department of that government which was, in many respects, national, and in all, supreme. It is a part of the very same instrument which was to act not merely upon individuals, but upon states; and to deprive them altogether of the exercise of some powers of sovereignty, and to restrain and regulate them in the exercise of others. . . .

Let this article be carefully weighed and considered. The language of the article throughout is manifestly designed to be mandatory upon the legislature. . . . The object of the constitution was to establish three great departments of government; the legislative, the executive and the judicial department. The first was to pass laws, the second to approve and execute them, and the third to expound and enforce them. Without the latter it would be impossible to carry into effect some of the express provisions of the constitution. How, otherwise, could crimes against the United States be tried and punished? How could causes between two states be heard and determined? The judicial power must, therefore, be vested in some court, by Congress; and to suppose that it was not an obligation binding on them, but might, at their pleasure, be omitted or declined, is to suppose that, under the sanction of the constitution they might defeat the constitution itself; a construction which would lead to such a result cannot be sound. . . .

If, then, it is the duty of Congress to vest the judicial power of the United States, it is a duty to vest the whole judicial power. . . .

It . . . being . . . established that the language . . . is imperative, the next question is as to the cases to which it shall apply. The answer is found in the constitution itself. The judicial power shall extend to all the cases enumerated in the constitution. As the mode is not limited, it may extend to all such cases, in any form in which judicial power may be exercised. It may, therefore, extend to them in the shape of original or appellate jurisdiction, or both; for there is nothing in the nature of the cases which binds to the exercise of the one in preference to the other. . . .

As . . . by the terms of the constitution, the appellate jurisdiction is not limited as to the Supreme Court, and as to this court it may be exercised in all other cases than those of which it has original cognizance, [then] what is there to restrain its exercise over state tribunals in the enumerated cases? The appellate power is not limited by the terms of the third article to any particular courts. The words are, "the judicial power (which includes appellate power) shall extend to all cases," etc., and "in all other cases before mentioned the Supreme Court shall have appellate jurisdiction." It is the case, then, and not the court, that gives the jurisdiction. If the judicial power extends to the case, it will be in vain to search in the letter of the constitution for any qualifications as to the tribunal where it depends. It is incumbent, then, upon those who assert such a qualification to show its existence by necessary implication. If the text be clear and distinct, no restriction upon its plain and obvious import ought to be admitted, unless the inference be irresistible. . . .

It is plain that the framers of the constitution did contemplate that cases within the judicial cognizance of the United States not only might but would arise in the state courts, in the exercise of their ordinary jurisdiction. With this view the sixth article declares, that "this constitution, and the laws of the United States which shall be made in pursuance thereof, and all treaties made, or which shall be made, under the authority of the United States, shall be the supreme law of the land, and the judges in every state shall be bound thereby, anything in the constitution or laws of any state to the contrary notwithstanding.'' It is obvious that this obligation is imperative upon the state judges in their official, and not merely in their private, capacities. From the very nature of their judicial duties they would be called upon to pronounce the law applicable to the case in judgment. They were not to decide merely according to the laws or constitution of the state, but according to the constitution, laws and treaties of the United States—"the supreme law of the land." . . .

It must be conceded that the constitution not only contemplated, but meant to provide for cases within the scope of the judicial power of the United States, which might yet defend before state tribunals. It was forseen that in the exercise of their ordinary jurisdiction, state courts would incidentally take cognizance of cases arising under the constitution, the laws and treaties of the United States. Yet to all these cases the judicial power, by the very terms of the constitution, is to extend. It cannot extend by original jurisdiction if that was already rightfully and exclusively attached in the state courts, which (as has been already shown) may occur, it must, therefore, extend by appellate jurisdiction, or not at all. It would seem to follow that the appellate power of the United States must, in such cases, extend to state tribunals; and if in such cases, there is no reason why it should not equally attach upon all others within the purview of the constitution.

It has been argued that such an appellate jurisdiction over state courts is inconsistent with the genius of our governments, and the spirit of the constitution. That the latter was never designed to act upon state sovereignties, but only upon the people, and that if the power exists, it will materially impair the sovereignty of the states, and the independence of their courts. We cannot yield to the force of this reasoning; it assumes principles which we cannot admit, and draws conclusions to which we do not yield our assent.

It is a mistake that the constitution was not designed to operate upon states, in their corporate capacities. It is crowded with provisions which restrain or annul the sovereignty of the states in some of the highest branches of their prerogatives. The tenth section of the first article contains a long list of disabilities and prohibitions imposed upon the states. Surely, when such essential portions of state sovereignty are taken away, or prohibited to be exercised, it cannot be correctly asserted that the constitution does not act upon the states. . . .

It is . . . argued that no great public mischief can result from a constitution which shall limit the appellate power of the United States to cases in their own courts . . . because state judges are bound by an oath to support the constitution of the United States, and must be presumed to be men of learning and integrity. . . . As to this reason—admitting that the judges of the state courts are, and always will be, of as much learning, integrity, and wisdom, as those of the courts of the United States (which we very cheerfully admit), it does not aid the argument. It is manifest that the constitution has proceeded upon a theory of its own, and given or withheld powers according to the judgment of the American people, by whom it was adopted. We can only construe its powers, and cannot inquire into the policy or principles which induced the grant of them. The constitution has presumed (whether rightly or wrongly we do not inquire) that state attachments, state prejudices, state jealousies, and state interests, might sometimes obstruct, or control, or be supposed to obstruct or control, the regular administration of justice. Hence, in controversies between states; between citizens of different states; between citizens claiming grants under different states; between a state and its citizens, or foreigners, and between citizens and foreigners, it enables the parties, under the authority of Congress, to have the controversies heard, tried, and determined before the national tribunals. No other reason than that which has been stated can be assigned, why some, at least, of those cases should not have been left to the cognizance of the state courts. In respect to the other enumerated cases— the cases arising under the constitution, laws, and treaties of the United States, cases affecting ambassadors and other public ministers, and cases of admiralty and maritime jurisdiction—reasons of a higher and more extensive nature, touching the safety, peace, and sovereignty of the nation, might well justify a grant of exclusive jurisdiction.

This is not all. A motive of another kind, perfectly compatible with the most sincere respect for state tribunals, might induce the grant of appellate power over their decisions. That motive is the importance, and even necessity of uniformity of decisions throughout the whole United States, upon all subjects within the purview of the constitution. Judges of equal learning and integrity, in different states, might differently interpret a statute, or a treaty of the United States, or even the constitution itself. If there were no revising authority to control these jarring and discordant judgments, and harmonize them into uniformity, the laws, the treaties, and the constitution of the United States would be different in different states, and might, perhaps, never have precisely the same construction, obligation, or efficacy, in any two states. The public mischiefs that would attend such a state of things would be truly deplorable; and it cannot be believed that they could have escaped the enlightened convention which formed the constitution. What, indeed, might then have been only prophecy, has now become fact; and the appellate jurisdiction must continue to be the only adequate remedy for such evils. . . .

On the whole, the court is of [the] opinion that the appellate power of the United States does extend to cases pending in the state courts; and that the 25th section of the judiciary act, which authorizes the exercise of this jurisdiction in the specified cases, by a writ of error, is supported by the letter and spirit of the constitution. We find no clause in that instrument which limits this power; and we dare not interpose a limitation where the people have not been disposed to create one. . . .

The next question which has been argued is, whether the case at bar be within the purview of the 25th section of the judiciary act, so that this court may rightfully sustain the present writ of error. . . .

That the present writ of error is founded upon a judgment of the court below, which drew in question and denied the validity of a statute of the United States, is incontrovertible, for it is apparent upon the face of the record. . . .

It is the opinion of the whole court that the judgment of the Court of Appeals of Virginia, rendered on the mandate in this cause, be reversed, and the judgment of the District Court, held at Winchester, be, and the same is hereby affirmed.

MR. JUSTICE JOHNSON [concurring]: [omitted]

BARRON v. BALTIMORE, 7 PETERS 243 (1833)

John Barron owned a wharf in the city of Baltimore. The city undertook civic improvements, including the paving of some of its streets. By so doing the city diverted the flow of some streams, and deposits of sand and gravel made Barron's wharf unfit for shipping. Barron claimed his property was taken from him without just compensation. He pointed to the just compensation guarantee of the Fifth Amendment, claiming that it applied to the states as well as to the federal government. The Supreme Court was faced with having to determine whether the Fifth Amendment and, by implication, other amendments in the Bill of Rights were appli-

cable to the states. This was another way of asking whether the Court had jurisdiction in the case (i.e., whether a federal right was involved). The decision by the Court was to have serious implications for civil liberties law.

Votes: Unanimous

MR. JUSTICE MARSHALL delivered the opinion of the Court:. . . .

The constitution was ordained and established by the people of the United States for themselves, for their own government and not for the government of the individual States. Each State established a constitution for itself, and, in that constitution, provided such limitations and restrictions on the powers of its particular government as its judgment dictated. The people of the United States framed such a government for the United States as they supposed best adapted to their situation, and best calculated to promote their interests. The powers they conferred on this government were to be exercised by itself; and the limitations on power, if expressed in general terms, are naturally, and, we think, necessarily applicable to the government created by the instrument. They are limitations of power granted in the instrument itself; not of distinct governments, framed by different persons and for different purposes.

If these propositions be correct, the 5th amendment must be understood as restraining the power of the general government, not as applicable to the States. . . .

The counsel for the plaintiff in error insists that the constitution was intended to secure the people of the several States against the undue exercise of power by their respective state governments; as well as against that which might be attempted by their general government. In support of this argument he relies on the inhibitions contained in the 10th section of the 1st article.

We think that section affords a strong if not a conclusive argument in support of the opinion already indicated by the court.

The preceding section contains restrictions which are obviously intended for the exclusive purpose of restraining the exercise of power, by the departments of the general government. Some of them use language applicable only to congress; others are expressed in general terms. The 3d clause, for example, declares that "no bill of attainder or *ex post facto* law shall be passed." No language can be more general; yet the demonstration is complete that it applies solely to the government of the United States. In addition to the general arguments furnished by the instrument itself, some of which have been already suggested, the succeeding section, the avowed purpose of which is to restrain state legislation, contains in terms the very prohibition. It declares that "no State shall pass any bill of attainder or *ex post facto* law." This provision, then, of the 9th section, however comprehensive its language, contains no restriction on state legislation.

The 9th section having enumerated, in the nature of a bill of rights, the limitations intended to be imposed on the powers of the general government, the 10th proceeds to enumerate those which were to operate on the state legislatures. These restrictions are brought together in the same section, and are by express words applied to the States. "No State shall enter into any treaty," &c. Perceiving that in a constitution framed by the people of the United States for the government of all, no limitation of the action of government on the people would apply to the state government, unless expressed in terms; the restrictions contained in the 10th section are in direct words so applied to the States. . . .

If the original constitution, in the 9th and 10th sections of the 1st article, draws this plain and marked line of discrimination between the limitations it imposes on the powers of the general government, and on those of the States; if in every inhibition intended to act on state power, words are employed which directly express that intent; some strong reason must be assigned for departing from this safe and judicious course in framing the amendments, before that departure can be assumed.

We search in vain for that reason.

Had the people of the several States, or any of them, required changes in their constitutions; had they required additional safeguards to liberty from the apprehended encroachments of their particular governments; the remedy was in their own hands, and would have been applied by themselves. A convention would have been assembled by the discontented State, and the required improvements would have been made by itself. The unwieldy and cumbrous machinery of procuring a recommendation from two thirds of congress, and the assent of three fourths of their sister States, could never have occurred to any human being as a mode of doing that which might be affected by the State itself. Had the framers of these amendments intended them to be limitations on the powers of the state governments, they would have imitated the framers of the original constitution, and have expressed that intention. Had congress engaged in the extraordinary occupation of improving the constitutions of the several States by affording the people additional protection from the exercise of power by their own governments in matters which concerned themselves alone, they would have declared this purpose in plain and intelligible language.

But it is universally understood, it is a part of the history of the day, that the great revolution which established the constitution of the United States, was not effected without immense opposition. Serious fears were extensively entertained that those powers which the patriot statesmen, who then watched over the interests of our country, deemed essential to union, and to the attainment of those invaluable objects for which union was sought, might be exercised in a manner dangerous to liberty. In almost every convention by which the constitution was adopted, amendments to guard against the abuse of power were recommended. These amendments demanded security against the apprehended encroachments of the general government, not against those of the local governments.

In compliance with a sentiment thus generally expressed to quiet fears thus extensively entertained, amendments were proposed by the required majority in congress, and adopted by the States. These amendments contain no expression indicating an intention to apply them to the state governments. This court cannot so apply them.

We are of opinion that the provision in the 5th amendment to the constitution, declaring that private property shall not be taken for public use without just compensation, is intended solely as a limitation on the exercise of power by the government of the United States, and is not applicable to the legislation of the States. We are therefore of opinion, that there is no repugnancy between the several acts of the general assembly of Maryland, given in evidence by the defendants at the trial of this cause, in the court of that State, and the constitution of the United States. This court, therefore, has no jurisdiction of the cause; and it is dismissed.

LUTHER v. BORDEN,
7 HOWARD 1 (1849)

The events culminating in this case before the Supreme Court concerned one of the most dramatic episodes in American history—a bona fide revolution. In 1841 Rhode Island had an archaic form of government, one that had survived almost intact from its original royal charter of 1663 through the American Revolution and even the Age of Jackson. Suffrage was severely restricted to those with substantial amounts of property. Widespread resentment of this singularly undemocratic form of government led to a people's convention that had no legal standing but nevertheless began meeting in October 1841 and soon drafted a democratic constitution. A referendum was held in late December, and the new constitution was approved. Elections were held on April 18, 1842, for state officers, and the leader of the rebellion, Thomas Dorr, was "elected" Governor. All these activities were undertaken without any official recognition by the authorities who were operating under the old charter. On May 17, Dorr and his followers unsuccessfully attempted to raid the state arsenal in Providence, after which Dorr fled the state. When rumors spread that Dorr was ready to invade the state with a volunteer army, on June 24 the old charter government declared martial law and called on President Tyler to send in federal troops to help put down the rebellion. When the President agreed to do so if an actual insurrection were to occur, the rebellion collapsed, arrests were made, and eventually Dorr was taken prisoner.

Martin Luther was a follower of Dorr; Borden, who was a member of the state militia, broke into Luther's house to arrest him. Luther, however, fled to Fall River, Massachusetts, where he claimed residence for diversity of citizenship jurisdiction purposes in order to sue in federal court. Luther subsequently sued Borden for trespass. At issue at the trial was whether the old charter government met the Article 4 Section 4 federal constitutional provision that "the United States shall guarantee to every State in this Union a Republican Form of Government." If the old charter government was not "a republican form of government," it was an illegal government, and all its acts including martial law were invalid. The Dorr Rebellion captured the imagination of much of the country, particularly Democrats whose sympathies were with Dorr and his followers. Nevertheless, the old charter government was clearly in control. The Taney Court was not anxious to decide this case, and through a series of delays managed to hold off until 1849 before rendering its decision.

Majority votes: 8
Dissenting votes: 1

MR. CHIEF JUSTICE TANEY delivered the opinion of the Court: . . .

Upon what ground could the Circuit Court of the United States which tried this case have . . . disregarded and overruled the decisions of the courts of Rhode Island? Undoubtedly the courts of the United States have certain powers under the Constitution and laws of the United States which do not belong to the State courts. But the power of deter-

mining that a state government has been lawfully established, which the courts of the State disown and repudiate, is not one of them. Upon such a question the courts of the United States are bound to follow the decisions of the state tribunals, and must therefore regard the charter government as the lawful and established government during the time of this contest.

Besides, if the Circuit Court had entered upon this inquiry, by what rule could it have determined the qualification of voters upon the adoption or rejection of the proposed constitution, unless there was some previous law of the State to guide it? It is the province of a court to expound the law, not to make it. And certainly it is no part of the judicial functions of any court of the United States to prescribe the qualification of voters in a State, giving the right to those to whom it is denied by the written and established constitution and laws of the State, or taking it away from those to whom it is given; nor has it the right to determine what political privileges the citizens of a State are entitled to, unless there is an established constitution or law to govern its decision. . . .

. . . . [T]he Constitution of the United States, as far as it has provided for an emergency of this kind, and authorized the general government to interfere in the domestic concerns of a State, has treated the subject as political in its nature, and placed the power in the hands of that department.

The fourth section of the fourth article of the Constitution of the United States provides that the United States shall guarantee to every state in the Union a republican form of government, and shall protect each of them against invasion; and on the application of the legislature or of the executive (when the legislature cannot be convened) against domestic violence.

Under this article of the Constitution it rests with Congress to decide what government is the established one in a State. For as the United States guarantee to each State a republican government, Congress must necessarily decide what government is established in the State before it can determine whether it is republican or not. And when the senators and representatives of a State are admitted into the councils of the Union, the authority of the government under which they are appointed, as well as its republican character, is recognized by the proper constitutional authority. And its decision is binding on every other department of the government, and could not be questioned in a judicial tribunal. It is true that the contest in this case did not last long enough to bring the matter to this issue, and as no senators or representatives were elected under the authority of the government of which Mr. Dorr was the head, Congress was not called upon to decide the controversy. Yet the right to decide is placed there, and not in the courts.

So, too, as relates to the clause in the above-mentioned article of the Constitution, providing for cases of domestic violence. It rested with Congress, too, to determine upon the means proper to be adopted to fulfill this guarantee. They might, if they had deemed it most advisable to do so, have placed it in the power of a court to decide when the contingency had happened which required the federal government to interfere. But Congress thought otherwise, and no doubt wisely; and by the act of February 28, 1795, provided, that, "in case of an insurrection in any State against the government thereof, it shall be lawful for the President of the United States, on application of the legislature of such State or of the executive (when the legislature cannot be convened), to call forth such number of the militia of any other State or States, as may be applied for, as he may judge sufficient to suppress such insurrection."

By this act, the power of deciding whether the exigency had arisen upon which the government of the United States is bound to interfere, is given to the President. He is to act upon the application of the legislature or of the executive, and consequently he must determine what body of men constitute the legislature, and who is the governor, before he can act. The fact that both parties claim the right to the government cannot alter the case, for both cannot be entitled to it. If there is an armed conflict, like the one of which we are speaking, it is a case of domestic violence, and one of the parties must be in insurrection against the lawful government. And the President must, of necessity, decide which is the government, and which party is unlawfully arrayed against it, before he can perform the duty imposed upon him by the act of Congress.

After the President has acted and called out the militia, is a Circuit Court of the United States authorized to inquire whether his decision was right? Could the court, while the parties were actually contending in arms for the possession of the government, call witnesses before it and inquire which party represented a majority of the people? If it could, then it would become the duty of the court (provided it came to the conclusion that the President had decided incorrectly) to discharge those who were arrested or detained by the troops in the service of the United States or the government which the President was endeavouring to maintain. If the judicial power extends so far, the guarantee contained in the Constitution of the United States is a guarantee of anarchy, and not of order. Yet if this right does not reside in the courts when the conflict is raging, if the judicial power is at the time bound to follow the decision of the political, it must be equally bound when the contest is over. It cannot, when peace is restored, punish as offences and crimes the acts which it before recognized, and was bound to recognize, as lawful.

It is true that in this case the militia were not called out by the President. But upon the application of the governor under the charter government, the President recognized him as the executive power of the State, and took measures to call out the militia to support his authority if it should be found necessary for the general government to interfere; and it is admitted in the argument, that it was the knowledge of this decision that put an end to the armed opposition to the charter government, and prevented any further efforts to establish by force the proposed constitution. The interference of the President, therefore, by announcing his determination, was as effectual as if the militia had been assembled under his orders. And it should be equally authoritative. For certainly no court of the United States, with a knowledge of this decision, would have been justified in recognizing the opposing party as the lawful government; or in treating as wrongdoers, or insurgents the officers of the government which the President had recognized, and was prepared to support by an armed force. . . .

It is said that this power in the President is dangerous to liberty, and may be abused. All power may be abused if placed in unworthy hands. But it would be difficult, we think, to point out any other hands in which this power would be more safe, and at the same time equally effectual. When citizens of the same State are in arms against each other, and the constituted authorities unable to execute the laws, the interposition of the United States must be prompt, or it is of little value. The ordinary course of proceedings in courts of justice would be utterly unfit for the crisis. And the elevated office of the President, chosen as he is by the people of the United States, and the high responsibility he could not fail to feel when acting in a case of so much moment, appear to furnish as strong safeguards against a wilful abuse of power as human prudence and foresight could well provide. At all events, it is conferred upon him by the Constitution and laws of the United States, and must therefore be respected and enforced in its judicial tribunals. . . .

Much of the argument on the part of the plaintiff turned upon political rights and political questions, upon which the court has been urged to express an opinion. We decline doing so. The high power has been conferred on this court of passing judgment upon the acts of the State sovereignties, and of the legislative and executive branches of the federal government, and of determining whether they are beyond the limits of power marked out for them respectively by the Constitution of the United States. This tribunal, therefore, should be the last to overstep the boundaries which limit its own jurisdiction. And while it should always be ready to meet any question confided to it by the Constitution, it is equally its duty not to pass beyond its appropriate sphere of action, and to take care not to involve itself in discussions which properly belong to other forums. No one, we believe, has ever doubted the proposition, that, according to the institutions of this country, the sovereignty in every State resides in the people of the State, and that they may alter and change their form of government at their own pleasure. But whether they have changed it or not by abolishing an old government, and establishing a new one in its place, is a question to be settled by the political power. And when that power has decided, the courts are bound to take notice of its decision, and to follow it.

The judgment of the Circuit Court must therefore be affirmed.

MR. JUSTICE WOODBURY, dissenting: [omitted]

EX PARTE McCARDLE, 7 WALLACE 506 (1869)

When Congress enacted the Reconstruction Acts, it also enacted the Habeas Corpus Act of 1867. The Habeas Corpus Act was broad sweeping in its language, and authorized the federal courts to issue writs of habeas corpus to "any person restrained of his or her liberty in violation of the Constitution, or of any treaty or law of the United States." The purpose was to prevent the state authorities from harassing by arresting the newly freed blacks, federal officials, and Republican politicians (the so-called carpetbaggers who went South to organize the black electorate). But instead the law was used by William H. McCardle, the racist editor of the Vicksburg (Mississippi) Times, *who was arrested by the military for having written and published articles critical of Reconstruction. He was charged with inciting to insurrection, disorder and violence, libel, and impeding Reconstruction. McCardle petitioned the United States Circuit Court for the District of Mississippi for a writ of*

habeas corpus, which was granted. McCardle appeared in federal court and argued that the Reconstruction Acts were unconstitutional and his arrest illegal. The federal judge did not agree with McCardle, whereupon McCardle under the provisions of the Habeas Corpus Act of 1867 appealed to the Supreme Court. The Court, it seemed, would be forced to rule on the constitutionality of the Reconstruction Acts in light of the Court's own contradictory open court rule of Ex Parte Milligan. *But the Radical Republicans in Congress did not want the Court to rule in this case; they therefore enacted legislation in 1868 which repealed the Court's appellate jurisdiction in all cases arising under the Habeas Corpus Act of 1867. The Supreme Court had its jurisdiction withdrawn to hear such appeals "which have been, or may hereafter be, taken." The Supreme Court eventually gave its reaction to this development in its unanimous decision in this case.*

Votes: Unanimous

MR. CHIEF JUSTICE CHASE delivered the opinion of the Court:

The first question necessarily is that of jurisdiction; for, if the act of March, 1868, takes away the jurisdiction defined by the act of February, 1867, it is useless, if not improper, to enter into any discussion of other questions.

It is quite true, as was argued by the counsel for the petitioner, that the appellate jurisdiction of this court is not derived from acts of Congress. It is, strictly speaking, conferred by the Constitution. But it is conferred "with such exceptions and under such regulations as Congress shall make." . . .

. . . [A]cts of Congress, providing for the exercise of jurisdiction . . . [are] spoken of as acts granting jurisdiction, and not as acts making exceptions to the constitutional grant of it.

The exception to appellate jurisdiction in the case before us, however, is not an inference from the affirmation of other appellate jurisdiction. It is made in terms. The provision of the act of 1867, affirming the appellate jurisdiction of this court in cases of *habeas corpus* is expressly repealed. It is hardly possible to imagine a plainer instance of positive exception.

We are not at liberty to inquire into the motives of the legislature. We can only examine into its power under the Constitution; and the power to make exceptions to the appellate jurisdiction of this court is given by express words.

What, then, is the effect of the repealing act upon the case before us? We cannot doubt as to this. Without jurisdiction the court cannot proceed at all in any cause. Jurisdiction is power to declare the law, and when it ceases to exist, the only function remaining to the court is that of announcing the fact and dismissing the cause. And this is not less clear upon authority than upon principle.

Several cases were cited by the counsel for the petitioner in support of the position that jurisdiction of this case is not affected by the repealing act. But none of them in our judgment, afford any support to it. . . .

On the other hand, the general rule, supported by the best elementary writers, is, that "when an act of the legislature is repealed, it must be considered, except as to transactions past and closed, as if it never existed." And the effect of repealing acts upon suits under acts repealed, has been determined by the adjudications of this court. . . .

It is quite clear . . . that this court cannot proceed to pronounce judgment in this case, for it has no longer jurisdiction of the appeal; and judicial duty is not less fitly performed by declining ungranted jurisdiction than in exercising firmly that which the Constitution and the laws confer.

Counsel seem to have supposed, if effect be given to the repealing act in question, that the whole appellate power of the court, in cases of *habeas corpus*, is denied. But this is an error. The act of 1868 does not except from that jurisdiction any cases but appeals from Circuit Courts under the act of 1867. It does not affect the jurisdiction which was previously exercised.

The appeal of the petitioner in this case must be

Dismissed for want of jurisdiction.

DRED SCOTT v. SANDFORD, 19 HOWARD 393 (1857)

Controversial constitutional questions surrounded the institution of Negro slavery. They included: What is the legal status of a slave who is taken to a free state where slavery is against the law? Does the slave's status then automatically change to that of a free person? What is the legal status of a slave taken to federal territory where slavery is prohibited by congressional legislation? Does such congressional legislation constitute an unconstitutional deprivation of the slaveowner's property by forbidding the slaveowner from living in "free" territory with his or her slaves (property)? The Dred Scott case came to the Supreme Court raising these issues and others. Dred Scott himself was born into slavery. He was owned by Dr. John Emerson, a surgeon in the United States Army, whose permanent residence was in the slave state of Missouri. Beginning in 1833 the doctor took

Scott with him on his army tour of duty into the state of Illinois, where slavery was forbidden by law; he later took him into the upper Louisiana Purchase (now Minnesota), where slavery was forever prohibited by Congress according to the Missouri Compromise of 1820. In 1843 Dr. Emerson died.

Scott, with the aid of abolitionist lawyers, began his suit for freedom in the Missouri state courts in 1846. These efforts ultimately proved unsuccessful. Mrs. Emerson remarried in 1850 and her new husband was an abolitionist; the ownership of Scott was transferred to John Sanford of New York, Mrs. Emerson's brother (note that the official Court records misspelled his name). Dred Scott began his suit for freedom in the United States Circuit Court in St. Louis in November of 1853. Scott claimed that his residence in free United States territory as well as in the free state of Illinois made him a free man. The Circuit Court accepted the case, assumed jurisdiction, but ruled against Scott's substantive claims. The case then came to the Supreme Court, which first delayed hearing and then delayed deciding the case. Finally, shortly after the inauguration of President Buchanan, the Court announced its opinion. Chief Justice Taney spoke for the majority in a 54-page opinion of the Court.

Majority votes: 7
Dissenting votes: 2

MR. CHIEF JUSTICE TANEY delivered the opinion of the Court:. . . .

The question is simply this: can a negro, whose ancestors were imported into this country and sold as slaves, become a member of the political community formed and brought into existence by the Constitution of the United States, and as such become entitled to all the rights, and privileges, and immunities, guarantied by that instrument to the citizen. One of these rights is the privilege of suing in a court of the United States in the cases specified in the Constitution. . . .

The words "people of the United States" and "citizens" are synonymous terms, and mean the same thing. They both describe the political body, who, according to our republican institutions, form the sovereignty, and who hold the power and conduct the government through their representatives. They are what we familiarly call the "sovereign people," and every citizen is one of this people, and a constituent member of this sovereignty. The question before us is, whether [negroes] . . . compose a portion of this people, and are constituent members of this sovereignty. We think they are not, and that they are not included, and were not intended to be included, under the word "citizens" in the Constitution, and can, therefore, claim none of the rights and privileges which that instrument provides for and secures to citizens of the United States. On the contrary, they were at that time considered as a subordinate and inferior class of beings, who had been subjugated by the dominant race, and whether emancipated or not yet remained subject to their authority, and had no rights or privileges but such as those who held the power and the government might choose to grant them. . . .

The question then arises, whether the provisions of the Constitution, in relation to the personal rights and privileges to which the citizen of a state should be entitled, embraced the negro African race, at that time in this country, or who might afterwards be imported, who had then or should afterwards be made free in any State; and to put it in the power of a single State to make him a citizen of the United States, and endow him with the full rights of citizenship in every other State without their consent. Does the Constitution of the United States act upon him whenever he shall be made free under the laws of a State, and raised there to the rank of a citizen, and immediately clothe him with all the privileges of a citizen in every other State, and in its own courts?

The court thinks the affirmative of these propositions cannot be maintained. And if it cannot, the plaintiff in error could not be a citizen of the State of Missouri, within the meaning of the Constitution of the United States, and, consequently, was not entitled to sue in its courts. . . .

In the opinion of the court, the legislation and histories of the times, and the language used in the Declaration of Independence, show, that neither the class of persons who had been imported as slaves, nor their descendants, whether they had become free or not, were then acknowledged as a part of the people, nor intended to be included in the general words used in that memorable instrument. . . . They had for more than a century before been regarded as beings of an inferior order; and altogether unfit to associate with the white race, either in social or political relations; and so far inferior, that they had no rights which the white man was bound to respect; and that the negro might justly and lawfully be reduced to slavery for his benefit. He was bought and sold, and treated as an ordinary article of merchandise and traffic, whenever a profit could be made by it. This opinion was at that time fixed and universal in the civilized portion of the white race. It was regarded as an axiom in morals as well as in politics, which no one thought of disputing, or supposed to be open to dispute; and men in every grade and position in society daily and habitually acted upon it in their private pursuits, as well as in matters of public

concern, without doubting for a moment the correctness of this opinion. . . .

The legislation of the different Colonies furnishes positive and indisputable proof of this fact. . . . They show that a perpetual and impassable barrier was intended to be erected between the white race and the one which they had reduced to slavery, and governed as subjects with absolute and despotic power, and which they then looked upon as so far below them in the scale of created beings, that intermarriages between white persons and negroes or mulattoes were regarded as unnatural and immoral, and punished as crimes, not only in the parties, but in the person who joined them in marriage. And no distinction in this respect was made between the free negro or mulatto and the slave, but this stigma, of the deepest degradation, was fixed upon the whole race.

We refer to these historical facts for the purpose of showing the fixed opinions concerning that race, upon which the statesmen of that day spoke and acted. It is necessary to do this, in order to determine whether the general terms used in the Constitution of the United States, as to the rights of man and the rights of the people, was intended to include them, or to give to them or their posterity the benefit of any of its provisions.

There are two clauses in the Constitution which point directly and specifically to the negro race as a separate class of persons, and show clearly that they were not regarded as a portion of the people or citizens of the government then formed.

One of these clauses reserves to each of the thirteen States the right to import slaves until the year 1808, if it thinks proper. And the importation which it thus sanctions was unquestionably of persons of the race of which we are speaking, as the traffic in slaves in the United States had always been confined to them. And by the other provision the States pledged themselves to each other to maintain the right of property of the master, by delivering up to him any slave who may have escaped from his service, and be found within their respective territories. By the first above-mentioned clause, therefore, the right to purchase and hold this property is directly sanctioned and authorized for twenty years by the people who framed the Constitution. And by the second, they pledge themselves to maintain and uphold the right of the master in the manner specified, as long as the government they then formed should endure. And these two provisions show, conclusively, that neither the description of persons therein referred to, nor their descendants, were embraced in any of the other provisions of the Constitution; for certainly these two clauses were not intended to confer on them or their posterity the blessings of liberty, or any of the personal rights so carefully provided for the citizen.

No one of that race had ever migrated to the United States voluntarily; all of them had been brought here as articles of merchandise. The number that had been emancipated at that time were but few in comparison with those held in slavery; and they were identified in the public mind with the race to which they belonged, and regarded as a part of the slave population rather than the free. It is obvious that they were not even in the minds of the framers of the Constitution when they were conferring special rights and privileges upon the citizens of a State in every other part of the Union.

Indeed, when we look to the condition of this race in the several States at the time, it is impossible to believe that these rights and privileges were intended to be extended to them. . . .

It would be impossible to enumerate and compress, in the space usually allotted to an opinion of a court, the various laws, marking the condition of this race, which were passed from time to time after the Revolution, and before and since the adoption of the Constitution of the United States. . . . It is sufficient to say that Chancellor Kent, whose accuracy and research no one will question, states in the sixth edition of his Commentaries, published in 1848, 2d vol. 258, note b, that in no part of the country, except Maine, did the African race, in point of fact, participate equally with the whites in the exercise of civil and political rights. . . .

To all this mass of proof we have still to add, that Congress has repeatedly legislated upon the same construction of the Constitution that we have given. . . . The Naturalization Law was passed at the second session of the first Congress, March 26, 1790, and confines the right of becoming citizens "to aliens being free white persons." . . .

Another is the first Militia Law, which was passed in 1792, at the first session of the second Congress. The language of this law is equally plain and significant with the one just mentioned. It directs that every "free able-bodied white male citizen" shall be enrolled in the militia. The word "white" is evidently used to exclude the African race, and the word "citizen" to exclude unnaturalized foreigners, the latter forming no part of the sovereignty; owing it no allegiance, and therefore under no obligation to defend it. The African race, however, born in the country, did owe allegiance to the government, whether they were slave or free; but it is repudiated, and rejected from the duties and obligations of citizenship in marked language. . . .

The conduct of the Executive Department of the government has been in perfect harmony upon this subject with this course of legislation. The question was brought officially before the late William Wirt, when he was the Attorney-General of the United States, in 1821, and he decided that the words "citizens of the United States" were used in the Acts of Congress in the same sense as in the Constitution; and that free persons of color were not citizens, within the meaning of the Constitution and laws; and this opinion has been confirmed by that of the late Attorney-General, Caleb Cushing, in a recent case, and acted upon by the Secretary of State, who refused to grant passports to them as "citizens of the United States." . . .

And upon a full and careful consideration of the subject, the court is of opinion that, upon the facts stated . . . Dred Scott was not a citizen of Missouri within the meaning of the Constitution of the United States, and not entitled as such to sue in its courts; and, consequently, that the Circuit Court had not jurisdiction of the case, and that the judgment [granting jurisdiction] is erroneous.

The correction of one error in the court below does not deprive the appellate court of the power of examining further into the record, and correcting any other material errors which may have been committed by the inferior court. . . . We proceed, therefore, to inquire whether the facts relied on by the plaintiff entitled him to his freedom. . . .

In considering this part of the controversy, two questions arise: 1st. Was he, together with his family, free in Missouri by reason of the stay in the [Upper Louisiana] territory of the United States . . .? And 2d. If they were not, is Scott himself free by reason of his removal to Rock Island, in the State of Illinois . . .?

We proceed to examine the first question.

The Act of Congress, upon which the plaintiff relies, declares that slavery and involuntary servitude, except as a punishment for crime, shall be forever prohibited in all that part of that territory ceded by France, under the name of Louisiana which lies north of thirty-six degrees thirty minutes north latitude, and not included within the limits of Missouri. And the difficulty which meets us at the threshold of this part of the injury is, whether Congress was authorized to pass this law under any of the powers granted to it by the Constitution; for if the authority is not given by that instrument, it is the duty of this court to declare it void and inoperative, and incapable of conferring freedom upon one who is held as a slave under the laws of any one of the States. . . .

. . . [I]t may be safely assumed that citizens of the United States who migrate to a territory belonging to the people of the United States, cannot be ruled as mere colonists, dependent upon the will of the general government, and to be governed by any laws it may think proper to impose. . . . A power, . . . in the general government to obtain and hold Colonies and dependent Territories, over which they might legislate without restriction, would be inconsistent with its own existence in its present form. . . . The territory being a part of the United States, the government and the citizen both enter it under the authority of the Constitution, with their respective rights defined and marked out; and the Federal Government can exercise no power over his person or property, beyond what that instrument confers, nor lawfully deny any right which it has reserved. . . .

These powers, and others in relation to rights of person, which it is not necessary here to enumerate, are, in express and positive terms, denied to the general government; and the rights of private property have been guarded with equal care. Thus the rights of property are united with the rights of person, and placed on the same ground by the fifth amendment to the Constitution, which provides that no person shall be deprived of life, liberty and property, without due process of law. And an Act of Congress which deprives a citizen of the United States of his liberty or property, merely because he came himself or brought his property into a particular Territory of the United States, and who had committed no offense against the laws, could hardly be dignified with the name of due process of law.

So, too, it will hardly be contended that Congress could . . . take private property for public use without just compensation.

The powers over person and property of which we speak are not only not granted to Congress, but are in express terms denied, and they are forbidden to exercise them. And this prohibition is not confined to the States, but the words are general, and extend to the whole territory over which the Constitution gives it power to legislate, including those portions of it remaining under territorial government, as well as that covered by States. It is a total absence of power everywhere within the dominion of the United States, and places the citizens of a territory, so far as these rights are concerned, on the same footing with citizens of the States, and guards them as firmly and plainly against any inroads which the general government might attempt under the plea of implied or incidental powers. And if Congress itself cannot do this—if it is beyond the powers conferred on the Federal Government—it will be admitted, we presume, that it could not authorize a territorial government to exercise them. It could confer no power on any local government,

established by its authority, to violate the provisions of the Constitution. . . .

Upon these considerations, it is the opinion of the court that the Act of Congress which prohibited a citizen from holding and owning property of this kind in the territory of the United States north of the line therein mentioned, is not warranted by the Constitution, and is therefore void: and that neither Dred Scott himself, nor any of his family, were made free by being carried into this territory; even if they had been carried there by the owner, with the intention of becoming a permanent resident.

We have so far examined the case, as it stands under the Constitution of the United States, and the powers thereby delegated to the Federal Government.

But there is another point in the case which depends on state power and state law. And it is contended, on the part of the plaintiff, that he is made free by being taken to Rock Island, in the State of Illinois, independently of his residence in the territory of the United States; and being so made free he was not again reduced to a state of slavery by being brought back to Missouri.

Our notice of this part of the case will be very brief; for the principle on which it depends was decided in this court, upon much consideration, in the case of *Strader et al.* v. *Graham,* reported in 10th Howard, 82. In that case, the slaves had been taken from Kentucky to Ohio, with the consent of the owner, and afterwards brought back to Kentucky. And this court held that their status or condition, as free or slave, depended upon the laws of Kentucky, when they were brought back into that State, and not of Ohio; and that this court had no jurisdiction to revise the judgment of a state court upon its own laws. This was the point directly before the court, and the decision that this court had not jurisdiction, turned upon it, as will be seen by the report of the case.

So in this case: as Scott was a slave when taken into the State of Illinois by his owner, and was there held as such, and brought back in that character, his status, as free or slave, depended on the laws of Missouri, and not of Illinois. . . . We are satisfied, upon a careful examination of all the cases decided in the State courts of Missouri that it is now firmly settled by the decisions of the highest court in the State, that Scott and his family upon their return were not free, but were, by the laws of Missouri the property of the defendant; and that the Circuit Court of the United States had no jurisdiction, when, by the laws of the State, the plaintiff was a slave and not a citizen. . . .

[Dismissed]

MR. JUSTICE WAYNE [concurring]: [omitted]
MR. JUSTICE NELSON [concurring]: [omitted]
MR. JUSTICE GRIER[concurring]: [omitted]
MR. JUSTICE DANIEL [concurring]: [omitted]
MR. JUSTICE CAMPBELL [concurring]: [omitted]
MR. JUSTICE CATRON [concurring]: [omitted]
MR. JUSTICE McLEAN, dissenting:. . . .

If Congress may establish a territorial government in the exercise of its discretion, it is a clear principle that a court cannot control that discretion. This being the case. I do not see on what ground the Act [Missouri Compromise] is held to be void. It did not purport to forfeit property, or take it for public purposes. It only prohibited slavery; in doing which, it followed the Ordinance of 1787. . . .

MR. JUSTICE CURTIS, dissenting:. . . .

It has been often asserted that the Constitution was made exclusively by and for the white race. It has already been shown that in five of the thirteen original States, colored persons then possessed the elective franchise, and were among those by whom the Constitution was ordained and established. If so, it is not true, in point of fact, that the Constitution was made exclusively for the white race. And that it was made exclusively for the white race, is, in my opinion, not only an assumption not warranted by anything in the Constitution, but contradicted by its opening declaration, that it was ordained and established by the people of the United States, for themselves and their posterity. And as free colored persons were then citizens of at least five States, and so in every sense part of the people of the United States, they were among those for whom and whose posterity the Constitution was ordained and established. . . .

Slavery being contrary to natural right, is created only by municipal law. This is not only plain in itself, and agreed by all writers on the subject, but is inferable from the Constitution, and has been explicitly declared by this court. The Constitution refers to slaves as "persons held to service in one State, under the laws thereof." Nothing can more clearly describe a status created by municipal law. In *Prigg* v. *Pennsylvania*, 16 Pet. 611, this court said: "The state of slavery is deemed to be a mere municipal regulation, founded on and limited to the range of territorial laws." I am not acquainted with any case or writer questioning the correctness of this doctrine. . . .

Is it conceivable that the Constitution has conferred the right on every citizen to become a resident on the Territory of the United States with his slaves, and there to hold them as such, but has neither made nor provided for any municipal regulations which are essential to the existence of slavery?

Is it not more rational to conclude that they who framed and adopted the Constitution were aware that persons held to service under the laws of a State are property only to the extent and under the conditions fixed by those laws; that they must cease to be available as property, when their owners voluntarily place them permanently within another jurisdiction, where no municipal laws on the subject of slavery exist; and that, being aware of these principles, and having said nothing to interfere with or displace them, or compel Congress to legislate in any particular manner on the subject, and having empowered Congress to make all needful rules and regulations respecting the Territory of the United States, it was their intention to leave to the discretion of Congress what regulations, if any, should be made concerning slavery therein? Moreover, if the right exists, what are its limits, and what are its conditions? If citizens of the United States have the right to take their slaves to a Territory, and hold them there as slaves, without regard to the laws of the Territory, I suppose this right is not to be restricted to the citizens of slave-holding States. A citizen of a State which does not tolerate slavery can hardly be denied the power of doing the same thing. And what law of slavery does either take with him to the Territory? If it be said to be those laws respecting slavery which existed in the particular State from which each slave last came, what an anomaly is this? Where else can we find, under the law of any civilized country, the power to introduce and permanently continue diverse systems of foreign municipal law, for holding persons in slavery?. . . Whatever theoretical importance may be now supposed to belong to the maintenance of such a right, I feel a perfect conviction that it would, if ever tried, prove to be as impracticable in fact, as it is, in my judgment, monstrous in theory. . . .

BAKER v. CARR,
369 U.S. 186 (1962)

The Supreme Court once before had faced a question similar to the one it faced in the Baker case. In 1946, in the case of Colegrove v. Green, *328 U.S. 549, the Supreme Court by a vote of four to three had ruled that malapportionment of congressional districts by the Illinois state legislature did not present a justiciable issue. Justice Frankfurter, speaking for three of the four justices, argued that the determination of what interests were to be represented, and in what proportions, was a political determination and not one appropriate for courts to consider. In the case from Tennessee,* Baker v. Carr, *the Court was again presented with a malapportionment issue. Tennessee had not reapportioned its state legislative districts since 1901 and the disparities were pronounced. Some 37 percent of the voters of Tennessee elected over 60 percent of the State Senate and 40 percent of the voters elected 64 percent of the members of the House. The Court reconsidered the question whether malapportionment was justiciable and concluded that it was, agreeing with Baker and other plaintiffs that the case raised a Fourteenth Amendment equal protection issue.*

Majority votes: 6
Dissenting votes: 2

MR. JUSTICE BRENNAN delivered the opinion of the Court:. . . .

In holding that the subject matter of this suit was not justiciable, the District Court relied on *Colegrove* v. *Green,* and subsequent *per curiam* cases. The court stated: "From a review of these decisions there can be no doubt that the federal rule . . . is that the federal courts . . . will not intervene in cases of this type to compel legislative reapportionment." 179 F. Supp., at 826. We understand the District Court to have read the cited cases as compelling the conclusion that since the appellants sought to have a legislative apportionment held unconstitutional, their suit presented a "political question" and was therefore nonjusticiable. We hold that this challenge to an apportionment presents no nonjusticiable "political question." The cited cases do not hold the contrary.

Of course the mere fact that the suit seeks protection of a political right does not mean it presents a political question. . . . Rather, it is argued that apportionment cases, whatever the actual wording of the complaint, can involve no federal constitutional right except one resting on the guaranty of a republican form of government, and that complaints based on that clause have been held to present political questions which are nonjusticiable.

We hold that the claim pleaded here neither rests upon nor implicates the Guaranty Clause and that its justiciability is therefore not foreclosed by our decisions of cases involving that clause. The District Court misinterpreted *Colegrove* v. *Green* and other decisions of this Court on which it relied. Appellants' claim that they are being denied equal protection is justiciable, and if "discrimination is sufficiently shown, the right to relief under the equal protection clause is not diminished by the fact that the discrimination relates to political rights." *Snowden* v. *Hughes,* 321 U.S. 1, 11. To show why we reject the argument based on the Guaranty Clause, we must examine the authorities under it.

But because there appears to be some uncertainty as to why those cases did present political questions, and specifically as to whether this apportionment case is like those areas, we deem it necessary first to consider the contours of the "political question" doctrine.

Our discussion, even at the price of extending this opinion, requires review of a number of political question cases, in order to expose the attributes of the doctrine—attributes which, in various settings, diverge, combine, appear, and disappear in seeming disorderliness. . . . [T]hat review . . . demonstrate[s] that neither singly nor collectively do these cases support a conclusion that this apportionment case is nonjusticiable; we of course do not explore their implications in other contexts. That review reveals that in the Guaranty Clause cases and in the other "political question" cases, it is the relationship between the judiciary and the coordinate branches of the Federal Government, and not the federal judiciary's relationship to the States, which gives rise to the "political question."

. . . . The nonjusticiability of a political question is primarily a function of the separation of powers. Much confusion results from the capacity of the "political question" label to obscure the need for case-by-case inquiry. Deciding whether a matter has in any measure been committed by the Constitution to another branch of government, or whether the action of that branch exceeds whatever authority has been committed, is itself a delicate exercise in constitutional interpretation, and is a responsibility of this Court as ultimate interpreter of the Constitution. . . .

We come, finally, to the ultimate inquiry whether our precedents as to what constitutes a nonjusticiable "political question" bring the case before us under the umbrella of that doctrine. A natural beginning is to note whether any of the common characteristics which we have been able to identify and label descriptively are present. We find none: The question here is the consistency of state action with the Federal Constitution. We have no question decided, or to be decided, by a political branch of government coequal with this Court. Nor do we risk embarrassment of our government abroad, or grave disturbance at home if we take issue with Tennessee as to the constitutionality of her action here challenged. Nor need the appellants, in order to succeed in this action, ask the Court to enter upon policy determinations for which judicially manageable standards are lacking. Judicial standards under the Equal Protection Clause are well developed and familiar, and it has been open to courts since the enactment of the Fourteenth Amendment to determine, if on the particular facts they must, that a discrimination reflects *no* policy, but simply arbitrary and capricious action. . . .

We conclude that the complaint's allegations of a denial of equal protection present a justiciable constitutional cause of action upon which appellants are entitled to a trial and a decision. The right asserted is within the reach of judicial protection under the Fourteenth Amendment.

The judgment of the District Court is reversed and the cause is remanded for further proceedings consistent with this opinion.

Reversed and remanded.

MR. JUSTICE WHITTAKER did not participate in the decision of this case.

MR. JUSTICE DOUGLAS, concurring: [omitted]
MR. JUSTICE CLARK, concurring: [omitted]
MR. JUSTICE STEWART, concurring: [omitted]
MR. JUSTICE FRANKFURTER, with whom MR. JUSTICE HARLAN joins, dissenting:

The Court today reverses a uniform course of decision established by a dozen cases, including one by which the very claim now sustained was unanimously rejected only five years ago. The impressive body of rulings thus cast aside reflected the equally uniform course of our political history regarding the relationship between population and legislative representation—a wholly different matter from denial of the franchise to individuals because of race, color, religion or sex. Such a massive repudiation of the experience of our whole past in asserting destructively novel judicial power demands a detailed analysis of the role of this Court in our constitutional scheme. Disregard of inherent limits in the effective exercise of the Court's "judicial Power" not only presages the futility of judicial intervention in the essentially political conflict of forces by which the relation between population and representation has time out of mind been and now is determined. It may well impair the Court's position as the ultimate organ of "the supreme Law of the Land" in that vast range of legal problems, often strongly entangled in popular feeling, on which this Court must pronounce. The Court's authority—possessed neither of the purse nor the sword—ultimately rests on sustained public confidence in its moral sanction. Such feeling must be nourished by the Court's complete detachment, in fact and in appearance, from political entanglements and by abstention from injecting itself into the clash of political forces in political settlements.

A hypothetical claim resting on abstract assumptions is now for the first time made the basis for affording illusory relief for a particular evil even though it foreshadows deeper and more pervasive difficulties in consequence. The claim is hypothetical and the assumptions are abstract because the Court does not vouchsafe the lower courts—state and federal—guidelines for formulating specific, definite, wholly unprecedented remedies for the inevitable litigations that today's umbrageous disposition is bound to stimulate in connection with politically motivated reapportionments in so many States. In such a setting, to promulgate jurisdiction in the abstract is meaningless. It is devoid of reality as "a brooding omnipresence in the sky" for it conveys no intimation what relief, if any, a District Court is capable of affording that would not invite legislatures to play ducks and drakes with the judiciary. For this Court to direct the District Court to enforce a claim to which the Court has over the years consistently found itself required to deny legal enforcement and at the same time to find it necessary to withhold any guidance to the lower court how to enforce this turnabout, new legal claim, manifests an odd—indeed an esoteric—conception of judicial propriety. One of the Court's supporting opinions, as elucidated by commentary, unwittingly affords a disheartening preview of the mathematical quagmire (apart from divers judicially inappropriate and elusive determinants), into which this Court today catapults the lower courts of the country without so much as adumbrating the basis for a legal calculus as a means of extrication. Even assuming the indispensable intellectual disinterestedness on the part of judges in such matters, they do not have accepted legal standards or criteria or even reliable analogies to draw upon for making judicial judgments. To charge courts with the task of accommodating the incommensurable factors of policy that underlie these mathematical puzzles is to attribute, however flatteringly, omnicompetence to judges. The Framers of the Constitution persistently rejected a proposal that embodied this assumption and Thomas Jefferson never entertained it.

Recent legislation, creating a district appropriately described as "an atrocity of ingenuity," is not unique. Considering the gross inequality among legislative electoral units within almost every State, the Court naturally shrinks from asserting that in districting at least substantial equality is a constitutional requirement enforceable by courts. Room continues to be allowed for weighting. This of course implies that geography, economics, urban-rural conflict, and all the other non-legal factors which have throughout our history entered into political districting are to some extent not to be ruled out in the undefined vista now opened up by review in the federal courts of state reapportionments. To some extent—aye, there's the rub. In effect today's decision empowers the courts of the country to devise what should constitute the proper composition of the legislatures of the fifty States. If state courts should for one reason or another find themselves unable to discharge this task, the duty of doing so is put on the federal courts or on this Court, if State views do not satisfy this Court's notion of what is proper districting.

We were soothingly told at the bar of this Court that we need not worry about the kind of remedy a court could effectively fashion once the abstract constitutional right to have courts pass on a statewide system of electoral districting is recognized as a matter of judicial rhetoric, because legislatures would heed the Court's admonition. This is not only an euphoric hope. It implies a sorry confession of judicial impotence in place of a frank acknowledgement that there is not under our Constitution a judicial remedy for every political mischief, for every undesirable exercise of legislative power. The Framers carefully and with deliberate forethought refused so to enthrone the judiciary. In this situation, as in others of like nature, appeal for relief does not belong here. Appeal must be to an informed, civically militant electorate. In a democratic society like ours, relief must come through an aroused popular conscience that sears the conscience of the people's representatives. . . .

Dissenting opinion of MR. JUSTICE HARLAN, whom MR. JUSTICE FRANKFURTER joins: [omitted]

FLAST v. COHEN,
392 U.S. 83 (1968)

Florence Flast and other taxpayers initiated litigation against federal officials including Wilbur J. Cohen, Secretary of Health, Education, and Welfare in the Johnson Administration. The suit challenged federal legislation that authorized the expenditure of federal funds to finance the teaching of secular subjects in, and the purchase of instructional materials including textbooks for, religious schools. Flast and the others sought to prevent the spending of tax money in ways that, they claimed, violated the First Amendment prohibition on the establishment of religion. The United States District Court for the Southern District of New York ruled that the taxpayers did not have standing following the well-established precedent of Frothingham v. Mellon. *Appeal was taken to the Supreme Court, and the sole question to be decided was whether Ms. Flast and other taxpayers had standing to sue in federal court.*

Majority votes: 8
Dissenting votes: 1

MR. CHIEF JUSTICE WARREN delivered the opinion of the Court: . . .

As we understand it, the Government's position is that the constitutional scheme of separation of powers, and the deference owed by the federal judiciary to the other two branches of government within that scheme, present an absolute bar to taxpayer suits challenging the validity of federal spending programs. The Government views such suits as involving no more than the mere disagreement by the taxpayer "with the uses to which tax money is put." According to the Government, the resolution of such disagreements is committed to other branches of the Federal Government and not to the judiciary. Consequently, the Government contends that, under no circumstances, should standing be conferred on federal taxpayers to challenge a federal taxing or spending program. An analysis of the function served by standing limitations compels a rejection of the Government's position.

Standing is an aspect of justiciability and, as such, the problem of standing is surrounded by the same complexities and vagaries that inhere in justiciability. Standing has been called one of "the most amorphous [concepts] in the entire domain of public law." Some of the complexities peculiar to standing problems result because standing "serves, on occasion, as a shorthand expression for all the various elements of justiciability." In addition, there are at work in the standing doctrine the many subtle pressures which tend to cause policy considerations to blend into constitutional limitations.

Despite the complexities and uncertainties, some meaningful form can be given to the jurisdictional limitations placed on federal court power by the concept of standing. The fundamental aspect of standing is that it focuses on the party seeking to get his complaint before a federal court and not on the issues he wishes to have adjudicated. The "gist of the question of standing" is whether the party seeking relief has "alleged such a personal stake in the outcome of the controversy as to assure that concrete adverseness which sharpens the presentation of issues upon which the court so largely depends for illumination of difficult constitutional questions." In other words, when standing is placed in issue in a case, the question is whether the person whose standing is challenged is a proper party to request an adjudication of a particular issue and not whether the issue itself is justiciable. Thus, a party may have standing in a particular case, but the federal court may nevertheless decline to pass on the merits of the case because, for example, it presents a political question. A proper party is demanded so that federal courts will not be asked to decide "ill-defined controversies over constitutional issues," or a case which is of "a hypothetical or abstract character." So stated, the standing requirement is closely related to, although more general than, the rule that federal courts will not entertain friendly suits, or those which are feigned or collusive in nature.

When the emphasis in the standing problem is placed on whether the person invoking a federal court's jurisdiction is a proper party to maintain the action, the weakness of the Government's argument in this case becomes apparent. The question whether a particular person is a proper party to maintain the action does not, by its own force, raise separation of powers problems related to improper judicial interference in areas committed to other branches of the Federal Government. Such problems arise, if at all, only from the substantive issues the individual seeks to have adjudicated. Thus, in terms of Article III limitations on federal court jurisdiction, the question of standing is related only to whether the dispute sought to be adjudicated will be presented in an adversary context and in a form historically viewed as capable of judicial resolution. It is for that reason that the emphasis in standing problems is on whether the party invoking federal court jurisdiction has "a personal stake in the outcome of the controversy," and whether the dispute touches upon "the legal relations of parties having adverse legal interests." A taxpayer may or may not have the requisite personal stake in the outcome, depending upon the circumstances of the particular case. Therefore, we find no absolute bar in Article III to suits by federal taxpayers challenging allegedly unconstitutional federal taxing and spending programs. There remains, however, the problem of determining the circumstances under which a federal taxpayer will be deemed to have the personal stake and interest that impart the necessary concrete adverseness to such litigation so that standing can be conferred on the taxpayer *qua* taxpayer consistent with the constitutional limitations of Article III. . . .

. . . [I]n ruling on standing, it is both appropriate and necessary to look to the substantive issues . . . to determine whether there is a logical nexus between the status asserted and the claim sought to be adjudicated. . . . The nexus demanded of federal taxpayers has two aspects to it. First, the taxpayer must establish a logical link between that status and the type of legislative enactment attacked. Thus, a taxpayer will be a proper party to allege the unconstitutionality only of exercises of congressional power under the taxing and spending clause of Art. I, §8, of the Constitution. It will not be sufficient to allege an incidental expenditure of tax funds in the administration of an essentially regulatory statute. . . . Secondly, the taxpayer must establish a nexus between that status and the precise nature of the constitutional infringement alleged. Under this requirement, the taxpayer must show that the challenged enactment exceeds specific constitutional limitations imposed upon the exercise of the congressional taxing and spending power and not simply that the enactment is generally beyond the powers delegated to Congress by Art. I, §8. When both nexuses are established, the litigant will have shown a taxpayer's stake in the outcome of the controversy and will be a proper and appropriate party to invoke a federal court's jurisdiction.

The taxpayer-appellants in this case have satisfied both nexuses to support their claim of standing under the test we announce today. . . . Our history vividly illustrates that one of the specific evils feared by those who drafted the Establishment Clause and fought for its adoption was that the taxing and spending power would be used to favor one religion over another or to support religion in general. . . .

The allegations of the taxpayer in *Frothingham* v. *Mellon* were quite different from those made in this case, and the result in *Frothingham* is consistent with the test of taxpayer standing announced today. The taxpayer in *Frothingham* attacked a federal spending program and she, therefore, established the first nexus required. However, she lacked standing because her constitutional attack was not based on an allegation that Congress, in enacting the Maternity Act of 1921, had breached a specific limitation upon its taxing and spending power. . . .

We have noted that the Establishment Clause of the First Amendment does specifically limit the taxing and spending power conferred by Art. I, §8. Whether the Constitution contains other specific limitations can be determined only in the context of future cases. However, whenever such specific limitations are found, we believe a taxpayer will have a clear stake as a taxpayer in assuring that they are not breached by Congress. Consequently, we hold that a taxpayer will have standing consistent with Article III to invoke federal judicial power when he alleges that congressional action under the taxing and spending clause is in derogation of those constitutional provisions which operate to restrict the exercise of the taxing and spending power. . . .

While we express no view at all on the merits of appellants' claims in this case, their complaint contains sufficient allegations under the criteria we have outlined to give them standing to invoke a federal court's jurisdiction for an adjudication on the merits.

Reversed.

MR. JUSTICE DOUGLAS, concurring:

While I have joined the opinion of the Court, I do not think that the test it lays down is a durable one for the reasons stated by my Brother Harlan. I think, therefore, that it will suffer erosion and in time result in the demise of *Frothingham* v. *Mellon*. It would therefore be . . . wis[e], as I see the problem, to be rid of *Frothingham* here and now. . . .

There need to be no inundation of the federal courts if taxpayers' suits are allowed. There is a wise judicial discretion that usually can distinguish between the frivolous question and the substantial question, between cases ripe for decision and cases that need prior administrative processes, and the like. . . .

MR. JUSTICE STEWART, concurring: [omitted]
MR. JUSTICE FORTAS, concurring: [omitted]
MR. JUSTICE HARLAN, dissenting:

The problems presented by this case are narrow and relatively abstract, but the principles by which they must be resolved involve nothing less than the proper functioning of the federal courts, and so run to the roots of our constitutional system. The nub of my view is that the end result of *Frothingham* v. *Mellon* was correct, even though, like others, I do not subscribe to all of its reasoning and premises. Although I therefore agree with certain of the conclusions reached today by the Court, I cannot accept the standing doctrine that it substitutes for *Frothingham* for it seems to me that this new doctrine rests on premises that do not withstand analysis. Accordingly, I respectfully dissent.

. . . I have not found, and the opinion of the Court has not adduced, historical evidence that properly permits the Court to distinguish, as it has here, among the Establishment Clause, the Tenth Amendment, and the Due Process Clause of the Fifth Amendment as limitations upon Congress' taxing and spending powers.

The Court's position is equally precarious if it is assumed that its premise is that the Establishment Clause is in some uncertain fashion a more "specific" limitation upon Congress' powers than are the various other constitutional commands. . . .

It seems to me clear that public actions, whatever the constitutional provisions on which they are premised, may involve important hazards for the continued effectiveness of the federal judiciary. Although I believe such actions to be within the jurisdiction conferred upon the federal courts by Article III of the Constitution, there surely can be little doubt that they strain the judicial function and press to the limit judicial authority. There is every reason to fear that unrestricted public actions might well alter the allocation of authority among the three branches of the Federal Government. It is not, I submit, enough to say that the present members of the Court would not seize these opportunities for abuse, for such actions would, even without conscious abuse, go far toward the final transformation of this Court into the Council of Revision which, despite Madison's support, was rejected by the Constitutional Convention. I do not doubt that there must be "some effectual power in the government to restrain or correct the infractions" of the Constitution's several commands, but neither can I suppose that such power resides only in the federal courts. . . . The powers of the federal judiciary will be adequate for the great burdens placed upon them only if they are employed prudently, with recognition of the strengths as well as the hazards that go with our kind of representative government.

Presumably the Court recognizes at least certain of these hazards, else it would not have troubled to impose limitations upon the situations in which, and purposes for which, such suits may be brought. Nonetheless, the limitations adopted by the Court are, as I have endeavored to indicate, wholly untenable. This is the more unfortunate because there is available a resolution of this problem that entirely satisfies the demands of the principle of separation of powers. This Court has previously held that individual litigants have standing to represent the public interest, despite their lack of economic or other personal interests, if Congress has appropriately authorized such suits. See especially *Oklahoma* v. *United States Civil Service Comm.*, 330 U.S. 127, 137–139. I would adhere to that principle. . . . The question here is not, despite the Court's unarticulated premise, whether the religious clauses of the First Amendment are hereafter to be enforced by the federal courts; the issue is simply whether plaintiffs of an *additional* category, heretofore excluded from those courts, are to be permitted to maintain suits. The recent history of this Court is replete with illustrations . . . that questions involving the religious clauses will not, if federal taxpayers are prevented from contesting federal expenditures, be left "unacknowledged, unresolved, and undecided."

Accordingly, for the reasons contained in this opinion, I would affirm the judgment of the District Court.

CALDER v. BULL,
3 DALLAS 386 (1798)

This case began with a contest over a will. A probate court in Connecticut disallowed Mr. and Mrs. Bull, the stated beneficiaries in the will of Normand Morrison, from receiving the inheritance. The court instead awarded it to Calder. The Bulls at first decided not to appeal the probate court ruling, but then, over a year and a half later, changed their minds, only to discover that Connecticut law only permits an appeal of probate court rulings made within 18-months of the original ruling. The Bulls went to their friends in the Connecticut legislature, who saw to it that legislation was passed that changed the 18-month rule and permitted the Bulls to appeal. The Bulls successfully appealed. The probate court ruling was overturned and Calder was denied the inheritance. Calder then appealed to the United States Supreme Court, claiming that the Connecticut legislation that permitted the Bulls to make their appeal was in violation of Article 1, Section 10, of the United States Constitution that prohibits states from enacting ex post facto laws.

Votes: Unanimous

MR. JUSTICE CHASE:. . . .

The counsel for the plaintiffs in error, contend, that the said resolution or law of the Legislature of Connecticut, granting a new hearing, in the above case, is an *ex post facto* law, prohibited by the Constitution of the United States; that any law of the federal government, or of any of the state governments, contrary to the constitution of the United States, is void; and that this court possesses the power to declare such law void. . . .

. . . The sole enquiry is, whether this resolution or law of Connecticut, having such operation, is an *ex post facto* law, within the prohibition of the federal constitution?. . . .

I shall endeavor to show what law is to be considered an *ex post facto* law, within the words and meaning of the prohibition in the Federal constitution. . . . The prohibition, in the letter, is not to pass any law concerning and after the fact; but the plain and obvious meaning and intention of the prohibition is this; that the Legislatures of the several states shall not pass laws, after a fact done by a subject or citizen, which shall have relation to such fact, and shall punish him for having done it. The prohibition considered in this light, is an additional bulwark in favor of the personal security of the subject, to protect his person from punishment by legislative acts, having a retrospective operation. I do not think it was inserted to secure the citizen in his private rights, of either property, or contracts. The prohibition not to make anything but gold and silver coin a tender in payment of debts, and not to pass any law impairing the obligation of contracts, were inserted to secure private rights; but the restriction not to pass any *ex post facto* law, was to secure the person of the subject from injury, or punishment, in consequence of such law. If the prohibition against making *ex post facto* laws was intended to secure personal rights from being affected, or injured, by such laws, and the prohibition is sufficiently extensive for that object, the other restraints, I have enumerated, were unnecessary, and therefore improper; for both of them are retrospective.

I will state what laws I consider *ex post facto* laws, within the words and the intent of the prohibition. 1st. Every law that makes an action done before the passing of the law; and which was innocent when done, criminal; and punishes such action. 2d. Every law that aggravates a crime, or makes it greater than it was, when committed. 3rd. Every law that changes the punishment, and inflicts a greater punishment, than the law annexed to the crime, when committed. 4th. Every law that alters the legal rules of evidence, and receives less, or different, testimony, than the law required at the time of the commission of the offense, in order to convict the offender. All these, and similar laws, are manifestly unjust and oppressive. In my opinion, the true distinction is between *ex post facto* laws, and retrospective laws. Every *ex post facto* law must necessarily be retrospective; but every retrospective law is not an *ex post facto* law: The former, only, are prohibited. Every law that takes away, or impairs, rights vested, agreeably to existing laws, is retrospective, and is generally unjust, and may be oppressive; and it is a good general rule, that a law should have no retrospect: but there are cases in which laws may justly, and for the benefit of the community, and also of individuals, relate to a time antecedent to their commencement; as statutes of oblivion, or of pardon. They are certainly retrospective, and literally both concerning, and after, the facts committed. But I do not consider any law *ex post facto* within the prohibition, that mollifies the rigor of the criminal law; but only those that create, or aggravate, the crime; or increase the punishment, or change the rules of evidence, for the purpose of conviction. Every law that is to have an operation before the making thereof, as to commence at an antecedent time; or to save time from the statute of limitations; or to excuse acts which were unlawful, and before committed, and the like; is retrospective. But such laws may be proper or necessary, as the case may be. There is a great and apparent difference between making an unlawful act lawful; and the making an innocent action criminal, and punishing it as a crime. The expressions "*ex post facto* laws," are technical, they had been in use long before the Revolution, and had acquired an appropriate meaning, by legislators, lawyers, and authors. . . .

I am under a necessity to give a construction, or explanation of the words "*ex post facto* laws," because they have not any certain meaning attached to them. But I will not go farther than I feel myself bound to do; and if I ever exercise the jurisdiction I will not decide any law to be void, but in a very clear case.

I am of opinion, that the decree of the supreme court of errors of Connecticut be affirmed, with costs.

MR. JUSTICE PATERSON:. . . .

It may, in general, be truly observed of retrospective laws of every description, that they neither accord with sound legislation, nor the fundamental principles of the social compact. But on full consideration, I am convinced, that *ex post facto* laws must be limited in the manner already expressed; they must be taken in their technical, which is also their common and general acceptation, and are not to be understood in their literal sense.

MR. JUSTICE IREDELL:. . . . I concur in the general result of the opinions, which have been delivered. . . .

MR. JUSTICE CUSHING: The case appears to me to be clear of all difficulty, taken either way. If the act is a judicial act, it is not touched by the federal constitution; and, if it is a legislative act, it is maintained and justified by the ancient and uniform practice of the state of Connecticut.

Judgment affirmed.

THE SLAUGHTERHOUSE CASES,
16 WALLACE 36 (1873)

The Slaughterhouse Cases provided the first test of the major provisions of the first section of the Fourteenth Amendment. Although the intent of the amendment had been at the very least to reverse the Dred Scott decision, and to provide basic civil rights and liberties for black Americans, the words of the first section were vague—"privileges or immunities," "due process," "equal protection of the laws"—and the scope of the amendment's protection was unclear. It was supreme irony that the first case to confront the Court with putting concrete meaning into the Fourteenth Amendment was brought by whites, not blacks, and argued on the grounds that the amendment should be broadly construed to limit the states from interfering with individual civil rights and liberties. The case had its genesis in the granting of a corporate charter by the Louisiana legislature in 1869 to the Crescent City Livestock Landing & Slaughterhouse Company, a slaughterhouse that was given an effective monopoly of the slaughterhouse business in New Orleans. The impact of this legislative action was to put over 1000 smaller-scale butchers and slaughterhouses out of business. The Louisiana monopoly was granted under the state's police power as a public health measure to remove the various slaughterhouses from the heavily populated sections of the city and centralize slaughtering operations. But the displaced butchers thought otherwise and brought suit claiming that their privileges or immunities as citizens of the United States were denied them. That is, they argued that the right to engage in a lawful occupation is one of the privileges or immunities of being a citizen of the United States. They also argued that the Louisiana legislature by, in effect, closing their businesses denied them their property without due process of law. In addition, they claimed that they were treated unequally in violation of the equal protection of the laws guarantee of the Fourteenth Amendment. A subsidiary claim was that by requiring all slaughtering of animals to be done by the monopoly, the other butchers were placed in a position of involuntary servitude forbidden by the Thirteenth Amendment. Justice Miller, speaking for a five-man majority, rejected these contentions as seen in the opinion that follows.

Majority votes: 5
Dissenting votes: 4

MR. JUSTICE MILLER delivered the opinion of the Court:. . . .

It cannot be denied that the statute under consideration is aptly framed to remove from the more densely populated part of the city, the noxious slaughterhouses, and large and offensive collections of animals necessarily incident to the slaughtering business of a large city, and to locate them where the convenience, health, and comfort of the people require they shall be located. And it must be conceded that the means adopted by the act for this purpose are appropriate, are stringent, and effectual. But it is said that in creating a corporation for this purpose, and conferring upon it exclusive privileges—privileges which it is said constitute a monopoly—the legislature has exceeded its power. If this statue had imposed on the city of New Orleans precisely the same duties, accompanied by the same privileges, which it has on the corporation which it created, it is believed that no question would have been raised as to its constitutionality. In that case the effect on the butchers in pursuit of their occupation and on the public would have been the same as it is now. Why cannot the legislature confer the same powers on another corporation, created for a lawful and useful public object, that it can on the municipal corporation already existing? That wherever a legislature has the right to accomplish a certain result, and that result is best attained by means of a corporation, it has the right to create such a corporation, and to endow it with the powers necessary to effect the desired and lawful purpose, seems hardly to admit of debate. The proposition is ably discussed and affirmed in the case of *McCulloch* v. *The State of Maryland*, in relation to the power of Congress to organize the Bank of the United States to aid in the fiscal operations of the government. . . .

It may, therefore, be considered as established, that the authority of the legislature of Louisiana to pass the present statute is ample, unless some restraint in the exercise of that power be found. . . .

The plaintiffs in error accepting this issue, allege that the statute is a violation of the Constitution of the United States in these several particulars:

That it creates an involuntary servitude forbidden by the thirteenth article of amendment;

That it abridges the privileges and immunities of citizens of the United States;

That it denies to the plaintiffs the equal protection of the laws; and,

That it deprives them of their property without due process of law; contrary to the provisions of the first section of the fourteenth article of amendment.

This court is thus called upon for the first time to give construction to these articles. . . .

The most cursory glance at these articles discloses a unity of purpose, when taken in connection with the history of the times, which cannot fail to have an important bearing on any question of doubt concerning their true meaning. . . .

. . . [O]n the most casual examination of the language of these amendments, no one can fail to be impressed with the one pervading purpose found in them all, lying at the foundation of each, and without which none of them would have been even suggested; we mean the freedom of the slave race, the security and firm establishment of that freedom, and the protection of the newly-made freeman and citizen from the oppressions of those who had formerly exercised unlimited dominion over him. It is true that only the fifteenth amendment, in terms, mentions the negro by speaking of his color and his slavery. But it is just as true that each of the other articles was addressed to the grievances of that race, and designed to remedy them as the fifteenth.

We do not say that no one else but the negro can share in this protection. . . . But what we do say, and what we wish to be understood is, that in any fair and just construction of any section or phrase of these amendments, it is necessary to look to the purpose which we have said was the pervading spirit of them all, the evil which they were designed to remedy, and the process of continued addition to the Constitution, until that purpose was supposed to be accomplished, as far as constitutional law can accomplish it.

The first section of the fourteenth article, to which our attention is more specially invited, opens with a definition of citizenship—not only citizenship of the United States, but citizenship of the States. . . .

The first observation we have to make on this clause is, that it puts at rest both the questions which we stated to have been the subject of differences of opinion. It declares that persons may be citizens of the United States without regard to their citizenship of a particular State, and it overturns the *Dred Scott* decision by making *all persons* born within the United States and subject to its jurisdiction citizens of the United States. . . .

The next observation is more important in view of the arguments of counsel in the present case. It is, that the distinction between citizenship of the United States and citizenship of a State is clearly recognized and established. Not only may a man be a citizen of the United States without being a citizen of a State, but an important element is necessary to convert the former into the latter. He must reside within the State to make him a citizen of it, but it is only necessary that he should be born or naturalized in the United States to be a citizen of the Union.

It is quite clear, then, that there is a citizenship of the United States, and a citizenship of a State, which are distinct from each other, and which depend upon different characteristics of circumstances in the individual.

We think this distinction and its explicit recognition in this amendment of great weight in this argument, because the next paragraph of this same section, which is the one mainly relied on by the plaintiffs in error, speaks only of privileges and immunities of citizens of the United States, and does not speak of those of citizens of the several States. The argument, however, in favor of the plaintiffs rests wholly on the assumption that the citizenship is the same, and the privileges and immunities guaranteed by the clause are the same.

The language is, "No State shall make or enforce any law which shall abridge the privileges or immunities of citizens of *the United States.*" It is a little remarkable, if this clause was intended as a protection to the citizen of a State against the legislative power of his own State, that the word citizen of the State should be left out when it is so carefully used, and used in contradistinction to citizens of the United States, in the very sentence which precedes it. It is too clear for argument that the change in phraseology was adopted understandingly and with a purpose. . . .

If, then, there is a difference between the privileges and immunities belonging to a citizen of the United States as such, and those belonging to the citizen of the State as such the latter must rest for their security and protection where they have heretofore rested; for they are not embraced by this paragraph of the amendment. . . .

In the Constitution of the United States . . . is found in section two of the fourth article, the following words: "The citizens of each State shall be entitled to all the privileges and immunities of citizens of the several States." . . .

Fortunately we are not without judicial construction of this clause of the Constitution. The leading case on the subject is that of *Corfield* v. *Coryell,* decided by Mr. Justice Washington in the Circuit Court for the District of Pennsylvania in 1823.

"The inquiry," he says, "is, what are the privileges and immunities of citizens of the several States? We feel no hesitation in confining these expressions to those privileges and immunities which are *fundamental;* which belong of right to the citizens of all free governments, and which have at all times been enjoyed by citizens of the several States which compose this Union, from the time of their becoming free, independent, and sovereign. What these fundamental principles are, it would be more tedious than difficult to enumerate. They may all, however, be comprehended under the following general heads: protection by the government, with the right to acquire and possess property of every kind, and to pursue and obtain happiness and

safety, subject, nevertheless, to such restraints as the government may prescribe for the general good of the whole." . . .

Was it the purpose of the fourteenth amendment, by the simple declaration that no State should make or enforce any law which shall abridge the privileges and immunities of *citizens of the United States,* to transfer the security and protection of all the civil rights which we have mentioned, from the States to the Federal government? And where it is declared that Congress shall have the power to enforce that article, was it intended to bring within the power of Congress the entire domain of civil rights heretofore belonging exclusively to the States?

All this and more must follow, if the proposition of the plaintiffs in error be sound. For not only are these rights subject to the control of Congress whenever in its discretion any of them are supposed to be abridged by State legislation, but that body may also pass laws in advance, limiting and restricting the exercise of legislative power by the States, in their most ordinary and usual functions, as in its judgment it may think proper on all such subjects. And still further, such a construction followed by the reversal of the judgments of the Supreme Court of Louisiana in these cases, would constitute this court a perpetual censor upon all legislation of the states, on the civil rights of their own citizens, with authority to nullify such as it did not approve as consistent with those rights, as they existed at the time of the adoption of this amendment. The argument we admit is not always the most conclusive which is drawn from the consequences urged against the adoption of a particular construction of an instrument. But when, as in the case before us, these consequences are so serious, so far reaching and pervading, so great a departure from the structure and spirit of our institutions; when the effect is to fetter and degrade the State governments by subjecting them to the control of Congress, in the exercise of powers heretofore universally conceded to them of the most ordinary and fundamental character; when in fact it radically changes the whole theory of the relations of the State and Federal governments to the people; the argument has a force that is irresistible, in the absence of language which expresses such a purpose too clearly to admit of doubt.

We are convinced that no such results were intended by the Congress which proposed these amendments, nor by the legislatures of the States which ratified them.

Having shown that the privileges and immunities relied on in the argument are those which belong to citizens of the States as such, and that they are left to the State governments for security and protection, and not by this article placed under the special care of the Federal government, we may hold ourselves excused from defining the privileges and immunities of citizens of the United States which no State can abridge, until some case involving those privileges may make it necessary to do so.

But lest it should be said that no such privileges and immunities are to be found if those we have been considering are excluded, we venture to suggest some which owe their existence to the Federal government, its National character, its Constitution, or its laws.

One of these is . . . the right of the citizen of this great country, protected by implied guarantees of its Constitution, "to come to the seat of government to assert any claim he may have upon that government, to transact any business he may have with it, to seek its protection, to share its offices, to engage in administering its functions. He has the right of free access to its seaports, through which all operations of foreign commerce are conducted, to the subtreasuries, land offices, and courts of justice in the several States." . . .

Another privilege of a citizen of the United States is to demand the care and protection of the Federal government over his life, liberty, and property when on the high seas or within the jurisdiction of a foreign government. Of this there can be no doubt, nor that the right depends upon his character as a citizen of the United States. The right to peaceably assemble and petition for redress of grievances, the privilege of the writ of *habeas corpus,* are rights of the citizen guaranteed by the Federal Constitution. The right to use the navigable waters of the United States, however they may penetrate the territory of the several States, all rights secured to our citizens by treaties with foreign nations, are dependent upon citizenship of the United States, and not citizenship of a State. One of these privileges is conferred by the very article under consideration. It is that a citizen of the United States can, of his own volition, become a citizen of any State of the Union by a *bona fide* residence therein, with the same rights as other citizens of that State. To these may be added the rights secured by the thirteenth and fifteenth articles of amendment, and by the other clause of the fourteenth, next to be considered.

But it is useless to pursue this branch of the inquiry, since we are of opinion that the rights claimed by these plaintiffs in error, if they have any existence, are not privileges and immunities of citizens of the United States within the meaning of the clause of the fourteenth amendment under consideration. . . .

The argument has not been much pressed in these cases that the defendant's charter deprives the plaintiffs of their property without due process of the law, or that it denies to them the equal protection of the law. The first of these paragraphs has been in the Constitution since the adoption of the fifth amendment, as a restraint upon the Federal power. It is also to be found in some form of expression in the constitutions of nearly all the States, as a restraint upon the power of the States. This law, then, has practically been the same as it now is during the existence of the government, except so far as the present amendment may place the restraining power over the States in this matter in the hands of the Federal government.

We are not without judicial interpretation, therefore, both State and National, of the meaning of this clause. And it is sufficient to say that under no construction of that provision that we have ever seen, or any that we deem admissible, can the restraint imposed by the State of Louisiana upon the exercise of their trade by the butchers of New Orleans be held to be a deprivation of property within the meaning of that provision.

"Nor shall any State deny to any person within its jurisdiction the equal protection of the laws."

In the light of the history of these amendments, and the pervading purpose of them, which we have already discussed, it is not difficult to give a meaning to this clause. The existence of laws in the States where the newly emancipated negroes resided, which discriminated with gross injustice and hardship against them as a class, was the evil to be remedied by this clause, and by it such laws are forbidden.

If, however, the States did not conform their laws to its requirements, then by the fifth section of the article of amendment Congress was authorized to enforce it by suitable legislation. We doubt very much whether any action of a State not directed by way of discrimination against the negroes as a class, or on account of their race, will ever be held to come within the purview of this provision. It is so clearly a provision for that race and that emergency, that a strong case would be necessary for its application to any other. . . .

The judgments of the Supreme Court of Louisiana in these cases are

Affirmed.

Mr. Justice Field, dissenting:. . . .

The question presented is . . . one of the gravest

importance, not merely to the parties here, but to the whole country. It is nothing less than the question whether the recent amendments to the Federal Constitution protect the citizens of the United States against the deprivation of their common rights by State legislation. In my judgment the fourteenth amendment does afford such protection, and was so intended by the Congress which framed and the States which adopted it. . . .

The first clause of this amendment determines who are citizens of the United States, and how their citizenship is created. . . . It recognizes in express terms, if it does not create, citizens of the United States, and it makes their citizenship dependent upon the place of their birth, or the fact of their adoption, and not upon the constitution or laws of any State or the condition of their ancestry. A citizen of a State is now only a citizen of the United States residing in that State. The fundamental rights, privileges, and immunities which belong to him as a free man and a free citizen, now belong to him as a citizen of the United States, and are not dependent upon his citizenship of any State. The exercise of these rights and privileges, and the degree of enjoyment received from such exercise, are always more or less affected by the condition and the local institutions of the State, or city, or town where he resides. . . . [But] they do not derive their existence from its legislation, and cannot be destroyed by its power.

The amendment does not attempt to confer any new privileges or immunities upon citizens, or to enumerate or define those already existing. It assumes that there are such privileges and immunities which belong of right to citizens as such, and ordains that they shall not be abridged by State legislation. If this inhibition has no reference to privileges and immunities of this character, but only refers, as held by the majority of the court in their opinion, to such privileges and immunities as were before its adoption specially designated in the Constitution or necessarily implied as belonging to citizens of the United States, it was a vain and idle enactment, which accomplished nothing, and most unnecessarily excited Congress and the people on its passage. With privileges and immunities thus designated or implied no State could ever have interfered by its laws, and no new constitutional provision was required to inhibit such interference. The supremacy of the Constitution and the laws of the United States always controlled any State legislation of that character. But if the amendment refers to the natural and inalienable rights which belong to all citizens, the inhibition has a profound significance and consequence.

What, then, are the privileges and immunities which are secured against abridgment by State legislation?

In the first section of the Civil Rights Act Congress has given its interpretation to these terms, or at least has stated some of the rights which, in its judgment, these terms include; the right "to make and enforce contracts, to sue, be parties and give evidence, to inherit, purchase, lease, sell, hold, and convey real and personal property, and to full and equal benefit of all laws and proceedings for the security of person and property." That act, it is true, was passed before the fourteenth amendment, but the amendment was adopted, as I have already said, to obviate objections to the act, or, speaking more accurately, I should say, to obviate objections to legislation of a similar character, extending the protection of the National government over the common rights of all citizens of the United States. Accordingly, after its ratification, Congress [in 1870] reenacted the act under the belief that whatever doubts may have previously existed of its validity, they were removed by the amendment.

The terms, privileges and immunities, are not new in the amendment; they were in the Constitution before the amendment was adopted. They are found in the second section of the fourth article, which declares that "the citizens of each State shall be entitled to all privileges and immunities of citizens in the several States." . . .

What the clause in question did for the protection of the citizens of one State against hostile and discriminating legislation of other States, the fourteenth amendment does for the protection of every citizen of the United States against hostile and discriminating legislation against him in favor of others, whether they reside in the same or in different States. If under the fourth article of the Constitution equality of privileges and immunities is secured between citizens of different States, under the fourteenth amendment the same equality is secured between citizens of the United States. . . .

Now, what the clause in question does for the protection of citizens of one State against the creation of monopolies in favor of citizens of other States, the fourteenth amendment does for the protection of every citizen of the United States against the creation of any monopoly whatever. . . .

In all these cases there is a recognition of the equality of right among citizens in the pursuit of the ordinary avocations of life, and a declaration that all grants of exclusive privileges, in contravention of this equality, are against common right, and void.

This equality of right, with exemption from all

disparaging and partial enactments, in the lawful pursuits of life, throughout the whole country, is the distinguishing privilege of citizens of the United States. To them, everywhere, all pursuits, all professions, all avocations are open without other restrictions than such as are imposed equally upon all others of the same age, sex, and condition. The State may prescribe such regulations for every pursuit and calling of life as will promote the public health, secure the good order and advance the general prosperity of society, but when once prescribed, the pursuit or calling must be free to be followed by every citizen who is within the conditions designated, and will conform to the regulations. This is the fundamental idea upon which our institutions rest, and unless adhered to in the legislation of the country, our government will be a republic only in name. The fourteenth amendment, in my judgment, makes it essential to the validity of the legislation of every State that this equality of right should be respected. . . .

I am authorized by CHIEF JUSTICE CHASE, MR. JUSTICE SWAYNE, and MR. JUSTICE BRADLEY, to state that they concur with me in this dissenting opinion.

MR. JUSTICE BRADLEY, also dissenting: . . . .

In my view, a law which prohibits a large class of citizens from adopting a lawful employment, or from following a lawful employment previously adopted, does deprive them of liberty as well as property, without due process of law. Their right of choice is a portion of their liberty; their occupation is their property. Such a law also deprives those citizens of the equal protection of the laws, contrary to the last clause of the section. . . .

It is futile to argue that none but persons of the African race are intended to be benefited by this amendment. They may have been the primary cause of the amendment, but its language is general, embracing all citizens, and I think it was purposely so expressed. . . .

. . . [E]ven if the business of the National courts should be increased [because of cases seeking to define the broad concept favored by Bradley of privileges or immunities], Congress could easily supply the remedy by increasing their number and efficiency. The great question is, What is the true construction of the amendment? When once we find that, we shall find the means of giving it effect. The argument from inconvenience ought not to have a very controlling influence in questions of this sort. The National will and National interest are of far greater importance. . . .

MR. JUSTICE SWAYNE, dissenting: [omitted]

GRISWOLD v. CONNECTICUT,
381 U.S. 479 (1965)

Connecticut's birth control statute made it a crime for "any person" married or unmarried to use "any drug, medicinal article or instrument for the purpose of preventing conception." Furthermore, the law specified that any person who assists another in violating the law shall be punished "as if he were the principal offender." Estelle Griswold, Executive Director of the Planned Parenthood League of Connecticut, and Dr. Buxton, a professor of medicine at the Yale Medical School, were arrested for having violated the state law by dispensing birth control information and advice to married persons. They were convicted and their convictions were upheld by the Connecticut courts. They claimed that the statute violated the Fourteenth Amendment.

Majority votes: 7
Dissenting votes: 2

MR. JUSTICE DOUGLAS delivered the opinion of the Court: . . . .

Coming to the merits, we are met with a wide range of questions that implicate the Due Process Clause of the Fourteenth Amendment. Overtones of some arguments suggest that *Lochner* v. *State of New York,* 198 U.S. 45, should be our guide. But we decline that invitation. . . . We do not sit as super-legislature to determine the wisdom, need, and propriety of laws that touch economic problems, business affairs, or social conditions. This law, however, operates directly on an intimate relation of husband and wife and their physician's role in one aspect of that relation.

The association of people is not mentioned in the Constitution nor in the Bill of Rights. The right to educate a child in a school of the parents' choice—whether public or private or parochial—is also not mentioned. Nor is the right to study any particular subject or any foreign language. Yet the First Amendment has been construed to include certain of those rights. . . .

In *NAACP* v. *State of Alabama,* 357 U.S. 449, we protected the "freedom to associate and privacy in one's associations," noting that freedom of association was a peripheral First Amendment right. Disclosure of membership lists of a constitutionally valid association, we held, was invalid "as entailing the likelihood of a substantial restraint upon the exercise by petitioner's members of their right to freedom of association." In other words, the First Amendment has a penumbra where privacy is protected from governmental intrusion. In like context, we have protected forms of "association" that are not political in the customary sense but pertain to the social, legal, and economic benefit of the members. In *Schware* v. *Board of Bar Examiners*, 353 U.S. 232, we held it not permissible to bar a lawyer from practice, because he had once been a member of the Communist Party. The man's "association with that Party" was not shown to be "anything more than a political faith in a political party" and was not action of a kind proving bad moral character.

Those cases involved more than the "right of assembly"—a right that extends to all irrespective of their race or ideology. The right of "association," like the right of belief is more than the right to attend a meeting; it includes the right to express one's attitudes or philosophies by membership in a group or by affiliation with it or by other lawful means. Association in that context is a form of expression of opinion; and while it is not expressly included in the First Amendment its existence is necessary in making the express guarantees fully meaningful.

The foregoing cases suggest that specific guarantees in the Bill of Rights have penumbras, formed by emanations from those guarantees that help give them life and substance. Various guarantees create zones of privacy. The right of association contained in the penumbra of the First Amendment is one, as we have seen. The Third Amendment in its prohibition against the quartering of soldiers "in any house" in time of peace without the consent of the owner is another facet of that privacy. The Fourth Amendment explicitly affirms the "right of the people to be secure in their persons, houses, papers, and effects, against unreasonable searches and seizures." The Fifth Amendment in its Self-Incrimination Clause enables the citizen to create a zone of privacy which government may not force him to surrender to his detriment. The Ninth Amendment provides: "The enumeration in the Constitution, of certain rights, shall not be construed to deny or disparage others retained by the people."

The Fourth and Fifth Amendments were described in *Boyd* v. *United States,* 116 U.S. 616, 630 as protection against all governmental invasions "of the sanctity of a man's home and the privacies of life." We recently referred in *Mapp* v. *Ohio,* 367 U.S. 643, 656 to the Fourth Amendment as creating a "right to privacy, no less important than any other right carefully and particularly reserved to the people." . . .

The present case, then, concerns a relationship lying within the zone of privacy created by several fundamental constitutional guarantees. And it concerns a law which, in forbidding the use of contraceptives rather than regulating their manufacture or sale, seeks to achieve its goals by means having a maximum destructive impact upon that relationship. Such a law cannot stand in light of the familiar principle, so often applied by this Court, that a "governmental purpose to control or prevent activities constitutionally subject to state regulation may not be achieved by means which sweep unnecessarily broadly and thereby invade the area of protected freedoms." *NAACP* v. *Alabama,* 377 U.S. 288, 307. Would we allow the police to search the sacred precincts of marital bedrooms for telltale signs of the use of contraceptives? The very idea is repulsive to the notions of privacy surrounding the marriage relationship.

We deal with a right to privacy older than the Bill of Rights—older than our political parties, older than our school system. Marriage is a coming together for better or for worse, hopefully enduring, and intimate to the degree of being sacred. It is an association that promotes a way of life, not causes; a harmony in living, not political faiths; a bilateral loyalty, not commercial or social projects. Yet it is an association for as noble a purpose as any involved in our prior decisions.

Reversed.

MR. JUSTICE GOLDBERG, whom CHIEF JUSTICE WARREN and MR. JUSTICE BRENNAN join, concurring:

I agree with the Court that Connecticut's birth-control law unconstitutionally intrudes upon the right of marital privacy, and I join in its opinion and judgment. Although I have not accepted the view that "due process" as used in the Fourteenth Amendment includes all of the first eight Amendments . . . I do agree that the concept of liberty protects those personal rights that are fundamental, and is not confined to the specific terms of the Bill of Rights. My conclusion that the concept of liberty is not so restricted and that it embraces the right of marital privacy though that right is not mentioned explicitly in the Constitution is supported both by numerous decisions of this Court, referred to in the Court's opinion, and by the language and history of the Ninth Amendment. In reaching the conclusion that the right of marital privacy is protected, as being within the protected penumbra of specific guarantees of the Bill of Rights, the Court refers to the Ninth Amendment. I add these words to emphasize the relevance of that Amendment to the Court's holding. . . . The Framers did not intend that the first eight amendments be construed to exhaust the basic and fundamental rights which the Constitution guaranteed to the people.

While this Court has had little occasion to interpret the Ninth Amendment "[i]t cannot be presumed that any clause in the constitution is intended to be without effect." *Marbury* v. *Madison,* 1 Cranch 137, 174, 2 L.Ed. 60. In interpreting the Constitution, "real effect should be given to all the words it uses." *Myers* v. *United States,* 272 U.S. 52, 151. The Ninth Amendment to the Constitution may be regarded by some as a recent discovery but since 1791 it has been a basic part of the Constitution which we are sworn to uphold. To hold that a right so basic and fundamental and so deep-rooted in our society as the right of privacy in marriage may be infringed because that right is not guaranteed in so many words by the first eight amendments to the Constitution is to ignore the Ninth Amendment and to give it no effect whatsoever. Moreover, a judicial construction that this fundamental right is not protected by the Constitution because it is not mentioned in explicit terms by one of the first eight amendments or elsewhere in the Constitution would violate the Ninth Amendment, which specifically states that "[t]he enumeration in the Constitution, of certain rights shall not be *construed* to deny or disparage others retained by the people." (Emphasis added.) . . . [T]he Ninth Amendment simply lends strong support to the view that the "liberty" protected by the Fifth and Fourteenth Amendments from infringement by the Federal Government or the States is not restricted to rights specifically mentioned in the first eight amendments. . . .

In sum, I believe that the right of privacy in the marital relation is fundamental and basic—a personal right "retained by the people" within the meaning of the Ninth Amendment. Connecticut cannot constitutionally abridge this fundamental right, which is protected by the Fourteenth Amendment from infringement by the States. I agree with the Court that petitioners' convictions must therefore be reversed.

MR. JUSTICE HARLAN, concurring in the judgment:. . . .

In my view, the proper constitutional inquiry in this case is whether this Connecticut statute infringes the Due Process Clause of the Fourteenth Amendment because the enactment violates basic values "implicit in the concept of ordered liberty," *Palko* v. *State of Connecticut,* 302 U.S. 319, 325. . . . I believe that it does. While the relevant inquiry may be aided by resort to one or more of the provisions of the Bill of Rights, it is not dependent on them or any of their radiations. The Due Process Clause of the Fourteenth Amendment stands, in my opinion, on its own bottom. . . .

MR. JUSTICE WHITE, concurring in the judgment: [omitted]

MR. JUSTICE BLACK, with whom MR. JUSTICE STEWART joins, dissenting:. . . .

The Court talks about a constitutional "right of privacy" as though there is some constitutional provision or provisions forbidding any law ever to be passed which might abridge the "privacy" of individuals. But there is not. . . .

One of the most effective ways of diluting or expanding a constitutionally guaranteed right is to substitute for the crucial word or words of a constitutional guarantee another word or words, more or less flexible and more or less restricted in meaning. This fact is well illustrated by the use of the term "right of privacy" as a comprehensive substitute for the Fourth Amendment's guarantee against "unreasonable searches and seizures." "Privacy" is a broad, abstract and ambiguous concept which can easily be shrunken in meaning but which can also, on the other hand, easily be interpreted as a constitutional ban against many things other than searches and seizures. I have expressed the view many times that First Amendment freedoms, for example, have suffered from a failure of the courts to stick to the simple language of the First Amendment in construing it, instead of invoking multitudes of words substituted for those the Framers used. For these reasons I get nowhere in this case by talk about a constitutional "right of privacy" as an emanation from one or more constitutional provisions. I like my privacy as well as the next one, but I am nevertheless compelled to admit that government has a right to invade it unless prohibited by some specific constitutional provision. For these reasons I cannot agree with the Court's judgment and the reasons it gives for holding this Connecticut law unconstitutional. . . .

My Brother Goldberg has adopted the recent discovery that the Ninth Amendment as well as the Due Process Clause can be used by this Court as authority to strike down all state legislation which this Court thinks violates "fundamental principles of liberty and justice," or is contrary to the "traditions and [collective] conscience of our people." He also states, without proof satisfactory to me, that in making decisions on this basis judges will not consider "their personal and private notions." One may ask how they can avoid considering them. Our Court certainly has no machinery with which to take a Gallup Poll. And the scientific miracles of this age have not yet produced a gadget which the Court can use to determine what traditions are rooted in the "[collective] conscience of our people." Moreover, one would certainly have to look far beyond the language of the Ninth Amendment to find that the Framers vested in this Court any such awesome veto powers over lawmaking, either by the States or by the Congress. Nor does anything in the history of the Amendment offer any support for such a shocking doctrine. The whole history of the adoption of the Constitution and Bill of Rights points the other way, and the very material quoted by my Brother Goldberg shows that the Ninth Amendment was intended to protect against the idea that "by enumerating particular exceptions to the grant of power" to the Federal Government, "those rights were not singled out, were intended to be assigned into the hands of the General Government [the United States], and were consequently insecure." That Amendment was passed, not to broaden the powers of this Court or any other department of "the General Government," but, as every student of history knows, to assure the people that the Constitution in all its provisions was intended to limit the Federal Government to the powers granted expressly or by necessary implication. If any broad, unlimited power to hold laws unconstitutional because they offend what this Court conceives to be the "[collective] conscience of our people" is vested in this Court by the Ninth Amendment, the Fourteenth Amendment, or any other provision of the Constitution, it was not given by the Framers, but rather has been bestowed on the Court by the Court. This fact is perhaps responsible for the peculiar phenomenon that for a period of a century and a half no serious suggestion was ever made that the Ninth Amendment, enacted to protect state powers against federal invasion, could be used as a weapon of federal power to prevent state legislatures from passing laws they consider appropriate to govern local affairs. Use of any such broad, unbounded judicial authority would make of this Court's members a day-to-day constitutional convention. . . .

MR. JUSTICE STEWART, whom MR. JUSTICE BLACK joins, dissenting: [omitted]

ROE v. WADE,
410 U.S. 113 (1973)

Jane Roe (not her real name) was single and pregnant and wanted to have an abortion. She lived in Dallas, Texas, but Texas, like other states, made abortion a state crime if performed for reasons other than saving the life of the mother. Roe went into federal district court in Dallas and asked the court to declare the Texas criminal abortion statute unconstitutional as an inherent deprivation of her liberty without due process of law which was in violation of the Fourteenth Amendment. She also asked the court to enjoin Dallas District Attorney Henry Wade from enforcing the statute. The federal district court ruled the statute unconstitutional, but did not issue an injunction against enforcement. Both sides appealed and the case came before the Supreme Court.

Majority votes: 7
Dissenting votes: 2

MR. JUSTICE BLACKMUN delivered the opinion of the Court:. . . .

It perhaps is not generally appreciated that the restrictive criminal abortion laws in effect in a majority of States today are of relatively recent vintage. Those laws, generally proscribing abortion or its attempt at any time during pregnancy except when necessary to preserve the pregnant woman's life, are not of ancient or even of common law origin. Instead, they derive from statutory changes effected, for the most part, in the latter half of the 19th century.

1. *Ancient attitudes*. These are not capable of precise determination. We are told that at the time of the Persian Empire abortifacients were known and that criminal abortions were severely punished. We are also told, however, that abortion was practiced in Greek times as well as in the Roman Era, and that "it was resorted to without scruple." . . . Greek and Roman law afforded little protection to the unborn. . . . Ancient religion did not bar abortion.

2. *The Hippocratic Oath*. What then of the famous Oath that has stood so long as the ethical guide of the medical profession and that bears the name of the Greek who has been described as the Father of Medicine. . . . The Oath varies somewhat according to the particular translation, but in any translation the content is clear: "I will give no deadly medicine to anyone if asked, nor suggest any such counsel; and in like manner I will not give to a woman a pessary to produce abortion." . . .

. . . . [T]he Oath [however] originated in a group representing only a small segment of Greek opinion and . . . it certainly was not accepted by all ancient physicians. . . . [M]edical writings down to Galen (130–200 A.D.) "give evidence of the violation of almost every one of its injunctions." But with the end of antiquity a decided change took place. Resistance against suicide and against abortion became common. The Oath came to be popular. The emerging teachings of Christianity were in agreement with the Pythagorean ethic. The Oath "became the nucleus of all medical ethics" and "was applauded as the embodiment of truth." . . .

This, it seems to us, is a satisfactory and acceptable explanation of the Hippocratic Oath's apparent rigidity. It enables us to understand, in historical context, a long accepted and revered statement of medical ethics.

3. *The Common Law.* It is undisputed that at the common law, abortion performed *before* "quickening"—the first recognizable movement of the fetus *in utero,* appearing usually from the 16th to the 18th week of pregnancy—was not an indictable offense. The absence of a common law crime for pre-quickening abortion appears to have developed from a confluence of earlier philosophical, theological, and civil and canon law concepts of when life begins. These disciplines variously approached the question in terms of the point at which the embryo or fetus became "formed" or recognizably human, or in terms of when a "person" came into being, that is, infused with a "soul" or "animated." A loose consensus evolved in early English law that these events occurred at some point between conception and live birth. . . . There was agreement that prior to this point the fetus was to be regarded as part of the mother and its destruction, therefore, was not homicide. . . . The significance of quickening was echoed by later common law scholars and found its way into the received common law in this country.

Whether abortion of a *quick* fetus was a felony at common law, or even a lesser crime, is still disputed. . . . [I]t now appears doubtful that abortion was ever firmly established as a common law crime even with respect to the destruction of a quick fetus.

4. *The English statutory law.* England's first criminal abortion statute, came in 1803. . . .

Recently Parliament enacted a new abortion law. This is the Abortion Act of 1967. The Act permits . . . a physician, to terminate a pregnancy where he is of the good faith opinion that the abortion "is immediately necessary to save the life or to prevent grave permanent injury to the physical or mental health of the pregnant woman."

5. *The American law.* In this country the law in effect in all but a few States until mid-19th century was the pre-existing English common law. . . . In 1828 New York enacted legislation that, in two respects, was to serve as a model for early antiabortion statutes. First, while barring destruction of an unquickened fetus as well as a quick fetus, it made the former only a misdemeanor, but the latter second-degree manslaughter. Second, it incorporated a concept of therapeutic abortion by providing that an abortion was excused if it "shall have been necessary to preserve the life of such mother, or shall have been advised by two physicians to be necessary for such purpose." By 1840, when Texas had received the common law, only eight American States had statutes dealing with abortion. It was not until after the War Between the States that legislation began generally to replace the common law. Most of these initial statutes dealt severely with abortion after quickening but were lenient with it before quickening. Most punished attempts equally with completed abortions. While many statutes included the exception for an abortion thought by one or more physicians to be necessary to save the mother's life, that provision soon disappeared and the typical law required that the procedure actually be necessary for that purpose.

Gradually, in the middle and late 19th century the quickening distinction disappeared from the statutory law of most States and the degree of the offense and the penalties were increased. By the end of the 1950's, a large majority of the States banned abortion, however and whenever performed, unless done to save or preserve the life of the mother. . . . Three other States permitted abortions that were not "unlawfully" performed or that were not "without lawful justification." In the past several years, however, a trend toward liberalization of abortion statutes has resulted in adoption, by about one-third of the States, of less stringent laws. . . .

It is thus apparent that at common law, at the time of the adoption of our Constitution, and throughout the major portion of the 19th century, abortion was viewed with less disfavor than under most American statutes currently in effect. Phrasing it another way, a woman enjoyed a substantially broader right to terminate a pregnancy than she does in most States today. At least with respect to the early stage of pregnancy, and very possibly without such a limitation, the opportunity to make this choice was present in this country well into the 19th century. Even later, the law continued for some time to treat less punitively an abortion procured in early pregnancy. . . .

Parties challenging state abortion laws have sharply disputed in some courts the contention that a purpose of these laws, when enacted, was to protect prenatal life. Pointing to the absence of legislative history to support the contention, they claim that most state laws were designed solely to protect the woman. Because medical advances have lessened this concern, at least with respect to abortion in early pregnancy, they argue that with respect to such abortions the laws can no longer be justified by any state interest. . . .

The Constitution does not explicitly mention any right of privacy. In a line of decisions, however, going back perhaps as far as *Union Pacific R. Co.* v. *Botsford*, 141 U.S. 250, 251 (1891), the Court has recognized that a right of personal privacy, or a guarantee of certain areas or zones of privacy, does exist under the Constitution. In varying contexts the Court or individual Justices have indeed found at least the roots of that right in the First Amendment, *Stanley* v. *Georgia*, 394 U.S. 557, 564 (1969); in the Fourth and Fifth Amendments, *Terry* v. *Ohio*, 392 U.S. 1, 8–9 (1968), *Katz* v. *United States*, 389 U.S. 347, 350 (1967). . . .; in the penumbras of the Bill of Rights, *Griswold* v. *Connecticut*, 381 U.S. 479, 484–485 (1965); in the Ninth Amendment, *id.*, at 486 (Goldberg, J., concurring); or in the concept of liberty guaranteed by the first section of the Fourteenth Amendment, see *Meyer* v. *Nebraska*, 262 U.S. 390, 399 (1923). These decisions make it clear that only personal rights that can be deemed "fundamental" or "implicit" in the "concept of ordered liberty," are included in this guarantee of personal privacy. They also make it clear that the right has some extension to activities relating to marriage, *Loving* v. *Virginia*, 388 U.S. 1, 12 (1967); procreation, *Skinner* v. *Oklahoma*, 316 U.S. 535, 541–542 (1942); contraception, *Eisenstadt* v. *Baird*, 405 U.S. 438, 453–454 (1972); family relationships, *Prince* v. *Massachusetts*, 321 U.S. 158, 166 (1944); and child rearing and education, *Pierce* v. *Society of Sisters*, 268 U.S. 510, 535 (1925), *Meyer* v. *Nebraska, supra.*

This right of privacy, whether it be founded in the Fourteenth Amendment's concept of personal liberty and restrictions upon state action, as we feel it is, or, as the District Court determined, in the Ninth Amendment's reservation of rights to the people, is broad enough to encompass a woman's decision whether or not to terminate her pregnancy. The detriment that the State would impose upon the pregnant woman by denying this choice altogether is apparent. Specific and direct harm medically diagnosable even in early pregnancy may be involved. Maternity, or additional offspring, may force upon the woman a distressful life and future. Psychological harm may be imminent. Mental and physical health may be taxed by child care. There is also the distress, for all concerned, associated with the unwanted child, and there is the problem of bringing a child into a family already unable, psychologically and otherwise, to care for it. In other cases, as in this one, the additional difficulties and continuing stigma of unwed motherhood may be involved. All these are factors the woman and her responsible physician necessarily will consider in consultation.

On the basis of elements such as these, appellants and some *amici* argue that the woman's right is absolute and that she is entitled to terminate her pregnancy at whatever time, in whatever way, and for whatever reason she alone chooses. With this we do not agree. Appellants' arguments that Texas either has no valid interest at all in regulating the abortion decision, or no interest strong enough to support any limitation upon the woman's sole determination, is unpersuasive. The Court's decisions recognizing a right of privacy also acknowledge that some state regulation in areas protected by that right is appropriate. As noted above, a state may properly assert important interests in safeguarding health, in maintaining medical standards, and in protecting potential life. At some point in pregnancy, these respective interests become sufficiently compelling to sustain regulation of the factors that govern the abortion decision. The privacy right involved, therefore, cannot be said to be absolute. In fact, it is not clear to us that the claim asserted by some *amici* that one has an unlimited right to do with one's body as one pleases bears a close relationship to the right of privacy previously articulated in the Court's decisions. The Court has refused to recognize an unlimited right of this kind in the past. *Jacobson* v. *Massachusetts*, 197 U.S. 11 (1905) (vaccination); *Buck* v. *Bell*, 274 U.S. 200 (1927) (sterilization).

We therefore conclude that the right of personal privacy includes the abortion decision, but that this right is not unqualified and must be considered against important state interests in regulation. . . .

The appellee and certain *amici* argue that the fetus is a "person" within the language and meaning of the Fourteenth Amendment. . . .

The Constitution does not define "person" in so many words. . . . [T]he use of the word is such that it has application only postnatally. . . .

All this, together with our observation, *supra*, that throughout the major portion of the 19th century prevailing legal abortion practices were far freer than they are today, persuades us that the word "person," as used in the Fourteenth Amendment, does not include the unborn. . . .

The pregnant woman cannot be isolated in her privacy. She carries an embryo and, later, a fetus. . . . The situation therefore is inherently different from marital intimacy, or bedroom possession of obscene material, or marriage, or procreation, or education. . . . As we have intimated above, it is reasonable and appropriate for a State to decide that at some point in time another interest, that of health of the mother or that of potential human life, becomes significantly involved. The woman's privacy is no longer sole and any right of privacy she possesses must be measured accordingly.

Texas urges that, apart from the Fourteenth Amendment, life begins at conception and is present throughout pregnancy, and that, therefore, the State has a compelling interest in protecting that life from and after conception. We need not resolve the difficult question of when life begins. When those trained in the respective disciplines of medicine, philosophy, and theology are unable to arrive at any consensus, the judiciary, at this point in the development of man's knowledge, is not in a position to speculate as to the answer.

It should be sufficient to note briefly the wide divergence of thinking on this most sensitive and difficult question. There has always been strong support for the view that life does not begin until live birth. This was the belief of the Stoics. It appears to be a predominant, though not the unanimous, attitude of the Jewish faith. It may be taken to represent also the position of a large segment of the Protestant community, insofar as that can be ascertained; organized groups that have taken a formal position on the abortion issue have generally regarded abortion as a matter for the conscience of the individual and her family. As we have noted, the common law found greater significance in quickening. Physicians and their scientific colleagues have regarded that event with less interest and have tended to focus either upon conception or upon live birth or upon the interim point at which the fetus becomes "viable," that is, potentially able to live outside the mother's womb, albeit with artificial aid. Viability is usually placed at about seven months (28 weeks) but may occur earlier, even at 24 weeks. . . .

In areas other than criminal abortion the law has been reluctant to endorse any theory that life, as we recognize it, begins before live birth or to accord legal rights to the unborn except in narrowly defined situations and except when the rights are contingent upon live birth. . . .

In view of all this, we do not agree that, by adopting one theory of life, Texas may override the rights of the pregnant woman that are at stake. . . .

With respect to the State's important and legitimate interest in the health of the mother, the "compelling" point, in the light of present medical knowledge, is at approximately the end of the first trimester. This is so because of the now established

medical fact . . . that until the end of the first trimester mortality in abortion is less than mortality in normal childbirth. It follows that, from and after this point, a State may regulate the abortion procedure to the extent that the regulation reasonably relates to the preservation and protection of maternal health. . . .

This means, on the other hand, that, for the period of pregnancy prior to this "compelling" point, the attending physician, in consultation with his patient, is free to determine, without regulation by the State, that in his medical judgment the patient's pregnancy should be terminated. If that decision is reached, the judgment may be effectuated by an abortion free of interference by the State.

With respect to the State's important and legitimate interest in potential life, the "compelling" point is at viability. This is so because the fetus then presumably has the capability of meaningful life outside the mother's womb. State regulation protective of fetal life after viability thus has both logical and biological justifications. If the State is interested in protecting fetal life after viability, it may go so far as to proscribe abortion during that period except when it is necessary to preserve the life or health of the mother. . . .

To summarize and to repeat:

1. A state criminal abortion statute of the current Texas type, that excepts from criminality only a *life saving* procedure on behalf of the mother, without regard to pregnancy state and without recognition of the other interests involved, is violative of the Due Process Clause of the Fourteenth Amendment.

(a) For the stage prior to approximately the end of the first trimester, the abortion decision and its effectuation must be left to the medical judgment of the pregnant woman's attending physician.

(b) For the stage subsequent to approximately the end of the first trimester, the State, in promoting its interest in the health of the mother, may, if it chooses, regulate the abortion procedure in ways that are reasonably related to maternal health.

(c) For the stage subsequent to viability, the State in promoting its interest in the potentiality of human life may, if it chooses, regulate, and even proscribe, abortion except where it is necessary, in appropriate medical judgment, for the preservation of the life or health of the mother.

2. The State may define the term "physician," . . . to mean only a physician currently licensed by the State, and may proscribe any abortion by a person who is not a physician as so defined. . . .

This holding, we feel, is consistent with the relative weights of the respective interests involved, with the lessons and examples of medical and legal history, with the lenity of the common law, and with the demands of the profound problems of the present day. The decision leaves the State free to place increasing restrictions on abortion as the period of pregnancy lengthens, so long as those restrictions are tailored to the recognized state interests. The decision vindicates the right of the physician to administer medical treatment according to his professional judgment up to the points where important state interests provide compelling justifications for intervention. Up to those points, the abortion decision in all its aspects is inherently, and primarily, a medical decision, and basic responsibility for it must rest with the physician. If an individual practitioner abuses the privilege of exercising proper medical judgment, the usual remedies, judicial and intra-professional, are available. . . .

It is so ordered.

MR. CHIEF JUSTICE BURGER, concurring: [omitted]
MR. JUSTICE DOUGLAS, concurring: [omitted]
MR. JUSTICE STEWART, concurring: [omitted]
MR. JUSTICE REHNQUIST, dissenting: . . . .

I have difficulty in concluding, as the Court does, that the right of "privacy" is involved in this case. Texas by the statute here challenged bars the performance of a medical abortion by a licensed physician on a plaintiff such as Roe. A transaction resulting in an operation such as this is not "private" in the ordinary usage of that word. Nor is the "privacy" which the Court finds here even a distant relative of the freedom from searches and seizures protected by the Fourth Amendment to the Constitution which the Court has referred to as embodying a right to privacy. . . . [T]he adoption of the compelling state interest standard will inevitably require this Court to examine the legislative policies and pass on the wisdom of these policies in the very process of deciding whether a particular state interest put forward may or may not be "compelling." The decision here to break the term of pregnancy into three distinct terms and to outline the permissible restrictions the State may impose in each one, for example, partakes more of judicial legislation than it does of a determination of the intent of the drafters of the Fourteenth Amendment.

The fact that a majority of the States, reflecting after all the majority sentiment in those States, have had restrictions on abortions for at least a century seems to me as strong an indication there is that the asserted right to an abortion is not "so rooted in the traditions and conscience of our people as to be ranked as fundamental." Even today,

when society's views on abortion are changing, the very existence of the debate is evidence that the "right" to an abortion is not so universally accepted as the appellants would have us believe.

To reach its result the Court necessarily has had to find within the scope of the Fourteenth Amendment a right that was apparently completely unknown to the drafters of the Amendment. . . .
MR. JUSTICE WHITE, with whom MR. JUSTICE REHNQUIST joins, dissenting:

At the heart of the controversy in these cases are those recurring pregnancies that pose no danger whatsoever to the life or health of the mother but are nevertheless unwanted for any one or more of a variety of reasons—convenience, family planning, economics, dislike of children, the embarrassment of illegitimacy, etc. The common claim before us is that for any one of such reasons, or for no reason at all, and without asserting or claiming any threat to life or health, any woman is entitled to an abortion at her request if she is able to find a medical advisor willing to undertake the procedure.

The Court for the most part sustains this position:

During the period prior to the time the fetus becomes viable, the Constitution of the United States values the convenience, whim or caprice of the putative mother more than the life or potential life of the fetus; the Constitution, therefore, guarantees the right to an abortion as against any state law or policy seeking to protect the fetus from an abortion not prompted by more compelling reasons of the mother.

With all due respect, I dissent. I find nothing in the language or history of the Constitution to support the Court's judgment. The Court simply fashions and announces a new constitutional right for pregnant mothers and, with scarcely any reason or authority for its action, invests that right with sufficient substance to override most existing state abortion statutes. The upshot is that the people and the legislatures of the 50 States are constitutionally disentitled to weigh the relative importance of the continued existence and development of the fetus on the one hand against a spectrum of possible impacts on the mother on the other hand. As an exercise of raw judicial power, the Court perhaps has authority to do what it does today; but in my view its judgment is an improvident and extravagant exercise of the power of judicial review which the Constitution extends to this Court. . . . In a sensitive area such as this, involving as it does issues over which reasonable men may easily and heatedly differ, I cannot accept the Court's exercise of its clear power of choice by interposing a constitutional barrier to state efforts to protect human life and by investing mothers and doctors with the constitutionally protected right to exterminate it. This issue, for the most part, should be left with the people and to the political processes the people have devised to govern their affairs. . . .

BOWERS v. HARDWICK,
478 U.S. 186 (1986)

Michael Hardwick, a 29-year-old homosexual living in Atlanta, brought this civil suit in federal district court. The suit had its genesis in the following facts. On August 3, 1982, a police officer went to Hardwick's home to serve Hardwick a warrant for failure to pay a fine for public drunkenness. The man answering the door was not sure if Hardwick was at home but allowed the officer to enter and pointed the way to Hardwick's bedroom. The officer walked down the hall to the bedroom where he found the door partly open and he observed Hardwick and another man engaged in oral sex. The officer then arrested both men and charged them with sodomy, an offense under Georgia criminal law punishable by a prison sentence as long as 20 years. Hardwick challenged his arrest as a violation of his rights, and the district attorney decided not to submit the charge to the grand jury unless there was additional evidence. This was unsatisfactory to Hardwick, who believed that the district attorney could, at his discretion, reinstitute the charges. Hardwick then decided to challenge the Georgia sodomy law under which he was originally arrested. The federal district judge, on motion of the state officials named in the suit, dismissed for failure to state a claim. The court of appeals reversed and remanded, holding that the Georgia statute violated Hardwick's fundamental rights. The Attorney General of Georgia, Michael J. Bowers, took the case to the Supreme Court.

Majority votes: 5
Dissenting votes: 4

JUSTICE WHITE delivered the opinion of the Court:
   In August 1982, respondent [Michael Hardwick] was charged with violating the Georgia statute criminalizing sodomy[1] by committing that act with another adult male in the bedroom of respondent's home. After a preliminary hearing, the District Attorney decided not to present the matter to the grand jury unless further evidence developed.

   Respondent then brought suit in the Federal District Court, challenging the constitutionality of the statute insofar as it criminalized consensual sodomy.[2] He asserted that he was a practicing homosexual, that the Georgia sodomy statute, as administered by the defendants, placed him in imminent danger of arrest, and that the statute for several reasons violates the Federal Constitution. The District Court granted the defendants' motion to dismiss for failure to state a claim, relying on *Doe* v. *Commonwealth's Attorney for the City of Richmond*, 425 U.S. 901 (1976).

   A divided panel of the Court of Appeals for the Eleventh Circuit reversed. The court first held that, because *Doe* was distinguishable and in any event had been undermined by later decisions, our summary affirmance in that case did not require affirmance of the District Court. Relying on our decisions in *Griswold* v. *Connecticut*, 381 U.S. 479 (1965), *Eisenstadt* v. *Baird*, 405 U.S. 438 (1972), *Stanley* v. *Georgia*, 394 U.S. 557 (1969), and *Roe* v. *Wade*, 410 U.S. 113 (1973), the court went on to hold that the Georgia statute violated respondent's fundamental rights because his homosexual activity is a private and intimate association that is beyond the reach of state regulation by reason of the Ninth Amendment and the Due Process Clause of the Fourteenth Amendment. The case was remanded for trial, at which, to prevail, the State would have to prove that the statute is supported by a compelling interest and is the most narrowly drawn means of achieving that end.

   Because other Courts of Appeals have arrived at judgments contrary to that of the Eleventh Circuit in this case, we granted the Attorney General's petition for certiorari questioning the holding that its sodomy statute violates the fundamental rights of homosexuals. We agree with the State that the Court of Appeals erred, and hence reverse its judgment.

   This case does not require a judgment on whether laws against sodomy between consenting adults in general, or between homosexuals in particular, are wise or desirable. It raises no question about the right or propriety of state legislative decisions to repeal their laws that criminalize homosex-

---

[1]GA. Code Ann. §16-6-2 (1984) provides, in pertinent part, as follows:
   "(a) A person commits the offense of sodomy when he performs or submits to any sexual act involving the sex organs of one person and the mouth or anus of another. . . ."
   "(b) A person convicted of the offense of sodomy shall be punished by imprisonment for not less than one nor more than 20 years. . . ."

[2]. . . The only claim properly before the Court . . . is Hardwick's challenge to the Georgia statute as applied to consensual homosexual sodomy. We express no opinion on the constitutionality of the Georgia statute as applied to other acts of sodomy.

ual sodomy, or of state court decisions invalidating those laws on state constitutional grounds. The issue presented is whether the Federal Constitution confers a fundamental right upon homosexuals to engage in sodomy and hence invalidates the laws of the many States that still make such conduct illegal and have done so for a very long time. The case also calls for some judgment about the limits of the Court's role in carrying out its constitutional mandate.

We first register our disagreement with the Court of Appeals and with respondent that the Court's prior cases have construed the Constitution to confer a right of privacy that extends to homosexual sodomy and for all intents and purposes have decided this case. The reach of this line of cases was sketched in *Carey* v. *Population Services International*, 431 U.S. 678, 685 (1977). *Pierce* v. *Society of Sisters*, 268 U.S. 510 (1925), and *Meyer* v. *Nebraska*, 262 U.S. 390 (1923), were described as dealing with child rearing and education; *Prince* v. *Massachusetts*, 321 U.S. 158 (1944), with family relationships; *Skinner* v. *Oklahoma ex rel Williamson*, 316 U.S. 535 (1942), with procreation; *Loving* v. *Virginia*, 388 U.S. 1 (1967), with marriage; *Griswold* v. *Connecticut*, and *Eisenstadt* v. *Baird*, with contraception; and *Roe* v. *Wade*, 410 U.S. 113 (1973), with abortion. The latter three cases were interpreted as construing the Due Process Clause of the Fourteenth Amendment to confer a fundamental individual right to decide whether or not to beget or bear a child.

Accepting the decisions in these cases and the above description of them, we think it evident that none of the rights announced in those cases bears any resemblance to the claimed constitutional right of homosexuals to engage in acts of sodomy that is asserted in this case. No connection between family, marriage, or procreation on the one hand and homosexual activity on the other has been demonstrated, either by the Court of Appeals or by respondent. Moreover, any claim that these cases nevertheless stand for the proposition that any kind of private sexual conduct between consenting adults is constitutionally insulated from state proscription is unsupportable. . . .

Precedent aside, however, respondent would have us announce, as the Court of Appeals did, a fundamental right to engage in homosexual sodomy. This we are quite unwilling to do. It is true that despite the language of the Due Process Clauses of the Fifth and Fourteenth Amendments, which appears to focus only on the processes by which life, liberty, or property is taken, the cases are legion in which those Clauses have been interpreted to have substantive content, subsuming

rights that to a great extent are immune from federal or state regulation or proscription. Among such cases are those recognizing rights that have little or no textual support in the constitutional language. *Meyer, Prince,* and *Pierce* fall in this category, as do the privacy cases from *Griswold* to *Carey*.

Striving to assure itself and the public that announcing rights not readily identifiable in the Constitution's text involves much more than the imposition of the Justices' own choice of values on the States and the Federal Government, the Court has sought to identify the nature of the rights qualifying for heightened judicial protection. In *Palko* v. *Connecticut,* 302 U.S. 319, 325, 326 (1937), it was said that this category includes those fundamental liberties that are "implicit in the concept of ordered liberty," such that "neither liberty nor justice would exist if [they] were sacrificed." A different description of fundamental liberties appeared in *Moore* v. *East Cleveland,* 431 U.S. 494, 503 (1977) (opinion of POWELL, J.), where they are characterized as those liberties that are "deeply rooted in this Nation's history and tradition." See also *Griswold* v. *Connecticut,* 381 U.S., at 506.

It is obvious to us that neither of these formulations would extend a fundamental right to homosexuals to engage in acts of consensual sodomy. Proscriptions against that conduct have ancient roots. Sodomy was a criminal offense at common law and was forbidden by the laws of the original thirteen States when they ratified the Bill of Rights. In 1868, when the Fourteenth Amendment was ratified, all but 5 of the 37 States in the Union had criminal sodomy laws. In fact, until 1961, all 50 States outlawed sodomy, and today, 24 States and the District of Columbia continue to provide criminal penalties for sodomy performed in private and between consenting adults. Against this background, to claim that a right to engage in such conduct is "deeply rooted in this Nation's history and tradition" or "implicit in the concept of ordered liberty" is, at best, facetious.

Nor are we inclined to take a more expansive view of our authority to discover new fundamental rights imbedded in the Due Process Clause. The Court is most vulnerable and comes nearest to illegitimacy when it deals with judge-made constitutional law having little or no cognizable roots in the language or design of the Constitution. That this is so was painfully demonstrated by the face-off between the Executive and the Court in the 1930's which resulted in the repudiation of much of the substantive gloss that the Court had placed on the Due Process Clause of the Fifth and Fourteenth Amendments. There should be, therefore, great resistance to expand the substantive reach of those

Clauses, particularly if it requires redefining the category of rights deemed to be fundamental. Otherwise, the Judiciary necessarily takes to itself further authority to govern the country without express constitutional authority. The claimed right pressed on us today falls far short of overcoming this resistance.

Respondent, however, asserts that the result should be different where the homosexual conduct occurs in the privacy of the home. He relies on *Stanley* v. *Georgia,* 394 U.S. 557 (1969), where the Court held that the First Amendment prevents conviction for possessing and reading obscene material in the privacy of one's home: "If the First Amendment means anything, it means that a State has no business telling a man, sitting alone in his house, what books he may read or what films he may watch." *Id.,* at 565.

Stanley did protect conduct that would not have been protected outside the home, and it partially prevented the enforcement of state obscenity laws; but the decision was firmly grounded in the First Amendment. The right pressed upon us here has no similar support in the text of the Constitution, and it does not qualify for recognition under the prevailing principles for construing the Fourteenth Amendment. Its limits are also difficult to discern. Plainly enough, otherwise illegal conduct is not always immunized whenever it occurs in the home. Victimless crimes, such as the possession and use of illegal drugs, do not escape the law where they are committed at home. *Stanley* itself recognized that its holding offered no protection for the possession in the home of drugs, firearms, or stolen goods. And if respondent's submission in limited to the voluntary sexual conduct between consenting adults, it would be difficult, except by fiat, to limit the claimed right to homosexual conduct while leaving exposed to prosecution adultery, incest, and other sexual crimes even though they are committed in the home. We are unwilling to start down that road.

Even if the conduct at issue here is not a fundamental right, respondent asserts that there must be a rational basis for the law and that there is none in this case other than the presumed belief of a majority of the electorate in Georgia that homosexual sodomy is immoral and unacceptable. This is said to be an inadequate rationale to support the law. The law, however, is constantly based on notions of morality, and if all laws representing essentially moral choices are to be invalidated under the Due Process Clause, the courts will be very busy indeed. Even respondent makes no such claim, but insists that majority sentiments about the morality of homosexuality should be declared inadequate.

We do not agree, and are unpersuaded that the sodomy laws of some 25 States should be invalidated on this basis.

Accordingly, the judgment of the Court of Appeals is

Reversed.

CHIEF JUSTICE BURGER, concurring:

I join the Court's opinion, but I write separately to underscore my view that in constitutional terms there is no such thing as a fundamental right to commit homosexual sodomy. . . .

JUSTICE POWELL, concurring:

I join the opinion of the Court. I agree with the Court that there is no fundamental right—i.e., no substantive right under the Due Process Clause—such as that claimed by respondent Hardwick, and found to exist by the Court of Appeals. This is not to suggest, however, that respondent may not be protected by the Eighth Amendment of the Constitution. The Georgia statute at issue in this case, Ga. Code Ann. §16-6-2 (1984), authorizes a court to imprison a person for up to 20 years for a single private, consensual act of sodomy. In my view, a prison sentence for such conduct—certainly a sentence of long duration—would create a serious Eighth Amendment issue. Under the Georgia statute a single act of sodomy, even in the private setting of a home, is a felony comparable in terms of the possible sentence imposed to serious felonies such as aggravated battery, first degree arson, and robbery.

In this case, however, respondent has not been tried, much less convicted and sentenced. Moreover, respondent has not raised the Eighth Amendment issue below. For these reasons this constitutional argument is not before us.

JUSTICE BLACKMUN, with whom JUSTICE BRENNAN, JUSTICE MARSHALL, and JUSTICE STEVENS join, dissenting:

This case is no more about "a fundamental right to engage in homosexual sodomy," as the Court purports to declare, than *Stanley* v. *Georgia* was about a fundamental right to watch obscene movies, or *Katz* v. *United States* was about a fundamental right to place interstate bets from a telephone booth. Rather, this case is about "the most comprehensive of rights and the right most valued by civilized men," namely, "the right to be let alone."

The statute at issue denies individuals the right to decide for themselves whether to engage in particular forms of private, consensual sexual activity. . . . I believe we must analyze Hardwick's claim in the light of the values that underlie the con-

stitutional right to privacy. If that right means anything, it means that, before Georgia can prosecute
its citizens for making choices about the most intimate aspects of their lives, it must do more than
assert that the choice they have made is an "abomi-
nable crime not fit to be named among Christians."
Herring v. *State,* 119 Ga. 709, 721 (1904).

"Our cases long have recognized that the Constitution embodies a promise that a certain private
sphere of individual liberty will be kept largely beyond the reach of government." *Thornburgh* v.
American Coll. of Obst. & Gyn. In construing the
right to privacy, the Court has proceeded along two
somewhat distinct, albeit complementary, lines.
First, it has recognized a privacy interest with reference to certain *decisions* that are properly for the
individual to make. *E.g., Roe v. Wade; Pierce* v.
Society of Sisters. Second, it has recognized a privacy interest with reference to certain *places* without regard for the particular activities in which the
individuals who occupy them are engaged. . . . The
case before us implicates both the decisional and
the spatial aspects of the right to privacy.

The Court concludes today that none of our
prior cases dealing with various decisions that individuals are entitled to make free of governmental
interference "bears any resemblance to the claimed
constitutional right of homosexuals to engage in
acts of sodomy that is asserted in this case." While
it is true that these cases may be characterized by
their connection to protection of the family, the
Court's conclusion that they extend no further than
this boundary ignores the warning in *Moore* v. *East
Cleveland,* 431 U.S. 494, 501 (1977) (plurality opinion), against "clos[ing] our eyes to the basic reasons why certain rights associated with the family
have been accorded shelter under the Fourteenth
Amendment's Due Process Clause." We protect
those rights not because they contribute, in some
direct and material way, to the general public welfare, but because they form so central a part of an
individual's life. "[T]he concept of privacy embodies the 'moral fact that a person belongs to himself
and not others nor to society as a whole.' " And so
we protect the decision whether to marry precisely
because marriage "is an association that promotes
a way of life, not causes; a harmony in living, not
political faiths; a bilateral loyalty, not commercial
or social projects." *Griswold* v. *Connecticut,* 381
U.S., at 486. We protect the decision whether to
have a child because parenthood alters so dramatically an individual's self-definition, not because of
demographic considerations or the Bible's command to be fruitful and multiply. And we protect
the family because it contributes so powerfully to
the happiness of individuals, not because of a pref-

erence for stereotypical households. The Court
[has] recognized . . . that the "ability independently to define one's identity that is central to any
concept of liberty" cannot truly be exercised in a
vacuum; we all depend on the "emotional enrichment from close ties with others."

Only the most willful blindness could obscure
the fact that sexual intimacy is "a sensitive, key
relationship of human existence, central to family
life, community welfare, and the development of
human personality." The fact that individuals define themselves in a significant way through their
intimate sexual relationships with others suggests,
in a Nation as diverse as ours, that there may be
many "right" ways of conducting those relationships, and that much of the richness of a relationship will come from the freedom an individual has
to *choose* the form and nature of these intensely
personal bonds.

In a variety of circumstances we have recognized that a necessary corollary of giving individuals freedom to choose how to conduct their lives is
acceptance of the fact that different individuals will
make different choices. For example, in holding
that the clearly important state interest in public education should give way to a competing claim by
the Amish to the effect that extended formal
schooling threatened their way of life, the Court declared: "There can be no assumption that today's
majority is 'right' and the Amish and others like
them are 'wrong.' A way of life that is odd or even
erratic but interferes with no rights or interest of
others is not to be condemned because it is different." *Wisconsin* v. *Yoder,* 406 U.S. 205, 223-224
(1972). The Court claims that its decision today
merely refuses to recognize a fundamental right to
engage in homosexual sodomy; what the Court
really has refused to recognize is the fundamental
interest all individuals have in controlling the nature of their associations with others.

The behavior for which Hardwick faces prosecution occurred in his own home, a place to which
the Fourth Amendment attaches special significance. The Court's treatment of this aspect of the
case is symptomatic of its overall refusal to consider the broad principles that have informed our
treatment of privacy in specific cases. Just as the
right to privacy is more than the mere aggregation
of a number of entitlements to engage in specific
behavior, so too, protecting the physical integrity
of the home is more than merely a means of protecting specific activities that often take place
there. . . .

The Court's interpretation of the pivotal case of
Stanley v. *Georgia,* 394 U.S. 557 (1969), is entirely
unconvincing. *Stanley* held that Georgia's un-

doubted power to punish the public distribution of constitutionally unprotected, obscene material did not permit the State to punish the private possession of such material. According to the majority here, *Stanley* relied entirely on the First Amendment, and thus, it is claimed, sheds no light on cases not involving printed materials. But that is not what *Stanley* said. Rather, the *Stanley* Court anchored its holding in the Fourth Amendment's special protection for the individual in his home. . . .

The central place that *Stanley* gives Justice Brandeis' dissent in *Olmstead,* a case raising *no* First Amendment claim, shows that *Stanley* rested as much on the Court's understanding of the Fourth Amendment as it did on the First. . . . Indeed, the right of an individual to conduct intimate relationships in the intimacy of his or her own home seems to me to be the heart of the Constitution's protection of privacy.

The Court's failure to comprehend the magnitude of the liberty interests at stake in this case leads it to slight the question whether petitioner, on behalf of the State, has justified Georgia's infringement on these interests. I believe that neither of the two general justifications for §16-6-2 that petitioner has advanced warrants dismissing respondent's challenge for failure to state a claim.

First, petitioner asserts that the acts made criminal by the statute may have serious adverse consequences for "the general public health and welfare," such as spreading communicable diseases or fostering other criminal activity. Inasmuch as this case was dismissed by the District Court on the pleadings, it is not surprising that the record before us is barren of any evidence to support petitioner's claim. . . . Nothing in the record before the Court provides any justification for finding the activity forbidden by §16-6-2 to be physically dangerous, either to the persons engaged in it or to others.

The core of petitioner's defense of §16-6-2, however, is that respondent and others who engage in the conduct prohibited by §16-6-2 interfere with Georgia's exercise of the "right of the Nation and of the States to maintain a decent society." Essentially, petitioner argues, and the Court agrees, that the fact that the acts described in §16-6-2 "for hundreds of years, if not thousands, have been uniformly condemned as immoral" is a sufficient reason to permit a State to ban them today.

I cannot agree that either the length of time a majority has held its convictions or the passions with which it defends them can withdraw legislation from this Court's scrutiny. . . .

The assertion that "traditional Judeo-Christian values proscribe" the conduct involved cannot provide an adequate justification for §16-6-2. That certain, but by no means all, religious groups condemn the behavior at issue gives the State no license to impose their judgments on the entire citizenry. The legitimacy of secular legislation depends instead on whether the State can advance some justification for its law beyond its conformity to religious doctrine. Thus, far from buttressing his case, petitioner's invocation of Leviticus, Romans, St. Thomas Aquinas, and sodomy's heretical status during the Middle Ages undermines his suggestion that §16-6-2 represents a legitimate use of secular coercive power. A State can no more punish private behavior because of religious intolerance than it can punish such behavior because of racial animus. . . . No matter how uncomfortable a certain group may make the majority of this Court, we have held that "[m]ere public intolerance or animosity cannot constitutionally justify the deprivation of a person's physical liberty."

Nor can §16-6-2 be justified as a "morally neutral" exercise of Georgia's power to "protect the public environment," *Paris Adult Theatre I,* 413, U.S., at 68–69. Certainly, some private behavior can affect the fabric of society as a whole. Reasonable people may differ about whether particular sexual acts are moral or immoral, but "we have ample evidence for believing that people will not abandon morality, will not think any better of murder, cruelty and dishonesty, merely because some private sexual practice which they abominate is not punished by the law." Petitioner and the Court fail to see the difference between laws that protect public sensibilities and those that enforce private morality. Statutes banning public sexual activity are entirely consistent with protecting the individual's liberty interest in decisions concerning sexual relations: the same recognition that those decisions are intensely private which justifies protecting them from governmental interference can justify protecting individuals from unwilling exposure to the sexual activities of others. But the mere fact that intimate behavior may be punished when it takes place in public cannot dictate how States can regulate intimate behavior that occurs in intimate places.

This case involves no real interference with the rights of others, for the mere knowledge that other individuals do not adhere to one's value system cannot be a legally cognizable interest let alone an interest that can justify invading the houses, hearts, and minds of citizens who choose to live their lives differently.

It took but three years for the Court to see the error in its analysis in *Minersville School District* v. *Gobitis,* 310 U.S. 586 (1940), and to recognize that the threat to national cohesion posed by a refusal to salute the flag was vastly outweighed by the threat to those same values by compelling such a salute. See *West Virginia Board of Education* v. *Barnette*, 319 U.S. 624 (1943). I can only hope that here, too, the Court soon will reconsider its analysis and conclude that depriving individuals of the right to choose for themselves how to conduct their intimate relationships poses a far greater threat to the values most deeply rooted in our Nations's history than tolerance of nonconformity could ever do. Because I think the Court today betrays those values, I dissent.

JUSTICE STEVENS, with whom JUSTICE BRENNAN and JUSTICE MARSHALL join, dissenting:

Like the statute that is challenged in this case, the rationale of the Court's opinion applies equally to the prohibited conduct regardless of whether the parties who engage in it are married or unmarried, or are of the same or different sexes. Sodomy was condemned as an odious and sinful type of behavior during the formative period of the common law. That condemnation was equally damning for heterosexual and homosexual sodomy. Moreover, it provided no special exemption for married couples. The license to cohabit and to produce legitimate offspring simply did not include any permission to engage in sexual conduct that was considered a "crime against nature."

The history of the Georgia statute before us clearly reveals this traditional prohibition of heterosexual, as well as homosexual, sodomy. Indeed, at one point in the 20th century, Georgia's law was constructed to permit certain sexual conduct between homosexual women even though such conduct was prohibited between heterosexuals. The history of the statutes cited by the majority as proof for the proposition that sodomy is not constitutionally protected, similarly reveals a prohibition on heterosexual, as well as homosexual, sodomy. . . .

[O]ur prior cases thus establish that a State may not prohibit sodomy within "the sacred precincts of marital bedrooms," or, indeed, between unmarried heterosexual adults. In all events, it is perfectly clear that the State of Georgia may not totally prohibit the conduct proscribed by §16-6-2 of the Georgia Criminal Code. . . .

The Court orders the dismissal of respondent's complaint even though the State's statute prohibits all sodomy; even though that prohibition is concededly unconstitutional with respect to heterosexuals; and even though the State's *post hoc* explanations for selective application are belied by the State's own actions. At the very least, I think it clear at this early stage of the litigation that respondent has alleged a constitutional claim sufficient to withstand a motion to dismiss.

I respectfully dissent.

INS v. CHADHA, 462 U.S. 919 (1983)

Mr. Chadha, of East Indian heritage, was born in Kenya and held a British passport. He was admitted to the United States on a nonimmigrant student visa in 1966. When his visa expired on June 30, 1972, he did not leave the country but remained illegally. The Immigration and Naturalization Service (INS) took steps to deport him, but he filed an application for suspension of deportation under the appropriate provision of the Immigration and Nationality Act. As a result of the evidence presented at his hearing and the findings of a character investigation conducted by the INS, the immigration judge on June 25, 1974, found that Chadha met the statutory requirements for suspension of deportation in that he had resided continuously in the United States for over seven years, was of good moral character, and would suffer "extreme hardship" if deported. Report of the suspension was transmitted to Congress as required by the immigration statute. Under Section 244(c)(2) of the act, either branch of Congress could pass a resolution that invalidated the decision of the executive branch to allow a particular deportable alien to remain in the United States. This is the so-called legislative veto that has appeared in numerous statutes over the last half century and has been employed by Congress when it delegates broad authority to the executive branch but wishes to retain some check on its exercise. In Mr. Chadha's case, the June 25, 1974, order in his favor by the immigration judge remained in effect for a year and a half until the House of Representatives, on December 16, 1975, approved a resolution from the House Judiciary Committee opposing the granting of permanent residence to six aliens including Chadha. The House voted after being informed by the Chairman of the Judiciary Subcommittee on Immigration, Citizenship, and International Law that the six, including Chadha, did not meet the statutory requirement as to hardship and therefore their deportations should not be suspended. Chadha then challenged the constitutionality of Section 244(c)(2), arguing that the legislative veto violated the Constitution. The U.S. Court of Appeals for the Ninth Circuit ruled that Section 244(c)(2) violated the constitutional doctrine of separation of powers and ordered the Attorney General to cease taking any steps to deport Chadha based on the House Resolution.

Majority votes: 7
Dissenting votes: 2

CHIEF JUSTICE BURGER delivered the opinion of the Court:. . . .

We turn to the question whether action of one House of Congress under §244(c)(2) violates strictures of the Constitution. We begin, of course, with the presumption that the challenged statute is valid. Its wisdom is not the concern of the courts; if a challenged action does not violate the Constitution, it must be sustained. . . .

By the same token, the fact that a given law or procedure is efficient, convenient, and useful in facilitating functions of government, standing alone, will not save it if it is contrary to the Constitution. Convenience and efficiency are not the primary objectives—or the hallmarks—of democratic government and our inquiry is sharpened rather than blunted by the fact that Congressional veto provisions are appearing with increasing frequency in statutes which delegate authority to executive and independent agencies. . . .

Explicit and unambiguous provisions of the Constitution prescribe and define the respective functions of the Congress and of the Executive in the legislative process. . . .

These provisions of Art. I are integral parts of the constitutional design for the separation of powers. . . . [W]e find that the purposes underlying the Presentment Clauses, Art. I, §7, cls. 2,3, and the bicameral requirement of Art. I, §1 and §7, cl. 2, guide our resolution of the important question presented in this case. The very structure of the articles delegating and separating powers under Arts. I, II, and III exemplify the concept of separation of powers and we now turn to Art. I.

THE PRESENTMENT CLAUSES

The records of the Constitutional Convention reveal that the requirement that all legislation be presented to the President before becoming law was uniformly accepted by the Framers. Presentment to the President and the Presidential veto were considered so imperative that the draftsmen took special pains to assure that these requirements could not be circumvented. During the final debate on Art. I, §7, cl. 2, James Madison expressed concern that it might easily be evaded by the simple expedient of calling a proposed law a "resolution" or "vote" rather than a "bill." As a consequence, Art. I, §7, cl. 3, was added.

The decision to provide the President with a limited and qualified power to nullify proposed legisla-

tion by veto was based on the profound conviction of the Framers that the powers conferred on Congress were the powers to be most carefully circumscribed. It is beyond doubt that lawmaking was a power to be shared by both Houses and the President. . . .

The President's role in the lawmaking process also reflects the Framers' careful efforts to check whatever propensity a particular Congress might have to enact oppressive, improvident, or ill-considered measures. . . .

BICAMERALISM

The bicameral requirement of Art. I, §§1, 7 was of scarcely less concern to the Framers than was the Presidential veto and indeed the two concepts are interdependent. By providing that no law could take effect without the concurrence of the prescribed majority of the Members of both Houses, the Framers reemphasized their belief, already remarked upon in connection with the Presentment Clauses, that legislation should not be enacted unless it has been carefully and fully considered by the Nation's elected officials. In the Constitutional Convention debates on the need for a bicameral legislature, James Wilson, later to become a Justice of this Court, commented:

> "Despotism comes on mankind in different shapes. Sometimes in an Executive, sometimes in a military, one. Is there danger of a Legislative despotism? Theory & practice both proclaim it. If the Legislative authority be not restrained, there can be neither liberty nor stability; and it can only be restrained by dividing it within itself, into distinct and independent branches. In a single house there is no check, but the inadequate one, of the virtue & good sense of those who compose it."

Hamilton argued that a Congress comprised of a single House was antithetical to the very purposes of the Constitution. . . .

This view was rooted in a general skepticism regarding the fallibility of human nature. . . .

However familiar, it is useful to recall that apart from their fear that special interests could be favored at the expense of public needs, the Framers were also concerned, although not of one mind, over the apprehensions of the smaller states. Those states feared a commonality of interest among the larger states would work to their disadvantage; representatives of the larger states, on the other hand, were skeptical of a legislature that could pass laws favoring a minority of the people. It need hardly be repeated here that the Great Compromise, under which one House was viewed as representing the people and the other the states, allayed the fears of both the large and small states.

We see therefore that the Framers were acutely conscious that the bicameral requirement and the Presentment Clauses would serve essential constitutional functions. The President's participation in the legislative process was to protect the Executive Branch from Congress and to protect the whole people from improvident laws. The division of the Congress into two distinctive bodies assures that the legislative power would be exercised only after opportunity for full study and debate in separate settings. The President's unilateral veto power, in turn, was limited by the power of two thirds of both Houses of Congress to overrule a veto thereby precluding final arbitrary action of one person. It emerges clearly that the prescription for legislative action in Art. I, § §1, 7 represents the Framers' decision that the legislative power of the Federal government be exercised in accord with a single, finely wrought and exhaustively considered procedure. . . .

Examination of the action taken here by one House pursuant to §244(c)(2) reveals that it was essentially legislative in purpose and effect. In purporting to exercise power defined in Art. I, §8, cl. 4 to "establish an uniform Rule of Naturalization," the House took action that had the purpose and effect of altering the legal rights, duties and relations of persons, including the Attorney General, Executive Branch officials and Chadha, all outside the legislative branch. Section 244(c)(2) purports to authorize one House of Congress to require the Attorney General to deport an individual alien whose deportation otherwise would be cancelled under §244. The one-House veto operated in this case to overrule the Attorney General and mandate Chadha's deportation; absent the House action, Chadha would remain in the United States. Congress has acted and its action has altered Chadha's status.

The legislative character of the one-House veto in this case is confirmed by the character of the Congressional action it supplants. Neither the House of Representatives nor the Senate contends that, absent the veto provision in §244(c)(2), either of them, or both of them acting together, could effectively require the Attorney General to deport an alien once the Attorney General, in the exercise of legislatively delegated authority, had determined the alien should remain in the United States. Without the challenged provision in §244(c)(2), this could have been achieved, if at all, only by legisla-

tion requiring deportation. Similarly, a veto by one House of Congress under §244(c)(2) cannot be justified as an attempt at amending the standards set out in §244(a)(1), or as a repeal of §244 as applied to Chadha. Amendment and repeal of statutes, no less than enactment, must conform with Art. I.

The nature of the decision implemented by the one-House veto in this case further manifests its legislative character. After long experience with the clumsy, time consuming private bill procedure, Congress made a deliberate choice to delegate to the Executive Branch, and specifically to the Attorney General, the authority to allow deportable aliens to remain in this country in certain specified circumstances. It is not disputed that this choice to delegate authority is precisely the kind of decision that can be implemented only in accordance with the procedures set out in Art. I. Disagreement with the Attorney General's decision on Chadha's deportation—that is, Congress' decision to deport Chadha—no less than Congress' original choice to delegate to the Attorney General the authority to make the decision, involves determinations of policy that Congress can implement in only one way; bicameral passage followed by presentment of the President. Congress must abide by its delegation of authority until that delegation is legislatively altered or revoked.

Finally, we see that when the Framers intended to authorize either House of Congress to act alone and outside of its prescribed bicameral legislative role, they narrowly and precisely defined the procedure for such action. There are but four provisions in the Constitution, explicit and unambiguous, by which one House may act alone with the unreviewable force of law, not subject to the President's veto:

(a) The House of Representatives alone was given the power to initiate impeachments. Art. I, §2, cl. 6;

(b) The Senate alone was given the power to conduct trials following impeachment on charges initiated by the House and to convict following trial. Art. I, §3, cl. 5;

(c) The Senate alone was given final unreviewable power to approve or to disapprove presidential appointments. Art. II, §2, cl. 2;

(d) The Senate alone was given unreviewable power to ratify treaties negotiated by the President. Art. II, §2, cl. 2.

Clearly, when the Draftsmen sought to confer special powers on one House, independent of the other House, or of the President, they did so in explicit, unambiguous terms. These carefully defined exceptions from presentment and bicameralism underscore the difference between the legislative functions of Congress and other unilateral but important and binding one-House acts provided for in the Constitution. These exceptions are narrow, explicit, and separately justified; none of them authorize the action challenged here. On the contrary, they provide further support for the conclusion that Congressional authority is not to be implied and for the conclusion that the veto provided for in §244(c)(2) is not authorized by the constitutional design of the powers of the Legislative Branch.

Since it is clear that the action by the House under §244(c)(2) was not within any of the express constitutional exceptions authorizing one House to act alone, and equally clear that it was an exercise of legislative power, that action was subject to the standards prescribed in Article I. The bicameral requirement, the Presentment Clauses, the President's veto, and Congress' power to override a veto were intended to erect enduring checks on each Branch and to protect the people from the improvident exercise of power by mandating certain prescribed steps. To preserve those checks, and maintain the separation of powers, the carefully defined limits on the power of each Branch must not be eroded. To accomplish what has been attempted by one House of Congress in this case requires action in conformity with the express procedures of the Constitution's prescription for legislative action: passage by a majority of both Houses and presentment to the President.

The veto authorized by §244(c)(2) doubtless has been in many respects a convenient shortcut; the "sharing" with the Executive by Congress of its authority over aliens in this manner is, on its face, an appealing compromise. In purely practical terms, it is obviously easier for action to be taken by one House without submission to the President; but it is crystal clear from the records of the Convention, contemporaneous writings and debates, that the Framers ranked other values higher than efficiency. The records of the Convention and debates in the States preceding ratification underscore the common desire to define and limit the exercise of the newly created federal powers affecting the states and the people. There is unmistakable expression of a determination that legislation by the national Congress be a step-by-step, deliberate and deliberative process.

The choices we discern as having been made in the Constitutional Convention impose burdens on governmental processes that often seem clumsy, inefficient, even unworkable, but those hard choices were consciously made by men who had lived under a form of government that permitted arbitrary governmental acts to go unchecked. There is no support in the Constitution or decisions of this Court for the proposition that the cumbersomeness and delays often encountered in complying with explicit Constitutional standards may be avoided, either by the Congress or by the President. See *Youngstown Sheet & Tube Co.* v. *Sawyer,* 343 U.S. 579 (1952). With all the obvious flaws of delay, untidiness, and potential for abuse, we have not yet found a better way to preserve freedom than by making the exercise of power subject to the carefully crafted restraints spelled out in the Constitution.

We hold that the Congressional veto provision in §244(c)(2) is severable from the Act and that it is unconstitutional. Accordingly, the judgment of the Court of Appeals is

Affirmed.

JUSTICE POWELL, concurring in the judgment:

The Court's decision, based on the Presentment Clauses, Art. I, §7, cls. 2 and 3, apparently will invalidate every use of the legislative veto. The breadth of this holding gives one pause. Congress has included the veto in literally hundreds of statutes, dating back to the 1930s. Congress clearly views this procedure as essential to controlling the delegation of power to administrative agencies. One reasonably may disagree with Congress' assessment of the veto's utility, but the respect due its judgment as a coordinate branch of Government cautions that our holding should be no more extensive than necessary to decide this case. In my view, the case may be decided on a narrower ground. When Congress finds that a particular person does not satisfy the statutory criteria for permanent residence in this country it has assumed a judicial function in violation of the principle of separation of powers. Accordingly, I concur only in the judgment. . . .

JUSTICE WHITE, dissenting:

Today the Court not only invalidates §244(c)(2) of the Immigration and Nationality Act, but also sounds the death knell for nearly 200 other statutory provisions in which Congress has reserved a "legislative veto." For this reason, the Court's decision is of surpassing importance. And it is for this reason that the Court would have been well-advised to decide the case, if possible, on the narrower grounds of separation of powers, leaving for full consideration the constitutionality of other congressional review statutes operating on such varied matters as war powers and agency rulemaking, some of which concern the independent regulatory agencies.

The prominence of the legislative veto mechanism in our contemporary political system and its importance to Congress can hardly be overstated. It has become a central means by which Congress secures the accountability of executive and independent agencies. Without the legislative veto, Congress is faced with the Hobson's choice: either to refrain from delegating the necessary authority, leaving itself with a hopeless task of writing laws with the requisite specificity to cover endless special circumstances across the entire policy landscape, or in the alternative, to abdicate its lawmaking function to the executive branch and independent agencies. To choose the former leaves major national problems unresolved; to opt for the latter risks unaccountable policymaking by those not elected to fill that role. Accordingly, over the past five decades, the legislative veto has been placed in nearly 200 statutes. The device is known in every field of governmental concern: reorganization, budgets, foreign affairs, war powers, and regulation of trade, safety, energy, the environment and the economy. . . .

The history of the legislative veto . . . makes clear that it has not been a sword with which Congress has struck out to aggrandize itself at the expense of the other branches—the concerns of Madison and Hamilton. Rather, the veto has been a means of defense, a reservation of ultimate authority necessary if Congress is to fulfill its designated role under Article I as the nation's lawmaker. While the President has often objected to particular legislative vetoes, generally those left in the hands of congressional committees, the Executive has more often agreed to legislative review as the price for a broad delegation of authority. To be sure, the President may have preferred unrestricted power, but that could be precisely why Congress thought it essential to retain a check on the exercise of delegated authority.

For all these reasons, the apparent sweep of the Court's decision today is regrettable. The Court's Article I analysis appears to invalidate all legislative vetoes irrespective of form or subject. Because the legislative veto is commonly found as a check upon rulemaking by administrative agencies and upon broad-based policy decisions of the Executive Branch, it is particularly unfortunate that the Court reaches its decision in a case involving the exercise of a veto over deportation decisions regarding particular individuals. Courts should always be wary of striking statutes as unconstitutional; to strike an entire class of statutes based on consideration of a somewhat atypical and more readily indictable exemplar of the class is irresponsible. . . .

If the legislative veto were as plainly unconstitutional as the Court strives to suggest, its broad ruling today would be more comprehensible. But, the constitutionality of the legislative veto is anything but clearcut. The issue divides scholars, courts, attorneys general, and the two other branches of the National Government. If the veto devices so flagrantly disregarded the requirements of Article I as the Court today suggests, I find it incomprehensible that Congress, whose members are bound by oath to uphold the Constitution, would have placed these mechanisms in nearly 200 separate laws over a period of 50 years.

The reality of the situation is that the constitutional question posed today is one of immense difficulty over which the executive and legislative branches—as well as scholars and judges—have understandably disagreed. That disagreement stems from the silence of the Constitution on the precise question: The Constitution does not directly authorize or prohibit the legislative veto. Thus, our task should be to determine whether the legislative veto is consistent with the purposes of Art. I and the principles of Separation of Powers which are reflected in that Article and throughout the Constitution. We should not find the lack of a specific constitutional authorization for the legislative veto surprising, and I would not infer disapproval of the mechanism from its absence. From the summer of 1787 to the present the government of the United States has become an endeavor far beyond the contemplation of the Framers. Only within the last half century has the complexity and size of the Federal Government's responsibilities grown so greatly that the Congress must rely on the legislative veto as the most effective if not the only means to insure their role as the nation's lawmakers. But the wisdom of the Framers was to anticipate that the nation would grow and new problems of governance would require different solutions. Accordingly, our Federal Government was intentionally chartered with the flexibility to respond to contemporary needs without losing sight of fundamental democratic principles. . . .

This is the perspective from which we should approach the novel constitutional questions presented by the legislative veto. In my view, neither Article I of the Constitution nor the doctrine of separation of powers is violated by this mechanism by which our elected representatives preserved their voice in the governance of the nation. . . .

The power to exercise a legislative veto is not

the power to write new law without bicameral approval or presidential consideration. The veto must be authorized by statute and may only negate what an executive department or independent agency has proposed. On its face, the legislative veto no more allows one House of Congress to make law than does the presidential veto confer such power upon the President. . . .

The Court's holding today that all legislative-type action must be enacted through the lawmaking process ignores that legislative authority is routinely delegated to the executive branch, to the independent regulatory agencies, and to private individuals and groups. . . .

JUSTICE REHNQUIST with whom JUSTICE WHITE joins, dissenting: [omitted]

Chapter

7

Powers of the President

DECISIONAL TRENDS

The first major Supreme Court decision in which the nature of presidential power was discussed was the landmark case of **Marbury v. Madison,** reprinted in the previous chapter. Chief Justice Marshall, although recognizing broad discretionary powers of the presidency, was insistent in making a distinction between those powers and merely ministerial-administrative functions. President Jefferson's order to his Secretary of State Madison to withhold the justice of the peace commissions to Marbury and others did not fall within the President's discretionary authority. Jefferson exceeded his authority and was duty bound to instruct his Secretary of State to deliver the duly signed and sealed commissions. It was "only" the little technicality of which court had the jurisdiction to issue the writ of mandamus to Madison that provided the occasion for the establishment of the principle of judicial review and the invalidation of a part of an act of Congress.

Not until the Civil War did the Supreme Court have to confront major issues of presidential power and authority. In one notorious incident at the outset of the war, Chief Justice Taney clashed with the Lincoln Administration over the issue of military imprisonment and trial of civilians. Chief Justice Taney in his capacity as circuit judge granted the writ of habeas corpus on behalf of John Merryman; but the military refused to honor the writ, thus provoking Taney to write *Ex Parte Merryman* (1861) in which he denied that the President had the power to suspend the writ of habeas corpus. By ignoring the Chief Justice's opinion, President Lincoln illuminated the severe limits on judicial power, particularly during wartime. Although Chief Justice Taney in *Ex Parte Merryman* had denied that the President has any inherent presidential power to suspend the writ of habeas corpus in the absence of congressional action, the full Court did not rule on this. Indeed, a bitterly divided Court, with Taney in dissent, approved a broad view of presidential power in the very important **Prize Cases.** At the outbreak of the Civil War, President Lincoln took a number of bold steps, including the imposition of a naval blockade of southern ports. Three months later Congress authorized the blockade, but the question before the Court in these cases was the validity of the President's actions *before* Congress had acted. Immediately after the blockade had been ordered, the federal government began seizing various neutral ships (mostly owned by British subjects) carrying products made in the rebel states and had them and their cargo condemned as prizes (or captured enemy property under international law). However, the Union government took the legal position that secession was illegal and that the war was the effort of the national government to put down civil disorder or rebellion, hence the South had no standing under international law (which would have also meant that the Union government had no legal basis for taking "prizes"). The South, on the other hand, considered the war as one between the states and held that under international law the Confederacy was entitled to belligerent status. The Union government, by instituting the blockade and then by taking "prizes," was acting as if the Confederacy was a belligerent under international law; yet the Union refused to concede that a state of war existed. President Lincoln took advantage of international law regarding the capture of prizes during war, but at the same time denied that there was a legal state of war. If no legal state of war existed, not only was the Lincoln Administration violating international law, but Lincoln's actions in instituting the blockade before Congress had acted would be patently illegal. A bare five-man majority ruled that under the circumstances the President could order a blockade and that Confederate property was enemy property subject to government seizure regardless of belligerent status. The majority took a realistic view of the Civil War and the necessity for the President to act as he did. At the same time the majority upheld the Union's legal position that the war was an insurrection and not one between sovereign powers.

After the war, in **Mississippi** v. **Johnson,** the Court further recognized the broad sweep of presidential power and the practical inability of the Court to order the President himself to obey its rulings.

Although the Civil War saw a marked increase in the powers of the presidency, the post–Civil War period saw the scaling back of presidential power, particularly with the confrontation between President Andrew Johnson and Congress. The climax of this confrontation was, of course, the impeachment of the President, trial in the Senate, and acquittal by a close vote. It is not until the twentieth century that we see much litigation concerning the powers of the presidency and the executive branch. Generally, wars and economic crises have been the greatest impetus to the expansion of presidential power and the legitimizing of that expanded role by the Court.

During the White and Taft Courts, the Court was generally supportive of the exercise of presidential-executive powers. For example, in *United States* v. *Grimaud,* 220 U.S. 506 (1911), the Court recognized that administrative rulings have the force of law and that if Congress so enacts, violations can be treated and punished as violations of criminal law. In *United States* v. *Midwest Oil Co.,* 236 U.S. 459 (1915), the Court upheld the power of the President, even in the absence of congressional authority, to issue an executive order removing from public sale valuable public lands. In 1919 the Court upheld President Wilson's seizure and operation of the railroads during World War I in the case of *Northern Pacific Railway Co.* v. *North Dakota,* 250 U.S. 135 (1919). The Court ruled this a valid exercise of the federal war power. The treaty-making power was also broadly construed in **Missouri** v. **Holland,** in which the Court ruled that a treaty with Great Britain for the protection of migratory birds and congressional legislation implementing it did not interfere with the rights reserved to the states under the Tenth Amendment.

The Taft Court in *Ex Parte Grossman,* 267

U.S. 87 (1925), ruled that the President has the constitutional power to pardon anyone convicted of criminal contempt of court. The most far-reaching decision of the Taft Court in favor of presidential power was the decision in the case of **Myers** v. **United States.** The Court ruled that the President has the power to remove subordinate executive officials without the consent of the Senate even though these same officials obtained their jobs with Senate confirmation. The case involved a postmaster summarily dismissed by President Wilson. The decision, squarely in favor of broad presidential powers and implicitly favoring presidential government, was curtailed by the Hughes Court in 1935 in **Humphrey's Executor** v. **United States** when the Court determined that members of independent federal regulatory agencies cannot be summarily removed by the President. Of course, the Court at this time was antagonistic toward the New Deal, and in the **Schechter Poultry Corp.** v. **United States** decision (chap. 8) ruled that Congress cannot delegate to the President such vast powers as it had in the National Industrial Recovery Act. The Court, however, was more permissive when it came to foreign policy and ruled that the conduct of foreign policy is, in effect, out of the hands of the Court (**United States** v. **Curtiss-Wright Export Corporation**). The power of the President was also said by the Court to include the power to enter into executive agreements (*United States* v. *Belmont,* 301 U.S. 324 [1937]).

Without doubt, it was the extreme emergency of World War II that expanded the powers of the presidency and executive branch even beyond those stemming from the economic crisis of the Great Depression. The executive branch assumed full war powers and took complete administrative control of the domestic economy as well as full responsibility for internal security. In terms of the domestic economy, the Court approved both the Emergency Price Control Act of 1942 and the Inflation Control Act of 1942 (in *Yakus* v. *United States* 321 U.S. 414 [1944]), which del-

egated wide-ranging economic powers to the executive branch. The Office of Price Administration was established and its power to administer sanctions was also upheld in *Steuart and Bros.* v. *Bowles,* 322 U.S. 398 (1944).

The exclusion of those of Japanese descent from the West Coast and their internment by the federal government in hastily constructed camps were perhaps the most extreme measures taken in the name of internal security against American citizens and lawfully residing aliens. The Court upheld the various facets of the anti-Japanese program in **Hirabayashi** v. **United States** and **Korematsu** v. **United States.** Only in *Ex Parte Endo,* 323 U.S. 283 (1944), did the Court restrict the executive branch. The Court upheld the federal government's use of military trials in several cases, although provable treason was made more difficult by the decision in *Cramer* v. *United States,* 325 U.S. 1 (1945). The Court restricted the federal government's power to strip citizenship from politically suspect naturalized Americans. In *Schneiderman* v. *United States,* 320 U.S. 118 (1943), the Court refused to allow the denaturalization of a Communist Party member because the government failed to prove that Schneiderman's citizenship had been illegally acquired. In *Baumgartner* v. *United States,* 322 U.S. 665 (1944), the Court similarly prevented the denaturalization of someone with strong pro-Nazi views on the ground that the government failed to prove that Baumgartner had mental reservations when he swore allegiance to the United States at the time of his naturalization in 1932—*before* Hitler had come to power. However, the Court in *Knauer* v. *United States,* 328 U.S. 654 (1946), allowed the denaturalization of a pro-Nazi individual who had sworn his allegiance to the United States at his naturalization ceremony in 1937—*after* Hitler seized control of Germany. The government in this instance had proved that Knauer had sworn falsely. In general, Congress gave the executive branch broad regulatory powers during the war that the Court upheld, the end effect being an expansion of the powers of the institutionalized presidency.

A leading decision stemming from wartime (the Korean War) relating to the powers of the presidency was the famous steel seizure case, **Youngstown Sheet and Tube Co.** v. **Sawyer.** That decision rejected a broad *inherent powers* concept of the presidency. The President may act only as authorized by law, and no congressional or constitutional provision had authorized President Truman to seize the steel mills. However, the Court continued to be deferential to the President in the conduct of foreign affairs. For example, in *Zemel* v. *Rusk,* 381 U.S. 1 (1965), the Court upheld the power of the Secretary of State to refuse issuing a passport that would be valid for travel to Cuba. Furthermore, during the Vietnam War the Court refused to consider the constitutionality of the war. For example, in the case of *Mora* v. *McNamara,* 389 U.S. 934 (1967), the Court denied review of a suit brought by three army privates who contended that the Vietnam War was illegal and that the Secretary of Defense and the Secretary of the Army should be prevented from carrying out orders transferring the men to active duty in Vietnam. The lower courts had dismissed the suit. The Court, however, did decide a number of Selective Service Act cases involving conscientious objectors, but it is doubtful that they affected the President's ability to exercise his power as commander-in-chief of the armed forces.

Only a small number of cases concerning the powers of the President were decided by the Burger Court, but in four major cases involving the Nixon Administration the Court, although dominated by Nixon appointees, decided against the claims of the administration. In **United States** v. **United States District Court** (chap. 16), a unanimous Court ruled that the President's responsibility for domestic security does not entitle him to ignore the Fourth Amendment. In **United States** v. **Nixon,** again a unanimous Court ruled that the legitimate

concerns of executive privilege cannot be stretched to permit the President to withhold evidence necessary for criminal proceedings. And in *Train* v. *City of New York,* 420 U.S. 35 (1975), the Court disallowed the Nixon Administration's practice of impounding funds appropriated by Congress. The President, said the Court, cannot choose *not* to spend monies that Congress has specifically appropriated for particular purposes. These decisions emphasized that the President is not above the law and that obvious violations would not be tolerated by the judiciary. Yet, in **Nixon** v. **Fitzgerald** the Court ruled that the President cannot be sued for damages in civil proceedings, in effect saying that insofar as the consequences of violating civil law are concerned, the President is above the law. However, the President's aides and cabinet officers may, in some circumstances, be held accountable for their actions in civil court (*Harlow* v. *Fitzgerald,* 457 U.S. 800 [1982]; *Mitchell* v. *Forsyth,* 472 U.S. 511 [1985]).

The Burger Court was generous in its interpretation of presidential power when there were no clear-cut violations of law. For example, in *Schick* v. *Reed,* 419 U.S. 256 (1974), the Court adopted a broad view of the presidential pardoning power, thereby permitting the President to attach conditions not specifically provided for by statute. In **INS** v. **Chadha** (chap. 6), the Court ruled unconstitutional the legislative veto over administration actions, and this can be read as a decision favorable to the President and executive branch. So, too, was the decision and reasoning of **Bowsher** v. **Synar** in which the Court, in effect, ruled that an agent of Congress (the Comptroller General) cannot order the President to make specific budget cuts. The Court in these last two decisions emphasized the separation of powers.

The Burger Court followed the tradition of deferring to the President in matters of foreign policy. In late 1979 the Court in *Goldwater* v. *Carter,* 444 U.S. 996 (1979), dismissed a suit by Senator Goldwater and others challenging President Carter's abrogation of the defense treaty with Taiwan without the advice and consent of the Senate. In June 1981 the Court within a three-week period granted certiorari, heard oral argument, and handed down the unanimous decision in *Dames & Moore* v. *Regan,* 453 U.S. 654, upholding the deal with Iran ending the hostage crisis. The upholding of the draft registration law by the Court in 1981 in **Rostker** v. **Goldberg** (chap. 19) can be seen as an example of the Court deferring to Congress and the executive branch in matters concerning foreign policy.

The Rehnquist Court thus far has had few major decisions concerning the powers of the President and the executive branch. The Court avoided deciding a suit concerning the President's ''pocket veto'' power by ruling that the case was moot (*Burke* v. *Barnes,* 479 U.S. 361 [1987]). In **Morrison** v. **Olson** the Court decided the constitutionality of the law providing for the appointment of special prosecutors (technically, independent counsel) and in so doing considered whether the law infringed upon the appointment powers of the President.

THE IMPACT OF THE COURT'S DECISIONS

Table 7.1 summarizes the impact of selected Court decisions concerning the powers of the President. The reprinted cases follow.

Table 7.1 THE IMPACT OF SELECTED COURT DECISIONS CONCERNING THE POWERS OF THE PRESIDENT

Case	Year	Impact on Parties	Short-Run Impact	Long-Run Impact
The Prize Cases	1863	Seizures of goods upheld except for goods bought and paid for before onset of war.	Upheld Lincoln Administration's extraordinary assumption of power during crisis.	Provides precedent for exercise of broad presidential powers in an emergency.
Mississippi v. Johnson	1867	Mississippi forced to accept military reconstruction.	Newly freed slaves protected by Union forces, participate in government; blacks elected to high office including U.S. Senate.	Precedent for exercise of broad presidential powers unchecked by the judicial system.
Missouri v. Holland	1920	Decision is for the birds.	Rejects Tenth Amendment claim of Missouri and provides precedent counter to prevalent dual federalism doctrine.	Provides precedent for broad treaty-making powers of the executive branch.
Myers v. United States	1926	Myers' estate loses as claim for $8,838.71 is rejected.	Upholds practice of awarding postmasterships as political patronage.	Provides precedent for President's removal power and a generous view of presidential discretion.
Humphrey's Executor v. United States	1935	Executor to Humphrey's estate collects salary due.	Decision seen as another assault on Roosevelt Administration by anti–New Deal Court.	Independent regulatory commissions strengthened. Curb on President's policymaking ability.
United States v. Curtiss-Wright Export Corporation	1936	United States wins and proceeds with criminal prosecution.	President Roosevelt's discretion in the foreign policy sphere upheld. Even though Court was locked in struggle with Roosevelt and the New Deal, Court conceded President's primacy in foreign affairs.	Although Court does not use political-questions doctrine it recognizes distinction between foreign and domestic affairs and accords the President considerably more discretion in the realm of foreign policy.

Hirabayashi v. *United States*	1943	Gordon Hirabayashi had to complete 30 remaining days of 90-day sentence.	Court seen as upholding racially restrictive regulation. Some civil libertarians upset, but most Americans seemed unconcerned by ruling. Was precedent for *Korematsu* ruling.	Stands as precedent for exercise of military discretion to maintain internal security even at the expense of civil rights of minority groups. However, Hirabayashi's conviction was overturned by federal district court in 1986.
Korematsu v. *United States*	1944	Korematsu had been given a suspended sentence and five years probation. He had been forcibly taken to a relocation camp. Decision had little impact on him.	Legitimized unprecedented harsh treatment of American citizens and lawfully residing aliens.	Precedent for placing American citizens accused of no crime in concentration camps on the basis of their race where internal security dictates this course of action. However, Korematsu's conviction was overturned by federal district court in 1983. Congress enacted legislation in 1988 in which the government officially apologized and voted restitution of $20,000 to all surviving Americans of Japanese descent who had been in the camps.
Youngstown Sheet and Tube Co. v. *Sawyer*	1952	Steel companies had plants returned to them. Steelworkers went on strike.	Political defeat for President Truman. Steel strike and subsequent settlement that resulted in higher steel prices contributed to nation's economic problems, making it easier for the Republicans to achieve victory in November 1952 elections.	Landmark precedent on limits of presidential power. Decision contributed to swing to strong Congress–weak President pattern that lasted until Lyndon Johnson's presidency.

(continued)

225

Table 7.1 *(continued)*

Case	Year	Impact on Parties	Short-Run Impact	Long-Run Impact
United States v. Nixon	1974	Within two weeks of decision, Nixon resigns the presidency. Tapes given to federal prosecutors.	Incriminating evidence from the tapes forced the resignation of the President and helped to convict the high government officials on trial for obstructing justice in the Watergate incident.	Provides precedent that the President is subject to the rule of law and the rulings of the Supreme Court.
Nixon v. Fitzgerald	1982	Fitzgerald loses and is not paid $28,000 Nixon would have paid him had Fitzgerald won.	Court places the President in special legal status so that President need not fear civil suits for damages.	Uncertain but appears to remove one potential set of restraints on the exercise of presidential power.
Bowsher v. Synar	1986	Named parties in suit not vitally affected by outcome.	Congress in temporary disarray until revised legislation enacted in 1987. Comptroller General now bypassed and mandatory budget cuts are ordered by the Office of Management and Budget.	Precedent for strict interpretation of separation of powers.
Morrison v. Olson	1988	Olson et al. must comply with subpoenas.	Convictions of former Reagan aides brought by special prosecutors stand. Investigations of other former members of executive branch continue.	Thought to have beneficial effect by encouraging ethical behavior.

THE PRIZE CASES,
2 BLACK 635 (1863)

At the onset of the Civil War, President Lincoln ordered a blockade of southern ports. Not until three months later did Congress authorize such action. During the interim the navy seized ships attempting to run the blockade and their contents were condemned as prizes of war under international law. However, war had not been declared and were the President so inclined he could not unilaterally declare war. As a matter of fact, the Lincoln Administration took the position that it was putting down a rebellion and that the southern states did not have the legal status of belligerents. Therefore, there was no legal state of war, a position which carried to its logical conclusion meant that the seizing of prizes was illegal under international law. The owners of seized ships and cargo instituted this series of cases known as The Prize Cases *and in their arguments confronted the Lincoln Administration's contradictory legal position under international law as well as the shaky basis for Lincoln's orders before Congress had acted. The Court had to consider not only international law but constitutional law in the context of the reality of an all-out Civil War, in which the survival of the nation was at stake, and the nature of presidential power under such extraordinary circumstances.*

Majority votes: 5
Dissenting votes: 4

MR. JUSTICE GRIER delivered the opinion of the Court:. . . .

Had the President a right to institute a blockade of ports in possession of persons in armed rebellion against the government, on the principles of international law, as known and acknowledged among civilized States? . . .

That a blockade *de facto* actually existed, and was formally declared and notified by the President on the 27th and 30th of April, 1861, is an admitted fact in these cases.

That the President, as the Chief Executive of the Government and Commander-in-Chief of the Army and Navy, was the proper person to make such notification, has not been, and cannot be disputed.

The right of prize and capture has its origin in the *"jus belli,"* and is governed and adjudged under the laws of nations. To legitimate the capture of a neutral vessel or property on the high seas, a war must exist *de facto*, and the neutral must have knowledge or notice of the intention of one of the parties belligerent to use this mode of coercion against a port, city or territory, in possession of the other.

Let us inquire whether, at the time this blockade was instituted, a state of war existed which would justify a resort to these means of subduing the hostile force. . . .

By the Constitution, Congress alone has the power to declare a national or foreign war. It cannot declare war against a State, or any number of States, by virtue of any clause in the Constitution. The Constitution confers on the President the whole executive power. He is bound to take care that the laws be faithfully executed. He is Commander-in-Chief of the Army and Navy of the United States, and of the militia of the several States when called into the actual service of the United States. He has no power to initiate or declare a war either against a foreign nation or a domestic State. But by the Acts of Congress of Feb. 28th, 1795, and 3d of March, 1807, he is authorized to call out the militia and use the military and naval forces of the United States in case of invasion by foreign nations, and to suppress insurrection against the government of a State or of the United States.

If a war be made by invasion of a foreign nation, the President is not only authorized but bound to resist force, by force. He does not initiate the war, but is bound to accept the challenge without waiting for any special legislative authority. And whether the hostile party be a foreign invader, or States organized in rebellion, it is none the less a war, although the declaration of it be *"unilateral."* . . .

It is not the less a civil war, with belligerent parties in hostile array, because it may be called an "insurrection" by one side, and the insurgents be considered as rebels or traitors. It is not necessary that the independence of the revolted province or State be acknowledged in order to constitute it a party belligerent in a war according to the law of nations. Foreign nations acknowledge it as war by a declaration of neutrality. The condition of neutrality cannot exist unless there be two belligerent parties. . . .

As soon as the news of the attack on Fort Sumter, and the organization of a government by the seceding States, assuming to act as belligerents, could become known in Europe, to wit: on the 13th of May, 1861, the Queen of England issued her proclamation of neutrality, "recognizing hostilities as existing between the Government of the United States of America and certain States styling themselves the Confederate States of America." This was immediately followed by similar declarations or silent acquiescence by other nations.

After such an official recognition by the sovereign, a citizen of a foreign State is estopped to deny the existence of a war, with all its consequences, as regards neutrals. They cannot ask a court to affect a technical ignorance of the existence of a war, which all the world acknowledges to be the greatest civil war known in the history of the human race, and thus cripple the arm of the government and paralyze its power by subtle definitions and ingenious sophisms.

The law of nations is also called the law of nature; it is founded on the common consent as well as the common sense of the world. It contains no such anomalous doctrines as that which this court are now for the first time desired to pronounce, to wit: That insurgents who have risen in rebellion against their sovereign, expelled her courts, established a revolutionary government, organized armies, and commenced hostilities, are not enemies because they are traitors; and a war levied on the government by traitors, in order to dismember and destroy it, is not a war because it is an "insurrection."

Whether the President in fulfilling his duties, as Commander-in-Chief, in suppressing an insurrection, has met with such armed hostile resistance, and a civil war of such alarming proportions as will compel him to accord to them the character of belligerents, is a question to be decided by him, and this court must be governed by the decisions and acts of the Political Department of the government to which this power was intrusted. "He must determine what degree of force the crisis demands." The proclamation of blockade is, itself, official and conclusive evidence to the court that a state of war existed which demanded and authorized a recourse to such a measure, under the circumstances peculiar to the case. . . .

If it were necessary to the technical existence of a war, that it should have a legislative sanction, we find it in almost every Act passed at the extraordinary session of the Legislature of 1861, which was wholly employed in enacting laws to enable the government to prosecute the war with vigor and efficiency. And finally, in 1861 we find Congress . . . passing an Act "approving, legalizing and making valid all the acts, proclamations, and orders of the President, &c., as if they had been issued and done under the previous express authority and direction of the Congress of the United States." . . .

On this first question, therefore, we are of the opinion that the President had a right, *jure belli,* to institute a blockade of ports in possession of the States in rebellion which neutrals are bound to regard. . . .

The decree below [upholding the seizure of the ships and cargo but returning property to a New York business purchased before the war]

is affirmed with costs. . . .

MR. JUSTICE NELSON [dissenting]:. . . .

The legal consequences resulting from a state of war between two countries at this day are well understood, and will be found described in every approved work on the subject of international law. . . .

By our Constitution this power is lodged in Congress. Congress shall have power "to declare war, grant letters of marque and reprisal, and make rules concerning captures on land and water." . . .

It has been argued that the authority conferred on the President by the Act of 1795 invests him with the war power. But the obvious answer is, that it proceeds from a different clause in the Constitution and which is given for different purposes and objects, namely: to execute the laws and preserve the public order and tranquillity of the country in a time of peace by preventing or suppressing any public disorder or disturbance by foreign or domestic enemies. . . .

The Acts of 1795 and 1807 did not, and could not, under the Constitution, confer on the President the power of declaring war against a State of this Union, or of deciding that war existed, and upon that ground authorize the capture and confiscation of the property of every citizen of the State whenever it was found on the waters. . . . It cannot be delegated or surrendered to the Executive. Congress alone can determine whether war exists or should be declared; and until they have acted, no citizen of the State can be punished in his person or property, unless he has committed some offense against a law of Congress passed before the act was committed, which made it a crime, and defined the punishment. The penalty of confiscation for the acts of others with which he had no concern cannot lawfully be inflicted. . . .

Upon the whole, . . . I am compelled to the conclusion that no civil war existed between this Government and the States in insurrection till recognized by the Act of Congress 13th July, 1861; that the President does not possess the power under the Constitution to declare war or recognize its existence within the meaning of the law of nations, which carries with it belligerent rights, and thus change the country and all its citizens from a state of peace to a state of War; that this power belongs exclusively to the Congress of the United States and, consequently, that the President had no power to set on foot a blockade under the law of nations, and the capture of the vessel and cargo in this case, and in all cases before us in which the capture occurred before the 13th July, 1861, for breach of blockade, or as enemies' property, are illegal and

void, and that the decrees of condemnation should be reversed and the vessel and cargo restored.
CHIEF JUSTICE TANEY AND JUSTICES CATRON, NELSON, and CLIFFORD dissented.

MISSISSIPPI v. JOHNSON, 4 WALLACE 475 (1867)

When the Supreme Court decided Ex Parte Milligan *and formulated the open court rule—that civilians may not be tried by military commissions when the civil courts are open and functioning—the Radical Republicans in control of Congress after the Civil War were furious. The open court rule was inconsistent with the concept of military reconstruction whereby the military would supervise the "reconstruction" of the South and military commissions would have jurisdiction over civilians who interfered with Reconstruction and the rights of blacks. Congress, despite the* Milligan *ruling, passed the Reconstruction Acts in 1867, and when President Johnson vetoed them, enacted them over his veto. State officials in Mississippi, in an effort to prevent the onset of Reconstruction, went directly to the Supreme Court on behalf of the state. The state asked for an injunction directed at President Johnson, ordering him not to carry out the Reconstruction Acts on the grounds that they were unconstitutional and if enforced would produce grave injury to the state. The Court was faced for the first time in its history with the prospect of issuing an injunction directed against the President personally. Even if, as in this case, the President would willingly obey (although he opposed in principle the attempt to enjoin him from carrying out an act of Congress), the Congress would clearly not permit its will to be frustrated—and the Radicals in the House of Representatives had the votes for impeachment, which the President himself was soon to discover.*

Votes: Unanimous

MR. CHIEF JUSTICE CHASE delivered the opinion of the Court:

A motion was made, some days since, in behalf of the State of Mississippi, for leave to file a bill in the name of the State, praying this court perpetually to enjoin and restrain Andrew Johnson, President of the United States, and E.O.C. Ord, general commanding in the District of Mississippi and Arkansas, from executing, or in any manner carrying out, certain acts of Congress therein named.

The acts referred to are those of March 2d and March 23d, 1867, commonly known as the Reconstruction Acts.

The Attorney-General objected to the leave asked for, upon the ground that no bill which makes a President a defendant, and seeks an injunction against him to restrain the performance of his duties as President, should be allowed to be filed in this court.

This point has been fully argued, and we will now dispose of it.

We shall limit our inquiry to the question presented by the objection, without expressing any opinion on the broader issues discussed in argument, whether, in any case, the President of the United States may be required, by the process of this court, to perform a purely ministerial act under a positive law, or may be held amenable, in any case, otherwise than by impeachment for crime.

The single point which requires consideration is this: Can the President be restrained by injunction from carrying into effect an act of Congress alleged to be unconstitutional?

It is assumed by the counsel for the State of Mississippi, that the President, in the execution of the Reconstruction Acts, is required to perform a mere ministerial duty. In this assumption there is, we think, a confounding of the terms ministerial and executive, which are by no means equivalent in import.

A ministerial duty, the performance of which may, in proper cases, be required of the head of a department, by judicial process, is one in respect to which nothing is left to discretion. It is a simple, definite duty, arising under conditions admitted or proved to exist, and imposed by law. . . .

Very different is the duty of the President in the exercise of the power to see that the laws are faithfully executed, and among these laws the acts named in the bill. By the first of these acts he is required to assign generals to command in the several military districts, and to detail sufficient military force to enable such officers to discharge their duties under the law. By the supplementary act, other duties are imposed on the several commanding generals, and these duties must necessarily be performed under the supervision of the President as commander-in-chief. The duty thus imposed on the President is in no just sense ministerial. It is purely executive and political.

An attempt on the part of the judicial department of the government to enforce the performance of such duties by the President might be justly characterized, in the language of Chief Justice Marshall, as "an absurd and excessive extravagance."

It is true that in the instance before us the interposition of the court is not sought to enforce action by the Executive under constitutional legislation, but to restrain such action under legislation alleged to be unconstitutional. But we are unable to perceive that this circumstance takes the case out of the general principles which forbid judicial interference with the exercise of Executive discretion.

It was admitted in the argument that the application now made to us is without a precedent; and this is of much weight against it. . . .

The fact that no such application was ever before made in any case indicates the general judgment of the profession that no such application should be entertained. . . .

The Congress is the legislative department of the government; the President is the executive department. Neither can be restrained in its action by the judicial department; though the acts of both, when performed, are, in proper cases, subject to its cognizance.

The impropriety of such interference will be clearly seen upon consideration of its possible consequences.

Suppose the bill filed and the injunction prayed for allowed. If the President refuse obedience, it is needless to observe that the court is without power to enforce its process. If, on the other hand, the President complies with the order of the court and refuses to execute the acts of Congress, is it not clear that a collision may occur between the executive and legislative departments of the government? May not the House of Representatives impeach the President for such refusal? And in that case could this court interfere, in behalf of the President, thus endangered by compliance with its mandate, and restrain by injunction the Senate of the United States from sitting as a court of impeachment? Would the strange spectacle be offered to the public world of an attempt by this court to arrest proceedings in that court?

These questions answer themselves.

It is true that a State may file an original bill in this court. And it may be true, in some cases, that such a bill may be filed against the United States. But we are fully satisfied that this court has no jurisdiction of a bill to enjoin the President in the performance of his official duties; and that no such bill ought to be received by us. . . .

The motion for leave to file the bill is, therefore,

Denied.

MISSOURI v. HOLLAND,
252 U.S. 416 (1920)

This little case is considered important because of what the majority had to say about the treaty-making power of the national government. It is also important because of its view of the state's powers under the Tenth Amendment. The decision is as relevant for what it says about executive power as for what it says about federalism. The relevant facts are recounted in the opinion. Because the subject of the treaty at issue was migratory birds, it gave flight to subtle humor on the part of Justice Holmes. Today, environmentalists would cry foul at any attempt to upset a treaty aimed at protecting endangered species.

Majority votes: 7
Dissenting votes: 2

Mr. Justice Holmes delivered the opinion of the Court:

This is a bill in equity brought by the State of Missouri to prevent a game warden of the United States from attempting to enforce the Migratory Bird Treaty Act of July 3, 1918, and the regulations made by the Secretary of Agriculture in pursuance of the same. . . . [T]he question raised is the general one whether the treaty and a statute are void as an interference with the rights reserved to the States.

To answer this question it is not enough to refer to the Tenth Amendment, reserving the powers not delegated to the United States, because by Article 2, Section 2, the power to make treaties is delegated expressly, and by Article 6 treaties made under the authority of the United States, along with the Constitution and laws of the United States made in pursuance thereof, are declared the supreme law of the land. If the treaty is valid there can be no dispute about the validity of the statute under Article 1, Section 8, as a necessary and proper means to execute the powers of the Government. The language of the Constitution as to the supremacy of treaties being general, the question before us is narrowed to an inquiry into the ground upon which the present supposed exception is placed.

It is said that a treaty cannot be valid if it infringes the Constitution, that there are limits, therefore, to the treaty-making power, and that one such limit is that what an act of Congress could not do unaided, in derogation of the powers reserved to the States, a treaty cannot do. An earlier act of Congress that attempted by itself and not in pursuance of a treaty to regulate the killing of migratory birds within the States had been held bad in the District Court. Those decisions were supported by arguments that migratory birds were owned by the States in their sovereign capacity for the benefit of their people, and that under cases like *Geer v. Connecticut,* 161 U.S. 519, this control was one that

Congress had no power to displace. The same argument is supposed to apply now with equal force.

Whether the . . . cases cited were decided rightly or not they cannot be accepted as a test of the treaty power. Acts of Congress are the supreme law of the land only when made in pursuance of the Constitution, while treaties are declared to be so when made under the authority of the United States. It is open to question whether the authority of the United States means more than the formal acts prescribed to make the convention. We do not mean to imply that there are no qualifications to the treaty-making power; best they must be ascertained in a different way. It is obvious that there may be matters of the sharpest exigency for the national well being that an act of Congress could not deal with but that a treaty followed by such an act could, and it is not lightly to be assumed that, in matters requiring national action, "a power which must belong to and somewhere reside in every civilized government" is not to be found. *Andrews* v. *Andrews,* 188 U.S. 14,33. What was said in that case with regard to the powers of the States applies with equal force to the powers of the nation in cases where the States individually are incompetent to act. We are not yet discussing the particular case before us but only are considering the validity of the test proposed. With regard to that we may add that when we are dealing with words that also are a constituent act, like the Constitution of the United States, we must realize that they have called into life a being the development of which could not have been foreseen completely by the most gifted of its begetters. It was enough for them to realize or to hope that they had created an organism; it has taken a century and has cost their successors much sweat and blood to prove that they created a nation. The case before us must be considered in the light of our whole experience and not merely in that of what was said a hundred years ago. The treaty in question does not contravene any prohibitory words to be found in the Constitution. The only question is whether it is forbidden by some invisible radiation from the general terms of the Tenth Amendment. We must consider what this country has become in deciding what that amendment has reserved.

The State as we have intimated founds its claim of exclusive authority upon an assertion of title to migratory birds, an assertion that is embodied in statute. No doubt it is true that as between a State and its inhabitants the State may regulate the killing and sale of such birds, but it does not follow that its authority is exclusive of paramount powers. To put the claim of the State upon title is to lean upon a slender reed. Wild birds are not in the possession of anyone; and possession is the beginning of ownership. The whole foundation of the State's rights is the presence within their jurisdiction of birds that yesterday had not arrived, tomorrow may be in another State and in a week a thousand miles away. If we are to be accurate we cannot put the case of the State upon higher ground than that the treaty deals with creatures that for the moment are within the state borders, that it must be carried out by officers of the United States within the same territory, and that but for the treaty the State would be free to regulate this subject itself. . . .

Here a national interest of very nearly the first magnitude is involved. It can be protected only by national action in concert with that of another power. The subject matter is only transitorily within the State and has no permanent habitat therein. But for the treaty and the statute there soon might be no birds for any powers to deal with. We see nothing in the Constitution that compels the Government to sit by while a food supply is cut off and the protectors of our forests and our crops are destroyed. It is not sufficient to rely upon the States. The reliance is vain, and were it otherwise, the question is whether the United States is forbidden to act. We are of opinion that the treaty and statute must be upheld.

Decree affirmed.

MR. JUSTICE VAN DEVANTER and MR. JUSTICE PITNEY dissent [without opinion].

MYERS v. UNITED STATES, 272 U.S. 52 (1926)

This case raised important questions of the President's power to remove from office members of the executive branch of government who had been appointed by the President with the advice and consent of the Senate. This case involved removal of postmasters, and as such was of special interest to the political parties because until 1970 when it was reorganized, the United States Postal Service (as it is now called) was run on a partisan basis. The Postmaster General was a member of the President's cabinet coming to Washington after having played a key role in the presidential election campaign. Postmasterships were considered prime political patronage. This also meant that by tradition a postmaster resigned when asked to do so by the President. Myers refused to resign, as is noted in the facts of the case as recounted by Chief Justice Taft in his opinion of the Court. Taft, the only justice in the history of the Court to have also been President, was particularly sensitive to the prerogatives of presidential office. Note that Myers died before the case came to Court but his widow, as administrator of the estate, continued the suit. Also note that in ruling as it did, the Court struck down as unconstitutional two separate acts of Congress.

Majority votes: 6
Dissenting votes: 3

MR. CHIEF JUSTICE TAFT delivered the opinion of the Court:

This case presents the question whether under the Constitution the President has the exclusive power of removing executive officers of the United States whom he has appointed by and with the advice and consent of the Senate.

Myers . . . was on July 21, 1917, appointed by the President, by and with the advice and consent of the Senate, to be a postmaster of the first class at Portland, Oregon, for a term of four years. On January 20, 1920, Myers' resignation was demanded. He refused the demand. On February 2, 1920, he was removed from office by order of the Postmaster General, acting by direction of the President. . . . On April 21, 1921, he brought this suit in the Court of Claims for his salary from the date of his removal, which, as claimed by supplemental petition filed after July 21, 1921, the end of his term, amounted to $8,838.71. . . .

The Court of Claims gave judgment against Myers and this is an appeal from that judgment. . . .

By the sixth section of the Act of Congress of July 12, 1876, under which Myers was appointed with the advice and consent of the Senate as a first-class postmaster, it is provided that:

"Postmasters of the first, second, and third classes shall be appointed and may be removed by the President by and with the advice and consent of the Senate, and shall hold their offices for four years unless sooner removed or suspended according to law."

The Senate did not consent to the President's removal of Myers during his term. If this statute in its requirement that his term should be four years unless sooner removed by the President by and with the consent of the Senate is valid, the appellant, Myers' administratrix, is entitled to recover his unpaid salary for his full term and the judgment of the Court of Claims must be reversed. The government maintains that that requirement is invalid, for the reason that under article 2 of the Constitution the President's power of removal of executive officers appointed by him with the advice and consent of the Senate is full and complete without consent of the Senate. If this view is sound, the removal of Myers by the President without the Senate's consent was legal, and the judgment of the Court of Claims against the appellant was correct, and must be affirmed, though for a different reason from that given by that court. We are therefore confronted by the constitutional question and cannot avoid it. . . .

The question where the power of removal of executive officers appointed by the President by and with the advice and consent of the Senate was vested, was presented early in the first session of the First Congress. There is no express provision respecting removals in the Constitution, except as section 4 of article 2 provides for removal from office by impeachment. The subject was not discussed in the Constitutional Convention. . . .

In the House of Representatives of the First Congress, on Tuesday, May 18, 1789, Mr. Madison moved in the committee of the whole that there should be established three executive departments, one of Foreign Affairs, another of the Treasury, and a third of War, at the head of each of which there should be a Secretary, to be appointed by the President by and with the advice and consent of the Senate, and to be removable by the President. The committee agreed to the establishment of a Department of Foreign Affairs, but a discussion ensued as to making the Secretary removable by the President. "The question was now taken and carried, by a considerable majority, in favor of declaring the power of removal to be in the President." . . .

It is very clear . . . that the exact question which the House voted upon was whether it should recognize and declare the power of the President under the Constitution to remove the Secretary of Foreign Affairs without the advice and consent of the Senate. That was what the vote was taken for. Some effort has been made to question whether the decision carries the result claimed for it, but there is not the slightest doubt, after an examination of the record, that the vote was, and was intended to be, a legislative declaration that the power to remove officers appointed by the President and the Senate vested in the President alone, and until the Johnson impeachment trial in 1868 its meaning was not doubted, even by those who questioned its soundness. . . .

Mr. Madison and his associates in the discussion in the House dwelt at length upon the necessity there was for construing article 2 to give the President the sole power of removal in his responsibility for the conduct of the executive branch, and enforced this by emphasizing his duty expressly declared in the third section of the article to "take care that the laws be faithfully executed."

The vesting of the executive power in the President was essentially a grant of the power to execute the laws. But the President alone and unaided could not execute the laws. He must execute them by the assistance of subordinates. This view has since been repeatedly affirmed by this court. . . . As he is charged specifically to take care that they be faithfully executed, the reasonable implication, even in the absence of express words, was that as part of his executive power he should select those who were to act for him under his direction in the execution of the laws. The further implication must be, in the absence of any express limitation respecting removals, that as his selection of administrative officers is essential to the execution of the laws by him, so must be his power of removing those for whom he cannot continue to be responsible. It was urged that the natural meaning of the term "executive power" granted the President included the appointment and removal of executive subordinates. If such appointments and removals were not an exercise of the executive power, what were they? They certainly were not the exercise of legislative or judicial power in government as usually understood. . . .

It was pointed out in this great debate that the power of removal, though equally essential to the executive power is different in its nature from that of appointment. A veto by the Senate—a part of the legislative branch of the government—upon removals is a much greater limitation upon the executive branch, and a much more serious blending of the legislative with the executive, than a rejection of a proposed appointment. It is not to be implied. The rejection of a nominee of the President for a particular office does not greatly embarrass him in the conscientious discharge of his high duties in the selection of those who are to aid him, because the President usually has an ample field from which to select for office, according to his preference, competent and capable men. The Senate has full power to reject newly proposed appointees whenever the President shall remove the incumbents. Such a check enables the Senate to prevent the filling of offices with bad or incompetent men, or with those against whom there is tenable objection.

The power to prevent the removal of an officer who has served under the President is different from the authority to consent to or reject his appointment. When a nomination is made, it may be presumed that the Senate is, or may become, as well advised as to the fitness of the nominee as the President, but in the nature of things the defects in ability or intelligence or loyalty in the administration of the laws of one who has served as an officer under the President are facts as to which the President, or his trusted subordinates, must be better informed than the Senate, and the power to remove him may therefore be regarded as confined for very sound and practical reasons, to the governmental authority which has administrative control. The power of removal is incident to the power of appointment, not to the power of advising and consenting to appointment, and when the grant of the executive power is enforced by the express mandate to take care that the laws be faithfully executed, it emphasizes the necessity for including within the executive powers as conferred the exclusive power of removal. . . .

A reference of the whole power of removal to general legislation by Congress is quite out of keeping with the plan of government devised by the framers of the Constitution. It could never have been intended to leave to Congress unlimited discretion to vary fundamentally the operation of the great independent executive branch of government and thus most seriously to weaken it. It would be a delegation by the convention to Congress of the function of defining the primary boundaries of another of the three great divisions of government. The inclusion of removals of executive officers in the executive power vested in the President by article 2 according to its usual definition, and the implication of his power of removal of such officers from the provision of section 2 expressly recognizing in him the power of their appointment, are a much more natural and appropriate source of the removing power.

It is reasonable to suppose also that had it been intended to give to Congress power to regulate or control removals in the manner suggested, it would have been included among the specifically enumerated legislative powers in article 1, or in the specified limitations on the executive power in article 2. The difference between the grant of legislative power under article 1 to Congress which is limited to powers therein enumerated, and the more general grant of the executive power to the President under article 2 is significant. The fact that the executive power is given in general terms strengthened by specific terms where emphasis is appropriate, and limited by direct expressions where limitation is needed, and that no express limit is placed on the power of removal by the executive is a convincing indication that none was intended. . . .

When on the merits we find our conclusion strongly favoring the view which prevailed in the

First Congress, we have no hesitation in holding that conclusion to be correct; and it therefore follows that the Tenure of Office Act of 1867, in so far as it attempted to prevent the President from removing executive officers who had been appointed by him by and with the advice and consent of the Senate, was invalid, and that subsequent legislation of the same effect was equally so.

For the reasons given, we must therefore hold that the provision of the law of 1876 by which the unrestricted power of removal of first-class postmasters is denied to the President is in violation of the Constitution and invalid. . . .

Judgment affirmed.

The separate opinion of MR. JUSTICE MCREYNOLDS [dissenting]: [omitted]

MR. JUSTICE BRANDEIS, dissenting:. . . .

. . . May the President, having acted under the statute in so far as it creates the office and authorizes the appointment, ignore, while the Senate is in session, the provision which prescribes the condition under which a removal may take place?

It is this narrow question, and this only, which we are required to decide. We need not consider what power the President, being Commander-in-Chief, has over officers in the Army and the Navy. We need not determine whether the President, acting alone, may remove high political officers. We need not even determine whether, acting alone, he may remove inferior civil officers when the Senate is not in session. It was in session when the President purported to remove Myers, and for a long time thereafter. All questions of statutory construction have been eliminated by the language of the act. It is settled that, in the absence of a provision expressly providing for the consent of the Senate to a removal, the clause fixing the tenure will be construed as a limitation, not as a grant, and that, under such legislation, the President, acting alone, has the power of removal. . . . But in defining the tenure, this statute used words of grant. Congress clearly intended to preclude a removal without the consent of the Senate. . . .

The separation of the powers of government did not make each branch completely autonomous. It left each in some measure, dependent upon the others, as it left to each power to exercise, in some respects, functions in their nature executive, legislative and judicial. Obviously the President cannot secure full execution of the laws, if Congress denies to him adequate means of doing so. Full execution may be defeated because Congress declines to create offices indispensable for that purpose; or be-cause Congress, having created the office, declines to make the indispensable appropriation; or because Congress, having both created the office and made the appropriation, prevents, by restrictions which it imposes, the appointment of officials who in quality and character are indispensable to the efficient execution of the law. If, in any such way, adequate means are denied to the President, the fault will lie with Congress. The President performs his full constitutional duty, if, with the means and instruments provided by Congress and within the limitations prescribed by it, he uses his best endeavors to secure the faithful execution of the laws enacted. . . .

Checks and balances were established in order that this should be "a government of laws and not of men." As . . . [was] said in the House in 1789, an uncontrollable power of removal in the Chief Executive "is a doctrine not to be learned in American governments." Such power had been denied in colonial charters, and even under proprietary grants and royal commissions. It had been denied in the thirteen states before the framing of the federal Constitution. The doctrine of the separation of powers was adopted by the convention of 1787 not to promote efficiency but to preclude the exercise of arbitrary power. The purpose was not to avoid friction, but, by means of the inevitable friction incident to the distribution of the governmental powers among three departments, to save the people from autocracy. In order to prevent arbitrary executive action, the Constitution provided in terms that presidential appointments be made with the consent of the Senate, unless Congress should otherwise provide; and this clause was construed by Alexander Hamilton in *The Federalist,* No. 77, as requiring like consent to removals. Limiting further executive prerogatives customary in monarchies, the Constitution empowered Congress to vest the appointment of inferior officers, "as we think proper, in the President alone, in the Courts of Law, or in the Heads of Departments." Nothing in support of the claim of uncontrollable power can be inferred from the silence of the convention of 1787 on the subject of removal. For the outstanding fact remains that every specific proposal to confer such uncontrollable power upon the President was rejected. In America, as in England, the conviction prevailed then that the people must look to representative assemblies for the protection of their liberties. And protection of the individual, even if he be an official, from the arbitrary or capricious exercise of power was then believed to be an essential of free government.

MR. JUSTICE HOLMES, dissenting:. . . .

The arguments drawn from the executive power of the President, and from his duty to appoint officers of the United States (when Congress does not vest the appointment elsewhere), to take care that the laws be faithfully executed, and to commission all officers of the United States, seem to me spiders' webs inadequate to control the dominant facts.

We have to deal with an office that owes its existence to Congress and that Congress may abolish tomorrow. Its duration and the pay attached to it while it lasts depend on Congress alone. Congress alone confers on the President the power to appoint to it and at any time may transfer the power to other hands. With such power over its own creation, I have no more trouble in believing that Congress has power to prescribe a term of life for it free from any interference than I have in accepting the undoubted power of Congress to decree its end. I have equally little trouble in accepting its power to prolong the tenure of an incumbent until Congress or the Senate shall have assented to his removal. The duty of the President to see that the laws be executed is a duty that does not go beyond the laws or require him to achieve more than Congress sees fit to leave within his power.

HUMPHREY'S EXECUTOR v. UNITED STATES, 295 U.S. 602 (1935)

William E. Humphrey was appointed to the Federal Trade Commission by President Herbert Hoover. This was Humphrey's second term, and, as before, he was confirmed by the Senate for a term of seven years expiring September 25, 1938. However, the year after this new appointment, Franklin D. Roosevelt was elected President and when he took office Roosevelt sought to bring new ways of thinking to solve the nation's problems. Humphrey was considered an obstructionist of the New Deal and was asked to resign. Humphrey refused and was then removed from office by the President. Humphrey challenged his removal from office but died about four months after he was purged from the federal payroll. The executor of Humphrey's estate pursued the claim for the salary that was not paid from the date of removal to the day of Humphrey's death. The Court of Claims when confronted with this dispute certified two questions to the Supreme Court.

Votes: Unanimous

MR. JUSTICE SUTHERLAND delivered the opinion of the Court:

Plaintiff brought suit in the Court of Claims against the United States to recover a sum of money alleged to be due the deceased for salary as a Federal Trade Commissioner from October 8, 1933, when the President undertook to remove him from office, to the time of his death on February 14, 1934. The court below has certified to this court two questions . . .:

"1. Do the provisions of section 1 of the Federal Trade Commission Act, stating that 'any commissioner may be removed by the President for inefficiency, neglect of duty, or malfeasance in office,' restrict or limit the power of the President to remove a commissioner except upon one or more of the causes named?

If the foregoing question is answered in the affirmative, then—

2. If the power of the President to remove a commissioner is restricted or limited as shown by the foregoing interrogatory and the answer made thereto, is such a restriction or limitation valid under the Constitution of the United States?"

The Federal Trade Commission Act creates a commission of five members to be appointed by the President by and with the advice and consent of the Senate, and section 1 provides: "Not more than three of the commissioners shall be members of the same political party. The . . . commissioners appointed shall continue in office for terms of seven years, except that any person chosen to fill a vacancy shall be appointed only for the unexpired term of the commissioner whom he shall succeed. . . . Any commissioner may be removed by the President for inefficiency, neglect of duty, or malfeasance in office. . . .

. . . The commission is to be nonpartisan; and it must, from the very nature of its duties, act with entire impartiality. It is charged with the enforcement of no policy except the policy of the law. Its duties are neither political nor executive, but predominantly quasi judicial and quasi legislative. Like the Interstate Commerce Commission, its members are called upon to exercise the trained judgment of a body of experts "appointed by law and informed by experience." . . .

The legislative reports in both houses of Congress clearly reflected the view that a fixed term was necessary to the effective and fair administration of the law. . . .

The debates in both houses demonstrate that the

prevailing view was that the Commission was not to be "subject to anybody in the government but *** only to the people of the United States"; free from "political domination or control" or the "probability or possibility of such a thing"; to be "separate and apart from any existing department of the government—not subject to the orders of the President." . . .

Thus, the language of the act, the legislative reports, and the general purposes of the legislation as reflected by the debates, all combine to demonstrate the congressional intent to create a body of experts who shall gain experience by length of service; a body which shall be independent of executive authority, *except in its selection,* and free to exercise its judgment without the leave or hindrance of any other official or any department of the government. To the accomplishment of these purposes, it is clear that Congress was of opinion that length and certainty of tenure would vitally contribute. And to hold that, nevertheless, the members of the commission continue in office at the mere will of the President, might be to thwart, in large measure, the very ends which Congress sought to realize by definitely fixing the term of office.

We conclude that the intent of the act is to limit the executive power of removal to the causes enumerated, the existence of none of which is claimed here; and we pass to the second question.

Second. To support its contention that the removal provision of section 1, as we have just construed it, is an unconstitutional interference with the executive power of the President, the government's chief reliance is *Myers* v. *United States.* . . . [T]he narrow point actually decided was only that the President had power to remove a postmaster of the first class, without the advice and consent of the Senate as required by act of Congress. In the course of the opinion of the court, expressions occur which tend to sustain the government's contention, but these are beyond the point involved and, therefore, do not come within the rule of *stare decisis*. In so far as they are out of harmony with the views here set forth, these expressions are disapproved. . . .

The office of a postmaster is so essentially unlike the office now involved that the decision in the Myers Case cannot be accepted as controlling our decision here. A postmaster is an executive officer restricted to the performance of executive functions. He is charged with no duty at all related to either the legislative or judicial power. The actual decision in the Myers Case finds support in the the-

ory that such an officer is merely one of the units in the executive department and, hence, inherently subject to the exclusive and illimitable power of removal by the Chief Executive, whose subordinate and aide he is. Putting aside dicta, which may be followed if sufficiently persuasive but which are not controlling, the necessary reach of the decision goes far enough to include all purely executive officers. It goes no farther; much less does it include an officer who occupies no place in the executive department and who exercises no part of the executive power vested by the Constitution in the President.

The Federal Trade Commission is an administrative body created by Congress to carry into effect legislative policies embodied in the statute in accordance with the legislative standard therein prescribed, and to perform other specified duties as a legislative or as a judicial aide. Such a body cannot in any proper sense be characterized as an arm or an eye of the executive. Its duties are performed without executive leave and, in the contemplation of the statute, must be free from executive control. In administering the provisions of the statute in respect of "unfair methods of competition," that is to say, in filling in and administering the details embodied by that general standard, the commission acts in part quasi-legislatively and in part quasi-judicially. In making investigations and reports thereon for the information of Congress under section 6, in aid of the legislative power, it acts as a legislative agency. Under section 7, which authorizes the commission to act as a master in chancery under rules prescribed by the court, it acts as an agency of the judiciary. To the extent that it exercises any executive function, as distinguished from executive power in the constitutional sense, it does so in the discharge and effectuation of its quasi-legislative or quasi-judicial powers, or as an agency of the legislative or judicial departments of the government.

If Congress is without authority to prescribe causes for removal of members of the trade commission and limit executive power of removal accordingly, that power at once becomes practically all-inclusive in respect of civil officers with the exception of the judiciary provided for by the Constitution. The Solicitor General, at the bar, apparently recognizing this to be true, with commendable candor, agreed that his view in respect of the removability of members of the Federal Trade Commission necessitated a like view in respect of the Interstate Commerce Commission and the Court of Claims. We are thus confronted with the serious question whether not only the members of these quasi-legislative and quasi-judicial bodies, but the judges of the legislative Court of Claims, exercising judicial power continue in office only at the pleasure of the President.

We think it plain under the Constitution that illimitable power of removal is not possessed by the President in respect of officers of the character of those just named. The authority of Congress, in creating quasi-legislative or quasi-judicial agencies, to require them to act in discharge of their duties independently of executive control cannot well be doubted; and that authority includes, as an appropriate incident, power to fix the period during which they shall continue, and to forbid their removal except for cause in the meantime. For it is quite evident that one who holds his office only during the pleasure of another cannot be depended upon to maintain an attitude of independence against the latter's will. . . .

In the light of the question now under consideration, we have re-examined the precedents referred to in the Myers Case, and find nothing in them to justify a conclusion contrary to that which we have reached. . . .

The result of what we now have said is this: Whether the power of the President to remove an officer shall prevail over the authority of Congress to condition the power by fixing a definite term and precluding a removal except for cause will depend upon the character of the office; the *Myers* decision, affirming the power of the President alone to make the removal, is confined to purely executive officers; and as to officers of the kind here under consideration, we hold that no removal can be made during the prescribed term for which the officer is appointed, except for one or more of the causes named in the applicable statute.

To the extent that, between the decision in the Myers Case, which sustains the unrestrictable power of the President to remove purely executive officers, and our present decision that such power does not extend to an office such as that here involved, there shall remain a field of doubt. We leave such cases as may fall within it for future consideration and determination as they may arise.

In accordance with the foregoing, the questions submitted are answered:

Question No. 1, Yes.
Question No. 2, Yes.

MR. JUSTICE MCREYNOLDS [concurring] agrees that both questions should be answered in the affirmative. . . .

UNITED STATES v. CURTISS-WRIGHT EXPORT CORPORATION, 299 U.S. 304 (1936)

The facts of the case are stated in Justice Sutherland's opinion. After the Curtiss-Wright Export Corporation was indicted, it successfully challenged the indictment in federal district court. The government took the case directly to the Supreme Court. Although the Court did not use the political-questions doctrine, it nevertheless was highly deferential to the President's exercise of foreign policy powers. Note the marked distinction the Court makes between domestic and foreign affairs.

Majority votes: 7
Dissenting votes: 1

MR. JUSTICE SUTHERLAND delivered the opinion of the Court:

On January 27, 1936, an indictment was returned in the court below, the first count of which charges that appellees, beginning with the 29th day of May, 1934, conspired to sell in the United States certain arms of war, namely, fifteen machine guns, to Bolivia, a country then engaged in armed conflict in the Chaco, in violation of the Joint Resolution of Congress approved May 28, 1934, and the provisions of a proclamation issued on the same day by the President of the United States pursuant to authority conferred by section 1 of the resolution. In pursuance of the conspiracy, the commission of certain overt acts was alleged, details of which need not be stated. . . .

. . . It is contended that by the Joint Resolution the going into effect and continued operation of the resolution was conditioned (a) upon the President's judgment as to its beneficial effect upon the re-establishment of peace between the countries engaged in armed conflict in the Chaco; (b) upon the making of a proclamation, which was left to his unfettered discretion, thus constituting an attempted substitution of the President's will for that of Congress; (c) upon the making of a proclamation putting an end to the operation of the resolution, which again was left to the President's unfettered discretion; and (d) further, that the extent of its operation in particular cases was subject to limitation and exception by the President, controlled by no standard. In each of these particulars, appellees urge that Congress abdicated its essential functions and delegated them to the Executive.

Whether, if the Joint Resolution had related solely to internal affairs, it would be open to the challenge that it constituted an unlawful delegation of legislative power to the Executive, we find it unnecessary to determine. The whole aim of the resolution is to affect a situation entirely external to the United States, and falling within the category of foreign affairs. The determination which we are called to make, therefore, is whether the Joint Resolution as applied to that situation, is vulnerable to attack under the rule that forbids a delegation of the lawmaking power. In other words, assuming (but not deciding) that the challenged delegation, if it were confined to internal affairs, would be invalid, may it nevertheless be sustained on the ground that its exclusive aim is to afford a remedy for a hurtful condition within foreign territory?

It will contribute to the elucidation of the question if we first consider the differences between the powers of the federal government in respect of foreign or external affairs and those in respect of domestic or internal affairs. That there are differences between them, and that these differences are fundamental, may not be doubted.

The two classes of powers are different, both in respect of their origin and their nature. The broad statement that the federal government can exercise no powers except those specifically enumerated in the Constitution, and such implied powers as are necessary and proper to carry into effect the enumerated powers, is categorically true only in respect of our internal affairs. In that field, the primary purpose of the Constitution was to crave from the general mass of legislative powers *then possessed by the states* such portions as it was thought desirable to vest in the federal government, leaving those not included in the enumeration still in the states. That this doctrine applies only to powers which the states had is self-evident. And since the states severally never possessed international powers, such powers could not have been carved from the mass of state powers but obviously were transmitted to the United States from some other source. . . .

As a result of the separation from Great Britain by the colonies, acting as a unit, the powers of external sovereignty passed from the Crown not to the colonies severally, but to the colonies in their collective and corporate capacity as the United States of America. Even before the Declaration, the colonies were a unit in foreign affairs, acting through a common agency—namely, the Continental Congress, composed of delegates from the thirteen colonies. That agency exercised the powers of war and peace, raised an army, created a navy, and finally adopted the Declaration of Independence. Rulers come and go; governments end and forms of government change; but sovereignty survives. . . .

It results that the investment of the federal government with the powers of external sovereignty did not depend upon the affirmative grants of the Constitution. The powers to declare and wage war, to conclude peace, to make treaties, to maintain diplomatic relations with other sovereignties, if they had never been mentioned in the Constitution, would have vested in the federal government as necessary concomitants of nationality. . . .

Not only, as we have shown, is the federal power over external affairs in origin and essential character different from that over internal affairs, but participation in the exercise of the power is significantly limited. In this vast external realm, with its important, complicated, delicate and manifold problems, the President alone has the power to speak or listen as a representative of the nation. He *makes* treaties with the advice and consent of the Senate; but he alone negotiates. Into the field of negotiation the Senate cannot intrude; and Congress itself is powerless to invade it. . . .

It is important to bear in mind that we are here dealing not alone with an authority vested in the President by an exertion of legislative power, but with such an authority plus the very delicate, plenary and exclusive power of the President as the sole organ of the federal government in the field of international relations—a power which does not require as a basis for its exercise an act of Congress, but which, of course, like every other governmental power, must be exercised in subordination to the applicable provisions of the Constitution. It is quite apparent that if, in the maintenance of our international relations, embarrassment—perhaps serious embarrassment—is to be avoided and success for our aims achieved, congressional legislation which is to be made effective through negotiation and inquiry within the international field must often accord to the President a degree of discretion and freedom from statutory restriction which would not be admissible were domestic affairs alone involved. Moreover, he, not Congress, has the better opportunity of knowing the conditions which prevail in foreign countries, and especially is this true in time of war. He has his confidential sources of information. He has his agents in the form of diplomatic, consular and other officials. Secrecy in respect of information gathered by them may be highly necessary, and the premature disclosure of it productive of harmful results. . . .

The marked difference between foreign affairs and domestic affairs in this respect is recognized by both houses of Congress in the very form of their requisitions for information from the executive departments. In the case of every department except the Department of State, the resolution *directs* the official to furnish the information. In the case of the State Department, dealing with foreign affairs, the President is *requested* to furnish the information "if not incompatible with the public interest." A statement that to furnish the information is not compatible with the public interest rarely, if ever, is questioned.

When the President is to be authorized by legislation to act in respect of a matter intended to affect a situation in foreign territory, the legislator properly bears in mind the important consideration that the form of the President's action—or, indeed, whether he shall act at all—may well depend, among other things, upon the nature of the confidential information which he has or may thereafter receive, or upon the effect which his action may have upon our foreign relations. This consideration, in connection with what we have already said on the subject discloses the unwisdom of requiring Congress in this field of governmental power to lay down narrowly defined standards by which the President is to be governed. . . .

In the light of the foregoing observations, it is evident that this court should not be in haste to apply a general rule which will have the effect of condemning legislation like that under review as constituting an unlawful delegation of legislative power. The principles which justify such legislation find overwhelming support in the unbroken legislative practice which has prevailed almost from the inception of the national government to the present day. . . .

The result of holding that the joint resolution here under attack is void and unenforceable as constituting an unlawful delegation of legislative power would be to stamp . . . [the] multitude of comparable acts and resolutions as likewise invalid. And while this court may not, and should not, hesitate to declare acts of Congress, however many times repeated, to be unconstitutional if beyond all rational doubt it finds them to be so, an impressive array of legislation . . . enacted by nearly every Congress from the beginning of our national existence to the present day, must be given unusual weight in the process of reaching a correct determination of the problem. A legislative practice such as we have here, evidenced not by only occasional instances, but marked by the movement of a steady stream for a century and a half of time, goes a long way in the direction of proving the presence of unassailable ground for the constitutionality of the practice, to be found in the origin and history of the power involved, or in its nature, or in both combined. . . .

. . . [T]o summarize . . . both upon principle and in accordance with precedent, we conclude there is sufficient warrant for the broad discretion vested in the President to determine whether the enforcement of the statute will have a beneficial effect upon the re-establishment of peace in the affected countries; whether he shall make proclamation to bring the resolution into operation; whether and when the resolution shall cease to operate and to make proclamation accordingly; and to prescribe limitations and exceptions to which the enforcement of the resolution shall be subject. . . .

The judgment of the court below must be reversed and the cause remanded for further proceedings in accordance with the foregoing opinion.

It is so ordered.

MR. JUSTICE MCREYNOLDS [dissenting] does not agree. He is of opinion that the court below reached the right conclusion and its judgment ought to be affirmed.

MR. JUSTICE STONE took no part in the consideration or decision of this case.

HIRABAYASHI v. UNITED STATES, 320 U.S. 81 (1943)

After Japan attacked Pearl Harbor on that day of infamy, December 7, 1941, the West Coast experienced widespread hysteria, fear, and anger directed toward Japanese Americans and Japanese resident aliens. The newspapers, nativist groups, politicians, and military personnel raised questions about the loyalty of persons of Japanese ancestry. They demanded that the federal government do something to protect West Coast Americans from the alleged subversion and treachery of those of Japanese descent, particularly because the fear was great that Japan was planning to invade the West Coast. President Roosevelt was finally persuaded to act and on February 19 and March 18, 1942, he issued executive orders, both of which Congress subsequently enacted into law. The first executive order authorized the Secretary of War to designate military areas from which any or all persons could be excluded in order to prevent sabotage or espionage. The second executive order authorized the establishment of the War Relocation Authority with responsibility for removing, relocating, maintaining, and supervising persons excluded under the first executive order. Under the authority provided by these executive orders, the West Coast states of California, Washington, and Oregon, and the southern part of Arizona were designated by the West Coast military commander to be military areas from which those of Japanese ancestry—some

70,000 American citizens and over 40,000 resident aliens—were to be excluded. But the military commander also ordered that these people were prohibited from leaving the military area. Rather, they were to be relocated in camps that were hastily constructed in the Arizona desert and in six other western states. Preparatory to the actual relocation, those of Japanese descent were subject to a curfew. They were forbidden to leave their residences after 8 P.M. until 6 A.M. Gordon Kiyoshi Hirabayashi, a college senior at the University of Washington, defied both the curfew and the order to report for registration preparatory to relocation; he was tried and convicted of violating both orders. Sentence for the two offenses was to run concurrently, a fact which the Supreme Court seized upon to provide the rationale for the Court's considering only the constitutionality of the curfew. Hirabayashi argued that Congress had unconstitutionally delegated its legislative power to the military commander and that the restrictions amounted to unconstitutional racial discrimination in violation of the Fifth Amendment.

Votes: Unanimous

MR. CHIEF JUSTICE STONE delivered the opinion of the Court:. . . .

The challenged orders were defense measures for the avowed purpose of safeguarding the military area in question, at a time of threatened air raids and invasion by the Japanese forces, from the danger of sabotage and espionage. As the curfew was made applicable to citizens residing in the area only if they were of Japanese ancestry, our inquiry must be whether in the light of all the facts and circumstances there was any substantial basis for the conclusion, in which Congress and the military commander united, that the curfew as applied was a protective measure necessary to meet the threat of sabotage and espionage which would substantially affect the war effort and which might reasonably be expected to aid a threatened enemy invasion. The alternative which appellant insists must be accepted is for the military authorities to impose the curfew on all citizens within the military area, or on none. In a case of threatened danger requiring prompt action, it is a choice between inflicting obviously needless hardship on the many, or sitting passive and unresisting in the presence of the threat. We think that constitutional government, in time of war, is not so powerless and does not compel so hard a choice if those charged with the responsibility of our national defense have reasonable ground for believing that the threat is real.

When the orders were promulgated there was a vast concentration, within Military Areas No. 1 and 2, of installations and facilities for the production of military equipment, especially ships and airplanes. Important Army and Navy bases were located in California and Washington. . . .

In the critical days of March, 1942, the danger to our war production by sabotage and espionage in this area seems obvious. The German invasion of the Western European countries had given ample warning to the world of the menace of the "fifth column." Espionage by persons in sympathy with the Japanese Government had been found to have been particularly effective in the surprise attack on Pearl Harbor. At a time of threatened Japanese attack upon this country, the nature of our inhabitants' attachments to the Japanese enemy was consequently a matter of grave concern. Of the 126,000 persons of Japanese descent in the United States, citizens and non-citizens, approximately 112,000 resided in California, Oregon and Washington at the time of the adoption of the military regulations. Of these approximately two-thirds are citizens because born in the United States. . . .

There is support for the view that social, economic and political conditions which have prevailed since the close of the last century, when the Japanese began to come to this country in substantial numbers, have intensified their solidarity and have in large measure prevented their assimilation as an integral part of the white population. In addition, large numbers of children of Japanese parentage are sent to Japanese language schools outside the regular hours of public schools in the locality. Some of these schools are generally believed to be sources of Japanese nationalistic propaganda, cultivating allegiance to Japan. . . .

Viewing these data in all their aspects, Congress and the Executive could reasonably have concluded that these conditions have encouraged the continued attachment of members of this group to Japan and Japanese institutions. These are only some of the many considerations which those charged with the responsibility for the national defense could take into account in determining the nature and extent of the danger of espionage and sabotage, in the event of invasion or air raid attack. The extent of that danger could be definitely known only after the event and after it was too late to meet it. Whatever views we may entertain regarding the loyalty to the country of the citizens of Japanese ancestry, we cannot reject as unfounded the judgment of the military authorities and of Congress that there were disloyal members of that population, whose number and strength could not be precisely and quickly ascertained. We cannot say that the war-making branches of the Government did not have ground for believing that in a critical hour such persons could not readily be isolated and separately dealt with. . . .

Appellant does not deny that, given the danger, a curfew was an appropriate measure against sabotage. It is obvious protection against the perpetration of sabotage most readily committed during the hours of darkness. If it was an appropriate exercise of the war power its validity is not impaired because it has restricted the citizen's liberty. Like every military control of the population of a dangerous zone in war time, it necessarily involves some infringement of individual liberty, just as does the police establishment of fire lines during a fire, or the confinement of people to their houses during an air raid alarm—neither of which could be thought to be an infringement of constitutional right. Like them, the validity of the restraints of the curfew order depends on all the conditions which obtain at the time the curfew is imposed and which support the order imposing it.

But appellant insists that the exercise of the power is inappropriate and unconstitutional because it discriminates against citizens of Japanese ancestry, in violation of the Fifth Amendment. The Fifth Amendment contains no equal protection clause and it restrains only such discriminatory legislation by Congress as amounts to a denial of due process. . . .

Distinctions between citizens solely because of their ancestry are by their very nature odious to a free people whose institutions are founded upon the doctrine of equality. For that reason, legislative classification or discrimination based on race alone has often been held to be a denial of equal protection. . . . We may assume that these considerations were controlling here were it not for the fact that the danger of espionage and sabotage, in time of war and of threatened invasion, calls upon the military authorities to scrutinize every relevant fact bearing on the loyalty of populations in the danger areas. Because racial discriminations are in most circumstances irrelevant and therefore prohibited, it by no means follows that, in dealing with the perils of war, Congress and the Executive are wholly precluded from taking into account those facts and circumstances which are relevant to measures for our national defense and for the successful prosecution of the war, and which may in fact place citizens of one ancestry in a different category from others. . . .

Here the aim of Congress and the Executive was the protection against sabotage of war materials and utilities in areas thought to be in danger of Japanese invasion and air attack. We have stated in detail facts and circumstances with respect to the American citizens of Japanese ancestry residing on the Pacific Coast which support the judgment of the war-waging branches of the Government that some restrictive measure was urgent. We cannot say that these facts and circumstances, considered in the particular war setting, could afford no ground for differentiating citizens of Japanese ancestry from other groups in the United States. The fact alone that attack on our shores was threatened by Japan rather than another enemy power set these citizens apart from others who have no particular associations with Japan.

Our investigation here does not go beyond the inquiry whether, in the light of all the relevant circumstances preceding and attending their promulgation, the challenged orders and statute afforded a reasonable basis for the action taken in imposing the curfew. We cannot close our eyes to the fact, demonstrated by experience, that in time of war residents having ethnic affiliations with an invading enemy may be a greater source of danger than those of a different ancestry. Nor can we deny that Congress, and the military authorities acting with its authorization, have constitutional power to appraise the danger in the light of facts of public notoriety. . . .

The military commander's appraisal of facts in the light of the authorized standard, and the inferences which he drew from those facts, involved the exercise of his informed judgment. But as we have seen, those facts, and the inferences which could be rationally drawn from them, support the judgment of the military commander, that the danger of espionage and sabotage to our military resources was imminent, and that the curfew order was an appropriate measure to meet it. . . .

The conviction under the second count is without constitutional infirmity. Hence we have no occasion to review the conviction on the first count since, as already stated, the sentences on the two counts are to run concurrently and conviction on the second is sufficient to sustain the sentence. For this reason also it is unnecessary to consider the Government's argument that compliance with the order to report at the Civilian Control Station did not necessarily entail confinement in a relocation center.

Affirmed.

MR. JUSTICE DOUGLAS, concurring: [omitted]
MR. JUSTICE MURPHY, concurring:. . . .

Distinctions based on color and ancestry are utterly inconsistent with our traditions and ideals. They are at variance with the principles for which we are now waging war. . . .

Today is the first time, so far I am aware, that we have sustained a substantial restriction of the personal liberty of citizens of the United States based upon the accident of race or ancestry. Under the curfew order here challenged no less than 70,000 American citizens have been placed under a special ban and deprived of their liberty because of their particular racial inheritance. In this sense it bears a melancholy resemblance to the treatment accorded to members of the Jewish race in Germany and in other parts of Europe. The result is the creation in this country of two classes of citizens for the purposes of a critical and perilous hour—to sanction discrimination between groups of United States citizens upon the basis of ancestry. In my opinion this goes to the very brink of constitutional power. . . .

In view, however, of the critical military situation which prevailed on the Pacific Coast area in the spring of 1942, and the urgent necessity of taking prompt and effective action to secure defense installations and military operations against the risk of sabotage and espionage, . . . the military authorities could have reasonably concluded at the time that determinations as to the loyalty and dependability of individual members of the large and widely scattered group of persons of Japanese extraction on the West Coast could not be made without delay that might have had tragic consequences. Modern war does not always wait for the observance of procedural requirements that are considered essential and appropriate under normal conditions. Accordingly I think that the military arm, confronted with the peril of imminent enemy attack and acting under the authority conferred by the Congress, made an allowable judgment at the time the curfew restriction was imposed. Whether such a restriction is valid today is another matter.

In voting for affirmance of the judgment I do not wish to be understood as intimating that the military authorities in time of war are subject to no restraints whatsoever, or that they are free to impose any restrictions they may choose on the rights and liberties of individual citizens or groups of citizens in those places which may be designated as "military areas." While this Court sits, it has the inescapable duty of seeing that the mandates of the Constitution are obeyed. That duty exists in time of war as well as in time of peace, and in its performance we must not forget that few indeed have been the invasions upon essential liberties which have not been accompanied by pleas of urgent necessity advanced in good faith by responsible men.

Nor do I mean to intimate that citizens of a particular racial group whose freedom may be curtailed within an area threatened with attack should be generally prevented from leaving the area and going at large in other areas that are not in danger of attack and where special precautions are not needed. Their status as citizens, though subject to requirements of national security and military necessity, should at all times be accorded the fullest consideration and respect. When the danger is past, the restrictions imposed on them should be promptly removed and their freedom of action fully restored.

MR. JUSTICE RUTLEDGE, concurring: [omitted]

KOREMATSU v. UNITED STATES,
323 U.S. 214 (1944)

By the time the Court handed down this decision at the end of 1944, the "relocation" camps for the detained American citizens of Japanese ancestry and Japanese resident aliens were in the process of being dismantled. The Court, nonetheless, dealt with the constitutionality of the exclusion order that, in conjunction with incarceration in relocation camps, represented the most sweeping abrogation of basic constitutional rights by the federal government in the history of the Republic. The Court was badly split and the dissenters bitterly attacked this first instance of American concentration camps. Some of those in the majority reluctantly joined the opinion of the Court, but did so in part because the Court that same day handed down its decision in Ex Parte Endo, *ruling that once the loyalty of an internee was determined, the War Relocation Authority no longer had any jurisdiction over that individual and that immediate release was required. Korematsu, an American citizen of Japanese descent, was convicted in a federal district court for remaining in San Leandro, California, a "military area," in defiance of the civilian exclusion order issued by the military commander of the Western Command of the U.S. Army. Korematsu challenged the constitutionality of the exclusion and detention program.*

Majority votes: 6
Dissenting votes: 3

MR. JUSTICE BLACK delivered the opinion of the Court:. . . .

In the light of the principles we announced in the *Hirabayashi* case, we are unable to conclude that it was beyond the war power of Congress and the Executive to exclude those of Japanese ancestry from the West Coast war area at the time they did. True, exclusion from the area in which one's home is located is a far greater deprivation than constant confinement to the home from 8 P.M. to 6 A.M. Nothing short of apprehension by the proper military authorities of the gravest imminent danger to the public safety can constitutionally justify either. But exclusion from a threatened area, no less than curfew, has a definite and close relationship to the prevention of espionage and sabotage. The military authorities, charged with the primary responsibility of defending our shores, concluded that curfew provided inadequate protection and ordered exclusion. They did so, as pointed out in our *Hirabayashi* opinion, in accordance with Congressional authority to the military to say who should, and who should not, remain in the threatened areas.

In this case the petitioner challenges the assumption upon which we rested our conclusions in the *Hirabayashi* case. He also urges that by May 1942, when Order No. 34 was promulgated, all danger of Japanese invasion of the West Coast had disappeared. After careful consideration of these contentions we are compelled to reject them. . . .

Like curfew, exclusion of those of Japanese origin was deemed necessary because of the presence of an unascertained number of disloyal members of the group, most of whom we have no doubt were loyal to this country. It was because we could not reject the finding of the military authorities that it was impossible to bring about an immediate segregation of the disloyal from the loyal that we sustained the validity of the curfew order as applying to the whole group. In the instant case, temporary exclusion of the entire group was rested by the military on the same ground. The judgment that exclusion of the whole group was for the same reason a military imperative answers the contention that the exclusion was in the nature of group punishment based on antagonism to those of Japanese origin. That there were members of the group who retained loyalties to Japan has been confirmed by investigations made subsequent to the exclusion. Approximately five thousand American citizens of Japanese ancestry refused to swear unqualified allegiance to the United States and to renounce allegiance to the Japanese Emperor, and several thousand evacuees requested repatriation to Japan.

We uphold the exclusion order as of the time it was made and when the petitioner violated it. In doing so, we are not unmindful of the hardships imposed by it upon a large group of American citizens. But hardships are part of war, and war is an aggregation of hardships. All citizens alike, both in and out of uniform, feel the impact of war in greater or lesser measure. Citizenship has its responsibilities as well as its privileges, and in time of war the burden is always heavier. Compulsory exclusion of large groups of citizens from their homes, except under circumstances of direst emergency and peril, is inconsistent with our basic governmental institutions. But when under conditions of modern warfare our shores are threatened by hostile forces, the power to protect must be commensurate with the threatened danger. . . .

It is said that we are dealing here with the case of imprisonment of a citizen in a concentration camp solely because of his ancestry, without evidence or inquiry concerning his loyalty and good disposition towards the United States. Our task would be simple, our duty clear, were this a case involving the imprisonment of a loyal citizen in a concentration camp because of racial prejudice. Regardless of the true nature of the assembly and relocation centers—and we deem it unjustifiable to call them concentration camps with all the ugly connotations that term implies—we are dealing specifically with nothing but an exclusion order. To cast this case into outlines of racial prejudice, without reference to the real military dangers which were presented, merely confuses the issue. Korematsu was not excluded from the Military Area because of hostility to him or his race. He was excluded because we are at war with the Japanese Empire, because the properly constituted military authorities feared an invasion of our West Coast and felt constrained to take proper security measures, because they decided that the military urgency of the situation demanded that all citizens of Japanese ancestry be segregated from the West Coast temporarily, and finally, because Congress, reposing its confidence in this time of war in our military leaders—as inevitably it must—determined that they should have the power to do just this. There was evidence of disloyalty on the part of some, the military authorities considered that the need for action was great, and time was short. We cannot—by availing ourselves of the calm perspective of hindsight—now say that at that time these actions were unjustified.

Affirmed.

MR. JUSTICE FRANKFURTER, concurring: [omitted]
MR. JUSTICE ROBERTS, dissenting:

I dissent, because I think the indisputable facts exhibit a clear violation of Constitutional rights.

This is not a case of keeping people off the

streets at night as was *Hirabayashi* v. *United States,* 320 U.S. 81, nor a case of temporary exclusion of a citizen from an area for his own safety or that of the community, nor a case of offering him an opportunity to go temporarily out of an area where his presence might cause danger to himself or to his fellows. On the contrary, it is the case of convicting a citizen as a punishment for not submitting to imprisonment in a concentration camp, based on his ancestry, and solely because of his ancestry, without evidence or inquiry concerning his loyalty and good disposition towards the United States. If this be a correct statement of the facts disclosed by this record, facts of which we take judicial notice, I need hardly labor the conclusion that Constitutional rights have been violated. . . .

MR. JUSTICE MURPHY, dissenting:

This exclusion of "all persons of Japanese ancestry, both alien and non-alien," from the Pacific Coast area on a plea of military necessity in the absence of martial law ought not to be approved. Such exclusion goes over "the very brink of constitutional power" and falls into the ugly abyss of racism. . . .

. . . [T]he exclusion order necessarily must rely for its reasonableness upon the assumption that all persons of Japanese ancestry may have a dangerous tendency to commit sabotage and espionage and to aid our Japanese enemy in other ways. It is difficult to believe that reason, logic or experience could be marshalled in support of such an assumption.

That this forced exclusion was the result in good measure of this erroneous assumption of racial guilt rather than bona fide military necessity is evidenced by the Commanding General's Final Report on the evacuation from the Pacific Coast area. In it he refers to all individuals of Japanese descent as "subversive," as belonging to "an enemy race" whose "racial strains are undiluted," and as constituting "over 112,000 potential enemies . . . at large today" along the Pacific Coast. In support of this blanket condemnation of all persons of Japanese descent, however, no reliable evidence is cited to show that such individuals were generally disloyal, or had generally so conducted themselves in this area as to constitute a special menace to defense installations or war industries, or had otherwise by their behavior furnished reasonable ground for their exclusion as a group. . . .

I dissent, therefore, from this legalization of racism. Racial discrimination in any form and in any degree has no justifiable part whatever in our democratic way of life. It is unattractive in any setting but it is utterly revolting among a free people who have embraced the principles set forth in the Constitution of the United States. All residents of this nation are kin in some way by blood or culture to a foreign land. Yet they are primarily and necessarily a part of the new and distinct civilization of the United States. They must accordingly be treated at all times as the heirs of the American experiment and as entitled to all the rights and freedoms guaranteed by the Constitution.

MR. JUSTICE JACKSON, dissenting:

Korematsu was born on our soil, of parents born in Japan. The Constitution makes him a citizen of the United States by nativity and a citizen of California by residence. No claim is made that he is not loyal to this country. There is no suggestion that apart from the matter involved here he is not law-abiding and well disposed. Korematsu, however, has been convicted of an act not commonly a crime. It consists merely of being present in the state whereof he is a citizen, near the place where he was born, and where all his life he has lived.

Even more unusual is the series of military orders which made this conduct a crime. They forbid such a one to remain, and they also forbid him to leave. They were so drawn that the only way Korematsu could avoid violation was to give himself up to the military authority. This meant submission to custody, examination, and transportation out of the territory, to be followed by indeterminate confinement in detention camps.

A citizen's presence in the locality, however, was made a crime only if his parents were of Japanese birth. Had Korematsu been one of four—the others being, say, a German alien enemy, an Italian alien enemy, and a citizen of American-born ancestors convicted of treason but out on parole—only Korematsu's presence would have violated the order. The difference between their innocence and his crime would result, not from anything he did, said, or thought, different than they, but only in that he was born of different racial stock.

Now, if any fundamental assumption underlies our system, it is that guilt is personal and not inheritable. Even if all of one's antecedents had been convicted of treason, the Constitution forbids its penalties to be visited upon him, for it provides that "no attainder of treason shall work corruption of blood, or forfeiture except during the life of the person attained." But here is an attempt to make an otherwise innocent act a crime merely because this prisoner is the son of parents as to whom he had no choice, and belongs to a race from which there is no way to resign. . . .

YOUNGSTOWN SHEET AND TUBE COMPANY v. SAWYER, 343 U.S. 579 (1952)

On April 8, 1952, when the nation was engaged in the Korean War, President Truman issued an Executive Order directing Secretary of Commerce Charles Sawyer to take possession of and operate the nation's steel mills. This came about after collective bargaining failed between the steel companies and the United Steelworkers of America, despite the efforts of the federal government; and a strike was called for April 9. President Truman asserted that it was in the vital national interest to keep the steel mills open in that it was essential for the successful prosecution of the war and that it was necessary for the health of the American economy. The companies subject to the takeover obeyed the subsequent implementation orders issued by Secretary Sawyer and promptly brought proceedings against him in the District Court of the District of Columbia. On April 30 the District Court ruled against the government, but the next day the Court of Appeals for the District of Columbia stayed the implementation of the District Court's decision. The Supreme Court granted certiorari on May 3 and the case was argued on May 12. On June 2 the Court announced its decision.

Majority votes: 6
Dissenting votes: 3

MR. JUSTICE BLACK delivered the opinion of the Court:

We are asked to decide whether the President was acting within his constitutional power when he issued an order directing the Secretary of Commerce to take possession of and operate most of the Nation's steel mills. The mill owners argue that the President's order amounts to lawmaking, a legislative function which the Constitution has expressly confided to the Congress and not to the President. The Government's position is that the order was made on findings of the President that his action was necessary to avert a national catastrophe which would inevitably result from a stoppage of steel production, and that in meeting this grave emergency the President was acting within the aggregate of his constitutional powers as the Nation's Chief Executive and the Commander in Chief of the Armed Forces of the United States. . . .

The President's power, if any, to issue the order must stem either from an act of Congress or from the Constitution itself. There is no statute that expressly authorizes the President to take possession of property as he did here. Nor is there any act of

Congress to which our attention has been directed from which such a power can fairly be implied. Indeed, we do not understand the Government to rely on statutory authorization for this seizure. There are two statutes which do authorize the President to take both personal and real property under certain conditions. However, the Government admits that these conditions were not met and that the President's order was not rooted in either of the statutes. The Government refers to the seizure provisions of one of these statutes (§ 201(b) of the Defense Production Act) as "much too cumbersome, involved, and time-consuming for the crisis which was at hand."

Moreover, the use of the seizure technique to solve labor disputes in order to prevent work stoppages was not only unauthorized by any congressional enactment; prior to this controversy, Congress had refused to adopt that method of settling labor disputes. When the Taft-Hartley Act was under consideration in 1947, Congress rejected an amendment which would have authorized such governmental seizures in cases of emergency. Apparently it was thought that the technique of seizure, like that of compulsory arbitration, would interfere with the process of collective bargaining. Consequently, the plan Congress adopted in that Act did not provide for seizure under any circumstances. Instead, the plan sought to bring about settlements by use of the customary devices of mediation, conciliation, investigation by boards of inquiry, and public reports. In some instances temporary injunctions were authorized to provide cooling-off periods. All this failing, unions were left free to strike after a secret vote by employees as to whether they wished to accept their employers' final settlement offer.

It is clear that if the President had authority to issue the order he did, it must be found in some provision of the Constitution. And it is not claimed that express constitutional language grants this power to the President. The contention is that presidential power should be implied from the aggregate of his powers under the Constitution. Particular reliance is placed on provisions in Article II which say that "The executive Power shall be vested in a President . . ."; that "he shall take Care that the Laws be faithfully executed"; and that he "shall be Commander in Chief of the Army and Navy of the United States."

The order cannot properly be sustained as an exercise of the President's military power as Commander in Chief of the Armed Forces. The Government attempts to do so by citing a number of cases upholding broad powers in military commanders engaged in day-to-day fighting in a theater of war. Such cases need not concern us here. Even though "theater of war" be an expanding concept, we cannot with faithfulness to our constitutional system hold that the Commander in Chief of the Armed Forces has the ultimate power as such to take possession of private property in order to keep labor disputes from stopping production. This is a job for the Nation's lawmakers not for its military authorities.

Nor can the seizure order be sustained because of the several constitutional provisions that grant executive power to the President. In the framework of our Constitution, the President's power to see that the laws are faithfully executed refutes the idea that he is to be a lawmaker. The Constitution limits his functions in the lawmaking process to the recommending of laws he thinks wise and the vetoing of laws he thinks bad. And the Constitution is neither silent nor equivocal about who shall make laws which the President is to execute. The first section of the first article says that "All legislative Powers herein granted shall be vested in a Congress of the United States. . . ." After granting many powers to the Congress, Article I goes on to provide that Congress may "make all Laws which shall be necessary and proper for carrying into Execution the foregoing Powers, and all other Powers vested by this Constitution in the Government of the United States, or in any Department or Officer thereof."

The President's order does not direct that a congressional policy be executed in a manner prescribed by Congress—it directs that a presidential policy be executed in a manner prescribed by the President. The preamble of the order itself, like that of many statutes, sets out reasons why the President believes certain policies should be adopted, proclaims these policies as rules of conduct to be followed, and again, like a statute, authorizes a government official to promulgate additional rules and regulations consistent with the policy proclaimed and needed to carry that policy into execution. The power of Congress to adopt such public policies as those proclaimed by the order is beyond question. It can authorize the taking of private property for public use. It can make laws regulating the relationships between employers and employees, prescribing rules designed to settle labor disputes, and fixing wages and working conditions in certain fields of our economy. The Constitution does not subject this lawmaking power of Congress to presidential or military supervision or control.

It is said that other Presidents without congressional authority have taken possession of private business enterprises in order to settle labor disputes. But even if this be true, Congress has not thereby lost its exclusive constitutional authority to make laws necessary and proper to carry out the powers vested by the Constitution "in the Government of the United States, or in any Department or Officer thereof."

The Founders of this Nation entrusted the lawmaking power to the Congress alone in both good and bad times. It would do no good to recall the historical events, the fears of power and the hopes for freedom that lay behind their choice. Such a review would but confirm our holding that this seizure order cannot stand.

The judgment of the District Court is

Affirmed.

MR. JUSTICE FRANKFURTER, concurring: [omitted]
MR. JUSTICE DOUGLAS, concurring:. . . .

The legislative nature of the action taken by the President seems to me to be clear. When the United States takes over an industrial plant to settle a labor controversy, it is condemning property. The seizure of the plant is a taking in the constitutional sense. A permanent taking would amount to the nationalization of the industry. A temporary taking falls short of that goal. But though the seizure is only for a week or a month, the condemnation is complete and the United States must pay compensation for the temporary possession.

The power of the Federal Government to condemn property is well established. It can condemn for any public purpose; and I have no doubt but that condemnation of a plant, factory, or industry in order to promote industrial peace would be constitutional. But there is a duty to pay for all property taken by the Government. The command of the Fifth Amendment is that no "private property be taken for public use, without just compensation." That constitutional requirement has an important bearing on the present case.

The President has no power to raise revenues. That power is in the Congress by Article I, Section 8 of the Constitution. The President might seize and the Congress by subsequent action might ratify the seizure. But until and unless Congress acted, no condemnation would be lawful. The branch of government that has the power to pay compensation for a seizure is the only one able to authorize a seizure or make lawful one that the President has effected. That seems to me to be the necessary result of the condemnation provision in the Fifth Amendment. It squares with the theory of checks and balances expounded by Mr. Justice Black in the opinion of the Court in which I join. . . .

MR. JUSTICE JACKSON, concurring in the judgment and opinion of the Court:. . . .

We may well begin by a somewhat over-simplified grouping of practical situations in which a President may doubt, or others may challenge, his powers, and by distinguishing roughly the legal consequences of this factor of relativity.

1. When the President acts pursuant to an express or implied authorization of Congress, his authority is at its maximum, for it includes all that he possesses in his own right plus all the Congress can delegate. In these circumstances, and in these only, may he be said (for what it may be worth) to personify the federal sovereignty. If his act is held unconstitutional under these circumstances, it usually means that the Federal Government as an undivided whole lacks power. A seizure executed by the President pursuant to an Act of Congress would be supported by the strongest of presumptions and the widest latitude of judicial interpretation, and the burden of persuasion would rest heavily upon any who might attack it.

2. When the President acts in absence of either a congressional grant or denial of authority, he can only rely upon his own independent powers, but there is a zone of twilight in which he and Congress may have concurrent authority, or in which its distribution is uncertain. Therefore, congressional inertia, indifference or quiescence may sometimes, at least as a practical matter, enable, if not invite, measures on independent presidential responsibility. In this area, any actual test of power is likely to depend on the imperatives of events and contemporary imponderables rather than on abstract theories of law.

3. When the President takes measures incompatible with the expressed or implied will of Congress, his power is at its lowest ebb, for then he can rely only upon his own constitutional powers minus any constitutional powers of Congress over the matter. Courts can sustain exclusive presidential control in such a case only by disabling the Congress from acting upon the subject. Presidential claim to a power at once so conclusive and preclusive must be scrutinized with caution, for what is at stake is the equilibrium established by our constitutional system.

Into which of these classifications does this executive seizure of the steel industry fit? It is eliminated from the first by admission, for it is conceded that no congressional authorization exists for this seizure. . . .

Can it then be defended under flexible tests available to the second category? It seems clearly eliminated from that class because Congress has not left seizure of private property an open field but has covered it by three statutory policies inconsistent with this seizure. . . .

This leaves the current seizure to be justified only by the severe tests under the third grouping, where it can be supported only by any remainder of executive power after subtraction of such powers as Congress may have over the subject. In short, we can sustain the President only by holding that seizure of such strike-bound industries is within his domain and beyond control by Congress.

[Jackson finds it is not.]

. . . In view of the ease, expedition and safety with which Congress can grant and has granted large emergency powers, certainly ample to embrace this crisis, I am quite unimpressed with the argument that we should affirm possession of them without statute. Such power either has no beginning or it has no end. If it exists, it need submit to no legal restraint. I am not alarmed that it would plunge us straightway into dictatorship, but it is at least a step in that wrong direction. . . .

MR. JUSTICE BURTON, concurring in both the opinion and judgment of the Court: [omitted]

MR. JUSTICE CLARK, concurring in the judgment of the Court: [omitted]

MR. CHIEF JUSTICE VINSON, with whom MR. JUSTICE REED and MR. JUSTICE MINTON join, dissenting:. . . .

The steel mills were seized for a public use. The power of eminent domain, invoked in this case, is an essential attribute of sovereignty and has long been recognized as a power of the Federal Government. Plaintiffs cannot complain that any provision in the Constitution prohibits the exercise of the power of eminent domain in this case. The Fifth Amendment provides: "nor shall private property be taken for public use, without just compensation." It is no bar to this seizure for, if the taking is not otherwise unlawful, plaintiffs are assured of receiving the required just compensation.

Admitting that the Government could seize the mills, plaintiffs claim that the implied power of eminent domain can be exercised only under an Act of Congress; under no circumstances, they say, can that power be exercised by the President unless he can point to an express provision in enabling legislation. This was the view adopted by the District Judge when he granted the preliminary injunction. Without an answer, without hearing evidence, he determined the issue on the basis of his "fixed conclusion . . . that defendant's acts are illegal" because the President's only course in the face of an emergency is to present the matter to Congress and await the final passage of legislation which will enable the Government to cope with threatened disaster.

Under this view, the President is left powerless at the very moment when the need for action may be most pressing and when no one, other than he, is immediately capable of action. Under this view, he is left powerless because a power not expressly given to Congress is nevertheless found to rest exclusively with Congress. . . .

A review of executive action demonstrates that our Presidents have on many occasions exhibited the leadership contemplated by the Framers when they made the President Commander in Chief, and imposed upon him the trust to "take Care that the Laws be faithfully executed." With or without explicit statutory authorization, Presidents have at such times dealt with national emergencies by acting promptly and resolutely to enforce legislative programs, at least to save those programs until Congress could act. Congress and the courts have responded to such executive initiative with consistent approval. . . .

Focusing . . . on the situation confronting the President on the night of April 8, 1952, we cannot but conclude that the President was performing his duty under the Constitution to "take Care that the Laws be faithfully executed"—a duty described by President Benjamin Harrison as "the central idea of the office."

The President reported to Congress the morning after the seizure that he acted because a work stoppage in steel production would immediately imperil the safety of the Nation by preventing execution of the legislative programs for procurement of military equipment. And, while a shutdown could be averted by granting the price concessions requested by plaintiffs, granting such concessions would disrupt the price stabilization program also enacted by Congress. Rather than fail to execute either legislative program, the President acted to execute both.

Much of the argument in this case has been directed at straw men. We do not now have before us the case of a President acting solely on the basis of his own notions of the public welfare. Nor is there any question of unlimited executive power in this case. The President himself closed the door to any such claim when he sent his Message to Congress stating his purpose to abide by any action of Congress, whether approving or disapproving his seizure action. Here, the President immediately made sure that Congress was fully informed of the temporary action he had taken only to preserve the legislative programs from destruction until Congress could act.

The absence of a specific statute authorizing seizure of the steel mills as a mode of executing the laws—both the military procurement program and the anti-inflation program—has not until today been thought to prevent the President from executing the laws. Unlike an administrative commission confined to the enforcement of the statute under which it was created, or the head of a department when administering a particular statute, the President is a constitutional officer charged with taking care that a "mass of legislation" be executed. Flexibility as to mode of execution to meet critical situations is a matter of practical necessity. . . .

The diversity of views expressed in the six opinions of the majority, the lack of reference to authoritative precedent, the repeated reliance upon prior dissenting opinions, the complete disregard of the uncontroverted facts showing the gravity of the emergency and the temporary nature of the taking all serve to demonstrate how far afield one must go to affirm the order of the District Court. . . .

UNITED STATES v. NIXON, 418 U.S. 683 (1974)

The famous Nixon Tapes case, of course, had its genesis in the "coverup" of the break-in at the Democratic Party headquarters located in the Watergate Hotel on June 17, 1972. Thanks to the investigative reporting of a few journalists and the probing of federal district court Judge John J. Sirica at the trial of the Watergate burglars, it became apparent that the coverup led directly to high government officials operating within the office of the President of the United States. The national scandal led to the formation of the Senate Watergate Committee that began its hearings in the spring of 1973. Former White House Counsel John W. Dean III directly implicated the President in the coverup. Subsequently, one witness revealed that President Nixon had installed an automatic taping system in the Oval Office and that all *conversations in that office, including Nixon's conversations with Dean and those that occurred right after the break-in, had been recorded. Archibald Cox, who had been appointed Special Prosecutor to investigate the Watergate affair, met with resistance from the White House when he tried to acquire certain of the tapes. President Nixon finally fired Cox, but the national outcry led the President to appoint a new Special Prosecutor, Leon Jaworski, who proceeded to obtain indictments of a number of high ranking administration officials, including the former Attorney General. For purposes of the trial of these officials, Jaworski subpoenaed certain tapes of conversations that appeared likely to contain incriminating evidence. Mr. Nixon refused to turn over the tapes, citing executive privilege and the need for confidentiality, and appealed Judge Sirica's order that he do so. At the request of the Special Prosecutor, the Supreme Court agreed to expedite the decision in this case by granting certiorari and bypassing the United States Court of Appeals. The question in this case was can the President of the United States, on the ground of executive privilege, withhold evidence needed for a criminal prosecution? The Court's decision was announced on July 24, 1974, the day when the House Judiciary Committee began hearings on whether to impeach the President.*

Votes: Unanimous

MR. CHIEF JUSTICE BURGER delivered the opinion of the Court:. . . .

On March 1, 1974, a grand jury of the United States District Court for the District of Columbia returned an indictment charging seven named individuals with various offenses, including conspiracy to defraud the United States and to obstruct justice. Although he was not designated as such in the indictment, the grand jury named the President, among others, as an unindicted coconspirator. On April 18, 1974, upon motion of the Special Prosecutor, a subpoena *duces tecum* was issued pursuant to Rule 17(c) [of the Federal Rules of Criminal Procedure] to the President by the United States District Court and made returnable on May 2, 1974. This subpoena required the production, in advance of the September 9 trial date, of certain tapes, memoranda, papers, transcripts of other writings relating to certain precisely identified meetings between the President and others. The Special Prosecutor was able to fix the time, place, and persons present at these discussions because the White House daily logs and appointment records had been delivered to him. On April 30, the President publicly released edited transcripts of 43 conversations; portions of 20 conversations subject to subpoena in the present case were included. On May 1, 1974, the President's counsel filed a "special appearance" and a motion to quash the subpoena under Rule 17(c). This motion was accompanied by a formal claim of privilege. At a subsequent hearing, further motions to expunge the grand jury's action naming the President as an unindicted coconspirator and for protective orders against the disclosure of the information were filed or raised orally by counsel for the President.

On May 20, 1974, the District Court denied the motion to quash and the motions to expunge and for protective orders. 377 F.Supp. 1326. It further ordered "the President or any subordinate officer, official, or employee with custody or control of the documents or objects subpoenaed," to deliver to the District Court, on or before May 31, 1974, the originals of all subpoenaed items, as well as an index and analysis of those items, together with tape copies of those portions of the subpoenaed recordings for which transcripts had been released to the public by the President on April 30. . . .

On May 24, 1974, the President filed a timely notice of appeal from the District Court order, and the certified record from the District Court was docketed in the United States Court of Appeals for the District of Columbia Circuit. On the same day, the President also filed a petition for writ of mandamus in the Court of Appeals seeking review of the District Court order.

Later on May 24, the Special Prosecutor also filed, in this Court, a petition for a writ of certiorari before judgment. On May 31, the petition was granted with an expedited briefing schedule. On June 6, the President filed, under seal, a cross-petition for writ of certiorari before judgment. This cross-petition was granted June 15, 1974, and the case was set for argument on July 8, 1974.

The threshold question presented is whether the May 20, 1974, order of the District Court was an appealable order and whether this case was properly "in" the Court of Appeals when the petition for certiorari was filed in this Court. . . . [The Court answers yes.]

In the District Court, the President's counsel argued that the court lacked jurisdiction to issue the subpoena because the matter was an intrabranch dispute between a subordinate and superior officer of the Executive Branch and hence not subject to judicial resolution. . . .

Our starting point is the nature of the proceeding for which the evidence is sought—here a pending criminal prosecution. It is a judicial proceeding in a federal court alleging violation of federal laws and is brought in the name of the United States as sovereign. Under the authority of Art. II, § 2, Congress has vested in the Attorney General the power to conduct the criminal litigation of the United States Government. 28 U.S.C. § 516. It has also vested in him the power to appoint subordinate officers to assist him in the discharge of his duties. 28 U.S.C. §§509, 510, 515, 533. Acting pursuant to those statutes, the Attorney General has delegated the authority to represent the United States in these particular matters to a Special Prosecutor with unique authority and tenure. The regulation gives the Special Prosecutor explicit power to contest the invocation of executive privilege in the process of seeking evidence deemed relevant to the performance of these specially delegated duties.

So long as this regulation is extant it has the force of law. . . .

Here, . . . it is theoretically possible for the Attorney General to amend or revoke the regulation defining the Special Prosecutor's authority. But he has not done so. So long as this regulation remains in force the Executive Branch is bound by it, and indeed the United States as the sovereign composed of the three branches is bound to respect and to enforce it. Moreover, the delegation of authority to the Special Prosecutor in this case is not an ordinary delegation by the Attorney General to a subordinate officer: with the authorization of the President, the Acting Attorney General provided in the regulation that the Special Prosecutor was not to be removed without the "consensus" of eight designated leaders of Congress. . . .

In light of the uniqueness of the setting in which the conflict arises, the fact that both parties are officers of the Executive Branch cannot be viewed as a barrier to justiciability. It would be inconsistent with the applicable law and regulation, and the unique facts of this case, to conclude other than that the Special Prosecutor has standing to bring this action and that a justiciable controversy is presented for decision. . . .

In a case such as this, . . . where a subpoena is directed to a President of the United States, appellate review, in deference to a coordinate branch of Government, should be particularly meticulous to ensure that the standards of Rule 17(c) have been correctly applied. From our examination of the materials submitted by the Special Prosecutor to the District Court in support of his motion for the subpoena, we are persuaded that the District Court's denial of the President's motion to quash the subpoena was consistent with Rule 17(c). We also conclude that the Special Prosecutor has made a sufficient showing to justify a subpoena for production before trial. The subpoenaed materials are not available from any other source, and their examination and processing should not await trial in the circumstances shown.

Having determined that the requirements of Rule 17(c) were satisfied, we turn to the claim that the subpoena should be quashed because it demands "confidential conversations between a President and his close advisors that it would be inconsistent with the public interest to produce." The first contention is a broad claim that the separation of powers doctrine precludes judicial review of a President's claim of privilege. The second contention is that if he does not prevail on the claim of absolute privilege, the court should hold as a matter of constitutional law that the privilege prevails over the subpoena *duces tecum*.

In the performance of assigned constitutional duties each branch of the Government must initially interpret the Constitution, and the interpretation of its powers by any branch is due great respect from the others. The President's counsel, as we have noted, reads the Constitution as providing an absolute privilege of confidentiality for all Presidential communications. Many decisions of this Court, however, have unequivocally reaffirmed the holding of *Marbury* v. *Madison,* 1 Cranch 137 (1803), that "[i]t is emphatically the province and duty of the judicial department to say what the law is."

No holding of the Court has defined the scope of judicial power specifically relating to the enforcement of a subpoena for confidential Presidential communications for use in a criminal prosecution, but other exercises of power by the Executive Branch and the Legislative Branch have been found invalid as in conflict with the Constitution. *Powell* v. *McCormack,* 395 U.S. 486 (1969); *Youngstown Sheet & Tube Co.* v. *Sawyer,* 343 U.S. 579 (1952). . . . Since this Court has consistently exercised the power to construe and delineate claims arising under express powers, it must follow that the Court has authority to interpret claims with respect to powers alleged to derive from enumerated powers. . . .

We therefore reaffirm that it is the province and duty of this Court "to say what the law is" with respect to the claim of privilege presented in this case.

In support of his claim of absolute privilege, the President's counsel urges two grounds, one of which is common to all governments and one of which is peculiar to our system of separation of powers. The first ground is the valid need for protection of communications between high Government officials and those who advise and assist them in the performance of their manifold duties; the importance of this confidentiality is too plain to require further discussion. Human experience teaches that those who expect public dissemination of their remarks may well temper candor with a concern for appearances and for their own interests to the detriments of the decision-making process. Whatever the nature of the privilege of confidentiality of Presidential communications in the exercise of Art. II powers, the privilege can be said to derive from the supremacy of each branch within its own assigned area of constitutional duties. Certain powers and privileges flow from the nature of enumerated powers; the protection of the confidentiality of Presidential communications has similar constitutional underpinnings.

The second ground asserted by the President's counsel in support of the claim of absolute privilege rests on the doctrine of separation of powers. Here it is argued that the independence of the Executive Branch within its own sphere, insulates a President from a judicial subpoena in an ongoing criminal prosecution, and thereby protects confidential Presidential communications.

However, neither the doctrine of separation of powers, nor the need for confidentiality of high-level communications, without more, can sustain an absolute, unqualified Presidential privilege of immunity from judicial process under all circumstances. The President's need for complete candor and objectivity from advisers calls for great deference from the courts. However, when the privilege depends solely on the broad, undifferentiated claim of public interest in the confidentiality of such conversations, a confrontation with other values arises. Absent a claim of need to protect military, diplomatic, or sensitive national security secrets, we find it difficult to accept the argument that even the very important interest in confidentiality of Presidential communications is significantly diminished by production of such material for *in camera* inspection with all the protection that a district court will be obliged to provide.

The impediment that an absolute, unqualified privilege would place in the way of the primary constitutional duty of the Judicial Branch to do justice in criminal prosecutions would plainly conflict with the function of the courts under Art. III. In designing the structure of our Government and dividing and allocating the sovereign power among three coequal branches, the Framers of the Constitution sought to provide a comprehensive system, but the separate powers were not intended to operate with absolute independence. . . .

To read the Art. II powers of the President as providing an absolute privilege as against a subpoena essential to enforcement of criminal statutes on no more than a generalized claim of the public interest in confidentiality of nonmilitary and non-diplomatic discussions would upset the constitutional balance of "a workable government" and gravely impair the role of the courts under Art. III. . . .

In this case the President challenges a subpoena

served on him as a third party requiring the production of materials for use in a criminal prosecution; he does so on the claim that he has a privilege against disclosure of confidential communications. He does not place his claim of privilege on the ground they are military or diplomatic secrets. As to these areas of Art. II duties the courts have traditionally shown the utmost deference to Presidential responsibilities. . . .

No case of the Court, however, has extended this high degree of deference to a President's generalized interest in confidentiality. Nowhere in the Constitution, as we have noted earlier, is there any explicit reference to a privilege of confidentiality, yet to the extent this interest relates to the effective discharge of a President's powers, it is constitutionally based.

The right to the production of all evidence at a criminal trial similarly has constitutional dimensions. The Sixth Amendment explicitly confers upon every defendant in a criminal trial the right "to be confronted with the witnesses against him" and "to have compulsory process for obtaining witnesses in his favor." Moreover, the Fifth Amendment also guarantees that no person shall be deprived of liberty without due process of law. It is the manifest duty of the courts to vindicate those guarantees, and to accomplish that it is essential that all relevant and admissible evidence be produced.

In this case we must weigh the importance of the general privilege of confidentiality of Presidential communications in performance of the President's responsibilities against the inroads of such a privilege on the fair administration of criminal justice. The interest in preserving confidentiality is weighty indeed and entitled to great respect. However, we cannot conclude that advisers will be moved to temper the candor of their remarks by the infrequent occasions of disclosure because of the possibility that such conversations will be called for in the context of a criminal prosecution.

On the other hand, the allowance of the privilege to withhold evidence that is demonstrably relevant in a criminal trial would cut deeply into the guarantee of due process of law and gravely impair the basic function of the courts. A President's acknowledged need for confidentiality in the communications of his office is general in nature, whereas the constitutional need for production of relevant evidence in a criminal proceeding is specific and central to the fair adjudication of a particular criminal case in the administration of justice. Without access to specific facts a criminal prosecution may be totally frustrated. The President's broad interest in confidentiality of communications will not be vitiated by disclosure of a limited number of conversations preliminarily shown to have some bearing on the pending criminal cases.

We conclude that when the ground for asserting privilege as to subpoenaed materials sought for use in a criminal trial is based only on the generalized interest in confidentiality, it cannot prevail over the fundamental demands of due process of law in the fair administration of criminal justice. The generalized assertion of privilege must yield to the demonstrated, specific need for evidence in a pending criminal trial. . . .

Here the District Court treated the material as presumptively privileged, proceeded to find that the Special Prosecutor had made a sufficient showing to rebut the presumption, and ordered an *in camera* examination of the subpoenaed material. On the basis of our examination of the record we are unable to conclude that the District Court erred in ordering the inspection. Accordingly we affirm the order of the District Court that subpoenaed materials be transmitted to that court. We now turn to the important question of the District Court's responsibilities in conducting the *in camera* examination of Presidential materials or communications delivered under the compulsion of the subpoena *duces tecum*.

. . . . It is elementary that *in camera* inspection of evidence is always a procedure calling for scrupulous protection against any release or publication of material not found by the court, at that stage, probably admissible in evidence and relevant to the issues of the trial for which it is sought. That being true of an ordinary situation, it is obvious that the District Court has a very heavy responsibility to see to it that Presidential conversations, which are either not relevant or not admissible, are accorded that high degree of respect due the President of the United States. . . . We have no doubt that the District Judge will . . . discharge his responsibility to see to it that until released to the Special Prosecutor no *in camera* material is revealed to anyone. This burden applies with even greater force to excised material; once the decision is made to excise, the material is restored to its privileged status and should be returned under seal to its lawful custodian.

Since this matter came before the Court during the pendency of a criminal prosecution, and on representations that time is of the essence, the mandate shall issue forthwith.

Affirmed.

MR. JUSTICE REHNQUIST took no part in the consideration or decision of these cases.

NIXON v. FITZGERALD,
457 U.S. 731 (1982)

A. Ernest Fitzgerald was a civilian management analyst with the United States Air Force. On November 13, 1968, Fitzgerald testified before the Subcommittee on Economy in Government of the Joint Economic Committee of Congress that cost overruns on the C-5A transport plane could approximate $2 billion. He also revealed that unexpected technical difficulties had arisen during the development of the aircraft. Fitzgerald's revelations were prominently covered by the mass media, and he was widely praised by the press and members of Congress as a man of courage who put the public interest before institutional loyalty. He was dubbed a "whistle-blower" who called attention to government waste and inefficiency. His testimony highly embarrassed and also angered his superiors in the Air Force. Within 14 months Fitzgerald was out of a job, technically because of a departmental reorganization and reduction in force but really because his superiors wanted to fire him because of his congressional testimony. Fitzgerald complained to the Civil Service Commission, which concluded that his dismissal offended applicable regulations because it was motivated by purely personal reasons. Fitzgerald then filed suit for damages in federal district court against various Department of Defense officials and White House aides allegedly responsible for his dismissal. After President Nixon publicly took responsibility for Fitzgerald's firing, Nixon was eventually named in the suit. The case moved very slowly and involved several preliminary judicial rulings and extensive pretrial discovery. Ultimately, on March 26, 1980, the district court ruled that Fitzgerald had a triable cause of action under two federal statutes and the First Amendment and that President Nixon was not entitled to claim absolute presidential immunity from civil suits for money damages. The former President appealed the immunity ruling to the Court of Appeals for the District of Columbia which summarily dismissed the appeal. Nixon then went to the Supreme Court. The Supreme Court granted certiorari to consider the scope of immunity available to a President of the United States. Interestingly, after the certiorari petition was filed and Fitzgerald entered his rejoinder to Nixon's petition, Nixon and Fitzgerald entered into an agreement whereby Nixon paid Fitzgerald $142,000 and would pay an additional $28,000 if the Court ruled that Nixon was not entitled to absolute immunity. If the Court ruled in Nixon's favor (as it did), Nixon would not have to pay the $28,000, and, in any *event, the suit for damages would be settled. Fitzgerald ultimately settled with the Air Force and he received back pay and his old job back effective June 21, 1982.*

Majority votes: 5
Dissenting votes: 4

JUSTICE POWELL delivered the opinion of the Court:

The plaintiff in this lawsuit seeks relief in civil damages from a former President of the United States. The claim rests on actions allegedly taken in the former President's official capacity during his tenure in office. The issue before us is the scope of the immunity possessed by the President of the United States. . . .

This Court consistently has recognized that government officials are entitled to some form of immunity from suits for civil damages. . . . [I]n *Butz* v. *Economou,* 438 U.S. 478 (1978), . . . we considered for the first time the kind of immunity possessed by *federal* executive officials who are sued for constitutional violations. In *Butz* the Court rejected an argument, based on decisions involving federal officials charged with common-law torts, that all high federal officials have a right to absolute immunity from constitutional damages actions. Concluding that a blanket recognition of absolute immunity would be anomalous in light of the qualified immunity standard applied to state executive officials, we held that federal officials generally have the same qualified immunity possessed by state officials in cases under §1983. In so doing we reaffirmed our holdings that some officials, notably judges and prosecutors, "because of the special nature of their responsibilities," *id.,* at 511, "require a full exemption from liability.' *Id.,* at 508. In *Butz* itself we upheld a claim of absolute immunity for administrative officials engaged in functions analogous to those of judges and prosecutors. We also left open the question whether other federal officials could show that "public policy requires an exemption of that scope." *Id.,* at 506. . . .

Here a former President asserts his immunity from civil damages claims of two kinds. He stands named as a defendant in a direct action under the Constitution and in two statutory actions under federal laws of general applicability. In neither case has Congress taken express legislative action to subject the President to civil liability for his official acts.

Applying the principles of our cases to claims of this kind, we hold that petitioner, as a former President of the United States, is entitled to absolute immunity from damages liability predicated on his official acts. We consider this immunity a functionally mandated incident of the President's unique office, rooted in the constitutional tradition of the separation of powers and supported by our history. . . .

In arguing that the President is entitled only to qualified immunity, the respondent relies on cases in which we have recognized immunity of this scope for governors and cabinet officers. We find these cases to be inapposite. The President's unique status under the Constitution distinguishes him from other executive officials.

Because of the singular importance of the President's duties, diversion of his energies by concern with private law suits would raise unique risks to the effective functioning of government. As is the case with prosecutors and judges—for whom absolute immunity now is established—a President must concern himself with matters likely to "arouse the most intense feelings." *Pierson* v. *Ray,* 386 U.S., at 554. Yet, as our decisions have recognized, it is in precisely such cases that there exists the greatest public interest in providing an official "the maximum ability to deal fearlessly and impartially with" the duties of his office. *Ferri* v. *Ackerman,* 444 U.S. 193, 203 (1979). This concern is compelling where the officeholder must make the most sensitive and far-reaching decisions entrusted to any official under our constitutional system. Nor can the sheer prominence of the President's office be ignored. In view of the visibility of his office and the effect of his actions on countless people, the President would be an easily identifiable target for suits for civil damages. Cognizance of this personal vulnerability frequently could distract a President from his public duties, to the detriment of not only the President and his office but also the Nation that the Presidency was designed to serve. . . .

Under the Constitution and laws of the United States the President has discretionary responsibilities in a broad variety of areas, many of them highly sensitive. In many cases it would be difficult to determine which of the President's innumerable "functions" encompassed a particular action. In this case, for example, respondent argues that he was dismissed in retaliation for his testimony to Congress—a violation of 5 U.S.C. §7211 (1976 ed., Supp. IV) and 18 U.S.C. §1505. The Air Force, however, has claimed that the underlying reorganization was undertaken to promote efficiency. Assuming that petitioner Nixon ordered the reorganization in which respondent lost his job, an inquiry into the President's motives could not be avoided under the kind of "functional" theory asserted both by respondent and the dissent. Inquiries of this kind could be highly intrusive.

Here respondent argues that petitioner Nixon would have acted outside the outer perimeter of his duties by ordering the discharge of an employee who was lawfully entitled to retain his job in the absence of " 'such cause as will promote the efficiency of the service.' " Because Congress has granted this legislative protection, respondent argues, no federal official could, within the outer perimeter of his duties of office, cause Fitzgerald to be dismissed without satisfying this standard in prescribed statutory proceedings.

This construction would subject the President to trial on virtually every allegation that an action was unlawful, or was taken for a forbidden purpose. Adoption of this construction thus would deprive absolute immunity of its intended effect. It clearly is within the President's constitutional and statutory authority to prescribe the manner in which the Secretary will conduct the business of the Air Force. Because this mandate of office must include the authority to prescribe reorganizations and reductions in force, we conclude that petitioner's alleged wrongful acts lay well within the outer perimeter of his authority.

A rule of absolute immunity for the President will not leave the Nation without sufficient protection against misconduct on the part of the Chief Executive. There remains the constitutional remedy of impeachment. In addition, there are formal and informal checks on Presidential action that do not apply with equal force to other executive officials. The President is subjected to constant scrutiny by the press. Vigilant oversight by Congress also may serve to deter Presidential abuses of office, as well as to make credible the threat of impeachment. Other incentives to avoid misconduct may include a desire to earn reelection, the need to maintain prestige as an element of Presidential influence, and a President's traditional concern for his historical stature.

The existence of alternative remedies and deterrents establishes that absolute immunity will not place the President "above the law." For the President, as for judges and prosecutors, absolute immunity merely precludes a particular private remedy for alleged misconduct in order to advance compelling public ends.

For the reasons stated in this opinion, the decision of the Court of Appeals is reversed, and the case is remanded for action consistent with this opinion.

So ordered.

CHIEF JUSTICE BURGER, concurring:

I join the Court's opinion, but I write separately to underscore that the Presidential immunity derives from and is mandated by the constitutional doctrine of separation of powers. . . .

JUSTICE WHITE, with whom JUSTICE BRENNAN, JUSTICE MARSHALL, and JUSTICE BLACKMUN join, dissenting:. . . .

Attaching absolute immunity to the Office of the President, rather than to particular activities that the President might perform, places the President above the law. It is a reversion to the old notion that the King can do no wrong. Until now, this concept had survived in this country only in the form of sovereign immunity. That doctrine forecloses suit against the Government itself and against Government officials, but only when the suit against the latter actually seeks relief against the sovereign. Suit against an officer, however, may be maintained where it seeks specific relief against him for conduct contrary to his statutory authority or to the Constitution. Now, however, the Court clothes the Office of the President with sovereign immunity, placing it beyond the law. . . .

Unfortunately, the Court now abandons basic principles that have been powerful guides to decision. It is particularly unfortunate since the judgment in this case has few, if any, indicia of a judicial decision; it is almost wholly a policy choice, a choice that is without substantial support and that in all events is ambiguous in its reach and import. . . . The Court casually, but candidly, abandons the functional approach to immunity that has run through all of our decisions. Indeed, the majority turns this rule on its head by declaring that because the functions of the President's office are so varied and diverse and some of them so profoundly important, the office is unique and must be clothed with officewide, absolute immunity. This is policy, not law, and in my view, very poor policy. . . .

I find it ironic, as well as tragic, that the Court would so casually discard its own role of assuring "the right of every individual to claim the protection of the laws," *Marbury* v. *Madison,* 1 Cranch, at 163, in the name of protecting the principle of separation of powers. Accordingly, I dissent.

JUSTICE BLACKMUN, with whom JUSTICE BRENNAN and JUSTICE MARSHALL join, dissenting: [omitted]

BOWSHER v. SYNAR,
478 U.S. 714 (1986)

This decision was one of the most awaited of those decided in 1986 because it concerned a novel device for cutting budget deficits that Congress de-

vised and that met with the reluctant approval of President Ronald Reagan. Under the Balanced Budget and Emergency Deficit Control Act of 1985, better known as the Gramm-Rudman-Hollings Act after its Senate sponsors, a maximum deficit amount for federal spending was set for each of the fiscal years 1986 through 1991. If in any fiscal year the budget deficit exceeds the maximum stipulated by the act, across-the-board cuts in federal spending are required. Because Congress preferred not to have to actually vote on cutting funds from programs, votes that could be politically harmful to individual members of Congress, Gramm-Rudman-Hollings provided for an automatic cutting scheme that would be administered by the Comptroller General. Under Section 251 of the act, the directors of the Office of Management and Budget (OMB) and the Congressional Budget Office (CBO) were required to submit their deficit estimates and their calculations for budget reductions for each federal program to the Comptroller General. The Comptroller General was then to make a final determination of the budgets cuts for each program and submit them to the President, who, under the law, was required to order the cuts. The act also contains Section 274(f), a "fallback" deficit reduction process in the event that Section 251's provisions were found to be unconstitutional. The fallback process eliminates the Comptroller General's role and provides for a congressional vote on the spending cuts determined to be necessary by the directors of OMB and CBO. Shortly after the President signed the act, Representative Mike Synar filed a court challenge to the act claiming it was unconstitutional. He was later joined by eleven other members of Congress. Named in the suit was Charles A. Bowsher, the Comptroller General of the United States. A three-judge federal district court struck down Section 251's provision for automatic spending cuts ordered by the Comptroller General and made mandatory on the President. Appeal was taken directly to the Supreme Court.

Majority votes: 7
Dissenting votes: 2

CHIEF JUSTICE BURGER delivered the opinion of the Court:

The question presented by these appeals is whether the assignment by Congress to the Comptroller General of the United States of certain functions under the Balanced Budget and Emergency Deficit Control Act of 1985 violates the doctrine of separation of powers. . . .

We noted recently that "[t]he Constitution sought to divide the delegated powers of the new Federal Government into three defined categories, Legislative, Executive, and Judicial." *INS* v. *Chadha,* 462 U.S. 919, 951 (1983). The declared purpose of separating and dividing the powers of government, of course, was to "diffus[e] power the better to secure liberty." Justice Jackson's words echo the famous warning of Montesquieu, quoted by James Madison in The Federalist No. 47, that " 'there can be no liberty where the legislative and executive powers are united in the same person, or body of magistrates'. . . ."

Even a cursory examination of the Constitution reveals the influence of Montesquieu's thesis that checks and balances were the foundation of a structure of government that would protect liberty. The Framers provided a vigorous Legislative branch and a separate and wholly independent Executive branch, with each branch responsible ultimately to the people. The Framers also provided for a Judicial branch equally independent with "[t]he judicial Power . . . extend[ing] to all Cases, in Law and Equity, arising under this Constitution, and the Laws of the United States." Article III, §2.

Other, more subtle, examples of separated powers are evident as well. . . .

That this system of division and separation of powers produces conflicts, confusion, and discordance at times is inherent, but it was deliberately so structured to assure full, vigorous and open debate on the great issues affecting the people and to provide avenues for the operation of checks on the exercise of governmental power.

The Constitution does not contemplate an active role for Congress in the supervision of officers charged with the execution of the laws it enacts. . . .

To permit the execution of the laws to be vested in an officer answerable only to Congress would, in practical terms, reserve in Congress control over the execution of the laws. . . . The structure of the Constitution does not permit Congress to execute the laws; it follows that Congress cannot grant to an officer under its control what it does not possess.

Our decision in *INS* v. *Chadha* supports this conclusion. In *Chadha,* we struck down a one house "legislative veto" provision by which each House of Congress retained the power to reserve a decision Congress had expressly authorized the Attorney General to make. . . . To permit an officer controlled by Congress to execute the laws would be, in essence, to permit a congressional veto. Congress could simply remove, or threaten to remove, an officer for executing the laws in any fashion found to be unsatisfactory to Congress.

This kind of congressional control over the execution of the laws, *Chadha* makes clear, is constitutionally impermissible. . . .

The critical factor lies in the provisions of the statute defining the Comptroller General's office relating to removability. Although the Comptroller General is nominated by the President from a list of three individuals recommended by the Speaker of the House of Representatives and the President pro tempore of the Senate, and confirmed by the Senate, he is removable only at the initiative of Congress. He may be removed not only by impeachment but also by Joint Resolution of Congress "at any time" resting on any one of the following bases:

"(i) permanent disability;
"(ii) inefficiency;
"(iii) neglect of duty;
"(iv) malfeasance; or
"(v) a felony or conduct involving moral turpitude."

This provision was included, as one Congressman explained in urging passage of the Act, because Congress "felt that [the Comptroller General] should be brought under the sole control of Congress, so that Congress at the moment when it found he was inefficient and was not carrying on the duties of his office as he should and as the Congress expected, could remove him without the long, tedious process of a trial by impeachment." 61 Cong. Rec. 1081 (1921). . . .

It is clear that Congress has consistently viewed the Comptroller General as an officer of the Legislative Branch. The Reorganization Acts of 1945 and 1949, for example, both stated that the Comptroller General and the GAO are "a part of the legislative branch of the Government." . . . Over the years, the Comptrollers General have also viewed themselves as part of the Legislative Branch. . . .

Against this background, we see no escape from the conclusion that, because Congress has retained removal authority over the Comptroller General, he may not be entrusted with executive powers. The remaining question is whether the Comptroller General has been assigned such powers in the Balanced Budget and Emergency Deficit Control Act of 1985.

The primary responsibility of the Comptroller General under the instant Act is the preparation of a "report." This report must contain detailed estimates of projected federal revenues and expenditures. The report must also specify the reductions, if any, necessary to reduce the deficit to the target for the appropriate fiscal year. The reductions must be set forth on a program-by-program basis.

In preparing the report, the Comptroller General is to have "due regard" for the estimates and reductions set forth in a joint report submitted to him by the Director of CBO [Congressional Budget Office] and the Director of OMB [the Office of Management and Budget], the President's fiscal and budgetary advisor. However, the Act plainly contemplates that the Comptroller General will exercise his independent judgment and evaluation with respect to those estimates. The Act also provides that the Comptroller General's report "shall explain fully any differences between the contents of such report and the report of the Directors."

Appellants suggest that the duties assigned to the Comptroller General in the Act are essentially ministerial and mechanical so that their performance does not constitute "execution of the law" in a meaningful sense. On the contrary, we view these functions as plainly entailing execution of the law in constitutional terms. Interpreting a law enacted by Congress to implement the legislative mandate is the very essence of "execution" of the law. Under §251, the Comptroller General must exercise judgment concerning facts that affect the application of the Act. He must also interpret the provisions of the Act to determine precisely what budgetary calculations are required. Decisions of that kind are typically made by officers charged with executing a statute.

The executive nature of the Comptroller General's functions under the Act is revealed in §252(a)(3) which gives the Comptroller General the ultimate authority to determine the budget cuts to be made. Indeed, the Comptroller General commands the President himself to carry out, without the slightest variation (with exceptions not relevant to the constitutional issues presented), the directive of the Comptroller General as to the budget reductions. . . .

No one can doubt that Congress and the President are confronted with fiscal and economic problems of unprecedented magnitude, but "the fact that a given law or procedure is efficient, convenient, and useful in facilitating functions of government, standing alone, will not save it if it is contrary to the Constitution. Convenience and efficiency are not the primary objectives—or the hallmarks—of democratic government. . . ." *Chadha, supra,* at 944.

We conclude the District Court correctly held that the powers vested in the Comptroller General under §251 violate the command of the Constitution that the Congress play no direct role in the execution of the laws. Accordingly, the judgment and order of the District Court are affirmed.

Our judgment is stayed for a period not to exceed 60 days to permit Congress to implement the fallback provisions.

[Affirmed.]

JUSTICE STEVENS, with whom JUSTICE MARSHALL joins, concurring in the judgment: [omitted]
JUSTICE WHITE, dissenting:

The Court, acting in the name of separation of powers, takes upon itself to strike down the Gramm-Rudman-Hollings Act, one of the most novel and far-reaching legislative responses to a national crisis since the New Deal. The basis of the Court's action is a solitary provision of another statute that was passed over sixty years ago and has lain dormant since that time. I cannot concur in the Court's action. Like the Court, I will not purport to speak to the wisdom of the policies incorporated in the legislation the Court invalidates; that is a matter for the Congress and the Executive, *both* of which expressed their assent to the statute barely half a year ago. I will, however, address the wisdom of the Court's willingness to interpose its distressingly formalistic view of separation of powers as a bar to the attainment of governmental objectives through the means chosen by the Congress and the President in the legislative process established by the Constitution. Twice in the past four years I have expressed my view that the Court's recent efforts to police the separation of powers have rested on untenable constitutional propositions leading to regrettable results. . . . Today's result is even more misguided. As I will explain, the Court's decision rests on a feature of the legislative scheme that is of minimal practical significance and that presents no substantial threat to the basic scheme of separation of powers. . . .

It is evident (and nothing in the Court's opinion is to the contrary) that the powers exercised by the Comptroller General under the Gramm-Rudman Act are not such that vesting them in an officer not subject to removal at will by the President would in itself improperly interfere with Presidential powers. Determining the level of spending by the Federal Government is not by nature a function central either to the exercise of the President's enumerated powers or to his general duty to ensure execution of the laws; rather, appropriating funds is a peculiarly legislative function, and one expressly committed to Congress by Article I, §9, which provides that "[n]o Money shall be drawn from the Treasury, but in Consequence of Appropriations made by Law."

In enacting Gramm-Rudman, Congress has chosen to exercise this legislative power to establish the level of federal spending by providing a detailed set of criteria for reducing expenditures below the level of appropriations in the event that certain conditions are met. Delegating the execution of this legislation—that is, the power to apply the Act's criteria and make the required calculations—to an officer independent of the President's will does not deprive the President of any power that he would otherwise have or that is essential to the performance of the duties of his office. Rather, the result of such a delegation, from the standpoint of the President, is no different from the result of more traditional forms of appropriation: under either system, the level of funds available to the Executive branch to carry out its duties is not within the President's discretionary control. . . .

[T]o strike down a statute posing no real danger of aggrandizement of congressional power is extremely misguided and insensitive to our constitutional role. The wisdom of vesting "executive" powers in an officer removable by joint resolution may indeed be debatable—as may be the wisdom of the entire scheme of permitting an unelected official to revise the budget enacted by Congress—but such matters are for the most part to be worked out between the Congress and the President through the legislative process, which affords each branch ample opportunity to defend its interests. The Act vesting budget-cutting authority in the Comptroller General represents Congress' judgment that the delegation of such authority to counteract ever-mounting deficits is "necessary and proper" to the exercise of the powers granted the Federal Government by the Constitution; and the President's approval of the statute signifies his unwillingness to reject the choice made by Congress. Under such circumstances, the role of this Court should be limited to determining whether the Act so alters the balance of authority among the branches of government as to pose a genuine threat to the basic division between the lawmaking power and the power to execute the law. Because I see no such threat, I cannot join the Court in striking down the Act.

I dissent.

JUSTICE BLACKMUN, dissenting:. . . .

The only relief sought in this case is nullification of the automatic budget-reduction provisions of the Deficit Control Act, and that relief should not be awarded even if the Court is correct that those provisions are constitutionally incompatible with Congress' authority to remove the Comptroller General by joint resolution. Any incompatibility, I feel, should be cured by refusing to allow congressional removal—if it ever is attempted—and not by striking down the central provisions of the Deficit Control Act. However wise or foolish it may be, that statute unquestionably ranks among the most important federal enactments of the past several decades. I cannot see the sense of invalidating legislation of this magnitude in order to preserve a cumbersome, 65-year-old removal power that has never been exercised and appears to have been all but forgotten until this litigation. . . .

MORRISON v. OLSON,
487 U.S. 654 (1988)

The dispute that underlay this case was between the House of Representatives and the executive branch in the course of a House investigation of the Environmental Protection Agency during the early years of the Reagan Administration. Theodore Olson was the Assistant Attorney General for the Office of Legal Counsel, Edward C. Schmults was Deputy Attorney General, and Carol E. Dinkins was Assistant Attorney General for the Land and Natural Resources Division. The House Judiciary Committee issued a report in which it suggested that Olson had given false and misleading testimony and that Schmults and Dinkins had obstructed the Committee's investigation by wrongfully withholding certain documents from the Committee. The Committee asked Attorney General Edwin Meese III to seek the appointment of an independent counsel under the provisions of the Ethics in Government Act to investigate the allegations. Alexia Morrison was eventually appointed independent counsel and sought to compel the testimony of Olson, Schmults, and Dinkins before a grand jury. In turn, these former government officials brought this suit challenging the constitutionality of the independent counsel provisions. The federal district court upheld the act's constitutionality. The Court of Appeals reversed and appeal was taken.

Majority votes: 7
Dissenting votes: 1

CHIEF JUSTICE REHNQUIST delivered the opinion of the Court:

This case presents us with a challenge to the independent counsel provisions of the Ethics in Government Act of 1978. We hold today that these provisions of the Act do not violate the Appointments Clause of the Constitution, Art. II, §2, cl. 2, or the limitations of Article III, nor do they impermissibly interfere with the President's authority under Arti-

cle II in violation of the constitutional principle of separation of powers. . . .

The Appointments Clause of Article II reads as follows:

"[The President] shall nominate, and by and with the Advice and Consent of the Senate, shall appoint Ambassadors, other public Ministers and Consuls, Judges of the Supreme Court, and all other Officers of the United States, whose Appointments are not herein otherwise provided for, and which shall be established by Law: but the Congress may by Law vest the Appointment of such inferior Officers, as they think proper, in the President alone, in the Courts of Law, or in the Heads of Departments." U.S. Const., Art. II, §2, cl. 2.

The parties do not dispute that "[t]he Constitution for purposes of appointment . . . divides all its officers into two classes." As we stated in *Buckley* v. *Valeo,* 424 U.S. 1, 132 (1976), "[p]rincipal officers are selected by the President with the advice and consent of the Senate. Inferior officers Congress may allow to be appointed by the President alone, by the heads of departments, or by the Judiciary." The initial question is, accordingly, whether appellant is an "inferior" or a "principal" officer. If she is the latter, as the Court of Appeals concluded, then the Act is in violation of the Appointments Clause.

The line between "inferior" and "principal" officers is one that is far from clear, and the Framers provided little guidance into where it should be drawn. . . . We need not attempt here to decide exactly where the line falls between the two types of officers, because in our view appellant clearly falls on the "inferior officer" side of that line. Several factors lead to this conclusion.

First, appellant is subject to removal by a higher Executive Branch official. Although appellant may not be "subordinate" to the Attorney General (and the President) insofar as she possesses a degree of independent discretion to exercise the powers delegated to her under the Act, the fact that she can be removed by the Attorney General indicates that she is to some degree "inferior" in rank and authority. Second, appellant is empowered by the Act to perform only certain, limited duties. An independent counsel's role is restricted primarily to investigation and, if appropriate, prosecution for certain federal crimes. Admittedly, the Act delegates to appellant "full power and independent authority to exercise all investigative and prosecutorial functions and powers of the Department of Justice," but this grant of authority does not include any authority to formulate policy for the Government or the Executive Branch, nor does it give appellant any administrative duties outside of those necessary to operate her office. The Act specifically provides that in policy matters appellant is to comply to the extent possible with the policies of the Department.

Third, appellant's office is limited in jurisdiction. Not only is the Act itself restricted in applicability to certain federal officials suspected of certain serious federal crimes, but an independent counsel can only act within the scope of the jurisdiction that has been granted by the Special Division pursuant to a request by the Attorney General. Finally, appellant's office is limited in tenure. There is concededly no time limit on the appointment of a particular counsel. Nonetheless, the office of independent counsel is "temporary" in the sense that an independent counsel is appointed essentially to accomplish a single task, and when that task is over the office is terminated, either by the counsel herself or by action of the Special Division. Unlike other prosecutors, appellant has no ongoing responsibilities that extend beyond the accomplishment of the mission that she was appointed for and authorized by the Special Division to undertake. In our view, these factors relating to the "ideas of tenure, duration . . . and duties" of the independent counsel are sufficient to establish that appellant is an "inferior" officer in the constitutional sense. . . .

This does not, however, end our inquiry under the Appointments Clause. Appellees argue that even if appellant is an "inferior" officer, the Clause does not empower Congress to place the power to appoint such an officer outside the Executive Branch. They contend that the Clause does not contemplate congressional authorization of "interbranch appointments," in which an officer of one branch is appointed by officers of another branch. The relevant language of the Appointments Clause is worth repeating. It reads: ". . . but the Congress may by Law vest the Appointment of such inferior Officers, as they think proper, in the President alone, in the courts of Law, or in the Heads of Departments." On its face, the language of this "excepting clause" admits of no limitation on interbranch appointments. Indeed, the inclusion of "as they think proper" seems clearly to give Congress significant discretion to determine whether it is "proper" to vest the appointment of, for example, executive officials in the "courts of Law." . . .

We also note that the history of the clause provides no support for appellees' position. . . . [T]here was little or no debate on the question of whether the Clause empowers Congress to provide for interbranch appointments, and there is nothing to suggest that the Framers intended to prevent Congress from having that power.

We do not mean to say that Congress' power to provide for interbranch appointments of "inferior officers" is unlimited. In addition to separation of powers concerns, which would arise if such provisions for appointment had the potential to impair the constitutional functions assigned to one of the branches, . . . Congress' decision to vest the appointment power in the courts would be improper if there was some "incongruity" between the functions normally performed by the courts and the performance of their duty to appoint. . . . In this case, however, we do not think it impermissible for Congress to vest the power to appoint independent counsels in a specially created federal court. We thus disagree with the Court of Appeals' conclusion that there is an inherent incongruity about a court having the power to appoint prosecutorial officers. We have recognized that courts may appoint private attorneys to act as prosecutor for judicial contempt judgments. . . . In *Go-Bart Importing Co.* v. *United States,* 282 U.S. 344 (1931), we approved court appointment of United States commissioners, who exercised certain limited prosecutorial powers. . . . Lower courts have also upheld interim judicial appointments of United States Attorneys, see *United States* v. *Solomon,* 216 F.Supp. 835 (SDNY 1963). . . Congress of course was concerned when it created the office of independent counsel with the conflicts of interest that could arise in situations when the Executive Branch is called upon to investigate its own high-ranking officers. If it were to remove the appointing authority from the Executive Branch, the most logical place to put it was in the Judicial Branch. In the light of the Act's provision making the judges of the Special Division ineligible to participate in any matters relating to an independent counsel they have appointed, we do not think that appointment of the independent counsels by the court runs afoul of the constitutional limitation on "incongruous" interbranch appointments.

. . .

We now turn to consider whether the Act is invalid under the constitutional principle of separation of powers. Two related issues must be addressed: The first is whether the provision of the Act restricting the Attorney General's power to remove the independent counsel to only those instances in which he can show "good cause," taken by itself, impermissibly interferes with the President's exercise of his constitutionally appointed functions. The second is whether, taken as a whole, the Act violates the separation of powers by reducing the President's ability to control the prosecutorial powers wielded by the independent counsel. . . . [O]ur present considered view is that the determination of whether the Constitution allows Congress to impose a "good cause"-type restriction on the President's power to remove an official cannot be made to turn on whether or not that official is classified as "purely executive." The analysis contained in our removal cases is designed not to define rigid categories of those officials who may or may not be removed at will by the President, but to ensure that Congress does not interfere with the President's exercise of the "executive power" and his constitutionally appointed duty to "take care that the laws be faithfully executed" under Article II. . . . [T]he real question is whether the removal restrictions are of such a nature that they impede the President's ability to perform his constitutional duty, and the functions of the officials in question must be analyzed in that light.

Considering for the moment the "good cause" removal provision in isolation from the other parts of the Act at issue in this case, we cannot say that the imposition of a "good cause" standard for removal by itself unduly trammels on executive authority. There is no real dispute that the functions performed by the independent counsel are "executive" in the sense that they are law enforcement functions that typically have been undertaken by officials within the Executive Branch. As we noted above, however, the independent counsel is an inferior officer under the Appointments Clause, with limited jurisdiction and tenure and lacking policymaking or significant administrative authority. Although the counsel exercises no small amount of discretion and judgment in deciding how to carry out her duties under the Act, we simply do not see how the President's need to control the exercise of that discretion is so central to the functioning of the Executive Branch as to require as a matter of constitutional law that the counsel be terminable at will by the President.

Nor do we think that the "good cause" removal provision at issue here impermissibly burdens the President's power to control or supervise the independent counsel, as an executive official, in the execution of her duties under the Act. This is not a case in which the power to remove an executive official has been completely stripped from the President, thus providing no means for the President to ensure the "faithful execution" of the laws. Rather,

because the independent counsel may be terminated for "good cause," the Executive, through the Attorney General, retains ample authority to assure that the counsel is competently performing her statutory responsibilities in a manner that comports with the provisions of the Act. . . . Here, as with the provision of the Act conferring the appointment authority of the independent counsel on the special court, the congressional determination to limit the removal power of the Attorney General was essential, in the view of Congress, to establish the necessary independence of the office. We do not think that this limitation as it presently stands sufficiently deprives the President of control over the independent counsel to interfere impermissibly with his constitutional obligation to ensure the faithful execution of the laws.

The final question to be addressed is whether the Act, taken as a whole, violates the principle of separation of powers by unduly interfering with the role of the Executive Branch. Time and again we have reaffirmed the importance in our constitutional scheme of the separation of governmental powers into the three coordinate branches. . . .

We observe first that this case does not involve an attempt by Congress to increase its own powers at the expense of the Executive Branch. . . . Unlike some of our previous cases, most recently *Bowsher* v. *Synar,* this case simply does not pose a "dange[r] of congressional usurpation of Executive Branch functions." . . . Indeed, with the exception of the power of impeachment—which applies to all officers of the United States—Congress retained for itself no powers of control or supervision over an independent counsel. The Act does empower certain members of Congress to request the Attorney General to apply for the appointment of an independent counsel, but the Attorney General has no duty to comply with the request, although he must respond within a certain time limit. Other than that, Congress' role under the Act is limited to receiving reports or other information and oversight of the independent counsel's activities, functions that we have recognized generally as being incidental to the legislative function of Congress.

Similarly, we do not think that the Act works any *judicial* usurpation of properly executive functions. . . .

Finally, we do not think that the Act "impermissibly undermine[s]" the powers of the Executive Branch, or "disrupts the proper balance between the coordinate branches [by] prevent[ing] the Executive Branch from accomplishing its constitutionally assigned functions." It is undeniable that the

Act reduces the amount of control or supervision that the Attorney General and, through him, the President exercises over the investigation and prosecution of a certain class of alleged criminal activity. The Attorney General is not allowed to appoint the individual of his choice; he does not determine the counsel's jurisdiction; and his power to remove a counsel is limited. Nonetheless, the Act does give the Attorney General several means of supervising or controlling the prosecutorial powers that may be wielded by an independent counsel. Most importantly, the Attorney General retains the power to remove the counsel for "good cause," a power that we have already concluded provides the Executive with substantial ability to ensure that the laws are "faithfully executed" by an independent counsel. No independent counsel may be appointed without a specific request by the Attorney General, and the Attorney General's decision not to request appointment if he finds "no reasonable grounds to believe that further investigation is warranted" is committed to his unreviewable discretion. The Act thus gives the Executive a degree of control over the power to initiate an investigation by the independent counsel. In addition, the jurisdiction of the independent counsel is defined with reference to the facts submitted by the Attorney General, and once a counsel is appointed, the Act requires that the counsel abide by Justice Department policy unless it is not "possible" to do so. Notwithstanding the fact that the counsel is to some degree "independent" and free from Executive supervision to a greater extent than other federal prosecutors, in our view these features of the Act give the Executive Branch sufficient control over the independent counsel to ensure that the President is able to perform his constitutionally assigned duties. . . .

The decision of the Court of Appeals is therefore

Reversed.

JUSTICE KENNEDY took no part in the consideration or decision of this case.

JUSTICE SCALIA, dissenting: . . .

That is what this suit is about. Power. The allocation of power among Congress, the President and the courts in such fashion as to preserve the equilibrium the Constitution sought to establish—so that "a gradual concentration of the several powers in the same department," Federalist No. 51, p. 321 (J. Madison), can effectively be resisted. Frequently an issue of this sort will come before the Court clad, so to speak, in sheep's clothing: the potential of the asserted principle to effect important change in the equilibrium of power is not immediately evident, and must be discerned by a careful and perceptive analysis. But this wolf comes as a wolf. . . .

[B]y the application of this statute in the present case, Congress has effectively compelled a criminal investigation of a high-level appointee of the President in connection with his actions arising out of a bitter power dispute between the President and the Legislative Branch. Mr. Olson may or may not be guilty of a crime; we do not know. But we do know that the investigation of him has been commenced, not necessarily because the President or his authorized subordinates believe it is in the interest of the United States, in the sense that it warrants the diversion of resources from other efforts, and is worth the cost in money and in possible damage to other governmental interests; and not even, leaving aside those normally considered factors, because the President or his authorized subordinates necessarily believe that an investigation is likely to unearth a violation worth prosecuting; but only because the Attorney General cannot affirm, as Congress demands, that there are *no reasonable grounds to believe* that further investigation is warranted. The decisions regarding the scope of that further investigation, its duration, and, finally, whether or not prosecution should ensue, are likewise beyond the control of the President and his subordinates. . . . It seems to me, . . . that the decision of the Court of Appeals invalidating the present statute must be upheld on fundamental separation-of-powers principles if the following two questions are answered affirmatively: (1) Is the conduct of a criminal prosecution (and of an investigation to decide whether to prosecute) the exercise of purely executive power? (2) Does the statute deprive the President of the United States of exclusive control over the exercise of that power? Surprising to say, the Court appears to concede an affirmative answer to both questions, but seeks to avoid the inevitable conclusion that since the statute vests some purely executive power in a person who is not the President of the United States it is void. . . . A system of separate and coordinate powers necessarily involves an acceptance of exclusive power that can theoretically be abused. . . . While the separation of powers may prevent us from righting every wrong, it does so in order to ensure that we do not lose liberty. The checks against any Branch's abuse of its exclusive powers are twofold: First, retaliation by one of the other Branch's use of *its* exclusive powers: Congress, for example, can impeach the Executive who willfully fails to enforce the laws; the Executive can decline to prosecute under unconstitutional statutes . . . and the courts can dismiss malicious prosecutions. Second, and ultimately, there is the political check that the people will replace those in the political branches . . . who are guilty of abuse. Political pressures produced special prosecutors—for Teapot Dome and for Watergate, for example—long before this statute created the independent counsel.

The Court has, nonetheless, replaced the clear constitutional prescription that the executive power belongs to the President with a "balancing test." What are the standards to determine how the balance is to be struck, that is, how much removal of presidential power is too much? . . . Once we depart from the text of the Constitution, just where short of that do we stop? The most amazing feature of the Court's opinion is that it does not even purport to give an answer. It simply *announces,* with no analysis, that the ability to control the decision whether to investigate and prosecute the President's closest advisors, and indeed the President himself, is not "so central to the functioning of the Executive Branch" as to be constitutionally required to be within the President's control. Apparently that is so because we say it is so. . . . Evi-

dently, the governing standard is to be what might be called the unfettered wisdom of a majority of this Court, revealed to an obedient people on a case-by-case basis. This is not only not the government of laws that the Constitution established; it is not a government of laws at all. . . .

The independent counsel is not even subordinate to the President. The Court essentially admits as much, noting that "appellant may not be 'subordinate' to the Attorney General (and the President) insofar as she possesses a degree of independent discretion to exercise the powers delegated to her under the Act." In fact, there is no doubt about it. As noted earlier, the Act specifically grants her the "*full* power and *independent* authority to exercise *all* investigative and prosecutorial functions of the Department of Justice," and makes her removable only for "good cause," a limitation specifically intended to ensure that she be *independent* of, not *subordinate* to, the President and the Attorney General.

Because appellant is not subordinate to another officer, she is not an "inferior" officer and her appointment other than by the President with the advice and consent of the Senate is unconstitutional. . . .

Chapter

8

Powers of Congress Under the Commerce Clause

DECISIONAL TRENDS

The commerce clause cases raise the issues of the nature of Congress' powers and the permissible range of action of the states in the commerce sphere. These questions were not to be resolved satisfactorily and definitively until the 1940s, and even today commerce clause issues come to the Court. The Marshall Court, in the first case to concern Congress' commerce power, **Gibbons** v. **Ogden,** offered a broad definition of commerce and the powers of Congress. In *Gibbons* as well as in the subsequent case of *Brown* v. *Maryland,* 12 Wheaton 419 (1827), the Court restricted the actions of the states in the commerce sphere. In the *Brown* case, the Court determined that a Maryland law requiring an importer of foreign goods to purchase a state license before being permitted to sell the imported goods impinged upon Congress' commerce power and was also a tax on imports forbidden by the Constitution. The Court ruled that as long as

the goods remain in their original form or package in which they were imported, the state may not tax those goods. But the Marshall Court justices were unable to agree among themselves just what commerce powers remained with the states. In **Willson** v. **Blackbird Creek Marsh Company** (chap. 10), instead of treating the case as a commerce case, Marshall considered it as raising the police powers issue. But that was clearly a way of avoiding the justices' differing views as to the commerce power. Interestingly, the concept of state police powers, the inherent power of the state to act in order to protect the health, safety, and welfare of its citizens, was to be developed by later courts and achieve great importance in the twentieth century.

Like its predecessor Court, the Taney Court was badly split on the question of whether the states could exercise the commerce power in the absence of its exercise by Congress. The Court majority in **Mayor of**

New York v. Miln (chap. 10) opted for the police powers doctrine as the basis for sustaining the disputed New York regulation. Twelve years later in two similar cases (including another one from New York) known as the *Passenger Cases*, 7 Howard 283 (1849), a 5–4 majority struck down the state regulation as an unconstitutional regulation of interstate and foreign commerce. The New York statute levied a tax on ships from abroad on the basis of the number of alien passengers aboard. The money raised was to help with their medical examination costs and to pay for treatment of those found to have communicable diseases. Chief Justice Taney could not see how this New York regulation was less an exercise of the state's police power than the one upheld in the *Miln* case, and as a consequence he led the dissenters. The decision of the majority must certainly have seemed all the more confusing to the public if not to the bench and bar of the nation, because just two years earlier in the three cases known as the *License Cases*, 5 Howard 504 (1847), the Court majority had utilized the police power doctrine to rule constitutional state statutes regulating and taxing the sale of alcoholic beverages brought in from outside the state. One state law (New Hampshire's) specifically taxed liquor that was still in the original package—in apparent violation of *Brown* v. *Maryland*.

The confusion in the commerce sphere was not to be resolved until 1852 when the Court by a 7–2 majority adopted the compromise formulation devised by the newest addition to the Court, Justice Benjamin Curtis, in **Cooley v. Board of Wardens.** By recognizing the necessity for exclusive congressional control over commerce when national uniformity demands it, the Court upheld the principle of federal supremacy and the broad reading of Congress' commerce powers first established by the Marshall Court. But by also acknowledging that there are circumstances in which local control in the absence of congressional regulation is desirable because of diverse local

conditions, the Court also recognized the need to be pragmatic and realistic. Involved in the *Cooley* case was the fact that Congress had empowered the states to regulate their own harbors; thus, if Congress' commerce powers were to be exercised only by Congress, the Court would have to strike down an act of Congress! It should be stressed that whenever Congress did in fact act under its commerce powers and its action was challenged, the Court unhesitatingly upheld Congress. (See, e.g., *Pennsylvania* v. *Wheeling and Belmont Bridge Company,* 18 Howard 421 [1856].)

The commerce clause figured prominently in the constitutional jurisprudence of the Court, particularly toward the end of the nineteenth century. For example, the Waite Court had first permitted railroad rate regulation in *Peik* v. *Chicago & N.W.R. Co.,* 94 U.S. 164 (1877). However, by 1886, the Court in *The Wabash Case,* 118 U.S. 557, felt obliged to consider the interstate commerce implications of state regulation of interstate railroad rates. Justice Miller, speaking for the majority, invoked the Cooley Rule (from *Cooley* v. *Board of Wardens*) and declared that only national rate regulation was permissible. Miller, himself ordinarily sympathetic to the state police power but realizing that here national uniformity was necessary, issued an explicit invitation to Congress to regulate the railroads under Congress' commerce powers. Congress did just that shortly after the *Wabash* decision was handed down. The Interstate Commerce Act established the Interstate Commerce Commission (ICC), and railroad rates were regulated by the federal government until the Fuller Court some ten years after *Wabash* emasculated the ICC in *The ICC Case,* 162 U.S. 184 (1896). In a series of subsequent cases, the Court systematically struck down the ICC's power. Even the ICC's fact-finding powers were scuttled by the Court (*ICC* v. *Alabama Midland Ry. Co.,* 168 U.S. 144 [1897]). However, after Congress enacted the Hepburn Act of 1906, clarifying the powers of the

ICC and plainly investing it with rate regulation powers, the Court generally upheld the agency.

It was in the area of the Sherman Anti-Trust Act cases that the Fuller Court formulated new (mostly negative) commerce clause doctrines. The case of *United States* v. *E.C. Knight Co.,* 156 U.S. 1 (1895), was the springboard for doctrines narrowing Congress' reach under the commerce clause. Yet the Court in **Swift** v. **United States** could and did enunciate positive commerce clause doctrines with which to uphold government regulation.

The commerce power can be used by government to promote moral values. When those values clashed with those of the Court majority, the Court did not hesitate to impose its own policy preferences. For example, the Waite Court was generally unsympathetic to the rights of blacks. When Louisiana's reconstructionist legislature enacted a civil rights statute requiring public carriers operating in the state to provide all passengers, regardless of race, with equal facilities, the Court struck the statute down as "a direct burden upon interstate commerce." *Hall* v. *DeCuir,* 95 U.S. 485 (1878), was the case. The Fuller Court, close to two decades later, however, upheld a mandatory state segregation law for public carriers in **Plessy** v. **Ferguson** (chap. 18) and did not find *that* to be a burden on interstate commerce. In contrast to black rights, the Court in the 1903 case of *Champion* v. *Ames,* 188 U.S. 321, approved legislation passed under Congress' commerce powers prohibiting lotteries through interstate commerce and via the United States mail.

The Court's antilabor bias was evident in *Loewe* v. *Lawlor,* 208 U.S. 274 (1908), in which the Court ruled that the Danbury Hatters' Union was guilty of a combination in restraint of trade in violation of the Sherman Anti-Trust Act by engaging in a labor boycott against a manufacturer whose goods were sold in interstate commerce. Also in the *First Employers' Liability Cases,* 207 U.S. 463 (1908),

the Court invalidated the Employers' Liability Act of 1906, which did away with the fellow servant rule by holding railroads liable for the death or injury of their employees because of the negligence of fellow workers or other railroad employees. The Court said that the legislation as written exceeded Congress' commerce power by including intrastate commerce. Subsequently, however, revised legislation explicitly limited to interstate commerce was upheld by the Court in the *Second Employers' Liability Cases,* 223 U.S. 1 (1912).

It is in the commerce area perhaps more than any other during the period between 1910 and 1937 that we see the Court developing alternative lines of precedent that enabled it to sustain or invalidate acts of Congress at will. The Court, beginning with *Champion* v. *Ames,* had recognized that Congress could use its commerce power for essentially police power purposes. In 1911 the Court upheld the Pure Food and Drug Act in *Hipolite Egg Co.* v. *United States,* 220 U.S. 45, once again reaffirming a broad view of Congress' commerce powers. In the *Second Employers' Liability Cases,* the Court upheld a 1908 workmen's compensation statute enacted by Congress and applicable to those employed by common carriers who are actually engaged in interstate commerce. The following year the Court in *Hoke* v. *United States,* 227 U.S. 308 (1913), upheld the Mann Act, aimed at interstate prostitution rings, which made it a federal crime to transport women across state lines for immoral purposes. In *Clark Distilling Co.* v. *Western Maryland R. R. Co.,* 242 U.S. 311 (1917), the Court upheld congressional legislation forbidding the shipment of alcoholic beverages in interstate commerce into dry states. Then, in a decision in marked contrast to these precedents, the Court struck down the 1916 Child Labor Law in **Hammer** v. **Dagenhart.** Congress may not prohibit anything it wishes, only that which is harmful in and of itself or produces harmful effects. The harmful effects of child labor, said the majority, occur only before the goods are shipped in interstate commerce. But this could not be said for the lottery tickets, the adulterated food, the dangerous drugs, the prostitutes, or alcoholic beverages. Along the lines of this reasoning, the Court shortly after the *Hammer* decision ruled that the Meat Inspection Act was constitutional and that uninspected, potentially harmful meat could be prohibited from interstate commerce (*Pittsburgh Melting Co.* v. *Totten,* 248 U.S. 1 [1918]). But the Court did not stand by this harmful goods/effect doctrine in *Brooks* v. *United States,* 267 U.S. 432 (1925), when it upheld the National Motor Vehicle Theft Act making it a federal crime to transport stolen automobiles across state lines. Later, in January 1937, the Court again ignored the distinction by allowing the prohibition of convict-made goods from interstate commerce (*Kentucky Whip and Collar Co.* v. *Illinois Central R. R. Co.,* 299 U.S. 334 [1937]).

The Court was somewhat more consistent in its treatment of railroad regulation. The White Court, in particular, established a record of support for railroad regulation under the Commerce Clause. In the *Minnesota Rate Case,* 230 U.S. 352 (1913), the Court, utilizing the Cooley Rule, recognized local diverse conditions and upheld the Minnesota Railroad and Warehouse Commission's order establishing intrastate railroad rates, even though they affected interstate rates, in the absence of federal railroad rate regulation. The *Shreveport Case,* 234 U.S. 342 (1914), concerned the ICC setting intrastate railroad rates in Texas, and the Court upheld this. The Court, indeed, had made it clear that Congress could confer on the ICC original rate-setting powers. The 1910 Mann-Elkins Act giving the ICC this power was upheld by the Court in *United States* v. *Atchison, Topeka and Santa Fe,* 234 U.S. 476 (1914). When Congress passed the Adamson Act in 1916 establishing an eight-hour day for railroad workers, the Court approved it in *Wilson* v. *New,* 243 U.S. 332 (1917). During World War I the federal government national-

ized the railroads. At the end of the war, Congress enacted the Transportation Act of 1920, returning the railroads to private ownership but providing for extensive federal government regulation of all railroad properties including intrastate railroads. The legislation also contained a recapture of excess profits provision whereby all profits above 6 percent were to be split between the railroads and the federal government. The government's share of the excess profits was to be placed in a fund to aid ailing railroads. Government regulation of intrastate railroad properties was upheld by the Court in *Railroad Commission of Wisconsin* v. *C.B. & Q. R. R. Co.,* 257 U.S. 563 (1922), and the recapture provision of the 1920 legislation was upheld in *Dayton–Goose Creek Railway Co.* v. *United States,* 263 U.S. 456 (1924).

The Court had a decidedly less favorable view of the federal government's antitrust activities. In *Standard Oil Co.* v. *United States,* 221 U.S. 1 (1910), the Court upheld the prosecution and conviction of Standard Oil officials for violating the Sherman Anti-Trust Act. But in so doing the Court established a doctrine known as the "rule of reason" that, in effect, qualified the Sherman Act to apply only to "unreasonable" trusts but not to trusts that served useful purposes. "Reasonable" monopolies, declared the Court, were not violations of the Sherman Act. The Court followed this doctrine in *United States* v. *American Tobacco Co.,* 221 U.S. 106 (1911), finding the combination not unreasonable and that therefore total dissolution was not warranted. In *United States* v. *Winslow,* 227 U.S. 202 (1913), the Court ruled that the shoe machinery trust was reasonable and that the government's antitrust prosecution was not justified. In *United States* v. *U.S. Steel Corp.,* 251 U.S. 417 (1920), the steel trust was also found to be reasonable and therefore the government's prosecution was struck down. Indeed, the 1920s was an era of unprecedented monopolistic activities.

The Court's permissive approach to business monopolies was conveniently abandoned when organized labor's activities were challenged as violations of the antitrust laws. In *Duplex Printing Press Co.* v. *Deering,* 254 U.S. 443 (1921), the Court ruled that secondary boycotts by labor unions violated the antitrust laws. In *Bedford Cut Stone Co.* v. *Journeymen Stone Cutters' Association,* 274 U.S. 37 (1927), the Court, ignoring its long-established distinction between manufacturing and commerce and direct-versus-indirect effects on commerce, ruled that the lower court should have granted the injunction against the stonecutters' union, because it had instructed its locals not to work on stone cut by nonunion workers. Although the stonecutters' work was local and only indirectly related to commerce, the antitrust laws at least for labor unions were far-reaching.

Of course, not all the Court's antitrust cases were antiregulatory or antiunion. For example, in *Stafford* v. *Wallace,* 258 U.S. 495 (1922), the Court upheld the Packers and Stockyards Act of 1921 regulating the meat trust and reaffirmed *Swift* v. *United States.* Thus, by the time of the Hughes Court and the Great Depression, the Court had both positive and negative commerce clause doctrines. The Court, during the first seven years under Chief Justice Hughes, opted for the negative restrictive doctrines as is evident from two of the major anti-New Deal decisions of the Court— **Schechter Poultry Corp.** v. **United States** and **Carter** v. **Carter Coal Company.**

The landmark case of **National Labor Relations Board** v. **Jones & Laughlin Steel Corp.,** along with companion NLRB cases handed down at the same time, swept away the old restrictive commerce clause doctrines that had been used to stifle economic regulation by the federal government. But it took several years of subsequent decisions to make clear the full sweep of the new constitutional order. In the labor relations area, to name one field, after the *Jones and Laughlin* and companion

decisions, the Court consistently ruled in favor of the NLRB whenever a question of coverage under the statute arose. For example, in *Consolidated Edison Co.* v. *NLRB,* 305 U.S. 197 (1938), the NLRB's jurisdiction was upheld over a utility that sold power entirely within one state. In the opinion of the Court by Chief Justice Hughes, a connection to interstate commerce was found in that power was sold to radio stations, airports, and railroads and *they* were directly engaged in interstate commerce. In *NLRB* v. *Fainblatt,* 306 U.S. 601 (1939), the Court applied the National Labor Relations Act (thereby upholding NLRB jurisdiction) to a small concern engaged in processing garments received from out-of-state but whose postprocessing delivery was entirely within the state in which the business was located. Even companies selling insurance were subject to the NLRB (*Polish National Alliance* v. *NLRB,* 322 U.S. 643 [1944]), a ruling consistent with the decision in *United States* v. *South-Eastern Underwriters Association,* 322 U.S. 533 (1944), in which the Court ruled that the insurance business was interstate commerce for purposes of congressional regulation under its commerce powers (the next year, however, Congress enacted legislation permitting the states to regulate insurance companies).

The Fair Labor Standards Act of 1938 was upheld in the classic **United States** v. **Darby** case that overturned *Hammer* v. *Dagenhart.* In subsequent cases the Court sought to determine whether various types of businesses were to be considered interstate commerce and thus held to the statutory standards. The Court's decisions were mixed. For example, in decisions handed down close together, the Court in one case, *Borden Company* v. *Borella,* 325 U.S. 679 (1945), ruled that elevator operators and other building service personnel of a New York office building owned by as well as containing the main offices of the Borden Company were subject to the wages and hours statute. But service workers in another

New York office building, owned by a New York real estate company, and housing tenants about a fourth of whom had manufacturing plants out of state, were not covered by the act (the decision was *10 East 40th St. Building* v. *Callus,* 325 U.S. 578 [1945]). However, in most instances the Court found a rationale for extending coverage under the statute.

Federal government regulation of agriculture, provided by the Agricultural Adjustment Act of 1938 and subsequent amendments, was sustained by the Court in *Mulford* v. *Smith,* 307 U.S. 38 (1939), and **Wickard** v. **Filburn.** Other cases also upheld government regulation of agriculture, including *United States* v. *Rock Royal Cooperative,* 307 U.S. 533 (1939), approving parity, price schedules, and marketing quotas.

What powers may the states exercise in the commerce sphere? This recurring question of constitutional law once again came before the Court. In general, after 1937, the Court was sympathetic to state economic regulation, but not when it interfered with federal regulation or burdened national commerce. In one of the relatively few decisions striking down state regulation as burdening commerce, *Southern Pacific Railroad* v. *Arizona,* 325 U.S. 761 (1945), the Court invalidated an Arizona law that limited the length of trains operating within the state to no more than 14 passenger cars or 70 freight cars. The Court also struck down anti–civil rights state laws on commerce clause grounds. In **Edwards** v. **California** (chap. 10), the Court declared unconstitutional, as impeding interstate commerce, a California law that made it a misdemeanor to transport a poor person into the state. The legislation was aimed at the poverty-stricken "Okies" (whose plight was dramatized by John Steinbeck in his great novel *The Grapes of Wrath*) who were flocking into the state during the Depression searching for nonexistent jobs. Another state statute struck down by the Court was Virginia's Jim Crow statute

that required racial segregation on all public motor carriers. Under the statute, it was a misdemeanor for a passenger to refuse to honor the driver's order to change seats. In *Morgan* v. *Virginia,* 328 U.S. 373 (1946), the Court struck down the Virginia statute as applied to interstate travel because it placed an impermissible burden on interstate commerce.

When examining the decisions of the Vinson and Warren Courts in which Congress' exercise of its powers was challenged, one is confronted by the reality that the Roosevelt Court's constitutional revolution so took hold that there was no instance when economic regulation was pronounced unconstitutional. Early in the Vinson Court, for example, the Court decided *Woods* v. *Miller,* 333 U.S. 138 (1948), which upheld national peacetime rent control legislation as a legitimate exercise of Congress' war powers. The unanimous Court reasoned that the war power does not necessarily end with the cessation of hostilities but rather permits Congress to deal with the domestic effects of the war during the postwar period. It should also be remembered that the **Youngstown Sheet & Tube Co.** v. **Sawyer** (chap. 7) decision, although it placed limits on the presidency, was essentially a pro-Congress and pro-congressional regulatory powers decision.

The Court was permissive, indeed expansive, in its interpretation of Congress' commerce powers even when they were clearly used for social purposes as in **Heart of Atlanta Motel** v. **United States** and **Katzenbach** v. **McClung,** which upheld the public accommodations provisions of the Civil Rights Act of 1964.

In recent years, during the Burger and Rehnquist Courts, the commerce clause has been at issue in cases in which the power of the states was also in question. The Burger Court demonstrated that it would not automatically defer to Congress' exercise of its commerce powers. In *Fry* v. *United States,* 421 U.S. 542 (1975), the Court held that wage increases for state employees *may* be regulated by Congress, but indicated in a footnote that in some circumstances the Tenth Amendment could limit federal regulation of the states. The next year, in **National League of Cities** v. **Usery** (chap. 10), the Court majority demonstrated that it took its footnote seriously and struck down an act of Congress applying federal minimum wage standards to certain state and local government employees because, said the Court, such regulation goes to the heart of state sovereignty. The *National League of Cities* ruling was the first time since the constitutional revolution of 1937 that a federal law enacted under Congress' commerce powers was struck down. Court observers wondered if the Court would now embark on a new line of constitutional rulings utilizing the Tenth Amendment and reining in Congress' commerce powers. However, in subsequent decisions, the Court pointedly narrowed *National League of Cities* by ruling, for example, in *Hodel* v. *Virginia Surface Mining and Reclamation Association,* 452 U.S. 264 (1981), and *Hodel* v. *Indiana,* 452 U.S. 314 (1981), that Congress validly used its commerce power in enacting the federal strip mining law that imposed stringent requirements on strip mine operators. In a 1983 decision, the Court further eroded the *National League of Cities* ruling by upholding the imposition of federal anti-age discrimination on the states vis-à-vis state employees in *Equal Employment Opportunity Commission* v. *Wyoming,* 460 U.S. 226. This was, said the majority, a valid exercise of Congress' commerce power that did not impinge upon the state's powers under the Tenth Amendment. Finally, in 1985, the Court by a 5–4 majority overturned *National League of Cities* in **Garcia** v. **San Antonio Metropolitan Transit Authority** (chap. 10). The commerce powers of Congress were restored to their pre–*National League of Cities* status but the close division on the Court hinted that some time in the future, when more states rights conservatives come to the Court, the Tenth

Amendment may again be revived at the expense of Congress' commerce powers. Interestingly, in another 1985 case, a criminal case that involved a federal conviction of unlawfully attempting to destroy by fire a building used in interstate commerce (a two-family home used as rental property), the Court unanimously upheld the conviction. In so doing it reaffirmed a broad definition of the commerce power (the case was *Russell* v. *United States,* 471 U.S. 858).

In 1979 the Court restricted the scope of Congress' commerce power in the labor relations area by ruling that the National Labor Relations Board (NLRB) did not have jurisdiction over teachers employed in parochial schools. That decision, *NLRB* v. *Catholic Bishop of Chicago,* 440 U.S. 490 (1979), technically a narrow construction of the National Labor Relations Act, suggested that NLRB involvement in labor-management disputes in which "management" was a religious institution would violate the separation of church and state demanded by the First Amendment. In 1980 the National Labor Relations Act was again given a narrow reading, this time denying NLRB jurisdiction over faculty efforts to bargain collectively with their private-university employer. The ruling, *NLRB* v. *Yeshiva University,* 444 U.S. 672, determined that the faculty exercised supervisory and managerial functions, thereby falling outside the scope of the labor relations law.

In commerce clause cases involving state legislation, however, the Court has reaffirmed the broad view of the federal commerce power. The Court, for example, in the 1978 case of *Raymond Motor Transport* v. *Rice,* 434 U.S. 429, struck down a Wisconsin regulation limiting the length of trucks using Wisconsin highways as an interference with national commerce. A similar Iowa law was struck down in *Kassel* v. *Consolidated Freightways Corp.,* 450 U.S. 662 (1981). In the 1977 case of *Douglas* v. *Seacoast Products, Inc.,* 431 U.S. 265, Virginia statutes prohibiting federally licensed vessels owned by nonresidents of Virginia from fishing in Chesapeake Bay and prohibiting ships owned by noncitizens from obtaining commercial fishing licenses to fish anywhere in Virginia were struck down as conflicting with federal law. The landmark case of *Gibbons* v. *Ogden* was heavily relied upon. In *Japan Line Ltd.* v. *County of Los Angeles,* 441 U.S. 434 (1979), the Court struck down a California property tax as applied to cargo containers owned by certain Japanese shipping companies as conflicting with Congress' power to regulate commerce with foreign nations. In 1980 the Court, in *Lewis* v. *BT Investment Managers,* 447 U.S. 27, struck down as a burden on interstate commerce a Florida statute that prohibited out-of-state banks and other non-Florida financial institutions from owning or controlling investment advisory service businesses within the state. The 1981 decision of *Maryland* v. *Louisiana,* 451 U.S. 725 (1981), in which the Court struck down on commerce clause grounds the Louisiana tax on natural gas for out-of-state customers, had widespread financial consequences for consumers. In 1982, in *New England Power Co.* v. *New Hampshire,* 455 U.S. 331, the Court struck down as a violation of the commerce clause a state order to the New England Power Company not to export hydroelectric power. Efforts by the state of Nebraska to prevent the transporting of groundwater into Colorado without a permit were rejected by the Court in *Sporhase* v. *Nebraska ex rel Douglas,* 458 U.S. 941 (1982) as an impermissible burden on interstate commerce. The state of Alaska's requirement that timber taken from state lands be processed within the state prior to export was found by the Court to have violated the commerce clause in *South-Central Timber Development, Inc.* v. *Wunnicke,* 467 U.S. 82 (1984). A state challenge on commerce clause grounds to federal public utility regulatory policies was rejected in *Federal Energy Regulatory Commission* v. *Mississippi,* 456 U.S. 742 (1982). State

or local taxes (or tax credits) were struck down as impinging on Congress' commerce powers in several cases including: *Xerox Corporation* v. *Harris County, Texas,* 459 U.S. 145 (1982); *Bacchus Imports, Ltd.* v. *Dias,* 468 U.S. 263 (1984); *Westinghouse* v. *Tully,* 466 U.S. 388 (1984); *Armco Inc.* v. *Hardesty,* 467 U.S. 638 (1984); and *Tyler Pipe Indus.* v. *Washington Dept. of Revenue,* 483 U.S. 232 (1987). In **New Energy Co. of Indiana** v. **Limbach** (chap. 10), the Rehnquist Court ruled that an Ohio statute that provided tax credits for ethanol producers from Ohio or from states with reciprocal tax credit exemptions for Ohio-produced ethanol discriminated against interstate commerce in violation of the commerce clause. However, in *D.H. Holmes Co. Ltd.* v. *McNamara,* 486 U.S. 24 (1988), the Court found that the imposition of a use tax on direct mail catalogues printed out of state did not violate the commerce clause. The Court reached a similar conclusion regarding a state tax on oil producers (*Ameranda Hess Corp.* v. *Director, Div. of Taxation,* 109 S. Ct. 1617 [1989]), and an excise tax on telecommunications (*Goldberg* v. *Sweet,* 109 S. Ct. 582 [1989]).

Recent decisions of the Court have shown that the validity of state regulation of business depends upon the Court's determination of the impact of such regulation on interstate commerce. For example, in *Brown-Forman Distillers* v. *New York,* 476 U.S. 573 (1986), the Court struck down as interfering with interstate commerce a New York law that prohibited distillers of hard liquor from charging higher prices to wholesalers in New York than they charged to out-of-state wholesalers. A similar Connecticut statute was invalidated in *Healy* v. *Beer Institute, Inc.,* 109 S. Ct. 2491 (1989), because the majority saw it as regulating liquor sales in other states. In contrast, in *White* v. *Mass. Council of Const. Employers,* 460 U.S. 204 (1983), the Court upheld as not violating the commerce clause an executive order of the mayor of Boston that required that all construction projects funded in whole or in part by city funds be performed by a work force of which at least half were bona fide residents of the city. Similarly, in *Wardair Canada, Inc.* v. *Florida Dept. of Revenue,* 477 U.S. 1 (1986), the Court upheld a Florida tax on aviation fuel sold within the state to all airlines, without regard to whether the fuel is used in instate or out-of-state air traffic. This was not inconsistent with Congress' commerce powers. The Rehnquist Court upheld a state law regulating corporate takeovers (*CTS Corp.* v. *Dynamics Corp. of America,* 481 U.S. 69 [1987]), and a state law regulating pipelines (*N. W. Cent. Pipeline* v. *State Corp. Commission of Kansas,* 109 S. Ct. 1262 [1989]). These laws did not violate the commerce clause.

When the actions of the states are challenged on commerce clause grounds, not only is the nature of the commerce power at issue but also the relationship of the national government to the states. That is why, as we shall see in Chapter 10, the issue of federalism is bound up in these cases. Chapter 10 will continue the discussion of commerce clause issues as they involve the actions of the states vis-à-vis the national government.

THE IMPACT OF THE COURT'S DECISIONS

Table 8.1 summarizes the impact of selected Court decisions concerning the powers of Congress under the commerce clause. The reprinted cases follow.

Table 8.1   THE IMPACT OF SELECTED COURT DECISIONS CONCERNING THE POWERS OF CONGRESS UNDER THE COMMERCE CLAUSE

Case	Year	Impact on Parties	Short-Run Impact	Long-Run Impact
Gibbons v. Ogden	1824	Gibbons back in business. New York monopoly struck down.	Decision ends devastating commercial warfare among states. Popular decision.	Congress' powers strengthened vis-à-vis states.
Cooley v. Board of Wardens	1852	Local harbor regulation upheld. Cooley paid fine.	Resolved legal conflict over commerce powers of state and federal governments, but in practical terms did not change status quo.	Court does not allow Congress full range of its commerce powers until after 1937.
Swift v. United States	1905	Beef trust, though technically dismantled, soon reorganized and retained monopolistic power.	Decision popular with progressives and farmers. Justice Department encouraged.	Stream of commerce doctrine provided precedent for upholding regulation.
Hammer v. Dagenhart	1918	Roland Dagenhart's young sons allowed to work at the cotton mill alongside their father. U.S. Attorney W. C. Hammer enjoined from enforcing Child Labor Act.	Child labor increased in the United States. Introduction of constitutional amendment to ban child labor. Congress tries to ban child labor through use of its taxing powers, but Court in *Bailey v. Drexel Furniture Co.* strikes down the new legislation.	Most states eventually adopted child labor standards similar to those of the 1916 act. Fair Labor Standards Act of 1938 incorporated these child labor provisions. Court upheld the 1938 Act in *United States v. Darby* (1941) and overturned *Hammer*.
Schechter Poultry Corp. v. United States	1935	Conviction reversed. Schechter brothers did not have to pay fine of $7425 and did not serve three-month jail sentences.	Decision permanently killed the National Industrial Recovery Act that Congress would otherwise have had to renew as the act was soon due to expire. Decision seen as anti–New Deal and contributed to constitutional crisis of 1936–1937.	Negative commerce clause doctrines had no long-run impact as Court in effect reversed itself in 1937 and beyond.

Carter v. Carter Coal Company	1936	Stockholder successful in preventing enforcement of the coal industry code as enacted by Congress in 1935.	Decision prevented the government from dealing with the coal industry crisis. Decision contributed to constitutional crisis of 1936–1937.	Narrow reading of commerce clause had no long-run impact in light of doctrinal reversal by Court in 1937 and after.
National Labor Relations Board v. Jones & Laughlin Steel Corp.	1937	NLRB's authority established.	Helped to undermine Roosevelt's Court-packing bill as Court no longer obstructed New Deal programs. Broad view of Congress' commerce powers encouraged further New Deal legislation based on commerce power.	Federal government control of American economy rests primarily on Congress' commerce powers.
Wickard v. Filburn	1942	Roscoe Filburn required to pay penalty of $117.11.	Federal government had complete control over agricultural production during World War II. Vast governmental economic powers exercised during the war.	One of series of decisions consolidating federal government control over the American economy.
United States v. Darby	1941	Darby Lumber Co. required to comply with Fair Labor Standards Act.	Congress' commerce powers broadly construed to permit wide-ranging labor legislation.	Major precedent for government regulation of labor.
Heart of Atlanta Motel v. United States; Katzenbach v. McClung	1964	Motel and restaurant under court order to obey Title 2 and accept black patronage.	Decision well received in most of nation. With Title 2 upheld, civil rights movement shifted attention from public accommodations to other civil rights concerns (voting, housing, employment).	Landmark decision upholding congressional power to deal with social problems through use of commerce power.

GIBBONS v. OGDEN,
9 WHEATON 1 (1824)

The state of New York granted a monopoly to Robert Livingston and Robert Fulton, the developers of the steamboat, whereby they were empowered to issue licenses to those who wished to operate steamboats in New York waters. Aaron Ogden bought a license and for a time was a partner with Thomas Gibbons in operating a steamboat between New York and New Jersey. The partners had a falling-out and Gibbons went into business for himself in competition with his former partner Ogden. Gibbons secured a federal coasting license issued under the provisions of a congressional statute enacted in 1793. However, only Ogden possessed the license authorized by the state of New York, and he argued that Gibbons could not legally operate a steamboat within the state. Ogden went to a New York court and obtained an injunction against Gibbons forbidding him to operate his steamboat on New York waters. When Gibbons defied the court order, his ship was seized. The case came to the Supreme Court and raised exceedingly important questions about the commerce clause of the Constitution (Article 1, Section 8, Clause 3) such as: What is the definition of commerce? What is the nature of Congress' commerce powers? What role if any can the states play in regulating commerce? The case had major implications for the economic health and development of the country, for the New York monopoly law had provoked retaliatory legislation by other states. If the Court were to construe narrowly Congress' commerce powers and uphold the steamboat monopoly, that would not only be a blow to the federal government in its struggle with the states' rights forces but it would also encourage the ominous trend toward destructive economic competition among the states and the resulting economic chaos.

Votes: Unanimous

MR. CHIEF JUSTICE MARSHALL delivered the opinion of the Court:. . . .

The words [of the Constitution] are, "congress shall have power to regulate commerce with foreign nations, and among the several states, and with the Indian tribes." The subject to be regulated is "commerce;" and our constitution being, as was aptly said at the bar, one of enumeration, and not of definition, to ascertain the extent of the power, it becomes necessary to settle the meaning of the word. The counsel for the appellee [Ogden] would limit it to traffic, to buying and selling, or the interchange of commodities, and do not admit that it comprehends navigation. This would restrict a general term, applicable to many objects, to one of its significations. Commerce, undoubtedly, is traffic, but it is something more—it is intercourse. It describes the commercial intercourse between nations, and parts of nations, in all its branches, and is regulated by prescribing rules for carrying on that intercourse. The mind can scarely conceive a system for regulating commerce between nations, which shall exclude all laws concerning navigation, which shall be silent on the admission of the vessels of the one nation into the ports of the other, and be confined to prescribing rules for the conduct of individuals, in the actual employment of buying and selling, or of barter. If commerce does not include navigation, the government of the Union has no direct power over that subject, and can make no law prescribing what shall constitute American vessels, or requiring that they shall be navigated by American seamen. Yet this power has been exercised from the commencement of the government, has been exercised with the consent of all, and has been understood by all to be a commercial regulation. All America understands, and has uniformly understood, the word "commerce," to comprehend navigation. It was so understood, and must have been so understood, when the constitution was framed. The power over commerce, including navigation, was one of the primary objects for which the people of America adopted their government, and must have been contemplated in forming it. The convention must have used the word in that sense, because all have understood it in that sense; and the attempt to restrict it comes too late. . . .

. . . The 9th section of the last article declares, that "no preference shall be given, by any regulation of commerce or revenue, to the ports of one state over those of another.". . . . [T]he subsequent part of the sentence is still more explicit. It is, "nor shall vessels bound to or from one state, be obliged to enter, clear or pay duties in another." These words have a direct reference to navigation. . . .

. . . To what commerce does this power extend? The constitution informs us, to commerce "with foreign nations, and among the several states, and with the Indian tribes." It has, we believe, been universally admitted, that these words comprehend every species of commercial intercourse between the United States and foreign nations. No sort of trade can be carried on between this country and any other, to which this power does not extend. It has been truly said, that commerce, as the word is used in the constitution, is a unit, every part of which is indicated by the term.

If this be the admitted meaning of the word, in

its application to foreign nations, it must carry the same meaning throughout the sentence, and remain a unit, unless there be some plain intelligible cause which alters it. The subject to which power is next applied, is to commerce, "among the several states." The word "among" means intermingled with. A thing which is among others, is intermingled with them. Commerce among the states, cannot stop at the external boundary line of each state, but may be introduced into the interior. It is not intended to say, that these words comprehend that commerce, which is completely internal, which is carried on between man and man in a state, or between different parts of the same state, and which does not extend to or affect other states. Such a power would be inconvenient, and is certainly unnecessary. Comprehensive as the word "among" is, it may very properly be restricted to that commerce which concerns more states than one. The phrase is not one which would probably have been selected to indicate the completely interior traffic of a state, because it is not an apt phrase for that purpose; and the enumeration of the particular classes of commerce to which the power was to be extended, would not have been made, had the intention been to extend the power to every description. The enumeration presupposes something not enumerated; and that something, if we regard the language or the subject of the sentence, must be the exclusively internal commerce of a state. The genius and character of the whole government seem to be, that its action is to be applied to all the external concerns of the nation, and to those internal concerns which affect the states generally; but not to those which are completely within a particular state, which do not affect other states, and with which it is not necessary to interfere, for the purpose of executing some of the general powers of the government. The completely internal commerce of a state, then, may be considered as reserved for the state itself. . . .

We are now arrived at the inquiry—what is this power? It is the power to regulate; that is, to prescribe the rule by which commerce is to be governed. This power, like all others vested in congress, is complete in itself, may be exercised to its utmost extent, and acknowledges no limitations, other than are prescribed in the constitution. . . .

But is has been urged, with great earnestness, that although the power of congress to regulate commerce with foreign nations, and among the several states, be co-extensive with the subject itself, and have no other limits than are prescribed in the constitution, yet the states may severally exercise the same power, within their respective jurisdictions. In support of this argument, it is said, that

they possessed it as an inseparable attribute of sovereignty, before the formation of the constitution, and still retain it, except so far as they have surrendered it by that instrument; that this principle results from the nature of the government, and is secured by the tenth amendment; that an affirmative grant of power is not exclusive, unless in its own nature it be such that the continued exercise of it by the former possessor is inconsistent with the grant and that this is not of that description. . . .

The grant of the power to lay and collect taxes is, like the power to regulate commerce, made in general terms, and has never been understood to interfere with the exercise of the same power by the states; and hence has been drawn an argument which has been applied to the question under consideration. But the two grants are not, it is conceived, similar in their terms or their nature. . . . In imposing taxes for state purposes, the states are not doing what congress is empowered to do. Congress is not empowered to tax for those purposes which are within the exclusive province of the states. When, then, each government exercises the power of taxation, neither is exercising the power of the other. But when a state proceeds to regulate commerce with foreign nations, or among the several states, it is exercising the very power that is granted to congress, and is doing the very thing which congress is authorized to do. There is no analogy, then, between the power of taxation and the power of regulating commerce.

In discussing the question, whether this power is still in the states, in the case under consideration, we may dismiss from it the inquiry, whether it is surrendered by the mere grant to congress, or is retained until congress shall exercise the power. We may dismiss that inquiry, because it has been exercised, and the regulations which congress deemed it proper to make, are now in full operation. The sole question is, can a state regulate commerce with foreign nations and among the states, while congress is regulating it? . . .

It has been contended by the counsel for the appellant, that, as the word "to regulate" implies in its nature, full power over the thing to be regulated, it excludes, necessarily, the action of all others that would perform the same operation on the same thing. That regulation is designed for the entire result, applying to those parts which remain as they were, as well as to those which are altered. It produces a uniform whole, which is as much disturbed and deranged by changing what the regulating power designs to leave untouched, as that on which it has operated. There is great force in this argument, and the court is not satisfied that it has been refuted.

Since, however, in exercising the power of regulating their own purely internal affairs, whether of trading or police, the states may sometimes enact laws, the validity of which depends on their interfering with, and being contrary to, an act of congress passed in pursuance of the constitution, the court will enter upon the inquiry, whether the laws of New York, as expounded by the highest tribunal of that state, have, in their application to this case, come into collision with an act of congress, and deprived a citizen of a right to which that act entitles him. Should this collision exist, it will be immaterial, whether those laws were passed in virtue of a concurrent power "to regulate commerce with foreign nations and among the several states," or, in virtue of a power to regulate their domestic trade and police. In one case and the other, the acts of New York must yield to the law of congress; and the decision sustaining the privilege they confer, against a right given by a law of the Union, must be erroneous. This opinion has been frequently expressed in this court, and is founded, as well on the nature of the government, as on the words of the constitution. In argument, however, it has been contended, that if a law passed by a state, in the exercise of its acknowledged sovereignty, comes into conflict with a law passed by congress in pursuance of the constitution, they affect the subject, and each other, like equal opposing powers. But the framers of our constitution foresaw this state of things, and provided for it, by declaring the supremacy not only of itself, but of the laws made in pursuance of it.

The nullity of any act, inconsistent with the constitution, is produced by the declaration, that the constitution is the supreme law. The appropriate application of that part of the clause which confers the same supremacy on laws and treaties, is to such acts of the state legislatures as do not transcend their powers, but though enacted in the execution of acknowledged state powers, interfere with, or are contrary to, the laws of congress, made in pursuance of the constitution, or some treaty made under the authority of the United States. In every such case, the act of congress, or the treaty, is supreme; and the law of the state, though enacted in the exercise of powers not controverted, must yield to it.

. . . .In the exercise of [the commerce] power, congress has passed "an act for enrolling or licensing ships or vessels to be employed in the coasting trade and fisheries, and for regulating the same." . . .

. . . To the court, it seems very clear, that the whole act on the subject of the coasting trade, ac-cording to those principles which govern the construction of statutes, implies, unequivocally, an authority to licensed vessels to carry on the coasting trade. . . .

. . . The act describes, with great minuteness, the various operations of a vessel engaged in it; and it cannot, we think, be doubted, that a voyage from New Jersey to New York, is one of those operations.

. . . .The laws of New York, which grant the exclusive privilege set up by the respondent, . . . relate only to the principle by which vessels are propelled . . . whether they are moved by steam or wind. If by the former, the waters of New York are closed against them. . . . If by the latter, those waters are free to them. . . . In conformity with the New York law, is the bill of the plaintiff Ogden in the state court. The bill . . . complains that the Bellona and the Stoudinger . . . are moved by steam. This is the injury of which he complains, and is the sole injury against the continuance of which he asks relief. . . . The answer avers only, that they were employed in the coasting trade, and insists on the right to carry on any trade authorized by the [federal] license. No testimony is taken, and the writ of injunction and decree restrain these licensed vessels . . . from being moved through the waters of New York by steam, for any purpose whatever. . . . The real and sole question seems to be, whether a steam-machine, in actual use, deprives a vessel of the privileges conferred by a [federal] license.

In considering this question, the first idea which presents itself is, that the laws of congress for the regulation of commerce, do not look to the principle by which vessels are moved. That subject is left entirely to individual discretion; and in that vast and complex system of legislative enactment concerning it, which embraces everything that the legislature thought it necessary to notice, there is not, we believe, one word respecting the peculiar principle by which vessels are propelled through the water, except what may be found in a single act, granting a particular privilege to steam-boats. With this exception, every act, either prescribing duties, or granting privileges, applies to every vessel, whether navigated by the instrumentality of wind or fire, of sails or machinery. The whole weight of proof, then, is thrown upon him who would introduce a distinction to which the words of the law give no countenance. . . .

But all inquiry into this subject seems to the court to be put completely at rest, by the act already mentioned, entitled, "an act for the enrolling and licensing of steam-boats." This act authorizes a steam-boat employed, or intended to be employed, only in a river or bay of the United States, owned wholly or in part by an alien, resident within the United States, to be enrolled and licensed as if the same belonged to a citizen of the United States. This act demonstrates the opinion of congress, that steam-boats may be enrolled and licensed, in common with vessels using sails. They are, of course, entitled to the same privileges, and can no more be restrained from navigating waters, and entering ports which are free to such vessels, than if they were wafted on their voyage by the winds, instead of being propelled by the agency of fire. The one element may be as legitimately used as the other, for every commercial purpose authorized by the laws of the Union; and the act of a state inhibiting the use of either, to any vessel having a license under the act of congress, comes, we think, in direct collision with that act. . . .

[*Reversed*]

MR. JUSTICE JOHNSON [concurring]:

The judgment entered by the court in this cause, has my entire approbation; but having adopted my conclusions on views of the subject materially different from those of my brethren, I feel it incumbent on me to exhibit those views. I also have another inducement: in questions of great importance and great delicacy, I feel my duty to the public best discharged, by an effort to maintain my opinions in my own way. . . .

The "power to regulate commerce" . . . meant to be granted, was that power to regulate commerce which previously existed in the states. But what was that power? The states were, unquestionably, supreme; and each possessed that power over commerce, which is acknowledged to reside in every sovereign state. The definition and limits of that power are to be sought among the features of international law. . . . The law of nations, regarding man as a social animal, pronounces all commerce legitimate, in a state of peace, until prohibited by positive law. The power of a sovereign state over commerce, therefore, amounts to nothing more than a power to limit and restrain it at pleasure. And since the power to prescribe the limits to its freedom, necessarily implies the power to determine what shall remain unrestrained, it follows, that the power must be exclusive; it can reside but in one potentate; and hence, the grant of this power carries with it the whole subject, leaving nothing for the state to act upon. . . .

Power to regulate foreign commerce, is given in the same words, and in the same breath, as it were,

with that over the commerce of the states and with the Indian tribes. But the power to regulate foreign commerce is necessarily exclusive. The states are unknown to foreign nations; their sovereignty exists only with relation to each other and the general government. Whatever regulations foreign commerce should be subjected to in the ports of the Union, the general government would be held responsible for them; and all other regulations, but those which congress had imposed, would be regarded by foreign nations as trespasses and violations of national faith and comity.

But the language which grants the power as to one description of commerce, grants it as to all; and, in fact, if ever the exercise of a right, or acquiescence in a construction, could be inferred from contemporaneous and continued assent, it is that of the exclusive effect of this grant. . . .

It is impossible . . . to concur in the view which this court takes of the effect of the coasting license in this case. . . . If there was any one object riding over every other in the adoption of the constitution, it was to keep the commercial intercourse among the states free from all invidious and partial restraints. And I cannot overcome the conviction, that if the licensing act was repealed tomorrow, the rights of the appellant to a reversal of the decision complained of, would be as strong as it is under this license. . . . The inferences to be correctly drawn . . . appear to me to be altogether in favor of the exclusive grant to congress of power over commerce, and the reverse of that which the appellee contends for.

[JUSTICE THOMPSON did not participate in the decision.]

COOLEY v. BOARD OF WARDENS, 12 HOWARD 299 (1852)

One of the first enactments of the first Congress in 1789 was legislation that had the effect of adopting all present and future state harbor and harbor pilot regulations until such time as Congress should enact further legislation. In 1803 the state of Pennsylvania enacted legislation that required that all ships entering and leaving the port of Philadelphia engage a local pilot. Ships that failed to hire a local pilot would be fined the equivalent of one-half the cost of pilotage. The fine would go into a fund for retired pilots and their dependents, which was administered by the Board of Wardens of the Port of Philadelphia. Aaron Cooley refused to hire a local pilot and to pay the fine. Action was subsequently brought before the Pennsylvania courts, where Cooley was ordered to pay. Cooley challenged the constitutionality of the Pennsylvania statute, arguing that the regulation of harbors involved commerce that only Congress could regulate. The case required the Supreme Court to confront this argument because if Cooley's position were correct, then not only would the Pennsylvania statute be unconstitutional but so would the 1789 act of Congress that delegated such regulatory authority to the states.

Majority votes: 6
Dissenting votes: 2

MR. JUSTICE CURTIS delivered the opinion of the Court:. . . .

[T]he objection [to the Pennsylvania statute of 1803 is] that it is repugnant to the third clause of the eighth section of the first article. "The congress shall have power to regulate commerce with foreign nations, and among the several States, and with the Indian tribes."

That the power to regulate commerce includes the regulation of navigation, we consider settled. And when we look to the nature of the service performed by pilots, to the relations which that service and its compensations bear to navigation between the several States, and between the ports of the United States and foreign countries, we are brought to the conclusion, that the regulation of the qualifications of pilots, of the modes and times of offering and rendering their services, of the responsibilities which shall rest upon them, of the powers they shall possess, of the compensation they may demand, and of the penalties by which their rights and duties may be enforced, do constitute regulations of navigation, and consequently of commerce, within the just meaning of this clause of the constitution.

The power to regulate navigation is the power to prescribe rules in conformity with which navigation must be carried on. It extends to the persons who conduct it, as well as to the instruments used. Accordingly, the first congress assembled under the constitution passed laws, requiring the masters of ships and vessels of the United States to be citizens of the United States, and established many rules for the government and regulation of officers and seamen. These have been from time to time added to and changed, and we are not aware that their validity has been questioned.

Now, a pilot, so far as respects the navigation of the vessel in that part of the voyage which is his pilotage-ground, is the temporary master charged with the safety of the vessel and cargo, and of the lives of those on board, and intrusted with the command of the crew. He is not only one of the persons engaged in navigation, but he occupies a most important and responsible place among those thus engaged. And if congress has power to regulate the seamen who assist the pilot in the management of the vessel, a power never denied, we can perceive no valid reason why the pilot should be beyond the reach of the same power. . . .

Nor should it be lost sight of, that this subject of the regulation of pilots and pilotage has an intimate connection with, and an important relation to, the general subject of commerce with foreign nations and among the several States, over which it was one main object of the constitution to create a national control. . . . [A] majority of the court are of opinion, that a regulation of pilots is a regulation of commerce, within the grant to congress of the commercial power, contained in the third clause of the eighth section of the first article of the constitution.

It becomes necessary, therefore, to consider whether this law of Pennsylvania, being a regulation of commerce, is valid.

The act of congress of the 7th of August, 1789, §4, is as follows:—

"That all pilots in the bays, inlets, rivers, harbors, and ports of the United States shall continue to be regulated in conformity with the existing laws of the States, respectively, wherein such pilots may be, or with such laws as the States may respectively hereafter enact for the purpose, until further legislative provision shall be made by congress." . . .

If the States were divested of the power to legislate on this subject by the grant of the commercial power to congress, it is plain this act could not confer upon them power thus to legislate. . . . We are brought directly and unavoidably to the consideration of the question, whether the grant of the commercial power to congress, did *per se* deprive the States of all power to regulate pilots. This question has never been decided by this court, nor, in our judgment, has any case depending upon all the considerations which must govern this one, come before this court. The grant of commercial power to congress does not contain any terms which expressly exclude the States from exercising an authority over its subject-matter. If they are excluded, it must be because the nature of the power, thus granted to congress, requires that a similar authority should not exist in the States. If it were conceded on the one side, that the nature of this power, like that to legislate for the District of Columbia, is absolutely and totally repugnant to the existence of similar power in the States, probably no one would deny that the grant of the power to congress, as effectually and perfectly excludes the States from all future legislation on the subject, as if express words had been used to exclude them. And on the other hand, if it were admitted that the existence of this power in congress, like the power of taxation, is compatible with the existence of a similar power in the States, then it would be in conformity with the contemporary exposition of the constitution, (Federalist, No. 32,) and with the judicial construction, given from time to time by this court, after the most deliberate consideration, to hold that the mere grant of such a power to congress, did not imply a prohibition on the States to exercise the same power; that it is not the mere existence of such a power, but its exercise by congress, which may be incompatible with the exercise of the same power by the States, and that the States may legislate in the absence of congressional regulations.

The diversities of opinion, therefore, which have existed on this subject, have arisen from the different views taken of the nature of this power. But when the nature of a power like this is spoken of, when it is said that the nature of the power requires that is should be exercised exclusively by congress, it must be intended to refer to the subjects of that power, and to say they are of such a nature as to require exclusive legislation by congress. Now, the power to regulate commerce, embraces a vast field, containing not only many, but exceedingly various subjects, quite unlike in their nature; some imperatively demanding a single uniform rule, operating equally on the commerce of the United States in every port; and some, like the subject now in question, as imperatively demanding that diversity, which alone can meet the local necessities of navigation.

Either absolutely to affirm, or deny that the nature of this power requires exclusive legislation by congress, is to lose sight of the nature of the subjects of this power, and to assert concerning all of them, what is really applicable but to a part. Whatever subjects of this power are in their nature national, or admit only of one uniform system, a plan of regulation, may justly be said to be of such a nature as to require exclusive legislation by congress. That this cannot be affirmed of laws for the regulation of pilots and pilotage, is plain. The act of 1789 contains a clear and authoritative declaration by the first congress, that the nature of this subject is such, that until congress should find it necessary to exert its power, it should be left to the legislation of the States; that it is local and not national; that it is likely to be the best provided for, not by one system, or plan of regulations, but by as many as the legislative discretion of the several States should deem applicable to the local peculiarities of the ports within their limits.

Viewed in this light, so much of this act of 1789, as declares that pilots shall continue to be regulated "by such laws as the States may respectively hereafter enact for that purpose," instead of being held to be inoperative, as an attempt to confer on the States a power to legislate, of which the constitution had deprived them, is allowed an appropriate and important signification. It manifests the understanding of congress, at the outset of the government, that the nature of this subject is not such as to require its exclusive legislation. The practice of the States, and of the national government, has been in conformity with this declaration, from the origin of the national government to this time; and the nature of the subject when examined, is such as to leave no doubt of the superior fitness and propriety, not to say the absolute necessity, of different systems of regulation, drawn from local knowledge and experience, and conformed to local wants. How, then, can we say, that by the mere grant of power to regulate commerce, the States are deprived of all the power to legislate on this subject, because from the nature of the power the legislation of congress must be exclusive. This would be to affirm, that the nature of the power is, in this case, something different from the nature of the subject to which, in such case, the power extends, and that the nature of the power necessarily demands, in all cases, exclusive legislation by congress, while the nature of one of the subjects of that power, not only does not require such exclusive legislation, but may be best provided for by many different systems enacted by the States, in conformity with the circumstances of the ports within their limits. In construing an instrument designed for the formation of a government, and in determining the extent of one of its important grants of power to legislate, we can make no such distinction between the nature of the power and the nature of the subject on which that power was intended practically to operate, nor consider the grant more extensive, by affirming of the power, what is not true of its subject now in question.

It is the opinion of a majority of the court that the mere grant to congress of the power to regulate commerce, did not deprive the States of power to regulate pilots, and that although congress has legislated on this subject, its legislation manifests an intention . . . not to regulate this subject, but to leave its regulation to the several States. To these precise questions, which are all we are called on to decide, this opinion must be understood to be confined. It does not extend to the question what other subjects, under the commercial power, are within the exclusive control of congress, or may be regulated by the States in the absence of all congressional legislation; nor to the general question, how far any regulation of a subject by congress, may be deemed to operate as an exclusion of all legislation by the States upon the same subject. We decide the precise questions before us, upon what we deem sound principles, applicable to this particular subject in the State in which the legislation of congress has left it. We go no further. . . .

We are of opinion that this state law was enacted by virtue of a power, residing in the State to legislate, that it is not in conflict with any law of congress; that it does not interfere with any system which congress has established by making regulations, or by intentionally leaving individuals to their own unrestricted action; that this law is therefore valid, and the judgment of the supreme court of Pennsylvania in each case must be affirmed.

[*Affirmed*]

MR. JUSTICES MCLEAN and WAYNE [dissented]: [omitted]
MR. JUSTICE DANIEL although concurring in the judgment of the court dissented from its reasoning: [omitted]
[MR. JUSTICE MCKINLEY did not participate.]

SWIFT v. UNITED STATES,
196 U.S. 375 (1905)

Although the Sherman Anti-Trust Act had been interpreted narrowly in the United States v. E. C. Knight *case, the Court in the* Swift *case made it clear that it could, if it wished, generously interpret the act. The case involved the meat trust that operated out of the stockyards of Chicago. The major dealers in fresh meat agreed not to bid against each other so that they could set the prices. They also pressured the railroads into charging them less than the established rates—to the detriment of the meat trust's competition. The Supreme Court agreed with the federal government that these were violations of the Sherman Act. In an opinion for a unanimous Court, Justice Holmes argued that the regulation of the meat trust fell within Congress' commerce power because the activities of the meat dealers, notably the purchase of cattle at the stockyards, were but part of a stream of commerce beginning at the cattle ranch and ending on the dinner plate. Justice Holmes made a distinction between a manufacturing monopoly (such as the sugar trust) with only an indirect effect on commerce and a sales monopoly (such as the meat trust) whose effect on commerce was direct.*

Votes: Unanimous

MR. JUSTICE HOLMES delivered the opinion of the Court:. . . .

. . . [T]he combination alleged embraces restraint and monopoly of trade within a single State, [and] its effect upon commerce among the States is not accidental, secondary, remote or merely probable. On the allegations of the bill [of charges against Swift and Co.] the latter commerce no less, perhaps even more, than commerce within a single State is an object of attack. Moreover, it is a direct object, it is that for the sake of which the several specific acts and courses of conduct are done and adopted. Therefore the case is not like *United States* v. *E. C. Knight Co.,* 156 U.S. 1, where the subject matter of the combination was manufacture and the direct object monopoly of manufacture within a State. However likely monopoly of commerce among the States in the article manufactured was to follow from the agreement it was not a necessary consequence nor a primary end. Here the subject matter is sales and the very point of the combination is to restrain and monopolize commerce among the States in respect of such sales. The two cases are near to each other, as sooner or later always must happen where lines are to be drawn, but the line between them is distinct. . . .

For the foregoing reasons we are of opinion that the carrying out of the scheme alleged, by the means set forth, properly may be enjoined. . . .

. . . [The case involves] a combination of independent dealers to restrict the competition of their agents when purchasing stock for them in the stock yards. The purchasers and their slaughtering establishments are largely in different States from those of the stock yards, and the sellers of the cattle, perhaps it is not too much to assume, largely in different States from either. The intent of the combination is not merely to restrict competition among the parties, but as we have said, by force of the general allegation at the end of the bill [of charges], to aid in an attempt to monopolize commerce among the States.

It is said that this charge is too vague and that it does not set forth a case of commerce among the States. Taking up the latter objection first, commerce among the States is not a technical legal conception, but a practical one, drawn from the course of business, When cattle are sent for sale from a place in one State, with the expectation that they will end their transit, after purchase, in another, and when in effect they do so, with only the interruption necessary to find a purchaser at the stock yards, and when this is a typical, constantly recurring course, the current thus existing is a current of commerce among the States, and the purchase of the cattle is a part and incident of such commerce. . . . The injunction against taking part in a combination, the effect of which will be a restraint of trade among the States by directing the defendants' agents to refrain from bidding against one another at the sales of live stock, is justified so far as the subject matter is concerned.

The injunction, however, refers not to trade among the States in cattle, concerning which there can be no question of original packages, but to trade in fresh meats, as the trade forbidden to be restrained, and it is objected that the trade in fresh meats described in the second and third sections of the bill is not commerce among the States, because the meat is sold at the slaughtering places, or when sold elsewhere may be sold in less than the original packages. But the allegations of the second section, even if they import a technical passing of title at the slaughtering places, also import that the sales are to persons in other States, and that the shipments to other States are part of the transaction—"pursuant to such sales"—and the third section imports that the same things which are sent to agents are sold by them, and sufficiently indicates that some at least of the sales are of the original packages. Moreover, the sales are by persons in one State to persons in another. . . .

We are of opinion, further, that the charge in the sixth section is not too vague. The charge is not of a single agreement but of a course of conduct intended to be continued. Under the act it is the duty of the court, when applied to, to stop the conduct. The thing done and intended to be done is perfectly definite: with the purpose mentioned, directing the defendants' agents and inducing each other to refrain from competition in bids. The defendants cannot be ordered to compete, but they properly can be forbidden to give directions or to make agreements not to compete. . . .

Decree modified and affirmed.

HAMMER v. DAGENHART, 247 U.S. 251 (1918)

Child labor was long one of the major industrial evils in the United States. Children worked long hours for low pay, often under dangerous working conditions. Their exploitation had obvious adverse effects on their health and overall welfare. Finally, in 1916, enough momentum was gained in Congress to lead to the enactment of the Keating-Owen Federal Child Labor Act. Utilizing its commerce powers, Congress forbade the shipment in interstate commerce of the products of factories, mines,

or quarries that employed children under the age of 14 or where children between the ages of 14 and 16 worked more than eight hours a day, six days a week, or worked at night. An employer would have to obey the standards set by the act or forego the interstate market. Hammer v. Dagenhart arose when Roland Dagenhart, who worked in a Charlotte, North Carolina, cotton mill with his two sons Reuben, 14, and John, 12, sought and obtained an injunction against enforcement of the act. The government unsuccessfully appealed. The Supreme Court had ample precedents to support this type of police power regulation of the actual transportation of goods. However, the Court not only frustrated this use of Congress' commerce power but also in the process weakened it.

Majority votes: 5
Dissenting votes: 4

Mr. Justice Day delivered the opinion of the Court:. . . .

The power essential to the passage of this act, the government contends, is found in the commerce clause of the Constitution which authorizes Congress to regulate commerce with foreign nations and among the states. . . . [I]t is insisted that adjudged cases in this court established the doctrine that the power to regulate given to Congress incidentally includes the authority to prohibit the movement of ordinary commodities and therefore that the subject is not open for discussion. The cases demonstrate the contrary. They rest upon the character of the particular subjects dealt with and the fact that the scope of governmental authority, state or national, possessed over them is such that the authority to prohibit is as to them but the exertion of the power to regulate.

The first of these cases is *Champion* v. *Ames,* 188 U.S. 321, the so-called Lottery Case, in which it was held that Congress might pass a law having the effect to keep the channels of commerce free from use in the transportation of tickets used in the promotion of lottery schemes. In *Hipolite Egg Co.* v. *United States,* 220 U.S. 45, this court sustained the power of Congress to pass the Pure Food and Drug Act, which prohibited the introduction into the states by means of interstate commerce of impure foods and drugs. In *Hoke* v. *United States,* 227 U.S. 308, this court sustained the constitutionality of the so-called "White Slave Traffic Act," whereby the transportation of a woman in interstate commerce for the purpose of prostitution was forbidden. . . .

In each of these instances the use of interstate

transportation was necessary to the accomplishment of harmful results. In other words, although the power over interstate transportation was to regulate, that could only be accomplished by prohibiting the use of the facilities of interstate commerce to effect the evil intended.

This element is wanting in the present case. The thing intended to be accomplished by this statute is the denial of the facilities of interstate commerce to those manufacturers in the states who employ children within the prohibited ages. The act in its effect does not regulate transportation among the states, but aims to standardize the ages at which children may be employed in mining and manufacturing within the states. The goods shipped are of themselves harmless. The act permits them to be freely shipped after thirty days from the time of their removal from the factory. When offered for shipment, and before transportation begins, the labor of their production is over, and the mere fact that they were intended for interstate commerce transportation does not make their production subject to federal control under the commerce power. . . .

Over interstate transportation, or its incidents, the regulatory power of Congress is ample, but the production of articles, intended for interstate commerce, is a matter of local regulation. . . . If it were otherwise, all manufacture intended for interstate shipment would be brought under federal control to the practical exclusion of the authority of the states, a result certainly not contemplated by the framers of the Constitution when they vested in Congress the authority to regulate commerce among the States.

It is further contended that the authority of Congress may be exerted to control interstate commerce in the shipment of childmade goods because of the effect of the circulation of such goods in other states where the evil of this class of labor has been recognized by local legislation, and the right to thus employ child labor has been more rigorously restrained than in the state of production. In other words, that the unfair competition, thus engendered, may be controlled by closing the channels of interstate commerce to manufacturers in those states where the local laws do not meet what Congress deems to be the more just standard of other states.

There is no power vested in Congress to require the states to exercise their police power so as to prevent possible unfair competition. . . . The grant of power to Congress over the subject of interstate commerce was to enable it to regulate such commerce, and not to give it authority to control the states in their exercise of the police power over local trade and manufacture.

The grant of authority over a purely federal matter was not intended to destroy the local power always existing and carefully reserved to the states in the Tenth Amendment to the Constitution. . . .

That there should be limitations upon the right to employ children in mines and factories in the interest of their own and the public welfare, all will admit. That such employment is generally deemed to require regulation is shown by the fact that the brief of counsel states that every state in the Union has a law upon the subject, limiting the right to thus employ children. In North Carolina, the state wherein is located the factory in which the employment was had in the present case, no child under twelve years of age is permitted to work.

It may be desirable that such laws be uniform, but our federal government is one of enumerated powers. . . . The maintenance of the authority of the states over matters purely local is as essential to the preservation of our institutions as is the conservation of the supremacy of the federal power in all matters entrusted to the nation by the federal Constitution. . . .

In our view the necessary effect of this act is, by means of a prohibition against the movement in interstate commerce of ordinary commercial commodities to regulate the hours of labor of children in factories and mines within the states, a purely state authority. Thus the act in a two-fold sense is repugnant to the Constitution. It not only transcends the authority delegated to Congress over commerce but also exerts a power as to a purely local matter to which the federal authority does not extend. The far-reaching result of upholding the act cannot be more plainly indicated than by pointing out that if Congress can thus regulate matters entrusted to local authority by prohibition of the movement of commodities in interstate commerce, all freedom of commerce will be at an end, and the power of the states over local matters may be eliminated, and thus our system of government be practically destroyed.

For these reasons we hold that this law exceeds the constitutional authority of Congress. It follows that the decree of the District Court must be

Affirmed.

MR. JUSTICE HOLMES [with whom MR. JUSTICE McKENNA, MR. JUSTICE BRANDEIS, and MR. JUSTICE CLARKE join], dissenting: . . . .

The first step in my argument is to make plain what no one is likely to dispute—that the statute in question is within the power expressly given to Congress if considered only as to its immediate effects and that if invalid it is so only upon some collateral ground. The statute confines itself to prohibiting the carriage of certain goods in interstate or foreign commerce. Congress is given power to regulate such commerce in unqualified terms. It would not be argued today that the power to regulate does not include the power to prohibit. Regulation means the prohibition of something, and when interstate commerce is the matter to be regulated I cannot doubt that the regulation may prohibit any part of such commerce that Congress sees fit to forbid. At all events it is established by the Lottery Case and others that have followed it that a law is not beyond the regulative power of Congress merely because it prohibits certain transportation out and out. . . .

The question then is narrowed to whether the exercise of its otherwise constitutional power by Congress can be pronounced unconstitutional because of its possible reaction upon the conduct of the States in a matter upon which I have admitted that they are free from direct control. I should have thought that that matter had been disposed of so fully as to leave no room for doubt. I should have thought that the most conspicuous decisions of this Court had made it clear that the power to regulate commerce and other constitutional powers could not be cut down or qualified by the fact that it might interfere with the carrying out of the domestic policy of any State. . . .

The notion that prohibition is any less prohibition when applied to things now thought evil I do not understand. But if there is any matter upon which civilized countries have agreed—far more unanimously than they have with regard to intoxicants and some other matters over which this country is now emotionally aroused—it is the evil of premature and excessive child labor. I should have thought that if we were to introduce our own moral conceptions where in my opinion they do not belong, this was preeminently a case for upholding the exercise of all its powers by the United States.

But I had thought that the propriety of the exercise of a power admitted to exist in some cases was for the consideration of Congress alone and that this Court always had disavowed the right to intrude its judgment upon questions of policy or morals. It is not for this Court to pronounce when prohibition is necessary to regulation if it ever may be necessary—to say that it is permissible as against strong drink but not as against the product of ruined lives.

The Act does not meddle with anything belonging to the States. They may regulate their internal affairs and their domestic commerce as they like. But when they seek to send their products across the State line they are no longer within their rights. If there were no Constitution and no Congress, their power to cross the line would depend upon their neighbors. Under the Constitution such commerce belongs not to the States but to Congress to regulate. It may carry out its views of public policy whatever indirect effect they may have upon the activities of the States. Instead of being encountered by a prohibitive tariff at her boundaries the State encounters the public policy of the United States which it is for Congress to express. The public policy of the United States is shaped with a view to the benefit of the nation as a whole. If, as has been the case within the memory of men still living, a State should take a different view of the propriety of sustaining a lottery from that which generally prevails, I cannot believe that the fact would require a different decision from that reached in *Champion* v. *Ames*. Yet in that case it would be said with quite as much force as in this that Congress was attempting to intermeddle with the State's domestic affairs. The national welfare as understood by congress may require a different attitude within its sphere from that of some self-seeking State. It seems to me entirely constitutional for Congress to enforce its understanding by all the means at its command. . . .

SCHECHTER POULTRY CORP. v. UNITED STATES, 295 U.S. 495 (1935)

One of the early measures of President Franklin Roosevelt's New Deal Administration was the National Industrial Recovery Act of 1933. The act was designed to deal with the problem of how to help American businesses recover from the greatest financial Depression this country had ever experienced. The measure, based on the exercise of Congress' commerce powers, created the National Recovery Administration (NRA), which was authorized to establish codes of fair competition for the nation's industries. These codes were to fix minimum wages and maximum hours, eliminate child labor, and regulate, even prohibit, competitive practices that were unfair or destructive. The codes were to be drawn up by representatives of each industry in consultation with the NRA. The President had the responsibility for giving final approval, and the law required that each code contain certain basic provisions for the protection of workers and safeguards against monopolistic actions. If an industry could not formulate a code for itself, the statute stipulated that the President could impose one. Once approved, these codes had the force of law, and they were mandatory on all businesses covered. Violations of the codes were punishable by civil process and criminal prosecution. By 1935 more than 700 industries had codes of fair competition. The Schechter Poultry Corporation case concerned one such code, the Live Poultry Code. The federal government charged the corporation, a wholesale poultry business, with violating the minimum wage, maximum hour, and trade practices provisions of the code. The corporation countered by arguing that the legislation exceeded Congress' commerce powers, thus being an unconstitutional invasion of the domain reserved to the states by the Tenth Amendment. The lower federal courts upheld only part of the conviction, and both the corporation and the government appealed. The Supreme Court was at the crossroads. It had positive commerce clause precedents that could have been used to justify such sweeping government regulation; it also had negative precedents available with which to strike down the act. The Court chose to go the negative route, partly because the statute was an unprecedented delegation of legislative authority to the executive branch of the government. Nevertheless, the decision signaled the head-on confrontation that was brewing between the Supreme Court and the New Deal President and Congress.

Votes: Unanimous

MR. CHIEF JUSTICE HUGHES delivered the opinion of the Court:. . . .

[Chief Justice Hughes analyzes the provisions of the National Industrial Recovery Act and concludes:]

Section 3 of the Recovery Act is without precedent. It supplies no standards for any trade, industry, or activity. It does not undertake to prescribe rules of conduct to be applied to particular states of fact determined by appropriate administrative procedure. Instead of prescribing rules of conduct, it authorizes the making of codes to prescribe them. For that legislative undertaking, section 3 sets up no standards, aside from the statement of the general aims of . . . [the legislation] described in section 1. In view of the scope of that broad declaration and of the nature of the few restrictions that are imposed, the discretion of the President in approving or prescribing codes, and thus enacting laws for the government of trade and industry throughout the country, is virtually unfettered. We think that the code-making authority thus conferred is an unconstitutional delegation of legislative power. . . .

[THE APPLICATION OF THE CODE TO INTERSTATE TRANSACTIONS]

Although the validity of the codes (apart from the question of delegation) rests upon the commerce clause of the Constitution, Section 3(a) of the act is not in terms limited to interstate and foreign commerce. From the generality of its terms, and from the argument of the government at the bar, it would appear that section 3(a) was designed to authorize codes without that limitation. But under section 3(f) of the act penalties are confined to violations of a code provision "in any transaction in or affecting interstate or foreign commerce." This aspect of the case presents the question whether the particular provisions of the Live Poultry Code, which the defendants were convicted for violating and for having conspired to violate, were within the regulating power of Congress.

These provisions relate to the hours and wages of those employed by defendants in their slaughterhouses in Brooklyn and to the sales there made to retail dealers and butchers.

Were these transactions "in" interstate commerce? Much is made of the fact that almost all the poultry coming to New York is sent there from other states. But the code provisions, as here applied, do not concern the transportation of the poultry from other states to New York, or the transactions of the commission men or others to whom it is consigned, or the sales made by such consignees to defendants. When defendants had made their purchases, whether at the West Washington Market in New York City or at the railroad terminals serving the city, or elsewhere, the poultry was trucked to their slaughterhouses in Brooklyn for local disposition. The interstate transactions in relation to that poultry then ended. Defendants held the poultry at their slaughterhouse markets for slaughter and local sale to retail dealers and butchers who in turn sold directly to consumers. Neither the slaughtering nor the sales by defendants were transactions in interstate commerce. . . .

The undisputed facts thus afford no warrant for the argument that the poultry handled by defendants at their slaughterhouse markets was in a "current" or "flow" of interstate commerce, and was thus subject to congressional regulation. The mere fact that there may be a constant flow of commodities into a state does not mean that the flow continues after the property has arrived and has become commingled with the mass of property within the state and is there held solely for local disposition and use. So far as the poultry here in question is concerned, the flow in interstate commerce had ceased. The poultry had come to a permanent rest within the state. It was not held, used, or sold by defendants in relation to any further transactions in interstate commerce and was not destined for transportation to other states. Hence decisions which deal with a stream of interstate commerce—where goods come to rest within a state temporarily and are later to go forward in interstate commerce—and with the regulations of transactions involved in that practical continuity of movement, are not applicable here. . . .

Did the defendants' transactions directly "affect" interstate commerce so as to be subject to federal regulation? The power of Congress extends, not only to the regulation of transactions which are part of interstate commerce, but to the protection of that commerce from injury. It matters not that the injury may be due to the conduct of those engaged in intrastate operations. Thus, Congress may protect the safety of those employed in interstate transportation, "no matter what may be the source of the dangers which threaten it." . . . We have held that, in dealing with common carriers engaged in both interstate and intrastate commerce, the dominant authority of Congress necessarily embraces the right to control their intrastate operations in all matters having such a close and substantial relation to interstate traffic that the control is essential or appropriate to secure the freedom of that traffic from interference or unjust discrimination and to promote the efficiency of the interstate service. . . .

The instant case is not of that sort. This is not a prosecution for a conspiracy to restrain or monopolize interstate commerce in violation of the Anti-Trust Act. Defendants have been convicted, not upon direct charges of injury to interstate commerce or of interference with persons engaged in that commerce, but of violations of certain provisions of the Live Poultry Code and of conspiracy to commit these violations. Interstate commerce is brought in only upon the charge that violations of these provisions—as to hours and wages of employees and local sales—"affected" interstate commerce.

In determining how far the federal government may go in controlling intrastate transactions upon the ground that they "affect" interstate commerce, there is a necessary and well-established distinction between direct and indirect effects. The precise line can be drawn only as individual cases arise, but the distinction is clear in principle. . . . [W]here the effect of intrastate transactions upon interstate commerce is merely indirect, such transactions remain within the domain of state power. If the commerce clause were construed to reach all enterprises and transactions which could be said to have an indirect effect upon interstate commerce, the federal authority would embrace practically all the activities of the people, and the authority of the state over its domestic concerns would exist only by sufferance of the federal government. Indeed, on such a theory, even the development of the state's commercial facilities would be subject to federal control. . . .

. . . [T]he distinction between direct and indirect effects of intrastate transactions upon interstate commerce must be recognized as a fundamental one, essential to the maintenance of our constitutional system. Otherwise, as we have said, there would be virtually no limit to the federal power, and for all practical purposes we should have a completely centralized government. We must consider the provisions here in question in the light of this distinction. . . .

We are of the opinion that the attempt through the provisions of the code to fix the hours and wages of employees of defendants in their intrastate business was not a valid exercise of federal power.

The other violations for which defendants were convicted related to the making of local sales. Ten counts, for violation of the provision as to "straight killing," were for permitting customers to make "selections of individual chickens taken from particular coops and half coops." Whether or not this practice is good or bad for the local trade, its effect, if any, upon interstate commerce was only indirect. The same may be said of violations of the code by intrastate transactions consisting of the sale "of an unfit chicken" and of sales which were not in accord with the ordinances of the city of New York. The requirement of reports as to prices and volumes of defendants' sales was incident to the effort to control their intrastate business. . . .

On both the grounds we have discussed, the attempted delegation of legislative power and the attempted regulation of intrastate transactions which affect interstate commerce only indirectly, we hold the code provisions here in question to be invalid and that the judgment of conviction must be reversed.

MR. JUSTICE CARDOZO (concurring):

The delegated power of legislation which has found expression in this code is not canalized within banks that keep it from overflowing. It is unconfined and vagrant. . . .

. . . [T]here is [a] conception of codes of fair competition, their significance and function, . . . that is struggling now for recognition and acceptance. By this . . . conception a code is not to be restricted to the elimination of business practices that would be characterized by general acceptance as oppressive or unfair. It is to include whatever ordinances may be desirable or helpful for the well-being or prosperity of the industry affected. In that view, the function of its adoption is not merely negative, but positive; the planning of improvements as well as the extirpation of abuses. What is fair, as thus conceived, is not something to be contrasted with what is unfair or fraudulent or tricky. The extension becomes as wide as the field of industrial regulation. If that conception shall prevail, anything that Congress may do within the limits of the commerce clause for the betterment of business may be done by the President upon the recommendation of a trade association by calling it a code. This is delegation running riot. No such plenitude of power is susceptible of transfer. The statute, however, aims at nothing less, as one can learn both from its terms and from the administrative practice under it. Nothing less is aimed at by the code now submitted to our scrutiny. . . .

But there is another objection, far-reaching and incurable, aside from any defect of unlawful delegation. . . .

I find no authority in that grant for the regulation of wages and hours of labor in the intrastate transactions that make up the defendant's business. As to this feature of the case, little can be added to the opinion of the court. There is a view of causation that would obliterate the distinction between what is national and what is local in the activities of commerce. Motion at the outer rim is communicated perceptibly, though minutely, to recording instruments at the center. . . . The law is not indifferent to considerations of degree. Activities local in their immediacy do not become interstate and national because of distant repercussions. What is near and what is distant may at times be uncertain. There is no penumbra of uncertainty obscuring judgment here. To find immediacy or directness here is to find it almost everywhere. If centripetal forces are to be isolated to the exclusion of the forces that oppose and counteract them, there will be an end to our federal system. . . .

I am authorized to state that MR. JUSTICE STONE joins in this opinion.

CARTER v. CARTER COAL COMPANY, 298 U.S. 238 (1936)

When the Supreme Court struck down the National Industrial Recovery Act in the Schechter case, it was true that the legislation had about run its course as a temporary emergency measure. Congress took very seriously the Court's criticism that the legislation had delegated too much power to the executive branch. The new approach of the Congress, working with the Roosevelt Administration, was to deal with particularly troubled industries separately. The coal industry was clearly in that category and Congress responded by enacting the Bituminous Coal Conservation Act of 1935 (also known as the Guffey Coal Act after Senator Guffey, the principal sponsor of the legislation). The act provided a code of fair practices and competition for the coal industry and stipulated minimum coal prices, minimum wages and maximum hours, a ban on child labor, and other regulation of certain practices. However, compliance with the code by coal producers was to be voluntary. The local coal producers, of course, were given an inducement to accept the code—a refund of 90 percent of the 15 percent tax imposed by the statute on sales at the mines. The case itself was a stockholder's suit whereby Carter sued his own company to prevent it from paying what Carter asserted was an unconstitutional tax. He argued that Congress exceeded its power by regulating the coal industry.

Majority votes: 5
Dissenting votes: 4

MR. JUSTICE SUTHERLAND delivered the opinion of the Court:. . . .

Since the validity of the act depends upon whether it is a regulation of interstate commerce, the nature and extent of the power conferred upon Congress by the commerce clause becomes the determinative question in this branch of the case. . . .

That commodities produced or manufactured within a state are intended to be sold or transported outside the state does not render their production or manufacture subject to federal regulation under the commerce clause. . . .

. . . [T]he word "commerce" is the equivalent of the phrase "intercourse for the purpose of trade." Plainly, the incidents leading up to and culminating in the mining of coal do not constitute such intercourse. The employment of men, the fixing of their wages, hours of labor and working conditions, the bargaining in respect of these things—whether carried on separately or collectively—each and all constitute intercourse for the purpose of production, not of trade. The latter is a thing apart from the relation of employer and employee, which in all producing occupations is purely local in character. Extraction of coal from the mine is the aim and the completed result of local activities. Commerce in the coal mined is not brought into being by force of these activities, but by negotiations, agreements, and circumstances entirely apart from production. Mining brings the subject matter of commerce into existence. Commerce disposes of it.

A consideration of the foregoing, and of many cases . . . renders inescapable the conclusion that the effect of the labor provisions of the act, including those in respect of minimum wages, wage agreements, collective bargaining, and the Labor Board and its powers, primarily falls upon production and not upon commerce; and confirms the further resulting conclusion that production is a purely local activity. It follows that none of these essential antecedents of production constitutes a transaction in or forms any part of interstate commerce. . . . Everything which moves in interstate commerce has had a local origin. Without local production somewhere, interstate commerce, as now carried on, would practically disappear. Nevertheless, the local character of mining, of manufacturing and of crop growing is a fact, and remains a fact, whatever may be done with the products. . . .

Swift & Co. v. *United States,* 196 U.S. 375 rest[s] upon the circumstance that the acts in question constituted direct interferences with the "flow" of commerce among the states. In the *Swift* case, livestock was consigned and delivered to stockyards—not as a place of final destination. . . . It was nowhere suggested . . . that the interstate commerce power extended to the growth or production of the things which, after production, entered the flow. If the court had held that the raising of the cattle, which were involved in the *Swift* case, including the wages paid to and working conditions of the herders and others employed in the business, could be regulated by Congress, that decision and decisions holding similarly would be in point; for it is that situation, and not the one with which the court actually dealt, which here concerns us. . . .

The restricted field covered by the *Swift* and kindred cases is illustrated by the *Schechter* case. . . . There the commodity in question, although shipped from another state, had come to rest in the state of its destination, and, as the Court pointed out, was no longer in a current or flow of interstate commerce. The *Swift* doctrine was rejected as inapposite. In the *Schechter* case the flow had ceased. Here it had not begun. The difference is not one of substance. The applicable principle is the same. . . .

Whether the effect of a given activity or condition is direct or indirect is not always easy to determine. The word "direct" implies that the activity or condition invoked or blamed shall operate proxi-

mately—not mediately, remotely, or collaterally—to produce the effect. It connotes the absence of an efficient intervening agency or condition. And the extent of the effect bears no logical relation to its character. The distinction between a direct and an indirect effect turns, not upon the magnitude of either the cause or the effect, but entirely upon the manner in which the effect has been brought about. If the production by one man of a single ton of coal intended for interstate sale and shipment, and actually so sold and shipped, affects interstate commerce indirectly, the effect does not become direct by multiplying the tonnage, or increasing the number of men employed, or adding to the expense or complexities of the business, or by all combined. It is quite true that rules of law are sometimes qualified by considerations of degree, as the government argues. But the matter of degree has no bearing upon the question here, since that question is not—What is the *extent* of the local activity or condition, or the *extent* of the effect produced upon interstate commerce? but—What is the *relation* between the activity or condition and the effect?

Much stress is put upon the evils which come from the struggle between employers and employees over the matter of wages, working conditions, the right of collective bargaining, etc., and the resulting strikes, curtailment and irregularity of production and effect on prices; and it is insisted that interstate commerce is greatly affected thereby. But, in addition to what has just been said, the conclusive answer is that the evils are all local evils over which the federal government has no legislative control. The relation of employer and employee is a local relation. At common law, it is one of the domestic relations. The wages are paid for the doing of local work. Working conditions are obviously local conditions. The employees are not engaged in or about commerce, but exclusively in producing a commodity. And the controversies and evils, which it is the object of the act to regulate and minimize, are local controversies and evils affecting local work undertaken to accomplish that local result. Such effect as they may have upon commerce, however extensive it may be, is secondary and indirect. An increase in the greatness of the effect adds to its importance. It does not alter its character. . . .

. . . [T]he primary contemplation of the [Bituminous Coal Conservation] Act is stabilization of the industry through the regulation of labor and the regulation of prices; for, since both were adopted, we must conclude that both were thought essential. The regulations of labor on the one hand and prices on the other furnish mutual aid and support; and their associated force—not one or the other but both combined—was deemed by Congress to be necessary to achieve the end sought. The statutory mandate for a code upheld by two legs at once suggests the improbability that Congress would have assented to a code supported by only one. . . . The conclusion is unavoidable that the price-fixing provisions of the code are so related to and dependent upon the labor provisions . . . as to make it clearly probably that the latter being held bad, the former would not have been passed. The fall of the latter, therefore, carries down with it the former. . . .

It is so ordered.

Separate opinion of MR. CHIEF JUSTICE HUGHES dissenting in part:

I agree that the stockholders were entitled to bring their suits; that, in view of the question whether any part of the Act could be sustained, the suits were not premature; that the so-called tax is not a real tax, but a penalty; that the constitutional power of the Federal Government to impose this penalty must rest upon the commerce clause, as the Government concedes; that production—in this case mining—which precedes commerce, is not itself commerce; and that the power to regulate commerce among the several States is not a power to regulate industry within the State. . . .

But that is not the whole case. The Act also provides for the regulation of the prices of bituminous coal sold in interstate commerce and prohibits unfair methods of competition in interstate commerce. Undoubtedly transactions in carrying on interstate commerce are subject to the federal power to regulate that commerce and the control of charges and the protection of fair competition in that commerce are familiar illustrations of the exercise of the power, as the Interstate Commerce Act, the Packers and Stockyards Act, and the Anti-Trust Acts abundantly show. The Court has repeatedly stated that the power to regulate interstate commerce among the several States is supreme and plenary. . . .

In this view, the Act, and the Code for which it provides, may be sustained in relation to the provisions for marketing in interstate commerce, and the decisions of the courts below, so far as they accomplish that result, should be affirmed.

MR. JUSTICE CARDOZO dissenting:. . . .

I am satisfied that the Act is within the power of the central government in so far as it provides for minimum and maximum prices upon sales of bituminous coal in the transactions of interstate commerce and in those of intrastate commerce where

interstate commerce is directly or intimately affected. . . . As a system of price fixing the Act is challenged upon three grounds: (1) because the governance of prices is not within the commerce clause; (2) because it is a denial of due process forbidden by the Fifth Amendment; and (3) because the standards for administrative action are indefinite, with the result that there has been an unlawful delegation of legislative power.

(1) With reference to the first objection, the obvious and sufficient answer is, so far as the Act is directed to interstate transactions, that sales made in such conditions constitute interstate commerce, and do not merely "affect" it. . . . Prices in interstate transactions may not be regulated by the states. They must therefore be subject to the power of the nation unless they are to be withdrawn altogether from governmental supervision. If such a vacuum were permitted, many a public evil incidental to interstate transactions would be left without a remedy. This does not mean, of course, that prices may be fixed for arbitrary reasons or in an arbitrary way. The commerce power of the nation is subject to the requirement of due process like the police power of the states. . . .

Regulation of prices being an exercise of the commerce power in respect of interstate transactions, the question remains whether it comes within that power as applied to intrastate sales where interstate prices are directly or intimately affected. Mining and agriculture and manufacture are not interstate commerce considered by themselves, yet their relation to that commerce may be such that for the protection of the one there is need to regulate the other. Sometimes it is said that the relation must be "direct" to bring that power into play. In many circumstances such a description will be sufficiently precise to meet the needs of the occasion. But a great principle of constitutional law is not susceptible of comprehensive statement in an adjective. The underlying thought is merely this, that "the law is not indifferent to considerations of degree." It cannot be indifferent to them without an expansion of the commerce clause that would absorb or imperil the reserved powers of the states. At times, as in . . . [*Schechter*] the waves of causation will have radiated so far that their undulatory motion, if discernible at all, will be too faint or obscure, too broken by cross-currents, to be heeded by the law. In such circumstances the holding is not directed at prices or wages considered in the abstract, but at prices or wages in particular conditions. The relation may be tenuous or the opposite according to the facts. Always the setting of the facts is to be viewed if one would know the closeness of the tie. Perhaps, if one group of adjectives is to be chosen in preference to another, "intimate" and "remote" will be found to be as good as any. At all events "direct" and "indirect," even if accepted as sufficient must not be read too narrowly. A survey of the cases shows that the words have been interpreted with suppleness of adaptation and flexibility of meaning. The power is as broad as the need that evokes it. . . .

(2) The commerce clause being accepted as a sufficient source of power, the next inquiry must be whether the power has been exercised consistently with the Fifth Amendment. In the pursuit of that inquiry, *Nebbia* v. *New York,* 291 U.S. 502, lays down the applicable principle. There a statute of New York prescribing a minimum price for milk was upheld against the objection that price-fixing was forbidden by the Fourteenth Amendment. We found it a sufficient reason to uphold the challenged system that "the conditions or practices in an industry make unrestricted competition an inadequate safeguard of the consumer's interest produce waste harmful to the public, threaten ultimately to cut off the supply of a commodity needed by the public, or portend the destruction of the industry itself." 291 U.S. at p. 538.

All this may be said, and with equal, if not greater force, of the conditions and practices in the bituminous coal industry, not only at the enactment of this statute in August, 1935, but for many years before. Overproduction was at a point where free competition had been degraded into anarchy. Prices had been cut so low that profit had become impossible for all except the lucky handful. Wages came down along with prices and with profits. There were strikes, at times nation-wide in extent, at other times spreading over broad areas and many mines, with the accompaniment of violence and bloodshed and misery and bitter feeling. The sordid tale is unfolded in many a document and treatise. During the twenty-three years between 1913 and 1935, there were nineteen investigations or hearings by Congress or by specially created commissions with reference to conditions in the coal mines. The hope of betterment was faint unless the industry could be subjected to the compulsion of a code. In the weeks immediately preceding the passage of this Act the country was threatened once more with a strike of ominous proportions. The plight of the industry was not merely a menace to owners and to mine workers: it was and had long been a menace to the public, deeply concerned in a steady and uniform supply of a fuel so vital to the national economy.

Congress was not condemned to inaction in the face of price wars and wage wars so pregnant with disaster. Commerce had been choked and burdened; its normal flow had been diverted from one state to another; there had been bankruptcy and waste and ruin alike for capital and for labor. The liberty protected by the Fifth Amendment does not include the right to persist in this anarchic riot. "When industry is grievously hurt, when production concerns fail, when unemployment mounts and communities dependent upon profitable production are prostrated, the wells of commerce go dry." . . .

(3) Finally, and in answer to the third objection to the statute in its price-fixing provisions, there has been no excessive delegation of legislative power. . . .

I am authorized to state that MR. JUSTICE BRANDEIS and MR. JUSTICE STONE join in this opinion.

NATIONAL LABOR RELATIONS BOARD v. JONES & LAUGHLIN STEEL CORP., 301 U.S. 1 (1937)

In the face of Supreme Court decisions invalidating efforts by the states to provide minimum wages for employees as well as attempts by the federal government to accomplish that purpose through codes of fair competition, the Roosevelt Administration adopted a new strategy. Congress enacted the National Labor Relations Act (also known as the Wagner Act, after New York Senator Wagner, the principal sponsor of the legislation), whose objective was to establish the rights of employees to organize into labor unions and to bargain collectively with their employers. Such collective bargaining, it was assumed, would enable the workers to obtain for themselves a living wage and reasonable working hours and conditions. The goal of the statute was to permit workers to be able to exercise meaningfully the freedom of contract to which the Court had paid so much lip service. Certain types of interference with union organizing and collective bargaining were unfair labor practices forbidden by law. The National Labor Relations Board (NLRB) was created to oversee the implementation of the rights guaranteed by the statute and was given the authority to compel employers to cease and desist from unfair labor practices. The constitutional basis for the Wagner Act was Congress' commerce power. The Jones & Laughlin Corporation, one of the nation's major steel producers, with its own mines, railroads, ships, and mills in a number of states throughout the country, was charged with having committed unfair labor practices in one of its plants in Pennsylvania. The

NLRB found that the corporation discriminated against union members in hiring and tenure of employment and that employees were being coerced and intimidated to keep them from joining the union. The corporation refused to comply with NLRB orders and the federal Court of Appeals for the Fifth Circuit refused to enforce the NLRB's order. The NLRB went to the Supreme Court.

Majority votes: 5
Dissenting votes: 4

MR. CHIEF JUSTICE HUGHES delivered the opinion of the Court:. . . .

First. The Scope of the Act.—The Act is challenged in its entirety as an attempt to regulate all industry, thus invading the reserved powers of the States over their local concerns. It is asserted that the references in the Act to interstate and foreign commerce are colorable at best; that the Act is not a true regulation of such commerce or of matters which directly affect it but on the contrary has the fundamental object of placing under the compulsory supervision of the federal government all industrial labor relations within the nation. . . .

We think it clear that the National Labor Relations Act may be construed so as to operate within the sphere of constitutional authority. . . .

There can be no question that the commerce . . . contemplated by the Act (aside from that within a Territory or District of Columbia) is interstate and foreign commerce in the constitutional sense. The Act also defines the term "affecting commerce" (§2 (7)):

"The term 'affecting commerce' means in commerce, or burdening or obstructing commerce or the free flow of commerce, or having led or tending to lead to a labor dispute burdening or obstructing commerce or the free flow of commerce."

This definition is one of exclusion as well as inclusion. The grant of authority to the Board does not purport to extend to the relationship between all industrial employees and employers. Its terms do not impose collective bargaining upon all industry regardless of effects upon interstate or foreign commerce. It purports to reach only what may be deemed to burden or obstruct that commerce and, thus qualified, it must be construed as contemplating the exercise of control within constitutional bounds. It is a familiar principle that acts which directly burden or obstruct interstate or foreign commerce, or its free flow, are within the reach of the congressional power. Acts having that effect are not rendered immune because they grow out of labor disputes. . . .

Second. The unfair labor practices in question.—. . . .

. . . [I]n its present application, the statute goes no further than to safeguard the right of employees to self-organization and to select representatives of their own choosing for collective bargaining or other mutual protection without restraint or coercion by their employer.

That is a fundamental right. Employees have as clear as right to organize and select their representatives for lawful purposes as the respondent has to organize its business and select its own officers and agents. Discrimination and coercion to prevent the free exercise of the right of employees to self-organization and representation is a proper subject for condemnation by competent legislative authority. . . .

Third. The application of the Act to employees engaged in production.—The principle involved.—Respondent says that whatever may be said of employees engaged in interstate commerce, the industrial relations and activities in the manufacturing department of respondent's enterprise are not subject to federal regulation. The argument rests upon the proposition that manufacturing in itself is not commerce. . . .

. . . The congressional authority to protect interstate commerce from burdens and obstructions is not limited to transactions which can be deemed to be an essential part of a "flow" of interstate or foreign commerce. Burdens and obstructions may be due to injurious action springing from other sources. The fundamental principle is that the power to regulate commerce is the power to enact "all appropriate legislation" for "its protection and advancement;" to adopt measures "to promote its growth and insure its safety;" "to foster, protect, control and restrain." That power is plenary and may be exerted to protect interstate commerce "no matter what the source of the dangers which threaten it." Although activities may be intrastate in character when separately considered, if they have such a close and substantial relation to interstate commerce that their control is essential or appropriate to protect that commerce from burdens and obstructions, Congress cannot be denied the power to exercise that control. Undoubtedly the scope of this power must be considered in the light of our dual system of government and may not be extended so as to embrace effects upon interstate commerce so indirect and remote that to embrace them, in view of our complex society, would effectually obliterate the distinction between what is national and what is local and create a completely centralized government. The question is necessarily one of degree. . . .

The close and intimate effect which brings the subject within the reach of federal power may be due to activities in relation to productive industry although the industry when separately viewed is local. This has been abundantly illustrated in the application of the federal Anti-Trust Act. In the *Standard Oil* and *American Tobacco* cases, 221 U.S. 1, 106, that statute was applied to combinations of employers engaged in productive industry. . . .

It is . . . apparent that the fact that the employees here concerned were engaged in production is not determinative. The question remains as to the effect upon interstate commerce of the labor practice involved. . . .

Fourth. Effects of the unfair labor practice in respondent's enterprise. . . . We are asked to shut our eyes to the plainest facts of our national life and to deal with the question of direct and indirect effects in an intellectual vacuum. Because there may be but indirect and remote effects upon interstate commerce in connection with a host of local enterprises throughout the country, it does not follow that other industrial activities do not have such a close and intimate relation to interstate commerce as to make the presence of industrial strife a matter of the most urgent national concern. When industries organize themselves on a national scale, making their relation to interstate commerce the dominant factor in their activities, how can it be maintained that their industrial labor relations constitute a forbidden field into which Congress may not enter when it is necessary to protect interstate commerce from the paralyzing consequences of industrial war? We have often said that interstate commerce itself is a practical conception. It is equally true that interferences with that commerce must be appraised by a judgment that does not ignore actual experience.

Experience has abundantly demonstrated that the recognition of the right of employees to self-organization and to have representatives of their own choosing for the purpose of collective bargaining is often an essential condition of industrial peace. Refusal to confer and negotiate has been one of the most prolific causes of strife. This is such an outstanding fact in the history of labor disturbances that it is a proper subject of judicial notice and requires no citation of instances. . . .

The steel industry is one of the great basic industries of the United States, with ramifying activities affecting interstate commerce at every point. The Government aptly refers to the steel strike of 1919–1920 with its far-reaching consequences. The fact that there appears to have been no major disturbance in that industry in the more recent period did not dispose of the possibilities of future and like dangers to interstate commerce which Congress was entitled to foresee and to exercise its protective power to forestall. It is not necessary again to detail the facts as to respondent's enterprise. Instead of being beyond the pale, we think that it presents in a most striking way the close and intimate relation which a manufacturing industry may have to interstate commerce and we have no doubt that Congress had constitutional authority to safeguard the right of respondent's employees to self-organization and freedom in the choice of representatives for collective bargaining. . . .

Our conclusion is that the order of the Board was within its competency and that the Act is valid as here applied. The judgment of the Circuit Court of Appeals is reversed and the cause is remanded for further proceedings in conformity with this opinion.

Reversed.

MR. JUSTICE MCREYNOLDS delivered a dissenting opinion in which MR. JUSTICE VAN DEVANTER, MR. JUSTICE SUTHERLAND, MR. JUSTICE BUTLER joined:

We conclude that these causes were rightly decided by the three Circuit Courts of Appeals and that their judgments should be affirmed. The opinions there given without dissent are terse, well-considered, and sound. . . .

WICKARD v. FILBURN,
317 U.S. 111 (1942)

Perhaps the most extreme regulations of American agriculture were the amendments to the Agricultural Adjustment Act of 1938, which authorized the Secretary of Agriculture to establish for each farm how much of what commodity could be grown including crops intended solely for on-the-farm consumption. In this case Filburn, a small farmer in Montgomery County, Ohio, was given a wheat acreage allotment of 11.1 acres for the following year. He was given notice before the fall planting and sent a reminder before the wheat was harvested. However, Filburn defied the Department of Agriculture and harvested almost 12 acres of wheat beyond his quota. Filburn wanted additional wheat for on-the-farm purposes including feed for his poultry and livestock. Nevertheless, the penalty provisions of the law were enforced against Filburn, who, in turn, argued that the excess wheat had nothing to do with commerce since it was grown for his own use. In upholding the quotas, a unanimous Court dramatically demonstrated how far the Court had come from the narrow view of Congress' commerce power as reflected in the Schechter *and* Carter Coal Company *decisions.*

Votes: Unanimous

MR. JUSTICE JACKSON delivered the opinion of the Court:. . . .

The general scheme of the Agricultural Adjustment Act of 1938 as related to wheat is to control the volume moving in interstate and foreign commerce in order to avoid surpluses and shortages and the consequent abnormally low or high wheat prices and obstructions to commerce. Within prescribed limits and by prescribed standards the Secretary of Agriculture is directed to ascertain and proclaim each year a national acreage allotment for the next crop of wheat, which is then apportioned to the states and their counties, and is eventually broken up into allotments for individual farms. . . .

It is urged that under the Commerce Clause of the Constitution, Article I, § 8, clause 3, Congress does not possess the power it has in this instance sought to exercise. The question would merit little consideration since our decision in *United States* v. *Darby,* 312 U.S. 100, sustaining the federal power to regulate production of goods for commerce, except for the fact that this Act extends federal regulation to production not intended in any part for commerce but wholly for consumption on the farm. The Act includes a definition of "market" and its derivatives, so that as related to wheat, in addition to its conventional meaning, it also means to dispose of "by feeding (in any form) to poultry or livestock which, or the products of which, are sold, bartered, or exchanged, or to be disposed of." Hence, marketing quotas not only embrace all that may be sold without penalty but also what may be consumed on the premises. Wheat produced on excess acreage is designated as "available for marketing" as so defined, and the penalty is imposed thereon. Penalties do not depend upon whether any part of the wheat, either within or without the quota, is sold or intended to be sold. The sum of this is that the Federal Government fixes a quota including all that the farmer may harvest for sale or for his own farm needs, and declares that wheat produced on excess acreage may neither be disposed of nor used except upon payment of the penalty, or except if it is stored as required by the Act or delivered to the Secretary of Agriculture.

Appellee says that this is a regulation of production and consumption of wheat. Such activities are, he urges, beyond the reach of Congressional power

under the Commerce Clause, since they are local in character, and their effects upon interstate commerce are at most "indirect." In answer the Government argues that the statute regulates neither production nor consumption, but only marketing; and, in the alternative, that if the Act does go beyond the regulation of marketing it is sustainable as a "necessary and proper" implementation of the power of Congress over interstate commerce.

The Government's concern lest the Act be held to be a regulation of production or consumption, rather than of marketing, is attributable to a few dicta and decisions of this Court which might be understood to lay it down that activities such as "production," "manufacturing," and "mining" are strictly "local" and, except in special circumstances which are not present here, cannot be regulated under the commerce power because their effects upon interstate commerce are, as matter of law, only "indirect." Even today, when this power has been held to have great latitude, there is no decision of this Court that such activities may be regulated where no part of the product is intended for interstate commerce or intermingled with the subjects thereof. We believe that a review of the course of decision under the Commerce Clause will make plain, however, that questions of the power of Congress are not to be decided by reference to any formula which would give controlling force to nomenclature such as "production" and "indirect" and foreclose consideration of the actual effects of the activity in question upon interstate commerce. . . .

. . . Once an economic measure of the reach of the power granted to Congress in the Commerce Clause is accepted, questions of federal power cannot be decided simply by finding the activity in question to be "production" nor can consideration of its economic effects be foreclosed by calling them "indirect.". . .

Whether the subject of the regulation in question was "production," "consumption," or "marketing" is . . . not material for purposes of deciding the question of federal power before us. That an activity is of local character may help in a doubtful case to determine whether Congress intended to reach it. . . . But even if appellee's activity be local and though it may not be regarded as commerce, it may still, whatever its nature, be reached by Congress if it exerts a substantial economic effect on interstate commerce, and this irrespective of whether such effect is what might at some earlier time have been defined as "direct" or "indirect." . . .

The effect of consumption of home-grown wheat on interstate commerce is due to the fact that it constitutes the most variable factor in the disappearance of the wheat crop. Consumption on the farm where grown appears to vary in an amount greater than 20 per cent of average production. The total amount of wheat consumed as food varies but relatively little, and use as seed is relatively constant.

The maintenance by government regulation of a price for wheat undoubtedly can be accomplished as effectively by sustaining or increasing the demand as by limiting the supply. The effect of the statute before us is to restrict the amount which may be produced for market and the extent as well to which one may forestall resort to the market by producing to meet his own needs. That appellee's own contribution to the demand for wheat may be trivial by itself is not enough to remove him from the scope of federal regulation where, as here, his contribution, taken together with that of many others similarly situated, is far from trivial. . . .

It is well established by decisions of this Court that the power to regulate commerce includes the power to regulate the prices at which commodities in that commerce are dealt in and practices affecting such prices. One of the primary purposes of the Act in question was to increase the market price of wheat, and to that end to limit the volume thereof that could affect the market. It can hardly be denied that a factor of such volume and variability as home-consumed wheat would have a substantial influence on price and market conditions. This may arise because being in marketable condition such wheat overhangs the market and, if induced by rising prices, tends to flow into the market and check price increases. But if we assume that it is never marketed, it supplies a need of the man who grew it which would otherwise be reflected by purchases in the open market. Home-grown wheat in this sense competes with wheat in commerce. The stimulation of commerce is a use of the regulatory function quite as definitely as prohibitions or restrictions thereon. This record leaves us in no doubt that Congress may properly have considered that wheat consumed on the farm where grown, if wholly outside the scheme of regulation, would have a substantial effect in defeating and obstructing its purpose to stimulate trade therein at increased prices.

It is said, however, that this Act, forcing some farmers into the market to buy what they could provide for themselves, is an unfair promotion of the markets and prices of specializing wheat growers. It is of the essence of regulation that it lays a restraining hand on the self-interest of the regulated and that advantages from the regulation commonly fall to others. The conflicts of economic interest between the regulated and those who advantage by it are wisely left under our system to resolution by the Congress under its more flexible and responsible legislative process. Such conflicts rarely lend themselves to judicial determination. And with the wisdom, workability, or fairness, of the plan of regulation we have nothing to do. . . .

Reversed.

UNITED STATES v. DARBY, 312 U.S. 100 (1941)

The Fair Labor Standards Act of 1938 was the most far-reaching labor legislation ever to pass Congress. It provided for minimum wages, maximum hours, and the regulation of child labor in all industries or businesses engaged in interstate commerce or in the production of goods for interstate commerce. The statute made it unlawful to send goods in interstate commerce made in violation of the act's standards. The Darby Lumber Company failed to comply, and the government sought enforcement. The company was indicted, but the federal district court threw out the case on the grounds that the federal legislation was unconstitutional. The government appealed to the Supreme Court.

Votes: Unanimous

MR. JUSTICE STONE delivered the opinion of the Court:

The two principal questions raised by the record in this case are, *first,* whether Congress has constitutional power to prohibit the shipment in interstate commerce of lumber manufactured by employees whose wages are less than a prescribed minimum or whose weekly hours of labor at that wage are greater than a prescribed maximum, and, *second,* whether it has power to prohibit the employment of workmen in the production of goods "for interstate commerce" at other than prescribed wages and hours. . . .

While manufacture is not of itself interstate commerce, the shipment of manufactured goods interstate is such commerce and the prohibition of such shipment by Congress is indubitably a regulation of the commerce. The power to regulate commerce is the power "to prescribe the rule by which commerce is governed." *Gibbons* v. *Ogden,* 9 Wheat. 1, 196. It extends not only to those regulations which aid, foster and protect the commerce, but embraces those which prohibit it. . . .

The power of Congress over interstate commerce "is complete in itself, may be exercised to its utmost extent, and acknowledges no limitations other than are prescribed in the Constitution." *Gib-*

bons v. *Ogden, supra,* 196. That power can neither be enlarged nor diminished by the exercise or non-exercise of state power. . . .

The motive and purpose of the present regulation are plainly to make effective the Congressional conception of public policy that interstate commerce should not be made the instrument of competition in the distribution of goods produced under substandard labor conditions, which competition is injurious to the commerce and to the states from and to which the commerce flows. The motive and purpose of a regulation of interstate commerce are matters for the legislative judgment upon the exercise of which the Constitution places no restriction and over which the courts are given no control. . . . [W]e conclude that the prohibition of the shipment interstate of goods produced under the forbidden substandard labor conditions is within the constitutional authority of Congress.

In the more than a century which has elapsed since the decision of *Gibbons* v. *Ogden,* these principles of constitutional interpretation have been so long and repeatedly recognized by this Court as applicable to the Commerce Clause, that there would be little occasion for repeating them now were it not for the decision of this Court twenty-two years ago in *Hammer* v. *Dagenhart,* 247 U.S. 251. In that case it was held by a bare majority of the Court over the powerful and now classic dissent of Mr. Justice Holmes setting forth the fundamental issues involved, that Congress was without power to exclude the products of child labor from interstate commerce. The reasoning and conclusion of the Court's opinion there cannot be reconciled with the conclusion which we have reached, that the power of Congress under the Commerce Clause is plenary to exclude any article from interstate commerce subject only to the specific prohibitions of the Constitution.

Hammer v. *Dagenhart* has not been followed. The distinction on which the decision was rested that Congressional power to prohibit interstate commerce is limited to articles which in themselves have some harmful or deleterious property—a distinction which was novel when made and unsupported by any provision of the Constitution—has long since been abandoned. . . . The thesis of the opinion that the motive of the prohibition or its effect to control in some measure the use or production within the states of the article thus excluded from the commerce can operate to deprive the regulation of its constitutional authority has long since ceased to have force. . . .

The conclusion is inescapable that *Hammer* v. *Dagenhart* was a departure from the principles which have prevailed in the interpretation of the Commerce Clause both before and since the decision and that such vitality, as a precedent, as it then had has long since been exhausted. It should be and now is overruled.

Validity of the wage and hour requirements. . . .
. . . The obvious purpose of the Act was not only to prevent the interstate transportation of the proscribed product, but to stop the initial step toward transportation, production with the purpose of so transporting it. Congress was not unaware that most manufacturing businesses shipping their product in interstate commerce make it in their shops without reference to its ultimate destination and then after manufacture select some of it for shipment interstate and some intrastate according to the daily demands of their business, and that it would be practically impossible, without disrupting manufacturing businesses, to restrict the prohibited kind of production to the particular pieces of lumber, cloth, furniture or the like which later move in interstate rather than intrastate commerce.

The recognized need of drafting a workable statute and the well known circumstances in which it was to be applied are persuasive of the conclusion, which the legislative history supports, that the "production for commerce" intended includes at least production of goods, which, at the time of production, the employer, according to the normal course of his business, intends or expects to move in interstate commerce although, through the exigencies of the business, all of the goods may not thereafter actually enter interstate commerce.

There remains the question whether such restriction on the production of goods for commerce is a permissible exercise of the commerce power. The power of Congress over interstate commerce is not confined to the regulation of commerce among the states. It extends to those activities intrastate which so affect interstate commerce or the exercise of the power of Congress over it as to make regulation of them appropriate means to the attainment of a legitimate end, the exercise of the granted power of Congress to regulate interstate commerce. . . .

Congress, having by the present Act adopted the policy of excluding from interstate commerce all goods produced for the commerce which do not conform to the specified labor standards, it may choose the means reasonably adapted to the attainment of the permitted end, even though they involve control of intrastate activities. Such legislation has often been sustained with respect to powers, other than the commerce power granted to the national government, when the means chosen, although not themselves within the granted power, were nevertheless deemed appropriate aids to the accomplishment of some purpose within an admitted power of the national government. . . .

. . . [T]he evils aimed at by the Act are the spread of substandard labor conditions through the use of the facilities of interstate commerce for competition by the goods so produced with those produced under the prescribed or better labor conditions; and the consequent dislocation of the commerce itself caused by the impairment or destruction of local business by competition made effective through interstate commerce. The Act is thus directed at the suppression of a method or kind of competition in interstate commerce which it has in effect condemned as "unfair," as the Clayton Act has condemned other "unfair methods of competition" made effective through interstate commerce. . . .

The Sherman Act and the National Labor Relations Act are familiar examples of the exertion of the commerce power to prohibit or control activities wholly intrastate because of their effect on interstate commerce. . . .

The means adopted by [the Act] for the protection of interstate commerce by the suppression of the production of the condemned goods for interstate commerce is so related to the commerce and so affects it as to be within the reach of the commerce power. Congress, to attain its objective in the suppression of nationwide competition in interstate commerce by goods produced under substandard labor conditions, has made no distinction as to the volume or amount of shipments in the commerce or of production for commerce by any particular shipper or producer. It recognized that in present day industry, competition by a small part may affect the whole and that the total effect of the competition of many small producers may be great. . . . The legislation aimed at a whole embraces all its parts.

Our conclusion is unaffected by the Tenth Amendment which provides: "The powers not delegated to the United States by the Constitution, nor prohibited by it to the States, are reserved to the States respectively, or to the people." The amendment states but a truism that all is retained which has not been surrendered. There is nothing in the history of its adoption to suggest that it was more than declaratory of the relationship between the national and state governments as it had been established by the Constitution before the amendment or that its purpose was other than to allay fears that the new national government might seek to exercise powers not granted, and that the states might not be able to exercise fully their reserved powers. . . .

From the beginning and for many years the amendment has been construed as not depriving the national government of authority to resort to all means for the exercise of a granted power which are appropriate and plainly adapted to the permitted end. . . . Whatever doubts may have arisen of the soundness of that conclusion, they have been put at rest by the decisions under the Sherman Act and the National Labor Relations Act. . . .

Validity of the wage and hour provisions under the Fifth Amendment. Both provisions are minimum wage requirements compelling the payment of a minimum standard wage with a prescribed increased wage for overtime of "not less than one and one-half times the regular rate" at which the worker is employed. Since our decision in *West Coast Hotel Co. v. Parrish,* 300 U.S. 379, it is no longer open to question that the fixing of a minimum wage is within the legislative power and that the bare fact of its exercise is not a denial of due process under the Fifth more than under the Fourteenth Amendment. Nor is it any longer open to question that it is within the legislative power to fix maximum hours. Similarly the statute is not objectionable because applied alike to both men and women.

The Act is sufficiently definite to meet constitutional demands. One who employs persons, without conforming to the prescribed wage and hour conditions, to work on goods which he ships or expects to ship across state lines, is warned that he may be subject to the criminal penalties of the Act. No more is required. . . .

Reversed.

HEART OF ATLANTA MOTEL v. UNITED STATES, 379 U.S. 241 (1964);
KATZENBACH v. McCLUNG,
379 U.S. 294 (1964)

These two cases involved the constitutionality of Title 2, the public accommodations section, of the Civil Rights Act of 1964. Title 2 forbade racial discrimination by any business that "is a place of public accommodation" if "its operations affect commerce." The Heart of Atlanta Motel located in Atlanta, Georgia, was found to have solicited patronage from out of state and to be easily accessible to two interstate highways. It was accepted as fact that approximately 75 percent of its registered guests came from other states. The motel refused black patronage and was charged with violating Title 2. The motel's lawyers argued that Title 2 exceeded Congress' commerce powers. In Katzenbach v. McClung, Ollie McClung had refused to allow blacks to patronize his family-owned restaurant, Ollie's Barbecue, located in Birmingham, Ala-

bama. The restaurant's only connection with inter-state commerce was the source of its food supply, particularly the meat that was bought from a local supplier who had obtained it from outside Alabama.

Votes: Unanimous

HEART OF ATLANTA MOTEL v. UNITED STATES

MR. JUSTICE CLARK delivered the opinion of the Court:

This is a declaratory judgment action [by the Heart of Atlanta Motel, Inc.] attacking the constitutionality of Title II of the Civil Rights Act of 1964. . . . Appellees counterclaimed for enforcement under §206(a) of the Act and asked for a three-judge district court under §206(b). A three-judge court . . . sustained the validity of the Act and issued a permanent injunction . . . restraining appellant from continuing to violate the Act. We affirm the judgment. . . .

The appellant contends that Congress in passing this Act exceeded its power to regulate commerce under Art. I. §8, cl. 3, of the Constitution of the United States; that the Act violates the Fifth Amendment because appellant is deprived of the right to choose its customers and operate its business as it wishes, resulting in a taking of its liberty and property without due process of law and a taking of its property without just compensation; and, finally, that by requiring appellant to rent available rooms to Negroes against its will, Congress is subjecting it to involuntary servitude in contravention of the Thirteenth Amendment.

The appellees counter that the unavailability to Negroes of adequate accommodations interferes significantly with interstate travel, and that Congress, under the Commerce Clause, has power to remove such obstructions and restraints; that the Fifth Amendment does not forbid reasonable regulation and that consequential damage does not constitute a "taking" within the meaning of that amendment; that the Thirteenth Amendment claim fails because it is entirely frivolous to say that an amendment directed to the abolition of human bondage and the removal of widespread disabilities associated with slavery places discrimination in public accommodations beyond the reach of both federal and state law. . . .

. . . The legislative history of [Title II of the Civil Rights Act of 1964] . . . indicates that Congress based the Act on §5 and the Equal Protection Clause of the Fourteenth Amendment as well as its power to regulate interstate commerce under Art. I, §8, cl. 3 of the Constitution.

The Senate Commerce Committee made it quite clear that the fundamental object of Title II was to vindicate "the deprivation of personal dignity that surely accompanies denials of equal access to public establishments." At the same time, however, it noted that such an objective has been and could be readily achieved "by congressional action based on the commerce power of the Constitution." Our study of the legislative record, made in the light of prior cases, has brought us to the conclusion that Congress possessed ample power in this regard, and we have therefore not considered the other grounds relied upon. This is not to say that the remaining authority upon which it acted was not adequate, a question upon which we do not pass, but merely that since the commerce power is sufficient for our decision here we have considered it alone. . . .

While the Act as adopted carried no congressional findings the record of its passage through each house is replete with evidence of the burdens that discrimination by race or color places upon interstate commerce. . . . This testimony included the fact that our people have become increasingly mobile with millions of people of all races traveling from State to State; that Negroes in particular have been the subject of discrimination in transient accommodations, having to travel great distances to secure the same; that often they have been unable to obtain accommodations and have had to call upon friends to put them overnight; and that these conditions had become so acute as to require the listing of available lodging for Negroes in a special guidebook which was itself "dramatic testimony to the difficulties" Negroes encounter in travel. These exclusionary practices were found to be nation-wide, the Under Secretary of Commerce testifying that there is "no question that this discrimination in the North still exists to a large degree" and in the West and Midwest as well. This testimony indicated a qualitative as well as quantitative effect on interstate travel by Negroes. The former was the obvious impairment of the Negro traveler's pleasure and convenience that resulted when he continually was uncertain of finding lodging. As for the latter, there was evidence that this uncertainty stemming from racial discrimination had the effect of discouraging travel on the part of a substantial portion of the Negro community. This was the conclusion not only of the Under Secretary of Commerce but also of the Administrator of the Federal Aviation Agency who wrote the Chairman of the Senate Commerce Committee that it was his "belief that air commerce is adversely affected by the denial to a substantial segment of the traveling public of adequate and desegregated public accommodations." We shall not burden this opinion with further details since the voluminous testimony presents overwhelming evidence that discrimination by hotels and motels impedes interstate travel.

The power of Congress to deal with these obstructions depends on the meaning of the Commerce Clause. Its meaning was first enunciated 140 years ago by the great Chief Justice John Marshall in *Gibbons* v. *Ogden*, 9 Wheat. 1 (1824). . . .

. . . [T]he determinative test of the exercise of power by the Congress under the Commerce Clause is simply whether the activity sought to be regulated is "commerce which concerns more States than one" and has a real and substantial relation to the national interest. Let us now turn to this facet of the problem.

That . . . [commerce] included the movement of persons through more States than one was settled as early as 1849, in the *Passenger Cases,* 7 How. 283. . . . Nor does it make any difference whether the transportation is commercial in character. *Caminetti* v. *United States*, 242 U.S. 470 (1917), at 484–486. . . .

The same interest in protecting interstate commerce . . . led Congress to deal with segregation in interstate carriers and the white-slave traffic [and] has prompted it to extend the exercise of its power to gambling, *Lottery Case,* 188 U.S. 321 (1903); to criminal enterprises, *Brooks* v. *United States,* 267 U.S. 432 (1925); to deceptive practices in the sale of products, *Federal Trade Comm'n* v. *Mandel Bros., Inc.,* 359 U.S. 385 (1959); to fraudulent security transactions, *Securities & Exchange Comm'n* v. *Ralston Purina Co.,* 346 U.S. 119 (1953); to misbranding of drugs, *Weeks* v. *United States,* 245 U.S. 618 (1918); . . . and to racial discrimination by owners and managers of terminal restaurants, *Boynton* v. *Virginia,* 364 U.S. 454 (1960).

That Congress was legislating against moral wrongs in many of these areas rendered its enactment no less valid. In framing Title II of this Act Congress was also dealing with what it considered a moral problem. But that fact does not detract from the overwhelming evidence of the disruptive effect that racial discrimination has had on commercial intercourse. It was this burden which empowered Congress to enact appropriate legislation, and, given this basis for the exercise of its power, Congress was not restricted by the fact that the particular obstruction to interstate commerce with which it was dealing was also deemed a moral and social wrong.

It is said that the operation of the motel here is of a purely local character. But, assuming this to be true, "[i]f it is interstate commerce that feels the pinch, it does not matter how local the operation which applies the squeeze." . . . Thus the power of Congress to promote interstate commerce also includes the power to regulate the local incidents thereof, including local activities in both the States of origin and destination, which might have a substantial and harmful effect upon that commerce. One need only examine the evidence which we have discussed above to see that Congress may—as it has—prohibit racial discrimination by motels serving travelers, however "local" their operations may appear.

Nor does the Act deprive appellant of liberty or property under the Fifth Amendment. The commerce power invoked here by the Congress is a specific and plenary one authorized by the Constitution itself. The only questions are: (1) whether Congress had a rational basis for finding that racial discrimination by motels affected commerce, and (2) if it had such a basis, whether the means it selected to eliminate that evil are reasonable and appropriate. If they are, appellant has no "right" to select its guests as it sees fit, free from governmental regulation.

There is nothing novel about such legislation. Thirty-two States now have it on their books either by statute or executive order and many cities provide such regulation. Some of these Acts go back fourscore years. It has been repeatedly held by this Court that such laws do not violate the Due Process Clause of the Fourteenth Amendment. . . .

As we have pointed out, 32 States now have such statutes and no case has been cited to us where the attack on a state statute has been successful, either in federal or state courts. . . .

. . . [W]e [do not] find any merit in the claim that the Act is a taking of property without just compensation.

We find no merit in the remainder of appellant's contentions, including that of "involuntary servitude." . . .

We, therefore, conclude that the action of the Congress in the adoption of the Act as applied here to a motel which concededly serves interstate travelers is within the power granted it by the Commerce Clause of the Constitution, as interpreted by this Court for 140 years. It may be argued that Congress could have pursued other methods to eliminate the obstructions it found in interstate commerce caused by racial discrimination. But this is a matter of policy that rests entirely with the Congress not with the courts. How obstructions in commerce may be removed—what means are to be employed—is within the sound and exclusive discretion of the Congress. It is subject only to one caveat—that the means chosen by it must be reasonably adapted to the end permitted by the Constitution. We cannot say that its choice here was not so adapted. The Constitution requires no more.

Affirmed.

MR. JUSTICE BLACK, concurring: [omitted]

MR. JUSTICE DOUGLAS, concurring:

Though I join the Court's opinion, I am somewhat reluctant here . . . to rest solely on the Commerce Clause. My reluctance is not due to any conviction that Congress lacks power to regulate commerce in the interests of human rights. It is rather my belief that the right of people to be free of state action that discriminates against them because of race, like the "right of persons to move freely from State to State" "occupies a more protected position in our constitutional system than does the movement of cattle, fruit, steel and coal across state lines." . . .

Hence I would prefer to rest on the assertion of legislative power contained in §5 of the Fourteenth Amendment. . . .

A decision based on the Fourteenth Amendment would have a more settling effect, making unnecessary litigation over whether a particular restaurant or inn is within the commerce definitions of the Act or whether a particular customer is an interstate traveler. Under my construction, the Act would apply to all customers in all the enumerated places of public accommodation. And that construction would put an end to all obstructionist strategies and finally close one door on a bitter chapter in American history. . . .

MR. JUSTICE GOLDBERG, concurring: [omitted]

KATZENBACH v. McCLUNG

MR. JUSTICE CLARK delivered the opinion of the Court:. . . .

Ollie's Barbecue admits that it is covered by the provisions of the Act. The Government makes no contention that the discrimination at the restaurant was supported by the State of Alabama. There is no claim that interstate travelers frequented the restaurant. The sole question, therefore, narrows down to whether Title II, as applied to a restaurant receiving about $70,000 worth of food which has moved in commerce, is a valid exercise of the power of Congress. The Government has contended that Congress had ample basis upon which to find that racial discrimination at restaurants which receive from out of state a substantial portion of the food served does, in fact, impose commercial burdens of national magnitude upon interstate commerce. The appellees' major argument is directed to this premise. They urge that no such basis existed. It is to that question that we now turn.

As we noted in *Heart of Atlanta Motel*, both Houses of Congress conducted prolonged hearings on the Act. . . . The record is replete with testimony of the burdens placed on interstate commerce by racial discrimination in restaurants. A comparison of per capita spending by Negroes in restaurants, theaters, and like establishments indicated less spending, after discounting income differences, in areas where discrimination is widely practiced. This condition, which was especially aggravated in the South, was attributed in the testimony of the Under Secretary of Commerce to racial segregation. . . . This diminutive spending springing from a refusal to serve Negroes and their total loss as customers has, regardless of the absence of direct evidence, a close connection to interstate commerce. The fewer customers a restaurant enjoys the less food it sells and consequently the less it buys. . . . In addition, the Attorney General testified that this type of discrimination imposed "an artificial restriction on the market" and interfered with the flow of merchandise. . . . In addition, there were many references to discriminatory situations causing wide unrest and having a depressant effect on general business conditions in the respective communities. . . .

We believe that this testimony afforded ample basis for the conclusion that established restaurants in such areas sold less interstate goods because of the discrimination, that interstate travel was obstructed directly by it, that business in general suffered and that many new businesses refrained from establishing there as a result of it. Hence the District Court was in error in concluding that there was no connection between discrimination and the movement of interstate commerce. The court's conclusion that such a connection is outside "common experience" flies in the face of stubborn fact. . . .

Confronted as we are with the facts laid before Congress, we must conclude that it had a rational basis for finding that racial discrimination in restaurants had a direct and adverse effect on the free flow of interstate commerce. . . . Congress prohibited discrimination only in those establishments having a close tie to interstate commerce, i.e., those, like the McClungs', serving food that has come from out of the State. We think in so doing that Congress acted well within its power to protect and foster commerce in extending the coverage of Title II only to those restaurants offering to serve interstate travelers or serving food, a substantial portion of which has been moved in interstate commerce. . . .

The judgment is therefore

Reversed.

Chapter

9

Powers of Congress: Taxing, Spending, Monetary

DECISIONAL TRENDS

In examining the Supreme Court's treatment of the fiscal powers of Congress including use of the taxing, spending, and monetary powers, we find that early on the Court was supportive of Congress. **Hylton** v. **United States** stands as the first case in which Congress' taxing power was broadly construed and a federal tax was upheld as constitutional. The case also required the justices to interpret what the Constitution means by a direct tax, which must be apportioned among the several states according to population, and what is meant by an excise tax. The justices seemed to think that a land tax and a head tax were direct taxes, and this definition stood as a precedent until 1895 for *not* treating an income tax as a direct tax.

Congress' monetary power over the currency was brought before the Court during the Civil War when the Legal Tender Acts were challenged. But in *Roosevelt* v. *Meyer,* 1 Wallace 512 (1863), the Court ruled that it had no

jurisdiction in the case. Finally, in 1870, in *Hepburn* v. *Griswold,* 8 Wallace 603, the Court confronted the issue of the retroactive application of the Legal Tender Acts and by a vote of four to three the majority ruled such retroactive application unconstitutional. The next year, in the *Second Legal Tender Cases,* 12 Wallace 457, with two new justices forming a new majority, the Court did an about-face. Congress ultimately was recognized as having broad war powers including the power to regulate the currency.

The Waite Court, in line with its generally sympathetic view of the exercise of Congress' powers, upheld the federal income tax that had been enacted during the Civil War (*Springer* v. *United States*, 102 U.S. 586 [1881]), and furthermore upheld the peacetime issuance of greenbacks by the U.S. Treasury in 1878 in the case of *Juilliard* v. *Greenman,* 110 U.S. 421 (1884). The record of the Fuller Court, however, was considerably less permissive. In 1895 in **Pollock** v. **Farmers' Loan**

and Trust Co., the Court invalidated the federal income tax and repudiated the Court's contrary precedents. But in **McCray** v. **United States** in 1904, the Court took an expansive view of Congress' taxing powers being used to accomplish social and economic ends.

In the *McCray* decision the Court seemed to establish the precedent that a tax that is ostensibly for revenue is within Congress' power to enact even if it serves to regulate. This was reaffirmed by the Court in *United States* v. *Doremus,* 249 U.S. 86 (1919), which upheld the Harrison Narcotic Drug Act of 1914. Yet the Court in **Bailey** v. **Drexel Furniture Co.** and during the Depression in **United States** v. **Butler** turned its back on these precedents and proceeded to make constitutional judgments about the *subject* of the taxation. The Court took the position that taxation could not be used by Congress as a means of regulating manufacturing, agriculture, or any local production activity. However, the Court in 1937 and later repudiated the negative taxation and spending doctrines used previously and it firmly established the broad power of Congress to tax and to spend its revenues for the general welfare. **Steward Machine Company** v. **Davis** was the vehicle of this new posture of the Court as was *Helvering* v. *Davis,* 301 U.S. 619 (1937), which upheld the old age social security taxes and program. The Court also in *Sonzinsky* v. *United States,* 300 U.S. 506 (1937), upheld the $200 annual license tax imposed on dealers in firearms under the National Firearms Act of 1934. In so doing, the Court asserted that Congress may use its taxing power to regulate and that as long as the tax is a revenue raiser, the Court may not speculate as to the motives of Congress in imposing the tax or the tax's effects. The Court in *Alabama Power Company* v. *Ickes,* 302 U.S. 464 (1938), upheld a congressional financial aid program to municipalities to help establish public power plants.

When examining the decisions of the Vinson and Warren Courts in which Congress'

exercise of its powers was challenged, one is struck by the fact that the Roosevelt Court's constitutional revolution so took hold that there was no instance when economic regulation was pronounced unconstitutional. Early in the Vinson Court, for example, the Court decided *Woods* v. *Miller,* 333 U.S. 138 (1948), which upheld national peacetime rent control legislation as a legitimate exercise of Congress' war powers. The unanimous Court reasoned that the war power does not necessarily end with the cessation of hostilities but rather permits Congress to deal with the domestic effects of the war during the postwar period. The Warren Court, however, invalidated taxes that Congress enacted for the purpose of prosecuting criminal activity. The taxes were such that to comply with them meant the violation of Fifth Amendment rights of the compliers. Thus in *Marchetti* v. *United States,* 390 U.S. 39 (1968), and *Grosso* v. *United States,* 390 U.S. 62 (1968), the federal tax on gamblers that also required their registration with the Internal Revenue Service was struck down as violating the Fifth Amendment right against self-incrimination. So, too, were taxes on firearms that were not registered (*Haynes* v. *United States,* 390 U.S. 85 [1968]) and taxes on the transfer of marijuana (*Leary* v. *United States,* 395 U.S. 6 [1969]). Congress, in other words, could not tax illegal activities that would force those complying with the tax to identify themselves and thus face federal prosecution. But in no way was the essential power of taxation to raise revenue or for the purpose of regulation of the economy adversely affected.

The Burger Court continued to uphold Congress' taxing and spending powers when they were challenged. In **Buckley** v. **Valeo** (chap. 13), while striking down some provisions limiting campaign spending of the Federal Election Campaign Act of 1971, the Court nevertheless upheld the program of public financing of presidential campaigns. Another congressional spending program upheld by the Court was the minority business enterprise provision of the Public Works Employment Act of 1977. That case was **Fullilove** v. **Klutznick,** a decision that also, in effect, gave the Court's approval to Congress' efforts at affirmative action by using race for benign purposes. The Court also approved Congress' decision to have federal funds under the Medicaid program pay for the delivery of babies but not for abortions (see **Harris** v. **McRae** [chap. 19]). In 1983 the Court upheld the oil windfall profits tax in *United States* v. *Ptasynski,* 462 U.S. 74. In 1987 the Court in **South Dakota** v. **Dole** upheld the federal statute conditioning state receipt of federal highway funds on adoption of a minimum drinking age of 21 on the grounds that this was a valid use of Congress' spending power. In the 1986 decision of **Bowsher** v. **Synar** (chap. 7), however, the Court ruled that Congress did not have the constitutional authority to delegate spending decisions to the Comptroller General of the United States even though those spending decisions followed the mandate of Con-gress. Spending decisions must be made by Congress itself. The administration of those decisions must be undertaken by the executive branch and not by an official of the legislative branch. In short, the powers of Congress to tax, spend, and regulate monetary policy are well established constitutionally, and challenges to Congress' exercise of these powers have met with little success over the past half century. Note that other powers of Congress are discussed in passing in chapter 7 (see the discussion of foreign affairs) and chapter 13 (see the discussion of Congress' investigatory powers and other powers to regulate in areas that may impinge on First Amendment freedoms).

THE IMPACT OF THE COURT'S DECISIONS

Table 9.1 summarizes the impact of selected Court decisions concerning the powers of Congress in taxing, spending, and monetary matters. The reprinted cases follow.

Table 9.1 THE IMPACT OF SELECTED COURT DECISIONS CONCERNING THE TAXING, SPENDING, AND MONETARY POWERS OF CONGRESS

Case	Year	Impact on Parties	Short-Run Impact	Long-Run Impact
Hylton v. United States	1796	Carriage tax enforced, but Daniel Hylton by prearrangement with government pays only $16, the tax and penalty for one carriage.	Court legitimates Hamilton's economic program.	Court promotes federal supremacy and a broad view of Congress' powers. Precedent that direct taxes are only head and land taxes. Judicial review precedent.
Pollock v. Farmers' Loan and Trust Co.	1895	Since suit was an arranged suit and both "sides" wanted the income tax struck down, both sides won.	Decision prevented the federal government from using income tax to raise revenue. Decision was heavily criticized by populists and progressives. Court denounced in 1896 Democratic party platform.	Led to the adoption of the Sixteenth Amendment that overturned the Pollock decision.
McCray v. United States	1904	McCray paid the statutory penalty of $50.	Dairy farmers pleased with decision. Led to further government regulation through taxation.	Provided positive precedent for Congress to use its taxing powers to regulate.

Case	Year	Decision		Significance
Bailey v. Drexel Furniture Co.	1922	Drexel Furniture Co. recovered $6,312.79 from the Internal Revenue Service.	Evil of child labor continued. Congress warned that it could not use its taxing powers to regulate that which the Court says it cannot.	By questioning Congress' motives in enacting the tax on employers of child labor, Court stifled the use of Congress' taxing power for police power purposes and provided a negative precedent.
United States v. Butler	1936	Butler, the receiver for Hoosac Mills, did not have to pay the processing tax.	Unpopular decision that suggested the federal government was impotent to deal with the devastating economic situation of the farmers. Contributed to the constitutional crisis of 1936–1937.	No long-range impact as the Court, in effect, reversed itself the next year and afterward.
Steward Machine Company v. Davis	1937	Steward Machine Company not entitled to refund of $46.14.	Social security program upheld. Widespread employer compliance. Harshest effects of Depression abated.	Precedent for broad federal government taxing and spending powers.
Fullilove v. Klutznick	1980	Fullilove and other contractors lose.	Decision legitimized program that greatly helped minority-owned companies. Decision praised by civil rights groups.	Provides precedent for affirmative action-type programs by Congress.
South Dakota v. Dole	1987	South Dakota loses.	States adopt 21 as minimum drinking age.	Another precedent for the use of Congress' spending power to regulate.

HYLTON v. UNITED STATES,
3 DALLAS 171 (1796)

Congress passed various measures that were part of the Washington Administration's economic program, a program that was essentially put together by the Secretary of the Treasury, Alexander Hamilton. The program resolved the long-standing controversial issue as to who would assume responsibility for paying the war bonds issued by the states to finance the Revolutionary War. The federal government would assume the burden, but in turn it would have to raise money with which to do so and, of course, revenue measures would continually be needed to finance the activities of government. One of the revenue measures passed by Congress was the Carriage Tax Act, which imposed throughout the country a graduated excise tax ranging from $10 for a coach to $1 per horse-drawn two-wheel carriage. Daniel Hylton of Richmond, Virginia, refused to pay, as did a number of Virginia notables. The administration wanted to test the tax's constitutionality, and with the cooperation of Hylton brought an action in the United States Circuit Court to recover the tax due. For purposes of the suit it was stated that Hylton owned 125 coaches. Hylton's lawyer argued that the tax was not an excise tax but a direct tax and that the Constitution specifies in Article 1, Section 2, Paragraph 3 (and also in Article 1, Section 9, Clause 4) that direct taxes "shall be apportioned among the several States . . . according to their respective Numbers, which shall be determined by adding to the whole Number of free Persons . . . three fifths of all other Persons." The three-fifths referred to the counting of slaves. The government countered by arguing that Article 1, Section 8, Clause 1 instructs that "all Duties, Imposts and Excises shall be uniform throughout the United States" and that the carriage tax was such a tax. The circuit court was divided on the constitutional issue and Hylton then asked the Supreme Court, in effect, to strike down an act of Congress as unconstitutional.

Votes: Unanimous

MR. JUSTICE CHASE:

By the case stated, only one question is submitted to the opinion of this court:—whether the law of congress of the 5th of June, 1794, entitled, "An act to lay duties upon carriages, for the conveyance of persons," is unconstitutional and void? . . .

The great object of the constitution was, to give congress a power to lay taxes, adequate to the exigencies of government; but they were to observe two rules in imposing them, namely, the rule of uni-formity, when they laid duties, imposts, or excises; and the rule of apportionment, according to the census, when they laid any direct tax. . . .

. . . The rule of apportionment is only to be adopted in such cases where it can reasonably apply; and the subject taxed, must ever determine the application of the rule.

If it is proposed to tax any specific article by the rule of apportionment, and it would evidently create great inequality and injustice, it is unreasonable to say, that the Constitution intended such tax should be laid by that rule.

It appears to me, that a tax on carriages cannot be laid by the rule of apportionment, without very great inequality and injustice. For example: Suppose two states, equal in census, to pay 80,000 dollars each, by a tax on carriages and in one state there are 100 carriages, and in the other 1000. The owner of carriages in one state, would pay ten times the tax of owners in the other. A. in one state, would pay for his carriage 8 dollars, but B. in the other state, would pay for his carriage, 80 dollars. . . .

I think, an annual tax on carriages, for the conveyance of persons, may be considered as within the power granted to Congress to lay duties. The term duty, is the most comprehensive next to the generical term tax; and practically in Great Britain (whence we take our general ideas of taxes, duties, imposts, excises, customs, etc.,) embraces taxes on stamps, tolls for passage, etc., etc., and is not confined to taxes on importation only. . . .

I am inclined to think, but of this I do not give a judicial opinion, that the direct taxes contemplated by the Constitution, are only two, to wit, a capitation, or poll tax, simply, without regard to property, profession, or any other circumstance; and a tax on land. I doubt whether a tax, by a general assessment of personal property, within the United States, is included within the term, direct tax.

As I do not think the tax on carriages is a direct tax, it is unnecessary, at this time, for me to determine, whether this court, constitutionally possesses the power to declare an act of Congress void, on the ground of its being made contrary to, and in violation of, the constitution; but if the court have such power, I am free to declare, that I will never exercise it, but in a very clear case.

MR. JUSTICE PATERSON:

What are direct taxes within the meaning of the constitution? The constitution declares that a capitation tax is a direct tax; and, both in theory and practice, a tax on land is deemed to be a direct tax. . . . The provision was made in favor of the southern states. They possessed a large number of slaves; they had extensive tracts of territory, thinly settled, and not very productive. A majority of the states had but few slaves, and several of them a limited territory, well settled, and in a high state of cultivation. The southern states, if no provision had been introduced in the constitution, would have been wholly at the mercy of the other states. Congress in such case, might tax slaves, at discretion or arbitrarily, and land in every part of the union after the same rate or measure; so much a head in the first instance, and so much an acre in the second. To guard them against imposition in these particulars, was the reason of introducing the clause in the constitution, which directs that representatives and direct taxes shall be apportioned among the states, according to their respective numbers.

On the part of the plaintiff in error, it has been contended, that the rule of apportionment is to be favored rather than the rule of uniformity; and, of course, that the instrument is to receive such a construction, as will extend the former and restrict the latter. I am not of that opinion. The constitution has been considered as an accommodating system; it was the effect of mutual sacrifices and concessions; it was the work of compromise. The rule of apportionment is of this nature; it is radically wrong; it cannot be supported by any solid reasoning. Why should slaves, who are a species of property, be represented more than any other property? The rule, therefore, ought not to be extended by construction. . . .

. . . A tax on carriages, if apportioned, would be oppressive and pernicious. . . . Apportionment is an operation on states, and involves valuations and assessments, which are arbitrary, and should not be restored to but in case of necessity. Uniformity is an instant operation on individuals, without the intervention of assessments, or any regard to states, and is at once easy, certain, and efficacious. All taxes on expenses or consumption are indirect taxes. A tax on carriages is of this kind, and of course is not a direct tax. . . .

MR. JUSTICE IREDELL: [omitted]

MR. JUSTICE WILSON:

As there were only four judges, including myself, who attended the argument of this cause, I should have thought it proper to join in the decision, though I had before expressed a judicial opinion on the subject, in the circuit court of Virginia, did not the unanimity of the other three judges relieve me from the necessity. I shall now, however, only add, that my sentiments, in favor of the constitutionality of the tax in question, have not been changed.

MR. JUSTICE CUSHING:

As I have been prevented, by indisposition, from attending to the argument, it would be improper to give an opinion on the merits of the cause. CHIEF JUSTICE ELLSWORTH not having heard the whole of the argument did not participate in the decision.

BY THE COURT:—Let the judgment of the circuit court be affirmed.

POLLOCK v. FARMERS' LOAN AND TRUST CO., 158 U.S. 601 (1895)

The Constitution refers to two different types of taxes. Direct taxes, the Constitution specifies in Article 1, Section 9, are to be apportioned among the several states by population. On the other hand, indirect taxes, such as excises, imposts, and duties, according to Article 1, Section 8, are to be uniform throughout the United States. In Hylton v. United States, the Court in 1796 had suggested that a head tax and a tax on land were direct taxes. When Congress enacted an income tax during the Civil War, it was therefore assumed that this was an indirect tax, and the Supreme Court in 1881 (Springer v. United States) upheld it. Congress again in 1894 enacted an income tax law. The new tax, modest by present-day standards, levied a tax of 2 percent on incomes over $4000; it was scheduled to become effective January 1, 1985. But the law provoked anxiety on the part of the well-to-do who saw it as the start of a social revolution. The Pollock case became the test case to challenge the income tax's constitutionality. Charles Pollock of Massachusetts was a stockholder in the Farmers' Loan and Trust Company, a New York state corporation. He sued the company on behalf of himself and fellow stockholders to prevent it from paying the income tax on the grounds that the tax was unconstitutional and that for the company to pay an illegal tax would be a breach of trust and bring economic harm to him (Pollock) and other stockholders. The Court handed down its decision on April 8, 1895, with a majority ruling that the income tax on income from land was unconstitutional as was the tax on the income from state and municipal bonds. But the Court split 4 to 4 on the constitutionality of the remainder of the income tax law. Justice Howell Jackson had not participated in the decision because of illness. One week later, a petition for a rehearing was filed and since Justice Jackson indicated he would return to the Court, the petition was granted. The case was reargued and the Court handed down its second decision in the Pollock case, which in part is reprinted here. Interestingly, one of the justices, either Shiras, Gray, or Brewer, shifted sides, producing the 5–4 majority, thus *striking down the income tax law in its entirety. As a result of this decision, the United States could not rely on income taxes until the Sixteenth Amendment became part of the Constitution some 18 years after* Pollock *was decided.*

Majority votes: 5
Dissenting votes: 4

MR. CHIEF JUSTICE FULLER delivered the opinion of the Court:. . . .

It is said that a tax on the whole income of property is not a direct tax in the meaning of the Constitution, but a duty, and, as a duty, leviable without apportionment, whether direct or indirect. We do not think so. Direct taxation was not restricted in one breath, and the restriction blown to the winds in another. . . .

The Constitution prohibits any direct tax, unless in proportion to numbers as ascertained by the census; and, in the light of the circumstances to which we have referred, is it not an evasion of that prohibition to hold that a general unapportioned tax, imposed upon all property owners as a body for or in respect of their property, is not direct, in the meaning of the Constitution, because confined to the income therefrom?

Whatever the speculative views of political economists or revenue reformers may be, can it be properly held that the Constitution, taken in its plain and obvious sense, and with due regard to the circumstances attending the formation of the government, authorizes a general unapportioned tax on the products of the farm and the rents of real estate, although imposed merely because of ownership and with no possible means of escape from payment, as belonging to a totally different class from that which includes the property from whence the income proceeds?

There can be but one answer, unless the constitutional restriction is to be treated as utterly illusory and futile, and the object of its framers defeated. We find it impossible to hold that a fundamental requisition, deemed so important as to be enforced by two provisions, one affirmative and one negative, can be refined away by forced distinctions between that which gives value to property, and the property itself.

Nor can we perceive any ground why the same reasoning does not apply to capital in personalty held for the purpose of income or ordinarily yielding income, and to the income therefrom. All the real estate of the country, and all its invested personal property, are open to the direct operation of the taxing power if an apportionment be made according to the Constitution. The Constitution does not say that no direct tax shall be laid by apportionment on any other property than land; on the contrary, it forbids all unapportioned direct taxes; and we know of no warrant for excepting personal property from the exercise of the power, or any reason why an apportioned direct tax cannot be laid and assessed. . . .

The stress of the argument is thrown, however, on the assertion that an income tax is not a property tax at all; that it is not a real estate tax, or a crop tax, or a bond tax; that it is an assessment upon the taxpayer on account of his money-spending power as shown by his revenue for the year preceding the assessment; that rents received, crops harvested, interest collected, have lost all connection with their origin, and although once not taxable have become transmuted in their new form into taxable subject-matter; in other words, that income is taxable irrespective of the source from whence it is derived. . . .

Admitting that this act taxes the income of property irrespective of its source, still we cannot doubt that such a tax is necessarily a direct tax in the meaning of the Constitution. . . .

The power to tax real and personal property and the income from both, there being an apportionment, is conceded; that such a tax is a direct tax in the meaning of the Constitution has not been, and, in our judgment, cannot be successfully denied; and yet we are thus invited to hesitate in the enforcement of the mandate of the Constitution, which prohibits Congress from laying a direct tax on the revenue from property of the citizen without regard to state lines, and in such manner that the States cannot intervene by payment in regulation of their own resources, lest a government of delegated powers should be found to be, not less powerful, but less absolute, than the imagination of the advocate had supposed.

We are not here concerned with the question whether an income tax be or be not desirable, nor whether such a tax would enable the government to diminish taxes on consumption and duties on imports, and to enter upon what may be believed to be a reform of its fiscal and commercial system. Questions of that character belong to the controversies of political parties, and cannot be settled by judicial decision. In these cases our province is to determine whether this income tax on the revenue from property does or does not belong to the class of direct taxes. If it does, it is, being unapportioned, in violation of the Constitution, and we must so declare. . . .

. . . [We are of the] opinion that so much of the

sections of this law as lays a tax on income from real and personal property is invalid. . . .

We are constrained to conclude that sections twenty-seven to thirty-seven, inclusive, of the act, which became a law without the signature of the President on August 28, 1894, are wholly inoperative and void.

Our conclusions may, therefore, be summed up as follows:

First. We adhere to the opinion already announced, that, taxes on real estate being indisputably direct taxes, taxes on the rents or income of real estate are equally direct taxes.

Second. We are of opinion that taxes on personal property, or on the income of personal property, are likewise direct taxes.

Third. The tax imposed by sections twenty-seven to thirty-seven, inclusive, of the act of 1894, so far as it falls on the income of real estate and of personal property, being a direct tax within the meaning of the Constitution, and, therefore, unconstitutional and void because not apportioned according to representation, all those sections, constituting one entire scheme of taxation, are necessarily invalid.

The decrees hereinbefore entered in this court will be vacated; the decrees below will be reversed, and the case remanded, with instructions to grant the relief prayed.

MR. JUSTICE HARLAN dissenting:. . . .

[JUSTICE HARLAN EXTENSIVELY REVIEWS THE CARRIAGE TAX CASE, *HYLTON* v. *UNITED STATES*, AND SUBSEQUENT TAXATION CASES.]

From this history of legislation and of judicial decisions it is manifest—

That, in the judgment of the members of this court as constituted when the *Hylton* case was decided—all of whom were statesmen and lawyers of distinction, two, Wilson and Paterson, being recognized as great leaders in the convention of 1787— the only taxes that could certainly be regarded as direct taxes, within the meaning of the Constitution, were capitation taxes and taxes on lands. . . .

That from the foundation of the government, until 1861, Congress following the declarations of the judges in the *Hylton* case, restricted direct taxation to real estate and slaves, and in 1861 to real estate exclusively, and has never, by any statute, indicated its belief that personal property, however assessed or valued, was the subject of "direct taxes" to be apportioned among the States;. . . .

That in 1861 and subsequent years Congress imposed, without apportionment among the States on the basis of numbers, but by the rule of uniformity, duties on *income* derived *from every kind of property, real and personal,* including income derived from *rents,* and from trades, professions, and employments, etc.; and, lastly,

That upon every occasion when it has considered the question whether a duty on *incomes* was a direct tax within the meaning of the Constitution, this court has, *without a dissenting voice,* determined it in the negative, always proceeding on the ground that capitation taxes and taxes on land were the only direct taxes contemplated by the framers of the Constitution. . . .

In its practical operation this decision withdraws from national taxation not only all incomes derived from real estate, but tangible personal property, "invested personal property, bonds, stocks, investments of all kinds," and the income that may be derived from such property. This results from the fact that by the decision of the court, all such personal property and all incomes from real estate and personal property, are placed beyond national taxation otherwise than by *apportionment* among the States *on the basis* simply of *population*. No such apportionment can possibly be made without doing gross injustice to the many for the benefit of the favored few in particular States. Any attempt upon the part of Congress to apportion among the States, upon the basis simply of their population, taxation of personal property or of incomes, would tend to arouse such indignation among the freemen of America that it would never be repeated. When, therefore, this court adjudges, as it does now adjudge, that Congress cannot impose a duty or tax upon personal property, or upon income arising either from rents of real estate or from personal property, including invested personal property, bonds, stocks, and investments of all kinds, except by apportioning the sum to be so raised among the States according to population, it *practically* decides that, *without an amendment of the Constitution*—two-thirds of both Houses of Congress and three-fourths of the States concurring—such property and incomes can never be made to contribute to the support of the national government. . . .

I cannot assent to an interpretation of the Constitution that impairs and cripples the just powers of the National Government in the essential matter of taxation. . . .

The practical effect of the decision to-day is to give to certain kinds of property a position of favoritism and advantage inconsistent with the fundamental principles of our social organization, and to invest them with power and influence that may be perilous to that portion of the American people upon whom rests the larger part of the burdens of the government, and who ought not to be subjected to the dominion of aggregated wealth any more than the property of the country should be at the mercy of the lawless.

I dissent from the opinion and judgment of the court.

MR. JUSTICE BROWN dissenting: [omitted]

MR. JUSTICE JACKSON dissenting: [omitted]

MR. JUSTICE WHITE dissenting: [omitted]

McCRAY v. UNITED STATES,
195 U.S. 27 (1904)

Can Congress use its taxing power for a regulatory or prohibitory purpose? The question arose in this case concerning an act of Congress passed at the urging of the nation's dairy farmers. A tax of 10 cents per pound was imposed on oleomargarine that was artificially colored yellow to resemble butter, but noncolored margarine was taxed only one-quarter of a cent per pound. The purpose of the tax was to restore the competitive advantage of butter, a product that was threatened by the more cheaply produced margarine. The tax, in effect, would drive yellow oleo off the market. McCray was accused by the government of violating the statute. McCray lost in the lower courts and appealed to the Supreme Court.

Majority votes: 6
Dissenting votes: 3

MR. JUSTICE WHITE delivered the opinion of the Court:. . . .

Did Congress in passing the acts which are assailed, exert a power not conferred by the Constitution?

That the acts in question on their face impose excise taxes which Congress had the power to levy is so completely established as to require only statement. . . .

The summary which follows embodies the propositions contained in the assignments of error, and the substance of the elaborate argument by which those assignments are deemed to be sustained. Not denying the general power of Congress to impose excise taxes, and conceding that the acts in question, on their face, purport to levy taxes of that character, the propositions are these:

(a) That the power of internal taxation which the Constitution confers on Congress is given to that body for the purpose of raising revenue, and that the tax on artificially colored oleomargarine is void because it is of such an onerous character as to make it manifest that the purpose of Congress in levying it was not to raise revenue but to suppress the manufacture of the taxed article.

(b) The power to regulate the manufacture and sale of oleomargarine being solely reserved to the several States, it follows that the acts in question, enacted by Congress for the purpose of suppressing the manufacture and sale of oleomargarine, when artificially colored, are void, because usurping the reserved power of the States, and therefore exerting an authority not delegated to Congress by the Constitution.

(c) Whilst it is true—so the argument proceeds—that Congress in exerting the taxing power conferred upon it may use all means appropriate to the exercise of such power, a tax which is fixed at such a high rate as to suppress the production of the article taxed, is not a legitimate means to the lawful end, and is therefore beyond the scope of the taxing power.

(d) As the tax levied by the acts which are assailed discriminates against oleomargarine artificially colored, and in favor of butter so colored, and creates an unwarranted and unreasonable distinction between the oleomargarine which is artificially colored and that which is not, and as the necessary operation and effect of the tax is to suppress the manufacture of artificially colored margarine, and to aid the butter industry, therefore the acts are void. And with this proposition in mind it is insisted that wherever the judiciary is called upon to determine whether a power which Congress has exerted is within the authority conferred by the Constitution, the duty is to test the validity of the act, not merely by its face, or to use the words of the argument, "by the label placed upon it by Congress," but by the necessary scope and effect of the assailed enactment. . . .

It is argued if a lawful power may be exerted for an unlawful purpose, and thus by abusing the power it may be made to accomplish a result not intended by the Constitution, all limitations of power must disappear, and the grave function lodged in the judiciary, to confine all the departments within the authority conferred by the Constitution, will be of no avail. This, when reduced to its last analysis, comes to this, that, because a particular department of the government may exert its lawful powers with the object or motive of reaching an end not justified, therefore it becomes the duty of the judiciary to restrain the exercise of a lawful power wherever it seems to the judicial mind that such lawful power has been abused. But this reduces itself to the contention that, under our constitutional system, the abuse by one department of the government of its lawful powers is to be corrected by the abuse of its powers by another department.

The proposition, if sustained, would destroy all distinction between the powers of the respective departments of the government, would put an end to that confidence and respect for each other which it was the purpose of the Constitution to uphold, and would thus be full of danger to the permanence of our institutions. . . .

It is, of course, true, as suggested, that if there be no authority in the judiciary to restrain a lawful exercise of power by another department of the government, where a wrong motive or purpose has impelled to the exertion of the power, that abuses of a power conferred may be temporarily effectual. The remedy for this, however, lies, not in the abuse by the judicial authority of its functions, but in the people, upon whom, after all, under our institutions, reliance must be placed for the correction of abuses committed in the exercise of a lawful power. . . .

The decisions of this court from the beginning lend no support whatever to the assumption that the judiciary may restrain the exercise of lawful power on the assumption that a wrongful purpose or motive has caused the power to be exerted. . . .

It being thus demonstrated that the motive or purpose of Congress in adopting the acts in question may not be inquired into, we are brought to consider the contentions relied upon to show that the acts assailed were beyond the power of Congress, putting entirely out of view all considerations based upon purpose or motive.

Undoubtedly, in determining whether a particular act is within a granted power, its scope and effect are to be considered. Applying this rule to the acts assailed, it is self-evident that on their face they levy an excise tax. That being their necessary scope and operation, it follows that the acts are within the grant of power. The argument to the contrary rests on the proposition that, although the tax be within the power, as enforcing it will destroy or restrict the manufacture of artificially colored oleomargarine, therefore the power to levy the tax did not obtain. This, however, is but to say that the question of power depends, not upon the authority conferred by the Constitution, but upon what may be the consequence arising from the exercise of the lawful authority.

Since . . . the taxing power conferred by the Constitution knows no limits except those expressly stated in that instrument, it must follow, if a tax be within the lawful power, the exertion of that power may not be judicially restrained because of the results to arise from its exercise. . . .

Let us concede, for the sake of argument only, . . . if by the perverted exercise of such power so great an abuse was manifested as to destroy fundamental rights which no free government could consistently violate, that it would be the duty of the judiciary to hold such acts to be void upon the assumption that the Constitution by necessary implication forbade them.

Such concession, however, is not controlling in this case. This follows when the nature of oleomargarine, artificially colored to look like butter, is recalled. . . . [I]t has been conclusively settled by this court that the tendency of that article to deceive the public into buying it for butter is such that the States, may, in the exertion of their police powers, without violating the due process clause of the Fourteenth Amendment, absolutely prohibit the manufacture of the article. It hence results, that even although it be true that the effect of the tax in question is to repress the manufacture of artificially colored oleomargarine, it cannot be said that such repression destroys rights which no free government could destroy, and, therefore, no ground exists to sustain the proposition that the judiciary may invoke an implied prohibition, upon the theory that to do so is essential to save such rights from destruction. And the same considerations dispose of the contention based upon the due process clause of the Fifth Amendment. That provision . . . does not withdraw or expressly limit the grant of power to tax conferred upon Congress by the Constitution. From this it follows, as we have previously declared, the judiciary is without authority to void an act of Congress exerting the taxing power even in a case where to the judicial mind it seems that Congress had in putting such power in motion abused its lawful authority by levying a tax which was unwise or oppressive, or the result of the enforcement of which might be to indirectly affect subjects not within the powers delegated to Congress.

Let us concede that if a case was presented where the abuse of the taxing power was so extreme as to be beyond the principles which we have previously stated, and where it was plain to the judicial mind that the power had been called into play not for revenue but solely for the purpose of destroying rights which could not be rightfully destroyed consistently with the principles of freedom and justice upon which the Constitution rests, that it would be the duty of the courts to say that such an arbitrary act was not merely an abuse of a delegated power, but was the exercise of an authority not conferred. This concession, however, like the one previously made, must be without influence upon the decision of this cause for the reasons previously stated; that is, that the manufacture of artificially colored oleomargarine may be prohibited by a free government without a violation of fundamental rights.

Affirmed.

MR. CHIEF JUSTICE FULLER, MR. JUSTICE BROWN, and MR. JUSTICE PECKHAM dissent.

BAILEY v. DREXEL FURNITURE CO.,
259 U.S. 20 (1922)

After the Supreme Court invalidated the federal Child Labor Act of 1916 in Hammer *v.* Dagenhart *on the ground that Congress exceeded its commerce powers, the opponents of child labor turned to Congress' taxing powers. There were precedents, including* McCray v. United States, *suggesting that the Court would not question Congress' motives, even were they regulatory, when Congress exercised its powers of taxation—as long as the tax on its face was for revenue purposes. Congress thus enacted the Revenue Act of 1919, otherwise known as the Child Labor Tax Law. Under the terms of the legislation, a 10 percent excise tax was to be imposed on the annual net profits of businesses that at any time during the year employed children contrary to the provisions of the act. The standards specified in the Revenue Act were identical to those of the previously invalidated federal Child Labor Act of 1916. Clearly Congress was attempting an end-run around* Hammer v. Dagenhart. *In this case challenging the Revenue Act, the Drexel Furniture Company employed a child under the age of 14 years during 1919. Bailey, the federal collector of internal revenue for the district, notified the furniture company that under the terms of the Revenue Act it was to be assessed 10 percent of its net profit for the year, a sum of over $6000. The company paid the tax under protest and began litigation to recover the tax. The U.S. District Court agreed with the company that the law was unconstitutional, and the federal government took the case directly to the Supreme Court.*

Majority votes: 8
Dissenting votes: 1

MR. CHIEF JUSTICE TAFT delivered the opinion of the Court:

This case presents the question of the constitutional validity of the Child Labor Tax Law. . . .

The law is attacked on the ground that it is a regulation of the employment of child labor in the states—an exclusively state function under the federal Constitution and within the reservations of the Tenth Amendment. It is defended on the ground that it is a mere excise tax levied by the Congress of the United States under its broad power of taxation conferred by section 8, article 1, of the federal Constitution. We must construe the law and interpret the intent and meaning of Congress from the language of the act. The words are to be given their ordinary meaning unless the context shows that they are differently used. Does this law impose a tax with only that incidental restraint and regulation which a tax must inevitably involve? Or does it regulate by the use of the so-called tax as a penalty? If a tax, it is clearly an excise. If it were an excise on a commodity or other thing of value, we might not be permitted under previous decisions of this court to infer solely from its heavy burden that the act intends a prohibition instead of a tax. But this act is more. It provides a heavy exaction for a departure from a detailed and specified course of conduct in business. . . . [A] court must be blind not to see that the so-called tax is imposed to stop the employment of children within the age limits prescribed. Its prohibitory and regulatory effect and purpose are palpable. All others can see and understand this. How can we properly shut our minds to it?

It is the high duty and function of this court in cases regularly brought to its bar to decline to recognize or enforce seeming laws of Congress, dealing with subjects not intrusted to Congress, but left or committed by the supreme law of the land to the control of the states. We cannot avoid the duty, even though it require us to refuse to give effect to legislation designed to promote the highest good. The good sought in unconstitutional legislation is an insidious feature, because it leads citizens and legislators of good purpose to promote it, without thought of the serious breach it will make in the ark of our covenant, or the harm which will come from breaking down recognized standards. In the maintenance of local self-government, on the one hand, and the national power, on the other, our country has been able to endure and prosper for near a century and a half.

Out of a proper respect for the acts of a coordinate branch of the government, this court has gone far to sustain taxing acts as such, even though there has been ground for suspecting, from the weight of the tax, it was intended to destroy its subject. But in the act before us the presumption of validity cannot prevail, because the proof of the contrary is found on the very face of its provisions. Grant the validity of this law, and all that Congress would need to do, hereafter, in seeking to take over to its control any one of the great number of subjects of public interest, jurisdiction of which the states have never parted with, and which are reserved to them by the Tenth Amendment, would be to enact a detailed measure of complete regulation of the subject and enforce it by a so-called tax upon departures from it. To give such magic to the word "tax" would be to break down all constitutional limitation of the powers of Congress and completely wipe out the sovereignty of the states. . . .

The case before us cannot be distinguished from that of *Hammer* v. *Dagenhart*, 247 U.S. 251. Congress there enacted a law to prohibit transportation in interstate commerce of goods made at a factory in which there was employment of children within the same ages and for the same number of hours a day and days in a week as are penalized by the act in this case. . . .

In the case at the bar, Congress in the name of a tax which on the face of the act is a penalty seeks to do the same thing, and the effort must be equally futile.

The analogy of the *Dagenhart Case* is clear. The congressional power over interstate commerce is, within its proper scope, just as complete and unlimited as the congressional power to tax, and the legislative motive in its exercise is just as free from judicial suspicion and inquiry. Yet when Congress threatened to stop interstate commerce in ordinary and necessary commodities, unobjectionable as subjects of transportation, and to deny the same to the people of a state in order to coerce them into compliance with Congress' regulation of state concerns, the court said this was not in fact regulation of interstate commerce, but rather that of state concerns and was invalid. So here the so-called tax is a penalty to coerce people of a state to act as Congress wishes them to act in respect of a matter completely the business of the state government under the federal Constitution. . . .

For the reasons given, we must hold the Child Labor Tax Law invalid and the judgment of the District Court is

Affirmed.

MR. JUSTICE CLARKE dissents.

UNITED STATES v. BUTLER,
297 U.S. 1 (1936)

The Depression struck the farmers especially hard. One of the first New Deal measures passing Congress was the Agricultural Adjustment Act of 1933, which attempted to deal with the problem of how to raise the prices of agricultural commodities in order to increase the farmers' standard of living. The device to accomplish this was a processing tax to be imposed on the processors of the basic agricultural commodities. The tax money collected was to be placed in a special fund for the compensation of farmers who reduced their acreage. Cutting down the supply of agricultural commodities was anticipated to cause the prices to rise, thus benefiting the farmers. This self-financing scheme was thought of as similar to the protective tariff, from which the revenues had been used to subsidize industry and which had been upheld by the Court. In this case Hoosac Mills, a Massachusetts cotton processor, went bankrupt. The receiver, Butler, refused to pay the processing tax on the ground that the tax exceeded Congress' powers; he argued that it was intended to finance a program of agricultural production regulation, and that this could only be done by the states. Thus not only was the taxing power of the federal government challenged but also its spending power. The federal District Court upheld the government, but in the Court of Appeals the government lost. By the time the case came to the Supreme Court, it seemed not only that the constitutionality of the processing tax was at stake, but the concept of the recently enacted social security taxes as well. Would the Court examine Congress' motives or would it accept the processing tax as, on its face, a valid revenue measure? Would the Court challenge the use of Congress' spending power? The Court delivered its answer in early 1936.

Majority votes: 6
Dissenting votes: 3

MR. JUSTICE ROBERTS delivered the opinion of the Court:. . . .

First. . . . The [processing] tax can only be sustained by ignoring the avowed purpose and operation of the act, and holding it a measure merely laying an excise upon processors to raise revenue for the support of government. Beyond cavil the sole object of the legislation is to restore the purchasing power of agricultural products to a parity with that prevailing in an earlier day; to take money from the processor and bestow it upon farmers who will reduce their acreage for the accomplishment of the proposed end, and, meanwhile to aid these farmers during the period required to bring the prices of their crops to the desired level. . . . The exaction cannot be wrested out of its setting, denominated an excise for raising revenue and legalized by ignoring its purpose as a mere instrumentality for bringing about a desired end. To do this would be to shut our eyes to what all others than we can see and understand.

We conclude that the act is one regulating agricultural production; that the tax is a mere incident of such regulation and that the respondents have standing to challenge the legality of the exaction. . . .

Second. The Government asserts that . . . Article 1, § 8 of the Constitution authorizes the contemplated expenditure of the funds raised by the tax. This contention presents the great and controlling question in the case. . . .

There should be no misunderstanding as to the function of this court in such a case. It is sometimes said that the court assumes a power to overrule or control the action of the people's representatives. This is a misconception. The Constitution is the supreme law of the land ordained and established by the people. All legislation must conform to the principles it lays down. When an act of Congress is appropriately challenged in the courts as not conforming to the constitutional mandate the judicial branch of the Government has only one duty,—to lay the article of the Constitution which is invoked beside the statute which is challenged and to decide whether the latter squares with the former. All the court does, or can do, is to announce its considered judgment upon the question. The only power it has, if such it may be called, is the power of judgment. This court neither approves nor condemns any legislative policy. Its delicate and difficult office is to ascertain and declare whether the legislation is in accordance with, or in contravention of, the provisions of the Constitution; and, having done that, its duty ends. . . .

The clause thought to authorize the legislation [Article 1, § 8] . . . confers upon the Congress power "to lay and collect Taxes, Duties, Imposts and Excises, to pay the Debts and provide for the common Defence and general Welfare of the United States. . . ." . . . [T]he Government asserts that warrant is found in this clause for the adoption of the Agricultural Adjustment Act. The argument is that Congress may appropriate and authorize the spending of moneys for the "general welfare"; that the phrase should be liberally construed to cover anything conducive to national welfare; that decision as to what will promote such welfare rests with Congress alone, and the courts may not review its determination; and finally that the appropriation under attack was in fact for the general welfare of the United States. . . .

We are not now required to ascertain the scope of the phrase "general welfare of the United States" or to determine whether an appropriation

in aid of agriculture falls within it. Wholly apart from that question, another principle embedded in our Constitution prohibits the enforcement of the Agricultural Adjustment Act. The act invades the reserved rights of the states. It is a statutory plan to regulate and control agricultural production, a matter beyond the powers delegated to the federal government. The tax, the appropriation of the funds raised and the direction for their disbursement, are but parts of the plan. They are but means to an unconstitutional end.

From the accepted doctrine that the United States is a government of delegated powers, it follows that those not expressly granted, or reasonably to be implied from such as are conferred, are reserved to the states or to the people. To forestall any suggestion to the contrary, the Tenth Amendment was adopted. The same proposition, otherwise stated, is that powers not granted are prohibited. None to regulate agricultural production is given, and therefore legislation by Congress for that purpose is forbidden. . . .

Third. . . . The Government asserts that whatever might be said against the validity of the plan if compulsory, it is constitutionally sound because the end is accomplished by voluntary cooperation. There are two sufficient answers to the contention. The regulation is not in fact voluntary. The farmer, of course, may refuse to comply, but the price of such refusal is the loss of benefits. The amount offered is intended to be sufficient to exert pressure on him to agree to the proposed regulation. The power to confer or withhold unlimited benefits is the power to coerce or destroy. If the cotton grower elects not to accept the benefits, he will receive less for his crops; those who receive payments will be able to undersell him. The result may well be financial ruin. The coercive purpose and intent of the statute is not obscured by the fact that it has not been perfectly successful. It is pointed out that, because there still remained a minority whom the rental and benefit payments were sufficient to induce to surrender their independence of action, the Congress has gone further and, in the Bankhead Cotton Act, used the taxing power in a more directly minatory fashion to compel submission. This progression only serves more fully to expose the coercive purpose of the so-called tax imposed by the present act. It is clear that the Department of Agriculture has properly described the plan as one to keep a non-cooperating minority in line. This is coercion by economic pressure. The asserted power of choice is illusory. . . .

A possible result of sustaining the claimed federal power would be that every business group which thought itself underprivileged might demand that a tax be laid on its vendors or vendees, the proceeds to be appropriated to the redress of its deficiency of income. . . .

Until recently no suggestion of the existence of any such power in the Federal Government has been advanced. The expressions of the framers of the Constitution, the decisions of this court interpreting that instrument, and the writings of great commentators will be searched in vain for any suggestion that there exists in the clause under discussion or elsewhere in the Constitution, the authority whereby every provision and every fair implication from that instrument may be subverted, the independence of the individual states obliterated, and the United States converted into a central government exercising uncontrolled police power in every state of the Union, superseding all local control or regulation of the affairs or concerns of the states.

Hamilton himself, the leading advocate of broad interpretation of the power to tax and to appropriate for the general welfare, never suggested that any power granted by the Constitution could be used for the destruction of local self-government in the states. . . .

The judgment [of the Court of Appeals striking down the Act as unconstitutional] is

Affirmed.

MR. JUSTICE STONE, dissenting:

I think the judgment should be reversed.

The present stress of widely held and strongly expressed differences of opinion of the wisdom of the Agricultural Adjustment Act makes it important, in the interest of clear thinking and sound result, to emphasize at the outset certain propositions which should have controlling influence in determining the validity of the Act. They are:

1. The power of courts to declare a statute unconstitutional is subject to two guiding principles of decision which ought never to be absent from judicial consciousness. One is that courts are concerned only with the power to enact statutes, not with their wisdom. The other is that while unconstitutional exercise of power by the executive and legislative branches of the government is subject to judicial restraint, the only check upon our own exercise of power is our sense of self-restraint. For the removal of unwise laws from the statute books appeal lies not to the courts but to the ballot and to the processes of democratic government.

2. The constitutional power of Congress to levy an excise tax upon the processing of agricultural products is not questioned. The present levy is held invalid, not for any want of power in Congress to lay such a tax to defray public expenditures, including those for the general welfare, but because the use to which its proceeds are put is disapproved.

3. As the present depressed state of agriculture is nationwide in its extent and effects, there is no basis for saying that the expenditure of public money in aid of farmers is not within the specifically granted power of Congress to levy taxes to "provide for the . . . general welfare." The opinion of the Court does not declare otherwise. . . .

It is upon the contention that state power is infringed by purchased regulation of agricultural production that chief reliance [by the Court] is placed. It is insisted that, while the Constitution gives to Congress, in specific and unambiguous terms, the power to tax and spend, the power is subject to limitations which do not find their origin in any express provision of the Constitution and to which other expressly delegated powers are not subject. . . .

Such a limitation is contradictory and destructive of the power to appropriate for the public welfare, and is incapable of practical application. The spending power of Congress is in addition to the legislative power and not subordinate to it. This independent grant of the power of the purse, and its very nature, involving in its exercise the duty to insure expenditure within the granted power, presuppose freedom of selection among divers ends and aims, and the capacity to impose such conditions as will render the choice effective. It is a contradiction in terms to say that there is power to spend for the national welfare, while rejecting any power to impose conditions reasonably adapted to the attainment of the end which alone would justify the expenditure.

The limitation now sanctioned must lead to absurd consequences. The government may give seeds to farmers, but may not condition the gift upon their being planted in places where they are most needed or even planted at all. The government may give money to the unemployed, but may not ask that those who get it shall give labor in return, or even use it to support their families. It may give money to sufferers from earthquake, fire, tornado, pestilence or flood, but may not impose conditions—health precautions designed to prevent the spread of disease, or induce the movement of population to safer or more sanitary areas. All that, because it is purchased regulation infringing state powers, must be left for the states, who are unable or unwilling to supply the necessary relief. . . . Do all its activities collapse because, in order to effect the permissible purpose, in myriad ways the money is paid out upon terms and conditions which influence action of the recipients within the states, which Congress cannot command? The answer would seem plain. If the expenditure is for a national public purpose, that purpose will not be thwarted because payment is on condition which will advance that purpose. The action which Congress induces by payments of money to promote the general welfare, but which it does not command or coerce, is but an incident to a specifically granted power, but a permissible means to a legitimate end. If appropriation in aid of a program of curtailment of agricultural production is constitutional, and it is not denied that it is, payment to farmers on condition that they reduce their crop acreage is constitutional. It is not any the less so because the farmer at his own option promises to fulfill the condition.

That the governmental power of the purse is a great one is not now for the first time announced. . . . The suggestion that it must now be curtailed by judicial fiat because it may be abused by unwise use hardly rises to the dignity of argument. So may judicial power be abused. . . .

A tortured construction of the Constitution is not to be justified by recourse to extreme examples of reckless congressional spending which might occur if courts could not prevent—expenditures which, even if they could be thought to effect any national purpose, would be possible only by action of a legislature lost to all sense of public responsibility. Such suppositions are addressed to the mind accustomed to believe that it is the business of courts to sit in judgment on the wisdom of legislative action. Courts are not the only agency of government that must be assumed to have capacity to govern. Congress and the courts both unhappily may falter or be mistaken in the performance of their constitutional duty. But interpretation of our great charter of government which proceeds on any assumption that the responsibility for the preservation of our institutions is the exclusive concern of any one of the three branches of government, or that it alone can save them from destruction is far more likely, in the long run, "to obliterate the constituent members" of "an indestructible union of indestructible states" than the frank recognition that language, even of a constitution, may mean what it says: that the power to tax and spend in-

cludes the power to relieve a nation-wide economic maladjustment by conditional gifts of money.

MR. JUSTICE BRANDEIS and MR. JUSTICE CARDOZO join in this opinion.

STEWARD MACHINE COMPANY v. DAVIS, 301 U.S. 548 (1937)

A major section of the Social Security Act was challenged here. The case concerned the unemployment compensation provisions that established a federal payroll tax on employers, the proceeds of which were to go into the federal treasury. Were employers to pay taxes into a state unemployment compensation fund, created under a state program that met federal standards, the employers could credit their state payments up to 90 percent of their federal tax. A companion case, Helvering v. Davis, *involved the old age benefits provision of social security. Both provisions were challenged as unconstitutional exercises of the taxing and spending powers of Congress. The Court met these arguments most extensively in the* Steward Machine Company *case, involving an Alabama corporation that sued to recover its federal payroll tax payment.*

Majority votes: 5
Dissenting votes: 4

MR. JUSTICE CARDOZO delivered the opinion of the Court:

The validity of the tax imposed by the Social Security Act on employers of eight or more is here to be determined. . . .

The assault on the statute proceeds on an extended front. Its assailants take the ground that the tax is not an excise; that it is not uniform throughout the United States as excises are required to be; that its exceptions are so many and arbitrary as to violate the Fifth Amendment; that its purpose was not revenue, but an unlawful invasion of the reserved powers of the states; and that the states in submitting to it have yielded to coercion and have abandoned governmental functions which they are not permitted to surrender.

The objections will be considered seriatim with such further explanation as may be necessary to make their meaning clear.

First. The tax, which is described in the statute as an excise, is laid with uniformity throughout the United States as a duty, an impost or an excise upon the relation of employment. . . .

Second. The excise is not invalid under the provisions of the Fifth Amendment by force of its exemptions. . . .

The classifications and exemptions directed by the statute now in controversy have support in considerations of policy and practical convenience that cannot be condemned as arbitrary. . . .

Third. The excise is not void as involving the coercion of the States in contravention of the Tenth Amendment or of restrictions implicit in our federal form of government.

The proceeds of the excise when collected are paid into the Treasury at Washington, and thereafter are subject to appropriation like public moneys generally. No presumption can be indulged that they will be misapplied or wasted. Even if they were collected in the hope or expectation that some other and collateral good would be furthered as an incident, that without more would not make the act invalid. This indeed is hardly questioned. The case for the petitioner is built on the contention that here an ulterior aim is wrought into the very structure of the act, and what is even more important that the aim is not only ulterior, but essentially unlawful. In particular, the 90 per cent credit is relied upon as supporting that conclusion. But before the statute succumbs to an assault upon these lines, two propositions must be made out by the assailant. There must be a showing in the first place that separated from the credit the revenue provisions are incapable of standing by themselves. There must be a showing in the second place that the tax and the credit in combination are weapons of coercion, destroying or impairing the autonomy of the states. The truth of each proposition being essential to the success of the assault, we pass for convenience to a consideration of the second, without pausing to inquire whether there has been a demonstration of the first.

To draw the line intelligently between duress and inducement there is need to remind ourselves of facts as to the problem of unemployment that are now matters of common knowledge. The relevant statistics are gathered in the brief of counsel for the Government. Of the many available figures a few only will be mentioned. During the years 1929 to 1936, when the country was passing through a cyclical depression, the number of the unemployed mounted to unprecedented heights. Often the average was more than 10 million; at times a peak was attained of 16 million or more. Disaster to the breadwinner meant disaster to dependents. Accordingly the roll of the unemployed, itself formidable enough, was only a partial roll of the destitute or needy. The fact developed quickly that the states were unable to give the requisite relief. The prob-

lem had become national in area and dimensions. There was need of help from the nation if the people were not to starve. It is too late today for the argument to be heard with tolerance that in a crisis so extreme the use of the moneys of the nation to relieve the unemployed and their dependents is a use for any purpose narrower than the promotion of the general welfare. . . . The nation responded to the call of the distressed. . . .

In the presence of this urgent need for some remedial expedient, the question is to be answered whether the expedient adopted has overlept the bounds of power. The assailants of the statute say that its dominant end and aim is to drive the state legislatures under the whip of economic pressure into the enactment of unemployment compensation laws at the bidding of the central government. Supporters of the statute say that its operation is not constraint, but the creation of a larger freedom, the states and the nation joining in a cooperative endeavor to avert a common evil. Before Congress acted, unemployment compensation insurance was still, for the most part, a project and no more. . . . But if states had been holding back before the passage of the federal law, inaction was not owing, for the most part, to the lack of sympathetic interest. Many held back through alarm lest, in laying such a toll upon their industries, they would place themselves in a position of economic disadvantage as compared with neighbors or competitors. . . .

The Social Security Act is an attempt to find a method by which all these public agencies may work together to a common end. Every dollar of the new taxes will continue in all likelihood to be used and needed by the nation as long as states are unwilling, whether through timidity or for other motives, to do what can be done at home. At least the inference is permissible that Congress so believed, though retaining undiminished freedom to spend the money as it pleased. On the other hand fulfilment of the home duty will be lightened and encouraged by crediting the taxpayer upon his account with the Treasury of the nation to the extent that his contributions under the laws of the locality have simplified or diminished the problem of relief and the probable demand upon . . . resources. . . .

United States v. *Butler* is cited by petitioner as a decision to the contrary. There a tax was imposed on processors of farm products, the proceeds to be paid to farmers who would reduce their acreage and crops under agreements with the Secretary of Agriculture, the plan of the act being to increase the price of certain farm products by decreasing the quantities produced. . . . The decision was by a divided court, a minority taking the view that the objections were untenable. None of them is applicable to the situation here developed.

(a) The proceeds of the tax in controversy are not earmarked for a special group.

(b) The unemployment compensation law which is a condition of the credit has had the approval of the state and could not be a law without it.

(c) The condition is not linked to an irrevocable agreement, for the state at its pleasure may repeal its unemployment law, terminate the credit, and place itself where it was before the credit was accepted.

(d) The condition is not directed to the attainment of an unlawful end, but to an end, the relief of unemployment, for which nation and state may lawfully cooperate.

Fourth. The statute does not call for a surrender by the states of powers essential to their quasi-sovereign existence. . . .

We are to keep in mind steadily that the conditions to be approved by the Board as the basis for a credit are not provisions of a contract, but terms of a statute, which may be altered or repealed. The state does not bind itself to keep the law in force. It does not even bind itself that the moneys paid into the federal fund will be kept there indefinitely or for any stated time. On the contrary, the Secretary of the Treasury will honor a requisition for the whole or any part of the deposit in the fund whenever one is made by the appropriate officials. . . .

These basic considerations are in truth a solvent of the problem. Subjected to their test, the several objections on the score of abdication are found to be unreal. . . .

The judgment is

Affirmed.

MR. JUSTICE MCREYNOLDS dissented: [omitted]
MR. JUSTICE SUTHERLAND dissented in an opinion joined by MR. JUSTICE VAN DEVANTER: [omitted]
MR. JUSTICE BUTLER, dissenting: [omitted]

FULLILOVE v. KLUTZNICK,
448 U.S. 448 (1980)

The Public Works Employment Act of 1977 contained a "minority business enterprise" (MBE) provision that required that at least 10 percent of the $4 billion appropriation for local public works projects must be used by the state or local grantee to obtain services or supplies from businesses owned by minority group members. The definition of MBE in the legislation is a business in which at least 50 percent is owned by minority group members or in case of a publicly owned business at least 51 percent of the stock is owned by minorities. The minority groups entitled to this 10 percent "set aside" were defined as "citizens of the United States who are Negroes, Spanish-speaking, Orientals, Indians, Eskimos, and Aleuts." The act also contained a proviso whereby the MBE requirement could be administratively waived on a case-by-case basis if infeasibility is demonstrated by a showing that, despite affirmative efforts, the 10 percent MBE participation cannot be achieved. H. Earl Fullilove and other construction contractors and subcontractors filed suit on November 30, 1977, for declaratory and injunctive relief in the United States District Court for the Southern District of New York. Named as defendants were the Secretary of Commerce as the program administrator and the state and the city of New York as actual and potential project grantees. The plaintiffs alleged that they had suffered economically due to enforcement of the 10 percent MBE requirement. The District Court, however, upheld the validity of the program and the United States Court of Appeals for the Second Circuit affirmed. The case came to the Supreme Court in the wake of the Bakke *and* Weber *decisions.*

Majority votes: 6
Dissenting votes: 3

MR. CHIEF JUSTICE BURGER announced the judgment of the Court and delivered an opinion in which MR. JUSTICE WHITE and MR. JUSTICE POWELL joined: . . . .

The clear objective of the MBE [Minority Business Enterprise] provision is disclosed by . . . review of its legislative and administrative background. The program was designed to ensure that, to the extent federal funds were granted under the Public Works Employment Act of 1977, grantees who elect to participate would not employ procurement practices that Congress had decided might result in perpetuation of the effects of prior discrimination which had impaired or foreclosed access by minority businesses to public contracting opportunities. The MBE program does not mandate the allocation of federal funds according to inflexible percentages solely based on race or ethnicity. . . .

In enacting the MBE provision, it is clear that Congress employed an amalgam of its specifically delegated powers. The Public Works Employment Act of 1977, by its very nature, is primarily an exercise of the Spending Power. U.S. Const., Art. I. § 8, cl. 1. This Court has recognized that the power to "provide for the . . . general Welfare" is an independent grant of legislative authority, distinct from other broad congressional powers. Congress has frequently employed the Spending Power to further broad policy objectives by conditioning receipt of federal monies upon compliance by the recipient with federal statutory and administrative directives. This Court has repeatedly upheld against constitutional challenge the use of this technique to induce governments and private parties to cooperate voluntarily with federal policy.

The MBE program is structured within this familiar legislative pattern. The program conditions receipt of public works grants upon agreement by the state or local governmental grantee that at least 10% of the federal funds will be devoted to contracts with minority businesses to the extent this can be accomplished by overcoming barriers to access and by awarding contracts to bona fide MBE's. It is further conditioned to require that MBE bids on these contracts are competitively priced, or might have been competitively priced but for the present effects of prior discrimination. Admittedly, the problems of administering this program with respect to these conditions may be formidable. Although the primary responsibility for ensuring minority participation falls upon the grantee, when the procurement practices of the grantee involve the award of a prime contract to a general or prime contractor, the obligations to assure minority participation devolve upon the contracting party; this is a contractual condition of eligibility for award of the prime contract.

Here we need not explore the outermost limitations on the objectives attainable through such an application of the Spending Power. The reach of the Spending Power, within its sphere, is at least as broad as the regulatory powers of Congress. If, pursuant to its regulatory powers, Congress could have achieved the objectives of the MBE program, then it may do so under the Spending Power. And we have no difficulty perceiving a basis for accomplishing the objectives of the MBE program through the Commerce Power insofar as the program objectives pertain to the action of private contracting parties, and through the power to enforce the equal protection guarantees of the Fourteenth Amendment insofar as the program objectives pertain to the action of state and local grantees. . . .

Any preference based on racial or ethnic criteria must necessarily receive a most searching examina-

tion to make sure that it does not conflict with constitutional guarantees. This case is one which requires, and which has received, that kind of examination. . . . The MBE provision of the Public Works Employment Act of 1977 does not violate the Constitution.

Affirmed.

MR. JUSTICE POWELL, concurring: [omitted]
MR. JUSTICE MARSHALL, with whom MR. JUSTICE BRENNAN and MR. JUSTICE BLACKMUN join, concurring in the judgment:

My resolution of the constitutional issue in this case is governed by the separate opinion I coauthored in *University of California Regents* v. *Bakke*. In my view, the 10% minority set-aside provision . . . passes constitutional muster under the standard announced in that opinion. . . .

MR. JUSTICE STEWART, with whom MR. JUSTICE REHNQUIST joins, dissenting:. . . .

Today, the Court upholds a statute that accords a preference to citizens who are "Negroes, Spanish-speaking, Orientals, Indians, Eskimos, and Aleuts." . . . I think today's decision is wrong for the same reason that *Plessy* v. *Ferguson* was wrong, and I respectfully dissent. . . .

On its face, the minority business enterprise (MBE) provision at issue in this case denies the equal protection of the law. . . . The statute, on its face and in effect, bars a class to which the petitioners belong from having the opportunity to receive a government benefit, and bars the members of that class solely on the basis of their race or ethnic background. This is precisely the kind of law that the guarantees of equal protection forbid. . . .

. . . [E]ven assuming that Congress has the power, under § 5 of the Fourteenth Amendment or some other constitutional provision, to remedy previous illegal racial discrimination, there is no evidence that Congress has in the past engaged in racial discrimination in its disbursement of federal contracting funds. . . .

MR. JUSTICE STEVENS, dissenting:
The 10% set-aside contained in the Public Works Employment Act of 1977 creates monopoly privileges in a $400,000,000 market for a class of investors defined solely by racial characteristics. The direct beneficiaries of these monopoly privileges are the relatively small number of persons within the racial classification who represent the entrepreneurial subclass—those who have, or can borrow, working capital. . . .

Although I do not dispute the validity of the assumption that each of the subclasses identified in the Act has suffered a severe wrong at some time in the past, I cannot accept this slapdash statute as a legitimate method of providing classwide relief. . . .

SOUTH DAKOTA v. DOLE,
438 U.S. 203 (1987)

In 1984 Congress enacted legislation (23 U.S.C. §158) directing the Secretary of Transportation to withhold a percentage of federal highway funds that otherwise would be allocated from States that allowed those under twenty-one years of age to purchase or publicly possess alcoholic beverages. Congress hoped that by this monetary inducement states would raise the drinking age to 21. South Dakota had a lower drinking age and stood to lose 5 percent of the federal funds to which it was otherwise entitled. The state sued Secretary of Transportation Elizabeth Dole in United States District Court seeking a declaratory judgment that the law violates the constitutional limitations on Congress' spending power and also the Twenty-first Amendment. The District Court rejected the claims of the state, and the Court of Appeals for the Eighth Circuit affirmed. The state took the case to the Supreme Court.

Majority Votes: 7
Dissenting votes: 2

CHIEF JUSTICE REHNQUIST delivered the opinion of the Court:. . . .

The Constitution empowers Congress to "lay and collect Taxes, Duties, Imposts, and Excises, to pay the Debts and provide for the common Defence and general Welfare of the United States." Art. I, § 8, cl. 1. Incident to this power, Congress may attach conditions on the receipt of federal funds, and has repeatedly employed the power "to further broad policy objectives by conditioning receipt of federal moneys upon compliance by the recipient with federal statutory and administrative directives." . . .

The spending power is of course not unlimited, but is instead subject to several general restrictions articulated in our cases. The first of these limitations is derived from the language of the Constitution itself: the exercise of the spending power must be in pursuit of "the general welfare." In considering whether a particular expenditure is intended to serve general public purposes, courts should defer substantially to the judgment of Congress. Second, we have required that if Congress desires to condi-

tion the States' receipt of federal funds, it "must do so unambiguously . . ., enabl[ing] the States to exercise their choice knowingly, cognizant of the consequences of their participation." Third, our cases have suggested (without significant elaboration) that conditions on federal grants might be illegitimate if they are unrelated "to the federal interest in particular national projects or programs." . . . Finally, we have noted that other constitutional provisions may provide an independent bar to the conditional grant of federal funds. . . .

South Dakota does not seriously claim that § 158 is inconsistent with any of the first three restrictions mentioned above. We can readily conclude that the provision is designed to serve the general welfare, especially in light of the fact that "the concept of welfare or the opposite is shaped by Congress. . . ." Congress found that the differing drinking ages in the States created particular incentives for young persons to combine their desire to drink with their ability to drive, and that this interstate problem required a national solution. The means it chose to address this dangerous situation were reasonably calculated to advance the general welfare. The conditions upon which States receive the funds, moreover, could not be more clearly stated by Congress. And the State itself, rather than challenging the germaneness of the condition to federal purposes, admits that it "has never contended that the congressional action was . . . unrelated to a national concern in the absence of the Twenty-first Amendment." Indeed, the condition imposed by Congress is directly related to one of the main purposes for which highway funds are expended—safe interstate travel. This goal of the interstate highway system had been frustrated by varying drinking ages among the States. A presidential commission appointed to study alcohol-related accidents and fatalities on the Nation's highways concluded that the lack of uniformity in the States' drinking ages created "an incentive to drink and drive" because "young persons commut[e] to border States where the drinking age is lower." By enacting § 158, Congress conditioned the receipt of federal funds in a way reasonably calculated to address this particular impediment to a purpose for which the funds are expended.

The remaining question about the validity of § 158—and the basic point of disagreement between the parties—is whether the Twenty-first Amendment constitutes an "independent constitutional bar" to the conditional grant of federal funds. Petitioner, relying on its view that the Twenty-first Amendment prohibits *direct* regulation of drinking ages by Congress, asserts that "Congress may not use the spending power to regulate that which it is prohibited from regulating directly under the Twenty-first Amendment." But our cases show that this "independent constitutional bar" limitation on the spending power is not of the kind petitioner suggests. . . .

We have also held that a perceived Tenth Amendment limitation on congressional regulation of state affairs did not concomitantly limit the range of conditions legitimately placed on federal grants. . . .

[W]e think that the language in our earlier opinions stands for the unexceptionable proposition that the power may not be used to induce the States to engage in activities that would themselves be unconstitutional. Thus, for example, a grant of federal funds conditioned on invidiously discriminatory state action or the infliction of cruel and unusual punishment would be an illegitimate exercise of the Congress' broad spending power. But no such claim can be or is made here. Were South Dakota to succumb to the blandishments offered by Congress and raise its drinking age to 21, the State's action in so doing would not violate the constitutional rights of anyone.

Our decisions have recognized that in some circumstances the financial inducement offered by Congress might be so coercive as to pass the point at which "pressure turns into compulsion." Here, however, Congress has directed only that a State desiring to establish a minimum drinking age lower than 21 lose a relatively small percentage of certain federal highway funds. Petitioner contends that the coercive nature of this program is evident from the degree of success it has achieved. We cannot conclude, however, that a conditional grant of federal money of this sort is unconstitutional simply by reason of its success in achieving the congressional objective.

When we consider, for a moment, that all South Dakota would lose if she adheres to her chosen course as to a suitable minimum drinking age is 5% of the funds otherwise obtainable under specified highway grant programs, the argument as to coercion is shown to be more rhetoric than fact. . . .

Here Congress has offered relatively mild encouragement to the States to enact higher minimum drinking ages than they would otherwise choose. But the enactment of such laws remains the prerogative of the States not merely in theory but in fact. Even if Congress might lack the power to impose a national minimum drinking age directly, we conclude that encouragement to state action found in § 158 is a valid use of the spending power. Accordingly, the judgment of the Court of Appeals is

Affirmed.

JUSTICE BRENNAN, dissenting:

I agree with JUSTICE O'CONNOR that regulation of the minimum age of purchasers of liquor falls squarely within the ambit of those powers reserved to the States by the Twenty-first Amendment. Since States possess this constitutional power, Congress can not condition a federal grant in a manner that abridges this right. The Amendment, itself, strikes the proper balance between federal and state authority. I therefore dissent.

JUSTICE O'CONNOR, dissenting: . . .

[A] condition that a State will raise its drinking age to 21 cannot fairly be said to be reasonably related to the expenditure of funds for highway construction. The only possible connection, highway safety, has nothing to do with how the funds Congress has appropriated are expended. Rather than a condition determining how federal highway money shall be expended, it is a regulation determining who shall be able to drink liquor. As such it is not justified by the Spending Power.

Of the other possible sources of congressional authority for regulating the sale of liquor only the Commerce Power comes to mind. But in my view, the regulation of the age of the purchasers of liquor, just as the regulation of the price at which liquor may be sold, falls squarely within the scope of those powers reserved to the States by the Twenty-first Amendment. . . . Because 23 U.S.C. § 158 cannot be justified as an exercise of any power delegated to the Congress, it is not authorized by the Constitution. The Court errs in holding it to be the law of the land, and I respectfully dissent.

Chapter

10

Federalism

DECISIONAL TRENDS

In a broad sense, the history of federalism in the United States is the history of the country. In that history the Supreme Court of the United States has played a leading role. It is the Supreme Court that has determined the powers of the national government under the Constitution of the United States and the powers that are left to the states. It is the Supreme Court that has determined what relationships the states may have with one another consistent with the federal Constitution. Many of the cases in this book are federalism cases in the sense that they deal with the division of power between the federal government and the states. This is particularly true in the realm of commerce but extends to other areas of law as well. The bottom line of federalism in the United States is the recognition of federal supremacy in powers accorded the national government by the Constitution. This was asserted by the Supreme Court in one of its early cases, *Ware* v. *Hylton,* 3 Dallas 199 (1796). The Court also made clear in the landmark case of **McCulloch** v. **Maryland** that Congress' powers were to be broadly construed and that the states were not to burden, retard, or impede their exercise.

An area of federalism the Court dealt with early in its history concerned the reach of federal judicial power over the states. As was seen in **Chisholm** v. **Georgia** (chap. 6), the Supreme Court assumed jurisdiction in a suit against a state by someone from another state. This decision, of course, provided the impetus for the passage of the Eleventh Amendment, thereby withdrawing jurisdiction of the federal courts from suits "commenced or prosecuted" against a state by citizens of another state or of a foreign country. But the matter did not end there. In **Cohens** v. **Virginia** the Court took an appeal of a criminal conviction that was technically before the Court in the form of a suit against a state. But the Court ruled that the Eleventh Amendment only prevents an individual from *initiating* a legal action against a state without its consent, *not* from appealing the outcome of a legal action initiated by the state. The Court went even further in **Osborn** v. **The Bank of the United States** when it ruled that a suit may be brought against a state official personally for carrying out an unconstitutional state "law," and that this was not a suit against a state. Later Courts reaffirmed this; see, e.g., *Ex Parte Young,* 209 U.S. 123 (1908). But more recently (see, for example, *Green* v. *Mansour,* 474 U.S. 64 [1985]) the Court considered certain suits by citizens of a state against a state official to be a suit against a state, forbidden by the Eleventh Amendment. With the *Cohens* and *Osborn* decisions, the Marshall Court in effect negated much of the intended effect of the Eleventh Amendment. What did remain in the Eleventh Amendment was not even explicitly stated in it but rather assumed—that a state may not be named in a suit and sued without its consent by one of its own citizens (see *Hans* v. *Louisiana,* 134 U.S. 1 [1890]). More recent Eleventh Amendment decisions protecting the states from being sued include *Welch* v. *State Dept. of Highways and Public Transp.,* 483 U.S. 468 (1987), and *Dellmuth* v. *Muth,* 109 S. Ct. 2397 (1989).

The record of the Taney and Civil War Courts was one of forceful assertion of federal judicial supremacy vis-à-vis the state courts but a considerably more restrained and cautious assertion vis-à-vis other branches and levels of government. In *Swift* v. *Tyson,* 16 Peters 1 (1842), the Court, in an opinion by Justice Story, ruled that the federal courts were not bound by state court precedents in deciding cases falling within the Court's diversity jurisdiction. This meant that identical issues would be decided differently, depending on whether they were heard in federal or state courts, and the litigants could choose to bring their cases to federal court if they saw federal common law more favorable to their interests than existing state law. Here was, in effect, a clash between national and state judiciaries. In the context of the broader nation-state cleavage that dominated American politics through the Civil War, the Court came down

strongly on the national (federal judicial) supremacy side. From then on, until close to a century later in *Erie Railroad Co.* v. *Tompkins,* 304 U.S. 64 (1938), when the Court overruled *Swift* v. *Tyson,* the federal courts developed a body of federal common law in the various areas of civil law coming to the courts under their diversity of citizenship jurisdiction.

While the Supreme Court has historically been vigorous in rejecting state judicial challenges to federal court power (also recall **Martin** v. **Hunter's Lessee** [chap. 6]), the Court *has* recognized the legitimacy of the state court decisions based solely on state law that grants more rights than under federal law and which does not conflict with federal law. Such state court decisions must be respected by the federal courts because there are independent and adequate state grounds for the decision. An example of such a state court decision being honored by the Supreme Court is **Pruneyard Shopping Center** v. **Robins** (chap. 13).

It is the realm of congressional power versus state authority that contains the bulk of the Court's federalism jurisprudence. Solicitude for state sovereignty seemed to underscore the Court's decision in **The Collector** v. **Day,** which also proved to be a tax break granted the state judiciaries by the Supreme Court. The burning issue of the 1960s, the civil rights of black Americans, was considered in the voting rights case of **South Carolina** v. **Katzenbach,** which required the Court to delineate the scope of federal power vis-à-vis state power in this area. But it is the commerce cases or those in which the commerce power of Congress is invoked that we find the most impressive and continuing line of constitutional law cases concerning a specific congressional power that also raises federalism issues.

As will be recalled from chapter 8, **Gibbons** v. **Ogden** gave a liberal interpretation to Congress' commerce powers and established the rule that when Congress invokes its commerce power, it is superior to the actions of the states. But the Court did not answer the question as to what happens when Congress has not acted. In **Willson** v. **Blackbird Creek Marsh Company** and in **Mayor of New York** v. **Miln,** the Court sidestepped the commerce issue and instead developed the police powers doctrine that allowed the states to act as an exercise of the state's inherent power to protect the public health, safety, and welfare. This was not considered a regulation of commerce. Little over a century after *Miln* was decided, the Court in **Edwards** v. **California** confronted another instance of a state trying to exclude "undesirables" from coming into the state. The Court's decision here is, in moral terms, light-years ahead of the *Miln* decision, but the underlying federalism question before the Court was remarkably similar, namely, May a state unilaterally act to prevent the influx of certain kinds of people (or goods) when that action has national consequences in the commerce sphere?

We saw in chapter 8 how the Court dealt with the exercise of the commerce power by the states and the federal government. In recent years, the Court or at least several of the justices have recognized that the federal government has for most intents and purposes overwhelmed the states in terms of the exercise of power and the assumption of responsibility for problems with a nationwide scope. In part this is unavoidable because of the structure of our national economy. But the net effect has been a serious erosion of state sovereignty. It was this that the majority had in mind when it handed down in 1976 its decision in **National League of Cities** v. **Usery.** What made this decision so remarkable was that the 5–4 majority defied Court precedent by invalidating a provision of the Fair Labor Standards Act. In so doing, the Court for the first time since 1937 ruled that Congress exceeded its commerce powers, thereby encroaching upon the powers reserved to the states under the Tenth Amendment. Congress may not, said the Court, apply federal standards (in-

cluding wages and overtime provisions) to state employees performing essential state functions, for this goes to the heart of state sovereignty. Yet this decision turned out to be an isolated attempt by the Court to restore states sovereignty at the expense of the exercise of Congress' commerce powers. In a series of subsequent decisions, the Court made it clear that the Court was not challenging federal economic regulation under the commerce clause. Finally, in 1985, by a 5–4 vote (with Justice Blackmun switching sides to the new majority), the Court overturned *National League of Cities* with its decision in **Garcia** v. **San Antonio Metropolitan Transit Authority.** Justice Blackmun in his opinion of the Court pointed out that Congress' commerce power cannot be checked by ambiguous, open-ended conceptions of state sovereignty created by the judiciary such as "traditional governmental functions." Rather, it is up to the national political process, which has built into it protection of state sovereign interests, to determine the limits of the federal commerce power. As with the decisions constituting the Court's about-face in the late 1930s, the Court in *Garcia* was, in effect, announcing that there were virtually no constitutional limits on the exercise of Congress' commerce powers.

In general, where state regulation results in an advantage for the state or for in-state businesses at the expense of other states or out-of-state based businesses, or if the regulation is deemed a burden on interstate commerce, the Court has taken a dim view of such state legislation. **New Energy Co. of Indiana** v. **Limbach** is a relatively recent example from the Rehnquist Court. But if the state regulation was not in direct conflict with an act of Congress and was primarily an inspection or safety law or providing remedies for damages, the Court has been more generous. Similarly, a state sales tax on a business carrying on interstate activities within the state was ruled constitutional in *Complete Auto Transit, Inc.* v. *Brady,* 430 U.S. 274 (1977).

Federalism concerns not only the division of power between the federal government and the states but also the relationships among the states. Article 4, Sections 1 and 2 of the Constitution, along with certain provisions in Articles 1 and 3, state the minimum constitutional requirements of interstate relationships. Article 4, Section 1, specifies that "full faith and credit shall be given in each State to the public acts, records, and judicial proceedings of every other State." Congress is authorized to implement this and in fact did so by legislation enacted in 1790. However, Supreme Court decisions interpreted the full faith and credit guarantee in the realm of civil law so as to undermine it and the implementing act of Congress. The key decision was *McElmoyle* v. *Cohen,* 13 Peters 312 (1839), in which the Court ruled that the guarantee was not intended to turn one state into an automatic enforcer of another's civil law to the detriment of the first state's own laws. Rather, when the judgment of a court of state A is being pursued in state B, there must be a new case brought under the laws of state B and subject to the remedies of state B. It is also necessary for state B to have jurisdiction over the parties to the suit; otherwise there may be a violation of due process (*McGee* v. *International Life Insurance Co., 355* U.S. 220 [1957]). Thus, the full faith and credit guarantee does not mean automatic enforcement of one state's laws and court judgments in another state, particularly if the other state's law conflicts with the first state's.

Article 4, Section 2, contains the requirement that persons charged with crime in one state who escape to another shall be returned to the state in which the alleged crime was committed when the governor of the state so requests. Congress in 1793 enacted legislation implementing this provision. However, the Supreme Court in *Kentucky* v. *Dennison,* 24 Howard 66 (1861), ruled that the governor of the state to which the accused fled, while having a legal duty to return (or extradite) the person, cannot be compelled by the federal courts to do so. Although in practice it was unusual for a governor to refuse an extradition request, sometimes that in fact occurred, as we see in **Puerto Rico** v. **Branstad,** a case in which the Court took the opportunity to overrule *Kentucky* v. *Dennison.*

Article 4, Section 2, contains the guarantee that "the Citizens of each State shall be entitled to all Privileges and Immunities of Citizens in the several States." This privilege and immunities clause came into play in the Court's discussion of **Dred Scott** v. **Sandford** and **The Slaughterhouse Cases** (chap. 6). A more direct and recent discussion of this guarantee is found in **Supreme Court of Virginia** v. **Friedman** concerning residency requirements for admission to the state bar.

THE IMPACT OF THE COURT'S DECISIONS

Table 10.1 summarizes the impact of most of the Court decisions concerning federalism that are reprinted following the table.

Table 10.1 THE IMPACT OF SELECTED COURT DECISIONS, FEDERALISM CASES

Case	Year	Impact on Parties	Short-Run Impact	Long-Run Impact
McCulloch v. Maryland	1819	Bank of the United States wins and is able to stay in business for duration of its charter.	Unpopular decision. Several states push for constitutional amendment to permit states to bar U.S. Bank. Ohio defies McCulloch ruling, leading to Osborn case.	Implied powers of Congress theory developed. Federal supremacy strengthened.
Cohens v. Virginia	1821	Cohen brothers' convictions upheld (fined $100 + $31.50 court costs).	Virginia officials/politicians outraged at Court's assumption of jurisdiction. Movement in states and Congress to repeal Sec. 25.	Eleventh Amendment weakened because states are forced to appear before Supreme Court in appeals from state court decisions.
Osborn v. The Bank of the United States	1824	Bank victorious. Money had been earlier returned. Osborn personally unaffected.	States' rights forces outraged at another decision strengthening federal and judicial supremacy at the expense of the states.	Eleventh Amendment undermined because states could be sued by having plaintiff sue state official personally and not technically the state. Increase in Court business also resulted.
The Collector v. Day	1871	Judge Day recovers $61.50.	Decision is conciliatory to the states and signals the Court's interest in rejuvenating state sovereignty at a time of national government ascendancy.	Provides precedent for interpreting Tenth Amendment so as to favor the states as opposed to the national government.
South Carolina v. Katzenbach	1966	South Carolina voter registration and participation comes under federal supervision.	Black registration and participation in the electoral process increases (as does registration of poor whites). Blacks elected to public office.	White politicians court black voters. Overt racism disappears from mainstream electoral process.
Willson v. Blackbird Creek Marsh Company	1829	Unknown if Marsh Company collected damages.	Favorably received by states' rights forces and Jacksonians.	Although provided Court with doctrinal flexibility in commerce area, decision also added uncertainty as to extensiveness of Congress' powers.

Case	Year			
Mayor of New York v. Miln	1837	New York state successful; subsequently enacts even stronger anti-alien legislation that is eventually invalidated in The Passenger Cases (1849). Miln fails to recover $7500 fine.	Encourages states to regulate influx of aliens; provides continued uncertainty as to extensiveness of states' commerce powers; decision seen as favoring states at expense of federal power.	Eventually the federal government assumed responsibility over immigration. Nation versus state controversy in the commerce area subsequently resolved.
Edwards v. California	1941	Edwards' misdemeanor conviction record expunged.	No adverse economic impact because America's involvement in World War II began within two weeks of decision, and war economy provided jobs for all.	Important precedent for freedom of movement or travel of American citizens.
National League of Cities v. Usery	1976	State and local governments able to decide for themselves the minimum wage and overtime to be paid to essential state and local employees.	Symbolic victory for state sovereignty, but little impact beyond saving the states below the federal standards some amount of money.	Decision overturned in 1985.
Garcia v. San Antonio Metropolitan Transit Authority	1985	Employees win. Federal overtime standards prevail.	In response to clamor from states and localities, Congress enacts legislation in November 1985 allowing public employers to provide time-and-a-half compensatory time off for workers who put in overtime instead of requiring pay for overtime. In all other respects public employees covered by Fair Labor Standards Act.	Not discernible at this time.

McCULLOCH v. MARYLAND, 4 WHEATON 316 (1819)

The Second Bank of the United States was chartered by Congress in 1816. It had branch banks in various states including Maryland. Although at the time it was chartered there seemed to be widespread recognition of its need, the bank was soon to become unpopular, for its operations were thought to be mismanaged, if not corrupt, and to have contributed to economic problems in Maryland (and elsewhere). Maryland enacted a law that, in effect, taxed the bank. McCulloch, the cashier of the Baltimore branch of the bank, refused to comply and a suit arose in the state courts. With the cooperation of state and federal officials considering this to be a test case, McCulloch appealed to the Supreme Court, arguing that the Maryland statute was an unconstitutional interference with a valid congressional entity. The state officials, wanting the Court to decide the issues, willingly appeared to argue that the bank was not constitutional in that it was not "necessary and proper" to carry out any of the enumerated powers of Congress stipulated in Article 1, Section 8, of the Constitution. Maryland further argued that as a sovereign state it had the power to tax and that its tax on the branch of the United States Bank was an essential exercise of state sovereignty. The case was to turn on the meaning of the "necessary and proper" clause of Article 1, Section 8, Clause 18, and confronted the Court with two conflicting theories: (1) the broad constructionist theory of interpreting the necessary-and-proper clause, which meant acceptance of a doctrine of Congress' implied powers; or (2) the strict constructionist theory, which had its roots in the Jeffersonian theory of the 1790s and considered the clause to be a limit on the powers of Congress, encompassing only those means that were absolutely essential for the carrying out of the enumerated powers.

Votes: Unanimous

MR. CHIEF JUSTICE MARSHALL delivered the opinion of the Court:

In the case now to be determined, the defendant, a sovereign state, denies the obligation of a law enacted by the legislature of the Union, and the plaintiff, on his part, contests the validity of an act which has been passed by the legislature of that state. The constitution of our country, in its most interesting and vital parts, is to be considered; the conflicting powers of the government of the Union and of its members, as marked in that constitution, are to be discussed; and an opinion given, which may essentially influence the great operations of the government. No tribunal can approach such a question without a deep sense of its importance, and of the awful responsibility involved in its decision. But it must be decided peacefully, or remain a source of hostile legislation, perhaps, of hostility of a still more serious nature; and if it is to be decided, by this tribunal alone can the decision be made. On the Supreme Court of the United States has the constitution of our country devolved this important duty.

The first question made in the cause is—has congress power to incorporate a bank?. . . .

The power now contested was exercised by the first congress elected under the present constitution. The bill for incorporating the Bank of the United States did not steal upon an unsuspecting legislature, and pass unobserved. Its principle was completely understood, and was opposed with equal zeal and ability. After being resisted, first, in the fair and open field of debate, and afterwards, in the executive cabinet, with as much persevering talent as any measure has ever experienced, and being supported by arguments which convinced minds as pure and as intelligent as this country can boast, it became a law. The original act was permitted to expire, but a short experience of the embarrassments to which the refusal to revive it exposed the government, convinced those who were most prejudiced against the measure of its necessity, and induced the passage of the present law. It would require no ordinary share of intrepidity, to assert that a measure adopted under these circumstances, was a bold and plain usurpation, to which the constitution gave no countenance. These observations belong to the cause; but they are not made under the impression, that, were the question entirely new, the law would be found irreconcilable with the constitution.

In discussing this question, the counsel for the state of Maryland have deemed it of some importance, in the construction of the constitution, to consider that instrument, not as emanating from the people, but as the act of sovereign and independent states. The powers of the general government, it has been said, are delegated by the states, who alone are truly sovereign; and must be exercised in subordination to the states, who alone possess supreme dominion. It would be difficult to sustain this proposition. The convention which framed the constitution was indeed elected by the state legislatures. But the instrument, when it came from their hands, was a mere proposal, without obligation, or pretensions to it. It was reported to the then existing congress of the United States, with a request that it might "be submitted to a convention of delegates, chosen in each state by the people thereof, under the recommendation of its legislature, for their assent and ratification.'' This mode of proceeding was adopted; and by the convention, by congress, and by the state legislatures, the instrument was submitted to the *people*. They acted upon it in the only manner in which they can act safely, effectively and wisely, on such a subject, by assembling in convention. It is true, they assembled in their several states—and where else should they have assembled? No political dreamer was ever wild enough to think of breaking down the lines which separate the states, and of compounding the American people into one common mass. Of consequence, when they act, they act in their states. But the measures they adopt do not, on that account, cease to be the measures of the people themselves, or become the measures of the state governments.

From these conventions, the constitution derives its whole authority. The government proceeds directly from the people; is ''ordained and established,'' in the name of the people; and is declared to be ordained, ''in order to form a more perfect union, establish justice, insure domestic tranquility, and secure the blessings of liberty to themselves and to their posterity.'' The assent of the states, in their sovereign capacity, is implied, in calling a convention, and thus submitting that instrument to the people. But the people were at perfect liberty to accept or reject it; and their act was final. It required not the affirmance, and could not be negatived, by the state governments. The constitution, when thus adopted, was of complete obligation, and bound the state sovereignties.

It has been said, that the people had already surrendered all their powers to the state sovereignties, and had nothing more to give. But, surely, the question whether they may resume and modify the powers granted to government, does not remain to be settled in this country. Much more might the legitimacy of the general government be doubted, had it been created by the states. The powers delegated to the state sovereignties were to be exercised by themselves, not by a distinct and independent sovereignty, created by themselves. To the formation of a league, such as was the confederation, the state sovereignties were certainly competent. But when ''in order to form a more perfect union,'' it was deemed necessary to change this alliance into an effective government, possessing great and sovereign powers, and acting directly on the people, the necessity of referring it to the people, and of deriving its powers directly from them, was felt and acknowledged by all. The government of the Union, then (whatever may be the influence of this fact on the case), is, emphatically and truly, a government of the people. In form, and in substance, it emanates from them. Its powers are granted by them, and are to be exercised directly on them, and for their benefit.

This government is acknowledged by all, to be one of enumerated powers. The principle, that it can exercise only the powers granted to it . . . is now universally admitted. But the question respecting the extent of the powers actually granted, is perpetually arising, and will probably continue to arise, so long as our system shall exist. In discussing these questions, the conflicting powers of the general and state governments must be brought into view, and the supremacy of their respective laws, when they are in opposition, must be settled.

If any one proposition could command the universal assent of mankind, we might expect it would be this—that the government of the Union, though limited in its powers, is supreme within its sphere of action. This would seem to result, necessarily, from its nature. It is the government of all; its powers are delegated by all; it represents all, and acts for all. Though any one state may be willing to control its operations, no state is willing to allow others to control them. The nation, on those subjects on which it can act, must necessarily bind its component parts. But this question is not left to mere reason: the people have, in express terms, decided it, by saying, ''this constitution, and the laws of the United States, which shall be made in pursuance thereof,'' ''shall be the supreme law of the land,'' and by requiring that the members of the state legislatures, and the officers of the executive and the judicial departments of the states, shall take the oath of fidelity to it. The government of the United States, then, though limited in its powers, is supreme; and its laws, when made in pursuance of the constitution, form the supreme law of the land, ''anything in the constitution or laws of any state to the contrary notwithstanding.''

Among the enumerated powers, we do not find that of establishing a bank or creating a corporation. But there is no phrase in the instrument which, like the articles of confederation, excludes incidental or implied powers; and which requires that everything granted shall be expressly and minutely described. Even the 10th amendment, which was framed for the purpose of quieting the excessive jealousies which had been excited, omits the word ''expressly,'' and declares only, that the powers ''not delegated to the United States, nor prohibited to the states, are reserved to the states or the people;'' thus leaving the question whether the particular power, which may become the subject of contest, has been delegated to the one government, or prohibited to the other, to depend on a fair construction of the whole instrument. The men who drew and adopted this amendment had experienced the embarrassments resulting from the insertion of this word in the articles of confederation, and probably omitted it, to avoid those embarrassments. A constitution, to contain an accurate detail of all the subdivisions of which its great powers will admit, and of all the means by which they may be carried into execution, would partake of the prolixity of a legal code, and could scarcely be embraced by the human mind. It would, probably, never be understood by the public. Its nature, therefore, requires, that only its great outlines should be marked, its important objects designated, and the minor ingredients which compose those objects, be deduced from the nature of the objects themselves. That this idea was entertained by the framers of the American constitution, is not only to be inferred from the nature of the instrument, but from the language. Why else were some of the limitations, found in the 9th section of the 1st article, introduced? It is also, in some degree, warranted, by their having omitted to use any restrictive term which might prevent its receiving a fair and just interpretation. In considering this question, then, we must never forget that it is a *constitution* we are expounding.

Although, among the enumerated powers of government, we do not find the word "bank" or "incorporation," we find the great powers, to lay and collect taxes; to borrow money; to regulate commerce; to declare and conduct a war; and to raise and support armies and navies. The sword and the purse, all the external relations, and no inconsiderable portion of the industry of the nation, are intrusted to its government. It can never be pretended, that these vast powers draw after them others of inferior importance, merely because they are inferior. Such an idea can never be advanced. But it may with great reason be contended, that a government, intrusted with such ample powers, on the due execution of which the happiness and prosperity of the nation so vitally depends, must also be intrusted with ample means for their execution. The power being given, it is the interest of the nation to facilitate its execution. . . . The government which has a right to do an act, and has imposed on it, the duty of performing that act, must, according to the dictates of reason, be allowed to select the means; and those who contend that it may not select any appropriate means, that one particular mode of effecting the object is excepted, take upon themselves the burden of establishing that exception. . . .

But the constitution of the United States has not left the right of congress to employ the necessary means, for the execution of the powers conferred on the government, to general reasoning. To its enumeration of powers is added, that of making "all laws which shall be necessary and proper, for carrying into execution the foregoing powers, and all other powers vested by this constitution, in the government of the United States, or in any department thereof." The counsel for the state of Maryland have urged various arguments, to prove that this clause, though, in terms, a grant of power, is not so, in effect; but is really restrictive of the general right, which might otherwise be implied, of selecting means for executing the enumerated powers. In support of this proposition, they have found it necessary to contend, that this clause was inserted for the purpose of conferring on congress the power of making laws. That, without it, doubts might be entertained, whether congress could exercise its powers in the form of legislation.

But could this be the object for which it was inserted? . . . Could it be necessary to say, that a legislature should exercise legislative powers, in the shape of legislation? After allowing each house to prescribe its own course of proceeding, after describing the manner in which a bill should become a law, would it have entered into the mind of a single member of the convention, that an express power to make laws was necessary, to enable the legislature to make them? That a legislature, endowed with legislative powers, can legislate, is a proposition too self-evident to have been questioned.

But the argument on which most reliance is placed, is drawn from that peculiar language of this clause. Congress is not empowered by it to make all laws, which may have relation to the powers conferred on the government, but such only as may be *necessary and proper* for carrying them into execution. The word *necessary* is considered as controlling the whole sentence, and as limiting the right to pass laws for the execution of the granted powers, to such as are indispensable, and without which the power would be nugatory. That it excludes the choice of means, and leaves to congress, in each case, that only which is most direct and simple.

Is it true, that this is the sense in which the word "necessary" is always used? Does it always import an absolute physical necessity, so strong, that one thing to which another may be termed necessary, cannot exist without that other? We think it does not. If reference be had to its use, in the common affairs of the world, or in approved authors, we find that it frequently imports no more than that one thing is convenient, or useful, or essential to another. To employ the means necessary to an end, is generally understood as employing any means calculated to produce the end, and not as being confined to those single means, without which the end would be entirely unattainable. Such is the character of human language, that no word conveys to the mind, in all situations, one single definite idea; and nothing is more common than to use words in a figurative sense. Almost all compositions contain words, which, taken in their rigorous sense, would convey a meaning different from that which is obviously intended. It is essential to just construction, that many words which import something excessive, should be understood in a more mitigated sense—in that sense which common usage justifies. The word "necessary" is of this description. It has not a fixed character, peculiar to itself. It admits of all degrees of comparison; and is often connected with other words, which increase or diminish the impression the mind receives of the urgency it imports. A thing may be necessary, very necessary, absolutely or indispensably necessary. To no mind would the same idea be conveyed by these several phrases. The comment on the word is well illustrated by the passage cited at the bar, from the 10th section of the 1st article of the constitution. It is, we think, impossible to compare the sentence which prohibits a state from laying "imposts, or duties on imports or exports, except what may be *absolutely* necessary for executing its inspection laws," with that which authorizes congress "to make all laws which shall be necessary and proper for carrying into execution" the powers of the general government, without feeling a conviction, that the convention understood itself to change materially the meaning of the word "necessary," by prefixing the word "absolutely." This word, then, like others, is used in various senses; and, in its construction, the subject, the context, the intention of the person using them, are all to be taken into view.

Let this be done in the case under consideration. The subject is the execution of those great powers on which the welfare of a nation essentially depends. It must have been the intention of those who gave these powers, to insure, so far as human prudence could insure, their beneficial execution. This could not be done, by confiding the choice of means to such narrow limits as not to leave it in the power of congress to adopt any which might be appropriate, and which were conducive to the end. This provision is made in a constitution, intended to endure for ages to come, and consequently, to be adapted to the various *crises* of human affairs. To have prescribed the means by which government

should, in all future time, execute its powers, would have been to change, entirely, the character of the instrument, and give it the properties of a legal code. It would have been an unwise attempt to provide, by immutable rules, for exigencies which, if foreseen at all, must have been seen dimly, and which can be best provided for as they occur. To have declared, that the best means shall not be used, but those alone, without which the power given would be nugatory, would have been to deprive the legislature of the capacity to avail itself of experience, to exercise its reason, and to accommodate its legislation to circumstances. . . .

But the argument which most conclusively demonstrates the error of the construction contended for by the counsel for the state of Maryland, is founded on the intention of the convention, as manifested in the whole clause. . . . We think so for the following reasons: 1st. The clause is placed among the powers of congress, not among the limitations on those powers. 2nd. Its terms purport to enlarge, not to diminish the powers vested in the government. It purports to be an additional power, not a restriction on those already granted. No reason has been, or can be assigned, for thus concealing an intention to narrow the discretion of the national legislature, under words which purport to enlarge it. The framers of the constitution wished its adoption, and well knew that it would be endangered by its strength, not by its weakness. Had they been capable of using language which would convey to the eye one idea, and, after deep reflection, impress on the mind, another, they would rather have disguised the grant of power, than its limitation. If, then, their intention had been, by this clause, to restrain the free use of means which might otherwise have been implied, that intention would have been inserted in another place, and would have been expressed in terms resembling these. "In carrying into execution the foregoing powers, and all others," &c., "no laws shall be passed but such as are necessary and proper." Had the intention been to make this clause restrictive, it would unquestionably have been so in form as well as in effect. . . .

We admit, as all must admit, that the powers of the government are limited, and that its limits are not to be transcended. But we think the sound construction of the constitution must allow to the national legislature that discretion, with respect to the means by which the powers it confers are to be carried into execution, which will enable that body to perform the high duties assigned to it, in the manner most beneficial to the people. Let the end be legitimate, let it be within the scope of the constitution, and all means which are appropriate, which are plainly adapted to that end, which are not prohibited, but consist with the letter and spirit of the constitution, are constitutional. . . .

After the most deliberate consideration, it is the unanimous and decided opinion of this court, that the act to incorporate the Bank of the United States is a law made in pursuance of the constitution, and is a part of the supreme law of the land.

The branches, proceeding from the same stock, and being conducive to the complete accomplishment of the object, are equally constitutional. It would have been unwise, to locate them in the charter, and it would be unnecessarily inconvenient, to employ the legislative power in making those subordinate arrangements. The great duties of the bank are prescribed; those duties required branches; and the bank itself may, we think, be safely trusted with the selection of places where those branches shall be fixed; reserving always to the government the right to require that a branch shall be located where it may be deemed necessary.

It being the opinion of the court, that the act incorporating the bank is constitutional; and that the power of establishing a branch in the state of Maryland might be properly exercised by the bank itself, we proceed to inquire—

Whether the state of Maryland may, without violating the constitution, tax that branch? That the power of taxation is one of vital importance; that it is retained by the states; that it is not abridged by the grant of a similar power to the government of the Union; that it is to be concurrently exercised by the two governments—are truths which have never been denied. But such is the paramount character of the constitution, that its capacity to withdraw any subject from the action of even this power, is admitted. The states are expressly forbidden to lay any duties on imports or exports, except what may be absolutely necessary for executing their inspection laws. If the obligation of this prohibition must be conceded—if it may restrain a state from the exercise of its taxing power on imports and exports—the same paramount character would seem to restrain, as it certainly may restrain, a state from such other exercise of this power, as is in its nature incompatible with, and repugnant to, the constitutional laws of the Union. A law, absolutely repugnant to another, as entirely repeals that other as if express terms of repeal were used.

On this ground, the counsel for the bank place its claim to be exempted from the power of a state to tax its operations. There is no express provision for the case, but the claim has been sustained on a principle which so entirely pervades the constitution, is so intermixed with the materials which compose it, so interwoven with its web, so blended with its texture, as to be incapable of being separated from it, without rending it into shreds. This great principle is, that the constitution and the laws made in pursuance thereof are supreme; that they control the constitution and laws of the respective states, and cannot be controlled by them. From this, which may be almost termed an axiom, other propositions are deduced as corollaries, on the truth or error of which, and on their application to this case, the cause has been supposed to depend. These are, 1st. That a power to create implies a power to preserve: 2d. That a power to destroy, if wielded by a different hand, is hostile to, and incompatible with these powers to create and to preserve: 3d. That where this repugnancy exists, that authority which is supreme must control, not yield to that over which it is supreme.

These propositions, as abstract truths, would, perhaps, never be controverted. Their application to this case, however, has been denied; and both in maintaining the affirmative and the negative, a splendor of eloquence, and strength of argument, seldom, if ever, surpassed, have been displayed.

The power of congress to create, and of course, to continue, the bank, was the subject of the preceding part of this opinion; and is no longer to be considered as questionable. That the power of taxing it by the states may be exercised so as to destroy it, is too obvious to be denied. But taxation is said to be an absolute power, which acknowledges no other limits than those expressly prescribed in the constitution, and like sovereign power of every other description, is intrusted to the discretion of those who use it. But the very terms of this argument admit, that the sovereignty of the state, in the article of taxation itself, is subordinate to, and may be controlled by the constitution of the United States. . . .

. . . That the power to tax involves the power to destroy; that the power to destroy may defeat and render useless the power to create; that there is a plain repugnance in conferring on one government a power to control the constitutional measures of another, which other, with respect to those very measures, is declared to be supreme over that which exerts the control, are propositions not to be denied. But all inconsistencies are to be reconciled by the magic of the word *confidence*. Taxation, it is said, does not necessarily and unavoidably destroy. To carry it to the excess of destruction, would be an abuse, to presume which, would banish that confidence which is essential to all government. But is this a case of confidence? Would the people of any one state trust those of another with a power to control the most insignificant operations of their state government? We know they would not. Why, then, should we suppose, that the people of any one state should be willing to trust those of another with a power to control the operations of a government to which they have confided their most important and most valuable interests? In the legislature of the Union alone, are all represented. The legislature of the Union alone, therefore, can be trusted by the people with the power of controlling measures which concern all, in the confidence that it will not be abused. This, then, is not a case of confidence, and we must consider it as it really is.

If we apply the principle for which the state of Maryland contends, to the constitution, generally, we shall find it capable of changing totally the character of that instrument. We shall find it capable of arresting all the measures of the government, and of prostrating it at the foot of the states. The American people have declared their constitution and the laws made in pursuance thereof, to be supreme; but this principle would transfer the supremacy, in fact, to the states. If the states may tax one instrument, employed by the government in the execution of its powers, they may tax any and every other instrument. They may tax the mail; they may tax the mint; they may tax patent-rights; they may tax the papers of the customhouse; they may tax judicial process; they may tax all the means employed by the government, to an excess which would defeat all the ends of government. This was not intended by the American people. They did not design to make their government dependent on the states. . . .

It has also been insisted, that, as the power of taxation in the general and state governments is acknowledged to be concurrent, every argument which would sustain the right of the general government to tax banks chartered by the states, will equally sustain the right of the states to tax banks chartered by the general government. But the two cases are not on the same reason. The people of all the states have created the general government, and have conferred upon it the general power of taxation. The people of all the states, and the states themselves, are represented in congress, and, by their representatives, exercise this power. When they tax the chartered institutions of the states, they tax their constituents; and these taxes must be uniform. But when a state taxes the operation of the government of the United States, it acts upon institutions created, not by their own constituents, but by people over whom they claim no control. It acts upon the measures of a government created by others as well as themselves, for the benefit of oth-

ers in common with themselves. The difference is that which always exists, and always must exist, between the action of the whole on the part, and the action of a part on the whole—between the laws of a government declared to be supreme, and those of a government which, when in opposition to those laws, is not supreme. . . .

The court has bestowed on this subject its most deliberate consideration. The result is a conviction that the states have no power, by taxation or otherwise, to retard, impede, burden, or in any manner control, the operations of the constitutional laws enacted by congress to carry into execution the powers vested in the general government. This is, we think, the unavoidable consequence of that supremacy which the constitution has declared. We are unanimously of opinion, that the law passed by the legislature of Maryland, imposing a tax on the Bank of the United States, is unconstitutional and void.

This opinion does not deprive the states of any resources which they originally possessed. It does not extend to a tax paid by the real property of the bank, in common with the other real property within the state, nor to a tax imposed on the interest which the citizens of Maryland may hold in this situation, in common with other property of the same description throughout the state. But this is a tax on the operations of the bank and is, consequently, a tax on the operation of an instrument employed by the government of the Union to carry its powers into execution. Such a tax must be unconstitutional.

[Reversed]

COHENS v. VIRGINIA, 6 WHEATON 264 (1821)

Congress passed legislation authorizing the District of Columbia to conduct a lottery that would raise funds to be used for civic improvements. The state of Virginia had a law forbidding lotteries and the sale of lottery tickets. The Cohen brothers went into Virginia and violated the state law by selling District of Columbia lottery tickets. The brothers were found guilty and fined $100 and, in addition, $31.50 for court costs. In their defense they argued that the federal law authorizing the lottery made their actions legal and that the Virginia law cannot be held applicable to the sale of District of Columbia lottery tickets. The Cohens appealed to the United States Supreme Court and the Court accepted the case. The state authorities asserted that

the Court had no jurisdiction in the case as it was
clearly a suit against a state forbidden by the Elev-
enth Amendment.

Votes: Unanimous

MR. CHIEF JUSTICE MARSHALL delivered the opinion of the Court:. . . .

The questions presented to the court . . . are of
great magnitude, and may be truly said vitally to
affect the Union. . . . The [state] maintains that the
constitution of the United States has provided no
tribunal for the final construction of itself, or of the
laws or treaties of the nation; but that this power
may be exercised in the last resort by the courts of
every state of the Union, and that the constitution,
laws, and treaties, may receive as many construc-
tions as there are states; and that this is not a mischief, or, if a mischief, is irremediable. . . .

If such be the constitution, it is the duty of the
court to bow with respectful submission to its provisions. If such be not the constitution, it is equally
the duty of this court to say so; and to perform that
task which the American people have assigned to
the judicial department.

1st. The first question to be considered is,
whether the jurisdiction of this court is excluded by
the character of the parties, one of them being a
state, and the other a citizen of that state?

The second section of the third article of the
constitution defines the extent of the judicial power
of the United States. Jurisdiction is given to the
courts of the Union in two classes of cases. In the
first, their jurisdiction depends on the character of
the cause, whoever may be the parties. This class
comprehends "all cases in law and equity arising
under this constitution, the laws of the United
States, and treaties made, or which shall be made,
under their authority." This clause extends the jurisdiction of the court to all the cases described,
without making in its terms any exception whatever, and without any regard to the condition of the
party. If there be any exception, it is to be implied
against the express words of the article.

In the second class, the jurisdiction depends entirely on the character of the parties. In this are
comprehended "controversies between two or
more states, between a state and citizens of another
state," "and between a state and foreign states, citizens or subjects." If these be the parties, it is entirely unimportant what may be the subject of controversy. Be it what it may, these parties have a
constitutional right to come into the courts of the
Union. . . .

One of the express objects, then, of which the

judicial department was established, is the decision
of controversies between states, and between a
state and individuals. The mere circumstance, that
a state is a party, gives jurisdiction to the court.
How, then, can it be contended, that the very same
instrument, in the very same section, should be so
construed as that this same circumstance should
withdraw a case from the jurisdiction of the court,
where the constitution or laws of the United States
are supposed to have been violated? The constitution gave to every person having a claim upon a
state, a right to submit his case to the court of the
nation. However unimportant his claim might be,
however little the community might be interested in
its decision, the framers of our constitution thought
it necessary, for the purposes of justice, to provide
a tribunal as superior to influence as possible, in
which that claim might be decided. Can it be imagined, that the same persons considered a case involving the constitution of our country and the maj-
esty of the laws—questions in which every
American citizen must be deeply interested—as
withdrawn from this tribunal, because a state is a
party? . . .

We think, then, that, as the constitution originally stood, the appellate jurisdiction of this court,
in all cases arising under the constitution, laws, or
treaties of the United States, was not arrested by
the circumstance that a state was a party.

This leads to a consideration of the 11th
amendment. . . .

The first impression made on the mind by this
amendment is, that it was intended for those cases,
and for those only, in which some demand against
a state is made by an individual in the courts of the
Union. If we consider the causes to which it is to be
traced, we are conducted to the same conclusion. A
general interest might well be felt in leaving to a
state the full power of consulting its convenience in
the adjustment of its debts, or of other claims upon
it; but no interest could be felt in so changing the
relations between the whole and its parts, as to strip
the government of the means of protecting, by the
instrumentality of its courts, the constitution and
laws from active violation. . . .

To commence a suit, is to demand something by
the institution of process in a court of justice; and
to prosecute the suit, is, according to the common
acceptation of language, to continue that demand.
By a suit commenced by an individual against a
state, we should understand process sued out by
that individual against the state, for the purpose of
establishing some claim against it by the judgment
of a court; and the prosecution of that suit is its
continuance. Whatever may be the stages of its

progress, the actor is still the same. . . . The object of the amendment was not only to prevent the commencement of future suits, but to arrest the prosecution of those which might be commenced when this article should form a part of the constitution. It therefore embraces both objects; and its meaning is, that the judicial power shall not be construed to extend to any suit which may be commenced, or which, if already commenced, may be prosecuted against a state by the citizen of another state. If a suit, brought in one court, and carried by legal process to a supervising court, be a continuation of the same suit, then this suit is not commenced nor prosecuted against a state. It is clearly in its commencement the suit of a state against an individual, which suit is transferred to this court, not for the purpose of asserting any claim against the state, but for the purpose of asserting a constitutional defense against a claim made by a state. . . .

Under the judiciary act, the effect of a writ of error is simply to bring the record into court, and submit the judgment of the inferior tribunal to reexamination. It does not in any manner act upon the parties; it acts only on the record. It removes the record into the supervising tribunal. Where, then, a state obtains a judgment against an individual, and the court, rendering such judgment, overrules a defense set up under the constitution or laws of the United States, the transfer of this record into the Supreme Court, for the sole purpose of inquiring whether the judgment violates the constitution or laws of the United States, can with no propriety, we think, be denominated a suit commenced or prosecuted against the state whose judgment is so far re-examined. Nothing is demanded from the state. No claim against it of any description is asserted or prosecuted. The party is not to be restored to the possession of anything. Essentially, it is an appeal on a single point; and the defendant who appeals from a judgment rendered against him, is never said to commence or prosecute a suit against the plaintiff who has obtained the judgment. . . .

It is, then, the opinion of the court, that the defendant who removes a judgment rendered against him by a state court into this court, for the purpose of re-examining the question, whether that judgment be in violation of the constitution or laws of the United States, does not commence or prosecute a suit against the state, whatever may be its opinion where the effect of the writ may be to restore the party to the possession of a thing which he demands.

. . . If this writ of error be a suit in the sense of the 11th amendment, it is not a suit commenced or prosecuted "by a citizen of another state, or by a citizen or subject of any foreign state." It is not, then, within the amendment, but is governed entirely by the constitution as originally framed, and we have already seen, that in its origin, the judicial power was extended to all cases arising under the constitution or laws of the United States, without respect to parties.

2d. The second objection to the jurisdiction of the court is, that its appellate power cannot be exercised, in any case, over the judgment of a state court. . . .

We think that in a government acknowledgedly supreme, with respect to objects of vital interest to the nation, there is nothing inconsistent with sound reason, nothing incompatible with the nature of government, in making all its departments supreme, so far as respects those objects, and so far as is necessary to their attainment. The exercise of the appellate power over those judgments of the state tribunals which may contravene the constitution or laws of the United States, is, we believe, essential to the attainment of those objects. . . .

Let the nature and objects of our Union be considered; let the great fundamental principles, on which the fabric stands, be examined; and we think the result must be, that there is nothing so extravagantly absurd in giving to the court of the nation the power of revising the decisions of local tribunals on questions which affect the nation, as to require that words which import this power should be restricted by a forced construction. The question, then, must depend on the words themselves; and on their construction we shall be the more readily excused for not adding to the observations already made, because the subject was fully discussed and exhausted in the case of *Martin* v. *Hunter*. . . .

The counsel for the state of Virginia have, in support of this motion, urged many arguments of great weight against the application of the act of Congress to such a case as this; but those arguments go to the construction of the constitution, or of the law, or of both; and seem, therefore, rather calculated to sustain their cause upon its merits, than to prove a failure of jurisdiction in the court.

After having bestowed upon this question the most deliberate consideration of which we are capable, the court is unanimously of opinion, that the objections to its jurisdiction are not sustained, and that the motion ought to be overruled.

. . . It now comes on to be decided on the question whether the Borough Court of Norfolk, in overruling the defense set up under the act of Congress, has misconstrued that act. . . .

The subject on which Congress was employed

when framing this act was a local subject; it was not the establishment of a lottery, but the formation of a separate body for the management of the internal affairs of the city [of Washington, D.C.], for its internal government, for its police. Congress must have considered itself as delegating to this corporate body powers for these objects, and for these objects solely. In delegating those powers, therefore, it seems reasonable to suppose that the mind of the legislature was directed to the city alone, to the action of the being they were creating within the city, and not to any extraterritorial operations. . . .

[I]n this case no lottery is established by law, no control is exercised by the government over any which may be established. The lottery emanates from a corporate power. The corporation may authorize, or not authorize it, and may select the purposes to which the proceeds are to be applied. This corporation is a being intended for local objects only. All its capacities are limited to the city. This, as well as every other law it is capable of making, is a by-law, and, from its nature, is only co-extensive with the city. . . .

Whether we consider the general character of a law incorporating a city, the objects for which such law is usually made, or the words in which this particular power is conferred, we arrive at the same result. The corporation was merely empowered to authorize the drawing of lotteries; and the mind of Congress was not directed to any provision for the sale of the tickets beyond the limits of the corporation. That subject does not seem to have been taken into view. It is the unanimous opinion of the court, that the law cannot be construed to embrace it.

Judgment affirmed.

OSBORN v. THE BANK OF THE UNITED STATES, 9 WHEATON 738 (1824)

The state of Ohio levied a $50,000 tax on each branch of the congressionally chartered United States Bank in Ohio. When the Court shortly thereafter ruled in McCulloch v. Maryland *that a similar tax by Maryland was unconstitutional, the Ohio officials decided to ignore the Court decision and to enforce the state law. The United States Bank then went to the United States Circuit Court and received an injunction prohibiting Ralph Osborn, the Ohio State Auditor, whose office had responsibility for collecting the tax, from collecting it. Osborn defied the injunction and personnel from his office forcibly seized funds from the bank. The bank sued Osborn and his colleagues for damages and they were ordered to repay the amount seized. Osborn*

and his colleagues appealed to the Supreme Court, arguing that the federal circuit court did not have jurisdiction in the case, because the suit was, in effect, an action commenced against the state of Ohio in violation of the Eleventh Amendment.

Majority votes: 6
Dissenting votes: 1

MR. CHIEF JUSTICE MARSHALL delivered the opinion of the Court:. . . .

The question . . . is, whether the constitution of the United States has provided a tribunal which can peacefully and rightfully protect those who are employed in carrying into execution the laws of the Union, from the attempts of a particular state to resist the execution of those laws.

The state of Ohio denies the existence of this power, and contends that no preventive proceedings whatever, or proceedings against the very property which may have been seized by the agent of a state, can be sustained against such agent, because they would be substantially against the state itself, in violation of the 11th amendment of the constitution.

That the courts of the Union cannot entertain a suit brought against a state by an alien, or the citizen of another state, is not to be controverted. Is a suit, brought against an individual for any cause whatever, a suit against a state, in the sense of the constitution? . . .

Do the provisions, then, of the American constitution, respecting controversies to which a state may be a party, extend, on a fair construction of that instrument, to cases in which the state is not a party on the record? . . .

It may, we think, be laid down as a rule which admits of no exception, that, in all cases where jurisdiction depends on the party, it is the party named in the record. Consequently, the 11th amendment, which restrains the jurisdiction granted by the constitution over suits against states, is, of necessity, limited to those suits in which a state is a party on the record. The amendment has its full effect, if the constitution be construed as it would have been construed, had the jurisdiction of the court never been extended to suits brought against a state, by the citizens of another state, or by aliens.

The state not being a party on the record, and the court having jurisdiction over those who are parties on the record, the true question is, not one of jurisdiction, but whether, in the exercise of its jurisdiction, the court ought to make a decree against the defendants; whether they are to be considered as having a real interest, or as being only nominal parties. . . . The parties must certainly have a real interest in the case, since their personal responsibility is acknowledged, and, if denied, could be demonstrated.

It was proper, then, to make a decree against the defendants in the Circuit Court, if the law of the state of Ohio be repugnant to the constitution, or to a law of the United States made in pursuance thereof, so as to furnish no authority to those who took, or to those who received, the money for which this suit was instituted.

Is that law constitutional?

This point was argued with great ability, and decided by this court, after mature and deliberate consideration, in the case of *McCulloch* v. *The State of Maryland*. . . . The whole opinion of the court, in the case of *McCulloch* v. *The State of Maryland*, is founded on, and sustained by, the idea that the bank is an instrument which is "necessary and proper for carrying into effect the powers vested in the government of the United States." . . .

Why is it that Congress can incorporate or create a bank? This question was answered in the case of *McCulloch* v. *The State of Maryland*. It is an instrument which is "necessary and proper" for carrying on the fiscal operations of government. . . . To tax its faculties, its trade and occupation, is to tax the bank itself. To destroy or preserve the one, is to destroy or preserve the other. . . .

It being then shown, we think conclusively, that the defendants could derive neither authority nor protection from the act which they executed, and that this suit is not against the state of Ohio within the view of the constitution, the state being no party on the record, the only real question in the cause is, whether the record contains sufficient matter to justify the court in pronouncing a decree against the defendants? That this question is attended with great difficulty, has not been concealed or denied. But when we reflect that the defendants, Osborn and Harper, are incontestably liable for the full amount of the money taken out of the bank; that the defendant, Currie, is also responsible for the sum received by him, it having come to his hands with full knowledge of the unlawful means by which it was acquired; that the defendant, Sullivan, is also responsible for the sum specifically delivered to him, with notice that it was the property of the bank, unless the form of having made an entry on the books of the treasury can countervail the fact, that it was, in truth, kept untouched, in a trunk, by itself, as a deposit, to await the event of the pending suit respecting it; we may lay it down

as a proposition, safely to be affirmed, that all the defendants in the cause were liable in an action at law for the amount of this decree. . . .

We think, then, that there is no error in the decree of the Circuit Court for the district of Ohio, so far as it directs restitution of [the money] . . . which was taken out of the bank unlawfully. . . .

[Affirmed]

MR. JUSTICE JOHNSON [dissenting]:. . . .

I cannot persuade myself . . . that . . . Congress ever could have intended to vest in the Bank of the United States the right of suit to the extent here claimed. And, notwithstanding the confidence with which this point has been argued, an examination of the terms of the act, and a consideration of them with a view to the context, will be found to leave it by no means a clear case, that such is the legal meaning of the act of incorporation. . . .

[W]hat state of facts have we exhibited here? Making a person, makes a case; and thus, a government which cannot exercise jurisdiction unless an alien or citizen of another state be a party, makes a party which is neither alien nor citizen, and then claims jurisdiction because it has made a case. . . .

Upon the whole, I feel compelled to dissent from the court, on the point of jurisdiction; and this renders it unnecessary for me to express my sentiments on the residue of the points in the cause. . . .

THE COLLECTOR v. DAY, 11 WALLACE 113 (1871)

In 1864 Congress enacted an income tax of 5 percent on income over $1000. It again did so in 1865, 1866, and 1867. Under these statutes, the collector of internal revenue for Massachusetts assessed the sum of $61.50 upon the salary of J. M. Day, a Massachusetts state judge of the Court of Probate and Insolvency for Barnstable County. This assessment covered the years 1866 and 1867. Day paid the tax under protest and brought suit in federal court to recover the $61.50. Day was successful and the government brought the case to the Supreme Court. The Court was faced with the question of the nature of state sovereignty and the permissible reach of the national government's power of taxation.

Majority votes: 7
Dissenting votes: 1

MR. JUSTICE NELSON delivered the opinion of the Court:

The case presents the question whether or not it

is competent for Congress, under the Constitution of the United States, to impose a tax upon the salary of a judicial officer of a State? . . .

It is a familiar rule of construction of the Constitution of the Union, that the sovereign powers vested in the State governments by their respective constitutions, remained unaltered and unimpaired, except so far as they were granted to the government of the United States. That the intention of the framers of the Constitution in this respect might not be misunderstood, this rule of interpretation is expressly declared in the tenth article of the amendments, namely: "The powers not delegated to the United States are reserved to the States respectively, or, to the people." The government of the United States, therefore, can claim no powers which are not granted to it by the Constitution, and the powers actually granted must be such as are expressly given, or given by necessary implication.

The general government, and the States, although both exist within the same territorial limits, are separate and distinct sovereignties, acting separately and independently of each other, within their respective spheres. The former in its appropriate sphere is supreme; but the States within the limits of their powers not granted, or, in the language of the tenth amendment, "reserved," are as independent of the general government as that government within its sphere is independent of the States. . . .

Two of the great departments of the government, the executive and legislative, depend upon the exercise of the powers, or upon the people of the States. The Constitution guarantees to the States a republican form of government, and protects each against invasion or domestic violence. Such being the separate and independent condition of the States in our complex system, as recognized by the Constitution, and the existence of which is so indispensable, that, without them, the general government itself would disappear from the family of nations, it would seem to follow, as a reasonable, if not a necessary consequence, that the means and instrumentalities employed for carrying on the operations of their governments, for preserving their existence, and fulfilling the high and responsible duties assigned to them in the Constitution, should be left free and unimpaired, should not be liable to be crippled, much less defeated by the taxing power of another government, which power acknowledges no limits but the will of the legislative body imposing the tax. And, more especially, those means and instrumentalities which are the creation of their sovereign and reserved rights, one of which is the establishment of the judicial department, and the appointment of officers to administer their laws.

Without this power, and the exercise of it, we risk nothing in saying that no one of the States under the form of government guaranteed by the Constitution could long preserve its existence. A despotic government might. We have said that one of the reserved powers was that to establish a judicial department; it would have been more accurate, and in accordance with the existing state of things at the time, to have said the power to maintain a judicial department. All of the thirteen States were in the possession of this power, and had exercised it at the adoption of the Constitution; and it is not pretended that any grant of it to the general government is found in that instrument. It is, therefore, one of the sovereign powers vested in the States by their constitutions, which remained unaltered and unimpaired, and in respect to which the State is as independent of the general government as that government is independent of the States.

The supremacy of the general government, therefore, so much relied on in the argument of the counsel for the plaintiff in error, in respect to the question before us, cannot be maintained. The two governments are upon an equality. . . . [I]n respect to the reserved powers, the State is as sovereign and independent as the general government. And if the means and instrumentalities employed by the government to carry into operation the powers granted to it are, necessarily, and for the sake of self-preservation, exempt from taxation by the States, why are not those of the States depending upon their reserved powers, for like reasons, equally exempt from Federal taxation? Their unimpaired existence in the one case is as essential as in the other. It is admitted that there is no express provision in the Constitution that prohibits the general government from taxing the means and instrumentalities of the States, nor is there any prohibiting the States from taxing the means and instrumentalities of that government. In both cases the exemption rests upon necessary implication, and is upheld by the great law of self-preservation; as any government, whose means employed in conducting its operations, if subject to the control of another and distinct government, can exist only at the mercy of that government. Of what avail are these means if another power may tax them at discretion? . . .

Judgment affirmed.

MR. JUSTICE BRADLEY, dissenting:

I dissent from the opinion of the court in this case, because, it seems to me that the general government has the same power of taxing the income of officers of the State governments as it has of taxing that of its own officers. It is the common government of all alike; and every citizen is presumed to trust his own government in the matter of taxation. No man ceases to be a citizen of the United States by being an officer under the State government. I cannot accede to the doctrine that the general government is to be regarded as in any sense foreign or antagonistic to the State governments, their officers, or people; nor can I agree that a presumption can be admitted that the general government will act in a manner hostile to the existence or functions of the State governments, which are constituent parts of the system or body politic forming the basis on which the general government is founded. The taxation by the State governments of the instruments employed by the general government in the exercise of its powers, is a very different thing. Such taxation involves an interference with the powers of a government in which other States and their citizens are equally interested with the State which imposes the taxation. In my judgment, the limitation of the power of taxation in general government, which the present decision establishes, will be found very difficult [to] control. Where are we to stop in enumerating the functions of the State governments which will be interfered with by Federal taxation? If a State incorporates a railroad to carry out its purposes of internal improvement, or a bank to aid its financial arrangements, reserving, perhaps, a percentage on the stock or profits, for the supply of its own treasury, will the bonds or stock of such an institution be free from Federal taxation? How can we now tell what the effect of this decision will be? I cannot but regard it as founded on a fallacy, and that it will lead to mischievous consequences. I am as much opposed as any one can be to any interference by the general government with the just powers of the State governments. But no concession of any of the just powers of the general government can easily be recalled. I, therefore, consider it my duty to at least record my dissent when such concession appears to be made. An extended discussion of the subject would answer no useful purpose.

[Chief Justice Chase did not participate in this decision.]

SOUTH CAROLINA v. KATZENBACH, 383 U.S. 301 (1966)

This case was taken by the Supreme Court under its original jurisdiction. The facts of the case are stated in the opinion of the Court. A major question in this case was at what point, when federally guaranteed rights are concerned and are found to have been consistently abridged, the national government can move into a domain previously administered by a state. And what is the reach of the national government's power under such circumstances? Can state sovereignty be, in effect, forfeited?

Majority votes: 8
Dissenting votes: 1

MR CHIEF JUSTICE WARREN delivered the opinion of the Court:

By leave of the Court, 382 U.S. 898, South Carolina has filed a bill of complaint, seeking a declaration that selected provisions of the Voting Rights Act of 1965 violate the Federal Constitution, and asking for an injunction against enforcement of these provisions by the Attorney General. Original jurisdiction is founded on the presence of a controversy between a State and a citizen of another State under Art. III, §2, of the Constitution. Because no issues of fact were raised in the complaint, and because of South Carolina's desire to obtain a ruling prior to its primary elections in June 1966, we . . . expedited our hearing of the case.

Recognizing that the questions presented were of urgent concern to the entire country, we invited all of the States to participate in this proceeding as friends of the Court. A majority responded by submitting or joining in briefs on the merits, some supporting South Carolina [five southern States] and others the Attorney General [21 States]. Seven of these States also requested and received permission to argue the case orally at our hearing. . . .

The Voting Rights Act was designed by Congress to banish the blight of racial discrimination in voting, which has infected the electoral process in parts of our country for nearly a century. The Act creates stringent new remedies for voting discrimination where it persists on a pervasive scale, and in addition the statute strengthens existing remedies for pockets of voting discrimination elsewhere in the country. Congress assumed the power to prescribe these remedies from §2 of the Fifteenth Amendment, which authorizes the National Legislature to effectuate by ''appropriate'' measures the constitutional prohibition against racial discrimination in voting. We hold that the sections of the Act which are properly before us are an appropriate means for carrying out Congress' constitutional responsibilities and are consonant with all other provisions of the Constitution. We therefore deny South Carolina's request that enforcement of these sections of the Act be enjoined. . . .

Two points emerge vividly from the voluminous legislative history of the Act contained in the committee hearings and floor debates. First: Congress felt itself confronted by an insidious and pervasive evil which had been perpetuated in certain parts of our country through unremitting and ingenious defiance of the Constitution. Second: Congress concluded that the unsuccessful remedies which it had prescribed in the past would have to be replaced by sterner and more elaborate measures in order to satisfy the clear commands of the Fifteenth Amendment. . . .

Congress exercised its authority under the Fifteenth Amendment in an inventive manner when it enacted the Voting Rights Act of 1965. First: The measure prescribes remedies for voting discrimination which go into effect without any need for prior adjudication. This was clearly a legitimate response to the problem, for which there is ample precedent under other constitutional provisions. Congress had found that case-by-case litigation was inadequate to combat widespread and persistent discrimination in voting, because of the inordinate amount of time and energy required to overcome the obstructionist tactics invariably encountered in these lawsuits. After enduring nearly a century of systematic resistance to the Fifteenth Amendment, Congress might well decide to shift the advantage of time and inertia from the perpetrators of the evil to its victims. . . .

Second: The Act intentionally confines these remedies to a small number of States and political subdivisions which in most instances were familiar to Congress by name. This, too, was a permissible method of dealing with the problem. Congress had learned that substantial voting discrimination presently occurs in certain sections of the country, and it knew no way of accurately forecasting whether the evil might spread elsewhere in the future. In acceptable legislative fashion, Congress chose to limit its attention to the geographic areas where immediate action seemed necessary. The doctrine of the equality of States, invoked by South Carolina, does not bar this approach, for that doctrine applies only to the terms upon which States are admitted to the Union, and not to the remedies for local evils which have subsequently appeared.

COVERAGE FORMULA.

We now consider the related question of whether the specific States and political subdivisions within §4 (b) of the Act were an appropriate target for the new remedies. South Carolina contends that the coverage formula is awkwardly designed in a number of respects and that it disregards various local conditions which have nothing to do with racial discrimination. These arguments, however, are largely beside the point. Congress began work with reliable evidence of actual voting discrimination in a great majority of the States and political subdivisions affected by the new remedies of the Act. The formula eventually evolved to describe these areas was relevant to the problem of voting discrimination, and Congress was therefore entitled to infer a significant danger of the evil in the few remaining States and political subdivisions covered by §4 (b) of the Act. No more was required to justify the application to these areas of Congress' express powers under the Fifteenth Amendment. . . .

The areas, . . . for which there was evidence of actual voting discrimination, share two characteristics incorporated by Congress into the coverage formula: the use of tests and devices for voter registration, and a voting rate in the 1964 presidential election at least 12 points below the national average. Tests and devices are relevant to voting discrimination because of their long history as a tool for perpetrating the evil; a low voting rate is pertinent for the obvious reason that widespread disenfranchisement must inevitably affect the number of actual voters. Accordingly, the coverage formula is rational in both practice and theory. It was therefore permissible to impose the new remedies on the few remaining States and political subdivisions covered by the formula, at least in the absence of proof that they have been free of substantial voting discrimination in recent years. . . .

SUSPENSION OF TESTS.

. . . The record shows that in most of the States covered by the Act, including South Carolina, various tests and devices have been instituted with the purpose of disenfranchising Negroes, have been framed in such a way as to facilitate this aim, and have been administered in a discriminatory fashion for many years. Under these circumstances, the Fifteenth Amendment has clearly been violated. . . .

The Act suspends literacy tests and similar devices for a period of five years from the last occurrence of substantial voting discrimination. This was a legitimate response to the problem, for which there is ample precedent in Fifteenth Amendment cases. . . . Underlying the response was the feeling that States and political subdivisions which had been allowing white illiterates to vote for years could not sincerely complain about "dilution" of their electorates through the registration of Negro illiterates. Congress knew that continuance of the tests and devices in use at the present time, no matter how fairly administered in the future, would freeze the effect of past discrimination in favor of unqualified white registrants. Congress permissibly rejected the alternative of requiring a complete re-registration of all voters, believing that this would be too harsh on many whites who had enjoyed the franchise for their entire adult lives.

REVIEW OF NEW RULES.

The Act suspends new voting regulations pending scrutiny by federal authorities to determine whether their use would violate the Fifteenth Amendment. This may have been an uncommon exercise of congressional power, as South Carolina contends, but the Court has recognized that exceptional conditions can justify legislative measures not otherwise appropriate. See *Home Bldg. & Loan Assn.* v. *Blaisdell; Wilson* v. *New*. Congress knew that some of the States covered by §4 (b) of the Act had resorted to the extraordinary stratagem of contriving new rules of various kinds for the sole purpose of perpetuating voting discrimination in the face of adverse federal court decrees. Congress had reason to suppose that these States might try similar maneuvers in the future in order to evade the remedies for voting discrimination contained in the Act itself. Under the compulsion of these unique circumstances, Congress responded in a permissibly decisive manner. . . .

FEDERAL EXAMINERS.

The Act authorizes the appointment of federal examiners to list qualified applicants who are thereafter entitled to vote, subject to an expeditious challenge procedure. This was clearly an appropriate response to the problem, closely related to remedies authorized in prior cases. In many of the political subdivisions covered by §4 (b) of the Act, voting officials have persistently employed a variety of procedural tactics to deny Negroes the franchise, often in direct defiance or evasion of federal court decrees. Congress realized that merely to suspend voting rules which have been misused or are subject to misuse might leave this localized evil undisturbed. . . .

After enduring nearly a century of widespread resistance to the Fifteenth Amendment, Congress has marshalled an array of potent weapons against the evil, with authority in the Attorney General to employ them effectively. Many of the areas directly affected by this development have indicated their

willingness to abide by any restraints legitimately imposed upon them. We here hold that the portions of the Voting Rights Act properly before us are a valid means for carrying out the commands of the Fifteenth Amendment. Hopefully, millions of non-white Americans will now be able to participate for the first time on an equal basis in the government under which they live. . . .

The bill of complaint is

Dismissed.

MR. JUSTICE BLACK, concurring [in part] and dissenting [in part]: . . .

Though . . . I agree with most of the Court's conclusions, I dissent from its holding that every part of §5 of the Act is constitutional. Section 4 (a), to which §5 is linked, suspends for five years all literacy tests and similar devices in those States coming within the formula of §4 (b). Section 5 goes on to provide that a State covered by §4 (b) can in no way amend its constitution or laws relating to voting without first trying to persuade the Attorney General of the United States or the Federal District Court for the District of Columbia that the new proposed laws do not have the purpose and will not have the effect of denying the right to vote to citizens on account of their race or color. I think this section is unconstitutional . . .

. . . Section 5, by providing that some of the States cannot pass state laws or adopt state constitutional amendments without first being compelled to beg federal authorities to approve their policies, so distorts our constitutional structure of government as to render any distinction drawn in the Constitution between state and federal power almost meaningless. One of the most basic premises upon which our structure of government was founded was that the Federal Government was to have certain specific and limited powers and no others, and all other power was to be reserved either "to the States respectively, or to the people." Certainly if all the provisions of our Constitution which limit the power of the Federal Government and reserve other power to the States are to mean anything, they mean at least that the States have power to pass laws and amend their constitutions without first sending their officials hundreds of miles away to beg federal authorities to approve them. Moreover, it seems to me that §5 which gives federal officials power to veto state laws they do not like is in direct conflict with the clear command of our Constitution that "The United States shall guarantee to every State in this Union a Republican Form of Government." I cannot help but believe that the inevitable effect of any such law which forces any one of the States to entreat federal authorities in far-away places for approval of local laws before they can become effective is to create the impression that the State or States treated in this way are little more than conquered provinces. . . . A federal law which assumes the power to compel the States to submit in advance any proposed legislation they have for approval by federal agents approaches dangerously near to wiping the States out as useful and effective units in the government of our country. I cannot agree to any constitutional interpretation that leads inevitably to such a result. . . .

WILLSON v. BLACKBIRD CREEK MARSH COMPANY, 2 PETERS 245 (1829)

This case had all the makings of another Gibbons v. Ogden. *Willson was the captain-owner of a vessel and had a federal coasting license secured under the same congressional statute of 1793 under which Gibbons had obtained his federal license. The state of Delaware had authorized the Blackbird Creek Marsh Company to build a dam across the Blackbird Creek. Although the purpose of the dam was to reclaim marshland, it had the effect of obstructing navigation on the creek. Willson's ship was traveling on the creek when it encountered the dam and subsequently broke through to continue on its journey. The Blackbird Creek Marsh Company successfully sued Willson in the state courts for trespass and damages. Willson appealed to the Supreme Court and argued that the Delaware legislation authorizing the building of the dam was an unconstitutional exercise of the commerce power that is the exclusive domain of Congress. But instead of making this case the vehicle for another great commerce clause decision, John Marshall took a different perspective and utilized the concept of the state police powers.*

Votes: Unanimous

MR. CHIEF JUSTICE MARSHALL delivered the opinion of the Court:. . . .

The Act of Assembly by which the plaintiffs were authorized to construct their dam, shows plainly that this is one of those many creeks, passing through a deep, level marsh adjoining the Delaware, up which the tide flows for some distance. The value of the property on its banks must be enhanced by excluding the water from the marsh, and the health of the inhabitants probably improved. Measures calculated to produce these objects, pro-

vided they do not come into collision with the powers of the general government, are undoubtedly within those which are reserved to the States. But the measure authorized by this Act stops a navigable creek, and must be supposed to abridge the rights of those who have been accustomed to use it. But this abridgment, unless it comes in conflict with the Constitution or a law of the United States, is an affair between the government of Delaware and its citizens, of which this court can take no cognizance.

The counsel for the plaintiffs in error insist that it comes in conflict with the power of the United States "to regulate commerce with foreign nations and among the several States."

If Congress had passed any Act which bore upon the case; any Act in execution of the power to regulate commerce, the object of which was to control State legislation over those small navigable creeks into which the tide flows, and which abound throughout the lower country of the Middle and Southern States, we should feel not much difficulty in saying that a State law coming in conflict with such Act would be void. But Congress has passed no such Act. The repugnancy of the law of Delaware to the Constitution is placed entirely on its repugnancy to the power to regulate commerce with foreign nations and among the several states; a power which has not been so exercised as to affect the question.

We do not think that the Act empowering the Black Bird Creek Marsh Company to place a dam across the creek, can, under all the circumstances of the case, be considered as repugnant to the power to regulate commerce in its dormant state, or as being in conflict with any law passed on the subject.

There is no error, and the judgment is *affirmed.*

MAYOR OF NEW YORK v. MILN, 11 PETERS 102 (1837)

The state of New York enacted the Passenger Act of 1824 which required that the captains of all incoming passengers ships to the port of New York provide the Mayor of New York with a list of all foreign passengers. The list was to include the name, place of birth, age, last legal residence, and occupation of the passenger. Bond was required to be posted to assure the accuracy of the information and fines were to be levied for noncompliance. The purpose of this legislation was to permit the New York authorities to bar foreigners who could not support themselves and who, if admitted, would become a financial burden on the public agencies of

New York. The law specified that the ship's captain had to assume the expense of transporting elsewhere those foreigners refused admission to the city by the mayor. George Miln, the owner of a passenger ship and himself an alien, refused to comply with the statute and was obliged to pay a fine of $7500. He then went to the federal circuit court and sued to have the fine refunded. Miln's main argument was that the New York legislation violated the federal Constitution because it was a regulation of foreign commerce that invaded the exclusive domain of Congress as specified in the commerce clause (Article 1, Section 8, Clause 3). New York argued that the law was merely a police power regulation. The circuit court was divided over the question of constitutionality and certified that question to the Supreme Court for determination. This case raised the question of whether Congress' commerce powers were exclusive, that is, only to be exercised by Congress and never by the states, or whether the states could exercise commerce powers in the absence of congressional action. The Court, just as it had done in the Blackbird Creek Marsh Company *case, avoided these issues and instead approached the case from the perspective of state police powers.*

Majority votes: 6
Dissenting votes: 1

MR. JUSTICE BARBOUR delivered the opinion of the Court:. . . .

We shall not enter into any examination of the question whether the power to regulate commerce be or not be exclusive of the States, because the opinion which we have formed renders it unnecessary; in other words, we are of opinion that the [New York] act is not a regulation of commerce, but of police; and that being thus considered, it was passed in the exercise of a power which rightfully belonged to the States. . . .

Now, in relation to the section in the act immediately before us, that is obviously passed [by the state] with a view to prevent her citizens from being oppressed by the support of multitudes of poor persons, who come from foreign countries without possessing the means of supporting themselves. There can be no mode in which the power to regulate internal police could be more appropriately exercised. New York, from her particular situation, is, perhaps, more than any other city in the Union, exposed to the evil of thousands of foreign emigrants arriving there, and the consequent danger of her citizens being subjected to a heavy charge in the maintenance of those who are poor. It is the

duty of the State to protect its citizens from this evil; they have endeavored to do so by passing, among other things, the section of the law in question. We should, upon principle, say that it had a right to do so. . . .

We think it as competent and as necessary for a State to provide precautionary measures against the moral pestilence of paupers, vagabonds, and possibly convicts, as it is to guard the physical pestilence which may arise from unsound and infectious articles imported, or from a ship, the crew of which may be laboring under an infectious disease. . . .

We are therefore of opinion, and do direct it to be certified to the Circuit Court for the Southern District of New York, that so much of the section of the act of the Legislature of New York as applies to the breaches assigned in the declaration, does not assume to regulate commerce between the port of New York and foreign ports, and that so much of said section is constitutional. . . .

MR. JUSTICE THOMPSON [concurring]:. . . .

The case of *Willson* v. *The Black Bird Creek Marsh Company,* is a strong case to show that a power admitted to fall within the power to regulate commerce may be exercised by the States until Congress assumes the exercise. . . .

Whether . . . the law of New York, so far as it is drawn in question in this case, be considered as relating purely to the police and internal government of the State, and as part of the system of poor laws in the city of New York, and in this view belonging exclusively to the legislation of the State; or whether the subject matter of the law be considered as belonging concurrently to the State and to Congress, but never having been exercised by the latter, no constitutional objection can be made to it. . . .

I have chosen to consider this question under this double aspect, because I do not find as yet laid down by this court any certain and defined limits to the exercise of this power to regulate commerce; or what shall be considered commerce with foreign nations, and what the regulations of domestic trade and police. And when it is denied that a State law, in requiring a list of the passengers arriving in the port of New York from a foreign country, to be reported to the police authority of the city, is unconstitutional and void, because embraced within that power, I am at a loss to say where its limits are to be found. It becomes, therefore, a very important principle to establish that the States retain the exercise of powers, which, although they may in some measure partake of the character of commercial regulations, until Congress asserts the exercise of the power under the grant of the power to regulate commerce.

MR. JUSTICE STORY, dissenting:. . . .

It has been argued that the act of New York is not a regulation of commerce, but is a mere police law upon the subject of paupers; and it has been likened to the cases of health laws, quarantine laws, ballast laws, gunpowder laws, and others of a similar nature. The nature and character of these laws were fully considered and the true answer given to them in the case of *Gibbons* v. *Ogden;* and though the reasoning there given might be expanded, it cannot in its grounds and distinctions be more pointedly illustrated or better expounded. . . . I admit the power of the State to pass such laws, and to use the proper means to effectuate the objects of them; but it is with this reserve, that these means are not exclusively vested in Congress. A State cannot make a regulation of commerce to enforce its health laws, because it is a means withdrawn from its authority. It may be admitted that it is a means adapted to the end, but it is quite a different question whether it be a means within the competency of the State jurisdiction. The States have a right to borrow money, and borrowing by the issue of bills of credit would certainly be an appropriate means; but we all know that the emission of bills of credit by a State is expressly prohibited by the Constitution. If the power to regulate commerce be exclusive in Congress, then there is no difference between an express and an implied prohibition upon the States.

But how can it be truly said that the act of New York is not a regulation of commerce? No one can well doubt that if the same act had been passed by Congress it would have been a regulation of commerce; and in that way, and in that only, would it be a constitutional act of Congress. The right of Congress to pass such an act has been expressly conceded at the argument. . . . If the act is a regulation of commerce, and that subject belongs exclusively to Congress, it is a means cut off from the range of State sovereignty and State legislation. . . .

It has been argued that the power of Congress to regulate commerce is not exclusive, but concurrent with that of the States. If this were a new question in this court, wholly untouched by doctrine or decision, I should not hesitate to go into a full examination of all the grounds upon which concurrent authority is attempted to be maintained. But in point of fact, the whole argument on this very question, as presented by the learned counsel on the present occasion, was presented by the learned counsel who argued the case of *Gibbons* v. *Ogden*, and it

was then deliberately examined and deemed inadmissible by the court. Mr. Chief Justice Marshall, with his accustomed accuracy and fullness of illustration, reviewed at that time the whole grounds of the controversy; and from that time to the present, the question has been considered (as far as I know) to be at rest. The power given to Congress to regulate commerce with foreign nations and among the States has been deemed exclusive, from the nature and objects of the power, and the necessary implications growing out of its exercise. Full power to regulate a particular subject implies the whole power, and leaves no residuum; and a grant of the whole to one, is incompatible with a grant to another of a part. When a State proceeds to regulate commerce with foreign nations, or among the States, it is doing the very thing which Congress is authorized to do . . .

Such is a brief view of the grounds upon which my judgment is that the act of New York is unconstitutional and void. In this opinion I have the consolation to know that I had the entire concurrence, upon the same grounds, of that great constitutional jurist, the late Mr. Chief Justice Marshall. Having heard the former arguments, his deliberate opinion was that the act of New York was unconstitutional. . . .

EDWARDS v. CALIFORNIA, 314 U.S. 160 (1941)

This case was an appeal from a judgment of the Superior Court of California which affirmed the misdemeanor conviction of Edwards. The Superior Court was the highest court to which an appeal could be taken under the laws of California. The facts of the case are contained within the opinion of the Court. The case raised important questions of the reach of the state's police powers, the status of the right to travel, and the nature of Congress' commerce powers. The case was also reminiscent of Miln *but was handled markedly differently, although the right to travel was tied to Congress' commerce powers and not to national citizenship.*

Votes: Unanimous

MR. JUSTICE BYRNES delivered the opinion of the Court:

The facts of this case are simple and are not disputed. Appellant is a citizen of the United States and a resident of California. In December, 1939, he left his home in Marysville, California, for Spur, Texas, with the intention of bringing back to Marysville his wife's brother, Frank Duncan, a citizen of the United States and a resident of Texas. When he arrived in Texas, appellant learned that Duncan had last been employed by the Works Progress Administration. Appellant thus became aware of the fact that Duncan was an indigent person and he continued to be aware of it throughout the period involved in this case. The two men agreed that appellant should transport Duncan from Texas to Marysville in appellant's automobile. Accordingly, they left Spur on January 1, 1940, entered California by way of Arizona on January 3, and reached Marysville on January 5. . . .

In Justice Court a complaint was filed against appellant under §2615 of the Welfare and Institutions Code of California, which provides: "Every person, firm or corporation or officer or agent thereof that brings or assists in bringing into the State any indigent person who is not a resident of the State, knowing him to be an indigent person, is guilty of a misdemeanor." On demurrer to the complaint, appellant urged that the Section violated several provisions of the Federal Constitution. The demurrer was overruled, the cause was tried, appellant was convicted and sentenced to six months imprisonment in the county jail, and sentence was suspended. . . . Consequently, the conviction was affirmed. . . .

Article I, §8 of the Constitution delegates to the Congress the authority to regulate interstate commerce. And it is settled beyond question that the transportation of persons is "commerce," within the meaning of that provision. It is nevertheless true, that the States are not wholly precluded from exercising their police power in matters of local concern even though they may thereby affect interstate commerce. The issue presented in this case, therefore, is whether the prohibition embodied in §2615 against the "bringing" or transportation of indigent persons into California is within the police power of that State. We think that it is not, and hold that it is an unconstitutional barrier to interstate commerce.

The grave and perplexing social and economic dislocation which this statute reflects is a matter of common knowledge and concern. We are not unmindful of it. We appreciate that the spectacle of large segments of our population constantly on the move has given rise to urgent demands upon the ingenuity of government. . . . The State asserts that the huge influx of migrants into California in recent years has resulted in problems of health, morals, and especially finance, the proportions of which are staggering. It is not for us to say that this is not true. We have repeatedly and recently affirmed, and we now reaffirm, that we do not con-

ceive it our function to pass upon "the wisdom, need, or appropriateness" of the legislative efforts of the States to solve such difficulties.

But this does not mean that there are no boundaries to the permissible area of State legislative activity. There are. And none is more certain than the prohibition against attempts on the part of any single State to isolate itself from difficulties common to all of them by restraining the transportation of persons and property across its borders. It is frequently the case that a State might gain a momentary respite from the pressure of events by the simple expedient of shutting its gates to the outside world. But, in the words of Mr. Justice Cardozo: "The Constitution was framed under the dominion of a political philosophy less parochial in range. It was framed upon the theory that the peoples of the several States must sink or swim together, and that in the long run prosperity and salvation are in union and not division." *Baldwin* v. *Seelig*, 294 U.S. 511, 523.

It is difficult to conceive of a statute more squarely in conflict with this theory than the Section challenged here. Its express purpose and inevitable effect is to prohibit the transportation of indigent persons across the California border. The burden upon interstate commerce is intended and immediate; it is the plain and sole function of the statute. Moreover, the indigent non-residents who are the real victims of the statute are deprived of the opportunity to exert political pressure upon the California legislature in order to obtain a change in policy. We think this statute must fail under any known test of the validity of State interference with interstate commerce. . . .

. . . [T]he social phenomenon of large-scale interstate migration is as certainly a matter of national concern as the provision of assistance to those who have found a permanent or temporary abode. Moreover, and unlike the relief problem, this phenomenon does not admit of diverse treatment by the several States. The prohibition against transporting indigent non-residents into one State is an open invitation to retaliatory measures, and the burdens upon the transportation of such persons become cumulative. Moreover, it would be a virtual impossibility of migrants and those who transport them to acquaint themselves with the peculiar rules of admission of many States. . . .

Whether an able-bodied but unemployed person like Duncan is a "pauper" within the historical meaning of the term is open to considerable doubt. But assuming that the term is applicable to him and to persons similarly situated, we do not consider ourselves bound by the language referred to [in]

City of New York v. *Miln* . . . decided in 1837. Whatever may have been the notion then prevailing, we do not think that it will now be seriously contended that because a person is without employment and without funds he constitutes a "moral pestilence." Poverty and immorality are not synonymous.

We are of the opinion that §2615 is not a valid exercise of the police power of California; that it imposes an unconstitutional burden upon interstate commerce, and that the conviction under it cannot be sustained. In the view we have taken it is unnecessary to decide whether the Section is repugnant to other provisions of the Constitution.

Reversed.

MR. JUSTICE DOUGLAS, concurring:. . . .

I am of the opinion that the right of persons to move freely from State to State occupies a more protected position in our constitutional system than does the movement of cattle, fruit, steel and coal across state lines. While the opinion of the Court expresses no view on that issue, the right involved is so fundamental that I deem it appropriate to indicate the reach of the constitutional question which is present.

The right to move freely from State to State is an incident of *national* citizenship protected by the privileges and immunities clause of the Fourteenth Amendment against state interference. . . . Yet before the Fourteenth Amendment it was recognized as a right fundamental to the national character of our Federal government. It was so decided in 1868 by *Crandall* v. *Nevada*, 6 Wall. 35. In that case this Court struck down a Nevada tax "upon every person leaving the State" by common carrier. Mr. Justice Miller writing for the Court held that the right to move freely throughout the nation was a right of *national* citizenship. That the right was implied did not make it any less "guaranteed" by the Constitution. . . .

So, when the Fourteenth Amendment was adopted in 1868, it had been squarely and authoritatively settled that the right to move freely from State to State was a right of *national* citizenship. As such it was protected by the privileges and immunities clause of the Fourteenth Amendment against state interference. . . .

The conclusion that the right of free movement is a right of *national* citizenship stands on firm historical ground. If a state tax on that movement, as in the *Crandall* case, is invalid, *a fortiori* a statute which obstructs or in substance prevents that movement must fall. That result necessarily follows unless perchance a State can curtail the right of free movement of those who are poor or destitute. But to allow such an exception to be engrafted on the rights of *national* citizenship would be to contravene every conception of national unity. It would also introduce a caste system utterly incompatible with the spirit of our system of government. It would permit those who were stigmatized by a State as indigents, paupers, or vagabonds to be relegated to an inferior class of citizenship. It would prevent a citizen because he was poor from seeking new horizons in other States. It might thus withhold from large segments of our people that mobility which is basic to any guarantee of freedom of opportunity. The result would be a substantial dilution of the rights of *national* citizenship, a serious impairment of the principles of equality. Since the state statute here challenged involves such consequences, it runs afoul of the privileges and immunities clause of the Fourteenth Amendment.

MR. JUSTICE BLACK and MR. JUSTICE MURPHY join in this opinion.

MR. JUSTICE JACKSON, concurring:

I concur in the result reached by the Court, and I agree that the grounds of its decision are permissible ones under applicable authorities. But the migrations of a human being, of whom it is charged that he possesses nothing that can be sold and has no wherewithal to buy, do not fit easily into my notions as to what is commerce. To hold that the measure of his rights is the commerce clause is likely to result eventually either in distorting the commercial law or in denaturing human rights. I turn, therefore, away from principles by which commerce is regulated to that clause of the Constitution by virtue of which Duncan is a citizen of the United States and which forbids any State to abridge his privileges or immunities as such. . . .

While instances of valid "privileges or immunities" must be but few, I am convinced that this is one. I do not ignore or belittle the difficulties of what has been characterized by this Court as an "almost forgotten" clause. But the difficulty of the task does not excuse us from giving these general and abstract words whatever of specific content and concreteness they will bear as we mark out their application, case by case. That is the method of the common law, and it has been the method of this Court with other no less general statements in our fundamental law. This Court has not been timorous about giving concrete meaning to such obscure and vagrant phrases as "due process," "general welfare," "equal protection," or even "commerce among the several States." But it has always hesitated to give any real meaning to the privileges and immunities clause lest it improvidently give too much.

This Court should, however, hold squarely that it is a privilege of citizenship of the United States, protected from state abridgment, to enter any state of the Union, either for temporary sojourn or for the establishment of permanent residence therein and for gaining resultant citizenship thereof. If national citizenship means less than this, it means nothing. . . .

Any measure which would divide our citizenry on the basis of property into one class free to move from state to state and another class that is poverty-bound to the place where it has suffered misfortune is not only at war with the habit and custom by which our country has expanded, but is also a short-sighted blow at the security of property itself. Property can have no more dangerous, even if unwitting, enemy than one who would make its possession a pretext for unequal or exclusive civil rights. Where those rights are derived from national citizenship no state may impose such a test, and whether the Congress could do so we are not called upon to inquire. . . . Rich or penniless, Duncan's citizenship under the Constitution pledges his strength to the defense of California as a part of the United States, and his right to migrate to any part of the land he must defend is something she must respect under the same instrument. Unless this Court is willing to say that citizenship of the United States means at least this much to the citizen, then our heritage of constitutional privileges and immunities is only a promise to the ear to be broken to the hope, a teasing illusion like a munificent bequest in a pauper's will.

NATIONAL LEAGUE OF CITIES v. USERY, 426 U.S. 833 (1976)

Since 1937 it had been an open question whether there were any limits at all on Congress' exercise of its commerce power other than such express prohibitions as are found in the Bill of Rights. Until this case was decided, the Court for almost four decades had consistently refused to limit Congress in its use of this power. And when the Court did move for the first time since before the constitutional revolution of 1937, it did so not to further economic laissez-faire but rather to preserve what the majority saw as the essentials of state sovereignty. The National League of Cities and others, including the state of California, challenged 1974 amendments to the Fair Labor Standards Act of 1938 that extended the statutory protection of minimum wages and maximum hours to state employ-ees performing traditional governmental functions. The act now covered fire fighters, law enforcement personnel, sanitation workers, and those employed in public health, recreation, and other state and local activities. The appellants had initiated the litigation by suing Secretary of Labor Usery and asking a three-judge district court to declare the 1974 amendments unconstitutional and to enjoin the Secretary of Labor from enforcing them. The district court dismissed the complaint and appeal was taken to the Supreme Court.

Majority votes: 5
Dissenting votes: 4

MR. JUSTICE REHNQUIST delivered the opinion of the Court:. . . .

This Court has never doubted that there are limits upon the power of Congress to override state sovereignty, even when exercising its otherwise plenary powers to tax or to regulate commerce which are conferred by Art. I of the Constitution. . . . Appellee Secretary in this case, both in his brief and upon oral argument, has agreed that our federal system of government imposes definite limits upon the authority of Congress to regulate the activities of the States as States by means of the commerce power. . . .

Appellee Secretary argues that the cases in which this Court has upheld sweeping exercises of authority by Congress, even though those exercises preempted state regulation of the private sector, have already curtailed the sovereignty of the States quite as much as the 1974 amendments to the Fair Labor Standards Act. We do not agree. It is one thing to recognize the authority of Congress to enact laws regulating individual businesses necessarily subject to the dual sovereignty of the government of the Nation and the State in which they reside. It is quite another to uphold a similar exercise of congressional authority directed not to private citizens, but to the States as States. We have repeatedly recognized that there are attributes of sovereignty attaching to every state government which may not be impaired by Congress, not because Congress may lack an affirmative grant of legislative authority to reach the matter, but because the Constitution prohibits it from exercising the authority in that manner. . . .

One undoubted attribute of state sovereignty is the States' power to determine the wages which shall be paid to those whom they employ in order to carry out their governmental functions, what hours those persons will work, and what compensation will be provided where these employees may be called upon to work overtime. The question we must resolve in this case, then, is whether these determinations are "functions essential to separate and independent existence," so that Congress may not abrogate the States' otherwise plenary authority to make them.

In their complaint appellants advanced estimates of substantial costs which will be imposed upon them by the 1974 amendments. . . .

Judged solely in terms of increased costs in dollars, these allegations show a significant impact on the functioning of the governmental bodies involved. . . .

The degree to which the amendments would interfere with traditional aspects of state sovereignty can be seen even more clearly upon examining the overtime requirements of the Act. The general effect of these provisions is to require the States to pay their employees at premium rates whenever their work exceeds a specified number of hours in a given period. . . .

This congressionally imposed displacement of state decisions may substantially restructure traditional ways in which the local governments have arranged their affairs. . . . The requirement imposing premium rates upon any employment in excess of what Congress has decided is appropriate for a governmental employee's workweek, for example, appears likely to have the effect of coercing the States to structure work periods in some employment areas, such as police and fire protection, in a manner substantially different from practices which have long been commonly accepted among local governments of this Nation. . . . Another example of congressional choices displacing those of the States in the area of what are without doubt essential governmental decisions may be found in the practice of using volunteer firemen, a source of manpower crucial to many of our smaller towns' existence. Under the regulations proposed by appellee, whether individuals are indeed "volunteers" rather than "employees" subject to the minimum wage provisions of the Act are questions to be decided in the courts. . . .

Our examination of the effect of the 1974 amendments, as sought to be extended to the States and their political subdivisions, satisfies us that both the minimum wage and the maximum hour provisions will impermissibly interfere with the integral governmental functions of these bodies. . . . This exercise of congressional authority does not comport with the federal system of government embodied in the Constitution. We hold that insofar as the challenged amendments operate to directly displace the States' freedom to structure integral operations in areas of traditional government functions, they are not within the authority granted Congress by Art. I, § 8, cl. 3. . . .

The judgment of the District Court is accordingly reversed and the case is remanded for further proceedings consistent with this opinion.

So ordered.

MR. JUSTICE BLACKMUN, concurring:

The Court's opinion and the dissents indicate the importance and significance of this litigation as it bears upon the relationship between the Federal Government and our States. Although I am not untroubled by certain possible implications of the Court's opinion—some of them suggested by the dissents—I do not read the opinion so despairingly as does my Brother Brennan. In my view, the result with respect to the statute under challenge here is necessarily correct. I may misinterpret the Court's opinion, but it seems to me that it adopts a balancing approach, and does not outlaw federal power in areas such as environmental protection, where the federal interest is demonstrably greater and where state facility compliance with imposed federal standards would be essential. With this understanding on my part of the Court's opinion, I join it.

MR. JUSTICE BRENNAN, with whom MR. JUSTICE WHITE and MR. JUSTICE MARSHALL join, dissenting:

The Court concedes, as of course it must, that Congress enacted the 1974 amendments pursuant to its exclusive power under Art. I, § 8, cl. 3, of the Constitution "To regulate Commerce . . . among the several States." It must therefore be surprising that my Brethren should choose this Bicentennial year of our independence to repudiate principles governing judicial interpretation of our Constitution settled since the time of Chief Justice John Marshall, discarding his postulate that the Constitution contemplates that restraints upon exercise by Congress of its plenary commerce power lie in the political process and not in the judicial process. . . .

The reliance of my Brethren upon the Tenth Amendment as "an express declaration of [a state sovereignty] limitation," not only suggests that they overrule governing decisions of this Court that address this question but must astound scholars of the Constitution. . . .

Today's repudiation of [the] unbroken line of precedents that firmly reject my Brethren's ill-conceived abstraction can only be regarded as a transparent cover for invalidating a congressional judgment with which they disagree. The only analysis even remotely resembling that adopted today is found in a line of opinions dealing with the Commerce Clause and the Tenth Amendment that ultimately provoked a constitutional crisis for the Court in the 1930's, e.g., *Carter* v. *Carter Coal Co.*, 298 U.S. 238; *United States* v. *Butler*, 297 U.S. 1; *Hammer* v. *Dagenhart*, 247 U.S. 251. We tend to forget that the Court invalidated legislation during the Great Depression, not solely under the Due Process Clause, but also and primarily under the Commerce Clause and the Tenth Amendment. It may have been the eventual abandonment of that overly restrictive construction of the commerce power that spelled defeat for the Court-packing plan, and preserved the integrity of this institution . . .

We are left . . . with a catastrophic judicial body blow at Congress' power under the Commerce Clause. Even if Congress may nevertheless accomplish its objectives—for example by conditioning grants of federal funds upon compliance with federal minimum wage and overtime standards, there is an ominous portent of disruption of our constitutional structure implicit in today's mischievous decision. I dissent.

MR. JUSTICE STEVENS, dissenting:

The Court holds that the Federal Government may not interfere with a sovereign state's inherent right to pay a substandard wage to the janitor at the state capitol. The principle on which the holding rests is difficult to perceive.

The Federal Government may, I believe, require the State to act impartially when it hires or fires the janitor, to withhold taxes from his pay check, to observe safety regulations when he is performing his job, to forbid him from burning too much soft coal in the capitol furnace, from dumping untreated refuse in an adjacent waterway, from overloading a state-owned garbage truck or from driving either the truck or the governor's limousine over 55 miles an hour. Even though these and many other activities of the capitol janitor are activities of the state qua state. I have no doubt that they are subject to federal regulation.

I agree that it is unwise for the Federal Government to exercise its power in the ways described in the Court's opinion. . . . My disagreement with the wisdom of this legislation may not, of course, affect my judgment with respect to its validity. On this issue there is no dissent from the proposition that the Federal Government's power over the labor market is adequate to embrace these employees. Since I am unable to identify a limitation on that federal power that would not also invalidate federal regulation of state activities that I consider unquestionably permissible, I am persuaded that this stat-

ute is valid. Accordingly, with respect and a great deal of sympathy for the views expressed by the Court, I dissent from its constitutional holding.

GARCIA v. SAN ANTONIO METROPOLITAN TRANSIT AUTHORITY, 469 U.S. 528 (1985)

The Supreme Court in National League of Cities v. Usery *had ruled that areas of traditional governmental functions were not subject to the minimum wage and overtime requirements of the Fair Labor Standards Act (FLSA). The San Antonio Metropolitan Transit Authority (SAMTA), the major provider of transportation in the San Antonio, Texas, metropolitan area, considered itself performing a traditional governmental function and therefore not subject to FLSA standards. The United States Department of Labor disagreed and noted that SAMTA received substantial federal financial assistance under the Urban Mass Transportation Act of 1964. SAMTA filed an action in federal district court seeking declaratory relief. Both the Secretary of Labor and Joe Garcia, a transit authority employee, took issue with SAMTA. The district court ruled for SAMTA, prompting Garcia and the Secretary of Labor to appeal. The Supreme Court took the case and also took the opportunity to reconsider the* National League of Cities *decision itself.*

Majority votes: 5
Dissenting votes: 4

JUSTICE BLACKMUN delivered the opinion of the Court: . . .

The controversy in the present cases has focused on the . . . requirement that the challenged federal statute trench on "traditional governmental functions." The District Court voiced a common concern: "Despite the abundance of adjectives, identifying which particular state functions are immune remains difficult." Just how troublesome the task has been is revealed by the results reached in other federal cases. Thus, courts have held that regulating ambulance services; licensing automobile drivers; operating a municipal airport; performing solid waste disposal; and operating a highway authority, are functions *protected* under *National League of Cities*. At the same time, courts have held that issuance of industrial development bonds; regulation of intrastate natural gas sales; regulation of traffic on public roads; regulation of air transportation; operation of a telephone system; leasing and sale of natural gas; operation of a mental health facility; and provision of in-house domestic services for the aged and handicapped, are *not* entitled to

The last two decades have seen an unprecedented growth of federal regulatory activity, as the majority itself acknowledges. . . .

The problems of federalism in an integrated national economy are capable of more responsible resolution than holding that the States as States retain no status apart from that which Congress chooses to let them retain. The proper resolution, I suggest, lies in weighing state autonomy as a factor in the balance when interpreting the means by which Congress can exercise its authority on the States as States. It is insufficient, in assessing the validity of congressional regulation of a State pursuant to the commerce power, to ask only whether the same regulation would be valid if enforced against a private party. That reasoning, embodied in the majority opinion, is inconsistent with the spirit of our Constitution. It remains relevant that a *State* is being regulated, as *National League of Cities* and every recent case have recognized. As far as the Constitution is concerned, a State should not be equated with any private litigant. Instead, the autonomy of a State is an essential component of federalism. If state autonomy is ignored in assessing the means by which Congress regulates matters affecting commerce, then federalism becomes irrelevant simply because the set of activities remaining beyond the reach of such a commerce power "may well be negligible."

It has been difficult for this Court to craft bright lines of defining the scope of the state autonomy protected by *National League of Cities*. Such difficulty is to be expected whenever constitutional concerns as important as federalism and the effectiveness of the commerce power come into conflict. Regardless of the difficulty, it is and will remain the duty of this Court to reconcile these concerns in the final instance. That the Court shuns the task today by appealing to the "essence of federalism" can provide scant comfort to those who believe our federal system requires something more than a unitary, centralized government. I would not shirk the duty acknowledged by *National League of Cities* and its progeny, and I share Justice Rehnquist's belief that this Court will in time again assume its constitutional responsibility.

I respectfully dissent.

NEW ENERGY CO. OF INDIANA v. LIMBACH,
486 U.S. 269 (1988)

The Ohio law described in Justice Scalia's opinion was challenged by an Indiana manufacturer of ethanol, the New Energy Company of Indiana, whose sales in Ohio were ineligible for an Ohio tax credit. Joanne Limbach, the Tax Commissioner of Ohio, was sued in the Ohio Court of Common Pleas of Franklin County on the ground that the Ohio law violated the Commerce Clause of the U.S. Constitution by discriminating against out-of-state ethanol producers. The Ohio court rejected this claim as did the Ohio Court of Appeals and the Ohio Supreme Court.

Votes: Unanimous

JUSTICE SCALIA delivered the opinion of the Court:

Appellant New Energy Company of Indiana has challenged the constitutionality of Ohio Rev. Code Ann. § 5735.145(B) (1986), a provision that awards a tax credit against the Ohio motor vehicle fuel sales tax for each gallon of ethanol sold (as a component of gasohol) by fuel dealers, but only if the ethanol is produced in Ohio or in a State that grants similar tax advantages to ethanol produced in Ohio. The question presented is whether § 5735.145(B) discriminates against interstate commerce in violation of the Commerce Clause, U.S. Const., Art. I, § 8, cl. 3. . . .

It has long been accepted that the Commerce Clause not only grants Congress the authority to regulate commerce among the States, but also directly limits the power of the States to discriminate against interstate commerce. . . . This "negative" aspect of the Commerce Clause prohibits economic protectionism—that is, regulatory measures designed to benefit in-state economic interests by burdening out-of-state competitors. . . . Thus, state statutes that clearly discriminate against interstate commerce are routinely struck down, unless the discrimination is demonstrably justified by a valid factor unrelated to economic protectionism.

The Ohio provision at issue here explicitly deprives certain products of generally available beneficial tax treatment because they are made in certain other States, and thus on its face appears to violate the cardinal requirement of nondiscrimination. Appellees argue, however, that the availability of the tax credit to some out-of-state manufacturers (those in States that give tax advantages to Ohio-produced ethanol) shows that the Ohio provision, far from discriminating against interstate commerce, is likely to promote it, by encouraging other States to enact similar tax advantages that will spur the interstate sale of ethanol. We rejected a similar contention in an earlier "reciprocity" case, *Great Atlantic & Pacific Tea Co.* v. *Cottrell,* 424 U.S. 366 (1976). The regulation at issue there permitted milk from out of State to be sold in Mississippi only if the State of origin accepted Mississippi milk on a reciprocal basis. Mississippi put forward, among other arguments, the assertion that "the reciprocity requirement is in effect a free-trade provision, advancing the identical national interest that is served by the Commerce Clause." In response, we said that "Mississippi may not use the threat of economic isolation as a weapon to force sister States to enter into even a desirable reciprocity agreement." More recently, we characterized a Nebraska reciprocity requirement for the export of ground water from the State as "facially discriminatory legislation" which merited " 'strictest scrutiny.' " *Sporhase* v. *Nebraska ex rel. Douglas,* 458 U.S. 941 (1982).

It is true that in *Cottrell* and *Sporhase* the effect of a State's refusal to accept the offered reciprocity was total elimination of all transport of the subject product into or out of the offering State; whereas in the present case the only effect of refusal is that the out-of-state product is placed at a substantial commercial disadvantage through discriminatory tax treatment. That makes no difference for purposes of Commerce Clause analysis. In the leading case of *Baldwin* v. *G.A.F. Seelig, Inc.,* 294 U.S. 511 (1935), the New York law excluding out-of-state milk did not impose an absolute ban, but rather allowed importation and sale so long as the initial purchase from the dairy farmer was made at or above the New York State-mandated price. In other words, just as the appellant here, in order to sell its product in Ohio, only has to cut its profits by reducing its sales price below the market price sufficiently to compensate the Ohio purchaser-retailer for the foregone tax credit, so also the milk wholesaler-distributor in *Baldwin,* in order to sell its product in New York, only had to cut its profits by increasing its purchase price above the market price sufficiently to meet the New York-prescribed minimum. We viewed the New York law as "an economic barrier against competition" that was "equivalent to a rampart of customs duties." Similarly, in *Hunt* v. *Washington Apple Advertising Comm'n,* 432 U.S. 333, 349–351 (1977), we found invalid under the Commerce Clause a North Carolina statute that did not exclude apples from other States, but merely imposed additional costs upon Washington sellers and deprived them of the commercial advantage of their distinctive grading system. The present law likewise imposes an economic disadvantage upon out-of-state sellers; and the promise to remove that if reciprocity is accepted no more justifies disparity of treatment than it would justify categorical exclusion. We have indicated that reciprocity requirements are not *per se* unlaw-

ful. *Kane* v. *New Jersey,* 242 U.S. 160, 167–168 (1916), discussed a context in which, if a State offered the reciprocity did not accept it, the consequence was, to be sure, *less favored* treatment for its citizens, but nonetheless treatment that complied with the minimum requirements of the Commerce Clause. Here, quite to the contrary, the threat used to induce Indiana's acceptance is, in effect, taxing a product made by its manufacturers at a rate higher than the same product made by Ohio manufacturers, without (as we shall see) justification for the disparity. . . .

It has not escaped our notice that the appellant here, which is eligible to receive a cash subsidy under Indiana's program for in-state ethanol producers, is the potential beneficiary of a scheme no less discriminatory than the one that it attacks, and no less effective in conferring a commercial advantage over out-of-state competitors. To believe the Indiana scheme is valid, however, is not to believe that the Ohio scheme must be valid as well. The Commerce Clause does not prohibit all state action designed to give its residents an advantage in the marketplace, but only action of that description *in connection with the State's regulation of interstate commerce.* Direct subsidization of domestic industry does not ordinarily run afoul of that prohibition; discriminatory taxation of out-of-state manufacturers does. Of course, even if the Indiana subsidy were invalid, retaliatory violation of the Commerce Clause by Ohio would not be acceptable. . . .

Our cases leave open the possibility that a State may validate a statute that discriminates against interstate commerce by showing that it advances a legitimate local purpose that cannot be adequately served by reasonable nondiscriminatory alternatives. . . . This is perhaps just another way of saying that what may appear to be a "discriminatory" provision in the constitutionally prohibited sense—that is, a protectionist enactment—may on closer analysis not be so. However it be put, the standards for such justification are high. . . .

Appellees advance two justifications for the clear discrimination in the present case: health and commerce. As to the first, they argue that the provision encourages use of ethanol (in replacement of lead as a gasoline octane-enhancer) to reduce harmful exhaust emissions, both in Ohio itself and in surrounding States whose polluted atmosphere may reach Ohio. Certainly the protection of health is a legitimate state goal, and we assume for purposes of this argument that use of ethanol generally furthers it. But § 5735.145(B) obviously does not, except perhaps by accident. As far as ethanol use in Ohio itself is concerned, there is no reason to suppose that ethanol produced in a State that does not offer tax advantages to ethanol produced in Ohio is less healthy, and thus should have its importation into Ohio suppressed by denial of the otherwise standard tax credit. And as far as ethanol use outside Ohio is concerned, surely that is just as effectively fostered by other States' subsidizing ethanol production or sale in some fashion other than giving a tax credit to Ohio-produced ethanol; but these helpful expedients do not qualify for the tax credit. It could not be clearer that health is not the purpose of the provision, but is merely an occasional and accidental effect of achieving what is its purpose, favorable tax treatment for *Ohio*-produced ethanol. Essentially the same reasoning also responds to appellees' second (and related) justification for the discrimination, that the reciprocity requirement is designed to increase commerce in ethanol by encouraging other States to enact ethanol subsidies. What is encouraged is not ethanol subsidies in general, but only favorable treatment for Ohio-produced ethanol. In sum, appellees' health and commerce justifications amount to no more than implausible speculation, which does not suffice to validate this plain discrimination against products of out-of-state manufacture.

For the reasons stated, the judgment of the Ohio Supreme Court is

Reversed.

PUERTO RICO v. BRANSTAD, 483 U.S. 219 (1987)

The events that gave rise to this case were tragic and dramatic. Ronald Calder, an Iowa native working in Puerto Rico as a civilian air traffic controller, became involved in an argument with a man and his pregnant wife in a grocery store parking lot. According to witnesses, Calder struck the couple, knocking down the woman, and then drove his car over the woman at least two times killing her and her unborn child and injuring her husband. Calder was arrested and charged with first degree murder and attempted murder. He was released on bail and fled to his family's home in Iowa. Puerto Rico officials notified local authorities in Iowa that Calder was wanted for first degree murder and Calder surrendered to the Iowa authorities. The governor of Puerto Rico submitted to the governor of Iowa a request for Calder's extradition. After a hearing conducted by the governor's counsel, and after unsuccessful attempts by Iowa officials to have Puerto Rico reduce the charges against Calder, Iowa's governor denied the extradition request.

Puerto Rico then filed suit in federal district court asking for a writ of mandamus ordering Iowa Governor Terry Branstad to turn over Calder. Puerto Rico also asked the court to declare that failure to deliver Calder upon presentation of proper extradition papers violated the extradition clause of the U.S. Constitution and the federal Extradition Act. The district court dismissed the complaint ruling that under the precedent of Kentucky v. Dennison *federal courts have no power to order a governor to extradite a fugitive from justice. The Court of Appeals for the Eighth Circuit affirmed and the case came before the Supreme Court.*

Votes: Unanimous

JUSTICE MARSHALL delivered the opinion of the Court:

This case requires that we reconsider the holding of *Kentucky* v. *Dennison,* 24 How. 66 (1861), that federal courts have no power to order the Governor of a State to fulfill the State's obligation under the Extradition Clause of the Constitution, Art. IV, § 2, to deliver up fugitives from justice. . . .

[F]or over 125 years, *Kentucky* v. *Dennison* has stood for two propositions: first, that the Extradition Clause creates a mandatory duty to deliver up fugitives upon proper demand; and second, that the federal courts have no authority under the Constitution to compel performance of this ministerial duty of delivery. As to the first of these conclusions, the passage of time has revealed no occasion for doubt. The language of the Clause is "clear and explicit." Its mandatory language furthers its intended purposes: "to enable each state to bring offenders to trial as swiftly as possible in the state where the alleged offense was committed," and "to preclude any state from becoming a sanctuary for fugitives from justice of another state." The Framers of the Constitution perceived that the frustration of these objectives would create a serious impediment to national unity, and the Extradition Clause responds to that perception. . . . We reaffirm the conclusion that the commands of the Extradition Clause are mandatory, and afford no discretion to the executive officers or courts of the asylum State.

The second, and dispositive, holding of *Kentucky* v. *Dennison* rests upon a foundation with which time and the currents of constitutional change have dealt much less favorably. If it seemed clear to the Court in 1861, facing the looming shadow of a Civil War, that "the Federal Government, under the Constitution, has no power to impose on a State officer, as such, any duty whatever, and compel him to perform it," 24 How., at 107, basic constitutional principles now point as clearly the other way. Within 15 years of the decision in *Dennison* it was said that "when a plain official duty, requiring no exercise of discretion, is to be performed, and performance is refused, any person who will sustain personal injury by such refusal may have a *mandamus* to compel its performance," and it was no objection that such an order might be sought in the federal courts against a state officer. *Board of Liquidation* v. *McComb,* 92 U.S. (2 Otto) 531, 541 (1876). It has long been a settled principle that federal courts may enjoin unconstitutional action by state officials. See *Ex Parte Young,* 209 U.S. 123, 155–156 (1908). It would be superfluous to restate all the occasions on which this Court has imposed upon state officials a duty to obey the requirements of the Constitution, or compelled the performance of such duties; it may suffice to refer to *Brown* v. *Board of Education,* 349 U.S. 294 (1955), and *Cooper* v. *Aaron,* 358 U.S. 1 (1958). The fundamental premise of the holding in *Dennison*—"that the States and the Federal Government in all circumstances must be viewed as co-equal sovereigns—is not representative of the law today." *FERC* v. *Mississippi,* 456 U.S. 742, 761 (1982).

Yet with respect to extradition the law has remained as it was more than a century ago. Considered *de novo,* there is no justification for distinguishing the duty to deliver fugitives from the many other species of constitutional duty enforceable in the federal courts. Indeed the nature of the obligation here is such as to avoid many of the problems with which federal courts must cope in other circumstances. That this is a ministerial duty precludes conflict with essentially discretionary elements of state governance, and eliminates the need for continuing federal supervision of state functions. The explicit and long-settled nature of the command, contained in a constitutional provision and a statute substantially unchanged for two hundred years, eliminates the possibility that state officers will be subjected to inconsistent direction. Because the duty is directly imposed upon the States by the Constitution itself, there can be no need to weigh the performance of the federal obligation against the powers reserved to the States under the Tenth Amendment.

Respondents contend, however, that an "executive common law" of extradition has developed through the efforts of governors to employ the discretion accorded them under *Dennison,* and that this "common law" provides a superior alternative to the "ministerial duty" to extradite provided for

by the Constitution. Even assuming the existence of this tradition of "executive common law," no weight can be accorded to it. Long continuation of decisional law or administrative practice incompatible with the requirements of the Constitution cannot overcome our responsibility to enforce those requirements. Though not articulated in these terms, respondents' argument is in essence a request that we reconsider our construction of the Extradition Clause to establish as a matter of constitutional interpretation a discretion which has hitherto been exercised solely because the Constitution's explicit command has gone unenforced. This, for the reasons previously stated, we decline to do.

Respondents further contend that even if the holding in *Kentucky* v. *Dennison* cannot withstand contemporary scrutiny, petitioner would not profit from its demise because Puerto Rico is not a State, and has no right to demand rendition of fugitives under the Extradition Clause. It is true that the words of the Clause apply only to "States," and we have never held that the Commonwealth of Puerto Rico is entitled to all the benefits conferred upon the States under the Constitution. We need not decide today what applicability the Extradition Clause may have to the Commonwealth of Puerto Rico, however, for the Extradition Act [of 1793] clearly applies. The Act requires rendition of fugitives at the request of a demanding "Territory," as well as State. It was decided long ago that Puerto Rico, as a Territory of the United States, could invoke the Act to reclaim fugitives from its justice, see *New York ex rel. Kopel* v. *Bingham,* 211 U.S. 468 (1909), and respondents do not challenge the correctness of that holding. The subsequent change to Commonwealth status through legislation did not remove from the Government of the Commonwealth any power to demand extradition which it had possessed as a Territory, for the intention of that legislation was "to accord to Puerto Rico the degree of autonomy and independence normally associated with States of the Union." Since the Act applies to Puerto Rico, the Commonwealth may invoke the power of federal courts to enforce against state officers rights created by federal statutes, including equitable relief to compel performance of federal statutory duties. Accordingly, Puerto Rico may predicate its mandamus action on the Act, without regard to the direct applicability of the Extradition Clause.

Kentucky v. *Dennison* is the product of another time. The conception of the relation between the States and the Federal Government there announced is fundamentally incompatible with more than a century of constitutional development. Yet this decision has stood while the world of which it was a part has passed away. We conclude that it may stand no longer. The decision of the Court of Appeals is

Reversed.

JUSTICE O'CONNOR, with whom Justice POWELL joins, concurring in part and concurring in the judgment: [omitted]
JUSTICE SCALIA, concurring in part and concurring in the judgment: [omitted]

SUPREME COURT OF VIRGINIA v. FRIEDMAN, 487 U.S. 59 (1988)

Virginia's residency requirement for admission to the state's bar without examination was challenged by Myrna Friedman, a lawyer who had recently accepted a job as associate general counsel for a firm located in Vienna, Virginia. Ms. Friedman lived in nearby Maryland. After being turned down by the Virginia Supreme Court, Ms. Friedman filed suit in federal district court arguing that the residency requirement violated the Privileges and Immunities Clause. The federal district court agreed and the Court of Appeals for the Fourth Circuit affirmed. The Supreme Court of Virginia appealed to the U.S. Supreme Court.

Majority votes: 7
Dissenting votes: 2

JUSTICE KENNEDY delivered the opinion of the Court:

Qualified lawyers admitted to practice in other States may be admitted to the Virginia bar "on motion," that is, without taking the bar examination which Virginia otherwise requires. The State conditions such admission on a showing, among other matters, that the applicant is a permanent resident of Virginia. The question for decision is whether this residency requirement violates the Privileges and Immunities Clause of the United States Constitution, Art. IV, § 2. We hold that it does. . . .

Article IV, § 2, of the Constitution provides that the "Citizens of each State shall be entitled to all Privileges and Immunities of Citizens in the several States." The provision was designed "to place the citizens of each State upon the same footing with citizens of other States, so far as the advantages resulting from citizenship in those States are concerned." *Paul* v. *Virginia,* 8 Wall. 168, 180

(1869). . . . The Clause "thus establishes a norm of comity without specifying the particular subjects as to which citizens of one State coming within the jurisdiction of another are guaranteed equality of treatment." *Austin* v. *New Hampshire,* 420 U.S. 656, 660 (1975).

While the Privileges and Immunities Clause cites the term "Citizens," for analytic purposes citizenship and residency are essentially interchangeable. When examining claims that a citizenship or residency classification offends privileges and immunities protections, we undertake a two-step inquiry. First, the activity in question must be " 'sufficiently basic to the livelihood of the Nation' . . . as to fall within the purview of the Privileges and Immunities Clause. . . ." For it is " '[o]nly with respect to those "privileges" and "immunities" bearing on the vitality of the Nation as a single entity' that a State must accord residents and nonresidents equal treatment." Second, if the challenged restriction deprives nonresidents of a protected privilege, we will invalidate it only if we conclude that the restriction is not closely related to the advancement of a substantial State interest. Appellants assert that the residency requirement offends neither part of this test. We disagree.

Appellants concede, as they must, that our decision in *Supreme Court of New Hampshire* v. *Piper* establishes that a nonresident who takes and passes an examination prescribed by the State, and who otherwise is qualified for the practice of law, has an interest in practicing law that is protected by the Privileges and Immunities Clause. Appellants contend, however, that the discretionary admission provided for by Rule 1A:1 is not a privilege protected by the Clause for two reasons. First, appellants argue that the bar examination "serves as an adequate, alternative means of gaining admission to the bar." In appellants' view, "[s]o long as any applicant may gain admission to a State's bar, without regard to residence, by passing the bar examination," the State cannot be said to have discriminated against nonresidents "as a matter of fundamental concern." Second, appellants argue that the right to admission on motion is not within the purview of the Clause because, without offense to the Constitution, the State could require all bar applicants to pass an examination. Neither argument is persuasive.

We cannot accept appellants' first theory because it is quite inconsistent with our precedents. We reaffirmed in *Piper* the well-settled principle that " 'one of the privileges which the Clause guarantees to citizens of State A is that of doing business in State B on terms of substantial equality with the citizens of that State.' " . . . After reviewing our precedents, we explicitly held that the practice of law, like other occupations considered in those cases, is sufficiently basic to the national economy to be deemed a privilege protected by the Clause. The clear import of *Piper* is that the Clause is implicated whenever, as is the case here, a State does not permit qualified nonresidents to practice law within its borders on terms of substantial equality with its own residents.

Nothing in our precedents, moreover, supports the contention that the Privileges and Immunities Clause does not reach a State's discrimination against nonresidents when such discrimination does not result in their total exclusion from the State. In *Ward* v. *Maryland,* 12 Wall. 418 (1871), for example, the Court invalidated a statute under which residents paid an annual fee of $12 to $150 for a license to trade foreign goods, while nonresidents were required to pay $300. . . .

Further, we find appellants' second theory— that Virginia could constitutionally require that all applicants to its bar take and pass an examination— quite irrelevant to the question whether the Clause is applicable in the circumstances of this case. A State's abstract authority to require from resident and nonresident alike that which it has chosen to demand from the nonresident alone has never been held to shield the discriminatory distinction from the reach of the Privileges and Immunities Clause. . . . The issue is . . . whether the State has burdened the right to practice law, a privilege protected by the Privileges and Immunities Clause, by discriminating among otherwise equally qualified applicants solely on the basis of citizenship or residency. We conclude it has. . . .

We acknowledge that a bar examination is one method of assuring that the admitted attorney has a stake in her professional licensure and a concomitant interest in the integrity and standards of the bar. A bar examination, as we know judicially and from our own experience, is not a casual or light-hearted exercise. The question, however, is whether lawyers who are admitted in other States and seek admission in Virginia are less likely to respect the bar and further its interests solely because they are nonresidents. We cannot say this is the case. While *Piper* relied on an examination requirement as an indicium of the nonresident's commitment to the bar and to the State's legal profession, it does not follow that when the State waives the examination it may make a distinction between residents and nonresidents. . . .

Further, to the extent that the State is justifiably concerned with ensuring that its attorneys keep abreast of legal developments, it can protect these interests through other equally or more effective means that do not themselves infringe constitutional protections. . . . The Supreme Court of Virginia could, for example, require mandatory attendance at periodic continuing legal education courses. The same is true with respect to the State's interest that the nonresident bar member does her share of volunteer and *pro bono* work. . . .

We also reject appellants' attempt to justify the residency restriction as a necessary aid to the enforcement of the full-time practice requirement of Rule 1A:1. Virginia already requires, pursuant to the full-time practice restriction of Rule 1A:1, that attorneys admitted on motion maintain an office for the practice of law in Virginia. As the Court of Appeals noted, the requirement that applicants maintain an office in Virginia facilitates compliance with the full-time practice requirement in nearly the identical manner that the residency restriction does, rendering the latter restriction largely redundant. The office requirement furnishes an alternative to the residency requirement that is not only less restrictive, but also is fully adequate to protect whatever interest the State might have in the full-time practice restriction.

We hold that Virginia's residency requirement for admission to the State's bar without examination violates the Privileges and Immunities Clause. The nonresident's interest in practicing law on terms of substantial equality with those enjoyed by residents is a privilege protected by the Clause. A State may not discriminate against nonresidents unless it shows that such discrimination bears a close relation to the achievement of substantial State objectives. Virginia has failed to make this showing. Accordingly, the judgment of the Court of Appeals is affirmed.

It is so ordered.

CHIEF JUSTICE REHNQUIST, with whom JUSTICE SCALIA joins, dissenting:

Three Terms ago the Court invalidated a New Hampshire Bar rule which denied admission to an applicant who had passed the state bar examination because she was not, and would not become, a resident of the State. *Supreme Court of New Hampshire* v. *Piper,* 470 U.S. 274 (1985). In the present case the Court extends the reasoning of *Piper* to invalidate a Virginia Bar rule allowing admission on motion without examination to qualified applicants, but restricting the privilege to those applicants who have become residents of the State.

For the reasons stated in my dissent in *Piper,* I also disagree with the Court's decision in this case. I continue to believe that the Privileges and Immunities Clause of Article IV, § 2, does not require States to ignore residency when admitting lawyers to practice. . . .

I think the effect of today's decision is unfortunate even apart from what I believe is its mistaken view of the Privileges and Immunities Clause. Virginia's rule allowing admission on motion is an ameliorative provision, recognizing the fact that previous practice in another State may qualify a new resident of Virginia to practice there without the necessity of taking another bar examination. The Court's ruling penalizes Virginia, which has at least gone part way towards accommodating the present mobility of our population, but of course leaves untouched the rules of those States which allow no reciprocal admission on motion. Virginia may of course retain the privilege of admission on motion without enforcing a residency requirement even after today's decision, but it might also decide to eliminate admission on motion altogether.

Chapter

11

The Contract Clause

DECISIONAL TRENDS

The contract clause figured prominently in nineteenth century constitutional law. With the doctrines developed and used by the Supreme Court, the actions of the states affecting private property rights were subject to the constitutional veto power of a majority of the justices. During much of the nineteenth century, when a state law was struck down, the likely reason was violation of the contract clause.

Among his many accomplishments in constitutional law, John Marshall must be given credit for his landmark rulings in the contract clause realm. John Marshall, in effect, rewrote the contract clause. He felt obliged to do so in the first major case concerning it—**Fletcher** v. **Peck**—because the ex post facto clause was not applicable to civil law thanks to **Calder** v. **Bull** (chap. 6). Thus the Georgia legislature's Rescinding Act could not be considered an ex post facto law, and Marshall therefore suggested that a public grant constitutes a contract and that the contract clause

applied to public as well as to private contracts. In **New Jersey** v. **Wilson,** two years later, the Court reinforced these new doctrines; and by the time of the **Dartmouth College** case not only were they taken for granted but the Court added still another—that a corporate charter constitutes a public contract whose obligation may not be impaired by the state. Just four years after the *Dartmouth College* case was decided, the Court took the contract clause even further and ruled in *Green* v. *Biddle,* 8 Wheaton 1 (1823), that the contract clause applies to compacts between states. In 1830, however, the Court appeared to retreat somewhat by holding in *Providence Bank* v. *Billings,* 4 Peters 514, that corporate charters must be strictly construed in favor of the public interest—a position that was to be elaborated upon about seven years later by Marshall's successor in office, Roger B. Taney, in the controversial **Charles River Bridge** v. **Warren Bridge.**

The contract clause was used by the Marshall Court in *Sturges* v. *Crowninshield,* 4 Wheaton 122 (1819), to bar the retroactive application of a state bankruptcy law to debts contracted before passage of the act. But the Court, in *Ogden* v. *Saunders,* 12 Wheaton 213 (1827), with Marshall himself dissenting along with two other colleagues, held that the contract clause was not violated by a bankruptcy law that applied to debts contracted *after* passage of the act. Thus, although the thrust of the Marshall Court was to protect property rights by creating contract clause doctrines, the Court nevertheless showed some flexibility in meeting legitimate governmental needs.

John Marshall's successor, Roger B. Taney, assumed the chief justiceship at a time of economic trouble. As will be recalled from the discussion in Chapter 2, the new Taney Court appeared to be undertaking a reversal of the Marshall Court. When the Taney Court announced its decision in *Charles River Bridge* v. *Warren Bridge,* the Whigs charged—and feared—that the contract clause doctrines of the Marshall Court were being eroded by a Court dominated by antibusiness agrarians. Of course, these fears were groundless, and opponents of the decision failed to appreciate the earlier Marshall Court *Providence Bank* v. *Billings* decision that had anticipated the major thrust of the Taney Court. As subsequent decisions made clear, the Taney Court subscribed to the Marshall Court doctrines and went even further than Marshall did in protecting corporations by, for example, allowing them the status of citizens of the state in which they were chartered for diversity jurisdiction purposes of suing in the federal courts. *Louisville etc. R.R.* v. *Letson,* 2 Howard 497 (1844), was the case that accomplished this. In *Bank of Augusta* v. *Earle,* 13 Peters 519 (1839), the Court ruled that a banking corporation chartered in Georgia could do business in bills of exchange in Alabama unless the state specifically enacted legislation excluding all "foreign" corporations from such dealings, which it had not. Since bills of exchange were important instruments of credit, this decision was considered a great victory for the nation's private banks and corporations, even though Alabama then proceeded to enact an exclusionary law.

Even more impressively probusiness was *Bronson* v. *Kinzie,* 1 Howard 311 (1843), in which the Court struck down as a violation of the contract clause an Illinois stay law enacted in 1841. The Illinois law placed restrictions on foreclosure sales (no forced sale of property was permitted unless it was sold for at least two-thirds of the appraised value) and gave debtors one year in which to repurchase their former property. The Court ruled that the law impaired the obligation of contracts when applied to mortgages on property obtained before passage of the Illinois law. *Piqua Branch of the State Bank* v. *Knoop,* 16 Howard 369 (1854) is another example of the orthodoxy of the Taney Court majority when the contract clause—and a Marshall Court precedent—was on the line. The Court ruled that Ohio cannot raise the tax rate of banks whose corporate charters stipulate a lower rate and exempt them from all other taxes. In *Dodge* v. *Woolsey,* 18 Howard 331 (1856), the Court ruled that an Ohio state constitutional amendment that attempted to circumvent the Court's *Piqua Branch* decision by repealing the previous tax exemptions contained in bank corporate charters nevertheless impaired the obligation of contracts in violation of the federal Constitution.

The *Charles River Bridge* case, however, did not stand by itself as a pro-state aberration of the Taney Court. Although not a contract clause case, *Briscoe* v. *The Bank of Kentucky,* 11 Peters 257 (1837), upheld the state's regulation of its own banking and currency and in particular the use of state instruments that are suspiciously like state bills of credit, which are outlawed by the federal Constitution. More to the point, the Court in *West River Bridge Co.* v. *Dix,* 6 Howard 507 (1848), ruled that the sovereign right of eminent domain in the public interest takes precedence over the sanctity of corporate charters. The police power, in this case the exercise of eminent domain (with compensation), is superior to the contract clause. The decision in *Christ Church Hospital* v. *County of Philadelphia,* 24 Howard 300 (1861), concerned a tax exemption contained within a grant that was subsequently repealed. Unlike *New Jersey* v. *Wilson* and the *Piqua Branch* case, the Court ruled that the original tax exemption was *not* perpetual but was temporary and linked to the special circumstances. The Taney Court, then, although generally respecting both the contract clause doctrines and the precedents of the Marshall Court, nevertheless placed its own distinctive stamp in this area by giving the states just a bit more than did predecessor courts.

The contract clause, however, became less of a basis to challenge state economic regulation of corporations when the states began inserting reservation clauses in corporate charters reserving to the states the right to change the terms of the charter to serve the public interest. By the end of the nineteenth century, the contract clause was a much less viable basis on which to mount a constitutional challenge to social and economic policies than was the due process clause (see the discussion in Chapter 12 of the development of substantive due process). Into the twentieth century, other actions of the states were occasionally challenged as violating the clause. None is more famous or as important as **Home Building and Loan Association** v. **Blaisdell,** decided at the height of the Great Depression. The Court, here, put the public welfare before a strict and narrow interpretation of the contract clause.

More recently, the Burger Court invoked the contract clause in several decisions. In *United States Trust Co.* v. *New Jersey,* 431

U.S. 1 (1977), the Court, for the first time since 1941, used the contract clause to strike down economic regulation by invalidating the efforts of the states of New York and New Jersey to repeal retroactively statutory covenants they had made to bondholders. The covenants limited the use of funds pledged to bondholders of the Port Authority of New York and New Jersey from being invested in railroad mass transit facilities. The Court majority took the position that contracts to which a state itself is a party must be subject to exacting review if the contract clause of the Constitution is to offer any protection. The Court found that repeal of the covenant was unreasonable. The next year, the Court in **Allied Structural Steel Co.** v. **Spannaus** went further and used the contract clause to overturn a Minnesota statute. Yet, in 1983, the Court upheld a portion of an Alabama statute increasing the severance tax on oil and gas extracted from Alabama wells as not violating the contract clause (*Exxon Corp.* v. *Eagerton,* 462 U.S. 176 [1983]). The Court, thus, can be seen as continuing to use its discretion even in such a relatively well-settled area of constitutional law as the contract clause. While it is unusual for the modern Court to strike down state economic and social welfare regulation on contract clause grounds, it can occur, as the *United States Trust Company* and *Allied Structural Steel* decisions suggest. It is more likely to occur when there is a conservative majority on the Court such as exists today.

THE IMPACT OF THE COURT'S DECISIONS

Table 11.1 summarizes the impact of selected Court decisions concerning the contract clause. The reprinted cases follow.

Table 11.1 THE IMPACT OF SELECTED COURT DECISIONS, CONTRACT CLAUSE CASES

Case	Year	Impact on Parties	Short-Run Impact	Long-Run Impact
Fletcher v. Peck	1810	Land titles on basis of original grant definitively upheld.	Complex long-simmering controversy resolved. States' rights advocates opposed.	Court develops contract clause doctrines that were to provide the legal protection for business enterprises against actions of the states. Decision helps cultivate constituency for Court among propertied interests.
New Jersey v. Wilson	1812	Although state is prohibited from taxing land, in later years land is subdivided and starting in 1826 taxes are paid. In 1886 Court rules that nontaxpaying status of the land had lapsed and was void by disuse.	Court reinforces Contract Clause doctrines announced in *Fletcher v. Peck*.	Decision in context of contract clause decisions that established doctrines conducive to corporate growth.
Dartmouth College v. Woodward	1819	New trustees disbanded by time of decision; old college trustees victorious and seize possession of school buildings upon learning of Court's decision.	Marshall Court reinforces its concern for property rights with the doctrines of this case.	Making a corporate charter a public contract subject to contract clause gave business the necessary protection to enable the economic development of the country. Led eventually to states placing reservation clauses in corporate charters reserving the right to change the terms in the public interest.

Case	Year			
Charles River Bridge v. *Warren Bridge*	1837	Charles River Bridge proprietors lose, bridge closes, state gives owners $25,000 settlement for surrender of charter and bridge.	Encourages state internal improvements and development of railroads; seen as a Jacksonian pro-states' rights and anti-corporate special interests decision.	Decision provided favorable legal climate for technological development and for state sponsorship in the public interest. Contract clause proved inadequate to insulate private corporations from public regulation.
Home Building and Loan Association v. *Blaisdell*	1934	Mr. & Mrs. Blaisdell given until May 1, 1935, under Minnesota law, in which to obtain a new loan of $4,258.82 to redeem their Minneapolis home.	Supreme Court seen as sympathetic to state efforts to lessen traumatic effects of the Depression.	Precedent for a liberal construction of the contract clause to enable the states to exercise their police powers for the common good.
Allied Structural Steel Co. v. *Spannaus*	1978	The company did not have to pay the $185,000 pension funding charge.	Demonstrated the probusiness orientation of the Burger Court.	One of the few post-1937 contract clause precedents for restraining state actions.

FLETCHER v. PECK,
6 CRANCH 87 (1810)

This case grew out of the so-called Yazoo Land Grant Scandal whereby some 35 million acres of land now in Alabama and Mississippi were sold to four land companies for the price of $500,000 (less than 1 1/2 cents an acre). The sale was accomplished by way of a grant by the Georgia legislature in 1795. However, it was soon discovered that almost all legislators voting in favor of the grant had been bribed to do so. Irate voters replaced the corrupt legislators at the next year's election and a new legislature in 1796 passed a Rescinding Act rendering the 1795 grant null and void. By the time the Rescinding Act was enacted, however, the land had been sold to many presumably innocent purchasers who had bought it in good faith. They refused to give up "their" land. Complicating the situation was the fact that the federal government claimed that it had original title to part of the land and that Georgia's sale of that land was illegal. The situation was complex and confusing, producing great uncertainty; yet land sales continued. Finally, by 1802, after extensive negotiations, the federal government came to an agreement with Georgia officials that provided that the federal government would in part reimburse Georgia and assume responsibility for straightening out the confusion. This would be done on the basis of the original grant. But the fact remained that the Rescinding Act was still on the law books in Georgia. John Peck of New Hampshire owned some of the land, and his title was upheld by the federal government. He sold a portion of it to Robert Fletcher from Massachusetts. Fletcher was eager to resolve any doubts regarding the legal status of the Georgia Rescinding Act and to accomplish this he sued Peck. The suit was to recover the money Fletcher paid for the land on the grounds that Peck's title was invalid due to the Georgia Rescinding Act of 1796. The United States Circuit Court for the District of Massachusetts in Boston ruled that Peck's title was valid and the Rescinding Act was of no standing. Fletcher then appealed to the Supreme Court.

Votes: Unanimous

MR. CHIEF JUSTICE MARSHALL delivered the opinion of the Court as follows:. . . .

If a suit be brought to set aside a conveyance obtained by fraud, and the fraud be clearly proved, the conveyance will be set aside, as between the parties; but the rights of third persons, who are purchasers without notice, for a valuable consideration, cannot be disregarded. Titles, which, according to every legal test, are perfect, are acquired with that confidence which is inspired by the opinion that the purchaser is safe. If there be any concealed defect, arising from the conduct of those who had held the property long before he acquired it, of which he had no notice, that concealed defect cannot be set up against him. He has paid his money for a title good at law; he is innocent, whatever may be the guilt of others, and equity will not subject him to the penalties attached to that guilt. All titles would be insecure, and the intercourse between man and man would be very seriously obstructed, if this principle be overturned. . . .

Is the power of the legislature competent to the annihilation of such title, and to a resumption of the property thus held?

The principle asserted is, that one legislature is competent to repeal any act which a former legislature was competent to pass; and that one legislature cannot abridge the powers of a succeeding legislature.

The correctness of this principle, so far as respects general legislation, can never be controverted. But if an act be done under a law, a succeeding legislature cannot undo it. The past cannot be recalled by the most absolute power. Conveyances have been made, those conveyances have vested legal estates, and, if those estates may be seized by the sovereign authority, still, that they originally vested is a fact, and cannot cease to be a fact.

When, then, a law is in its nature a contract, when absolute rights have vested under that contract, a repeal of the law cannot devest those rights; and the act of annulling them, if legitimate, is rendered so by a power applicable to the case of every individual in the community.

It may well be doubted whether the nature of society and of government does not prescribe some limits to the legislative power; and if any be prescribed, where are they to be found, if the property of an individual, fairly and honestly acquired, may be seized without compensation.

To the legislature all legislative power is granted; but the question, whether the act of transferring the property of an individual to the public, be in the nature of the legislative power, is well worthy of serious reflection.

It is the peculiar province of the legislature to prescribe general rules for the government of society; the application of those rules to individuals in society would seem to be the duty of other departments. How far the power of giving the law may involve every other power, in cases where the constitution is silent, never has been, and perhaps never can be, definitely stated.

The validity of this rescinding act, then, might well be doubted, were Georgia a single sovereign power. But Georgia cannot be viewed as a single, unconnected, sovereign power, on whose legislature no other restrictions are imposed than may be found in its own constitution. She is a part of a large empire; she is a member of the American Union; and that union has a constitution the supremacy of which all acknowledge, and which imposes limits to the legislatures of the several States, which none claim a right to pass. The constitution of the United States declares that no State shall pass any bill of attainder, *ex post facto law,* or law impairing the obligation of contracts.

Does the case now under consideration come within this prohibitory section of the constitution?

In considering this very interesting question, we immediately ask ourselves what is a contract? Is a grant a contract?

A contract is a compact between two or more parties, and is either executory or executed. An executory contract is one in which a party binds himself to do, or not to do, a particular thing. . . . A contract executed is one in which the object of contract is performed; and this, says Blackstone, differs in nothing from a grant. The contract between Georgia and the purchasers was executed by the grant. A contract executed, as well as one which is executory, contains obligations binding on the parties. A grant, in its own nature, amounts to an extinguishment of the right of the grantor, and implies a contract not to reassert that right. A party is, therefore, always estopped by his own grant.

Since, then, in fact, a grant is a contract executed, the obligation of which still continues, and since the constitution uses the general term contract, without distinguishing between those which are executory and those which are executed, it must be construed to comprehend the latter as well as the former. A law annulling conveyances between individuals, and declaring that the grantors should stand seized of their former estates, notwithstanding those grants, would be as repugnant to the constitution as a law discharging the vendors of property from the obligation of executing their contracts by conveyances. It would be strange if a contract to convey was secured by the constitution, while an absolute conveyance remained unprotected.

If, under a fair construction of the constitution, grants are comprehended under the term contracts, is a grant from the State excluded from the operation of the provision? Is the clause to be considered as inhibiting the State from impairing the obligation of contracts between two individuals, but as excluding from that inhibition contracts made with itself?

The words themselves contain no such distinction. They are general, and are applicable to contracts of every description. If contracts made with the State are to be exempted from their operation, the exception must arise from the character of the contracting party, not from the words which are employed.

Whatever respect might have been felt for the state sovereignties, it is not to be disguised that the framers of the constitution viewed, with some apprehension, the violent acts which might grow out of the feelings of the moment; and that the people of the United States, in adopting that instrument, have manifested a determination to shield themselves and their property from the effects of those sudden and strong passions to which men are exposed. The restrictions on the legislative power of the States are obviously founded in this sentiment; and the Constitution of the United States contains what may be deemed a bill of rights for the people of each State.

No State shall pass any bill of attainder, *ex post facto* law, or law impairing the obligation of contracts.

A bill of attainder may affect the life of an individual, or may confiscate his property, or may do both.

In this form the power of the legislature over the lives and fortunes of individuals is expressly restrained. What motive, then, for implying, in words which import a general prohibition to impair the obligation of contracts, an exception in favor of the right to impair the obligation of those contracts into which the State may enter?

The State legislatures can pass no *ex post facto* law. An *ex post facto* law is one which renders an act punishable in a manner in which it was not punishable when it was committed. Such a law may inflict penalties on the person, or may inflict pecuniary penalties which swell the public treasury. The legislature is then prohibited from passing a law by which a man's estate, or any part of it, shall be seized for a crime which was not declared, by some previous law, to render him liable to that punishment. Why, then, should violence be done to the natural meaning of words for the purpose of leaving to the legislature the power of seizing, for public use, the estate of an individual in the form of a law annulling the title by which he holds that estate? The court can perceive no sufficient grounds for making that distinction. This rescinding act would

*ward, the secretary-treasurer of Dartmouth (and
Wheelock's nephew), who sided with the new trustees. The suit was for the recovery of the college
charter and seal, college records, and the account
books. The New Hampshire courts upheld Woodward and the college appealed to the Supreme
Court. The principal issue before the Court was
whether a state may unilaterally change the terms
of a corporate charter once it has been granted by
the state (note that royal charters were accepted as
having full validity when New Hampshire shed its
colonial status). A subsidiary issue was whether the
old trustees had a vested beneficial interest—a material or financial stake in Dartmouth College—that
would support the argument that the change in
Dartmouth's corporate charter impaired the obligation of the original contract (corporate charter)
in violation of the federal Constitution.*

*Majority votes: 6
Dissenting votes: 1*

MR. CHIEF JUSTICE MARSHALL delivered the opinion of the Court:. . . .

It can require no argument to prove, that the circumstances of this case constitute a contract. An
application is made to the crown for a charter to
incorporate a religious and literary institution. In
the application, it is stated, that large contributions
have been made for the object, which will be conferred on the corporation, as soon as it shall be created. The charter is granted, and on its faith the
property is conveyed. Surely, in this transaction
every ingredient of a complete and legitimate contract is to be found. The points for consideration
are 1. Is this contract protected by the constitution
of the United States? 2. Is it impaired by the acts
under which the defendant holds?

1. . . . [T]he term "contract" must be understood in a . . . limited sense. . . . [A]nterior to the
formation of the constitution, a course of legislation
had prevailed in many, if not in all, of the states,
which weakened the confidence of man in man, and
embarrassed all transactions between individuals,
by dispensing with a faithful performance of en-
gagements. To correct this mischief, by restraining
the power which produced it, the state legislatures
were forbidden "to pass any law impairing the obligation of contracts," that is, of contracts respecting
property, under which some individual could claim
a right to something beneficial to himself; and that,
since the clause in the constitution must in construction receive some limitation, it may be confined, and ought to be confined, to cases of this description; to cases within the mischief it was
intended to remedy. . . .

The parties in this case differ less on general
principles, less on the true construction of the constitution in the abstract, than on the application of
those principles to this case, and on the true construction of the charter of 1769. This is the point on
which the cause essentially depends. If the act of
incorporation be a grant of political power, if it creates a civil institution, to be employed in the administration of the government, or if the funds of the
college be public property, or if the state of New
Hampshire, as a government, be alone interested
in its transactions, the subject is one in which the
legislature of the state may act according to its own
judgment, unrestrained by any limitation of its
power imposed by the constitution of the United
States.

But if this be a private eleemosynary institution,
endowed with a capacity to take property, for objects unconnected with government, whose funds
are bestowed by individuals, on the faith of the
charter; if the donors have stipulated for the future
disposition and management of those funds, in the
manner prescribed by themselves; there may be
more difficulty in the case, although neither the persons who have made these stipulations, nor those
for whose benefit they were made, should be parties to the cause. Those who are no longer interested in the property, may yet retain such an interest in the preservation of their own arrangements,
as to have a right to insist, that those arrangements
shall be held sacred. Or, if they have themselves
disappeared, it becomes a subject of serious and
anxious inquiry, whether those whom they have legally empowered to represent them forever, may
not assert all the rights which they possessed, while
in being; whether, if they be without personal representatives, who may feel injured by a violation of
the compact, the trustees be not so completely their
representatives, in the eye of the law, as to stand
in their place, not only as respects the government
of the college, but also as respects the maintenance
of the college charter. . . .

Whence, . . . can be derived the idea, that Dartmouth College has become a public institution, and
its trustees public officers, exercising powers conferred by the public for public objects? Not from
the source whence its funds were drawn; for its
foundation is purely private and eleemosynary—
not from the application of those funds; for money
may be given for education, and the persons receiving it do not, by being employed in the education
of youth, become members of the civil government.
Is it from the act of incorporation? Let this subject
be considered.

A corporation is an artificial being, invisible, intangible, and existing only in contemplation of law.

Being the mere creature of law, it possesses only those properties which the charter of its creation confers upon it, either expressly, or as incidental to its very existence. These are such as are supposed best calculated to effect the object for which it was created. Among the most important are immortality, and, if the expression may be allowed, individuality; properties, by which a perpetual succession of many persons are considered as the same, and may act as a single individual. They enable a corporation to manage its own affairs, and to hold property, without the perplexing intricacies, the hazardous and endless necessity, of perpetual conveyances for the purpose of transmitting it from hand to hand. It is chiefly for the purpose of clothing bodies of men, in succession, with these qualities and capacities, that corporations were invented, and are in use. By these means, a perpetual succession of individuals are capable of acting for the promotion of the particular object, like one immortal being. But this being does not share in the civil government of the country, unless that be the purpose for which it was created. Its immortality no more confers on it political power, or a political character, than immortality would confer such power or character on a natural person. It is no more a state instrument, than a natural person exercising the same powers would be. If, then, a natural person, employed by individuals in the education of youth, or for the government of a seminary in which youth is educated, would not become a public officer, or be considered as a member of the civil government, how is it, that this artificial being, created by law, for the purpose of being employed by the same individuals, for the same purposes, should become a part of the civil government of the country? Is it because its existence, its capacities, its powers, are given by law? Because the government has given it the power to take and to hold property, in a particular form, and for particular purposes, has the government a consequent right substantially to change that form, or to vary the purposes to which the property is to be applied? This principle has never been asserted or recognised, and is supported by no authority. Can it derive aid from reason? . . .

From the fact . . . that a charter of incorporation has been granted, nothing can be inferred, which changes the character of the institution, or transfers to the government any new power over it. The character of civil institutions does not grow out of their incorporation, but out of the manner in which they are formed, and the objects for which they are created. The right to change them is not founded on their being incorporated, but on their being the instruments of government, created for its pur-

poses. The same institutions, created for the same objects, though not incorporated, would be public institutions, and, of course, be controllable by the legislature. The incorporating act neither gives nor prevents this control. Neither, in reason, can the incorporating act change the character of a private eleemosynary institution. . . .

From this review of the charter, it appears, that Dartmouth College is an eleemosynary institution, incorporated for the purpose of perpetuating the application of the bounty of the donors, to the specified objects of that bounty; that its trustees or governors were originally named by the founder, and invested with the power of perpetuating themselves; that they are not public officers, nor is it a civil institution, participating in the administration of government; but a charity-school, or a seminary of education, incorporated for the preservation of its property, and the perpetual application of that property to the objects of its creation.

Yet a question remains to be considered, of more real difficulty, on which more doubt has been entertained, than on all that have been discussed. The founders of the college, at least, those whose contributions were in money, have parted with the property bestowed upon it, and their representatives have no interest in that property. The donors of land are equally without interest, so long as the corporation shall exist. Could they be found, they are unaffected by any alteration in its constitution, and probably regardless of its form, or even of its existence. The students are fluctuating, and no individual among our youth has a vested interest in the institution, which can be asserted in a court of justice. Neither the founders of the college, nor the youth for whose benefit it was founded, complain of the alteration made in its charter, or think themselves injured by it. The trustees alone complain, and the trustees have no beneficial interest to be protected. Can this be such a contract, as the constitution intended to withdraw from the power of state legislation? Contracts, the parties to which have a vested beneficial interest, and those only, it has been said, are the objects about which the constitution is solicitous, and to which its protection is extended.

The court has bestowed on this argument the most deliberate consideration, and the result will be stated. Dr. Wheelock, acting for himself, and for those who, at his solicitation, had made contributions to his school, applied for this charter, as the instrument which should enable him, and them, to perpetuate their beneficent intention. It was granted. An artificial, immortal being, was created by the crown, capable of receiving and distributing forever, according to the will of the donors, the donations which should be made to it. On this being, the contributions which had been collected were immediately bestowed. These gifts were made, not indeed to make a profit for the donors, or their posterity, but for something in their opinion, of inestimable value; for something which they deemed a full equivalent for the money with which it was purchased. The consideration for which they stipulated, is the perpetual application of the fund to its object, in the mode prescribed by themselves. Their descendants may take no interest in the preservation of this consideration. But in this respect their descendants are not their representatives; they are represented by the corporation. The corporation is the assignee of their rights, stands in their place, and distributes their bounty, as they would themselves have distributed it, had they been immortal. So, with respect to the students who are to derive learning from this source; the corporation is a trustee for them also. Their potential rights, which, taken distributively, are imperceptible, amount collectively to a most important interest. These are, in the aggregate, to be exercised, asserted and protected, by the corporation. They were as completely out of the donors, at the instant of their being vested in the corporation, and as incapable of being asserted by the students, as at present.

According to the theory of the British constitution, their parliament is omnipotent. To annul corporate rights might give a shock to public opinion, which that government has chosen to avoid; but its power is not questioned. Had parliament, immediately after the emanation of this charter, and the execution of those conveyances which followed it, annulled the instrument, so that the living donors would have witnessed the disappointment of their hopes, the perfidy of the transaction would have been universally acknowledged. Yet, then, as now, the donors would have no interest in the property; then, as now, those who might be students would have had no rights to be violated; then, as now, it might be said, that the trustees, in whom the rights of all were combined, possessed no private individual, beneficial interests in the property confided to their protection. Yet the contract would, at that time, have been deemed sacred by all. What has since occurred, to strip it of its inviolability? Circumstances have not changed it. In reason, in justice, and in law, it is now, what it was in 1769.

This is plainly a contract to which the donors, the trustees and the crown (to whose rights and obligations New Hampshire succeeds) were the original parties. It is a contract made on a valuable consideration. It is a contract for the security and disposition of property. It is a contract, on the faith of which, real and personal estate has been conveyed to the corporation. It is, then, a contract within the letter of the constitution, and within its spirit also . . . the obligation of which cannot be impaired, without violating the constitution of the United States. This opinion appears to us to be equally supported by reason, and by the former decisions of this court.

2. We next proceed to the inquiry, whether its obligation has been impaired by those acts of the legislature of New Hampshire, to which the special verdict refers?

From the review of this charter, which has been taken, it appears that the whole power of governing the college, of appointing and removing tutors, of fixing their salaries, of directing the course of study to be pursued by the students, and of filling up vacancies created in their own body, was vested in the trustees. . . . [I]t was expressly stipulated, that this corporation, thus constituted, should continue forever; and that the number of trustees should forever consist of twelve, and no more. By this contract, the crown was bound, and could have made no violent alteration in its essential terms, without impairing its obligation.

By the revolution, the duties, as well as the powers, of government devolved on the people of New Hampshire. . . . It is too clear, to require the support of argument, that all contracts and rights respecting property, remained unchanged by the revolution. The obligations, then, which were created by the charter to Dartmouth College, were the same in the new, that they had been in the old government. . . .

. . . [T]he act "to amend the charter, and enlarge and improve the corporation of Dartmouth College," increases the number of trustees to twenty-one, gives the appointment of the additional members to the executive of the state, and creates a board of overseers, to consist of twenty-five persons, of whom twenty-one are also appointed by the executive of New Hampshire, who have power to inspect and control the most important acts of the trustees.

On the effect of this law, two opinions cannot be entertained. . . . The charter of 1769 exists no longer. It is reorganized; and reorganized in such a manner, as to convert a literary institution, moulded according to the will of its founders, and placed under the control of private literary men, into a machine entirely subservient to the will of government. This may be for the advantage of this college in particular, and may be for the advantage of literature in general; but it is not according to the will of the donors and is subversive of that contract, on the faith of which their property was given.

In the view which has been taken of this interesting case, the court has confined itself to the rights possessed by the trustees, as the assignees and representatives of the donors and founders, for the benefit of religion and literature. . . . [I]n these private eleemosynary institutions, the body corporate, as possessing the whole legal and equitable interest, and completely representing the donors, for the purpose of executing the trust, has rights which are protected by the constitution.

It results from this opinion, that the acts of the legislature of New Hampshire, which are stated in the special verdict found in this cause, are repugnant to the constitution of the United States; and that the judgment on this special verdict ought to have been for the plaintiffs. The judgment of the state court must, therefore, be reversed.

Reversed.

MR. JUSTICE WASHINGTON: [concurring opinion omitted]

MR. JUSTICE JOHNSON: concurred, for the reasons stated by the Chief Justice.

MR. JUSTICE LIVINGSTON: concurred, for the reasons stated by CHIEF JUSTICE MARSHALL and JUSTICES WASHINGTON and STORY.

MR. JUSTICE STORY: [concurring opinion omitted]

MR. JUSTICE DUVALL: dissented [with no opinion].

CHARLES RIVER BRIDGE v. WARREN BRIDGE, 11 PETERS 420 (1837)

In 1785 the Massachusetts legislature granted a corporate charter to the Charles River Bridge Company. The corporate charter authorized the company to build a bridge over the Charles River and to charge a toll for a period of 40 years. The charter also specified that the company would make an annual payment to Harvard College as compensation for Harvard's surrender of an exclusive ferry right granted by an earlier legislature for the purpose of transporting passengers across the Charles River. Nothing in the charter explicitly stated that the Charles River Bridge Company would have the exclusive right to build a bridge over the river, but that seemed to be implied. Only seven years later the Massachusetts legislature amended the corporate charter and extended by some 30 years the time period in which the company could charge a toll. However, in 1828 the Massachusetts legislature chartered the Warren Bridge Company and gave it the right to build another bridge across the

Charles River. The Warren Bridge Company would be able to charge a toll, but only for up to six years, after which the bridge would revert to the state and become part of the state's public highway system with no toll charged. The Charles River Bridge Company went to court complaining that its charter was violated by the Warren Bridge charter. The proprietors of the Charles River Bridge Company argued that their corporate charter constituted a contract on the part of the state and that it clearly implied that they had an exclusive right to operate a bridge across the Charles River. The Warren Bridge Company charter thus constituted an impairment of the obligation of their contract in violation of the contract clause of the Constitution. The case raised the important question of whether the doctrine of implied contracts applies to public grants. This was a question that had profound social and economic policy consequences.

Majority votes: 4
Dissenting votes: 3

MR. CHIEF JUSTICE TANEY delivered the opinion of the Court:. . . .

The plaintiffs in error insist, . . . that by virtue of the grant of 1650, Harvard College was entitled, in perpetuity, to the right of keeping a ferry between Charlestown and Boston; that this right was exclusive, and that . . . the ferry rights of the college have been transferred to the proprietors of the Charles River Bridge. . . . The petition to the Legislature in 1785, on which the charter was granted, does not suggest an assignment, nor any agreement or consent on the part of the college; and the petitioners do not appear to have regarded the wishes of that institution, as by any means necessary to insure their success. They place their application entirely on considerations of public interest and public convenience, and the superior advantages of a communication across the Charles River by a bridge instead of a ferry. . . . [T]he State, by virtue of its sovereign powers and eminent domain, had a right to take away the franchise of the ferry; because in their judgment, the public interest and convenience would be better promoted by a bridge in the same place; and upon that principle they proceed to make a pecuniary compensation to the college for the franchise thus taken away, and as there is an express reservation of a continuing pecuniary compensation to the college when the bridge shall become the property of the State, and no provision whatever for the restoration of the ferry right, it is evident that no such right was intended to be reserved or continued. The ferry, with all its privileges, was intended to be forever at an end, and a compensation in money was given in lieu of it. . . .

We are not now left to determine, for the first time, the rules by which public grants are to be construed in this country. The subject has already been considered in this court . . . and the principle recognized, that in grants by the public nothing passes by implication. . . .

Adopting the rule of construction above stated as the settled one, we proceed to apply it to the charter of 1785, to the proprietors of the Charles River Bridge. This act of incorporation is in the usual form, and the privileges such as are commonly given to corporations of that kind. It confers on them the ordinary faculties of a corporation, for the purpose of building the bridge; and establishes certain rates of toll, which the company are authorized to take. This is the whole grant. There is no exclusive privilege given to them over the waters of Charles River, above or below their bridge. No right to erect another bridge themselves, nor to prevent other persons from erecting one. No engagement from the State that another shall not be erected, and no undertaking not to sanction competition, nor to make improvements that may diminish the amount of its income. Upon all these subjects the charter is silent, and nothing is said in it about a line of travel, so much insisted on in the argument, in which they are to have exclusive privileges. No words are used from which an intention to grant any of these rights can be inferred. If the plaintiff is entitled to them, it must be implied simply from the nature of the grant, and cannot be inferred from the words by which the grant is made. . . .

. . . In order, then, to entitle themselves to relief, it is necessary to show that the Legislature contracted not to do the act of which they complain; and that they impaired, or in other words violated, that contract, by the erection of the Warren Bridge.

The inquiry then is, does the charter contain such a contract on the part of the State? Is there any such stipulation to be found in that instrument? It must be admitted on all hands, that there is none—no words that even relate to another bridge, or to the diminution of their tolls, or to the line of travel. If a contract on that subject can be gathered from the charter, it must be by implication, and cannot be found in the words used. Can such an agreement be implied? The rule of construction before stated is an answer to the question. In charters of this description, no rights are taken from the public or given to the corporation, beyond those which the words of the charter, by their natural and proper construction, purport to convey. There are no words which import such a contract as the plaintiffs in error contend for, and none can be implied. . . .

The practice and usage of almost every State in the Union, old enough to have commenced the work of internal improvement, is opposed to the doctrine contended for on the part of the plaintiffs in error. . . .

And what would be the fruits of this doctrine of implied contracts on the part of the States, and of property in a line of travel by a corporation, if it should now be sanctioned by this court? To what results would it lead us? If it is to be found in the charter to this bridge, the same process of reasoning must discover it in the various acts which have been passed within the last forty years, for turnpike companies. And what is to be the extent of the privileges of exclusion on the different sides of the road? How far must the new improvement be distant from the old one? How near may you approach without invading its rights in the privileged line? If this court should establish the principles now contended for, what is to become of the numerous railroads established on the same line of travel with turnpike companies; and which have rendered the franchise of the turnpike corporations of no value? Let it once be understood that such charters carry with them these implied contracts, and give this unknown and undefined property in a line of traveling, and you will soon find the old turnpike corporations awakening from their sleep, and calling upon this court to put down the improvements which have taken their place. The millions of property which have been invested in railroads and canals, upon lines of travel which have been before occupied by turnpike corporations, will be put in jeopardy. We shall be thrown back to the improvements of the last century, and obliged to stand still until the claims of the old turnpike corporations shall be satisfied, and they shall consent to permit these States to avail themselves of the lights of modern science, and to partake of the benefit of those improvements which are now adding to the wealth and prosperity, and the convenience and comfort, of every other part of the civilized world. Nor is this all. This court will find itself compelled to fix, by some arbitrary rule, the width of this new kind of property in a line of travel; for if such a right of property exists, we have no lights to guide us in marking out its extent, unless, indeed, we resort to the old feudal grants, and to the exclusive rights of ferries, by prescription, between towns; and are prepared to decide that when a turnpike road from one town to another had been made, no railroad or canal, between these two points, could afterwards be established. This court is not prepared to sanction principles which must lead to such results. . . .

The judgment of the Supreme Judicial Court of the Commonwealth of Massachusetts, dismissing the plaintiffs' bill, must, therefore, be affirmed with costs.

[*Affirmed*]

MR. JUSTICE MCLEAN: [dissenting] [omitted]
MR. JUSTICE STORY, dissenting:. . . .

. . .I do not insist upon any extraordinary liberality in interpreting this charter. All I contend for is that it shall receive a fair and reasonable interpretation, so as to carry into effect the legislative intention, and secure to the grantees a just security for their privileges. . . .

Let us now enter upon the consideration of the terms of the charter. In my judgment, nothing can be more plain than that it is a grant of a right to erect a bridge between Boston and Charlestown, in the place where the ferry between those towns was kept. It has been said that the charter itself does not describe the bridge as between Charlestown and Boston, but grants an authority to erect "a bridge over the Charles River, in the place where the old ferry was then kept;" and that these towns are not named, except for the purpose of describing the then ferry. Now, this seems to me, with all due deference, to be a distinction without a difference. The bridge is to be erected in the place where the old ferry then was. But where was it to begin, and where was it to terminate? Boston and Charlestown are the only possible terminals, for the ferryways were there; and it was to be built between Boston and Charlestown, because the ferry was between them. . . .

The argument of the defendants is that the plaintiffs are to take nothing by implication. Either (say they) the exclusive grant extends only to the local limits of the bridge, or it extends the whole length of the river, or at least up to old Cambridge Bridge. The latter construction would be absurd and monstrous, and therefore the former must be the true one. Now, I utterly deny the alternatives involved in the dilemma. The right to build a bridge over a river, and to take toll, may well include an exclusive franchise beyond the local limits of the bridge, and yet not extend through the whole course of the river, or even to any considerable distance on the river. There is no difficulty in common sense, or in law, in maintaining such a doctrine. But then, it is asked, what limits can be assigned to such a franchise? The answer is obvious; the grant carries with it an exclusive franchise to a reasonable distance

on the river, so that the ordinary travel to the bridge shall not be diverted by any new bridge to the injury or ruin of the franchise. A new bridge, which would be a nuisance to the old bridge, would be within the reach of its exclusive right. . . .

Let us see what is the result of the narrow construction contended for by the defendants. If that result be such as is inconsistent with all reasonable presumptions growing out of the case; if it be repugnant to the principles of equal justice; if it will defeat the whole objects of the grant; it will not, I trust, be insisted on that this court is bound to adopt it. . . .

Now, I put it to the common sense of every man, whether if at the moment of granting the charter the Legislature had said to the proprietors—you shall build the bridge; you shall bear the burdens; you shall be bound by the charges; and your sole reimbursement shall be from the tolls of forty years; and yet we will not even guaranty you any certainty of receiving any tolls. On the contrary, we reserve to ourselves the full power and authority to erect other bridges, toll or free bridges, according to our own free will and pleasure, contiguous to yours, and having the same termini with yours; and if you are successful we may thus supplant you, divide, destroy your profits, and annihilate your tolls, without annihilating your burdens; if, I say, such had been the language of the Legislature, is there a man living of ordinary discretion or prudence, who would have accepted such a charter upon such terms? I fearlessly answer no. There would have been such a gross inadequacy of consideration, and such a total insecurity of all the rights of property, under such circumstances, that the project would have dropped, stillborn. And I put the question further, whether any Legislature, meaning to promote a project of permanent public utility (such as this confessedly was), would ever have dreamed of such a qualification of its own grant, when it sought to enlist private capital and private patronage to insure the accomplishment of it? . . .

To sum up, then, the whole argument on this head, I maintain that, upon the principles of common reason and legal interpretation, the present grant carries with it a necessary implication that the Legislature shall do no act to destroy or essentially to impair the franchise; that (as one of the learned judges of the State court expressed it) there is an implied agreement that the State will not grant another bridge between Boston and Charlestown, so near as to draw away the custom from the old one; and (as another learned judge expressed it) that there is an implied agreement of the State to grant the undisturbed use of the bridge and its tolls, so

Chapter

12

Due Process: Economic Rights

FROM PROCEDURAL TO SUBSTANTIVE DUE PROCESS

State constitutions and the Fifth and Fourteenth Amendments to the U.S. Constitution contain a due process guarantee that neither life, liberty, nor property can be denied any person without due process of law. The meaning of due process was widely understood at the time these provisions became part of the state and federal constitutions to provide a guarantee against arbitrary governmental action not covered by law; that is, no government official can take any action against anyone without being authorized by law to do so. Furthermore, due process of law was thought to mean that any law that potentially can deprive one of life, liberty, or property should contain certain basic procedures to assure fairness in carrying out the law. Such procedures as an impartial hearing, the right to appeal, the right to call witnesses on one's behalf, and the right to have a lawyer argue one's case were generally considered to be the sorts of safeguards needed to assure fairness

in carrying out laws that could have devastating consequences for an individual. Although what precisely constituted "due process" was generally not defined in the constitutions and was probably fuzzy in the minds of the framers themselves, the essential thrust of the concept was toward fair procedures and away from government arbitrariness in dealing with individuals. Certainly due process was *not* seen as a limitation on government's ability to act. Rather, when government acted it was obliged to do so under the authority of law and to carry out the law in each instance in a fair manner. This is *procedural due process*.

In the creative hands of lawyers and judges over the last half of the nineteenth century, due process of law was transformed into a substantive barrier to enacting certain laws. *Substantive due process* is the concept that government may not enact a particular law because that law is inherently unfair and unjust and therefore can never meet the requirement of due process of law. The substance of the law must be just and must not unfairly deny persons their life, liberty, or property. Substantive due process thus becomes the vehicle for a natural law jurisprudence. Judges determine what they think is morally right or wrong and equate that with due process of law. Due process of law, then, was originally a procedural limitation on government—procedural due process. But by the beginning of the twentieth century it had also become a substantive limitation on the enactment of legislation—substantive due process. How this came about is one of the most fascinating chapters in American constitutional law. Some of the highlights of the transformation follow.

One of the earliest and best known instances of a law itself being invalidated on due process grounds was in the 1856 decision of the New York Court of Appeals, *Wynehamer* v. *New York,* 13 N.Y. 378, involving the New York state constitution's due process guarantee. The case concerned the validity of a liquor prohibition law enacted by the New York legislature in 1855 "for the prevention of intemperance, pauperism and crime." Under the provisions of the statute, all owners of intoxicating liquors were forbidden to sell *and* to store them except for medicinal usages. Violation of the law was a misdemeanor, and the liquor was considered a nuisance to be destroyed by summary process. Liquor merchants were thus faced with having to destroy their property themselves or risk misdemeanor charges being brought against them, thus having the state destroy their merchandise. Wynehamer violated the law and was convicted—and on his appeal challenged the validity of the law. The majority of New York's highest court sided with Wynehamer and struck down the statute as a deprivation of property without due process of law. Judge Comstock, speaking for the majority, emphasized that any law requiring the destruction of private property (that before enactment of the law was legally protected) is by definition an unjust law that can never meet the requirements of due process. Comstock stressed that there are some absolute private rights beyond

the reach of legislatures, and the right to own and possess property is one of those rights.

The *Wynehamer* decision attracted much attention in legal circles because of the unusual use of due process. That due process was being used to protect property rights was also not lost on the legal profession. Interestingly, the Supreme Court, the same year as the *Wynehamer* decision, decided a due process case, *Murray* v. *Hoboken,* 18 Howard 272, and offered the conventional procedural due process interpretation of the Fifth Amendment guarantee. However, just one year later, Chief Justice Taney in his **Dred Scott** (chap. 6) opinion observed with reference to the Missouri Compromise of 1820 prohibiting slavery in certain of the federal territories: "[A]n Act of Congress which deprives a citizen of the United States of his liberty or property, merely because he came himself or brought his property [i.e., slaves] into a particular Territory of the United States, and who had committed no offense against the laws, could hardly be dignified with the name of due process of law." The influence of the *Wynehamer* decision seems apparent. But the justices did not immediately make much of this novel view of due process.

The next major use by the Court of a substantive concept of due process occurred in the majority opinion of Chief Justice Chase in *Hepburn* v. *Griswold,* 8 Wallace 603 (1870). Here, Chase desperately sought to find a constitutional basis for setting aside the retroactive provisions of the Legal Tender Act of 1862. Among other arguments, Chase offered his view that the retroactive application of the law denied creditors their property without due process of law.

In 1868 the Fourteenth Amendment, with its own due process clause applicable to the states, became part of the federal Constitution. That year was also the publication date of a major constitutional law treatise entitled *Constitutional Limitations* by Thomas Cooley. In it Cooley argued for substantive due process as a way of protecting property rights. This was particularly important at this time, because the contract clause no longer was a viable barrier to government economic regulation; states were routinely inserting clauses in corporate charters reserving to the state the right to change the terms for the public welfare. Substantive due process was thus offered as a much-needed barrier to unwarranted government interference with private enterprise.

In **The Slaughterhouse Cases** (chap. 6), Justice Miller speaking for the Court rejected substantive due process, observing that due process was traditionally a procedural concept and that no other interpretation of due process was recognized by the Court. Although the Waite Court was generally sympathetic to state regulation, the new thinking about due process as a substantive limit on government legislation and activity gradually began to infiltrate the thinking of the justices. This can be seen in the **Munn** v. **Illinois** opinion of the Court by Chief Justice Waite. While upholding the challenged legislation as a valid exercise of the state police power because grain elevators were "a business affected with a public interest," Waite observed offhandedly that statutes regulating the use and the price of the use of private property do not ordinarily deprive an owner of due process of law. "Under some circumstances they may, but not under all." Waite, without realizing it, was giving due process a substantive flavor, suggesting that even justices who (like himself) opposed using substantive due process were nonetheless intellectually affected by the arguments its advocates made.

One year after the *Munn* case was decided, Justice Miller in the case of *Davidson* v. *New Orleans,* 96 U.S. 97 (1878), expressed astonishment that the due process clause of the Fourteenth Amendment had provoked such extensive legal argument as the basis for limiting state economic regulation. He pointed out that the same due process clause was con-

tained in the Fifth Amendment, but for close to a century it had never created any serious limitation on the substance of federal legislation. Be that as it may, the concept of substantive due process was taking root even with justices who supported state regulation. From 1877 to 1890 no state law was invalidated on due process grounds. However, in the process of sustaining state economic regulation, the justices, whether subconsciously or not, moved closer to recognizing substantive due process. For example, in the 1884 case of *Spring Valley Water-Works* v. *Schottler,* 110 U.S. 347, Chief Justice Waite in upholding California legislation regulating the price that water companies could charge observed that such legislation does not deny property without due process of law. But "What may be done if the municipal authorities do not exercise an honest judgment, or if they fix upon a price which is manifestly unreasonable, need not now be considered. . . ." The clear implication was that a dishonest judgment or unreasonable price would be a due process violation.

Three years later in *Mugler* v. *Kansas,* 123 U.S. 623 (1887), the Court, while upholding a Kansas prohibition law, noted, "It does not at all follow that every statute enacted ostensibly for the promotion of these ends [public health, safety, welfare] is to be accepted as a legitimate exertion of the police powers of the state." Rather, the legitimacy of regulatory legislation is to be determined by the judiciary. "The courts are not bound by mere forms, nor are they to be misled by mere pretenses. They are at liberty—indeed, are under a solemn duty—to look at the substance of things."

By 1890 the Court had a new chief justice and a new majority ready to utilize substantive due process to limit government economic regulation. The turning point was the **Minnesota Rate Case.** However, although the Court began to use substantive due process to limit governmental regulatory legislation, the large majority of legislation brought before the Court, as pointed out earlier, did pass the muster of the majority. Even though, as Justice Bradley in dissent argued, the **Minnesota Rate Case** seemed to reverse *Munn* v. *Illinois,* the Court two years later in *Budd* v. *New York,* 143 U.S. 517 (1892), upheld a New York law regulating grain elevator rates and did so on the authority of *Munn.*

In 1886 the Court accepted the proposition argued before it one year earlier by Roscoe Conkling that corporations were legal persons entitled to Fourteenth Amendment protection and that the framers purposely used the term "person" in the amendment in order to extend protection to corporations. Conkling had spoken with special authority, for he had served in Congress on the Joint Committee on Reconstruction. In his appearance before the Court, he produced, for the first time, a journal of committee proceedings, and he quoted selectively from that document to prove that the intent of the framers was to include corporations under the umbrella of Fourteenth Amendment rights. However, historical research has subsequently revealed that Conkling deceived the justices; the term *person* was really used in the Due Process Clause in order to protect blacks who were not born in the United States and other aliens. Furthermore, note that the entire Due Process Clause, including use of the term *person,* was lifted directly from the Fifth Amendment. But before accusing the Court of excessive gullibility, we should recognize that since 1844 corporations had been considered citizens for purposes of the federal courts' diversity jurisdiction. In addition, Congress in 1871 legislation had specifically included corporations within the term *persons;* thus Conkling's argument had the ring of plausibility.

The final triumph of substantive due process as a vehicle with which to protect businessmen and corporations occurred with **Allgeyer** v. **Louisiana** in 1897, which defined the liberty of the Due Process Clause in economic terms. Liberty was held to include liberty of contract. State legislation regulating the contractual affairs of businesses and corporations, if a majority of the justices believed it to be unfair or unjust, could now be struck down as violating liberty of contract without due process of law.

The Fourteenth Amendment became almost worthless as a protection of civil rights and civil liberties, and the Court suggested in such cases as **Hurtado** v. **California** (chap. 16) that the Due Process Clause did not incorporate any of the rights contained within the Bill of Rights. Despite this, the Court in *Chicago B. & Q. R. Co.* v. *Chicago,* 166 U.S. 226 (1897), implied that the Fifth Amendment's just compensation guarantee to property owners *was* incorporated within the Fourteenth Amendment's Due Process Clause—an obvious doctrinal inconsistency blithely glossed over by most justices. But it was substantive due process that gave the justices the constitutional tool they needed to become the superlegislature of the nation. As the Court observed in the case of *Holden* v. *Hardy,* 169 U.S. 366 (1898), in which the Court upheld a Utah statute limiting to eight hours a day the hours of coal workers and others employed in underground mines: "The question in each case is whether the legislature had adopted the statute in exercise of a reasonable discretion, or whether its actions be a mere excuse for an unjust discrimination, or the oppression, or spoliation of a particular class."

The Fuller Court's record in upholding hours legislation was generally a good one, although the Court is best known for its reactionary antilabor decision in 1905 in the closely decided **Lochner** v. **New York** case. The *Lochner* decision dramatically demonstrated the perils substantive due process could hold for social legislation. But just three years later in 1908 in **Muller** v. **Oregon,** the Court upheld hours legislation and acted as if *Lochner* had never been decided. However, as if to confound students of the Court, the

Court, with a majority opinion written by Justice Harlan, produced **Adair** v. **United States,** which was a great setback for organized labor. Substantive due process was to be much used to promote economic laissez-faire, particularly by the Court of the 1920s.

The transformation of due process from a procedural to a substantive concept had its roots in the 1850s, but took a long time before becoming accepted by the Court. By the late 1880s substantive due process had become acknowledged and in 1890 was used by the Court for the first time to invalidate legislation. Although the Court for the remainder of Chief Justice Fuller's tenure was to use the concept sparingly as the basis for exercising a constitutional veto power, when the veto *was* used (as in *Lochner* and *Adair*) its impact was great. This use of the veto, along with other antiregulatory decisions involving other provisions of the Constitution, gave the Fuller Court the reputation of being the first Court to enshrine economic laissez-faire in the United States Constitution.

SUBSTANTIVE ECONOMIC DUE PROCESS

Substantive due process was generally used by the Court to disallow state labor legislation (with the important exception of hours legislation) and to strike down other attempts at business regulation. Hours legislation for women, first approved in *Muller* v. *Oregon,* was reaffirmed by the Court in *Miller* v. *Wilson,* 236 U.S. 373 (1915), and an even broader hours and wages state statute was approved two years later in **Bunting** v. **Oregon.** In *Bunting,* the Court approved of Oregon's overtime provision, but professed to see it as a mechanism for regulating hours and not wages. Another Oregon statute legislating a minimum wage for women workers also came to the Court. Because Justice Brandeis did not participate in the decision, for he had helped with preparing the brief in favor of the statute before coming to the Court, only eight justices

participated in the decision, and they were evenly divided. The practical effect of the decision, *Stettler* v. *O'Hara,* 243 U.S. 629 (1917), was to affirm the Oregon Supreme Court ruling sustaining the act's constitutionality. Clearly, there were five justices on the Court in favor of wages legislation and a precedent of sorts had been established. Nevertheless, when a newly constituted Court under the leadership of Chief Justice Taft once again considered minimum wage legislation for women, this time enacted by Congress for the District of Columbia, the Court in **Adkins** v. **Children's Hospital** did an about-face and in the process resurrected *Lochner.* Even compulsory arbitration of wage controversies was struck down by the Court (see *Wolff Packing Co.* v. *Court of Industrial Relations,* 262 U.S. 522 [1923]).

The Court in *Murphy* v. *Sardell,* 269 U.S. 530 (1925), made it plain that state minimum wage laws for women violated the liberty of contract guarantee within the Fourteenth Amendment's Due Process Clause, and in 1936 at the height of the Depression the Court insisted on maintaining this position in **Morehead** v. **New York ex rel. Tipaldo.** The Court indicated its lack of sympathy for labor in other cases such as *Coppage* v. *Kansas,* 236 U.S. 1 (1915), in which it struck down a Kansas law prohibiting the use of the yellow-dog contract. The reasoning followed that of *Adair* v. *United States.* In *Truax* v. *Corrigan,* 257 U.S. 312 (1921), the Court struck down a pro-labor Arizona statute. That statute had prohibited Arizona courts from issuing injunctions against picketing.

The Court, in a series of decisions in the 1920s and early 1930s, justified striking down state regulation of business practices on the ground that the businesses regulated were not affected with a public interest; thus such regulation denied due process of law that was protected by the Fourteenth Amendment. Under this reasoning the Court struck down the following: a Nebraska law establishing a standard weight for bread [*Burns Baking Co.* v. *Bryan,* 264 U.S. 504 (1924)]; a New York law prohibiting ticket scalping by theater ticket brokers [*Tyson & Brother* v. *Banton,* 273 U.S. 418 (1927)]; a New Jersey statute fixing rates that could be charged by employment agencies [*Ribnik* v. *McBride,* 277 U.S. 350 (1928)]; a Tennessee statute that set gasoline prices [*Williams* v. *Standard Oil Co.,* 278 U.S. 235 (1929)]; and an Oklahoma statute regulating the ice business [*New State Ice Co.* v. *Liebmann,* 285 U.S. 262 (1932)]. However, in 1934 the Court abandoned the business-affected-with-a-public-interest doctrine as a bar to state regulation and upheld a New York state milk price control law in *Nebbia* v. *New York,* 291 U.S. 502. The Court said that the doctrine formed "an unsatisfactory test of the constitutionality of legislation directed at business practices or prices" and that "It is clear that there is no closed class or category of businesses affected with a public interest. . . ."

When the Court in 1936 handed down *Morehead* v. *New York ex rel. Tipaldo,* that unpopular decision was in the context of the Court's battle with the New Deal, as will be recalled from chapter 3. The turning point came with a decision that did an about-face on the issue of a minimum wage for women, the case of **West Coast Hotel** v. **Parrish** that was a landmark in several respects. Coming as it did at the height of the controversy over President Roosevelt's court reform bill, the decision served to lessen, in part, the urgency with which the administration and its congressional supporters approached the bill. The decision also accomplished, in one fell swoop, the reversal of such unpopular precedents as *Adkins* v. *Children's Hospital, Lochner* v. *New York,* and *Morehead* v. *Tipaldo.* The Court undid the liberty of contract doctrine as an obstacle to economic and social legislation and, most importantly, the Court signaled an end to using substantive due process to strike down economic and social welfare policy. In only one more case after 1937, *Connecticut Gen-*

eral Life Insurance Company v. *Johnson,* 303 U.S. 77 (1938), was the Court to use substantive economic due process to invalidate state legislation. As Justice Black was to observe in *Ferguson* v. *Skrupa,* 372 U.S. 726 (1963), with reference to the Due Process Clause, "Courts no longer substitute their social and economic beliefs for the judgment of legislative bodies." In *Driscoll* v. *Edison Light and Power Co.,* 307 U.S. 104 (1939), the Court upheld a state commission's utility rates and suggested that the Court was disengaging itself from its previous preoccupation with formulas for setting rates favorable to the utilities. In *Olsen* v. *Nebraska,* 313 U.S. 236 (1941), the Court unanimously upheld a Nebraska statute that fixed maximum fees that could be charged by employment agencies. In so doing, it reversed the previous Court decision of *Ribnik* v. *McBride* and the opinion of the Court noted simply that "the drift away from *Ribnik* v. *McBride* has been so great that it can no longer be deemed a controlling authority." In **Williamson** v. **Lee Optical Co.,** the Court upheld the regulation of the optometry business. The Rehnquist Court rejected the due process claims of a landlord seeking to invalidate a city rent control law in **Pennell** v. **City of San Jose.**

Today, due process in the realm of economic rights is essentially confined to procedures, not the substance of the law. For example, in *Green* v. *Lindsey,* 456 U.S. 444 (1982), the Court struck down a Kentucky law regulating landlord-tenant relations which permitted a landlord to post an eviction notice in a conspicuous place on the premises. The tenant claimed that the notice was never received and therefore was unable to legally challenge it, thereby being deprived of property. The Court agreed that the notice provision was faulty, thus the law deprived the tenant of property without due process of law. Notice by the U.S. mail, suggested the Court, would satisfy due process.

While there is no longer a doctrinal legitimacy for the use of substantive due process for the purpose of vetoing state or federal economic legislation, the Court in 1985 hinted that another provision of the Fourteenth Amendment had potential for such use, the Equal Protection Clause. In the case of *Metropolitan Life Insurance Co.* v. *Ward,* 470 U.S. 869, a 5–4 majority invalidated an Alabama law that gave tax advantages to domestically based Alabama insurance companies not given to out-of-state companies doing business in the state. The Commerce Clause was not an issue because Congress has authorized the states to regulate the insurance industry (and this previously had met with the Court's approval). The Court in this case ruled that the Alabama law violated equal protection of the laws by using an impermissible classification based solely on residence. This was the first time that the equal protection clause was used for economic reasons to protect the rights of businesses. The dissenters, an unusual coalition of justices (O'Connor, Brennan, Marshall, and Rehnquist) saw this decision as a precedent for a future Court to once again superlegislate in matters of economic regulation.

THE IMPACT OF THE COURT'S DECISIONS

Table 12.1 summarizes the impact of selected Court decisions concerning economic rights under due process. The reprinted cases follow.

Table 12.1 THE IMPACT OF SELECTED COURT DECISIONS, DUE PROCESS-ECONOMIC RIGHTS CASES

Case	Year	Impact on Parties	Short-Run Impact	Long-Run Impact
Munn v. Illinois	1877	Some financial impact on grain elevators and railroads as they lowered their rates and began cooperating with Illinois Railroad and Warehouse Commission.	State railroad and grain elevator rate regulation encouraged. Conservative newspapers attack decision. Temporary panic by holders of railroad securities.	Business-affected-with-a-public-interest doctrine established. Was later used to restrict regulation. Opinion of the Court *seemed* to concede *some* scope for the concept of substantive due process.
Chicago, Milwaukee and St. Paul R.R. Co. v. Minnesota (Minnesota Rate Case)	1890	Railroad wins.	Called into question legality of railroad and grain elevator rate regulation legislation. Uncertainty over whether *Munn v. Illinois* was overturned.	Substantive due process used to restrict government economic regulation.
Allgeyer v. Louisiana	1897	Allgeyer & Co. wins. Does not have to pay $1000 fine.	States cannot regulate mail-order insurance industry.	Liberty of contract established as Fourteenth Amendment due process clause doctrine.
Lochner v. New York	1905	By winning case Lochner does not have to pay $50 fine.	Many state court decisions declared state labor legislation unconstitutional on authority of *Lochner* precedent.	Extreme defense of liberty of contract used in later years by Court in *Adkins v. Children's Hospital* (1923).
Muller v. Oregon	1908	Muller required to pay fine of $10.	Following this decision and over the subsequent nine years, 39 states enacted new or toughened existing laws regulating the work of women.	Provided positive precedent for sustaining social legislation. Launched the Brandeis brief as a strategy for arguing validity of social legislation before the Court.
Adair v. United States	1908	Adair did not have to pay the $100 fine. The Louisville and Nashville Railroad Co. continued to fire employees who joined unions.	Some states sought to outlaw yellow dog contracts, but Court in *Coppage v. Kansas* (1915) put a halt to that.	Provided antiunion precedent. Contributed to labor unrest on the railroads, climaxed by federal government intervention in 1916 with passage of Adamson Act.

(continued)

Table 12.1 *(continued)*

Case	Year	Impact on Parties	Short-Run Impact	Long-Run Impact
Bunting v. Oregon	1917	Bunting fined $50.	*Lochner v. New York* implicitly overruled. Hours legislation upheld.	Provided a precedent for treating social legislation as valid exercise of state police power.
Adkins v. Children's Hospital	1923	Minimum Wage Board of the District of Columbia permanently enjoined from enforcing orders fixing minimum wages.	The *Lochner* doctrine was resurrected. States prevented from enacting minimum wage legislation.	Provided negative precedent used in 1936 that helped spark the constitutional crisis of 1936–1937.
Morehead v. Tipaldo	1936	State Industrial Commissioner barred from setting minimum wages for women employees. Tipaldo not tried because statute under which he was indicted is struck down.	Decision greeted unfavorably. Court majority seen as insensitive to the hardships caused by the Depression. Ruling helped provoke constitutional crisis of 1936–1937.	No long-run impact. With *West Coast Hotel* decision of 1937, Court renounced the *Morehead* ruling.
West Coast Hotel v. Parrish	1937	Elsie Parrish received wages owed her.	Popular decision. Signaled the Court's retreat from economic laissez-faire. Helped to undermine Roosevelt's court bill. Encouraged states to enact minimum wage legislation for all workers. Paved the way for the Fair Labor Standards Act of 1938.	Court began withdrawal from substantive economic due process. Liberty of contract no longer a viable device for stifling social legislation. Both state and federal governments enacted far-reaching labor laws.
Williamson v. Lee Optical Co.	1955	Adverse business effect on opticians.	Decision consistent with Court's post-1937 disengagement from substantive due process in economic matters.	States given continued go-ahead to economically regulate free from the exercise of the judicial veto under substantive due process.

MUNN v. ILLINOIS,
94 U.S. 113 (1877)

Illinois, like other midwestern states, took action in the 1870s to regulate the rates charged by railroads and grain elevators. These laws were enacted at the behest of the farmers' organizations, known as the Granges, to correct widespread abuses. Illinois' Constitution of 1870 contained an article declaring grain elevators to be public warehouses and giving the legislature the power to regulate them. The Munn *case involved a statute enacted in 1871 that established a commission with power to set the maximum rates owners of grain elevators could charge. Because this legislation was based upon a specific provision of the Illinois Constitution, it could only be challenged as violating the federal and not the state constitution. Ira Munn and associates, owners of grain elevators in Chicago, argued that setting the rates they could charge denied them the full use of their property, and of the income they would otherwise derive from it, without due process of law. The Court majority answered this contention by rejecting it; but in so doing it seemed to hint that not all state regulation of rates charged by businesses would meet the requirements of the Fourteenth Amendment's due process clause.*

Majority votes: 7
Dissenting votes: 2

MR. CHIEF JUSTICE WAITE delivered the opinion of the Court: . . .

When one becomes a member of society, he necessarily parts with some rights or privileges which, as an individual not affected by his relations to others, he might retain. "A body politic," as aptly defined in the preamble of the Constitution of Massachusetts, "is a social compact by which the whole people covenants with each citizen, and each citizen with the whole people, that all shall be governed by certain laws for the common good." This does not confer power upon the whole people to control rights which are purely and exclusively private, . . . but it does authorize the establishment of laws requiring each citizen to so conduct himself, and so use his own property, as not unnecessarily to injure another. This is the very essence of government. . . . From this source come the police powers, which, as was said by Mr. Chief Justice Taney in the *License Cases,* 5 How. 583, "are nothing more or less than the powers of government inherent in every sovereignty, . . . that is to say, . . . the power to govern men and things." Under these powers the government regulates the conduct of its citizens one towards another, and the manner in which each shall use his own property, when such regulation becomes necessary for the public good. In their exercise it has been customary in England from time immemorial, and in this country from its first colonization, to regulate ferries, common carriers, hackmen, bakers, millers, wharfingers, innkeepers, etc., and in so doing to fix a maximum of charge to be made for services rendered, accommodations furnished, and articles sold. To this day, statutes are to be found in many of the States upon some or all these subjects; and we think it has never yet been successfully contended that such legislation came within any of the constitutional prohibitions against interference with private property. . . .

From this it is apparent that, down to the time of the adoption of the Fourteenth Amendment, it was not supposed that statutes regulating the use, or even the price of the use, of private property necessarily deprived an owner of his property without due process of law. Under some circumstances they may, but not under all. The amendment does not change the law in this particular: it simply prevents the States from doing that which will operate as such a deprivation.

This brings us to inquire as to the principles upon which this power of regulation rests, in order that we may determine what is within and what without its operative effect. Looking, then, to the common law, from whence came the right which the Constitution protects, we find that when private property is "affected with a public interest, it ceases to be *juris privati* only." This was said by Lord Chief Justice Hale more than two hundred years ago, in his treatise *De Portibus Maris* and has been accepted without objection as an essential element in the law of property ever since. Property does become clothed with a public interest when used in a manner to make it of public consequence, and affect the community at large. When, therefore, one devotes his property to a use in which the public has an interest, he, in effect, grants to the public an interest in that use, and must submit to be controlled by the public for the common good, to the extent of the interest he has thus created. He may withdraw his grant by discontinuing the use; but, so long as he maintains the use, he must submit to the control. . . .

. . . The grain warehouses or elevators in Chicago are immense structures, holding from 300,000 to 1,000,000 bushels at one time, according to size. . . . They are located with the river harbor on one side and the railway tracks on the other; and the grain is run through them from car to vessel, or boat to car, as may be demanded in the course of business."

. . . [I]t is apparent that all the elevating facilities through which these vast productions "of seven or eight great States of the West" must pass on the way "to four or five of the States on the seashore" may be a "virtual" monopoly.

Under such circumstances it is difficult to see why, if the common carrier, or the miller, or the ferryman, or the innkeeper, or the wharfinger, or the baker, or the cartman, or the hackney-coach-man, pursues a public employment and exercises "a sort of public office," these plaintiffs in error do not. They stand, to use again the language of their counsel, in the very "gateway of commerce," and take toll from all who pass. Their business most certainly "tends to a common charge, and is become a thing of public interest and use." . . . Certainly, if any business can be clothed "with a public interest, and cease to be *juris privati* only," this has been. It may not be made so by the operation of the Constitution of Illinois or this statute, but it is by the facts. . . .

We conclude, therefore, that the statute in question is not repugnant to the Constitution of the United States, and that there is no error in the judgment. . . .

Judgment affirmed.

MR. JUSTICE FIELD [with whom concurred MR. JUSTICE STRONG dissenting]:

I am compelled to dissent from the decision of the court in this case, and from the reasons upon which that decision is founded. The principle upon which the opinion of the majority proceeds is, in my judgment, subversive of the rights of private property, heretofore believed to be protected by constitutional guarantees against legislative interference, and is in conflict with the authorities cited in its support. . . . One might as well attempt to change the nature of colors, by giving them a new designation. The defendants were no more public warehousemen, as justly observed by counsel, than the merchant who sells his merchandise to the public is a public merchant, or the blacksmith who shoes horses for the public is a public blacksmith; and it was a strange notion that by calling them so they would be brought under legislative control. . . .

. . . There is hardly an enterprise or business engaging the attention and labor of any considerable portion of the community, in which the public has not an interest in the sense in which that term is used by the court in its opinion; and the doctrine which allows the legislature to interfere with and

regulate the charges which the owners of property thus employed shall make for its use, that is, the rates at which all these different kinds of business shall be carried on, has never before been asserted, so far as I am aware, by any judicial tribunal in the United States. . . .

CHICAGO, MILWAUKEE AND ST. PAUL R.R. CO. v. MINNESOTA (MINNESOTA RATE CASE), 134 U.S. 418 (1890)

Despite the protestations of Justice Miller and some of his colleagues, the Court during the 1880s began to accept the concept of substantive due process as distinct from procedural due process. The Court was putting the states on notice that their police powers, that is, their powers to enact regulatory legislation to promote the public health, safety, and welfare, were not unlimited. But the justices did not use substantive due process to strike down state regulation until the Minnesota Rate Case. This case evolved as follows: The state of Minnesota enacted a statute in 1887 that created a railroad and warehouse commission for the purpose of determining and setting reasonable railroad and warehouse rates. A complaint was filed with the commission that the Chicago, Milwaukee and St. Paul Railroad Co. was charging dairy farmers unreasonable rates to ship milk. A hearing was held by the commission, and a lawyer for the railroad defended his client's rates. The commission, however, ruled in favor of the complainants, finding that a lower rate for the shipment of milk was reasonable. After the railroad refused to comply, the commission obtained a writ of mandamus from the Minnesota Supreme Court; the railroad then appealed to the United States Supreme Court, arguing that the Minnesota statute deprived the railroad of its property without due process of law, which was in violation of the Fourteenth Amendment. The Court used both procedural due process (questioning the procedures used by the commission) and substantive due process (claiming that the courts have the constitutional obligation to pass on the reasonableness of the rates themselves).

Majority votes: 6
Dissenting votes: 3

MR. JUSTICE BLATCHFORD delivered the opinion of the Court:. . . .

The construction put upon the [Minnesota] statute by the Supreme Court of Minnesota must be accepted by this court, for the purposes of the present case, as conclusive and not to be reexamined here as to its propriety or accuracy. The Supreme Court authoritatively declares that it is the expressed intention of the legislature of Minnesota, by the statute, that the rates recommended and published by the commission, if it proceeds in the manner pointed out by the act, are not simply advisory, nor merely *prima facie* equal and reasonable, but final and conclusive as to what are equal and reasonable charges; that the law neither contemplates nor allows any issue to be made or inquiry to be had as to their equality or reasonableness in fact; that, under the statute, the rates published by the commission are the only ones that are lawful, and, therefore, in contemplation of law the only ones that are equal and reasonable; and that, in a proceeding for a mandamus under the statute, there is no fact to traverse except the violation of law in not complying with the recommendations of the commission. In other words, although the railroad company is forbidden to establish rates that are not equal and reasonable, there is no power in the courts to stay the hands of the commission, if it chooses to establish rates that are unequal and unreasonable.

This being the construction of the statute by which we are bound in considering the present case, we are of opinion that, so construed, it conflicts with the Constitution of the United States in the particulars complained of by the railroad company. It deprives the company of its right to a judicial investigation, by due process of law, under the forms and with the machinery provided by the wisdom of successive ages for the investigation judicially of the truth of a matter in controversy, and substitutes therefore, as an absolute finality, the action of a railroad commission which, in view of the powers conceded to it by the state court, cannot be regarded as clothed with judicial functions or possessing the machinery of a court of justice.

Under section 8 of the statute, which the Supreme Court of Minnesota says is the only one which relates to the matter of the fixing by the commission of general schedules of rates, and which section, it says, fully and exclusively provides for that subject, and is complete in itself, all that the commission is required to do is, on the filing with it by a railroad company of copies of its schedules of charges, to "find" that any part thereof is in any respect unequal or unreasonable, and then it is authorized and directed to compel the company to change the same and adopt such charge as the commission "shall declare to be equal and reasonable," and, to that end, it is required to inform the company in writing in what respect its charges are unequal and unreasonable. No hearing is provided for, no summons or notice to the company before the commission has found what it is to find and declared what it is to declare, no opportunity provided for the company to introduce witnesses before the commission, in fact, nothing which has the semblance of due process of law; and although, in the present case, it appears that, prior to the decision of the commission, the company appeared before it by its agent, and the commission investigated the rates charged by the company for transporting milk, yet it does not appear what the character of the investigation was or how the result was arrived at.

By the second section of the statute in question, it is provided that all charges made by a common carrier for the transportation of passengers or property shall be equal and reasonable. Under this provision, the carrier has a right to make equal and reasonable charges for such transportation. In the present case, the return alleged that the rate of charge fixed by the commission was not equal or reasonable, and the Supreme Court held that the statute deprived the company of the right to show that judicially. The question of the reasonableness of a rate of charge for transportation by a railroad company, involving as it does the element of reasonableness both as regards the public, is eminently a question for judicial investigation, requiring due process of law for its determination. If the company is deprived of the power of charging reasonable rates for the use of its property, and such deprivation takes place in the absence of an investigation by judicial machinery, it is deprived of the lawful use of its property, and thus, in substance and effect, of the property itself, without due process of law and in violation of the Constitution of the United States; and in so far as it is thus deprived, while other persons are permitted to receive reasonable profits upon their invested capital, the company is deprived of the equal protection of the laws. . . .

The issuing of the peremptory writ of mandamus in this case was, therefore, unlawful, because in violation of the Constitution of the United States; and it is necessary that the relief administered in favor of the plaintiff in error should be a reversal of the judgment of the [Minnesota] Supreme Court awarding that writ, and an instruction for further proceedings by it not inconsistent with the opinion of this court. . . .

[Reversed and remanded]

MR. JUSTICE MILLER concurring: [omitted]
MR. JUSTICE BRADLEY [with whom concurred MR. JUSTICE GRAY and MR. JUSTICE LAMAR] dissenting:
I cannot agree to the decision of the court in this

case. It practically overrules *Munn* v. *Illinois*, 94 U.S. 113, and the several railroad cases that were decided at the same time. . . .

ALLGEYER v. LOUISIANA,
165 U.S. 578 (1897)

In this case the Supreme Court made it clear that the "liberty" of the due process clause of the Fourteenth Amendment meant economic liberty, including liberty to enter into contracts. The case stemmed from a Louisiana statute that forbade persons and businesses from buying insurance on property from firms that did not have a license to do business in the state and did not have a representative in the state on whom legal papers could be served. This legislation was an exercise of the state's police powers to protect the people of the state from unscrupulous insurance companies. But Allgeyer and Company disregarded this statute, buying insurance from a mail order firm based in New York. The Company was prosecuted for violating the Louisiana law, and its appeal was taken to the Supreme Court. Allgeyer and Company argued that the Louisiana statute interfered with its liberty to enter into contracts, a liberty guaranteed by the due process clause of the Fourteenth Amendment.

Votes: Unanimous

MR. JUSTICE PECKHAM delivered the opinion of the Court:

There is no doubt of the power of the State to prohibit foreign insurance companies from doing business within its limits. The State can impose such conditions as it pleases upon the doing of any business by those companies within its borders, and unless the conditions be complied with, the prohibition may be absolute. . . .

A conditional prohibition in regard to foreign insurance companies doing business within the State of Louisiana is to be found in article 236 of the constitution of that State, which reads as follows: "No foreign corporation shall do any business in this State without having one or more known places of business, and an authorized agent or agents in the State, upon whom process may be served."

It is not claimed in this suit that the Atlantic Mutual Insurance Company has violated this provision of the constitution by doing business within the State.

. . . In this case the only act which it is claimed was a violation of the statute in question consisted in sending the letter through the mail notifying the company of the property to be covered by the pol-

icy already delivered. We have then a contract which it is conceded was made outside and beyond the limits of the jurisdiction of the State of Louisiana, being made and to be performed within the State of New York, where the premiums were to be paid and losses, if any, adjusted. . . .

It is natural that the state court should have remarked that there is in this "statute an apparent interference with the liberty of defendants in restricting their rights to place insurance on property of their own whenever and in what company they desired." Such interference is not only apparent, but it is real, and we do not think that it is justified for the purpose of upholding what the State says is its policy with regard to foreign insurance companies which had not complied with the laws of the State for doing business within its limits. In this case the company did no business within the State, and the contracts were not therein made.

The Supreme Court of Louisiana says that the act of writing within that State, the letter of notification, was an act therein done to effect an insurance on property then in the State, in a marine insurance company which had not complied with its laws, and such act was, therefore, prohibited by the statute. As so construed we think the statute is a violation of the Fourteenth Amendment of the Federal Constitution, in that it deprives the defendants of their liberty without due process of law. The statute which forbids such act does not become due process of law, because it is inconsistent with the provisions of the Constitution of the Union. The liberty mentioned in that amendment means not only the right of the citizen to be free from the mere physical restraint of his person, as by incarceration, but the term is deemed to embrace the right of the citizen to be free in the enjoyment of all his faculties; to be free to use them in all lawful ways; to live and work where he will; to earn his livelihood by any lawful calling; to pursue any livelihood or avocation, and for that purpose to enter into all contracts which may be proper, necessary and essential to his carrying out to a successful conclusion the purposes above mentioned. . . .

The Atlantic Mutual Insurance Company of New York has done no business of insurance within the State of Louisiana and has not subjected itself to any provisions of the statute in question. It had the right to enter into a contract in New York with citizens of Louisiana for the purpose of insuring the property of its citizens, even if that property were in the State of Louisiana, and correlatively the citizens of Louisiana had the right without the State of entering into contract with an insurance company for the same purpose. Any act of the state legislature which should prevent the entering into such a contract, or the mailing within the State of Louisiana of such a notification as is mentioned in this case, is an improper and illegal interference with the conduct of the citizen, although residing in Louisiana, in his right to contract and to carry out the terms of a contract validly entered into outside and beyond the jurisdiction of the State. . . .

Reversed, and the case remanded to the Supreme Court of Louisiana for further proceedings not inconsistent with this opinion.

LOCHNER v. NEW YORK,
198 U.S. 45 (1905)

The state of New York, exercising its police powers to act to protect the public welfare, enacted legislation that placed a maximum on the number of hours per day (10) and week (60) that employees of bakeries and confectionery establishments would be allowed to work. Lochner owned a bakery in Utica, New York, and violated the provisions of the law. He unsuccessfully challenged the constitutionality of the law in the courts of New York and then appealed to the U.S. Supreme Court. Lochner argued that the New York law restricted his liberty to enter into a contract with his employees, in violation of the Fourteenth Amendment guarantee that no state shall deny any person liberty without due process of law. The Supreme Court, in a sharply divided decision, agreed with Lochner in an opinion of the Court that is perhaps the most extreme statement ever made by the Court of the right of business to be free from government regulation.

Majority votes: 5
Dissenting votes: 4

MR. JUSTICE PECKHAM delivered the opinion of the Court:

The indictment, it will be seen, charges that the plaintiff in error violated the one hundred and tenth section of article 8, chapter 415, of the Laws of 1897, known as the labor law of the State of New York, in that he wrongfully and unlawfully required and permitted an employee working for him to work more than sixty hours in one week. . . .

The mandate of the statute that "no employee shall be required or permitted to work," is the substantial equivalent of an enactment that "no employee shall contract or agree to work," more than ten hours per day, and as there is no provision for special emergencies the statute is mandatory in all cases. It is not an act merely fixing the number of

hours which shall constitute a legal day's work, but an absolute prohibition upon the employer, permitting, under any circumstances, more than ten hours work to be done in his establishment. The employee may desire to earn the extra money, which would arise from his working more than the prescribed time, but this statute forbids the employer from permitting the employee to earn it.

The statute necessarily interferes with the right of contract between the employer and employees, concerning the number of hours in which the latter may labor in the bakery of the employer. The general right to make a contract in relation to his business is part of the liberty of the individual protected by the Fourteenth Amendment of the Federal Constitution. *Allgeyer* v. *Louisiana,* 165 U.S. 578. Under that provision no State can deprive any person of life, liberty or property without due process of law. The right to purchase or to sell labor is part of the liberty protected by this amendment, unless there are circumstances which exclude the right. There are, however, certain powers, existing in the sovereignty of each State in the Union, somewhat vaguely termed police powers, the exact description and limitation of which have not been attempted by the courts. Those powers, broadly stated and without, at present, any attempt at a more specific limitation, relate to the safety, health, morals and general welfare of the public. Both property and liberty are held on such reasonable conditions as may be imposed by the governing power of the State in the exercise of those powers, and with such conditions the Fourteenth Amendment was not designed to interfere. . . .

It must, of course, be conceded that there is a limit to the valid exercise of the police power by the State. There is no dispute concerning this general proposition. Otherwise the Fourteenth Amendment would have no efficacy and the legislatures of the States would have unbounded power, and it would be enough to say that any piece of legislation was enacted to conserve the morals, the health or the safety of the people; such legislation would be valid, no matter how absolutely without foundation the claim might be. The claim of the police power would be a mere pretext—become another and delusive name for the supreme sovereignty of the State to be exercised free from constitutional restraint. This is not contended for. In every case that comes before this court, therefore, where legislation of this character is concerned and where the protection of the Federal Constitution is sought, the question necessarily arises: Is this a fair, reasonable and appropriate exercise of the police power of the State, or is it an unreasonable, unnecessary and arbitrary interference with the right of the individual to his personal liberty or to enter into those contracts in relation to labor which may seem to him appropriate or necessary for the support of himself and his family? Of course the liberty of contract relating to labor includes both parties to it. The one has as much right to purchase as the other to sell labor. . . .

The question whether this act is valid as a labor law, pure and simple, may be dismissed in a few words. There is no reasonable ground for interfering with the liberty of person or the right of free contract, by determining the hours of labor, in the occupation of a baker. There is no contention that bakers as a class are not equal in intelligence and capacity to men in other trades or manual occupations, or that they are not able to assert their rights and care for themselves without the protecting arm of the State, interfering with their independence of judgment and of action. They are in no sense wards of the State. Viewed in the light of a purely labor law, with no reference whatever to the question of health, we think that a law like the one before us involves neither the safety, the morals nor the welfare of the public, and that the interest of the public is not in the slightest degree affected by such an act. The law must be upheld, if at all, as a law pertaining to the health of the individual engaged in the occupation of a baker. It does not affect any other portion of the public than those who are engaged in that occupation. Clean and wholesome bread does not depend upon whether the baker works but ten hours per day or only sixty hours a week. The limitation of the hours of labor does not come within the police power on that ground.

It is a question of which of two powers or rights shall prevail—the power of the State to legislate or the right of the individual to liberty of person and freedom of contract. The mere assertion that the subject relates though but in a remote degree to the public health does not necessarily render the enactment valid. The act must have a more direct relation, as a means to an end, and the end itself must be appropriate and legitimate, before an act can be held to be valid which interferes with the general right of an individual to be free in his person and in his power to contract in relation to his own labor. . . .

We think the limit of the police power has been reached and passed in this case. There is, in our judgment, no reasonable foundation for holding this to be necessary or appropriate as a health law to safeguard the public health or the health of the individuals who are following the trade of a baker. If this statute be valid, and if, therefore, a proper case is made out in which to deny the right of an individual . . . to make contracts . . . there would seem to be no length to which legislation of this nature might not go. . . .

We think that there can be no fair doubt that the trade of a baker, in and of itself, is not an unhealthy one to that degree which would authorize the legislature to interfere with the right to labor, and with the right of free contract on the part of the individual, either as employer or employee. In looking through statistics regarding all trades and occupations, it may be true that the trade of a baker does not appear to be as healthy as some other trades, and is also vastly more healthy than still others. To the common understanding the trade of a baker has never been regarded as an unhealthy one. Very likely physicians would not recommend the exercise of that or of any other trade as a remedy for ill health. Some occupations are more healthy than others, but we think there are none which might not come under the power of the legislature to supervise and control the hours of working therein, if the mere fact that the occupation is not absolutely and perfectly healthy is to confer that right upon the legislative department of the Government. It might be safely affirmed that almost all occupations more or less affect the health. There must be more than the mere fact of the possible existence of some small amount of unhealthiness to warrant legislative interference with liberty. It is unfortunately true that labor, even in any department, may possibly carry with it the seeds of unhealthiness. But are we all, on that account, at the mercy of legislative majorities? . . .

. . . Statutes of the nature of that under review, limiting the hours in which grown and intelligent men may labor to earn their living, are mere meddlesome interferences with the rights of the individual, and they are not saved from condemnation by the claim that they are passed in the exercise of the police power and upon the subject of the health of the individual whose rights are interfered with, unless there be some fair ground, reasonable in and of itself, to say that there is material danger to the public health or to the health of the employees, if the hours of labor are not curtailed. . . .

It was further urged on the argument that restricting the hours of labor in the case of bakers was valid because it tended to cleanliness on the part of the workers, as a man was more apt to be cleanly when not overworked, and if cleanly then his "output" was also more likely to be so. . . . In our judgment it is not possible in fact to discover the connection between the number of hours a baker may work in the bakery and the healthful quality of the bread made by the workman. The connection, if any exists, is too shadowy and thin to build any argument for the interference of the legislature. If the man works ten hours a day it is all right, but if ten and a half or eleven his health is in danger and his bread may be unhealthful, and, therefore, he shall not be permitted to do it. This, we think, is unreasonable and entirely arbitrary. When assertions such as we have adverted to become necessary in order to give, if possible, a plausible foundation for the contention that the law is a "health law," it gives rise to at least a suspicion that there was some other motive dominating the legislature than the purpose to subserve the public health or welfare.

This interference on the part of the legislatures of the several States with the ordinary trades and occupations of the people seems to be on the increase. . . .

It is impossible for us to shut our eyes to the fact that many of the laws of this character, while passed under what is claimed to be the police power for the purpose of protecting the public health or welfare, are, in reality, passed from other motives. We are justified in saying so when, from the character of the law and the subject upon which it legislates, it is apparent that the public health or welfare bears but the most remote relation to the law. . . .

It is manifest to us that the limitation of the hours of labor as provided for in this section of the statute under which the indictment was found, and the plaintiff in error convicted, has no such direct relation to and no such substantial effect upon the health of the employee, as to justify us in regarding the section as really a health law. It seems to us that the real object and purpose were simply to regulate the hours of labor between the master and his employees in a private business, not dangerous in any degree to morals or in any real and substantial degree, to the health of the employees. Under such circumstances the freedom of master and employee to contract with each other in relation to their employment, and in defining the same, cannot be prohibited or interfered with, without violating the federal Constitution.

The judgment of the Court of Appeals of New York as well as that of the Supreme Court and of the County Court of Oneida County must be reversed and the case remanded to the County Court for further proceedings not inconsistent with this opinion.

Reversed.

MR. JUSTICE HARLAN, with whom MR. JUSTICE WHITE and MR. JUSTICE DAY concurred, dissenting: . . . .

Granting . . . that there is a liberty of contract which cannot be violated even under the sanction of direct legislative enactment, but assuming, as according to settled law we may assume, that such liberty of contract is subject to such regulations as the State may reasonably prescribe for the common good and the well-being of society, what are the conditions under which the judiciary may declare such regulations to be in excess of legislative authority and void? Upon this point there is no room for dispute; for, the rule is universal that a legislative enactment, Federal or state, is never to be disregarded or held invalid unless it be, beyond question, plainly and palpably in excess of legislative power. . . . If there be doubt as to the validity of the statute, that doubt must therefore be resolved in favor of its validity, and the courts must keep their hands off, leaving the legislature to meet the responsibility for unwise legislation. . . .

It is plain that this statute was enacted in order to protect the physical well-being of those who work in baker and confectionery establishments. It may be that the statute had its origin, in part, in the belief that employers and employees in such establishments were not upon an equal footing, and that the necessities of the latter often compelled them to submit to such exactions as unduly taxed their strength. Be this as it may, the statute must be taken as expressing the belief of the people of New York that, as a general rule, and in the case of the average man, labor in excess of sixty hours during a week in such establishments may endanger the health of those who thus labor. Whether or not this be wise legislation it is not the province of the court to inquire. Under our systems of government the courts are not concerned with the wisdom or policy of legislation. So that in determining the question of power to interfere with liberty of contract, the court may inquire whether the means devised by the State are germane to an end which may be lawfully accomplished and have a real or substantial relation to the protection of health, as involved in the daily work of the persons, male and female, engaged in bakery and confectionery establishments. But when this inquiry is entered upon I find it impossible, in view of common experience, to say that there is here no real or substantial relation between the means employed by the State and the end sought to be accomplished by its legislation. Nor can I say that the statute has no appropriate or direct connection with that protection to health which each State owes to her citizens or that it is not promotive of the health of the employees in question or that the regulation prescribed by the State is utterly unreasonable and extravagant or wholly arbitrary. Still less can I say that the statute is, beyond question, a plain, palpable invasion of rights secured by the fundamental law. . . .

[JUSTICE HARLAN quotes in some detail from various authoritative sources concerning the hazards of the occupation of a baker.]

. . . We are not to presume that the State of New York has acted in bad faith. Nor can we assume that its legislature acted without due deliberation, or that it did not determine this question upon the fullest attainable information, and for the common good. We cannot say that the State has acted without reason nor ought we to proceed upon the theory that its action is a mere sham. Our duty, I submit, is to sustain the statute as not being in conflict with the Federal Constitution, for the reason—and such is an all-sufficient reason—it is not shown to be plainly and palpably inconsistent with that instrument. Let the State alone in the management of its purely domestic affairs, so long as it does not appear beyond all question that it has violated the Federal Constitution. This view necessarily results from the principle that the health and safety of the people of a State are primarily for the State to guard and protect. . . .

MR. JUSTICE HOLMES dissenting:. . . .

This case is decided upon an economic theory which a large part of the country does not entertain. If it were a question whether I agreed with that theory, I should desire to study it further and long before making up my mind. But I do not conceive that to be my duty, because I strongly believe that my agreement or disagreement has nothing to do with the right of a majority to embody their opinions in law. It is settled by various decisions of this court that state constitutions and state laws may regulate life in many ways which we as legislators might think as injudicious or if you like as tyrannical as this, and which equally with this interfere with the liberty to contract. Sunday laws and usury laws are ancient examples. A more modern one is the prohibition of lotteries. The liberty of the citizen to do as he likes so long as he does not interfere with the liberty of others to do the same, which has been a shibboleth for some well-known writers, is interfered with by school laws, by the Post Office, by every state or municipal institution which takes his money for purposes thought desirable, whether he likes it or not. The Fourteenth Amendment does not enact Mr. Herbert Spencer's Social Statics. The other day we sustained the Massachusetts vaccination law. *Jacobson* v. *Massachusetts,* 197 U.S. 11. United States and state statutes and decisions cutting down the liberty to contract by way of com-

bination are familiar to this court. *Northern Securities Co.* v. *United States,* 193 U.S. 197. Two years ago we upheld the prohibition of sales of stock on margins or for future delivery in the constitution of California. *Otis* v. *Parker,* 187 U.S. 606. The decision sustaining an eight hour law for miners is still recent. *Holden* v. *Hardy,* 169 U.S. 366. Some of these laws embody convictions or prejudices which judges are likely to share. Some may not. But a constitution is not intended to embody a particular economic theory, whether of paternalism and the organic relation of the citizen to the State or of laissez-faire. It is made for people of fundamentally differing views, and the accident of our finding certain opinions natural and familiar or novel and even shocking ought not to conclude our judgment upon the question whether statutes embodying them conflict with the Constitution of the United States.

General propositions do not decide concrete cases. The decision will depend on a judgment or intuition more subtle than any articulate major premise. But I think that the proposition just stated, if it is accepted, will carry us far toward the end. Every opinion tends to become a law. I think that the word liberty in the Fourteenth Amendment is perverted when it is held to prevent the natural outcome of a dominant opinion, unless it can be said that a rational and fair man necessarily would admit that the statute proposed would infringe fundamental principles as they have been understood by the traditions of our people and our law. It does not need research to show that no such sweeping condemnation can be passed upon the statute before us. A reasonable man might think it is a proper measure on the score of health. Men whom I certainly could not pronounce unreasonable would uphold it as a first instalment of a general regulation of the hours of work. Whether in the latter aspect it would be open to the charge of inequality I think it unnecessary to discuss.

MULLER v. OREGON,
208 U.S. 412 (1908)

Substantive due process was not always associated with antiregulatory Court decisions. The Muller *case dramatically demonstrated this. The state of Oregon enacted legislation providing for a ten-hour maximum workday for women who were factory or laundry workers. Curt Muller, owner of a laundry, was convicted of violating the statute. He challenged the law as violating his liberty to enter into a labor contract over the hours to be worked by his female employees. When the state's attorneys went before the Supreme Court they were joined by the well-known lawyer, Louis D. Bran-*

deis, hired by the National Consumers League, a progressive organization that favored social welfare legislation. Brandeis gave the Court a novel brief. Instead of the traditional legal arguments, Brandeis' brief contained, for the most part, a multitude of facts, tables, and statistics drawn from various government studies and reports, all of which strongly suggested that long working hours are detrimental to the health, safety, and well-being of women. Brandeis' brief, then, presented a solid factual basis for the Oregon legislature's exercise of its police powers in enacting the disputed legislation. This tactic worked, and the Court unanimously upheld the Oregon law in an opinion of the Court that is as sexist a Court opinion as any that has ever been written.

Votes: Unanimous

MR. JUSTICE BREWER delivered the opinion of the Court:. . . .

The single question is the constitutionality of the statute under which the defendant was convicted so far as it affects the work of a female in a laundry. . . .

. . . It may not be amiss, in the present case, before examining the constitutional question, to notice the course of legislation as well as expressions of opinion from other than judicial sources. In the brief filed by Mr. Louis D. Brandeis, for the defendant in error, is a very copious collection of all these matters. . . .

The legislation and opinions referred to . . . may not be, technically speaking, authorities, and in them is little or no discussion of the constitutional question presented to us for determination, yet they are significant of a widespread belief that woman's physical structure, and the functions she performs in consequence thereof, justify special legislation restricting or qualifying the conditions under which she should be permitted to toil. Constitutional questions, it is true, are not settled by even a consensus of present public opinion, for it is the peculiar value of a written constitution that it places in unchanging form limitations upon legislative action, and thus gives a permanence and stability to popular government which otherwise would be lacking. At the same time, when a question of fact is debated and debatable, and the extent to which a special constitutional limitation goes is affected by the truth in respect to that fact, a widespread and long continued belief concerning it is worthy of consideration. We take judicial cognizance of all matters of general knowledge.

It is undoubtedly true, as more than once declared by this court, that the general right to contract in relation to one's business is part of the liberty of the individual, protected by the Fourteenth Amendment to the Federal Constitution; yet it is equally well settled that this liberty is not absolute and extending to all contracts, and that a State may, without conflicting with the provisions of the Fourteenth Amendment, restrict in many respects the individual's power of contract. . . .

That woman's physical structure and the performance of maternal functions place her at a disadvantage in the struggle for subsistence is obvious. This is especially true when the burdens of motherhood are upon her. Even when they are not, by abundant testimony of the medical fraternity continuance for a long time on her feet at work, repeating this from day to day, tends to injurious effects upon the body, and as healthy mothers are essential to vigorous offspring, the physical well-being of woman becomes an object of public interest and care in order to preserve the strength and vigor of the race.

Still again, history discloses the fact that woman has always been dependent upon man. He established his control at the outset by superior physical strength, and this control in various forms, with diminishing intensity, has continued to the present. As minors, though not to the same extent, she has been looked upon in the courts as needing especial care that her rights may be preserved. Education was long denied her, and while now the doors of the school room are opened and her opportunities for acquiring knowledge are great, yet even with that and the consequent increase of capacity for business affairs it is still true that in the struggle for subsistence she is not an equal competitor with her brother. Though limitations upon personal and contractual rights may be removed by legislation there is that in her disposition and habits of life which will operate against a full assertion of those rights. She will still be where some legislation to protect her seems necessary to secure a real equality of right. Doubtless there are individual exceptions, and there are many respects in which she has an advantage over him; but looking at it from the viewpoint of the effort to maintain an independent position in life, she is not upon an equality. Differentiated by these matters from the other sex, she is properly placed in a class by herself, and legislation designed for her protection may be sustained, even when like legislation is not necessary for men and could not be sustained. It is impossible to close one's eyes to the fact that she still looks to her brother and depends upon him. Even though all restrictions on political, personal and contractual rights were taken away, and she stood, so far as statutes are concerned, upon an absolutely equal plane with him, it would still be true that she is so constituted that she will rest upon and look to him for protection; that her physical structure and a proper discharge of her maternal functions—having in view not merely her own health, but the well-being of the race—justify legislation to protect her from the greed as well as the passion of man. The limitations which this statute places upon her con-tractual powers, upon her right to agree with her employer as to the time she shall labor, are not im-posed solely for her benefit, but also largely for the benefit of all. Many words cannot make this plainer. The two sexes differ in structure of body, in the functions to be performed by each, in the amount of physical strength, in the capacity for long-continued labor, particularly when done standing, the influence of vigorous health upon the future well-being of the race, the self-reliance which enables one to assert full rights, and in the capacity to maintain the struggle for subsistence. This difference justifies a difference in legislation and upholds that which is designed to compensate for some of the burdens which rest upon her. . . .

For these reasons, and without questioning in any respect the decision in *Lochner* v. *New York,* we are of the opinion that it cannot be adjudged that the act in question is in conflict with the Federal Constitution, so far as it respects the work of a fe-male in a laundry, and the judgment of the Supreme Court of Oregon is

Affirmed.

ADAIR v. UNITED STATES,
208 U.S. 161 (1908)

In 1898 Congress, asserting its commerce power, enacted legislation that made it a federal crime for an interstate railroad to place in its labor contracts a provision stipulating that the employee will not join a labor union. Under the terms of such a contract, derisively called "a yellow dog con-tract" by the labor movement, if the employee joined a union, the contract would become null and void and the employee would be summarily dis-charged. William Adair, acting for the Louisville and Nashville Railroad Company, fired a locomo-tive fireman employed by the railroad who had joined a labor union known as The Order of Loco-motive Firemen. Adair was prosecuted for violating the 1898 law and was found guilty. On appeal to the Court, the congressional law outlawing the yel-low dog contract was challenged by Adair on the grounds that the law interfered with the liberty to enter into a contract without due process of law in

violation of the Fifth Amendment. The Supreme Court agreed with Adair and utilized substantive due process as the principal constitutional basis for striking down the legislation.

Majority votes: 6
Dissenting votes: 2

MR. JUSTICE HARLAN delivered the opinion of the Court:. . . .

The first inquiry is whether the part of the tenth section of the act of 1898 upon which the first count of the indictment was based is repugnant to the Fifth Amendment of the Constitution declaring that no person shall be deprived of liberty or property without due process of law. In our opinion that sec-tion, in the particular mentioned, is an invasion of the personal liberty, as well as of the right of prop-erty, guaranteed by that Amendment. Such liberty and right embraces the right to make contracts for the purchase of the labor of others and equally the right to make contracts for the sale of one's own labor; each right, however, being subject to the fun-damental condition that no contract, whatever its subject matter, can be sustained which the law, upon reasonable grounds, forbids as inconsistent with the public interests or as hurtful to the public order or as detrimental to the common good. . . . Without stopping to consider what would have been the rights of the railroad company under the Fifth Amendment, had it been indicted under the act of Congress, it is sufficient in this case to say that as agent of the railroad company and as such responsible for the conduct of the business of one of its departments, it was the defendant Adair's right—and that right inhered in his personal liberty, and was also a right of property—to serve his em-ployer as best he could, so long as he did nothing that was reasonably forbidden by law as injurious to the public interests. It was the right of the defen-dant to prescribe the terms upon which the services of Coppage [the employee] would be accepted, and it was the right of Coppage to become or not, as he chose, an employee of the railroad company upon the terms offered to him. . . .

While, as already suggested, the rights of liberty and property guaranteed by the Constitution against deprivation without due process of law, is subject to such reasonable restraints as the com-mon good or the general welfare may require, it is not within the functions of government—at least in the absence of contract between the parties—to compel any person in the course of his business and against his will to accept or retain the personal ser-vices of another, or to compel any person, against his will, to perform personal services for another. The right of a person to sell his labor upon such terms as he deems proper is, in its essence, the same as the right of the purchaser of labor to prescribe the conditions upon which he will accept such labor from the person offering to sell it. So the right of the employee to quit the service of the employer, for whatever reason, is the same as the right of the employer, for whatever reason, to dispense with the services of such employee. It was the legal right of the defendant Adair—however unwise such a course might have been—to discharge Coppage because of his being a member of a labor organization, as it was the legal right of Coppage, if he saw fit to do so—however unwise such a course on his part might have been—to quit the service in which he was engaged, because the defendant employed some persons who were not members of a labor organization. In all such particulars the employer and the employee have equality of right, and any legislation that disturbs that equality is an arbitrary interference with the liberty of contract which no government can legally justify in a free land. . . .

Looking alone at the words of the statute for the purpose of ascertaining its scope and effect, and of determining its validity, we hold that there is no such connection between interstate commerce and membership in a labor organization as to authorize Congress to make it a crime against the United States for an agent of an interstate carrier to discharge an employee because of such membership on his part. . . .

. . . [T]he provision of the statute under which the defendant was convicted must be held to be repugnant to the Fifth Amendment and as not embraced by nor within the power of Congress to regulate interstate commerce, but under the guise of regulating interstate commerce and as applied to this case it arbitrarily sanctions an illegal invasion of the personal liberty as well as the right of property of the defendant Adair. . . .

The judgment must be reversed, with directions to set aside the verdict and judgment of conviction, sustain the demurrer to the indictment, and dismiss the case.

It is so ordered.

MR. JUSTICE MOODY did not participate in the decision of this case.
MR. JUSTICE MCKENNA, dissenting: [omitted]
MR. JUSTICE HOLMES, dissenting: . . . .
The ground on which this particular law is held bad is not so much that it deals with matters remote

from commerce among the States, as that it interferes with the paramount individual rights, secured by the Fifth Amendment. The section is, in substance, a very limited interference with freedom of contract, no more. It does not require the carriers to employ any one. It does not forbid them to refuse to employ any one, for any reason they deem good, even where the notion of a choice of persons is a fiction and wholesale employment is necessary upon general principles that it might be proper to control. The section simply prohibits the more powerful party to exact certain undertakings, or to threaten dismissal or unjustly discriminate on certain grounds against those already employed. I hardly can suppose that the grounds on which a contract lawfully may be made to end are less open to regulation than other terms. So I turn to the general question whether the employment can be regulated at all. I confess that I think that the right to make contracts at will that has been derived from the word liberty in the amendments has been stretched to its extreme by the decisions; but they agree that sometimes the right may be restrained. Where there is, or generally is believed to be, an important ground of public policy for restraint the Constitution does not forbid it, whether this court agrees or disagrees with the policy pursued. It cannot be doubted that to prevent strikes, and, so far as possible, to foster its scheme of arbitration, might be deemed by Congress an important point of policy, and I think it impossible to say that Congress might not reasonably think that the provision in question would help a good deal to carry its policy along. But suppose the only effect really were to tend to bring about the complete unionizing of such railroad laborers as Congress can deal with, I think that object alone would justify the act. I quite agree that the question what and how much good labor unions do, is one on which intelligent people may differ,—I think that laboring men sometimes attribute to them advantages, as many attribute to combinations of capital disadvantages, that really are due to economic conditions of a far wider and deeper kind—but I could not pronounce it unwarranted if Congress should decide that to foster a strong union was for the best interest, not only of the men, but of the railroads and the country at large.

BUNTING v. OREGON,
243 U.S. 426 (1917)

An Oregon hours of employment statute was challenged in this case. The Oregon law provided for a ten-hour maximum working day for all em-

ployees in mills, factories, and manufacturing industries. Employees were permitted to work up to three hours beyond the ten-hour limit but only if the workers were paid time and a half for overtime. Bunting violated the overtime provision and in his defense argued that the Oregon law was regulating wages as well as hours in violation of his liberty to enter into contracts with his employees. Because the Oregon law encompassed the baking industry and was applicable to men as well as to women, the Court could have invoked the Lochner v. New York *precedent. But the Court majority chose to uphold the statute and furthermore entirely ignore the* Lochner *precedent.*

Majority votes: 5
Dissenting votes: 3

MR. JUSTICE MCKENNA delivered the opinion of the Court:. . . .

The consonance of the Oregon law with the Fourteenth Amendment is the question in the case, and this depends upon whether it is a proper exercise of the police power of the State, as the Supreme Court of the State decided that it is. . . .

Section I of the law expresses the policy that impelled its enactment to be the interest of the State in the physical well-being of its citizens and that it is injurious to their health for them to work "in any mill, factory or manufacturing establishment" more than ten hours in any one day; and §2 . . . forbids their employment in those places for a longer time. If, therefore, we take the law at its word there can be no doubt of its purpose, and the Supreme Court of the State has added the confirmation of its decision, by declaring that "the aim of the statute is to fix the maximum hours of service in certain industries. The act makes no attempt to fix the standard of wages. No maximum or minimum wage is named. That is left wholly to the contracting parties." . . .

First, as to plaintiff in error's attack upon the law. . . .

There is a certain verbal plausibility in the contention that it was intended to permit 13 hours' work if there be 14 1/2 hours' pay, but the plausibility disappears upon reflection. The provision for overtime is permissive, in the same sense that any penalty may be said to be permissive. Its purpose is to deter by its burden and its adequacy for this was a matter of legislative judgment under the particular circumstances. It may not achieve its end, but its insufficiency cannot change its character from penalty to permission. Besides, it is to be borne in mind that the legislature was dealing with

a matter in which many elements were to be considered. It might not have been possible, it might not have been wise, to make a rigid prohibition. We can easily realize that the legislature deemed it sufficient for its policy to give to the law an adaptation to occasions different from special cases of emergency for which it provided, occasions not of such imperative necessity, and yet which should have some accommodation—abuses prevented by the requirement of higher wages. Or even a broader contention might be made that the legislature considered it a proper policy to meet the conditions long existent by a tentative restraint of conduct rather than by an absolute restraint, and achieve its purpose through the interest of those affected rather than by the positive fiat of the law. . . .

But we need not cast about for reasons for the legislative judgment. We are not required to be sure of the precise reasons for its exercise or be convinced of the wisdom of its exercise. It is enough for our decision if the legislation under review was passed in the exercise of an admitted power of government; and that it is not as complete as it might be, not as rigid in its prohibitions as it might be, gives perhaps evasion too much play, is lighter in its penalties than it might be, is no impeachment of its legality. This may be a blemish, giving opportunity for criticism and difference in characterization, but the constitutional validity of legislation cannot be determined by the degree of exactness of its provisions or remedies. New policies are usually tentative in their beginnings, advance in firmness as they advance in acceptance. They do not at a particular moment of time spring full-perfect in extent or means from the legislative brain. Time may be necessary to fashion them to precedent customs and conditions and as they justify themselves or otherwise they pass from militancy to triumph or from question to repeal.

But passing general considerations and coming back to our immediate concern, which is the validity of the particular exertion of power in the Oregon law, our judgment of it is that it does not transcend constitutional limits. . . .

There is a contention made that the law . . . is not either necessary or useful "for preservation of the health of employees in mills, factories and manufacturing establishments." The record contains no facts to support the contention, and against it is the judgment of the legislature and the Supreme Court. . . .

The next contention of plaintiff in error is that the law discriminates against mills, factories and manufacturing establishments in that it requires that a manufacturer, without reason other than the fiat of the legislature, shall pay for a commodity, meaning labor, one and one-half times the market value thereof while other people purchasing labor in like manner in the open market are not subjected to the same burden. But the basis of the contention is that which we have already disposed of, that is, that the law regulates wages, not hours of service. Regarding it as the latter, there is a basis for the classification.

Further discussion we deem unnecessary.

Judgment affirmed.

CHIEF JUSTICE WHITE, MR. JUSTICE VAN DEVANTER and MR. JUSTICE MCREYNOLDS dissented without opinion.
MR. JUSTICE BRANDEIS took no part in the consideration and decision of the case.

ADKINS v. CHILDREN'S HOSPITAL,
261 U.S. 525 (1923)

In 1918 Congress enacted a minimum wage law for women workers and minors employed in the District of Columbia. The law was challenged in this case as violating the rights of women and their employers to enter into a labor contract, thus constituting a violation of their liberty without the due process of law guaranteed by the Fifth Amendment. A Brandeis-type factual brief was submitted to demonstrate that the law was a reasonable exercise of Congress' police powers. But, as is seen in Justice Sutherland's opinion of the Court that follows, the response of the majority was that such facts are "interesting, but only mildly persuasive." Instead, the majority went back to Lochner v. New York *and approvingly restated its basic assumptions and doctrines. The imposition of minimum wages by the government amounts to the fixing of prices and unconstitutionally restricts the liberty to enter into a contract. The parties to the case included Adkins and others constituting the Minimum Wage Board of the District of Columbia who were permanently enjoined by the lower courts from enforcing the minimum wages under the statute. The Children's Hospital and a 21-year-old woman hotel elevator operator were the parties that sought the injunctions.*

Majority votes: 5
Dissenting votes: 3

MR. JUSTICE SUTHERLAND delivered the opinion of the Court:
The question presented for determination by

these appeals is the constitutionality of the Act of September 19, 1918, providing for the fixing of minimum wages for women and children in the District of Columbia. . . .

The statute now under consideration is attacked upon the ground that it authorizes an unconstitutional interference with the freedom of contract included within the guaranties of the due process clause of the Fifth Amendment. That the right to contract about one's affairs is a part of the liberty of the individual protected by this clause, is settled by the decisions of this Court and is no longer open to question. . . . Within this liberty are contracts of employment of labor. In making such contracts, generally speaking, the parties have an equal right to obtain from each other the best terms they can as the result of private bargaining. . . .

There is, of course, no such thing as absolute freedom of contract. It is subject to a great variety of restraints. But freedom of contract is, nevertheless, the general rule and restraint the exception; and the exercise of legislative authority to abridge it can be justified only by the existence of exceptional circumstances. Whether these circumstances exist in the present case constitutes the question to be answered. . . .

[The Court reviews several past decisions and places special emphasis on the reasoning used in *Lochner* v. *New York*. Attention is then turned to the *Muller* case.]

In the *Muller* v. *Oregon* Case the validity of an Oregon statute, forbidding the employment of any female in certain industries more than ten hours during any one day was upheld. The decision proceeded upon the theory that the difference between the sexes may justify a different rule respecting hours of labor in the case of women than in the case of men. It is pointed out that these consist in differences of physical structure, especially in respect of the maternal functions, and also in the fact that historically woman has always been dependent upon man, who has established his control by superior physical strength. . . . But the ancient inequality of the sexes, otherwise than physical, as suggested in the *Muller* Case has continued "with diminishing intensity." In view of the great—not to say revolutionary—changes which have taken place since that utterance, in the contractual, political and civil status of women, culminating in the Nineteenth Amendment, it is not unreasonable to say that these differences have now come almost, if not quite, to the vanishing point. In this aspect of the matter, while the physical differences must be recognized in appropriate cases, and legislation fixing hours or conditions of work may properly take them into account, we cannot accept the doctrine that women of mature age require or may be subjected to restrictions upon their liberty of contract which could not lawfully be imposed in the case of men under similar circumstances. To do so would be to ignore all the implications to be drawn from the present day trend of legislation, as well as that of common thought and usage, by which woman is accorded emancipation from the old doctrine that she must be given special protection or be subjected to special restraint in her contractual and civil relationships. . . .

. . . [W]e examine and analyze the statute in question. . . . It is not a law dealing with any business charged with a public interest or with public work, or to meet and tide over a temporary emergency. It has nothing to do with the character, methods or periods of wage payments. It does not prescribe hours of labor or conditions under which labor is to be done. It is not for the protection of persons under legal disability or for the prevention of fraud. It is simply and exclusively a price-fixing law, confined to adult women (for we are not now considering the provisions relating to minors), who are legally as capable of contracting for themselves as men. It forbids two parties having lawful capacity—under penalties as to the employer—to freely contract with one another in respect of the price for which one shall render service to the other in a purely private employment where both are willing, perhaps anxious, to agree, even though the consequence may be to oblige one to surrender a desirable engagement and the other to dispense with the services of a desirable employee. The price fixed by the board need have no relation to the capacity or earning power of the employee, the number of hours which may happen to constitute the day's work, the character of the place where the work is to be done, or the circumstances or surroundings of the employment; and, while it has no other basis to support its validity than the assumed necessities of the employee, it takes no account of any independent resources she may have. It is based wholly on the opinions of the members of the board and their advisers—perhaps an average of their opinions, if they do not precisely agree—as to what will be necessary to provide a living for a woman, keep her in health and preserve her morals. It applies to any and every occupation in the District, without regard to its nature or the character of the work.

The standard furnished by the statute for the guidance of the board is so vague as to be impossible of practical application with any reasonable degree of accuracy. . . .

The law takes account of the necessities of only one party to the contract. . . . It takes no account of periods of stress and business depression, of crippling losses, which may leave the employer himself without adequate means of livelihood. To the extent that the sum fixed exceeds the fair value of the services rendered, it amounts to a compulsory exaction from the employer for the support of a partially indigent person, for whose condition there rests upon him no peculiar responsibility, and therefore, in effect, arbitrarily shifts to his shoulders a burden which, if it belongs to anybody, belongs to society as a whole.

The feature of this statute which, perhaps more than any other, puts upon it the stamp of invalidity is that it exacts from the employer an arbitrary payment for a purpose and upon a basis having no causal connection with his business, or the contract or the work the employee engages to do. The declared basis, as already pointed out, is not the value of the service rendered, but the extraneous circumstance that the employee needs to get a prescribed sum of money to insure her subsistence, health and morals. . . . The moral requirement implicit in every contract of employment, viz, that the amount to be paid and the service to be rendered shall bear to each other some relation of just equivalence, is completely ignored. . . . A statute which prescribes payment . . . solely with relation to circumstances apart from the contract of employment, the business affected by it and the work done under it, is so clearly the product of a naked, arbitrary exercise of power that it cannot be allowed to stand under the Constitution of the United States. . . .

It is said that great benefits have resulted from the operation of such statutes, not alone in the District of Columbia but in the several States, where they have been in force. A mass of reports, opinions of special observers and students of the subject, and the like, has been brought before us in support of this statement, all of which we have found interesting but only mildly persuasive. That the earnings of women now are greater than they were formerly and that conditions affecting women have become better in other respects may be conceded, but convincing indications of the logical relation of these desirable changes to the law in question are significantly lacking. They may be, and quite probably are, due to other causes. . . .

Affirmed.

MR. JUSTICE BRANDEIS took no part in the consideration or decision of these cases.

MR. CHIEF JUSTICE TAFT, dissenting:

I regret much to differ from the Court in these cases. . . .

Legislatures in limiting freedom of contract between employee and employer by a minimum wage proceed on the assumption that employees, in the class receiving least pay, are not upon a full level of equality of choice with their employer and in their necessitous circumstances are prone to accept pretty much anything that is offered. They are peculiarly subject to the overreaching of the harsh and greedy employer. The evils of the sweatshop system and of the long hours and low wages which are characteristic of it are well known. Now, I agree that it is a disputable question in the field of political economy how far a statutory requirement of maximum hours or minimum wages may be a useful remedy for these evils, and whether it may not make the case of the oppressed employee worse than it was before. But it is not the function of this Court to hold congressional acts invalid simply because they are passed to carry out economic views which the Court believes to be unwise or unsound. . . .

[CHIEF JUSTICE TAFT reviews previous decisions and observes that *Bunting* v. *Oregon* cannot be reconciled with *Lochner* v. *New York* and that "I have always supposed that the *Lochner Case* was thus overruled *sub silentio*." Taft objects to the majority relying on the reasoning in *Lochner*.]

I am authorized to say that MR. JUSTICE SANFORD concurs in this opinion.

MR. JUSTICE HOLMES, dissenting:. . . .

I confess that I do not understand the principle on which the power to fix a minimum for the wages of women can be denied by those who admit the power to fix a maximum for their hours of work. I fully assent to the proposition that here as elsewhere the distinctions of the law are distinctions of degree, but I perceive no difference in the kind or degree of interference with liberty, the only matter with which we have any concern, between the one case and the other. The bargain is equally affected whichever half you regulate. *Muller* v. *Oregon,* I take it, is as good law today as it was in 1908. It will need more than the Nineteenth Amendment to convince me that there are no differences between men and women, or that legislation cannot take those differences into account. . . .

MOREHEAD v. NEW YORK ex rel. TIPALDO, 298 U.S. 587 (1936)

In Adkins v. Children's Hospital *one of the objections that the majority had to the District of Columbia minimum wage law was that it failed to take into account the value-for-service principle. That is, some jobs of a menial nature may not be worth the minimum wage, and if forced to pay it, the employer would suffer an enforced deprivation of his property. Alternatively, the employer might eliminate the job entirely. A New York state minimum wage law for women that took into account this principle was challenged before the Supreme Court. Tipaldo, manager of a laundry, had disobeyed the New York law and was actually sent to jail to await trial. Despite the fact that the New York law incorporated a provision authorizing minimum wages to be set only after consideration of the value of the service to be rendered in return, the Court majority struck it down as a violation of liberty of contract protected by the Fourteenth Amendment.*

Majority votes: 5
Dissenting votes: 4

MR. JUSTICE BUTLER delivered the opinion of the Court:

This is a habeas corpus case originating in the Supreme Court of New York. Relator was indicted in the county court of Kings county and sent to jail to await trial upon the charge that as manager of a laundry he failed to obey the mandatory order of the state industrial commissioner prescribing minimum wages for women employees.

The relator's petition for the writ avers that the statute under which the commissioner made the order, insofar as it purports to authorize him to fix women's wages, is repugnant to the due process clause of the constitution of the State and the due process clause of the Fourteenth Amendment to the Constitution of the United States. The application for the writ is grounded upon the claim that the state statute is substantially identical with the minimum wage law enacted by Congress for the District of Columbia, which in 1923 was condemned by this court as repugnant to the due process clause of the Fifth Amendment. *Adkins* v. *Children's Hospital,* 261 U.S. 525. . . .

Relator took the case to the [New York] Court of Appeals. It held the Act repugnant to the due process clauses of the state and federal constitutions . . . [and] directed that the order appealed from be reversed, the writ sustained and the prisoner discharged; it certified that the federal constitutional question was presented and necessarily passed on. . . . We granted a writ of certiorari. . . .

The *Adkins* case, unless distinguishable, requires affirmance of the judgment below. The petition for the writ sought review upon the ground that this case is distinguishable from that one. No application has been made for reconsideration of the constitutional question there decided. The validity of the principles upon which that decision rests is not challenged. This court confines itself to the ground upon which the writ was asked or granted. Here the review granted was no broader than that sought by the petitioner. He is not entitled and does not ask to be heard upon the question whether the *Adkins* case should be overruled. He maintains that it may be distinguished on the ground that the statutes are vitally dissimilar. . . .

The minimum wage provided for in the District Act was one not less than adequate "to supply the necessary cost of living to any such women workers to maintain them in good health and to protect their morals." The New York Act defines an oppressive and unreasonable wage as containing two elements. The one first mentioned is: "less than the fair and reasonable value of the services rendered." The other is: "less than sufficient to meet the minimum cost of living necessary for health." The basis last mentioned is not to be distinguished from the living wage defined in the District Act. The exertion of the granted power to prescribe minimum wages is by the State Act conditioned upon a finding by the commissioner or other administrative agency that a substantial number in any occupation are receiving wages that are oppressive and unreasonable, i.e., less than value of the service and less than a living wage. That finding is essential to jurisdiction of the commissioner. In the state court there was controversy between the parties as to whether the "minimum fair wage rates" are required to be established solely upon value of service or upon that value and the living wage. Against the contention of the attorney general, the Court of Appeals held that the minimum wage must be based on both elements.

Speaking through its chief judge, that court said: "We find no material difference between the act of Congress and this act of the New York State Legislature. . . ."

There is no blinking the fact that the state court construed the prescribed standard to include cost of living or that petitioner here refuses to accept that construction. Petitioner's contention that the Court of Appeals misconstrued the Act cannot be entertained. This court is without power to put a different construction upon the state enactment from that adopted by the highest court of the State. We are not at liberty to consider petitioner's argument based on the construction repudiated by that court. The meaning of the statute as fixed by its decision must be accepted here as if the meaning had been specifically expressed in the enactment. . . .

The state court rightly held that the *Adkins* case controls this one and requires that relator be discharged upon the ground that the legislation under which he was indicted and imprisoned is repugnant to the due process clause of the Fourteenth Amendment. . . . [T]he restraint imposed by the due process clause of the Fourteenth Amendment upon legislative power of the State is the same as that imposed by the corresponding provision of the Fifth Amendment upon the legislative power of the United States. . . .

The [*Adkins*] decision and the reasoning upon which it rests clearly show that the State is without power by any form of legislation to prohibit, change or nullify contracts between employers and adult women workers as to the amount of wages to be paid. . . .

The New York court's decision conforms to ours in the *Adkins* case, and the later rulings that we have made on the authority of that case. . . . [T]he judgment in the case now before us must be

Affirmed.

MR. CHIEF JUSTICE HUGHES [with whom MR. JUSTICE BRANDEIS, MR. JUSTICE STONE, and MR. JUSTICE CARDOZO join], dissenting: [omitted]
MR. JUSTICE STONE [with whom MR. JUSTICE BRANDEIS and MR. JUSTICE CARDOZO join], dissenting: [omitted]

WEST COAST HOTEL v. PARRISH, 300 U.S. 379 (1937)

In 1936 the Court in Morehead v. Tipaldo *reaffirmed the* Adkins v. Children's Hospital *doctrine that freedom of contract prohibited state minimum wage legislation interfering with labor contracts between employers and employees. But by 1937, the political situation for the Court had changed dramatically. A reelected President Roosevelt was promoting his court "reform" plan, and public opinion clearly opposed the Court's obstructionism. The* West Coast Hotel *decision then assumed great moment not only because of the doctrine emerging from the decision, significant as it was, but also from the symbolic importance of a new majority approving social and economic reform. The case concerned the validity of legislation from the state of Washington mandating a minimum wage for women and minors. Elsie Parrish had been paid below the minimum wage and sued her employer, the West Coast Hotel Company, to recover wages owed her under Washington law. Her employer challenged the act's constitutionality, but the Washington courts sustained it. The hotel appealed to the Supreme Court.*

Majority votes: 5
Dissenting votes: 4

MR. CHIEF JUSTICE HUGHES delivered the opinion of the Court:

This case presents the question of the constitutional validity of the minimum wage law of the State of Washington. . . .

. . . The appellant challenged the act as repugnant to the due process clause of the Fourteenth Amendment of the Constitution of the United States. The Supreme Court of the State, reversing the trial court, sustained the statute and directed judgment for the plaintiffs. The case is here on appeal.

The appellant relies upon the decision of this Court in *Adkins* v. *Children's Hospital,* 261 U.S. 525, which held invalid the District of Columbia Minimum Wage Act, which was attacked under the due process clause of the Fifth Amendment. . . .

The recent case of *Morehead* v. *New York ex rel. Tipaldo,* 298 U.S. 587, came here on certiorari to the New York court, which had held the New York minimum wage act for women to be invalid. A minority of this Court thought that the New York statute was distinguishable in a material feature from that involved in the *Adkins* case, and that for that and other reasons the New York statute should be sustained. But the Court of Appeals of New York had said that it found no material difference between the two statutes. . . . That view led to the affirmance by this Court of the judgment in the *Morehead* case, as the Court considered that the only question before it was whether the *Adkins* case was distinguishable and that reconsideration of that decision had not been sought. . . .

We think that the question which was not deemed to be open in the *Morehead* case is open and is necessarily presented here. The Supreme Court of Washington has upheld the minimum wage statute of that State. It has decided that the statute is a reasonable exercise of the police power of the State. In reaching that conclusion the state court has invoked principles long established by this Court in the application of the Fourteenth Amendment. The state court has refused to regard the decision in the *Adkins* case as determinative and has pointed to our decisions both before and since that case as justifying its position. We are of the opinion that this ruling of the state court demands on our part a reexamination of the *Adkins* case. The importance of the question, in which many states having similar laws are concerned, the close division by which the decision in the *Adkins* case was reached, and the economic conditions which have super-

vened, and in the light of which the reasonableness of the exercise of the protective power of the State must be considered, make it not only appropriate, but we think imperative, that in deciding the present case the subject should receive fresh consideration. . . .

The principle which must control our decision is not in doubt. The constitutional provision invoked is the due process clause of the Fourteenth Amendment governing the States, as the due process clause invoked in the *Adkins* case governed Congress. In each case the violation alleged by those attacking minimum wage regulation for women is deprivation of freedom of contract. What is this freedom? The Constitution does not speak of freedom of contract. It speaks of liberty and prohibits the deprivation of liberty without due process of law. In prohibiting that deprivation the Constitution does not recognize an absolute and uncontrollable liberty. Liberty in each of its phases has its history and connotation. But the liberty safeguarded is liberty in a social organization which requires the protection of law against the evils which menace the health, safety, morals and welfare of the people. Liberty under the Constitution is thus necessarily subject to the restraints of due process, and regulation which is reasonable in relation to its subject and is adopted in the interests of the community is due process.

This essential limitation of liberty in general governs freedom of contract in particular. . . .

This power under the Constitution to restrict freedom of contract has had many illustrations. That it may be exercised in the public interest with respect to contracts between employer and employee is undeniable. Thus statutes have been sustained limiting employment in underground mines and smelters to eight hours a day (*Holden* v. *Hardy,* 169 U.S. 366); . . . in prohibiting contracts limiting liability for injuries to employees (*Chicago, B. & Q. R. Co.* v. *McGuire,* 219 U.S. 549); in limiting hours of work of employees in manufacturing establishments (*Bunting* v. *Oregon,* 243 U.S. 426); and in maintaining workmen's compensation laws (*New York Central R. Co.* v. *White,* 243 U.S. 188; *Mountain Timber Co.* v. *Washington,* 243 U.S. 219). In dealing with the relation of employer and employed, the legislature has necessarily a wide field of discretion in order that there may be suitable protection of health and safety, and that peace and good order may be promoted through regulations designed to insure wholesome conditions of work and freedom from oppression. . . .

The point that has been strongly stressed that adult employees should be deemed competent to make their own contracts was decisively met nearly forty years ago in *Holden* v. *Hardy, supra,* where we pointed out the inequality in the footing of the parties. . . .

The array of precedents and the principles they applied were thought by the dissenting Justices in the *Adkins* case to demand that the minimum wage statute be sustained. The validity of the distinction made by the Court between a minimum wage and a maximum of hours in limiting liberty of contract was especially challenged. That challenge persists and is without any satisfactory answer. . . .

We think that the . . . decision in the *Adkins* case was a departure from the true application of the principles governing the regulation by the State of the relation of employer and employed. . . .

. . . What can be closer to the public interest than the health of women and their protection from unscrupulous and overreaching employers? And if the protection of women is a legitimate end of the exercise of state power, how can it be said that the requirement of the payment of a minimum wage fairly fixed in order to meet the very necessities of existence is not an admissible means to that end? The legislature of the State was clearly entitled to consider the situation of women in employment, the fact that they are in the class receiving the least pay, that their bargaining power is relatively weak, and that they are the ready victims of those who would take advantage of their necessitous circumstances. The legislature was entitled to adopt measures to reduce the evils of the "sweating system," the exploiting of workers at wages so low as to be insufficient to meet the bare cost of living, thus making their very helplessness the occasion of a most injurious competition. . . . Legislative response to that conviction cannot be regarded as arbitrary or capricious, and that is all we have to decide. Even if the wisdom of the policy be regarded as debatable and its effects uncertain, still the legislature is entitled to its judgment.

There is an additional and compelling consideration which recent economic experience has brought into a strong light. The exploitation of a class of workers who are in an unequal position with respect to bargaining power and are thus relatively defenseless against the denial of a living wage is not only detrimental to their health and well being but casts a direct burden for their support upon the community. What these workers lose in wages the taxpayers are called upon to pay. The bare cost of living must be met. We may take judicial notice of the unparalleled demands for relief which arose during the recent period of depression and still continue to an alarming extent despite the degree of economic recovery which has been achieved. It is unnecessary to cite official statistics to establish what is of common knowledge through the length and breadth of the land. While in the instant case no factual brief has been presented, there is no reason to doubt that the State of Washington has encountered the same social problem that is present elsewhere. The community is not bound to provide what is in effect a subsidy for unconscionable employers. The community may direct its law-making power to correct the abuse which springs from their selfish disregard of the public interest. The argument that the legislation in question constitutes an arbitrary discrimination, because it does not extend to men, is unavailing. This Court has frequently held that the legislative authority, acting within its proper field, is not bound to extend its regulation to all cases which it might possibly reach. The legislature "is free to recognize degrees of harm and it may confine its restrictions to those classes of cases where the need is deemed to be clearest." If "the law presumably hits the evil where it is most felt, it is not to be overthrown because there are other instances to which it might have been applied." There is no "doctrinaire requirement" that the legislation should be couched in all embracing terms. . . .

Our conclusion is that the case of *Adkins* v. *Children's Hospital, supra,* should be, and it is, overruled. The judgment of the Supreme Court of the State of Washington is

Affirmed.

MR. JUSTICE SUTHERLAND, dissenting:

MR. JUSTICE VAN DEVANTER, MR. JUSTICE McREYNOLDS, MR. JUSTICE BUTLER and I think the judgment of the court below should be reversed.

The principles and authorities relied upon to sustain the judgment, were considered in *Adkins* v. *Children's Hospital,* and *Morehead* v. *New York ex rel. Tipaldo;* and their lack of application to cases like the one in hand was pointed out. A sufficient answer to all that is now said will be found in the opinions of the Court in those cases. . . .

WILLIAMSON v. LEE OPTICAL COMPANY, 384 U.S. 483 (1955)

This case concerned a challenge to an Oklahoma statute that among its provisions made it unlawful for any person not a licensed optometrist or ophthalmologist to fit lenses for eyeglasses or to duplicate or replace into frames lenses or other optical appliances except with a written prescription

*from an Oklahoma licensed ophthalmologist or op-
tometrist. The effect of the law was to forbid opticians from fitting or duplicating lenses without a
prescription. An optician firm, the Lee Optical
Company of Oklahoma, Inc., and others went into
federal district court for an injunction against Oklahoma law enforcement authorities, including state
Attorney General Mac Q. Williamson, from enforcing the law. A three-judge district court agreed with
the opticians and ruled key provisions, including
the provision just mentioned (but not the entire
statute), as violating the due process guarantee of
the Fourteenth Amendment. Appeal was then taken
to the Supreme Court.*

Votes: Unanimous

MR. JUSTICE DOUGLAS delivered the opinion of the
Court:

This suit was instituted in the District Court to
have an Oklahoma law declared unconstitutional
and to enjoin state officials from enforcing it for the
reason that it allegedly violated various provisions
of the Federal Constitution. . . .

The Oklahoma law may exact a needless, wasteful requirement in many cases. But it is for the legislature, not the courts, to balance the advantages
and disadvantages of the new requirement. . . . It
is enough that there is an evil at hand for correction, and that it might be thought that the particular
legislative measure was a rational way to correct it.

The day is gone when this Court uses the Due
Process Clause of the Fourteenth Amendment to
strike down state laws, regulatory of business and
industrial conditions, because they may be unwise,
improvident, or out of harmony with a particular
school of thought. . . . We emphasize again what
Chief Justice Waite said in *Munn* v. *Illinois:* "For
protection against abuses by legislatures the people
must resort to the polls, not to the courts." . . .

Affirmed in part and reversed in part.

MR. JUSTICE HARLAN took no part in the consideration or decision of these cases.

PENNELL v. CITY OF SAN JOSE,
485 U.S. 1 (1988)

*San Jose, California, enacted a rent control or-
dinance under which a landlord may automatically
raise the annual rent up to eight percent, but if a
tenant objects a hearing is required to determine
whether the landlord's proposed increase is "reasonable under the circumstances." The hearing of-*

*ficer is directed to consider certain factors, includ-
ing "the hardship to a tenant." Richard Pennell, a
landlord, along with a landlord's association, went
into state court seeking to invalidate the ordinance
as a violation of various provisions of the U.S.
Constitution including the due process clause of the
Fourteenth Amendment. The lower state courts
ruled in favor of the landlords but the California
Supreme Court reversed.*

Majority votes: 6
Dissenting votes: 2

CHIEF JUSTICE REHNQUIST delivered the opinion of
the Court:. . . .

The City of San Jose enacted its rent control ordinance (Ordinance) in 1979 with the stated purpose
of "alleviat[ing] some of the more immediate needs
created by San Jose's housing situation. These
needs include but are not limited to the prevention
of excessive and unreasonable rent increases, the
alleviation of undue hardships upon individual tenants, and the assurance to landlords of a fair and
reasonable return on the value of their property."
San Jose Municipal Ordinance 19696, § 5701.2.

At the heart of the Ordinance is a mechanism for
determining the amount by which landlords subject
to its provisions may increase the annual rent which
they charge their tenants. A landlord is automatically
entitled to raise the rent of a tenant in possession by
as much as eight percent; if a tenant objects to an
increase greater than eight percent, a hearing is required before a "Mediation Hearing Officer" to determine whether the landlord's proposed increase is
"reasonable under the circumstances." The Ordinance sets forth a number of factors to be considered
by the hearing officer in making this determination,
including "the hardship to a tenant." . . .

Appellants . . . urge that the mere provision in
the Ordinance that a Hearing Officer may *consider*
the hardship of the tenant in finally fixing a reasonable rent renders the Ordinance "facially invalid"
under the Due Process and Equal Protection
Clauses, even though no landlord ever has its rent
diminished by as much as one dollar because of the
application of this provision. The standard for determining whether a state price-control regulation
is constitutional under the Due Process Clause is
well established: "Price control is 'unconstitutional
. . . if arbitrary, discriminatory, or demonstrably irrelevant to the policy the legislature is free to
adopt. . . .' " In other contexts we have recognized that the Government may intervene in the
marketplace to regulate rates or prices that are artificially inflated as a result of the existence of a mo-

nopoly or near monopoly . . . or a discrepancy between supply and demand in the market for a certain product, see, *e.g., Nebbia* v. *New York* 291 U.S., at 530, 538, (allowing a minimum price for milk to offset a "flood of surplus milk"). Accordingly, appellants do not dispute that the Ordinance's asserted purpose of "prevent[ing] excessive and unreasonable rent increases" caused by the "growing shortage of and increasing demand for housing in the City of San Jose," is a legitimate exercise of appellees' police powers. . . . They do argue, however, that it is "arbitrary, discriminatory, or demonstrably irrelevant," for appellees to attempt to accomplish the additional goal of reducing the burden of housing costs on low-income tenants by requiring that "hardship to a tenant" be considered in determining the amount of excess rent increase that is "reasonable under the circumstances" pursuant to § 5703.28. As appellants put it, "The objective of alleviating individual tenant hardship is . . . not a 'policy the legislature is free to adopt' in a rent control ordinance."

We reject this contention, however, because we have long recognized that a legitimate and rational goal of price or rate regulation is the protection of consumer welfare. . . . Here, the Ordinance establishes a scheme in which a Hearing Officer considers a number of factors in determining the reasonableness of a proposed rent increase which exceeds eight percent *and* which exceeds the amount deemed reasonable under either §§ 5703.28(a) or 5703.28(b). The first six factors of § 5703.28(c) focus on the individual landlord—the Hearing Officer examines the history of the premises, the landlord's costs, and the market for comparable housing. Section 5703.28(c)(5) also allows the landlord to bring forth any other financial evidence—including presumably evidence regarding his own financial status—to be taken into account by the Hearing Officer. It is in only this context that the Ordinance allows tenant hardship to be considered and, under § 5703.29, "balance[d]" with the other factors set out in § 5703.28(c). Within this scheme, § 5703.28(c) represents a rational attempt to accommodate the conflicting interests of protecting tenants from burdensome rent increases while at the same time ensuring that landlords are guaranteed a fair return on their investment. . . . We accordingly find that the Ordinance, which so carefully considers both the individual circumstances of the landlord and the tenant before determining whether to allow an *additional* increase in rent over and above certain amounts that are deemed reasonable, does not on its face violate the Fourteenth Amendment's Due Process Clause. . . .

The judgment of the Supreme Court of California is accordingly

Affirmed.

JUSTICE KENNEDY took no part in the consideration or decision of this case.

JUSTICE SCALIA, with whom JUSTICE O'CONNOR joins, concurring in part and dissenting in part:

I agree that the tenant hardship provision of the Ordinance does not, on its face, violate either the Due Process Clause or the Equal Protection Clause of the Fourteenth Amendment. I disagree, however, with the Court's conclusion that appellants' takings claim is premature. I would decide that claim on the merits, and would hold that the tenant hardship provision of the Ordinance effects a taking of private property without just compensation in violation of the Fifth and Fourteenth Amendments. . . .

Appellants do not contest the validity of rent regulation in general. . . . Appellants' only claim is that a reduction of a rent increase below what would otherwise be a "reasonable rent" under this scheme may not, consistently with the Constitution, be based on consideration of the seventh factor—the hardship to the tenant as defined in § 5703.29. I think they are right.

Once the other six factors of the ordinance have been applied to a landlord's property, so that he is receiving only a reasonable return, he can no longer be regarded as a "cause" of exorbitantly priced housing; nor is he any longer reaping distinctively high profits from the housing shortage. The seventh factor, the "hardship" provision, is invoked to meet a quite different social problem: the existence of some renters who are too poor to afford even reasonably priced housing. But *that* problem is no more caused or exploited by landlords than it is by the grocers who sell needy renters their food, or the department stores that sell them their clothes, or the employers who pay them their wages, or the citizens of San Jose holding the higher-paying jobs from which they are excluded. And even if the neediness of renters could be regarded as a problem distinctively attributable to landlords in general, it is not remotely attributable to the *particular* landlords that the ordinance singles out—namely, those who happen to have a "hardship" tenant at the present time, or who may happen to rent to a "hardship" tenant in the future, or whose current or future affluent tenants may happen to decline into the "hardship" category.

The traditional manner in which American government has met the problem of those who cannot pay reasonable prices for privately sold necessities—a problem caused by the society at large—has been the distribution to such persons of funds raised from the public at large through taxes, either in cash (welfare payments) or in goods (public housing, publicly subsidized housing, and food stamps). Unless we are to abandon the guiding principle of the Takings Clause that "public burdens . . . should be borne by the public as a whole," this is the only manner that our Constitution permits. The fact that government acts through the landlord-tenant relationship does not magically transform general public welfare, which must be supported by all the public, into mere "economic regulation," which can disproportionately burden particular individuals. Here the City is not "regulating" rents in the relevant sense of preventing rents that are excessive; rather, it is using the occasion of rent regulation (accomplished by the rest of the Ordinance) to establish a welfare program privately funded by those landlords who happen to have "hardship" tenants. . . .

PART
THREE

CIVIL LIBERTIES

Chapter

13

The First Amendment: Political Free Speech and Association

DECISIONAL TRENDS

The guarantees of the First Amendment meant something to the framers but precisely *what* has been cause for debate. The words of the amendment themselves are unequivocal and eloquently speak of fundamental personal and political freedoms. How seriously the framers of the First Amendment meant those guarantees to be taken was put to the test less than a decade after the amendment was ratified and became a part of the Constitution at the head of the Bill of Rights. Congress in 1798 enacted the Alien and Sedition Acts in order to protect the political interests of the Federalist Party, which was then in control of both the presidency and Congress, against the growing political opposition led by Jefferson. These wide-sweeping laws, which for most intents and purposes made criticism of the President or Congress, whether written or spoken, to be federal crimes, were to be in effect for a limited time period. Nevertheless, they were

used as the basis for federal prosecutions. The laws themselves were not challenged before the Supreme Court, and it was not until 1964 in **New York Times Co.** v. **Sullivan** (chap. 14) that the Court expressed an opinion about the validity of those laws.

It is noteworthy that the Federalist party proponents of the Alien and Sedition Acts, many of whom were framers of the Constitution, used an argument that has become familiar to those who advocate limitations on speech. The argument is that the threat to national security or to the public welfare justifies temporary limitations on speech because preservation of the country or the public order must assume the highest priority. If the country is destroyed or anarchy prevails, no rights will be able to be exercised. This logic can be and has been used to argue for a restrictive interpretation of the Constitution's criminal procedures guarantees. Obviously this line of thinking can potentially be used to justify the evisceration of all fundamental freedoms. And the idea that limitations are of a temporary nature can easily get lost in the shuffle.

Recall from **Barron** v. **Baltimore** (chap. 6) that the states were under no federal constitutional obligation to honor the Bill of Rights because these guarantees were clearly meant to be limitations on the acts of Congress. States, thus, could enact their own laws limiting or even prohibiting altogether political or any other kind of speech without raising a federal constitutional issue. However, it should be kept in mind that each state had its own constitution with its own guaranteed rights. Indeed, the impetus for the Bill of Rights being added to the federal Constitution came from the states. Thus, while state abridgment of speech did not violate the First Amendment, it would have violated the states' own constitutions. However, such alleged violations would not have raised a federal question and would not have come to the United States Supreme Court. And, in fact, no such freedom of speech cases came to the Court before the adoption of the Fourteenth Amendment changed the nature of the relationship between the federal government and the states concerning personal rights and freedoms.

After the Alien and Sedition Acts, neither the Congress nor the executive branch was responsible for alleged violations of First Amendment freedom of speech until the Civil War. And then, as *Ex Parte Vallandigham,* 1 Wallace 243 (1864), made clear, the Court refused to get involved. Indeed, not until the period of World War I did the Court directly confront an alleged congressional violation of the First Amendment speech guarantee.

As for the relationship of the states to First Amendment freedoms, the Fourteenth Amendment in 1868 provided a potential for both congressional and Supreme Court involvement to protect those guarantees against encroachment by the states. But, as we saw in chapters 2 and 12, the Fourteenth Amendment, while intended by its framers and ratifiers to protect basic civil rights and liberties, instead became the vehicle to protect the economic rights of businesses and businessmen. The liberty of the Fourteenth Amendment's due process clause became economic liberty.

As we saw in chapter 12, substantive due process was used by the Court in the late nineteenth century and during the first three and one-half decades of the twentieth century to strike down legislation impairing economic liberty. But it was not clear, even though the Court at first rejected freedom of speech claims on other grounds, that the Court could or would take the position that the liberty referred to in the Fourteenth Amendment *only* meant economic liberty and *not* freedom of speech or other personal rights spelled out in the Bill of Rights. What in fact happened was that eventually the Court did recognize that the liberty of the due process clause "incorporated" freedom of speech and press and other freedoms that are explicitly guaranteed in the Bill of Rights so that these guarantees applied to the states as well as the federal government. By the process of incorporation, as we shall see in this and subsequent chapters, most of the freedoms contained in the Bill of Rights became applicable to the states (with most of the decisions coming after 1937). The Supreme Court took the due process clause of the Fourteenth Amendment and gave life to that guarantee by incorporating specific rights and freedoms.

The first major First Amendment decisions in the twentieth century grew out of the events surrounding Word War I. Congress enacted the Espionage Act of 1917, which was the basis of a conviction that was challenged on First Amendment grounds in **Schenck** v. **United States.** The *Schenck* decision launched the *clear-and-present danger doctrine,* which held open the potential for narrowing governmental encroachment on freedom of speech, although the decision itself sustained Schenck's conviction and rejected his argument that his First Amendment rights were violated. The Sedition Law of 1918, which more broadly punished speech, was also challenged on First Amendment grounds, but in **Abrams** v. **United States** the Court upheld the statute and the conviction obtained under it. The Court majority ignored the clear and present danger test (that only speech that created a clear and immediate danger of bringing about some evil that government has a right to prevent can be regulated to the point of prohibition). The next year, in *Pierce* v. *United States,* 252 U.S. 239 (1920), the Court developed the *bad tendency test* that the Court was later to use in **Gitlow** v. **New York.** The bad tendency test of whether speech could be punished by government was whether the content of the speech would tend to promote an evil that government had the right if not the duty to prevent. If the speech had a bad tendency to bring about the evil, no matter how remote the possibility of this coming about, then government could act and not be in violation of the First Amendment.

Although the Court upheld federal convictions and rejected First Amendment claims in several cases in 1919–1920, freedom of speech became a more salient issue and one that the justices had thrust upon their collective consciousness. It was perhaps inevitable, considering the development of the Fourteenth Amendment's due process clause by the turn of the century, that freedom of speech would be claimed as a *liberty* that no state could deny without due process of law. In a 1920 case, *Gilbert* v. *Minnesota,* 254 U.S. 325, Justice McKenna, for the majority, assumed for the sake of argument that freedom of speech guaranteed in the First Amendment was applicable to the states. The decision, however, upheld the state. Justice Brandeis in dissent recited the long list of cases in which due process was used to protect property rights and pointedly observed: "I cannot believe that the liberty guaranteed by the Fourteenth Amendment includes only liberty to acquire and to enjoy property." (254 U.S. at 343). He wanted the

Court to assert unequivocally that freedom of speech was a liberty guaranteed by the due process clause. Three years later in *Meyer* v. *Nebraska,* 262 U.S. 390, the Court began to look more favorably on First Amendment rights and in *Gitlow* v. *New York* the majority conceded that "freedom of speech and of the press—which are protected by the First Amendment from abridgment by Congress— are among the fundamental personal rights and 'liberties' protected by the due process clause of the Fourteenth Amendment from impairment by the States."

In *Fiske* v. *Kansas,* 274 U.S. 380 (1927), the Court for the first time overturned a criminal anarchy conviction. That same year the Court upheld a conviction under California's Criminal Syndicalism Statute in **Whitney** v. **California,** but Justice Brandeis, in a famous concurrence, promoted the value of freedom of speech and redefined the clear and present danger test so that it would be better able to protect speech from abridgment by the states. Justice Brandeis' concept of clear and present danger eventually was accepted by the Court in 1937.

In the 1930s before the constitutional turnaround of 1937 in the economic sphere, the Court decided several cases favorable to First Amendment claims. In the 1931 decision of *Stromberg* v. *California,* 283 U.S. 359, the Court invalidated a California law forbidding the display of "a red flag . . . or any flag . . . of any color . . . as a sign, symbol or emblem of opposition to organized government. . . ." Other cases were favorable to freedom of the press, and they will be considered in the next chapter.

As hopeful as these early decisions were for the protection of First Amendment freedoms, it was not until 1937 and beyond that the value of First Amendment freedoms became a high priority of the Court. This was an area in which the post-1937 Court made distinctive and creative constitutional interpretations. The new approach to First Amendment freedoms was evident in 1937 in *Herndon* v. *Lowry,* 301 U.S. 242 (1937), in which the Court protected Herndon's First Amendment rights, giving a new civil libertarian life to the clear and present danger test. It was also evident in *DeJonge* v. *Oregon,* 299 U.S. 353 (1937), in which the Court overturned De-Jonge's conviction for taking part in a Communist Party meeting in violation of Oregon's Criminal Syndicalism Act. DeJonge's rights of freedom of speech and assembly had been violated. The Court followed through with other decisions affecting these political freedoms. In the famous second flag salute case, **West Virginia State Board of Education** v. **Barnette** (chap. 15), the opinion of the Court by Justice Jackson provides one of the most eloquent defenses of the broad range of First Amendment freedoms ever to grace the pages of the *U.S. Reports.* In *Taylor* v. *Mississippi,* 319 U.S. 583 (1943), the Court overturned three convictions that were based on a Mississippi sedition statute. No clear and present danger was found. Furthermore, in several denaturalization decisions (e.g., *Schneiderman* v. *United States,* 320 U.S. 118 [1943]), the Court, by requiring strict proof that citizenship had been illegally acquired and by not finding that to have occurred, seemed to be defending the First Amendment rights of communists and even Nazi sympathizers. The case of *Hartzel* v. *United States,* 322 U.S. 680 (1944), certainly a high point along these lines, saw the Court protect the freedom of speech of those with racist views. Yet, the Court in *In Re Summers,* 325 U.S. 561 (1945), upheld the Illinois Supreme Court decision refusing a conscientious objector (to military service) admission to the state bar.

The scope of First Amendment political freedoms widened in the 1938 decision of *Lovell* v. *Griffin,* 303 U.S. 444, when the Court unanimously struck down the municipal ordinance of Griffin, Georgia, forbidding the distribution of pamphlets and circulars without the written consent of the city manager.

The next year in *Schneider* v. *State,* 308 U.S. 147 (1939), the Court invalidated various municipal ordinances that forbade the distribution of circulars or pamphlets without a license or other form of permission from the authorities. The Court also disapproved a Jersey City municipal ordinance in the case of *Hague* v. *CIO,* 307 U.S. 496 (1939), which had prohibited assemblies in the public streets, parks, or buildings without a permit from the Director of Public Safety. The ordinance was the basis for harassing the union workers engaging in labor organizing in the city. Another labor case worthy of note is *Bridges* v. *California,* 314 U.S. 252 (1941), in which union leader Harry Bridges and a newspaper company were both convicted of contempt of court for criticizing the state judge before whom a labor dispute was being tried. The Supreme Court reversed the convictions on First Amendment grounds.

It should be stressed that as liberal as the Court was in the First Amendment sphere, there was never a majority of justices who adopted the view that no law whatsoever could restrain First Amendment rights. This meant that some restrictions on First Amendment rights were, on occasion, sustained. For example, in *Cox* v. *New Hampshire,* 312 U.S. 569 (1941), the Court approved, as a reasonable police power regulation, a New Hampshire statute requiring parade organizers to secure a special license in order to conduct a parade or procession. The Court in *Chaplinsky* v. *New Hampshire,* 315 U.S. 568 (1942), upheld another New Hampshire statute, this one making it a crime to call anyone offensive or derisive names in public. Such "fighting words," said the Court, are not protected by the First Amendment. Neither is obscenity or libel.

The First Amendment rights of organized labor were given a major boost by the landmark decision of **Thornhill** v. **Alabama** in which peaceful picketing was brought under the umbrella of the First Amendment. But the

Court was to emphasize in later decisions that picketing that was not peaceful *could* be enjoined (see *Milk Wagon Drivers Union* v. *Meadowmoor Dairies,* 312 U.S. 287 [1941]) and so could picketing at a location having no direct relation to the labor dispute involved (see *Carpenters and Joiners Union* v. *Ritter's Cafe,* 315 U.S. 722 [1942]).

The Vinson and Warren Courts were heavily involved in developing constitutional law in the First Amendment area. Cases involving alleged subversives, communists, radicals, or other political dissidents came before the Court and the reception given First Amendment claims by the Vinson Court was typically chilly—befitting the Cold War politics of the era. In *American Communications Association* v. *Douds,* 339 U.S. 382 (1950), the Vinson Court upheld Section 9(h) of the Taft-Hartley Act (the Labor-Management Relations Act of 1947) that denied certain benefits of the National Labor Relations Act to unions whose officers would not sign an affidavit that they were not communists and that they did not advocate the overthrow of the United States government by violence or other illegal means. The practical effect of this provision was to force union officials to take the oath or lose their union jobs. This provision had been enacted under Congress' commerce powers to prevent subversive union officials from conducting political strikes, thereby obstructing the flow of commerce. But the provision obviously infringed upon the First Amendment rights of union officials; that is, certain political beliefs could not be held on pain of losing one's job. The Vinson Court, however, balanced the evil of political strikes disrupting commerce against the evil of impinging upon political speech and found the former a more formidable evil. The Court was able to bypass the clear and present danger test. However, the next year in **Dennis** v. **United States** the Court was forced to confront that issue, that is, to determine whether restraints on certain kinds of advocacy and teaching violated the

First Amendment because no clear and present danger had occurred.

The Vinson Court grappled with the First Amendment rights of political dissidents, sometimes upholding them—as in *Terminiello* v. *Chicago,* 337 U.S. 1 (1949), involving a disorderly conduct conviction of an anti-Semitic speaker who nearly caused a riot—but usually denying them. In *Feiner* v. *New York,* 340 U.S. 315 (1951), the Court upheld the breach of the peace conviction of a Syracuse University student who had addressed a street meeting and had angered some listeners in the crowd. Perhaps the most serious assaults on First Amendment freedoms lay with such state laws as that of New York which required the Board of Regents to make a list of organizations that it found advocated or taught the doctrine of illegal overthrow of the government. Membership in such a subversive organization meant an automatic disqualification for employment in public schools. Anyone fired or denied employment had the right to a full hearing with the right to counsel and the right to judicial review. The Vinson Court upheld this law in *Adler* v. *Board of Education of the City of New York,* 342 U.S. 485 (1952). However, the Court in the case of *Wieman* v. *Updegraff,* 344 U.S. 183 (1952), struck down an Oklahoma statute that excluded from state employment anyone who was or had been a member of a so-called subversive organization regardless of the individual's knowledge about the organization. The Court found that this inhibited First Amendment rights by arbitrarily punishing innocent along with knowing associational activity.

The first part of the Warren Court era saw an easing of the more restrictive attitude of the Vinson Court in the area of the rights of political dissidents. In *Pennsylvania* v. *Nelson,* 350 U.S. 497 (1956), Steve Nelson, an acknowledged member of the Communist Party, was convicted of violating the Pennsylvania Sedition Act and sentenced to imprisonment and fine. The Court invalidated the Pennsylvania statute on the ground that the federal government had taken over the sedition field with various pieces of legislation starting with the Smith Act of 1940. Although the Court refrained from bringing in the First Amendment, clearly by stymying state regulation of sedition, political free speech was given fewer restraints. A similar cautious yet civil libertarian oriented approach was evident in *Cole* v. *Young,* 351 U.S. 536 (1956), in which the Court sharply narrowed the scope of the federal loyalty program by ruling that it applied only to employees directly working in sensitive national security positions. Then, in 1957, the Court in **Yates** v. **United States** cautiously but distinctly backtracked from the *Dennis* decision. The Court also handed down a ruling in the 1956 Term in *Watkins* v. *United States,* 354 U.S. 178 (1957), that implicitly reaffirmed First Amendment freedoms against the predations of congressional investigatory committees. In *Sweezy* v. *New Hampshire,* 354 U.S. 234 (1957), the Court did the same with regard to state investigations. The New Hampshire state legislature had directed the state attorney general to investigate whether "subversive persons are presently located" in the state. Sweezy was one of those questioned, and he refused to answer queries about his association with the Progressive party and also concerning a lecture he had delivered in 1954 at the University of New Hampshire. The Court, in reversing Sweezy's contempt conviction, emphasized the First Amendment rights of academic freedom and political expression.

The course of the rights of political dissidents suffered some setbacks in the period between 1959 and 1961, but in the 1962 Term, with a firm civil liberties majority, the Warren Court reasserted the primacy of First Amendment values. For example in *Dombrowski* v. *Pfister,* 380 U.S. 479 (1965), the Court struck down the Louisiana Subversive Activities Criminal Control Act. In *Elfbrandt* v. *Russell,* 384 U.S. 11 (1966), the Court invalidated the Arizona loyalty oath for state employees. And in **Keyishian** v. **Board of Regents** the Court gave one of its most eloquent defenses of academic freedom and First Amendment rights. New York State's loyalty certification program was struck down as violating the First and Fourteenth Amendments and, in the process, the Court overruled the Vinson Court decision in *Adler* v. *Board of Education,* 342 U.S. 485 (1952). One of the last of the Warren Court decisions was **Brandenburg** v. **Ohio,** in which the Court, seeming to be using the clear and present danger standard, invalidated an Ohio criminal syndicalism statute that made advocacy of illegal force and violence a state crime. The Court said that only "incitement to imminent lawless action" can be prohibited. And in so ruling, the Court rather offhandedly overturned *Whitney* v. *California.*

The Warren Court limited Congress' ability to regulate the civil liberties of suspected subversives. Not all of the decisions were decided on First Amendment grounds. An example was the decision in *United States* v. *Brown,* 381 U.S. 437 (1965), in which the Court ruled unconstitutional as a bill of attainder the statutory provision making it a federal crime for a member of the Communist Party to become an officer or employee of a labor union. Another non–First Amendment decision with political free speech overtones was the decision in *Aptheker* v. *Secretary of State,* 378 U.S. 500 (1964), in which a section of the Subversive Activities Control Act of 1950 (that forbade the issuance of a United States passport to, or use of a passport by, any member of an organization found by the Subversive Activities Control Board to be communist dominated or infiltrated) was declared a violation of the liberty to travel guaranteed by the Fifth Amendment. Another provision of the same act, which made it unlawful for a member of the Communist Party to work in a defense plant, however, was struck down as violating the freedom of association guaranteed by the First Amendment. That decision was *United States*

v. *Robel,* 389 U.S. 258 (1967). In 1965 the Court struck down a provision of a 1962 act that authorized the tampering with other than first class mail from abroad that was deemed to be communist propaganda. The provision specified that the intended recipient could have the mail delivered only by specifically requesting it in writing. This, said the Court in *Lamont* v. *Postmaster-General,* 381 U.S. 301, violated the First Amendment guarantee of freedom of speech. This was also the first time that the Supreme Court invalidated an act of Congress on First Amendment grounds.

The Warren Court sought to limit Congress' exercise of its investigatory powers in *Watkins* v. *United States,* 354 U.S. 178 (1957). The Court ruled that John T. Watkins, a witness before a subcommittee of the House Committee on Un-American Activities, could not be convicted of contempt of Congress for refusal to answer pertinent questions because the committee had never defined the "question under inquiry" or explained the pertinence to it of the questions that had been asked. Chief Justice Warren took the opportunity to criticize severely the committee and to decry exposure "for the sake of exposure," a committee tactic that had wrecked careers and caused much individual suffering by stigmatizing persons as "un-American." However, two years later, a new Court majority beat a retreat in *Barenblatt* v. *United States,* 360 U.S. 109 (1959), and upheld the House Un-American Activities Committee's investigatory authority. Not until 1962, when the Court had experienced a change in personnel, did the Court strike down the House Committee's fishing expedition in *Russell* v. *United States,* 369 U.S. 749.

The Vietnam War placed great strains on America's social and political fabric. Antiwar protesters resorted to a variety of means to capture media and hence public attention, and one of the devices used was the public burning of draft cards at antiwar rallies. Congress promptly enacted a statute making it a federal crime to mutilate or destroy one's draft card. This was challenged in *United States* v. *O'Brien,* 391 U.S. 367 (1968), but the Court upheld the statute. The majority made the distinction between speech and conduct, with draft card burning going beyond the protective mantle of symbolic speech. However, schoolchildren wearing black armbands to protest the war had their First Amendment rights upheld in *Tinker* v. *Des Moines Independent Community School District,* 393 U.S. 503 (1969). But note that one of the last Burger Court decisions severely restricted the way ideas are expressed by schoolchildren. *Bethel School District, No. 403* v. *Fraser,* 478 U.S. 675 (1986), distinguished the *Tinker* decision and permitted school authorities to discipline students whose speech in their judgment is offensively lewd and indecent.

The Rehnquist Court has also had to confront political free speech claims and its decisions have tended to be liberal (but often by only 5 to 4 margins). In **Rankin** v. **McPherson** the Court gave protection to public employees from being penalized for the private expression of their political views. In **Boos** v. **Barry** the Court was sympathetic to the rights of those protesting against the policies of foreign governments near or in front of their embassies. And in the most controversial political free speech case of the Rehnquist Court, the Court in **Texas** v. **Johnson** struck down a flag-burning statute and ruled that burning the American flag as a political statement in the context of a political demonstration was protected by the First Amendment. President Bush expressed great outrage at the decision and pushed for a constitutional amendment to overturn it. Congress, instead, enacted a new flag-burning law which was promptly challenged before the Court in **U.S.** v. **Eichman** (reprinted at the end of this book). The Court, in the *Eichman* case, reaffirmed, *Texas* v. *Johnson.*

The cases discussed thus far primarily involved the First Amendment rights of political dissidents or suspected subversives. Another category of First Amendment cases concerned political expression in conflict with the law of libel. The Vinson Court in *Beauharnais* v. *Illinois*, 343 U.S. 250 (1952), upheld the Illinois conviction of Joseph Beauharnais, head of the White Circle League, who had circulated anti-black pamphlets on the streets of Chicago. This violated an Illinois statute proscribing the publication of material portraying any class of citizens of any race, color, creed, or religion as depraved, criminal, or unchaste, and exposing them to contempt, derision, or obloquy. The Court treated the statute as a group libel law that did not impinge upon the First Amendment. The Warren Court, however, took a much different view of libel (see the discussion in the next chapter) particularly as it affected the press.

Another area of political speech is that of peaceful picketing. The Court in the landmark *Thornhill* v. *Alabama* decision had brought peaceful labor picketing under the protection of the First Amendment. The Vinson Court, however, backed away from considering picketing to be an exercise of a preferred First Amendment freedom and instead balanced the rights of organized labor with competing social interests. In *Giboney* v. *Empire Storage & Ice Co.*, 336 U.S. 490 (1949), the Court established the principle that peaceful picketing to achieve an unlawful objective could be prohibited by the state—in this case, violation of the state's antitrust statutes. The Vinson Court even went further in the case of *International Brotherhood of Teamsters* v. *Hanke*, 339 U.S. 470 (1950), when it upheld the enjoining of peaceful picketing simply because the state court had disapproved of the union's objectives. The majority of the United States Supreme Court suggested that it was appropriate for the state court to balance competing economic interests. It was the early Warren Court, however, in *International Brotherhood of Teamsters* v. *Vogt*, 354 U.S. 284 (1957), that made it evident how much First Amend-

ment ground organized labor had lost concerning peaceful picketing. The Court ruled that the state may prevent unions from coercing employers to coerce their employees to join a union. In such instances, picketing by organized labor may be enjoined. The later Warren Court reclaimed some of the First Amendment for labor picketing in the case of *Amalgamated Food Employees Union* v. *Logan Valley Plaza Inc.*, 391 U.S. 308 (1968). The Court ruled that labor union pickets have a First Amendment right to picket on private property that is open to the public. A privately owned shopping center could not exclude pickets from communicating to the public the facts of a labor dispute. But this liberal interpretation of labor's rights under the First Amendment was not to last long. Eight years later, in *Hudgens* v. *NLRB*, 424 U.S. 507 (1976), the Burger Court overturned it.

Political free speech issues during the Burger Court of the early 1970s tended to stem from the opposition to the Vietnam War. In 1971 the Court in *Cohen* v. *California*, 403 U.S. 15, handed down a favorable civil liberties decision ruling that the words emblazoned on Cohen's jacket, ''Fuck the Draft,'' which he wore in the corridors of a county courthouse, were protected by the First Amendment. But the next year in *Lloyd Corporation* v. *Tanner*, 407 U.S. 551 (1972), the Court found that the property rights of a shopping mall owner were more important than the free speech rights of anti–Vietnam War protesters. The Court in the Tanner case, however, assured that the 1968 Warren Court precedent in *Logan Valley* stood and that First Amendment rights in privately owned shopping centers could still be exercised by those protesting the labor policies of businesses located in the centers themselves. But this concession was eventually dropped in *Hudgens* v. *NLRB*. Yet the Court four years later allowed the California Supreme Court interpreting the California constitution to accomplish in **Prune-Yard Shopping Center** v. **Robins** what the

Court itself refused to do under the First Amendment in *Tanner*.

In several cases unrelated to the war or property rights, the Burger Court asserted the primacy of the First Amendment. For example, *Wooley* v. *Maynard*, 430 U.S. 705 (1977), upheld the right of individuals to obscure or remove from their license plates mottos with which they disagreed. In *Village of Schaumburg* v. *Citizens for a Better Environment*, 444 U.S. 620 (1980), the Court struck down a municipal ordinance restricting solicitation of charitable contributions to organizations that use at least 75 percent of their receipts for "charitable purposes." *Board of Education, Island Trees Community School District* v. *Pico*, 457 U.S. 853 (1982), reasserted the principle that no officials can prescribe what shall be orthodox in politics, nationalism, religion, or other matters of opinion and therefore may not seek the removal of books from public school libraries which contain ideas with which they disagree. A portion of a federal law prohibiting picketing on the public sidewalks surrounding the Supreme Court building was struck down by the Court in *United States* v. *Grace*, 461 U.S. 171 (1983). A lawyer's suspension from practicing law, ordered by a federal judge because the lawyer criticized the court, was overturned by the Supreme Court in *In Re Snyder*, 472 U.S. 634 (1985). The Burger Court even used the First Amendment to protect the NAACP from being held responsible for the economic losses of white merchants who were subject to a civil rights boycott led by that organization (*NAACP* v. *Claiborne Hardware Co.*, 458 U.S. 886 [1982]).

The Rehnquist Court decided in favor of First Amendment claims in cases other than those previously mentioned. In *City of Houston, Texas* v. *Hill*, 482 U.S. 451 (1987), the Court struck down as unconstitutionally overbroad under the First Amendment a Houston ordinance making it unlawful to interrupt a police officer in the performance of duties. The ordinance had been used to punish a gay rights activist who verbally protested to a police officer when the officer used violence to make an arrest. In *Meyer* v. *Grant*, 486 U.S. 414 (1988), the Court invalidated a Colorado statute that prohibited paying people to circulate initiative petitions on the ground that it violated the First Amendment right to engage in political speech. In *Riley* v. *National Federation of the Blind of North Carolina*, 487 U.S. 781 (1988), the Court ruled as an unconstitutional infringement of freedom of speech the North Carolina Charitable Solicitations Act that placed limits on fundraiser's fees and the ability to solicit. The solicitation of charitable contributions is protected speech, asserted the Court.

The post–Warren Court was concerned with a variety of issues related to the electoral process or political practices in which the First Amendment was the basis for decision. Campaign promises were given First Amendment protection in *Brown* v. *Hartlage*, 456 U.S. 45 (1982), a case that involved a county commissioner candidate who promised if elected to work to lower commissioners' salaries and whose electoral victory had been challenged as having, in effect, bribed voters in violation of state law. **Buckley** v. **Valeo** saw the Court strike down certain restrictions on candidate expenditures in political campaigns as violations of the First Amendment. In *Citizens Against Rent Control* v. *City of Berkeley*, 454 U.S. 290 (1981), the Court invalidated a Berkeley, California, ordinance that placed a $250 limit on contributions to committees formed to support or oppose ballot measures submitted to the electorate. The Court ruled that this violated the First Amendment guarantees of expression and association. In 1985 the Court, continuing this line of decisions, decided *Federal Election Commission* v. *National Conservative Political Action Committee*, 470 U.S. 480 in which restrictions on political action committees independent of the political parties or political candidates were struck down. This decision, in particular, has great implications for the political parties by undermining their ability to coordinate and conduct political campaigns. The decision in *Branti* v. *Finkel,* 445 U.S. 507 (1980), was also a victory for First Amendment claims that has an adverse effect on the political parties. Here, the Court undermined the political patronage reward system used by party organizations. The Court ruled that a public employee at the nonpolicymaking level cannot be fired for political reasons. The Rehnquist Court went even further in **Rutan** v. **Republican Party of Illinois** (reprinted at the end of this book) and ruled that promotion, transfer, recall, and hiring decisions are governed by the First Amendment principles established in *Branti*. The political association guarantee of the First Amendment, however, was used to the benefit of the national parties.

In *Democratic Party of the United States* v. *LaFollette,* 450 U.S. 107 (1981), the Court found that the rules of the Democratic National Convention validly barred the delegate selection process of the state of Wisconsin, which utilized the open primary. Wisconsin cannot infringe upon the national party's right of political association. Similarly, First Amendment associational rights were violated by an Ohio statute that required an independent candidate for the office of President of the United States to file a statement of candidacy and nominating petition in the month of March in order to appear on the general election ballot the following November. This, said the Court in *Anderson* v. *Celebrezze,* 460 U.S. 780 (1983), places an unconstitutional burden on the associational rights of the supporters of the independent candidate. Another Ohio law relevant for the electoral process was struck down for violating the associational rights of supporters of minor political parties. This was the law that required the listing of the names and addresses of campaign contributors as that law was applied to the Socialist Workers party. The Court in *Brown* v. *Socialist Workers '74 Campaign*

Committee, 459 U.S. 87 (1982), ruled that the First Amendment prohibits a state from compelling such disclosure by minor political parties as would subject those persons so identified to the reasonable probability of threats, harassment, or reprisals.

More recently, the Rehnquist Court also decided First Amendment cases concerning political parties and it, too, favored freedom of political association. In *Tashjian* v. *Republican Party of Connecticut,* 479 U.S. 208 (1986), the Supreme Court upheld the Republican party of Connecticut's claim that the Connecticut closed primary law that limited voting in the primary to only those registered with the party interfered with the party's rule that permitted independents to vote in the Republican primary. The Connecticut law interfered with the party's First Amendment right to define its associational boundaries. In *Eu* v. *San Francisco Cty. Democratic Cent. Comm.,* 109 S. Ct. 1013 (1989), the Court struck down a California election law regulating the parties, including: the provisions forbidding the official governing bodies of political parties from endorsing or opposing candidates in primary elections; limits on terms of office for state central committee chairs; and the requirement that such chairs rotate between residents of northern and southern California. These regulations, said the Court, burden the First Amendment associational rights of the parties. However, the Court in **Austin** v. **Michigan Chamber of Commerce** (reprinted at the end of this book), ruled that the states and the federal government may prohibit corporations from contributing to political parties and political candidates with corporate funds. This, said the majority, is a valid regulation of campaign expenditures and not a denial of a corporation's freedom of political speech.

First Amendment claims involving political speech are, as suggested by some of the cases just mentioned, often raised in new and complex contexts. Although the Burger Court had a record of support for many of those claims, there were some important claims that did not receive such support. Earlier we discussed the cases concerning freedom of speech in shopping malls. Some other cases of note in which First Amendment political speech claims were rejected include *Connick* v. *Myers,* 461 U.S. 138 (1983), which concerned the firing of an assistant district attorney in New Orleans who strongly opposed her transfer to a different section of criminal court and subsequently prepared and distributed a questionnaire to other assistant district attorneys concerning office transfer policy. She challenged her dismissal claiming that her First Amendment rights were thereby violated. A 5–4 majority ruled that her rights were not violated and that the First Amendment did not provide immunity for employee grievances. Another rejected First Amendment claim that was even more political, in the sense that it concerned the furthering of a public policy position, was in **Clark** v. **Community for Creative Non-Violence,** which raised questions of symbolic speech. In *Wayte* v. *United States,* 470 U.S. 598 (1985), the Court rejected, among other claims, the political speech argument. This case concerned a challenge to the federal government's passive enforcement policy of the draft registration requirement. That is, the Government only prosecutes those who publicly report themselves as having violated the law by not registering (typically in the context of opposition to United States foreign policy in, for example, Latin America) or who were reported by others as being in violation of the registration law. Such selective prosecution does not violate the Constitution.

The Rehnquist Court, too, has handed down some decisions rejecting political free speech claims. In *Lyng* v. *International Union, UAW,* 485 U.S. 360 (1988), the Court rejected the First Amendment claim of union members and their union challenging a 1981 Amendment to the Food Stamp Act that bars a household from receiving food stamps if a member of the household is on strike. In *Ward* v. *Rock Against Racism,* 109 S. Ct. 2746

(1989), the Court ruled as constitutional the New York City ordinance requiring performers in outdoor band shells to use a sound system and sound technicians provided by the city. The Court found that this regulation was a reasonable time, place, and manner regulation that was designed to ensure that music performances do not disturb surrounding residents. The six-person majority found that the political free speech rights of the Rock Against Racism performers were not violated. In *U.S.* v. *Kokinda,* 110 S.Ct. 3115 (1990), the Court upheld a post office ban on all soliciting on post office property. The 5–4 decision upheld the convictions of two political activists who refused to stop soliciting donations on a post office walkway. The restriction, said the majority, is reasonable and does not concern a traditional public forum.

In summary, there will always be some ambiguity to the status of political free speech because the First Amendment guarantee has never been interpreted as being absolute. However, it would appear that the current Court does accept the clear and present danger standard (however it may be phrased) so that political speech divorced from illegal conduct may not be regulated. The political content of speech may not be regulated except insofar as it relates to the time, place, or manner of its exercise. Speech plus conduct or symbolic speech, however, raises a more troublesome issue, as *Clark* v. *Community for Creative Non-Violence* and *Texas* v. *Johnson* illustrate. Whether the conduct component is seen as subject to reasonable regulation by government as a valid exercise of its police powers will in large part rest on the balance struck by justices with differing attitudes and values as to the competing claims of individuals and governmental authorities.

THE IMPACT OF THE COURT'S DECISIONS

Table 13.1 summarizes the impact of selected Court decisions concerning political free speech and association. The reprinted cases follow.

Table 13.1   THE IMPACT OF SELECTED COURT DECISIONS, POLITICAL FREE SPEECH AND ASSOCIATION CASES

Case	Year	Impact on Parties	Short-Run Impact	Long-Run Impact
Schenck v. United States	1919	Schenck and codefendant sent to prison.	By upholding Espionage Act of 1917, decision encouraged continued prosecutions and discouraged appeals to the Supreme Court.	The clear and present danger doctrine was launched and was used after 1937 as a civil liberties doctrine.
Abrams v. United States	1919	Abrams and four codefendants sent to prison to serve 20-year sentences. Sentences subsequently commuted upon deportation to the Soviet Union.	Court seemingly abandons the clear and present danger test. The Sedition Act amendments of 1918 to the Espionage Act of 1917 upheld. Encouraged official federal government action against alien subversives. Palmer raids followed within two months of decision.	Civil libertarians alerted by Holmes' eloquent dissent to the need for doctrines capable of protecting First Amendment freedoms. After 1937 the preferred freedoms doctrine developed.
Gitlow v. New York	1925	Benjamin Gitlow sent to prison, but given pardon by Governor Al Smith in December, 1925.	Although New York statute and Gitlow's conviction upheld, decision, by conceding incorporation of freedoms of speech and press within the Fourteenth Amendment, made it somewhat more difficult to achieve criminal anarchy convictions. Court in 1927, *Fiske v. Kansas*, overturned such a conviction.	Freedom of speech and press brought under the "liberty" of the Fourteenth Amendment due process clause. Provided precedent for later Court involvement in and protection of First Amendment freedoms against the actions of the state.
Whitney v. California	1927	Charlotte Anita Whitney's conviction upheld.	Court reveals continuing hostility to communists and appears to give the go-ahead for prosecution of internationally organized American "subversives."	Justice Brandeis' concurring opinion redefining the clear and present danger standard is eventually adopted and used by the Court to prevent people from being sent to jail for their political views. *Whitney* specifically overruled in *Brandenburg v. Ohio.*

(continued)

Table 13.1 *(continued)*

Case	Year	Impact on Parties	Short-Run Impact	Long-Run Impact
Thornhill v. *Alabama*	1940	Byron Thornhill did not have to serve 73-day prison sentence.	Organized labor given a boost because one of its major weapons was accorded First Amendment protection.	Stands as precedent for liberal interpretation of scope of First Amendment freedoms and consequent limits on state police power.
Dennis v. *United States*	1951	The Communist Party leaders were sent to prison to serve their five-year sentences. Each was fined $10,000.	Prosecution of lesser party functionaries undertaken. Publicity fanned anticommunist hysteria.	Although decision stands as a negative civil liberties precedent, its doctrines have not as yet been used again by the Court.
Yates v. *United States*	1957	Five of the 14 convictions reversed. The Justice Department eventually quashed the indictments against the nine others. Sentences of five years' imprisonment and $10,000 fines not carried out.	The strict evidentiary requirements led to the dropping of indictments or the reversal of convictions.	Signaled the Warren Court's civil liberties thrust. Decision attacked by right-wingers and was one of several that led to erosion of public support for the Court in the 1960s.
Keyishian v. *Board of Regents*	1967	Keyishian and three others vindicated by the Court although the State University had ended the certificate and statement requirement before the case was tried.	By 1972 almost all loyalty oaths for teachers eliminated nationwide.	Major First Amendment precedent and landmark academic freedom case.
Brandenburg v. *Ohio*	1969	Brandenburg did not serve the 1–10 year sentence nor did he pay the $1,000 fine.	Decision reaffirmed the primacy of First Amendment values and discouraged prosecutions for "mere advocacy" of unpopular views.	Clear and present danger test relaunched as "inciting or producing imminent lawless action" as the standard under which speech may be punished.

Case	Year			
PruneYard Shopping Center v. Robins	1980	Little effect on students who won case. Minimal effect on PruneYard Shopping Center.	Decision praised by press and liberals. Signal to state courts that they are free to be more liberal than the Supreme Court in protecting freedom of speech under the state constitutions.	Encouraged some state supreme courts to rely on their state constitutions rather than on the federal Constitution to protect certain rights.
Buckley v. Valeo	1976	Candidates for federal office free to spend unlimited amounts of their own money.	Cost of political campaigns continues to increase. Campaign spending reform dealt a major blow. Public financing of presidential campaigns accepted by public.	Decision likely has accelerated the influence of special interests in the electoral process. Has also made it more likely than would otherwise have occurred under the provisions of the statute that the wealthy have a pronounced edge when it comes to running for public office.
Clark v. Community for Creative Non-Violence	1984	No impact on demonstrators because decision came long after dates of demonstration.	Court continues its less than full support of symbolic speech and gives new emphasis to time-place-manner doctrine.	Precedent for restricted view of symbolic speech even when it concerns important public issues.
Texas v. Johnson	1989	Johnson does not have to serve jail sentence nor pay fine.	Tremendous political controversy as President Bush opposes the decision and campaigns for a constitutional amendment prohibiting desecration of the American flag. Congress enacts new flag-burning law that is challenged and struck down in *U.S. v. Eichman*.	Important political freedom precedent. If proposed constitutional amendment overturning decision becomes part of the Constitution, it will seriously erode the First Amendment and will be the first constitutional amendment to curb civil liberties.

SCHENCK v. UNITED STATES,
249 U.S. 47 (1919)

Schenck was prosecuted for having violated the Espionage Act of 1917. This law made it a federal crime to interfere with military recruitment or the draft or to affect adversely military morale. The intent of the speaker or writer was a crucial element of the offense. Schenck, the General Secretary of the Socialist party, along with his colleagues, published and distributed leaflets that opposed the United States' entry into World War I as well as the military draft. The draft was likened to slave labor and the pamphlet vigorously urged the repeal of the draft law. Schenck was convicted of conspiring to obstruct the draft, and of other violations of the Espionage Act. In his defense his lawyers argued that he was within his right of freedom of speech and that the Espionage Act violated the First Amendment by punishing speech.

Votes: Unanimous

MR. JUSTICE HOLMES delivered the opinion of the Court:

This is an indictment in three counts. The first charges a conspiracy to violate the Espionage Act of June 15, 1917, by causing and attempting to cause insubordination, in the military and naval forces of the United States, and to obstruct the recruiting and enlistment service of the United States, when the United States was at war with the German Empire, to-wit, that the defendants wilfully conspired to have printed and circulated to men who had been called and accepted for military service under the Act of May 18, 1917, a document set forth and alleged to be calculated to cause such insubordination and obstruction. The count alleges overt acts in pursuance of the conspiracy, ending in the distribution of the document set forth. The second count alleges a conspiracy to commit an offence against the United States, to-wit, to use the mails for the transmission of . . . the above mentioned document. . . . The third count charges an unlawful use of the mails for the transmission of the same matter and otherwise as above. The defendants were found guilty on all the counts. They set up the First Amendment to the Constitution forbidding Congress to make any law abridging the freedom of speech, or of the press, and bringing the case here on that ground have argued some other points also of which we must dispose. . . .

The document in question upon its first printed side recited the first section of the Thirteenth Amendment, said that the idea embodied in it was violated by the Conscription Act and that a conscript is little better than a convict. In impassioned language it intimated that conscription was despotism in its worst form and a monstrous wrong against humanity in the interest of Wall Street's chosen few. It said "Do not submit to intimidation," but in form at least confined itself to peaceful measures such as a petition for the repeal of the act. The other and later printed side of the sheet was headed "Assert Your Rights." . . . It denied the power to send our citizens away to foreign shores to shoot up the people of other lands, and added that words could not express the condemnation such cold-blooded ruthlessness deserves, &c., &c., winding up "You must do your share to maintain, support and uphold the rights of the people of this country." Of course the document would not have been sent unless it had been intended to have some effect, and we do not see what effect it could be expected to have upon persons subject to the draft except to influence them to obstruct the carrying of it out. The defendants do not deny that the jury might find against them on this point.

But it is said, suppose that that was the tendency of this circular, it is protected by the First Amendment to the Constitution. . . . We admit that in many places and in ordinary times the defendants in saying all that was said in the circular would have been within their constitutional rights. But the character of every act depends upon the circumstances in which it is done. The most stringent protection of free speech would not protect a man in falsely shouting fire in a theatre and causing a panic. It does not even protect a man from an injunction against uttering words that may have all the effect of force. The question in every case is whether the words used are used in such circumstances and are of such a nature as to create a clear and present danger that they will bring about the substantive evils that Congress has a right to prevent. It is a question of proximity and degree. When a nation is at war many things that might be said in time of peace are such a hindrance to its effort that their utterance will not be endured so long as men fight and that no Court could regard them as protected by any constitutional right. It seems to be admitted that if an actual obstruction of the recruiting service were proved, liability for words that produced that effect might be enforced. The statute of 1917 in § 4 punishes conspiracies to obstruct as well as actual obstruction. If the act, (speaking, or circulating a paper,) its tendency and the intent with which it is done are the same, we perceive no ground for saying that success alone warrants making the act a crime. . . .

Judgments affirmed.

ABRAMS v. UNITED STATES,
250 U.S. 616 (1919)

Jacob Abrams and his colleagues were charged with violation of the Sedition Act of 1918, the first American sedition act in 120 years. The act made it a federal crime to speak in "disloyal, profane, scurrilous or abusive language about the form of government, the Constitution, soldiers and sailors, flag or uniform of the armed forces" and to speak or act in favor of the German Empire or opposed to the United States. Abrams and four others, all resident aliens and all anarchist-socialists, threw pamphlets from a window in the lower East Side of New York City one day in August, 1918. The pamphlets attacked the Allied incursion into Russia to attempt to put down the Russian Revolution, and, utilizing inflammatory prose, attacked United States policy. Abrams and his associates were tried, convicted, and sentenced to 20 years imprisonment for their actions.

Majority votes: 7
Dissenting votes: 2

MR. JUSTICE CLARKE delivered the opinion of the Court: . . .

It was admitted on the trial that the defendants had united to print and distribute the described circulars and that five thousand of them had been printed and distributed about the 22d day of August, 1918. . . . [T]he language of these circulars was obviously intended to provoke and to encourage resistance to the United States in the war, as the third count runs, and, the defendants, in terms, plainly urged and advocated a resort to a general strike of workers in ammunition factories for the purpose of curtailing the production of ordnance and munitions necessary and essential to the prosecution of the war as is charged in the fourth count. Thus it is clear not only that some evidence but that much persuasive evidence was before the jury tending to prove that the defendants were guilty as charged in both the third and fourth counts of the indictment. . .

Affirmed.

MR. JUSTICE HOLMES dissenting: . . . .

I do not doubt for a moment that . . . the United States constitutionally may punish speech that produces or is intended to produce a clear and imminent danger that it will bring about forthwith certain substantive evils that the United States constitutionally may seek to prevent. The power undoubtedly is greater in time of war than in time of peace because war opens dangers that do not exist at other times.

But as against dangers peculiar to war, as against others, the principle of the right to free speech is always the same. It is only the present danger of immediate evil or an intent to bring it about that warrants Congress in setting a limit to the expression of opinion where private rights are not concerned. Congress certainly cannot forbid all effort to change the mind of the country. Now nobody can suppose that the surreptitious publishing of a silly leaflet by an unknown man, without more, would present any immediate danger that its opinions would hinder the success of the government arms or have any appreciable tendency to do so. . . .

In this case sentences of twenty years imprisonment have been imposed for the publishing of two leaflets that I believe the defendants had as much right to publish as the Government has to publish the Constitution of the United States now vainly invoked by them. Even if I am technically wrong and enough can be squeezed from these poor and puny anonymities to turn the color of legal litmus paper; I will add, even if what I think the necessary intent were shown; the most nominal punishment seems to me all that possibly could be inflicted, unless the defendants are to be made to suffer not for what the indictment alleges but for the creed that they avow—a creed that I believe to be the creed of ignorance and immaturity when honestly held, as I see no reason to doubt that it was held here, but which, although made the subject of examination at the trial, no one has a right even to consider in dealing with the charges before the Court.

Persecution for the expression of opinions seems to me perfectly logical. If you have no doubt of your premises or your power and want a certain result with all your heart you naturally express your wishes in law and sweep away all opposition. To allow opposition by speech seems to indicate that you think the speech impotent, as when a man says that he has squared the circle, or that you do not care wholeheartedly for the result, or that you doubt either your power or your premises. But when men have realized that time has upset many fighting faiths, they may come to believe even more than they believe the very foundations of their own conduct that the ultimate good desired is better reached by free trade in ideas—that the best test of truth is the power of the thought to get itself accepted in the competition of the market, and that truth is the only ground upon which their wishes safely can be carried out. That at any rate is the theory of our Constitution. It is an experiment, as all life is an experiment. Every year if not every day we have to wager our salvation upon some prophecy based upon imperfect knowledge. While that experiment is part of our system I think that we should be eternally vigilant against attempts to check the expression of opinions that we loathe and believe to be fraught with death, unless they so imminently threaten immediate interference with the lawful and pressing purposes of the law that an immediate check is required to save the country. . . . MR. JUSTICE BRANDEIS concurs with the foregoing opinion.

GITLOW v. NEW YORK,
268 U.S. 652 (1925)

Benjamin Gitlow was a member of the Left Wing Section of the Socialist Party. He published and circulated "The Left Wing Manifesto" as a part of the Left Wing's newspaper, The Revolutionary Age. *The manifesto advocated revolutionary mass action to overthrow the government by force, violence, and other unlawful means. He was convicted of violating the New York State Criminal Anarchy Act of 1902 by advocating, advising, teaching, and publishing his views of the necessity of overthrowing the government by illegal force and violence. Gitlow's lawyer argued that the New York statute deprived Gitlow of his "liberty" of speech and press without due process of law in violation of the Fourteenth Amendment.*

Majority votes: 6
Dissenting votes: 2

MR. JUSTICE SANFORD delivered the opinion of the Court: . . .

The precise question presented, and the only question which we can consider under this writ of error, then is, whether the statute, as construed and applied in this case by the state courts, deprived the defendant of his liberty of expression in violation of the due process clause of the Fourteenth Amendment.

The statute does not penalize the utterance or publication of abstract "doctrine" or academic discussion having no quality of incitement to any concrete action. It is not aimed against mere historical or philosophical essays. It does not restrain the advocacy of changes in the form of government by constitutional and lawful means. What it prohibits is language advocating, advising, or teaching the overthrow of organized government by unlawful means. . . .

The Manifesto, plainly, is neither the statement

of abstract doctrine nor, as suggested by counsel, mere prediction that industrial disturbances and revolutionary mass strikes will result spontaneously in an inevitable process of evolution in the economic system. It advocates and urges in fervent language mass action which shall progressively foment industrial disturbances and through political mass strikes and revolutionary mass action overthrow and destroy organized parliamentary government. . . .

For present purposes we may and do assume that freedom of speech and of the press—which are protected by the First Amendment from abridgment by Congress—are among the fundamental personal rights and "liberties" protected by the due process clause of the Fourteenth Amendment from impairment by the States. . . .

It is a fundamental principle, long established, that the freedom of speech and of the press which is secured by the Constitution, does not confer an absolute right to speak or publish, without responsibility, whatever one may choose, or an unrestricted and unbridled license that gives immunity for every possible use of language and prevents the punishment of those who abuse this freedom. . . .

That a State in the exercise of its police power may punish those who abuse this freedom by utterances inimical to the public welfare, tending to corrupt public morals, incite to crime, or disturb the public peace, is not open to question. . . .

And, for yet more imperative reasons, a State may punish utterances endangering the foundations of organized government and threatening its overthrow by unlawful means. These imperil its own existence as a constitutional State. Freedom of speech and press . . . does not protect disturbances to the public peace or the attempt to subvert the government. It does not protect publications or teachings which tend to subvert or imperil the government or to impede or hinder it in the performance of its governmental duties. . . . In short this freedom does not deprive a State of the primary and essential right of self preservation; which, so long as human governments endure, they cannot be denied. . . .

By enacting the present statute the State has determined, through its legislative body, that utterances advocating the overthrow of organized government by force, violence and unlawful means, are so inimical to the general welfare and involve such danger of substantive evil that they may be penalized in the exercise of its police power. That determination must be given great weight. Every presumption is to be indulged in favor of the validity of the statute. . . . [T]he immediate danger is none the less real and substantial, because the effect of a given utterance cannot be accurately foreseen. The State cannot reasonably be required to measure the danger from every such utterance in the nice balance of a jeweler's scale. A single revolutionary spark may kindle a fire that, smouldering for a time, may burst into a sweeping and destructive conflagration. It cannot be said that the State is acting arbitrarily or unreasonably when in the exercise of its judgment as to the measures necessary to protect the public peace and safety, it seeks to extinguish the spark without waiting until it has enkindled the flame or blazed into the conflagration. It cannot reasonably be required to defer the adoption of measures for its own peace and safety until the revolutionary utterances lead to actual disturbances of the public peace or imminent and immediate danger of its own destruction; but it may, in the exercise of its judgment, suppress the threatened danger in its incipiency. . . .

We cannot hold that the present statute is an arbitrary or unreasonable exercise of the police power of the State unwarrantably infringing the freedom of speech or press; and we must and do sustain its constitutionality.

This being so it may be applied to every utterance—not too trivial to be beneath the notice of the law—which is of such a character and used with such intent and purpose as to bring it within the prohibition of the statute. . . . In other words, when the legislative body has determined generally, in the constitutional exercise of its discretion, that utterances of a certain kind involve such danger of substantive evil that they may be punished, the question whether any specific utterance coming within the prohibited class is likely, in and of itself, to bring about the substantive evil, is not open to consideration. It is sufficient that the statute itself be constitutional and that the use of the language comes within its prohibition. . . . [T]he general provisions of the statute may be constitutionally applied to the specific utterance of the defendant if its natural tendency and probable effect was to bring about the substantive evil which the legislative body might prevent. . . .

It was not necessary, within the meaning of the statute, that the defendant should have advocated "some definitive or immediate act or acts" of force, violence or unlawfulness. It was sufficient if such acts were advocated in general terms; and it was not essential that their immediate execution should have been advocated. Nor was it necessary that the language should have been "reasonably and ordinarily calculated to incite certain persons" to acts of force, violence or unlawfulness. The advocacy need not be addressed to specific persons. Thus the publication and circulation of a newspaper article may be an encouragement or endeavor to persuade to murder, although not addressed to any person in particular.

And finding, for the reasons stated, that the statute is not in itself unconstitutional, and that it has not been applied in the present case in derogation of any constitutional right, the judgment of the Court of Appeals is

Affirmed.

MR. JUSTICE HOLMES, dissenting:

MR. JUSTICE BRANDEIS and I are of opinion that this judgment should be reversed. The general principle of free speech, it seems to me, must be taken to be included in the Fourteenth Amendment, in view of the scope that has been given to the word 'liberty' as there used, although perhaps it may be accepted with a somewhat larger latitude of interpretation than is allowed to Congress by the sweeping language that governs or ought to govern the laws of the United States. If I am right, then I think that the criterion sanctioned by the full Court in *Schenck* v. *United States,* 249 U.S. 47, 52, applies. "The question in every case is whether the words used are used in such circumstances and are of such a nature as to create a clear and present danger that they will bring about the substantive evils that [the State] has a right to prevent." It is true that in my opinion this criterion was departed from in *Abrams* v. *United States,* 250 U.S. 616, but the convictions that I expressed in that case are too deep for it to be possible for me as yet to believe that it and *Schaefer* v. *United States,* 251 U.S. 466, have settled the law. If what I think the correct test is applied, it is manifest that there was no present danger of an attempt to overthrow the government by force on the part of the admittedly small minority who shared the defendant's views. It is said that this manifesto was more than a theory, that it was an incitement. Every idea is an incitement. It offers itself for belief and if believed it is acted on unless some other belief outweighs it or some failure of energy stifles the movement at its birth. The only difference between the expression of an opinion and an incitement in the narrower sense is the speaker's enthusiasm for the result. Eloquence may set fire to reason. But whatever may be thought of the redundant discourse before us it had no chance of starting a present conflagration. If in the long run the beliefs expressed in proletarian dictatorship are destined to be accepted by the dominant forces of the community, the only meaning of free speech is that they should be given their chance and have their way.

If the publication of this document had been laid as an attempt to induce an uprising against government at once and not at some indefinite time in the future it would have presented a different question. The object would have been one with which the law might deal, subject to the doubt whether there was any danger that the publication could produce any result, or in other words, whether it was not futile and too remote from possible consequences. But the indictment alleges the publication and nothing more.

[MR. JUSTICE STONE did not participate in the decision.]

WHITNEY v. CALIFORNIA, 274 U.S. 357 (1927)

The essential facts of the case are stated in Justice Brandeis' concurring opinion. It is this opinion rather than the opinion of the Court that has stood as distinguishing this case. By concurring rather than dissenting, Justice Brandeis sought to exert influence on the majority to protect, at least in principle, freedom of speech and assembly. The clear and present danger test as reformulated by Brandeis was offered as the means to accomplish this, although for reasons stated by the Justice, that test could not be applied to help Ms. Whitney.

Votes: Unanimous

MR. JUSTICE SUTHERLAND delivered the opinion of the Court: [omitted]

MR. JUSTICE BRANDEIS, concurring:

Miss Whitney was convicted of the felony of assisting in organizing, in the year 1919, the Communist Labor Party of California, of being a member of it, and of assembling with it. These acts are held to constitute a crime, because the party was formed to teach criminal syndicalism. The statute which made these acts a crime restricted the right of free speech and of assembly theretofore existing. The claim is that the statute, as applied, denied to Miss Whitney the liberty guaranteed by the 14th Amendment. . . .

Despite arguments to the contrary which had seemed to me persuasive, it is settled that the due process clause of the 14th Amendment applies to matters of substantive law as well as to matters of procedure. Thus all fundamental rights comprised within the term "liberty" are protected by the Federal Constitution from invasion by the states. The right of free speech, the right to teach, and the right of assembly are, of course, fundamental rights. . . .

These may not be denied or abridged. But, although the rights of free speech and assembly are fundamental, they are not in their nature absolute. Their exercise is subject to restriction, if the particular restriction proposed is required in order to protect the state from destruction or from serious injury, political, economic or moral. That the necessity which is essential to a valid restriction does not exist unless speech would produce, or is intended to produce, a clear and imminent danger of some substantive evil which the state constitutionally may seek to prevent has been settled. See *Schenck* v. *United States,* 249 U.S. 47, 52.

It is said to be the function of the legislature to determine whether at a particular time and under the particular circumstances the formation of, or assembly with, a society organized to advocate criminal syndicalism constitutes a clear and present danger of substantive evil; and that by enacting the law here in question the legislature of California determined that question in the affirmative. Compare *Gitlow* v. *New York.* The legislature must obviously decide, in the first instance, whether a danger exists which calls for a particular protective measure. But where a statute is valid only in case certain conditions exist, the enactment of the statute cannot alone establish the facts which are essential to its validity. Prohibitory legislation has repeatedly been held invalid, because unnecessary, where the denial of liberty involved was that of engaging in a particular business. The power of the courts to strike down an offending law are no less when the interests involved are not property rights, but the fundamental personal rights of free speech and assembly.

This court has not yet fixed the standard by which to determine when a danger shall be deemed clear; how remote the danger may be and yet be deemed present; and what degree of evil shall be deemed sufficiently substantial to justify resort to abridgment of free speech and assembly as the means of protection. To reach sound conclusions on these matters, we must bear in mind why a state is, ordinarily, denied the power to prohibit dissemination of social, economic and political doctrine which a vast majority of its citizens believes to be false and fraught with evil consequence.

Those who won our independence believed that the final end of the state was to make men free to develop their faculties; and that in its government the deliberative forces should prevail over the arbitrary. They valued liberty both as an end and as a means. They believed liberty to be the secret of happiness and courage to be the secret of liberty. They believed that freedom to think as you will and to speak as you think are means indispensable to the discovery and spread of political truth; that without free speech and assembly discussion would be futile; that with them, discussion affords ordinarily adequate protection against the dissemination of noxious doctrine; that the greatest menace to freedom is an inert people; that public discussion is a political duty; and that this should be a fundamental principle of the American government. They recognized the risks to which all human institutions are subject. But they knew that order cannot be secured merely through fear of punishment for its infraction; that it is hazardous to discourage thought, hope and imagination; that fear breeds repression; that repression breeds hate; that hate menaces stable government; that the path of safety lies in the opportunity to discuss freely supposed grievances and proposed remedies; and that the fitting remedy for evil counsels is good ones. Believing in the power of reason as applied through public discussion, they eschewed silence coerced by law—the argument of force in its worst form. Recognizing the occasional tyrannies of governing majorities, they amended the Constitution so that free speech and assembly should be guaranteed.

Fear of serious injury cannot alone justify suppression of free speech and assembly. Men feared witches and burned women. It is the function of speech to free men from the bondage of irrational fears. To justify suppression of free speech there must be reasonable ground to fear that serious evil will result if free speech is practiced. There must be reasonable ground to believe that the danger apprehended is imminent. There must be reasonable ground to believe that the evil to be prevented is a serious one. Every denunciation of existing law tends in some measure to increase the probability that there will be violation of it. Condonation of a breach enhances the probability. Expressions of approval add to the probability. Propagation of the criminal state of mind by teaching syndicalism increases it. Advocacy of law-breaking heightens it still further. But even advocacy of violation, however reprehensible morally, is not a justification for denying free speech where the advocacy falls short of incitement and there is nothing to indicate that the advocacy would be immediately acted on. The wide difference between advocacy and incitement, between preparation and attempt, between assembling and conspiracy, must be borne in mind. In order to support a finding of clear and present danger it must be shown either that immediate serious violence was to be expected or was advocated, or that the past conduct furnished reason to believe that such advocacy was then contemplated.

Those who won our independence by revolution were not cowards. They did not fear political change. They did not exalt order at the cost of liberty. To courageous, self-reliant men, with confidence in the power of free and fearless reasoning applied through the processes of popular government, no danger flowing from speech can be deemed clear and present, unless the incidence of the evil apprehended is so imminent that it may befall before there is opportunity for full discussion. If there be time to expose through discussion the falsehood and fallacies, to avert the evil by the processes of education, the remedy to be applied is more speech, not enforced silence. Only an emergency can justify repression. Such must be the rule if authority is to be reconciled with freedom. Such, in my opinion, is the command of the Constitution. It is, therefore, always open to Americans to challenge a law abridging free speech and assembly by showing that there was no emergency justifying it.

Moreover, even imminent danger cannot justify resort to prohibition of these functions essential to effective democracy, unless the evil apprehended is relatively serious. Prohibition of free speech and assembly is a measure so stringent that it would be inappropriate as the means for averting a relatively trivial harm to society. A police measure may be unconstitutional merely because the remedy, although effective as means of protection, is unduly harsh or oppressive. Thus, a state might, in the exercise of its police power, make any trespass upon the land of another a crime, regardless of the results or of the intent or purpose of the trespasser. It might, also, punish an attempt, a conspiracy, or an incitement to commit the trespass. But it is hardly conceivable that this court would hold constitutional a statute which punished as a felony the mere voluntary assembly with a society formed to teach that pedestrians had the moral right to cross unenclosed, unposted, waste lands and to advocate their doing so, even if there was imminent danger that advocacy would lead to a trespass. The fact that speech is likely to result in some violence or in destruction of property is not enough to justify its suppression. There must be the probability of serious injury to the state. Among freemen, the deterrents ordinarily to be applied to prevent crime are education and punishment for violations of the law, not abridgment of the rights of free speech and assembly. . . .

Whether, in 1919, when Miss Whitney did the things complained of, there was in California such clear and present danger of serious evil, might have been made the important issue in the case. She might have required that the issue be determined either by the court or the jury. She claimed below that the statute as applied to her violated the Federal Constitution; but she did not claim that it was void because there was no clear and present danger of serious evil, nor did she request that the existence of these conditions of a valid measure thus restricting the rights of free speech and assembly be passed upon by the court or a jury. On the other hand, there was evidence on which the court or jury might have found that such danger existed. I am unable to assent to the suggestion in the opinion of the Court that assembling with a political party, formed to advocate the desirability of a proletarian revolution by mass action at some date necessarily far in the future, is not a right within the protection of the 14th Amendment. In the present case, however, there was other testimony which tended to establish the existence of a conspiracy, on the part of members of the International Workers of the World, to commit present serious crimes; and likewise to show that such a conspiracy would be furthered by the activity of the society of which Miss Whitney was a member. Under these circumstances the judgment of the state court cannot be disturbed. . . . Because we may not inquire into the errors now alleged, I concur in affirming the judgment of the state court.

MR. JUSTICE HOLMES joins in this opinion.

THORNHILL v. ALABAMA,
310 U.S. 88 (1940)

Section 3448 of the Alabama State Code made picketing a misdemeanor. However, Byron Thornhill joined a picket line that was picketing his former employer, the Brown Wood Preserving Company. He was arrested, tried, and convicted of violating the Alabama law. He was fined $100 plus court costs, but refused to pay and was sentenced to serve a jail sentence in default of payment. Thornhill was the union president and he was the only picketer against whom the law was enforced. The American Federation of Labor, with which Thornhill's union was affiliated, helped Thornhill take the case to the Supreme Court in order to challenge the constitutionality of the statute.

Majority votes: 8
Dissenting votes: 1

MR. JUSTICE MURPHY delivered the opinion of the Court:. . . .

We think that § 3448 is invalid on its face. The freedom of speech and of the press guaranteed by the Constitution embraces at the least the liberty to discuss publicly and truthfully all matters of public concern without previous restraint or fear of subsequent punishment. . . . Freedom of discussion, if it would fulfill its historic function in this nation, must embrace all issues about which information is needed or appropriate to enable the members of society to cope with the exigencies of their period.

In the circumstances of our times the dissemination of information concerning the facts of a labor dispute must be regarded as within that area of free discussion that is guaranteed by the Constitution. . . . The merest glance at state and federal legislation on the subject demonstrates the force of the argument that labor relations are not matters of mere local or private concern. Free discussion concerning the conditions in industry and the causes of labor disputes appears to us indispensable to the effective and intelligent use of the processes of popular government to shape the destiny of modern industrial society. The issues raised by regulations, such as are challenged here, infringing upon the right of employees effectively to inform the public of the facts of a labor dispute are part of this larger problem. . . .

It is true that the rights of employers and employees to conduct their economic affairs and to compete with others for a share in the products of industry are subject to modification or qualification in the interests of the society in which they exist. This is but an instance of the power of the State to set the limits of permissible contest open to industrial combatants. . . . It does not follow that the State in dealing with the evils arising from industrial disputes may impair the effective exercise of the right to discuss freely industrial relations which are matters of public concern. A contrary conclusion could be used to support abridgment of freedom of speech and of the press concerning almost every matter of importance to society.

The range of activities proscribed by §3448, whether characterized as picketing or loitering or otherwise, embraces nearly every practicable, effective means whereby those interested—including the employees directly affected—may enlighten the public on the nature and causes of a labor dispute. The safeguarding of these means is essential to the securing of an informed and educated public opinion with respect to a matter which is of public concern. It may be that effective exercise of the means of advancing public knowledge may persuade some of those reached to refrain from entering into advantageous relations with the business establishment which is the scene of the dispute. Every expression of opinion on matters that are important has the potentiality of inducing action in the interests of one rather than another group in society. But the group in power at any moment may not impose penal sanctions on peaceful and truthful discussion of matters of public interest merely on a showing that others may thereby be persuaded to take action inconsistent with its interests. Abridgment of the liberty of such discussion can be justified only where the clear danger of substantive evils arises under circumstances affording no opportunity to test the merits of ideas by competition for acceptance in the market of public opinion. We hold that the danger of injury to an industrial concern is neither so serious nor so imminent as to justify the sweeping proscription of freedom of discussion embodied in §3448.

The State urges that the purpose of the challenged statute is the protection of the community from the violence and breaches of the peace, which, it asserts, are the concomitants of picketing. The power and the duty of the State to take adequate steps to preserve the peace and to protect the privacy, the lives, and the property of its residents cannot be doubted. But no clear and present danger of destruction of life or property, or invasion of the right of privacy, or breach of the peace can be thought to be inherent in the activities of every person who approaches the premises of an employer and publicizes the facts of a labor dispute involving the latter. We are not now concerned with picketing *en masse* or otherwise conducted which might occasion such imminent and aggravated danger to these interests as to justify a statute narrowly drawn to cover the precise situation giving rise to the danger. . . . Section 3448 in question here does not aim specifically at serious encroachments on these interests and does not evidence any such care in balancing these interests against the interest of the community and that of the individual in freedom of discussion on matters of public concern.

It is not enough to say that §3448 is limited or restricted in its application to such activity as takes place at the scene of the labor dispute. . . . The danger of breach of the peace or serious invasion of rights of property or privacy at the scene of a labor dispute is not sufficiently imminent in all cases to warrant the legislature in determining that such place is not appropriate for the range of activities outlawed by §3448.

Reversed.

MR. JUSTICE MCREYNOLDS is of opinion that the judgment below should be affirmed.

DENNIS v. UNITED STATES,
341 U.S. 494 (1951)

Under political pressure from conservative Republicans, the Democratic Truman Administration in the 1948 presidential election year began a highly publicized prosecution of the 11 principal Commu- *nist Party leaders in the United States. They were charged with violating Sections 2 and 3 of the Alien Registration Act of 1940, also known as the Smith Act, that made it a federal crime knowingly to advocate, advise, teach, print, or distribute written material advocating, or knowingly to become a member of a group advocating, the overthrow or destruction by force or violence of any government in the United States. Conspiring to do any of these forbidden activities was also illegal. These Smith Act provisions were the first peacetime sedition laws since the Alien and Sedition Acts of 1798. The communist leaders were accused of conspiring to teach and advocate the violent overthrow of the government of the United States, and to organize the Communist Party in the United States for the purpose of teaching and advocating that doctrine. However, they were not charged with any overt act designed to bring about the communist revolution. They were convicted in federal district court and the convictions were upheld on appeal. The Supreme Court was faced with reconciling the broad First Amendment doctrines protecting freedom of speech, press, and association with the harsh and unprecedented action taken by the federal government against individuals for exercising those freedoms.*

Majority votes: 6
Dissenting votes: 2

MR. CHIEF JUSTICE VINSON announced the judgment of the Court and an opinion in which MR. JUSTICE REED, MR. JUSTICE BURTON and MR. JUSTICE MINTON join:. . . .

We granted certiorari, limited to the following two questions: (1) Whether either §2 or §3 of the Smith Act, inherently or as construed and applied in the instant case, violates the First Amendment and other provisions of the Bill of Rights; (2) whether either § 2 or § 3 of the Act, inherently or as construed and applied in the instant case, violates the First and Fifth Amendments because of indefiniteness. . . .

The obvious purpose of the statute is to protect existing Government, not from change by peaceable, lawful and constitutional means, but from change by violence, revolution and terrorism. That it is within the power of the Congress to protect the Government of the United States from armed rebellion is a proposition which requires little discussion. Whatever theoretical merit there may be to the argument that there is a "right" to rebellion against dictatorial governments is without force where the existing structure of the government provides for peaceful and orderly change. We reject any principle of governmental helplessness in the face of preparation for revolution, which principle, carried to its logical conclusion, must lead to anarchy. No one could conceive that it is not within the power of Congress to prohibit acts intended to overthrow the Government by force and violence. The question with which we are concerned here is not whether Congress has such power, but whether the means which it has employed conflict with the First and Fifth Amendments to the Constitution.

One of the bases for the contention that the means which Congress has employed are invalid takes the form of an attack on the face of the statute on the grounds that by its terms it prohibits academic discussion of the merits of Marxism-Leninism, that it stifles ideas and is contrary to all concepts of free speech and a free press. . . .

The very language of the Smith Act negates the interpretation which petitioners would have us impose on that Act. It is directed at advocacy, not discussion. Thus, the trial judge properly charged the jury that they could not convict if they found that petitioners did "no more than pursue peaceful studies and discussions or teaching and advocacy in the realm of ideas." He further charged that it was not unlawful "to conduct in an American college and university a course explaining the philosophical theories set forth in the books which have been placed in evidence." Such a charge is in strict accord with the statutory language, and illustrates the meaning to be placed on those words. Congress did not intend to eradicate the free discussion of political theories, to destroy the traditional rights of Americans to discuss and evaluate ideas without fear of governmental sanction. Rather Congress was concerned with the very kind of activity in which the evidence showed these petitioners engaged. . . .

In this case we are squarely presented with the application of the "clear and present danger" test, and must decide what that phrase imports. We first note that many of the cases in which this Court has reversed convictions by use of this or similar tests have been based on the fact that the interest which the State was attempting to protect was itself too insubstantial to warrant restriction of speech. . . .

Overthrow of the Government by force and violence is certainly a substantial enough interest for the Government to limit speech. Indeed, this is the ultimate value of any society, for if a society cannot protect its very structure from armed internal attack, it must follow that no subordinate value can be protected. If, then, this interest may be protected, the literal problem which is presented is what has been meant by the use of the phrase "clear and present danger" of the utterances bring-

ing about the evil within the power of Congress to punish.

Obviously, the words cannot mean that before the Government may act, it must wait until the *putsch* is about to be executed, the plans have been laid and the signal is awaited. If Government is aware that a group aiming at its overthrow is attempting to indoctrinate its members and to commit them to a course whereby they will strike when the leaders feel the circumstances permit, action by the Government is required. The argument that there is no need for Government to concern itself, for Government is strong, it possesses ample powers to put down a rebellion, it may defeat the revolution with ease needs no answer. For that is not the question. Certainly an attempt to overthrow the Government by force, even though doomed from the outset because of inadequate numbers or power of the revolutionists, is a sufficient evil for Congress to prevent. The damage which such attempts create both physically and politically to a nation makes it impossible to measure the validity in terms of the probability of success, or the immediacy of a successful attempt. In the instant case the trial judge charged the jury that they could not convict unless they found that petitioners intended to overthrow the Government "as speedily as circumstances would permit." This does not mean, and could not properly mean, that they would not strike until there was certainty of success. What was meant was that the revolutionists would strike when they thought the time was ripe. We must therefore reject the contention that success or probability of success is the criterion. . . .

Chief Judge Learned Hand, writing for the majority below, interpreted the phrase as follows: "In each case [courts] must ask whether the gravity of the 'evil,' discounted by its improbability, justifies such invasion of free speech as is necessary to avoid the danger." We adopt this statement of the rule. As articulated by Chief Judge Hand, it is as succinct and inclusive as any other we might devise at this time. It takes into consideration those factors which we deem relevant, and relates their significances. More we cannot expect from words.

Likewise, we are in accord with the court below, which affirmed the trial court's finding that the requisite danger existed. The mere fact that from the period 1945 to 1948 petitioners' activities did not result in an attempt to overthrow the Government by force and violence is of course no answer to the fact that there was a group that was ready to make the attempt. The formation by petitioners of such a highly organized conspiracy, with rigidly disciplined members subject to call when the leaders, these petitioners, felt that the time had come for action, coupled with the inflammable nature of world conditions, similar uprisings in other countries, and the touch-and-go nature of our relations with countries with whom petitioners were in the very least ideologically attuned, convince us that their convictions were justified on this score. And this analysis disposes of the contention that a conspiracy to advocate, as distinguished from the advocacy itself, cannot be constitutionally restrained, because it comprises only the preparation. It is the existence of the conspiracy which creates the danger. If the ingredients of the reaction are present, we cannot bind the Government to wait until the catalyst is added. . . .

We hold that §§ 2(a) (1), 2(a) (3) and 3 of the Smith Act, do not inherently, or as construed or applied in the instant case, violate the First Amendment and other provisions of the Bill of Rights, or the First and Fifth Amendments because of indefiniteness. Petitioners intended to overthrow the Government of the United States as speedily as the circumstances would permit. Their conspiracy to organize the Communist Party and to teach and advocate the overthrow of the Government of the United States by force and violence created a "clear and present danger" of an attempt to overthrow the Government by force and violence. They were properly and constitutionally convicted for violation of the Smith Act. The judgments of conviction are affirmed.

Affirmed.

MR.. JUSTICE CLARK took no part in the consideration or decision of this case.

MR. JUSTICE FRANKFURTER, concurring in affirmance of the judgment:. . . .

[H]ow are competing interests to be assessed? Since they are not subject to quantitative ascertainment, the issue necessarily resolves itself into asking, who is to make the adjustment?—who is to balance the relevant factors and ascertain which interest is in the circumstances to prevail? Full responsibility for the choice cannot be given to the courts. Courts are not representative bodies. They are not designed to be a good reflex of a democratic society. Their judgment is best informed, and therefore most dependable, within narrow limits. Their essential quality is detachment, founded on independence. History teaches that the independence of the judiciary is jeopardized when courts become embroiled in the passions of the day and assume primary responsibility in choosing between competing political, economic and social pressures.

Primary responsibility for adjusting the interests which compete in the situation before us of neces-

sity belongs to the Congress. . . . We are to set aside the judgment of those whose duty it is to legislate only if there is no reasonable basis for it. . . . [W]e must scrupulously observe the narrow limits of judicial authority even though self-restraint is alone set over us. Above all we must remember that this Court's power of judicial review is not "an exercise of the powers of a super-Legislature". . . .

Free-speech cases are not an exception to the principle that we are not legislators, that direct policy-making is not our province. How best to reconcile competing interests is the business of legislatures, and the balance they strike is a judgment not to be displaced by ours, but to be respected unless outside the pale of fair judgment.

On occasion we have strained to interpret legislation in order to limit its effect on interests protected by the First Amendment. In some instances we have denied to States the deference to which I think they are entitled. . . .

But in no case has a majority of the Court held that legislative judgment, even as to freedom of utterance, may be overturned merely because the Court would have made a different choice between the competing interests had the initial legislative judgment been for it to make. . . .

[T]here is ample justification for a legislative judgment that the conspiracy now before us is a substantial threat to national order and security. If the Smith Act is justified at all, it is justified precisely because it may serve to prohibit the type of conspiracy for which these defendants were convicted. . . .

It is a familiar experience in the law that new situations do not fit neatly into legal conceptions that arose under different circumstances to satisfy different needs. So it was when the injunction was tortured into an instrument of oppression against labor in industrial conflicts. So it is with the attempt to use the direction of thought lying behind the criterion of "clear and present danger" wholly out of the context in which it originated, and to make of it an absolute dogma and definitive measuring rod for the power of Congress to deal with assaults against security through devices other than overt physical attempts. . . .

It were far better that the phrase be abandoned than that it be sounded once more to hide from the believers in an absolute right of free speech the plain fact that the interest in speech, profoundly important as it is, is no more conclusive in judicial review than other attributes of democracy or than a determination of the people's representatives that a measure is necessary to assure the safety of government itself.

Not every type of speech occupies the same position on the scale of values. There is no substantial public interest in permitting certain kinds of utterances: "the lewd and obscene, the profane, the libelous, and the insulting or 'fighting' words—those which by their very utterance inflict injury or tend to incite an immediate breach of the peace." *Chaplinsky* v. *State of New Hampshire*, 315 U.S. 568, 572. We have frequently indicated that the interest in protecting speech depends on the circumstances of the occasion. It is pertinent to the decision before us to consider where on the scale of values we have in the past placed the type of speech now claiming constitutional immunity.

The defendants have been convicted of conspiring to organize a party of persons who advocate the overthrow of the Government by force and violence. The jury has found that the object of the conspiracy is advocacy as "a rule or principle of action," by language reasonably and ordinarily calculated to incite persons to such action," and with the intent to cause the overthrow "as speedily as circumstances would permit."

On any scale of values which we have hitherto recognized, speech of this sort ranks low.

Throughout our decisions there has recurred a distinction between the statement of an idea which may prompt its hearers to take unlawful action, and advocacy that such action be taken. The distinction has its root in the conception of the common law, supported by principles of morality, that a person who procures another to do an act is responsible for that act as though he had done it himself. . . .

MR. JUSTICE JACKSON, concurring: . . .

The authors of the clear and present danger test never applied it to a case like this, nor would I. If applied as it is proposed here, it means that the Communist plotting is protected during its period of incubation; its preliminary states of organization and preparation are immune from the law; the Government can move only after imminent action is manifest, when it would, of course, be too late. . . .

Of course, it is not always easy to distinguish teaching or advocacy in the sense of incitement from teaching or advocacy in the sense of exposition or explanation. It is a question of fact in each case. . . .

MR. JUSTICE BLACK, dissenting: . . . .

At the outset I want to emphasize what the crime involved in this case is, and what it is not. These petitioners were not charged with an attempt to `overthrow the Government. They were not charged with overt acts of any kind designed to overthrow the Government. They were not even charged with saying anything or writing anything designed to overthrow the Government. The charge

was that they agreed to assemble and to talk and publish certain ideas at a later date: The indictment is that they conspired to organize the Communist Party and to use speech or newspapers and other publications in the future to teach and advocate the forcible overthrow of the Government. No matter how it is worded, this is a virulent form of prior censorship of speech and press, which I believe the First Amendment forbids. I would hold §3 of the Smith Act authorizing this prior restraint unconstitutional on its face and as applied.

But let us assume, contrary to all constitutional ideas of fair criminal procedure, that petitioners although not indicted for the crime of actual advocacy, may be punished for it. Even on this radical assumption, the other opinions in this case show that the only way to affirm these convictions is to repudiate directly or indirectly the established "clear and present danger" rule. This the Court does, in a way which greatly restricts the protections afforded by the First Amendment. The opinions for affirmance indicate that the chief reason for jettisoning the rule is the expressed fear that advocacy of Communist doctrine endangers the safety of the Republic. Undoubtedly, a governmental policy of unfettered communication of ideas does entail dangers. To the Founders of this Nation, however, the benefits derived from free expression were worth the risk. They embodied this philosophy in the First Amendment's command that "Congress shall make no law *** abridging the freedom of speech, or of the press ***." I have always believed that the First Amendment is the keystone of our Government, that the freedoms it guarantees provide the best insurance against destruction of all freedom. . . .

. . . I cannot agree that the First Amendment permits us to sustain laws suppressing freedom of speech and press on the basis of Congress' or our own notions of mere "reasonableness." Such a doctrine waters down the First Amendment so that it amounts to little more than an admonition to Congress. The Amendment as so construed is not likely to protect any but those "safe" or orthodox views which rarely need its protection. . . .

Public opinion being what it now is, few will protest the conviction of these Communist petitioners. There is hope, however, that in calmer times, when present pressures, passions and fears subside, this or some later Court will restore the First Amendment liberties to the high preferred place where they belong in a free society.

MR. JUSTICE DOUGLAS, dissenting:

If this were a case where those who claimed protection under the First Amendment were teaching the techniques of sabotage, the assassination of the President, the filching of documents from public files, the planting of bombs, the art of street warfare, and the like, I would have no doubts. The freedom to speak is not absolute; the teaching of methods of terror and other seditious conduct should be beyond the pale along with obscenity and immorality. This case was argued as if those were the facts. The argument imported much seditious conduct into the record. That is easy and it has popular appeal, for the activities of Communists in plotting and scheming against the free world are common knowledge. But the fact is that no such evidence was introduced at the trial. There is a statute which makes a seditious conspiracy unlawful. Petitioners, however, were not charged with a "conspiracy to overthrow" the Government. They were charged with a conspiracy to form a party and groups and assemblies of people who teach and advocate the overthrow of our Government by force or violence and with a conspiracy to advocate and teach its overthrow by force and violence. It may well be that indoctrination in the techniques of terror to destroy the Government would be indictable under either statute. But the teaching which is condemned here is of a different character.

So far as the present record is concerned, what petitioners did was to organize people to teach and themselves teach the Marxist-Leninist doctrine contained chiefly in four books: Foundations of Leninism by Stalin (1924); The Communist Manifesto by Marx and Engels (1848); State and Revolution by Lenin (1917); History of the Communist Party of the Soviet Union (1939). . . .

The vice of treating speech as the equivalent of overt acts of a treasonable or seditious character is emphasized by a concurring opinion, which by invoking the law of conspiracy makes speech do service for deeds which are dangerous to society. The doctrine of conspiracy has served divers and oppressive purposes and in its broad reach can be made to do great evil. But never until today has anyone seriously thought that the ancient law of conspiracy could constitutionally be used to turn speech into seditious conduct. Yet that is precisely what is suggested. I repeat that we deal here with speech alone, not with speech plus acts of sabotage or unlawful conduct. Not a single seditious act is charged in the indictment. To make a lawful speech unlawful because two men conceive it is to raise the law of conspiracy to appalling proportions. That course is to make a radical break with the past and to violate one of the cardinal principles of our constitutional scheme. . . .

There comes a time when even speech loses its constitutional immunity. Speech innocuous one year may at another time fan such destructive flames that it must be halted in the interests of the safety of the Republic. That is the meaning of the clear and present danger test. When conditions are so critical that there will be no time to avoid the evil that the speech threatens, it is time to call a halt. Otherwise, free speech which is the strength of the Nation will be the cause of its destruction.

Yet free speech is the rule, not the exception. The restraint to be constitutional must be based on more than fear, on more than passionate opposition against the speech, on more than a revolted dislike for its contents. There must be some immediate injury to society that is likely if speech is allowed. . . .

How it can be said that there is a clear and present danger that this advocacy will succeed is . . . a mystery. Some nations less resilient than the United States, where illiteracy is high and where democratic traditions are only budding, might have to take drastic steps and jail those men for merely speaking their creed. But in America they are miserable merchants of unwanted ideas; their wares remain unsold. The fact that their ideas are abhorrent does not make them powerful. . . . Free speech—the glory of our system of government—should not be sacrificed on anything less than plain and objective proof of danger that the evil advocated is imminent. On this record no one can say that petitioners and their converts are in such a strategic position as to have even the slightest chance of achieving their aims. . . .

YATES v. UNITED STATES,
354 U.S. 298 (1957)

After the successful prosecution of the major Communist Party leaders in Dennis v. United States, *the federal government prosecuted lower level party functionaries and met with continued success until the* Yates *case. Mrs. Oleta O'Connor Yates and 13 other communists who were based in California were charged with violations of the Smith Act. The Supreme Court not only reversed the convictions of 5 of the 14 defendants but also made it much more difficult to secure Smith Act convictions in the future. It did so by narrowing the meaning of "organizing" as well as "advocacy," and requiring hard evidence of a call to action beyond the standard Marxist-Leninist texts.*

Majority votes: 6
Dissenting votes: 1

MR. JUSTICE HARLAN delivered the opinion of the Court:. . . .

In the view we take of this case, it is necessary for us to consider only the following of petitioners' contentions: (1) that the term "organize" as used in the Smith Act was erroneously construed by the two lower courts; (2) that the trial court's instructions to the jury erroneously excluded from the case the issue of "incitement to action"; (3) that the evidence was so insufficient as to require this Court to direct the acquittal of these petitioners. . . . For reasons given hereafter, we conclude that these convictions must be reversed and the case remanded to the District Court with instructions to enter judgments of acquittal as to certain of the petitioners, and to grant a new trial as to the rest.

I. THE TERM "ORGANIZE." . . .

We are . . . left to determine for ourselves the meaning of [the organizing] provision of the Smith Act, without any revealing guides as to the intent of Congress. In these circumstances we should follow the familiar rule that criminal statutes are to be strictly construed and give to "organize" its narrow meaning, that is, that the word refers only to acts entering into the creation of a new organization, and not to acts thereafter performed in carrying on its activities, even though such acts may loosely be termed "organizational." Such indeed is the normal usage of the word "organize," and until the decisions below in this case the federal trial courts in which the question had arisen uniformly gave it that meaning. We too think this statute should be read "according to the natural and obvious import of the language, without resorting to subtle and forced construction for the purpose of either limiting or extending its operation." *United States* v. *Temple,* 105 U.S. 97, 99.

The Government contends that even if the trial court was mistaken in its construction of the statute, the error was harmless because the conspiracy charged embraced both "advocacy" of violent overthrow and "organizing" the Communist Party, and the jury was instructed that in order to convict it must find a conspiracy extending to both objectives. Hence, the argument is, the jury must in any event be taken to have found petitioners guilty of conspiring to advocate, and the convictions are supportable on that basis alone. We cannot accept this proposition for a number of reasons. The portions of the trial court's instructions relied on by the Government are not sufficiently clear or specific to warrant our drawing the inference that the

jury understood it must find an agreement extending to *both* "advocacy" and "organizing" in order to convict. Further, in order to convict, the jury was required, as the court charged, to find an overt act which was "knowingly done in furtherance of an object or purpose of the conspiracy charged in the indictment," and we have no way of knowing whether the overt act found by the jury was one which it believed to be in furtherance of the "advocacy" rather than the "organizing" objective of the alleged conspiracy. The character of most of the overt acts alleged associates them as readily with "organizing" as with "advocacy." In these circumstances we think the proper rule to be applied is that which requires a verdict to be set aside in cases where the verdict is supportable on one ground but not on another, and it is impossible to tell which ground the jury selected.

We conclude, therefore, that since the Communist Party came into being in 1945, and the indictment was not returned until 1951, the three year statute of limitations had run on the "organizing" charge, and required the withdrawal of that part of the indictment from the jury's consideration.

II. INSTRUCTIONS TO THE JURY. . . .

We are . . . faced with the question whether the Smith Act prohibits advocacy and teaching of forcible overthrow as an abstract principle, divorced from any effort to instigate action to that end, so long as such advocacy or teaching is engaged in with evil intent. We hold that it does not.

The distinction between advocacy of abstract doctrine and advocacy directed at promoting unlawful action is one that has been consistently recognized in the opinions of this Court. . . .

We need not . . . decide the issue before us in terms of constitutional compulsion, for our first duty is to construe this statute. In doing so we should not assume that Congress chose to disregard a constitutional danger zone so clearly marked, or that it used the words "advocate" and "teach" in their ordinary dictionary meanings when they had already been construed as terms of art carrying a special and limited connotation. . . . The statute was aimed at the advocacy and teaching of concrete action for the forcible overthrow of the Government, and not of principles divorced from action. . . .

We recognize that distinctions between advocacy or teaching of abstract doctrines, with evil intent, and that which is directed to stirring people to action, are often subtle and difficult to grasp. . . . But the very subtlety of these distinctions required the most clear and explicit instructions with reference to them, for they concerned an issue which went to the very heart of the charges against these petitioners. The need for precise and understandable instructions on this issue is further emphasized by the equivocal character of the evidence in this record, with which we deal in Part III of this opinion. Instances of speech that could be considered to amount to "advocacy of action" are so few and far between as to be almost completely overshadowed by the hundreds of instances in the record in which overthrow, if mentioned at all, occurs in the course of doctrinal disputation so remote from action as to be almost wholly lacking in probative value. Vague references to "revolutionary" or "militant" action of an unspecified character, which are found in the evidence, might in addition be given too great weight by the jury in the absence of more precise instructions. Particularly in light of this record, we must regard the trial court's charge in this respect as furnishing wholly inadequate guidance to the jury on this central point in the case. We cannot allow a conviction to stand on such "an equivocal direction to the jury on a basic issue."

III. The evidence. . . .

. . . [W]e have concluded that the evidence against [5] petitioners . . . is so clearly insufficient that their acquittal should be ordered, but that as to [9] petitioners . . . we would not be justified in closing the way to their retrial. . . .

As to the nine . . . while the record contains evidence of little more than a general program of educational activity by the Communist Party which included advocacy of violence as a theoretical matter, we are not prepared to say, at this stage of the case, that it would be impossible for a jury, resolving all conflicts in favor of the Government and giving the evidence . . . its utmost sweep, to find that advocacy of action was also engaged in when the group involved was thought particularly trustworthy, dedicated, and suited for violent tasks.

Nor can we say that the evidence linking these nine petitioners to that sort of advocacy, with the requisite specific intent, is so tenuous as not to justify their retrial under proper legal standards. . . .

The judgment of the Court of Appeals is reversed, and the case remanded to the District Court for further proceedings consistent with this opinion.

It is so ordered.

Mr. Justice Burton, concurring in the result: [omitted]
Mr. Justice Brennan and Mr. Justice Whittaker took no part in the consideration or decision of this case.
Mr. Justice Black, with whom Mr. Justice Douglas joins, concurring in part and dissenting in part:

I would reverse every one of these convictions and direct that all the defendants be acquitted. In my judgment the statutory provisions on which these prosecutions are based abridge freedom of speech, press and assembly in violation of the First Amendment to the United States Constitution. . . .
Mr. Justice Clark, dissenting: [omitted; he would affirm all the convictions]

KEYISHIAN v. BOARD OF REGENTS,
385 U.S. 589 (1967)

In 1917 the New York state legislature enacted a law that made speaking or acting treasonably or seditiously a ground for dismissal from the public school system. In 1939 another statute went further and disqualified from employment in the public educational system anyone advocating, publishing material advocating, or joining any group advocating, the overthrow of government by force, violence, or any unlawful means. The state legislature in 1949 passed what became known as the Feinberg Law, which charged the New York State Board of Regents with the duty of issuing rules and regulations in implementing the 1917 and 1939 laws. The board of regents was also instructed to make a list, after notice and hearing, of "subversive" groups that advocated the doctrine of overthrowing the government by force, violence, or any unlawful means. The board was directed to include in its rules and regulations that membership in any listed "subversive" organization would constitute prima facie evidence of disqualification for appointment to or retention in any office or position in New York's public schools. The Supreme Court in Adler v. Board of Education, *342 U.S. 485 (1952), upheld the Feinberg Law. In 1953, an amendment to the Feinberg Law extended its reach to public higher education. Subsequently, the board of regents listed the Communist Party of the United States and of the state of New York as "subversive organizations."*

The board in 1956 issued a regulation requiring that each applicant for an appointment or the renewal of an appointment sign a certificate declaring that the person had read the regents' rules and understood that the rules and the statutes consti-

tuted terms of employment. Furthermore, the certificate certified that the person was not now a member of the Communist Party and that the fact of any past membership had been communicated to the president of the state university. Keyishian, an instructor in English at the State University of New York at Buffalo, along with others, refused to sign the certificate. His one-year-term contract was not renewed. Keyishian and his colleagues challenged the state program under the Feinberg Law. Before the trial, the board rescinded the certificate and statement requirement. The Court, nevertheless, faced the issues that were raised in the case.

Majority votes: 5
Dissenting votes: 4

MR. JUSTICE BRENNAN delivered the opinion of the Court:. . . .

Appellants brought this action for declaratory and injunctive relief alleging that the state program violated the Federal Constitution in various respects. A three-judge federal court held that the program was constitutional. . . . We reverse.

We considered some aspects of the constitutionality of the New York plan 15 years ago in *Adler* v. *Board of Education,* 342 U.S. 485. . . . *Adler* was a declaratory judgment suit in which the Court held, in effect, that there was no constitutional infirmity . . . in the Feinberg Law. . . . [T]o the extent that *Adler* sustained the provision of the Feinberg Law constituting membership in an organization advocating forceful overthrow of government a ground for disqualification, pertinent constitutional doctrines have since rejected the premises upon which that conclusion rested. *Adler* is therefore not dispositive of the constitutional issues we must decide in this case. . . .

[The New York Education Law] required removal for "treasonable or seditious" utterances or acts. . . . [T]he Civil Service Law provides that the terms "treasonable word or act" shall mean "treason" as defined in the Penal Law and the term "seditious word or act" shall mean "criminal anarchy" as defined in the Penal Law. . . . [U]nder [the] Penal Law, one commits the felony of advocating criminal anarchy if he ". . . publicly displays any book . . . containing or advocating, advising or teaching the doctrine that organized government should be overthrown by force, violence or any unlawful means." Does the teacher who carries a copy of the Communist Manifesto on a public street thereby advocate criminal anarchy? It is no answer to say that the statute would not be applied in such a case. We cannot gainsay the potential effect of

this obscure wording on "those with a conscientious and scrupulous regard for such undertakings." . . . The teacher cannot know the extent, if any, to which a "seditious" utterance must transcend mere statement about abstract doctrine, the extent to which it must be intended to and tend to indoctrinate or incite to action in furtherance of the defined doctrine. The crucial consideration is that no teacher can know just where the line is drawn between "seditious" and nonseditious utterances and acts.

Other provisions of [the law] also have the same defect of vagueness. Subdivision 1(a) of §105 [of the Civil Service Law] bars employment of any person who "by word of mouth or writing wilfully and deliberately advocates, advises or teaches the doctrine" of forceful overthrow of government. This provision is plainly susceptible of sweeping and improper application. . . . Does the teacher who informs his class about the precepts of Marxism or the Declaration of Independence violate this prohibition?

Similar uncertainty arises as to the application of subdivision 1(b) of §105. That subsection requires the disqualification of an employee involved with the distribution of written material "containing or advocating, advising or teaching the doctrine" of forceful overthrow, and who himself "advocates, advises, teaches, or embraces the duty, necessity or propriety of adopting the doctrine contained therein." Here again, mere advocacy of abstract doctrine is apparently included. And does the prohibition of distribution of matter "containing" the doctrine bar histories of the evolution of Marxist doctrine or tracing the background of the French, American, or Russian revolutions? . . .

. . . It would be a bold teacher who would not stay as far as possible from utterances or acts which might jeopardize his living by enmeshing him in this intricate machinery. The uncertainty as to the utterances and acts proscribed increases that caution in "those who believe the written law means what it says." . . . The result must be to stifle "that free play of the spirit which all teachers ought especially to cultivate and practice. . . ."

There can be no doubt of the legitimacy of New York's interest in protecting its education system from subversion. But "even though the governmental purpose be legitimate and substantial, that purpose cannot be pursued by means that broadly stifle fundamental personal liberties when the end can be more narrowly achieved." . . . The principle is not inapplicable because the legislation is aimed at keeping subversives out of the teaching ranks. . . .

Our Nation is deeply committed to safeguarding

academic freedom, which is of transcendant value to all of us and not merely to the teachers concerned. That freedom is therefore a special concern of the First Amendment, which does not tolerate laws that cast a pall of orthodoxy over the classroom. "The vigilant protection of constitutional freedoms is nowhere more vital than in the community of American schools." The classroom is peculiarly the "marketplace of ideas." The Nation's future depends upon leaders trained through wide exposure to that robust exchange of ideas which discovers truth "out of a multitude of tongues, [rather] than through any kind of authoritative selection." . . .

We emphasize once again that "[p]recision of regulation must be the touchstone in an area so closely touching our most precious freedoms," . . . "[f]or standards of permissible statutory vagueness are strict in the area of free expression. . . . Because First Amendment freedoms need breathing space to survive, government may regulate in the area only with narrow specificity." . . . New York's complicated and intricate scheme plainly violates that standard. When one must guess what conduct or utterance may lose him his position, one necessarily will "steer far wider of the unlawful zone. . . ." . . . . For "[t]he threat of sanctions may deter . . . almost as potently as the actual application of sanctions." . . . The danger of that chilling effect upon the exercise of vital First Amendment rights must be guarded against by sensitive tools which clearly inform teachers what is being proscribed. . . .

The regulatory maze created by New York is wholly lacking in "terms susceptible of objective measurement." . . . Vagueness of wording is aggravated by prolixity and profusion of statutes, regulations, and administrative machinery, and by manifold cross-references to interrelated enactments and rules.

We therefore hold that §3021 of the Education Law and subdivisions 1(a), 1(b) and 3 of §105 of the Civil Service Law as implemented by the machinery created pursuant to §3022 of the Education Law [the Feinberg Law] are unconstitutional.

We proceed . . . to the question of the validity of the provisions of subdivision 1(c) of §105 and subdivision 2 of §3022, barring employment to members of listed organizations. Here again constitutional doctrine has developed since *Adler*. Mere knowing membership without a specific intent to further the unlawful aims of an organization is not a constitutionally adequate basis for exclusion from such positions as those held by appellants. . . .

. . . *Elfbrandt* v. *Russell*, 384 U.S. 11 (1966), and *Aptheker* v. *Secretary of State*, 378 U.S. 500 (1964),

state the governing standard: legislation which sanctions membership unaccompanied by specific intent to further the unlawful goals of the organization or which is not active membership violates constitutional limitations. . . .

We therefore hold that Civil Service Law §105, subd. 1(c), and Education Law §3022, subd. 2, are invalid insofar as they proscribe mere knowing membership without any showing of specific intent to further the unlawful aims of the Communist Party of the United States or of the State of New York.

The judgment of the District Court is reversed and the case is remanded for further proceedings consistent with this opinion.

Reversed and remanded.

Mr Justice Clark, with whom Mr. Justice Harlan, Mr. Justice Stewart and Mr. Justice White join, dissenting:

The blunderbuss fashion in which the majority couches "its artillery of words," together with the morass of cases it cites as authority and the obscurity of their application to the question at hand, makes it difficult to grasp the true thrust of its decision. At the outset, it is therefore necessary to focus on its basis.

This is a declaratory judgment action testing the *application* of the Feinberg Law to appellants. The certificate and statement once required by the Board of Trustees of the State University and upon which appellants base their attack were, before the case was tried, abandoned by the Board and are no longer required to be made. Despite this fact the majority proceeds to its decision striking down New York's Feinberg Law and other statutes as applied to appellants on the basis of the old certificate and statement. It does not explain how the statute can be applied to appellants under procedures which have been for almost two years a dead letter. The issues posed are, therefore, purely abstract and entirely speculative in character. The Court under such circumstances has in the past refused to pass upon such constitutional questions. . . .

This Court has again and again, since at least 1951, approved procedures either identical or at the least similar to the ones the Court condemns today. . . .

In view of [the] long list of decisions covering over 15 years of this Court's history, in which no opinion of this Court even questioned the validity of the *Adler* line of cases, it is strange to me that the Court now finds that the "constitutional doctrine which has emerged since, . . . has rejected [*Adler's*] major premise." With due respect, as I read them, our cases have done no such thing. . . .

. . . The majority makes much over the horribles that might arise from subdivision 1(b) of §105 which condemns the printing, publishing, selling, etc., of matter containing such [violent overthrow of Government] doctrine. But the majority fails to state that this action is condemned only *when and if* the teacher also personally advocates, advises, teaches, etc., the necessity or propriety of adopting such doctrine. . . . And the same is true of subdivision 1(c) where a teacher organizes, helps to organize or becomes a member of an organization which teaches or advocates such doctrine. . . . Moreover, membership is only prima facie evidence of disqualification and could be rebutted, leaving the burden of proof on the State. Furthermore, all of these procedures are protected by an adversary hearing with full judicial review.

In the light of these considerations the strained and unbelievable suppositions that the majority poses could hardly occur. . . .

The majority says that the Feinberg Law is bad because it has an "overbroad sweep." I regret to say—and I do so with deference—that the majority has by its broadside swept away one of our most precious rights, namely, the right of self-preservation. Our public educational system is the genius of our democracy. The minds of our youth are developed there and the character of that development will determine the future of our land. Indeed, our very existence depends upon it. The issue here is a very narrow one. It is not freedom of speech, freedom of thought, freedom of press, freedom of assembly, or of association, even in the Communist Party. It is simply this: May the State provide that one who, after a hearing with full judicial review, is found to have wilfully and deliberately advocated, advised, or taught that our Government should be overthrown by force or violence or other unlawful means; or to have wilfully and deliberately printed, published, etc., any book or paper that so advocated *and to have personally* advocated such doctrine himself; or to have wilfully and deliberately become a member of an organization that advocates such doctrine, is prima facie disqualified from teaching in its university? My answer, in keeping with all of our cases up until today, is "Yes"!

I dissent.

BRANDENBURG v. OHIO,
395 U.S. 444 (1969)

The facts of the case are stated in the Court's opinion. The decision once again points up the fact that political freedom, if it is to mean anything,

must apply not only to those with whom we agree but to those with whom we most vigorously take issue. It is perhaps curious that the Court chose a per curiam opinion in which to rather summarily dispose of the issues as well as to restate the clear and present danger test albeit with different phraseology. One can speculate that the justices believed the principles behind the decision were so well accepted that to give the case a full-dress signed opinion would have been belaboring the obvious. Yet an argument can be made that the issues raised by the case were deserving of more elaborate treatment particularly because they have a tendency to recur. It is always difficult for people to be tolerant of views they despise or speech that, while not "inciting or producing imminent lawless action," nevertheless provides a rationalization or gives moral support for acts of terror.

Votes: Unanimous

PER CURIAM.

The appellant, a leader of a Ku Klux Klan group, was convicted under the Ohio Criminal Syndicalism statute for "advocat[ing] . . . the duty, necessity, or propriety of crime, sabotage, violence, or unlawful methods of terrorism as a means of accomplishing industrial or political reform" and for "voluntarily assembl[ing] with any society, group, or assemblage of persons formed to teach or advocate the doctrines of criminal syndicalism." He was fined $1,000 and sentenced to one to 10 years' imprisonment. The appellant challenged the constitutionality of the criminal syndicalism statute under the First and Fourteenth Amendments to the United States Constitution, but the intermediate appellate court of Ohio affirmed his conviction without opinion. The Supreme Court of Ohio dismissed his appeal "for the reason that no substantial constitutional question exists herein." It did not file an opinion or explain its conclusions. . . .

The record shows that a man, identified at trial as the appellant, telephoned an announcer-reporter on the staff of a Cincinnati television station and invited him to come to a Ku Klux Klan "rally" to be held at a farm in Hamilton County. With the cooperation of the organizers, the reporter and a cameraman attended the meeting and filmed the events. Portions of the films were later broadcast on the local station and on a national network.

The prosecution's case rested on the films and on testimony identifying the appellant as the person who communicated with the reporter and who spoke at the rally. The State also introduced into evidence several articles appearing in the film, including a pistol, a rifle, a shotgun, ammunition, a Bible, and a red hood worn by the speaker in the films.

One film showed 12 hooded figures, some of whom carried firearms. They were gathered around a large wooden cross, which they burned. No one was present other than the participants and the newsmen who made the film. Most of the words uttered during the scene were incomprehensible when the film was projected, but scattered phrases could be understood that were derogatory of Negroes and, in one instance, of Jews. Another scene on the same film showed the appellant in Klan regalia, making a speech. The speech, in full, was as follows:

> "This is an organizers' meeting. We have had quite a few members here today which are—we have hundreds and hundreds of members throughout the state of Ohio. I can quote from a newspaper clipping from the Columbus, Ohio Dispatch, five weeks ago Sunday morning. The Klan has more members in the State of Ohio than does any other organization. We're not a revengent organization, but if our President, our Congress, our Supreme Court, continues to suppress the white, Caucasian race, it's possible that there might have to be some revengeance taken.
>
> "We are marching on Congress July the Fourth, four hundred thousand strong. From there we are dividing into two groups, one group to march on St. Augustine, Florida, the other group to march into Mississippi. Thank you." . . .

The Ohio Criminal Syndicalism Statute was enacted in 1919. From 1917 to 1920, identical or quite similar laws were adopted by 20 States and two territories. In 1927, this Court sustained the constitutionality of California's Criminal Syndicalism Act, the text of which is quite similar to that of the laws of Ohio. *Whitney* v. *California*. The Court upheld the statute on the ground that, without more, "advocating" violent means to effect political and economic change involves such danger to the security of the State that the State may outlaw it. But *Whitney* has been thoroughly discredited by later decisions. These later decisions have fashioned the principle that the constitutional guarantees of freedom of speech and free press do not permit a State to forbid or proscribe advocacy of the use of force or of law violation except where such advocacy is directed to inciting or producing imminent lawless action and is likely to incite or produce such action.

As we said in *Noto* v. *United States*, 367 U.S. 290, 297–298 (1961), "the mere abstract teaching . . . of the moral propriety or even moral necessity for a resort to force and violence, is not the same as preparing a group for violent action and steeling it to such action." See also *Herndon* v. *Lowry*, 301 U.S. 242, 259–261 (1937); *Bond* v. *Floyd*, 385 U.S. 116, 134 (1966). A statute which fails to draw this distinction impermissibly intrudes upon the freedoms guaranteed by the First and Fourteenth Amendments. It sweeps within its condemnation speech which our Constitution has immunized from governmental control.

Measured by this test, Ohio's Criminal Syndicalism Act cannot be sustained. The Act punishes persons who "advocate or teach the duty, necessity, or propriety" of violence "as a means of accomplishing industrial or political reform"; or who publish or circulate or display any book or paper containing such advocacy; or who "justify" the commission of violent acts "with intent to exemplify, spread or advocate the propriety of the doctrines of criminal syndicalism"; or who "voluntarily assemble" with a group formed "to teach or advocate the doctrines of criminal syndicalism." Neither the indictment nor the trial judge's instructions to the jury in any way refined the statute's bald definition of the crime in terms of mere advocacy not distinguished from incitement to imminent lawless action.

Accordingly, we are here confronted with a statute which, by its own words and as applied, purports to punish mere advocacy and to forbid, on pain of criminal punishment, assembly with others merely to advocate the described type of action. Such a statute falls within the condemnation of the First and Fourteenth Amendments. The contrary teaching of *Whitney* v. *California* cannot be supported, and that decision is therefore overruled.

Reversed.

MR. JUSTICE BLACK, concurring: [omitted]
MR. JUSTICE DOUGLAS, concurring: [omitted]

PRUNEYARD SHOPPING CENTER v. ROBINS, 447 U.S. 74 (1980)

One Saturday afternoon Michael Robins, a high school student, along with other students, set up a card table in a corner of the PruneYard Shopping Center and proceeded to distribute pamphlets and to ask passersby to sign petitions protesting a United Nations resolution they believed to be anti-Semitic. Shortly after they had begun their activi-

ties, a security guard informed them that they would have to leave because their activity violated shopping center regulations prohibiting any visitor or tenant from engaging in any publicly expressive activity, including circulating petitions not directly related to the Center's commercial purposes. The students immediately left the premises and later filed suit in a California state court to enjoin the shopping center and its owner, Fred Sahadi, from denying them access to the Center for the purpose of circulating their petitions. The trial court held that the students were not entitled under either the federal or California Constitution to exercise their asserted rights on the shopping center property, and the California Court of Appeal affirmed. The California Supreme Court, however, reversed, holding that the California Constitution protects speech and petitioning, reasonably exercised, in shopping centers even when the center is privately owned, and that this does not infringe property rights that are protected by the United States Constitution.

This case raised the same issue as in Lloyd Corporation *v.* Tanner, *described in Justice Rehnquist's opinion; the important difference is that it was the state constitution that was offered as the basis for protecting free speech over the asserted right of the property owner to have exclusive control over the speech activities on his property. Interestingly, Mr. Sahadi argued before the Supreme Court not only that the California Constitution as interpreted by the California Supreme Court violated his federal property rights under the Fifth and Fourteenth Amendments, but also that his federal free speech rights were violated.*

Votes: Unanimous

MR. JUSTICE REHNQUIST delivered the opinion of the Court:

We postponed jurisdiction of this appeal from the Supreme Court of California to decide the important federal constitutional questions it presented. Those are whether state constitutional provisions, which permit individuals to exercise free speech and petition rights on the property of a privately owned shopping center to which the public is invited, violate the shopping center owner's property rights under the Fifth and Fourteenth Amendments or his free speech rights under the First and Fourteenth Amendments. . . .

Appellants first contend that *Lloyd* v. *Tanner*, 407 U.S. 551 (1972), prevents the State from requiring a private shopping center owner to provide access to persons exercising their state constitutional

rights of free speech and petition when adequate alternative avenues of communication are available. *Lloyd* dealt with the question whether under the Federal Constitution a privately owned shopping center may prohibit the distribution of handbills on its property when the handbilling is unrelated to the shopping center's operations. . . . Respondents in *Lloyd* argued that because the shopping center was open to the public, the First Amendment prevents the private owner from enforcing the handbilling restriction on shopping center premises. In rejecting this claim we substantially repudiated the rationale of *Logan Valley*, which was later overruled in *Hudgens* v. *NLRB*, 424 U.S. 507 (1976). We stated that property does not "lose its private character merely because the public is generally invited to use it for designated purposes," and that "[t]he essentially private character of a store and its privately owned abutting property does not change by virtue of being large or clustered with other stores in a modern shopping center." 407 U.S., at 569.

Our reasoning in *Lloyd,* however, does not limit the authority of the State to exercise its police power or its sovereign right to adopt in its own Constitution individual liberties more expansive than those conferred by the Federal Constitution. In *Lloyd* there was no state constitutional or statutory provision that had been construed to create rights to the use of private property by strangers, comparable to those found to exist by the California Supreme Court here. It is, of course, well-established that a State in the exercise of its police power may adopt reasonable restrictions on private property so long as the restrictions do not amount to a taking without just compensation or contravene any other federal constitutional provision. . . .

Appellants next contend that a right to exclude others underlies the Fifth Amendment guarantee against the taking of property without just compensation. . . .

It is true that one of the essential sticks in the bundle of property rights is the right to exclude others. And here there has literally been a "taking" of that right to the extent that the California Supreme Court has interpreted the state constitution to entitle its citizens to exercise free expression and petition rights on shopping center property. But it is well established that "not every destruction or injury to property by governmental action has been held to be a 'taking' in the constitutional sense." . . .

Here the requirement that appellants permit appellees to exercise state-protected rights of free expression and petition on shopping center property clearly does not amount to an unconstitutional infringement of appellants' property rights under the Taking Clause. There is nothing to suggest that preventing appellants from prohibiting this sort of activity will unreasonably impair the value or use of their property as a shopping center. The PruneYard is a large commercial complex that covers several city blocks, contains numerous separate business establishments, and is open to the public at large. The decision of the California Supreme Court makes it clear that the PruneYard may restrict expressive activity by adopting time, place and manner regulations that will minimize any interference with its commercial functions. Appellees were orderly, and they limited their activity to the common areas of the shopping center. In these circumstances, the fact that they may have "physically invaded" appellants' property cannot be viewed as determinative. . . .

Appellants finally contend that a private property owner has a First Amendment right not to be forced by the State to use his property as a forum for the speech of others. They state that in *Wooley* v. *Maynard*, 430 U.S. 705 (1977), this Court concluded that a State may not constitutionally require an individual to participate in the dissemination of an ideological message by displaying it on his private property in a manner and for the express purpose that it be observed and read by the public. This rationale applies here, they argue, because the message of *Wooley* is that the State may not force an individual to display any message at all.

Wooley, however, was a case in which the government itself prescribed the message, required it to be displayed openly on appellee's personal property that was used "as part of his daily life," and refused to permit him to take any measures to cover up the motto even though the Court found that the display of the motto served no important state interest. Here, by contrast, there are a number of distinguishing factors. Most important, the shopping center by choice of its owner is not limited to the personal use of appellants. It is instead a business establishment that is open to the public to come and go as they please. The views expressed by members of the public in passing out pamphlets or seeking signatures for a petition thus will not likely be identified with those of the owner. Second, no specific message is dictated by the State to be displayed on appellants' property. There consequently is no danger of governmental discrimination for or against a particular message. Finally, as far as appears here appellants can expressly disavow any connection with the message by simply posting signs in the area where the speakers or handbillers

stand. Such signs, for example, could disclaim any sponsorship of the message and could explain that the persons are communicating their own messages by virtue of state law. . . .

We conclude that neither appellants' federally recognized property rights nor their First Amendment rights have been infringed by the California Supreme Court's decision recognizing a right of appellees to exercise state protected rights of expression and petition on appellants' property. The judgment of the Supreme Court of California is therefore

Affirmed.

MR. JUSTICE MARSHALL, concurring: [omitted]
MR. JUSTICE WHITE, concurring in part and concurring in the judgment: [omitted]
MR. JUSTICE POWELL, with whom MR. JUSTICE WHITE joins, concurring in part and in the judgment: [omitted]

BUCKLEY v. VALEO,
424 U.S. 1 (1976)

As recounted in the per curiam opinion, this litigation contained a challenge to the Federal Election Campaign Act of 1971 as amended in 1974, which was the culmination of years of effort aimed at reforming the way money is raised and spent in federal election campaigns for Congress and the presidency. It was hoped that restrictions on contributions and expenditures would call a halt to the ever-increasing cost of running for public office and remove federal office from a growing dependence on special interests or on wealthy individuals who are able to afford to run. The challenge to the legislation was mounted by Senator James Buckley (now a federal appeals court judge on the same court from which he appealed this case to the Supreme Court), who was running for reelection, by a potential contributor, by a candidate for President of the United States, and by an unlikely coalition of groups including the Mississippi Republican party, the Conservative party of the State of New York, and the New York Civil Liberties Union, Inc. The United States Court of Appeals for the District of Columbia upheld, with one exception, the substantive provisions of the act with respect to contributions, expenditures, and public disclosure. The appeals court also upheld the constitutionality of the newly created Federal Election Commission created to carry out the provisions of the act. The provisions concerning public funding of the presidential selection process were upheld in a related case by a three-judge district court. The cases came before the Supreme Court, and the justices could not agree as to the constitutionality of all portions of the act, and so the Court used the device of a per curiam *opinion to render its decision and its reasoning in each of the major provisions of the statute.*

Majority votes: 3
Dissenting in part and concurring in part (different provisions): 5

PER CURIAM.

These appeals present constitutional challenges to the key provisions of the Federal Election Campaign Act of 1971 (Act), and related provisions of the Internal Revenue Code of 1954, all as amended in 1974. . . . The statutes at issue summarized in broad terms, contain the following provisions: (a) individual political contributions are limited to $1,000 to any single candidate per election, with an overall annual limitation of $25,000 by any contributor; independent expenditures by individuals and groups "relative to a clearly identified candidate" are limited to $1,000 a year; campaign spending by candidates for various federal offices and spending for national conventions by political parties are subject to prescribed limits; (b) contributions and expenditures above certain threshold levels must be reported and publicly disclosed; (c) a system for public funding of Presidential campaign activities is established by Subtitle H of the Internal Revenue Code; and (d) a Federal Election Commission is established to administer and enforce the legislation. . . .

I. CONTRIBUTION AND EXPENDITURE
LIMITATIONS. . . .
A. GENERAL PRINCIPLES

The Act's contribution and expenditure limitations operate in an area of the most fundamental First Amendment activities. Discussion of public issues and debate on the qualifications of candidates are integral to the operation of the system of government established by our Constitution. The First Amendment affords the broadest protection to such political expression in order "to assure [the] unfettered interchange of ideas for the bringing about of political and social changes desired by the people." . . .

The First Amendment protects political association as well as political expression. . . .

It is with these principles in mind that we consider the primary contentions of the parties with respect to the Act's limitations upon the giving and spending of money in political campaigns. Those conflicting contentions could not more sharply define the basic issues before us. Appellees contend that what the Act regulates is conduct, and that its effect on speech and association is incidental at most. Appellants respond that contributions and expenditures are at the very core of political speech, and that the Act's limitations thus constitute restraints on First Amendment liberty that are both gross and direct. . . .

A restriction on the amount of money a person or group can spend on political communication during a campaign necessarily reduces the quantity of expression by restricting the number of issues discussed, the depth of their exploration, and the size of the audience reached. This is because virtually every means of communicating ideas in today's mass society requires the expenditure of money. The distribution of the humblest handbill or leaflet entails printing, paper, and circulation costs. Speeches and rallies generally necessitate hiring a hall and publicizing the event. The electorate's increasing dependence on television, radio, and other mass media for news and information has made these expensive modes of communication indispensable instruments of effective political speech.

The expenditure limitations contained in the Act represent substantial rather than merely theoretical restrains on the quantity and diversity of political speech. . . .

By contrast with a limitation upon expenditures for political expression, a limitation upon the amount that any one person or group may contribute to a candidate or political committee entails only a marginal restriction upon the contributor's ability to engage in free communication. . . . A limitation on the amount of money a person may give to a candidate or campaign organization involves little direct restraint on his political communication, for it permits the symbolic expression of support evidenced by a contribution but does not in any way infringe the contributor's freedom to discuss candidates and issues. . . .

Given the important role of contributions in financing political campaigns, contribution restrictions could have a severe impact on political dialogue if the limitations prevented candidates and political committees from amassing the resources necessary for effective advocacy. There is no indication, however, that the contribution limitations imposed by the Act would have any dramatic adverse effect on the funding of campaigns and political associations. The overall effect of the Act's contribution ceilings is merely to require candidates and political committees to raise funds from a greater number of persons and to compel people who would otherwise contribute amounts greater than the statutory limits to expend such funds on direct political expression, rather than to reduce the total amount of money potentially available to promote political expression.

The Act's contribution and expenditure limitations also impinge on protected associational freedoms. Making a contribution, like joining a political party, serves to affiliate a person with a candidate. In addition, it enables like-minded persons to pool their resources in furtherance of common political goals. The Act's contribution ceilings thus limit one important means of associating with a candidate or committee, but leave the contributor free to become a member of any political association and to assist personally in the association's efforts on behalf of candidates. And the Act's contribution limitations permit associations and candidates to aggregate large sums of money to promote effective advocacy. By contrast, the Act's $1,000 limitation on independent expenditures "relative to a clearly identified candidate" precludes most associations from effectively amplifying the voice of their adherents, the original basis for the recognition of First Amendment protection of the freedom of association. . . .

In sum, although the Act's contribution and expenditure limitations both implicate fundamental First Amendment interests, its expenditure ceilings impose significantly more severe restrictions on protected freedoms of political expression and association than do its limitations on financial contributions.

B. Contribution Limitations
1. The $1,000 limitation on contributions
by individuals and groups to candidates
and authorized campaign committees

It is unnecessary to look beyond the Act's primary purpose—to limit the actuality and appearance of corruption resulting from large individual financial contributions—in order to find a constitutionally sufficient justification for the $1,000 contribution limitation. Under a system of private financing of elections, a candidate lacking immense personal or family wealth must depend on financial contributions from others to provide the resources necessary to conduct a successful campaign. The increasing importance of the communications media and sophisticated mass-mailing and polling operations to effective campaigning make the raising of large sums of money an ever more essential ingredi-

ent of an effective candidacy. To the extent that large contributions are given to secure a political *quid pro quo* from current and potential office holders, the integrity of our system of representative democracy is undermined. Although the scope of such pernicious practices can never be reliably ascertained, the deeply disturbing examples surfacing after the 1972 election demonstrate that the problem is not an illusory one.

Of almost equal concern as the danger of actual *quid pro quo* arrangements is the impact of the appearance of corruption stemming from public awareness of the opportunities for abuse inherent in a regime of large individual financial contributions. . . .

The Act's $1,000 contribution limitation focuses precisely on the problem of large campaign contributions—the narrow aspect of political association where the actuality and potential for corruption have been identified—while leaving persons free to engage in independent political expression, to associate actively through volunteering their services, and to assist to a limited but nonetheless substantial extent in supporting candidates and committees with financial resources. Significantly, the Act's contribution limitations in themselves do not undermine to any material degree the potential for robust and effective discussion of candidates and campaign issues by individual citizens, associations, the institutional press, candidates, and political parties.

We find that, under the rigorous standard of review established by our prior decisions, the weighty interests served by restricting the size of financial contributions to political candidates are sufficient to justify the limited effect upon First Amendment freedoms caused by the $1,000 contribution ceiling. . . .

[The $5,000 limitation on contributions by political committees, limitations on volunteers' incidental expenses, and the $25,000 limitation on total contributions during any calendar year were upheld by the Court using similar reasoning.]

C. Expenditure Limitations

The Act's expenditure ceilings impose direct and substantial restraints on the quantity of political speech. . . . It is clear that a primary effect of these expenditure limitations is to restrict the quantity of campaign speech by individuals, groups, and candidates. The restrictions, while neutral as to the ideas expressed, limit political expression "at the core of our electoral process and of the First Amendment freedoms."

1. THE $1,000 LIMITATION ON EXPENDITURES "RELATIVE TO A CLEARLY IDENTIFIED CANDIDATE"

Section 608(e)(1) provides that "[n]o person may make any expenditure . . . relative to a clearly identified candidate during a calendar year which, when added to all other expenditures made by such person during the year advocating the election or defeat of such candidate, exceeds $1,000." The plain effect of §608(e)(1) is to prohibit all individuals, who are neither candidates nor owners of institutional press facilities, and all groups, except political parties and campaign organizations, from voicing their views "relative to a clearly identified candidate" through means that entail aggregate expenditures of more than $1,000 during a calendar year. The provision, for example, would make it a federal criminal offense for a person or association to place a single one-quarter page advertisement "relative to a clearly identified candidate" in a major metropolitan newspaper. . . .

We find that the governmental interest in preventing corruption and the appearance of corruption is inadequate to justify §608(e)(1)'s ceiling on independent expenditures. First, assuming *arguendo,* that large independent expenditures pose the same dangers of actual or apparent *quid pro quo* arrangements as do large contributions, §608(e)(1) does not provide an answer that sufficiently relates to the elimination of those dangers. Unlike the contribution limitations' total ban on the giving of large amounts of money to candidates, §608(e)(1) prevents only some large expenditures. So long as persons and groups eschew expenditures that in express terms advocate the election or defeat of a clearly identified candidate, they are free to spend as much as they want to promote the candidate and his views. The exacting interpretation of the statutory language necessary to avoid unconstitutional vagueness thus undermines the limitation's effectiveness as a loophole-closing provision by facilitating circumvention by those seeking to exert improper influence upon a candidate or officeholder. It would naively underestimate the ingenuity and resourcefulness of persons and groups desiring to buy influence to believe that they would have much difficulty devising expenditures that skirted the restriction on express advocacy of election or defeat but nevertheless benefited the candidate's campaign. Yet no substantial societal interest would be served by a loophole-closing provision designed to check corruption that permitted unscrupulous persons and organizations to expend unlimited sums of money in order to obtain improper influence over candidates for elective office.

Second, quite apart from the shortcomings of §608(e)(1) in preventing any abuses generated by large independent expenditures, the independent advocacy restricted by the provision does not presently appear to pose dangers of real or apparent corruption comparable to those identified with large campaign contributions. . . .

While the independent expenditure ceiling thus fails to serve any substantial governmental interest in stemming the reality or appearance of corruption in the electoral process, it heavily burdens core First Amendment expression. . . . Advocacy of the election or defeat of candidates for federal office is no less entitled to protection under the First Amendment than the discussion of political policy generally or advocacy of the passage or defeat of legislation.

It is argued, however, that the ancillary governmental interest in equalizing the relative ability of individuals and groups to influence the outcome of elections serves to justify the limitation on express advocacy of the election or defeat of candidates imposed by §608(e)(1)'s expenditure ceiling. But the concept that government may restrict the speech of some elements of our society in order to enhance the relative voice of others is wholly foreign to the First Amendment, which was designed "to secure 'the widest possible dissemination of information from diverse and antagonistic sources,' " and " 'to assure unfettered interchange of ideas for the bringing about of political and social changes desired by the people.' " The First Amendment's protection against governmental abridgment of free expression cannot properly be made to depend on a person's financial ability to engage in public discussion. . . .

For the reasons stated, we conclude that §608(e)(1)'s independent expenditure limitation is unconstitutional under the First Amendment

2. LIMITATION ON EXPENDITURES BY CANDIDATES FROM PERSONAL OR FAMILY RESOURCES . . .

The primary governmental interest served by the Act—the prevention of actual and apparent corruption of the political process—does not support the limitation on the candidate's expenditure of his own personal funds. . . . Indeed, the use of personal funds reduces the candidate's dependence on outside contributions and thereby counteracts the coercive pressures and attendant risks of abuse to which the Act's contribution limitations are directed.

The ancillary interest in equalizing the relative financial resources of candidates competing for elective office, therefore, provides the sole relevant rationale for §608(a)'s expenditure ceiling. That interest is clearly not sufficient to justify the provision's infringement of fundamental First Amendment rights. First, the limitation may fail to promote financial equality among candidates. A candidate who spends less of his personal resources on his campaign may nonetheless outspend his rival as a result of more successful fundraising efforts. Indeed, a candidate's personal wealth may impede his efforts to persuade others that he needs their financial contributions or volunteer efforts to conduct an effective campaign. Second, and more fundamentally, the First Amendment simply cannot tolerate §608(a)'s restriction upon the freedom of a candidate to speak without legislative limit on behalf of his own candidacy. We therefore hold that §608(a)'s restriction on a candidate's personal expenditures is unconstitutional.

3. LIMITATIONS ON CAMPAIGN EXPENDITURES

. . .

No governmental interest that has been suggested is sufficient to justify the restriction on the quantity of political expression imposed by §608(c)'s campaign expenditure limitations. The major evil associated with rapidly increasing campaign expenditures is the danger of candidate dependence on large contributions. The interest in alleviating the corrupting influence of large contributions is served by the Act's contribution limitations and disclosure provisions rather than by §608(c)'s campaign expenditure ceilings. . . .

The campaign expenditure ceilings appear to be designed primarily to serve the governmental interests in reducing the allegedly skyrocketing costs of political campaigns. . . . In any event, the mere growth in the cost of federal election campaigns in and of itself provides no basis for governmental restrictions on the quantity of campaign spending and the resulting limitation on the scope of federal campaigns. The First Amendment denies government the power to determine that spending to promote one's political views is wasteful, excessive, or unwise. In the free society ordained by our Constitution it is not the government, but the people—individually as citizens and candidates and collectively as associations and political committees—who must retain control over the quantity and range of debate on public issues in a political campaign.

For these reasons we hold that §608(c) is constitutionally invalid. . . .

II. REPORTING AND DISCLOSURE REQUIREMENTS

. . . [W]e find no constitutional infirmities in the re cordkeeping reporting, and disclosure provisions of the Act.

III. PUBLIC FINANCING OF PRESIDENTIAL ELECTION CAMPAIGNS

[Public financing of presidential election campaigns is found to be constitutional.]

. . . .

CONCLUSION

In summary, we sustain the individual contribution limits, the disclosure and reporting provisions, and the public financing scheme. We conclude, however, that the limitations on campaign expenditures, on independent expenditures by individuals and groups, and on expenditures by a candidate from his personal funds are constitutionally infirm. Finally, we hold that most of the powers conferred by the Act upon the Federal Election Commission can be exercised only by "Officers of the United States," appointed in conformity with Art. II, §2, cl. 2, of the Constitution, and therefore cannot be exercised by the Commission as presently constituted.

. . . .

So ordered.

MR. JUSTICE STEVENS took no part in the consideration or decision of these cases.
MR. CHIEF JUSTICE BURGER joined in the opinion in part and dissented in part and filed an opinion. [omitted]
MR. JUSTICE WHITE joined in the opinion in part and dissented in part and filed an opinion. [omitted]
MR. JUSTICE MARSHALL joined in the opinion in part and dissented in part and filed an opinion. [omitted]
MR. JUSTICE REHNQUIST joined in the opinion in part and dissented in part and filed an opinion. [omitted]
MR. JUSTICE BLACKMUN joined in the opinion in part and dissented in part and filed an opinion. [omitted]

CLARK v. COMMUNITY FOR CREATIVE NON-VIOLENCE, 468 U.S. 288 (1984) ·

The facts of this case are set out in Justice White's opinion of the Court. William P. Clark, then Secretary of the Interior, was named in the suit because the National Park Service comes under the Department of Interior. The case raises im-

portant questions concerning symbolic speech and its priority when it comes in conflict with other values.

Majority votes: 7
Dissenting votes: 2

JUSTICE WHITE delivered the opinion of the Court:

The issue in this case is whether a National Park Service regulation prohibiting camping in certain parks violates the First Amendment when applied to prohibit demonstrators from sleeping in Lafayette Park and the Mall in connection with a demonstration intended to call attention to the plight of the homeless. We hold that it does not and reverse the contrary judgment of the Court of Appeals. . . .

In 1982, the Park Service issued a renewable permit to respondent Community for Creative Non-Violence (CCNV) to conduct a wintertime demonstration in Lafayette Park and the Mall for the purpose of demonstrating the plight of the homeless. The permit authorized the erection of two symbolic tent cities: 20 tents in Lafayette Park that would accommodate 50 people and 40 tents in the Mall with a capacity of up to 100. The Park Service, however, relying on . . . [its] regulations, specifically denied CCNV's request that demonstrators be permitted to sleep in the symbolic tents.

CCNV and several individuals then filed an action to prevent the application of the anticamping regulations to the proposed demonstration, which, it was claimed, was not covered by the regulation. It was also submitted that the regulations were unconstitutionally vague, had been discriminatorily applied, and could not be applied to prevent sleeping in the tents without violating the First Amendment. The District Court granted summary judgment in favor of the Park Service. The Court of Appeals, sitting *en banc,* reversed. The eleven judges produced six opinions. Six of the judges believed that application of the regulations so as to prevent sleeping in the tents would infringe the demonstrator's First Amendment right of free expression. The other five judges disagreed and would have sustained the regulations as applied to CCNV's proposed demonstration. We granted the Government's petition for certiorari, and now reverse.

We need not differ with the view of the Court of Appeals that overnight sleeping in connection with the demonstration is expressive conduct protected to some extent by the First Amendment. We assume for present purposes, but do not decide, that such is the case, but this assumption only begins the inquiry. Expression, whether oral or written or symbolized by conduct, is subject to reasonable time, place, and manner restrictions. We have often noted that restrictions of this kind are valid provided that they are justified without reference to the content of the regulated speech, that they are narrowly tailored to serve a significant governmental interest, and that they leave open ample alternative channels for communication of the information. . . .

The United States submits, as it did in the Court of Appeals, that the regulation forbidding sleeping is defensible either as a time, place, or manner restriction or as a regulation of symbolic conduct. We agree with that assessment. The permit that was issued authorized the demonstration but required compliance with 36 CFR §50.19, which prohibits "camping" on park lands, that is, the use of park lands for living accommodations, such as sleeping, storing personal belongings, making fires, digging, or cooking. These provisions, including the ban on sleeping, are clearly limitations on the manner in which the demonstration could be carried out. That sleeping, like the symbolic tents themselves, may be expressive and part of the message delivered by the demonstration does not make the ban any less a limitation on the manner of demonstrating, for reasonable time, place, and manner regulations normally have the purpose and direct effect of limiting expression but are nevertheless valid. Neither does the fact that sleeping, *arguendo,* may be expressive conduct, rather than oral or written expression, render the sleeping prohibition any less a time, place, or manner regulation. To the contrary, the Park Service neither attempts to ban sleeping generally nor to ban it everywhere in the Parks. It has established areas for camping and forbids it elsewhere, including Lafayette Park and the Mall. Considered as such, we have very little trouble concluding that the Park Service may prohibit overnight sleeping in the parks involved here.

The requirement that the regulation be content neutral is clearly satisfied. . . . Neither was the regulation faulted, nor could it be, on the ground that without overnight sleeping the plight of the homeless could not be communicated in other ways. The regulation otherwise left the demonstration intact, with its symbolic city, signs, and the presence of those who were willing to take their turns in a day-and-night vigil. Respondents do not suggest that there was, or is, any barrier to delivering to the media, or to the public by other means, the intended message concerning the plight of the homeless.

It is also apparent to us that the regulation narrowly focuses on the Government's substantial interest in maintaining the parks in the heart of our capital in an attractive and intact condition, readily available to the millions of people who wish to see and enjoy them by their presence. To permit camping—using these areas as living accommodations—would be totally inimical to these purposes, as would be readily understood by those who have frequented the National Parks across the country and observed the unfortunate consequences of the activities of those who refuse to confine their camping to designated areas. . . .

Accordingly, the judgment of the Court of Appeals is

Reversed.

CHIEF JUSTICE BURGER, concurring: [omitted]
JUSTICE MARSHALL, with whom JUSTICE BRENNAN joins, dissenting:

The Court's disposition of this case is marked by two related findings. First, the majority is either unwilling or unable to take seriously the First Amendment claims advanced by respondents. Contrary to the impression given by the majority, respondents are not supplicants seeking to wheedle an undeserved favor from the Government. They are citizens raising issues of profound public importance who have properly turned to the courts for the vindication of their constitutional rights. Second, the majority misapplies the test for ascertaining whether a restraint on speech qualifies as a reasonable time, place, and manner regulation. In determining what constitutes a sustainable regulation, the majority fails to subject the alleged interests of the Government to the degree of scrutiny required to ensure that expressive activity protected by the First Amendment remains free of unnecessary limitations.

The proper starting point for analysis of this case is a recognition that the activity in which respondents seek to engage—sleeping in a highly public place, outside, in the winter for the purpose of protesting homelessness—is symbolic speech protected by the First Amendment. The majority assumes, without deciding, that the respondents' conduct is entitled to constitutional protection. The problem with this assumption is that the Court thereby avoids examining closely the reality of respondents' planned expression. The majority's approach denatures respondents' asserted right and thus makes all too easy identification of a government interest sufficient to warrant its abridgement. A realistic appraisal of the competing interests at stake in this case requires a closer look at the nature of the expressive conduct at issue and the context in which that conduct would be displayed. . . .

The primary purpose for making *sleep* an integral part of the demonstration was "to re-enact the central reality of homelessness," and to impress upon public consciousness, in as dramatic a way as possible, that homelessness is a widespread problem, often ignored, that confronts its victims with life-threatening deprivations. As one of the homeless men seeking to demonstrate explained: "Sleeping in Lafayette Park or on the Mall, for me, is to show people that conditions are so poor for the homeless and poor in this city that we would actually sleep *outside* in the winter to get the point across." . . .

Although sleep in the context of this case is symbolic speech protected by the First Amendment, it is nonetheless subject to reasonable time, place, and manner restrictions. I agree with the standard enunciated by the majority. . . . I conclude, however, that the regulations at issue in this case, as applied to respondents, fail to satisfy this standard.

According to the majority, the significant government interest advanced by denying respondents' request to engage in sleep-speech is the interest in "maintaining the parks in the heart of our capital in an attractive and intact condition, readily available to the millions of people who wish to see and enjoy them by their presence." That interest is indeed significant. However, neither the Government nor the majority adequately explains how prohibiting respondents' planned activity will substantially further that interest.

The majority's attempted explanation begins with the curious statement that it seriously doubts that the First Amendment requires the Park Service to permit a demonstration in Lafayette Park and the Mall involving a 24-hour vigil and the erection of tents to accommodate 150 people. I cannot perceive why the Court should have "serious doubts" regarding this matter and it provides no explanation for its uncertainty. Furthermore, even if the majority's doubts were well-founded, I cannot see how such doubts relate to the problem at hand. The issue posed by this case is not whether the Government is constitutionally compelled to permit the erection of tents and the staging of a continuous 24-hour vigil; rather, the issue is whether any substantial government interest is served by banning sleep that is part of a political demonstration. . . .

The majority's second argument is comprised of the suggestion that, although sleeping contains an element of expression, "its major value to [respondents'] demonstration would have been facilitative." While this observation does provide a hint of the weight the Court attached to respondents' First Amendment claims, it is utterly irrelevant to whether the Government's ban on sleeping advances a substantial government interest.

The majority's third argument is based upon two claims. The first is that the ban on sleeping relieves the Government of an administrative burden because, without the flat ban, the process of issuing and denying permits to other demonstrators asserting First Amendment rights to sleep in the parks "would present difficult problems for the Park Service." The second is that the ban on sleeping will increase the probability that "some around-the-clock demonstrations for days on end will not materialize, [that] others will be limited in size and duration, and that the purpose of the regulations will thus be materially served," that purpose being "to limit the wear and tear on park properties."

The flaw in these two contentions is that neither is supported by a factual showing that evinces a real, as opposed to a merely speculative, problem. The majority fails to offer any evidence indicating that the absence of an absolute ban on sleeping would present administrative problems to the Park Service that are substantially more difficult than those it ordinarily confronts. A mere apprehension of difficulties should not be enough to overcome the right to free expression. . . . The majority cites no evidence indicating that sleeping engaged in as symbolic speech will cause *substantial* wear and tear on park property. Furthermore, the Government's application of the sleeping ban in the circumstances of this case is strikingly underinclusive. The majority acknowledges that a proper time, place, and manner restriction must be "narrowly tailored." Here, however, the tailoring requirement is virtually forsaken inasmuch as the Government offers no justification for applying its absolute ban on sleeping yet is willing to allow respondents to engage in activities—such as feigned sleeping—that is no less burdensome.

In short, there are no substantial government interests advanced by the Government's regulations as applied to respondents. All that the Court's decision advances are the prerogatives of a bureaucracy that over the years has shown an implacable hostility toward citizens' exercise of First Amendment rights. . . .

. . . [G]overnment agencies by their very nature are driven to over-regulate public forums to the detriment of First Amendment rights, . . . facial viewpoint-neutrality is no shield against unnecessary restrictions on unpopular ideas or modes of expression, and . . . in this case in particular there was evidence readily available that should have impelled the Court to subject the Government's restrictive policy to something more than minimal scrutiny.

For the foregoing reasons, I respectfully dissent.

RANKIN v. McPHERSON,
483 U.S. 378 (1987)

Ardith McPherson, a 19-year-old black woman, began work on January 12, 1981, as a clerical employee in the Harris County, Texas, constable's office. On March 30, 1981, Ms. McPherson and some fellow employees heard on an office radio that there had been an attempt to assassinate President Ronald Reagan. Her co-worker and boyfriend Lawrence Jackson remarked to her privately when they thought they were alone that Reagan was cutting back on medicaid and food stamps, thereby causing greater hardship to poor black people, to which she responded, "If they go for him again, I hope they get him." Unknown to the couple, another co-worker was in the room when McPherson made her comment and the co-worker reported it to Constable Walter H. Rankin. Rankin confronted McPherson, who admitted having made the remark but insisted that she meant no harm. She nevertheless was fired. McPherson then brought suit against Rankin in federal district court, alleging that her discharge violated her First Amendment right to free speech. The court denied her claim, but the Court of Appeals for the Fifth Circuit reversed ruling in favor of McPherson's First Amendment rights. The Supreme Court granted certiorari.

Majority votes: 5
Dissenting votes: 4

JUSTICE MARSHALL delivered the opinion of the Court:

The issue in this case is whether a clerical employee in a county constable's office was properly discharged for remarking, after hearing of an attempt on the life of the President, "If they go for him again, I hope they get him.". . .

It is clearly established that a State may not discharge an employee on a basis that infringes that employee's constitutionally protected interest in freedom of speech. Even though McPherson was merely a probationary employee, and even if she could have been discharged for any reason or for no reason at all, she may nonetheless be entitled to reinstatement if she was discharged for exercising her constitutional right to freedom of expression.

The determination whether a public employer has properly discharged an employee for engaging in speech requires "a balance between the interests of the [employee], as a citizen, in commenting upon matters of public concern and the interest of the State, as an employer, in promoting the efficiency of the public services it performs through its employees." This balancing is necessary in order to accommodate the dual role of the public employer as a provider of public services and as a government entity operating under the constraints of the First Amendment. On one hand, public employers are *employers,* concerned with the efficient function of their operations; review of every personnel decision made by a public employer could, in the long run, hamper the performance of public functions. On the other hand, "the threat of dismissal from public employment is . . . a potent means of inhibiting speech." Vigilance is necessary to ensure that public employers do not use authority over employees to silence discourse, not because it hampers public functions but simply because superiors disagree with the content of employees' speech.

The threshold question in applying this balancing test is whether McPherson's speech may be "fairly characterized as constituting speech on a matter of public concern." "Whether an employee's speech addresses a matter of public concern must be determined by the content, form, and context of a given statement, as revealed by the whole record." The District Court apparently found that McPherson's speech did not address a matter of public concern. The Court of Appeals rejected this conclusion, finding that "the life and death of the President are obviously matters of public concern." Our view of these determinations of the courts below is limited in this context by our constitutional obligation to assure that the record supports this conclusion . . .

Considering the statement in context discloses that it plainly dealt with a matter of public concern. The statement was made in the course of a conversation addressing the policies of the President's administration. It came on the heels of a news bulletin regarding what is certainly a matter of heightened public attention: an attempt on the life of the President. While a statement that amounted to a threat to kill the President would not be protected by the First Amendment, the District Court concluded, and we agree, that McPherson's statement did not amount to a threat . . . . The inappropriate or controversial character of a statement is irrelevant to the question whether it deals with a matter of public concern. "[D]ebate on public issues should be uninhibited, robust, and wide-open, and . . . may well include vehement, caustic, and sometimes unpleasantly sharp attacks on government and public officials." . . .

Because McPherson's statement addressed a matter of public concern, . . . we [must] balance McPherson's interest in making her statement against "the interest of the State, as an employer, in promoting the efficiency of the public services it performs through its employees." The State bears a burden of justifying the discharge on legitimate grounds. . . .

In performing the balancing, the statement will not be considered in a vacuum; the manner, time, and place of the employee's expression are relevant, as is the context in which the dispute arose. We have previously recognized as pertinent considerations whether the statement impairs discipline by superiors or harmony among coworkers, has a detrimental impact on close working relationships for which personal loyalty and confidence are necessary, or impedes the performance of the speaker's duties or interferes with the regular operation of the enterprise.

These considerations, and indeed the very nature of the balancing test, make apparent that the state interest element of the test focuses on the effective functioning of the public employer's enterprise. Interference with work, personnel relationships, or the speaker's job performance can detract from the public employer's function; avoiding such interference can be a strong state interest. From this perspective, however, petitioner fails to demonstrate a state interest that outweighs McPherson's First Amendment rights. While McPherson's statement was made at the workplace, there is no evidence that it interfered with the efficient functioning of the office. The Constable was evidently not afraid that McPherson had disturbed or interrupted other employees—he did not inquire to whom respondent had made the remark and testified that he "was not concerned who she had made it to." In fact, Constable Rankin testified that the possibility of interference with the functions of the Constable's office had *not* been a consideration in his discharge of respondent and that he did not even inquire whether the remark had disrupted the work of the office.

Nor was there any danger that McPherson had discredited the office by making her statement in public. McPherson's speech took place in an area to which there was ordinarily no public access; her remark was evidently made in a private conversation with another employee. There is no suggestion that any member of the general public was present or heard McPherson's statement. Nor is there any evidence that employees other than Jackson who worked in the room even heard the remark. Not only was McPherson's discharge unrelated to the functioning of the office, it was not based on any assessment by the constable that the remark demonstrated a character trait that made respondent unfit to perform her work.

While the facts underlying Rankin's discharge of McPherson are, despite extensive proceedings in the District Court, still somewhat unclear, it is undisputed that he fired McPherson based on the *content* of her speech. Evidently because McPherson had made the statement, and because the constable believed that she "meant it," he decided that she was not a suitable employee to have in a law enforcement agency. But in weighing the State's interest in discharging an employee based on any claim that the content of a statement made by the employee somehow undermines the mission of the public employer, some attention must be paid to the responsibilities of the employee within the agency. The burden of caution employees bear with respect to the words they speak will vary with the extent of authority and public accountability the employee's role entails. Where, as here, an employee serves no confidential, policymaking, or public contact role, the danger to the agency's successful function from that employee's private speech is minimal. We cannot believe that every employee in Constable Rankin's office, whether computer operator, electrician, or file clerk, is equally required, on pain of discharge, to avoid any statement susceptible of being interpreted by the Constable as an indication that the employee may be unworthy of employment in his law enforcement agency. At some point, such concerns are so removed from the effective function of the public employer that they cannot prevail over the free speech rights of the public employee.

This is such a case. McPherson's employment-related interaction with the Constable was apparently negligible. Her duties were purely clerical and were limited solely to the civil process function of the constable's office. There is no indication that she would ever be in a position to further—or indeed to have any involvement with—the minimal law enforcement activity engaged in by the constable's office. Given the function of the agency, McPherson's position in the office, and the nature of her statement, we are not persuaded that Rankin's interest in discharging her outweighed her rights under the First Amendment.

Because we agree with the Court of Appeals that McPherson's discharge was improper, the judgment of the Court of Appeals is

Affirmed.

JUSTICE POWELL, concurring. [omitted]
JUSTICE SCALIA, with whom THE CHIEF JUSTICE, JUSTICE WHITE, and JUSTICE O'CONNOR join, dissenting:
I agree with the proposition, felicitously put by Constable Rankin's counsel, that no law enforcement agency is required by the First Amendment to permit one of its employees to "ride with the cops and cheer for the robbers." The issue in this case is whether Constable Rankin, a law enforcement official, is prohibited by the First Amendment from preventing his employees from saying of the attempted assassination of President Reagan—on the job and within hearing of other employees—"If they go for him again, I hope they get him." The Court, applying the two-prong analysis of *Connick v. Myers,* 461 U.S. 138 (1983), holds that McPherson's statement was protected by the First Amendment because (1) it "addressed a matter of public concern," and (2) McPherson's interest in making the statement outweighs Rankin's interest in suppressing it. In so doing, the Court significantly and irrationally expands the definition of "public concern"; it also carves out a new and very large class of employees—*i.e.,* those in "nonpolicymaking" positions—who, if today's decision is to be believed, can never be disciplined for statements that fall within the Court's expanded definition. Because I believe the Court's conclusions rest upon a distortion of both the record and the Court's prior decisions, I dissent. . . .

BOOS v. BARRY,
485 U.S. 312 (1988)

Michael Boos and Bridget Brooker wanted to carry signs critical of the Soviet Union in front of its Washington, D.C. embassy. J. Michael Waller wanted to display a sign reading "Stop the Killing" within 500 feet of the Nicaraguan Embassy. They brought a suit challenging a District of Columbia provision prohibiting display of signs within 500 feet of an embassy when the sign or signs bring that foreign government into disrepute. Congregating within 500 feet of the embassy is also prohibited by the statute. District of Columbia Mayor Marion S. Barry, Jr., was named in the suit. The U.S. District Court for the District of Columbia denied the claims and the Court of Appeals for the District of Columbia Circuit affirmed.

Majority votes: 5
Dissenting votes: 3

JUSTICE O'CONNOR delivered the opinion of the Court:
The question presented in this case is whether a provision of the District of Columbia Code, § 22–1115, violates the First Amendment. This section prohibits the display of any sign within 500 feet of

a foreign embassy if that sign tends to bring that foreign government into "public odium" or "public disrepute." It also prohibits any congregation of three or more persons within 500 feet of a foreign embassy. . . .

Our cases indicate that as a *content-based* restriction on *political speech* in a *public forum,* § 22–1115 must be subjected to the most exacting scrutiny. Thus, we have required the State to show that the "regulation is necessary to serve a compelling state interest and that it is narrowly drawn to achieve that end." . . .

We first consider whether the display clause serves a compelling governmental interest in protecting the dignity of foreign diplomatic personnel. Since the dignity of foreign officials will be affronted by signs critical of their governments or governmental policies, we are told, these foreign diplomats must be shielded from such insults in order to fulfill our country's obligations under international law.

As a general matter, we have indicated that in public debate our own citizens must tolerate insulting, and even outrageous, speech in order to provide "adequate 'breathing space' to the freedoms protected by the First Amendment." A "dignity" standard, like the "outrageousness" standard that we rejected in *Hustler,* is so inherently subjective that it would be inconsistent with "our longstanding refusal to [punish speech] because the speech in question may have an adverse emotional impact on the audience." *Hustler Magazine,* 108 S.Ct., at 882.

We are not persuaded that the differences between foreign officials and American citizens require us to deviate from these principles here. The dignity interest is said to be compelling in this context primarily because its recognition and protection is part of the United States' obligations under international law. . . .

As a general proposition, it is of course correct that the United States has a vital national interest in complying with international law. The Constitution itself attempts to further this interest by expressly authorizing Congress "[t]o define and punish Piracies and Felonies committed on the high Seas, and Offenses against the Law of Nations." U.S. Const., Art. I, § 8, cl. 10. Moreover, protecting foreign emissaries has a long history and noble purpose. . . .

The need to protect diplomats is grounded in our Nation's important interest in international relations. . . . In addition, in light of the concept of reciprocity that governs much of international law in this area, we have a more parochial reason to protect foreign diplomats in this country. Doing so ensures that similar protections will be accorded those that we send abroad to represent the United States, and thus serves our national interest in protecting our own citizens. . . .

At the same time, it is well-established that "no agreement with a foreign nation can confer power on the Congress, or on any other branch of Government, which is free from the restraints of the Constitution." . . .

Thus, the fact that an interest is recognized in international law does not automatically render that interest "compelling" for purposes of First Amendment analysis. We need not decide today whether, or to what extent, the dictates of international law could ever require that First Amendment analysis be adjusted to accommodate the interests of foreign officials. Even if we assume that international law recognizes a dignity interest and that it should be considered sufficiently "compelling" to support a content-based restriction on speech, we conclude that § 22–1115 is not narrowly tailored to serve that interest. . . . In § 1302 of the Omnibus Diplomatic Security and Anti-Terrorism Act of 1986, Congress said:

"(1) [T]he District law concerning demonstrations near foreign missions in the District of Columbia (D.C. Code, sec. 22–1115) may be inconsistent with the reasonable exercise of the rights of free speech and assembly, that law may have been selectively enforced, and peaceful demonstrators may have been unfairly arrested under the law;

"(2) the obligation of the United States to provide adequate security for the missions and personnel of foreign governments must be balanced with the reasonable exercise of the rights of free speech and assembly; and

"(3) therefore, the Council of the District of Columbia should review and, if appropriate, make revisions in the laws of the District of Columbia concerning demonstrations near foreign missions, in consultation with the Secretary of State and the Secretary of the Treasury." . . .

The District of Columbia government has responded to the congressional request embodied in the Omnibus Act by repealing § 22–1115. The repeal is contingent, however, on Congress' first acting to extend § 112 [of 1972 federal legislation that prohibits intimidating, coercing, or harassing foreign officials or obstructing them in the performance of their duties] to the District. . . .

While this most recent round of legislative action concerning § 22–1115 has not yet led to making the repeal of that provision effective, it has undercut significantly respondents' defense of the display clause. When considered together with earlier congressional action implementing the Vienna Convention, the claim that the display clause is sufficiently narrowly tailored is gravely weakened: if ever it did so, Congress no longer considers this statute necessary to comply with our international obligations. Relying on congressional judgment in this delicate area, we conclude that the availability of alternatives such as § 112 amply demonstrates that the display clause is not crafted with sufficient precision to withstand First Amendment scrutiny. It may serve an interest in protecting the dignity of foreign missions, but it is not narrowly tailored; a less restrictive alternative is readily available. Thus, even assuming for present purposes that the dignity interest is "compelling," we hold that the display clause of § 22–1115 is inconsistent with the First Amendment.

Petitioners initially attack the congregation clause by arguing that it confers unbridled discretion upon the police. . . .

The Court of Appeals, we must first observe, read the congregation clause as distinct from the display clause, so the constitutional infirmity of the latter need not affect the former. Second, the Court of Appeals followed the lead of several earlier decisions . . . and concluded that the statute permits the dispersal only of congregations that are directed at an embassy; it does not grant "police the power to disperse for reasons having nothing to do with the nearby embassy." Finally, the Court of Appeals further circumscribed police discretion by holding that the statute permits dispersal "only when the police reasonably believe that a threat to the security or peace of the embassy is present."
. . .

So narrowed, the congregation clause withstands First Amendment overbreadth scrutiny. It does not reach a substantial amount of constitutionally protected conduct; it merely regulates the place and manner of certain demonstrations. Unlike a general breach of the peace statute, the congregation clause is site-specific; it applies only within 500 feet of foreign embassies. . . . Moreover, the congregation clause does not prohibit peaceful congregations; its reach is limited to groups posing a security threat. As we have noted, "where demonstrations turn violent, they lose their protected quality as expression under the First Amendment." These two limitations prevent the congregation clause from reaching a substantial amount of constitutionally protected conduct and make the clause consistent with the First Amendment.

Petitioners argue that even as narrowed by the Court of Appeals, the congregation clause is invalid because it is impermissibly vague. In particular, petitioners focus on the word "peace," which is not further defined or limited. . . . Section 22–1115 . . . is crafted for a particular context and given that context, it is apparent that the "prohibited quantum of disturbance" is whether normal embassy activities have been or are about to be disrupted. The statute communicates its reach in words of common understanding, and it accordingly withstands petitioners' vagueness challenge. . . .

We conclude that the display clause of § 22–1115 is unconstitutional on its face. It is a content-based restriction on political speech in a public forum, and it is not narrowly tailored to serve a compelling state interest. We also conclude that the congregation clause, as narrowed by the Court of Appeals, is not facially unconstitutional. Accordingly, the judgment of the Court of Appeals is reversed in part and affirmed in part.

It is so ordered.

JUSTICE KENNEDY took no part in the consideration or decision of this case.

JUSTICE BRENNAN, with whom Justice MARSHALL joins, concurring in part and concurring in the judgment: [omitted]

CHIEF JUSTICE REHNQUIST, with whom Justices WHITE and BLACKMUN join, concurring in part and dissenting in part:

For the reasons stated by Judge Bork in his majority opinion below, I would uphold that portion of § 22–1115 of the District of Columbia Code that prohibits the display of any sign within 500 feet of a foreign embassy if that sign tends to bring that foreign government into "public odium" or "public disrepute." However, I agree with Justice O'CONNOR that § 22–1115's congregation clause is not unconstitutional . . .

TEXAS v. JOHNSON,
109 S.Ct. 2533 (1989)

Gregory Lee Johnson participated in a political demonstration during the 1984 Republican National Convention protesting the policies of the Reagan Administration and several Dallas-based defense-industry corporations. During a march through the streets of Dallas, a fellow protestor stole an American flag from a flag pole outside one of the targeted buildings and gave it to Johnson. The demonstration ended in front of Dallas City Hall where Johnson doused the flag with kerosene and set it on fire while about 100 demonstrators *chanted "America, the red, white, and blue, we spit on you." No one present was physically injured or threatened with injury although some observers of the protest were angry. Johnson was convicted of desecration of a venerated object in violation of Texas law and sentenced to one year in prison and fined $2000. A state court of appeals affirmed but the Texas Court of Criminal Appeals reversed, holding that Johnson's punishment was a violation of the First Amendment. Texas took the case to the U.S. Supreme Court.*

Majority votes: 5
Dissenting votes: 4

JUSTICE BRENNAN delivered the opinion of the Court:

After publicly burning an American flag as a means of political protest, Gregory Lee Johnson was convicted of desecrating a flag in violation of Texas law. This case presents the question whether his conviction is consistent with the First Amendment. We hold that it is not. . . .

The State of Texas conceded for purposes of its oral argument in this case that Johnson's conduct was expressive conduct. . . .

The Government generally has a freer hand in restricting expressive conduct than it has in restricting the written or spoken word. . . . It may not, however, proscribe particular conduct *because* it has expressive elements. . . . It is . . . not simply the verbal or nonverbal nature of the expression, but the governmental interest at stake, that helps to determine whether a restriction on that expression is valid. [W]e must decide whether Texas has asserted an interest in support of Johnson's conviction that is unrelated to the suppression of expression. . . . The State offers two separate interests to justify this conviction: preventing breaches of the peace, and preserving the flag as a symbol of nationhood and national unity. We hold that the first interest is not implicated on this record and that the second is related to the suppression of expression.

Texas claims that its interest in preventing breaches of the peace justifies Johnson's conviction for flag desecration. However, no disturbance of the peace actually occurred or threatened to occur because of Johnson's burning of the flag. . . .

[W]e have not permitted the Government to assume that every expression of a provocative idea will incite a riot, but have instead required careful consideration of the actual circumstances surrounding such expression, asking whether the expression "is directed to inciting or producing imminent lawless action and is likely to incite or produce such action." *Brandenburg* v. *Ohio,* (1969). . . . To

accept Texas' arguments that it need only demonstrate "the potential for a breach of the peace," and that every flag-burning necessarily possesses that potential, would be to eviscerate our holding in *Brandenburg.* This we decline to do.

Nor does Johnson's expressive conduct fall within that small class of "fighting words" that are "likely to provoke the average person to retaliation, and thereby cause a breach of the peace." *Chaplinsky* v. *New Hampshire,* (1942). No reasonable onlooker would have regarded Johnson's generalized expression of dissatisfaction with the policies of the Federal Government as a direct personal insult or an invitation to exchange fisticuffs. . . .

We thus conclude that the State's interest in maintaining order is not implicated on these facts. The State need not worry that our holding will disable it from preserving the peace. We do not suggest that the First Amendment forbids a State to prevent "imminent lawless action." And, in fact, Texas already has a statute specifically prohibiting breaches of the peace which tends to confirm that Texas need not punish this flag desecration in order to keep the peace. . . .

The State also asserts an interest in preserving the flag as a symbol of nationhood and national unity. . . . We are . . . persuaded that this interest is related to expression in the case of Johnson's burning of the flag. The State, apparently, is concerned that such conduct will lead people to believe either that the flag does not stand for nationhood and national unity, but instead reflects other, less positive concepts, or that the concepts reflected in the flag do not in fact exist, that is, we do not enjoy unity as a Nation. These concerns blossom only when a person's treatment of the flag communicates some message, and thus are related "to the suppression of free expression". . . .

It remains to consider whether the State's interest in preserving the flag as a symbol of nationhood and national unity justifies Johnson's conviction. . . .

Johnson was not, we add, prosecuted for the expression of just any idea; he was prosecuted for his expression of dissatisfaction with the policies of this country, expression situated at the core of our First Amendment values.

Moreover, Johnson was prosecuted because he knew that his politically charged expression would cause "serious offense." If he had burned the flag as a means of disposing of it because it was dirty or torn, he would not have been convicted of flag desecration under this Texas law; federal law designates burning as the preferred means of disposing of a flag "when it is in such condition that it is no longer a fitting emblem for display," 36 U. S. C. §

176(k), and Texas has no quarrel with this means of disposal. The Texas law is thus not aimed at protecting the physical integrity of the flag in all circumstances, but is designed instead to protect it only against impairments that would cause serious offense to others. Texas concedes as much. . . .

Whether Johnson's treatment of the flag violated Texas law thus depended on the likely communicative impact of his expressive conduct. Our decision in *Boos* v. *Barry* tells us that this restriction on Johnson's expression is content-based. In *Boos,* we considered the constitutionality of a law prohibiting "the display of any sign within 500 feet of a foreign embassy if that sign tends to bring that foreign government into 'public odium' or 'public disrepute.' " Rejecting the argument that the law was content-neutral because it was justified by "our international law obligation to shield diplomats from speech that offends their dignity," we held that "[t]he emotive impact of speech on its audience is not a 'secondary effect' " unrelated to the content of the expression itself. . . .

According to the principles announced in *Boos,* Johnson's political expression was restricted because of the content of the message he conveyed. We must therefore subject the State's asserted interest in preserving the special symbolic character of the flag to "the most exacting scrutiny."

Texas argues that its interest in preserving the flag as a symbol of nationhood and national unity survives this close analysis. Quoting extensively from the writings of this Court chronicling the flag's historic and symbolic role in our society, the State emphasizes the " 'special place' " reserved for the flag in our Nation. The State's argument is not that it has an interest simply in maintaining the flag as a symbol of *something,* no matter what it symbolizes; indeed, if that were the State's position, it would be difficult to see how that interest is endangered by highly symbolic conduct such as Johnson's. Rather, the State's claim is that it has an interest in preserving the flag as a symbol of *nationhood* and *national unity,* a symbol with a determinate range of meanings. According to Texas, if one physically treats the flag in a way that would tend to cast doubt on either the idea that nationhood and national unity are the flag's referents or that national unity actually exists, the message conveyed thereby is a harmful one and therefore may be prohibited.

If there is a bedrock principle underlying the First Amendment, it is that the Government may not prohibit the expression of an idea simply because society finds the idea itself offensive or disagreeable. . . .

We have not recognized an exception to this principle even where our flag has been involved. In *Street* v. *New York,* 394 U. S. 576 (1969), we held that a State may not criminally punish a person for uttering words critical of the flag. Rejecting the argument that the conviction could be sustained on the ground that Street had "failed to show the respect for our national symbol which may properly be demanded of every citizen," we concluded that "the constitutionally guaranteed 'freedom to be intellectually . . . diverse or even contrary,' and the 'right to differ as to things that touch the heart of the existing order,' encompass the freedom to express publicly one's opinions about our flag, including those opinions which are defiant or contemptuous." . . .

In short, nothing in our precedents suggests that a State may foster its own view of the flag by prohibiting expressive conduct relating to it. To bring its argument outside our precedents, Texas attempts to convince us that even if its interest in preserving the flag's symbolic role does not allow it to prohibit words or some expressive conduct critical of the flag, it does permit it to forbid the outright destruction of the flag. The State's argument cannot depend here on the distinction between written or spoken words and nonverbal conduct. That distinction, we have shown, is of no moment where the nonverbal conduct is expressive, as it is here, and where the regulation of that conduct is related to expression, as it is here. . . .

Texas' focus on the precise nature of Johnson's expression, moreover, misses the point of our prior decisions: their enduring lesson, that the Government may not prohibit expression simply because it disagrees with its message, is not dependent on the particular mode in which one chooses to express an idea. If we were to hold that a State may forbid flag-burning wherever it is likely to endanger the flag's symbolic role, but allow it wherever burning a flag promotes that role—as where, for example, a person ceremoniously burns a dirty flag—we would be saying that when it comes to impairing the flag's physical integrity, the flag itself may be used as a symbol—as a substitute for the written or spoken word or a "short cut from mind to mind"— only in one direction. We would be permitting a State to "prescribe what shall be orthodox" by saying that one may burn the flag to convey one's attitude toward it and its referents only if one does not endanger the flag's representation of nationhood and national unity.

We never before have held that the Government may ensure that a symbol be used to express only one view of that symbol or its referents. Indeed, in

Schacht v. *United States,* we invalidated a federal statute permitting an actor portraying a member of one of our armed forces to " 'wear the uniform of that armed force if the portrayal does not tend to discredit that armed force.' " This proviso, we held, "which leaves Americans free to praise the war in Vietnam but can send persons like Schacht to prison for opposing it, cannot survive in a country which has the First Amendment."

We perceive no basis on which to hold that the principle underlying our decision in *Schacht* does not apply to this case. To conclude that the Government may permit designated symbols to be used to communicate only a limited set of messages would be to enter territory having no discernible or defensible boundaries. Could the Government, on this theory, prohibit the burning of state flags? Of copies of the Presidential seal? Of the Constitution? In evaluating these choices under the First Amendment, how would we decide which symbols were sufficiently special to warrant this unique status? To do so, we would be forced to consult our own political preferences, and impose them on the citizenry, in the very way that the First Amendment forbids us to do.

There is, moreover, no indication—either in the text of the Constitution or in our cases interpreting it—that a separate juridical category exists for the American flag alone. Indeed, we would not be surprised to learn that the persons who framed our Constitution and wrote the Amendment that we now construe were not known for their reverence for the Union Jack. The First Amendment does not guarantee that other concepts virtually sacred to our Nation as a whole—such as the principle that discrimination on the basis of race is odious and destructive—will go unquestioned in the marketplace of ideas. See *Brandenburg* v. *Ohio* (1969). We decline, therefore, to create for the flag an exception to the joust of principles protected by the First Amendment.

It is not the State's ends, but its means, to which we object. It cannot be gainsaid that there is a special place reserved for the flag in this Nation, and thus we do not doubt that the Government has a legitimate interest in making efforts to "preserv[e] the national flag as an unalloyed symbol of our country." We reject the suggestion, urged at oral argument by counsel for Johnson, that the Government lacks "any state interest whatsoever" in regulating the manner in which the flag may be displayed. Congress has, for example, enacted precatory regulations describing the proper treatment of the flag and we cast no doubt on the legitimacy of its interest in making such recommenda-

tions. To say that the Government has an interest in encouraging proper treatment of the flag, however, is not to say that it may criminally punish a person for burning a flag as a means of political protest. . . .

We are fortified in today's conclusion by our conviction that forbidding criminal punishment for conduct such as Johnson's will not endanger the special role played by our flag or the feelings it inspires. To paraphrase Justice Holmes, we submit that nobody can suppose that this one gesture of an unknown man will change our Nation's attitude towards its flag. Indeed, Texas' argument that the burning of an American flag " 'is an act having a high likelihood to cause a breach of the peace,' " and its statute's implicit assumption that physical mistreatment of the flag will lead to "serious offense," tend to confirm that the flag's special role is not in danger; if it were, no one would riot or take offense because a flag had been burned.

We are tempted to say, in fact, that the flag's deservedly cherished place in our community will be strengthened, not weakened, by our holding today. Our decision is a reaffirmation of the principles of freedom and inclusiveness that the flag best reflects, and of the conviction that our toleration of criticism such as Johnson's is a sign and source of our strength. Indeed, one of the proudest images of our flag, the one immortalized in our own national anthem, is of the bombardment it survived at Fort McHenry. It is the Nation's resilience, not its rigidity, that Texas sees reflected in the flag—and it is that resilience that we reassert today.

The way to preserve the flag's special role is not to punish those who feel differently about these matters. It is to persuade them that they are wrong. . . .

[P]recisely because it is our flag that is involved, one's response to the flag-burner may exploit the uniquely persuasive power of the flag itself. We can imagine no more appropriate response to burning a flag than waving one's own, no better way to counter a flag-burner's message than by saluting the flag that burns, no surer means of preserving the dignity even of the flag that burned than by—as one witness here did—according its remains a respectful burial. We do not consecrate the flag by punishing its desecration, for in doing so we dilute the freedom that this cherished emblem represents.

Johnson was convicted for engaging in expressive conduct. The State's interest in preventing breaches of the peace does not support his conviction because Johnson's conduct did not threaten to disturb the peace. Nor does the State's interest in preserving the flag as a symbol of nationhood and national unity justify his criminal conviction for engaging in political expression. The judgment of the Texas Court of Criminal Appeals is therefore

Affirmed.

JUSTICE KENNEDY, concurring:

I write not to qualify the words JUSTICE BRENNAN chooses so well, for he says with power all that is necessary to explain our ruling. I join his opinion without reservation, but with a keen sense that this case, like others before us from time to time, exacts its personal toll. This prompts me to add to our pages these few remarks.

The case before us illustrates better than most that the judicial power is often difficult in its exercise. We cannot here ask another branch to share responsibility, as when the argument is made that a statute is flawed or incomplete. For we are presented with a clear and simple statute to be judged against a pure command of the Constitution. The outcome can be laid at no door but ours.

The hard fact is that sometimes we must make decisions we do not like. We make them because they are right, right in the sense that the law and the Constitution, as we see them, compel the result. And so great is our commitment to the process that, except in the rare case, we do not pause to express distaste for the result, perhaps for fear of undermining a valued principle that dictates the decision. This is one of those rare cases.

Our colleagues in dissent advance powerful arguments why respondent may be convicted for his expression, reminding us that among those who will be dismayed by our holding will be some who have had the singular honor of carrying the flag in battle. And I agree that the flag holds a lonely place of honor in an age when absolutes are distrusted and simple truths are burdened by unneeded apologetics.

With all respect to those views, I do not believe the Constitution gives us the right to rule as the dissenting members of the Court urge, however painful this judgment is to announce. Though symbols often are what we ourselves make of them, the flag is constant in expressing beliefs Americans share, beliefs in law and peace and that freedom which sustains the human spirit. The case here today forces recognition of the costs to which those beliefs commit us. It is poignant but fundamental that the flag protects those who hold it in contempt.

For all the record shows, this respondent was not a philosopher and perhaps did not even possess the ability to comprehend how repellent his statements must be to the Republic itself. But whether or not he could appreciate the enormity of the offense he gave, the fact remains that his acts were speech, in both the technical and the fundamental meaning of the Constitution. So I agree with the Court that he must go free.

CHIEF JUSTICE REHNQUIST, with whom JUSTICE WHITE and JUSTICE O'CONNOR join, dissenting: . . .

The flag symbolizes the Nation in peace as well as in war. It signifies our national presence on battleships, airplanes, military installations, and public buildings from the United States Capitol to the thousands of county courthouses and city halls throughout the country. Two flags are prominently placed in our courtroom. Countless flags are placed by the graves of loved ones each year on what was first called Decoration Day, and is now called Memorial Day. The flag is traditionally placed on the casket of deceased members of the Armed Forces, and it is later given to the deceased's family. Congress has provided that the flag be flown at half-staff upon the death of the President, Vice President, and other government officials "as a mark of respect to their memory." The flag identifies United States merchant ships, and "[t]he laws of the Union protect our commerce wherever the flag of the country may float."

No other American symbol has been as universally honored as the flag. . . .

Both Congress and the States have enacted numerous laws regulating misuse of the American flag. . . . Congress has also prescribed detailed rules for the design of the flag, the time and occasion of the flag's display, the position and manner of its display, and conduct during hoisting, lowering and passing of the flag. With the exception of Alaska and Wyoming, all of the States now have statutes prohibiting the burning of the flag. . . .

The American flag, then, throughout more than 200 years of our history, has come to be the visible symbol embodying our Nation. It does not represent the views of any particular political party, and it does not represent any particular political philosophy. The flag is not simply another "idea" or "point of view" competing for recognition in the marketplace of ideas. Millions and millions of Americans regard it with an almost mystical reverence regardless of what sort of social, political, or philosophical beliefs they may have. I cannot agree that the First Amendment invalidates the Act of Congress, and the laws of 48 of the 50 States, which make criminal the public burning of the flag. . . .

[T]he Court insists that the Texas statute prohibiting the public burning of the American flag infringes on respondent Johnson's freedom of expression. Such freedom, of course, is not absolute. See *Schenck* v. *United States,* 249 U.S. 47 (1919). In *Chaplinsky* v. *New Hampshire,* 315 U.S. 568 (1942), a unanimous Court said:

> "Allowing the broadest scope to the language and purpose of the Fourteenth Amendment, it is well understood that the right of free speech is not absolute at all times and under all circumstances. There are certain well-defined and narrowly limited classes of speech, the prevention and punishment of which have never been thought to raise any Constitutional problem. These include the lewd and obscene, the profane, the libelous, and the insulting or 'fighting' words—those which by their very utterance inflict injury or tend to incite an immediate breach of the peace. It has been well observed that such utterances are no essential part of any exposition of ideas, and are of such slight social value as a step to truth that any benefit that may be derived from them is clearly outweighed by the social interest in order and morality." *Id.,* at 571–572 (footnotes omitted).

The Court upheld Chaplinsky's conviction under a state statute that made it unlawful to "address any offensive, derisive or annoying word to any person who is lawfully in any street or other public place." Chaplinsky had told a local Marshal, "You are a God dammed racketeer" and a "damned Fascist and the whole government of Rochester are Fascists or agents of Fascists."

Here it may equally well be said that the public burning of the American flag by Johnson was no essential part of any exposition of ideas, and at the same time it had a tendency to incite a breach of the peace. Johnson was free to make any verbal denunciation of the flag that he wished; indeed, he was free to burn the flag in private. He could publicly burn other symbols of the Government or effigies of political leaders. He did lead a march through the streets of Dallas, and conducted a rally in front of the Dallas City Hall. He engaged in a "die-in" to protest nuclear weapons. He shouted out various slogans during the march, including: "Reagan, Mondale which will it be? Either one means World War III"; "Ronald Reagan, killer of the hour, Perfect example of U.S. power"; and "red, white and blue, we spit on you, you stand for plunder, you will go under." For none of these acts was he arrested or prosecuted; it was only when he proceeded to burn publicly an American flag stolen from its rightful owner that he violated the Texas statute.

The Court could not, and did not, say that Chaplinsky's utterances were not expressive phrases—they clearly and succinctly conveyed an extremely low opinion of the addressee. The same may be said of Johnson's public burning of the flag in this case; it obviously did convey Johnson's bitter dislike of his country. But his act, like Chaplinsky's provocative words, conveyed nothing that could not have been conveyed and was not conveyed just as forcefully in a dozen different ways. As with "fighting words," so with flag burning, for purposes of the First Amendment: It is "no essential part of any exposition of ideas, and [is] of such slight social value as a step to truth that any benefit that may be derived from [it] is clearly outweighed" by the public interest in avoiding a probable breach of the peace. . . .

The Court concludes its opinion with a regrettably patronizing civics lecture. . . . The Court's role as the final expositor of the Constitution is well established, but its role as a platonic guardian admonishing those responsible to public opinion as if they were truant school children has no similar place in our system of government. The cry of "no taxation without representation" animated those who revolted against the English Crown to found our Nation—the idea that those who submitted to government should have some say as to what kind of laws would be passed. Surely one of the high purposes of a democratic society is to legislate against conduct that is regarded as evil and profoundly offensive to the majority of people—whether it be murder, embezzlement, pollution, or flag burning.

Our Constitution wisely places limits on powers of legislative majorities to act, but the declaration of such limits by this Court "is, at all times, a question of much delicacy, which ought seldom, if ever, to be decided in the affirmative, in a doubtful case." Uncritical extension of constitutional protection to the burning of the flag risks the frustration of the very purpose for which organized governments are instituted. The Court decides that the American flag is just another symbol, about which not only must opinions pro and con be tolerated, but for which the most minimal public respect may not be enjoined. The government may conscript men into the Armed Forces where they must fight and perhaps die for the flag, but the government may not prohibit the public burning of the banner under which they fight. I would uphold the Texas statute as applied in this case.

JUSTICE STEVENS, dissenting:. . . .

It is appropriate to emphasize certain propositions that are not implicated by this case. The statutory prohibition of flag desecration does not "prescribe what shall be orthodox in politics, nationalism, religion, or other matters of opinion or force citizens to confess by word or act their faith therein.'' The statute does not compel any conduct or any profession of respect for any idea or any symbol.

Nor does the statute violate ''the government's paramount obligation of neutrality in its regulation of protected communication.'' The content of respondent's message has no relevance whatsoever to the case. . . . The case has nothing to do with ''disagreeable ideas.'' It involves disagreeable conduct that, in my opinion, diminishes the value of an important national asset.

The Court is therefore quite wrong in blandly asserting that respondent ''was prosecuted for his expression of dissatisfaction with the policies of this country, expression situated at the core of our First Amendment values.'' Respondent was prosecuted because of the method he chose to express his dissatisfaction with those policies. Had he chosen to spray paint—or perhaps convey with a motion pic-

ture projector—his message of dissatisfaction on the facade of the Lincoln Memorial, there would be no question about the power of the Government to prohibit his means of expression. The prohibition would be supported by the legitimate interest in preserving the quality of an important national asset. Though the asset at stake in this case is intangible, given its unique value, the same interest supports a prohibition on the desecration of the American flag.

The ideas of liberty and equality have been an irresistible force in motivating leaders like Patrick Henry, Susan B. Anthony, and Abraham Lincoln, schoolteachers like Nathan Hale and Booker T. Washington, the Philippine Scouts who fought at Bataan, and the soldiers who scaled the bluff at Omaha Beach. If those ideas are worth fighting for—and our history demonstrates that they are— it cannot be true that the flag that uniquely symbolizes their power is not itself worthy of protection from unnecessary desecration.

I respectfully dissent.

Chapter

14

Freedom of the Press, Commercial Free Speech, Obscenity

We continue in this chapter a consideration of other important aspects of First Amendment freedoms with a focus on freedom of the press, the extent to which the First Amendment is applicable to commercial advertising, and the issue of obscenity (which is sometimes an issue of artistic free expression in the representation or depiction of sexual matters). All three aspects involve the use of the communications media.

FREEDOM OF THE PRESS

The right of the news media to publish or broadcast goes to the heart of an open society. Without a free and independent press, it is impossible for democracy to flourish. Total control of information and state control of the media are the hallmarks of a totalitarian political system. Americans traditionally pride themselves on the freedoms they enjoy, particularly a free press. But the press in the United States has grown so powerful and influential,

with control of the national media in relatively few hands, that the press itself and the uses of its power have become issues in recent years. The power of the press is such that it is sometimes referred to as the fourth branch of government. But these are not issues that have faced the Supreme Court, nor are we concerned with them here outside of mentioning them at the outset. Rather, what the Court has dealt with, particularly in the twentieth century, is the constitutional nature and extensiveness of the press' freedom.

The First Amendment states unequivocally that Congress may not abridge freedom of the press. This has been interpreted by the Court as meaning that only in extraordinary circumstances (such as wartime when a newspaper is about to publish top secret troop movements) may government literally stop the presses. The freedom to publish free from censorship is almost, but not quite, absolute. There is a heavy burden on government to demonstrate that a newspaper cannot publish or a news program cannot be broadcast. This is what the Supreme Court, in the landmark 1931 decision in **Near** v. **Minnesota,** referred to as the guarantee against *prior restraint* or preventing publication. On the other hand, if the press publishes or broadcasts something and by so doing violates a law, such as obscenity or libel, it may be subject to what is known as *subsequent punishment.* That is, the editor or publisher may, if found guilty, be heavily fined and/or sent to prison. *But the presses may not be stopped.* In *Near* the Court applied the First Amendment's guarantee of freedom of the press to the states as part of the liberty that may not be denied without due process of law as provided by the Fourteenth Amendment. Forty years later, in the famous Pentagon Papers case, **New York Times Co.** v. **United States,** the Court reaffirmed *Near* v. *Minnesota's* presumption against prior restraint. The federal government unsuccessfully tried to stop publication of newspaper articles that included excerpts from the Pentagon's massive history of American involvement in Vietnam.

There have been other cases that have concerned the press' ability to publish. For example, in *Grosjean* v. *American Press Co.,* 297 U.S. 233 (1936), the Court struck down a Louisiana state gross receipts tax that had been enacted by demagogue Huey Long's political machine to get back at Louisiana newspapers that opposed Long. Some 37 years later the Burger Court struck down another special tax on newspapers, although this particular tax had not been aimed at punishing the press. The case was *Minneapolis Star & Tribune* v. *Minnesota,* 460 U.S. 575 (1983). The Rehnquist Court struck down a state sales tax that taxed general interest magazines but exempted religious, professional, trade, and sports journals. The Court ruled that the selective tax required state officials to scrutinize the contents of publications and that was incompatible with the First Amendment (*Arkansas Writers' Project, Inc.* v. *Ragland,* 481

U.S. 221 [1987]). Another Rehnquist Court decision favorable to the press was *City of Lakewood* v. *Plain Dealer Pub. Co.,* 486 U.S. 750 (1988) that concerned a municipal ordinance granting the mayor the authority to grant or deny applications for annual permits to place newsracks on public property. The Court found this to be unbridled discretion given a public official over the fortunes of the press and as such in violation of the First Amendment.

Another aspect of the press being able to publish concerns editorial control of the content of newspapers. In 1973 the Court ruled in *Pittsburgh Press Company* v. *Pittsburgh Commission on Human Relations,* 413 U.S. 376, that the order to the paper by the Pittsburgh Commission on Human Relations to classify its help-wanted advertisements without reference to gender did not violate the First Amendment. The Court majority took the position that no editorial judgment or public policy views of the newspaper were involved and that all that was concerned was pure commercial speech, which a 1942 precedent, *Valentine* v. *Chrestensen,* 316 U.S. 52, held to be unprotected by the First Amendment. In the case of *Miami Herald Publishing Company* v. *Tornillo,* 418 U.S. 241 (1974), the Court struck down a state enactment that clearly dictated editorial policy. This case involved a Florida law granting a political candidate the right of reply in any newspaper that published material assailing his or her personal character or official record. In the case of *Smith* v. *Daily Mail Publishing Company,* 443 U.S. 97 (1979), the Court struck down a West Virginia statute making it a crime for a newspaper to publish the names of juvenile offenders. In *The Florida Star* v. *B.J.F.,* 109 S.Ct. 2603 (1989), the Court considered a Florida statute that made it unlawful to "print, publish, or broadcast . . . in any instrument of mass communication" the name of the victim of a sexual offense. In this case a weekly newspaper, *The Florida Star,* was found civilly liable and the rape victim (B.J.F.) was awarded $100,000 because the Star published her name, which it had obtained from a publicly released police report. The Court ruled that imposing damages on the Star for publishing B.J.F.'s name violates the First Amendment. The Court suggested that where a newspaper publishes truthful information lawfully obtained, the state has the burden of demonstrating that subsequent punishment is narrowly tailored to a state interest of the highest order, which was not demonstrated in this case.

The broadcast media, however, fared less well, with the Court supporting the FCC's position that the broadcasting networks and stations must sell "reasonable" amounts of air time to congressional and presidential candidates (*CBS* v. *FCC*, 453 U.S. 367 [1981]). A related decision concerned regulation of motion pictures under the Foreign Agents Registration Act. The Court in *Meese* v. *Keene*, 481 U.S. 465 (1987), ruled that it was constitutional for the federal government to require two Canadian documentaries dealing with the environment ("If You Love This Planet" and "Acid Rain") to be labeled "political propaganda" under the act, before they could be shown in the United States.

Two decisions of the Burger Court were unfavorable to the print media's discretion in the editorial realm. In *Regan* v. *Time Inc.*, 468 U.S. 641 (1984), the Court upheld in part the federal law governing the publication or production of illustrations of federal currency. The publisher of *Time* magazine had challenged the law as restricting freedom of the press. The other decision concerned a suit by Harper & Row (also the publisher of this book) against *The Nation* magazine for violating copyright law. What had happened was that *The Nation* magazine obtained a copy of a manuscript in press, a book by former President Gerald Ford about his presidency, and ran a news story that contained unauthorized quotes from the manuscript and paraphrased

and summarized the juiciest revelations. When *The Nation's* article was published, *Time* (which had contracted with Harper & Row to have exclusive rights to publish excerpts from the manuscript in exchange for the sum of $12,500) claimed that the contract was now void. Harper & Row then sued *The Nation* for damages, claiming that the use of the quotations along with the paraphrasing and summary of Ford's revelations were not a "fair use" of material protected by copyright, and a majority of the Burger Court agreed. The dissenters in the case, *Harper & Row, Publishers* v. *Nation Enterprises*, 471 U.S. 539 (1985), argued that the magazine had run a legitimate news story and as a result of this decision newspaper and magazine editors will practice self-censorship for fear of being sued for violation of copyright law and that public discussion of public issues will be inhibited.

A Rehnquist Court decision unfavorable to the press was complicated by the fact that it concerned the student press. The sharply divided Court in **Hazelwood School District** v. **Kuhlmeier** raised serious questions concerning editorial control of the press and suggested the limits the majority would impose in the name of freedom of the press. A decision more favorable to editorial control was rendered in **FCC** v. **League of Women Voters of California.** The Court, by striking down a congressional provision on First Amendment grounds, enhanced the editorial discretion of public broadcasting.

Freedom of the press, historically, has not meant the right to libel. The press has been held accountable in courts of law for having printed libel and has been subject to payment of damages both actual and punitive. The Warren Court, in the landmark 1964 decision of **New York Times Co.** v. **Sullivan,** changed the law of libel and ruled that a public official is not entitled to damages for the publication of defamatory statements unless "actual malice" can be proved, that is, that the statement was made "with knowledge that it was false or with reckless disregard of whether it was false or not." This replaced the previous standard whereby the defendant was obliged to prove the truth of the alleged defamatory statement. The *New York Times* doctrine was a major extension of First Amendment freedoms and lifted a burden from the nation's press. The Warren Court extended the "actual malice" formula in *Time* v. *Hill,* 385 U.S. 374 (1967), to encompass any "newsworthy" story regardless of the privacy of those involved. Only when a publisher resorts to "deliberate falsity or a reckless disregard for the truth" does the First Amendment cease to protect. The Rehnquist Court strongly reaffirmed *New York Times Co.* v. *Sullivan* and extended the protection of the press in its ruling in **Hustler Magazine** v. **Falwell** that a public figure may not recover damages for the intentional infliction of emotional distress by being lampooned in print.

The Court, however, in several rulings, made modifications of the law of libel making it somewhat easier for private individuals to win a libel judgment against the media. In *Gertz* v. *Robert Welch, Inc.,* 418 U.S. 323 (1974), and *Wolston* v. *Reader's Digest Association,* 443 U.S. 157 (1979), the Court ruled that private individuals, including convicted criminals, were not public figures and therefore can sue for libel without having to prove "actual malice." Private individuals such as Gertz or Wolston need only prove negligence in defamation suits against the media. Similarly, in *Dun & Bradstreet, Inc.* v. *Greenmoss Builders, Inc.,* 472 U.S. 749 (1985), the Court permitted personal and punitive damages in defamation suits without a showing of "actual malice" when the defamatory statements do not involve matters of public concern (involved here was a false credit report issued to a contractor's creditors). But note that the Court, in *Philadelphia Newspapers, Inc.* v. *Hepps,* 475 U.S. 767 (1986), held that when the alleged defamation of a private individual involves a matter of public concern, the com-

mon law presumption that defamatory speech is false cannot stand and the private figure has the burden of proving the falsity of the statements at issue.

In *Herbert* v. *Lando,* 441 U.S. 153 (1979), the Court ruled that in determining whether there was "actual malice" in a media attack on a public figure, it was permissible to question reporters and editors as to their state of mind including their conversations and beliefs at the time they made the editorial decisions that resulted in the alleged libel. The Court was kinder to the publishers of *Consumer Reports* when it affirmed a court of appeals decision overturning a federal district court finding that the magazine had made a false disparaging statement with "actual malice." The Court, in *Bose Corporation* v. *Consumers Union of U.S., Inc.,* 466 U.S. 485 (1984), ruled that in libel suits, appellate courts could independently examine the record to determine if "actual malice" occurred. The Court, like the appeals court, found no "actual malice." In 1986 the Court ruled that at the trial court level, libel suits brought by public figures are subject to dismissal by the federal district judge on a motion by the media defendants if the plaintiff cannot prove "actual malice" with "clear and convincing evidence" to the satisfaction of the judge. The press hailed this ruling, in *Anderson* v. *Liberty Lobby,* 477 U.S. 242, as a victory that would relieve them of the heavy litigation costs involved in going to trial in cases where the plaintiff has a weak claim. However, the Court has not hesitated to examine the facts of a case to determine if "actual malice" has occurred and, for example in *Harte-Hanks Communications, Inc.* v. *Connaughton,* 109 S.Ct. 2678 (1989), found that there was actual malice that supported the verdict of libel and the award of compensatory and punitive damages.

Because of the importance of the press to an open society, the issue arises whether or not the press should have special access to the institutions of government. Without such access, the press cannot inform Americans how their institutions are working or what policies and practices are being implemented in their name. Without such access, it can be argued, there may be inadequate debate over policy, and as a consequence government officials may not be alerted to certain problems with current or contemplated policy and may fail to consider alternative policies that would be more effective. This issue came before the Supreme Court in *Houchins* v. *KQED,* 438 U.S. 1 (1978), and also in *Gannett Co., Inc.* v. *DePasquale,* 443 U.S. 368 (1979), but the Court refused to interpret the freedom of the press guarantee as granting the press any *special* right of access to governmental institutions. Neither has the Court seen fit to interpret the First Amendment free press guarantee as containing any presumption of confidentiality of news sources even though without such confidentiality the ability of journalists to investigate and report the workings of American institutions would be seriously impaired. The Court in *Branzburg* v. *Hayes,* 408 U.S. 665 (1972), refused to recognize the right of a reporter to protect sources by withholding information from a grand jury. The Burger Court did not see the need for the confidentiality of the reporter-source relationship in relation to the free press guarantee. Indeed, in *Zurcher* v. *Stanford Daily,* 436 U.S. 547 (1978), involving a college newspaper, the Court took the position that if there is probable cause to believe that the newspaper office harbors evidence relating to the commission of a crime by third parties, then law enforcement officials do not have to rely on subpoenas to obtain such evidence. They can obtain a search warrant and go up to the newspaper office and actually search the office. This decision outraged the nation's press and in 1980 led to federal legislation prohibiting this practice.

Sometimes freedom of the press clashes with another important civil liberty such as the right of an accused to a fair trial. The Warren Court in *Sheppard* v. *Maxwell,* 384 U.S. 333 (1966), overturned a murder conviction on the ground that the sensationalistic newspaper reporting of the trial made a fair trial impossible. The Court has not been sympathetic, however, to court orders forbidding the press from publishing details of criminal cases such as confessions (see, for example, *Nebraska Press Association* v. *Stuart,* 427 U.S. 539 [1976]). Although the Court ruled in *Gannett Co., Inc.* v. *DePasquale* that the press and the public could be excluded from pretrial proceedings if both prosecution and defense agree, the Court also subsequently ruled in **Richmond Newspapers, Inc.** v. **Virginia** that the public and the press have a First Amendment right to attend trials. This was extended, in 1986, to cover pretrial criminal hearings. The decision, *Press-Enterprise Co.* v. *Superior Court,* 478 U.S. 1, was careful to acknowledge the right of a defendant to a fair trial. It conceded that the public and the press may be excluded as a last resort to protect the rights of the defendant, but noted that the burden is on the trial judge to justify such an extreme action detrimental to First Amendment rights. States may even permit broadcast coverage of criminal trials, which the Court ruled in *Chandler* v. *Florida,* 449 U.S. 560 (1981), is not inherently a denial of due process. The Court has emphasized that the burden of providing a fair trial falls on the judge and that the judge has the authority to see to it that the accused has a fair trial. This can be accomplished, the Court has insisted, without banning the press from the courtroom or censoring its reporting.

COMMERCIAL FREE SPEECH

Paid commercial advertisements in the media were not considered to be protected by the First Amendment, or so the 1942 Supreme Court decision of *Valentine* v. *Chrestensen,* 316 U.S. 52, seemed to suggest. Although it is true that the *New York Times* v. *Sullivan* decision actually concerned a paid advertisement, the Court did not treat it as commercial speech since neither a product nor a service were being offered to the public. The Supreme Court in the mid-1970s, however, began to reconsider commercial speech and in *Bigelow* v. *Virginia,* 421 U.S. 809 (1975), lifted the bar to First Amendment protection of commercial advertising. *Bigelow* concerned the managing editor of a college-town newspaper who published an advertisement for a New York State abortion referral service. This occurred before the Court's decision in **Roe** v. **Wade** (chap. 6) in 1973. By publishing the advertisement, the editor was charged and then convicted of violating a Virginia law prohibiting the dissemination of information having the effect of encouraging abortion. The Supreme Court, however, overturned the conviction and suggested that whether or not speech in a commercial context is protected by the Constitution requires a balancing of the public interest in such speech with the objectives of state regulation. In so framing the question, the Court ruled that its precedents should not be read as automatically excluding commercial advertising from First Amendment protection. In this particular case the Court rejected the objective of the state regulation—preventing the citizens of Virginia from having access to information about lawful activities in another state. On the other hand, the public had a right to know about such lawful out-of-state activities. Thus, this type of advertising, truthful information about lawful out-of-state activities, was indeed protected by the First Amendment.

Subsequent cases involving commercial advertising followed. The Court in *Virginia State Board of Pharmacy* v. *Virginia Citizens Consumer Council, Inc.,* 425 U.S. 748 (1976), struck down a Virginia law that forbade the advertising of prescription drug prices, suggesting that consumers had a First Amendment right to receive truthful information by way of commercial advertising. In so doing

the Court seemed to (although it did not explicitly) overturn *Valentine* v. *Chrestensen.* The Court ruled along these lines in *Bates* v. *State Bar,* 433 U.S. 350 (1977), that Arizona cannot forbid newspaper advertising by lawyers of their fees for certain standard legal services. Again, the Court invoked a First Amendment right of consumers to have access to information contained in commercial advertising. In another case concerning lawyer advertising, *In Re R.M.J.,* 455 U.S. 191 (1982), the Court ruled that various restrictions on the kind of advertising that lawyers may undertake were violations of consumers' First Amendment rights. The Court stated explicitly that "truthful advertising related to lawful activities is entitled to the protections of the First Amendment." The Court went so far as to rule in *Shapero* v. *Kentucky Bar Ass'n,* 486 U.S. 466 (1988) that a state cannot categorically prohibit lawyers from soliciting legal business by sending truthful and nondeceptive letters to potential clients known to face particular legal problems. Advertising of contraceptives cannot be barred by the federal government from the United States mail, ruled the Court in *Bolger* v. *Youngs Drug Product Corp.,* 463 U.S. 60 (1983). In so ruling the Court unanimously struck down a federal statute and firmly protected this form of commercial speech under the First Amendment. But in a major ruling that brought to a halt the trend of the previous decade, the Court, by a 5–4 vote in *Posados de Puerto Rico* v. *Tourism Co.,* 478 U.S. 328 (1986), decided that truthful advertising related to lawful activities is not necessarily entitled to First Amendment protection. Justice Rehnquist, in his opinion of the Court, found that government can prohibit or otherwise regulate the advertisement of products or services if government officials believe either to be "harmful" to the public. If it would be constitutional for government to exercise its police powers by prohibiting the sale of a product or service, it can take the less severe action of regulating, or even prohibiting, the advertising of that product or service. This decision upheld Puerto Rico's prohibition of local advertising of a legal activity—lucrative, tourist-attracting casino gambling—which the authorities claimed was necessary to protect the morals and well-being of local residents. Under the regulations, however, casino operators were permitted to advertise in media that reached potential tourists. Justice Rehnquist, in upholding this, also suggested that truthful cigarette and alcoholic beverage advertising can also be regulated or even banned without a violation of the First Amendment.

Do corporations have free speech rights? The Court said "yes" in two 1980 cases from New York involving utilities. In one, *Consolidated Edison* v. *Public Service Commission,* 447 U.S. 530, the Court struck down the New York State Public Service Commission policy prohibiting utilities from enclosing statements of their views on public issues along with the monthly bill. This was considered to be political free speech and subject to the traditional high standards used to protect such speech. The other decision, *Central Hudson Gas* v. *Public Service Commission,* 447 U.S. 557, saw the Court invalidate the Public Service Commission's absolute ban on utility advertising promoting the use of electricity. The ban had been imposed during the severe energy crisis of the 1970s, but the Court saw this as restricting the flow of information to consumers. The Court went even further in 1986 in *Pacific Gas & Electric* v. *Public Utilities Commission of California,* 475 U.S. 1, when it struck down an order from the California Commission to the utility to stop using billing envelopes to distribute political editorials and instead give space four times a year to fundraising appeals by consumer advocacy groups. This, said the Court, impermissibly burdened Pacific Gas & Electric's First Amendment rights because the order was not a legitimate time-place-or-manner regulation and was not narrowly tailored to serve a compelling state interest. Business, however, has no absolute right to advertise on billboards. The Court ruled in *Metromedia* v. *San Diego,* 453 U.S. 490 (1981), that localities may exercise their police powers to the extent that they can ban billboards that carry commercial advertising. And the Rehnquist Court went further than the Burger Court in limiting commercial free speech rights by its ruling in *Bd. of Trustees of State Univ. of N.Y.* v. *Fox,* 109 S.Ct. 3028 (1989), when it ruled that governmental restrictions upon commercial speech need not be the absolute least restrictive means of achieving the governmental interests asserted. Governmental decision makers have much more regulatory leeway with commercial speech than they have with noncommercial speech. The Court pulled back considerably from its earlier *Central Hudson Gas* decision. Also in **Austin** v. **Michigan Chamber of Commerce** (reprinted at the end of this book) the Court treated political free speech of corporations differently than other kinds of political free speech when it upheld a Michigan statute that prohibits using corporate treasury funds for supporting or opposing candidates for state office. The Court found that Michigan has a compelling state interest in preventing corruption or the appearance of corruption in the political process.

OBSCENITY

Political free expression goes to the heart of a democratic political order. That right is strained to the limit when exercised by those who would deny such freedom to others or whose printed or oral message is that of hate and violence. Artistic free expression, on the other hand, touches other raw nerves of a culture, particularly in its representation of sex and sexual behavior. Here, the fear is not the debasing of the political system but the debasing of the society's ethics, morals, and culture in terms of how men and women treat each other and themselves. Those who want society to protect itself from unbridled immorality and violent sexism have favored censorship and the suppression of certain sexually oriented material considered obscene. But this has also meant that First Amendment questions are ultimately raised because censorship and the suppression of ideas run counter to the philosophy of the First Amendment, which values complete freedom of thought and the free trade in ideas with the faith that in the contest of ideas the vile and the hateful will ultimately be rejected.

Traditionally, "obscenity" (leaving aside the problem of definition) was a crime and not considered an exercise of freedom of expression. With motion pictures, whether a film was obscene or not was not even an issue because the Supreme Court in the 1915 decision of *Mutual Film Corporation* v. *Ohio Industrial Commission,* 236 U.S. 230, ruled that motion pictures were not part of the press and thus were not entitled to First Amendment protection. Movie censorship was upheld in that case. Not until 1952 with *Burstyn* v. *Wilson,* 343 U.S. 495, did the Court extend the scope of the First Amendment to cover motion pictures. But although the Court dealt with a censorship law that included obscenity, the particular case concerned a violation of the "sacrilegious" provision of the New York law; thus the Court did not specifically grapple with obscenity. In **Roth** v. **United States** the Court explicitly noted that obscenity was not protected by the First Amendment, but the Court also sought to define it in a way that would not unduly inhibit legitimate artistic expression in the sexual realm. Obscene material, said the Court, is "utterly without redeeming social importance." A work may be considered obscene if "to the average person, applying contemporary community standards, the dominant theme of the material taken as a whole appeals to prurient interest." In a subsequent case, *Jacobellis* v. *Ohio,* 378 U.S. 184 (1964), a plurality ruled that a *national* standard is to be used in determining

"contemporary community standards." Defining obscenity proved troublesome for the Warren Court, and by the mid-1960s in order for a work of art, a book, a magazine, or motion picture to be adjudged obscene it had to be shown that the work was "*utterly* without redeeming social value," something quite difficult to demonstrate. The Court's more permissive approach was noted in **Memoirs** v. **Massachusetts** although, the same day that *Memoirs* was handed down, the Court also ruled that when there was doubt as to whether a work was legally obscene, evidence of the merchandising or advertising would then be examined to determine whether or not there was sexual pandering (the case was *Ginzburg* v. *United States,* 383 U.S. 463 [1966]).

The 1960s was a decade of massive social change and part of that change included the liberalization of artistic standards in terms of representation of sex, sexual behavior, and language. The strict privately enforced codes that governed motion pictures were abandoned and replaced by a movie rating system in which R-rated films could have uncensored language and some nudity along with simulated sex acts. Books no longer were self-censored or subject to prosecution as written descriptions of sex and sexual behavior met with what appeared to be absolute constitutional protection. Photographic representation of sex, although somewhat more troublesome, passed the muster of the Warren Court's looser standards. In one of the last decisions of the Warren Court, **Stanley** v. **Georgia,** the Court for the first time gave obscenity some constitutional protection.

The Burger Court undertook to reverse the more liberal Warren Court policy on obscenity. The Court's new policy was offered in two major obscenity decisions, **Miller** v. **California** and **Paris Adult Theatre** v. **Slaton.** Under the Court's new definition of obscenity, *local* communities could impose their standards as to what representations of sex were patently offensive and appealed to the prurient interest in sex. State statutes were directed to be explicit and precise as to the representations of sex to be considered obscene. And the Court directed that no longer must the challenged work be *utterly* without redeeming social value. Rather, a work can be considered legally obscene if the work, taken as a whole, lacks artistic, literary, scientific, or political value. These new standards caused some initial confusion that the Court found necessary to correct the following year in **Jenkins** v. **Georgia.** The Court seemed to be defining obscenity in the realm of "hard-core pornography." The Court clearly was more supportive of efforts to suppress certain sexually oriented material but the Court's policy did not, in fact, result in a nationwide crackdown on the billion-dollar pornography industry. But the legal tools are there if and when public opinion and government officials wish to stifle hard-core pornography (although there surely would be extensive litigation concerning borderline materials or those that were more "soft-core" than "hard-core"). In 1986 the Court was supportive of local officials who used zoning laws to contain and regulate pornography shops and theaters (*City of Renton* v. *Playtime Theatres, Inc.,* 475 U.S. 41). The Court found the zoning ordinance at issue to be content-neutral and a valid time-place-and-manner regulation. The Court also found in *New York* v. *P.J. Video Inc.,* 475 U.S. 868 (1986), that no higher standard of probable cause for the issuance of a search warrant for allegedly obscene videocassettes is needed than for the search and seizure of evidence involving criminal statutes not raising First Amendment issues. And in *Arcara* v. *Cloud Books, Inc.,* 478 U.S. 697 (1986), the Court upheld a New York statute under which an "adult" bookstore was closed for one year when the premises were found to be a public nuisance because they were used for prostitution and lewd behavior (such as masturbation in the "private" projection booths). The Court found that this activity has no element of protected expression and

can justify the closing of a bookstore. However, in *Fort Wayne Books, Inc.* v. *Indiana,* 109 S.Ct. 916 (1989), the Rehnquist Court found that the First Amendment was violated by the padlocking of an adult bookstore and the seizure of its contents prior to a trial determination that the materials were obscene or that racketeering violations had occurred.

With the rise of the women's movement, the obscenity issue assumed a new perspective. The hard-core sex industry has shamelessly exploited and degraded women's bodies, often equating sex and violence. Some civil libertarians have rethought their position on censorship as it applies to these materials and have sought to distinguish erotic, nonsexist sexual material from exploitative, sexist, violent pornography. But this distinction has met with objections from doctrinaire defenders of the First Amendment such as the American Civil Liberties Union, who are fearful that censors are unable to make such distinctions (one person's erotica is another's pornography) and believe, furthermore, that adult members of society should be free to decide for themselves what they wish to read, see, or hear as long as they are not imposing their choices on others or otherwise impinging on another's rights.

There should also be mention of the special status of the broadcast media (radio and television) as distinct from the print media and also from live theater or from motion pictures that are theatrically exhibited. Although the broadcast media, including cable television (see *City of Los Angeles* v. *Preferred Communications,* 476 U.S. 488 [1986]), have First Amendment protection, the airwaves are subject to certain content control in the realm of sex and language by the Federal Communications Commission (FCC). In *FCC* v. *Pacifica Foundation,* 438 U.S. 726 (1978), the Court upheld government regulation of the content of broadcasts found by the FCC to be "indecent but not obscene." The FCC was empowered by Congress in 1988 to crack down on the dial–a–porn industry and this led to the case and decision in **Sable Communications of California, Inc.** v. **FCC** in which the Court allowed regulation of obscene phone messages but not ''indecent'' ones. The Court, in **New York** v. **Ferber,** also treated sympathetically a New York law aimed at the so-called kiddie-porn industry that punished the distributors of sexually oriented materials that used children under the age of 16. Here, too, the materials involved did not have to meet the legal definition of obscenity in order for them to be regulated. Possession of child pornography in the privacy of one's home may be made a state crime, ruled the Court in **Osborne** v. **Ohio** (reprinted at the end of this book). In this case, the Court made a major exception to the *Stanley* v. *Georgia* policy that placed privacy values on a higher plane than regulation of obscenity.

THE IMPACT OF THE COURT'S DECISIONS

Table 14.1 summarizes the impact of selected Court decisions concerning freedom of the press, commercial free speech, and obscenity. The reprinted cases follow.

Table 14.1 THE IMPACT OF SELECTED COURT DECISIONS, FIRST AMENDMENT CASES

Case	Year	Impact on Parties	Short-Run Impact	Long-Run Impact
Near v. *Minnesota*	1931	Injunction lifted. Near able to publish *The Saturday Press*.	Newspapers encouraged to investigate governmental corruption. Decision well received by the press and civil libertarians.	Provided solid precedent for protection of press freedom. Landmark case continually cited in subsequent press freedom cases.
New York Times Co. v. *United States*	1971	*New York Times* and *Washington Post* permitted to publish the Pentagon Papers.	Helped to shift public opinion against the Vietnam War. Embarrassed the Nixon Administration.	First Amendment, free press precedent. Encouraged press and public skepticism of government.
New York Times Co. v. *Sullivan*	1964	*New York Times* did not have to pay L. B. Sullivan $500,000 in damages.	Decision seen as big victory for the press. Decision also a victory for civil rights forces against harassment by their opponents.	By making libel suits more difficult against the press, encouraged more investigative reporting of the actions of public officials.
FCC v. *League of Women Voters of California*	1984	Pacifica Foundation stations begin to broadcast editorials.	Decision seen as victory for press but no discernible impact on the status of public broadcasting.	Uncertain.
Richmond Newspapers, Inc. v. *Virginia*	1980	The press wins on principle, but decision has no effect on original circumstances because trial long over.	Decision praised by press and liberals. Considered by some to be a watershed case.	Uncertain, but has potential for being used as foundation for a liberally construed right of access. First Amendment precedent.
Roth v. *United States; Alberts* v. *California*	1957	Convictions of Roth and Alberts upheld.	Reopened the issue of artistic free expression in the sexual realm.	Landmark case establishing obscenity as outside the pale of First Amendment protection. Attempt at defining obscenity influenced course of future decisions, particularly the criterion of obscenity as being *"utterly* without redeeming social importance."

(continued)

Table 14.1 *(continued)*

Case	Year	Impact on Parties	Short-Run Impact	Long-Run Impact
Memoirs v. Massachusetts	1966	The book *Fanny Hill* judged not obscene. G. P. Putnam's sold a lot of books.	By liberalizing the legal definition of obscenity, which still remained imprecise, the Court provoked much additional litigation. Decision unpopular with political conservatives.	Although severely modified in 1973, still stands as First Amendment precedent on behalf of artistic free speech. Decision played a part in the sexual revolution of the 1960s as the media had greater freedom to deal with matters of sex.
Stanley v. Georgia	1969	Stanley's conviction reversed. Did not have to serve prison sentence.	Reinforced Court's popular image as being pro-pornography. Decision itself had little impact.	Precedent for right to privacy with First Amendment implications. Would seem to offer protection to those possessing and viewing obscene videocassettes in the privacy of their own homes. But in 1990 child pornography was excluded from in-home protection (*Osborne v. Ohio*).
Miller v. California; Paris Adult Theatre I v. Slaton	1973	Miller's misdemeanor conviction upheld. Paris Adult Theatre unaffected.	Emboldened some local officials to crack down on adult theaters and bookstores, but effect of decision temporary and enforcement of similar obscenity statutes spotty.	Little long-run impact as sex industry continues to flourish, particularly as a broad new market of videocassettes opens up, which, ironically, diminishes the business of adult theaters.
Jenkins v. Georgia	1974	Jenkins did not have to pay $750 fine.	By clothing non-hard-core, sexual-oriented material with First Amendment protection, Court tacitly encouraged the continuation of the sexual revolution in the arts.	Decision provoked some confusion as to what is obscene and what are the powers of local communities in this area. As a result of confusion, as well as the continued demand for its product, the pornography business remains a major industry.
New York v. Ferber	1982	Paul Ferber's conviction upheld.	Encouraged crackdown on sex industry's use and abuse of children.	Uncertain. Little evidence that kiddie-porn industry has been permanently damaged.

NEAR v. MINNESOTA,
283 U.S. 697 (1931)

This was the landmark case in which the Supreme Court, by incorporating freedom of the press within the liberty protected by the Fourteenth Amendment's due process clause, invalidated a state statute as violating the free press guarantee. The statute in question was enacted in 1925 by the Minnesota legislature; it provided that any newspaper, magazine, or other periodical publishing "malicious, scandalous and defamatory," or "obscene" matter was a public nuisance that could be abated by a court order forbidding continued publication. Near published a weekly newspaper, The Saturday Press, *that was hysterically anti-Semitic and hurled serious charges of corruption and other wrong-doing on the part of public officials. Under the provisions of the statute, the county attorney successfully brought an action against Near to enjoin publication of his newspaper. The Minnesota courts upheld the constitutionality of the law and the injunction that had been issued.*

Majority votes: 5
Dissenting votes: 4

MR. CHIEF JUSTICE HUGHES delivered the opinion of the Court:

Chapter 285 of the Session Laws of Minnesota for the year 1925 provides for the abatement, as a public nuisance, of a "malicious, scandalous and defamatory newspaper, magazine or other periodical." . . .

This statute, for the suppression as a public nuisance of a newspaper or periodical, is unusual, if not unique, and raises questions of grave importance transcending the local interests involved in the particular action. It is no longer open to doubt that the liberty of the press and of speech, is within the liberty safeguarded by the due process clause of the Fourteenth Amendment from invasion by state action. . . . It is thus important to note precisely the purpose and effect of the statute as the state court has construed it.

First. The statute is not aimed at the redress of individual or private wrongs. Remedies for libel remain available and unaffected. . . . It [the statute] is aimed at the distribution of scandalous matter as "detrimental to public morals and to the general welfare," tending "to disturb the peace of the community" and "to provoke assaults and the commission of crime." In order to obtain an injunction to suppress the future publication of the newspaper or periodical, it is not necessary to prove the falsity of the charges that have been made in the publication

condemned. . . . It is alleged, and the statute requires the allegation, that the publication was "malicious." But, as in prosecutions for libel, there is no requirement of proof by the State of malice in fact as distinguished from malice inferred from the mere publication of the defamatory matter. The judgment in this case proceeded upon the mere proof of publication. The statute permits the defense, not of the truth alone, but only that the truth was published with good motives and for justifiable ends. It is apparent that under the statute the publication is to be regarded as defamatory if it injures reputation, and that it is scandalous if it circulates charges of reprehensible conduct, whether criminal or otherwise, and the publication is thus deemed to invite public reprobation and to constitute a public scandal. . . .

Second. The statute is directed not simply at the circulation of scandalous and defamatory statements with regard to private citizens, but at the continued publication by newspapers and periodicals of charges against public officers of corruption, malfeasance in office, or serious neglect of duty. Such charges by their very nature create a public scandal. They are scandalous and defamatory within the meaning of the statute, which has its normal operation in relation to publications dealing prominently and chiefly with the alleged derelictions of public officers.

Third. The object of the statute is not punishment, in the ordinary sense, but suppression of the offending newspaper or periodical. The reason for the enactment, as the state court has said, is that prosecutions to enforce penal statutes for libel do not result in "efficient repression or suppression of the evils of scandal." Describing the business of publication as a public nuisance, does not obscure the substance of the proceeding which the statute authorizes. It is the continued publication of scandalous and defamatory matter that constitutes the business and the declared nuisance. In the case of public officers, it is the reiteration of charges of official misconduct, and the fact that the newspaper or periodical is principally devoted to that purpose, that exposes it to suppression. In the present instance, the proof was that nine editions of the newspaper or periodical in question were published on successive dates, and that they were chiefly devoted to charges against public officers and in relation to the prevalence and protection of crime. In such a case, these officers are not left to their ordinary remedy in a suit for libel, or the authorities to a prosecution for criminal libel. Under this statute, a publisher of a newspaper or periodical, undertaking to conduct a campaign to expose and to censure official derelictions, and devoting his publication principally to that purpose, must face not simply the possibility of a verdict against him in a suit or prosecution for libel, but a determination that his newspaper or periodical is a public nuisance to be abated, and that this abatement and suppression will follow unless he is prepared with legal evidence to prove the truth of the charges and also to satisfy the court that, in addition to being true, the matter was published with good motives and for justifiable ends.

This suppression is accomplished by enjoining publication and that restraint is the object and effect of the statute. . . .

If we cut through mere details of procedure, the operation and effect of the statute in substance is that public authorities may bring the owner or publisher of a newspaper or periodical before a judge upon a charge of conducting a business of publishing scandalous and defamatory matter—in particular that the matter consists of charges against public officers of official dereliction—and unless the owner or publisher is able and disposed to bring competent evidence to satisfy the judge that the charges are true and are published with good motives and for justifiable ends, his newspaper or periodical is suppressed and further publication is made punishable as a contempt. This is of the essence of censorship.

The question is whether a statute authorizing such proceedings in restraint of publication is consistent with the conception of the liberty of the press as historically conceived and guaranteed. In determining the extent of the constitutional protection, it has been generally, if not universally, considered that it is the chief purpose of the guaranty to prevent restraints upon publication. . . . [I]t is recognized that punishment for the abuse of the liberty accorded to the press is essential to the protection of the public, and that the common law rules that subject the libeler to responsibility for the public offense, as well as for the private injury, are not abolished by the protection extended in our constitutions. The law of criminal libel rests upon that secure foundation. There is also the conceded authority of courts to punish for contempt when publications directly tend to prevent the proper discharge of judicial functions. In the present case, we have no occasion to inquire as to the permissible scope of subsequent punishment. For whatever wrong the appellant has committed or may commit, by his publications, the State appropriately affords both public and private redress by its libel laws. As has been noted, the statute in question does not deal with punishments; it provides for no punishment, except in case of contempt for violation of the court's order, but for suppression and injunction, that is, for restraint upon publication.

The objection has also been made that the principle as to immunity from previous restraint is stated too broadly, if every such restraint is deemed to be prohibited. That is undoubtedly true; the protection even as to previous restraint is not absolutely unlimited. But the limitation has been recognized only in exceptional cases: "When a nation is at war many things that might be said in time of peace are such a hindrance to its effort that their utterance will not be endured so long as men fight and that no Court could regard them as protected by any constitutional right." *Schenck* v. *United States,* 249 U.S. 47, 52. No one would question but that a government might prevent actual obstruction to its recruiting service or the publication of the sailing dates of transports or the number and location of troops. On similar grounds, the primary requirements of decency may be enforced against obscene publications. The security of the community life may be protected against incitements to acts of violence and the overthrow by force of orderly government. . . . These limitations are not applicable here. . . .

. . . [T]he administration of government has become more complex, the opportunities for malfeasance and corruption have multiplied, crime has grown to most serious proportions, and the danger of its protection by unfaithful officials and of the impairment of the fundamental security of life and property by criminal alliances and official neglect, emphasizes the primary need of a vigilant and courageous press, especially in great cities. The fact that the liberty of the press may be abused by miscreant purveyors of scandal does not make any the less necessary the immunity of the press from previous restraint in dealing with official misconduct. Subsequent punishment for such abuses as may exist is the appropriate remedy, consistent with constitutional privilege. . . .

For these reasons we hold the statute . . . to be an infringement of the liberty of the press guaranteed by the Fourteenth Amendment. . . .

Judgment reversed.

MR. JUSTICE BUTLER, dissenting:. . . .

The Minnesota statute does not operate as a *previous* restraint on publication within the proper meaning of that phrase. It does not authorize administrative control in advance such as was formerly exercised by the licensers and censors but prescribes a remedy to be enforced by a suit in equity. In this case there was previous publication made in the course of the business of regularly producing malicious, scandalous and defamatory periodicals. The business and publications unquestionably constitute an abuse of the right of free press.

The statute denounces the things done as a nuisance on the ground, as stated by the state supreme court, that they threaten morals, peace and good order. There is no question of the power of the State to denounce such transgressions. The restraint authorized is only in respect of continuing to do what has been duly adjudged to constitute a nuisance. . . . It is fanciful to suggest similarity between the granting or enforcement of the decree authorized by this statute to prevent *further* publication of malicious, scandalous and defamatory articles and the *previous restraint* upon the press by licensers as referred to by Blackstone and described in the history of the times to which he alludes.

The opinion seems to concede that under clause (a) of the Minnesota law the business of regularly publishing and circulating an obscene periodical may be enjoined as a nuisance. It is difficult to perceive any distinction, having any relation to constitutionality, between clause (a) and clause (b) under which this action was brought. Both nuisances are offensive to morals, order and good government. As that resulting from lewd publications constitutionally may be enjoined it is hard to understand why the one resulting from a regular business of malicious defamation may not.

It is well known, as found by the state supreme court, that existing libel laws are inadequate effectively to suppress evils resulting from the kind of business and publications that are shown in this case. The doctrine that measures such as the one before us are invalid because they operate as previous restraints to infringe freedom of press exposes the peace and good order of every community and the business and private affairs of every individual to the constant and protracted false and malicious assaults of any insolvent publisher who may have purpose and sufficient capacity to contrive and put into effect a scheme or program for oppression, blackmail or extortion.

The judgment should be affirmed.

MR. JUSTICE VAN DEVANTER, MR. JUSTICE MCREYNOLDS, and MR. JUSTICE SUTHERLAND concur in this opinion.

NEW YORK TIMES CO. v. UNITED STATES, 403 U.S. 713 (1971)

This case, better known as the Pentagon Papers Case, was in many ways extraordinary. During the Vietnam War, when opposition to the war was growing, Daniel Ellsberg, a former Pentagon official, gave the New York Times and Washington Post a classified 47-volume study conducted by the Pentagon entitled "History of U.S. Decision Making Process on Viet Nam Policy." The study con-tained memos, letters, and numerous other documents as well as analyses of every step in United States involvement with Vietnam. The newspapers assigned their top reporters to read, digest, and prepare selections and summaries from what became known as the "Pentagon Papers." It took several months for the reporters to prepare the series of articles that the Times began publishing on June 13, 1971. The Washington Post also began publishing articles based on the Pentagon Papers on June 18. Federal government officials quickly reacted by asserting that continued publication would constitute a serious threat to national security. The New York Times was asked voluntarily to stop publishing the articles. When the publisher of the Times refused, government lawyers went to the federal district court in Manhattan, and on June 15 obtained a temporary restraining order preventing the publication of the articles and giving the government time to prepare and present arguments before the judge. After hearing the government's position, the judge on June 19 denied the request for a permanent injunction. The government appealed to the Court of Appeals for the Second Circuit, which immediately heard the appeal and, on June 23, sent the case back to the district judge with instructions to determine whether the publication of any of the particular items in the Pentagon Papers would constitute a grave and immediate threat to the security of the United States. The New York Times then took the case to the Supreme Court. The District of Columbia courts ruled in favor of the Washington Post and the government asked the Court also to hear this case. The Court responded quickly. On June 25, it granted certiorari and, in an unprecedented move, scheduled oral argument for the following day, Saturday, June 26. On June 30 the Court announced its decision and each justice wrote an opinion of his own. The case commenced and went through the entire federal judicial system in a record 18 days.

Majority votes: 6
Dissenting votes: 3

PER CURIAM. . . .

"Any system of prior restraints of expression comes to this Court bearing a heavy presumption against its constitutional validity." *Bantam Books, Inc.* v. *Sullivan*, 372 U.S. 58, 70 (1963); see also *Near* v. *Minnesota ex rel. Olson*, 283 U.S. 697 (1931). The Government "thus carries a heavy burden of showing justification for the imposition of such a restraint." *Organization for a Better Austin* v. *Keefe*, 402 U.S. 415, 419 (1971). The District Court for the Southern District of New York in the

New York Times case, and the District Court for the District of Columbia and the Court of Appeals for the District of Columbia Circuit, in the *Washington Post* case held that the Government had not met that burden. We agree.

The judgment of the Court of Appeals for the District of Columbia Circuit is therefore affirmed. The order of the Court of Appeals for the Second Circuit is reversed, and the case is remanded with directions to enter a judgment affirming the judgment of the District Court for the Southern District of New York. The stays entered June 25, 1971, by the Court are vacated. The judgments shall issue forthwith.

So ordered.

MR. JUSTICE BLACK, with whom MR. JUSTICE DOUGLAS joins, concurring:. . . .

I believe that every moment's continuance of the injunctions against these newspapers amounts to a flagrant, indefensible, and continuing violation of the First Amendment. . . . In my view it is unfortunate that some of my Brethren are apparently willing to hold that the publication of news may sometimes be enjoined. Such a holding would make a shambles of the First Amendment.

Our Government was launched in 1789 with the adoption of the Constitution. The Bill of Rights, including the First Amendment, followed in 1791. Now, for the first time in the 182 years since the founding of the Republic, the federal courts are asked to hold that the First Amendment does not mean what it says, but rather means that the Government can halt the publication of current news of vital importance to the people of this country.

In seeking injunctions against these newspapers and in its presentation to the Court, the Executive Branch seems to have forgotten the essential purpose and history of the First Amendment. . . . Both the history and language of the First Amendment support the view that the press must be free to publish news, whatever the source, without censorship, injunctions, or prior restraints.

In the First Amendment the Founding Fathers gave the free press the protection it must have to fulfill its essential role in our democracy. The press was to serve the governed, not the governors. The Government's power to censor the press was abolished so that the press would remain forever free to censure the Government. . . . In revealing the workings of government that led to the Vietnam war, the newspapers nobly did precisely that which the Founders hoped and trusted they would do. . . .

. . . [W]e are asked to hold that despite the First Amendment's emphatic command, the Executive Branch, the Congress, and the Judiciary can make laws enjoining publication of current news and abridging freedom of the press in the name of "national security." The Government does not even attempt to rely on any act of Congress. Instead it makes the bold and dangerously far-reaching contention that the courts should take it upon themselves to "make" a law abridging freedom of the press in the name of equity, presidential power and national security, even when the representatives of the people in Congress have adhered to the command of the First Amendment and refused to make such a law. . . . To find that the President has "inherent power" to halt the publication of news by resort to the courts would wipe out the First Amendment and destroy the fundamental liberty and security of the very people the Government hopes to make "secure." . . .

MR. JUSTICE DOUGLAS, with whom MR. JUSTICE BLACK joins, concurring:. . . .

The dominant purpose of the First Amendment was to prohibit the widespread practice of governmental suppression of embarrassing information. . . . The present cases will, I think, go down in history as the most dramatic illustration of that principle. A debate of large proportions goes on in the Nation over our posture in Vietnam. That debate antedated the disclosure of the contents of the present documents. The latter are highly relevant to the debate in progress.

Secrecy in government is fundamentally antidemocratic, perpetuating bureaucratic errors. Open debate and discussion of public issues are vital to our national health. On public questions there should be "uninhibited, robust, and wide-open" debate. . . .

The stays in these cases that have been in effect for more than a week constitute a flouting of the principles of the First Amendment as interpreted in *Near* v. *Minnesota ex rel. Olson.*

MR. JUSTICE BRENNAN, concurring:

I write separately in these cases only to emphasize what should be apparent: that our judgments in the present cases may not be taken to indicate the propriety, in the future, of issuing temporary stays and restraining orders to block the publication of material sought to be suppressed by the Government. . . . [T]he First Amendment stands as an absolute bar to the imposition of judicial restraints in circumstances of the kind presented by these cases. . . .

MR. JUSTICE STEWART, with whom MR. JUSTICE WHITE joins, concurring:. . .

[I]t is elementary that the successful conduct of international diplomacy and the maintenance of an effective national defense require both confidentiality and secrecy. Other nations can hardly deal with this Nation in an atmosphere of mutual trust unless they can be assured that their confidences will be kept. And within our own executive departments, the development of considered and intelligent international policies would be impossible if those charge with their formulation could not communicate with each other freely, frankly, and in confidence. In the area of basic national defense the frequent need for absolute secrecy is, of course, self-evident.

I think there can be but one answer to this dilemma, if dilemma it be. The responsibility must be where the power is. If the Constitution gives the Executive a large degree of unshared power in the conduct of foreign affairs and the maintenance of our national defense, then under the Constitution the Executive must have the largely unshared duty to determine and preserve the degree of internal security necessary to exercise that power successfully. It is an awesome responsibility, requiring judgment and wisdom of a high order. I should suppose that moral, political, and practical considerations would dictate that a very first principle of that wisdom would be an insistence upon avoiding secrecy for its own sake. For when everything is classified, then nothing is classified, and the system becomes one to be disregarded by the cynical or the careless, and to be manipulated by those intent on self-protection or self-promotion. I should suppose, in short, that the hallmark of a truly effective internal security system would be the maximum possible disclosure, recognizing that secrecy can best be preserved only when credibility is truly maintained. But be that as it may, it is clear to me that it is the constitutional duty of the Executive—as a matter of sovereign prerogative and not as a matter of law as the courts know law—through the promulgation and enforcement of executive regulations, to protect the confidentiality necessary to carry out its responsibilities in the fields of international relations and national defense.

This is not to say that Congress and the courts have no role to play. Undoubtedly Congress has the power to enact specific and appropriate criminal laws to protect government property and preserve government secrets. Congress has passed such laws, and several of them are of very colorable relevance to the apparent circumstances of these cases. And if a criminal prosecution is instituted, it will be the responsibility of the courts to decide the applicability of the criminal law under which the charge is brought. Moreover, if Congress should pass a specific law authorizing civil proceedings in this field, the courts would likewise have the duty to decide the constitutionality of such a law as well as its applicability to the facts proved.

But in the cases before us we are asked neither to construe specific regulations nor to apply specific laws. We are asked, instead, to perform a function that the Constitution gave to the Executive, not the Judiciary. We are asked, quite simply, to prevent the publication by two newspapers of material that the Executive Branch insists should not, in the national interest, be published. I am convinced that the Executive is correct with respect to some of the documents involved. But I cannot say that disclosure of any of them will surely result in direct, immediate, and irreparable damage to our Nation or its people. That being so, there can under the First Amendment be but one judicial resolution of the issues before us. I join the judgments of the Court.

Mr. Justice White, with whom Mr. Justice Stewart joins, concurring: [omitted]

Mr. Justice Marshall, concurring: [omitted]

Mr. Chief Justice Burger, dissenting:. . . .

These cases are not simple. . . . We do not know the facts of the cases. No District Judge knew all the facts. No Court of Appeals Judge knew all the facts. No member of this Court knows all the facts. . . . An issue of this importance should be tried and heard in a judicial atmosphere conducive to thoughtful, reflective deliberation, especially when haste, in terms of hours, is unwarranted in light of the long period the *Times,* by its own choice, deferred publication. . . .

Mr. Justice Harlan, with whom the Chief Justice and Mr. Justice Blackmun join, dissenting:. . . .

It is plain to me that the scope of the judicial function in passing upon the activities of the Executive Branch of the Government in the field of foreign affairs is very narrowly restricted. This view is, I think, dictated by the concept of separation of powers upon which our constitutional system rests. . . .

Even if there is some room for the judiciary to override the executive determination [of national security], it is plain that the scope of review must be exceedingly narrow. I can see no indication in the opinions of either the District Court or the Court of Appeals in the Post litigation that the conclusions of the Executive were given even the deference owing to an administrative agency, much less that owing to a co-equal branch of the Government operating within the field of its constitutional prerogative.

Accordingly, I would vacate the judgment of the Court of Appeals for the District of Columbia Circuit on this ground and remand the case for further proceedings in the District Court. . . .

MR. JUSTICE BLACKMUN, dissenting:. . . .

. . . I hope that damage has not already been done. If, however, damage has been done, and if, with the Court's action today, these newspapers proceed to publish the critical documents and there results therefrom "the death of soldiers, the destruction of alliances, the greatly increased difficulty of negotiation with our enemies, the inability of our diplomats to negotiate," to which list I might add the factors of prolongation of the war and of further delay in the freeing of United States prisoners, then the Nation's people will know where the responsibility for these sad consequences rests.

NEW YORK TIMES CO. v. SULLIVAN,
376 U.S. 254 (1964)

L. B. Sullivan, an elected Commissioner of Montgomery, Alabama, brought a civil libel action against the New York Times *for having published an advertisement soliciting funds for the civil rights movement. The advertisement alleged various racist actions hostile to the civil rights of black Americans taken by unnamed Alabama officials. Sullivan claimed that as Commissioner his duties included supervision of the Police Department and that the advertisement thus libeled him. The advertisement was published on March 29, 1960, and approximately 394 copies of the newspaper were circulated in the entire state of Alabama. The total circulation of the* Times *for that day was about 650,000 copies. An Alabama jury agreed with Sullivan that he was libeled under the definition of libel according to Alabama law and awarded him $500,000. The Supreme Court of Alabama affirmed and the case came to the United States Supreme Court. The suit had originated at a crucial turning point in the civil rights struggle when southern white opposition to the racial equality demands of blacks turned to violence. Some southern whites blamed outsiders from the North for stirring up discontent with the southern way of life. The* New York Times *was clearly a symbol for these whites of northern white establishment holier-than-thou troublemakers, and the charges made in the advertisement, some of which were indeed inaccurate, were seen as typical of the fuel added to the fires of discontent. Sullivan's lawsuit therefore assumed an importance in Alabama far exceeding an individual public official's concern with his reputation. The suit was seen as the white South fighting back against those intent on forcing unwanted change on the region.*

Votes: Unanimous

MR. JUSTICE BRENNAN delivered the opinion of the Court:. . . .

The question before us is whether [the Alabama libel law] . . . as applied to an action brought by a public official against critics of his official conduct, abridges the freedom of speech and of the press that is guaranteed by the First and Fourteenth Amendments.

Respondent relies heavily, as did the Alabama courts, on statements of this Court to the effect that the Constitution does not protect libelous publications. Those statements do not foreclose our inquiry here. None of the cases sustained the use of libel laws to impose sanctions upon expression critical of the official conduct of public officials. . . . In the only previous case that did present the question of constitutional limitations upon the power to award damages for libel of a public official, the Court was equally divided and the question was not decided. *Schenectady Union Pub. Co.* v. *Sweeney*, 316 U.S. 642. In deciding the question now, we are compelled by neither precedent nor policy to give any more weight to the epithet "libel" than we have to other "mere labels" of state law. Like insurrection, contempt, advocacy of unlawful acts, breach of the peace, obscenity, solicitation of legal business, and the various other formulae for the repression of expression that have been challenged in this court, libel can claim no talismanic immunity from constitutional limitations. It must be measured by standards that satisfy the First Amendment.

The general proposition that freedom of expression upon public questions is secured by the First Amendment has long been settled by our decisions. . . . Thus we consider this case against the background of a profound national commitment to the principle that debate on public issues should be uninhibited, robust, and wide-open, and that it may well include vehement, caustic, and sometimes unpleasantly sharp attacks on government and public officials.

The present advertisement, as an expression of grievance and protest on one of the major public issues of our time, would seem clearly to qualify for the constitutional protection. The question is whether it forfeits that protection by the falsity of some of its factual statements and by its alleged defamation of respondent.

Authoritative interpretations of the First Amendment guarantees have consistently refused to recognize an exception for any test of truth—whether administered by judges, juries, or administrative officials—and especially one that puts the burden of proving truth on the speaker. The constitutional protection does not turn upon "the truth, popularity, or social utility of the ideas and beliefs which are offered." As Madison said, "Some degree of abuse is inseparable from the proper use of every thing; and in no instance is this more true than in that of the press." . . . [E]rroneous statement is inevitable in free debate, and it must be protected if the freedoms of expression are to have the "breathing space" that they "need . . . to survive." . . .

Injury to official reputation affords no more warrant for repressing speech that would otherwise be free than does factual error. Where judicial officers are involved, this Court has held that concern for the dignity and reputation of the courts does not justify the punishment as criminal contempt of criticism of the judge or his decision. *Bridges* v. *California*, 314 U.S. 252. This is true even though the utterance contains "half-truths" and "misinformation." Such repression can be justified, if at all, only by a clear and present danger of the obstruction of justice. . . .

If neither factual error nor defamatory contents suffices to remove the constitutional shield from criticism of official conduct, the combination of the two elements is no less inadequate. This is the lesson to be drawn from the great controversy over the Sedition Act of 1798 which first crystallized a national awareness of the central meaning of the First Amendment. . . . That statute made it a crime punishable by a $5,000 fine and five years in prison, "if any person shall write, print, utter, or publish . . . any false, scandalous and malicious writing or writings against the government of the United States, or either house of the Congress . . . , or the President . . . , with intent to defame . . . or to bring them, or either of them, into contempt or disrepute; or to excite against them, or either or any of them, the hatred of the good people of the United States." The Act allowed the defendant the defense of truth, and provided that the jury were to be judges both of the law and the facts. Despite these qualifications, the Act was vigorously condemned as unconstitutional in an attack joined in by Jefferson and Madison. . . .

Although the Sedition Act was never tested in this Court, the attack upon its validity has carried the day in the court of history. Fines levied in its prosecution were repaid by Act of Congress on the ground that it was unconstitutional. See, *e.g.,* Act of July 4, 1840, c. 45, 6 Stat. 802, accompanied by H.R. Rep. No. 86, 26th Cong., 1st Sess. (1840). Calhoun, reporting to the Senate on February 4, 1836, assumed that its invalidity was a matter "which no one now doubts." Jefferson, as President, pardoned those who had been convicted and sentenced under the Act and remitted their fines, stating: "I discharged every person under punishment or prosecution under the sedition law, because I considered, and now consider, that law to be a nullity, as absolute and as palpable as if Congress had ordered us to fall down and worship a golden image." The invalidity of the Act has also been assumed by Justices of this Court. . . . These views reflect a broad consensus that the Act, because of the restraint it imposed upon criticism of government and public officials, was inconsistent with the First Amendment. . . .

What a state may not constitutionally bring about by means of a criminal statute is likewise beyond the reach of its civil law of libel. The fear of damage awards under a rule such as that invoked by the Alabama courts here may be markedly more inhibiting than the fear of prosecution under a criminal statute. . . .

The state rule of law is not saved by its allowance of the defense of truth. . . . A rule compelling the critic of official conduct to guarantee the truth of all his factual assertions—and to do so on pain of libel judgments virtually unlimited in amount—leads to a comparable "self-censorship." Allowance of the defense of truth, with the burden of proving it on the defendant, does not mean that only false speech will be deterred. Even courts accepting this defense as an adequate safeguard have recognized the difficulties of adducing legal proofs that the alleged libel was true in all its factual particulars. Under such a rule, would-be critics of official conduct may be deterred from voicing their criticism, even though it is believed to be true and even though it is in fact true, because of doubt whether it can be proved in court or fear of the expense of having to do so. They tend to make only statements which "steer far wider of the unlawful zone." The rule thus dampens the vigor and limits the variety of public debate. It is inconsistent with the First and Fourteenth Amendments.

The constitutional guarantees require, we think, a federal rule that prohibits a public official from recovering damages for a defamatory falsehood relating to his official conduct unless he proves that the statement was made with "actual malice"—that is, with knowledge that it was false or with reckless disregard of whether it was false or not. . . .

Such a privilege for criticism of official conduct is appropriately analogous to the protection accorded a public official when he is sued for libel by a private citizen. In *Barr* v. *Matteo,* 360 U.S. 564, 575, this Court held the utterance of a federal official to be absolutely privileged if made "within the outer perimeter'' of his duties. The States accord the same immunity to statements of their highest officers, although some differentiate their lesser officials and qualify the privilege they enjoy. But all hold that all officials are protected unless actual malice can be proved. The reason for the official privilege is said to be that the threat of damage suits would otherwise "inhibit the fearless, vigorous, and effective administration of policies of government" and "dampen the ardor of all but the most resolute, or the most irresponsible, in the unflinching discharge of their duties." Analogous considerations support the privilege for the citizen-critic of government. It is as much his duty to criticize as it is the official's duty to administer. . . . It would give public servants an unjustified preference over the public they serve, if critics of official conduct did not have a fair equivalent of the immunity granted to the officials themselves.

We conclude that such a privilege is required by the First and Fourteenth Amendments.

We hold today that the Constitution delimits a State's power to award damages for libel in actions brought by public officials against critics of their official conduct. Since this is such an action, the rule requiring proof of actual malice is applicable. . . .

Applying these standards, we consider that the proof presented to show actual malice lacks the convincing clarity which the constitutional standard demands, and hence that it would not constitutionally sustain the judgment for respondent under the proper rule of law. . . . The statement by the *Times'* Secretary that he thought the advertisement was "substantially correct," affords no constitutional warrant for the Alabama Supreme Court's conclusion. . . . The statement does not indicate malice at the time of the publication; even if the advertisement was not "substantially correct"—although respondent's own proofs tend to show that it was—that opinion was at least a reasonable one, and there was no evidence to impeach the witness' good faith in holding it. . . . [T]here is evidence that the *Times* published the advertisement without checking its accuracy against the news stories in the *Times'* own files. The mere presence of the stories in the files does not, of course, establish that the *Times* "knew" the advertisement was false, since the state of mind required for actual malice would have to be brought home to the persons in the *Times'* organization having responsibility for the publication of the advertisement. . . . We think the evidence against the *Times* supports at most a finding of negligence in failing to discover the misstatements, and is constitutionally insufficient to

show the recklessness that is required for a finding of actual malice. . . .

We also think the evidence was constitutionally defective in another respect: it was incapable of supporting the jury's finding that the allegedly libelous statements were made "of and concerning" respondent. . . . There was no reference to respondent in the advertisement, either by name or official position. . . .

There is no legal alchemy by which a State may thus create the cause of action that would otherwise be denied for a publication which, as respondent himself said of the advertisement, "reflects not only on me but on the other Commissioners and the community." Raising as it does the possibility that a good-faith critic of government will be penalized for his criticism, the proposition relied on by the Alabama courts strikes at the very center of the constitutionally protected area of free expression. We hold that such a proposition may not constitutionally be utilized to establish that an otherwise impersonal attack on governmental operations was a libel of an official responsible for those operations. . . .

Reversed and remanded.

MR. JUSTICE BLACK, with whom MR. JUSTICE DOUGLAS joins, concurring:

. . . I base my vote to reverse on the belief that the First and Fourteenth Amendments not merely "delimit" a State's power to award damages to "public officials against critics of their official conduct" but completely prohibit a State from exercising such a power. The Court goes on to hold that a State can subject such critics to damages if "actual malice" can be proved against them. "Malice," even as defined by the Court, is an elusive, abstract concept, hard to prove and hard to disprove . . . and certainly does not measure up to the sturdy safeguard embodied in the First Amendment. Unlike the Court, therefore, I vote to reverse exclusively on the ground that the *Times* and the individual defendants had an absolute, unconditional constitutional right to publish in the *Times* advertisement their criticisms of the Montgomery agencies and officials. . . . An unconditional right to say what one pleases about public affairs is what I consider to be the minimum guarantee of the First Amendment.

I regret that the Court has stopped short of this holding indispensable to preserve our free press from destruction.

MR. JUSTICE GOLDBERG, with whom MR. JUSTICE DOUGLAS joins, concurring in the result:

. . . In my view, the First and Fourteenth Amendments to the Constitution afford to the citizen and to the press an absolute, unconditional privilege to criticize official conduct despite the harm which may flow from excesses and abuses. . . . The right should not depend upon a probing by the jury of the motivation of the citizen or press. . . . It necessarily follows that in a case such as this, where all agree that the allegedly defamatory statements related to official conduct, the judgments for libel cannot constitutionally be sustained.

FCC v. LEAGUE OF WOMEN VOTERS OF CALIFORNIA, 468 U.S. 364 (1984)

The Public Broadcasting Act of 1967 established the Corporation for Public Broadcasting (CPB) to financially support noncommercial public radio and television stations. Under section 399 of the act, stations receiving government grants were forbidden to editorialize. Pacifica Foundation, a nonprofit corporation that owns and operates several noncommercial educational broadcasting stations that receive grants from the CPB, brought suit in federal district court along with the League of Women Voters of California and an individual listener and viewer of public broadcasting. The suit challenged the constitutionality of section 399 as a violation of the First Amendment. The district court agreed with the challengers of section 399 that it violated the Constitution, and the case came before the Supreme Court.

Majority votes: 5
Dissenting votes: 4

JUSTICE BRENNAN delivered the opinion of the Court:. . . .

In seeking to defend the prohibition on editorializing imposed by §399, the Government urges that the statute was aimed at preventing two principal threats to the overall success of the Public Broadcasting Act of 1967. According to this argument, the ban was necessary, first, to protect noncommercial educational broadcasting stations from being coerced, as a result of federal financing, into becoming vehicles for government propagandizing or the objects of governmental influence; and, second, to keep these stations from becoming convenient targets for capture by private interest groups wishing to express their own partisan viewpoints. By seeking to safeguard the public's right to a balanced presentation of public issues through the prevention of either governmental or private bias,

these objectives are, of course, broadly consistent with the goals identified in our earlier broadcast regulation cases. But, in sharp contrast to the restrictions upheld in *Red Lion* or in *Columbia Broadcasting System, Inc.* v. *FCC*, which left room for editorial discretion and simply required broadcast editors to grant others access to the microphone, §399 directly prohibits the broadcaster from speaking out on public issues even in a balanced and fair manner. The Government insists, however, that the hazards posed in the "special" circumstances of noncommercial educational broadcasting are so great that §399 is an indispensable means of preserving the public's First Amendment interests. We disagree.

When Congress first decided to provide financial support for the expansion and development of noncommercial educational stations, all concerned agreed that this step posed some risk that these traditionally independent stations might be pressured into becoming forums devoted solely to programming and views that were acceptable to the Federal government. That Congress was alert to these dangers cannot be doubted. It sought through the Public Broadcasting Act to fashion a system that would provide local stations with sufficient funds to foster their growth and development while preserving their tradition of autonomy and community-orientation. A cardinal objective of the Act was the establishment of a private corporation that would "facilitate the development of educational radio and television broadcasting and . . . afford maximum protection to such broadcasting from extraneous interference and control."

The intended role of §399 in achieving these purposes, however, is not as clear. The provision finds no antecedent in the Carnegie Report, which generally provided the model for most other aspects of the Act. It was not part of the Administration's original legislative proposal. And it was not included in the original version of the Act passed by the Senate. The provision found its way into the Act only as a result of an amendment in the House. Indeed, it appears that, as the House Committee Report frankly admits, §399 was added not because Congress thought it was essential to preserving the autonomy and vitality of local stations, but rather "out of an abundance of caution." . . .

In sum, §399's broad ban on all editorializing by every station that receives CPB funds far exceeds what is necessary to protect against the risk of governmental interference or to prevent the public from assuming that editorials by public broadcasting stations represent the official view of government. The regulation impermissibly sweeps within its prohibition a wide range of speech by wholly private stations on topics that do not take a directly partisan stand or that have nothing whatever to do with federal, state or local government.

Assuming that the Government's second asserted interest in preventing noncommercial stations from becoming a "privileged outlet for the political and ideological opinions of station owners and management," is legitimate, the substantiality of this asserted interest is dubious. The patent over- and underinclusiveness of §399's ban "undermines the likelihood of a genuine [governmental] interest" in preventing private groups from propagating their own views via public broadcasting. If it is true, as the government contends, that noncommercial stations remain free, despite §399, to broadcast a wide variety of controversial views through their power to control program selection, to select which persons will be interviewed, and to determine how news reports will be presented, then it seems doubtful that §399 can fairly be said to advance any genuinely substantial government interest in keeping controversial or partisan opinions from being aired by noncommercial stations. Indeed, since the very same opinions that cannot be expressed by the station's management may be aired so long as they are communicated by a commentator or by a guest appearing at the invitation of the station during an interview, §399 clearly "provides only ineffective and remote support for the government's purpose." . . .

Finally, the public's interest in preventing public broadcasting stations from becoming forums for lopsided presentations of narrow partisan positions is already secured by a variety of other regulatory means that intrude far less drastically upon the "journalistic freedom" of noncommercial broadcasters. The requirements of the FCC's fairness doctrine, for instance, which apply to commercial and noncommercial stations alike, ensure that such editorializing would maintain a reasonably balanced and fair presentation of controversial issues. Thus, even if the management of a noncommercial educational station were inclined to seek to further only its own partisan views when editorializing, it simply could not do so. . . . Rather than requiring noncommercial broadcasters who express editorial opinions on controversial subjects to permit more speech on such subjects to ensure that the public's First Amendment interest in receiving a balanced account of the issue is met, §399 simply silences all editorial speech by such broadcasters. Since the breadth of §399 extends so far beyond what is necessary to accomplish the goals identified by the Government, it fails to satisfy the First Amendment standards that we have applied in this area.

We therefore hold that even if some of the hazards at which §399 was aimed are sufficiently substantial, the restriction is not crafted with sufficient precision to remedy those dangers that may exist to justify the significant abridgement of speech worked by the provision's broad ban on editorializing. The statute is not narrowly tailored to address any of the government's suggested goals. Moreover, the public's "paramount right" to be fully and broadly informed on matters of public importance through the medium of noncommercial educational broadcasting is not well served by the restriction, for its effect is plainly to diminish rather than augment "the volume and quality of coverage" of controversial issues. Nor do we see any reason to deny noncommercial broadcasters the right to address matters of public concern on the basis of merely speculative fears of adverse public or governmental reactions to such speech. . . .

In conclusion, we emphasize that our disposition of this case rests upon a narrow proposition. We do not hold that the Congress or the FCC are without power to regulate the content, timing, or character of speech by noncommercial educational broadcasting stations. Rather, we hold only that the specific interests sought to be advanced by §399's ban on editorializing are either not sufficiently substantial or are not served in a sufficiently limited manner to justify the substantial abridgement of important journalistic freedoms which the First Amendment jealously protects. Accordingly, the judgment of the District Court is

Affirmed.

JUSTICE REHNQUIST, with whom CHIEF JUSTICE BURGER and JUSTICE WHITE join, dissenting:

All but three paragraphs of the Court's lengthy opinion in this case are devoted to the development of a scenario in which the government appears as the "Big Bad Wolf," and the appellee Pacifica [Foundation] as "Little Red Riding Hood." In the Court's scenario the Big Bad Wolf cruelly forbids Little Red Riding Hood from taking to her grandmother some of the food that she is carrying in her basket. Only three paragraphs are used to delineate a truer picture of the litigants, wherein it appears that some of the food in the basket was given to Little Red Riding Hood by the Big Bad Wolf himself, and that the Big Bad Wolf had told Little Red Riding Hood in advance that if she accepted his food she would have to abide by his conditions. Congress in enacting §399 of the Public Broadcasting Act . . . has simply determined that public funds shall not be used to subsidize noncommercial, educational broadcasting stations which engage in "editorializing" or which support or oppose any political candidate. I do not believe that anything in the First Amendment to the United States Constitution prevents Congress from choosing to spend public monies in that manner. Perhaps a more appropriate analogy than that of Little Red Riding Hood and the Big Wolf is that of Faust and Mephistopheles; Pacifica, well aware of §399's condition on its receipt of public money, nonetheless accepted the public money and now seeks to avoid the conditions which Congress legitimately has attached to receipt of that funding. . . .

JUSTICE STEVENS, dissenting:

The court jester who mocks the King must choose his words with great care. An artist is likely to paint a flattering portrait of his patron. The child who wants a new toy does not preface his request with a comment on how fat his mother is. Newspaper publishers have been known to listen to their advertising managers. Elected officials may remember how their elections were financed. By enacting the statutory provision that the Court invalidates today, a sophisticated group of legislators expressed a concern about the potential impact of government funds on pervasive and powerful organs of mass communication. One need not have heard the raucous voice of Adolph Hitler over Radio Berlin to appreciate the importance of that concern. . . .

RICHMOND NEWSPAPERS, INC. v. VIRGINIA, 448 U.S. 555 (1980)

A criminal defendant tried in the Circuit Court of Hanover County, Virginia, for killing a hotel manager was convicted of second-degree murder, but the Virginia Supreme Court reversed, holding that a blood-stained shirt purportedly belonging to the defendant was improperly admitted into evidence. He was retried in the same court, but the second trial ended in a mistrial. A third trial did not make much progress when it, too, was terminated in a mistrial, for a prospective juror who had read about the previous trials informed other prospective jurors about the case. At the start of the fourth trial, two newspaper reporters for Richmond Newspapers, Inc., were present in the courtroom. Counsel for the defendant moved that the trial be closed to the public, and the prosecutor indicated no objection. The judge, asserting that he was empowered by Virginia law, ordered the closure of the trial. Later that day Richmond Newspapers, Inc., sought a hearing on a motion to vacate the judge's order. The hearing itself was closed to the press and the judge denied the motion. When the closed trial resumed the next day, defense counsel moved

that the judge strike the state's evidence—which he did and then proceeded to find the accused "not guilty." Richmond Newspapers, Inc., appealed the trial court's closure order to the Virginia Supreme Court, but the petition for appeal was denied. Appeal was then taken to the Supreme Court. Note that just one year earlier in Gannett Co., Inc. v. DePasquale, 443 U.S. 368 (1979), the Court in a 5–4 decision ruled that members of the public have no Sixth Amendment right to attend criminal trials and pretrial proceedings. This ruling produced a roar of disapproval from the nation's press. Now, in the context of intense criticism of Gannett, the Court came to grips with the First Amendment issue of public and press access to criminal judicial proceedings.

Majority votes: 7
Dissenting votes: 1

MR. CHIEF JUSTICE BURGER announced the judgment of the Court and delivered an opinion in which MR. JUSTICE WHITE and MR. JUSTICE STEVENS joined:

The narrow question presented in this case is whether the right of the public and press to attend criminal trials is guaranteed under the United States Constitution. . . .

In prior cases the Court has treated questions involving conflicts between publicity and a defendant's right to a fair trial. . . . But here for the first time the Court is asked to decide whether a criminal trial itself may be closed to the public upon the unopposed request of a defendant, without any demonstration that closure is required to protect the defendant's superior right to a fair trial, or that some other overriding consideration requires closure.

The origins of the proceeding which has become the modern criminal trial in Anglo-American justice can be tracked back beyond reliable historical records. We need not here review all details of its development. . . . What is significant for present purposes is that throughout its evolution, the trial has been open to all who cared to observe. . . .

We have found nothing to suggest that the presumptive openness of the trial, which English courts were later to call "one of the essential qualities of a court of justice," was not also an attribute of the judicial systems of colonial America. In Virginia, for example, such records as there are of early criminal trials indicate that they were open, and nothing to the contrary has been cited. . . .

Despite the history of criminal trials being presumptively open since long before the Constitution, the State presses its contention that neither the Constitution nor the Bill of Rights contains any provision which by its terms guarantees to the public the right to attend criminal trials. Standing alone, this is correct, but there remains the question whether, absent an explicit provision, the Constitution affords protection against exclusion of the public from criminal trials. . . .

The Bill of Rights was enacted against the backdrop of the long history of trials being presumptively open. Public access to trials was then regarded as an important aspect of the process itself. . . . In guaranteeing freedoms such as those of speech and press, the First Amendment can be read as protecting the right of everyone to attend trials so as to give meaning to those explicit guarantees. . . . Free speech carries with it some freedom to listen. "In a variety of contexts this Court has referred to a First Amendment right to 'receive information and ideas.' " *Kleindienst* v. *Mandel,* 408 U.S. 753, 762 (1972). What this means in the context of trials is that the First Amendment guarantees of speech and press, standing alone, prohibit government from summarily closing courtroom doors which had long been open to the public at the time that amendment was adopted. "For the First Amendment does not speak equivocally. . . . It must be taken as a command of the broadest scope that explicit language, read in the context of a liberty-loving society, will allow." *Bridges* v. *California,* 314 U.S. 252, 263 (1941).

It is not crucial whether we describe this right to attend criminal trials to hear, see, and communicate observations concerning them as a "right of access," or a "right to gather information," for we have recognized that "without some protection for seeking out the news, freedom of the press could be eviscerated." *Branzburg* v. *Hayes,* 408 U.S. 665, 681 (1972). The explicit guaranteed rights to speak and to publish concerning what takes place at a trial would lose much meaning if access to observe the trial could, as it was here, be foreclosed arbitrarily. . . .

We hold that the right to attend criminal trials is implicit in the guarantees of the First Amendment; without the freedom to attend such trials, which people have exercised for centuries, important aspects of freedom of speech and "of the press could be eviscerated." . . .

Having concluded there was a guaranteed right of the public under the First and Fourteenth Amendments to attend the trial of [the defendant in this case] . . . we return to the closure order challenged by appellants. . . . Despite the fact that this was the fourth trial of the accused, the trial judge made no findings to support closure; no inquiry was made as to whether alternative solutions would have met the need to ensure fairness; there was no recognition of any right under the Constitution for the public or press to attend the trial. In contrast to the pretrial proceeding dealt with in *Gannett,* there exist in the context of the trial itself various tested alternatives to satisfy the constitutional demands of fairness. There was no suggestion that any problems with witnesses could not have been dealt with by their exclusion from the courtroom or their sequestration during the trial. Nor is there anything to indicate that sequestration of the jurors would not have guarded against their being subjected to any improper information. All of the alternatives admittedly present difficulties for trial courts, but none of the factors relied on here was beyond the realm of the manageable. Absent an overriding interest articulated in findings, the trial of a criminal case must be open to the public. Accordingly, the judgment under review is reversed.

Reversed.

MR. JUSTICE POWELL took no part in the consideration or decision of this case.

MR. JUSTICE WHITE, concurring:

This case would have been unnecessary had *Gannett Co.* v. *DePasquale* construed the Sixth Amendment to forbid excluding the public from criminal proceedings except in narrowly defined circumstances. But the Court there rejected the submission of four of us to this effect, thus requiring that the First Amendment issue involved here be addressed. On this issue, I concur in the opinion of the Chief Justice.

MR. JUSTICE STEVENS, concurring:

This is a watershed case. Until today the Court has accorded virtually absolute protection to the dissemination of information or ideas, but never before has it squarely held that the acquisition of newsworthy matter is entitled to any constitutional protection whatsoever. . . . Today, . . . for the first time, the Court unequivocally holds that an arbitrary interference with access to important information is an abridgment of the freedoms of speech and of the press protected by the First Amendment. . . .

MR. JUSTICE BRENNAN, with whom MR. JUSTICE MARSHALL joins, concurring in the judgment:. . . .

Because I believe that the First Amendment—of itself and as applied to the States through the Fourteenth Amendment—secures . . . a public right of access, I agree with those of my Brethren who hold that, without more, agreement of the trial judge and the parties cannot constitutionally close a trial to the public. . . .

MR. JUSTICE STEWART, concurring in the judgment:. . . .

. . . Just as a legislature may impose reasonable time, place, and manner restrictions upon the exercise of First Amendment freedoms, so may a trial judge impose reasonable limitations upon the unrestricted occupation of a courtroom by representatives of the press and members of the public. Much more than a city street, a trial courtroom must be a quiet and orderly place. Moreover, every courtroom has a finite physical capacity, and there may be occasions when not all who wish to attend a trial may do so. And while there exist many alternative ways to satisfy the constitutional demands of a fair trial, those demands may also sometimes justify limitations upon the unrestricted presence of spectators in the courtroom.

Since in the present case the trial judge appears to have given no recognition to the right of representatives of the press and members of the public to be present at the Virginia murder trial over which he was presiding, the judgment under review must be reversed. . . .

MR. JUSTICE BLACKMUN, concurring in the judgment:. . . .

The Court's ultimate ruling in *Gannett*, with such clarification as is provided by the opinions in this case today, apparently is now to the effect that there is no *Sixth* Amendment right on the part of the public—or the press—to an open hearing on a motion to suppress. I, of course, continue to believe that *Gannett* was in error, both in its interpretation of the Sixth Amendment generally, and in its application to the suppression hearing, for I remain convinced that the right to a public trial is to be found where the Constitution explicitly placed it—in the Sixth Amendment. . . .

Having said all this, and with the Sixth Amendment set to one side in this case, I am driven to conclude, as a secondary position, that the First Amendment must provide some measure of protection for public access to the trial. . . . It is clear and obvious to me, on the approach the Court has chosen to take, that by closing this criminal trial, the trial judge abridged these First Amendment interests of the public. . . .

MR. JUSTICE REHNQUIST, dissenting: [omitted]

HAZELWOOD SCHOOL DIST. v.
KUHLMEIER,
484 U.S. 260 (1988)

Cathy Kuhlmeier and two other former students of Hazelwood East High School began the litigation. During the 1982–1983 school year they were *staff members of* Spectrum, *the school newspaper, which was written and edited by the Journalism II class at the high school and published and distributed about every three weeks. The practice was for the journalism teacher to submit page proofs of each issue of the newspaper to the principal, Robert E. Reynolds, for his review prior to publication. On May 10, 1983, Reynolds received the page proofs for the May 13 issue. Reynolds objected to two of the articles, one of which described three Hazelwood East students' experiences with pregnancy and another which discussed the impact of divorce on students at the school. His objections to the pregnancy article were that the pregnant students, although not named, might be identified from the text, and that the article's references to sexual activity and birth control were inappropriate for some of the younger students. The principal objected to the divorce article because he felt that the parents of one of the students quoted in the article should have been given an opportunity to respond to the remarks. Believing that there was no time to make the necessary changes in the articles if the paper was to be issued before the end of the school year, Reynolds directed that the two pages on which the articles appeared (which also contained other unobjectionable articles) be withheld from publication. He informed his superiors, including officials of the Hazelwood school district, of the decision, and they approved. Ms. Kuhlmeier and two of her colleagues subsequently sued in federal district court seeking a declaration that their First Amendment rights had been violated and asking for injunctive relief and monetary damages. The district judge ruled that no First Amendment violation had occurred and the students appealed. The Court of Appeals for the Eighth Circuit reversed. The school officials in turn went to the United States Supreme Court, which granted certiorari.*

Majority votes: 5
Dissenting votes: 3
[one vacancy on the Court]

JUSTICE WHITE delivered the opinion of the Court:

This case concerns the extent to which educators may exercise editorial control over the contents of a high school newspaper produced as part of the school's journalism curriculum. . . .

The question whether the First Amendment requires a school to tolerate particular student speech—the question that we addressed in *Tinker* [v. Des Moines Independent Community School Dist., 393 U.S. 503 (1969)]—is different from the question whether the First Amendment requires a school affirmatively to promote particular student speech. The former question addresses educators' ability to silence a student's personal expression that happens to occur on the school premises. The latter question concerns educators' authority over school-sponsored publications, theatrical productions, and other expressive activities that students, parents, and members of the public might reasonably perceive to bear the imprimatur of the school. These activities may fairly be characterized as part of the school curriculum, whether or not they occur in a traditional classroom setting, so long as they are supervised by faculty members and designed to impart particular knowledge or skills to student participants and audiences.

Educators are entitled to exercise greater control over this second form of student expression to assure that participants learn whatever lessons the activity is designed to teach, that readers or listeners are not exposed to material that may be inappropriate for their level of maturity, and that the views of the individual speaker are not erroneously attributed to the school. Hence, a school may in its capacity as publisher of a school newspaper or producer of a school play "disassociate itself," not only from speech that would "substantially interfere with [its] work . . . or impinge upon the rights of other students," but also from speech that is, for example, ungrammatical, poorly written, inadequately researched, biased or prejudiced, vulgar or profane, or unsuitable for immature audiences. A school must be able to set high standards for the student speech that is disseminated under its auspices—standards that may be higher than those demanded by some newspaper publishers or theatrical producers in the "real" world—and may refuse to disseminate student speech that does not meet those standards. In addition, a school must be able to take into account the emotional maturity of the intended audience in determining whether to disseminate student speech on potentially sensitive topics, which might range from the existence of Santa Claus in an elementary school setting to the particulars of teenage sexual activity in a high school setting. A school must also retain the authority to refuse to sponsor student speech that might reasonably be perceived to advocate drug or alcohol use, irresponsible sex, or conduct otherwise inconsistent with "the shared values of a civilized social order," or to associate the school with any position other than neutrality on matters of political controversy. Otherwise, the schools would be unduly constrained from fulfilling their role as "a principal instrument in awakening the child to cultural values, in preparing him for later profes-

sional training, and in helping him to adjust normally to his environment."

Accordingly, we conclude that the standard articulated in *Tinker* for determining when a school may punish student expression need not also be the standard for determining when a school may refuse to lend its name and resources to the dissemination of student expression. Instead, we hold that educators do not offend the First Amendment by exercising editorial control over the style and content of student speech in school-sponsored expressive activities so long as their actions are reasonably related to legitimate pedagogical concerns. . . .

We also conclude that Principal Reynolds acted reasonably in requiring the deletion from the May 13 issue of Spectrum of the pregnancy article, the divorce article, and the remaining articles that were to appear on the same pages of the newspaper.

The initial paragraph of the pregnancy article declared that "[a]ll names have been changed to keep the identity of these girls a secret." The principal concluded that the students' anonymity was not adequately protected, however, given the other identifying information in the article and the small number of pregnant students at the school. Indeed, a teacher at the school credibly testified that she could positively identify at least one of the girls and possibly all three. It is likely that many students at Hazelwood East would have been at least as successful in identifying the girls. Reynolds therefore could reasonably have feared that the article violated whatever pledge of anonymity had been given to the pregnant students. In addition, he could reasonably have been concerned that the article was not sufficiently sensitive to the privacy interests of the students' boyfriends and parents, who were discussed in the article but who were given no opportunity to consent to its publication or to offer a response. The article did not contain graphic accounts of sexual activity. The girls did comment in the article, however, concerning their sexual histories and their use or nonuse of birth control. It was not unreasonable for the principal to have concluded that such frank talk was inappropriate in a school-sponsored publication distributed to 14-year-old freshmen and presumably taken home to be read by students' even younger brothers and sisters. . . .

In sum, we cannot reject as unreasonable Principal Reynolds' conclusion that neither the pregnancy article nor the divorce article was suitable for publication in Spectrum. Reynolds could reasonably have concluded that the students who had written and edited these articles had not sufficiently mastered those portions of the Journalism II curriculum that pertained to the treatment of controversial issues and personal attacks, the need to protect the privacy of individuals whose most intimate concerns are to be revealed in the newspaper, and "the legal, moral, and ethical restrictions imposed upon journalists within [a] school community" that includes adolescent subjects and readers. Finally, we conclude that the principal's decision to delete two pages of Spectrum, rather than to delete only the offending articles or to require that they be modified, was reasonable under the circumstances as he understood them. Accordingly, no violation of First Amendment rights occurred.

The judgment of the Court of Appeals for the Eighth Circuit is therefore

Reversed.

JUSTICE BRENNAN, with whom JUSTICE MARSHALL and JUSTICE BLACKMUN join, dissenting:

When the young men and women of Hazelwood East High School registered for Journalism II, they expected a civics lesson. Spectrum, the newspaper they were to publish, "was not just a class exercise in which students learned to prepare papers and hone writing skills, it was a . . . forum established to give students an opportunity to express their views while gaining an appreciation of their rights and responsibilities under the First Amendment to the United States Constitution. . . ." "[A]t the beginning of each school year," the student journalists published a Statement of Policy—tacitly approved each year by school authorities—announcing their expectation that "*Spectrum,* as a student-press publication, accepts all rights implied by the First Amendment. . . . Only speech that 'materially and substantially interferes with the requirements of appropriate discipline' can be found unacceptable and therefore prohibited."

The school board itself affirmatively guaranteed the students of Journalism II an atmosphere conducive to fostering such an appreciation and exercising the full panoply of rights associated with a free student press. "School sponsored student publications," it vowed, "will not restrict free expression or diverse viewpoints within the rules of responsible journalism."

This case arose when the Hazelwood East administration breached its own promise, dashing its students' expectations. The school principal, without prior consultation or explanation, excised six articles—comprising two full pages—of the May 13, 1983, issue of Spectrum. He did so not because any of the articles would "materially and substantially interfere with the requirements of appropriate

discipline," but simply because he considered two of the six "inappropriate, personal, sensitive, and unsuitable" for student consumption.

In my view the principal broke more than just a promise. He violated the First Amendment's prohibitions against censorship of any student expression that neither disrupts classwork nor invades the rights of others, and against any censorship that is not narrowly tailored to serve its purpose . . . .

Even if we were writing on a clean slate, I would reject the Court's rationale for abandoning *Tinker* in this case. The Court offers no more than an obscure tangle of three excuses to afford educators "greater control" over school-sponsored speech than the *Tinker* test would permit: the public educator's prerogative to control curriculum; the pedagogical interest in shielding the high school audience from objectionable viewpoints and sensitive topics; and the school's need to dissociate itself from student expression. None of the excuses, once disentangled, supports the distinction that the Court draws. *Tinker* fully addresses the first concern; the second is illegitimate; and the third is readily achievable through less oppressive means. . . .

I fully agree with the Court that the First Amendment should afford an educator the prerogative not to sponsor the publication of a newspaper article that is "ungrammatical, poorly written, inadequately researched, biased or prejudiced," or that falls short of the "high standards for . . . student speech that is disseminated under [the school's] auspices. . . ." But we need not abandon *Tinker* to reach that conclusion; we need only apply it. The enumerated criteria reflect the skills that the curricular newspaper "is designed to teach." The educator may, under *Tinker,* constitutionally "censor" poor grammar, writing, or research because to reward such expression would "materially disrup[t]" the newspaper's curricular purpose.

The same cannot be said of official censorship designed to shield the *audience* or dissociate the *sponsor* from the expression. Censorship so motivated might well serve . . . some other school purpose. But it in no way furthers the curricular purposes of a student *newspaper,* unless one believes that the purpose of the school newspaper is to teach students that the press ought never report bad news, express unpopular views, or print a thought that might upset its sponsors. Unsurprisingly, Hazelwood East claims no such pedagogical purpose.

The Court relies on bits of testimony to portray the principal's conduct as a pedagogical lesson to Journalism II students who "had not sufficiently mastered those portions of the . . . curriculum that pertained to the treatment of controversial issues and personal attacks, the need to protect the privacy of individuals . . . , and 'the legal, moral, and ethical restrictions imposed upon journalists. . . .' " In that regard, the Court attempts to justify censorship of the article on teenage pregnancy on the basis of the principal's judgment that (1) "the [pregnant] students' anonymity was not adequately protected," despite the article's use of aliases; and (2) the judgment "that the article was not sufficiently sensitive to the privacy interests of the students' boyfriends and parents. . . ." Similarly, the Court finds in the principal's decision to censor the divorce article a journalistic lesson that the author should have given the father of one student an "opportunity to defend himself" against her charge that (in the Court's words) he "chose 'playing cards with the guys' over home and family. . . ."

But the principal never consulted the students before censoring their work. "[T]hey learned of the deletions when the paper was released. . . ." Further, he explained the deletions only in the broadest of generalities. In one meeting called at the behest of seven protesting Spectrum staff members (presumably a fraction of the full class), he characterized the articles as " 'too sensitive' for 'our immature audience of readers,' " and in a later meeting he deemed them simply "inappropriate, personal, sensitive and unsuitable for the newspaper." The Court's supposition that the principal intended (or the protesters understood) those generalities as a lesson on the nuances of journalistic responsibility is utterly incredible. If he did, a fact that neither the District Court nor the Court of Appeals found, the lesson was lost on all but the psychic Spectrum staffer.

The Court's second excuse for deviating from precedent is the school's interest in shielding an impressionable high school audience from material whose substance is "unsuitable for immature audiences." . . .

Tinker teaches us that the state educator's undeniable, and undeniably vital, mandate to inculcate moral and political values is not a general warrant to act as "thought police" stifling discussion of all but state-approved topics and advocacy of all but the official position. Otherwise educators could transform students into "closed-circuit recipients of only that which the State chooses to communicate," and cast a perverse and impermissible "pall of orthodoxy over the classroom.". . . .

The mere fact of school sponsorship does not, as the Court suggests, license such thought control

in the high school, whether through school suppression of disfavored viewpoints or through official assessment of topic sensitivity. . . .

The sole concomitant of school sponsorship that might conceivably justify the distinction that the Court draws between sponsored and nonsponsored student expression is the risk "that the views of the individual speaker [might be] erroneously attributed to the school." Of course, the risk of erroneous attribution inheres in any student expression, including "personal expression" that, like the Tinkers' armbands, "happens to occur on the school premises." Nevertheless, the majority is certainly correct that indicia of school sponsorship increase the likelihood of such attribution, and that state educators may therefore have a legitimate interest in dissociating themselves from student speech.

But "[e]ven though the governmental purpose be legitimate and substantial, that purpose cannot be pursued by means that broadly stifle fundamental personal liberties when the end can be more narrowly achieved.' " Dissociative means short of censorship are available to the school. It could, for example, require the student activity to publish a disclaimer, such as the "Statement of Policy" that *Spectrum* published each school year announcing that "[a]ll . . . editorials appearing in this newspaper reflect the opinions of the *Spectrum* staff, which are not necessarily shared by the administrators or faculty of Hazelwood East," or it could simply issue its own response clarifying the official position on the matter and explaining why the student position is wrong. Yet, without so much as acknowledging the less oppressive alternatives, the Court approves of brutal censorship.

Since the censorship served no legitimate pedagogical purpose, it cannot by any stretch of the imagination have been designed to prevent "materia[l] disrup[tion of] classwork." Nor did the censorship fall within the category that *Tinker* described as necessary to prevent student expression from "inva[ding] the rights of others." . . .

The Court opens its analysis in this case by purporting to reaffirm *Tinker*'s time-tested proposition that public school students " 'do not shed their constitutional rights to freedom of speech or expression at the schoolhouse gate.' " That is an ironic introduction to an opinion that denudes high school students of much of the First Amendment protection that *Tinker* itself prescribed. . . .

The young men and women of Hazelwood East expected a civics lesson, but not the one the Court teaches them today.

I dissent.

HUSTLER MAGAZINE v. FALWELL,
485 U.S. 46 (1988)

The inside front cover of the November 1983 issue of Hustler Magazine featured an advertisement "parody" that, among other things, portrayed Reverend Jerry Falwell as having engaged in a drunken incestuous encounter with his mother in an outhouse. Falwell sued Hustler Magazine and its publisher Larry C. Flynt for libel, invasion of privacy, and intentional infliction of emotional distress. The jury ruled in Falwell's favor on the emotional distress claim and stated that he should be awarded $100,000 in compensatory damages and $100,000 in punitive damages. The Court of Appeals for the Fourth Circuit affirmed.

Votes: Unanimous

CHIEF JUSTICE REHNQUIST delivered the opinion of the Court:

Petitioner Hustler Magazine, Inc., is a magazine of nationwide circulation. Respondent Jerry Falwell, a nationally known minister who has been active as a commentator on politics and public affairs, sued petitioner and its publisher, petitioner Larry Flynt, to recover damages for invasion of privacy, libel, and intentional infliction of emotional distress. The District Court directed a verdict against respondent [Falwell] on the privacy claim, and submitted the other two claims to a jury. The jury found for petitioners on the defamation claim, but found for respondent on the claim for intentional infliction of emotional distress and awarded damages. We now consider whether this award is consistent with the First and Fourteenth Amendments of the United States Constitution. . . .

Respondent would have us find that a State's interest in protecting public figures from emotional distress is sufficient to deny First Amendment protection to speech that is patently offensive and is intended to inflict emotional injury, even when that speech could not reasonably have been interpreted as stating actual facts about the public figure involved. This we decline to do.

At the heart of the First Amendment is the recognition of the fundamental importance of the free flow of ideas and opinions on matters of public interest and concern. . . . We have therefore been particularly vigilant to ensure that individual expressions of ideas remain free from governmentally imposed sanctions. The First Amendment recognizes no such thing as a "false" idea. . . .

The sort of robust political debate encouraged by the First Amendment is bound to produce speech that is critical of those who hold public office or those public figures who are "intimately involved in the resolution of important public questions or, by reason of their fame, shape events in areas of concern to society at large.". . . Justice Frankfurter put it succinctly in *Baumgartner v. United States,* 322 U.S. 665, 673–674 (1944), when he said that "[o]ne of the prerogatives of American citizenship is the right to criticize public men and measures." Such criticism, inevitably, will not always be reasoned or moderate; public figures as well as public officials will be subject to "vehement, caustic, and sometimes unpleasantly sharp attacks.". . .

Of course, this does not mean that *any* speech about a public figure is immune from sanction in the form of damages. Since *New York Times Co. v. Sullivan,* we have consistently ruled that a public figure may hold a speaker liable for the damage to reputation caused by publication of a defamatory falsehood, but only if the statement was made "with knowledge that it was false or with reckless disregard of whether it was false or not." False statements of fact are particularly valueless; they interfere with the truth-seeking function of the marketplace of ideas, and they cause damage to an individual's reputation that cannot easily be repaired by counterspeech, however persuasive or effective. But even though falsehoods have little value in and of themselves, they are "nevertheless inevitable in free debate," and a rule that would impose strict liability on a publisher for false factual assertions would have an undoubted "chilling" effect on speech relating to public figures that does have constitutional value. "Freedoms of expression require 'breathing space.' " . . . This breathing space is provided by a constitutional rule that allows public figures to recover for libel or defamation only when they can prove *both* that the statement was false and that the statement was made with the requisite level of culpability.

Respondent argues, however, that a different standard should apply in this case because here the State seeks to prevent not reputational damage, but the severe emotional distress suffered by the person who is the subject of an offensive publication. . . . In respondent's view, and in the view of the Court of Appeals, so long as the utterance was intended to inflict emotional distress, was outrageous, and did in fact inflict serious emotional distress, it is of no constitutional import whether the statement was a fact or an opinion, or whether it was true or false. It is the intent to cause injury that is the gravamen of the tort, and the State's interest in preventing emotional harm simply out-weighs whatever interest a speaker may have in speech of this type.

Generally speaking the law does not regard the intent to inflict emotional distress as one which should receive much solicitude, and it is quite un-derstandable that most if not all jurisdictions have chosen to make it civilly culpable where the con-duct in question is sufficiently "outrageous." But in the world of debate about public affairs, many things done with motives that are less than admira-ble are protected by the First Amendment. In *Gar-rison* v. *Louisiana,* 379 U.S. 64 (1964), we held that even when a speaker or writer is motivated by ha-tred or ill-will his expression was protected by the First Amendment. . . . Thus while such a bad mo-tive may be deemed controlling for purposes of tort liability in other areas of the law, we think the First Amendment prohibits such a result in the area of public debate about public figures.

Were we to hold otherwise, there can be little doubt that political cartoonists and satirists would be subjected to damages awards without any show-ing that their work falsely defamed its subject. . . . The appeal of the political cartoon or caricature is often based on exploration of unfortunate physical traits or politically embarrassing events—an explo-ration often calculated to injure the feelings of the subject of the portrayal. The art of the cartoonist is often not reasoned or evenhanded, but slashing and one-sided. . . .

Despite their sometimes caustic nature, from the early cartoon portraying George Washington as an ass down to the present day, graphic depictions and satirical cartoons have played a prominent role in public and political debate. Nast's castigation of the Tweed Ring, Walt McDougall's characterization of presidential candidate James G. Blaine's banquet with the millionaires at Delmonico's as "The Royal Feast of Belshazzar," and numerous other efforts have undoubtedly had an effect on the course and outcome of contemporaneous debate. Lincoln's tall, gangling posture, Teddy Roosevelt's glasses and teeth, and Franklin D. Roosevelt's jutting jaw and cigarette holder have been memorialized by po-litical cartoons with an effect that could not have been obtained by the photographer or the portrait artist. From the viewpoint of history it is clear that our political discourse would have been consider-ably poorer without them.

Respondent contends, however, that the carica-ture in question here was so "outrageous" as to distinguish it from more traditional political car-toons. There is no doubt that the caricature of re-spondent and his mother published in Hustler is at

best a distant cousin of the political cartoons de-scribed above, and a rather poor relation at that. If it were possible by laying down a principled stan-dard to separate the one from the other, public dis-course would probably suffer little or no harm. But we doubt that there is any such standard, and we are quite sure that the pejorative description "out-rageous" does not supply one. "Outrageousness" in the area of political and social discourse has an inherent subjectiveness about it which would allow a jury to impose liability on the basis of the jurors' tastes or views, or perhaps on the basis of their dis-like of a particular expression. An "outrageous-ness" standard thus runs afoul of our longstanding refusal to allow damages to be awarded because the speech in question may have an adverse emotional impact on the audience. . . . [A]s we stated in *FCC* v. *Pacifica Foundation,* 438 U.S. 726, (1978):

"[T]he fact that society may find speech offen-sive is not a sufficient reason for suppressing it. Indeed, if it is the speaker's opinion that gives offense, that consequence is a reason for accord-ing it constitutional protection. For it is a central tenet of the First Amendment that the govern-ment must remain neutral in the marketplace of ideas." *Id.,* at 745–746. . . .

Admittedly, these oft-repeated First Amend-ment principles, like other principles, are subject to limitations. We recognized in *Pacifica Foundation,* that speech that is " 'vulgar,' 'offensive,' and 'shocking' " is "not entitled to absolute constitu-tional protection under all circumstances." In *Chaplinsky* v. *New Hampshire,* 315 U.S. 568 (1942), we held that a state could lawfully punish an individual for the use of insulting " 'fighting' words—those which by their very utterance inflict injury or tend to incite an immediate breach of the peace." These limitations are but recognition of the observation in *Dun & Bradstreet, Inc.* v. *Green-moss Builders, Inc.,* 472 U.S. 749, 758 (1985), that this Court has "long recognized that not all speech is of equal First Amendment importance." But the sort of expression involved in this case does not seem to us to be governed by any exception to the general First Amendment principles stated above.

We conclude that public figures and public offi-cials may not recover for the tort of intentional in-fliction of emotional distress by reason of publica-tions such as the one here at issue without showing in addition that the publication contains a false statement of fact which was made with "actual mal-ice," *i.e.,* with knowledge that the statement was false or with reckless disregard as to whether or not it was true. This is not merely a "blind application" of the *New York Times* standard, it reflects our considered judgment that such a standard is necessary to give adequate "breathing space" to the freedoms protected by the First Amendment.

Here it is clear that respondent Falwell is a "public figure" for purposes of First Amendment law. The jury found against respondent on his libel claim when it decided that the Hustler ad parody could not "reasonably be understood as describing actual facts about [respondent] or actual events in which [he] participated." The Court of Appeals interpreted the jury's finding to be that the ad parody "was not reasonably believable," and in accordance with our custom we accept this finding. Respondent is thus relegated to his claim for damages awarded by the jury for the intentional infliction of emotional distress by "outrageous" conduct. But for reasons heretofore stated this claim cannot, consistently with the First Amendment, form a basis for the award of damages when the conduct in question is the publication of a caricature such as the ad parody involved here. The judgment of the Court of Appeals is accordingly

Reversed.

JUSTICE KENNEDY took no part in the consideration or decision of this case.

JUSTICE WHITE, concurring in the judgment: [omitted]

ROTH v. UNITED STATES, ALBERTS v. CALIFORNIA, 354 U.S. 476 (1957)

The facts of these cases are contained in the opinion of the Court written by Justice Brennan. The Court for the first time directly addressed the question of whether obscene matter was protected by the First Amendment. Ruling that it was not, the majority sought to fashion a standard for defining obscenity that would not carry with it into the realm of the forbidden all material with a sexual content. Justice Brennan's thinking on this subject was to evolve as subsequent obscenity decisions in Memoirs v. Massachusetts and Miller v. California indicate.

Majority votes: 6
Dissenting votes: 3

MR. JUSTICE BRENNAN delivered the opinion of the Court:

The constitutionality of a criminal obscenity statute is the question in each of these cases. In *Roth,* the primary constitutional question is whether the federal obscenity statute violates the provision of the First Amendment that "Congress shall make no law . . . abridging the freedom of speech, or of the press. . . ." In *Alberts,* the primary constitutional question is whether the obscenity provisions of the California Penal Code invade the freedoms of speech and press as they may be incorporated in the liberty protected from state action by the Due Process Clause of the Fourteenth Amendment. . . .

Roth conducted a business in New York in the publication and sale of books, photographs and magazines. He used circulars and advertising matter to solicit sales. He was convicted by a jury in the District Court for the Southern District of New York upon 4 counts of a 26-count indictment charging him with mailing obscene circulars and advertising, and an obscene book, in violation of the federal obscenity statute. . . .

Alberts conducted a mail-order business from Los Angeles. He was convicted by the Judge of the Municipal Court of the Beverly Hills Judicial District (having waived a jury trial) under a misdemeanor complaint which charged him with lewdly keeping for sale obscene and indecent books, and with writing, composing and publishing an obscene advertisement of them, in violation of the California Penal Code. . . .

The dispositive question is whether obscenity is utterance within the area of protected speech and press. Although this is the first time the question has been squarely presented to this Court, either under the First Amendment or under the Fourteenth Amendment, expressions found in numerous opinions indicated that this Court has always assumed obscenity is not protected by the freedoms of speech and press. . . .

The guaranties of freedom of expression in effect in 10 of the 14 states which by 1792 had ratified the Constitution, gave no absolute protection for every utterance. Thirteen of the 14 states provided for the prosecution of libel, and all of those States made either blasphemy or profanity, or both, statutory crimes. As early as 1712, Massachusetts made it criminal to publish "any filthy, obscene, or profane song, pamphlet, libel or mock sermon" in imitation or mimicking of religious services. Thus, profanity and obscenity were related offenses.

In light of this history, it is apparent that the unconditional phrasing of the First Amendment was not intended to protect every utterance. This phrasing did not prevent this Court from concluding that libelous utterances are not within the area of constitutionally protected speech. *Beauharnais* v. *Illi-*

nois, 343 U.S. 250, 266. At the time of the adoption of the First Amendment, obscenity law was not as fully developed as libel law, but there is sufficiently contemporaneous evidence to show that obscenity, too, was outside the protection intended for speech and press.

The protection given speech and press was fashioned to assure unfettered interchange of ideas for the bringing about of political and social changes desired by the people. . . . All ideas having even the slightest redeeming social importance—unorthodox ideas, controversial ideas, even ideas hateful to the prevailing climate of opinion—have the full protection of the guaranties, unless excludable because they encroach upon the limited area of more important interests. But implicit in the history of the First Amendment is the rejection of obscenity as utterly without redeeming social importance. This rejection for that reason is mirrored in the universal judgment that obscenity should be restrained, reflected in the international agreement of over 50 nations, in the obscenity laws of all of the 48 States, and in the 20 obscenity laws enacted by the Congress from 1842 to 1956. This is the same judgment expressed by this Court in *Chaplinsky* v. *New Hampshire,* 315 U.S. 568, 571–572.

" . . . There are certain well-defined and narrowly limited classes of speech, the prevention and punishment of which have never been thought to raise any Constitutional problem. *These include the lewd and obscene. . . . It has been well observed that such utterances are no essential part of any exposition of ideas, and are of such slight social value as a step to truth that any benefit that may be derived from them is clearly outweighed by the social interest in order and morality. . . .*" [Emphasis added.]

We hold that obscenity is not within the area of constitutionally protected speech or press.

It is strenuously urged that these obscenity statutes offend the constitutional guaranties because they punish incitation to impure sexual *thoughts,* not shown to be related to any overt antisocial conduct which is or may be incited in the persons stimulated to such *thoughts.* . . . It is insisted that the constitutional guaranties are violated because convictions may be had without proof either that obscene material will perceptibly create a clear and present danger of antisocial conduct, or will probably induce its recipients to such conduct. But, in light of our holding that obscenity is not protected speech, the complete answer to this argument is in the holding of this Court in *Beauharnais* v. *Illinois:*

"Libelous utterances not being within the area of constitutionally protected speech, it is unnecessary, either for us or for the State courts, to consider the issues behind the phrase 'clear and present danger.' Certainly no one would contend that obscene speech, for example, may be punished only upon a showing of such circumstances. Libel, as we have seen, is in the same class."

However, sex and obscenity are not synonymous. Obscene material is material which deals with sex in a manner appealing to prurient interest. The portrayal of sex, *e. g.,* in art, literature and scientific works, is not itself sufficient reason to deny material the constitutional protection of freedom of speech and press. Sex, a great and mysterious motive force in human life, has indisputably been a subject of absorbing interest to mankind through the ages; it is one of the vital problems of human interest and public concern. . . .

The fundamental freedoms of speech and press have contributed greatly to the development and well-being of our free society and are indispensable to its continued growth. Ceaseless vigilance is the watchword to prevent their erosion by Congress or by the States. The door barring federal and state intrusion into this area cannot be left ajar; it must be kept tightly closed and opened only the slightest crack necessary to prevent encroachment upon more important interests. It is therefore vital that the standards for judging obscenity safeguard the protection of freedom of speech and press for material which does not treat sex in a manner appealing to prurient interest.

The early leading standard of obscenity allowed material to be judged merely by the effect of an isolated excerpt upon particularly susceptible persons. *Regina* v. *Hicklin* [1868]. Some American courts adopted this standard but later decisions have rejected it and substituted this test: whether to the average person, applying contemporary community standards, the dominant theme of the material taken as a whole appeals to prurient interest. The *Hicklin* test, judging obscenity by the effect of isolated passages upon the most susceptible persons, might well encompass material legitimately treating with sex, and so it must be rejected as unconstitutionally restrictive of the freedoms of speech and press. On the other hand, the substituted standard provides safeguards adequate to withstand the charge of constitutional infirmity.

Both trial courts below sufficiently followed the proper standard. Both courts used the proper definition of obscenity. . . .

Many decisions have recognized that these terms of obscenity statutes are not precise. This

Court, however, has consistently held that lack of precision is not itself offensive to the requirements of due process. ". . . [T]he Constitution does not require impossible standards"; all that is required is that the language "conveys sufficiently definite warning as to the proscribed conduct when measured by common understanding and practices. . . ." These words, applied according to the proper standard for judging obscenity, already discussed, give adequate warning of the conduct proscribed and mark ". . . boundaries sufficiently distinct for judges and juries fairly to administer the law. . . . That there may be marginal cases in which it is difficult to determine the side of the line on which a particular fact situation falls is no sufficient reason to hold the language too ambiguous to define a criminal offense. . . ."

In summary, then, we hold that these statutes applied according to the proper standard for judging obscenity, do not offend constitutional safeguards against convictions based upon protected material, or fail to give men in acting adequate notice of what is prohibited. . . .

The judgments are

Affirmed.

MR. CHIEF JUSTICE WARREN, concurring in the result:. . .

The defendants in both these cases were engaged in the business of purveying textual or graphic matter openly advertised to appeal to the erotic interest of their customers. They were plainly engaged in the commercial exploitation of the morbid and shameful craving for materials with prurient effect. I believe that the State and Federal Governments can constitutionally punish such conduct. That is all that these cases present to us, and that is all we need to decide. . . .

MR. JUSTICE HARLAN, concurring in the result in [Alberts] and dissenting in [Roth]:. . . .

I dissent in *Roth* v. *United States.*

We are faced here with the question whether the federal obscenity statute, as construed and applied in this case, violates the First Amendment to the Constitution. To me this question is of quite a different order than one where we are dealing with state legislation under the Fourteenth Amendment. I do not think it follows that state and federal powers in this area are the same, and that just because the State may suppress a particular utterance, it is automatically permissible for the Federal Government to do the same. I agree with Mr. Justice Jackson that the historical evidence does not bear out the claim that the Fourteenth Amendment "incorporates" the First in any literal sense. But laying

aside any consequences which might flow from that conclusion, I prefer to rest my views about this case on broader and less abstract grounds.

The Constitution differentiates between those areas of human conduct subject to the regulation of the States and those subject to the powers of the Federal Government. The substantive powers of the two governments, in many instances, are distinct. And in every case where we are called upon to balance the interest in free expression against other interests, it seems to me important that we should keep in the forefront the question of whether those other interests are state or federal. Since under our constitutional scheme the two are not necessarily equivalent, the balancing process must . . . often produce different results. Whether a particular limitation on speech or press is to be upheld because it subserves a paramount governmental interest must, to a large extent, I think, depend on whether that government has under the Constitution, a direct substantive interest, that is the power to act, in the particular area involved. . . . [T]he interests which obscenity statutes purportedly protect are primarily entrusted to the care, not of the Federal Government, but of the States. Congress had no substantive power over sexual morality. Such powers as the Federal Government has in this field are but incidental to its other powers, here the postal power, and are not of the same nature as those possessed by the States, which bear direct responsibility for the protection of the local moral fabric. . . .

Not only is the federal interest in protecting the Nation against pornography attenuated, but the dangers of federal censorship in this field are far greater than anything the States may do. It has often been said that one of the great strengths of our federal system is that we have, in the forty-eight States, forty-eight experimental social laboratories. . . . Different States will have different attitudes toward the same work of literature. The same book which is freely read in one State might be classed as obscene in another. And it seems to me that no overwhelming danger to our freedom to experiment and to gratify our tastes in literature is likely to result from the suppression of a borderline book in one of the States, so long as there is no uniform nation-wide suppression of the book, and so long as other States are free to experiment with the same or bolder books.

Quite a different situation is presented, however, where the Federal Government imposes the ban. . . .

It is no answer to say, as the Court does, that obscenity is not protected speech. The point is that this statute, as here constructed, defines obscenity so widely that it encompasses matters which might very well be protected speech. I do not think that the federal statute can be constitutionally constructed to reach other than what the Government has termed as "hard-core" pornography. Nor do I think the statute can fairly be read as directed only at *persons* who are engaged in the business of catering to the prurient minded, even though their wares fall short of hard-core pornography. Such a statute would raise constitutional questions of a different order. That being so, and since in my opinion the material here involved cannot be said to be hard-core pornography, I would reverse this case with instructions to dismiss the indictment.

MR. JUSTICE DOUGLAS, with whom MR. JUSTICE BLACK concurs, dissenting:

When we sustain these convictions, we make the legality of a publication turn on the purity of thought which a book or tract instills in the mind of the reader. I do not think we can approve that standard and be faithful to the command of the First Amendment, which by its terms is a restraint on Congress and which by the Fourteenth is a restraint on the States. . . . This issue cannot be avoided by saying that obscenity is not protected by the First Amendment. The question remains, what is the constitutional test of obscenity?

The tests by which these convictions were obtained require only the arousing of sexual thoughts. . . . The test of obscenity the Court endorses today gives the censor free range over a vast domain. To allow the State to step in and punish mere speech or publication that the judge or the jury thinks has an *undesirable* impact on thoughts but that is not shown to be a part of unlawful action is drastically to curtail the First Amendment. . . .

If we were certain that impurity of sexual thoughts impelled to action, we would be on less dangerous ground in punishing the distributors of this sex literature. But it is by no means clear that obscene literature, as so defined, is a significant factor in influencing substantial deviations from the community standards. . . . The absence of dependable information on the effect of obscene literature on human conduct should make us wary. It should put us on the side of protecting society's interest in literature, except and unless it can be said that the particular publication has an impact on action that the government can control. . . .

I reject too the implication that problems of freedom of speech and of the press are to be resolved by weighing against the values of free expression, the judgment of the Court that a particular form of that expression has "no redeeming social importance." The First Amendment, its prohibition in

terms absolute, was designed to preclude courts as well as legislatures from weighing the values of speech against silence. The First Amendment puts free speech in the preferred position.

Freedom of expression can be suppressed if, and to the extent that, it is so closely brigaded with illegal action as to be an inseparable part of it. As a people, we cannot afford to relax that standard. For the test that suppresses a cheap tract today can suppress a literary gem tomorrow. All it need do is to incite a lascivious thought or arouse a lustful desire. The list of books that judges or juries can place in that category is endless.

I would give the broad sweep of the First Amendment full support. I have the same confidence in the ability of our people to reject noxious literature as I have in their capacity to sort out the truth from the false in theology, economics, politics, or any other field.

MEMOIRS v. MASSACHUSETTS,
383 U.S. 413 (1966)

The Warren Court in the mid-1960s sought to come to grips with the obscenity issue. In this case, the Court was asked to rule on a decision that came from the Massachusetts state courts. Under a special provision of Massachusetts law, the Attorney General of Massachusetts instituted civil proceedings to have adjudged obscene the book known as Fanny Hill *or* Memoirs of a Woman of Pleasure *written by John Cleland in the mid-eighteenth century. The book was placed on trial before a Massachusetts Superior Court justice. Defending the book was its publisher and copyright holder, G. P. Putnam's Sons. The Superior Court ruled the book obscene and the Massachusetts Supreme Judicial Court agreed.*

Majority votes: 6
Dissenting votes: 3

MR. JUSTICE BRENNAN announced the judgment of the Court and delivered an opinion in which THE CHIEF JUSTICE and MR. JUSTICE FORTAS join:

This is an obscenity case in which *Memoirs of a Woman of Pleasure* (commonly known as *Fanny Hill*), written by John Cleland in about 1750, was adjudged obscene in a proceeding that put on trial the book itself, and not its publisher or distributor. The proceeding was a civil equity suit brought by the Attorney General of Massachusetts. . . .

As authorized by [Massachusetts law], G. P. Putnam's Sons [the publisher and copyright holder of the book] intervened in the proceedings in behalf of the book. . . . At the hearing before a justice of the Superior Court . . . the court received the book in evidence and also . . . heard the testimony of experts and accepted other evidence, such as book reviews, in order to assess the literary, cultural, or educational character of the book. This constituted the entire evidence. . . . The trial justice entered a final decree, which adjudged *Memoirs* obscene and declared that the book "is not entitled to the protection of the First and Fourteenth Amendments to the Constitution of the United States against action by the Attorney General or other law enforcement officer. . . ." The Massachusetts Supreme Judicial Court affirmed the decree. . . . We reverse.

. . . We defined obscenity in *Roth* v. *United States,* 354 U.S. 476 (1957), in the following terms: "[W]hether to the average person, applying contemporary community standards, the dominant theme of the material taken as a whole appeals to prurient interest." . . . Under this definition, as elaborated in subsequent cases, three elements must coalesce: it must be established that (a) the dominant theme of the material taken as a whole appeals to a prurient interest in sex; (b) the material is patently offensive because it affronts contemporary community standards relating to the description or representation of sexual matters; and (c) the material is utterly without redeeming social value.

The Supreme Judicial Court purported to apply the *Roth* definition of obscenity and held all three criteria satisfied. We need not consider the claim that the court erred in concluding that *Memoirs* satisfied the prurient appeal and patent offensiveness criteria; for reversal is required because the court misinterpreted the social value criterion. The court applied the criterion in this passage:

> "But the fact that the testimony may indicate this book has some minimal literary value does not mean it is of any social importance. We do not interpret the 'social importance' test as requiring that a book which appeals to prurient interest and is patently offensive must be unqualifiedly worthless before it can be deemed obscene.". . .

The Supreme Judicial Court erred in holding that a book need not be "unqualifiedly worthless before it can be deemed obscene." A book cannot be proscribed unless it is found to be *utterly* without redeeming social value. This is so even though the book is found to possess the requisite prurient appeal and to be patently offensive. Each of the three federal constitutional criteria is to be applied independently; the social value of the book can neither be weighed against nor canceled by its prurient appeal or patent offensiveness. Hence, even on the view of the court below that *Memoirs* possessed only a modicum of social value, its judgment must be reversed as being founded on an erroneous interpretation of a federal constitutional standard. . . .

Reversed.

MR. JUSTICE BLACK and MR. JUSTICE STEWART concur in the reversal. . . .

MR. JUSTICE DOUGLAS, concurring in the judgment:. . . .

We are judges, not literary experts or historians or philosophers. We are not competent to render an independent judgment as to the worth of this or any other book, except in our capacity as private citizens. . . .

. . . The Constitution forbids abridgment of "freedom of speech, or of the press." Censorship is the most notorious form of abridgment. It substitutes majority rule where minority tastes or viewpoints were to be tolerated. . . .

The censor is always quick to justify his function in terms that are protective of society. But the First Amendment, written in terms that are absolute, deprives the States of any power to pass on the value, the propriety, or the morality of a particular expression. . . . Perhaps the most frequently assigned justification for censorship is the belief that erotica produce antisocial sexual conduct. But that relationship has yet to be proven. Indeed, if one were to make judgments on the basis of speculation, one might guess that literature of the most pornographic sort would, in many cases, provide a substitute—not a stimulus—for antisocial sexual conduct. . . . As I read the First Amendment, judges cannot gear the literary diet of an entire nation to whatever tepid stuff is incapable of triggering the most demented mind. The First Amendment demands more than a horrible example or two of the perpetrator of a crime of sexual violence, in whose pocket is found a pornographic book, before it allows the Nation to be saddled with a regime of censorship. . . .

MR. JUSTICE CLARK, dissenting:

It is with regret that I write this dissenting opinion. However, the public should know of the continuous flow of pornographic material reaching this Court and the increasing problem States have in controlling it. *Memoirs of a Woman of Pleasure,* the book involved here, is typical. I have "stomached" past cases for almost 10 years without much outcry. Though I am not known to be a purist—or a shrinking violet—this book is too much even for me. It is important that the Court has refused to declare it obscene and thus affords it further circulation. . . .

Memoirs is nothing more than a series of minutely and vividly described sexual episodes. . . . There can be no doubt that the whole purpose of the book is to arouse the prurient interest. Likewise the repetition of sexual episode after episode and the candor with which they are described renders the book "patently offensive." These facts weigh heavily in any appraisal of the book's claims to "redeeming social importance." . . . In my view, the book's repeated and unrelieved appeals to the prurient interest of the average person leave it utterly without redeeming social importance.

In his separate concurrence, my Brother Douglas asserts that there is no proof that obscenity produces antisocial conduct. I had thought that this question was foreclosed by the determination in *Roth* that obscenity was not protected by the First Amendment. . . .

MR. JUSTICE HARLAN, dissenting:. . . .

My premise is that in the area of obscenity the Constitution does not bind the States and the Federal Government in precisely the same fashion. This approach is plainly consistent with the language of the First and Fourteenth Amendments and in my opinion, more responsive to the proper functioning of a federal system of government in this area. . . .

Federal suppression of allegedly obscene matter should, in my view, be constitutionally limited to that often described as "hard-core pornography." To be sure, that rubric is not a self-executing standard, but it does describe something that most judges and others will "know . . . when they see it" . . . and that leaves the smallest room for disagreement between those of varying tastes. To me it is plain, for instance, that "Fanny Hill" does not fall within this class and could not be barred from the federal mails. If further articulation is meaningful, I would characterize as "hard-core" that prurient material that is patently offensive or whose indecency is self-demonstrating. . . . The Federal Government may be conceded a limited interest in excluding from the mails such gross pornography, almost universally condemned in this country. But I believe the dangers of national censorship and the existence of primary responsibility at the state level amply justify drawing the line at this point. . . .

. . . I think it more satisfactory to acknowledge that on this record the book has been shown to have some quantum of social value, that it may at the same time be deemed offensive and salacious, and that the State's decision to weigh these elements

and to ban this particular work does not exceed constitutional limits.

MR. JUSTICE WHITE, dissenting:. . . .

To say that material within the *Roth* definition of obscenity is nevertheless not obscene if it has some redeeming social value is to reject one of the basic propositions of the *Roth* case—that such material is not protected *because* it is inherently and utterly without social value.

If "social importance" is to be used as the prevailing opinion uses it today, obscene material, however far beyond customary limits of candor, is immune if it has any literary style, if it contains any historical references or language characteristic of a bygone day, or even if it is printed or bound in an interesting way. Well written, especially effective obscenity is protected; the poorly written is vulnerable. And why shouldn't the fact that some people buy and read such material prove its "social value"?

A fortiori, if the predominant theme of the book appeals to the prurient interest as stated in *Roth* but the book nevertheless contains here and there a passage descriptive of character, geography or architecture, the book would not be "obscene" under the social importance test. I had thought that *Roth* counseled the contrary: that the character of the book is fixed by its predominant theme and is not altered by the presence of minor themes of a different nature. . . .

STANLEY v. GEORGIA,
394 U.S. 557 (1969)

This is perhaps the most permissive decision in the realm of obscenity ever handed down by the Supreme Court. Here, the Warren Court, in its waning days, ruled that possession of obscene matter is a constitutionally protected right. The case began when police officers searched the home of Robert Eli Stanley, pursuant to a search warrant, looking for evidence of bookmaking. They did not find what they came for, but came across three rolls of allegedly pornographic 8-mm film. Stanley was arrested, tried, and convicted for possessing obscene material in violation of a Georgia statute making possession a state crime. The conviction was upheld by the Georgia Supreme Court and the United States Supreme Court granted certiorari.

Votes: Unanimous

MR. JUSTICE MARSHALL delivered the opinion of the Court:. . . .

Appellant raises several challenges to the validity of his conviction. We find it necessary to consider only one. Appellant argues here, and argued below, that the Georgia obscenity statute, insofar as it punishes mere private possession of obscene matter, violates the First Amendment, as made applicable to the States by the Fourteenth Amendment. For reasons set forth below, we agree that the mere private possession of obscene matter cannot constitutionally be made a crime. . . .

It is true that *Roth* v. *United States,* 354 U.S. 476, does declare, seemingly without qualification, that obscenity is not protected by the First Amendment. That statement has been repeated in various forms in subsequent cases. However, neither *Roth* nor any subsequent decision of this Court dealt with the precise problem involved in the present case. . . . None of the statements cited by the Court in *Roth* for the proposition that "this Court has always assumed that obscenity is not protected by the freedoms of speech and press" were made in the context of a statute punishing mere private possession of obscene material; the cases cited deal for the most part with use of the mails to distribute objectionable material or with some form of public distribution or dissemination. Moreover, none of this Court's decisions subsequent to *Roth* involved prosecution for private possession of obscene materials. Those cases dealt with the power of the State and Federal Governments to prohibit or regulate certain public actions taken or intended to be taken with respect to obscene matter. Indeed, with one exception, we have been unable to discover any case in which the issue in the present case has been fully considered.

In this context, we do not believe that this case can be decided simply by citing *Roth*. *Roth* and its progeny certainly do mean that the First and Fourteenth Amendments recognize a valid governmental interest in dealing with the problem of obscenity. But the assertion of that interest cannot, in every context, be insulated from all constitutional protections. Neither *Roth* nor any other decision of this Court reaches that far. . . .

That holding cannot foreclose an examination of the constitutional implications of a statute forbidding mere private possession of such material.

It is now well established that the Constitution protects the right to receive information and ideas. . . . This right to receive information and ideas, regardless of their social worth . . . is fundamental to our free society. Moreover, in the context of this case—a prosecution for mere possession of printed or filmed matter in the privacy of a person's own home—that right takes on an added dimension. For also fundamental is the right to be free,

except in very limited circumstances, from unwanted governmental intrusions into one's privacy. . . .

These are the rights that appellant is asserting in the case before us. He is asserting the right to read or observe what he pleases—the right to satisfy his intellectual and emotional needs in the privacy of his own home. He is asserting the right to be free from state inquiry into the contents of his library. Georgia contends that appellant does not have these rights, that there are certain types of materials that the individual may not read or even possess. Georgia justifies this assertion by arguing that the films in the present case are obscene. But we think that mere categorization of these films as "obscene" is insufficient justification for such a drastic invasion of personal liberties guaranteed by the First and Fourteenth Amendments. Whatever may be the justifications for other statutes regulating obscenity, we do not think they reach into the privacy of one's own home. If the First Amendment means anything, it means that a State has no business telling a man sitting alone in his own house, what books he may read or what films he may watch. Our whole constitutional heritage rebels at the thought of giving government the power to control men's minds.

And yet, in the face of these traditional notions of individual liberty, Georgia asserts the right to protect the individual's mind from the effects of obscenity. We are not certain that this argument amounts to anything more than the assertion that the State has the right to control the moral content of a person's thoughts. To some, this may be a noble purpose, but it is wholly inconsistent with the philosophy of the First Amendment. . . .

Perhaps recognizing this, Georgia asserts that exposure to obscene materials may lead to deviant sexual behavior or crimes of sexual violence. There appears to be little empirical basis for that assertion. . . . Given the present state of knowledge, the State may no more prohibit mere possession of obscene matter on the ground that it may lead to antisocial conduct than it may prohibit possession of chemistry books on the ground that they may lead to the manufacture of homemade spirits.

It is true that in *Roth* this Court rejected the necessity of proving that exposure to obscene material would create a clear and present danger of antisocial conduct or would probably induce its recipients to such conduct. But that case dealt with public distribution of obscene materials and such distribution is subject to different objections. For example, there is always the danger that obscene material might fall into the hands of children . . . or that it might intrude upon the sensibilities or privacy of the general public. No such dangers are present in this case.

Finally, we are faced with the argument that prohibition of possession of obscene materials is a necessary incident to statutory schemes prohibiting distribution. That argument is based on alleged difficulties of proving an intent to distribute or in producing evidence of actual distribution. We are not convinced that such difficulties exist, but even if they did we do not think that they would justify infringement of the individual's right to read or observe what he pleases. Because that right is so fundamental to our scheme of individual liberty, its restriction may not be justified by the need to ease the administration of otherwise valid criminal laws.

We hold that the First and Fourteenth Amendments prohibit making mere private possession of obscene material a crime. *Roth* and the cases following that decision are not impaired by today's holding. As we have said, the States retain broad power to regulate obscenity; that power simply does not extend to mere possession by the individual in the privacy of his own home. Accordingly, the judgment of the court below is reversed and the case is remanded for proceedings not inconsistent with this opinion. . . .

Judgment reversed and case remanded.

MR. JUSTICE BLACK, concurring: [omitted]
MR. JUSTICE STEWART, with whom MR. JUSTICE BRENNAN, and MR. JUSTICE WHITE, join, concurring in the result:

Before the commencement of the trial in this case, the appellant filed a motion to suppress the films as evidence upon the ground that they had been seized in violation of the Fourth and Fourteenth Amendments. The motion was denied, and the films were admitted in evidence at the trial. In affirming the appellant's conviction, the Georgia Supreme Court specifically determined that the films had been lawfully seized. The appellant correctly contends that this determination was clearly wrong under established principles of constitutional law. But the Court today disregards this preliminary issue in its hurry to move on to newer constitutional frontiers. I cannot so readily overlook the serious inroads upon Fourth Amendment guarantees countenanced in this case by the Georgia courts. . . .

Because the films were seized in violation of the Fourth and Fourteenth Amendments, they were inadmissible in evidence at the appellant's trial. *Mapp* v. *Ohio*, 367 U.S. 643. Accordingly, the judgment of conviction must be reversed.

MILLER v. CALIFORNIA,
413 U.S. 15 (1973)
PARIS ADULT THEATRE I v. SLATON,
413 U.S. 49 (1973)

The Burger Court grappled with the obscenity issue in a number of cases coming to the Court in 1973. In two of these, the Miller *and the* Paris Theatre *cases, the Court majority fashioned its own new obscenity policy. Marvin Miller owned a mail-order pornographic materials business in California and solicited customers by sending through the mails a brochure vividly advertising his wares. One of Miller's brochures was sent to the manager of a Newport Beach restaurant and his mother. Both were deeply offended by the brochure and its description of such works as "Sex Orgies Illustrated" and "Man-Woman." They complained to the police and Miller was subsequently prosecuted for violating the California law that makes it a misdemeanor knowingly to distribute obscene matter. The conviction was upheld by the California courts. Clearly, the original complainants in this case were unwilling recipients of the obscene matter.*

In contrast, the Paris Adult Theatre in Atlanta, Georgia, catered only to consenting adults. The theater had very low-key advertising that nevertheless made it unmistakably clear that the films shown dealt explicitly with sex. The District Attorney for Atlanta, Lewis Slaton, went to a local trial court and requested an injunction restraining the Paris Adult Theatre from continuing to show two allegedly obscene movies. The trial court ruled in favor of the theater because it showed the films only to consenting adult audiences, but the Georgia Supreme Court reversed. In these two decisions the Court majority offered new criteria for defining obscenity.

Majority votes: 5
Dissenting votes: 4

MILLER v. CALIFORNIA

MR. CHIEF JUSTICE BURGER delivered the opinion of the Court:. . . .

This much has been categorically settled by the Court, that obscene material is unprotected by the First Amendment. . . . We acknowledge, however, the inherent dangers of undertaking to regulate any form of expression. State statutes designed to regulate obscene materials must be carefully limited. As a result, we now confine the permissible scope of such regulation to works which depict or describe sexual conduct. That conduct must be specifically defined by the applicable state law, as written or authoritatively construed. A state offense must also be limited to works which, taken as a whole, appeal to the prurient interest in sex, which portray sexual conduct in a patently offensive way, and which, taken as a whole, do not have serious literary, artistic, political, or scientific value.

The basic guidelines for the trier of fact must be: (a) whether ''the average person, applying contemporary community standards'' would find that the work, taken as a whole, appeals to the prurient interest, (b) whether the work depicts or describes, in a patently offensive way, sexual conduct specifically defined by the applicable state law, and (c) whether the work, taken as a whole, lacks serious literary, artistic, political, or scientific value. We do not adopt as a constitutional standard the ''*utterly* without redeeming social value'' test of *Memoirs* v. *Massachusetts,* 383 U.S. 413, at 419; that concept has never commanded the adherence of more than three Justices at one time. If a state law that regulates obscene material is thus limited, as written or construed, the First Amendment values applicable to the States through the Fourteenth Amendment are adequately protected by the ultimate power of appellate courts to conduct an independent review of constitutional claims when necessary.

We emphasize that it is not our function to propose regulatory schemes for the States. That must await their concrete legislative efforts. It is possible, however, to give a few plain examples of what a state statute could define for regulation under the second part (b) of the standard announced in this opinion, supra:

(a) Patently offensive representations or descriptions of ultimate sexual acts, normal or perverted, actual or simulated.

(b) Patently offensive representation or descriptions of masturbation, excretory functions, and lewd exhibition of the genitals.

Sex and nudity may not be exploited without limit by films or pictures exhibited or sold in places of public accommodation any more than live sex and nudity can be exhibited or sold without limit in such public places. At a minimum, prurient, patently offensive depiction or description of sexual conduct must have serious literary, artistic, political, or scientific value to merit First Amendment protection. For example, medical books for the education of physicians and related personnel necessarily use graphic illustrations and descriptions of human anatomy. In resolving the inevitably sensitive questions of fact and law, we must continue to rely on the jury system, accompanied by the safeguards that judges, rules of evidence, presumption of innocence and other protective features provide, as we do with rape, murder and a host of other offenses against society and its individual members. . . .

Under the holdings announced today, no one will be subject to prosecution for the sale or exposure of obscene materials unless these materials depict or describe patently offensive ''hard core'' sexual conduct specifically defined by the regulating state law, as written or construed. We are satisfied that these specific prerequisites will provide fair notice to a dealer in such materials that his public and commercial activities may bring prosecution. . . .

Under a National Constitution, fundamental First Amendment limitations on the powers of the States do not vary from community to community, but this does not mean that there are, or should or can be, fixed, uniform national standards of precisely what appeals to the ''prurient interest'' or is ''patently offensive.'' These are essentially questions of fact, and our nation is simply too big and too diverse for this Court to reasonably expect that such standards could be articulated for all 50 States in a single formulation, even assuming the prerequisite consensus exists. When triers of fact are asked to decide whether ''the average person, applying contemporary community standards'' would consider certain materials ''prurient,'' it would be unrealistic to require that the answer be based on some abstract formulation. The adversary system, with lay jurors as the usual ultimate factfinders in criminal prosecutions, has historically permitted triers-of-fact to draw on the standards of their community, guided always by limiting instructions on the law. To require a State to structure obscenity proceedings around evidence of a *national* ''community standard'' would be an exercise in futility.

As noted before, this case was tried on the theory that the California obscenity statute sought to incorporate the tripartite test of *Memoirs*. This, a ''national'' standard of First Amendment protection enumerated by a plurality of this Court, was correctly regarded at the time of trial as limiting state prosecution under the controlling case law. The jury, however, was explicitly instructed that, in determining whether the ''dominant theme of the material as a whole . . . appeals to the prurient interest'' and in determining whether the material ''goes substantially beyond customary limits of candor and affronts contemporary community standards of decency,'' it was to apply ''contemporary community standards of the State of California.''

During the trial, both the prosecution and the defense assumed that the relevant ''community standards'' in making the factual determination of obscenity were those of the State of California, not some hypothetical standard of the entire United

States of America. Defense counsel at trial never objected to the testimony of the State's expert on community standards or to the instructions of the trial judge on "state-wide" standards. On appeal to the Appellate Department, Superior Court of California, County of Orange, appellant for the first time contended that application of state, rather than national, standards violated the First and Fourteenth Amendments.

We conclude that neither the State's alleged failure to offer evidence of "national standards," nor the trial court's charge that the jury consider state community standards, were constitutional errors. . . .

The dissenting Justices sound the alarm of repression. But, in our view, to equate the free and robust exchange of ideas and political debate with commercial exploitation of obscene material demeans the grand conception of the First Amendment and its high purposes in the historic struggle for freedom. . . .

In sum we (a) reaffirm the *Roth* holding that obscene material is not protected by the First Amendment, (b) hold that such material can be regulated by the States, subject to the specific safeguards enunciated above, without a showing that the material is "*utterly* without redeeming social value," and (c) hold that obscenity is to be determined by applying "contemporary community standards," not "national standards." The judgment of the Appellate Department of the Superior Court, Orange County, California, is vacated and the case remanded to that court for further proceedings not inconsistent with the First Amendment standards established by this opinion.

Vacated and remanded for further proceedings.

MR. JUSTICE DOUGLAS, dissenting:

Today we leave open the way for California to send a man to prison for distributing brochures that advertise books and a movie under freshly written standards defining obscenity which until today's decision were never the part of any law.

The Court has worked hard to define obscenity and concededly has failed. . . .

We deal with highly emotional, not rational, questions. To many the Song of Solomon is obscene. I do not think we, the judges, were ever given the constitutional power to make definitions of obscenity. If it is to be defined, let the people debate and decide by a constitutional amendment what they want to ban as obscene and what standards they want the legislatures and the courts to apply. Perhaps the people will decide that the path

towards a mature, integrated society requires that all ideas competing for acceptance must have no censor. Perhaps they will decide otherwise. Whatever the choice, the courts will have some guidelines. Now we have none except our own predilections.

MR. JUSTICE BRENNAN, with whom MR. JUSTICE STEWART and MR. JUSTICE MARSHALL join, dissenting: [omitted]

PARIS ADULT THEATRE I V. SLATON

MR. CHIEF JUSTICE BURGER delivered the opinion of the Court:. . . .

We categorically disapprove the theory, apparently adopted by the trial judge, that obscene, pornographic films acquire constitutional immunity from state regulation simply because they are exhibited for consenting adults only. This holding was properly rejected by the Georgia Supreme Court. Although we have often pointedly recognized the high importance of the state interest in regulating the exposure of obscene materials to juveniles and unconsenting adults, this Court has never declared these to be the only legitimate state interests permitting regulation of obscene material. The States have a long-recognized legitimate interest in regulating the use of obscene material in local commerce and in all places of public accommodation, as long as these regulations do not run afoul of specific constitutional prohibitions. . . .

In particular, we hold that there are legitimate state interests at stake in stemming the tide of commercialized obscenity, even assuming it is feasible to enforce effective safeguards against exposure to juveniles and to the passersby. Rights and interests "other than those of the advocates are involved." These include the interest of the public in the quality of life and the total community environment, the tone of commerce in the great city centers, and, possibly, the public safety itself. The Hill-Link Minority Report of the Commission on Obscenity and Pornography indicates that there is at least an arguable correlation between obscene material and crime. Quite apart from sex crimes, however, there remains one problem of large proportions aptly described by Professor Bickel:

"It concerns the tone of the society, the mode, or to use terms that have perhaps greater currency, the style and quality of life, now and in the future. A man may be entitled to read an obscene book in his room, or expose himself indecently there. . . . We should protect his privacy. But if he demands a right to obtain the books and pictures he wants in the market, and to foregather in public places—

discreet, if you will, but accessible to all—with others who share his tastes, *then to grant him his right is to affect the world about the rest of us and to impinge on other privacies.* Even supposing that each of us can, if he wishes, effectively avert the eye and stop the ear (which, in truth, we cannot), what is commonly read and seen and heard and done intrudes upon us all, want it or not." 22 *The Public Interest* 25–26 (Winter, 1971). (Emphasis added.) . . .

But, it is argued, there is no scientific data which conclusively demonstrates that exposure to obscene materials adversely affects men and women or their society. It is urged on behalf of the petitioner that, absent such a demonstration, any kind of state regulation is "impermissible." We reject this argument. It is not for us to resolve empirical uncertainties underlying state legislation, save in the exceptional case where that legislation plainly impinges upon rights protected by the Constitution itself. . . . Although there is no conclusive proof of a connection between antisocial behavior and obscene material, the legislature of Georgia could quite reasonably determine that such a connection does or might exist. In deciding *Roth*, this Court implicitly accepted that a legislature could legitimately act on such a conclusion to protect "*the social interest in order and morality*."

From the beginning of civilized societies, legislators and judges have acted on various unprovable assumptions. Such assumptions underlie much lawful state regulation of commercial and business affairs. The same is true of the federal securities, antitrust laws and a host of other federal regulations. . . . The sum of experience, including that of the past two decades, affords an ample basis for legislatures to conclude that a sensitive, key relationship of human existence, central to family life, community welfare, and the development of human personality, can be debased and distorted by crass commercial exploitation of sex. Nothing in the Constitution prohibits a State from reaching such a conclusion and acting on it legislatively simply because there is no conclusive evidence or empirical data. . . .

The States, of course, may follow . . . a "laissez faire" policy and drop all controls on commercialized obscenity, if that is what they prefer, just as they can ignore consumer protection in the market place, but nothing in the Constitution *compels* the States to do so with regard to matters falling within state jurisdiction. . . .

It is asserted, however, that standards for evaluating state commercial regulations are inapposite in the present context, as state regulation of access by consenting adults to obscene material violates the constitutionally protected right to privacy enjoyed by petitioners' customers. . . . Our prior decisions recognizing a right to privacy guaranteed by the Fourteenth Amendment included "only those personal rights that can be deemed 'fundamental' or 'implicit in the concept of ordered liberty.'" This privacy right encompasses and protects the personal intimacies of the home, the family, marriage, motherhood, procreation, and child rearing. Nothing, however, in this Court's decisions intimates that there is any "fundamental" privacy right "implicit in the concept of ordered liberty" to watch obscene movies in places of public accommodation. . . .

The idea of a "privacy" right and a place of public accommodation are, in this context, mutually exclusive. Conduct or depictions of conduct that the state police power can prohibit on a public street does not become automatically protected by the Constitution merely because the conduct is moved to a bar or a "live" theatre stage, any more than a "live" performance of a man and woman locked in a sexual embrace at high noon in Times Square is protected by the Constitution because they simultaneously engage in a valid political dialogue. . . .

. . . The States have the power to make a morally neutral judgment that public exhibition of obscene material, or commerce in such material, has a tendency to injure the community as a whole, to endanger the public safety, or to jeopardize, in Chief Justice Warren's words, the States' "right . . . to maintain a decent society."

To summarize, we have today reaffirmed the basic holding of *Roth* v. *United States* that obscene material has no protection under the First Amendment. We have directed our holdings, not at thoughts or speech, but at depiction and description of specifically defined sexual conduct that States may regulate within limits designed to prevent infringement of First Amendment rights. We have also reaffirmed the holdings of *United States* v. *Reidel* and *United States* v. *Thirty-Seven Photographs* that commerce in obscene material is unprotected by any constitutional doctrine of privacy. In this case we hold that the States have a legitimate interest in regulating commerce in obscene material and in regulating exhibition of obscene material in places of public accommodation, including so-called "adult" theatres from which minors are excluded. In light of these holdings, nothing precludes the State of Georgia from the regulation of the allegedly obscene materials exhibited in Paris Adult Theatre I or II, provided that the applicable Georgia law, as written or authoritatively interpreted by the Georgia courts, meets the First Amendment standards set forth in *Miller* v. *California*. The judgment is vacated and the case remanded to the Georgia Supreme Court for further proceedings not inconsistent with this opinion and *Miller* v. *California*.

Vacated and remanded for further proceedings.

MR. JUSTICE BRENNAN, with whom MR. JUSTICE STEWART and MR. JUSTICE MARSHALL join, dissenting:

This case requires the Court to confront once again the vexing problem of reconciling state efforts to suppress sexually oriented expression with the protections of the First Amendment, as applied to the States through the Fourteenth Amendment. No other aspect of the First Amendment has, in recent years, demanded so substantial a commitment of our time, generated such disharmony of views, and remained so resistant to the formulation of stable and manageable standards. I am convinced that the approach initiated 15 years ago in *Roth* v. *United States* and culminating in the Court's decision today, cannot bring stability to this area of the law without jeopardizing fundamental First Amendment values, and I have concluded that the time has come to make a significant departure from that approach. . . .

Our experience with the *Roth* approach has certainly taught us that the outright suppression of obscenity cannot be reconciled with the fundamental principles of the First and Fourteenth Amendments. For we have failed to formulate a standard that sharply distinguishes protected from unprotected speech, and out of necessity, we have resorted to the approach which resolves cases as between the parties but offers only the most obscure guidance to legislation, adjudication by other courts, and primary conduct. . . . [A]fter 16 years of experimentation and debate I am reluctantly forced to the conclusion that none of the available formulas, including the one announced today, can reduce the vagueness to a tolerable level while at the same time striking an acceptable balance between the protections of the First and Fourteenth Amendments, on the one hand, and on the other the asserted state interest in regulating the dissemination of certain sexually oriented materials. Any effort to draw a constitutionally acceptable boundary on state power must resort to such indefinite concepts as "prurient interest," "patent offensiveness," "serious literary value," and the like. The meaning of these concepts necessarily varies with the experience, outlook, and even idiosyncracies of the person defining them. Although we have assumed that obscenity does exist and that we "know it when [we] see it," *Jacobellis* v. *Ohio,* 378 U.S. 184, 197, (Stewart, J., concurring), we are manifestly unable to describe it in advance except by reference to concepts so elusive that they fail to distinguish clearly between protected and unprotected speech. . . . No one definition, no matter how precisely or narrowly drawn, can possibly suffice for all situations, or carve out fully suppressible expression from all media without also creating a substantial risk of encroachment upon the guarantees of the Due Process Clause and the First Amendment. . . .

Because we assumed—incorrectly, as experience has proven—that obscenity could be separated from the sexually oriented expression without significant costs either to the First Amendment or to the judicial machinery charged with the task of safeguarding First Amendment freedoms, we had no occasion in *Roth* to probe the asserted state interest in curtailing unprotected, sexually oriented speech. Yet as we have increasingly come to appreciate the vagueness of the concept of obscenity, we have begun to recognize and articulate the state interests at stake. . . . [S]tate interests in protecting children and in protecting unconsenting adults may stand on a different footing from the other asserted state interests. It may well be, as one commentator has argued, the "exposure to [erotic material] is for some persons an intense emotional experience. A communication of this nature, imposed upon a person contrary to his wishes, has all the characteristics of a physical assault. . . . [And it] constitutes an invasion of his privacy. . . ." Similarly, if children are "not possessed of that full capacity for individual choice which is the presupposition of the First Amendment guarantees," then the State may have a substantial interest in precluding the flow of obscene materials even to consenting juveniles.

But whatever the strength of the state interests in protecting juveniles and unconsenting adults from exposure to sexually oriented materials, those interests cannot be asserted in defense of the holding of the Georgia Supreme Court in this case. That court assumed for the purposes of its decision that the films in issue were exhibited only to persons over the age of 21 who viewed them willingly and with prior knowledge of the nature of their contents. And on that assumption the state court held that the films could still be suppressed. The justification for the suppression must be found, therefore, in some independent interest in regulating the reading and viewing habits of consenting adults.

At the outset it should be noted that virtually all of the interests that might be asserted in defense of suppression, laying aside the special interests associated with distribution to juveniles and unconsenting adults, were also posited in *Stanley* v. *Georgia* where we held that the State could not make the "mere private possession of obscene material a crime." That decision presages the conclusions I reach here today. . . .

In short, while I cannot say that the interests of the State—apart from the question of juveniles and unconsenting adults—are trivial or nonexistent, I am compelled to conclude that these interests cannot justify the substantial damage to constitutional rights and to this Nation's judicial machinery that inevitably results from state efforts to bar the distribution even of unprotected material to consenting adults. I would hold, therefore, that at least in the absence of distribution to juveniles or obtrusive exposure to unconsenting adults, the First and Fourteenth Amendments prohibit the state and federal governments from attempting wholly to suppress sexually oriented materials on the basis of their allegedly "obscene" contents. Nothing in this approach precludes those governments from taking action to serve what may be strong and legitimate interests through regulation of the manner of distribution of sexually oriented material. . . . Since the Supreme Court of Georgia erroneously concluded that the State has power to suppress sexually oriented material even in the absence of distribution to juveniles or exposure to unconsenting adults, I would reverse that judgment and remand the case to that court for further proceedings not inconsistent with this opinion.

MR. JUSTICE DOUGLAS, dissenting: [omitted]

JENKINS v. GEORGIA,
418 U.S. 153 (1974)

The difficulties inherent in applying the new obscenity standards of Miller v. California *and* Paris Adult Theatre v. Slaton *became apparent in the Jenkins case. This case concerned the well-known and highly acclaimed motion picture "Carnal Knowledge." The film starred Jack Nicholson and Ann-Margret, was directed by Mike Nichols, and was nominated for Academy Awards. It was a social satire on sex roles and sexual mores. Billy Jenkins, manager of a movie theater in Albany, Georgia, was convicted of the crime of distributing obscene material by showing the movie. Two weeks after the United States Supreme Court announced its new obscenity policy in* Miller *and in* Paris Theatre, *the Georgia Supreme Court seemingly applied these new standards to "Carnal Knowledge," finding the film to be obscene and affirming Jenkins' conviction. The Supreme Court was thus faced with the question whether juries have unbridled discretion in using local community standards to ban a work of art that elsewhere has been found to have serious artistic value.*

Votes: Unanimous

MR. JUSTICE REHNQUIST delivered the opinion of the Court:. . . .

We conclude here that the film "Carnal Knowledge" is not obscene under the constitutional standards announced in *Miller* v. *California,* 413 U.S. 15, and that the First and Fourteenth Amendments therefore require that the judgment of the Supreme Court of Georgia affirming appellant's conviction be reversed. . . .

There is little to be found in the record about the film "Carnal Knowledge" other than the film itself. However, appellant has supplied a variety of information and critical commentary, the authenticity of which appellee does not dispute. The film appeared on many "Ten Best" lists for 1971, the year in which it was released. Many but not all of the reviews were favorable. . . .

Miller states that the questions of what appeals to the "prurient interest" and what is "patently offensive" under the obscenity test which it formulates are "essentially questions of fact.". . . But all of this does not lead us to agree with the Supreme Court of Georgia's apparent conclusion that the jury's verdict against appellant virtually precluded all further appellate review of appellant's assertion that his exhibition of the film was protected by the First and Fourteenth Amendments. Even though questions of appeal to the "prurient interest" or of patent offensiveness are "essentially questions of fact," it would be a serious misreading of *Miller* to conclude that juries have unbridled discretion in determining what is "patently offensive." Not only did we there say that "the First Amendment values applicable to the States through the Fourteenth Amendment are adequately protected by the ultimate power of appellate courts to conduct an independent review of constitutional claims when necessary," 413 U.S., at 25, but we made it plain that under that holding "no one will be subject to prosecution for the sale or exposure of obscene materials unless these materials depict or describe patently offensive 'hard core' sexual conduct. . . ." 413 U.S., at 27. . . .

Our viewing of the film satisfies us that "Carnal Knowledge" could not be found under the *Miller* standards to depict sexual conduct in a patently of-fensive way. Nothing in the movie falls within either of the two examples given in *Miller* of material which may constitutionally be found to meet the "patently offensive" element of those standards, nor is there anything sufficiently similar to such material to justify similar treatment. While the subject matter of the picture is, in a broader sense, sex, and there are scenes in which sexual conduct including "ultimate sexual acts" is to be understood to be taking place, the camera does not focus on the bodies of the actors at such times. There is no exhibition whatever of the actors' genitals, lewd or otherwise, during these scenes. There are occasional scenes of nudity, but nudity alone is not enough to make material legally obscene under the *Miller* standards.

Appellant's showing of the film "Carnal Knowledge" is simply not the "public portrayal of hard core sexual conduct for its own sake, and for ensuing commercial gain" which we said was punishable in *Miller*. We hold that the film could not, as a matter of constitutional law, be found to depict sexual conduct in a patently offensive way, and that it is therefore not outside the protection of the First and Fourteenth Amendments because it is obscene. No other basis appearing in the record upon which the judgment of conviction can be sustained, we reverse the judgment of the Supreme Court of Georgia.

Reversed.

MR. JUSTICE BRENNAN, with whom MR. JUSTICE STEWART and MR. JUSTICE MARSHALL join, concurring in result:. . . .

After the Court's decision today, there can be no doubt that *Miller* requires appellate courts—including this Court—to review independently the constitutional fact of obscenity. . . .

[I]t is clear that as long as the *Miller* test remains in effect "one cannot say with certainty that material is obscene until at least five members of this Court, applying inevitably obscure standards, have pronounced it so." Because of the attendant uncertainty of such a process and its inevitable institutional stress upon the judiciary, I continue to adhere to my view that, "at least in the absence of distribution to juveniles or obtrusive exposure to unconsenting adults, the First and Fourteenth Amendments prohibit the State and Federal Governments from attempting wholly to suppress sexually oriented materials on the basis of their allegedly 'obscene' contents." *Paris Adult Theatre* v. *Slaton,* 413 U.S., at 113. (Brennan, J. dissenting.)

It is clear that, tested by that constitutional standard, the Georgia obscenity statutes under which appellant Jenkins was convicted are constitutionally overbroad and therefore facially invalid. I therefore concur in the result in the Court's reversal of Jenkins' conviction.

MR. JUSTICE DOUGLAS, being of the view that any ban on obscenity is prohibited by the First Amendment, made applicable to the States through the Fourteenth, concurs in the reversal of this conviction.

NEW YORK v. FERBER,
458 U.S. 747 (1982)

The facts of this case are contained in Justice White's opinion of the Court. This case concerned the nefarious practice of sexual exploitation of children in the production of sexually oriented materials and the range of permissible actions that can be taken by the authorities to punish those who profit from such exploitation. This case was decided at a time of growing recognition of the massive problem of child abuse. Because of the seriousness of the evil, not one justice dissented, despite significant First Amendment issues raised by the case.

Votes: Unanimous

JUSTICE WHITE delivered the opinion of the Court:

At issue in this case is the constitutionality of a New York criminal statute which prohibits persons from knowingly promoting sexual performances by children under the age of 16 by distributing material which depicts such performances.

In recent years, the exploitive use of children in the production of pornography has become a serious national problem. The Federal Government and 47 States have sought to combat the problem with statutes specifically directed at the production of child pornography. At least half of such statutes do not require that the materials produced be legally obscene. Thirty-five States and the United States Congress have also passed legislation prohibiting the distribution of such materials; 20 States prohibit the distribution of material depicting children engaged in sexual conduct without requiring that the material be legally obscene.

New York is one of the 20. In 1977, the New York Legislature enacted Article 263 of its Penal Law. Section 263.05 criminalizes as a class C felony the use of a child in a sexual performance:

"A person is guilty of the use of a child in a sexual performance if knowing the character and content thereof he employs, authorizes or induces a child less than sixteen years of age to engage in a sexual performance or being a parent, legal guardian or custodian of such child, he consents to the participation by such child in a sexual performance.''

A ''[s]exual performance'' is defined as ''any performance or part thereof which includes sexual conduct by a child less than sixteen years of age.'' §263.00(1). ''Sexual conduct'' is in turn defined in §263.00(3):

'' 'Sexual conduct' means actual or simulated sexual intercourse, deviate sexual intercourse, sexual bestiality, masturbation, sado-masochistic abuse, or lewd exhibition of the genitals.''

A performance is defined as ''any play, motion picture, photograph or dance'' or ''any other visual representation exhibited before an audience.'' §263.00(4).

At issue in this case is §263.15, defining a class D felony:

''A person is guilty of promoting a sexual performance by a child when, knowing the character and content thereof, he produces, directs or promotes any performance which includes sexual conduct by a child less than sixteen years of age.''

To ''promote'' is also defined:

'' 'Promote' means to procure, manufacture, issue, sell, give, provide, lend, mail, deliver, transfer, transmute, publish, distribute, circulate, disseminate, present, exhibit or advertise, or to offer or agree to do the same.'' §263.00(5).

A companion provision bans only the knowing dissemination of obscene material. §263.10.

This case arose when Paul Ferber, the proprietor of a Manhattan bookstore specializing in sexually oriented products, sold two films to an undercover police officer. The films are devoted almost exclusively to depicting young boys masturbating. Ferber was indicted on two counts of violating §263.10 and two counts of violating §263.15, the two New York laws controlling dissemination of child pornography. After a jury trial, Ferber was acquitted of the two counts of promoting an obscene sexual performance, but found guilty of the two counts under §263.15, which did not require

proof that the films were obscene. Ferber's convictions were affirmed without opinion by the Appellate Division of the New York State Supreme Court.

The New York Court of Appeals reversed, holding that §263.15 violated the First Amendment. . . . This case . . . constitutes our first examination of a statute directed at and limited to depictions of sexual activity involving children. We believe our inquiry should begin with the question of whether a State has somewhat more freedom in proscribing works which portray sexual acts or lewd exhibitions of genitalia by children. . . .

. . . Like obscenity statutes, laws directed at the dissemination of child pornography run the risk of suppressing protected expression by allowing the hand of the censor to become unduly heavy. For the following reasons, however, we are persuaded that the States are entitled to greater leeway in the regulation of pornographic depictions of children.

First. It is evident beyond the need for elaboration that a State's interest in ''safeguarding the physical and psychological well-being of a minor'' is ''compelling.'' . . .

The prevention of sexual exploitation and abuse of children constitutes a government objective of surpassing importance. . . .

Suffice it to say that virtually all of the States and the United States have passed legislation proscribing the production of or otherwise combating ''child pornography.'' The legislative judgment, as well as the judgment found in the relevant literature, is that the use of children as subjects of pornographic materials is harmful to the physiological, emotional, and mental health of the child. That judgment, we think, easily passes muster under the First Amendment.

Second. The distribution of photographs and films depicting sexual activity by juveniles is intrinsically related to the sexual abuse of children in at least two ways. First, the materials produced are a permanent record of the children's participation and the harm to the child is exacerbated by their circulation. Second, the distribution network for child pornography must be closed if the production of material which requires the sexual exploitation of children is to be effectively controlled. Indeed, there is no serious contention that the legislature was unjustified in believing that it is difficult, if not impossible, to halt the exploitation of children by pursuing only those who produce the photographs and movies. While the production of pornographic materials is a low-profile, clandestine industry, the need to market the resulting products requires a visible apparatus of distribution. The most expeditious if not the only practical method of law enforcement may be to dry up the market for this material by imposing severe criminal penalties on persons selling, advertising, or otherwise promoting the product. Thirty-five States and Congress have concluded that restraints on the distribution of pornographic materials are required in order to effectively combat the problem, and there is a body of literature and testimony to support these legislative conclusions. . . .

Respondent does not contend that the State is unjustified in pursuing those who distribute child pornography. Rather, he argues that it is enough for the State to prohibit the distribution of materials that are legally obscene under the *Miller* test. While some States may find that this approach properly accommodates its interests, it does not follow that the First Amendment prohibits a State from going further. The *Miller* standard, like all general definitions of what may be banned as obscene, does not reflect the State's particular and more compelling interest in prosecuting those who promote the sexual exploitation of children. Thus, the question under the *Miller* test of whether a work, taken as a whole, appeals to the prurient interest of the average person bears no connection to the issue of whether a child has been physically or psychologically harmed in the production of the work. Similarly, a sexually explicit depiction need not be "patently offensive" in order to have required the sexual exploitation of a child for its production. In addition, a work which, taken on the whole, contains serious literary, artistic, political, or scientific value may nevertheless embody the hardest core of child pornography. . . . We therefore cannot conclude that the *Miller* standard is a satisfactory solution to the child pornography problem.

Third. The advertising and selling of child pornography provide an economic motive for and are thus an integral part of the production of such materials, an activity illegal throughout the Nation. . . .

Fourth. The value of permitting live performances and photographic reproductions of children engaged in lewd sexual conduct is exceedingly modest, if not de minimis. We consider it unlikely that visual depictions of children performing sexual acts or lewdly exhibiting their genitals would often constitute an important and necessary part of a literary performance or scientific or educational work. As a state judge in this case observed, if it were necessary for literary or artistic value, a person over the statutory age who perhaps looked younger could be utilized. Simulation outside of the prohibition of the statute could provide another

alternative. Nor is there any question here of censoring a particular literary theme or portrayal of sexual activity. The First Amendment interest is limited to that of rendering the portrayal somewhat more "realistic" by utilizing or photographing children.

Fifth. Recognizing and classifying child pornography as a category of material outside the protection of the First Amendment is not incompatible with our earlier decisions. . . . When a definable class of material, such as that covered by §263.15, bears so heavily and pervasively on the welfare of children engaged in its production, we think the balance of competing interests is clearly struck and that it is permissible to consider these materials as without the protection of the First Amendment. . . .

We hold that §263.15 sufficiently describes a category of material the production and distribution of which is not entitled to First Amendment protection. It is therefore clear that there is nothing unconstitutionally "underinclusive" about a statute that singles out this category of material for proscription. It also follows that the State is not barred by the First Amendment from prohibiting the distribution of unprotected materials produced outside the State.

It remains to address the claim that the New York statute is unconstitutionally overbroad because it would forbid the distribution of material with serious literary, scientific, or educational value or material which does not threaten the harms sought to be combated by the State. Respondent prevailed on that ground below, and it is to that issue that we now turn. . . .

We consider this the paradigmatic case of a state statute whose legitimate reach dwarfs its arguably impermissible applications. New York, as we have held, may constitutionally prohibit dissemination of material specified in §263.15. While the reach of the statute is directed at the hard core of child pornography, the Court of Appeals was understandably concerned that some protected expression, ranging from medical textbooks to pictorials in the *National Geographic* would fall prey to the statute. How often, if ever, it may be necessary to employ children to engage in conduct clearly within the reach of §263.15 in order to produce educational, medical, or artistic works cannot be known with certainty. Yet we seriously doubt, and it has not been suggested, that these arguably impermissible applications of the statute amount to more than a tiny fraction of the materials within the statute's reach. Nor will we assume that the New York courts will widen the possibly invalid reach of the statute by giving an expansive construction to the proscription on "lewd exhibition[s] of the genitals." Under these circumstances, §263.15 is "not substantially overbroad and . . . whatever overbreadth may exist should be cured through case-by-case analysis of the fact situations to which its sanctions, assertedly, may not be applied."

Because §263.15 is not substantially overbroad, it is unnecessary to consider its application to material that does not depict sexual conduct of a type that New York may restrict consistent with the First Amendment. As applied to Paul Ferber and to others who distribute similar material, the statute does not violate the First Amendment as applied to the States through the Fourteenth. The decision of the New York Court of Appeals is reversed, and the case is remanded to that court for further proceedings not inconsistent with this opinion.

So ordered.

JUSTICE BLACKMUN concurs in the result.
JUSTICE O'CONNOR, concurring: [omitted]
JUSTICE BRENNAN, with whom JUSTICE MARSHALL joins, concurring in the judgment: [omitted]
JUSTICE STEVENS, concurring in the judgment: [omitted]

SABLE COMMUNICATIONS OF CALIFORNIA, INC. v. FCC
109 S.Ct. 2829 (1989)

In 1983, Sable Communications, Inc., based in Los Angeles, went into the dial-a-porn business. Those calling Sable's special telephone number were charged a fee and provided a sexually oriented pre-recorded telephone message. In 1988 Congress amended the Communications Act of 1934 and outlawed indecent as well as obscene phone messages in interstate telephone commerce in order to protect children from exposure to indecent as well as obscene dial-a-porn messages. Sable Communications brought suit in federal district court asking it to declare that this provision was unconstitutional under the First and Fourteenth Amendments and seeking an injunction enjoining the FCC and the Justice Department from initiating any action against Sable under the statute. The judge rejected the claim as to obscene telephone messages but agreed with Sable as to those that were merely indecent. The judge issued an injunction with regard to the indecent speech provision and both the FCC and Sable went to the United States Supreme Court.

Majority votes: 6
Dissenting (in part): 3

JUSTICE WHITE delivered the opinion of the Court:
The issue before us is the constitutionality of §223(b) of the Communications Act of 1934. The statute, as amended in 1988, imposes an outright ban on indecent as well as obscene interstate commercial telephone messages. The District Court upheld the prohibition against obscene interstate telephone communications for commercial purposes, but enjoined the enforcement of the statute insofar as it applied to indecent messages. We affirm the District Court in both respects. . . .

In the ruling at issue in No. 88–515, the District Court upheld §223(b)'s prohibition of obscene telephone messages as constitutional. We agree with that judgment. In contrast to the prohibition on indecent communications, there is no constitutional barrier to the ban on obscene dial-a-porn recordings. We have repeatedly held that the protection of the First Amendment does not extend to obscene speech. See, *e.g., Paris Adult Theatre I* v. *Slaton,* 413 U.S. 49, 69 (1973). The case before us today does not require us to decide what is obscene or what is indecent but rather to determine whether Congress is empowered to prohibit transmission of obscene telephonic communications.

In its facial challenge to the statute, Sable argues that the legislation creates an impermissible national standard of obscenity, and that it places message senders in a "double bind" by compelling them to tailor all their messages to the least tolerant community.

We do not read §223(b) as contravening the "contemporary community standards" requirement of *Miller* v. *California,* 413 U.S. 15 (1973). Section 223(b) no more establishes a "national standard" of obscenity than do federal statutes prohibiting the mailing of obscene materials . . . or the broadcasting of obscene messages. . . . In *United States* v. *Reidel,* 402 U.S. 351 (1971), we said that Congress could prohibit the use of the mails for commercial distribution of materials properly classifiable as obscene, even though those materials were being distributed to willing adults who stated that they were adults. Similarly, we hold today that there is no constitutional stricture against Congress' prohibiting the interstate transmission of obscene commercial telephone recordings.

We stated in *United States* v. *12 200-ft. Reels of Film,* 413 U.S. 123 (1973), that the *Miller* standards, including the "contemporary community standards" formulation, apply to federal legislation. As we have said before, the fact that "distributors of allegedly obscene materials may be subjected to varying community standards in the various federal judicial districts into which they transmit the materials does not render a federal statute unconstitutional because of the failure of application of uniform national standards of obscenity."

Furthermore, Sable is free to tailor its messages, on a selective basis, if it so chooses, to the communities it chooses to serve. While Sable may be forced to incur some costs in developing and implementing a system for screening the locale of incoming calls, there is no constitutional impediment to enacting a law which may impose such costs on a medium electing to provide these messages. Whether Sable chooses to hire operators to determine the source of the calls or engages with the telephone company to arrange for the screening and blocking of out-of-area calls or finds another means for providing messages compatible with community standards is a decision for the message provider to make. There is no constitutional barrier under *Miller* to prohibiting communications that are obscene in some communities under local standards even though they are not obscene in others. If Sable's audience is comprised of different communities with different local standards, Sable ultimately bears the burden of complying with the prohibition on obscene messages.

In No. 88–525, the District Court concluded that while the government has a legitimate interest in protecting children from exposure to indecent dial-a-porn messages, § 223(b) was not sufficiently narrowly drawn to serve that purpose and thus violated the First Amendment. We agree.

Sexual expression which is indecent but not obscene is protected by the First Amendment; and the government does not submit that the sale of such materials to adults could be criminalized solely because they are indecent. The government may, however, regulate the content of constitutionally protected speech in order to promote a compelling interest if it chooses the least restrictive means to further the articulated interest. We have recognized that there is a compelling interest in protecting the physical and psychological well-being of minors. This interest extends to shielding minors from the influence of literature that is not obscene by adult standards. *Ginsberg* v. *New York,* 390 U.S. 629, 639–640 (1968); *New York* v. *Ferber,* 458 U.S. 747, 756–757 (1982). The government may serve this legitimate interest, but to withstand constitutional scrutiny, "it must do so by narrowly drawn regulations designed to serve those interests without unnecessarily interfering with First Amendment

freedoms. . . . It is not enough to show that the government's ends are compelling; the means must be carefully tailored to achieve those ends.

In *Butler* v. *Michigan,* 352 U.S. 380 (1957), a unanimous Court reversed a conviction under a statute which made it an offense to make available to the general public materials found to have a potentially harmful influence on minors. The Court found the law to be insufficiently tailored since it denied adults their free speech rights by allowing them to read only what was acceptable for children. As Justice Frankfurter said in that case, "Surely this is to burn the house to roast the pig." In our judgment, this case, like *Butler,* presents us with "legislation not reasonably restricted to the evil with which it is said to deal."

In attempting to justify the complete ban and criminalization of the indecent commercial telephone communications with adults as well as minors, the government relies on *FCC* v. *Pacifica Foundation,* 438 U.S. 726 (1978), a case in which the Court considered whether the FCC has the power to regulate a radio broadcast that is indecent but not obscene. In an emphatically narrow holding, the *Pacifica* Court concluded that special treatment of indecent broadcasting was justified.

Pacifica is readily distinguishable from this case, most obviously because it did not involve a total ban on broadcasting indecent material. . . .

The *Pacifica* opinion also relied on the "unique" attributes of broadcasting, noting that broadcasting is "uniquely pervasive," can intrude on the privacy of the home without prior warning as to program content, and is "uniquely accessible to children, even those too young to read." . . . The private commercial telephone communications at issue here are substantially different from the public radio broadcast at issue in *Pacifica*. In contrast to public displays, unsolicited mailings and other means of expression which the recipient has no meaningful opportunity to avoid, the dial-in medium requires the listener to take affirmative steps to receive the communication. There is no "captive audience" problem here; callers will generally not be unwilling listeners. The context of dial-in services, where a caller seeks and is willing to pay for the communication, is manifestly different from a situation in which a listener does not want the received message. Placing a telephone call is not the same as turning on a radio and being taken by surprise by an indecent message. Unlike an unexpected outburst on a radio broadcast, the message received by one who places a call to a dial-a-porn service is not so invasive or surprising that it prevents an unwilling listener from avoiding exposure to it. . . .

The Government nevertheless argues that the total ban on indecent commercial telephone communications is justified because nothing less could prevent children from gaining access to such messages. We find the argument quite unpersuasive. The FCC, after lengthy proceedings, determined that its credit card, access code, and scrambling rules were a satisfactory solution to the problem of keeping indecent dial-a-porn messages out of the reach of minors. The Court of Appeals, after careful consideration, agreed that these rules represented a "feasible and effective" way to serve the Government's compelling interest in protecting children.

The Government now insists that the rules would not be effective enough—that enterprising youngsters could and would evade the rules and gain access to communications from which they should be shielded. There is no evidence in the record before us to that effect, nor could there be since the FCC's implementation of § 223(b) prior to its 1988 amendment has never been tested over time. In this respect, the Government asserts that in amending § 223(b) in 1988, Congress expressed its view that there was not a sufficiently effective way to protect minors short of the total ban that it enacted. The Government claims that we must give deference to that judgment.

To the extent that the Government suggests that we should defer to Congress' conclusion about an issue of constitutional law, our answer is that while we do not ignore it, it is our task in the end to decide whether Congress has violated the Constitution. This is particularly true where the legislature has concluded that its product does not violate the First Amendment. . . . The Government, however, also urges us to defer to the factual findings by Congress relevant to resolving the constitutional issue. . . . Beyond the fact that whatever deference is due legislative findings would not foreclose our independent judgment of the facts bearing on an issue of constitutional law, our answer is that the congressional record contains no legislative findings that would justify us in concluding that there is no constitutionally acceptable less restrictive means, short of a total ban, to achieve the Government's interest in protecting minors.

There is no doubt Congress enacted a total ban on both obscene and indecent telephone communications. But aside from conclusory statements during the debates by proponents of the bill, as well as similar assertions in hearings on a substantially identical bill the year before, that under the FCC regulations minors could still have access to dial-a-porn messages, the Congressional record presented to us contains no evidence as to *how* effective or ineffective the FCC's most recent regulations were or might prove to be. It may well be that there is no fail-safe method of guaranteeing that never will a minor be able to access the dial-a-porn system. The bill that was enacted, however, was introduced on the floor, nor was there a committee report on the bill from which the language of the enacted bill was taken. No Congressman or Senator purported to present a considered judgment with respect to how often or to what extent minors could or would circumvent the rules and have access to dial-a-porn messages. . . .

For all we know from this record, the FCC's technological approach to restricting dial-a-porn messages to adults who seek them would be extremely effective, and only a few of the most enterprising and disobedient young people will manage to secure access to such messages. If this is the case, it seems to us that § 223(b) is not a narrowly tailored effort to serve the compelling interest of preventing minors from being exposed to indecent telephone messages. Under our precedents, § 223(b), in its present form, has the invalid effect of limiting the content of adult telephone conversations to that which is suitable for children to hear. It is another case of "burn[ing] up the house to roast the pig." *Butler* v. *Michigan,* 352 U. S., at 383.

Because the statute's denial of adult access to telephone messages which are indecent but not obscene far exceeds that which is necessary to limit the access of minors to such messages, we hold that the ban does not survive constitutional scrutiny.

Accordingly, we affirm the judgments of the District Court in No. 88–515 and No. 88–525.

It is so ordered.

JUSTICE SCALIA, concurring: [omitted]

JUSTICE BRENNAN, with whom JUSTICE MARSHALL and JUSTICE STEVENS join, concurring in part and dissenting in part:

I agree that a statute imposing criminal penalties for making, or for allowing others to use a telephone under one's control to make, any indecent telephonic communication for a commercial purpose is patently unconstitutional. . . .

In my view, however, § 223(b)(1)(A)'s parallel criminal prohibition with regard to obscene commercial communications likewise violates the First Amendment. I have long been convinced that the exaction of criminal penalties for the distribution of obscene materials to consenting adults is constitutionally intolerable. In my judgment, "the concept of 'obscenity' cannot be defined with sufficient specificity and clarity to provide fair notice to persons who create and distribute sexually oriented materials, to prevent substantial erosion of protected speech as a byproduct of the attempt to suppress unprotected speech, and to avoid very costly institutional harms.'' *Paris Adult Theatre I* v. *Slaton,* 413 U.S. 49, 103 (1973) (BRENNAN, J., dissenting). To be sure, the Government has a strong interest in protecting children against exposure to pornographic material that might be harmful to them. . . . But a complete criminal ban on obscene telephonic messages for profit is ''unconstitutionally overbroad, and therefore invalid on its face,'' as a means for achieving this end. . . .

Section 223(b)(1)(A) unambiguously proscribes all obscene commercial messages, and thus admits of no construction that would render it constitutionally permissible. Because this criminal statute curtails freedom of speech far more radically than the Government's interest in preventing harm to minors could possibly license on the record before us, I would reverse the District Court's decision in No. 88–515 and strike down the statute on its face. . . .

Chapter

15

The Religion Guarantees

It is significant that the guarantees first mentioned in the First Amendment are not the guarantees of speech and press, but rather the guarantees of free exercise of religion and against the establishment of religion. The significance lies in the fact that religious freedom was a running theme for much of colonial history and was considered by the framers of the Constitution to be a fundamental right. It is significant also that both religion guarantees were linked in that the framers believed that an established church, that is, a state-sponsored religion, would inevitably jeopardize the free exercise of religion and was thus incompatible with religious freedom. The Supreme Court decisions in the religion sphere historically first dealt with the free exercise guarantee, but over the last four decades, the establishment guarantee has occupied much of the Court's attention in terms of religious freedom. Although we will examine the free exercise clause and then the establishment guarantee, it is well to keep in mind that these two interlinked rights are sometimes merged in the

Court's decisions. On occasion, a free exercise claim will be decided as a more generalized First Amendment claim.

FREE EXERCISE OF RELIGION

Historically, the Supreme Court had few cases that raised questions of the free exercise of religion. The most important nineteenth-century decision concerning this issue involved the Mormons and their religious practice of polygamy (having more than one wife). In *Reynolds* v. *United States,* 98 U.S. 145 (1879), the Court confronted the claim of Mormons in the territory of Utah that the federal law prohibiting the practice of polygamy in federal territories violated the free exercise of their religion. The Court rejected the claim of the Mormons and ruled that the criminal law was superior to religious doctrines.

The Jehovah's Witnesses were involved in several cases that came to the Supreme Court in the early 1940s that established certain principles of free exercise and religious freedom that hold true today. The Court incorporated the free exercise guarantee as part of the liberty that the states may not deny. This was done in *Cantwell* v. *Connecticut,* 310 U.S. 296 (1940), which struck down a state statute that required a state certificate of approval before solicitation for funds for religious or charitable causes could be undertaken. But in *Jones* v. *Opelika,* 316 U.S. 584 (1942), the Court upheld an Alabama peddler's license requirement as applied to Jehovah's Witnesses. However, the next year as a result of personnel changes, a new Court majority reversed the *Opelika* ruling in *Murdock* v. *Pennsylvania,* 319 U.S. 105 (1943). The *Murdock* decision was notable also for the explicit declaration of what became known as the *preferred position doctrine.* That is, that First Amendment freedoms were the foundation of a free society and as such the framers placed them at the head of the Bill of Rights. They were placed in a preferred position, which means that any abridgment of such fundamental rights is suspect, with the heavy burden on the authorities for demonstrating the public policy considerations that justify compromising First Amendment rights. In the words of the Court: "Freedom of press, freedom of speech, freedom of religion are in a preferred position."

The Court invalidated a broadly written statute that was used to punish a Jehovah's Witness for ringing doorbells or otherwise summoning the occupants to their doors so that they could receive an announcement of a prayer meeting. That decision was *Martin* v. *Struthers,* 319 U.S. 141 (1943). A licensing statute applicable to book vendors and used against the Jehovah's Witnesses was struck down in *Follet* v. *Town of McCormick,* 321 U.S. 573 (1944). In *Marsh* v. *Alabama,* 326 U.S. 501 (1946), the Jehovah's Witnesses won a victory. The Court, in this decision, recognized that First Amendment rights were to be protected in company-owned towns from invasion by those acting in a governmental capacity. *Tucker* v. *Texas,* 326 U.S. 517 (1946),

recognized First Amendment rights of the Jehovah's Witnesses who were involved in this case on the property of a federal government housing project.

Jehovah's Witnesses were involved in some cases decided by the Vinson Court that were favorable to First Amendment rights. *Saia* v. *New York,* 334 U.S. 558 (1948), concerned a Jehovah's Witnesses minister who gave Sunday lectures in a public park in Lockport, New York. He used a loudspeaker placed on his car in order to attract attention and have his sermon reach a larger audience. Sound amplification devices were permitted in Lockport only if a permit were issued by the chief of police. Saia's permit expired and the chief of police refused to renew it because there had been complaints. Saia continued to use the loudspeaker even without the necessary permit, and he was eventually convicted of violating the Lockport ordinance. In the *Saia* decision, the Court struck down the ordinance as a previous restraint on the right of free speech. The Court the following year, however, in *Kovacs* v. *Cooper,* 336 U.S. 77 (1949), refused to strike down a Trenton, New Jersey, ordinance that effectively banned sound trucks or other sound amplifying devices from the public streets. The case did not involve religion but rather a labor dispute and the Court interpreted the statute as prohibiting only "loud and raucous" sound equipment. However, it was not clear that sound amplifying equipment could ever not be "loud" if not "raucous"; thus the Court, having first protected the rights of Jehovah's Witnesses, backed off from the underlying principle of the decision in a subsequent decision not involving religion.

Similarly, the Vinson Court decision in *Breard* v. *City of Alexandria,* 341 U.S. 622 (1951), which did not directly involve Jehovah's Witnesses, upheld a municipal ordinance that banned all door-to-door solicitation. This seemingly undermined the principle of the Jehovah's Witnesses case of *Martin* v.

Struthers. However, it should be pointed out that these decisions, including those involving the Jehovah's Witnesses, were not decided on the basis of the specific religion guarantees of the First Amendment. When those guarantees were the basis for decision, the Court tended to be generous in its reading of them. For example, the Vinson Court in *Kunz* v. *New York,* 340 U.S. 290 (1951), struck down the New York City ordinance requiring a permit obtained from the city police commissioner in order to hold a public worship meeting on the city streets.

Perhaps the most famous of the Jehovah's Witnesses cases concerned the compulsory flag salute, which violates the religious beliefs of that sect. The Court in **Minersville** v. **Gobitis** upheld the compulsory flag salute, but three years later reversed itself in **West Virginia State Board of Education** v. **Barnette** in an opinion that can only be seen as a ringing declaration of the virtues of First Amendment freedoms. The free exercise of religion was placed in a broader First Amendment context by Justice Robert Jackson, author of the Court's opinion. Some 34 years later, the Burger Court reaffirmed this precedent in *Wooley* v. *Maynard,* 430 U.S. 705 (1977), a case involving New Hampshire Jehovah's Witnesses who were convicted of obscuring the state motto "Live Free or Die" on their license plates in violation of New Hampshire state law. The Witnesses argued that the state motto conflicted with their political and religious beliefs, and the Court struck down the convictions relying heavily on *West Virginia* v. *Barnette.*

The Warren Court, too, furthered the free exercise guarantee by ruling in *Sherbert* v. *Verner,* 374 U.S. 398 (1963), that state unemployment compensation may not be denied a Seventh Day Adventist who refused employment that would require her to work on Saturday, her sabbath day, in violation of her religious beliefs. However, the Warren Court in *Gallagher* v. *Crown Kosher Super Market,*

366 U.S. 617 (1961), found no violation of the free exercise guarantee in Sunday closing laws that made no exception for those businesses whose proprietors (here Orthodox Jews) celebrated a different sabbath. Government has the right to use its police powers to promote a day of relative tranquility, and this does not prevent the free exercise of anyone's religion. Similarly, in **Goldman** v. **Weinberger,** the Burger Court in 1986 rejected the free exercise claim of an air force captain, Simcha Goldman, an Orthodox Jew, concerning an order forbidding him to wear a yarmulke. The Court found that the Air Force regulation, upon which the order to Goldman was based, reasonably and evenhandedly regulated military dress in the interest of the military's perceived need for uniformity. Goldman was not prevented from praying, celebrating his holidays, or even from wearing nonvisible religious garb. A legitimate governmental objective can therefore override a free exercise of religion claim. Prison inmates, like members of the military, are subject to restrictions on their free exercise of religion in deference to institutional needs. In *O'Lone* v. *Estate of Shabazz,* 482 U.S. 342 (1987), the Court rejected the claim that the free exercise rights of certain Islamic state prison inmates were violated when they were precluded from attending weekly Friday religious services.

The Rehnquist Court has continued the tradition of sympathy for the free exercise claims of those denied unemployment benefits because the state authorities did not recognize their religious claims. In *Hobbie* v. *Unemployment Appeals Commission of Florida,* 480 U.S. 136 (1987), the Court reaffirmed *Sherbert* v. *Verner* and ruled that a Seventh Day Adventist who was fired when she refused to work on her sabbath could not be denied unemployment compensation benefits by the state. In *Frazee* v. *Illinois Dept. of Employment Sec.,* 109 S.Ct. 1514 (1989), the state had denied unemployment benefits to a worker who refused a job because it would have required him to work on Sunday. Illinois officials had ruled that the refusal to work was not based on tenets or dogmas of an established religion. The Court, however, determined that it was not for Illinois to give its stamp of approval to religious beliefs. Frazee's claim that work on Sunday violated his religious beliefs meant that Illinois' denial of benefits violated his free exercise rights.

The Amish have been involved in litigation that raised free exercise claims that came before the Court. In **Wisconsin** v. **Yoder,** the Burger Court weighed the free exercise claim of Jonas Yoder and other Amish litigants against the state's interest in having Amish youth attend secondary school and found the Amish claim to be superior. Not so, however, with the Amish claim that as employers, to pay social security taxes violates their religious beliefs. In *United States* v. *Lee,* 455 U.S. 252 (1982), the Court unanimously turned down the free exercise claim and noted that while the Amish as individuals are exempt by federal statute from paying social security taxes for themselves, there is no exemption for Amish as employers from paying into the system for their employees. The integrity of the social security system depends upon all employers supporting the system and this legitimate governmental interest overrides any incidental infringement on the free exercise of religion of Amish employers. In *Bowen* v. *Roy,* 476 U.S. 693 (1986), the Court rejected the free exercise claim of a family of Abenaki Indians who objected to being assigned social security numbers. They had argued that the use of numbers to identify people was contrary to their religious beliefs. However, the Court ruled that the family could receive food stamp benefits even if they refused to use their numbers. Free exercise claims of Native Americans were also rejected in **Lyng** v. **Northwest Indian Cemetery Protective Ass'n** and in **Oregon Employment Division** v. **Smith** (reprinted at the end of this book). The free exercise of religion, asserted the

Court in *Smith,* is bound by criminal law. There is no constitutional right to ingest an illegal drug as part of Native American religious ceremonies. The Court rejected the free exercise claims of another minority religion in **Heffron** v. **International Society for Krishna Consciousness.** The free exercise of religion, suggested the Court, may be subject to reasonable time-place-and-manner regulations.

The free exercise guarantee can be seen as being in some conflict with the establishment guarantee insofar as the question arises: What may government do to enable persons to freely exercise their religion? Can government facilitate the free exercise guarantee by providing for prayers in the public schools or does that *establish* religion? Does a moment of silent meditation in the public schools facilitate the free exercise guarantee or a more generalized First Amendment right, or does *that* violate the establishment guarantee? Can government give tax credits to parents who send their children to parochial school in furtherance of their free exercise right or does this amount to government financing of religion in violation of the establishment clause? (We will discuss cases raising these questions shortly). There are numerous other issues as well. There is little doubt that government's payment of chaplains for the armed forces falls within the permissible range of government activity. The Court also said in *Zorach* v. *Clauson,* 343 U.S. 306 (1952), that released-time programs for religious instruction that occur off the public school's premises do not violate the establishment clause and, by implication, promote the free exercise of religion. Let us turn to the establishment clause decisions for a better perspective on the scope of religious freedom in the United States.

ESTABLISHMENT OF RELIGION

The Supreme Court, in the leading case of **Everson** v. **Board of Education** decided in 1947, ruled for the first time that the establishment guarantee of the First Amendment was an obligation on the states through the Fourteenth Amendment due process clause. Yet in the same decision, in which the Court used the metaphor of a wall separating church and state, the majority approved a New Jersey statute that reimbursed parents of all schoolchildren, including parochial school students, for their transportation costs in sending their children to school. The majority ruled that this did not violate the establishment guarantee and did not breach the wall of separation. With this ruling the Court became even more involved in state practices and programs that concerned religion.

The Court, in 1948, ruled in *McCollum* v. *Board of Education,* 333 U.S. 203 (1948), that it violated the establishment clause to use the public schools for religious instruction under a released-time program whereby religious teachers came to the public schools once a week to provide instruction to students who, with parental consent, were released from the regular school program. However, in the subsequent decision of *Zorach* v. *Clauson* (mentioned earlier), the Court approved a released-time program whereby the religious instruction did *not* take place on public property. The Warren Court, in the 1961 decision of *McGowan* v. *Maryland,* 366 U.S. 420, and companion cases, found that various state Sunday closing laws whereby certain businesses were forbidden to operate on Sunday did *not* violate the establishment guarantee. A New York state law that provided loan without charge of textbooks in secular subjects to private and parochial schools was upheld by the Warren Court when challenged on establishment grounds (the decision was *Board of Education* v. *Allen,* 392 U.S. 236 [1968]). The Court in these cases in which the establishment claim was rejected found valid secular purposes in the legislation under challenge.

When religion was clearly the motivating factor behind government legislation, the Warren Court generally took an unfavorable

view of such official action. For example, in the case of *Epperson* v. *Arkansas,* 393 U.S. 97 (1968), the Court invalidated as constituting establishment of religion an Arkansas statute that forbade the teaching of evolution in the public schools. About two decades later, the Rehnquist Court in **Edwards** v. **Aguillard** struck down a Louisiana law that *required* public schools to teach the biblical version of creation whenever evolution was also taught.

However, the most controversial line of establishment decisions has concerned prayer in the public schools. The Warren Court first ruled on this matter in 1962 in the case of *Engel* v. *Vitale,* 370 U.S. 421, when it invalidated a benign, nondenominational prayer approved by the New York State Board of Regents for use in those public schools in which the school officials wished to have students say a prayer. The next year the Court made a broader ruling in the famous **Abington School District** v. **Schempp** decision when it struck down as a violation of the establishment clause the reading of prayers including the Lord's Prayer and reading from the Bible as part of religious ceremonies in the public schools. Even though students who did not wish to participate were not forced to do so, the Court found that this amounted to state-sponsored religion that clearly breached the wall separating church and state. The Burger Court refused to overturn the *Schempp* precedent, but suggested that a moment of silent meditation in the public schools might prove constitutional although the particular Alabama statute before the Court in **Wallace** v. **Jaffree** was struck down.

Early in the Burger Court, there were several important church-state rulings in which establishment claims were considered. In an important early decision in 1970, *Walz* v. *Tax Commission of the City of New York,* 397 U.S. 664, the Court upheld property tax exemptions for church-owned property used for religious purposes. The tax exemptions, reasoned the Court, were in recognition of the charitable and social welfare activities of religious organizations and not designed to support religion. But the most significant of its early establishment decisions occurred the next year in **Lemon** v. **Kurtzman,** where the Court offered a three-pronged test to determine whether the establishment clause had been violated. For a law not to violate the establishment clause it must not have a religious purpose; the effect of the law on religion must be neutral—that is, the law must neither promote nor inhibit religion; and the law must not be seen as fostering excessive government entanglement with religion. This three-pronged test was used to invalidate two state statutes that provided financial aid to parochial elementary and secondary schools (subsidies or partial salary payments for teaching secular subjects). But this same test resulted in the Court upholding in **Tilton** v. **Richardson** federal aid to church-related colleges and universities by way of construction grants to build secular academic facilities.

The *Lemon* three-pronged test became the framework used by the Court in subsequent establishment cases. The Court followed the *Tilton* precedent in *Roemer* v. *Board of Public Works,* 426 U.S. 736 (1976), by upholding a Maryland law that provided lump-sum grants for secular purposes to church-affiliated colleges and universities. The *Lemon* ruling itself, in terms of the relationship of the state to elementary and secondary parochial school education, was followed up by the Court in such cases as *Essex* v. *Wolman,* 409 U.S. 808 (1972), invalidating an Ohio program of direct tuition rebates to parents of children attending parochial schools, and *Committee for Public Education and Religious Liberty* v. *Nyquist,* 413 U.S. 756 (1973), which struck down New York programs of various forms of aid to parochial schools including tuition reimbursement and tax credits to parents of children attending such schools. Consistent with the Warren Court precedent in *Board of Education* v. *Allen,* the Burger Court upheld the loan

of secular textbooks to parochial schools in *Meek* v. *Pittenger,* 421 U.S. 349 (1975), but it struck down in the same case other similar forms of aid—including the loan of visual aids such as maps and charts. In *Wolman* v. *Walter,* 433 U.S. 229 (1977), the Court conceded the inconsistency of this, but defended its ruling in *Meek* as adhering to stare decisis. In *Committee for Public Education and Religious Liberty* v. *Regan,* 444 U.S. 646 (1980), the Court upheld the use of public funds to reimburse church schools for performing various testing and reporting tasks required by state law of all schools. In the eyes of the dissenters, this ruling promoted confusion in this area of law where clarity had begun to take shape. The Court in 1985 attempted to clear up at least some of the confusion in *Grand Rapids School District* v. *Ball,* 473 U.S. 373, and *Aguilar* v. *Felton,* 473 U.S. 402. In these cases, the Court used the *Lemon* test to strike down different public-sponsored programs for the enrichment of the secular curriculum and the provision of remedial instruction and clinical and guidance services for students in parochial schools. Interestingly, in 1986 the Court unanimously permitted state financial assistance to a blind student attending a private Christian college and pursuing a religious calling. The Court in *Witters* v. *Washington Department of Services for the Blind,* 474 U.S. 481, found that such vocational rehabilitation assistance from the Washington Commission for the Blind did not fall within any of the three prongs of *Lemon* and that thus there was no violation of the establishment clause. Likewise, the Court found no violation of the establishment clause by the provisions of the Adolescent Family Life Act, under which religious groups received federal funding for a variety of purposes including (in the words of the statute) "educational services relating to family life and problems associated with adolescent premarital sexual relations." The five-person majority in *Bowen* v. *Kendrick,* 487 U.S. 589 (1988), applied the *Lemon* test and found no religious purpose of the statute, no primary effect of advancing religion, and no excessive entanglement.

The Court, in **Mueller** v. **Allen,** approved a Minnesota law that permitted parents of all schoolchildren including those in parochial schools to take a state tax deduction for the cost of tuition and other educational expenses. In *Marsh* v. *Chambers,* 463 U.S. 783 (1983), the Court rejected the establishment of religion claim in the practice of the hiring of chaplains by legislatures. In *Hernandez* v. *C.I.R.,* 109 S.Ct. 2136 (1989), the Court rejected the argument that by *not* allowing a tax deduction for fixed payments to the Church of Scientology for courses it conducted that the establishment and free exercise guarantees were violated. The Court also rejected the religious freedom claims of Jimmy Swaggart who challenged California's sales tax as imposed on sales of religious materials. California had no First Amendment obligation to grant Swaggart a tax exemption (*Jimmy Swaggart Ministries* v. *Board of Equalization,* 110 S. Ct. 688 [1990]). And in 1990, the Court upheld the federal Equal Access Act against the challenge that it violated the establishment clause. The Court, in *Board of Education of Westside Community Schools* v. *Mergens,* 110 S.Ct. 2356, thus legitimated the requirement that public schools receiving federal funds must allow student religious groups the same access to school facilities as it offers other extracurricular activities. But in other decisions the Court was sympathetic to the establishment claim. For example, in *NLRB* v. *Catholic Bishop of Chicago,* 440 U.S. 490 (1979), the Court, using statutory interpretation, denied the National Labor Relations Board jurisdiction over parochial school teachers and suggested that were such jurisdiction mandated by Congress it would violate the separation of church and state. In *Larkin* v. *Grendel's Den, Inc.,* 459 U.S. 116 (1982), the Court invalidated a Massachusetts statute that gave churches a veto over applications for liquor licenses by establishments within a 500-foot radius of the church. This, said the Court, violated the establishment clause and impermissibly made a church a governmental decision maker in the dispensing of liquor licenses. In *Estate of Thornton* v. *Caldor, Inc.,* 472 U.S. 703 (1985), the Court invalidated a Connecticut statute that provided sabbath observers with an absolute and unqualified right *not* to work on their sabbath. This law violated the establishment clause and the Court came to that conclusion by analyzing the law in terms of the three-pronged *Lemon* test. The Court also used the *Lemon* test to invalidate the Louisiana Balanced Treatment for Creation Science in Public School Instruction Act (in *Edwards* v. *Aguillard*).

In one of the most controversial and widely publicized establishment decisions, the Court in 1984, in **Lynch** v. **Donnelly,** ruled that the city of Pawtucket, Rhode Island, did not violate the religion guarantees by sponsoring a crèche in the context of a Christmas display in a city park. In the opinion of the Court, written by Chief Justice Burger, there was the clear suggestion that the three-pronged *Lemon* test was merely useful as a guide but need not necessarily be mechanically or rigidly applied in every case. What also made this case of particular interest was not only what seemed to be the majority's slight backing away from the *Lemon* test, but also the suggestion of Chief Justice Burger that the no-establishment-of-religion guarantee means simply that no particular religious denomination may become the official religion. This view, along with a view of the free exercise guarantee that permits the government to act to facilitate free exercise, led some observers to believe that the Supreme Court would approve a moment of silent prayer or meditation. But, in *Wallace* v. *Jaffree,* over Chief Justice Burger's dissent and the dissents of two other justices, a new majority reaffirmed the *Lemon* test and found Alabama's public school moment-of-silent-prayer statute an establishment of religion.

The majority found a clearly religious purpose to the Alabama statute, but hinted that a simple moment-of-silent-meditation law that had secular justification would likely be approved by the Court.

The Rehnquist Court faced continuing litigation over holiday displays. The Court was badly divided in **County of Allegheny** v. **American Civil Liberties U.,** but it nevertheless used the *Lemon* test to strike down the display of a crèche standing alone in a county courthouse but upheld the display of a Chanukah menorah placed outside a city building next to a Christmas tree.

As we have seen, the First Amendment guarantees both the free exercise of religion and no established religion. But these clauses do not necessarily mean that government has no role to play vis-à-vis religion. The wall of separation metaphor is misleading and does not accurately convey the relationship of church and state. Furthermore, as the decisions themselves reveal, there are few absolutes in this realm. If the Court eventually follows Chief Justice Rehnquist's view that the establishment guarantee should be taken as preventing the imposition of one official religion, but not the fostering of all religion, then the law of church and state surely will evolve and American society may well experience change in some fundamental ways.

THE IMPACT OF THE COURT'S DECISIONS

Table 15.1 summarizes the impact of selected Court decisions concerning the religion guarantees. The reprinted cases follow.

Table 15.1 THE IMPACT OF SELECTED SUPREME COURT DECISIONS, THE RELIGION GUARANTEES

Case	Year	Impact on Parties	Short-Run Impact	Long-Run Impact
Minersville v. Gobitis	1940	Lillian and William Gobitis kept out of the Minersville public school.	Decision attacked by liberals. Violence aimed at Jehovah's Witnesses followed decision. West Virginia enacted new legislation and regulations making flag salute compulsory. Over 2,000 Witness children expelled from public schools across the country.	No long-run impact because Court reversed itself three years later.
West Virginia State Board of Education v. Barnette	1943	Jehovah's Witnesses children were not required to salute flag and their parents no longer feared fines and jail sentences.	Decision favorable to rights of Jehovah's Witnesses. Seen as contrasting America's commitment to civil liberties with the fascist regimes we were fighting. Justice Department pushed compliance with ruling. Witness children returned to public schools.	Stands as great civil liberties precedent.
Wisconsin v. Yoder	1972	Convictions of Jonas Yoder, Wallace Miller, and Adin Yutzy overturned. They each did not have to pay $5 fine.	Rights of Amish vindicated. End of long-standing harassment and prosecution of Amish by state and local officials in as many as nine states.	Important free exercise of religion precedent.
Heffron v. International Society for Krishna Consciousness	1981	ISKCON subject to Rule 6.05	ISKCON subject to Rule 6.05. Court seen as unsympathetic to ISKCON. Raises questions about the right of offbeat religions to "freely exercise" their religion when in conflict with other values.	Precedent for a generous reading of state interests when free exercise claims are made.
Everson v. Board of Education	1947	New Jersey program upheld.	Church-state issues gain new saliency. Stimulated some new litigation.	Decision had mixed impact. Precedent for pragmatic handling of church-state issues although doctrinally extended the establishment of religion prohibition to the states.

(continued)

Table 15.1 (continued)

Case	Year	Impact on Parties	Short-Run Impact	Long-Run Impact
Abington School District v. Schempp	1963	Parents of schoolchildren vindicated.	Unpopular decision with conservative groups. Public opinion confused and mixed. Widespread evasion of ruling in South and Midwest and uneven self-enforcement elsewhere. But some surveys show high compliance rate.	Stands as definitive ruling on the separation of church and state in matters of school prayer. May have contributed to broader cultural trends eroding religious beliefs/practices and the authority of religious institutions.
Wallace v. Jaffree	1985	Alabama school prayer and meditation statute struck down.	Gave rise in some states to new moment-of-silent-meditation legislation that ostensibly had no religious purpose.	Supporters of school prayer press for constitutional amendment and also appointments to federal courts of judges in sympathy with their views.
Tilton v. Richardson; Lemon v. Kurtzman	1971 1971	Taxpayers lose suit against federal government but win suits against Pennsylvania and Rhode Island.	Church-related colleges aided by decision, but parochial school aid programs of 33 states called into question. Church-run elementary and secondary schools continue to face financial problems.	Precedent for governmental aid to church-related colleges. *Lemon* three-pronged test becomes framework for analyzing establishment claims.
Mueller v. Allen	1983	Van D. Mueller and June Noyes lose their taxpayer suit.	Gave encouragement to other efforts to enact tax deductions for the tuition, textbooks, and transportation expenses of taxpayers' children's elementary and secondary schooling.	Uncertain because Court was split 5–4, and decision, despite protestations by majority, was contrary to *Committee for Public Education v. Nyquist* (1973).
Lynch v. Donnelly	1984	Mayor of Pawtucket, Rhode Island, Dennis Lynch, wins.	Popular decision with Moral Majority and like groups. Civil libertarians dismayed.	Opinion's narrow reading of establishment guarantee holds potential for providing rationale for overturning previous rulings favorable to establishment claims, perhaps even *Abington School District v. Schempp*.

MINERSVILLE v. GOBITIS,
310 U. S. 586 (1940)

Pennsylvania law required that all public schoolchildren salute the flag and recite the pledge of allegiance. Lillian Gobitis, age 12, and her 10-year-old brother, William, both Jehovah's Witnesses, refused to salute the flag because that would violate their religious beliefs. Jehovah's Witnesses interpret the Bible literally, and one of their tenets is that they are forbidden to worship a "graven image." And saluting a flag is considered worshiping a graven image. The school authorities of Minersville, Pennsylvania, however, insisted that the children salute the flag or face expulsion. The Gobitis children were expelled and Walter Gobitis, their father, sought to enjoin the Minersville school authorities from continuing to exact participation in the flag-salute ceremony as a condition of his children's attendance. Both the federal district court and the court of appeals decided in favor of Gobitis. An appeal was taken to the Supreme Court by the Minersville authorities.

Majority votes: 8
Dissenting votes: 1

MR. JUSTICE FRANKFURTER delivered the opinion of the Court: . . .

In the judicial enforcement of religious freedom we are concerned with a historic concept. The religious liberty which the Constitution protects has never excluded legislation of general scope not directed against doctrinal loyalties of particular sects. Judicial nullification of legislation cannot be justified by attributing to the framers of the Bill of Rights views for which there is no historic warrant. Conscientious scruples have not, in the course of the long struggle for religious toleration, relieved the individual from obedience to a general law not aimed at the promotion or restriction of religious beliefs. The mere possession of religious convictions which contradict the relevant concerns of a political society does not relieve the citizen from the discharge of political responsibilities. The necessity for this adjustment has again and again been recognized. . . . [T]he question remains whether school children, like the Gobitis children, must be excused from conduct required of all the other children in the promotion of national cohesion. We are dealing with an interest inferior to none in the hierarchy of legal values. National unity is the basis of national security. To deny the legislature the right to select appropriate means for its attainment presents a totally different order of prob-

lem from that of the propriety of subordinating the possible ugliness of littered streets to the free expression of opinion through distribution of handbills. . . .

. . . The ultimate foundation of a free society is the binding tie of cohesive sentiment. Such a sentiment is fostered by all those agencies of the mind and spirit which may serve to gather up the traditions of a people, transmit them from generation to generation, and thereby create that continuity of a treasured common life which constitutes a civilization. "We live by symbols." The flag is the symbol of our national unity, transcending all internal differences, however large, within the framework of the Constitution. . . . The precise issue, then, for us to decide is whether the legislatures of the various states and the authorities in a thousand counties and school districts of this country are barred from determining the appropriateness of various means to evoke that unifying sentiment without which there can ultimately be no liberties, civil or religious. To stigmatize legislative judgment in providing for this universal gesture of respect for the symbol of our national life in the setting of the common school as a lawless inroad on that freedom of conscience which the Constitution protects, would amount to no less than the pronouncement of pedagogical and psychological dogma in a field where courts possess no marked and certainly no controlling competence. The influences which help toward a common feeling for the common country are manifold. Some may seem harsh and others no doubt are foolish. Surely, however, the end is legitimate. And the effective means for its attainment are still so uncertain and so unauthenticated by science as to preclude us from putting the widely prevalent belief in flag-saluting beyond the pale of legislative power. . . .

The wisdom of training children in patriotic impulses by those compulsions which necessarily pervade so much of the educational process is not for our independent judgment. Even were we convinced of the folly of such a measure, such belief would be no proof of its unconstitutionality. For ourselves, we might be tempted to say that the deepest patriotism is best engendered by giving unfettered scope to the most crotchety beliefs. Perhaps it is best, even from the standpoint of those interests which ordinances like the one under review seek to promote, to give to the least popular sect leave from conformities like those here in issue. But the courtroom is not the arena for debating issues of educational policy. It is not our province to choose among competing considerations in the subtle process of securing effective loyalty to the

owed it are overruled, and the judgment enjoining enforcement of the West Virginia Regulation is

Affirmed.

MR. JUSTICE ROBERTS and MR. JUSTICE REED adhere to the views expressed by the Court in *Minersville School District* v. *Gobitis,* 310 U.S. 586, and are of the opinion that the judgment below should be reversed.

MR. JUSTICE BLACK and MR. JUSTICE DOUGLAS, concurring: [omitted]

MR. JUSTICE MURPHY, concurring: [omitted]

MR. JUSTICE FRANKFURTER, dissenting:

One who belongs to the most vilified and persecuted minority in history is not likely to be insensible to the freedoms guaranteed by our Constitution. Were my purely personal attitude relevant I should wholeheartedly associate myself with the general libertarian views in the Court's opinion, representing as they do the thought and action of a lifetime. But as judges we are neither Jew nor Gentile, neither Catholic nor agnostic. We owe equal attachment to the Constitution and are equally bound by our judicial obligations whether we derive our citizenship from the earliest or the latest immigrants to these shores. As a member of this Court I am not justified in writing my private notions of policy into the Constitution, no matter how deeply I may cherish them or how mischievous I may deem their disregard. The duty of a judge who must decide which of two claims before the Court shall prevail, that of a State to enact and enforce laws within its general competence or that of an individual to refuse obedience because of the demands of his conscience, is not that of the ordinary person. It can never be emphasized too much that one's own opinion about the wisdom or evil of a law should be excluded altogether when one is doing one's duty on the bench. The only opinion of our own even looking in that direction that is material is our opinion whether legislators could in reason have enacted such a law. In the light of all the circumstances, including the history of this question in this Court, it would require more daring than I possess to deny that reasonable legislators could have taken the action which is before us for review. Most unwillingly, therefore, I must differ from my brethren with regard to legislation like this. I cannot bring my mind to believe that the "liberty" secured by the Due Process Clause gives this Court authority to deny to the State of West Virginia the attainment of that which we all recognize as a legitimate legislative end, namely, the promotion of good citizenship, by employment of the means here chosen. . . .

WISCONSIN v. YODER, 406 U.S. 205 (1972)

The parents of Frieda Yoder and Barbara Miller, both 15 years of age, and Vernon Yutzy, 14 years of age, were convicted of violating Wisconsin's compulsory school attendance law which requires schooling until age 16. The parents, Jonas Yoder and Wallace Miller, and their families, are members of the Old Order Amish religion. Parent Adin Yutzy and his family belong to the Conservative Amish Mennonite Church. The defendants declined to send their children to public or private school after they had graduated from the eighth grade because the Amish believe that high school attendance is contrary to the Amish religion and way of life and that they would endanger their own salvation and that of their children by complying with the law. The Wisconsin Supreme Court reversed the convictions, and the state took the case to the United States Supreme Court.

Majority votes: 6
Dissenting votes: 1

MR. CHIEF JUSTICE BURGER delivered the opinion of the Court:. . . .

We come . . . to the quality of the claims of the respondents concerning the alleged encroachment of Wisconsin's compulsory school-attendance statute on their rights and the rights of their children to the free exercise of the religious beliefs they and their forbears have adhered to for almost three centuries. . . .

. . . [W]e see that the record in this case abundantly supports the claim that the traditional way of life of the Amish is not merely a matter of personal preference, but one of deep religious conviction, shared by an organized group, and intimately related to daily living. . . .

As the society around the Amish has become more populous, urban, industrialized, and complex, particularly in this century, government regulation of human affairs has correspondingly become more detailed and pervasive. The Amish mode of life has thus come into conflict increasingly with requirements of contemporary society exerting a hydraulic insistence on conformity to majoritarian standards. So long as compulsory education laws were confined to eight grades of elementary basic education imparted in a nearby rural schoolhouse, with a large proportion of students of the Amish faith, the Old Order Amish had little basis to fear that school attendance would expose their children to the worldly influence they reject. But modern compulsory secondary education in rural areas is now largely carried on in a consolidated school, often remote from the student's home and alien to his daily home life. As the record so strongly shows, the values and programs of the modern secondary school are in sharp conflict with the fundamental mode of life mandated by the Amish religion; modern laws requiring compulsory secondary education have accordingly engendered great concern and conflict. The conclusion is inescapable that secondary schooling, by exposing Amish children to worldly influences in terms of attitudes, goals, and values contrary to beliefs, and by substantially interfering with the religious development of the Amish child and his integration into the way of life of the Amish faith community at the crucial adolescent stage of development, contravenes the basic religious tenets and practice of the Amish faith, both as to the parent and the child. . . .

We turn, then, to the State's broader contention that its interest in its system of compulsory education is so compelling that even the established religious practices of the Amish must give way. Where fundamental claims of religious freedom are at stake, however, we cannot accept such a sweeping claim; despite its admitted validity in the generality of cases, we must searchingly examine the interests that the State seeks to promote by its requirement for compulsory education to age 16, and the impediment to those objectives that would flow from recognizing the claimed Amish exemption.

The State advances two primary arguments in support of its system of compulsory education. It notes, as Thomas Jefferson pointed out early in our history, that some degree of education is necessary to prepare citizens to participate effectively and intelligently in our open political system if we are to preserve freedom and independence. Further, education prepares individuals to be self-reliant and self-sufficient participants in society. We accept these propositions.

However, the evidence adduced by the Amish in this case is persuasively to the effect that an additional one or two years of formal high school for Amish children in place of their long-established program of informal vocational education would do little to serve those interests. . . .

The State . . . supports its interest in providing an additional one or two years of compulsory high school education to Amish children because of the possibility that some such children will choose to leave the Amish community, and that if this occurs they will be ill-equipped for life. The State argues that if Amish children leave their church they should not be in the position of making their way in the world without the education available in the one

or two additional years the State requires. However, on this record, that argument is highly speculative. There is no specific evidence of the loss of Amish adherents by attrition, nor is there any showing that upon leaving the Amish community Amish children, with their practical agricultural training and habits of industry and self-reliance, would become burdens on society because of educational shortcomings. Indeed, this argument of the State appears to rest primarily on the State's mistaken assumption, already noted, that the Amish do not provide any education for their children beyond the eighth grade, but allow them to grow in "ignorance." To the contrary, not only do the Amish accept the necessity for formal schooling through the eighth grade level, but continue to provide what has been characterized by the undisputed testimony of expert educators as an "ideal" vocational education for their children in the adolescent years.

There is nothing in this record to suggest that the Amish qualities of reliability, self-reliance, and dedication to work would fail to find ready markets in today's society. Absent some contrary evidence supporting the State's position, we are unwilling to assume that persons possessing such valuable vocational skills and habits are doomed to become burdens on society should they determine to leave the Amish faith, nor is there any basis in the record to warrant a finding that an additional one or two years of formal school education beyond the eighth grade would serve to eliminate any such problem that might exist. . . .

Finally, the State, on authority of *Prince* v. *Massachusetts,* argues that a decision exempting Amish children from the State's requirement fails to recognize the substantive right of the Amish child to a secondary education, and fails to give due regard to the power of the State as *parens patriae* to extend the benefit of secondary education to children regardless of the wishes of their parents. . . .

Contrary to the suggestion of the dissenting opinion of MR. JUSTICE DOUGLAS, our holding today in no degree depends on the assertion of the religious interest of the child as contrasted with that of the parents. It is the parents who are subject to prosecution here for failing to cause their children to attend school, and it is their right of free exercise, not that of their children, that must determine Wisconsin's power to impose criminal penalties on the parent. The dissent argues that a child who expresses a desire to attend public high school in conflict with the wishes of his parents should not be prevented from doing so. There is no reason for the Court to consider that point since it is not an issue in the case. The children are not parties to this litigation. The State has at no point tried this case on the theory that respondents were preventing their children from attending school against their expressed desires, and indeed the record is to the contrary. The State's position from the outset has been that it is empowered to apply its compulsory-attendance law to Amish parents in the same manner as to other parents—that is, without regard to the wishes of the child. That is the claim we reject today. . . .

For the reasons stated we hold, with the Supreme Court of Wisconsin, that the First and Fourteenth Amendments prevent the State from compelling respondents to cause their children to attend formal high school to age 16. . . .

Affirmed.

MR. JUSTICE POWELL and MR. JUSTICE REHNQUIST took no part in the consideration or decision of this case.

MR. JUSTICE STEWART, with whom MR. JUSTICE BRENNAN joins, concurring: [omitted]

MR. JUSTICE WHITE, with whom MR. JUSTICE BRENNAN and MR. JUSTICE STEWART join, concurring: [omitted]

MR. JUSTICE DOUGLAS, dissenting in part:

I agree with the Court that the religious scruples of the Amish are opposed to the education of their children beyond the grade schools, yet I disagree with the Court's conclusion that the matter is within the dispensation of parents alone. The Court's analysis assumes that the only interests at stake in the case are those of the Amish parents on the one hand, and those of the State on the other. The difficulty with this approach is that, despite the Court's claim, the parents are seeking to vindicate not only their own free exercise claims, but also those of their high-school-age children. . . .

If the parents in this case are allowed a religious exemption, the inevitable effect is to impose the parents' notions of religious duty upon their children. Where the child is mature enough to express potentially conflicting desires, it would be an invasion of the child's rights to permit such an imposition without canvassing his views. . . . As the child has no other effective forum, it is in this litigation that his rights should be considered. And, if an Amish child desires to attend high school, and is mature enough to have that desire respected, the State may well be able to override the parents' religiously motivated objections. Frieda Yoder has in fact testified that her own religious views are opposed to high-school education. I therefore join the judgment of the Court as to respondent Jonas Yoder.

But Frieda Yoder's views may not be those of Vernon Yutzy or Barbara Miller. I must dissent, therefore, as to respondents Adin Yutzy and Wallace Miller as their motion to dismiss also raised the question of their children's religious liberty. . . .

On this important and vital matter of education, I think the children should be entitled to be heard. . . . [T]he education of the child is a matter on which the child will often have decided views. He may want to be a pianist or an astronaut or an oceanographer. To do so he will have to break from the Amish tradition.

It is the future of the student, not the future of the parents, that is imperiled by today's decision. . . . It is the student's judgment, not his parents', that is essential if we are to give full meaning to what we have said about the Bill of Rights and of the right of students to be masters of their own destiny. If he is harnessed to the Amish way of life by those in authority over him and if his education is truncated, his entire life may be stunted and deformed. The child, therefore, should be given an opportunity to be heard before the State gives the exemption which we honor today.

HEFFRON v. INTERNATIONAL SOCIETY FOR KRISHNA CONSCIOUSNESS, 452 U.S. 640 (1981)

Each year the Minnesota Agricultural Society, a public corporation, sponsors and operates a state fair. The fair takes place on a 125-acre state-owned tract located in St. Paul and attracts well over 1 million persons during its 12-day run. Under Minnesota law the Society is authorized to make all rules and regulations "not inconsistent with law, which it may deem necessary or proper for the government of the fair grounds." Minnesota State Fair Rule 6.05 was issued providing that sale or distribution of any merchandise, including printed or written material, except from a duly licensed fixed location on the fairgrounds, shall be a misdemeanor. Rule 6.05 is applicable to nonprofit, charitable, and commercial enterprises. Space in the fairgrounds is rented in a nondiscriminatory fashion on a first-come, first-served basis. This case arose when the International Society for Krishna Consciousness, Inc. (abbreviated in the Court opinion as ISKCON) challenged the constitutionality of Rule 6.05 in the Minnesota courts. The Krishna religious organization argued that the rule suppressed the practice of Sankirtan, a religious ritual that requires its members to go into public places to distribute or sell religious literature and to solicit donations for the support of the Krishna religion. It was alleged that by requiring that ISKCON confine its activities to a booth in the fairgrounds, Rule 6.05 violated the religious liberty of the Krishna followers that was protected by the First Amendment. The trial court upheld the constitutionality of Rule 6.05, but the Minnesota Supreme Court reversed. The United States Supreme Court granted the state officials' (including Michael Heffron's) petition for the writ of certiorari.

Majority votes: 5
Dissenting votes: 4

JUSTICE WHITE delivered the opinion of the Court:

The question presented for review is whether a State, consistent with the First and Fourteenth Amendments, may require a religious organization desiring to distribute and sell religious literature and to solicit donations at a state fair to conduct those activities only at an assigned location within the fairgrounds even though application of the rule limits the religious practices of the organization. . . .

The State does not dispute that the oral and written dissemination of the Krishna's religious views and doctrines is protected by the First Amendment. Nor does it claim that this protection is lost because the written materials sought to be distributed are sold rather than given away or because contributions or gifts are solicited in the course of propagating the faith. Our cases indicate as much. *Murdock* v. *Pennsylvania,* 319 U.S. 105, 111 (1943); *Village of Schaumburg* v. *Citizens for a Better Environment,* 444 U.S. 620, 632 (1980). See *Cantwell* v. *Connecticut,* 310 U.S. 296 (1940).

It is also common ground, however, that the First Amendment does not guarantee the right to communicate one's views at all times and places or in any manner that may be desired. *Adderley* v. *Florida,* 385 U.S. 39, 47–48 (1966). . . . As the Minnesota Supreme Court recognized, the activities of ISKCON [International Society for Krishna Consciousness], like those of others protected by the First Amendment, are subject to reasonable time, place, and manner restrictions. The issue here, as it was below, is whether Rule 6.05 is a permissible restriction on the place and manner of communicating the views of the Krishna religion, more specifically, whether the Society may require the members of ISKCON who desire to practice Sankirtan at the State Fair to confine their distribution, sales, and solicitation activities to a fixed location.

A major criterion for a valid time, place, and manner restriction is that the restriction "may not be based upon either the content or subject matter of the speech." *Consolidated Edison Co.* v. *Public Service Commission,* 447 U.S., at 536. Rule 6.05 qualifies in this respect, since, as the Supreme Court of Minnesota observed, the Rule applies evenhandedly to all who wish to distribute and sell written materials or to solicit funds. No person or organization, whether commercial or charitable, is permitted to engage in such activities except from a booth rented for those purposes.

Nor does Rule 6.05 suffer from the more covert forms of discrimination that may result when arbitrary discretion is vested in some governmental authority. The method of allocating space is a straightforward first-come, first-served system. . . .

A valid time, place, and manner regulation must also "serve a significant governmental interest." *Virginia Board* v. *Citizens Council,* 425 U.S., at 771. Here, the principal justification asserted by the State in support of Rule 6.05 is the need to maintain the orderly movement of the crowd given the large number of exhibitors and persons attending the Fair.

The fairgrounds comprise a relatively small area of 125 acres, the bulk of which is covered by permanent buildings, temporary structures, parking lots, and connecting thoroughfares. There were some 1400 exhibitors and concessionaires renting space for the 1977 and 1978 Fairs, chiefly in permanent and temporary buildings. . . . Because the Fair attracts large crowds—an average of 115,000 patrons on weekdays and 160,000 on Saturdays and Sundays—it is apparent that the State's interest in the orderly movement and control of such an assembly of persons is a substantial consideration.

As a general matter, it is clear that a State's interest in protecting the "safety and convenience" of persons using a public forum is a valid governmental objective. . . . [R]espondents make a number of analogies between the fairgrounds and city streets. . . . But it is clear that there are significant differences between a street and the fairgrounds. A street is continually open, often uncongested, and constitutes not only a necessary conduit in the daily affairs of a locality's citizens, but also a place where people may enjoy the open air or the company of friends and neighbors in a relaxed environment. The Minnesota Fair, as described above, is a temporary event attracting great numbers of visitors who come to the event for a short period to see and experience the host of exhibits and attractions at the Fair. The flow of the crowd and demands of safety are more pressing in the context of the Fair. As such, any comparisons to public streets are necessarily inexact. . . .

As we see it, the Minnesota Supreme Court took

too narrow a view of the State's interest in avoiding congestion and maintaining the orderly movement of fair patrons on the fairgrounds. The justification for the Rule should not be measured by the disorder that would result from granting an exemption solely to ISKCON. That organization and its ritual of Sankirtan have no special claim to First Amendment protection as compared to that of other religions who also distribute literature and solicit funds. . . .

. . . [T]he court below agreed that without Rule 6.05 there would be widespread disorder at the fairgrounds. The court also recognized that some disorder would inevitably result from exempting the Krishnas from the Rule. Obviously, there would be a much larger threat to the State's interest in crowd control if all other religious, nonreligious, and noncommercial organizations could likewise move freely about the fairgrounds distributing and selling literature and soliciting funds at will.

Given these considerations, we hold that the State's interest in confining distribution, selling, and fund solicitation activities to fixed locations is sufficient to satisfy the requirement that a place or manner restriction must serve a substantial state interest. By focusing on the incidental effect of providing an exemption from Rule 6.05 to ISKCON, the Minnesota Supreme Court did not take into effect the fact that any such exemption cannot be meaningfully limited to ISKCON, and as applied to similarly situated groups would prevent the State from furthering its important concern with managing the flow of the crowd. In our view, the [Minnesota Agricultural] Society may apply its Rule and confine the type of transactions at issue to designated locations without violating the First Amendment. . . .

For Rule 6.05 to be valid as a place and manner restriction, it must also be sufficiently clear that alternative forums for the expression of respondents' protected speech exist despite the effects of the Rule. Rule 6.05 is not vulnerable on this ground. First, the Rule does not prevent ISKCON from practicing Sankirtan anywhere outside the fairgrounds. More importantly, the Rule has not been shown to deny access within the forum in question. Here, the Rule does not exclude ISKCON from the fairgrounds, nor does it deny that organization the right to conduct any desired activity at some point within the forum. Its members may mingle with the crowd and orally propagate their views. The organization may also arrange for a booth and distribute and sell literature and solicit funds from that location on the fairgrounds itself. The Minnesota State Fair is a limited public forum in that it exists to pro-

vide a means for a great number of exhibitors temporarily to present their products or views, be they commercial, religious, or political, to a large number of people in an efficient fashion. Considering the limited functions of the Fair and the combined area within which it operates, we are unwilling to say that Rule 6.05 does not provide ISKCON and other organizations with an adequate means to sell and solicit on the fairgrounds. The First Amendment protects the right of every citizen to "reach the minds of willing listeners and to do so there must be opportunity to win their attention." *Kovacs* v. *Cooper,* 336 U.S. 77, 87 (1949). Rule 6.05 does not unnecessarily limit that right within the fairgrounds.

The judgment of the Supreme Court of Minnesota is reversed and the case is remanded for further proceedings not inconsistent with this opinion.

So ordered.

JUSTICE BRENNAN, with whom JUSTICE MARSHALL and JUSTICE STEVENS join, concurring in part and dissenting in part:

As the Court recognizes, the issue in this case is whether Minnesota State Fair Rule 6.05 constitutes a reasonable time, place, and manner restriction on respondents' exercise of protected First Amendment rights. In deciding this issue, the Court considers, *inter alia,* whether the regulation serves a significant governmental interest and whether that interest can be served by a less intrusive restriction. The Court errs, however, in failing to apply its analysis separately to each of the protected First Amendment activities restricted by Rule 6.05. Thus, the Court fails to recognize that some of the State's restrictions may be reasonable while others may not.

Rule 6.05 restricts three types of protected First Amendment activity: distribution of literature, sale of literature, and solicitation of funds. No individual or group is permitted to engage in these activities at the Minnesota State Fair except from preassigned, rented booth locations. Violation of this rule constitutes a misdemeanor, and violators are subject to arrest and expulsion from the fairgrounds. . . .

I quite agree with the Court that the State has a significant interest in maintaining crowd control on its fairgrounds. I also have no doubt that the State has a significant interest in protecting its fairgoers from fraudulent or deceptive solicitation practices. Indeed, because I believe on this record that this latter interest is substantially furthered by a Rule that restricts sales and solicitation activities to fixed booth locations, where the State will have the greatest opportunity to police and prevent possible deceptive practices, I would hold that Rule 6.05's restriction on those particular forms of First Amendment expression is justified as an antifraud measure. Accordingly, I join the judgment of the Court insofar as it upholds Rule 6.05's restriction on sales and solicitations. However, because I believe that the booth rule is an overly intrusive means of achieving the State's interest in crowd control, and because I cannot accept the validity of the State's asserted justification that it has an interest in protecting its fairgoers from annoyance and harassment, I dissent from the Court's approval of Rule 6.05's restriction on the distribution of literature. . . .

Because of Rule 6.05 . . . as soon as a proselytizing member of ISKCON hands out a free copy of the Bhagavad-Gita to an interested listener, or a political candidate distributes his campaign brochure to a potential voter, he becomes subject to arrest and removal from the fairgrounds. This constitutes a significant restriction on First Amendment rights. By prohibiting distribution of literature outside the booths, the fair officials sharply limit the number of fairgoers to whom the proselytizers and candidates can communicate their messages. Only if a fairgoer affirmatively seeks out such information by approaching a booth does Rule 6.05 fully permit potential communicators to exercise their First Amendment rights.

In support of its crowd control justification, the State contends that if fairgoers are permitted to distribute literature, large crowds will gather, blocking traffic lanes and causing safety problems. . . .

But the State has failed to provide any support for these assertions. It has made no showing that relaxation of its booth rule would create additional disorder in a fair that is already characterized by the robust and unrestrained participation of hundreds of thousands of wandering fairgoers. If fairgoers can make speeches, engage in face-to-face proselytizing, and buttonhole prospective supporters, they can surely distribute literature to members of their audience without significantly adding to the State's asserted crowd control problem. The record is devoid of any evidence that the 125-acre fairgrounds could not accommodate peripatetic distributors of literature just as easily as it now accommodates peripatetic speechmakers and proselytizers.

Relying on a general, speculative fear of disorder, the State of Minnesota has placed a significant restriction on respondents' ability to exercise core First Amendment rights. This restriction is not narrowly drawn to advance the State's interests, and

for that reason is unconstitutional. . . . If the State had a reasonable concern that distribution in certain parts of the fairgrounds—for example, entrances and exits—would cause disorder, it could have drafted its rule to prohibit distribution of literature at those points. If the State felt it necessary to limit the number of persons distributing an organization's literature, it could, within reason, have done that as well. It had no right, however, to ban all distribution of literature outside the booths. . . .

Because I believe that the State could have drafted a more narrowly-drawn restriction on the right to distribute literature without undermining its interest in maintaining crowd control on the fairgrounds, I would affirm that part of the judgment below that strikes down Rule 6.05 as it applies to distribution of literature.

JUSTICE BLACKMUN, concurring in part and dissenting in part: [omitted]

GOLDMAN v. WEINBERGER,
475 U.S. 503 (1986)

S. Simcha Goldman, an Orthodox Jew, was ordered not to wear a yarmulke (skullcap) while on duty and in uniform as a commissioned officer in the United States Air Force. Goldman was stationed at March Air Force Base in Riverside, California, and served as a clinical psychologist at the mental health clinic on the base. Until 1981 Goldman was not prevented from wearing his yarmulke on the base. But in April, 1981, after he had testified as a defense witness at a court-martial wearing his yarmulke, opposing counsel lodged a complaint with the Hospital Commander arguing that Goldman's practice of wearing his yarmulke violated Air Force Regulation 35-10. Goldman refused the order to comply with the regulation and subsequently brought a suit in federal district court claiming that the application of the regulation to prevent him from wearing his yarmulke infringed upon his First Amendment freedom to exercise his religious beliefs. The district court permanently enjoined the Air Force from enforcing the regulation against Goldman. The court of appeals reversed, and the Supreme Court was asked to determine whether the free exercise guarantee of the First Amendment was violated by the Air Force.

Majority votes: 5
Dissenting votes: 4

JUSTICE REHNQUIST delivered the opinion of the Court: . . . .

Petitioner argues that AFR 35-10, as applied to

him, prohibits religiously motivated conduct and should therefore be analyzed under the standard enunciated in *Sherbert* v. *Verner,* 374 U.S. 398, 406 (1963). But we have repeatedly held that "the military is, by necessity, a specialized society separate from civilian society," *Parker* v. *Levy,* 417 U.S. 733, 743 (1974). "[T]he military must insist upon a respect for duty and a discipline without counterpart in civilian life," in order to prepare for and perform its vital role.

Our review of military regulations challenged on First Amendment grounds is far more deferential than constitutional review of similar laws or regulations designed for civilian society. The military need not encourage debate or tolerate protest to the extent that such tolerance is required of the civilian state by the First Amendment; to accomplish its mission the military must foster instinctive obedience, unity, commitment, and esprit de corps. The essence of military service "is the subordination of the desires and interests of the individual to the needs of the service."

These aspects of military life do not, of course, render entirely nugatory in the military context the guarantees of the First Amendment. But "within the military community there is simply not the same [individual] autonomy as there is in the larger civilian community." *Parker* v. *Levy, supra,* at 751. In the context of the present case, when evaluating whether military needs justify a particular restriction on religiously motivated conduct, courts must give great deference to the professional judgment of military authorities concerning the relative importance of a particular military interest. Not only are courts " 'ill-equipped to determine the impact upon discipline that any particular intrusion upon military authority might have," but the military authorities have been charged by the Executive and Legislative Branches with carrying out our Nation's military policy. "Judicial deference . . . is at its apogee when legislative action under the congressional authority to raise and support armies and make rules and regulations for their governance is challenged." *Rostker* v. *Goldberg,* 453 U.S. 57, 70 (1981).

The considered professional judgment of the Air Force is that the traditional outfitting of personnel in standardized uniforms encourages the subordination of personal preferences and identities in favor of the overall group mission. Uniforms encourage a sense of hierarchical unity by tending to eliminate outward individual distinctions except for those of rank. The Air Force considers them as vital during peacetime as during war because its personnel must be ready to provide an effective defense on a moment's notice; the necessary habits of discipline

and unity must be developed in advance of trouble. We have acknowledged that "[t]he inescapable demands of military discipline and obedience to orders cannot be taught in battlefields; the habit of immediate compliance with military procedures and orders must be virtually reflex with no time for debate or reflection." . . .

Petitioner Goldman contends that the Free Exercise Clause of the First Amendment requires the Air Force to make an exception to its uniform dress requirements for religious apparel unless the accoutrements create a "clear danger" of undermining discipline and esprit de corps. He asserts that in general, visible but "unobtrusive" apparel will not create such a danger and must therefore be accommodated. He argues that the Air Force failed to prove that a specific exception for his practice of wearing an unobtrusive yarmulke would threaten discipline. He contends that the Air Force's assertion to the contrary is mere *ipse dixit,* with no support from actual experience or a scientific study in the record, and is contradicted by expert testimony that religious exceptions to AFR 35-10 are in fact desirable and will increase morale by making the Air Force a more humane place.

But whether or not expert witnesses may feel that religious exceptions to AFR 35-10 are desirable is quite beside the point. The desirability of dress regulations in the military is decided by the appropriate military officials, and they are under no constitutional mandate to abandon their considered professional judgment. Quite obviously, to the extent the regulations do not permit the wearing of religious apparel such as a yarmulke, a practice described by petitioner as silent devotion akin to prayer, military life may be more objectionable for petitioner and probably others. But the First Amendment does not require the military to accommodate such practices in the face of its view that they would detract from the uniformity sought by the dress regulations. The Air Force has drawn the line essentially between religious apparel which is visible and that which is not, and we hold that those portions of the regulations challenged here reasonably and evenhandedly regulate dress in the interest of the military's perceived need for uniformity. The First Amendment therefore does not prohibit them from being applied to petitioner even though their effect is to restrict the wearing of the headgear required by his religious beliefs.

The judgment of the Court of Appeals is

Affirmed.

JUSTICE STEVENS, with whom JUSTICE WHITE and JUSTICE POWELL join, concurring:. . . .

As the Court demonstrates, the rule that is challenged in this case is based on a neutral, completely objective standard—visibility. It was not motivated by hostility against, or any special respect for, any religious faith. An exception for yarmulkes would represent a fundamental departure from the true principle of uniformity that supports that rule. For that reason, I join the Court's opinion and its judgment.

JUSTICE BRENNAN, with whom JUSTICE MARSHALL joins, dissenting:

Simcha Goldman invokes this Court's protection of his First Amendment right to fulfill one of the traditional religious obligations of a male Orthodox Jew—to cover his head before an omnipresent God. The Court's response to Goldman's request is to abdicate its role as principal expositor of the Constitution and protector of individual liberties in favor of credulous deference to unsupported assertions of military necessity. I dissent. . . .

. . . The contention that the discipline of the armed forces will be subverted if Orthodox Jews are allowed to wear yarmulkes with their uniforms surpasses belief. It lacks support in the record of this case and the Air Force offers no basis for it as a general proposition. While the perilous slope permits the services arbitrarily to refuse exceptions requested to satisfy mere personal preferences, before the Air Force may burden free exercise rights it must advance, at the *very least*, a rational reason for doing so. . . .

The dress code . . . allows men to wear up to three rings and one identification bracelet of "neat and conservative," but non-uniform, design. This jewelry is apparently permitted even if, as is often the case with rings, it associates the wearer with a denominational school or a religious or secular fraternal organization. If these emblems of religious, social, and ethnic identity are not deemed to be unacceptably divisive, the Air Force cannot rationally justify its bar against yarmulkes on that basis. . . .

Finally, the Air Force argues that while Dr. Goldman describes his yarmulke as an "unobtrusive" addition to his uniform, obtrusiveness is a purely relative, standardless judgment. The Government notes that while a yarmulke might not seem obtrusive to a Jew, neither does a turban to a Sikh, a saffron robe to a Satchidananda Ashram-Integral Yogi, nor do dreadlocks to a Rastafarian. If the Court were to require the Air Force to permit yarmulkes, the service must also allow all of these other forms of dress and grooming.

The Government dangles before the Court a classic parade of horribles, the specter of a brightly-colored, "rag-tag band of soldiers." Although turbans, saffron robes, and dreadlocks are not before

us in this case and must each be evaluated against the reasons a service branch offers for prohibiting personnel from wearing them while in uniform, a reviewing court could legitimately give deference to dress and grooming rules that have a *reasoned* basis in, for example, functional utility, health and safety considerations, and the goal of a polished, professional appearance. It is the lack of any reasoned basis for prohibiting yarmulkes that is so striking here. . . .

. . . The Court and the military services have presented patriotic Orthodox Jews with a painful dilemma—the choice between fulfilling a religious obligation and serving their country. Should the draft be reinstated, compulsion will replace choice. Although the pain the services inflict on Orthodox Jewish servicemen is clearly the result of insensitivity rather than design, it is unworthy of our military because it is unnecessary. The Court and the military have refused these servicemen their constitutional rights; we must hope that Congress will correct this wrong.

JUSTICE BLACKMUN, dissenting: [omitted]

JUSTICE O'CONNOR, with whom JUSTICE MARSHALL joins, dissenting:. . . .

I believe that the Court should attempt to articulate and apply an appropriate standard for a free exercise claim in the military context, and should examine Captain Goldman's claim in light of that standard.

Like the Court today in this case involving the military, the Court in the past has had some difficulty, even in the civilian context, in articulating a clear standard for evaluating free exercise claims that result from the application of general state laws burdening religious conduct. . . . One can, however, glean at least two consistent themes from th[e] Court's precedents. First, when the Government attempts to deny a free exercise claim, it must show that an unusually important interest is at stake, whether that interest is denominated "compelling," "of the highest order," or "overriding." Second, the Government must show that granting the requested exemption will do substantial harm to that interest, whether by showing that the means adopted is the "least restrictive" or "essential," or that the interest will not "otherwise be served." These two requirements are entirely sensible in the context of the assertion of a free exercise claim. First, because the Government is attempting to override an interest specifically protected by the Bill of Rights, the Government must show that the opposing interest it asserts is of especial importance before there is any chance that its claim can prevail. Second, since the Bill of Rights is expressly designed to protect the individual against the aggregated and sometimes intolerant powers of the state, the Government must show that the interest asserted will in fact be substantially harmed by granting the type of exemption requested by the individual.

There is no reason why these general principles should not apply in the military, as well as the civilian, context. . . .

I have no doubt that there are many instances in which the unique fragility of military discipline and esprit de corps necessitates rigidity by the Government when similar rigidity to preserve an assertedly analogous interest would not pass constitutional muster in the civilian sphere. Nonetheless, as JUSTICE BRENNAN persuasively argues, the Government can present no sufficiently convincing proof in *this* case to support an assertion that granting an exemption of the type requested here would do substantial harm to military discipline and esprit de corps. . . .

LYNG v. NORTHWEST INDIAN CEMETERY PROTECTIVE ASS'N, 485 U.S. 439 (1988)

Officials of the United States Forest Service were seriously considering constructing a paved road that would cut through the Chimney Rock area of the Six Rivers National Forest. It was also considering timber harvesting in the same area. The Forest Service commissioned a study that reported that the Chimney Rock area has historically been used by certain Native Americans for religious rituals that depend upon privacy, silence, and an undisturbed natural setting. The study recommended that no road be constructed through the Chimney Rock area because it would irreparably damage the sacred areas. The Forest Service, however, rejected the recommendation and selected a route that was as far as possible from the sites used for religious purposes. After appealing in vain, the Northwest Indian Cemetery Protective Ass'n and others filed suit in federal district court against Secretary of Agriculture Lyng, whose jurisdiction includes the Forest Service. The court issued a permanent injunction prohibiting the Forest Service from constructing the Chimney Rock section of the road and from allowing timber harvesting in that area. The court found that to do otherwise would violate the free exercise rights of the Indians. The Court of Appeals for the Ninth Circuit affirmed, and the federal government went to the Supreme Court, which granted certiorari.

Majority votes: 5
Dissenting votes: 3

JUSTICE O'CONNOR delivered the opinion of the Court:

This case requires us to consider whether the First Amendment's Free Exercise Clause forbids the Government from permitting timber harvesting in, or constructing a road through, a portion of a National Forest that has traditionally been used for religious purposes by members of three American Indian tribes in northwestern California. We conclude that it does not. . . .

It is undisputed that the Indian respondents' beliefs are sincere and that the Government's proposed actions will have severe adverse effects on the practice of their religion. Respondents contend that the burden on their religious practices is heavy enough to violate the Free Exercise Clause unless the Government can demonstrate a compelling need. . . . We disagree.

In *Bowen* v. *Roy,* 476 U.S. 693 (1986), we considered a challenge to a federal statute that required the States to use Social Security numbers in administering certain welfare programs. Two applicants for benefits under these programs contended that their religious beliefs prevented them from acceding to the use of a Social Security number for their two-year-old daughter because the use of a numerical identifier would " 'rob the spirit' of [their] daughter and prevent her from attaining greater spiritual power." Similarly, in this case, it is said that disruption of the natural environment caused by the road will diminish the sacredness of the area in question and create distractions that will interfere with "training and ongoing religious experience of individuals using [sites within] the area for personal medicine and growth . . . and as integrated parts of a system of religious belief and practice which correlates ascending degrees of personal power with a geographic hierarchy of power." The Court rejected this kind of challenge in *Roy*. . . .

The building of a road or the harvesting of timber on publicly owned land cannot meaningfully be distinguished from the use of a Social Security number in *Roy*. In both cases, the challenged government action would interfere significantly with private persons' ability to pursue spiritual fulfillment according to their own religious beliefs. In neither case, however, would the affected individuals be coerced by the Government's action into violating their religious beliefs; nor would either governmental action penalize religious activity by denying any person an equal share of the rights, benefits, and privileges enjoyed by other citizens.

We are asked to distinguish this case from *Roy* on the ground that the infringement on religious liberty here is "significantly greater." In this case . . .

it is said that the proposed road will "physically destro[y] the environmental conditions and the privacy without which the [religious] practices cannot be conducted."

These efforts to distinguish *Roy* are unavailing. This Court cannot determine the truth of the underlying beliefs that led to the religious objections here or in *Roy,* and accordingly cannot weigh the adverse effects on the Roys and compare them with the adverse effects on respondents. Without the ability to make such comparisons, we cannot say that the one form of incidental interference with an individual's spiritual activities should be subjected to a different constitutional analysis than the other.

Respondents insist, nonetheless, that the courts below properly relied on a factual inquiry into the degree to which the Indians' spiritual practices would become ineffectual if the road were built. They rely on several cases in which this Court has sustained free exercise challenges to government programs that interfered with individuals' ability to practice their religion. See *Wisconsin* v. *Yoder* (1972) (compulsory school-attendance law); *Sherbert* v. *Verner,* (1963) (denial of unemployment benefits to applicant who refused to accept work requiring her to violate the Sabbath); *Thomas* v. *Review Board, Indiana Employment Security Div.,* (1981) (denial of unemployment benefits to applicant whose religion forbade him to fabricate weapons).

Even apart from the inconsistency between *Roy* and respondents' reading of these cases, their interpretation will not withstand analysis. It is true that this Court has repeatedly held that indirect coercion or penalties on the free exercise of religion, not just outright prohibitions, are subject to scrutiny under the First Amendment. Thus, for example, ineligibility for unemployment benefits, based solely on a refusal to violate the Sabbath, has been analogized to a fine imposed on Sabbath worship. This does not and cannot imply that incidental effects of government programs, which may make it more difficult to practice certain religions but which have no tendency to coerce individuals into acting contrary to their religious beliefs, require government to bring forward a compelling justification for its otherwise lawful actions. The crucial word in the constitutional text is "prohibit": "For the Free Exercise Clause is written in terms of what the government cannot do to the individual, not in terms of what the individual can exact from the government."

Even if we assume that we should accept the Ninth Circuit's prediction, according to which the road will "virtually destroy the Indians' ability to practice their religion," the Constitution simply does not provide a principle, that could justify upholding respondents' legal claims. However much we might wish that it were otherwise, government simply could not operate if it were required to satisfy every citizen's religious needs and desires. A broad range of government activities—from social welfare programs to foreign aid to conservation projects—will always be considered essential to the spiritual well-being of some citizens, often on the basis of sincerely held religious beliefs. Others will find the very same activities deeply offensive, and perhaps incompatible with their own search for spiritual fulfillment and with the tenets of their religion. The First Amendment must apply to all citizens alike, and it can give to none of them a veto over public programs that do not prohibit the free exercise of religion. The Constitution does not, and courts cannot, offer to reconcile the various competing demands on government, many of them rooted in sincere religious belief, that inevitably arise in so diverse a society as ours. That task, to the extent that it is feasible, is for the legislatures and other institutions.

The dissent proposes an approach to the First Amendment that is fundamentally inconsistent with the principles on which our decision rests. Notwithstanding the sympathy that we all must feel for the plight of the Indian respondents, it is plain that the approach taken by the dissent cannot withstand analysis. On the contrary, the path towards which it points us is incompatible with the text of the Constitution, with the precedents of this Court, and with a responsible sense of our own institutional role.

The dissent begins by asserting that the "constitutional guarantee we interpret today . . . is directed against *any* form of government action that frustrates or inhibits religious practice." The Constitution, however, says no such thing. Rather, it states: "Congress shall make no law . . . *prohibiting* the free exercise [of religion]." U.S. Const., Amdt. 1 (emphasis added).

As we explained above, *Bowen* v. *Roy* rejected a First Amendment challenge to government activities that the religious objectors sincerely believed would " 'rob the spirit' of [their] daughter and prevent her from attaining greater spiritual power."

The dissent now offers to distinguish that case by saying that the Government was acting there "in a purely internal manner," whereas land-use decisions "are likely to have substantial external effects." Whatever the source or meaning of the dissent's distinction, it has no basis in *Roy.* Robbing the spirit of a child, and preventing her from attaining greater spiritual power, is both a "substantial external effect" and one that is remarkably similar to the injury claimed by respondents in the case before us today. The dissent's reading of *Roy* would effectively overrule that decision, without providing any compelling justification for doing so.

The dissent also misreads *Wisconsin* v. *Yoder*. The Court acknowledged that the statute might be constitutional, *despite* its coercive nature, if the state could show with sufficient "particularity how its admittedly strong interest in compulsory education would be adversely affected by granting an exemption to the Amish." The dissent's out-of-context quotations notwithstanding, there is nothing whatsoever in the *Yoder* opinion to support the proposition that the "impact" on the Amish religion would have been constitutionally problematic if the statute at issue had not been coercive in nature.

Seeing the Court as the arbiter, the dissent proposes a legal test under which it would decide which public lands are "central" or "indispensable" to which religions, and by implication which are "dispensable" or "peripheral," and would then decide which government programs are "compelling" enough to justify "infringement of those practices." We would accordingly be required to weigh the value of every religious belief and practice that is said to be threatened by any government program. Unless a "showing of 'centrality,' " is nothing but an assertion of centrality, dissent thus offers us the prospect of this Court holding that some sincerely held religious beliefs and practices are not "central" to certain religions, despite protestations to the contrary from the religious objectors who brought the lawsuit. In other words, the dissent's approach would require us to rule that some religious adherents misunderstand their own religious beliefs. We think such an approach cannot be squared with the Constitution or with our precedents, and that it would cast the judiciary in a role that we were never intended to play.

The decision of the court below, according to which the First Amendment precludes the Government from completing the road or from permitting timber harvesting in the Chimney Rock area, is reversed. In order that the District Court's injunction may be reconsidered in light of this holding, and in the light of any other relevant events that may have intervened since the injunction issued, the case is remanded for further proceedings consistent with this opinion.

It is so ordered.

JUSTICE KENNEDY took no part in the consideration or decision of this case.

JUSTICE BRENNAN, with whom JUSTICE MARSHALL and JUSTICE BLACKMUN join, dissenting:. . . .

[T]he Court concludes that even where the Government uses federal land in a manner that threatens the very existence of a Native American religion, the Government is simply not *"doing"* anything to the practitioners of that faith. Instead, the Court believes that Native Americans who request that the Government refrain from destroying their religion effectively seek to exact from the Government *de facto* beneficial ownership of federal property. These two astonishing conclusions follow naturally from the Court's determination that federal land-use decisions that render the practice of a given religion impossible do not burden that religion in a manner cognizable under the Free Exercise Clause, because such decisions neither coerce conduct inconsistent with religious belief nor penalize religious activity. The constitutional guarantee we interpret today, however, draws no such fine distinctions between types of restraints on religious exercise, but rather is directed against any form of governmental action that frustrates or inhibits religious practice. Because the Court today refuses even to acknowledge the constitutional injury respondents will suffer, and because this refusal essentially leaves Native Americans with absolutely no constitutional protection against perhaps the gravest threat to their religious practices, I dissent. . . .

As the Forest Service's commissioned study, the Theodoratus Report, explains, for Native Americans religion is not a discrete sphere of activity separate from all others, and any attempt to isolate the religious aspects of Indian life "is in reality an exercise which forces Indian concepts into non-Indian categories." Thus, for most Native Americans, "[t]he area of worship cannot be delineated from social, political, cultur[al], and other areas o[f] Indian lifestyle."

A pervasive feature of this life-style is the individual's relationship with the natural world; this relationship, which can accurately though somewhat incompletely be characterized as one of stewardship, forms the core of what might be called, for want of a better nomenclature, the Indian religious experience. While traditional western religions view creation as the work of a deity "who institutes natural laws which then govern the operation of physical nature," tribal religions regard creation as an on-going process in which they are morally and religiously obligated to participate. Native Americans fulfill this duty through ceremonies and rituals designed to preserve and stabilize the earth and to protect humankind from disease and other catastrophes. Failure to conduct these ceremonies in the manner and place specified, adherents believe, will result in great harm to the earth and to the people whose welfare depends upon it.

For respondent Indians, the most sacred of lands is the high country where, they believe, prehuman spirits moved with the coming of humans to the earth. Because these spirits are seen as the source of religious power, or "medicine," many of the tribes' rituals and practices require frequent journeys to the area. . . .

The Court does not for a moment suggest that the interests served by the road are in any way compelling, or that they outweigh the destructive effect construction of the road will have on respondents' religious practices. Instead, the Court embraces the Government's contention that its prerogative as landowner should always take precedence over a claim that a particular use of federal property infringes religious practices. Attempting to justify this rule, the Court argues that the First Amendment bars only outright prohibitions, indirect coercion, and penalties on the free exercise of religion. . . .

Since our recognition nearly half a century ago that restraints on religious conduct implicate the concerns of the Free Exercise Clause, see *Prince* v. *Massachusetts,* (1944), we have never suggested that the protections of the guarantee are limited to so narrow a range of governmental burdens. The land-use decision challenged here will restrain respondents from practicing their religion as surely and as completely as any of the governmental actions we have struck down in the past, and the Court's efforts simply to define away respondents' injury as nonconstitutional is both unjustified and ultimately unpersuasive. . . .

In the final analysis, the Court's refusal to recognize the constitutional dimension of respondents' injuries stems from its concern that acceptance of respondents' claim could potentially strip the Government of its ability to manage and use vast tracts of federal property. In addition, the nature of respondent's site-specific religious practices raises the specter of future suits in which Native Americans seek to exclude all human activity from such areas. These concededly legitimate concerns lie at the very heart of this case, which represents yet another stress point in the longstanding conflict between two disparate cultures—the dominant western culture, which views land in terms of ownership and use, and that of Native Americans, in which concepts of private property are not only alien, but contrary to a belief system that holds land sacred. Rather than address this conflict in any meaningful fashion, however, the Court disclaims all responsibility for balancing these competing and potentially irreconcilable interests, choosing instead to turn this difficult task over to the federal legislature. Such an abdication is more than merely indefensible as an institutional matter: by defining respondents' injury as "nonconstitutional," the Court has effectively bestowed on one party to this conflict the unilateral authority to resolve all future disputes in its favor, subject only to the Court's toothless exhortation to be "sensitive" to affected religions. In my view, however, Native Americans deserve—and the Constitution demands—more than this.

Prior to today's decision, several courts of appeals had attempted to fashion a test that accommodates the competing "demands" placed on federal property by the two cultures. Recognizing that the Government normally enjoys plenary authority over federal lands, the Courts of Appeals required Native Americans to demonstrate that any land-use decisions they challenged involved lands that were "central" or "indispensable" to their religious practices. . . .

Although this requirement limits the potential number of free exercise claims that might be brought to federal land management decisions, and thus forestalls the possibility that the Government will find itself ensnared in a host of lilliputian lawsuits, it has been criticized as inherently ethnocentric, for it incorrectly assumes that Native American belief systems ascribe religious significance to land in a traditionally western hierarchical manner.

It is frequently the case in constitutional litigation, however, that courts are called upon to balance interests that are not readily translated into rough equivalents. At their most absolute, the competing claims that both the Government and Native Americans assert in federal land are fundamentally incompatible, and unless they are tempered by compromise, mutual accommodation will remain impossible.

I believe it appropriate, therefore, to require some showing of "centrality" before the Government can be required either to come forward with a compelling justification for its proposed use of federal land or to forego that use altogether. "Centrality," however, should not be equated with the survival or extinction of the religion itself. In *Yoder,* for example, we treated the objection to the compulsory school attendance of adolescents as "central" to the Amish faith even though such attendance did not prevent or otherwise render the practice of that religion impossible, and instead simply threatened to "undermine" that faith. Because of their perceptions of and relationship with the natural world, Native Americans consider all land sacred. Nevertheless, the Theodoratus Report reveals that respondents here deemed certain lands more powerful and more directly related to their religious practices than others. Thus, in my view, while Native Americans need not demonstrate, as respondents did here, that the Government's land-use decision will assuredly eradicate their faith, I do not think it is enough to allege simply that the land in question is held sacred. Rather, adherents challenging a proposed use of federal land should be required to show that the decision poses a substantial and realistic threat of frustrating their religious practices. Once such a showing is made, the burden should shift to the Government to come forward with a compelling state interest sufficient to justify the infringement of those practices.

The Court today suggests that such an approach would place courts in the untenable position of deciding which practices and beliefs are "central" to a given faith and which are not, and invites the prospect of judges advising some religious adherents that they "misunderstand their own religious beliefs." In fact, however, courts need not undertake any such inquiries: like all other religious adherents, Native Americans would be the arbiters of which practices are central to their faith, subject only to the normal requirement that their claims be genuine and sincere. The question for the courts, then, is not whether the Native American claimants understand their own religion, but rather, whether they have discharged their burden of demonstrating, as the Amish did with respect to the compulsory school law in *Yoder,* that the land-use decision poses a substantial and realistic threat of undermining or frustrating their religious practices. Ironically, the Court's apparent solicitude for the integrity of religious belief and its desire to forestall the possibility that courts might second-guess the claims of religious adherents leads to far greater inequities than those the Court postulates: today's ruling sacrifices a religion at least as old as the Nation itself, along with the spiritual well-being of its approximately 5,000 adherents, so that the Forest Service can build a 6-mile segment of road that two lower courts found had only the most marginal and speculative utility, both to the Government itself and to the private lumber interests that might conceivably use it.

Similarly, the Court's concern that the claims of Native Americans will place "religious servitudes" upon vast tracts of federal property cannot justify its refusal to recognize the constitutional injury respondents will suffer here. It is true, as the Court notes, that respondents' religious use of the high country requires privacy and solitude. The fact remains, however, that respondents have never asked the Forest Service to exclude others from the area. Should respondents or any other group seek to force the Government to protect their religious practices from the interference of private parties, such a demand would implicate not only the concerns of the Free Exercise Clause, but those of the Establishment Clause as well. That case, however, is most assuredly not before us today, and in any event cannot justify the Court's refusal to acknowledge that the injuries respondents will suffer as a result of the Government's proposed activities are sufficient to state a constitutional cause of action. . . .

EVERSON v. BOARD OF EDUCATION,
330 U.S. 1 (1947)

The Supreme Court in the Everson *case for the first time dealt extensively with the obligation of the states to obey the command of the First Amendment against the establishment of religion. The case involved a New Jersey statute that provided for the payment of public funds to the parents of all schoolchildren, including parochial school students, to cover the costs of transporting the children to school. Everson, a taxpayer, challenged the statute on the ground that such aid to parents of parochial school students was subsidizing religion, thereby violating the First Amendment prohibition against the establishment of religion.*

Majority votes: 5
Dissenting votes: 4

Mr. Justice Black delivered the opinion of the Court:. . . .

The appellant, in his capacity as a district taxpayer, filed suit in a state court challenging the right of the Board to reimburse parents of parochial school students. He contended that the statute and the resolution passed pursuant to it violated both the State and the Federal Constitutions. That court held that the legislature was without power to authorize such payment under the state constitution. The New Jersey Court of Errors and Appeals reversed, holding that neither the statute nor the resolution passed pursuant to it was in conflict with the

State constitution or the provisions of the Federal Constitution in issue. The case is here on appeal. . . .

The New Jersey statute is challenged as a "law respecting an establishment of religion." The First Amendment, as made applicable to the states by the Fourteenth, commands that a state "shall make no law respecting an establishment of religion, or prohibiting the free exercise thereof. . . ." These words of the First Amendment reflected in the minds of early Americans a vivid mental picture of conditions and practices which they fervently wished to stamp out in order to preserve liberty for themselves and for their posterity. Doubtless their goal has not been entirely reached; but so far has the Nation moved toward it that the expression "law respecting an establishment of religion," probably does not so vividly remind present-day Americans of the evils, fears, and political problems that caused that expression to be written into our Bill of Rights. . . .

No one locality and no one group throughout the Colonies can rightly be given entire credit for having aroused the sentiment that culminated in adoption of the Bill of Rights' provisions embracing religious liberty. But Virginia, where the established church had achieved a dominant influence in political affairs and where many excesses attracted wide public attention, provided a great stimulus and able leadership for the movement. The people there, as elsewhere, reached the conviction that individual religious liberty could be achieved best under a government which was stripped of all power to tax, to support, or otherwise to assist any or all religions, or to interfere with the beliefs of any religious individual or group. . . .

In recent years, so far as the provision against the establishment of a religion is concerned, the question has most frequently arisen in connection with proposed state aid to church schools and efforts to carry on religious teachings in the public schools in accordance with the tenets of a particular sect. Some churches have either sought or accepted state financial support for their schools. Here again the efforts to obtain state aid or acceptance of it have not been limited to any one particular faith. The state courts, in the main, have remained faithful to the language of their own constitutional provisions designed to protect religious freedom and to separate religions and governments. Their decisions, however, show the difficulty in drawing the line between tax legislation which provides funds for the welfare of the general public and that which is designed to support institutions which teach religion.

The meaning and scope of the First Amendment, preventing establishment of religion or prohibiting the free exercise thereof, in the light of its history and the evils it was designed forever to suppress, have been several times elaborated by the decisions of this Court prior to the application of the First Amendment to the states by the Fourteenth. The broad meaning given the amendment by these earlier cases has been accepted by this Court in its decisions concerning an individual's religious freedom rendered since the Fourteenth Amendment was interpreted to make the prohibitions of the First applicable to state action abridging religious freedom. There is every reason to give the same application and broad interpretation to the "establishment of religion" clause. . . .

The "establishment of religion" clause of the First Amendment means at least this: Neither a state nor the Federal Government can set up a church. Neither can pass laws which aid one religion, aid all religions, or prefer one religion over another. Neither can force nor influence a person to go to or to remain away from church against his will or force him to profess a belief or disbelief in any religion. No person can be punished for entertaining or professing religious beliefs or disbeliefs, for church attendance or non-attendance. No tax in any amount, large or small, can be levied to support any religious activities or institutions, whatever they may be called, or whatever form they may adopt to teach or practice religion. Neither a state nor the Federal Government can, openly or secretly, participate in the affairs of any religious organizations or groups and vice versa. In the words of Jefferson, the clause against establishment of religion by law was intended to erect "a wall of separation between church and State."

We must consider the New Jersey statute in accordance with the foregoing limitations imposed by the First Amendment. But we must not strike that state statute down if it is within the State's constitutional power even though it approaches the verge of that power. New Jersey cannot consistently with the "establishment of religion" clause of the First Amendment contribute tax-raised funds to the support of an institution which teaches the tenets and faith of any church. On the other hand, other language of the amendment commands that New Jersey cannot hamper its citizens in the free exercise of their own religion. Consequently, it cannot exclude individual Catholics, Lutherans, Mohammedans, Baptists, Jews, Methodists, Nonbelievers, Presbyterians, or the members of any other faith, *because of their faith,* or *lack of it,* from receiving the benefits of public welfare legislation. While we do not mean to intimate that a state could not provide transportation only to children attending public schools, we must be careful, in protecting the citizens of New Jersey against state-established churches, to be sure that we do not inadvertently prohibit New Jersey from extending its general state law benefits to all its citizens without regard to their religious belief.

Measured by these standards, we cannot say that the First Amendment prohibits New Jersey from spending tax-raised funds to pay the bus fares of parochial school pupils as a part of a general program under which it pays the fares of pupils attending public and other schools. It is undoubtedly true that children are helped to get to church schools. There is even a possibility that some of the children might not be sent to the church schools if the parents were compelled to pay their children's bus fares out of their own pockets when transportation to a public school would have been paid for by the State. The same possibility exists where the state requires a local transit company to provide reduced fares to school children including those attending parochial schools, or where a municipally owned transportation system undertakes to carry all school children free of charge. Moreover, state-paid policemen, detailed to protect children going to and from church schools from the very real hazards of traffic, would serve much the same purpose and accomplish much the same result as state provisions intended to guarantee free transportation of a kind which the state deems to be best for the school children's welfare. And parents might refuse to risk their children to the serious danger of traffic accidents going to and from parochial schools, the approaches to which were not protected by policemen. Similarly, parents might be reluctant to permit their children to attend schools which the state had cut off from such general government services as ordinary police and fire protection, connections for sewage disposal, public highways and sidewalks. Of course, cutting off church schools from these services, so separate and so indisputably marked off from the religious function, would make it far more difficult for the schools to operate. But such is obviously not the purpose of the First Amendment. That Amendment requires the state to be a neutral in its relations with groups of religious believers and nonbelievers; it does not require the state to be their adversary. State power is no more to be used so as to handicap religions than it is to favor them.

This Court has said that parents may, in the discharge of their duty under state compulsory education laws, send their children to a religious rather than a public school if the school meets the secular educational requirements which the state has power to impose. It appears that these parochial schools meet New Jersey's requirements. The State contributes no money to the schools. It does not support them. Its legislation, as applied, does no more than provide a general program to help parents get their children, regardless of their religion, safely and expeditiously to and from accredited schools.

The First Amendment has erected a wall between church and state. That wall must be kept high and impregnable. We could not approve the slightest breach. New Jersey has not breached it here.

Affirmed.

MR. JUSTICE JACKSON, dissenting:

I find myself, contrary to first impressions, unable to join in this decision. I have a sympathy, though it is not ideological, with Catholic citizens who are compelled by law to pay taxes for public schools, and also feel constrained by conscience and discipline to support other schools for their own children. Such relief to them as this case involves is not in itself a serious burden to taxpayers and I had assumed it to be as little serious in principle. Study of this case convinces me otherwise. The Court's opinion marshals every argument in favor of state aid and puts the case in its most favorable light, but much of its reasoning confirms my conclusions that there are no good grounds upon which to support the present legislation. In fact, the undertones of the opinion, advocating complete and uncompromising separation of Church from State, seem utterly discordant with its conclusion yielding support to their commingling in educational matters. The case which irresistibly comes to mind as the most fitting precedent is that of Julia who, according to Byron's reports, "whispering 'I will ne'er consent,'—consented." . . .

I should be surprised if any Catholic would deny that the parochial school is a vital, if not the most vital, part of the Roman Catholic Church. If put to the choice, that venerable institution, I should expect, would forego its whole service for mature persons before it would give up education of the young, and it would be a wise choice. Its growth and cohesion, discipline and loyalty, spring from its schools. Catholic education is the rock on which the whole structure rests, and to render tax aid to its Church school is indistinguishable to me from rendering the same aid to the Church itself.

It is of no importance in this situation whether

the beneficiary of this expenditure of tax-raised funds is primarily the parochial school and incidentally the pupil, or whether the aid is directly bestowed on the pupil with indirect benefits to the school. The state cannot maintain a Church and it can no more tax its citizens to furnish free carriage to those who attend a Church. The prohibition against establishment of religion cannot be circumvented by a subsidy, bonus or reimbursement of expense to individuals for receiving religious instruction and indoctrination. . . .

MR. JUSTICE RUTLEDGE, with whom MR. JUSTICE FRANKFURTER, MR. JUSTICE JACKSON and MR. JUSTICE BURTON agree, dissenting:. . . .

Does New Jersey's action furnish support for religion by use of the taxing power? Certainly it does, if the test remains undiluted as Jefferson and Madison made it, that money taken by taxation from one is not to be used or given to support another's religious training or belief, or indeed one's own. Today as then the furnishing of "contributions of money for the propagation of opinions which he disbelieves" is the forbidden exaction; and the prohibition is absolute for whatever measure brings that consequence and whatever amount may be sought or given to that end.

The funds used here were raised by taxation. The Court does not dispute, nor could it, that their use does in fact give aid and encouragement to religious instruction. It only concludes that this aid is not "support" in law. But Madison and Jefferson were concerned with aid and support in fact, not as a legal conclusion "entangled in precedents." Here parents pay money to send their children to parochial schools and funds raised by taxation are used to reimburse them. This not only helps the children to get to school and the parents to send them. It aids them in a substantial way to get the very thing which they are sent to the particular school to secure, namely, religious training and teaching. . . .

But we are told that the New Jersey statute is valid in its present application because the appropriation is for a public, not private purpose, namely, the promotion of education, and the majority accept this idea in the conclusion that all we have here is "public welfare legislation." If that is true and the Amendment's force can be thus destroyed, what has been said becomes all the more pertinent. For then there could be no possible objection to more extensive support of religious education by New Jersey.

If the fact alone be determinative that religious schools are engaged in education, thus promoting the general and individual welfare, together with the legislature's decision that the payment of public moneys for their aid makes their work a public function, then I can see no possible basis, except one of dubious legislative policy, for the state's refusal to make full appropriation for support of private, religious schools, just as is done for public instruction. There could not be, on that basis, valid constitutional objection. . . .

We have here then one substantial issue, not two. To say that New Jersey's appropriation and her use of the power of taxation for raising the funds appropriated are not for public purposes but are for private ends, is to say that they are for the support of religion and religious teaching. Conversely, to say that they are for public purposes is to say that they are not for religious ones.

This is precisely for the reason that education which includes religious training and teaching, and its support, have been made matters of private right and function, not public, by the very terms of the First Amendment. That is the effect not only in its guaranty of religion's free exercise, but also in the prohibition of establishments. It was on this basis of the private character of the function of religious education that this Court held parents entitled to send their children to private, religious schools. Now it declares in effect that the appropriation of public funds to defray part of the cost of attending those schools is for a public purpose. If so, I do not understand why the state cannot go farther or why this case approaches the verge of its power.

In truth this view contradicts the whole purpose and effect of the First Amendment as heretofore conceived. The "public function"-"public welfare"-"social legislation" argument seeks, in Madison's words, to "employ Religion [that is, here, religious education] as an engine of Civil policy." It is of one piece with the Assessment Bill's preamble, although with the vital difference that it wholly ignores what that preamble explicitly states.

Our constitutional policy is exactly the opposite. It does not deny the value or the necessity for religious training, teaching or observance. Rather it secures their free exercise. But to that end it does deny that the state can undertake or sustain them in any form or degree. For this reason the sphere of religious activity, as distinguished from the secular intellectual liberties, has been given the twofold protection and, as the state cannot forbid, neither can it perform or aid in performing the religious function. The dual prohibition makes that function altogether private. It cannot be made a public one by legislative act. . . . But most important is that this approach, if valid, supplies a ready method for nullifying the Amendment's guaranty, not only for this case and others involving small grants in aid for religious education, but equally for larger ones. The only thing needed will be for the Court again to transplant the ''public welfare-public function'' view from its proper nonreligious due process bearing to First Amendment application, holding that religious education is not ''supported'' though it may be aided by the appropriation, and that the cause of education generally is furthered by helping the pupil to secure that type of training.

This is not therefore just a little case over bus fares. In paraphrase of Madison, distant as it may be in its present form from a complete establishment of religion, it differs from it only in degree; and is the first step in that direction. . . .

The realm of religious training and belief remains, as the Amendment made it, the kingdom of the individual man and his God. It should be kept inviolately private, not ''entangled . . . in precedents'' or confounded with what legislatures legitimately may take over into the public domain. . . .

ABINGTON SCHOOL DISTRICT v. SCHEMPP, 374 U.S. 203 (1963)

The state of Pennsylvania enacted a statute in 1959 requiring the reading of at least ten verses from the Bible at the opening of each public school on each school day. The law specified that upon the written request of a parent or guardian any child "shall be excused" from the devotional exercise. The School District of Abington Township, Pennsylvania, in conformity with state law had a morning program in each public school in which the Bible reading was followed by recitation by all students of the Lord's Prayer. Edward Schempp and his wife Sidney, both Unitarians, on behalf of their children, Roger and Donna, students at the Abington Senior High School, brought suit to enjoin enforcement of the Pennsylvania statute and the Abington devotional exercise program. They contended that their First and Fourteenth Amendment rights were violated. A federal three-judge district court agreed and an appeal was taken to the Court. A companion case, Murray v. Curlett, *involved a Maryland statute similar to the Pennsylvania law. Mrs. Madalyn Murray and her son, William J. Murray III, both atheists, challenged the devotional Bible reading and Lord's Prayer exercises of the Baltimore public school that William attended. Mrs. Murray took her suit through the state courts, and the highest state court was divided four to three in favor of the state requirement. Mrs. Murray petitioned the Supreme Court for certiorari, which was granted.*

Majority votes: 8
Dissenting votes: 1

MR. JUSTICE CLARK delivered the opinion of the Court: . . .

It is true that religion has been closely identified with our history and government. . . . The fact that the Founding Fathers believed devotedly that there was a God and that the unalienable rights of man were rooted in Him is clearly evidenced in their writings, from the Mayflower Compact to the Constitution itself. . . .

This is not to say, however, that religion has been so identified with our history and government that religious freedom is not likewise as strongly imbedded in our public and private life. Nothing but the most telling of personal experiences in religious persecution suffered by our forebears could have planted our belief in liberty of religious opinion any more deeply in our heritage. . . .

. . . [T]his Court has decisively settled that the First Amendment's mandate that ''Congress shall make no law respecting an establishment of religion, or prohibiting the free exercise thereof'' has been made wholly applicable to the States by the Fourteenth Amendment. *Cantwell* v. *Connecticut,* 310 U.S. 296, 303 (1940). . . .

. . . [T]his Court has rejected unequivocally the contention that the Establishment Clause forbids only governmental preference of one religion over another. Almost 20 years ago in *Everson* v. *Board of Education* the Court said that ''[n]either a state nor the Federal Government can set up a church. Neither can pass laws which aid one religion, aid all religions, or prefer one religion over another.'' . . .

The wholesome ''neutrality'' of which this Court's cases speak . . . stems from a recognition of the teachings of history that powerful sects or groups might bring about a fusion of governmental and religious functions or a concert or dependency of one upon the other to the end that official support of the State or Federal Government would be placed behind the tenets of one or of all orthodoxies. This the Establishment Clause prohibits. And a further reason for neutrality is found in the Free Exercise Clause, which recognizes the value of religious training, teaching and observance and, more particularly, the right of every person to freely choose his own course with reference thereto, free of any compulsion from the state. This the Free Exercise Clause guarantees. Thus, as we have seen, the two clauses may overlap. . . . [T]he Establishment Clause has been directly considered by this

Court eight times in the past score of years and, with only one Justice dissenting on the point, it has consistently held that the clause withdrew all legislative power respecting religious belief or the expression thereof. The test may be stated as follows: what are the purpose and the primary effect of the enactment? If either is the advancement or inhibition of religion then the enactment exceeds the scope of legislative power as circumscribed by the Constitution. That is to say that to withstand the strictures of the Establishment Clause there must be a secular legislative purpose and a primary effect that neither advances nor inhibits religion. The Free Exercise Clause, likewise considered many times here, withdraws from legislative power, state and federal, the exertion of any restraint on the free exercise of religion. Its purpose is to secure religious liberty in the individual by prohibiting any invasions thereof by civil authority. Hence it is necessary in a free exercise case for one to show the coercive effect of the enactment as it operates against him in the practice of his religion. The distinction between the two clauses is apparent—a violation of the Free Exercise Clause is predicated on coercion while the Establishment Clause violation need not be so attended.

Applying the Establishment Clause principles to the cases at bar we find that the states are requiring the selection and reading at the opening of the school day of verses from the Holy Bible and the recitation of the Lord's Prayer by the students in unison. These exercises are prescribed as part of the curricular activities of students who are required by law to attend school. They are held in the school buildings under the supervision and with the participation of teachers employed in those schools. . . . The trial court has found that such an opening exercise is a religious ceremony and was intended by the State to be so. We agree with the trial court's finding as to the religious character of the exercises. Given that finding the exercises and the law requiring them are in violation of the Establishment Clause. . . .

[I]n both cases the laws require religious exercises and such exercises are being conducted in direct violation of the rights of the appellees and petitioners. Nor are these required exercises mitigated by the fact that individual students may absent themselves upon parental request, for that fact furnishes no defense to a claim of unconstitutionality under the Establishment Clause. Further, it is no defense to urge that the religious practices here may be relatively minor encroachments on the First Amendment. The breach of neutrality that is today

a trickling stream may all too soon become a raging torrent and, in the words of Madison, "it is proper to take alarm at the first experiment on our liberties."

It is insisted that unless these religious exercises are permitted a "religion of secularism" is established in the schools. We agree of course that the State may not establish a "religion of secularism" in the sense of affirmatively opposing or showing hostility to religion, thus "preferring those who believe in no religion over those who do believe." We do not agree, however, that this decision in any sense has that effect. In addition, it might well be said that one's education is not complete without a study of comparative religion or the history of religion and its relationship to the advancement of civilization. It certainly may be said that the Bible is worthy of study for its literary and historic qualities. Nothing we have said here indicates that such study of the Bible or of religion, when presented objectively as part of a secular program of education, may not be effected consistent with the First Amendment. But the exercises here do not fall into those categories. They are religious exercises, required by the States in violation of the command of the First Amendment that the Government maintain strict neutrality, neither aiding nor opposing religion.

Finally, we cannot accept that the concept of neutrality, which does not permit a State to require a religious exercise even with the consent of the majority of those affected, collides with the majority's right to free exercise of religion. While the Free Exercise Clause clearly prohibits the use of state action to deny the rights of free exercise to anyone, it has never meant that a majority could use the machinery of the State to practice its beliefs. . . .

The place of religion in our society is an exalted one, achieved through a long tradition of reliance on the home, the church and the inviolable citadel of the individual heart and mind. We have come to recognize through bitter experience that it is not within the power of government to invade that citadel, whether its purpose or effect be to aid or oppose, to advance or retard. In the relationship between man and religion, the State is firmly committed to a position of neutrality. Though the application of that rule requires interpretation of a delicate sort, the rule itself is clearly and concisely stated in the words of the First Amendment. Applying that rule to the facts of these cases, we affirm the judgment in No. 142. In No. 119, the judgment is reversed and the cause remanded to the Maryland Court of Appeals for further proceedings consistent with this opinion.

It is so ordered.

MR. JUSTICE DOUGLAS, concurring: [omitted]
MR. JUSTICE BRENNAN, concurring:. . . .

The line between permissible and impermissible forms of involvement between government and religion has already been considered by the lower federal and state courts. I think a brief survey of certain of these forms of accommodation will reveal that the First Amendment commands not official hostility toward religion, but only a strict neutrality in matters of religion. Moreover, it may serve to suggest that the scope of our holding today is to be measured by the special circumstances under which these cases have arisen, and by the particular dangers to church and state which religious exercises in the public schools present. It may be helpful for purposes of analysis to group these other practices and forms of accommodation into several rough categories.

A. *The Conflict Between Establishment and Free Exercise.*—There are certain practices, conceivably violative of the Establishment Clause, the striking down of which might seriously interfere with certain religious liberties also protected by the First Amendment. Provisions for churches and chaplains at military establishments for those in the armed services may afford one such example. The like provision by state and federal governments for chaplains in penal institutions may afford another example. It is argued that such provisions may be assumed to contravene the Establishment Clause, yet be sustained on constitutional grounds as necessary to secure to the members of the Armed Forces and prisoners those rights of worship guaranteed under the Free Exercise Clause. Since government has deprived such persons of the opportunity to practice their faith at places of their choice, the argument runs, government may, in order to avoid infringing the free exercise guarantees, provide substitutes where it requires such persons to be. Such a principle might support, for example, the constitutionality of draft exemptions for ministers and divinity students, of the excusal of children from school on their respective religious holidays; and of the allowance by government of temporary use of public buildings by religious organizations when their own churches have become unavailable because of a disaster or emergency.

Such activities and practices seem distinguishable from the sponsorship of daily Bible reading and prayer recital. For one thing, there is no element of coercion present in the appointment of military or prison chaplains; the soldier or convict who declines the opportunities for worship would not ordinarily subject himself to the suspicion or obloquy of his peers. Of special significance to this distinction is the fact that we are here usually dealing with adults, not with impressionable children as in the public schools. Moreover, the school exercises are not designed to provide the pupils with general opportunities for worship denied them by the legal obligation to attend school. The student's compelled presence in school for five days a week in no way renders the regular religious facilities of the community less accessible to him than they are to others. The situation of the school child is therefore plainly unlike that of the isolated soldier or the prisoner.

The State must be steadfastly neutral in all matters of faith, and neither favor nor inhibit religion. In my view, government cannot sponsor religious exercises in the public schools without jeopardizing that neutrality. On the other hand, hostility, not neutrality, would characterize the refusal to provide chaplains and places of worship for prisoners and soldiers cut off by the State from all civilian opportunities for public communion, the withholding of draft exemptions for ministers and conscientious objectors, or the denial of the temporary use of an empty public building to a congregation whose place of worship has been destroyed by fire or flood. I do not say that government must provide chaplains or draft exemptions or that the courts should intercede if it fails to do so.

B. *Establishment and Exercises in Legislative Bodies.*—The saying of invocational prayers in legislative chambers, state or federal, and the appointment of legislative chaplains, might well represent no involvements of the kind prohibited by the Establishment Clause. Legislators, federal and state, are mature adults who may presumably absent themselves from such public and ceremonial exercises without incurring any penalty, direct or indirect. . . .

C. *Non-Devotional Use of the Bible in the Public School.*—The holding of the Court today plainly does not foreclose teaching about the Holy Scriptures or about the differences between religious sects in classes in literature or history. Indeed, whether or not the Bible is involved, it would be impossible to teach meaningfully many subjects in the social sciences or the humanities without some mention of religion. To what extent, and at what points in the curriculum, religious materials should be cited are matters which the courts ought to entrust very largely to the experienced officials who superintend our Nation's public schools. They are experts in such matters, and we are not. . . .

D. *Uniform Tax Exemptions Incidentally Avail-*

able to Religious Institutions.—Nothing we hold today questions the propriety of certain tax deductions or exemptions which incidentally benefit churches and religious institutions, along with many secular charities and nonprofit organizations. If religious institutions benefit, it is in spite of rather than because of their religious character. For religious institutions simply share benefits which government makes generally available to educational, charitable, and eleemosynary groups. There is no indication that taxing authorities have used such benefits in any way to subsidize worship or foster belief in God. And as among religious beneficiaries, the tax exemption or deduction can be truly nondiscriminatory, available on equal terms to small as well as large religious bodies, to popular and unpopular sects, and to those organizations which reject as well as those which accept a belief in God. . . .

[E]. *Activities Which, Though Religious in Origin, Have Ceased to Have Religious Meaning.* . . . [N]early every criminal law on the books can be traced to some religious principle or inspiration. But that does not make the present enforcement of the criminal law in any sense an establishment of religion, simply because it accords with widely held religious principles. . . . This rationale suggests that the use of the motto "In God We Trust" on currency, on documents and public buildings and the like may not offend the clause. It is not that the use of those four words can be dismissed as "de minimis"—for I suspect there would be intense opposition to the abandonment of that motto. The truth is that we have simply interwoven the motto so deeply into the fabric of our civil polity that its present use may well not present that type of involvement which the First Amendment prohibits.

This general principle might also serve to insulate the various patriotic exercises and activities used in the public schools and elsewhere which, whatever may have been their origins, no longer have a religious purpose or meaning. The reference to divinity in the revised pledge of allegiance, for example, may merely recognize the historical fact that our Nation was believed to have been founded "under God." Thus reciting the pledge may be no more of a religious exercise than the reading aloud of Lincoln's Gettysburg Address, which contains an allusion to the same historical fact.

The principles which we reaffirm and apply today can hardly be thought novel or radical. They are, in truth, as old as the Republic itself, and have always been as integral a part of the First Amendment as the very words of that charter of religious liberty. . . .

MR. JUSTICE GOLDBERG, with whom MR. JUSTICE HARLAN joins, concurring: [omitted]
MR. JUSTICE STEWART, dissenting: [omitted]

LEMON v. KURTZMAN,
EARLEY v. DiCENSO,
403 U.S. 602 (1971)

Two state statutes that provided financial aid to parochial schools came before the Court in Lemon v. Kurtzman *and* Earley v. DiCenso. *A Pennsylvania statute established a state fund from which subsidies were made to nonpublic schools to help support the teaching of certain secular subjects. In order to be eligible for the subsidy, it was necessary for the content of the subsidized courses to correspond with similar courses in the public schools and for the courses to include only state-approved texts and materials. Religious instruction was not permitted in such courses. The Rhode Island statute (challenged in* DiCenso) *provided for the payment of 15 percent of the salaries of nonpublic schoolteachers who taught only secular subjects, used state-approved texts and materials, agreed not to teach religion, and were state certified. However, no salary subsidies were given to schools whose per pupil expenditure in secular subjects exceeded the average expenditures for the teaching of those subjects in the public schools.*

Majority votes: 8, 8
Dissenting votes: 0, 1

MR. CHIEF JUSTICE BURGER delivered the opinion of the Court:. . . .

The language of the Religion Clauses of the First Amendment is at best opaque, particularly when compared with other portions of the Amendment. Its authors did not simply prohibit the establishment of a state church or a state religion, an area history shows they regarded as very important and fraught with great dangers. Instead they commanded that there should be "no law *respecting* an establishment of religion." A law may be one "respecting" the forbidden objective while falling short of its total realization. A law "respecting" the proscribed result, that is, the establishment of religion, is not always easily identifiable as one violative of the clause. A given law might not *establish* a state religion but nevertheless be one "respecting" that end in the sense of being a step that could lead to such establishment and hence offend the First Amendment.

In the absence of precisely stated constitutional prohibitions, we must draw lines with reference to the three main evils against which the Establishment Clause was intended to afford protection: "sponsorship, financial support, and active involvement of the sovereign in religious activity."

Every analysis in this area must begin with consideration of the cumulative criteria developed by the Court over many years. Three such tests may be gleaned from our cases. First, the statute must have a secular legislative purpose; second, its principal or primary effect must be one that neither advances nor inhibits religion; finally, the statute must not foster "an excessive government entanglement with religion." . . .

(a) Rhode Island program

The District Court made extensive findings on the grave potential for excessive entanglement that inheres in the religious character and purpose of the Roman Catholic elementary schools of Rhode Island, to date the sole beneficiaries of the Rhode Island Salary Supplement Act. . . .

We need not and do not assume that teachers in parochial schools will be guilty of bad faith or any conscious design to evade the limitations imposed by the statute and the First Amendment. We simply recognize that a dedicated religious person, teaching in a school affiliated with his or her faith and operated to inculcate its tenets, will inevitably experience great difficulty in remaining religiously neutral. Doctrines and faith are not inculcated or advanced by neutrals. With the best of intentions such a teacher would find it hard to make a total separation between secular teaching and religious doctrine. . . .

The Rhode Island Legislature has not, and could not, provide state aid on the basis of a mere assumption that secular teachers under religious discipline can avoid conflicts. The State must be certain, given the Religion Clauses, that subsidized teachers do not inculcate religion—indeed the State here has undertaken to do so. To ensure that no trespass occurs, the State has therefore carefully conditioned its aid with pervasive restrictions. An eligible recipient must teach only those courses that are offered in the public schools and use only those texts and materials that are found in the public schools. In addition the teacher must not engage in teaching any course in religion.

A comprehensive, discriminating, and continuing state surveillance will inevitably be required to ensure that these restrictions are obeyed and the First Amendment otherwise respected. Unlike a book, a teacher cannot be inspected once so as to determine the extent and intent of his or her personal beliefs and subjective acceptance of the limitations imposed by the First Amendment. These

prophylactic contacts will involve excessive and enduring entanglement between state and church. . . .

(b) Pennsylvania program

The Pennsylvania statute also provides state aid to church-related schools for teachers' salaries. . . .

As we noted earlier, the very restrictions and surveillance necessary to ensure that teachers play a strictly nonideological role give rise to entanglements between church and state. The Pennsylvania statute, like that of Rhode Island, fosters this kind of relationship. Reimbursement is not only limited to courses offered in the public schools and materials approved by state officials, but the statute excludes "any subject matter expressing religious teaching, or the morals or forms of worship of any sect." In addition, schools seeking reimbursement must maintain accounting procedures that require the State to establish the cost of the secular as distinguished from the religious instruction.

The Pennsylvania statute, moreover, has the further defect of providing state financial aid directly to the church-related schools. . . . The history of government grants of a continuing cash subsidy indicates that such programs have almost always been accompanied by varying measures of control and surveillance. The government cash grants before us now provide no basis for predicting that comprehensive measures of surveillance and controls will not follow. In particular the government's post-audit power to inspect and evaluate a church-related school's financial records and to determine which expenditures are religious and which are secular creates an intimate and continuing relationship between church and state.

A broader base of entanglement of yet a different character is presented by the divisive political potential of these state programs. In a community where such a large number of pupils are served by church-related schools, it can be assumed that state assistance will entail considerable political activity. Partisans of parochial schools, understandably concerned with rising costs and sincerely dedicated to both the religious and secular educational missions of their schools, will inevitably champion this cause and promote political action to achieve their goals. Those who oppose state aid, whether for constitutional, religious, or fiscal reasons, will inevitably respond and employ all of the usual political campaign techniques to prevail. Candidates will be forced to declare and voters to choose. It would be unrealistic to ignore the fact that many people confronted with issues of this kind will find their votes aligned with their faith. . . .

The judgment of the Rhode Island District Court is affirmed. The judgment of the Pennsylvania District Court is reversed, and the case is remanded for further proceedings consistent with this opinion.

MR. JUSTICE MARSHALL took no part in the consideration or decision of *Lemon* v. *Kurtzman*.

MR. JUSTICE DOUGLAS, whom MR. JUSTICE BLACK joins, concurring: [omitted]

MR. JUSTICE MARSHALL, who took no part in the consideration or decision of *Lemon* v. *Kurtzman,* concurs in Mr. JUSTICE DOUGLAS' opinion [in *Tilton* v. *Richardson*] covering *Earley* v. *DiCenso*. . . .

MR. JUSTICE BRENNAN:

I agree that the judgments in *DiCenso* must be affirmed. In my view the judgment in *Lemon* v. *Kurtzman* must be reversed outright. I dissent in *Tilton* v. *Richardson* insofar as the plurality opinion and the opinion of my Brother White sustain the constitutionality, as applied to sectarian institutions, of the Federal Higher Education Facilities Act of 1963, as amended. In my view that Act is unconstitutional insofar as it authorizes grants of federal tax monies to sectarian institutions, but is unconstitutional only to that extent. I therefore think that our remand of the case should be limited to the direction of a hearing to determine whether the four institutional appellees here are sectarian institutions. . . .

The common feature of all three statutes before us is the provision of a direct subsidy from public funds for activities carried on by sectarian educational institutions. . . .

. . . [F]or more than a century, the consensus, enforced by legislatures and courts with substantial consistency, has been that public subsidy of sectarian schools constitutes an impermissible involvement of secular with religious institutions. . . . All three of these statutes require "too close a proximity" of government to the subsidized sectarian institutions and in my view create real dangers of "the secularization of a creed."

The Rhode Island statute requires Roman Catholic teachers to surrender their right to teach religion courses and to promise not to "inject" religious teaching into their secular courses. This has led at least one teacher to stop praying with his classes, a concrete testimonial to the self-censorship that inevitably accompanies state regulation of delicate First Amendment freedoms. . . . Both the Rhode Island and Pennsylvania statutes prescribe extensive standardization of the content of secular courses, and of the teaching materials and textbooks to be used in teaching the courses. And the regulations to implement those requirements necessarily require policing of instruction in the schools. The picture of state inspectors prowling the halls of parochial schools and auditing classroom instruction surely raises more than an imagined specter of governmental "secularization of a creed."

The same dangers attend the federal subsidy even if less obviously. . . .

MR. JUSTICE WHITE, concurring in the judgments in *Tilton* and *Lemon* and dissenting in *DiCenso*:. . . .

I would sustain both the federal and the Rhode Island programs at issue in these cases, and I therefore concur in the judgment in *Tilton* and dissent from the judgment in *DiCenso*. Although I would also reject the facial challenge to the Pennsylvania statute, I concur in the judgment in *Lemon*. . . .

I would reverse the judgment of the District Court and remand the case for trial, thereby holding the Pennsylvania legislation valid on its face but leaving open the question of its validity as applied to the particular facts of this case.

I find it very difficult to follow the distinction between the federal and state programs in terms of their First Amendment acceptability. . . . I find it even more difficult . . . to understand how the Court can accept the considered judgment of Congress that its program is constitutional and yet reject the equally considered decisions of the Rhode Island and Pennsylvania legislatures that their programs represent a constitutionally acceptable accommodation between church and state.

TILTON v. RICHARDSON,
403 U.S. 672 (1971)

This case concerned the question of federal aid to church-related colleges and universities. At issue was a provision of the federal Higher Education Facilities Act of 1963 that provided for construction grants to church-related higher educational institutions for the purpose of building secular academic facilities. There was also a provision in the statute to the effect that, 20 years after completion of construction, the colleges would be able to use the buildings for any purpose at all.

Majority votes: 5
Dissenting votes: 4

MR. CHIEF JUSTICE BURGER announced the judgment of the Court and an opinion in which MR. JUSTICE HARLAN, MR. JUSTICE STEWART and MR. JUSTICE BLACKMUN join:. . . .

The simplistic argument that every form of financial aid to church-sponsored activity violates the Religion Clauses was rejected long ago. . . .

The crucial question is not whether some benefit accrues to a religious institution as a consequence of the legislative program, but whether its principal or primary effect advances religion. . . .

The [Higher Education Facilities] Act itself was carefully drafted to ensure that the federally subsidized facilities would be devoted to the secular and not the religious function of the recipient institutions. It authorizes grants and loans only for academic facilities that will be used for defined secular purposes and expressly prohibits their use for religious instruction, training, or worship. . . .

Finally, this record fully supports the findings of the District Court that none of the four church-related institutions in this case has violated the statutory restrictions. The institutions presented evidence that there had been no religious services or worship in the federally financed facilities, that there are no religious symbols or plaques in or on them, and that they had been used solely for nonreligious purposes. On this record, therefore, these buildings are indistinguishable from a typical state university facility. Appellants presented no evidence to the contrary. . . .

Although we reject appellants' broad constitutional arguments we do perceive an aspect in which the statute's enforcement provisions are inadequate to ensure that the impact of the federal aid will not advance religion. If a recipient institution violates any of the statutory restrictions on the use of a federally financed facility, §754(b)(2) permits the Government to recover an amount equal to the proportion of the facility's present value that the federal grant bore to its original cost.

This remedy, however, is available to the Government only if the statutory conditions are violated "within twenty years after completion of construction." This 20-year period is termed by the statute as "the period of Federal interest" and reflects Congress' finding that after 20 years "the public benefit accruing to the United States" from the use of the federally financed facility "will equal or exceed in value" the amount of the federal grant.

Under §754(b)(2), therefore, a recipient institution's obligation not to use the facility for sectarian instruction or religious worship would appear to expire at the end of 20 years. . . .

Limiting the prohibition for religious use of the structure to 20 years obviously opens the facility to use for any purpose at the end of that period. It cannot be assumed that a substantial structure has no value after that period and hence the unrestricted use of a valuable property is in effect a contribution of some value to a religious body. Congress did not base the 20-year provision on any

contrary conclusion. If, at the end of 20 years, the building is, for example, converted into a chapel or otherwise used to promote religious interests, the original federal grant will in part have the effect of advancing religion.

To this extent the Act therefore trespasses on the Religion Clauses. The restrictive obligations of a recipient institution cannot, compatibly with the Religion Clauses, expire while the building has substantial value. This circumstance does not require us to invalidate the entire Act, however. . . .

We have found nothing in the statute or its objectives intimating that Congress considered the 20-year provision essential to the statutory program as a whole. In view of the broad and important goals that Congress intended this legislation to serve, there is no basis for assuming that the Act would have failed of passage without this provision; nor will its excision impair either the operation or administration of the Act in any significant respect.

We next turn to the question of whether excessive entanglements characterize the relationship between government and church under the Act. . . .

There are generally significant differences between the religious aspects of church-related institutions of higher learning and parochial elementary and secondary schools. The "affirmative if not dominant policy" of the instruction in pre-college church schools is "to assure future adherents to a particular faith by having control of their total education at an early age." There is substance to the contention that college students are less impressionable and less susceptible to religious indoctrination. Common observation would seem to support that view, and Congress may well have entertained it. The skepticism of the college student is not an inconsiderable barrier to any attempt or tendency to subvert the congressional objectives and limitations. Furthermore, by their very nature, college and postgraduate courses tend to limit the opportunities for sectarian influence by virtue of their own internal disciplines. Many church-related colleges and universities are characterized by a high degree of academic freedom and seek to evoke free and critical responses from their students.

The record here would not support a conclusion that any of these four institutions departed from this general pattern. . . .

Since religious indoctrination is not a substantial purpose or activity of these church-related colleges and universities, there is less likelihood than in primary and secondary schools that religion will permeate the area of secular education. This reduces the risk that government aid will in fact serve to support religious activities. Correspondingly, the necessity for intensive government surveillance is diminished and the resulting entanglements between government and religion lessened. . . .

The entanglement between church and state is also lessened here by the nonideological character of the aid that the Government provides. Our cases from *Everson* to *Allen* have permitted church-related schools to receive government aid in the form of secular, neutral, or nonideological services, facilities, or materials that are supplied to all students regardless of the affiliation of the school that they attend. . . .

Finally, government entanglements with religion are reduced by the circumstance that . . . the Government aid here is a one time, single-purpose construction grant. There are no continuing financial relationships or dependencies, no annual audits, and no government analysis of an institution's expenditures on secular as distinguished from religious activities. Inspection as to use is a minimal contact. . . .

We think that cumulatively these three factors substantially lessen the potential for divisive religious fragmentation in the political arena. This conclusion is admittedly difficult to document, but neither have appellants pointed to any continuing religious aggravation on this matter in the political processes. Possibly this can be explained by the character and diversity of the recipient colleges and universities and the absence of any intimate continuing relationship or dependency between government and religiously affiliated institutions. The potential for divisiveness inherent in the essentially local problems of primary and secondary schools is significantly less with respect to a college or university whose student constituency is not local but diverse and widely dispersed. . . .

We conclude that the Act does not violate the Religion Clauses of the First Amendment except that part of §754(b)(2) providing a 20-year limitation on the religious use restrictions contained in §751(a)(2). We remand to the District Court with directions to enter a judgment consistent with this opinion.

Vacated and remanded.

[MR. JUSTICE WHITE concurred.]
MR. JUSTICE DOUGLAS, with whom MR. JUSTICE BLACK and MR. JUSTICE MARSHALL concur, dissenting in part: . . .

The Federal Government is giving religious schools a block grant to build certain facilities. The fact that money is given once at the beginning of a program rather than apportioned annually as in *Lemon* and *DiCenso* is without constitutional significance. The First Amendment bars establishment of a religion. And as I noted today in *Lemon* and *DiCenso,* this bar has been consistently interpreted . . . as meaning: "No tax in any amount, large or small, can be levied to support any religious activities or institutions, whatever they may be called, or whatever form they may adopt to teach or practice religion." Thus it is hardly impressive that rather than giving a smaller amount of money annually over a long period of years, Congress instead gives a large amount all at once. The plurality's distinction is in effect that small violations of the First Amendment over a period of years are unconstitutional (see *Lemon* and *DiCenso*) while a huge violation occurring only once is *de minimis.* I cannot agree with such sophistry. . . .
[MR. JUSTICE BRENNAN dissented.]

WALLACE v. JAFFREE,
472 U.S. 38 (1985)

Ishmael Jaffree, a resident of Mobile County, Alabama, filed a complaint on behalf of his three children who were then in the second grade (two children) and kindergarten (one child). The complaint against various school officials and Alabama state officials, including Governor George C. Wallace, challenged the constitutionality of an Alabama school moment of silence for voluntary prayer or meditation statute. The federal district judge, William Brevard Hand, upheld the statute because in his opinion the state of Alabama has the power to establish a state religion if it chooses to do so. This incredible misreading of the Constitution and Court precedents was overturned by the Court of Appeals. The United States Supreme Court accepted the appeal brought by Alabama.

Majority votes: 6
Dissenting votes: 3

JUSTICE STEVENS delivered the opinion of the Court:. . . .

. . . [T]he narrow question for decision is whether [Alabama statute] §16-1-20.1, which authorizes a period of silence for "meditation or voluntary prayer," is a law respecting the establishment of religion within the meaning of the First Amendment. . . .

When the Court has been called upon to construe the breadth of the Establishment Clause, it has examined the criteria developed over a period of many years. Thus, in *Lemon* v. *Kurtzman,* (1971), we wrote:

"Every analysis in this area must begin with consideration of the cumulative criteria developed by the Court over many years. Three such tests may be gleaned from our cases. First, the statute must have a secular legislative purpose; second, its principal or primary effect must be one that neither advances nor inhibits religion; finally, the statute must not foster 'an excessive government entanglement with religion.' "

It is the first of these three criteria that is most plainly implicated by this case. As the District Court correctly recognized, no consideration of the second or third criteria is necessary if a statute does not have a clearly secular purpose. For even though a statute that is motivated in part by a religious purpose may satisfy the first criterion, the First Amendment requires that a statute must be invalidated if it is entirely motivated by a purpose to advance religion.

In applying the purpose test, it is appropriate to ask "whether government's actual purpose is to endorse or disapprove of religion." In this case, the answer to that question is dispositive. For the record not only provides us with an unambiguous affirmative answer, but it also reveals that the enactment of §16-1-20.1 was not motivated by any clearly secular purpose—indeed, the statute had *no* secular purpose.

The sponsor of the bill that became §16-1-20.1, Senator Donald Holmes, inserted into the legislative record—apparently without dissent—a statement indicating that the legislation was an "effort to return voluntary prayer" to the public schools. Later Senator Holmes confirmed this purpose before the District Court. In response to the question whether he had any purpose for the legislation other than returning voluntary prayer to public schools, he stated, "No, I did not have no other purpose in mind." The State did not present evidence of *any* secular purpose. . . .

The legislative intent to return prayer to the public schools is, of course, quite different from merely protecting every student's right to engage in voluntary prayer during an appropriate moment of silence during the school day. The 1978 statute already protected that right, containing nothing that prevented any student from engaging in voluntary prayer during a silent minute of meditation. Appellants have not identified any secular purpose that was not fully served by §16-1-20 before the enactment of §16-1-20.1. Thus, only two conclusions are consistent with the text of §16-1-20.1: (1) the statute was enacted to convey a message of State endorsement and promotion of prayer; or (2) the statute

was enacted for no purpose. No one suggests that the statute was nothing but a meaningless or irrational act.

We must, therefore, conclude that the Alabama Legislature intended to change existing law. . . .

Keeping in mind, as we must, "both the fundamental place held by the Establishment Clause in our constitutional scheme and the myriad, subtle ways in which Establishment Clause values can be eroded," we conclude that §16-1-20.1 violates the First Amendment.

The judgment of the Court of Appeals is affirmed.

It is so ordered.

JUSTICE POWELL, concurring: [omitted]
JUSTICE O'CONNOR, concurring in the judgment:

Nothing in the United States Constitution as interpreted by this Court or in the laws of the State of Alabama prohibits public school students from voluntarily praying at any time before, during, or after the school day. Alabama has facilitated voluntary silent prayers of students who are so inclined by enacting Ala. Code §16-1-20, which provides a moment of silence in appellees' schools each day. The parties to these proceedings concede the validity of this enactment. At issue in these appeals is the constitutional validity of an additional and subsequent Alabama statute, Ala. Code §16-1-20.1, which both the District Court and the Court of Appeals concluded was enacted solely to officially encourage prayer during the moment of silence. I agree with judgment of the Court that, in light of the findings of the Courts below and the history of its enactment, §16-1-20.1 of the Alabama Code violates the Establishment Clause of the First Amendment. In my view, there can be little doubt that the purpose and likely effect of this subsequent enactment is to endorse and sponsor voluntary prayer in the public schools. . . .

A state sponsored moment of silence in the public schools is different from state sponsored vocal prayer or Bible reading. First, a moment of silence is not inherently religious. Silence, unlike prayer or Bible reading, need not be associated with a religious exercise. Second, a pupil who participates in a moment of silence need not compromise his or her beliefs. During a moment of silence, a student who objects to prayer is left to his or her own thoughts, and is not compelled to listen to the prayers or thoughts of others. For these simple reasons, a moment of silence statute does not stand or fall under the Establishment Clause according to how the Court regards vocal prayer or Bible reading. . . . It is difficult to discern a serious threat to religious liberty from a room of silent, thoughtful schoolchildren. . . .

The relevant issue is whether an objective observer, acquainted with the text, legislative history, and implementation of . . . [a moment-of-silence] statute, would perceive it as a state endorsement of prayer in public schools. A moment-of-silence law that is clearly drafted and implemented so as to permit prayer, meditation, and reflection within the prescribed period, without endorsing one alternative over the others should pass this test.

The analysis above suggests that moment-of-silence laws in many States should pass Establishment Clause scrutiny. . . . The Court holds only that Alabama has intentionally crossed the line between creating a quiet moment during which those so inclined may pray, and affirmatively endorsing the particular religious practice of prayer. This line may be a fine one, but our precedents and the principles of religious liberty require that we draw it. In my view, the judgment of the Court of Appeals must be affirmed.

CHIEF JUSTICE BURGER, dissenting: [omitted]

JUSTICE WHITE, dissenting: . . . .

. . . As I read the filed opinions, a majority of the Court would approve statutes that provided for a moment of silence but did not mention prayer. But if a student asked whether he could pray during that moment, it is difficult to believe that the teacher could not answer in the affirmative. If that is the case, I would not invalidate a statute that at the outset provided the legislative answer to the question "May I pray?" This is so even if the Alabama statute is infirm, which I do not believe it is, because of its peculiar legislative history. . . .

JUSTICE REHNQUIST, dissenting: . . . .

It is impossible to build sound constitutional doctrine upon a mistaken understanding of constitutional history, but unfortunately the Establishment Clause has been expressly freighted with Jefferson's misleading metaphor [of a wall of separation between church and State] for nearly forty years. . . .

On the basis of the record of . . . proceedings in the House of Representatives, James Madison was undoubtedly the most important architect among the members of the House of the amendments which became the Bill of Rights, but it was James Madison speaking as an advocate of sensible legislative compromise. . . . During the ratification debate in the Virginia Convention, Madison had actually opposed the idea of any Bill of Rights. His sponsorship of the amendments in the House was obviously not that of a zealous believer in the necessity of the Religion Clauses, but of one who felt it might do some good, could do no harm, and would satisfy those who had ratified the Constitution on the condition that Congress propose a Bill of Rights. His original language "nor shall any national religion be established" obviously does not conform to the "wall of separation" between church and State idea which latter day commentators have ascribed to him. His explanation on the floor of the meaning of his language—"that Congress should not establish a religion, and enforce the legal observation of it by law" is of the same ilk. When he replied to [Representative] Huntington in the debate over the proposal which came from the Select Committee of the House, he urged that the language "no religion shall be established by law" should be amended by inserting the word "national" in front of the word "religion."

It seems indisputable from these glimpses of Madison's thinking, as reflected by actions on the floor of the House in 1789, that he saw the amendment as designed to prohibit the establishment of a national religion, and perhaps to prevent discrimination among sects. He did not see it as requiring neutrality on the part of government between religion and irreligion. . . .

None of the other Members of Congress who spoke during the August 15th debate expressed the slightest indication that they thought the language before them from the Select Committee, or the evil to be aimed at, would require that the Government be absolutely neutral as between religion and irreligion. The evil to be aimed at, so far as those who spoke were concerned, appears to have been the establishment of a national church, and perhaps the preference of one religious sect over another; but it was definitely not concern about whether the Government might aid all religions evenhandedly. If one were to follow the advice of JUSTICE BRENNAN, concurring in *Abington School District* v. *Schempp,* and construe the Amendment in the light of what particular "practices . . . challenged threaten those consequences which the Framers deeply feared; whether, in short, they tend to promote that type of interdependence between religion and state which the First Amendment was designed to prevent," one would have to say that the First Amendment Establishment Clause should be read no more broadly than to prevent the establishment of a national religion or the governmental preference of one religious sect over another. . . .

. . . [T]he *Lemon* test has no more grounding in the history of the First Amendment than does the wall theory upon which it rests. The three-part test represents a determined effort to craft a workable rule from an historically faulty doctrine; but the rule can only be as sound as the doctrine it attempts to service. The three-part test has simply not provided adequate standards for deciding Establishment Clause cases, as this Court has slowly come to realize. Even worse, the *Lemon* test has caused this Court to fracture into unworkable plurality opinions, depending upon how each of the three factors applies to a certain state action. The results from our school services cases show the difficulty we have encountered in making the *Lemon* test yield principled results. . . .

If a constitutional theory has no basis in the history of the amendment it seeks to interpret, it is difficult to apply and yields unprincipled results, I see little use in it. The "crucible of litigation," has produced only consistent unpredictability, and today's effort is just a continuation of "the sisyphean task of trying to patch together the 'blurred, indistinct and variable barrier' described in *Lemon* v. *Kurtzman*." We have done much straining since 1947, but still we admit that we can only "dimly perceive" the *Everson* wall. Our perception has been clouded not by the Constitution but by the mists of an unnecessary metaphor. . . .

The Court strikes down the Alabama statute in *Wallace* v. *Jaffree*, because the State wished to "endorse prayer as a favored practice." It would come as much of a shock to those who drafted the Bill of Rights as it will to a large number of thoughtful Americans today to learn that the Constitution, as construed by the majority, prohibits the Alabama Legislature from "endorsing" prayer. George Washington himself, at the request of the very Congress which passed the Bill of Rights, proclaimed a day of "public thanksgiving and prayer, to be observed by acknowledging with grateful hearts the many and signal favors of Almighty God." History must judge whether it was the father of his country in 1789, or a majority of the Court today, which has strayed from the meaning of the Establishment Clause.

The State surely has a secular interest in regulating the manner in which public schools are conducted. Nothing in the Establishment Clause of the First Amendment, properly understood, prohibits any such generalized "endorsement" of prayer. I would therefore reverse the judgment of the Court of Appeals in *Wallace* v. *Jaffree*.

MUELLER v. ALLEN,
463 U.S. 388 (1983)

Minnesota enacted legislation allowing state taxpayers to deduct on their state income tax expenses incurred in providing tuition, textbooks, and *transportation for their children's elementary or secondary school education. Van Mueller and June Noyes, both Minnesota taxpayers, brought suit in federal district court against Clyde Allen, the Commissioner of the Department of Revenue of Minnesota, and several parents who had taken the tax deduction for expenses incurred in sending their children to parochial school. Mueller and Noyes argued that the Minnesota tax deduction violated the establishment clause of the First Amendment by providing financial assistance to religious institutions. The district court rejected this argument and upheld the Minnesota law. The Court of Appeals for the Eighth Circuit affirmed, and the case came before the Supreme Court.*

Majority votes: 5
Dissenting votes: 4

JUSTICE REHNQUIST delivered the opinion of the Court:

Minnesota allows taxpayers, in computing their state income tax, to deduct certain expenses incurred in providing for the education of their children. Minn. Stat. §290.09(22). . . . In this case we are asked to decide whether Minnesota's tax deduction bears greater resemblance to those types of assistance to parochial schools we have approved, or to those we have struck down. Petitioners place particular reliance on our decision in *Committee for Public Education* v. *Nyquist*, where we held invalid a New York statute providing public funds for the maintenance and repair of the physical facilities of private schools and granting thinly disguised "tax benefits," actually amounting to tuition grants, to the parents of children attending private schools. As explained below, we conclude that §290.09(22) bears less resemblance to the arrangement struck down in *Nyquist* than it does to assistance programs upheld in our prior decisions and those discussed with approval in *Nyquist*.

The general nature of our inquiry in this area has been guided, since the decision in *Lemon* v. *Kurtzman*, by the "three-part" test laid down in that case. . . .

Little time need be spent on the question of whether the Minnesota tax deduction has a secular purpose. Under our prior decisions, governmental assistance programs have consistently survived this inquiry even when they have run afoul of other aspects of the *Lemon* framework. . . . This reflects, at least in part, our reluctance to attribute unconstitutional motives to the states, particularly when a plausible secular purpose for the state's program may be discerned from the face of the statute.

The state's decision to defray the cost of educational expenses incurred by parents—regardless of the type of schools their children attend—evidences a purpose that is both secular and understandable. An educated populace is essential to the political and economic health of any community, and a state's efforts to assist parents in meeting the rising cost of educational expenses plainly serves this secular purpose of ensuring that the state's citizenry is well-educated. Similarly, Minnesota, like other states, could conclude that there is a strong public interest in assuring the continued financial health of private schools, both sectarian and non-sectarian. By educating a substantial number of students such schools relieve public schools of a correspondingly great burden—to the benefit of all taxpayers. In addition, private schools may serve as a benchmark for public schools. . . . All these justifications are readily available to support §290.09(22), and each is sufficient to satisfy the secular purpose inquiry of *Lemon*.

We turn therefore to the more difficult but related question whether the Minnesota statute has "the primary effect of advancing the sectarian aims of the non-public schools." In concluding that it does not, we find several features of the Minnesota tax deduction particularly significant. First, an essential feature of Minnesota's arrangement is the fact that §290.09(22) is only one among many deductions—such as those for medical expenses, and charitable contributions, available under the Minnesota tax laws. Our decisions consistently have recognized that traditionally "[l]egislatures have especially broad latitude in creating classifications and distinctions in tax statutes," in part because the "familiarity with local conditions" enjoyed by legislators especially enables them to "achieve an equitable distribution of the tax burden." Under our prior decisions, the Minnesota legislature's judgment that a deduction for educational expenses fairly equalizes the tax burden of its citizens and encourages desirable expenditures for educational purposes is entitled to substantial deference.

Other characteristics of §290.09(22) argue equally strongly for the provision's constitutionality. Most importantly, the deduction is available for educational expenses incurred by *all* parents, including those whose children attend public schools and those whose children attend non-sectarian private schools or sectarian private schools. Just as in *Widmar* v. *Vincent,* 454 U.S. 263 (1981), where we concluded that the state's provision of a forum neutrally "open to a broad class of nonreligious as well as religious speakers" does not "confer any primatur of State approval," so here: "the provision of benefits to so broad a spectrum of groups is an important index of secular effect."

In this respect, as well as others, this case is vitally different from the scheme struck down in *Nyquist*. There, public assistance amounting to tuition grants, was provided only to parents of children in *non-public* schools. This fact had considerable bearing on our decision striking down the New York statute at issue; we explicitly distinguished both *Allen* and *Everson* on the grounds that "In both cases the class of beneficiaries included *all* schoolchildren, those in public as well as those in private schools." . . . Moreover, we intimated that "public assistance (e.g., scholarships) made available generally without regard to the sectarian-non-sectarian or public-nonpublic nature of the institution benefited" might not offend the Establishment Clause. We think the tax deduction adopted by Minnesota is more similar to this latter type of program than it is to the arrangement struck down in *Nyquist*. Unlike the assistance at issue in *Nyquist,* §290.09(22) permits *all* parents—whether their children attend public school or private—to deduct their children's educational expenses. As *Widmar* and our other decisions indicate, a program, like §290.09(22), that neutrally provides state assistance to a broad spectrum of citizens is not readily subject to challenge under the Establishment Clause. . . .

Petitioners argue that, notwithstanding the facial neutrality of §290.09(22), in application the statute primarily benefits religious institutions. Petitioners rely , as they did below, on a statistical analysis of the type of persons claiming the tax deduction. They contend that most parents of public school children incur no tuition expenses, and that other expenses deductible under §290.09(22) are negligible in value; moreover, they claim that 96% of the children in private schools in 1978–1979 attended religiously-affiliated institutions. Because of all this, they reason, the bulk of deductions taken under §290.09(22) will be claimed by parents of children in sectarian schools. Respondents reply that petitioners have failed to consider the impact of deductions for items such as transportation, summer school tuition, tuition paid by parents whose children attended schools outside the school districts in which they resided, rental or purchase costs for a variety of equipment, and tuition for certain types of instruction not ordinarily provided in public schools.

We need not consider these contentions in detail. We would be loath to adopt a rule grounding the constitutionality of a facially neutral law on an-

of commencing a lawsuit, however, create the appearance of divisiveness and then exploit it as evidence of entanglement.

We are satisfied that the City has a secular purpose for including the creche, that the City has not impermissibly advanced religion, and that including the creche does not create excessive entanglement between religion and government.

IV

JUSTICE BRENNAN describes the creche as a "recreation of an event that lies at the heart of Christian faith." The creche, like a painting, is passive; admittedly it is a reminder of the origins of Christmas. Even the traditional, purely secular displays extant at Christmas, with or without a creche, would inevitably recall the religious nature of the Holiday. The display engenders a friendly community spirit of good will in keeping with the season. The creche may well have special meaning to those whose faith includes the celebration of religious masses, but none who sense the origins of the Christmas celebration would fail to be aware of its religious implications. That the display brings people into the central city, and serves commercial interest and benefits merchants and their employees, does not, as the dissent points out, determine the character of the display. That a prayer invoking Divine guidance in Congress is preceded and followed by debate and partisan conflict over taxes, budgets, national defense, and myriad mundane subjects, for example, has never been thought to demean or taint the sacredness of the invocation.

Of course the creche is identified with one religious faith but no more so than the examples we have set out from prior cases in which we found no conflict with the Establishment Clause. It would be ironic, however, if the inclusion of a single symbol of a particular historic religious event, as part of a celebration acknowledged in the Western World for 20 centuries, and in this country by the people, by the Executive Branch, by the Congress, and the courts for two centuries, would so "taint" the City's exhibit as to render it violative of the Establishment Clause. To forbid the use of this one passive symbol—the creche—at the very time people are taking note of the season with Christmas hymns and carols in public schools and other public places, and while the Congress and Legislatures open sessions with prayers by paid chaplains would be a stilted over-reaction contrary to our history and to our holdings. If the presence of the creche in this display violates the Establishment Clause, a host of other forms of taking official note of Christ-

mas, and of our religious heritage, are equally offensive to the Constitution. . . . Any notion that these symbols pose a real danger of establishment of a state church is far-fetched indeed. . . .

We hold that, notwithstanding the religious significance of the creche, the City of Pawtucket has not violated the Establishment Clause of the First Amendment. Accordingly, the judgment of the Court of Appeals is reversed.

It is so ordered.

JUSTICE O'CONNOR, concurring: [omitted]
JUSTICE BRENNAN, with whom JUSTICE MARSHALL, JUSTICE BLACKMUN and JUSTICE STEVENS join, dissenting:

The principles announced in the compact phrases of the Religion Clauses have, as the Court today reminds us, proven difficult to apply. Faced with that uncertainty, the Court properly looks for guidance to the settled test announced in *Lemon* v. *Kurtzman,* for assessing whether a challenged governmental practice involves an impermissible step toward the establishment of religion. Applying that test to this case, the Court reaches an essentially narrow result which turns largely upon the particular holiday context in which the City of Pawtucket's nativity scene appeared. The Court's decision implicitly leaves open questions concerning the constitutionality of the public display on public property of a creche standing alone, or the public display of other distinctively religious symbols such as a cross. Despite the narrow contours of the Court's opinion, our precedents in my view compel the holding that Pawtucket's inclusion of a lifesized display depicting the biblical description of the birth of Christ as part of its annual Christmas celebration is unconstitutional. Nothing in the history of such practices or the setting in which the City's creche is presented obscures or diminishes the plain fact that Pawtucket's action amounts to an impermissible governmental endorsement of a particular faith. . . .

In my view, Pawtucket's maintenance and display at public expense of a symbol as distinctively sectarian as a creche simply cannot be squared with our prior cases. And it is plainly contrary to the purposes and values of the Establishment Clause to pretend, as the Court does, that the otherwise secular setting of Pawtucket's nativity scene dilutes in some fashion the creche's singular religiosity, or that the City's annual display reflects nothing more than an "acknowledgment" of our shared national heritage. Neither the character of the Christmas holiday itself, nor our heritage of religious expression supports this result. Indeed, our remarkable and precious religious diversity as a nation, which the Establishment Clause seeks to protect, runs directly counter to today's decision. . . .

Applying the three-part test to Pawtucket's creche, I am persuaded that the City's inclusion of the creche in its Christmas display simply does not reflect a "clearly secular purpose." . . . Plainly, the City's interest in celebrating the holiday and in promoting both retail sales and goodwill are fully served by the elaborate display of Santa Claus, reindeer, and wishing wells that are already a part of Pawtucket's annual Christmas display. More importantly, the nativity scene, unlike every other element of the Hodgson Park display, reflects a sectarian exclusivity that the avowed purposes of celebrating the holiday season and promoting retail commerce simply do not encompass. To be found constitutional, Pawtucket's seasonal celebration must at least be non-denominational and not serve to promote religion. The inclusion of a distinctively religious element like the creche, however, demonstrates that a narrower sectarian purpose lay behind the decision to include a nativity scene. That the creche retained this religious character for the people and municipal government of Pawtucket is suggested by the Mayor's testimony at trial in which he stated that for him as well as others in the City, the effort to eliminate the nativity scene from Pawtucket's Christmas celebration "is a step towards establishing another religion, non-religion that it may be." Plainly, the City and its leaders understood that the inclusion of the creche in its display would serve the wholly religious purpose of "keep[ing] 'Christ in Christmas.' ". . .

The "primary effect" of including a nativity scene in the City's display is, as the District Court found, to place the government's imprimatur of approval on the particular religious beliefs exemplified by the creche. . . . The effect on minority religious groups, as well as on those who may reject all religion, is to convey the message that their views are not similarly worthy of public recognition nor entitled to public support. It was precisely this sort of religious chauvinism that the Establishment Clause was intended forever to prohibit. . . .

Finally, it is evident that Pawtucket's inclusion of a creche as part of its annual Christmas display does pose a significant threat of fostering "excessive entanglement.". . . Jews and other non-Christian groups, prompted perhaps by the Mayor's remark that he will include a Menorah in future displays, can be expected to press government for inclusion of their symbols, and faced with such requests, government will have to become involved in accommodating the various demands. Furthermore, the Court should not blind itself to the fact that because communities differ in religious composition, the controversy over whether local governments may adopt religious symbols will continue to fester. In many communities, non-Christian groups can be expected to combat practices similar to Pawtucket's; this will be so especially in areas where there are substantial non-Christian minorities. . . .

I refuse to accept the notion implicit in today's decision that non-Christians would find that the religious content of the creche is eliminated by the fact it appears as part of the City's otherwise secular celebration of the Christmas holiday. The nativity scene is clearly distinct in its purpose and effect from the rest of the Hodgson Park display for the simple reason that it is the only one rooted in a biblical account of Christ's birth. . . . Unlike such secular figures as Santa Claus, reindeer and carolers, a nativity scene represents far more than a mere "traditional" symbol of Christmas. The essence of the creche's symbolic purpose and effect is to prompt the observer to experience a sense of simple awe and wonder appropriate to the contemplation of one of the central elements of Christian dogma—that God sent His son into the world to be a Messiah. Contrary to the Court's suggestion, the creche is far from a mere representation of a "particular historic religious event." It is, instead, best understood as a mystical recreation of an event that lies at the heart of Christian faith. To suggest, as the Court does, that such a symbol is merely "traditional" and therefore no different from Santa's house or reindeer is not only offensive to those for whom the creche has profound significance, but insulting to those who insist for religious or personal reasons that the story of Christ is in no sense a part of "history" nor an unavoidable element of our national "heritage.". . .

In this case, . . . the angels, shepherds, Magi and infant of Pawtucket's nativity scene can only be viewed as symbols of a particular set of religious beliefs. . . .

Despite this body of case law, the Court has never comprehensively addressed the extent to which government may acknowledge religion by, for example, incorporating religious references into public ceremonies and proclamations, and I do not presume to offer a comprehensive approach. Nevertheless, it appears from our prior decisions that at least three principles—tracing the narrow channels which government acknowledgments must follow to satisfy the Establishment Clause—may be identified. First, although the government may not be compelled to do so by the Free Exercise Clause, it may, consistently with the Establishment Clause, act to accommodate to some extent the opportunities of individuals to practice their religion. For me that principle would justify government's decision to declare December 25th a public holiday.

Second, our cases recognize that while a particular governmental practice may have derived from religious motivations and retain certain religious connotations, it is nonetheless permissible for the government to pursue the practice when it is continued today solely for secular reasons. As this Court noted with reference to Sunday Closing Laws in *McGowan* v. *Maryland,* the mere fact that a governmental practice coincides to some extent with certain religious beliefs does not render it unconstitutional. Thanksgiving Day, in my view, fits easily within this principle, for despite its religious antecedents, the current practice of celebrating Thanksgiving is unquestionably secular and patriotic. We all may gather with our families on that day to give thanks both for personal and national good fortune, but we are free, given the secular character of the holiday, to address that gratitude either to a divine beneficence or to such mundane sources as good luck or the country's abundant natural wealth.

Finally, we have noted that government cannot be completely prohibited from recognizing in its public actions the religious beliefs and practices of the American people as an aspect of our national history and culture. While I remain uncertain about these questions, I would suggest that such practices as the designation of "In God We Trust" as our national motto, or the references to God contained in the Pledge of Allegiance can best be understood, in Dean Rostow's apt phrase, as a form of "ceremonial deism," protected from Establishment Clause scrutiny chiefly because they have lost through rote repetition any significant religious content. Moreover, these references are uniquely suited to serve such wholly secular purposes as solemnizing public occasions, or inspiring commitment to meet some national challenge in a manner that simply could not be fully served in our culture if government were limited to purely non-religious phrases. The practices by which the government has long acknowledged religion are therefore probably necessary to serve certain secular functions, and that necessity, coupled with their long history, gives those practices an essentially secular meaning.

The creche fits none of these categories. Inclusion of the creche is not necessary to accommodate individual religious expression. . . . Nor is the inclusion of the creche necessary to serve wholly sec-

ular goals; it is clear that the City's secular purposes of celebrating the Christmas holiday and promoting retail commerce can be fully served without the creche. And the creche, because of its unique association with Christianity, is clearly more sectarian than those references to God that we accept in ceremonial phrases or in other contexts that assure neutrality. The religious works on display at the National Gallery, Presidential references to God during an Inaugural Address, or the national motto present no risk of establishing religion. To be sure, our understanding of these expressions may begin in contemplation of some religious element, but it does not end here. Their message is dominantly secular. In contrast, the message of the creche begins and ends with reverence for a particular image of the divine. . . .

The intent of the Framers with respect to the public display of nativity scenes is virtually impossible to discern primarily because the widespread celebration of Christmas did not emerge in its present form until well into the nineteenth century. . . .

I dissent.

JUSTICE BLACKMUN, with whom JUSTICE STEVENS joins, dissenting: [omitted]

EDWARDS v. AGUILLARD,
482 U.S. 578 (1987)

At issue in this case was the constitutionality of Louisiana's Balanced Treatment for Creation-Science and Evolution-Science in Public School Instruction Act. The Act did not require the teaching of creation-science, i.e., the biblical version of creation, except when the theory of evolution was taught. Don Aguillard and other Louisiana parents, teachers, and religious leaders filed suit in federal district court against Governor Edwin W. Edwards and other state government officials seeking an injunction against the implementation of the statute and a declaration of its unconstitutionality. The district court held the statute to be a violation of the establishment clause and the Court of Appeals for the Fifth Circuit affirmed. The Supreme Court agreed to hear the case.

Majority votes: 7
Dissenting votes: 2

JUSTICE BRENNAN delivered the opinion of the Court:

The question for decision is whether Louisiana's "Balanced Treatment for Creation-Science and Evolution-Science in Public School Instruction"

Act is facially invalid as violative of the Establishment Clause of the First Amendment. . . .

The Establishment Clause forbids the enactment of any law "respecting an establishment of religion." The Court has applied a three-pronged test to determine whether legislation comports with the Establishment Clause. First, the legislature must have adopted the law with a secular purpose. Second, the statute's principal or primary effect must be one that neither advances nor inhibits religion. Third, the statute must not result in an excessive entanglement of government with religion. *Lemon v. Kurtzman,* 403 U.S. 602, 612–613 (1971). State action violates the Establishment Clause if it fails to satisfy any of these prongs. . . .

[I]n employing the three-pronged *Lemon* test, we must do so mindful of the particular concerns that arise in the context of public elementary and secondary schools. We now turn to the evaluation of the Act under the *Lemon* test.

Lemon's first prong focuses on the purpose that animated adoption of the Act. . . . A governmental intention to promote religion is clear when the State enacts a law to serve a religious purpose. . . . In this case, the petitioners have identified no clear secular purpose for the Louisiana Act.

True, the Act's stated purpose is to protect academic freedom. This phrase might, in common parlance, be understood as referring to enhancing the freedom of teachers to teach what they will. The Court of Appeals, however, correctly concluded that the Act was not designed to further that goal. We find no merit in the State's argument that the "legislature may not [have] use[d] the terms 'academic freedom' in the correct legal sense. They might have [had] in mind, instead, a basic concept of fairness; teaching all of the evidence." Even if "academic freedom" is read to mean "teaching all of the evidence" with respect to the origin of human beings, the Act does not further this purpose. The goal of providing a more comprehensive science curriculum is not furthered either by outlawing the teaching of evolution or by requiring the teaching of creation science. . . .

While the Court is normally deferential to a State's articulation of a secular purpose, it is required that the statement of such purpose be sincere and not a sham. . . .

It is clear from the legislative history that the purpose of the legislative sponsor, Senator Bill Keith, was to narrow the science curriculum. During the legislative hearings, Senator Keith stated: "My preference would be that neither [creationism nor evolution] be taught." Such a ban on teaching does not promote—indeed, it undermines—the provision of a comprehensive scientific education.

It is equally clear that requiring schools to teach creation science with evolution does not advance academic freedom. The Act does not grant teachers a flexibility that they did not already possess to supplant the present science curriculum with the presentation of theories, besides evolution, about the origin of life. Indeed, the Court of Appeals found that no law prohibited Louisiana public schoolteachers from teaching any scientific theory. . . .

Furthermore, the goal of basic "fairness" is hardly furthered by the Act's discriminatory preference for the teaching of creation science and against the teaching of evolution. While requiring that curriculum guides be developed for creation science, the Act says nothing of comparable guides for evolution. Similarly, research services are supplied for creation science but not for evolution. Only "creation scientists" can serve on the panel that supplies the resource services. The Act forbids school boards to discriminate against anyone who "chooses to be a creation-scientist" or to teach "creationism," but fails to protect those who choose to teach evolution or any other noncreation science theory, or who refuse to teach creation science.

If the Louisiana legislature's purpose was solely to maximize the comprehensiveness and effectiveness of science instruction, it would have encouraged the teaching of all scientific theories about the origins of humankind. But under the Act's requirements, teachers who were once free to teach any and all facets of this subject are now unable to do so. Moreover, the Act fails even to ensure that creation science will be taught, but instead requires the teaching of this theory only when the theory of evolution is taught. Thus we agree with the Court of Appeals' conclusion that the Act does not serve to protect academic freedom, but has the distinctly different purpose of discrediting "evolution by counterbalancing its teaching at every turn with the teaching of creation science. . . ."

The legislative history documents that the Act's primary purpose was to change the science curriculum of public schools in order to provide persuasive advantage to a particular religious doctrine that rejects the factual basis of evolution in its entirety. . . .

The Louisiana Creationism Act advances a religious doctrine by requiring either the banishment of the theory of evolution from public school classrooms or the presentation of a religious viewpoint that rejects evolution in its entirety. The Act vio-

County Building, next to a Christmas tree and a sign saluting liberty. The Court of Appeals for the Third Circuit ruled that each display violates the Establishment Clause of the First Amendment because each has the impermissible effect of endorsing religion. We agree that the crèche display has that unconstitutional effect but reverse the Court of Appeals' judgment regarding the menorah display. . . .

We turn first to the county's crèche display. There is no doubt, of course, that the crèche itself is capable of communicating a religious message. . . . Indeed, the crèche in this lawsuit uses words, as well as the picture of the nativity scene, to make its religious meaning unmistakably clear. "Glory to God in the Highest!" says the angel in the crèche—Glory to God because of the birth of Jesus. This praise to God in Christian terms is indisputably religious—indeed sectarian—just as it is when said in the Gospel or in a church service.

Under the Court's holding in *Lynch,* the effect of a crèche display turns on its setting. Here, unlike in *Lynch,* nothing in the context of the display detracts from the crèche's religious message. The *Lynch* display comprised a series of figures and objects, each group of which had its own focal point. Santa's house and his reindeer were objects of attention separate from the crèche, and had their specific visual story to tell. Similarly, whatever a "talking" wishing well may be, it obviously was a center of attention separate from the crèche. Here, in contrast, the crèche stands alone: it is the single element of the display on the Grand Staircase.

The floral decoration surrounding the crèche cannot be viewed as somehow equivalent to the secular symbols in the overall *Lynch* display. The floral frame, like all good frames, serves only to draw one's attention to the message inside the frame. The floral decoration surrounding the crèche contributes to, rather than detracts from, the endorsement of religion conveyed by the crèche. It is as if the county had allowed the Holy Name Society to display a cross on the Grand Staircase at Easter, and the county had surrounded the cross with Easter lilies. The county could not say that surrounding the cross with traditional flowers of the season would negate the endorsement of Christianity conveyed by the cross on the Grand Staircase. Its contention that the traditional Christmas greens negate the endorsement effect of the crèche fares no better. . . . [T]he county sends an unmistakable message that it supports and promotes the Christian praise to God that is the crèche's religious message.

The fact that the crèche bears a sign disclosing its ownership by a Roman Catholic organization does not alter this conclusion. On the contrary, the sign simply demonstrates that the government is endorsing the religious message of that organization, rather than communicating a message of its own. But the Establishment Clause does not limit only the religious content of the government's own communications. It also prohibits the government's support and promotion of religious communications by religious organizations. . . . Indeed, the very concept of "endorsement" conveys the sense of promoting someone else's message. Thus, by prohibiting government endorsement of religion, the Establishment Clause prohibits precisely what occurred here: the government's lending its support to the communication of a religious organization's religious message.

Finally, the county argues that it is sufficient to validate the display of the crèche on the Grand Staircase that the display celebrates Christmas, and Christmas is a national holiday. This argument obviously proves too much. It would allow the celebration of the Eucharist inside a courthouse on Christmas Eve. While the county may have doubts about the constitutional status of celebrating the Eucharist inside the courthouse under the government's auspices, this court does not. The government may acknowledge Christmas as a cultural phenomenon, but under the First Amendment it may not observe it as a Christian holy day by suggesting that people praise God for the birth of Jesus.

In sum, *Lynch* teaches that government may celebrate Christmas in some manner and form, but not in a way that endorses Christian doctrine. Here, Allegheny County has transgressed this line. It has chosen to celebrate Christmas in a way that has the effect of endorsing a patently Christian message: Glory to God for the birth of Jesus Christ. Under *Lynch,* and the rest of our cases, nothing more is required to demonstrate a violation of the Establishment Clause. The display of the crèche in this context, therefore, must be permanently enjoined.

JUSTICE KENNEDY and the three Justices who join him would find the display of the crèche consistent with the Establishment Clause. He argues that this conclusion necessarily follows from the Court's decision in *Marsh* v. *Chambers,* 463 U. S. 783 (1983), which sustained the constitutionality of legislative prayer. He also asserts that the crèche, even in this setting, poses "no realistic risk" of "represent[ing] an effort to proselytize," having repudiated the Court's endorsement inquiry in favor of a "proselytization" approach. The Court's analysis of the crèche, he contends, "reflects an unjustified hostility toward religion."

JUSTICE KENNEDY's reasons for permitting the

crèche on the Grand Staircase and his condemnation of the Court's reasons for deciding otherwise are so far-reaching in their implications that they require a response in some depth:

In *Marsh,* the Court relied specifically on the fact that Congress authorized legislative prayer at the same time that it produced the Bill of Rights. JUSTICE KENNEDY, however, argues that *Marsh* legitimates all "practices with no greater potential for an establishment of religion" than those "accepted traditions dating back to the Founding." Otherwise, the Justice asserts, such practices as our national motto ("In God We Trust") and our Pledge of Allegiance (with the phrase "under God") are in danger of invalidity.

Our previous opinions have considered in dicta the motto and the pledge, characterizing them as consistent with the proposition that government may not communicate an endorsement of religious belief. . . . We need not return to the subject of "ceremonial deism," because there is an obvious distinction between crèche displays and references to God in the motto and the pledge. However history may affect the constitutionality of nonsectarian references to religion by the government, history cannot legitimate practices that demonstrate the government's allegiance to a particular sect or creed.

Indeed, in *Marsh* itself, the Court recognized that not even the "unique history" of legislative prayer can justify contemporary legislative prayers that have the effect of affiliating the government with any one specific faith or belief. The legislative prayers involved in *Marsh* did not violate this principle because the particular chaplain had "removed all references to Christ." Thus, *Marsh* plainly does not stand for the sweeping proposition JUSTICE KENNEDY apparently would ascribe to it, namely, that all accepted practices 200 years old and their equivalents are constitutional today. Nor can *Marsh,* given its facts and its reasoning, compel the conclusion that the display of the crèche involved in this lawsuit is constitutional. Although JUSTICE KENNEDY says that he "cannot comprehend" how the crèche display could be invalid after *Marsh,* surely he is able to distinguish between a specifically Christian symbol, like a crèche, and more general religious references, like the legislative prayers in *Marsh.*

JUSTICE KENNEDY's reading of *Marsh* would gut the core of the Establishment Clause, as this Court understands it. . . .

Although JUSTICE KENNEDY repeatedly accuses the Court of harboring a "latent hostility" or "callous indifference" toward religion, nothing could be further from the truth, and the accusation could be said to be as offensive as they are absurd. JUSTICE KENNEDY apparently has misperceived a respect for religious pluralism, a respect commanded by the Constitution, as hostility or indifference to religion. No misperception could be more antithetical to the values embodied in the Establishment Clause.

JUSTICE KENNEDY's accusations are shot from a weapon triggered by the following proposition: if government may celebrate the secular aspects of Christmas, then it must be allowed to celebrate the religious aspects as well because, otherwise, the government would be discriminating against citizens who celebrate Christmas as a religious, and not just a secular, holiday. This proposition, however, is flawed at its foundation. The government does not discriminate against any citizen on the basis of the citizen's religious faith if the government is secular in its functions and operations. On the contrary, the Constitution mandates that the government remain secular, rather than affiliating itself with religious beliefs or institutions, precisely in order to avoid discriminating among citizens on the basis of their religious faiths.

A secular state, it must be remembered, is not the same as an atheistic or antireligious state. A secular state establishes neither atheism nor religion as its official creed. JUSTICE KENNEDY thus has it exactly backwards when he says that enforcing the Constitution's requirement that government remain secular is a prescription of orthodoxy. It follows directly from the Constitution's proscription against government affiliation with religious beliefs or institutions that there is no orthodoxy on religious matters in the secular state. Although JUSTICE KENNEDY accuses the Court of "an Orwellian rewriting of history," perhaps it is JUSTICE KENNEDY himself who has slipped into a form of Orwellian newspeak when he equates the constitutional command of secular government with a prescribed orthodoxy.

To be sure, in a pluralistic society there may be some would-be theocrats, who wish that their religion were an established creed, and some of them perhaps may be even audacious enough to claim that the lack of established religion discriminates against their preferences. But this claim gets no relief, for it contradicts the fundamental premise of the Establishment Clause itself. The antidiscrimination principle inherent in the Establishment Clause necessarily means that would-be discriminators on the basis of religion cannot prevail.

For this reason, the claim that prohibiting government from celebrating Christmas as a religious holiday discriminates against Christians in favor of nonadherents must fail. Celebrating Christmas as a religious, as opposed to a secular, holiday, necessarily entails professing, proclaiming or believing that Jesus of Nazareth, born in a manger in Bethlehem, is the Christ, the Messiah. If the government celebrates Christmas as a religious holiday (for example, by issuing an official proclamation saying: "We rejoice in the glory of Christ's birth!"), it means that the government really is declaring Jesus to be the Messiah, a specifically Christian belief. In contrast, confining the government's own celebration of Christmas to the holiday's secular aspects does *not* favor the religious beliefs of non-Christians over those of Christians. Rather, it simply permits the government to acknowledge the holiday without expressing an allegiance to Christian beliefs, an allegiance that would truly favor Christians over non-Christians. To be sure, some Christians may wish to see the government proclaim its allegiance to Christianity in a religious celebration of Christmas, but the Constitution does not permit the gratification of that desire, which would contradict the " 'the logic of secular liberty' " it is the purpose of the Establishment Clause to protect. . . .

Of course, not all religious celebrations of Christmas located on government property violate the Establishment Clause. It obviously is not unconstitutional, for example, for a group of parishioners from a local church to go caroling through a city park on any Sunday in Advent or for a Christian club at a public university to sing carols during their Christmas meeting. The reason is that activities of this nature do not demonstrate the government's allegiance to, or endorsement of, the Christian faith.

Equally obvious, however, is the proposition that not all proclamations of Christian faith located on government property are permitted by the Establishment Clause just because they occur during the Christmas holiday season, as the example of a Mass in the courthouse surely illustrates. And once the judgment has been made that a particular proclamation of Christian belief, when disseminated from a particular location on government property, has the effect of demonstrating the government's endorsement of Christian faith, then it necessarily follows that the practice must be enjoined to protect the constitutional rights of those citizens who follow some creed other than Christianity. It is thus incontrovertible that the Court's decision today, premised on the determination that the crèche display on the Grand Staircase demonstrates the county's endorsement of Christianity, does not represent a hostility or indifference to religion but, instead, the respect for religious diversity that the Constitution requires. . . .

Lynch v. *Donnelly* confirms, and in no way repudiates, the longstanding constitutional principle that government may not engage in a practice that has the effect of promoting or endorsing religious beliefs. The display of the crèche in the County Courthouse has this unconstitutional effect. The display of the menorah in front of the City-County Building, however, does not have this effect, given its "particular physical setting."

The judgment of the Court of Appeals is affirmed in part and reversed in part, and the cases are remanded for further proceedings.

It is so ordered.

JUSTICE O'CONNOR concurring in part and concurring in the judgment: [omitted]
JUSTICE BRENNAN, with whom JUSTICE MARSHALL and JUSTICE STEVENS join, concurring in part and dissenting in part:

I have previously explained at some length my views on the relationship between the Establishment Clause and government-sponsored celebrations of the Christmas holiday. See *Lynch* v. *Donnelly,* 465 U.S. 668, 694–726 (1984) (dissenting opinion). I continue to believe that the display of an object that "retains a specifically Christian [or other] religious meaning," is incompatible with the separation of church and state demanded by our Constitution. I therefore agree with the Court that Allegheny County's display of a crèche at the county courthouse signals an endorsement of the Christian faith in violation of the Establishment Clause . . . I cannot agree, however, that the city's display of a 45-foot Christmas tree and an 18-foot Chanukah menorah at the entrance to the building housing the Mayor's office shows no favoritism towards Christianity, Judaism, or both. Indeed, I should have thought that the answer as to the first display supplied the answer to the second.

According to the Court, the crèche display sends a message endorsing Christianity because the crèche itself bears a religious meaning, because an angel in the display carries a banner declaring "Glory to God in the highest!," and because the floral decorations surrounding the crèche highlighted it rather than secularized it. The display of a Christmas tree and Chanukah menorah, in contrast, is said to show no endorsement of a particular faith or faiths, or of religion in general, because the Christmas tree is a secular symbol which brings out the secular elements of the menorah. And, JUSTICE BLACKMUN concludes, even though the menorah has religious aspects, its display reveals no endorsement of religion because no other symbol could have been used to represent the secular aspects of the holiday of Chanukah without mocking its celebration. Rather than endorsing religion, therefore, the display merely demonstrates that "Christmas is not the only traditional way of observing the winter-holiday season," and confirms our "cultural diversity."

Thus, the decision as to the menorah rests on three premises: the Christmas tree is a secular symbol; Chanukah is a holiday with secular dimensions, symbolized by the menorah; and the government may promote pluralism by sponsoring or condoning displays having strong religious associations on its property. None of these is sound. . . .

The . . . premise on which today's decision rests is the notion that Chanukah is a partly secular holiday, for which the menorah can serve as a secular symbol. It is no surprise and no anomaly that Chanukah has historical and societal roots that range beyond the purely religious. I would venture that most, if not all, major religious holidays have beginnings and enjoy histories studded with figures, events, and practices that are not strictly religious. It does not seem to me that the mere fact that Chanukah shares this kind of background makes it a secular holiday in any meaningful sense. The menorah is indisputably a religious symbol, used ritually in a celebration that has deep religious significance. That, in my view, is all that need be said. Whatever secular practices the holiday of Chanukah has taken on in its contemporary observance are beside the point. . . .

The uncritical acceptance of a message of religious pluralism . . . ignores the extent to which even that message may offend. Many religious faiths are hostile to each other, and indeed, refuse even to participate in ecumenical services designed to demonstrate the very pluralism JUSTICES BLACK-MUN and O'CONNOR extol. To lump the ritual objects and holidays of religions together without regard to their attitudes toward such inclusiveness, or to decide which religions should be excluded because of the possibility of offense, is not a benign or beneficent celebration of pluralism: it is instead an interference in religious matters precluded by the Establishment Clause. . . .

Those religions that have no holiday at all during the period between Thanksgiving and New Year's Day will not benefit, even in a second-class manner, from the city's once-a-year tribute to "liberty" and "freedom of belief." This is not "pluralism" as I understand it.

JUSTICE STEVENS, with whom JUSTICE BRENNAN and JUSTICE MARSHALL join, concurring in part and dissenting in part: [omitted]

JUSTICE KENNEDY, with whom THE CHIEF JUSTICE, JUSTICE WHITE, and JUSTICE SCALIA join, concurring in the judgment in part and dissenting in part:

The majority holds that the County of Allegheny violated the Establishment Clause by displaying a crèche in the county courthouse, because the "principal or primary effect" of the display is to advance religion within the meaning of *Lemon* v. *Kurtzman,* 403 U.S. 602, 612–613 (1971). This view of the Establishment Clause reflects an unjustified hostility toward religion, a hostility inconsistent with our history and our precedents, and I dissent from this holding. The crèche display is constitutional, and, for the same reasons, the display of a menorah by the city of Pittsburgh is permissible as well. On this latter point, I concur in the result, but not the reasoning . . . of JUSTICE BLACKMUN's opinion.

In keeping with the usual fashion of recent years, the majority applies the *Lemon* test to judge the constitutionality of the holiday displays here in question. I am content for present purposes to remain within the *Lemon* framework, but do not wish to be seen as advocating, let alone adopting, that test as our primary guide in this difficult area. Persuasive criticism of *Lemon* has emerged. Our cases often question its utility in providing concrete answers to Establishment Clause questions, calling it but a 'helpful signpos[t]' " or " 'guidelin[e]' " to assist our deliberations rather than a comprehensive test. . . . Substantial revision of our Establishment Clause doctrine may be in order, but it is unnecessary to undertake that task today, for even the *Lemon* test, when applied with proper sensitivity to our traditions and our caselaw, supports the conclusion that both the crèche and the menorah are permissible displays in the context of the holiday season.

The only *Lemon* factor implicated in this case directs us to inquire whether the "principal or primary effect" of the challenged government practice is "one that neither advances nor inhibits religion." . . .

Government policies of accommodation, acknowledgment, and support for religion are an accepted part of our political and cultural heritage. As Chief Justice Burger wrote for the Court in *Walz* v. *Tax Comm'n,* 397 U.S. 664 (1970), we must be careful to avoid "[t]he hazards of placing too much weight on a few words or phrases of the Court," and so we have "declined to construe the Religion Clauses with a literalness that would undermine the ultimate constitutional objective as illuminated by history."

Rather than requiring government to avoid any action that acknowledges or aids religion, the Establishment Clause permits government some latitude in recognizing and accommodating the central role religion plays in our society. Any approach less sensitive to our heritage would border on latent hostility toward religion, as it would require government in all its multifaceted roles to acknowledge only the secular, to the exclusion and so to the detriment of the religious. A categorical approach would install federal courts as jealous guardians of an absolute "wall of separation," sending a clear message of disapproval. In this century, as the modern administrative state expands to touch the lives of its citizens in such diverse ways and redirects their financial choices through programs of its own, it is difficult to maintain the fiction that requiring government to avoid all assistance to religion can in fairness be viewed as serving the goal of neutrality. . . .

The ability of the organized community to recognize and accommodate religion in a society with a pervasive public sector requires diligent observance of the border between accommodation and establishment. Our cases disclose two limiting principles: government may not coerce anyone to support or participate in any religion or its exercise; and it may not, in the guise of avoiding hostility or callous indifference, give direct benefits to religion in such a degree that it in fact "establishes a [state] religion or religious faith, or tends to do so." These two principles, while distinct, are not unrelated, for it would be difficult indeed to establish a religion without some measure of more or less subtle coercion, be it in the form of taxation to supply the substantial benefits that would sustain a state-established faith, direct compulsion to observance, or governmental exhortation to religiosity that amounts in fact to proselytizing.

It is no surprise that without exception we have invalidated actions that further the interests of religion through the coercive power of government. . . .

[C]oercion need not be a direct tax in aid of religion or a test oath. Symbolic recognition or accommodation of religious faith may violate the Clause in an extreme case. I doubt not, for example, that the Clause forbids a city to permit the permanent erection of a large Latin cross on the roof of city hall. This is not because government speech about religion is *per se* suspect, as the majority would have it, but because such an obtrusive year-round religious display would place the government's weight behind an obvious effort to proselytize on behalf of a particular religion. . . .

Absent coercion, the risk of infringement of religious liberty by passive or symbolic accommodation is minimal. Our cases reflect this reality by requiring a showing that the symbolic recognition or accommodation advances religion to such a degree that it actually "establishes a religion or religious faith, or tends to do so." . . .

Non-coercive government action within the realm of flexible accommodation or passive acknowledgment of existing symbols does not violate the Establishment Clause unless it benefits religion in a way more direct and more substantial than practices that are accepted in our national heritage.

These principles are not difficult to apply to the facts of the case before us. In permitting the displays on government property of the menorah and the crèche, the city and county sought to do no more than "celebrate the season," and to acknowledge, along with many of their citizens, the historical background and the religious as well as secular nature of the Chanukah and Christmas holidays. This interest falls well within the tradition of government accommodation and acknowledgment of religion that has marked our history from the beginning. It cannot be disputed that government, if it chooses, may participate in sharing with its citizens the joy of the holiday season, by declaring public holidays, installing or permitting festive displays, sponsoring celebrations and parades, and providing holiday vacations for its employees. All levels of our government do precisely that. As we said in *Lynch,* "Government has long recognized—indeed it has subsidized—holidays with religious significance."

If government is to participate in its citizens' celebration of a holiday that contains both a secular and a religious component, enforced recognition of only the secular aspect would signify the callous indifference toward religious faith that our cases and traditions do not require; for by commemorating the holiday only as it is celebrated by nonadherents, the government would be refusing to acknowledge the plain fact, and the historical reality, that many of its citizens celebrate its religious aspects as well. Judicial invalidation of government's attempts to recognize the religious underpinnings of the holiday would signal not neutrality but a pervasive intent to insulate government from all things religious. The Religion Clauses do not require government to acknowledge these holidays or their religious component; but our strong tradition of government accommodation and acknowledgment permits government to do so.

There is no suggestion here that the government's power to coerce has been used to further the interests of Christianity or Judaism in any way. No one was compelled to observe or participate in any religious ceremony or activity. Neither the city nor the county contributed significant amounts of tax money to serve the cause of one religious faith. The crèche and the menorah are purely passive symbols of religious holidays. Passersby who disagree with the message conveyed by these displays are free to ignore them, or even to turn their backs, just as they are free to do when they disagree with any other form of government speech.

There is no realistic risk that the crèche or the menorah represent an effort to proselytize or are otherwise the first step down the road to an establishment of religion. *Lynch* is dispositive of this claim with respect to the crèche, and I find no reason for reaching a different result with respect to the menorah. Both are the traditional symbols of religious holidays that over time have acquired a secular component. Without ambiguity, *Lynch* instructs that "the focus of our inquiry must be on the [religious symbol] in the context of the [holiday] season," In that context, religious displays that serve "to celebrate the Holiday and to depict the origins of that Holiday" give rise to no Establishment Clause concern. If Congress and the state legislatures do not run afoul of the Establishment Clause when they begin each day with a state-sponsored prayer for divine guidance offered by a chaplain whose salary is paid at government expense, I cannot comprehend how a menorah or a crèche, displayed in the limited context of the holiday season, can be invalid.

Respondents say that the religious displays involved here are distinguishable from the crèche in *Lynch* because they are located on government property and are not surrounded by the candy canes, reindeer, and other holiday paraphernalia that were a part of the display in *Lynch*. Nothing in Chief Justice Burger's opinion for the Court in *Lynch* provides support for these purported distinctions. After describing the facts, the *Lynch* opinion makes no mention of either of these factors. It concentrates instead on the significance of the crèche as part of the entire holiday season. Indeed, it is clear that the Court did not view the secular aspects of the display as somehow subduing the religious message conveyed by the crèche, for the majority expressly rejected the dissenters' suggestion that it sought " 'to explain away the clear religious import of the crèche' " or had "equated the crèche with a Santa's house or reindeer." Crucial to the Court's conclusion was not the number, prominence, or type of secular items contained in the holiday display but the simple fact that, when displayed by

government during the Christmas season, a crèche presents no realistic danger of moving government down the forbidden road toward an establishment of religion. Whether the crèche be surrounded by poinsettias, talking wishing wells, or carolers, the conclusion remains the same, for the relevant context is not the items in the display itself but the season as a whole.

The fact that the crèche and menorah are both located on government property, even at the very seat of government, is likewise inconsequential. In the first place, the *Lynch* Court did not rely on the fact that the setting for Pawtucket's display was a privately owned park, and it is difficult to suggest that anyone could have failed to receive a message of government sponsorship after observing Santa Claus ride the city fire engine to the park to join with the Mayor of Pawtucket in inaugurating the holiday season by turning on the lights of the city-owned display. . . .

Our cases do not suggest, moreover, that the use of public property necessarily converts otherwise permissible government conduct into an Establishment Clause violation. To the contrary, in some circumstances the First Amendment may *require* that government property be available for use and even where not required, such use has long been permitted. The prayer approved in *Marsh* v. *Chambers,* for example, was conducted in the legislative chamber of the State of Nebraska, surely the single place most likely to be thought the center of state authority.

Nor can I comprehend why it should be that placement of a government-owned crèche on private land is lawful while placement of a privately owned crèche on public land is not. If anything, I should have thought government ownership of a religious symbol presented the more difficult question under the Establishment Clause, but as *Lynch* resolved that question to sustain the government action, the sponsorship here ought to be all the easier to sustain. In short, nothing about the religious displays here distinguishes them in any meaningful way from the crèche we permitted in *Lynch*.

If *Lynch* is still good law—and until today it was—the judgment below cannot stand. I accept and indeed approve both the holding and the reasoning of Chief Justice Burger's opinion in *Lynch*, and so I must dissent from the judgment that the crèche display is unconstitutional. On the same reasoning, I agree that the menorah display is constitutional. . . .

In addition to disregarding precedent and historical fact, the majority's approach to government use of religious symbolism threatens to trivialize constitutional adjudication. By mischaracterizing the Court's opinion in *Lynch* as an endorsement-in-context test, the majority embraces a jurisprudence of minutiae. A reviewing court must consider whether the city has included Santas, talking wishing wells, reindeer or other secular symbols as "a center of attention separate from the crèche." After determining whether these centers of attention are sufficiently "separate" that each "had their specific visual story to tell," the court must then measure their proximity to the crèche. A community that wishes to construct a constitutional display must also take care to avoid floral frames or other devices that might insulate the crèche from the sanitizing effect of the secular portions of the display. The majority also notes the presence of evergreens near the crèche that are identical to two small evergreens placed near official county signs. After today's decision, municipal greenery must be used with care.

Another important factor will be the prominence of the setting in which the display is placed. In this case, the Grand Staircase of the county courthouse proved too resplendent. . . .

My description of the majority's test, though perhaps uncharitable, is intended to illustrate the inevitable difficulties with its application. This test could provide workable guidance to the lower courts, if ever, only after this Court has decided a long series of holiday display cases, using little more than intuition and a tape measure. Deciding cases on the basis of such an unguided examination of marginalia is irreconcilable with the imperative of applying neutral principles in constitutional adjudication. . . .

The approach adopted by the majority contradicts important values embodied in the Clause. Obsessive, implacable resistance to all but the most carefully scripted and secularized forms of accommodation requires this Court to act as a censor, issuing national decrees as to what is orthodox and

what is not. What is orthodox, in this context, means what is secular; the only Christmas the State can acknowledge is one in which references to religion have been held to a minimum. The Court thus lends its assistance to an Orwellian rewriting of history as many understand it. I can conceive of no judicial function more antithetical to the First Amendment.

A further contradiction arises from the majority's approach, for the Court also assumes the difficult and inappropriate task of saying what every religious symbol means. Before studying this case, I had not known the full history of the menorah, and I suspect the same was true of my colleagues. . . .

The case before us is admittedly a troubling one. It must be conceded that, however neutral the purpose of the city and county, the eager proselytizer may seek to us these symbols for his own ends. The urge to use them to teach or to taunt is always present. It is also true that some devout adherents of Judaism or Christianity may be as offended by the holiday display as are nonbelievers, if not more so. To place these religious symbols in a common hallway or sidewalk, where they may be ignored or even insulted, must be distasteful to many who cherish their meaning.

For these reasons, I might have voted against installation of these particular displays were I a local legislative official. But we have no jurisdiction over matters of taste within the realm of constitutionally permissible discretion. Our role is enforcement of a written Constitution. In my view, the principles of the Establishment Clause and our Nation's historic traditions of diversity and pluralism allow communities to make reasonable judgments respecting the accommodation or acknowledgement of holidays with both cultural and religious aspects. No constitutional violation occurs when they do so by displaying a symbol of the holiday's religious origins.

I dissent.

Chapter

16

Fourth and Fifth Amendment Issues

Procedural guarantees are of a different order than the substantive guarantees contained in the First Amendment that we examined in chapters 13, 14, and 15. Procedural rights concern guarantees of fairness on the part of government when government acts to deprive us of our liberty, property, or even lives and are applicable to both criminal and noncriminal processes. However, it is in the criminal sphere that the Constitution provides the most detailed and explicit inventory of rights to assure fairness, and it is the major criminal procedural guarantees to which we devote our attention in this and the following chapter.

FOURTH AMENDMENT RIGHTS

The Fourth Amendment guarantees "the right of the people to be secure in their persons, houses, papers, and effects, against unreasonable searches and seizures." The Amendment specifies that no warrants shall be issued "but upon probable cause, supported by Oath or af-

firmation, and particularly describing the place to be searched, and the persons or things to be seized." Clearly the Fourth Amendment contains both a substantive right of privacy protecting individuals from general open-ended searches as well as a procedural guarantee concerned with the circumstances under which searches can be conducted, evidence seized, or persons arrested.

The Supreme Court had only a few occasions in the first 150 years of its existence to rule on searches and seizures involving the actions of the federal government. But when it did consider such issues the Court tended to be sympathetic to Fourth Amendment claims as, for example, in the ruling in *Boyd* v. *United States,* 116 U.S. 616 (1886), when the Fourth Amendment guarantee was liberally construed and linked with the Fifth Amendment guarantee against self-incrimination. In *Boyd,* the Court decided that compulsory production of the private books and papers of the owner of goods the government sought to have forfeited was the equivalent of an unreasonable search and seizure because it compelled the owner to be a witness against himself in violation of the Fifth Amendment. The search was unreasonable as a violation of the Fourth Amendment, and the use of the evidence seized violated the Fifth Amendment's guarantee against self-incrimination. It was not until 1914, however, in *Weeks* v. *United States,* 232 U.S. 383, that the Court established a more firm basis for the exclusion of evidence seized by federal officials in violation of the Fourth Amendment. The Court in *Weeks* ruled that evidence seized in violation of the Fourth Amendment's explicit standards could not be introduced as evidence in a federal trial court because to do so would negate the intended effect of the Amendment. It would provide an incentive for law enforcement officers to violate rights and would enable government to profit from the commission of illegal acts. The suppression of illegally obtained evidence became known as the *Weeks* rule or the exclusionary rule. The Court strongly suggested that the exclusionary rule must be considered as part of the Fourth Amendment.

In 1928, another Fourth Amendment case, *Olmstead* v. *United States,* 277 U.S. 438, raised the question whether the use of noninvasive eavesdropping devices to gather incriminating evidence was a search and seizure subject to Fourth Amendment standards. This case concerned evidence acquired by telephone wiretaps. The Court ruled that a search and seizure must be a physical one in which something tangible can be searched and seized. Wiretapping did not, said the Court, involve a physical search and seizure as the evidence was gathered strictly by the use of the sense of hearing. *Olmstead* was reaffirmed in *Goldman* v. *United States,* 316 U.S. 129 (1942), as applied to any nonintrusive eavesdropping devices. Not until 1967, in **Katz** v. **United States,** did the Court overturn *Olmstead*. This was one of the expansive Warren

Court criminal procedures rulings, and the Court made it clear that electronic eavesdropping or bugging was subject to Fourth Amendment standards and that the Amendment protects people wherever they have a reasonable expectation of privacy. The Burger Court, although more restrictive in its interpretation of Fourth Amendment rights than the Warren Court, nevertheless defended the Amendment's mandate with regard to wiretaps and eavesdropping in **United States** v. **United States District Court.** In that decision, the Court unanimously struck down the Nixon Administration's view of the guarantees of the amendment. Had the Court upheld the government's position, it would have marked a fatal blow to the Fourth Amendment's guarantees and the legal cornerstone of a police state would have been set in place.

As we saw with First Amendment cases, the Court began incorporating specific guarantees of the Bill of Rights beginning in 1925. Criminal procedural guarantees began to be incorporated in 1932 with **Powell** v. **Alabama** (chap. 17). In *Wolf* v. *Colorado,* 338 U.S. 25 (1949), the Court faced the question of whether the guarantee against unreasonable searches and seizures, along with the exclusionary rule, were applicable to the states via the Fourteenth Amendment's due process clause. The Court said yes insofar as concerns the basic guarantee, but no to the exclusionary rule. However, in the landmark case of **Mapp** v. **Ohio,** the Warren Court overturned *Wolf* in terms of its position with regard to the exclusionary rule and found that the exclusionary rule was applicable to the states through the Fourteenth Amendment's Due Process Clause. The states along with the federal government must respect the requirements of the Fourteenth Amendment, and if either does not, any evidence so acquired must be thrown out of court.

The Fourth Amendment has raised a number of continuing issues and the constitutional status of these issues is rarely clear-cut. The exclusionary rule itself has been under attack for allowing criminals to go free on "a technicality." Some have attacked the exclusionary rule as being contrary to the intent of the framers. But realizing that the exclusionary rule has been attached to the Fourth Amendment since the 1914 *Weeks* case, opponents of the rule, including some justices of the Supreme Court among whom must be counted Chief Justice Warren Burger and William Rehnquist, his successor, have taken an incremental approach so as gradually to erode it. The Burger Court's decisions have weakened the exclusionary rule. For example, in *United States* v. *Calandra,* 414 U.S. 338 (1974), the Court decided that the exclusionary rule does not apply to grand jury proceedings, and held that the rule was not a "personal constitutional right" of an accused but merely a means of deterring police violations of the Fourth Amendment. Thus, evidence obtained in violation of Fourth Amendment requirements may be introduced before a grand jury. In 1976, in *United States* v. *Janis,* 428 U.S. 433, the Court ruled that evidence illegally seized by state authorities was admissible in federal *civil* proceedings such as, in the *Janis* case, a civil action by the Internal Revenue Service for collecting back taxes. In *United States* v. *Havens,* 446 U.S. 620 (1980), the Court permitted the admission of illegally seized evidence (in violation of the Fourth Amendment) at a trial to impeach the credibility of the defendant's testimony on cross-examination. In *Stone* v. *Powell,* 428 U.S. 465 (1976), the Court abruptly withdrew federal district court supervision of how state courts were handling the exclusionary rule. The Burger Court was asked to establish a good-faith exception to the exclusionary rule to allow evidence illegally seized to be used as evidence in court as long as the police acted in good faith that they were obeying the law. In the 1984 decision of **United States** v. **Leon** and a companion case applicable to the states (*Massachusetts* v. *Sheppard,* 468 U.S. 981 [1984]), the Burger

Court took that step with regard to defective search warrants. That is, evidence secured by use of a defective warrant, that the police in good faith thought was valid, is admissible in a court of law. This can be seen as the first major step on the road not only to a general good-faith exception rule but to the eventual demise of the exclusionary rule. Significantly, the majority in *Leon* refused to tie the exclusionary rule to the Fourth Amendment as an integral part of the guarantee.

The Rehnquist Court has continued the trend of finding exceptions to the applicability of the Fourth Amendment. For example, in *Colorado* v. *Bertine,* 479 U.S. 367 (1987), the police arrested Bertine for drunk driving and in the process of conducting an inventory of the contents of his van opened a closed backpack and found cocaine and a large amount of cash. He was subsequently convicted of drug offenses but the Colorado Supreme Court overturned the conviction on Fourth Amendment grounds. The Rehnquist Court, however, said that the inventory search was reasonable and that there is an inventory exception to the Fourth Amendment. In a later case, however, the Court insisted that there must be an official police policy governing which closed containers are to be opened during inventory searches. In the absence of such a policy, a particular search was found to violate the Fourth Amendment (*Florida* v. *Wells,* 110 S.Ct. 1632 [1990]). In *New York* v. *Burger,* 482 U.S. 691 (1987), the Court upheld a New York statute authorizing warrantless searches of vehicle-dismantling businesses. This, said the Court, comes within the exception to the warrant requirement because it is an administrative inspection of a closely regulated business. *Murray* v. *U.S.,* 487 U.S. 533 (1988), concerned an unlawful police entry into a warehouse where the police observed marijuana in plain view. They then secured a search warrant and seized the drugs. The Supreme Court said that was constitutional provided that there was an independent source for obtaining the search warrant (independent of what was observed in the first illegal entry). This is the independent source exception doctrine to the exclusionary rule. In **California** v. **Greenwood,** a person's garbage was found to be unprotected from a warrantless search. And in *U.S.* v. *Verdugo-Urquidez,* 110 U.S. 1056 (1990), the Court ruled that the Fourth Amendment does not operate outside the United States on behalf of non-resident aliens. What happened was that U.S. agents without a warrant searched the Mexican residence of a Mexican citizen believed to be a leader of a drug gang that smuggles narcotics into the U.S. The Mexican police brought the Mexican across the border and turned him over to U.S. authorities. He was brought to trial using the incriminating evidence that had been obtained in violation of the Fourth Amendment. The Court's decision means that under certain circumstances the Fourth Amendment can be disregarded by federal trial courts.

The automobile has provided particular problems with regard to the Fourth Amendment. Under what circumstances can an automobile or its occupants be searched and evidence seized without a search warrant? After some confusing and contradictory decisions, the Burger Court came up with a policy for stopping, searching and seizing. In **United States** v. **Ross,** the Court ruled that where there is probable cause to believe an automobile is transporting contraband, the automobile may be stopped and thoroughly searched only insofar as the places or containers searched could potentially contain the contraband. Of course, any time a person consents to be searched or consents to a search of his or her home, automobile, or possessions, that individual, by consenting, has waived his or her Fourth Amendment rights. In *Schneckloth* v. *Bustamonte,* 412 U.S. 218 (1973), the Court ruled that consent to search of an automobile can be considered "voluntary" even though the person consenting was unaware of having

a constitutional right to withhold consent. In *United States* v. *Robinson,* 414 U.S. 218 (1973), the Court broadened the search and seizure authority of the police when a motorist is stopped for a traffic law violation. However, the Court ruled in *Delaware* v. *Prouse,* 440 U.S. 648 (1979), that police may not, without probable cause, randomly stop automobiles in order to check drivers' licenses and automobile registrations. But stopping *all* drivers at roadside checkpoints to catch drunk drivers does not violate the Fourth Amendment (**Michigan** v. **Sitz** [reprinted at the end of this book]).

The Court has emphasized that the Fourth Amendment applies where an individual has a reasonable expectation of privacy. This means that a warrant must be obtained based on probable cause to search a home. For example, in *Payton* v. *New York,* 445 U.S. 573 (1980), the Court ruled that a warrant is needed for the routine arrest of a suspect in his or her place of residence. Any evidence seized in the absence of a warrant is inadmissible. The Court even applied this ruling to all similarly obtained convictions that were not yet final at the time *Payton* was handed down (the case was *United States* v. *Johnson,* 457 U.S. 537 [1982]). A warrant is also needed for the arrest of an overnight guest in a private residence. Overnight guests, said the Court in *Minnesota* v. *Olson,* 110 S.Ct. 1684 (1990), have a legitimate expectation of privacy in a host's home and enjoy the same Fourth Amendment rights as the host. The Court invalidated as a violation of the Fourth Amendment a warrantless night entry into a home to arrest an individual for drunk driving even where the guilt of the individual was clear (see *Welsh* v. *Wisconsin,* 466 U.S. 740 [1984]). Similarly, when the police have a valid arrest warrant, they may not search for the suspect in another's home without a warrant (*Steagald* v. *United States,* 451 U.S. 204 [1981]). But when they have a valid warrant to search a home, police officers may detain the occupants of the premises while the search is conducted (*Michigan* v. *Summers,* 452 U.S. 692 [1981]). Also, if the officer has a right to be in a place of residence and observes contraband, he may seize it and arrest the owner. This ruling came in the case of *Washington* v. *Chrisman,* 455 U.S 1 (1982), which concerned a police officer at a state university who observed an apparently underage student leaving his dormitory with a bottle of gin. The student was asked for his identification card but did not have it on his person. The officer then accompanied the student back to the student's dormitory room to get the card, and once in the room the officer observed in plain view narcotics on the roommate's desk which the officer seized and which the Court said could lawfully be introduced at the narcotics violation trial. On the other hand, in another case in which a police officer lawfully present in an apartment but without probable cause moved stereo equipment to locate serial numbers, the Court ruled that the evidence should be suppressed because it was not in plain view (*Arizona* v. *Hicks,* 480 U.S. 321 [1987]).

The Burger Court in the 1985 decision of *California* v. *Carney,* 471 U.S. 386, ruled that a mobile motor home that can be easily driven on the highway and is not being used as a fixed dwelling place (that is, not mounted on blocks and attached to utilities) is not to be given the protection given a traditional home. Rather, that sort of mobile home is to be considered the same way automobiles are considered under the Fourth Amendment. That is, an exception is made and a search without a warrant can be made on probable cause. Also, the Court ruled in *Oliver* v. *United States,* 466 U.S. 170 (1984), that an open field, even when fenced in and with posted "No Trespassing" signs, does not protect its owner (who happened to have been growing marijuana) under the Fourth Amendment because in an open field there is no reasonable expectation of privacy. An owner of a fenced-in backyard ordinarily does have a reasonable expectation of

privacy. Yet even here, the owner who was growing marijuana could not claim a Fourth Amendment violation when his backyard was viewed and photographed by police officers from a private airplane that flew over his house, which provided the justification for the issuance of a search warrant and the seizure of the marijuana plants (see *California* v. *Ciraolo,* 476 U.S. 207 (1986). Two cases from the Rehnquist Court have continued this line of decisions. In *U.S.* v. *Dunn,* 480 U.S. 294 (1987), police officers were in an open field, aimed their flashlights inside a barn, and saw evidence that led to a conviction of manufacturing illegal drugs. The Court determined that even if the defendant had a reasonable expectation of privacy in the barn, the use of a flashlight to illuminate the inside of the barn was not unreasonable. In *Florida* v. *Riley,* 109 S.Ct. 693 (1989), police officers in a helicopter flew some 400 feet over defendant's partially covered greenhouses in his backyard and on the basis of their observations secured a search warrant and subsequently seized marijuana plants. In this 5–4 decision the Court ruled that no search warrant was needed for the viewing by helicopter.

The Court found in *Hudson* v. *Palmer,* 468 U.S. 517 (1984), that a prisoner does not have a reasonable expectation of privacy in his or her cell and is consequently not protected by the Fourth Amendment from surprise searches. Neither does the bookstore seller of obscene material have a legitimate expectation of privacy; thus a county detective can enter such a bookstore, observe the materials on the magazine racks, purchase some material, and then promptly arrest the seller without a warrant. The magazines may be introduced at the trial as they did not constitute a Fourth Amendment seizure when they were purchased and the detective's perusal of the wares did not constitute a search within the meaning of the Fourth Amendment (see *Maryland* v. *Macon,* 472 U.S. 463 [1985]). In *United States* v. *Knotts,* 460 U.S. 276 (1983),

The big setback to incorporation was the decision in **Hurtado** v. **California.** The *Hurtado* case concerned the grand jury indictment guarantee of the Fifth Amendment, and the Court in this 1884 decision refused to consider this right as part of the due process the states must honor under the Fourteenth Amendment. Of course, as will be recalled from the discussion in Chapter 2, this decision must be seen in the context of the post-Civil War Court's narrow reading of the Fourteenth Amendment so that the Fourteenth did not offer much by way of the protection of the rights of blacks. In *Hurtado,* the Court's reasoning seemed to be reading out of the Fourteenth Amendment's due process clause any civil liberties content whatsoever. The antiredundancy argument of the Court meant that whatever rights were specified in the Fifth Amendment and by implication in the rest of the Bill of Rights could not possibly be included within the Fourteenth Amendment's due process guarantee because the wording of the due process clause was precisely the same as that found in the due process clause of the Fifth Amendment, and the Constitution may not be interpreted as being redundant. That is, if the grand jury indictment right was part of due process, there was no need for the framers to explicitly mention that guarantee as well as the due process guarantee in the Fifth Amendment. Thus, using the antiredundancy rationale, the Court reasoned that the due process clause of the Fifth Amendment meant something other than the grand jury indictment, the double jeopardy, or self-incrimination guarantees that were explicitly mentioned in the same amendment. Since the Fourteenth Amendment due process guarantee is the same as the Fifth Amendment's due process guarantee, it, too, must mean something other than those rights explicitly spelled out in the Fifth Amendment (and by implication elsewhere in the Bill of Rights).

Despite the Court's position and reasoning in *Hurtado,* the Court in 1897 made a conspic-uous exception to the *Hurtado* doctrine when it suggested in *Chicago, Burlington & Quincy Railroad Co.* v. *Chicago,* 166 U.S. 226 (1897), that the just compensation guarantee of the Fifth Amendment was part of the due process of the Fourteenth Amendment applicable to the states. As for the criminal procedural guarantees of due process, the Court slowly began moving away from *Hurtado* in such cases as *Twining* v. *New Jersey,* 211 U.S. 78 (1908). In *Twining,* the Court hinted that the Fourteenth Amendment due process clause did mean something for criminal defendants, although the Court rejected the argument that the Fifth Amendment guarantee against self-incrimination was part of the due process protected by the Fourteenth Amendment. But it was not until 1925 that the Court clearly abandoned the *Hurtado* reasoning when it brought freedom of speech and press under the aegis of the Fourteenth Amendment's due process clause in **Gitlow** v. **New York** (chap. 13). The Court explicitly rejected the *Hurtado* reasoning in *Powell* v. *Alabama* (chap. 17) in 1932 and incorporated the Sixth Amendment guarantee of the right to the assistance of counsel under the Fourteenth Amendment. But the Court was to move cautiously with regard to incorporating other criminal procedural guarantees. In *Brown* v. *Mississippi,* 297 U.S. 278 (1936), the Court threw out a confession based on physical coercion and ruled that the due process guaranteed by the Fourteenth Amendment does not permit the use of torture in the administration of criminal law. But the Court did not incorporate the self-incrimination guarantee until the 1964 Warren Court decision in *Malloy* v. *Hogan,* 378 U.S. 1. Rather, the Court's cautious approach was explicated in **Palko** v. **Connecticut.** The Court indicated its view as to what rights of the accused stated in the Bill of Rights were incorporated by the due process clause of the Fourteenth Amendment and thus applied to the states. In effect, the post-1937 Hughes through Vinson Courts recognized a double standard of criminal justice. When a *federal* prosecution was involved, the Court sympathetically considered and frequently accepted criminal procedural claims based on the Bill of Rights applicable to the federal government. However, when practices in the *states* were at issue, there was considerably less Court support for extending to the states specific guarantees of the Bill of Rights. In *Palko,* the Court, in an opinion by Justice Cardozo, refused to incorporate the double jeopardy guarantee, arguing that it was not essential to the concept of ordered liberty (in contrast to freedoms of speech and press and the right to counsel, which are). Not until the Warren Court's 1969 decision in *Benton* v. *Maryland,* 395 U.S. 784, was the double jeopardy guarantee incorporated. Curiously, one of the few rights not incorporated by the Warren Court and remaining unincorporated today is the grand jury indictment guarantee. Thus, although the *Hurtado* doctrine or reasoning has long since been abandoned by the Court, the bottom-line ruling of *Hurtado,* that the grand jury guarantee of the Fifth Amendment is not part of the due process guarantee of the Fourteenth Amendment, remains law today.

The self-incrimination guarantee has proved to be the most controversial of the Fifth Amendment rights, particularly since its incorporation in 1964. There were few early cases involving the federal government. One notable case was *Counselman* v. *Hitchcock,* 142 U.S. 547 (1892), in which the Court gave a generous reading of the guarantee although the case itself concerned a grand jury investigation of violations of the Interstate Commerce Act and the practical effect of the case was to protect businessmen from investigation by the ICC. Before 1964, and starting with *Brown* v. *Mississippi,* the Court would reverse state court convictions using confessions obtained through the use of physical or extreme psychological coercion (see, for example, *Chambers* v. *Florida,* 309 U.S. 227 [1940], *Ward* v. *Texas,* 316 U.S. 547 [1942], and *Ashcraft* v. *Tennessee,* 322 U.S. 143 [1944]). But

neither the Roosevelt Court nor the Vinson Court would incorporate the self-incrimination guarantee.

The Vinson Court was decidedly unsympathetic to the incorporation claim. An important example of this was *Adamson* v. *California,* 332 U.S. 46 (1947), where the Court considered a California law that permitted the judge and counsel to comment on the failure of a defendant to testify and defend himself against the damaging evidence presented, thus permitting the jury to take that silence into consideration while reaching a verdict. It was claimed that this violated the Fifth Amendment guarantee. The Vinson Court, however, ruled that the Fifth Amendment guarantee against self-incrimination was not incorporated into the due process clause of the Fourteenth Amendment and thus not applicable to the states. The decision was also important because of Justice Black's dissent, in which he argued (and presented historical evidence) that the framers of the Fourteenth Amendment had intended to incorporate the entire Bill of Rights into the Fourteenth Amendment through the due process clause. As it turned out, Justice Black lost the battle (and constitutional historians see the evidence as much more ambiguous than Black would have it), but virtually won the war because almost all of the important guarantees of the Bill of Rights were subsequently "incorporated" during the 1960s. In *Malloy* v. *Hogan,* the Court incorporated the Fifth Amendment privilege against self-incrimination and then began the task of enunciating objective standards that could be used to determine if incriminating statements or confessions were involuntary and thus were obtained in violation of the Fifth Amendment guarantee. In the case of *Escobedo* v. *Illinois,* 378 U.S. 478 (1964), the Court seemed to be suggesting that it could not accept the constitutional validity of a confession or incriminating statements obtained under circumstances whereby the accused was refused permission to consult with his lawyer and also was not advised of his right to remain silent. The climax of this line of decisions was reached with **Miranda** v. **Arizona,** where the criteria for implementing the constitutional guarantee were explicitly spelled out.

The Court took the not unreasonable position that a confession or a statement that is used as evidence at the trial of the person who made it is, by definition, being "a witness against himself" or self-incrimination, which the Fifth Amendment forbids unless it was not "compelled." *Miranda* v. *Arizona* spelled out the conditions under which a confession or statement would not be considered "compelled" (the famous *Miranda* rules). Any statement or confession made by the suspect must be truly voluntary (by definition, not compelled) and made with full knowledge of one's constitutional rights.

The Court also made clear that if questioning occurs without an attorney being present and a statement is taken or confession made, "a heavy burden rests on the government to demonstrate that the defendant knowingly and intelligently waived his privilege against self-incrimination and his right to retained or appointed counsel." Statements or confessions made in violation of the *Miranda* rules are considered to be "compelled" and may not be used in any manner at the trial. Chief Justice Warren in his opinion for the Court also pointed out, "In fact, statements merely intended to be exculpatory by the defendant [intended by the suspect to demonstrate innocence] are often used to impeach his testimony at trial or to demonstrate untruths in the statement given under interrogation and thus to prove guilt by implication. These statements are incriminating in any meaningful sense of the word and may not be used without the full warnings and effective waiver required for any other statement."

The Burger and Rehnquist Courts, unlike the Warren Court, have not been known for their generosity in interpreting criminal proce-

dural guarantees and the *Miranda* policy has been one policy about which the Court has not hid its general antipathy. Early in the Burger Court era, the Court ruled in **Harris** v. **New York** that statements made without the *Miranda* warnings can nevertheless be introduced at the trial in order to impeach the credibility of the defendant's testimony. The *Miranda* v. *Arizona* statement to the contrary, quoted in the previous paragraph, was considered a mere judicial aside and not a controlling precedent. Thus, *Miranda* v. *Arizona* was not overruled, but rather distinguished—and undermined. In *Oregon* v. *Hass,* 420 U.S. 714 (1975), the Court reversed a more generous interpretation of the Fifth Amendment self-incrimination guarantee by the Oregon Supreme Court and reaffirmed its *Harris* v. *New York* ruling. In *Michigan* v. *Tucker,* 417 U.S. 433 (1974), the Court deemed admissible, in a trial held *after* the *Miranda* case had been decided, the evidence obtained as a result of an interrogation without the *Miranda* warnings that was conducted *before* the decision in *Miranda*. In another decision, *Wainwright* v. *Sykes,* 433 U.S. 72 (1977), the Court cut off federal habeas corpus proceedings to a state criminal defendant who claimed a violation of his *Miranda* rights, but who failed to comply with his state's contemporaneous objection rule (requiring any objection to be raised before or during the trial itself). The Court in *Jenkins* v. *Anderson,* 447 U.S. 231 (1980), ruled that a criminal defendant's pre-arrest silence can be used in the prosecutor's argument to impeach the credibility of the defendant's assertion that he killed in self-defense (the prosecutor stressed that if the defendant killed in self-defense, why did he keep silent during the two weeks after the killing before he surrendered to the police?) This, said the Court, does not violate the Fifth Amendment.

In **Rhode Island** v. **Innis** the Court defined what is meant by "interrogation" for use in *Miranda*-type cases as encompassing any interchange with the accused (words or actions on the part of the police) that the police should know is reasonably likely to elicit an incriminating statement. But then the Court proceeded to apply this definition to the case at hand and overturned a Rhode Island Supreme Court decision favoring the criminal defendant. The Court found no violation of *Miranda* rights. Similarly, no violation of *Miranda* was found in a case in which the confession was made to a probation officer who had not given any prior *Miranda* warnings. In its decision in *Minnesota* v. *Murphy,* 465 U.S. 420 (1984), the Court observed that the defendant was not in custody at the time and voluntarily chose to answer the probation officer's questions. In another decision, *Oregon* v. *Elstad,* 470 U.S. 298 (1985), the Court faced the situation where the police had obtained an earlier voluntary but unwarned incriminating admission from the suspect. Later the defendant was read the *Miranda* warnings but waived his Fifth Amendment rights and again confessed. The Court ruled that the later confession is admissible and that no Fifth Amendment violation occurred.

In 1984, in a major departure from *Miranda,* the Court determined in **New York** v. **Quarles** that when the public safety is immediately and directly threatened, *Miranda* warnings need not be given before the questioning of a suspect. This public safety exception to *Miranda,* like the good-faith warrant exception to the exclusionary rule, is a signpost down the road whose end is the overturning of Court precedent. This does not necessarily mean that *Miranda* will be overturned in the near future. But the logic of a public safety exception can be stretched to cover nonphysically coercive custodial interrogation without *Miranda* warnings of suspected terrorists, suspected murderers, suspected violent rapists, all of whom, it could be argued, represent a grave threat to the public safety. Another departure from *Miranda* with major implications for the Sixth Amendment right to counsel was the decision in *Moran* v. *Burbine,* 475 U.S.

412 (1986). In this case the defendant did not know that his sister had hired a lawyer to defend him. The police did not inform the defendant of the efforts of the attorney to reach him, and in fact the police deliberately misled the attorney. The Court found that these events did not invalidate a confession and did not violate the Fifth and Sixth Amendments. The Court also ruled in 1986 in the case of *Allen* v. *Illinois,* 478 U.S. 364, that the guarantee against self-incrimination did not apply to commitment proceedings to a psychiatric prison. In this case Terry Allen was committed indefinitely under the Illinois Sexually Dangerous Persons Act. He was committed on the basis of responses he made to questions by psychiatrists after the judge ordered him to answer the questions! Justice Rehnquist in his opinion of the Court argued that the commitment proceeding was not a criminal proceeding and that the Fifth Amendment guarantee thus was not applicable. Although Allen was indeed subject to lengthy incarceration, was sent to a maximum-security psychiatric prison, and became part of a prison population, he was, nevertheless, entitled under Illinois law (unlike convicted criminals) to be given psychiatric care and treatment. Commitment was for the purpose of treatment and not punishment. Needless to say, the four justices in dissent strenuously disagreed with this analysis.

The Rehnquist Court ruled that a voluntary confession by an individual suffering from psychosis (the Colorado Supreme Court had found the confession as not a product of "free will") was not a violation of the guarantee against self-incrimination (*Colorado* v. *Connelly,* 479 U.S. 157 [1986]). The Court also determined that the statements of drunk drivers stopped for ordinary traffic offenses can be used against them without the *Miranda* warnings having to be read. Such traffic stops do not involve custody for purposes of *Miranda,* said the Court in *Pennsylvania* v. *Bruder,* 109 S.Ct. 205 (1988). When drunk drivers are arrested and taken to the police station, videotapes of their answers to questions at the time they are booked that show slurred speech and other signs of intoxication can be introduced at their trial even though the defendants were not given the *Miranda* warnings. The video-taped answers are physical and not testimonial evidence, said the Court, in *Pennsylvania* v. *Muniz,* 110 S.Ct. 2638 (1990). But in the same decision the majority also ruled that questions aimed at eliciting answers showing the extent of mental alertness are testimonial evidence and as such are governed by *Miranda*. In *Duckworth* v. *Eagan,* 109 S.Ct. 2875 (1989), the Court in a 5–4 decision held that the *Miranda* warnings need not be given in the exact form described in *Miranda* but simply must convey to the suspect, in a reasonable way, the suspect's rights.

The Court's record in the *Miranda* sphere, has not been consistently negative. In the Spring of 1981, the Burger Court, defying its deserved reputation for undermining *Miranda,* handed down two decisions that were seen as extending the Fifth Amendment rights of criminal defendants. In one, *Estelle* v. *Smith,* 451 U.S. 454, the Court set aside a sentence of death because at the penalty stage of the trial the jury heard testimony from a court psychiatrist who had interviewed the defendant without any *Miranda* warnings having been given and whose testimony doomed the defendant. The defendant's statements, in effect, had been used to seal his fate and this violated his Fifth Amendment guarantee. In the other decision, *Edwards* v. *Arizona,* 451 U.S. 477, the Court ruled that after the defendant asked for an attorney, questioning could not resume the following day even with the defendant again being apprised of his rights. However, the Court subsequently decided, in *Solem* v. *Stumes,* 465 U.S. 638 (1984), that *Edwards* should not be retroactively applied because the principle that once the suspect has invoked the right to counsel no further questioning may occur (unless initiated by the suspect) has little to do with the truth-finding

function of the criminal trial. Two decisions in 1986 favored the self-incrimination claim. In *Wainwright* v. *Greenfield,* 474 U.S. 284, the Court unanimously ruled that the fact that the defendant remained silent after his arrest and after being given the *Miranda* warnings *cannot* be used as evidence of his sanity (the defendant's sanity was at issue in the trial). In *Crane* v. *Kentucky,* 476 U.S. 683, the Court also unanimously ruled that a defendant has the right at his jury trial to offer testimony before the jury demonstrating that the confession he gave was coerced and not voluntary. In *Arizona* v. *Roberson,* 486 U.S. 675 (1988), the Court ruled that when a suspect requests a lawyer, an incriminating statement made during a second interrogation concerning a different unrelated charge conducted by another officer unaware of the suspect's earlier request for a lawyer, is nevertheless inadmissible as a violation of the self-incrimination guarantee. And in **James** v. **Illinois** (reprinted at the end of this book) a closely divided Court ruled that illegally obtained statements cannot be used to impeach the credibility of defense witnesses.

Other decisions of the Court reveal its more typical unsympathetic reading of the self-incrimination guarantee. *Fisher* v. *United States,* 425 U.S. 391 (1976), *Andresen* v. *Maryland,* 427 U.S. 463 (1976), and *United States* v. *Doe,* 465 U.S. 605 (1984), undercut the 1886 precedent of *Boyd* v. *United States,* 116 U.S. 616, in which the Court had held that the self-incrimination guarantee in the Fifth Amendment protected an individual from being compelled to produce his books and papers for use at his trial. In *Fisher,* the Court said that a taxpayer can be compelled to produce an accountant's work papers used to prepare the contested returns. The accountant's work papers, said the Court, were not the taxpayer's "private papers" and therefore were subject to subpoena. In *Andresen,* the Court approved of introducing papers, lawfully seized, containing incriminating statements. The Burger Court majority disingenuously argued that the papers and statements had been voluntarily written and not compelled and therefore their lawful seizure made them acceptable as evidence. In *Doe,* the Court ruled that the contents of subpoenaed records and papers are not protected by the Fifth Amendment from disclosure as long as the government grants "use immunity," that is, the government promises not to use what it finds in those records and papers against the individual. The Court in *United States* v. *Euge,* 444 U.S. 707 (1980), determined that the Internal Revenue Service can compel a taxpayer to provide handwriting samples without violating the Fifth Amendment. The Court also established, in *United States* v. *Ward,* 448 U.S. 242 (1980), that the Federal Water Pollution Act provision requiring polluters to report oil spills and subjecting them to civil punishment did not violate the self-incrimination guarantee. Along similar lines, the Court in *Selective Service System* v. *Minnesota Public Interest Research Group,* 468 U.S. 841 (1984), concluded that there was no self-incrimination violation in the federal student loan provision requiring male recipients to have registered for the draft in order to receive federal financial aid. The provision permitted late draft registration. Opponents argued that by registering late, the registrant was subject to criminal penalties for having failed to have registered for the draft within 30 days of his eighteenth birthday. In *Baltimore City Dept. of Social Services* v. *Bouknight,* 110 S.Ct. 900 (1990), the Court ruled that a mother who is the custodian of her child pursuant to a court order may not invoke the Fifth Amendment privilege against self-incrimination to resist a later court order to produce the child. This case raised the issue of child abuse. In **Illinois** v. **Perkins** (reprinted at the end of this book), the Court decided that an undercover law enforcement officer posing as a fellow inmate was not required to give *Miranda* warnings to a jailed suspect before asking leading questions designed to elicit an incriminating response.

The guarantee against double jeopardy has been involved in several Court decisions. In *United States* v. *Lanza,* 260 U.S. 377 (1922), the Court ruled that both a state and the federal government can try someone for the same illegal act and that this does not constitute double jeopardy. *Palko* v. *Connecticut* also saw the Court reject the claim that the double jeopardy guarantee was applicable to the states. Not until the 1969 Warren Court decision in *Benton* v. *Maryland,* 395 U.S. 784, was *Palko* overturned. Among the more recent double jeopardy decisions of the Court are *Garrett* v. *United States,* 471 U.S. 773 (1985), *Heath* v. *Alabama,* 474 U.S. 82 (1985), *Jones* v. *Thomas,* 109 S.Ct. 2522 (1989), and *Grady* v. *Corbin,* 110 S.Ct. 2084 (1990). In *Garrett,* the Court found no double jeopardy violation by a federal prosecution for continuing criminal enterprise based on the same criminal activity that formed the basis of an earlier prosecution for marijuana importation. In *Heath,* the Court determined that there is no double jeopardy violation when two states try a person for the same criminal act that violated the laws of each state. In *Jones,* a state prisoner did not have his right against double jeopardy violated when a state court that erroneously sentenced him for two felonies when he should have been sentenced for one "corrected" its mistake. But in *Grady,* in a 5–4 decision in an opinion of the Court by Justice Brennan, the Court found that the double jeopardy guarantee bars subsequent prosecution of an essential element of the offense for which the defendant was already prosecuted. In this case, the decision meant that the state could not bring a homicide prosecution against someone who already had pleaded guilty to (and was convicted of) drunk driving in the accident that caused the death.

THE IMPACT OF THE COURT'S DECISIONS

Table 16.1 summarizes the impact of selected Court decisions concerning Fourth and Fifth Amendment issues. The reprinted cases follow.

Table 16.1 THE IMPACT OF SELECTED COURT DECISIONS, FOURTH AND FIFTH AMENDMENT ISSUES

Case	Year	Impact on Parties	Short-Run Impact	Long-Run Impact
Katz v. United States	1967	Katz's conviction reversed.	Congress in 1968 repealed Section 605 of the Federal Communications Act.	Decision thought to have brought bugging by law enforcement agencies under judicial control.
United States v. United States District Court	1972	District Judge Damon J. Keith's order upheld. Federal prosecutors required to turn over to criminal defendants electronic surveillance information illegally obtained.	Decision rejected the Nixon Administration's claim of discretionary power to protect national security.	Precedent for limiting the discretion of the executive branch in the domestic subversion area. Precedent supporting Fourth Amendment guarantees.
Mapp v. Ohio	1961	Ms. Mapp's conviction overturned. Did not have to serve a sentence of from one to seven years in the Ohio State Women's Reformatory.	Law enforcement officials and conservatives oppose decision. Compliance is uneven.	One of the major cases signaling the Warren Court's criminal due process revolution. Although far from being fully implemented, decision is thought to have raised standards of police conduct and increased law enforcement sensitivity to constitutional rights.
United States v. Leon	1984	Alberto Antonio Leon and associates failed in having incriminating evidence suppressed.	Gave impetus to attack on exclusionary rule. Reagan Justice Department pleased, civil liberties groups upset.	Decision considered a major step on the road to the reversal of *Weeks v. United States* and *Mapp v. Ohio*. Rehnquist Court expected to build on this.
United States v. Ross	1982	Albert Ross, Jr.'s conviction upheld.	Legitimated warrantless searches of contents of automobiles.	Decision part of Burger Court's trend adopting a stronger law-enforcement posture toward Fourth Amendment guarantees.
New Jersey v. T.L.O.	1985	Unknown whether delinquency finding was reinstated against T.L.O., who was 14 years old when first brought to court but 19 when Supreme Court decided case.	Strengthened hand of school officials.	By offering a watered-down version of the Fourth Amendment for the nation's schools, youngsters may be taught to find acceptable an eroded Fourth Amendment in adult nonschool settings.

Case	Year	Outcome	Doctrine / Ruling	Significance
Hurtado v. *California*	1884	Although Joseph Hurtado was scheduled to hang, he died in his prison cell from tuberculosis which he had contracted in jail.	States seemingly given carte blanche in devising criminal procedures.	Hurtado doctrine provides basis for excluding noneconomic liberties from the due process clause of the Fourteenth Amendment.
Palko v. *Connecticut*	1937	Palko executed.	Consolidated First Amendment protection under the Fourteenth Amendment, but limited the scope of criminal procedural guarantees incorporated under due process.	Provided rationale for selective incorporation of Bill of Rights under the Fourteenth Amendment due process clause. Double jeopardy ruling reversed in 1969.
Miranda v. *Arizona*	1966	Miranda's kidnapping and rape conviction reversed. But Miranda remained in prison serving sentence on unrelated robbery conviction. Retried and convicted on kidnapping and rape charges. He was paroled in 1972 and killed in a barroom fight in 1976.	Decision condemned by most law enforcement officials and by conservatives. Most police forces offered little more than token compliance. Efforts in Congress to "overturn" *Miranda*.	Greatest impact may have been on sensitizing police agencies as to meaning of Fifth Amendment self-incrimination guarantee. Full compliance never achieved nationwide.
Harris v. *New York*	1971	Harris' conviction and sentence upheld.	*Miranda* decision undermined. Police less concerned with violating *Miranda* rules.	One of several Burger Court decisions narrowing if not eroding *Miranda*.
Rhode Island v. *Innis*	1980	Thomas Innis' conviction upheld.	Decision seen by some civil liberties groups as continuation of trend of decisions weakening *Miranda*.	Uncertain.
New York v. *Quarles*	1984	Evidence admissible in Benjamin Quarles' trial.	Public safety exception to the *Miranda* rule applauded by conservatives but condemned by civil libertarians.	Uncertain but may be seen as a major step in the erosion of *Miranda* v. *Arizona* and so used by Rehnquist Court.

KATZ v. UNITED STATES,
389 U.S. 347 (1967)

The Fourth Amendment's search and seizure guarantee (until the Court's ruling in this case) was applicable only to that which could be physically searched and seized. The old doctrine, first announced in 1928 in Olmstead v. United States, meant that wiretapping and other electronic eavesdropping devices were not subject to constitutional regulation. Although Congress in 1934 made wiretapping a federal crime (Section 605 of the Federal Communications Act), the law did not encompass other electronic devices. In this case, Charles Katz, a gambler, was under surveillance by the FBI. He made a telephone call on a pay phone that was electronically bugged to record his end of the conversation. On the basis of this and other evidence, Katz was convicted in a federal district court. The appeals court affirmed the conviction and the case was taken to the Supreme Court, which granted certiorari. Katz's lawyers argued that obtaining the bugging evidence without a search warrant violated the Fourth Amendment search and seizure guarantee and the Supreme Court agreed. The Olmstead doctrine was explicitly overturned. In 1968 Congress repealed Section 605; thus wiretapping and other bugging devices are now treated alike. Congress also provided in Title III of the Omnibus Crime Control and Safe Streets Act of 1968 that the Attorney General or an Assistant Attorney General designated by him may authorize an application to a federal judge for an order "authorizing or approving the interception of wire or oral communications."

Majority votes: 7
Dissenting votes: 1

MR. JUSTICE STEWART delivered the opinion of the Court: . . . .

. . . [T]he Fourth Amendment cannot be translated into a general constitutional "right to privacy." That Amendment protects individual privacy against certain kinds of governmental intrusion, but its protections go further, and often have nothing to do with privacy at all. Other provisions of the Constitution protect personal privacy from other forms of governmental invasion. But the protection of a person's *general* right—his right to be let alone by other people—is, like the protection of his property and of his very life, left largely to the law of the individual States.

Because of the misleading way the issues have been formulated, the parties have attached great significance to the characterization of the telephone booth from which the petitioner placed his calls. The petitioner has strenuously argued that the booth was a "constitutionally protected area." The Government has maintained with equal vigor that it was not. But this effort to decide whether or not a given "area," viewed in the abstract, is "constitutionally protected" deflects attention from the problem presented by this case. For the Fourth Amendment protects people, not places. What a person knowingly exposes to the public, even in his own home or office, is not a subject of Fourth Amendment protection. . . . But what he seeks to preserve as private, even in an area accessible to the public, may be constitutionally protected. . . .

The Government stresses the fact that the telephone booth from which the petitioner made his calls was constructed partly of glass, so that he was as visible after he entered it as he would have been if he had remained outside. But what he sought to exclude when he entered the booth was not the intruding eye—it was the uninvited ear. He did not shed his right to do so simply because he made his calls from a place where he might be seen. No less than an individual in a business office, in a friend's apartment, or in a taxicab, a person in a telephone booth may rely upon the protection of the Fourth Amendment. One who occupies it, shuts the door behind him, and pays the toll that permits him to place a call, is surely entitled to assume that the words he utters into the mouthpiece will not be broadcast to the world. To read the Constitution more narrowly is to ignore the vital role that the public telephone has come to play in private communication.

The Government contends, however, that the activities of its agents in this case should not be tested by Fourth Amendment requirements, for the surveillance technique they employed involved no physical penetration of the telephone booth from which the petitioner placed his calls. It is true that the absence of such penetration was at one time thought to foreclose further Fourth Amendment inquiry, *Olmstead* v. *United States,* 277 U.S. 438 [1928]; *Goldman* v. *United States,* 316 U.S. 129 [1942], for that Amendment was thought to limit only searches and seizures of tangible property. But "[t]he premise that property interests control the right of the Government to search and seize has been discredited." Thus, although a closely divided Court supposed in *Olmstead* that surveillance without any trespass and without the seizure of any material object fell outside the ambit of the Constitution, we have since departed from the narrow view on which that decision rested. Indeed, we have expressly held that the Fourth Amendment governs not only the seizure of tangible items, but extends as well to the recording of oral statements, overheard without any "technical trespass under . . . local property law." . . . Once this much is acknowledged, and once it is recognized that the Fourth Amendment protects people—and not simply "areas"—against unreasonable searches and seizures, it becomes clear that the reach of that Amendment cannot turn upon the presence or absence of a physical intrusion into any given enclosure.

We conclude that the underpinnings of *Olmstead* and *Goldman* have been so eroded by our subsequent decisions that the "trespass" doctrine there enunciated can no longer be regarded as controlling. The Government's activities in electronically listening to and recording the petitioner's words violated the privacy upon which he justifiably relied while using the telephone booth and thus constituted a "search and seizure" within the meaning of the Fourth Amendment. The fact that the electronic device employed to achieve that end did not happen to penetrate the wall of the booth can have no constitutional significance.

The question remaining for decision, then, is whether the search and seizure conducted in this case complied with constitutional standards. In that regard, the Government's position is that its agents acted in an entirely defensible manner: They did not begin their electronic surveillance until investigation of the petitioner's activities had established a strong probability that he was using the telephone in question to transmit gambling information to persons in other states, in violation of federal law. Moreover, the surveillance was limited, both in scope and in duration, to the specific purpose of establishing the contents of the petitioner's unlawful telephonic communications. The agents confined their surveillance to the brief periods during which he used the telephone booth, and they took great care to overhear only the conversations of the petitioner himself.

Accepting this account of the Government's actions as accurate, it is clear that this surveillance was so narrowly circumscribed that a duly authorized magistrate, properly notified of the need for such investigation, specifically informed of the basis on which it was to proceed, and clearly apprised of the precise intrusion it would entail, could constitutionally have authorized, with appropriate safeguards, the very limited search and seizure that the Government asserts in fact took place. . . .

The Government . . . argues that surveillance of a telephone booth should be exempted from the usual requirement of advance authorization by a magistrate upon a showing of probable cause. We cannot agree. . . .

These considerations do not vanish when the search in question is transferred from the setting of a home, an office, or a hotel room, to that of a telephone booth. Wherever a man may be, he is entitled to know that he will remain free from unreasonable searches and seizures. The government agents here ignored "the procedure of antecedent justification . . . that is central to the Fourth Amendment," a procedure that we hold to be a constitutional precondition of the kind of electronic surveillance involved in this case. Because the surveillance here failed to meet that condition, and because it led to the petitioner's conviction, the judgment must be reversed.

It is so ordered.

MR. JUSTICE MARSHALL took no part in the consideration or decision of this case.
MR. JUSTICE WHITE, concurring: [omitted]
MR. JUSTICE DOUGLAS, with whom MR. JUSTICE BRENNAN joins, concurring: [omitted]
MR. JUSTICE HARLAN, concurring:

I join the opinion of the Court, which I read to hold only (a) that an enclosed telephone booth is an area where, like a home . . . a person has a constitutionally protected reasonable expectation of privacy; (b) that electronic as well as physical intrusion into a place that is in this sense private may constitute a violation of the Fourth Amendment; and (c) that the invasion of a constitutionally protected area by federal authorities is, as the Court has long held, presumptively unreasonable in the absence of a search warrant. . . .
MR. JUSTICE BLACK, dissenting:

If I could agree with the Court that eavesdropping carried on by electronic means (equivalent to wiretapping) constitutes a "search" or "seizure," I would be happy to join the Court's opinion. . . .

My basic objection is twofold: (1) I do not believe that the words of the Amendment will bear the meaning given them by today's decision, and (2) I do not believe that it is the proper role of this Court to rewrite the Amendment in order "to bring it into harmony with the times" and thus reach a result that many people believe to be desirable.

While I realize that an argument based on the meaning of words lacks the scope, and no doubt the appeal, of broad policy discussions and philosophical discourses on such nebulous subjects as privacy, for me the language of the Amendment is the crucial place to look in construing a written document such as our Constitution. . . . The first clause of the Fourth Amendment protects "persons, houses, papers, and effects, against unreasonable searches and seizures. . . ." These words connote the idea of tangible things with size, form, and weight, things capable of being searched, seized, or both. The second clause of the Amendment still further establishes its Framers' purpose to limit its protection to tangible things by providing that no warrants shall issue but those "particularly describing the place to be searched and the person or things to be seized." A conversation overheard by eavesdropping, whether by plain snooping or wiretapping, is not tangible and, under the normally accepted meanings of the words, can neither be searched nor seized. In addition the language of the second clause indicates that the Amendment refers to something not only tangible so it can be seized but to something already in existence so it can be described. Yet the Court's interpretation would have the Amendment apply to overhearing future conversations which by their very nature are nonexistent until they take place. How can one "describe" a future conversation, and if not, how can a magistrate issue a warrant to eavesdrop one in the future? It is argued that information showing what is expected to be said is sufficient to limit the boundaries of what later can be admitted into evidence; but does such general information really meet the specific language of the Amendment which says "particularly describing"? Rather than using language in a completely artificial way, I must conclude that the Fourth Amendment simply does not apply to eavesdropping. . . .

Since I see no way in which the words of the Fourth Amendment can be construed to apply to eavesdropping, that closes the matter for me. In interpreting the Bill of Rights, I willingly go as far as a liberal construction of the language takes me, but I simply cannot in good conscience give a meaning to words which they have never before been thought to have and which they certainly do not have in common ordinary usage. I will not distort the words of the Amendment in order to "keep the Constitution up to date" or "to bring it into harmony with the times." It was never meant for this Court to have such power, which in effect would make us a continuously functioning constitutional convention. . . .

UNITED STATES v. UNITED STATES DISTRICT COURT, 407 U.S. 297 (1972)

Lawrence Plamondon was charged with the dynamite bombing of an office of the Central Intelligence Agency in Ann Arbor, Michigan. Along with two cohorts, he was also charged with conspiracy to destroy government property. In response to the defendants' pretrial motion for disclosure of electronic surveillance information, the Government admitted that it had wiretapped without having secured search warrants. But the Government claimed that the surveillance was a lawful exercise of presidential power to protect the national security. Federal District Judge Damon J. Keith held that the wiretaps violated the Fourth Amendment and ordered the Government to make full disclosure to Plamondon of his overheard conversations. Plamondon's lawyers would then be able to move to exclude all evidence derived from the wiretaps and the likely result would be the dismissal of the cases. The Government, in response to Judge Keith's order, petitioned the Court of Appeals for the Sixth Circuit for a writ of mandamus ordering Judge Keith to set aside his order. The court of appeals held that the surveillance was unlawful and that the district court had properly required disclosure of the overheard conversations. The case went to the Supreme Court, raising questions concerning the scope of executive power to prevent domestic subversion as well as the extent to which the Fourth Amendment protects individual privacy rights.

Votes: Unanimous

MR. JUSTICE POWELL delivered the opinion of the Court:

The issue before us is an important one for the people of our country and their Government. It involves the delicate question of the President's power, acting through the Attorney General, to authorize electronic surveillance in internal security matters without prior judicial approval. Successive Presidents for more than one-quarter of a century have authorized such surveillance in varying degrees, without guidance from the Congress or a definitive decision of this Court. This case brings the issue here for the first time. Its resolution is a matter of national concern, requiring sensitivity both to the Government's right to protect itself from unlawful subversion and attack and to the citizen's right to be secure in his privacy against unreasonable Government intrusion. . . .

As the Fourth Amendment is not absolute in its terms, our task is to examine and balance the basic values at stake in this case: the duty of Government to protect the domestic security, and the potential danger posed by unreasonable surveillance to individual privacy and free expression. If the legitimate need of Government to safeguard domestic security requires the use of electronic surveillance, the question is whether the needs of citizens for privacy and free expression may not be better protected by requiring a warrant before such surveillance is undertaken. We must also ask whether a warrant requirement would unduly frustrate the efforts of Government to protect itself from acts of subversion and overthrow directed against it. . . .

The very heart of the Fourth Amendment directive is that, where practical, a governmental search and seizure should represent both the efforts of the officer to gather evidence of wrongful acts and the judgment of the magistrate that the collected evidence is sufficient to justify invasion of a citizen's private premises or conversation. Inherent in the concept of a warrant is its issuance by a "neutral and detached magistrate." The further requirement of "probable cause" instructs the magistrate that baseless searches shall not proceed.

These Fourth Amendment freedoms cannot properly be guaranteed if domestic security surveillances may be conducted solely within the discretion of the Executive Branch. The Fourth Amendment does not contemplate the executive officers of Government as neutral and disinterested magistrates. Their duty and responsibility are to enforce the laws, to investigate, and to prosecute. But those charged with this investigative and prosecutorial duty should not be the sole judges of when to utilize constitutionally sensitive means in pursuing their tasks. The historical judgment, which the Fourth Amendment accepts, is that unreviewed executive discretion may yield too readily to pressures to obtain incriminating evidence and overlook potential invasions of privacy and protected speech.

The Government argues that the special circumstances applicable to domestic security surveillances necessitate a further exception to the warrant requirement. It is urged that the requirement of prior judicial review would obstruct the President in the discharge of his constitutional duty to protect domestic security. We are told further that these surveillances are directed primarily to the collecting and maintaining of intelligence with respect to subversive forces, and are not an attempt to gather evidence for specific criminal prosecutions. It is said that this type of surveillance should not be subject to traditional warrant requirements which were established to govern investigation of criminal activity, not ongoing intelligence gathering.

The Government further insists that courts "as a practical matter would have neither the knowledge nor the techniques necessary to determine whether there was probable cause to believe that surveillance was necessary to protect national security." These security problems, the Government contends, involve "a large number of complex and subtle factors" beyond the competence of courts to evaluate.

As a final reason for exemption from a warrant requirement, the Government believes that disclosure to a magistrate of all or even a significant portion of the information involved in domestic security surveillances "would create serious potential dangers to the national security and to the lives of informants and agents. . . . Secrecy is the essential ingredient in intelligence gathering; requiring prior judicial authorization would create a greater 'danger of leaks . . . , because in addition to the judge, you have the clerk, the stenographer and some other officer like a law assistant or bailiff who may be apprised of the nature' of the surveillance."

These contentions in behalf of a complete exemption from the warrant requirement, when urged on behalf of the President and the national security in its domestic implications, merit the most careful consideration. We certainly do not reject them lightly, especially at a time of worldwide ferment and when civil disorders in this country are more prevalent than in the less turbulent periods of our history. There is, no doubt, pragmatic force to the Government's position.

But we do not think a case has been made for the requested departure from Fourth Amendment standards. The circumstances described do not justify complete exemption of domestic security surveillance from prior judicial scrutiny. Official surveillance, whether its purpose be criminal investigation or ongoing intelligence gathering, risks infringement of constitutionally protected privacy of speech. Security surveillances are especially sensitive because of the inherent vagueness of the domestic security concept, the necessarily broad and continuing nature of intelligence gathering, and the temptation to utilize such surveillances to oversee political dissent. We recognize, as we have before, the constitutional basis of the President's domestic security role, but we think it must be exercised in a manner compatible with the Fourth Amendment. In this case we hold that this requires an appropriate prior warrant procedure.

We cannot accept the Government's argument that internal security matters are too subtle and complex for judicial evaluation. Courts regularly deal with the most difficult issues of our society. There is no reason to believe that federal judges will be insensitive to or uncomprehending of the issues involved in domestic security cases. Certainly courts can recognize that domestic security surveillance involves different consideration from the surveillance of "ordinary crime." If the threat is too subtle or complex for our senior law enforcement officers to convey its significance to a court, one may question whether there is probable cause for surveillance.

Nor do we believe prior judicial approval will fracture the secrecy essential to official intelligence gathering. The investigation of criminal activity has long involved imparting sensitive information to judicial officers who have respected the confidentialities involved. Judges may be counted upon to be especially conscious of security requirements in national security cases. Title III of the Omnibus Crime Control and Safe Streets Act already has imposed this responsibility on the judiciary in connection with such crimes as espionage, sabotage, and treason, § 2516 (1) (a) and (c), each of which may involve domestic as well as foreign security threats. Moreover, a warrant application involves no public or adversary proceedings: it is an *ex parte* request before a magistrate or judge. Whatever security dangers clerical and secretarial personnel may pose can be minimized by proper administrative measures, possibly to the point of allowing the Government itself to provide the necessary clerical assistance.

Thus, we conclude that the Government's concerns do not justify departure in this case from the customary Fourth Amendment requirement of judicial approval prior to initiation of a search or surveillance. Although some added burden will be imposed upon the Attorney General, this inconvenience is justified in a free society to protect constitutional values. Nor do we think the Government's domestic surveillance powers will be impaired to any significant degree. A prior warrant establishes presumptive validity of the surveillance and will minimize the burden of justification in post-surveillance judicial review. By no means of least importance will be the reassurance of the public generally that indiscriminate wiretapping and bugging of law-abiding citizens cannot occur. . . .

As the surveillance of Plamondon's conversations was unlawful, because conducted without prior judicial approval, the courts below correctly held that disclosure to the accused of his own impermissibly intercepted conversations [is required]. . . .

The judgment of the Court of Appeals is hereby affirmed.

Affirmed.

CHIEF JUSTICE BURGER concurs in the result.
MR. JUSTICE REHNQUIST took no part in the consideration or decision of this case.

MR. JUSTICE DOUGLAS, concurring: [omitted]
MR. JUSTICE WHITE, concurring in the judgment: [omitted]

MAPP v. OHIO,
367 U.S. 643 (1961)

Although the Supreme Court had ruled in Wolf v. Colorado *that the Fourth Amendment search and seizure guarantee was part of the due process of law specified in the Fourteenth Amendment as an obligation of the states, the Court had specifically exempted the states from having to adopt the exclusionary rule followed by the federal courts. In the* Mapp *case, the Court reversed the state exemption and ruled that the exclusionary rule is an essential component of the Fourth Amendment and that it is a part of Fourteenth Amendment due process. The case began when Ms. Dollree Mapp's back door was forced open by Cleveland police looking for a suspect wanted for questioning. Ms. Mapp had refused to admit the police to her home and insisted that they produce a search warrant. A search warrant was never produced, the police handcuffed her, ransacked her apartment, end eventually found some pornographic pamphlets and photos. Ms. Mapp was arrested for violating the Ohio statute making it a criminal offense to possess obscene matter. It was this statute that she challenged in the Ohio courts. However, it was the illegal search and seizure and the admissibility of the evidence at her trial on which the Court majority chose to focus their attention.*

Majority votes: 6
Dissenting votes: 3

MR. JUSTICE CLARK delivered the opinion of the Court:. . . .

. . . [I]n the year 1914, in the *Weeks* case, this Court "for the first time" held that "in a federal prosecution the Fourth Amendment barred the use of evidence secured through an illegal search and seizure." This Court has ever since required of federal law officers a strict adherence to that command which this Court has held to be a clear, specific, and constitutionally required—even if judicially implied—deterrent safeguard without insistence upon which the Fourth Amendment would have been reduced to "a form of words." . . . It meant, quite simply, that "conviction by means of unlawful seizures and enforced confessions . . . should find no sanction in the judgments of the courts. . . ." and that such evidence "shall not be used at all." . . .

In 1949, 35 years after *Weeks* was announced,

this Court, in *Wolf* v. *Colorado,* again for the first time, discussed the effect of the Fourth Amendment upon the States through the operation of the Due Process Clause of the Fourteenth Amendment. . . . [A]fter declaring that the "security of one's privacy against arbitrary intrusion by the police" is "implicit in 'the concept of ordered liberty' and as such enforceable against the States through the Due Process Clause," and announcing that it "stoutly adhere[d]" to the *Weeks* decision, the Court decided that the *Weeks* exclusionary rule would not then be imposed upon the States as "an essential ingredient of the right." The Court's reasons for not considering essential to the right to privacy, as a curb imposed upon the States by the Due Process Clause, that which decades before had been posited as part and parcel of the Fourth Amendment's limitation upon federal encroachment of individual privacy, were bottomed on factual considerations. . . .

The Court in *Wolf* first stated that "[t]he contrariety of views of the States" on the adoption of the exclusionary rule of *Weeks* was "particularly impressive"; and, in this connection, that it could not "brush aside the experience of States which deem the incidence of such conduct by the police too slight to call for a deterrent remedy . . . by overriding the States' relevant rules of evidence." While in 1949, prior to the *Wolf* case, almost two-thirds of the States were opposed to the use of the exclusionary rule, now, despite the *Wolf* case, more than half of those since passing upon it, by their own legislative or judicial decision, have wholly or partly adopted or adhered to the *Weeks* rule. . . . [W]e note that the second basis elaborated in *Wolf* in support of its failure to enforce the exclusionary doctrine against the States was that "other means of protection" have been afforded "the right to privacy." . . . [T]hat such other remedies have been worthless and futile is buttressed by the experience of [the] States. . . .

It, therefore, plainly appears that the factual considerations supporting the failure of the *Wolf* Court to include the *Weeks* exclusionary rule when it recognized the enforceability of the right to privacy against the States in 1949, while not basically relevant to the constitutional consideration, could not, in any analysis, now be deemed controlling. . . .

. . . Today we examine *Wolf's* constitutional documentation of the right to privacy free from unreasonable state intrusion, and, after its dozen years on our books, are led by it to close the only courtroom door remaining open to evidence secured by official lawlessness in flagrant abuse of that basic right, reserved to all persons as a specific guarantee against that very same unlawful conduct. We hold that all evidence obtained by searches and seizures in violation of the Constitution is, by that same authority, inadmissible in a state court.

Since the Fourth Amendment's right of privacy has been declared enforceable against the States through the Due Process Clause of the Fourteenth, it is enforceable against them by the same sanction of exclusion as is used against the Federal Government. Were it otherwise, then just as without the *Weeks* rule the assurance against unreasonable federal searches and seizures would be "a form of words," valueless and undeserving of mention in a perpetual charter of inestimable human liberties, so too, without that rule the freedom from state invasions of privacy would be so ephemeral and so neatly severed from its conceptual nexus with the freedom from all brutish means of coercing evidence as not to merit this Court's high regard as a freedom "implicit in the concept of ordered liberty". . . .

. . . This Court has not hesitated to enforce as strictly against the States as it does against the Federal Government the rights of free speech and of a free press, the rights to notice and to a fair, public trial, including, as it does, the right not to be convicted by use of a coerced confession, however logically relevant it be, and without regard to its reliability. And nothing could be more certain than that when a coerced confession is involved, "the relevant rules of evidence" are overridden without regard to "the incidence of such conduct by the police," slight or frequent. Why should not the same rule apply to what is tantamount to coerced testimony by way of unconstitutional seizure of goods, papers, effects, documents, etc.? . . .

. . . [O]ur holding [is] that the exclusionary rule is an essential part of both the Fourth and Fourteenth Amendments. . . . There is no war between the Constitution and common sense. Presently, a federal prosecutor may make no use of evidence illegally seized, but a State's attorney across the street may, although he supposedly is operating under the enforceable prohibitions of the same Amendment. Thus the State, by admitting evidence unlawfully seized, serves to encourage disobedience to the Federal Constitution which it is bound to uphold. . . .

Federal-state cooperation in the solution of crime under constitutional standards will be promoted, if only by recognition of their now mutual obligation to respect the same fundamental criteria in their approaches. . . .

There are those who say, as did Justice (then

Judge) Cardozo, that under our constitutional exclusionary doctrine "[t]he criminal is to go free because the constable has blundered." In some cases this will undoubtedly be the result. But, "there is another consideration—the imperative of judicial integrity." The criminal goes free, if he must, but it is the law that sets him free. Nothing can destroy a government more quickly than its failure to observe its own laws, or worse, its disregard of the charter of its own existence. . . .

. . . Having once recognized that the right to privacy embodied in the Fourth Amendment is enforceable against the States, and that the right to be secure against rude invasions of privacy by state officers is, therefore, constitutional in origin, we can no longer permit that right to remain an empty promise. Because it is enforceable in the same manner and to like effect as other basic rights secured by the Due Process Clause, we can no longer permit it to be revocable at the whim of any police officer who, in the name of law enforcement itself, chooses to suspend its enjoyment. Our decision, founded on reason and truth, gives to the individual no more than that which the Constitution guarantees him, to the police officer no less than that to which honest law enforcement is entitled, and, to the courts, that judicial integrity so necessary in the true administration of justice.

The judgment of the Supreme Court of Ohio is reversed and the cause remanded for further proceedings not inconsistent with this opinion.

Reversed and remanded.

MR. JUSTICE BLACK, concurring:. . . .

I am still not persuaded that the Fourth Amendment, standing alone, would be enough to bar the introduction into evidence against an accused of papers and effects seized from him in violation of its commands. For the Fourth Amendment does not itself contain any provision expressly precluding the use of such evidence, and I am extremely doubtful that such a provision could properly be inferred from nothing more than the basic command against unreasonable searches and seizures. Reflection on the problem, however, in the light of cases coming before the Court since *Wolf,* has led me to conclude that when the Fourth Amendment's ban against unreasonable searches and seizures is considered together with the Fifth Amendment's ban against compelled self-incrimination, a constitutional basis emerges which not only justifies but actually requires the exclusionary rule. . . .

MR. JUSTICE DOUGLAS, concurring: [omitted]
Memorandum of MR. JUSTICE STEWART:

. . . I express no view as to the merits of the constitutional issue which the Court today decides. I would, however, reverse the judgment in this case, because I am persuaded that the provision of § 2905.34 of the Ohio Revised Code, upon which the petitioner's conviction was based, is, in the words of MR. JUSTICE HARLAN, not "consistent with the rights of free thought and expression assured against state action by the Fourteenth Amendment."

MR. JUSTICE HARLAN, whom MR. JUSTICE FRANKFURTER and MR. JUSTICE WHITTAKER join, dissenting:

In overruling the *Wolf* case the Court, in my opinion, has forgotten the sense of judicial restraint which, with due regard for *stare decisis,* is one element that should enter into deciding whether a past decision of this Court should be overruled. Apart from that I also believe that the *Wolf* rule represents sounder Constitutional doctrine than the new rule which now replaces it. . . .

The occasion which the Court has taken here is in the context of a case where the question was briefed not at all and argued only extremely tangentially. The unwisdom of overruling *Wolf* without full-dress argument is aggravated by the circumstance that that decision is a comparatively recent one (1949) to which three members of the present majority have at one time or other expressly subscribed, one to be sure with explicit misgivings. . . . It certainly has never been a postulate of judicial power that mere altered disposition, or subsequent membership on the Court, is sufficient warrant for overturning a deliberately decided rule of Constitutional law. . . .

At the heart of the majority's opinion in this case is the following syllogism: (1) the rule excluding in federal criminal trials evidence which is the product of an illegal search and seizure is "part and parcel" of the Fourth Amendment; (2) *Wolf* held that the "privacy" assured against federal action by the Fourth Amendment is also protected against state action by the Fourteenth Amendment; and (3) it is therefore "logically and constitutionally necessary" that the *Weeks* exclusionary rule should also be enforced against the States. . . .

. . . [W]hat the Court is now doing is to impose upon the States not only federal substantive standards of "search and seizure" but also the basic federal remedy for violation of those standards. For I think it entirely clear that the *Weeks* exclusionary rule is but a remedy which, by penalizing past official misconduct, is aimed at deterring such conduct in the future.

I would not impose upon the States this federal exclusionary remedy. The reasons given by the majority for now suddenly turning its back on *Wolf* seem to me notably unconvincing.

First, it is said that "the factual grounds upon which *Wolf* was based" have since changed, in that more States now follow the *Weeks* exclusionary rule than was so at the time *Wolf* was decided. While that is true, a recent survey indicates that at present one-half of the States still adhere to the common-law non-exclusionary rule. . . .

The preservation of a proper balance between state and federal responsibility in the administration of criminal justice demands patience on the part of those who might like to see things move faster among the States in this respect. Problems of criminal law enforcement vary widely from State to State. One State, in considering the totality of its legal picture, may conclude that the need for embracing the *Weeks* rule is pressing because other remedies are unavailable or inadequate to secure compliance with the substantive Constitutional principle involved. Another, though equally solicitous of Constitutional rights, may choose to pursue one purpose at a time, allowing all evidence relevant to guilt to be brought into a criminal trial, and dealing with Constitutional infractions by other means. Still another may consider the exclusionary rule too rough-and-ready a remedy, in that it reaches only unconstitutional intrusions which eventuate in criminal prosecution of the victims. Further, a State after experimenting with the *Weeks* rule for a time may, because of unsatisfactory experience with it, decide to revert to a non-exclusionary rule. And so on. . . . For us the question remains, as it has always been, one of the state power, not one of passing judgment on the wisdom of one state course or another. In my view this Court should continue to forbear from fettering the States with an adamant rule which may embarrass them in coping with their own peculiar problems in criminal law enforcement. . . .

UNITED STATES v. LEON,
468 U.S. 897 (1984)

In this landmark case, the Court carved out an exception to the exclusionary rule and in so doing provided a major precedent for weakening Fourth Amendment protection. This case had its genesis in a surveillance by the Burbank, California, Police Department of the activities of Albert Antonio Leon and associates, which in turn was based on informants' tips. The police officers prepared an affidavit summarizing their observations which was used by Officer Rombach to justify his application for a warrant to search three residences (including

Leon's) and the suspects' automobiles. The application was approved by several deputy district attorneys before it was taken to a state court judge. The judge issued the search warrant and the ensuing searches produced large quantities of drugs and other evidence. Leon and associates were indicted for federal drug offenses and their lawyers filed motions to suppress (exclude) the evidence thus obtained. After an evidentiary hearing, the federal district court concluded that the affidavit was insufficient to establish probable cause necessary for the issuance of a search warrant. Although recognizing that Officer Rombach had acted in good faith, the court rejected the Government's position that the Fourth Amendment exclusionary rule should not apply when evidence is seized in reasonable, good-faith reliance on the part of the police on a search warrant issued by a judge. The United States Court of Appeals for the Ninth Circuit affirmed, and the Supreme Court was asked to determine whether a good-faith exception to the exclusionary rule should be established.

Majority votes: 6
Dissenting votes: 3

JUSTICE WHITE delivered the opinion of the Court:

The Fourth Amendment contains no provision expressly precluding the use of evidence obtained in violation of its commands, and an examination of its origin and purposes makes clear that the use of fruits of a past unlawful search or seizure "work[s] no new Fourth Amendment wrong." The wrong condemned by the Amendment is "fully accomplished" by the unlawful search or seizure itself, and the exclusionary rule is neither intended nor able to "cure the invasion of the defendant's rights which he has already suffered." The rule thus operates as "a judicially created remedy designed to safeguard Fourth Amendment rights generally through its deterrent effect, rather than a personal constitutional right of the person aggrieved." *United States* v. *Calandra,* 414 U.S., at 348 (1974).

Whether the exclusionary sanction is appropriately imposed in a particular case, our decisions make clear, is "an issue separate from the question whether the Fourth Amendment rights of the party seeking to invoke the rule were violated by police conduct." Only the former question is currently before us, and it must be resolved by weighing the costs and benefits of preventing the use in the prosecution's case-in-chief of inherently trustworthy tangible evidence obtained in reliance on a search warrant issued by a detached and neutral magistrate that ultimately is found to be defective.

The substantial social costs exacted by the exclusionary rule for the vindication of Fourth Amendment rights have long been a source of concern. "Our cases have consistently recognized that unbending application of the exclusionary sanction to enforce ideals of governmental rectitude would impede unacceptably the truth-finding functions of judge and jury." *United States* v. *Payner,* 447 U.S. 727, 734 (1980). An objectionable collateral consequence of this interference with the criminal justice system's truth-finding function is that some guilty defendants may go free or receive reduced sentences as a result of favorable plea bargains. Particularly when law enforcement officers have acted in objective good faith or their transgressions have been minor, the magnitude of the benefit conferred on such guilty defendants offends basic concepts of the criminal justice system. Indiscriminate application of the exclusionary rule, therefore, may well "generat[e] disrespect for the law and the administration of justice." Accordingly, "[a]s with any remedial device, the application of the rule has been restricted to those areas where its remedial objectives are thought most efficaciously served." *United States* v. *Calandra,* 414 U.S., at 348.

Close attention to those remedial objectives has characterized our recent decisions concerning the scope of the Fourth Amendment exclusionary rule. The Court has, to be sure, not seriously questioned, "in the absence of a more efficacious sanction, the continued application of the rule to suppress evidence from the prosecution's case where a Fourth Amendment violation has been substantial and deliberate. . . ." *Franks* v. *Delaware,* 438 U.S. 154, 171 (1978). Nevertheless, the balancing approach that has evolved in various contexts—including criminal trials—"forcefully suggest[s] that the exclusionary rule be more generally modified to permit the introduction of evidence obtained in the reasonable good-faith belief that a search or seizure was in accord with the Fourth Amendment." *Illinois* v. *Gates,* (WHITE, J., concurring in the judgment). . . .

When considering the use of evidence obtained in violation of the Fourth Amendment in the prosecution's case-in-chief, moreover, we have declined to adopt a *per se* or *but for* rule that would render inadmissible any evidence that came to light through a chain of causation that began with an illegal arrest. We also have held that a witness' testimony may be admitted even when his identity was discovered in an unconstitutional search. The perception underlying these decisions—that the connection between police misconduct and evidence of crime may be sufficiently attenuated to permit the

use of that evidence at trial—is a product of considerations relating to the exclusionary rule and the constitutional principles it is designed to protect. In short, the "dissipation of the taint" concept that the Court has applied in deciding whether exclusion is appropriate in a particular case "attempts to mark the point at which the detrimental consequences of illegal police action become so attenuated that the deterrent effect of the exclusionary rule no longer justifies its cost." *Brown* v. *Illinois,* 422 U.S., at 609 (1975), (POWELL J. concurring in part). Not surprisingly in view of this purpose, an assessment of the flagrancy of the police misconduct constitutes an important step in the calculus. . . .

The same attention to the purposes underlying the exclusionary rule also has characterized decisions not involving the scope of the rule itself. We have not required suppression of the fruits of a search incident to an arrest made in good-faith reliance on a substantive criminal statute that subsequently is declared unconstitutional. *Michigan* v. *DeFillippo,* 443 U.S. 31 (1979). . . .

As yet, we have not recognized any form of good-faith exception to the Fourth Amendment exclusionary rule. But the balancing approach that has evolved during the years of experience with the rule provides strong support for the modification currently urged upon us. As we discuss below, our evaluation of the costs and benefits of suppressing reliable physical evidence seized by officers reasonably relying on a warrant issued by a detached and neutral magistrate leads to the conclusion that such evidence should be admissible in the prosecution's case-in-chief. . . .

Deference to the magistrate, however, is not boundless. It is clear, first, that the deference accorded to a magistrate's finding of probable cause does not preclude inquiry into the knowing or reckless falsity of the affidavit on which that determination was based. *Franks* v. *Delaware,* 438 U.S. 154 (1978). Second, the courts must also insist that the magistrate purport to "perform his 'neutral and detached' function and not serve merely as a rubber stamp for the police." A magistrate failing to "manifest that neutrality and detachment demanded of a judicial officer when presented with a warrant application" and who acts instead as "an adjunct law enforcement officer" cannot provide valid authorization for an otherwise unconstitutional search.

Third, reviewing courts will not defer to a warrant based on an affidavit that does not "provide the magistrate with a substantial basis for determining the existence of probable cause." "Sufficient information must be presented to the magistrate to allow that official to determine probable cause; his action cannot be a mere ratification of the bare conclusions of others." . . . Even if the warrant application was supported by more than a "bare bones" affidavit, a reviewing court may properly conclude that, notwithstanding the deference that magistrates deserve, the warrant was invalid because the magistrate's probable-cause determination reflected an improper analysis of the totality of the circumstances or because the form of the warrant was improper in some respect.

Only in the first of these three situations, however, has the Court set forth a rationale for suppressing evidence obtained pursuant to a search warrant; in the other areas, it has simply excluded such evidence without considering whether Fourth Amendment interests will be advanced. To the extent that proponents of exclusion rely on its behavioral effects on judges and magistrates in these areas, their reliance is misplaced. First, the exclusionary rule is designed to deter police misconduct rather than to punish the errors of judges and magistrates. Second, there exists no evidence suggesting that judges and magistrates are inclined to ignore or subvert the Fourth Amendment or that lawlessness among these actors requires application of the extreme sanction of exclusion.

Third, and most important, we discern no basis, and are offered none, for believing that exclusion of evidence seized pursuant to a warrant will have a significant deterrent effect on the issuing judge or magistrate. Many of the factors that indicate that the exclusionary rule cannot provide an effective "special" or "general" deterrent for individual offending law enforcement officers apply as well to judges or magistrates. And, to the extent that the rule is thought to operate as a "systemic" deterrent on a wider audience, it clearly can have no such effect on individuals empowered to issue search warrants. Judges and magistrates are not adjuncts to the law enforcement team; as neutral judicial officers, they have no stake in the outcome of particular criminal prosecutions. The threat of exclusion thus cannot be expected significantly to deter them. Imposition of the exclusionary sanction is not necessary meaningfully to inform judicial officers of their errors, and we cannot conclude that admitting evidence obtained pursuant to a warrant while at the same time declaring that the warrant was somehow defective will in any way reduce judicial officers' professional incentives to comply with the Fourth Amendment, encourage them to repeat their mistakes, or lead to the granting of all colorable warrant requests. . . .

. . . [W]hen an officer acting with objective good faith has obtained a search warrant from a judge or magistrate and acted within its scope, [i]n most such cases, there is no police illegality and thus nothing to deter. It is the magistrate's responsibility to determine whether the officer's allegations establish probable cause and, if so, to issue a warrant comporting in form with the requirements of the Fourth Amendment. In the ordinary case, an officer cannot be expected to question the magistrate's probable-cause determination or his judgment that the form of the warrant is technically sufficient. . . . Penalizing the officer for the magistrate's error, rather than his own, cannot logically contribute to the deterrence of Fourth Amendment violations.

We conclude that the marginal or nonexistent benefits produced by suppressing evidence obtained in objectively reasonable reliance on a subsequently invalidated search warrant cannot justify the substantial costs of exclusion. . . .

. . . The good-faith exception for searches conducted pursuant to warrants is not intended to signal our unwillingness strictly to enforce the requirements of the Fourth Amendment, and we do not believe that it will have this effect. As we have already suggested, the good-faith exception, turning as it does on objective reasonableness, should not be difficult to apply in practice. When officers have acted pursuant to a warrant, the prosecution should ordinarily be able to establish objective good faith without a substantial expenditure of judicial time. . . .

When the principles we have enunciated today are applied to the facts of this case, it is apparent that the judgment of the Court of Appeals cannot stand. The Court of Appeals applied the prevailing legal standards to Officer Rombach's warrant application and concluded that the application could not support the magistrate's probable-cause determination. In so doing, the court clearly informed the magistrate that he had erred in issuing the challenged warrant. This aspect of the court's judgment is not under attack in this proceeding.

Having determined that the warrant should not have issued, the Court of Appeals understandably declined to adopt a modification of the Fourth Amendment exclusionary rule that this Court had not previously sanctioned. Although the modification finds strong support in our previous cases, the Court of Appeals' commendable self-restraint is not to be criticized. We have now re-examined the purposes of the exclusionary rule and the propriety of its application in cases where officers have relied on a subsequently invalidated search warrant. Our conclusion is that the rule's purposes will only rarely be served by applying it in such circumstances.

In the absence of an allegation that the magistrate abandoned his detached and neutral role, suppression is appropriate only if the officers were dishonest or reckless in preparing their affidavit or could not have harbored an objectively reasonable belief in the existence of probable cause. Only respondent Leon has contended that no reasonably well-trained police officer could have believed that there existed probable cause to search his house; significantly, the other respondents advance no comparable argument. Officer Rombach's application for a warrant clearly was supported by much more than a ''bare bones'' affidavit. The affidavit related the results of an extensive investigation and, as the opinions of the divided panel of the Court of Appeals make clear, provided evidence sufficient to create disagreement among thoughtful and competent judges as to the existence of probable cause. Under these circumstances, the officers' reliance on the magistrate's determination of probable cause was objectively reasonable, and application of the extreme sanction of exclusion is inappropriate.

Accordingly, the judgment of the Court of Appeals is

Reversed.

JUSTICE BLACKMUN, concurring: [omitted]
JUSTICE BRENNAN, with whom JUSTICE MARSHALL joins, dissenting:

Ten years ago in *United States* v. *Calandra,* 414 U.S. 338 (1974), I expressed the fear that the Court's decision ''may signal that a majority of my colleagues have positioned themselves to reopen the door [to evidence secured by official lawlessness] still further and abandon altogether the exclusionary rule in search-and-seizure cases.'' (BRENNAN, J., dissenting). Since then, in case after case, I have witnessed the Court's gradual but determined strangulation of the rule. It now appears that the Court's victory over the Fourth Amendment is complete. That today's decision represents the *pièce de résistance* of the Court's past efforts cannot be doubted, for today the Court sanctions the use in the prosecution's case-in-chief of illegally obtained evidence against the individual whose rights have been violated—a result that had previously been thought to be foreclosed.

The Court seeks to justify this result on the ground that the ''costs'' of adhering to the exclusionary rule in cases like those before us exceed the ''benefits.'' But the language of deterrence and of cost/benefit analysis, if used indiscriminately, can have a narcotic effect. It creates an illusion of technical precision and ineluctability. It suggests that not only constitutional principle but also empirical data supports the majority's result. When the Court's analysis is examined carefully, however, it is clear that we have not been treated to an honest assessment of the merits of the exclusionary rule, but have instead been drawn into a curious world where the ''costs'' of excluding illegally obtained evidence loom to exaggerated heights and where the ''benefits'' of such exclusion are made to disappear with a mere wave of the hand.

The majority ignores the fundamental constitutional importance of what is at stake here. While the machinery of law enforcement and indeed the nature of crime itself have changed dramatically since the Fourth Amendment became part of the Nation's fundamental law in 1791, what the Framers understood then remains true today—that the task of combatting crime and convicting the guilty will in every era seem of such critical and pressing concern that we may be lured by the temptations of expediency into forsaking our commitment to protecting individual liberty and privacy. It was for that very reason that the Framers of the Bill of Rights insisted that law enforcement efforts be permanently and unambiguously restricted in order to preserve personal freedoms. In the constitutional scheme they ordained, the sometimes unpopular task of ensuring that the government's enforcement efforts remain within the strict boundaries fixed by the Fourth Amendment was entrusted to the courts. . . . If those independent tribunals lose their resolve, however, as the Court has done today, and give way to the seductive call of expediency, the vital guarantees of the Fourth Amendment are reduced to nothing more than a ''form of words.''. . .

At the outset, the Court suggests that society has been asked to pay a high price—in terms either of setting guilty persons free or of impeding the proper functioning of trials—as a result of excluding relevant physical evidence in cases where the police, in conducting searches and seizing evidence, have made only an ''objectively reasonable'' mistake concerning the constitutionality of their actions. But what evidence is there to support such a claim?

Significantly, the Court points to none, and, indeed, as the Court acknowledges, recent studies have demonstrated that the ''costs'' of the exclusionary rule—calculated in terms of dropped prosecutions and lost convictions—are quite low. Contrary to the claims of the rule's critics that exclusion leads to "the release of countless guilty criminals," these studies have demonstrated that federal and state prosecutors very rarely drop cases because of potential search and seizure problems. For example, a 1979 study prepared at the request of Congress by the General Accounting Office reported that only 0.4% of all cases actually declined for prosecution by federal prosecutors were declined primarily because of illegal search problems. . . . If the GAO data are restated as a percentage of *all* arrests, the study shows that only 0.2% of all felony arrests are declined for prosecution because of potential exclusionary rule problems. . . .

What then supports the Court's insistence that this evidence be admitted? Apparently, the Court's only answer is that even though the costs of exclusion are not very substantial, the potential deterrent effect in these circumstances is so marginal that exclusion cannot be justified. The key to the Court's conclusion in this respect is its belief that the prospective deterrent effect of the exclusionary rule operates only in those situations in which police officers, when deciding whether to go forward with some particular search, have reason to know that their planned conduct will violate the requirements of the Fourth Amendment. . . .

The flaw in the Court's argument, however, is that its logic captures only one comparatively minor element of the generally acknowledged deterrent purposes of the exclusionary rule. To be sure, the rule operates to some extent to deter future misconduct by individual officers who have had evidence suppressed in their own cases. But what the Court overlooks is that the deterrence rationale for the rule is not designed to be, nor should it be thought of as, a form of "punishment" of individual police officers for their failures to obey the restraints imposed by the Fourth Amendment. Instead, the chief deterrent function of the rule is its tendency to promote institutional compliance with Fourth Amendment requirements on the part of law enforcement agencies generally. Thus, as the Court has previously recognized, "over the long term, [the] demonstration [provided by the exclusionary rule] that our society attaches serious consequences to violation of constitutional rights is thought to encourage those who formulate law enforcement policies, and the officers who implement them, to incorporate Fourth Amendment ideals into their value system." *Stone* v. *Powell*, 428 U.S., at 492. It is only through such an institutionwide mechanism that information concerning Fourth Amendment standards can be effectively communicated to rank and file officers. . . .

After today's decision, however, that institutional incentive will be lost. Indeed, the Court's "reasonable mistake" exception to the exclusionary rule will tend to put a premium on police ignorance of the law. Armed with the assurance provided by today's decision that evidence will always be admissible whenever an officer has "reasonably" relied upon a warrant, police departments will be encouraged to train officers that if a warrant has simply been signed, it is reasonable, without more, to rely on it. Since in close cases there will no longer be any incentive to err on the side of constitutional behavior, police would have every reason to adopt a "let's-wait-until-it's-decided" approach in situations in which there is a question about a warrant's validity or the basis for its issuance. . . .

JUSTICE STEVENS, dissenting:. . . .

The Court assumes that the searches in these cases violated the Fourth Amendment, yet refuses to apply the exclusionary rule because the Court concludes that it was "reasonable" for the police to conduct them. In my opinion an official search and seizure cannot be both "unreasonable" and "reasonable" at the same time. . . .

The majority's . . . conclusion rests on the notion that it must be reasonable for a police officer to rely on a magistrate's finding. Until today that has plainly not been the law; it has been well-settled that even when a magistrate issues a warrant there is no guarantee that the ensuing search and seizure is constitutionally reasonable. Law enforcement officers have long been on notice that despite the magistrate's decision a warrant will be invalidated if the officers did not provide sufficient facts to enable the magistrate to evaluate the existence of probable cause responsibly and independently. Reviewing courts have always inquired into whether the magistrate acted properly in issuing the warrant—not merely whether the officers acted properly in executing it. . . .

. . . [T]he Framers of the Fourth Amendment were deeply suspicious of warrants; in their minds the paradigm of an abusive search was the execution of a warrant not based on probable cause. The fact that colonial officers had magisterial authorization for their conduct when they engaged in general searches surely did not make their conduct "reasonable." The Court's view that it is consistent with our Constitution to adopt a rule that it is presumptively reasonable to rely on a defective warrant is the product of constitutional amnesia. . . .

. . . Today, for the first time, this Court holds that although the Constitution has been violated, no court should do anything about it at any time and in

them in life. One of our most cherished ideals is the one contained in the Fourth Amendment: that the Government may not intrude on the personal privacy of its citizens without a warrant or compelling circumstance. The Court's decision today is a curious moral for the Nation's youth. Although the search of T.L.O.'s purse does not trouble today's majority, I submit that we are not dealing with "matters relatively trivial to the welfare of the Nation. There are village tyrants as well as village Hampdens, but none who acts under color of law is beyond the reach of the Constitution." *West Virginia State Board of Education* v. *Barnette,* 319 U.S. 624 (1943).

I respectfully dissent.

CALIFORNIA v. GREENWOOD,
486 U.S. 35 (1988)

Local police received information that Billy Greenwood might be dealing drugs from his home. They did not have enough information to constitute probable cause necessary for obtaining a search warrant. Instead, they decided to take the opaque garbage bags Greenwood left at the curbside for regular trash pickup and search them. Sure enough the police found evidence of narcotic use and as a result they obtained search warrants to search Greenwood's house. A search turned up illegal substances and Greenwood was arrested on felony narcotics charges. The state superior court dismissed the charges because the search warrant had been based on evidence illegally obtained under the Fourth Amendment and the California Constitution. The California Court of Appeals affirmed. California took the case to the United States Supreme Court.

Majority votes: 6
Dissenting votes: 2

JUSTICE WHITE delivered the opinion of the Court:. . . .

The warrantless search and seizure of the garbage bags left at the curb outside the Greenwood house would violate the Fourth Amendment only if respondents manifested a subjective expectation of privacy in their garbage that society accepts as objectively reasonable. Respondents do not disagree with this standard.

They assert, however, that they had, and exhibited, an expectation of privacy with respect to the trash that was searched by the police: The trash, which was placed on the street for collection at a fixed time, was contained in opaque plastic bags, which the garbage collector was expected to pick up, mingle with the trash of others, and deposit at the garbage dump. The trash was only temporarily on the street, and there was little likelihood that it would be inspected by anyone.

It may well be that respondents did not expect that the contents of their garbage bags would become known to the police or other members of the public. An expectation of privacy does not give rise to Fourth Amendment protection, however, unless society is prepared to accept that expectation as objectively reasonable.

Here, we conclude that respondents exposed their garbage to the public sufficiently to defeat their claim to Fourth Amendment protection. It is common knowledge that plastic garbage bags left on or at the side of a public street are readily accessible to animals, children, scavengers, snoops, and other members of the public. Moreover, respondents placed their refuse at the curb for the express purpose of conveying it to a third party, the trash collector, who might himself have sorted through respondents' trash or permitted others, such as the police, to do so. Accordingly, having deposited their garbage "in an area particularly suited for public inspection and, in a manner of speaking, public consumption, for the express purpose of having strangers take it," respondents could have had no reasonable expectation of privacy in the inculpatory items that they discarded.

Furthermore, as we have held, the police cannot reasonably be expected to avert their eyes from evidence of criminal activity that could have been observed by any member of the public. Hence, "[w]hat a person knowingly exposes to the public, even in his own home or office, is not a subject of Fourth Amendment protection." *Katz* v. *United States, supra,* 389 U.S. at 351. We held in *Smith* v. *Maryland,* 442 U.S. 735 (1979), for example, that the police did not violate the Fourth Amendment by causing a pen register to be installed at the telephone company's offices to record the telephone numbers dialed by a criminal suspect. An individual has no legitimate expectation of privacy in the numbers dialed on his telephone, we reasoned, because he voluntarily conveys those numbers to the telephone company when he uses the telephone. Again, we observed that "a person has no legitimate expectation of privacy in information he voluntarily turns over to third parties." . . .

Our conclusion that society would not accept as reasonable respondents' claim to an expectation of privacy in trash left for collection in an area accessible to the public is reinforced by the unanimous rejection of similar claims by the Federal Courts of

Appeals. . . . In addition, of those state appellate courts that have considered the issue, the vast majority have held that the police may conduct warrantless searches and seizures of garbage discarded in public areas. . . .

The judgment of the California Court of Appeal is therefore reversed, and this case is remanded for further proceedings not inconsistent with this opinion.

It is so ordered.

JUSTICE KENNEDY took no part in the consideration or decision of this case.

JUSTICE BRENNAN, with whom JUSTICE MARSHALL joins, dissenting:

Every week for two months, and at least once more a month later, the Laguna Beach police clawed through the trash that respondent Greenwood left in opaque, sealed bags on the curb outside his home. Complete strangers minutely scrutinized their bounty, undoubtedly dredging up intimate details of Greenwood's private life and habits. The intrusions proceeded without a warrant, and no court before or since has concluded that the police acted on probable cause to believe Greenwood was engaged in any criminal activity.

Scrutiny of another's trash is contrary to commonly accepted notions of civilized behavior. I suspect, therefore, that members of our society will be shocked to learn that the Court, the ultimate guarantor of liberty, deems unreasonable our expectation that the aspects of our private lives that are concealed safely in a trash bag will not become public. . . .

The Framers of the Fourth Amendment understood that "unreasonable searches" of "paper[s] and effects"—no less than "unreasonable searches" of "person[s] and houses"—infringe privacy. As early as 1878, this Court acknowledged that the contents of "[l]etters and sealed packages . . . in the mail are as fully guarded from examination and inspection . . . as if they were retained by the parties forwarding them in their own domiciles." In short, so long as a package is "closed against inspection," the Fourth Amendment protects its contents, "wherever they may be," and the police must obtain a warrant to search it just "as is required when papers are subjected to search in one's own household."

With the emergence of the reasonable-expectation-of-privacy analysis, we have reaffirmed this fundamental principle. In *Robbins* v. *California,* 453 U.S. 420 (1981), for example, Justice Stewart, writing for a plurality of four, pronounced that "un-less the container is such that its contents may be said to be in plain view, those contents are fully protected by the Fourth Amendment," and soundly rejected any distinction for Fourth Amendment purposes among various opaque, sealed containers . . . With only one exception, every Justice who wrote in that case eschewed any attempt to distinguish "worthy" from "unworthy" containers. . . .

Our precedent, therefore, leaves no room to doubt that had respondents been carrying their personal effects in opaque, sealed plastic bags—identical to the ones they placed on the curb—their privacy would have been protected from warrantless police intrusion. So far as Fourth Amendment protection is concerned, opaque plastic bags are every bit as worthy as "packages wrapped in green opaque plastic" and "double-locked footlocker[s]." . . . Respondents deserve no less protection just because Greenwood used the bags to discard rather than to transport his personal effects. Their contents are not inherently any less private, and Greenwood's decision to discard them, at least in the manner in which he did, does not diminish his expectation of privacy. . . .

A single bag of trash testifies eloquently to the eating, reading, and recreational habits of the person who produced it. A search of trash, like a search of the bedroom, can relate intimate details about sexual practices, health, and personal hygiene. Like rifling through desk drawers or intercepting phone calls, rummaging through trash can divulge the target's financial and professional status, political affiliations and inclinations, private thoughts, personal relationships, and romantic interests. It cannot be doubted that a sealed trash bag harbors telling evidence of the "intimate activity associated with the 'sanctity of a man's home and the privacies of life,' " which the Fourth Amendment is designed to protect. . . .

In evaluating the reasonableness of Greenwood's expectation that his sealed trash bags would not be invaded, the Court has held that we must look to "understandings that are recognized and permitted by society." Most of us, I believe, would be incensed to discover a meddler—whether a neighbor, a reporter, or a detective—scrutinizing our sealed trash containers to discover some detail of our personal lives. That was, quite naturally, the reaction to the sole incident on which the Court bases its conclusion that "snoops" and the like defeat the expectation of privacy in trash. When a tabloid reporter examined then-Secretary of State Henry Kissinger's trash and published his findings, Kissinger was "really revolted" by the intrusion and his wife suffered "grave anguish." The public response roundly condemning the reporter demonstrates that society not only recognized those reactions as reasonable, but shared them as well. Commentators variously characterized his conduct as "disgusting" . . .; "indefensible . . . as civilized behavior;" and contrary to "the way decent people behave in relation to each other."

Beyond a generalized expectation of privacy, many municipalities, whether for reasons of privacy, sanitation, or both, reinforce confidence in the integrity of sealed trash containers by "prohibit[ing] anyone, except authorized employees of the Town . . ., to rummage into, pick up, collect, move or otherwise interfere with articles or materials placed on . . . any public street for collection." In fact, the California Constitution, as interpreted by the State's highest court, guarantees a right of privacy in trash vis-à-vis government officials. . . .

That is not to deny that isolated intrusions into opaque, sealed trash containers occur. When, acting on their own, "animals, children, scavengers, snoops, [or] other members of the general public," *actually* rummage through a bag of trash and expose its contents to plain view, "police cannot reasonably be expected to avert their eyes from evidence of criminal activity that could have been observed by any member of the public."

Had Greenwood flaunted his intimate activity by strewing his trash all over the curb for all to see, or had some nongovernmental intruder invaded his privacy and done the same, I could accept the Court's conclusion that an expectation of privacy would have been unreasonable. Similarly, had police searching the city dump run across incriminating evidence that, despite commingling with the trash of others, still retained its identity as Greenwood's, we would have a different case. But all that Greenwood "exposed . . . to the public," were the exteriors of several opaque, sealed containers. Until the bags were opened by police, they hid their contents from the public's view . . .

Faithful application of the warrant requirement . . . requires them [police] to adhere to norms of privacy that members of the public plainly acknowledge.

The mere *possibility* that unwelcome meddlers *might* open and rummage through the containers does not negate the expectation of privacy in its contents any more than the possibility of a burglary negates an expectation of privacy in the home; or the possibility of a private intrusion negates an expectation of privacy in an unopened package; or the possibility that an operator will listen in on a telephone conversation negates an expectation of privacy in the words spoken on the telephone. . . .

Nor is it dispositive that "respondents placed their refuse at the curb for the express purpose of conveying it to a third party, . . . who might himself have sorted through respondents' trash or permitted others, such as police, to do so." In the first place, Greenwood can hardly be faulted for leaving trash on his curb when a county ordinance commanded him to do so . . . Unlike in other circumstances where privacy is compromised, Greenwood could not "avoid exposing personal belongings . . . by simply leaving them at home." More importantly, even the voluntary relinquishment of possession or control over an effect does not necessarily amount to a relinquishment of a privacy expectation in it. Were it otherwise, a letter or package would lose all Fourth Amendment protection when placed in a mail box or other depository with the "express purpose" of entrusting it to the postal officer or a private carrier; those bailees are just as likely as trash collectors (and certainly have greater incentive) to "sor[t] through" the personal effects entrusted to them, "or permi[t] others, such as police to do so." Yet, it has been clear for at least 110 years that the possibility of such an intrusion does not justify a warrantless search by police in the first instance.

In holding that the warrantless search of Greenwood's trash was consistent with the Fourth Amendment, the Court paints a grim picture of our society. It depicts a society in which local authorities may command their citizens to dispose of their personal effects in the manner least protective of the "sanctity of [the] home and the privacies of life," and then monitor them arbitrarily and without judicial oversight—a society that is not prepared to recognize as reasonable an individual's expectation of privacy in the most private of personal effects sealed in an opaque container and disposed of in a manner designed to commingle it imminently and inextricably with the trash of others. The American society with which I am familiar "chooses to dwell in reasonable security and freedom from surveillance," and is more dedicated to individual liberty and more sensitive to intrusions on the sanctity of the home than the Court is willing to acknowledge.

I dissent.

NATIONAL TREASURY EMPLOYEES UNION v. VON RAAB
109 S. Ct. 1384 (1989)

This case concerned the constitutionality of the federal government's drug testing program on employees of the United States Customs Service implemented in May 1986. The employees affected are those who are directly involved in rooting out drug smuggling into the United States or who carry firearms or handle classified material. The National Treasury Employees Union sued on behalf of Customs Service employees and asked the federal district court to stop the program on the ground that it violated the Fourth Amendment. William Von Raab, head of the Customs Service, was named in the suit. The District Court agreed with the union and issued an injunction. The Court of Appeals for the Fifth Circuit vacated the injunction and the union took the case to the United States Supreme Court.

Majority votes: 5
Dissenting votes: 4

JUSTICE KENNEDY delivered the opinion of the Court:

We granted certiorari to decide whether it violates the Fourth Amendment for the United States Customs Service to require a urinalysis test from employees who seek transfer or promotion to certain positions. . . .

. . . [T]he Customs Service's drug testing program is not designed to serve the ordinary needs of law enforcement. Test results may not be used in a criminal prosecution of the employee without the employee's consent. The purposes of the program are to deter drug use among those eligible for promotion to sensitive positions within the Service and to prevent the promotion of drug users to those positions. These substantial interests, no less than the Government's concern for safe rail transportation at issue in *Railway Labor Executives,* present a special need that may justify departure from the ordinary warrant and probable cause requirements. . . .

We think the Government's need to conduct the suspicionless searches required by the Customs program outweighs the privacy interests of employees engaged directly in drug interdiction, and of those who otherwise are required to carry firearms.

The Customs Service is our Nation's first line of defense against one of the greatest problems affecting the health and welfare of our population. We have adverted before to "the veritable national crisis in law enforcement caused by smuggling of illicit narcotics." Our cases also reflect the traffickers' seemingly inexhaustible repertoire of deceptive practices and elaborate schemes for importing narcotics. The record in this case confirms that, through the adroit selection of source locations, smuggling routes, and increasingly elaborate methods of concealment, drug traffickers have managed to bring into this country increasingly large quantities of illegal drugs. The record also indicates, and it is well known, that drug smugglers do not hesitate to use violence to protect their lucrative trade and avoid apprehension.

Many of the Service's employees are often exposed to this criminal element and to the controlled substances they seek to smuggle into the country. The physical safety of these employees may be threatened, and many may be tempted not only by bribes from the traffickers with whom they deal, but also by their own access to vast sources of valuable contraband seized and controlled by the Service. The Commissioner indicated below that "Customs [o]fficers have been shot, stabbed, run over, dragged by automobiles, and assaulted with blunt objects while performing their duties." At least nine officers have died in the line of duty since 1974. He also noted that Customs officers have been the targets of bribery by drug smugglers on numerous occasions, and several have been removed from the Service for accepting bribes and other integrity violations. . . .

It is readily apparent that the Government has a compelling interest in ensuring that front-line interdiction personnel are physically fit, and have unimpeachable integrity and judgment. Indeed, the Government's interest here is at least as important as its interest in searching travelers entering the country. We have long held that travelers seeking to enter the country may be stopped and required to submit to a routine search without probable cause, or even founded suspicion, "because of national self protection reasonably requiring one entering the country to identify himself as entitled to come in, and his belongings as effects which may be lawfully brought in." This national interest in self protection could be irreparably damaged if those charged with safeguarding it were, because of their own drug use, unsympathetic to their mission of interdicting narcotics. A drug user's indifference to the Service's basic mission or, even worse, his active complicity with the malefactors, can facilitate importation of sizable drug shipments or block apprehension of dangerous criminals. The public interest demands effective measures to bar drug users from positions directly involving the interdiction of illegal drugs.

The public interest likewise demands effective measures to prevent the promotion of drug users to positions that require the incumbent to carry a firearm, even if the incumbent is not engaged directly in the interdiction of drugs. Customs employees who may use deadly force plainly "discharge duties fraught with such risks of injury to others

ments to include liberty of the mind as well as liberty of action. The extension became, indeed, a logical imperative when once it was recognized, as long ago it was, that liberty is something more than exemption from physical restraint, and that even in the field of substantive rights and duties the legislative judgment if oppressive and arbitrary, may be overridden by the courts. Fundamental too in the concept of due process, and so in that of liberty, is the thought that condemnation shall be rendered only after trial. The hearing, moreover, must be a real one, not a sham or a pretense. For that reason, ignorant defendants in a capital case were held to have been condemned unlawfully when in truth, though not in form, they were refused the aid of counsel. The decision did not turn upon the fact that the benefit of counsel would have been guaranteed to the defendants by the provisions of the Sixth Amendment if they had been prosecuted in a federal court. The decision turned upon the fact that in the particular situation laid before us in the evidence the benefit of counsel was essential to the substance of a hearing.

Our survey of the cases serves, we think, to justify the statement that the dividing line between them, if not unfaltering throughout its course, has been true for the most part to a unifying principle. On which side of the line the case made out by the appellant has appropriate location must be the next inquiry and the final one. Is that kind of double jeopardy to which the statute has subjected him a hardship so acute and shocking that our polity will not endure it? Does it violate those "fundamental principles of liberty and justice which lie at the base of all our civil and political institutions"? The answer surely must be "no." What the answer would have to be if the state were permitted after a trial free from error to try the accused over again or to bring another case against him, we have no occasion to consider. We deal with the statute before us and no other. The state is not attempting to wear the accused out by a multitude of cases with accumulated trials. It asks no more than this, that the case against him shall go on until there shall be a trial free from the corrosion of substantial legal error. This is not cruelty at all, nor even vexation in any immoderate degree. If the trial had been infected with error adverse to the accused, there might have been review at his instance, and as often as necessary to purge the vicious taint. A reciprocal privilege, subject at all times to the discretion of the presiding judge, has now been granted to the state. There is here no seismic innovation. The edifice of justice stands, its symmetry, to many, greater than before. . . .

The judgment is

Affirmed.

MR. JUSTICE BUTLER dissents [without opinion].

MIRANDA v. ARIZONA,
384 U.S. 436 (1966)

The Miranda *decision is perhaps the most controversial criminal procedures decision of the Warren Court. It was the culmination of a series of decisions concerning the admissibility of confessions and the Warren Court's attempt to see to it that the Fifth Amendment guarantee against self-incrimination would be honored by the states. Essentially, the narrow five-man majority indicated a profound distrust of confessions obtained during the course of detention. To the majority, even an interrogation free from physical coercion was bound to be psychologically coercive and thus conducive to self-incrimination. In this case, Ernesto Miranda, a 23-year-old drifter, was arrested at his home and charged with the kidnapping and rape of an 18-year-old woman. Miranda was taken to the police station where the victim picked him out of a lineup. Two officers then took him into a separate interrogation room where he confessed in less than two hours. No force, threats, or promises were given and neither was he given any effective warnings about his rights. The confession was introduced at his trial and used to convict him. The Supreme Court of Arizona upheld the conviction, and the United States Supreme Court was then faced with Miranda's claim that the confession was self-incrimination in violation of his constitutional rights. The* Miranda *opinion also disposed of three other similar cases.*

Majority votes: 5
Dissenting votes: 4

MR. CHIEF JUSTICE WARREN delivered the opinion of the Court:

The cases before us raise questions which go to the roots of our concepts of American criminal jurisprudence: the restraints society must observe consistent with the Federal Constitution in prosecuting individuals for crime. More specifically, we deal with the admissibility of statements obtained from an individual who is subjected to custodial police interrogation and the necessity for procedures which assure that the individual is accorded his privilege under the Fifth Amendment to the Constitution not to be compelled to incriminate himself. . . .

We start here, as we did in *Escobedo* v. *Illinois*, 378 U.S. 478 (1964), with the premise that our holding is not an innovation in our jurisprudence, but is an application of principles long recognized and applied in other settings. . . . That case was but an explication of basic rights that are enshrined in our Constitution—that "No person . . . shall be compelled in any criminal case to be a witness against himself," and that "the accused shall . . . have the Assistance of Counsel"—rights which were put in jeopardy in that case through official overbearing. These precious rights were fixed in our Constitution only after centuries of persecution and struggle. And in the words of Chief Justice Marshall, they were secured "for ages to come, and . . . designed to approach immortality as nearly as human institutions can approach it," *Cohens* v. *Virginia*, 6 Wheat. 264, 387 (1821). . . .

I.

The constitutional issue we decide in each of these cases is the admissibility of statements obtained from a defendant questioned while in custody and deprived of his freedom of action. In each, the defendant was questioned by police officers, detectives, or a prosecuting attorney in a room in which he was cut off from the outside world. In none of these cases was the defendant given a full and effective warning of his rights at the outset of the interrogation process. In all the cases, the questioning elicited oral admissions, and in three of them, signed statements as well which were admitted at their trials. They all thus share salient features—incommunicado interrogation of individuals in a police-dominated atmosphere, resulting in self-incriminating statements without full warnings of constitutional rights.

An understanding of the nature and setting of this in-custody interrogation is essential to our decisions today. The difficulty in depicting what transpires at such interrogations stems from the fact that in this country they have largely taken place incommunicado. From extensive factual studies undertaken in the early 1930's, including the famous Wickersham Report to Congress by a Presidential Commission, it is clear that police violence and the "third degree" flourished at that time. In a series of cases decided by this Court long after these studies, the police resorted to physical brutality—beating, hanging, whipping—and to sustained and protracted questioning incommunicado in order to extort confessions. The 1961 Commission on Civil Rights found much evidence to indicate that "some policemen still resort to physical force to

obtain confessions," 1961 Comm'n on Civil Rights Rep., Justice, pt. 5, 17. The use of physical brutality and violence is not, unfortunately, relegated to the past or to any part of the country. Only recently in Kings County, New York, the police brutally beat, kicked and placed lighted cigarette butts on the back of a potential witness under interrogation for the purpose of securing a statement incriminating a third party. *People* v. *Portelli*, 205 N.E. 2d 857 (1965).

The examples given above are undoubtedly the exception now, but they are sufficiently widespread to be the object of concern. Unless a proper limitation upon custodial interrogation is achieved—such as these decisions will advance—there can be no assurance that practices of this nature will be eradicated in the forseeable future. . . .

Again we stress that the modern practice of in-custody interrogation is psychologically rather than physically oriented. As we have stated before, "Since *Chambers* v. *Florida*, 309 U.S. 227, this Court has recognized that coercion can be mental as well as physical, and that the blood of the accused is not the only hallmark of an unconstitutional inquisition." *Blackburn* v. *Alabama*, 361 U.S. 199, 206 (1960). Interrogation still takes place in privacy. Privacy results in secrecy and this in turn results in a gap in our knowledge as to what in fact goes on in the interrogation rooms. A valuable source of information about present police practices, however, may be found in various police manuals and texts which document procedures employed with success in the past, and which recommend various other effective tactics. These texts are used by law enforcement agencies themselves as guides. It should be noted that these texts professedly present the most enlightened and effective means presently used to obtain statements through custodial interrogation. By considering these texts and other data, it is possible to describe procedures observed and noted around the country. . . .

[Several texts are examined and the Chief Justice then concludes:]

From these representative samples of interrogation techniques, the setting prescribed by the manuals and observed in practice becomes clear. In essence, it is this: To be alone with the subject is essential to prevent distraction and to deprive him of any outside support. The aura of confidence in his guilt undermines his will to resist. He merely confirms the preconceived story the police seek to have him describe. Patience and persistence, at times relentless questioning, are employed. To obtain a confession, the interrogator must "patiently maneuver himself or his quarry into a position from which the desired objective may be attained.'' When normal procedures fail to produce the needed result, the police may resort to deceptive stratagems such as giving false legal advice. It is important to keep the subject off balance, for example, by trading on his insecurity about himself or his surroundings. The police then persuade, trick, or cajole him out of exercising his constitutional rights. . . .

II.

We sometimes forget how long it has taken to establish the privilege against self-incrimination, the sources from which it came and the fervor with which it was defended. Its roots go back into ancient times. . . .

. . . [W]e may view the historical development of the privilege as one which groped for the proper scope of governmental power over the citizen. . . . We have recently noted that the privilege against self-incrimination—the essential mainstay of our adversary system—is founded on a complex of values. All these policies point to one overriding thought: the constitutional foundation underlying the privilege is the respect a government—state or federal—must accord to the dignity and integrity of its citizens. . . . [O]ur accusatory system of criminal justice demands that the government seeking to punish an individual produce the evidence against him by its own independent labors, rather than by the cruel, simple expedient of compelling it from his own mouth. In sum, the privilege is fulfilled only when the person is guaranteed the right ''to remain silent unless he chooses to speak in the unfettered exercise of his own will.''

The question in these cases is whether the privilege is fully applicable during a period of custodial interrogation. . . . We are satisfied that all principles embodied in the privilege apply to informal compulsion exerted by law-enforcement officers during in-custody questioning. An individual swept from familiar surroundings into police custody, surrounded by antagonistic forces, and subjected to the techniques of persuasion described above cannot be otherwise than under compulsion to speak. As a practical matter, the compulsion to speak in the isolated setting of the police station may well be greater than in courts or other official investigations, where there are often impartial observers to guard against intimidation or trickery. . . .

III.

Today, then, there can be no doubt that the Fifth Amendment privilege is available outside of criminal court proceedings and serves to protect persons in all settings in which their freedom of action is curtailed from being compelled to incriminate themselves. We have concluded that without proper safeguards the process of in-custody interrogation of persons suspected or accused of crime contains inherently compelling pressures which work to undermine the individual's will to resist and to compel him to speak where he would not otherwise do so freely. In order to combat these pressures and to permit a full opportunity to exercise the privilege against self-incrimination, the accused must be adequately and effectively apprised of his rights and the exercise of those rights must be fully honored.

It is impossible for us to foresee the potential alternatives for protecting the privilege which might be devised by Congress or the States in the exercise of their creative rule-making capacities. Therefore we cannot say that the Constitution necessarily requires adherence to any particular solution for the inherent compulsions of the interrogation process as it is presently conducted. Our decision in no way creates a constitutional straitjacket which will handicap sound efforts at reform, nor is it intended to have this effect. We encourage Congress and the States to continue their laudable search for increasingly effective ways of protecting the rights of the individual while promoting efficient enforcement of our criminal laws. However, unless we are shown other procedures which are at least as effective in apprising accused persons of their right of silence and in assuring a continuous opportunity to exercise it, the following safeguards must be observed.

At the outset, if a person in custody is to be subjected to interrogation, he must first be informed in clear and unequivocal terms that he has the right to remain silent. For those unaware of the privilege, the warning is needed simply to make them aware of it—the threshold requirement for an intelligent decision as to its exercise. More important, such a warning is an absolute prerequisite in overcoming the inherent pressures of the interrogation atmosphere. . . .

The warning of the right to remain silent must be accompanied by the explanation that anything said can and will be used against the individual in court. This warning is needed in order to make him aware not only of the privilege, but also of the consequences of foregoing it. It is only through an awareness of these consequences that there can be any assurance of real understanding and intelligent exercise of the privilege. Moreover, this warning may serve to make the individual more acutely aware that he is faced with a phase of the adversary system—that he is not in the presence of persons acting solely in his interest.

The circumstances surrounding in-custody interrogation can operate very quickly to overbear the will of one merely made aware of his privilege by his interrogators. Therefore, the right to have counsel present at the interrogation is indispensable to the protection of the Fifth Amendment privilege under the system we delineate today. Our aim is to assure that the individual's right to choose between silence and speech remains unfettered throughout the interrogation process. A once-stated warning, delivered by those who will conduct the interrogation, cannot itself suffice to that end among those who most require knowledge of their rights. A mere warning given by the interrogators is not alone sufficient to accomplish that end. . . . Even preliminary advice given to the accused by his own attorney can be swiftly overcome by the secret interrogation process. . . . Thus, the need for counsel to protect the Fifth Amendment privilege comprehends not merely a right to consult with counsel prior to questioning, but also to have counsel present during any questioning if the defendant so desires. . . .

Accordingly we hold that an individual held for interrogation must be clearly informed that he has the right to consult with a lawyer and to have the lawyer with him during interrogation under the system for protecting the privilege we delineate today. As with the warnings of the right to remain silent and that anything stated can be used in evidence against him, this warning is an absolute prerequisite to interrogation. No amount of circumstantial evidence that the person may have been aware of this right will suffice to stand in its stead. Only through such a warning is there ascertainable assurance that the accused was aware of this right.

In order fully to apprise a person interrogated of the extent of his rights under this system . . . it is necessary to warn him not only that he has the right to consult with an attorney, but also that if he is indigent a lawyer will be appointed to represent him. Without this additional warning, the admonition of the right to consult with counsel would often be understood as meaning only that he can consult with a lawyer if he has one or has the funds to obtain one. The warning of a right to counsel would be hollow if not couched in terms that would convey to the indigent—the person most often subjected to interrogation—the knowledge that he too has a right to have counsel present. As with the warnings of the right to remain silent and of the general right to counsel, only by effective and express explanation to the indigent of this right can there be assurance that he was truly in a position to exercise it.

Once warnings have been given, the subsequent procedure is clear. If the individual indicates in any manner, at any time prior to or during questioning, that he wishes to remain silent, the interrogation must cease. At this point he has shown that he intends to exercise his Fifth Amendment privilege; any statement taken after the person invokes his privilege cannot be other than the product of compulsion, subtle or otherwise. Without the right to cut off questioning, the setting of in-custody interrogation operates on the individual to overcome free choice in producing a statement after the privilege has been once invoked. If the individual states that he wants an attorney, the interrogation must cease until an attorney is present. At that time, the individual must have an opportunity to confer with the attorney and to have him present during any subsequent questioning. If the individual cannot obtain an attorney and he indicates that he wants one before speaking to police, they must respect his decision to remain silent.

. . . If authorities conclude that they will not provide counsel during a reasonable period of time in which investigation in the field is carried out, they may do so without violating the person's Fifth Amendment privilege so long as they do not question him during that time.

If the interrogation continues without the presence of an attorney and a statement is taken, a heavy burden rests on the government to demonstrate that the defendant knowingly and intelligently waived his privilege against self-incrimination and his right to retained or appointed counsel. . . .

An express statement that the individual is willing to make a statement and does not want an attorney followed closely by a statement could constitute a waiver. But a valid waiver will not be presumed simply from the silence of the accused after warnings are given or simply from the fact that a confession was in fact eventually obtained. . . .

Whatever the testimony of the authorities as to waiver of rights by an accused, the fact of lengthy interrogation or incommunicado incarceration before a statement is made is strong evidence that the accused did not validly waive his rights. In these circumstances the fact that the individual eventually made a statement is consistent with the conclusion that the compelling influence of the interrogation finally forced him to do so. It is inconsistent with any notion of a voluntary relinquishment of the privilege. Moreover, any evidence that the accused was threatened, tricked, or cajoled into a waiver will, of course, show that the defendant did not voluntarily waive his privilege. The requirement of warnings and waiver of rights is a fundamental with respect to the Fifth Amendment privilege and not simply a preliminary ritual to existing methods of interrogation.

The warnings required and the waiver necessary in accordance with our opinion today are, in the absence of a fully effective equivalent, prerequisites to the admissibility of any statement made by a defendant. No distinction can be drawn between statements which are direct confessions and statements which amount to "admissions" of part or all of an offense. The privilege against self-incrimination protects the individual from being compelled to incriminate himself in any manner; it does not distinguish degrees of incrimination. Similarly, for precisely the same reason, no distinction may be drawn between inculpatory statements and statements alleged to be merely "exculpatory." If a statement made were in fact truly exculpatory it would, of course, never be used by the prosecution. In fact, statements merely intended to be exculpatory by the defendant are often used to impeach his testimony at trial or to demonstrate untruths in the statement given under interrogation and thus to prove guilt by implication. These statements are incriminating in any meaningful sense of the word and may not be used without the full warnings and effective waiver required for any other statement. . . .

The principles announced today deal with the protection which must be given to the privilege against self-incrimination when the individual is first subjected to police interrogation while in custody at the station or otherwise deprived of his freedom of action in any way. It is at this point that our adversary system of criminal proceedings commences, distinguishing itself at the outset from the inquisitorial system recognized in some countries. Under the system of warnings we delineate today or under any other system which may be devised and found effective, the safeguards to be erected about the privilege must come into play at this point.

Our decision is not intended to hamper the traditional function of police officers in investigating crime. When an individual is in custody on probable cause, the police may, of course, seek out evidence in the field to be used at trial against him. Such investigation may include inquiry of persons not under restraint. General on-the-scene questioning as to facts surrounding a crime or other general questioning of citizens in the fact-finding process is not affected by our holding. It is an act of responsible citizenship for individuals to give whatever information they may have to aid in law enforcement. In such situations the compelling atmosphere inherent in the process of in-custody interrogation is not necessarily present.

In dealing with statements obtained through interrogation, we do not purport to find all confessions inadmissible. Confessions remain a proper element in law enforcement. Any statement given freely and voluntarily without any compelling influences is, of course, admissible in evidence. . . . There is no requirement that police stop a person who enters a police station and states that he wishes to confess to a crime, or a person who calls the police to offer a confession or any other statement he desires to make. Volunteered statements of any kind are not barred by the Fifth Amendment and their admissibility is not affected by our holding today. . . .

Because of the nature of the problem and because of its recurrent significance in numerous cases, we have to this point discussed the relationship of the Fifth Amendment privilege to police interrogation without specific concentration on the facts of the cases before us. We turn now to these facts to consider the application to these cases of the constitutional principles discussed above. In each instance, we have concluded that statements were obtained from the defendant under circumstances that did not meet constitutional standards for protection of the privilege. . . .

It is so ordered.

MR. JUSTICE CLARK, dissenting: [omitted]
MR. JUSTICE HARLAN, whom MR. JUSTICE STEWART and MR. JUSTICE WHITE join, dissenting:

I believe the decision of the Court represents poor constitutional law and entails harmful consequences for the country at large. How serious these consequences may prove to be only time can tell. But the basic flaws in the Court's justification seem to me readily apparent now once all sides of the problem are considered.

At the outset, it is well to note exactly what is required by the Court's new constitutional code of rules for confessions. . . . [T]he thrust of the new rules is to negate all pressures, to reinforce the nervous or ignorant suspect, and ultimately to discourage any confession at all. The aim in short is toward "voluntariness" in a utopian sense, or to view it from a different angle, voluntariness with a vengeance.

To incorporate this notion into the Constitution requires a strained reading of history and precedent and a disregard of the very pragmatic concerns that alone may on occasion justify such strains. I believe that reasoned examination will show that the Due Process Clauses provide an adequate tool for coping with confessions and that, even if the Fifth Amendment privilege against self-incrimination be invoked, its precedents taken as a whole do not sustain the present rules. Viewed as a choice based on pure policy, these new rules prove to be highly debatable if not one-sided appraisal of the competing interests, imposed over widespread objection, at the very time when judicial restraint is most called for by the circumstances. . . .

The Fifth Amendment . . . has never been thought to forbid *all* pressure to incriminate one's self in the situations covered by it. . . . This is not to say that short of jail or torture any sanction is permissible in any case; policy and history alike may impose sharp limits. . . . However, the Court's unspoken assumption that *any* pressure violates the privilege is not supported by the precedents and it has failed to show why the Fifth Amendment prohibits that relatively mild pressure the Due Process Clause permits. . . .

Examined as an expression of public policy, the Court's new regime proves so dubious that there can be no due compensation for its weakness in constitutional law. . . . [P]recedent reveals that the Fourteenth Amendment in practice has been construed to strike a different balance, that the Fifth Amendment gives the Court little solid support in this context, and that the Sixth Amendment should have no bearing at all. Legal history has been stretched before to satisfy deep needs of society. In this instance, however, the Court has not and cannot make the powerful showing that its new rules are plainly desirable in the context of our society, something which is surely demanded before those rules are engrafted onto the Constitution and imposed on every State and county in the land.

Without at all subscribing to the generally black picture of police conduct painted by the Court, I think it must be frankly recognized at the outset that police questioning allowable under due process precedents may inherently entail some pressure on the suspect and may seek advantage in his ignorance or weaknesses. . . . Until today, the rule of the Constitution has been only to sift out *undue* pressure, not to assure spontaneous confessions.

The Court's new rules aim to offset these minor pressures and disadvantages intrinsic to any kind of police interrogation. The rules do not serve due process interests in preventing blatant coercion . . . they do nothing to contain the policeman who is prepared to lie from the start. The rules work for reliability in confessions almost only in the Pickwickian sense that they can prevent some from being given at all. In short, the benefit of this new regime is simply to lessen or wipe out the inherent compulsion and inequalities to which the Court devotes some nine pages of description.

What the Court largely ignores is that its rules impair, if they will not eventually serve wholly to frustrate, an instrument of law enforcement that has long and quite reasonably been thought worth the price paid for it. There can be little doubt that the Court's new code would markedly decrease the number of confessions. To warn the suspect that he may remain silent and remind him that his confession may be used in court are minor obstructions. To require also an express waiver by the suspect and an end to questioning whenever he demurs must heavily handicap questioning. And to suggest or provide counsel for the suspect simply invites the end of the interrogation.

How much harm this decision will inflict on law enforcement cannot fairly be predicted with accuracy. Evidence on the role of confessions is notoriously incomplete. . . . We do know that some crimes cannot be solved without confessions, that ample expert testimony attests to their importance in crime control, and that the Court is taking a real risk with society's welfare in imposing its new regime on the country. The social costs of crime are too great to call the new rules anything but a hazardous experimentation.

While passing over the costs and risks of its experiment, the Court portrays the evils of normal police questioning in terms which I think are exaggerated. Albeit stringently confined by the due process standards interrogation is no doubt often inconvenient and unpleasant for the suspect. However, it is no less so for a man to be arrested and jailed, to have his house searched, or to stand trial in court, yet all this may properly happen to the most innocent given probable cause, a warrant, or an indictment. Society has always paid a stiff price for law and order, and peaceful interrogation is not one of the dark moments of the law. . . .

MR. JUSTICE WHITE, with whom MR. JUSTICE HARLAN and MR. JUSTICE STEWART join, dissenting: [omitted]

HARRIS v. NEW YORK,
401 U.S. 222 (1971)

In Miranda v. Arizona, *the Supreme Court ruled that statements or confessions made by the criminal defendant during in-custody interrogation could be introduced at the trial only if certain warnings were given the defendant prior to the questioning. This was to ensure that the defendant knew his or her rights under the Fifth and Sixth Amendments as incorporated through the due process clause of the Fourteenth Amendment, and that any statement or confession made was truly voluntary. In the* Harris *case, the Supreme Court undermined the* Miranda *ruling. The case began when Harris was arrested for selling heroin twice to an undercover police officer. After his arrest, Harris claimed that he had made both sales at the request of the undercover officer. Harris made this statement without having received the full* Miranda *warnings—in particular, the warning that he had a right to the assistance of counsel. Because the statement was made in violation of the* Miranda *standards, it was not introduced at the trial as evidence. However, during the trial, Harris took the stand and denied making the first sale and claimed that, although he did make the second sale, he sold the officer baking soda and not heroin. On cross-examination, the prosecution attempted to impeach Harris' credibility by reading the statement that Harris had made after the arrest. The trial judge permitted the prosecutor to read the statement, and the judge instructed the jury to consider the statement only for the purpose of assessing Harris' credibility and not as evidence of guilt. Harris was found guilty of the second sale and he unsuccessfully appealed through the New York state courts. The case came to the Supreme Court, raising the question of whether the use of Harris' post-arrest statement violated his Fifth, Sixth, and Fourteenth Amendment rights as spelled out in* Miranda v. Arizona.

Majority votes: 5
Dissenting votes: 4

MR. CHIEF JUSTICE BURGER delivered the opinion of the Court:

We granted the writ in this case to consider petitioner's claim that a statement made by him to police under circumstances rendering it inadmissible to establish the prosecution's case in chief under *Miranda* v. *Arizona,* 384 U.S. 436 (1966), may not be used to impeach his credibility. . . .

At trial the prosecution made no effort in its case in chief to use the statements allegedly made by petitioner, conceding that they were inadmissible under *Miranda* v. *Arizona*. The transcript of the interrogation used in the impeachment, but not given to the jury, shows that no warning of a right to appointed counsel was given before questions were put to petitioner when he was taken into custody. . . .

Some comments in the *Miranda* opinion can indeed be read as indicating a bar to use of an uncounseled statement for any purpose, but discussion of that issue was not at all necessary to the Court's holding and cannot be regarded as controlling. *Miranda* barred the prosecution from making its case with statements of an accused made while in custody prior to having or effectively waiving counsel. It does not follow from *Miranda* that evi-

dence inadmissible against an accused in the prosecution's case in chief is barred for all purposes, provided of course that the trustworthiness of the evidence satisfies legal standards.

In *Walder* v. *United States,* 347 U.S. 62 (1954), the Court permitted physical evidence, inadmissible in the case in chief, to be used for impeachment purposes. . . . It is true that Walder was impeached as to collateral matters included in his direct examination, whereas petitioner here was impeached as to testimony bearing more directly on the crimes charged. We are not persuaded that there is a difference in principle that warrants a result different from that reached by the Court in *Walder* [v. *United States*]. Petitioner's testimony in his own behalf . . . contrasted sharply with what he told the police shortly after his arrest. The impeachment process here undoubtedly provided valuable aid to the jury in assessing petitioner's credibility, and the benefits of this process should not be lost, in our view, because of the speculative possibility that impermissible police conduct will be encouraged thereby. Assuming that the exclusionary rule has a deterrent effect on proscribed police conduct, sufficient deterrence flows when the evidence in question is made unavailable to the prosecution in its case in chief.

Every criminal defendant is privileged to testify in his own defense, or to refuse to do so. But that privilege cannot be construed to include the right to commit perjury. Having voluntarily taken the stand, petitioner was under an obligation to speak truthfully and accurately, and the prosecution here did no more than utilize the traditional truth-testing devices of the adversary process. Had inconsistent statements been made by the accused to some third person, it could hardly be contended that the conflict could not be laid before the jury by way of cross-examination and impeachment.

The shield provided by *Miranda* cannot be perverted into a license to use perjury by way of a defense, free from the risk of confrontation with prior inconsistent utterances. We hold, therefore, that petitioner's credibility was appropriately impeached by use of his earlier conflicting statements.

Affirmed.

MR. JUSTICE BLACK dissents [without opinion].
MR. JUSTICE BRENNAN, with whom MR. JUSTICE DOUGLAS and MR. JUSTICE MARSHALL join, dissenting:

It is conceded that the question-and-answer statement used to impeach petitioner's direct testimony was, under *Miranda* v. *Arizona,* constitutionally inadmissible as part of the State's direct case against petitioner. I think that the Constitution also denied the State the use of the statement on cross-examination to impeach the credibility of petitioner's testimony given in his own defense. The decision in *Walder* v. *United States* is not, as the Court today holds, dispositive to the contrary. Rather, that case supports my conclusion. . . .

Walder v. *United States* was not a case where tainted evidence was used to impeach an accused's direct testimony on matters directly related to the case against him. In *Walder* the evidence was used to impeach the accused's testimony on matters *collateral* to the crime charged. Walder had been indicted in 1950 for purchasing and possessing heroin. When his motion to suppress use of the narcotics as illegally seized was granted, the Government dismissed the prosecution. Two years later Walder was indicted for another narcotics violation completely unrelated to the 1950 one. Testifying in his own defense . . . he denied that law enforcement officers had seized narcotics from his home two years earlier. The Government was then permitted to introduce the testimony of one of the officers involved in the 1950 seizure, that when he had raided Walder's home at that time he had seized narcotics there. The Court held that on facts where "the defendant went beyond a mere denial of complicity in the crimes of which he was charged and made the sweeping claim that he had never dealt in or possessed any narcotics," 347 U.S., at 65, the exclusionary rule of *Weeks* v. *United States*, 232 U.S. 383 (1914), would not extend to bar the Government from rebutting this testimony with evidence, although tainted, that petitioner had in fact possessed narcotics two years before. The Court was careful, however, to distinguish the situation of an accused whose testimony, as in the instant case, was a "denial of complicity in the crimes of which he was charged," that is, where illegally obtained evidence was used to impeach the accused's direct testimony on matters directly related to the case against him. As to that situation, the Court said:

> "Of course, the Constitution guarantees a defendant the fullest opportunity to meet the accusation against him. He must be free to deny all the elements of the case against him without thereby giving leave to the Government to introduce by way of rebuttal evidence illegally secured by it, and therefore not available for its case in chief." 347 U.S., at 65.

From this recital of facts it is clear that the evidence used for impeachment in *Walder* was related to the earlier 1950 prosecution and had no direct bearing on "the elements of the case" being tried in 1952. The evidence tended solely to impeach the credibility of the defendant's direct testimony that he had never in his life possessed heroin. But that evidence was completely unrelated to the indictment on trial and did not in any way interfere with his freedom to deny all elements of that case against him. In contrast, here, the evidence used for impeachment, a statement concerning the details of the very sales alleged in the indictment, was directly related to the case against petitioner.

. . . [T]he Fifth Amendment's privilege against self-incrimination . . . has been extended against the States . . . [I]n *Miranda* . . . we said:

> "The privilege against self-incrimination protects the individual from being compelled to incriminate himself in *any* manner. . . . [S]tatements merely intended to be exculpatory by the defendant are often *used to impeach his testimony at trial. These statements are incriminating in any meaningful sense of the word and may not be used without the full warnings and effective waiver required for any other statement."* 384 U.S., at 476–477 (emphasis added).

This language completely disposes of any distinction between statements used on direct as opposed to cross-examination. . . . [I]t is monstrous that courts should aid or abet the law-breaking police officer. . . . The Court today tells the police that they may freely interrogate an accused incommunicado and without counsel and know that although any statement they obtain in violation of *Miranda* can't be used on the State's direct case, it may be introduced if the defendant has the temerity to testify in his own defense. This goes far toward undoing much of the progress made in conforming police methods to the Constitution. I dissent.

RHODE ISLAND v. INNIS,
446 U.S. 291 (1980)

Thomas J. Innis was arrested on the streets of Providence, Rhode Island, shortly after his picture had been identified by a taxicab driver as the person who had robbed him while wielding a sawed-off shotgun. Innis, however, was unarmed when arrested. He was advised of his Miranda *rights. When other police officers arrived at the arrest scene, Innis was twice again told his rights and at that point he stated that he wanted to speak with a lawyer. Innis was then placed in a police car in the company of three officers who were instructed not to question Innis nor intimidate him in any way. While en route to the central police station, two of the officers began conversing between themselves concerning the missing shotgun. One of the officers stated that there were "a lot of handicapped children running around in this area" due to the location nearby of a school for such children and "God forbid one of them might find a weapon with shells and they might hurt themselves." Innis interrupted the conversation, stating that the officers should turn the car around so that he could show them where the gun was located. Upon returning to the scene of the arrest where a search for the shotgun was in progress, Innis was again reminded of his* Miranda *rights, but he replied that although he understood those rights, he "wanted to get the gun out of the way because of the kids in the area in the school." Innis led the police to the shotgun.*

Innis was subsequently tried and convicted, but the Rhode Island Supreme Court set aside the conviction, concluding that Innis had invoked his Miranda *right to counsel and that all custodial interrogation had to cease. The police officers in the car had "interrogated" Innis by way of their "conversation," thereby violating his* Miranda *rights. The key questions before the Supreme Court were how to define an "interrogation" and whether the officers' colloquy in the context in which it occurred constituted forbidden "interrogation."*

Majority votes: 6
Dissenting votes: 3

MR. JUSTICE STEWART delivered the opinion of the Court:. . . .

In the present case, the parties are in agreement that the respondent was fully informed of his *Miranda* rights and that he invoked his *Miranda* right to counsel when he told Captain Leyden that he wished to consult with a lawyer. It is also uncontested that the respondent was "in custody" while being transported to the police station.

The issue, therefore, is whether the respondent was "interrogated" by the police officers in violation of the respondent's undisputed right under *Miranda* to remain silent until he had consulted with a lawyer. In resolving this issue, we first define the term "interrogation" under *Miranda* before turning to a consideration of the facts of this case.

The starting point of defining "interrogation" in this context is, of course, the Court's *Miranda* opinion. There the Court observed that "[b]y custodial interrogation, we mean *questioning* initiated by law enforcement officers after a person has been taken into custody or otherwise deprived of his freedom of action in any significant way." 384

U.S., at 444 (emphasis added). This passage and other references throughout the opinion to "questioning" might suggest that the *Miranda* rules were to apply only to those police interrogation practices that involve express questioning of a defendant while in custody.

We do not, however, construe the *Miranda* opinion so narrowly. The concern of the Court in *Miranda* was that the "interrogation environment" created by the interplay of interrogation and custody would "subjugate the individual to the will of his examiner" and thereby undermine the privilege against compulsory self-incrimination. . . . The Court in *Miranda* also included in its survey of interrogation practices the use of psychological ploys. . . . It is clear . . . that the special procedural safeguards outlined in *Miranda* are required not where a suspect is simply taken into custody, but rather where a suspect in custody is subjected to interrogation. "Interrogation," as conceptualized in the *Miranda* opinion, must reflect a measure of compulsion above and beyond that inherent in custody itself.

We conclude that the *Miranda* safeguards come into play whenever a person in custody is subjected to either express questioning or its functional equivalent. That is to say, the term "interrogation" under *Miranda* refers not only to express questioning, but also to any words or actions on the part of the police (other than those normally attendant to arrest and custody) that the police should know are reasonably likely to elicit an incriminating response from the suspect. The latter portion of this definition focuses primarily upon the perceptions of the suspect, rather than the intent of the police. This focus reflects the fact that the *Miranda* safeguards were designed to vest a suspect in custody with an added measure of protection against coercive police practices, without regard to objective proof of the underlying intent of the police. A practice that the police should know is reasonably likely to evoke an incriminating response from a suspect thus amounts to interrogation. But, since the police surely cannot be held accountable for the unforeseeable results of their words or actions, the definition of interrogation can extend only to words or actions on the part of police officers that they *should have known* were reasonably likely to elicit an incriminating response.

Turning to the facts of the present case, we conclude that the respondent was not "interrogated" within the meaning of *Miranda*. . . .

The case . . . boils down to whether, in the context of a brief conversation, the officers should have known that the respondent would suddenly be moved to make a self-incriminating response. Given the fact that the entire conversation appears to have consisted of no more than a few off-hand remarks, we cannot say that the officers should have known that it was reasonably likely that Innis would so respond. This is not a case where the police carried on a lengthy harangue in the presence of the suspect. Nor does the record support the respondent's contention that, under the circumstances, the officers' comments were particularly "evocative." It is our view, therefore, that the respondent was not subjected by the police to words or actions that the police should have known were reasonably likely to elicit an incriminating response from him.

The Rhode Island Supreme Court erred, in short, in equating "subtle compulsion" with interrogation. That the officers' comments struck a responsive chord is readily apparent. Thus, it may be said, as the Rhode Island Supreme Court did say, that the respondent was subjected to "subtle compulsion." But that is not the end of the inquiry. It must also be established that a suspect's incriminating response was the product of words or actions on the part of the police that they should have known were reasonably likely to elicit an incriminating response. This was not established in the present case.

For the reasons stated, the judgment of the Supreme Court of Rhode Island is vacated, and the case is remanded to that court for further proceedings not inconsistent with this opinion.

It is so ordered.

MR. JUSTICE WHITE, concurring: [omitted]
MR. CHIEF JUSTICE BURGER, concurring in the judgment: [omitted]
MR. JUSTICE MARSHALL, with whom MR. JUSTICE BRENNAN joins, dissenting:

I am substantially in agreement with the Court's definition of "interrogation" within the meaning of *Miranda* v. *Arizona*. . . . [T]he Court requires an objective inquiry into the likely effect of police conduct on a typical individual, taking into account any special susceptibility of the suspect to certain kinds of pressure of which the police know or have reason to know.

I am utterly at a loss, however, to understand how this objective standard as applied to the facts before us can rationally lead to the conclusion that there was no interrogation. Innis was arrested at 4:30 A.M., handcuffed, searched, advised of his rights, and placed in the back seat of a patrol car. Within a short time he had been twice more advised of his rights and driven away in a four door sedan

with three police officers. Two officers sat in the front seat and one sat beside Innis in the back seat. Since the car traveled no more than a mile before Innis agreed to point out the location of the murder weapon, Officer Gleckman must have begun almost immediately to talk about the search for the shotgun.

The Court attempts to characterize Gleckman's statements as "no more than a few off-hand remarks" which could not reasonably have been expected to elicit a response. If the statements had been addressed to petitioner, it would be impossible to draw such a conclusion. The simple message of the "talking back and forth" between Gleckman and McKenna was that they had to find the shotgun to avert a child's death.

One can scarcely imagine a stronger appeal to the conscience of a suspect—any suspect—than the assertion that if the weapon is not found an innocent person will be hurt or killed. And not just any innocent person, but an innocent child—a little girl—a helpless, handicapped little girl on her way to school. The notion that such an appeal could not be expected to have any effect unless the suspect were known to have some special interest in handicapped children verges on the ludicrous. As a matter of fact, the appeal to a suspect to confess for the sake of others, to "display some evidence of decency and honor," is a classic interrogation technique. . . .
MR. JUSTICE STEVENS, dissenting:. . . .

As the Court recognizes, *Miranda* v. *Arizona* makes it clear that, once respondent requested an attorney, he had an absolute right to have any type of interrogation cease until an attorney was present. As it also recognizes, Miranda requires that the term "interrogation" be broadly construed to include "either express questioning or its functional equivalent." In my view any statement that would normally be understood by the average listener as calling for a response is the functional equivalent of a direct question, whether or not it is punctuated by a question mark. The Court, however, takes a much narrower view. It holds that police conduct is not the "functional equivalent" of direct questioning unless the police should have known that what they were saying or doing was likely to elicit an incriminating response from the suspect. This holding represents a plain departure from the principles set forth in *Miranda*. . . .

NEW YORK v. QUARLES,
467 U.S. 649 (1984)

Benjamin Quarles was charged in a New York state court with criminal possession of a weapon. On September 11, 1980, shortly after midnight, a woman approached two police officers and told them that she had just been raped. She described her assailant and noted that the man had just entered a nearby supermarket and was carrying a gun. While one of the officers radioed for assistance, the other, Officer Kraft, entered the store and spotted Quarles, who matched the description given by the woman. Upon seeing Officer Kraft, Quarles ran toward the rear of the store. Kraft pursued Quarles, ordered him to stop and to put his hands over his head. Kraft frisked Quarles and discovered an empty shoulder holster. After handcuffing Quarles, Kraft asked where the gun was. Quarles nodded toward some empty cartons and responded, that "the gun is over there." Officer Kraft then retrieved the gun from one of the cartons, formally arrested Quarles, and read him his Miranda *rights. Quarles said he would answer questions without an attorney being present and admitted that he owned the gun. Quarles was originally charged with rape and with criminal possession of a weapon. The rape charge was dropped for reasons not revealed in the record. At the trial on the weapons charge the trial judge excluded Quarles' initial statement "the gun is over there" and the gun itself because Quarles had not yet been given the* Miranda *warnings. The trial judge excluded Quarles' other statements as evidence tainted by the* Miranda *violation. Both the state intermediate- and highest-level appellate courts affirmed and the State of New York petitioned for a writ of certiorari from the United States Supreme Court which was granted.*

Majority votes: 6 (including 1 concurrence in part)
Dissenting votes: 3

JUSTICE REHNQUIST delivered the opinion of the Court:

Respondent Benjamin Quarles was charged in the New York trial court with criminal possession of a weapon. The trial court suppressed the gun in question, and a statement made by respondent, because the statement was obtained by police before they read respondent his "*Miranda* rights." That ruling was affirmed on appeal through the New York Court of Appeals. We granted certiorari. We conclude that under the circumstances involved in this case, overriding considerations of public safety justify the officer's failure to provide *Miranda* warnings before he asked questions devoted to locating the abandoned weapon. . . .

We hold that . . . there is a "public safety" exception to the requirement that *Miranda* warnings be given before a suspect's answers may be admitted

into evidence, and that the availability of that exception does not depend upon the motivation of the individual officers involved. In a kaleidoscopic situation such as the one confronting these officers, where spontaneity rather than adherence to a police manual is necessarily the order of the day, the application of the exception which we recognize today should not be made to depend on *post hoc* findings at a suppression hearing concerning the subjective motivation of the arresting officer. Undoubtedly most police officers, if placed in Officer Kraft's position, would act out of a host of different, instinctive, and largely unverifiable motives—their own safety, the safety of others, and perhaps as well the desire to obtain incriminating evidence from the suspect.

Whatever the motivation of individual officers in such a situation, we do not believe that the doctrinal underpinnings of *Miranda* require that it be applied in all its rigor to a situation in which police officers ask questions reasonably prompted by a concern for the public safety. The *Miranda* decision was based in large part on this Court's view that the warnings which it required police to give to suspects in custody would fall victim to constitutionally impermissible practices of police interrogation in the presumptively coercive environment of the station house. . . .

The police in this case, in the very act of apprehending a suspect, were confronted with the immediate necessity of ascertaining the whereabouts of a gun which they had every reason to believe the suspect had just removed from his empty holster and discarded in the supermarket. So long as the gun was concealed somewhere in the supermarket, with its actual whereabouts unknown, it obviously posed more than one danger to the public safety: an accomplice might make use of it, a customer or employee might later come upon it.

In such a situation, if the police are required to recite the familiar *Miranda* warnings before asking the whereabouts of the gun, suspects in Quarles' position might well be deterred from responding. Procedural safeguards which deter a suspect from responding were deemed acceptable in *Miranda* in order to protect the Fifth Amendment privilege; when the primary social cost of those added protections is the possibility of fewer convictions, the *Miranda* majority was willing to bear that cost. Here, had *Miranda* warnings deterred Quarles from responding to Officer Kraft's question about the whereabouts of the gun, the cost would have been something more than merely the failure to obtain evidence useful in convicting Quarles. Officer Kraft needed an answer to his question not simply to make his case against Quarles but to insure that further danger to the public did not result from the concealment of the gun in a public area.

We conclude that the need for answers to questions in a situation posing a threat to the public safety outweighs the need for the prophylactic rule protecting the Fifth Amendment's privilege against self-incrimination. We decline to place officers such as Officer Kraft in the untenable position of having to consider, often in a matter of seconds, whether it best serves society for them to ask the necessary questions without the *Miranda* warnings and render whatever probative evidence they uncover inadmissible, or for them to give the warnings in order to preserve the admissibility of evidence they might uncover but possibly damage or destroy their ability to obtain that evidence and neutralize the volatile situation confronting them.

In recognizing a narrow exception to the *Miranda* rule in this case, we acknowledge that to some degree we lessen the desirable clarity of that rule. . . . The exception will not be difficult for police officers to apply because in each case it will be circumscribed by the exigency which justifies it. We think police officers can and will distinguish almost instinctively between questions necessary to secure their own safety or the safety of the public and questions designed solely to elicit testimonial evidence from a suspect.

The facts of this case clearly demonstrate that distinction and an officer's ability to recognize it. Officer Kraft asked only the question necessary to locate the missing gun before advising respondent of his rights. It was only after securing the loaded revolver and giving the warnings that he continued with investigatory questions about the ownership and place of purchase of the gun. The exception which we recognize today, far from complicating the thought processes and the on-the-scene judgments of police officers, will simply free them to follow their legitimate instincts when confronting situations presenting a danger to the public safety.

We hold that the Court of Appeals in this case erred in excluding the statement, "the gun is over there," and the gun because of the officer's failure to read respondent his *Miranda* rights before attempting to locate the weapon. Accordingly we hold that it also erred in excluding the subsequent statements as illegal fruits of a *Miranda* violation. We therefore reverse and remand for further proceedings not inconsistent with this opinion.

It is so ordered.

JUSTICE O'CONNOR, concurring in part in the judgment and dissenting in part:

In *Miranda* v. *Arizona,* the Court held unconstitutional, because inherently compelled, the admission of statements derived from in-custody questioning not preceded by an explanation of the privilege against self-incrimination and the consequences of foregoing it. Today, the Court concludes that overriding considerations of public safety justify the admission of evidence—oral statements and a gun—secured without the benefit of such warnings. In so holding, the Court acknowledges that it is departing from prior precedent and that it is "lessen[ing] the desirable clarity of [the *Miranda*] rule." Were the Court writing from a clean slate, I could agree with its holding. But *Miranda* is now the law and, in my view, the Court has not provided sufficient justification for departing from it or for blurring its now clear strictures. Accordingly, I would require suppression of the initial statement taken from respondent in this case. On the other hand, nothing in *Miranda* or the privilege itself requires exclusion of nontestimonial evidence derived from informal custodial interrogation, and I therefore agree with the Court that admission of the gun in evidence is proper. . . .

JUSTICE MARSHALL, with whom JUSTICE BRENNAN and JUSTICE STEVENS join, dissenting:

The police in this case arrested a man suspected of possessing a firearm in violation of New York law. Once the suspect was in custody and found to be unarmed, the arresting officer initiated an interrogation. Without being advised of his right not to respond, the suspect incriminated himself by locating the gun. The majority concludes that the State may rely on this incriminating statement to convict the suspect of possessing a weapon. I disagree. The arresting officers had no legitimate reason to interrogate the suspect without advising him of his rights to remain silent and to obtain assistance of counsel. By finding on these facts justification for unconsented interrogation, the majority abandons the clear guidelines enunciated in *Miranda* v. *Arizona,* and condemns the American judiciary to a new era of *post hoc* inquiry into the propriety of custodial interrogations. More significantly and in direct conflict with this Court's long-standing interpretation of the Fifth Amendment, the majority has endorsed the introduction of coerced self-incriminating statements in criminal prosecutions. I dissent.

The majority's entire analysis rests on the factual assumption that the public was at risk during Quarles' interrogation. This assumption is completely in conflict with the facts as found by New York's highest court. . . .

Earlier this Term, the four members of the majority joined an opinion stating: "[Q]uestions of historical fact . . . must be determined, in the first instance, by state courts and deferred to, in the absence of 'convincing evidence' to the contrary, by the federal courts.'' In this case, there was convincing, indeed almost overwhelming, evidence to support the New York court's conclusion that Quarles' hidden weapon did not pose a risk either to the arresting officers or to the public. The majority ignores this evidence and sets aside the factual findings of the New York Court of Appeals. More cynical observers might well conclude that a state court's findings of fact "deserve[d] a 'high measure of deference,' '' only when deference works against the interests of a criminal defendant. . . .

In fashioning its "public-safety" exception to *Miranda,* the majority makes no attempt to deal with the constitutional presumption established by that case. The majority does not argue that police questioning about issues of public safety is any less coercive than custodial interrogations into other matters. The majority's only contention is that police officers could more easily protect the public if *Miranda* did not apply to custodial interrogations concerning the public's safety. But *Miranda* was not a decision about public safety; it was a decision about coerced confessions. Without establishing that interrogations concerning the public's safety are less likely to be coercive than other interrogations, the majority cannot endorse the "public-safety" exception and remain faithful to the logic of *Miranda* v. *Arizona.* . . .

The irony of the majority's decision is that the public's safety can be perfectly well protected without abridging the Fifth Amendment. If a bomb is about to explode or the public is otherwise imminently imperiled, the police are free to interrogate suspects without advising them of their constitutional rights. Such unconsented questioning may take place not only when police officers act on instinct but also when higher faculties lead them to believe that advising a suspect of his constitutional rights mights decrease the likelihood that the suspect would reveal life-saving information. If trickery is necessary to protect the public, then the police may trick a suspect into confessing. While the Fourteenth Amendment sets limits on such behavior, nothing in the Fifth Amendment or our decision in *Miranda* v. *Arizona* proscribes this sort of emergency questioning. All the Fifth Amendment forbids is the introduction of coerced statements at trial. . . .

The Fifth Amendment prohibits compelled self-incrimination. As the Court has explained on numerous occasions, this prohibition is the mainstay of our adversarial system of criminal justice. Not only does it protect us against the inherent unreliability of compelled testimony, but it also ensures that criminal investigations will be conducted with integrity and that the judiciary will avoid the taint of official lawlessness. The policies underlying the Fifth Amendment's privilege against self-incrimination are not diminished simply because testimony is compelled to protect the public's safety. The majority should not be permitted to elude the Amendment's absolute prohibition simply by calculating special costs that arise when the public's safety is at issue. Indeed, were constitutional adjudication always conducted in such an *ad hoc* manner, the Bill of Rights would be a most unreliable protector of individual liberties.

Having determined that the Fifth Amendment renders inadmissible Quarles' response to Officer Kraft's questioning, I have no doubt that our precedents require that the gun discovered as a direct result of Quarles' statement must be presumed inadmissible as well. The gun was the direct product of a coercive custodial interrogation. . . . When they ruled on the issue, the New York courts were entirely correct in deciding that Quarles' gun was the tainted fruit of a nonconsensual interrogation and therefore was inadmissible under our precedents.

However, since the New York Court of Appeals issued its opinion, the scope of the . . . doctrine has changed. . . . In its briefs before this Court and before the New York courts, petitioner has argued that the "inevitable-discovery" rule, if applied to this case, would permit the admission of Quarles' gun. Although I have not joined the Court's opinion in *Nix* v. *Williams* (1984) and although I am not wholly persuaded that New York law would permit the application of the "inevitable-discovery" rule to this case, I believe that the proper disposition of the matter is to vacate the order of the New York Court of Appeals to the extent that it suppressed Quarles' gun and remand the matter to the New York Court of Appeals for further consideration in light of *Nix* v. *Williams.*

Accordingly, I would affirm the order of the Court of Appeals to the extent that it found Quarles' testimony inadmissible under the Fifth Amendment, would vacate the order to the extent that it suppressed Quarles' gun, and would remand the matter for reconsideration in light of *Nix* v. *Williams.*

Chapter

17

Sixth and Eighth Amendment Issues

SIXTH AMENDMENT RIGHTS

The Sixth Amendment contains numerous guarantees including "the right to a speedy and public trial, by an impartial jury of the State and district wherein the crime shall have been committed"; "to be informed of the nature and cause of the accusation; to be confronted with the witnesses against him; to have compulsory process for obtaining witnesses in his favor, and to have the Assistance of Counsel for his defense." These are the core rights of what constitutes a fair trial and they have been involved in cases at both the federal and state levels.

The most famous nineteenth-century decision concerning the Sixth Amendment in which the federal government was concerned was **Ex Parte Milligan,** which, as will be recalled from the discussion in Chapter 2, stemmed out of the Civil War and had implications for military reconstruction. Sixth Amendment guarantees, however, were not

made applicable to the states along the lines of the reasoning contained in **Hurtado** v. **California** (chap. 16).

During the first decade of the twentieth century, the Court began moving away from the restrictive *Hurtado* doctrine in that it was willing to consider claims in appeals from the states that were based on the criminal procedural guarantees in the Bill of Rights. During the second decade, however, that movement stopped, and the Court refused to consider even the basic fairness of a state trial in a habeas corpus proceeding where the question of the fairness of the trial had already been litigated in the state court—but there was good reason to believe that prejudice permeated the proceedings (*Frank* v. *Mangum,* 237 U.S. 309 [1915]). Not until *Moore* v. *Dempsey,* 261 U.S. 86 (1923), in 1923 did the Court begin to consider favorably the basic fairness of a state trial in terms of the Fourteenth Amendment's due process requirement. The Court in *Tumey* v. *Ohio,* 273 U.S. 510 (1927), again found that basic procedural fairness was absent. *Tumey* concerned an Ohio scheme that permitted Ohio mayors to try prohibition act offenders. If a conviction was obtained, the defendant was required to pay court fees out of which the mayor received his salary. This, said the Court, violated due process of law. Finally, with the 1932 case of **Powell** v. **Alabama** the Court incorporated a specific procedural right of the Bill of Rights within the Fourteenth Amendment's due process clause. *Norris* v. *Alabama* 294 U.S. 587 (1935), saw the Court assert the right to a trial by a jury selected by a process that did not exclude black people. In *Brown* v. *Mississippi,* 297 U.S. 278 (1936), the Court threw out a confession based on physical coercion as inconsistent with due process.

The Vinson Court, aside from incorporating the Fourth Amendment search and seizure guarantee (but not the exclusionary rule), incorporated the public trial guarantee in 1948 in *In Re Oliver,* 333 U.S. 257. It was the Warren Court in the 1960s that incorporated all but two of the remaining criminal procedural guarantees of the Bill of Rights. The guarantees that were not incorporated and remain unincorporated today are the Fifth Amendment right not to be brought to trial on a felony charge unless first indicted by a grand jury and the Eighth Amendment guarantee against excessive bail and fines. All the Sixth Amendment guarantees are incorporated. The decisions in which various Sixth Amendment rights were incorporated by the Warren Court include *Pointer* v. *Texas,* 380 U.S. 400 (1965) [the right to confront adverse witnesses]; *Parker* v. *Gladden,* 385 U.S. 363 (1966) [the right to a trial by a jury that is impartial]; *Washington* v. *Texas,* 388 U.S. 14 (1967) [the right to have compulsory process for obtaining favorable witnesses]; *Klopfer* v. *North Carolina,* 386 U.S. 213 (1967) [the right to a speedy trial]; and *Duncan* v. *Louisiana,* 391 U.S. 145 (1968) [the right to a trial by jury in a criminal case]. Of course, **Gideon** v. **Wainwright** in

1963 was a landmark right-to-counsel case (and we look at this right shortly). The Warren Court was also responsible for extending basic criminal procedural guarantees (including certain Sixth Amendment rights) to juveniles in the case of **In Re Gault.** Since the right to counsel, of all the Sixth Amendment guarantees, has generated the most litigation, we briefly turn our attention to that right.

It is significant that the first of the specific criminal procedural guarantees made applicable to the states was the right to counsel. Even the conservative majority, in 1932, agreed that without the right to assistance of one's own lawyer at a criminal trial, fundamental unfairness can result. Our system of justice is an adversarial one, and denial of counsel necessarily handicaps the party so denied. In this landmark 1932 case, *Powell* v. *Alabama,* the illiterate, poor, black teenage defendants in Scottsboro, Alabama, were charged with the rape of two white girls, a capital crime (punishable by death). They could not afford to hire a lawyer. The Court not only ruled that the Sixth Amendment counsel guarantee, as applied to the states through the Fourteenth Amendment, requires that one has the right to assistance of a privately retained lawyer, but also that defendants such as these, on trial with their lives at stake, are entitled to a lawyer provided free of charge by the state. This was, indeed, a major breakthrough. The Court, however, in 1942, in *Betts* v. *Brady,* 316 U.S. 455, rejected the argument that *all* poor criminal defendants (not just those on trial for capital offenses) were entitled to a court-appointed lawyer free of charge. The Court reasoned that as long as the trial is a fair one, the state need not be financially burdened by paying lawyers to represent poor criminal defendants. However, this decision was inconsistent with the rationale of the *Powell* decision. During the Vinson Court, in 6 out of 12 counsel cases the Court ruled that the lack of counsel resulted in unfair trials. During the course of the Warren Court until

Gideon v. *Wainwright,* not once did the Court affirm a felony conviction of an indigent tried without counsel. Finally in *Gideon* the Court acted and explicitly overturned *Betts* v. *Brady.*

Gideon v. *Wainwright* established the right under the Sixth and Fourteenth Amendments of any state criminal defendant accused of having committed a felony to a free court-appointed lawyer. In a companion case, *Douglas* v. *California,* 372 U.S. 353, the Court also ruled that indigents are entitled to a free lawyer, paid for by the state, through the first appeal of a criminal conviction. The Warren Court, in 1967, held in *Mempa* v. *Rhay,* 389 U.S. 128, that an indigent state criminal defendant was entitled to a court-appointed lawyer at probation revocation proceedings. In two other 1967 decisions, *United States* v. *Wade,* 388 U.S. 218, and *Gilbert* v. *California,* 388 U.S. 263, the Court ruled that federal and state officials must allow an attorney to be present when the defendant is placed in a pretrial lineup for purposes of eyewitness identification.

The Burger and Rehnquist Courts' record in the right-to-counsel area has been one in which generous readings of the guarantee are counterbalanced by narrow, conservative ones. On the narrow side, the Court undermined the *Wade* and *Gilbert* precedents in *Kirby* v. *Illinois,* 406 U.S. 682 (1972), when it professed to draw a distinction between pre- and post-indictment lineups. The Court in *Kirby* ruled that if the lineup occurs *before* the indictment has been handed down, there is no right to have an attorney present. But even this dubious distinction was bypassed the following year in *United States* v. *Ashe,* 413 U.S. 300, when the Court ruled that the Sixth Amendment does not grant an accused the right to have counsel present when the government conducts a postindictment photographic lineup (where the witness is asked to look at photographs for the purpose of identifying the offender). In two 5–4 decisions (*Caplin & Drysdale Chartered* v. *U.S.,* 109 S.

Ct. 2646 [1989] and *U.S.* v. *Monsanto,* 109 S. Ct. 2657 [1989]), the Court upheld provisions of the federal drug forfeiture statute that authorizes district courts to enter pretrial orders freezing assets and forfeiting property. By so doing, the Court rejected the claims of defendants that without access to their assets and property their Sixth Amendment right to counsel was impermissibly burdened because they could not pay attorney fees. The Court, however, took a more liberal view of the right to counsel in *United States* v. *Henry,* 447 U.S. 264 (1980), ruling that the government's use of the testimony of a paid informer in the same cellblock as Billy Gale Henry violated Henry's right to the assistance of counsel. Although the informer had been instructed not to initiate a conversation with Henry or to ask direct questions, the Court ruled that the government had intentionally created a situation likely to induce the incriminating admissions. The Court, however, seemed to backtrack on this in the 1986 decision of *Kuhlmann* v. *Wilson,* 477 U.S. 436, when it ruled that prosecutors may use incriminating statements made by indicted defendants to informers planted in the same cell as long as the informers did nothing beyond merely listening and took no action to elicit the incriminating remarks. The Court, however, was more liberal in its ruling in *Coleman* v. *Alabama,* 399 U.S. 1 (1970) that indigents are entitled to a court-appointed lawyer at the preliminary hearing at which time the state introduces the evidence and the judge determines whether it is sufficient to hold the accused for prosecution. Another liberal ruling was in 1986 that a convicted defendant is entitled to a federal habeas corpus hearing to review the claim that his right to effective assistance of counsel was violated because his lawyer failed to file in time a motion at the trial to exclude a key piece of evidence that was illegally obtained in violation of the Fourth Amendment. The decision was *Kimmelman* v. *Morrison,* 477 U.S. 365. The Sixth Amendment is also violated by a psychiatric examination of a defendant without notice to the lawyer and warning to the defendant that the testimony of the psychiatrist could be used in a capital sentencing proceeding on the issue of future dangerousness (see *Satterwhite* v. *Texas,* 486 U.S. 249 [1988], and *Powell* v. *Texas,* 109 S.Ct. 3146 [1989]). The Court also took a liberal view in *Michigan* v. *Jackson,* 475 U.S. 625 (1986), by ruling that when an indigent criminal defendant asks for the appointment of counsel at arraignment, the police may not subsequently initiate questioning. Any statement made by the defendant and any waiver of rights for that police-initiated interrogation are both invalid as violating the Sixth Amendment. However, the Court subsequently ruled in 1990 that such illegally obtained statements may be introduced at the trial to impeach the defendant's false or inconsistent testimony (*Michigan* v. *Harvey,* 110 S.Ct. 1176 [1990]).

As for the trial itself, the Court in **Argersinger** v. **Hamlin** generously extended the right of a poor person to a free lawyer when accused of a *misdemeanor* punishable by a jail sentence (remember *Gideon* applied only to felonies). But the Court later made clear that the state need not appoint a free lawyer for an indigent accused of a misdemeanor if, in fact, the defendant is not sentenced to jail (see *Scott* v. *Illinois,* 440 U.S. 367 [1979]). Thus, any judge refusing to appoint counsel for an indigent defendant in a misdemeanor trial is relinquishing discretion to impose a jail sentence as punishment. By so ruling, the Court majority ignored the potential negative consequences of a misdemeanor conviction (other than imprisonment) such as a damaged reputation or damage to future employment prospects. But the Court did rule, in the 1980 decision *Baldasar* v. *Illinois,* 446 U.S. 222, that a previous uncounseled misdemeanor conviction may not be used to enhance the penalty of a subsequent counseled misdemeanor conviction that then results in a prison term.

The Court also made it clear that the right to free counsel is limited to the trial itself and to those appeals that are provided by the state as a matter of right, but not such appeals as may be available at the discretion of the reviewing court. The states, said the Court in *Ross* v. *Moffitt,* 417 U.S. 600 (1974), are under no constitutional obligation to furnish indigent defendants with lawyers to pursue appeals to the highest state court, if that court has discretion to refuse to hear the appeal, or to the United States Supreme Court. Neither are they obliged to provide a lawyer for post-conviction proceedings. That is, once a conviction has gone through the appellate process and has become final, there is no right to a court-appointed lawyer for new attempts to overturn the conviction (*Pennsylvania* v. *Finley,* 481 U.S. 551 [1987]). Nor are the states obliged to provide a poor parent with free counsel at a court proceeding involving an action by the state to assume legal custody of that indigent's child. In this 1981 decision, *Lassiter* v. *Department of Social Services of Durham County, North Carolina,* 452 U.S. 18, the Court emphasized that the states are *required* to provide a poor person with the assistance of counsel *only* when the indigent faces loss of physical liberty. Even when an indigent criminal defendant is entitled to a court-appointed lawyer, there is no Sixth Amendment guarantee of a meaningful relationship between the accused and counsel (*Morris* v. *Slappy,* 461 U.S. 1 [1983]). Court-appointed as well as privately retained lawyers do not deny their clients the right to assistance of counsel by refusing to cooperate in presenting perjured testimony by the accused. Indeed, said the Court in the unanimous ruling in *Nix* v. *Whiteside,* 475 U.S. 157 (1986), counsel is precluded from taking steps or in any way assisting the client in presenting false evidence or otherwise violating the law. Furthermore, defense counsel assigned to handle the appeal from a criminal conviction does not have a constitutional obligation to raise every nonfrivolous issue requested by the defendant

(*Jones* v. *Barnes,* 463 U.S. 745 [1983]). However, the criminal defendant is entitled to effective assistance of counsel on the first appeal as a right (*Evitts* v. *Lucey,* 469 U.S. 387 [1985]).

In *Walters* v. *National Association of Radiation Survivors,* 473 U.S 305 (1985), the Burger Court upheld an act of Congress from the Civil War era which places a $10 maximum fee that may be paid an attorney who represents a veteran before the Veterans Administration for service-connected death or disability. The six-person majority rejected a number of constitutional objections to the statute that were made including the claim that the statute was a denial of the right to counsel of one's choice. In his separate dissent, Justice Stevens bitterly lamented, "The Court does not appreciate the value of individual liberty." Whether this is a too-harsh assessment or an accurate reflection of the Burger Court's jurisprudence in the right-to-counsel area is something students may well wish to consider.

Some additional Sixth Amendment issues that have attracted attention and were considered by the contemporary Court deserve brief mention. First, is the Sixth Amendment guarantee to the accused of a public trial. Recall from chapter 14 that the Court in *Gannett Co., Inc.* v. *DePasquale* found that this Sixth Amendment guarantee is for the benefit of the accused and does not grant the public and the media a right of access to pretrial proceedings if both the accused and the prosecution wish them closed. However, the Court subsequently in **Richmond Newspapers, Inc.** v. **Virginia** (chap. 14) found that the public and the press have a First Amendment right of access to the trial itself. In still another case, the Court found no inherent denial of a fair trial (or due process) by a state law permitting trial judges at their discretion and under their supervision to allow radio, television, and photographers into the courtroom during a trial (*Chandler* v. *Florida,* 449 U.S. 560 [1981]).

Another Sixth Amendment issue concerns the nature of trial by jury. Traditionally, the jury consisted of 12 persons who could deliver a verdict only if they were unanimous. However, the Court ruled in *Williams* v. *Florida,* 399 U.S. 78 (1970), that six-person juries as provided by Florida law in all but capital cases met the Sixth Amendment trial by jury requirement. And two years later in *Apodaca* v. *Oregon,* 406 U.S. 404, and *Johnson* v. *Louisiana,* 406 U.S. 356, the Court approved nonunanimous jury verdicts of 10 to 2 and 9 to 3 respectively. But the Court refused to approve a nonunanimous jury verdict of 5 to 1 in the case of *Burch* v. *Louisiana,* 441 U.S. 130 (1979), as well as a jury with only 5 members in *Ballew* v. *Georgia,* 435 U.S. 223 (1978). The Court, however, ruled in *Baldwin* v. *New York,* 399 U.S. 66 (1970), that the jury trial guarantee of the Sixth Amendment, applicable to the states through the Fourteenth Amendment, included the right to trial by jury for misdemeanors punishable by a jail sentence of at least six months. But the states are under no Sixth Amendment obligation to provide a trial by jury for petty crimes such as driving under the influence for which the maximum jail sentence is six months (*Blanton* v. *City of North Las Vegas, Nevada,* 109 S. Ct. 1289 [1989]). Also, juveniles processed by the juvenile courts are not entitled to trial by jury (see *McKeiver* v. *Pennsylvania,* 403 U.S. 528 [1971]).

The Sixth Amendment right to a jury trial is, more precisely, the right to an *impartial* jury, and the issue of how to obtain an impartial jury has been before the Court. For example, the following decisions in which this issue was raised involved criminal defendants convicted by juries and sentenced to death. In *Turner* v. *Murray,* 476 U.S. 28 (1986), the Court ruled that a defendant accused of an interracial capital crime is entitled to have prospective jurors informed of the victim's race and questioned to determine if they are racially biased. In *Lockhart* v. *McCree,* 476

U.S. 162 (1986), however, a majority of the Court ruled that in trials of capital offenses the guarantee of an impartial jury is not violated by removal for cause of prospective jurors opposed to the death penalty. This is so even when there is a two-stage jury process—the determination of guilt and then the death penalty determination. Potential jurors who express reservations about the death penalty may be removed for cause from the guilt phase of a capital trial, and this does not violate the impartial jury requirement of the Sixth Amendment. However, when there is impermissible exclusion of a juror in a capital case, the Court has ruled that this can never be treated as harmless error. The Court in *Gray* v. *Mississippi*, 481 U.S. 648 (1987), reiterated that the right to an impartial jury is basic to a fair trial.

The Sixth Amendment right of the accused to confront adverse witnesses was involved in several Rehnquist Court decisions. In *Kentucky* v. *Stincer*, 482 U.S. 730 (1987), the Court found no Sixth Amendment violation had occurred by excluding Sergio Stincer from a hearing to determine the competency-to-testify of two young children he was accused of (and later convicted of) sodomizing. But in *Coy* v. *Iowa*, 487 U.S. 1012 (1988), the Court found a violation of the right to confront witnesses when a screen had been placed between the defendant, John Coy, and the two thirteen-year-old girls he was accused of (and later convicted of) sexually assaulting. Two years later, in **Maryland** v. **Craig** (reprinted at the end of this book), the Court made it clear that persons charged with child abuse do not have an absolute right to a face-to-face confrontation with their child accusers. The Court approved the use of testimony by the children over one-way, closed-circuit television. But in *Idaho* v. *Wright*, 110 S.Ct. 3139 (1990), the Court found for the accused child-abuse defendant when the alleged victim did not testify but instead a doctor who had interviewed the child testified what the child had revealed.

Also, in *Olden* v. *Kentucky*, 109 S.Ct. 480 (1988), the Court ruled that the trial court's refusal to allow the defendant to impeach the rape victim's testimony by introducing evidence supporting a motive to lie deprived the defendant of this Sixth Amendment right.

EIGHTH AMENDMENT RIGHTS

The Eighth Amendment guarantees that "excessive bail shall not be required, nor excessive fines imposed, nor cruel and unusual punishment inflicted." Only the cruel and unusual punishment guarantee is imposed on the states through the Fourteenth Amendment, and this, like so many other guarantees in the Bill of Rights, came about through a decision of the Warren Court.

Because the Eighth Amendment guarantee against excessive bail does not apply to the states, state judges may impose excessive bail as a form of preventive detention (unless prevented by their state constitutions). That is, a judge may want to keep the accused incarcerated until tried because the judge believes the suspect to be dangerous. The judge therefore sets bail at such a level that it cannot be posted. More recently, Congress, in 1984, enacted the Bail Reform Act that permits federal judges to refuse to set bail and to preventively detain suspects for whom certain objective criteria would determine that they pose a potential menace to the community. While this is a more straightforward approach rather than using high bail to preventively detain, there are serious constitutional issues. These issues were addressed in **U.S.** v. **Salerno.** This decision upholding preventive detention has serious implications for those who are innocent. If the preventively detained individual is subsequently acquitted or the charges dropped, then a grave injustice will have been committed. This is all the more important because the Burger Court in *Bell* v. *Wolfish*, 441 U.S. 520 (1979), established that persons incarcerated because they cannot afford bail or the bail bond premium are subject to such prison practices, rules, and regulations as strip searches including inspection of body cavities after contact visits with outsiders, no packages or books from private parties including family, placement of two persons in a cell meant for one, surprise searches of cells, and so forth.

The Eighth Amendment guarantee against excessive fines was raised in an important civil suit decided by the Rehnquist Court. In a private antitrust suit, the jury awarded $6 million in punitive damages that the federal district court imposed. The antitrust defendant argued that such an amount of money was an excessive fine in violation of the Eighth Amendment. The Court, however, in *Browning-Ferris Industries* v. *Kelco Disposal Inc.*, 109 S. Ct. 2909 (1989), ruled that the excessive fine guarantee does not apply to awards of punitive damages in cases between private parties.

The cruel and unusual punishment guarantee has primarily, but not exclusively, been centered on the death penalty. The Vinson Court, in the 1947 case of *Louisiana ex rel Francis* v. *Resweber*, 329 U.S. 459, was asked to apply the cruel and unusual punishment guarantee to the state of Louisiana in a bizarre set of circumstances. What happened was that 17-year-old Willie Francis was scheduled to be executed by way of the electric chair, but when the procedure was underway the machine malfunctioned and Francis was shocked but not killed. The state sought again to electrocute Francis at a later date. His lawyers argued, in vain, that to subject Francis to a second electrocution was cruel and unusual punishment. The Vinson Court refused to incorporate the guarantee and did not consider a second electrocution to be cruel and unusual. Interestingly, when the guarantee *was* incorporated, it was not done so in the context of the death penalty. Rather, it was incorporated in a case that involved the conviction of a drug addict for violating the California law that made it a crime to *be* an addict. The Warren

Court ruled in *Robinson* v. *California,* 370 U.S. 660 (1962), that the cruel and unusual punishment guarantee was incorporated by the Fourteenth Amendment and that the challenged California statute violated that guarantee by imposing a punishment on a person merely for having an illness.

It was the Burger Court that confronted the issue of whether the death penalty, as imposed throughout the country, constituted cruel and unusual punishment. At the time the Court first considered the issue, there were relatively few death sentences pronounced by judges, and in practice, no one had been executed for at least several years, largely because of the Warren Court's liberalization of criminal procedures that gave rise to a variety of legal actions from death row. The first death penalty decision of the Court was in the 1972 decision of *Furman* v. *Georgia,* 408 U.S. 238. The justices ruled, in a cacophony of opinions, that at the very least, the capricious and arbitrary manner in which the death sentence was imposed and the lack of uniform nation–wide standards for its imposition constituted cruel and unusual punishment. But four years later, in a series of five cases, **The Death Penalty Cases of 1976,** the Court ruled that the death penalty in and of itself did not constitute cruel and unusual punishment. The majority were responding to a variety of death penalty statutes that had been enacted after the *Furman* decision. The Court suggested that mandatory death penalty statutes that did not consider mitigating circumstances were not constitutional but those that did were. In subsequent death penalty decisions the Court has clarified its death penalty policy. The Court ruled in **Coker** v. **Georgia** that the death penalty may not be imposed for the crime of rape. In the subsequent decision of *Enmund* v. *Florida,* 458 U.S. 782 (1982), it emphasized that only a person who kills, intends to kill, or tries to kill, can be punished by the death penalty— but determination of intent may be found by an appellate court if the trial court and the jury did not address this issue (*Cabana* v. *Bullock*, 474 U.S. 376 [1986]). The Rehnquist Court loosened this standard in *Tison* v. *Arizona*, 481 U.S. 137 (1987), when it ruled that the death penalty may be imposed on a defendant who neither killed, intended to kill, or tried to kill but whose participation in a crime in which murder was committed is major and whose mental state is one of reckless indifference to human life. Death penalty statutes must take into account a wide variety of mitigating circumstances, as suggested by *Lockett* v. *Ohio*, 438 U.S. 586 (1978), and must be precise and not broad and vaguely written or interpreted by state courts (see, for example, *Godfrey* v. *Georgia*, 446 U.S. 420 [1980] and *Maynard* v. *Cartwright*, 486 U.S. 356 [1988]). The Court in *Sumner* v. *Shuman*, 483 U.S. 66 (1987), ruled that a statute imposing a mandatory death penalty on prison inmates convicted of murder while serving a life sentence, without the possibility of parole, violates the Eighth Amendment. Mitigating factors must be taken into account even for hardened prisoners. And a state cannot restrict the mitigating circumstances to those only found by a unanimous jury. The requirement of unanimity impermissibly limited the jurors' consideration of mitigating evidence in violation of the Eighth Amendment (*McKoy* v. *North Carolina*, 110 S.Ct. 1227 [1990]. But a state appellate court can uphold a death sentence based in part on an invalid or improperly defined aggravating circumstance by reweighing the aggravating and mitigating evidence (*Clemons* v. *Mississippi*, 110 S.Ct. 1441 [1990]). But state courts are under *no* obligation, the Court made clear in *Pulley* v. *Harris*, 465 U.S. 37 (1984), to review the convictions of others for the same crimes to determine if consistency and fairness in the imposition of the death penalty is taking place. And in **McCleskey** v. **Kemp,** the Court rejected statistical evidence demonstrating the lack of fairness in Georgia's imposition of the death penalty (the death penalty was shown as being imposed more often

on black defendants and killers of white victims than on white defendants and killers of black victims).

The victims' rights movement in recent years has resulted in some states allowing the introduction of a victim impact statement at the sentencing stage of criminal proceedings. The victim or the victim's family give vivid proof of the havoc perpetrated on the lives of innocent people by the convicted criminal. However, the Court in *Booth* v. *Maryland*, 482 U.S. 496 (1987), by a 5–4 vote, struck down the introduction of victim impact statements at the sentencing phase of a capital murder trial. Such information, said the Court, is irrelevant to a capital sentencing decision and creates the risk that the jury may impose the death penalty in an arbitrary and capricious manner. So, too, in *South Carolina* v. *Gathers*, 109 S.Ct. 2207 (1989), a 5–4 vote overturned a death sentence because during the sentencing phase the prosecutor read at length from a religious tract the victim was carrying and commented on the victim's personal qualities that were inferred from the victim's possession of the tract. But new rules of constitutional law that favor those facing the death penalty are not to be retroactively applied, the Court ruled in *Sawyer* v. *Smith*, 110 S.Ct. 2822 (1990). The lower courts were instructed not to grant habeas corpus relief in such cases, which led the four dissenters in the decision to charge that the majority's overriding concern was "speeding defendants . . . to the executioner."

The Court has ruled that, those executed must be sane at the time of execution. It is cruel and unusual punishment to execute a convicted murderer who is so insane at the time of execution that he or she is unaware that the ultimate penalty is about to be inflicted and unknowing of the reason for it. The ruling was in *Ford* v. *Wainwright*, 477 U.S. 399 (1986). However, it is not cruel and unusual punishment to execute a mentally retarded person convicted of a capital offense, the Court ruled in **Penry** v. **Lynaugh.** Similarly, it is not cruel and unusual punishment to impose the death sentence on an individual for a crime committed at 16 or 17 years of age (**Stanford** v. **Kentucky**). But the Court in *Thompson* v. *Oklahoma,* 487 U.S. 815 (1988), refused to allow the execution of an individual for a first degree murder he had committed when he was 15 years old.

The Court has considered claims of a cruel and unusual punishment violation in several non-death penalty cases. In the case of *Ingraham* v. *Wright,* 430 U.S. 651 (1977), the Court determined that corporal punishment of schoolchildren did not constitute cruel and unusual punishment. The Court emphasized that the guarantee applies only to criminal punishments. In **Rummel** v. **Estelle,** the Court found no cruel and unusual punishment in a Texas mandatory life sentence statute applied to a man thrice convicted of fraud-type offenses that added up to a small monetary amount. Following *Rummel,* the Court subsequently upheld as not constituting cruel and unusual punishment a sentence of 40 years' imprisonment and a $20,000 fine imposed on a defendant convicted of possession of a small amount of marijuana (street value of $200) with intent to distribute (the decision was *Hutto* v. *Davis,* 454 U.S. 370 [1982]). *Rummel,* however, appeared to be but was not technically reversed three years later in **Solem** v. **Helm.** In *Solem,* the Court struck down a mandatory life sentence with no parole for a chronic recidivist who committed a series of petty nonviolent property crimes. The Court suggested that there is a concept of proportionality inherent in the cruel and unusual punishment guarantee. A life sentence without the possibility of parole in that case was disproportionate to the offenses committed.

As far as the rights of prisoners to be protected from cruel and unusual punishment are concerned, the Court ruled in *Carlson* v. *Green,* 446 U.S. 14 (1980), that the Eighth Amendment gives federal prisoners a direct right to sue prison officials for alleged mistreatment. In *Smith* v. *Wade,* 461 U.S. 30 (1983), the Court determined that a guard in a Missouri reformatory for youthful first offenders could be held liable for punitive damages upon a finding of reckless or careless disregard or indifference to inmate rights or safety. In this case the guard failed to protect a youth from being raped. However, in general, the Court has taken a dim view of most cruel and unusual claims made by inmates. For example, in *Rhodes* v. *Chapman,* 452 U.S. 337 (1981), the Court ruled that placing two prisoners in cells designed for one did not constitute cruel and unusual punishment. Also, in *Whitley* v. *Albers,* 475 U.S. 312 (1986), the Court found no cruel and unusual punishment inflicted on a prisoner shot in the leg without any warning by a guard in the quelling of a prison riot. This, determined the Court, was not an unnecessary and wanton infliction of pain.

THE IMPACT OF THE COURT'S DECISIONS

Table 17.1 summarizes the impact of selected Court decisions concerning Sixth and Eighth Amendment issues. The reprinted cases follow.

Table 17.1 THE IMPACT OF SELECTED COURT DECISIONS, SIXTH AND EIGHTH AMENDMENT ISSUES

Case	Year	Impact on Parties	Short-Run Impact	Long-Run Impact
Ex Parte Milligan	1866	Milligan freed.	Democrats applaud, Republicans appalled. Congress saw ruling as threat to military reconstruction of South. Stage set for potential confrontation.	Well-known civil liberties precedent—may have influenced actions of government during subsequent wars. Reaffirmed in 1946.
Powell v. Alabama	1932	Defendants retried with counsel and again sentenced to death. Although entitled to court-appointed lawyers, they needed none, because four eminent lawyers volunteered their services and international defense fund was established. Defendants were retried and convicted. They were eventually released or escaped. Clarence Norris received a full pardon from Alabama Governor George C. Wallace on October 25, 1976.	Case seen as major step toward protecting rights of criminal defendants in the states. Popular decision. Court seen as defender of the racially oppressed.	Start of incorporation of specific criminal procedural guarantees from the Bill of Rights under the due process clause of the Fourteenth Amendment.
Gideon v. Wainwright	1963	Gideon retried with assistance of counsel and acquitted.	Decision generally well received. Stimulated growth of public defenders offices. At time case was argued, only 5 states did not provide free lawyers for indigent felony defendants. Impact greatest in these states (Florida, Alabama, Mississippi, North Carolina, and South Carolina).	Did not significantly increase the number of trials but is thought to have raised standards of criminal justice. One of the great Warren Court landmarks with at least symbolic significance, although some have questioned its impact on the day-to-day workings of the typical courthouse bureaucracy in large metropolitan areas.
In Re Gault	1967	Gerald Gault had been released in November 1964. Court decision led to juvenile court records being expunged.	Juvenile courts began to provide procedural safeguards. Decision generally applauded. Called attention to inadequacies of juvenile justice	Landmark Warren Court decision. Influenced development of children's rights movement with focus on prevention of child abuse.

				No discernible long-run impact on the workings of criminal justice.
Argersinger v. *Hamlin*	1972	Jon Richard Argersinger vindicated.	No evidence that decision added to court backlogs or excessively strained resources of courts. Decision may have been of more symbolic importance than practical significance.	
Death Penalty Cases	1976	Troy Gregg, Jerry Jurek, and Charles Proffitt were not executed despite Court decision. Death sentences of James Woodson, Luby Waxton, and Stanislaus Roberts set aside and sentences of life imprisonment imposed.	Little short-run impact because states reluctant to resume actual executions. As of 1981 only one person had been involuntarily executed.	Executions eventually resumed. By 1991 dozens of executions had taken place.
Coker v. *Georgia*	1977	E. Anthony Coker saved from the death penalty.	Little national impact because only the state of Georgia authorized death sentence when the rape victim was an adult woman. Decision saved 34 convicted rapists from execution.	Eighth Amendment precedent concerning concepts of proportionality and excessive punishment.
Rummel v. *Estelle*	1980	William Rummel lost but was nevertheless released within eight months of the Court's decision.	Decision condemned by civil liberties groups. Narrow reading of cruel and unusual punishment guarantee.	Uncertain, because decision appeared to be reversed (although was not technically) three years later in *Solem* v. *Helm.*

EX PARTE MILLIGAN,
4 WALLACE 2 (1866)

Lambdin P. Milligan was a Peace Democrat and member of an underground group, the Sons of Liberty, operating in Indiana during the Civil War which advocated an end to the war by recognizing Confederate independence. The group planned to storm military prisons, freeing the Confederate prisoners of war, and to attack government arsenals and storehouses. The plot was exposed and Milligan, an unsuccessful candidate for the Democratic gubernatorial nomination, was arrested along with others and charged with providing aid to the rebels, inciting insurrection, practicing disloyalty and violating the laws of war. Milligan was convicted by a military commission and sentenced to death. However, several weeks before he was scheduled to die, the Civil War ended and President Lincoln was assassinated. President Johnson at the last moment commuted the death sentence in favor of life imprisonment. Meanwhile, Milligan's lawyers came before the United States Circuit Court for Indiana asking it to issue a writ of habeas corpus. Among their arguments perhaps the most persuasive was that Milligan as a civilian had a constitutional right to be tried by a civil tribunal and before a jury. The circuit court judges were divided over several questions and therefore certified them to the Supreme Court.

Majority Votes: 5
Dissenting votes: 4

Mr. Justice Davis delivered the opinion of the Court:. . . .

The opinions of the judges of the circuit court were opposed on three questions, which are certified to the Supreme Court:

1st. "On the facts stated in said petition and exhibits, ought a writ of habeas corpus to be issued?"

2d. "On the facts stated in said petition and exhibits, ought the said Lambdin P. Milligan to be discharged from custody as in said petition prayed?"

3d. "Whether, upon the facts stated in said petition and exhibits, the Military Commission mentioned therein had jurisdiction legally to try and sentence said Milligan in manner and form as in said petition and exhibits is stated." . . .

. . .The Constitution of the United States is a law for rulers and people, equally in war and in peace, and covers with the shield of its protection all classes of men, at all times, and under all circumstances. No doctrine, involving more pernicious consequences, was ever invented by the wit of man than that any of its provisions can be suspended during any of the great exigencies of government. Such a doctrine leads directly to anarchy or despotism, but the theory of necessity on which it is based is false; for the government, within the Constitution, has all the powers granted to it which are necessary to preserve its existence, as has been happily proved by the result of the great effort to throw off its just authority.

Have any of the rights guaranteed by the Constitution been violated in the case of Milligan? and if so, what are they?

Every trial involves the exercise of judicial power; and from what source did the Military Commission that tried him derive their authority? Certainly no part of the judicial power of the country was conferred on them; because the Constitution expressly vests it "in one Supreme Court and such inferior courts as the Congress may from time to time ordain and establish," and it is not pretended that the commission was a court ordained and established by Congress. They cannot justify on the mandate of the President; because he is controlled by law, and has his appropriate sphere of duty, which is to execute, not to make, the laws; and here is "no unwritten criminal code to which resort can be had as a source of jurisdiction."

But it is said that the jurisdiction is complete under the "laws and usages of war."

It can serve no useful purpose to inquire what those laws and usages are, whence they originated, where found, and on whom they operate; they can never be applied to citizens in states which have upheld the authority of the government, and where the courts are open and their process unobstructed. This court has judicial knowledge that in Indiana the Federal authority was always unopposed, and its courts always open to hear criminal accusations and redress grievances; and no usage of war could sanction a military trial there for any offense whatever of a citizen in civil life, in nowise connected with the military service. Congress could grant no such power; and to the honor of our national legislature be it said, it has never been provoked by the state of the country even to attempt its exercise. One of the plainest constitutional provisions was, therefore, infringed when Milligan was tried by a court not ordained and established by Congress, and not composed of judges appointed during good behavior.

Why was he not delivered to the circuit court of

Indiana to be proceeded against according to law? No reason of necessity could be urged against it; because Congress had declared penalties against the offenses charged, provided for their punishment, and directed that court to hear and determine them. And soon after this military tribunal was ended, the circuit court met, peacefully transacted its business, and adjourned. It needed no bayonets to protect it, and required no military aid to execute its judgments. It was held in a state, eminently distinguished for patriotism, by judges commissioned during the Rebellion, who were provided with juries, upright, intelligent, and selected by a marshal appointed by the President. The government had no right to conclude that Milligan, if guilty, would receive in that court merited punishment; for its records disclose that it was constantly engaged in the trial of similar offenses, and was never interrupted in its administration of criminal justice. If it was dangerous, in the distracted condition of affairs, to leave Milligan unrestrained of his liberty, the law said arrest him, confine him closely, render him powerless to do further mischief; and then present his case to the grand jury of the district, with proofs of his guilt and, if indicted, try him according to the course of the common law. If this had been done, the Constitution would have been vindicated, the law of 1863 enforced, and the securities for personal liberty preserved and defended.

Another guarantee of freedom was broken when Milligan was denied a trial by jury. . . . [C]itizens of states where the courts are open, if charged with crime, are guaranteed the inestimable privilege of trial by jury. This privilege is a vital principle, underlying the whole administration of criminal justice; it is not held by sufferance, and cannot be frittered away on any plea of state or political necessity. . . .

It is essential to the safety of every government that, in a great crisis, like the one we have just passed through, there should be a power somewhere of suspending the writ of habeas corpus. . . . [But] the Constitution . . . does not say after a writ of habeas corpus is denied a citizen, that he shall be tried otherwise than by the course of common law. If it had intended this result, it was easy by the use of direct words to have accomplished it. The illustrious men who framed that instrument were guarding the foundations of civil liberty against the abuses of unlimited power; they were full of wisdom, and the lessons of history informed them that a trial by an established court, assisted by an impartial jury, was the only sure way of protecting the citizen against oppression and wrong. Knowing this, they limited the suspension to one great right,

and left the rest to remain forever inviolable. . . .

It will be borne in mind that this is not a question of the power to proclaim martial law, when war exists in a community and the courts and civil authorities are overthrown. Nor is it a question what rule a military commander, at the head of his army, can impose on States in rebellion to cripple their resources and quell the insurrection. . . . [But] martial law cannot arise from a threatened invasion. The necessity must be actual and present; the invasion real, such as effectually closes the courts and deposes the civil administration. . . .

It follows, from what has been said on this subject, that there are occasions when martial rule can be properly applied. If, in foreign invasion or civil war, the courts are actually closed, and it is impossible to administer criminal justice according to law, then, on the theater of actual military operations, where war really prevails, there is a necessity to furnish a substitute for the civil authority, thus overthrown, to preserve the safety of the army and society; and as no power is left but the military, it is allowed to govern by martial rule until the laws can have their free course. As necessity creates the rule, so it limits its duration; for, if this government is continued after the courts are reinstated, it is a gross usurpation of power. Martial rule can never exist where the courts are open, and in the proper and unobstructed exercise of their jurisdiction. It is also confined to the locality of actual war. . . . And so in the case of a foreign invasion, martial rule may become a necessity, in one state, when, in another, it would be "mere lawless violence." . . .

To the third question, then, on which the judges below were opposed in opinion, an answer in the negative must be returned.

It is proper to say, although Milligan's trial and conviction by a military commission was illegal, yet, if guilty of the crimes imputed to him, and his guilt had been ascertained by an established court and impartial jury, he deserved severe punishment. . . .

The two remaining questions in this case must be answered in the affirmative. The suspension of the privilege of the writ of habeas corpus does not suspend the writ itself. The writ issues as a matter of course; and on the return made to it the court decides whether the party applying is denied the right of proceeding any further with it.

If the military trial of Milligan was contrary to law, then he was entitled, on the facts stated in his petition, to be discharged from custody by the terms of the act of Congress of March 3d, 1863. . . .

But it is insisted that Milligan was a prisoner of war, and, therefore excluded from the privileges of the statute. It is not easy to see how he can be treated as a prisoner of war, when he lived in Indiana for the past twenty years, was arrested there, and had not been, during the late troubles, a resident of any of the states in rebellion. If in Indiana he conspired with bad men to assist the enemy, he is punishable for it in the courts of Indiana; but, when tried for the offense, he cannot plead the rights of war; for he was not engaged in legal acts of hostility against the government, and only such persons, when captured, are prisoners of war. If he cannot enjoy the immunities attaching to the character of a prisoner of war, how can he be subject to their pains and penalties? . . .

MR. CHIEF JUSTICE CHASE concurring in part delivered the following opinion:. . . .

We agree, that the first two questions certified must receive affirmative answers and the last a negative. We do not doubt that the positive provisions of the act of Congress [1863] require such answers. We do not think it necessary to look beyond these provisions. In them we find sufficient and controlling reasons for our conclusions.

But the opinion which has just been read goes further; and as we understand it, asserts not only that the Military Commission held in Indiana was not authorized by Congress, but that it was not in the power of Congress to authorize it; from which it may be thought to follow, that Congress had no power to indemnify the officers who composed the commission against liability in civil courts for acting as members of it.

We cannot agree to this. . . .

We think that Congress had power, though not exercised, to authorize the Military Commission which was held in Indiana. . . .

Mr. Justice Wayne, Mr. Justice Swayne, and Mr Justice Miller, concur with me in these views.

POWELL v. ALABAMA,
287 U.S. 45 (1932)

This landmark case was the vehicle by which the Supreme Court brought for the first time a specific criminal procedural guarantee from the Bill of Rights under the umbrella of the due process clause of the Fourteenth Amendment. The case involved the "Scottsboro boys," as the defendants became known both in the United States and abroad. The defendants were nine young, illiterate, black youths whose ages ranged from 12 to 19. They were accused of raping two white girls in an open gondola car of a freight train. They were taken from the train outside Scottsboro, Alabama, and charged with having committed the crime of rape, an offense punishable by death in Alabama. The youths *protested their innocence to no avail. There was reason to doubt the truthfulness of the alleged victims, but that did not deter a wave of hysteria and racial hostility from infecting the citizens of Scottsboro and the surrounding communities. Brought before a judge, the youths were without a lawyer, and although the Alabama Constitution required the appointment of counsel for indigents accused of capital crimes, the judge merely appointed all members of the Alabama bar as counsel. That produced no takers; only on the day of the trial did a lawyer (from out of state) arrive to represent the black youngsters. Convictions were obtained, and all but the 12-year-old boy were sentenced to death. Eventually the two youngest were transferred to the juvenile authorities. The convictions of Ozie Powell and the others were unsuccessfully appealed through the Alabama courts. By the time the case was appealed to the U.S. Supreme Court, it had become a cause, not just a case, and the best legal talent was now working on the appeal.*

Majority votes: 7
Dissenting votes: 2

MR. JUSTICE SUTHERLAND delivered the opinion of the Court:. . . .

. . . The sole inquiry which we are permitted to make is whether the federal Constitution was contravened and as to that, we confine ourselves . . . to the inquiry whether the defendants were in substance denied the right of counsel, and if so, whether such denial infringes the due process clause of the Fourteenth Amendment.

First. The record shows that immediately upon the return of the indictment defendants were arraigned and pleaded not guilty. Apparently they were not asked whether they had, or were able to employ, counsel, or wished to have counsel appointed; or whether they had friends or relatives who might assist in that regard if communicated with. That it would not have been an idle ceremony to have given the defendants reasonable opportunity to communicate with their families and endeavor to obtain counsel is demonstrated by the fact that very soon after conviction, able counsel appeared in their behalf. . . .

It is hardly necessary to say that the right to counsel being conceded, a defendant should be afforded a fair opportunity to secure counsel of his own choice. Not only was that not done here, but such designation of counsel as was attempted was either so indefinite or so close upon the trial as to amount to a denial of effective and substantial aid in that regard. . . .

It . . . [is] seen that until the very morning of the

trial no lawyer had been named or definitely designated to represent the defendants. Prior to that time, the trial judge had "appointed all the members of the bar" for the limited "purpose of arraigning the defendants." Whether they would represent the defendants thereafter, if no counsel appeared in their behalf, was a matter of speculation only, or, as the judge indicated, of mere anticipation on the part of the court. Such a designation, even if made for all purposes, would, in our opinion, have fallen far short of meeting, in any proper sense, a requirement for the appointment of counsel. How many lawyers were members of the bar does not appear; but, in the very nature of things, whether many or few, they would not, thus collectively named, have been given that clear appreciation of responsibility or impressed with that individual sense of duty which should and naturally would accompany the appointment of a selected member of the bar, specifically named and assigned.

That this action of the trial judge in respect of appointment of counsel was little more than an expansive gesture, imposing no substantial or definite obligation upon any one, is borne out by the fact that prior to the calling of the case for trial on April 6, a leading member of the local bar accepted employment on the side of the prosecution and actively participated in the trial. . . . In any event, the circumstance lends emphasis to the conclusion that during perhaps the most critical period of the proceedings against these defendants, that is to say, from the time of their arraignment until the beginning of their trial, when consultation, thoroughgoing investigation and preparation were vitally important, the defendants did not have the aid of counsel in any real sense, although they were as much entitled to such aid during that period as at the trial itself. . . .

. . . The defendants, young, ignorant, illiterate, surrounded by hostile sentiment, haled back and forth under guard of soldiers, charged with an atrocious crime regarded with especial horror in the community where they were to be tried, were . . . put in peril of their lives within a few moments after counsel for the first time charged with any degree of responsibility began to represent them. . . .

Second. . . . The question, . . . which it is our duty, and within our power, to decide, is whether the denial of the assistance of counsel contravenes the due process clause of the Fourteenth Amendment to the Federal Constitution. . . .

We do not overlook the case of *Hurtado* v. *California,* 110 U.S. 516, where this court determined that due process of law does not require an indictment by a grand jury as a prerequisite to prosecution by a state for murder. In support of that conclu-

sion the court referred to the fact that the Fifth Amendment, in addition to containing the due process of law clause, provides in explicit terms that "no person shall be held to answer for a capital, or otherwise infamous crime, unless on a presentment or indictment of a Grand Jury," and said that since no part of this important amendment could be regarded as superfluous, the obvious inference is that in the sense of the Constitution due process of law was not intended to include, *ex vi termini,* the institution and procedure of a grand jury in any case; and that the same phrase, employed in the Fourteenth Amendment to restrain the action of the states, was to be interpreted as having been used in the same sense and with no greater extent; and that if it had been the purpose of that Amendment to perpetuate the institution of the grand jury in the states, it would have embodied, as did the Fifth Amendment, an express declaration to that effect.

The Sixth Amendment, in terms, provides that in all criminal prosecutions the accused shall enjoy the right "to have the Assistance of Counsel for his defence." In the face of the reasoning of the *Hurtado Case,* if it stood alone, it would be difficult to justify the conclusion that the right to counsel, being thus specifically granted by the Sixth Amendment, was also within the intendment of the due process of law clause. But the *Hurtado Case* does not stand alone. In the later case of *Chicago, Burlington & Q.R. Co.* v. *Chicago,* 166 U.S. 226, this court held that a judgment of a state court, even though authorized by statute, by which private property was taken for public use without just compensation, was in violation of the due process of law required by the Fourteenth Amendment, notwithstanding that the Fifth Amendment explicitly declares that private property shall not be taken for public use without just compensation. . . .

Likewise, this court has considered that freedom of speech and of the press are rights protected by the due process clause of the Fourteenth Amendment, although in the First Amendment, Congress is prohibited in specific terms from abridging the right.

These later cases establish that notwithstanding the sweeping character of the language in the *Hurtado Case,* the rule laid down is not without exceptions. The rule is an aid to construction, and in some instances may be conclusive; but it must yield to more compelling considerations whenever such considerations exist. The fact that the right involved is of such a character that it cannot be denied without violating those "fundamental principles of liberty and justice which lie at the base of all our civil and political institutions" is obviously one of those compelling considerations which must prevail in determining whether it is embraced within the due process clause of the Fourteenth Amendment, although it be specifically dealt with in another part of the Federal Constitution. Evidently this court, in the later cases . . . regarded the rights there under consideration as of this fundamental character. . . . While the question has never been categorically determined by this court, a consideration of the nature of the right and a review of the expressions of this and other courts makes it clear that the right to the aid of counsel is of this fundamental character.

It never has been doubted by this court, or any other so far as we know, that notice and hearing are preliminary steps essential to the passing of an enforceable judgment, and that they, together with a legally competent tribunal having jurisdiction of the case, constitute basic elements of the constitutional requirement of due process of law. . . .

What, then, does a hearing include? Historically and in practice, in our country at least, it has always included the right to the aid of counsel when desired and provided by the party asserting the right. The right to be heard would be, in many cases, of little avail if it did not comprehend the right to be heard by counsel. Even the intelligent and educated layman has small and sometimes no skill in the science of law. If charged with crime, he is incapable, generally, of determining for himself whether the indictment is good or bad. He is unfamiliar with the rules of evidence. Left without the aid of counsel he may be put on trial without a proper charge, and convicted upon incompetent evidence, or evidence irrelevant to the issue or otherwise inadmissible. He lacks both the skill and knowledge adequately to prepare his defense, even though he have a perfect one. He requires the guiding hand of counsel at every step in the proceedings against him. Without it, though he be not guilty, he faces the danger of conviction because he does not know how to establish his innocence. If that be true of men of intelligence, how much more true is it of the ignorant and illiterate, or those of feeble intellect. If in any case, civil or criminal, a state or federal court were arbitrarily to refuse to hear a party by counsel, employed by and appearing for him, it reasonably may not be doubted that such a refusal would be a denial of a hearing, and, therefore, of due process in the constitutional sense. . . .

In the light of the facts outlined in the forepart of this opinion—the ignorance and illiteracy of the defendants, their youth, the circumstances of public hostility, the imprisonment and the close surveillance of the defendants by the military forces, the fact that their friends and families were all in other states and communication with them necessarily

difficult, and above all that they stood in deadly peril of their lives—we think the failure of the trial court to give them reasonable time and opportunity to secure counsel was a clear denial of due process.

But passing that, and assuming their inability, even if opportunity had been given, to employ counsel, as the trial court evidently did assume, we are of opinion that, under the circumstances just stated, the necessity of counsel was so vital and imperative that the failure of the trial court to make an effective appointment of counsel was likewise a denial of due process within the meaning of the Fourteenth Amendment. Whether this would be so in other criminal prosecutions, or under other circumstances, we need not determine. All that it is necessary now to decide, as we do decide, is that in a capital case, where the defendant is unable to employ counsel, and is incapable adequately of making his own defense because of ignorance, feeblemindedness, illiteracy, or the like, it is the duty of the court, whether requested or not, to assign counsel for him as a necessary requisite of due process of law; and that duty is not discharged by an assignment at such a time or under such circumstances as to preclude the giving of effective aid in the preparation and trial of the case. To hold otherwise would be to ignore the fundamental postulate "that there are certain immutable principles of justice which inhere in the very idea of free government which no member of the Union may disregard." In a case such as this, whatever may be the rule in other cases, the right to have counsel appointed, when necessary, is a logical corollary from the constitutional right to be heard by counsel. . . .

The judgments must be reversed and the causes remanded for further proceedings not inconsistent with this opinion.

Judgments reversed.

MR. JUSTICE BUTLER [with whom MR. JUSTICE McREYNOLDS concurs], dissenting: [omitted]

GIDEON v. WAINWRIGHT, 372 U.S. 335 (1963)

The Gideon *case, along with* Miranda, *stands as one of the best known of the Warren Court criminal procedures decisions—in part, because of Anthony Lewis' masterful account of the case,* Gideon's Trumpet *(New York: Random House, 1964). But unlike* Miranda, *the Court here was unanimous in ruling that the Sixth Amendment right to counsel, as incorporated by the due process clause of the Fourteenth Amendment and thus to be honored by the states, means that poor people accused of fel-*

*onies are entitled to be provided, free of charge,
with a lawyer. The case came from Florida. Clarence Earl Gideon was charged with breaking and
entering a poolroom with intent to commit a misdemeanor. Under Florida law this was a felony. Gideon insisted that he was innocent and went to trial.
He could not afford to hire a lawyer and his request
for one was turned down by the trial judge. Gideon
was convicted and sentenced to serve five years in
the state prison. His habeas corpus petition
brought no satisfaction from the Florida Supreme
Court and Gideon ultimately petitioned the United
States Supreme Court for a hearing. The Court
granted certiorari and appointed a noted Washington lawyer and eventual Supreme Court Justice,
Abe Fortas, to represent Gideon.*

Votes: Unanimous

MR. JUSTICE BLACK delivered the opinion of the
Court:. . . .

. . . Since 1942, when *Betts* v. *Brady,* 316 U.S.
455, was decided by a divided Court, the problem
of a defendant's federal constitutional right to counsel in a state court has been a continuing source of
controversy and litigation in both state and federal
courts. To give this problem another review here,
we granted certiorari. Since Gideon was proceeding
in forma pauperis, we appointed counsel to represent him and requested both sides to discuss in their
briefs and oral arguments the following: "Should
this Court's holding in *Betts* v. *Brady,* 316 U.S. 455,
be reconsidered?" . . .

We think the Court in *Betts* had ample precedent
for acknowledging that those guarantees of the Bill
of Rights which are fundamental safeguards of liberty immune from federal abridgment are equally
protected against state invasion by the Due Process
Clause of the Fourteenth Amendment. This same
principle was recognized, explained, and applied in
Powell v. *Alabama,* 287 U.S. 45 (1932), a case upholding the right of counsel, where the Court held
that despite sweeping language to the contrary in
Hurtado v. *California,* 110 U.S. 516 (1884), the
Fourteenth Amendment "embraced" those " 'fundamental principles of liberty and justice which lie
at the base of all our civil and political institutions,' " even though they had been "specifically
dealt with in another part of the federal Constitution." In many cases other than *Powell* and *Betts,*
this Court has looked to the fundamental nature of
original Bill of Rights guarantees to decide whether
the Fourteenth Amendment makes them obligatory
on the States. . . .

We accept *Betts* v. *Brady*'s assumption, based
as it was on our prior cases, that a provision of the
Bill of Rights which is "fundamental and essential
to a fair trial" is made obligatory upon the States
by the Fourteenth Amendment. We think the Court
in *Betts* was wrong, however, in concluding that the
Sixth Amendment's guarantee of counsel is not one
of these fundamental rights. Ten years before *Betts*
v. *Brady,* this Court, after full consideration of all
the historical data examined in *Betts,* had unequivocally declared that "the right to the aid of counsel
is of this fundamental character." *Powell* v. *Alabama,* 287 U.S. 45, 68 (1932). While the Court at
the close of its *Powell* opinion did by its language,
as this Court frequently does, limit its holding to
the particular facts and circumstances of that case,
its conclusions about the fundamental nature of the
right to counsel are unmistakable. . . .

In light of . . . many other prior decisions of this
Court, it is not surprising that the *Betts* Court,
when faced with the contention that "one charged
with crime, who is unable to obtain counsel, must
be furnished counsel by the State," conceded that
"[e]xpressions in the opinions of this court lend
color to the argument. . . ." 316 U.S., at 462–463.
The fact is that in deciding as it did—that "appointment of counsel is not a fundamental right, essential
to a fair trial"—the Court in *Betts* v. *Brady* made
an abrupt break with its own well-considered precedents. In returning to these old precedents, sounder
we believe than the new, we but restore constitutional principles established to achieve a fair system of justice. Not only these precedents but also
reason and reflection require us to recognize that in
our adversary system of criminal justice, any person haled into court, who is too poor to hire a lawyer, cannot be assured a fair trial unless counsel is
provided for him. This seems to us to be an obvious
truth. Governments, both state and federal, quite
properly spend vast sums of money to establish machinery to try defendants accused of crime. Lawyers to prosecute are everywhere deemed essential
to protect the public's interest in an orderly society.
Similarly, there are few defendants charged with
crime, few indeed, who fail to hire the best lawyers
they can get to prepare and present their defenses.
That government hires lawyers to prosecute and
defendants who have the money hire lawyers to defend are the strongest indications of the widespread
belief that lawyers in criminal courts are necessities, not luxuries. The right of one charged with
crime to counsel may not be deemed fundamental
and essential to fair trials in some countries, but it
is in ours. From the very beginning, our state and
national constitutions and laws have laid great emphasis on procedural and substantive safeguards
designed to assure fair trials before impartial tribunals in which every defendant stands equal before

the law. This noble ideal cannot be realized if the poor man charged with crime has to face his accusers without a lawyer to assist him. . . . The Court in *Betts* v. *Brady* departed from the sound wisdom upon which the Court's holding in *Powell* v. *Alabama* rested. Florida, supported by two other States, has asked that *Betts* v. *Brady* be left intact. Twenty-two States, as friends of the Court, argue that *Betts* was "an anachronism when handed down" and that it should now be overruled. We agree.

The judgment is reversed and the cause is remanded to the Supreme Court of Florida for further action not inconsistent with this opinion.

Reversed.

MR. JUSTICE DOUGLAS, concurring: [omitted]
MR. JUSTICE CLARK, concurring in the result: [omitted]
MR. JUSTICE HARLAN, concurring:

I agree that *Betts* v. *Brady* should be overruled, but consider it entitled to a more respectful burial than has been accorded, at least on the part of those of us who were not on the Court when that case was decided.

I cannot subscribe to the view that *Betts* v. *Brady* represented "an abrupt break with its own well-considered precedents." In 1932, in *Powell* v. *Alabama,* 287 U.S. 45, a capital case, this Court declared that under the particular facts there presented—"the ignorance and illiteracy of the defendants, their youth, the circumstances of public hostility . . . and above all that they stood in deadly peril of their lives"—the state court had a duty to assign counsel for the trial as a necessary requisite of due process of law. It is evident that these limiting facts were not added to the opinion as an afterthought; they were repeatedly emphasized, and were clearly regarded as important to the result.

Thus when this Court, a decade later, decided *Betts* v. *Brady,* it did no more than to admit of the possible existence of special circumstances in noncapital as well as capital trials, while at the same time insisting that such circumstances be shown in order to establish a denial of due process. The right to appointed counsel had been recognized as being considerably broader in federal prosecutions, see *Johnson* v. *Zerbst,* 304 U.S. 458, but to have imposed these requirements on the States would indeed have been "an abrupt break" with the almost immediate past. The declaration that the right to appointed counsel in state prosecutions, as established in *Powell* v. *Alabama,* was not limited to capital cases was in truth not a departure from, but an extension of, existing precedent.

The principles declared in *Powell* and in *Betts,* however, have had a troubled journey throughout the years that have followed first the one case and then the other. Even by the time of the *Betts* decision, dictum in at least one of the Court's opinions had indicated that there was an absolute right to the services of counsel in the trial of state capital cases. Such dicta continued to appear in subsequent decisions and any lingering doubts were finally eliminated by the holding of *Hamilton* v. *Alabama,* 368 U.S. 52.

In noncapital cases, the "special circumstances" rule has continued to exist in form while its substance has been substantially and steadily eroded. In the first decade after *Betts,* there were cases in which the Court found special circumstances to be lacking, but usually by a sharply divided vote. However, no such decision has been cited to us, and I have found none, after *Quicksall* v. *Michigan,* 339 U.S. 660, decided in 1950. At the same time, there have been not a few cases in which special circumstances were found in little or nothing more than the "complexity" of the legal questions presented, although those questions were often of only routine difficulty. The Court has come to recognize, in other words, that the mere existence of a serious criminal charge constituted in itself special circumstances requiring the services of counsel at trial. In truth the *Betts* v. *Brady* rule is no longer a reality.

This evolution, however, appears not to have been fully recognized by many state courts, in this instance charged with the front-line responsibility for the enforcement of constitutional rights. To continue a rule which is honored by this Court only with lip service is not a healthy thing and in the long run will do disservice to the federal system.

The special circumstances rule has been formally abandoned in capital cases, and the time has now come when it should be similarly abandoned in noncapital cases, at least as to offenses which, as the one involved here, carry the possibility of a substantial prison sentence. (Whether the rule should extend to *all* criminal cases need not now be decided.) This indeed does no more than to make explicit something that has long since been foreshadowed in our decisions. . . .

IN RE GAULT,
387 U.S. 1 (1967)

Gerald Francis Gault, 15 years old, was good friends with trouble. Months before the incident that resulted in this Arizona case, Gerald was with a boy who stole a wallet from a woman's purse. For that, Gerald was placed on six months' proba-

tion. Now Gerald and a friend, Ronald Lewis, were in trouble for having made a lewd phone call to a neighbor, Mrs. Cook. The boys were taken into custody and placed in a detention home. The Juvenile Judge found Gerald to be "a delinquent child" and he was committed to the State Industrial School until the age of 21. Had he been an adult, Arizona law would have provided for a fine of not more than $50 or imprisonment for not more than two months. A petition for a writ of habeas corpus was filed and dismissed by the Arizona Superior Court. The Arizona Supreme Court affirmed the dismissal of the writ and the United States Supreme Court took the case.

Majority votes: 7 + 1 (in part)
Dissenting votes: 1

MR. JUSTICE FORTAS delivered the opinion of the Court:. . . .

The Juvenile Court movement began in this country at the end of the last century. . . .

The early reformers were appalled by adult procedures and penalties, and by the fact that children could be given long prison sentences and mixed in jails with hardened criminals. . . . They believed that society's role was not to ascertain whether the child was "guilty" or "innocent," but "What is he, how has he become what he is, and what had best be done in his interest and in the interest of the state to save him from a downward career." The child—essentially good, as they saw it—was to be made "to feel that he is the object of [the state's] care and solicitude," not that he was under arrest or on trial. The rules of criminal procedure were therefore altogether inapplicable. . . . The idea of crime and punishment was to be abandoned. The child was to be "treated" and "rehabilitated" and the procedures, from apprehension through institutionalization, were to be "clinical" rather than punitive.

These results were to be achieved, without coming to conceptual and constitutional grief, by insisting that the proceedings were not adversary, but that the state was proceeding as *parens patriae*. The Latin phrase proved to be a great help to those who sought to rationalize the exclusion of juveniles from the constitutional scheme; but its meaning is murky and its historic credentials are of dubious relevance. . . . On this basis, proceedings involving juveniles were described as "civil," not "criminal" and therefore not subject to the requirements which restrict the state when it seeks to deprive a person of his liberty.

Accordingly, the highest motives and most enlightened impulses led to a peculiar system for juveniles, unknown to our law in any comparable context. The constitutional and theoretical basis for this peculiar system is—to say the least—debatable. And in practice . . . the results have not been entirely satisfactory. Juvenile Court history has again demonstrated that unbridled discretion, however benevolently motivated, is frequently a poor substitute for principle and procedure. . . . Departures from established principles of due process have frequently resulted not in enlightened procedure, but in arbitrariness. . . .

It is claimed that juveniles obtain benefits from the special procedures applicable to them which more than offset the disadvantages of denial of the substance of normal due process. . . .

Ultimately, however, we confront the reality of that portion of the Juvenile Court process with which we deal in this case. A boy is charged with misconduct. The boy is committed to an institution where he may be restrained of liberty for years. It is of no constitutional consequence—and of limited practical meaning—that the institution to which he is committed is called an Industrial School. The fact of the matter is that, however euphemistic the title, a "receiving home" or an "industrial school" for juveniles is an institution of confinement in which the child is incarcerated for a greater or lesser time. . . . Instead of mother and father and sisters and brothers and friends and classmates, his world is peopled by guards, custodians, state employees, and "delinquents" confined with him for anything from waywardness to rape and homicide.

In view of this, it would be extraordinary if our Constitution did not require the procedural regularity and the exercise of care implied in the phrase "due process." Under our Constitution, the condition of being a boy does not justify a kangaroo court. The traditional ideas of Juvenile Court procedure, indeed, contemplated that time would be available and care would be used to establish precisely what the juvenile did and why he did it—was it a prank of adolescence or a brutal act threatening serious consequences to himself or society unless corrected? Under traditional notions, one would assume that in a case like that of Gerald Gault, where the juvenile appears to have a home, a working mother and father, and an older brother, the Juvenile Judge would have made a careful inquiry and judgment as to the possibility that the boy could be disciplined and dealt with at home, despite his previous transgressions. Indeed, so far as appears in the record before us, except for some conversation with Gerald about his school work and his "wanting to go to *** Grand Canyon with his father," the points to which the judge directed his attention were little different from those that would be involved in determining any charge of violation of a penal statute. The essential difference between Gerald's case and a normal criminal case is that safeguards available to adults were discarded in Gerald's case. The summary procedure as well as the long commitment was possible because Gerald was 15 years of age instead of over 18.

If Gerald had been over 18, he would not have been subject to Juvenile Court proceedings. For the particular offense immediately involved, the maximum punishment would have been a fine of $5 to $50, or imprisonment in jail for not more than two months. Instead, he was committed to custody for a maximum of six years. If he had been over 18 and had committed an offense to which such a sentence might apply, he would have been entitled to substantial rights under the Constitution of the United States as well as under Arizona's laws and constitution. . . .

We now turn to the specific issues which are presented to us in the present case.

NOTICE OF CHARGES. . . .

We cannot agree with the [Arizona] court's conclusion that adequate notice was given in this case. Notice, to comply with due process requirements, must be given sufficiently in advance of scheduled court proceedings so that reasonable opportunity to prepare will be afforded, and it must "set forth the alleged misconduct with particularity." . . . The "initial hearing" in the present case was a hearing on the merits. Notice at that time is not timely; and even if there were a conceivable purpose served by the deferral proposed by the court below, it would have to yield to the requirements that the child and his parents or guardian be notified, in writing, of the specific charge or factual allegations to be considered at the hearing, and that such written notice be given at the earliest practicable time, and in any event sufficiently in advance of the hearing to permit preparation. Due process of law requires notice of the sort we have described—that is, notice which would be deemed constitutionally adequate in a civil or criminal proceeding. It does not allow a hearing to be held in which a youth's freedom and his parents' right to his custody are at stake without giving them timely notice, in advance of the hearing, of the specific issues that they must meet. Nor, in the circumstances of this case, can it reasonably be said that the requirement of notice was waived.

RIGHT TO COUNSEL. . . .

We conclude that the Due Process Clause of the Fourteenth Amendment requires that in respect of proceedings to determine delinquency which may result in commitment to an institution in which the juvenile's freedom is curtailed, the child and his parents must be notified of the child's right to be represented by counsel retained by them, or if they are unable to afford counsel, that counsel will be appointed to represent the child.

At the habeas corpus proceeding, Mrs. Gault testified that she knew that she could have appeared with counsel at the juvenile hearing. This knowledge is not a waiver of the right to counsel which she and her juvenile son had, as we have defined it. They had a right expressly to be advised that they might retain counsel and to be confronted with the need for specific consideration of whether they did or did not choose to waive the right. If they were unable to afford to employ counsel, they were entitled in view of the seriousness of the charge and the potential commitment, to appointed counsel, unless they chose waiver. Mrs. Gault's knowledge that she could employ counsel was not an "intentional relinquishment or abandonment" of a fully known right.

CONFRONTATION, SELF-INCRIMINATION, CROSS-EXAMINATION. . . .

We conclude that the constitutional privilege against self-incrimination is applicable in the case of juveniles as it is with respect to adults. We appreciate that special problems may arise with respect to waiver of the privilege by or on behalf of children and that there may well be some differences in technique—but not in principle—depending upon the age of the child and the presence and competence of parents. The participation of counsel will, of course, assist the police, Juvenile Courts and appellate tribunals in administering the privilege. If counsel was not present for some permissible reason when an admission was obtained, the greatest care must be taken to assure that the admission was voluntary, in the sense not only that it was not coerced or suggested, but also that it was not the product of ignorance of rights or of adolescent fantasy, fright or despair.

The "confession" of Gerald Gault was first obtained by Officer Flagg, out of the presence of Gerald's parents, without counsel and without advising him of his right to silence, as far as appears. The judgment of the Juvenile Court was stated by the judge to be based on Gerald's admissions in court. Neither "admission" was reduced to writing, and, to say the least, the process by which the "admissions" were obtained and received must be characterized as lacking the certainty and order which are required of proceedings of such formidable consequences. Apart from the "admission," there was nothing upon which a judgment or finding might be based. There was no sworn testimony. Mrs. Cook, the complainant, was not present. . . . No reason is suggested or appears for a different rule in respect of sworn testimony in juvenile courts than in adult tribunals. Absent a valid confession adequate to support the determination of the Juvenile Court, confrontation and sworn testimony by witnesses available for cross-examination were essential for a finding of "delinquency" and an order committing Gerald to a state institution for a maximum of six years. . . .

As we said in *Kent* v. *United States,* 383 U.S. 541, 554 (1966), with respect to waiver proceedings, "there is no place in our system of law for reaching a result of such tremendous consequences without ceremony ***." We now hold that, absent a valid confession, a determination of delinquency and an order of commitment to a state institution cannot be sustained in the absence of sworn testimony subjected to the opportunity for cross-examination in accordance with our law and constitutional requirements. . . .

For the reasons stated, the judgment of the Supreme Court of Arizona is reversed and the cause remanded for further proceedings not inconsistent with this opinion. It is so ordered.

Judgment reversed and cause remanded with directions.

MR. JUSTICE BLACK, concurring: [omitted]
MR. JUSTICE WHITE, concurring: [omitted]
MR. JUSTICE HARLAN, concurring in part and dissenting in part: [omitted]
MR. JUSTICE STEWART, dissenting:

The Court today uses an obscure Arizona case as a vehicle to impose upon thousands of juvenile courts throughout the Nation restrictions that the Constitution made applicable to adversary criminal trials. I believe the Court's decision is wholly unsound as a matter of constitutional law, and sadly unwise as a matter of judicial policy. . . .

I possess neither the specialized experience nor the expert knowledge to predict with any certainty where may lie the brightest hope for progress in dealing with the serious problems of juvenile delinquency. But I am certain that the answer does not lie in the Court's opinion in this case, which serves to convert a juvenile proceeding into a criminal prosecution.

The inflexible restrictions that the Constitution so wisely made applicable to adversary criminal tri-

als have no inevitable place in the proceedings of those public social agencies known as juvenile or family courts. And to impose the Court's long catalog of requirements upon juvenile proceedings in every area of the country is to invite a long step backwards into the nineteenth century. . . .

A State in all its dealings must, of course, accord every person due process of law. And due process may require that some of the same restrictions which the Constitution has placed upon criminal trials must be imposed upon juvenile proceedings. For example, I suppose that all would agree that a brutally coerced confession could not constitutionally be considered in a juvenile court hearing. But it surely does not follow that the testimonial privilege against self-incrimination is applicable in all juvenile proceedings. Similarly, due process clearly requires timely notice of the purpose and scope of any proceedings affecting the relationship of parent and child. But it certainly does not follow that notice of a juvenile hearing must be framed with all the technical niceties of a criminal indictment.

In any event, there is no reason to deal with issues such as these in the present case. The Supreme Court of Arizona found that the parents of Gerald Gault "knew of their right to counsel, to subpoena and cross examine witnesses, of the right to confront the witnesses against Gerald and the possible consequences of a finding of delinquency." It further found that "Mrs. Gault knew the exact nature of the charge against Gerald from the day he was taken to the detention home." And . . . no issue of compulsory self-incrimination is presented by this case.

I would dismiss the appeal.

ARGERSINGER v. HAMLIN,
407 U.S. 25 (1972)

Gideon v. Wainwright *made it incumbent upon the states, through the due process clause of the Fourteenth Amendment, to provide a lawyer free of charge if a person accused of a serious crime could not afford one. The decision left unclear whether poor defendants accused of committing misdemeanors were also entitled to a free lawyer. The* Argersinger *decision made it clear that they are, at least if a jail sentence is imposed. The case involved Jon Argersinger, an indigent, who was charged in Florida with carrying a concealed weapon, an offense punishable by imprisonment for up to six months, a $1000 fine, or both. At the conclusion of a bench trial where he was unrepresented by counsel, he was sentenced to serve 90* *days in jail. The Supreme Court of Florida ruled that he had no right to court-appointed counsel. The United States Supreme Court granted Argersinger's petition for certiorari.*

Votes: Unanimous

MR. JUSTICE DOUGLAS delivered the opinion of the Court:. . . .

The Sixth Amendment, which in enumerated situations has been made applicable to the States by reason of the Fourteenth Amendment . . . provides specified standards for "all criminal prosecutions.". . .

The Sixth Amendment . . . extended the right to counsel beyond its common-law dimensions. . . .

The assistance of counsel is often a requisite to the very existence of a fair trial. . . . In *Gideon* v. *Wainwright,* 372 U.S. 335 (overruling *Betts* v. *Brady,* 316 U.S. 455), we dealt with a felony trial. But we did not so limit the need of the accused for a lawyer. . . .

Both *Powell* v. *Alabama,* 287 U.S. 45, and *Gideon* involved felonies. But their rationale has relevance to any criminal trial, where an accused is deprived of his liberty. . . .

The requirement of counsel may well be necessary for a fair trial even in a petty-offense prosecution. We are by no means convinced that legal and constitutional questions involved in a case that actually leads to imprisonment even for a brief period are any less complex than when a person can be sent off for six months or more. . . .

The trial of vagrancy cases is illustrative. While only brief sentences of imprisonment may be imposed, the cases often bristle with thorny constitutional questions. . . .

[A] problem which looms large in misdemeanor as well as in felony cases [is that of the guilty plea]. Counsel is needed so that the accused may know precisely what he is doing, so that he is fully aware of the prospect of going to jail or prison, and so that he is treated fairly by the prosecution.

In addition, the volume of misdemeanor cases, far greater in number than felony prosecutions, may create an obsession for speedy dispositions, regardless of the fairness of the result. . . .

There is evidence of the prejudice which results to misdemeanor defendants from . . . "assembly-line justice." One study concluded that "[m]isdemeanants represented by attorneys are five times as likely to emerge from police court with all charges dismissed as are defendants who face similar charges without counsel." American Civil Liberties Union, Legal Counsel for Misdemeanants, Preliminary Report 1 (1970).

We must conclude . . . that the problems associated with misdemeanor and petty offenses often require the presence of counsel to insure the accused a fair trial. Mr. Justice Powell suggests that these problems are raised even in situations where there is no prospect of imprisonment. We need not consider the requirements of the Sixth Amendment as regards the right to counsel where loss of liberty is not involved, however, for here petitioner was in fact sentenced to jail. And, as we said in *Baldwin* v. *New York,* 399 U.S., at 73, "the prospect of imprisonment for however short a time will seldom be viewed by the accused as a trivial or 'petty' matter and may well result in quite serious repercussions affecting his career and his reputation."

We hold, therefore, that absent a knowing and intelligent waiver, no person may be imprisoned for any offense, whether classified as petty, misdemeanor, or felony, unless he was represented by counsel at his trial. . . .

We do not sit as an ombudsman to direct state courts how to manage their affairs but only to make clear the federal constitutional requirement. How crimes should be classified is largely a state matter. The fact that traffic charges technically fall within the category of "criminal prosecutions" does not necessarily mean that many of them will be brought into the class where imprisonment actually occurs. . . .

Under the rule we announce today, every judge will know when the trial of a misdemeanor starts that no imprisonment may be imposed, even though local law permits it, unless the accused is represented by counsel. He will have a measure of the seriousness and gravity of the offense and therefore know when to name a lawyer to represent the accused before the trial starts.

The run of misdemeanors will not be affected by today's ruling. But in those that end up in the actual deprivation of a person's liberty, the accused will receive the benefit of "the guiding hand of counsel" so necessary when one's liberty is in jeopardy.

Reversed.

MR. CHIEF JUSTICE BURGER, concurring in the result: [omitted]

MR. JUSTICE BRENNAN, with whom MR. JUSTICE DOUGLAS and MR. JUSTICE STEWART join, concuring: [omitted]

MR. JUSTICE POWELL, with whom MR. JUSTICE REHNQUIST joins, concurring in the result:. . . .

Serious consequences . . . may result from convictions not punishable by imprisonment. Stigma may attach to a drunken-driving conviction or a hit-and-run escapade. Losing one's driver's license is more serious for some individuals than a brief stay in jail. . . . When the deprivation of property rights and interest is of sufficient consequence, denying the assistance of counsel to indigents who are incapable of defending themselves is a denial of due process. . . .

[A]lthough the new rule is extended today only to the imprisonment category of cases, the Court's opinion foreshadows the adoption of a broad prophylactic rule applicable to all petty offenses. No one can foresee the consequences of such a drastic enlargement of the constitutional right to free counsel. But even today's decision could have a seriously adverse impact upon the day-to-day functioning of the criminal justice system. We should be slow to fashion a new constitutional rule with consequences of such unknown dimensions, especially since it is supported neither by history nor precedent. . . .

THE DEATH PENALTY CASES OF 1976, 428 U.S. 153 (1976)

Five southern states' death penalty statutes came under the scrutiny of the Supreme Court. The statutes were of two kinds—mandatory (Louisiana and North Carolina) and those that allow consideration of mitigating circumstances to determine whether life imprisonment or death is to be the penalty (Georgia, Texas, and Florida). In each of the cases, the defendants had been convicted of first-degree murder. The Court was split three ways and the Stewart-Powell-Stevens group took the "middle" position.

Majority votes: 7, 5
Dissenting votes: 2, 4

Gregg v. *Georgia*
MR. JUSTICE STEWART, MR. JUSTICE POWELL, and MR. JUSTICE STEVENS announced the judgment of the Court and filed an opinion delivered by MR. JUSTICE STEWART:. . . .

. . . [U]ntil *Furman* v. *Georgia,* 408 U.S. 238 (1972), the Court never confronted squarely the fundamental claim that the punishment of death always, regardless of the enormity of the offense or the procedure followed in imposing the sentence, is cruel and unusual punishment in violation of the Constitution. Although this issue was presented and addressed in *Furman,* it was not resolved by the Court. Four justices would have held that capital punishment is not unconstitutional *per se;* two Justices would have reached the opposite conclusion; and three Justices, while agreeing that the statutes then before the Court were invalid as ap-

plied, left open the question whether such punishment may ever be imposed. We now hold that the punishment of death does not invariably violate the Constitution. . . .

The imposition of the death penalty for the crime of murder has a long history of acceptance both in the United States and in England. . . .

It is apparent from the text of the Constitution itself that the existence of capital punishment was accepted by the Framers. At the time the Eighth Amendment was ratified, capital punishment was a common sanction in every State. . . . The Fourteenth Amendment, adopted over three-quarters of a century later, similarly contemplates the existence of the capital sanction in providing that no State shall deprive any person of "life, liberty, or property" without due process of law.

For nearly two centuries, this Court, repeatedly and often expressly, has recognized that capital punishment is not invalid *per se.* . . . Despite the continuing debate, dating back to the 19th century, over the morality and utility of capital punishment, it is now evident that a large proportion of American society continues to regard it as an appropriate and necessary criminal sanction.

The most marked indication of society's endorsement of the death penalty for murder is the legislative response to *Furman.* The legislatures of at least 35 States have enacted new statutes that provide for the death penalty for at least some crimes that result in the death of another person. And the Congress of the United States, in 1974, enacted a statute providing the death penalty for aircraft piracy that results in death. These recently adopted statutes have attempted to address the concerns expressed by the Court in *Furman* primarily (i) by specifying the factors to be weighed and the procedures to be followed in deciding when to impose a capital sentence, or (ii) by making the death penalty mandatory for specified crimes. But all of the post-*Furman* statutes make clear that capital punishment itself has not been rejected by the elected representatives of the people.

In the only statewide referendum occurring since *Furman* and brought to our attention, the people of California adopted a constitutional amendment that authorized capital punishment, in effect negating a prior ruling by the Supreme Court of California, that the death penalty violated the California Constitution. . . .

The death penalty is said to serve two principal social purposes: retribution and deterrence of capital crimes by prospective offenders.

In part, capital punishment is an expression of society's moral outrage at particularly offensive conduct. This function may be unappealing to many, but it is essential in an ordered society that asks its citizens to rely on legal processes rather than self-help to vindicate their wrongs. . . . Indeed, the decision that capital punishment may be the appropriate sanction in extreme cases is an expression of the community's belief that certain crimes are themselves so grievous an affront to humanity that the only adequate response may be the penalty of death.

Statistical attempts to evaluate the worth of the death penalty as a deterrent to crimes by potential offenders have occasioned a great deal of debate. The results simply have been inconclusive. . . .

Although some of the studies suggest that the death penalty may not function as a significantly greater deterrent than lesser penalties, there is no convincing empirical evidence either supporting or refuting this view. . . .

In sum, we cannot say that the judgment of the Georgia legislature that capital punishment may be necessary in some cases is clearly wrong. Considerations of federalism, as well as respect for the ability of a legislature to evaluate, in terms of its particular state, the moral consensus concerning the death penalty and its social utility as a sanction, require us to conclude in the absence of more convincing evidence that the infliction of death as a punishment for murder is not without justification and thus is not unconstitutionally severe.

Finally, we must consider whether the punishment of death is disproportionate in relation to the crime for which it is imposed. There is no question that death as a punishment is unique in its severity and irrevocability. But we are concerned here only with the imposition of capital punishment for the crime of murder, and when a life has been taken deliberately by the offender, we cannot say that the punishment is invariably disproportionate to the crime. It is an extreme sanction, suitable to the most extreme of crimes.

We hold that the death penalty is not a form of punishment that may never be imposed, regardless of the circumstances of the offense, regardless of the character of the offender, and regardless of the procedure followed in reaching the decision to impose it.

We now consider whether Georgia may impose the death penalty on the petitioner in this case. . . .

[T]he concerns expressed in *Furman* that the penalty of death not be imposed in an arbitrary or capricious manner can be met by a carefully drafted statute that ensures that the sentencing authority is given adequate information and guidance. As a general proposition these concerns are best met by a system that provides for a bifurcated proceeding at which the sentencing authority is apprised of the information relevant to the imposition of sentence and provided with standards to guide its use of the information. . . .

. . . Georgia's new sentencing procedures require as a prerequisite to the imposition of the death penalty, specific jury findings as to the circumstances of the crime or the character of the defendant. Moreover to guard further against a situation comparable to that presented in *Furman* the Supreme Court of Georgia compares each death sentence with the sentences imposed on similarly situated defendants to ensure that the sentence of death in a particular case is not disproportionate. On their face these procedures seem to satisfy the concerns of *Furman*. . . .

The petitioner contends, however, that the changes in the Georgia sentencing procedures are only cosmetic, that the arbitrariness and capriciousness condemned by *Furman* continue to exist in Georgia—both in traditional practices that still remain and in the new sentencing procedures adopted in response to *Furman*.

First, the petitioner focuses on the opportunities for discretionary action that are inherent in the processing of any murder case under Georgia law. He notes that the state prosecutor has unfettered authority to select those persons whom he wishes to prosecute for a capital offense and to plea bargain with them. Further, at the trial the jury may choose to convict a defendant of a lesser included offense rather than find him guilty of a crime punishable by death, even if the evidence would support a capital verdict. And finally, a defendant who is convicted and sentenced to die may have his sentence commuted by the Governor of the State and the Georgia Board of Pardons and Paroles.

The existence of these discretionary stages is not determinative of the issues before us. At each of these stages an actor in the criminal justice system makes a decision which may remove a defendant from consideration as a candidate for the death penalty. *Furman,* in contrast, dealt with the decision to impose the death sentence on a specific individual who had been convicted of a capital offense. Nothing in any of our cases suggests that the decision to afford an individual defendant mercy violates the Constitution. *Furman* held only that, in order to minimize the risk that the death penalty would be imposed on a capriciously selected group of offenders, the decision to impose it had to be guided by standards so that the sentencing authority would focus on the particularized circumstances of the crime and the defendant. . . .

The provision for appellate review in the Georgia capital-sentencing system serves as a check against the random or arbitrary imposition of the death penalty. In particular, the proportionality review substantially eliminates the possibility that a person will be sentenced to die by the action of an aberrant jury. If a time comes when juries generally do not impose the death sentence in a certain kind of murder case, the appellate review procedures assures that no defendant convicted under such circumstances will suffer a sentence of death.

The basic concern of *Furman* centered on those defendants who were being condemned to death capriciously and arbitrarily. Under the procedures before the Court in that case, sentencing authorities were not directed to give attention to the nature or circumstances of the crime committed or to the character or record of the defendant. Left unguided, juries imposed the death sentence in a way that could only be called freakish. The new Georgia sentencing procedures, by contrast, focus the jury's attention on the particularized nature of the crime and the particularized characteristics of the individual defendant. While the jury is permitted to consider any aggravating or mitigating circumstances, it must find and identify at least one statutory aggravating factor before it may impose a penalty of death. In this way the jury's discretion is channeled. No longer can a jury wantonly and freakishly impose the death sentence; it is always circumscribed by the legislative guidelines. In addition, the review function of the Supreme Court of Georgia affords additional assurance that the concerns that prompted our decision in *Furman* are not present to any significant degree in the Georgia procedure applied here.

For the reasons expressed in this opinion, we hold that the statutory system under which Gregg was sentenced to death does not violate the Constitution. Accordingly, the judgment of the Georgia Supreme Court is affirmed.

It is so ordered.

MR. JUSTICE WHITE, with whom CHIEF JUSTICE BURGER and MR. JUSTICE REHNQUIST join, concurring in the judgment:. . . .

. . . Petitioner has argued in effect that no matter how effective the death penalty may be as a punishment, government, created and run as it must be by humans, is inevitably incompetent to administer it. This cannot be accepted as a proposition of constitutional law. . . . I decline to interfere with the manner in which Georgia has chosen to enforce [criminal laws against murder] . . . on what is simply an assertion of lack of faith in the ability of the

system of justice to operate in a fundamentally fair manner. . . .

MR. JUSTICE BLACKMUN concurs in the judgment.

[In *Jurek* v. *Texas* the Court, with the same voting lineup, upheld the State of Texas' capital sentencing procedure. Also in *Proffitt* v. *Florida* that State's procedure for the imposition of capital punishment was upheld.]

MR. JUSTICE BRENNAN, dissenting:

The Cruel and Unusual Punishments Clause "must draw its meaning from the evolving standards of decency that mark the progress of a maturing society" . . .

[M]y view . . . [is that] the Clause forbidding cruel and unusual punishments under our constitutional system of government embodies in unique degree moral principles restraining the punishments that our civilized society may impose on those persons who transgress its laws. . . .

This Court inescapably has the duty, as the ultimate arbiter of the meaning of our Constitution, to say whether, when individuals condemned to death stand before our Bar, "moral concepts" require us to hold that the law has progressed to the point where we should declare that the punishment of death, like punishments on the rack, the screw and the wheel, is no longer morally tolerable in our civilized society. My opinion in *Furman* v. *Georgia* concluded that our civilization and the law had progressed to this point and that therefore the punishment of death, for whatever crime and under all circumstances, is "cruel and unusual" in violation of the Eighth and Fourteenth Amendments of the Constitution. I shall not again canvass the reasons that led to that conclusion. I emphasize only that foremost among the "moral concepts" recognized in our cases and inherent in the Clause is the primary moral principle that the State, even as it punishes, must treat its citizens in a manner consistent with their intrinsic worth as human beings—a punishment must not be so severe as to be degrading to human dignity. A judicial determination whether the punishment of death comports with human dignity is therefore not only permitted but compelled by the Clause.

I do not understand that the Court disagrees that "[i]n comparison to all other punishments today . . . the deliberate extinguishment of human life by the State is uniquely degrading to human dignity." For three of my Brethren hold today that mandatory infliction of the death penalty constitutes the penalty cruel and unusual punishment. I perceive no principled basis for this limitation. Death for whatever crime and under all circumstances "is truly an awesome punishment. The calculated killing of a human being by the State involves, by its very nature, a denial of the executed person's humanity. . . . An executed person has indeed 'lost the right to have rights.' " Death is not only an unusually severe punishment, unusual in its pain, in its finality, and in its enormity, but it serves no penal purpose more effectively than a less severe punishment; therefore the principle inherent in the Clause that prohibits pointless infliction of excessive punishment when less severe punishment can adequately achieve the same purposes invalidates the punishment.

The fatal constitutional infirmity in the punishment of death is that it treats "members of the human race as nonhumans, as objects to be toyed with and discarded. [It is] thus inconsistent with the fundamental premise of the Clause that even the vilest criminal remains a human being possessed of common human dignity." As such it is a penalty that "subjects the individual to a fate forbidden by the principle of civilized treatment guaranteed by the [Clause]." I therefore would hold, on that ground alone, that death is today a cruel and unusual punishment prohibited by the Clause. "Justice of this kind is obviously no less shocking than the crime itself, and the new 'official' murder, far from offering redress for the offense committed against society, adds instead a second defilement to the first." . . .

I dissent . . . from the judgments in *Gregg* v. *Georgia, Proffitt* v. *Florida,* and *Jurek* v. *Texas,* insofar as each upholds the death sentences challenged in those cases. I would set aside the death sentences imposed in those cases as violative of the Eighth and Fourteenth Amendments.

MR. JUSTICE MARSHALL, dissenting:. . . .

. . . The evidence I reviewed in *Furman* remains convincing, in my view that "capital punishment is not necessary as a deterrent to crime in our society." The justification for the death penalty must be found elsewhere.

The other principal purpose said to be served by the death penalty is retribution. The notion that retribution can serve as a moral justification for the sanction of death finds credence in the opinion of my Brothers Stewart, Powell, and Stevens, and that of my Brother White in *Roberts* v. *Louisiana.* It is this notion that I find to be the most disturbing aspect of today's unfortunate decision. . . . It simply defies belief to suggest that the death penalty is necessary to prevent the American people from taking the law into their own hands. . . .

The death penalty, unnecessary to promote the goal of deterrence or to further any legitimate notion of retribution, is an excessive penalty forbidden by the Eighth and Fourteenth Amendments. I respectfully dissent from the Court's judgment upholding the sentences of death imposed upon the petitioners in these cases.

Woodson v. *North Carolina*

MR. JUSTICE STEWART, MR. JUSTICE POWELL, and MR. JUSTICE STEVENS announced the judgment of the Court and filed an opinion delivered by MR. JUSTICE STEWART:

The question in this case is whether the imposition of a death sentence for the crime of first-degree murder under the [mandatory death penalty] law of North Carolina violates the Eighth and Fourteenth Amendments. . . .

North Carolina, unlike Florida, Georgia, and Texas, . . . responded to the *Furman* decision by making death the mandatory sentence for all persons convicted of first-degree murder. In ruling on the constitutionality of the sentences imposed on the petitioners under this North Carolina statute, the Court now addresses for the first time the question whether a death sentence returned pursuant to a law imposing a mandatory death penalty for a broad category of homicidal offenses constitutes cruel and unusual punishment within the meaning of the Eighth and Fourteenth Amendments. The issue, like that explored in *Furman,* involves the procedure employed by the State to select persons for the unique and irreversible penalty of death. . . .

The history of mandatory death penalty statutes in the United States . . . reveals that the practice of sentencing to death all persons convicted of a particular offense has been rejected as unduly harsh and unworkably rigid. The two crucial indicators of evolving standards of decency respecting the imposition of punishment in our society—jury determinations and legislative enactments—both point conclusively to the repudiation of automatic death sentences. At least since the Revolution, American jurors have, with some regularity, disregarded their oaths and refused to convict defendants where a death sentence was the automatic consequence of a guilty verdict. . . . [T]he initial movement to reduce the number of capital offenses and to separate murder into degrees was prompted in part by the reaction of jurors as well as by reformers who objected to the imposition of death as the penalty for any crime. Nineteenth century journalists, statesmen, and jurists repeatedly observed that jurors were often deterred from convicting palpably guilty men of first-degree murder under mandatory statutes. Thereafter, continuing evidence of jury reluctance to convict persons of capital offenses in mandatory death penalty jurisdictions resulted in legislative authorization of discretionary jury sentencing—by Congress for federal crimes in 1897, by North Carolina in 1949, and by Congress for the District of Columbia in 1962. . . .

Although it seems beyond dispute that, at the time of the *Furman* decision in 1972, mandatory death penalty statutes had been renounced by American juries and legislatures, there remains the question whether the mandatory statutes adopted by North Carolina and a number of other States following *Furman* evince a sudden reversal of societal values regarding the imposition of capital punishment. In view of the persistent and unswerving legislative rejection of mandatory death penalty statutes beginning in 1838 and continuing for more than 130 years until *Furman*, it seems evident that the post-*Furman* enactments reflect attempts by the States to retain the death penalty in a form consistent with the Constitution, rather than a renewed societal acceptance of mandatory death sentencing. The fact that some States have adopted mandatory measures following *Furman* while others have legislated standards to guide jury discretion appears attributable to diverse readings of this Court's multi-opinioned decision in that case. . . .

It is now well established that the Eighth Amendment draws much of its meaning from "the evolving standards of decency that mark the progress of a maturing society." *Trop* v. *Dulles,* 356 U.S., at 101. . . . [O]ne of the most significant developments in our society's treatment of capital punishment has been the rejection of the common-law practice of inexorably imposing a death sentence upon every person convicted of a specified offense. North Carolina's mandatory death penalty statute for first-degree murder departs markedly from contemporary standards respecting the imposition of the punishment of death and thus cannot be applied consistently with the Eighth and Fourteenth Amendments' requirement that the State's power to punish "be exercised within the limits of civilized standards."

A separate deficiency of North Carolina's mandatory death sentence statute is its failure to provide a constitutionally tolerable response to Furman's rejection of unbridled jury discretion in the imposition of capital sentences. Central to the limited holding in *Furman* was the conviction that the vesting of standardless sentencing power in the jury violated the Eighth and Fourteenth Amendments. . . . North Carolina's mandatory death penalty statute provides no standards to guide the jury in its inevitable exercise of the power to determine which first-degree murderers shall live and which

shall die. And there is no way under the North Carolina law for the judiciary to check arbitrary and capricious exercise of that power through a review of death sentences. Instead of rationalizing the sentencing process, a mandatory scheme may well exacerbate the problem identified in *Furman* by resting the penalty determination on the particular jury's willingness to act lawlessly. While a mandatory death penalty statute may reasonably be expected to increase the number of persons sentenced to death, it does not fulfill *Furman's* basic requirement by replacing arbitrary and wanton jury discretion with objective standards to guide, regularize, and make rationally reviewable the process for imposing a sentence of death.

A third constitutional shortcoming of the North Carolina statute is its failure to allow the particularized consideration of relevant aspects of the character and record of each convicted defendant before the imposition upon him of a sentence of death. In *Furman*, members of the Court acknowledge what cannot fairly be denied—that death is a punishment different from all other sanctions in kind rather than degree. A process that accords no significance to relevant facets of the character and record of the individual offender or the circumstances of the particular offense excludes from consideration in fixing the ultimate punishment of death the possibility of compassionate or mitigating factors stemming from the diverse frailties of humankind. It treats all persons convicted of a designated offense not as uniquely individual human beings, but as members of a faceless, undifferentiated mass to be subjected to the blind infliction of the penalty of death. . . . Consideration of both the offender and the offense in order to arrive at a just and appropriate sentence has been viewed as a progressive and humanizing development. While the prevailing practice of individualizing sentencing determinations generally reflects simply enlightened policy rather than a constitutional imperative, we believe that in capital cases the fundamental respect for humanity underlying the Eighth Amendment requires consideration of the character and record of the individual offender and the circumstances of the particular offense as a constitutionally indispensable part of the process of inflicting the penalty of death.

This conclusion rests squarely on the predicate that the penalty of death is qualitatively different from a sentence of imprisonment, however long. Death, in its finality, differs more from life imprisonment than a 100-year prison term differs from one of only a year or two. Because of that qualitative difference, there is a corresponding difference in the need for reliability in the determination that death is the appropriate punishment in a specific case.

For the reasons stated, we conclude that the death sentences imposed upon the petitioners under North Carolina's mandatory death sentence statute violated the Eighth and Fourteenth Amendments and therefore must be set aside. The judgment of the Supreme Court of North Carolina is reversed insofar as it upheld the death sentences imposed upon the petitioners, and the case is remanded for further proceedings not inconsistent with this opinion.

It is so ordered.

MR. JUSTICE BRENNAN, concurring in the judgment: [omitted]

MR. JUSTICE MARSHALL, concurring in the judgment: [omitted]

MR. JUSTICE WHITE, with whom CHIEF JUSTICE BURGER and MR. JUSTICE REHNQUIST join, dissenting:. . . .

I reject petitioners' arguments that the death penalty in any circumstances is a violation of the Eighth Amendment and that the North Carolina statute, although making the imposition of the death penalty mandatory upon proof of guilt and a verdict of first-degree murder, will nevertheless result in the death penalty being imposed so seldom and arbitrarily that it is void under *Furman* v. *Georgia.* . . .

MR. JUSTICE BLACKMUN, dissenting: [omitted]

MR. JUSTICE REHNQUIST, dissenting:. . . .

The introduction of discretionary sentencing . . . creates no inference that contemporary society had rejected the mandatory system as unduly severe. . . . The plurality concedes, as they must, that following *Furman* 10 States enacted laws providing for mandatory capital punishment. These enactments the plurality seeks to explain as due to a wrong-headed reading of the holding in *Furman.* But this explanation simply does not wash. While those States may be presumed to have preferred their prior systems reposing sentencing discretion in juries or judges, they indisputably preferred mandatory capital punishment to no capital punishment at all. Their willingness to enact statutes providing that penalty is utterly inconsistent with the notion that they regarded mandatory capital sentencing as beyond "evolving standards of decency." The plurality's glib rejection of *these* legislative decisions as having little weight on the scale which it finds in the Eighth Amendment seems to me more an instance of their desire to save the people from themselves than a conscientious effort to ascertain the content of any "evolving standard of decency." . . .

I agree with the conclusion of the plurality, and with that of Mr. Justice White, that death is not a cruel and unusual punishment for the offense of which these petitioners were convicted. Since no member of the Court suggests that the trial which led to those convictions in any way fell short of the standards mandated by the Constitution, the judgments of conviction should be affirmed. . . .

[In *Roberts* v. *Louisiana,* the Court invalidated the Louisiana mandatory death penalty statute. Voting was the same as in *Woodson.*]

COKER v. GEORGIA,
433 U.S. 584 (1977)

Ehrlich Anthony Coker was serving various sentences in Georgia for murder, rape, kidnapping, and aggravated assault when he escaped from prison on September 2, 1974. That night he entered the home of Allen and Elnita Carver, tied up Mr. Carver, raped Mrs. Carver, and stole money and the family car, taking Mrs. Carver with him. Coker was soon apprehended and Mrs. Carver was released, otherwise unharmed. Coker was convicted of various offenses and sentenced to death on the rape charge. The jury had found present two of the statutorily required aggravating circumstances for the imposition of capital punishment. The Georgia Supreme Court affirmed the conviction and the sentence.

Majority votes: 7
Dissenting votes: 2

MR. JUSTICE WHITE announced the judgment of the Court and filed an opinion in which MR. JUSTICE STEWART, MR. JUSTICE BLACKMUN, and MR JUSTICE STEVENS joined:. . . .

That question, with respect to rape of an adult woman, is now before us. We have concluded that a sentence of death is grossly disproportionate and excessive punishment for the crime of rape and is therefore forbidden by the Eighth Amendment as cruel and unusual punishment.

As advised by recent cases, we seek guidance in history and from the objective evidence of the country's present judgment concerning the acceptability of death as a penalty for rape of an adult woman. At no time in the last 50 years has a majority of the States authorized death as a punishment for rape. In 1925, 18 States, the District of Columbia, and the Federal Government authorized capital punishment for the rape of an adult female. By 1971 just prior to the decision in *Furman* v. *Georgia,* that number had declined, but not substantially, to 16 States plus the Federal Government. *Furman* then invalidated most of the capital punishment statutes in this country, including the rape statutes, because, among other reasons, of the manner in which the death penalty was imposed and utilized under those laws.

With their death penalty statutes for the most part invalidated, the States were faced with the choice of enacting modified capital punishment laws in an attempt to satisfy the requirements of *Furman* or of being satisfied with life imprisonment as the ultimate punishment for any offense. . . .

[But] [i]n reviving death penalty laws to satisfy *Furman's* mandate, none of the States that had not previously authorized death for rape chose to include rape among capital felonies. Of the 16 States in which rape had been a capital offense, only three provided the death penalty for rape of an adult woman in their revised statutes—Georgia, North Carolina, and Louisiana. In the latter two States, the death penalty was mandatory for those found guilty, and those laws were invalidated by *Woodson* and *Roberts*. When Louisiana and North Carolina, responding to those decisions, again revised their capital punishment laws, they reenacted the death penalty for murder but not for rape; none of the seven other legislatures that to our knowledge have amended or replaced their death penalty statutes since July 2, 1976, including four States (in addition to Louisiana and North Carolina) that had authorized the death sentence for rape prior to 1972 and had reacted to *Furman* with mandatory statutes, included rape among the crimes for which death was an authorized punishment. . . .

Georgia is the sole jurisdiction in the United States at the present time that authorizes a sentence of death when the rape victim is an adult woman, and only two other jurisdictions provide capital punishment when the victim is a child.

The current judgment with respect to the death penalty for rape is not wholly unanimous among state legislatures, but it obviously weighs very heavily on the side of rejecting capital punishment as a suitable penalty for raping an adult woman. . . .

We do not discount the seriousness of rape as a crime. It is highly reprehensible, both in a moral sense and in its almost total contempt for the personal integrity and autonomy of the female victim and for the latter's privilege of choosing those with whom intimate relationships are to be established. Short of homicide, it is the "ultimate violation of self." It is also a violent crime because it normally involves force, or the threat of force or intimida-

tion, to overcome the will and the capacity of the victim to resist. Rape is very often accompanied by physical injury to the female and can also inflict mental and psychological damage. Because it undermines the community's sense of security, there is public injury as well.

Rape is without doubt deserving of serious punishment; but in terms of moral depravity and of the injury to the person and to the public, it does not compare with murder, which does involve the unjustified taking of human life. Although it may be accompanied by another crime, rape by definition does not include the death or even the serious injury to another person. The murderer kills; the rapist, if no more than that, does not. Life is over for the victim of the murderer; for the rape victim, life may not be nearly so happy as it was, but it is not over and normally is not beyond repair. We have the abiding conviction that the death penalty, which "is unique in its severity and revocability," is an excessive penalty for the rapist who, as such, does not take human life. . . .

The judgment of the Georgia Supreme Court upholding the death sentence is reversed and the case is remanded to that court for further proceedings not inconsistent with this opinion.

So ordered.

Mr. Justice Brennan, concurring in the judgment: [omitted]
Mr. Justice Marshall, concurring in the judgment of the Court: [omitted]
Mr. Justice Powell, concurring in part and dissenting in part: . . . .

The plurality draws a bright line between murder and all rapes—regardless of the degree of brutality of the rape or the effect upon the victim. I dissent because I am not persuaded that such a bright line is appropriate. . . . Rape is never an act committed accidentally. Rarely can it be said to be unpremeditated. There also is wide variation in the effect on the victim. The plurality opinion says that "[l]ife is over for the victim of the murderer; for the rape victim, life may not be nearly so happy as it was, but it is not over and normally is not beyond repair." But there is indeed "extreme variation" in the crime of rape. Some victims are so grievously injured physically or psychologically that life *is* beyond repair.

Thus it may be that the death penalty is not disproportionate punishment for the crime of aggravated rape. . . .

Mr. Chief Justice Burger, with whom Mr. Justice Rehnquist joins, dissenting: . . . .

. . . I accept that the Eighth Amendment's concept of disproportionality bars the death penalty for minor crimes. But rape is not a minor crime; hence the Cruel and Unusual Punishment Clause does not give the Members of this Court license to engraft their conceptions of proper public policy onto the considered legislative judgments of the States. Since I cannot agree that Georgia lacked the constitutional power to impose the penalty of death for rape, I dissent from the Court's judgment. . . .

McCLESKEY v. KEMP,
481 U.S. 279 (1987)

In 1978 Warren McCleskey, a black man, was convicted in a Georgia trial court of armed robbery and murder of a white police officer during the robbery. At the penalty hearing, the jury recommended the death penalty on the murder charge and the trial judge followed the recommendation. The Georgia Supreme Court affirmed. McCleskey challenged his conviction in a federal habeas corpus proceeding arguing that capital punishment sentencing in Georgia was racially discriminatory in violation of the Eighth and Fourteenth Amendments. In support of his claim, McCleskey's lawyers introduced a statistical study of the imposition of capital punishment in Georgia conducted by Professor David C. Baldus and associates that demonstrated that there was a disparity in the imposition of the death sentence based on the race of the murder victim and to a lesser extent the race of the defendant. The federal district court rejected the claim and the Court of Appeals for the Eleventh circuit affirmed. McCleskey took his case to the Supreme Court, which granted certiorari.

Majority votes: 5
Dissenting votes: 4

JUSTICE POWELL delivered the opinion of the Court:

This case presents the question whether a complex statistical study that indicates a risk that racial considerations enter into capital sentencing determinations proves that petitioner McCleskey's capital sentence is unconstitutional under the Eighth or Fourteenth Amendment. . . .

In support of his claim, McCleskey proffered a statistical study performed by Professors David C. Baldus, George Woodworth, and Charles Pulaski (the Baldus study) that purports to show a disparity in the imposition of the death sentence in Georgia based on the race of the murder victim and, to a lesser extent, the race of the defendant. The Baldus

study is actually two sophisticated statistical studies that examine over 2,000 murder cases that occurred in Georgia during the 1970s. The raw numbers collected by Professor Baldus indicate that defendants charged with killing white persons received the death penalty in 11% of the cases, but defendants charged with killing blacks received the death penalty in only 1% of the cases. The raw numbers also indicate a reverse racial disparity according to the race of the defendant: 4% of the black defendants received the death penalty, as opposed to 7% of the white defendants.

Baldus also divided the cases according to the combination of the race of the defendant and the race of the victim. He found that the death penalty was assessed in 22% of the cases involving black defendants and white victims; 8% of the cases involving white defendants and white victims; 1% of the cases involving black defendants and black victims; and 3% of the cases involving white defendants and black victims. Similarly, Baldus found that prosecutors sought the death penalty in 70% of the cases involving black defendants and white victims; 32% of the cases involving white defendants and white victims; 15% of the cases involving black defendants and black victims; and 19% of the cases involving white defendants and black victims.

Baldus subjected his data to an extensive analysis, taking account of 230 variables that could have explained the disparities on nonracial grounds. One of his models concludes that, even after taking account of 39 nonracial variables, defendants charged with killing white victims were 4.3 times as likely to receive a death sentence as defendants charged with killing blacks. According to this model, black defendants were 1.1 times as likely to receive a death sentence as other defendants. Thus, the Baldus study indicates that black defendants, such as McCleskey, who kill white victims have the greatest likelihood of receiving the death penalty. . . .

McCleskey argues that the Baldus study demonstrates that the Georgia capital sentencing system violates the Eighth Amendment. . . .

To evaluate McCleskey's challenge, we must examine exactly what the Baldus study may show. Even Professor Baldus does not contend that his statistics *prove* that race enters into any capital sentencing decisions or that race was a factor in McCleskey's particular case. Statistics at most may show only a likelihood that a particular factor entered into some decisions. There is, of course, some risk of racial prejudice influencing a jury's decision in a criminal case. There are similar risks that other kinds of prejudice will influence other criminal trials. The question "is at what point that risk becomes constitutionally unacceptable.'' McCleskey asks us to accept the likelihood allegedly shown by the Baldus study as the constitutional measure of an unacceptable risk of racial prejudice influencing capital sentencing decisions. This we decline to do. . . .

McCleskey's argument that the Constitution condemns the discretion allowed decisionmakers in the Georgia capital sentencing system is antithetical to the fundamental role of discretion in our criminal justice system. Discretion in the criminal justice system offers substantial benefits to the criminal defendant. Not only can a jury decline to impose the death sentence, it can decline to convict, or choose to convict of a lesser offense. Whereas decisions against a defendant's interest may be reversed by the trial judge or on appeal, these discretionary exercises of leniency are final and unreviewable. Similarly, the capacity of prosecutorial discretion to provide individualized justice is ''firmly entrenched in American law.'' As we have noted, a prosecutor can decline to charge, offer a plea bargain, or decline to seek a death sentence in any particular case. Of course, ''the power to be lenient [also] is the power to discriminate,'' but a capital-punishment system that did not allow for discretionary acts of leniency ''would be totally alien to our notions of criminal justice.''

At most, the Baldus study indicates a discrepancy that appears to correlate with race. Apparent disparities in sentencing are an inevitable part of our criminal justice system. The discrepancy indicated by the Baldus study is ''a far cry from the major systemic defects identified in *Furman*.'' . . . In light of the safeguards designed to minimize racial bias in the process, the fundamental value of jury trial in our criminal justice system, and the benefits that discretion provides to criminal defendants, we hold that the Baldus study does not demonstrate a constitutionally significant risk of racial bias affecting the Georgia capital-sentencing process. The Constitution does not require that a State eliminate any demonstrable disparity that correlates with a potentially irrelevant factor in order to operate a criminal justice system that includes capital punishment. As we have stated specifically in the context of capital punishment, the Constitution does not ''plac[e] totally unrealistic conditions on its use.'' *Gregg* v. *Georgia,* 428 U.S., at 199, n. 50. Despite McCleskey's wide ranging arguments that basically challenge the validity of capital punishment in our multi-racial society, the only question before us is whether in his case, the law of Georgia was properly applied. We agree with the District Court and the Court of Appeals for the Eleventh Circuit that this was carefully and correctly done in this case.

Accordingly, we affirm the judgment of the Court of Appeals for the Eleventh Circuit.

It is so ordered.

JUSTICE BRENNAN, with whom Justice MARSHALL, JUSTICE BLACKMUN and JUSTICE STEVENS join, dissenting:. . . .

At some point in this case, Warren McCleskey doubtless asked his lawyer whether a jury was likely to sentence him to die. A candid reply to this question would have been disturbing. First, counsel would have to tell McCleskey that few of the details of the crime or of McCleskey's past criminal conduct were more important than the fact that his victim was white. Furthermore, counsel would feel bound to tell McCleskey that defendants charged with killing white victims in Georgia are 4.3 times as likely to be sentenced to death as defendants charged with killing blacks. In addition, frankness would compel the disclosure that it was more likely than not that the race of McCleskey's victim would determine whether he received a death sentence: 6 of every 11 defendants convicted of killing a white person would not have received the death penalty if their victims had been black, while, among defendants with aggravating and mitigating factors comparable to McCleskey, 20 of every 34 would not have been sentenced to die if their victims had been black. Finally, the assessment would not be complete without the information that cases involving black defendants and white victims are more likely to result in a death sentence than cases featuring any other racial combination of defendant and victim. The story could be told in a variety of ways, but McCleskey could not fail to grasp its essential narrative line: there was a significant chance that race would play a prominent role in determining if he lived or died. . . .

It is important to emphasize at the outset that the Court's observation that McCleskey cannot prove the influence of race on any particular sentencing decision is irrelevant in evaluating his Eighth Amendment claim. Since *Furman* v. *Georgia,* 408 U.S. 238 (1972), the Court has been concerned with the *risk* of the imposition of an arbitrary sentence, rather than the proven fact of one. *Furman* held that the death penalty ''may not be imposed under sentencing procedures that create a substantial risk that the punishment will be inflicted in an arbitrary and capricious manner.'' . . . This emphasis on risk acknowledges the difficulty of divining the jury's motivation in an individual case.

In addition, it reflects the fact that concern for arbitrariness focuses on the rationality of the system as a whole, and that a system that features a significant probability that sentencing decisions are influenced by impermissible considerations cannot be regarded as rational. . . .

Defendants challenging their death sentences thus never have had to prove that impermissible considerations have actually infected sentencing decisions. We have required instead that they establish that the system under which they were sentenced posed a significant risk of such an occurrence. McCleskey's claim does differ, however, in one respect from these earlier cases: it is the first to base a challenge not on speculation about how a system *might* operate, but on empirical documentation of how it *does* operate.

The Court assumes the statistical validity of the Baldus study and acknowledges that McCleskey has demonstrated a risk that racial prejudice plays a role in capital sentencing in Georgia. Nonetheless, it finds the probability of prejudice insufficient to create constitutional concern. Close analysis of the Baldus study, however, in light of both statistical principles and human experience, reveals that the risk that race influenced McCleskey's sentence is intolerable by any imaginable standard. . . .

The statistical evidence in this case thus relentlessly documents the risk that McCleskey's sentence was influenced by racial considerations. . . .

Evaluation of McCleskey's evidence cannot rest solely on the numbers themselves. We must also ask whether the conclusion suggested by those numbers is consonant with our understanding of history and human experience. Georgia's legacy of a race-conscious criminal justice system, as well as this Court's own recognition of the persistent danger that racial attitudes may affect criminal proceedings, indicate that McCleskey's claim is not a fanciful product of mere statistical artifice. . . .

The Court cites four reasons for shrinking from the implications of McCleskey's evidence: the desirability of discretion for actors in the criminal-justice system, the existence of statutory safeguards against abuse of that discretion, the potential consequences for broader challenges to criminal sentencing, and an understanding of the contours of the judicial role. While these concerns underscore the need for sober deliberation, they do not justify rejecting evidence as convincing as McCleskey has presented. . . .

[T]he Court's fear of the expansive ramifications of a holding for McCleskey in this case is unfounded because it fails to recognize the uniquely sophisticated nature of the Baldus study. Mc-

Cleskey presents evidence that is far and away the most refined data ever assembled on any system of punishment, data not readily replicated through casual effort. Moreover, that evidence depicts not merely arguable tendencies, but striking correlations, all the more powerful because nonracial explanations have been eliminated. Acceptance of petitioner's evidence would therefore establish a remarkably stringent standard of statistical evidence unlikely to be satisfied with any frequency.

The Court's projection of apocalyptic consequences for criminal sentencing is thus greatly exaggerated. The Court can indulge in such speculation only by ignoring its own jurisprudence demanding the highest scrutiny on issues of death and race. As a result, it fails to do justice to a claim in which both those elements are intertwined—an occasion calling for the most sensitive inquiry a court can conduct. Despite its acceptance of the validity of Warren McCleskey's evidence, the Court is willing to let his death sentence stand because it fears that we cannot successfully define a different standard for lesser punishments. This fear is baseless. . . .

[I]t has been scarcely a generation since this Court's first decision striking down racial segregation, and barely two decades since the legislative prohibition of racial discrimination in major domains of national life. These have been honorable steps, but we cannot pretend that in three decades we have completely escaped the grip of an historical legacy spanning centuries. Warren McCleskey's evidence confronts us with the subtle and persistent influence of the past. His message is a disturbing one to a society that has formally repudiated racism, and a frustrating one to a Nation accustomed to regarding its destiny as the product of its own will. Nonetheless, we ignore him at our peril, for we remain imprisoned by the past as long as we deny its influence in the present.

It is tempting to pretend that minorities on death row share a fate in no way connected to our own, that our treatment of them sounds no echoes beyond the chambers in which they die. Such an illusion is ultimately corrosive, for the reverberations of injustice are not so easily confined. . . .

The Court's decision today will not change what attorneys in Georgia tell other Warren McCleskeys about their chances of execution. Nothing will soften the harsh message they must convey, nor alter the prospect that race undoubtedly will continue to be a topic of discussion. McCleskey's evidence will not have obtained judicial acceptance, but that will not affect what is said on death row. However many criticisms of today's decision may be rendered, these painful conversations will serve as the most eloquent dissents of all.

JUSTICE BLACKMUN, with whom JUSTICE MARSHALL and JUSTICE STEVENS join and with whom JUSTICE BRENNAN joins, dissenting: [omitted]

JUSTICE STEVENS, with whom JUSTICE BLACKMUN joins, dissenting: [omitted]

PENRY v. LYNAUGH,
109 S. Ct. 2934 (1989)

Is it cruel and unusual punishment to execute a mentally retarded murderer? This was the question before the Court in this case. Johnny Paul Penry had the mental age of a child of six-and-a-half years old. He had been repeatedly physically abused as a child. And he was convicted of having brutally raped, beaten, and murdered Pamela Carpenter. Penry was sentenced to death and his sentence was affirmed by the Texas Court of Criminal Appeals. After the United States Supreme Court denied certiorari on direct review, Penry began habeas corpus proceedings in federal district court naming James A. Lynaugh, the Director of the Texas Department of Corrections. Penry's lawyers argued that at the penalty stage mitigating evidence of Penry's mental retardation and childhood abuse should have been taken into account and that it is cruel and unusual punishment to execute a mentally retarded person with Penry's mental ability. The district court denied relief as did the Court of Appeals for the Fifth Circuit although the appeals court found considerable merit in the contention that the jury should have been able to consider Penry's mental retardation and history of childhood abuse. The Supreme Court's decision was twofold in that while it found that the execution of mentally retarded people convicted of capital offenses is not cruel and unusual punishment, it also found that Penry's death sentence was cruel and unusual because the jury was not instructed that it could consider the mitigating evidence of Penry's mental retardation and abused background in considering whether to impose the death penalty.

Majority votes: 5
Dissenting votes: 4

JUSTICE O'CONNOR delivered the opinion of the Court:

In this case, we must decide whether the petitioner, Johnny Paul Penry, was sentenced to death in violation of the Eighth Amendment because the jury was not instructed that it could consider and give effect to his mitigating evidence in imposing its sentence. We must also decide whether the Eighth Amendment categorically prohibits Penry's execution because he is mentally retarded. . . .

Although Penry offered mitigating evidence of his mental retardation and abused childhood as the basis for a sentence of life imprisonment rather than death, the jury that sentenced him was only able to express its views on the appropriate sentence by answering three questions: Did Penry act deliberately when he murdered Pamela Carpenter? Is there a probability that he will be dangerous in the future? Did he act unreasonably in response to provocation? The jury was never instructed that it could consider the evidence offered by Penry as *mitigating* evidence and that it could give mitigating effect to that evidence in imposing sentence. . . .

In this case, in the absence of instructions informing the jury that it could consider and give effect to the mitigating evidence of Penry's mental retardation and abused background by declining to impose the death penalty, we conclude that the jury was not provided with a vehicle for expressing its "reasoned moral response" to that evidence in rendering its sentencing decision. Our reasoning in *Lockett* and *Eddings* thus compels a remand for resentencing so that we do not "risk that the death penalty will be imposed in spite of factors which may call for a less severe penalty." "When the choice is between life and death, that risk is unacceptable and incompatible with the commands of the Eighth and Fourteenth Amendments."

Penry's second claim is that it would be cruel and unusual punishment, prohibited by the Eighth Amendment, to execute a mentally retarded person like himself with the reasoning capacity of a 7 year old. He argues that because of their mental disabilities, mentally retarded people do not possess the level of moral culpability to justify imposing the death sentence. He also argues that there is an emerging national consensus against executing the mentally retarded. The State responds that there is insufficient evidence of a national consensus against executing the retarded, and that existing procedural safeguards adequately protect the interests of mentally retarded persons such as Penry. . . .

The Eighth Amendment categorically prohibits the infliction of cruel and unusual punishments. At a minimum, the Eighth Amendment prohibits punishment considered cruel and unusual at the time the Bill of Rights was adopted. The prohibitions of the Eighth Amendment are not limited, however, to those practices condemned by the common law in 1789. The prohibition against cruel and unusual punishments also recognizes the "evolving standards of decency that mark the progress of a maturing society.'' In discerning those ''evolving standards,'' we have looked to objective evidence of how our society views a particular punishment today. The clearest and most reliable objective evidence of contemporary values is the legislation enacted by the country's legislatures. We have also looked to data concerning the actions of sentencing juries. . . .

It was well settled at common law that ''idiots,'' together with ''lunatics,'' were not subject to punishment for criminal acts committed under those incapacities. . . .

There was no one definition of idiocy at common law, but the term ''idiot'' was generally used to describe persons who had a total lack of reason or understanding, or an inability to distinguish between good and evil. . . .

The common law prohibition against punishing ''idiots'' and ''lunatics'' for criminal acts was the precursor of the insanity defense, which today generally includes ''mental defect'' as well as ''mental disease'' as part of the legal definition of insanity. . . .

In its emphasis on a permanent, congenital mental deficiency, the old common law notion of ''idiocy'' bears some similarity to the modern definition of mental retardation. The common law prohibition against punishing ''idiots'' generally applied, however, to persons of such severe disability that they lacked the reasoning capacity to form criminal intent or to understand the difference between good and evil. In the 19th and early 20th centuries, the term ''idiot'' was used to describe the most retarded of persons, corresponding to what is called ''profound'' and ''severe'' retardation today. . . .

The common law prohibition against punishing ''idiots'' for their crimes suggests that it may indeed be ''cruel and unusual'' punishment to execute persons who are profoundly or severely retarded and wholly lacking the capacity to appreciate the wrongfulness of their actions. Because of the protections afforded by the insanity defense today, such a person is not likely to be convicted or face the prospect of punishment. . . . Moreover, under *Ford* v. *Wainwright,* 477 U.S. 399 (1986), someone who is ''unaware of the punishment they are about to suffer and why they are to suffer it'' cannot be executed. . . .

Such a case is not before us today. Penry was found competent to stand trial. In other words, he was found to have the ability to consult with his lawyer with a reasonable degree of rational understanding, and was found to have a rational as well as factual understanding of the proceedings against him. In addition, the jury rejected his insanity defense, which reflected their conclusion that Penry knew that his conduct was wrong and was capable of conforming his conduct to the requirements of the law.

Penry argues, however, that there is objective evidence today of an emerging national consensus against execution of the mentally retarded, reflecting the ''evolving standards of decency that mark the progress of a maturing society.'' The federal Anti-Drug Abuse Act of 1988, prohibits execution of a person who is mentally retarded. Only one State, however, explicitly bans execution of retarded persons who have been found guilty of a capital offense.

In contrast, in *Ford* v. *Wainwright,* which held that the Eighth Amendment prohibits execution of the insane, considerably more evidence of a national consensus was available. No State permitted the execution of the insane, and 26 States had statutes explicitly requiring suspension of the execution of a capital defendant who became insane. Other States had adopted the common law prohibition against executing the insane. Moreover, in examining the objective evidence of contemporary standards of decency in *Thompson* v. *Oklahoma,* the plurality noted that 18 States expressly established a minimum age in their death penalty statutes, and all of them required that the defendant have attained at least the age of 16 at the time of the offense. In our view, the single state statute prohibiting execution of the mentally retarded, even when added to the 14 States that have rejected capital punishment completely, does not provide sufficient evidence at present of a national consensus. . . .

There is insufficient evidence of a national consensus against executing mentally retarded people convicted of capital offenses for us to conclude that it is categorically prohibited by the Eighth Amendment. . . .

In sum, mental retardation is a factor that may well lessen a defendant's culpability for a capital offense. But we cannot conclude today that the Eighth Amendment precludes the execution of any mentally retarded person of Penry's ability convicted of a capital offense simply by virtue of their mental retardation alone. So long as sentencers can consider and give effect to mitigating evidence of mental retardation in imposing sentence, an individualized determination of whether ''death is the appropriate punishment'' can be made in each particular case. While a national consensus against execution of the mentally retarded may someday emerge reflecting the ''evolving standards of decency that mark the progress of a maturing society,'' there is insufficient evidence of such a consensus today.

Accordingly, the judgment below is affirmed in part and reversed in part, and the case is remanded for further proceedings consistent with this opinion.

It is so ordered.

JUSTICE BRENNAN, with whom JUSTICE MARSHALL joins, concurring in part and dissenting in part:

I agree that the jury instructions given at sentencing in this case deprived petitioner of his constitutional right to have a jury consider all mitigating evidence that he presented before sentencing him to die. I would also hold, however, that the Eighth Amendment prohibits the execution of offenders who are mentally retarded and who thus lack the full degree of responsibility for their crimes that is a predicate for the constitutional imposition of the death penalty. . . .

In my judgment, . . . particularly the summary of the arguments advanced in the brief of the American Association on Mental Retardation and other *amici curiae,* compels the conclusion that such executions [of mentally retarded persons] are unconstitutional. I would therefore reverse the judgment of the Court of Appeals in its entirety.

JUSTICE SCALIA, with whom THE CHIEF JUSTICE, JUSTICE WHITE, and JUSTICE KENNEDY join, concurring in part and dissenting in part:. . . .

I disagree with the holding . . . of the Court's opinion that petitioner's . . . sentencing was unconstitutional because the Texas jury was not permitted fully to consider and give effect to the mitigating evidence of his mental retardation and background of abuse . . . I also disagree with the disposition of the merits of this contention . . .

It could not be clearer that *Jurek* v. *Texas* adopted the constitutional rule that the instructions had to render all mitigating circumstances relevant to the jury's verdict, but that the precise manner of their relevance—the precise *effect* of their consideration—could be channeled by law. The [*Jurek*] opinion approved the Texas statute expressly because it "focuses the jury's objective consideration of the particularized circumstances of the individual offense and the individual offender." . . . Special Issue One required the jury to determine whether " 'the conduct of the defendant that caused the death of the deceased was committed deliberately and with the reasonable expectation that the death of the deceased or another would result.' " . . . Evidence of Penry's mental retardation and abused childhood was relevant to that point. He was permitted to introduce all that evidence, relied upon it in urging the jury to answer "no" to the Special Issues, and had the benefit of an instruction

specifically telling the jury to consider all evidence for that purpose. Thus, the only available contention here, and the basis on which the Court decides the case, is that this evidence "has relevance to . . . moral culpability beyond the scope of the special issues." That contention was considered and rejected by *Jurek's* holding that the statute's "focus[-ing of] the jury's objective consideration" was constitutional. . . .

In providing for juries to consider all mitigating circumstances insofar as they bear upon (1) deliberateness, (2) future dangerousness, and (3) provocation, it seems to me Texas had adopted a rational scheme that meets the two concerns of our Eighth Amendment jurisprudence. The Court today demands that it be replaced, however, with a scheme that simply dumps before the jury all sympathetic factors bearing upon the defendant's background and character, and the circumstances of the offense, so that the jury may decide without further guidance whether he "lacked the moral culpability to be sentenced to death," "did not deserve to be sentenced to death," or "was not sufficiently culpable to deserve the death penalty." The Court seeks to dignify this by calling it a process that calls for a "reasoned moral response," but reason has nothing to do with it, the Court having eliminated the structure that required reason. It is an unguided, emotional "moral response" that the Court demands be allowed.

The Court cannot seriously believe that rationality and predictability can be achieved, and capriciousness avoided, by " 'narrow[ing] a sentencer's discretion to *impose* the death sentence,' " but expanding his discretion " *'to decline to impose the death sentence.' "* The decision whether to impose the death penalty is a unitary one; unguided discretion not to impose is unguided discretion to impose as well. In holding that the jury had to be free to deem Penry's mental retardation and sad childhood relevant for whatever purpose it wished, the Court has come full circle, not only permitting but requiring what *Furman* once condemned. "Freakishly" and "wantonly," *Furman,* 408 U.S., at 310 (Stewart, J. concurring), have been rebaptized "reasoned moral response." I do not think the Constitution forbids what the court imposes here, but I am certain it does not require it.

I respectfully dissent.

STANFORD v. KENTUCKY,
109 S. Ct. 2969 (1989)

Kevin Stanford was 17 years old when he and an accomplice robbed a gas station, raped and sodomized 20-year-old Baerbel Poore who worked as an attendant, and then abducted her and drove to a secluded area where Kevin shot her point-blank in the face, killing her. Heath Wilkins was 16 when he and an accomplice robbed a convenience store and Heath stabbed to death Nancy Allen, a 26-year-old mother of two who was working behind the counter of the store she owned with her husband. Kevin and Heath were sentenced to death and their convictions and sentences were affirmed by their state supreme courts. The United States Supreme Court took these cases to answer the question whether it is cruel and unusual punishment to execute individuals for capital offenses committed at 16 or 17 years of age.

Majority votes: 5
Dissenting votes: 4

JUSTICE SCALIA announced the judgment of the Court and delivered the opinion of the Court with respect to Parts I, II, III, and IV-A, and an opinion with respect to Parts IV-B and V, in which THE CHIEF JUSTICE, JUSTICE WHITE and JUSTICE KENNEDY join:

These two consolidated cases require us to decide whether the imposition of capital punishment on an individual for a crime committed at 16 or 17 years of age constitutes cruel and unusual punishment under the Eighth Amendment.

I. . . . [THE FACTS OF THE CASES ARE PRESENTED]

II

The thrust of both Wilkins' and Stanford's arguments is that imposition of the death penalty on those who were juveniles when they committed their crimes falls within the Eighth Amendment's prohibition against "cruel and unusual punishments." Wilkins would have us define juveniles as individuals 16 years of age and under; Stanford would draw the line at 17. . . .

[P]etitioners argue that their punishment is contrary to the "evolving standards of decency that mark the progress of a maturing society." They are correct in asserting that this Court has "not confined the prohibition embodied in the Eighth Amendment to 'barbarous' methods that were generally outlawed in the 18th century," but instead has interpreted the Amendment "in a flexible and dynamic manner." In determining what standards have "evolved," however, we have looked not to our own conceptions of decency, but to those of modern American society as a whole. As we have said, "Eighth Amendment judgments should not be, or appear to be, merely the

subjective views of individual Justices; judgment should be informed by objective factors to the maximum possible extent." . . .

III

"[F]irst" among the " 'objective indicia that reflect the public attitude toward a given sanction' " are statutes passed by society's elected representatives. Of the 37 States whose laws permit capital punishment, 15 decline to impose it upon 16-year-old offenders and 12 decline to impose it on 17-year-old offenders. This does not establish the degree of national consensus this Court has previously thought sufficient to label a particular punishment cruel and unusual. In invalidating the death penalty for rape of an adult woman, we stressed that Georgia was the *sole* jurisdiction that authorized such a punishment. See *Coker* v. *Georgia,* 433 U. S., at 595–596. In striking down capital punishment for participation in a robbery in which an accomplice takes a life, we emphasized that only eight jurisdictions authorized similar punishment. *Enmund* v. *Florida,* 458 U.S., at 792. In finding that the Eighth Amendment precludes execution of the insane and thus requires an adequate hearing on the issue of sanity, we relied upon (in addition to the common-law rule) the fact that "no State in the Union" permitted such punishment. *Ford* v. *Wainwright,* 477 U.S., at 408. And in striking down a life sentence without parole under a recidivist statute, we stressed that "[i]t appears that [petitioner] was treated more severely than he would have been in any other State." *Solem* v. *Helm,* 463 U.S. 277, 300 (1983).

Since a majority of the States that permit capital punishment authorize it for crimes committed at age 16 or above, petitioners' cases are more analogous to *Tison* v. *Arizona,* 481 U.S. 137, (1987) than *Coker, Enmund, Ford,* and *Solem.* In *Tison,* which upheld Arizona's imposition of the death penalty for major participation in a felony with reckless indifference to human life, we noted that only 11 of those jurisdictions imposing capital punishment rejected its use in such circumstances. As we noted earlier, here the number is 15 for offenders under 17, and 12 for offenders under 18. We think the same conclusion as in *Tison* is required in this case. . . .

IV
A

Wilkins and Stanford argue, however, that even if the laws themselves do not establish a settled consensus, the application of the laws does. That contemporary society views capital punishment of 16- and 17-year-old offenders as inappropriate is demonstrated, they say, by the reluctance of juries to impose, and prosecutors to seek, such sentences. Petitioners are quite correct that a far smaller number of offenders under 18 than over 18 have been sentenced to death in this country. . . . These statistics, however, carry little significance. Given the undisputed fact that a far smaller percentage of capital crimes is committed by persons under 18 than over 18, the discrepancy in treatment is much less than might seem. Granted, however, that a substantial discrepancy exists, that does not establish the requisite proposition that the death sentence for offenders under 18 is categorically unacceptable to prosecutors and juries. To the contrary, it is not only possible but overwhelmingly probable that the very considerations which induce petitioners and their supporters to believe that death should *never* be imposed on offenders under 18 cause prosecutors and juries to believe that it should *rarely* be imposed.

B

This last point suggests why there is also no relevance to the laws cited by petitioners and their *amici* which set 18 or more as the legal age for engaging in various activities, ranging from driving to drinking alcoholic beverages to voting. It is, to begin with, absurd to think that one must be mature enough to drive carefully, to drink responsibly, or to vote intelligently, in order to be mature enough to understand that murdering another human being is profoundly wrong, and to conform one's conduct to that most minimal of all civilized standards. But even if the requisite degrees of maturity were comparable, the age-statutes in question would still not be relevant. They do not represent a social judgment that all persons under the designated ages are not responsible enough to drive, to drink, or to vote, but at most a judgment that the vast majority are not. These laws set the appropriate ages for the operation of a system that makes its determinations in gross, and that does not conduct individualized maturity tests for each driver, drinker, or voter. The criminal justice system, however, does provide individualized testing. . . .

V

Having failed to establish a consensus against capital punishment for 16- and 17-year-old offenders through state and federal statutes and the behavior of prosecutors and juries, petitioners seek to demonstrate it through other indicia, including public opinion polls, the views of interest groups and the positions adopted by various professional associations. We decline the invitation to rest constitutional law upon such uncertain foundations. A revised national consensus so broad, so clear and so enduring as to justify a permanent prohibition upon all units of democratic government must appear in the operative acts (laws and the application of laws) that the people have approved. . . . To say, as the dissent says, that "it is for *us* ultimately to judge whether the Eighth Amendment permits imposition of the death penalty," . . . and to mean that as the dissent means it, *i.e.,* that it is for *us* to judge, not on the basis of what we perceive the Eighth Amendment originally prohibited, or on the basis of what we perceive the society through its democratic processes now overwhelmingly disapproves, but on the basis of what we think "proportionate" and "measurably contributory to acceptable goals of punishment"—to say and mean that, is to replace judges of the law with a committee of philosopher-kings. . . .

We discern neither a historical nor a modern societal consensus forbidding the imposition of capital punishment on any person who murders at 16 or 17 years of age. Accordingly, we conclude that such punishment does not offend the Eighth Amendment's prohibition against cruel and unusual punishment.

The judgments of the Supreme Court of Kentucky and the Supreme Court of Missouri are therefore

Affirmed.

JUSTICE O'CONNOR, concurring in part and concurring in the judgment: . . .

I conclude that the death sentences for capital murder imposed by Missouri and Kentucky on petitioners Wilkins and Stanford respectively should not be set aside because it is sufficiently clear that no national consensus forbids the imposition of capital punishment on 16 or 17-year-old capital murderers. . . . The day may come when there is such general legislative rejection of the execution of 16 or 17-year-old capital murderers that a clear national consensus can be said to have developed. Because I do not believe that day has yet arrived, I concur in Parts I-IV-A of the plurality's opinion and I concur in its judgment.

I am unable, however, to join the remainder of the plurality's opinion . . . Part V of the plurality's opinion "emphatically reject[s]," the suggestion that, beyond an assessment of the specific enactments of American legislatures, there remains a constitutional obligation imposed upon this Court to judge whether the " 'nexus between the punishment imposed and the defendant's blameworthiness' " is proportional. . . . Part IV-B of the plurality's opinion specifically rejects as irrelevant to Eighth Amendment considerations state statutes that distinguish juveniles from adults for a variety of other purposes. In my view, this Court does have a constitutional obligation to conduct proportionality analysis. . . . In *Thompson* I specifically identified age-based statutory classifications as "relevant to Eighth Amendment proportionality analysis." Thus, although I do not believe that these particular cases can be resolved through proportionality analysis, . . . I reject the suggestion that the use of such analysis is improper as a matter of Eighth Amendment jurisprudence. Accordingly, I join all but Parts IV-B and V of the Court's opinion.

JUSTICE BRENNAN, with whom JUSTICE MARSHALL, JUSTICE BLACKMUN, and JUSTICE STEVENS join, dissenting:

I believe that to take the life of a person as punishment for a crime committed when below the age of 18 is cruel and unusual and hence is prohibited by the Eighth Amendment.

The method by which this Court assesses a claim that a punishment is unconstitutional because it is cruel and unusual is established by our precedents, and it bears little resemblance to the method four Members of the Court apply in this case. To be sure, we *begin* the task of deciding whether a punishment is unconstitutional by reviewing legislative enactments and the work of sentencing juries relating to the punishment in question, to determine whether our Nation has set its face against a punishment to an extent that it can be concluded that the punishment offends our "evolving standards of decency." The Court undertakes such an analysis in this case. But JUSTICE SCALIA, in his separate opinion on this point, would treat the Eighth Amendment inquiry as *complete* with this investigation. I agree with JUSTICE O'CONNOR, that a more searching inquiry is mandated by our precedents interpreting the Cruel and Unusual Punishment Clause. In my view, that inquiry must in this case go beyond age-based statutory classifications relating to matters other than capital punishment, . . . and must also encompass what JUSTICE SCALIA calls, with evident but misplaced disdain, "ethico-scientific" evidence. Only then can we be in a position to judge, as our cases require, whether a punishment is unconstitutionally excessive, either because it is disproportionate given the culpability

of the offender, or because it serves no legitimate penal goal. . . .

The Court's discussion of state laws concerning capital sentencing gives a distorted view of the evidence of contemporary standards that these legislative determinations provide. . . . [A]ccuracy demands that the baseline for our deliberations should be that 27 States refuse to authorize a sentence of death in the circumstances of petitioner Stanford's case, and 30 would not permit Wilkins' execution; that 18 States have not squarely faced the question; and that only the few remaining jurisdictions have explicitly set an age below 18 at which a person may be sentenced to death. . . .

Both in absolute and in relative terms, imposition of the death penalty on adolescents is distinctly unusual. Adolescent offenders make up only a small proportion of the current death row population: 30 out of a total of 2,186 inmates, or 1.37 percent. . . . Forty-one, or 2.3 percent, of the 1,813 death sentences imposed between January 1, 1982, and June 30, 1988, were for juvenile crimes. And juvenile offenders are significantly less likely to receive the death penalty than adults. During the same period, there were 97,086 arrests of adults for homicide, and 1,772 adult death sentences, or 1.8 percent; and 8,911 arrests of minors for homicide, compared to 41 juvenile death sentences, or 0.5 percent. . . .

Further indicators of contemporary standards of decency that should inform our consideration of the Eighth Amendment question are the opinions of respected organizations. Where organizations with expertise in a relevant area have given careful consideration to the question of a punishment's appropriateness, there is no reason why that judgment should not be entitled to attention as an indicator of contemporary standards. There is no dearth of opinion from such groups that the state-sanctioned killing of minors is unjustified. A number, indeed, have filed briefs *amicus curiae* in these cases, in support of petitioners. The American Bar Association has adopted a resolution opposing the imposition of capital punishment upon any person for an offense committed while under age 18, as has the National Council of Juvenile and Family Court Judges. The American Law Institute's Model Penal Code similarly includes a lower age limit of 18 for the death sentence. And the National Commission on Reform of the Federal Criminal Laws also recommended that 18 be the minimum age. . . .

Together, the rejection of the death penalty for juveniles by a majority of the States, the rarity of the sentence for juveniles, both as an absolute and a comparative matter, the decisions of respected organizations in relevant fields that this punishment is unacceptable, and its rejection generally throughout the world, provide to my mind a strong grounding for the view that it is not constitutionally tolerable that certain States persist in authorizing the execution of adolescent offenders. It is unnecessary, however, to rest a view that the Eighth Amendment prohibits the execution of minors solely upon a judgment as to the meaning to be attached to the evidence of contemporary values outlined above, for the execution of juveniles fails to satisfy two well-established and independent Eighth Amendment requirements—that a punishment not be disproportionate, and that it make a contribution to acceptable goals of punishment. . . .

Proportionality analysis requires that we compare "the gravity of the offense," understood to include not only the injury caused, but also the defendant's culpability, with "the harshness of the penalty." In my view, juveniles so generally lack the degree of responsibility for their crimes that is a predicate for the constitutional imposition of the death penalty that the Eighth Amendment forbids that they receive that punishment. . . .

But the factors discussed above indicate that 18 is the dividing line that society has generally drawn, the point at which it is thought reasonable to assume that persons have an ability to make and a duty to bear responsibility for their judgments. Insofar as age 18 is a necessarily arbitrary social choice as a point at which to acknowledge a person's maturity and responsibility, given the different developmental rates of individuals, it is in fact "a conservative estimate of the dividing line between adolescence and adulthood. Many of the psychological and emotional changes that an adolescent experiences in maturing do not actually occur until the early 20s." . . .

Excluding juveniles from the class of persons eligible to receive the death penalty will have little effect on any deterrent value capital punishment may have for potential offenders who are over 18: these adult offenders may of course remain eligible for a death sentence. The potential deterrent effect of juvenile executions on adolescent offenders is also insignificant. The deterrent value of capital punishment rests "on the assumption that we are rational beings who always think before we act, and then base our actions on a careful calculation of the gains and losses involved." Gardiner, The Purposes of Criminal Punishment, 21 Mod. L. Rev. 117, 122 (1958). As the plurality noted in *Thomp-*

son, "[t]he likelihood that the teenage offender has made the kind of cost-benefit analysis that attaches any weight to the possibility of execution is so remote as to be virtually nonexistent." First, juveniles "have less capacity . . . to think in long-range terms than adults," and their careful weighing of a distant, uncertain, and indeed highly unlikely consequence prior to action is most improbable. In addition, juveniles have little fear of death, because they have "a profound conviction of their own omnipotence and immortality." . . . Because imposition of the death penalty on persons for offenses committed under the age of 18 makes no measurable contribution to the goals of either retribution or deterrence, it is "nothing more than the purposeless and needless imposition of pain and suffering," and is thus excessive and unconstitutional.

There are strong indications that the execution of juvenile offenders violates contemporary standards of decency: a majority of States decline to permit juveniles to be sentenced to death; imposition of the sentence upon minors is very unusual even in those States that permit it; and respected organizations with expertise in relevant areas regard the execution of juveniles as unacceptable, as does international opinion. These indicators serve to confirm in my view my conclusion that the Eighth Amendment prohibits the execution of persons for offenses they committed while below the age of 18, because the death penalty is disproportionate when applied to such young offenders, and fails measurably to serve the goals of capital punishment. I dissent.

RUMMEL v. ESTELLE,
445 U.S. 263 (1980)

William James Rummel got into trouble with the Texas authorities once too often. In 1964 he was convicted of his first felony, fraudulent use of a credit card to obtain $80 worth of goods (for which he was sentenced to three years' imprisonment). His second felony conviction occurred in 1969 and that was for passing a forged check in the amount of $28.36 (for which he was sentenced to four years in a state penitentiary). His third felony conviction was for obtaining $120.75 by false pretenses, but this time he received a life sentence mandated by a Texas recidivist statute. Rummel sought a writ of habeas corpus in federal district court claiming that his life sentence was so disproportionate to the crimes he had committed as to constitute cruel and unusual punishment in violation of the Eighth and Fourteenth Amendments. The district court re-

jected this claim and the Court of Appeals for the Fifth Circuit affirmed. The Supreme Court was thus faced with deciding whether three nonviolent criminal offenses involving fraud with a monetary value of $229.11 added up to a constitutionally viable mandatory life sentence.

Majority votes: 5
Dissenting votes: 4

MR. JUSTICE REHNQUIST delivered the opinion of the Court:. . . .

In this case . . . we need not decide whether Texas could impose a life sentence upon Rummel merely for obtaining $120.75 by false pretenses. Had Rummel only committed that crime, under the law enacted by the Texas Legislature he could have been imprisoned for no more than 10 years. In fact, at the time that he obtained the $120.75 by false pretenses, he already had committed and had been imprisoned for two other felonies, crimes that Texas and other States felt were serious enough to warrant significant terms of imprisonment even in the absence of prior offenses. Thus the interest of the State of Texas here is not simply that of making criminal the unlawful acquisition of another person's property; it is in addition the interest, expressed in all recidivist statutes, in dealing in a harsher manner with those who by repeated criminal acts have shown that they are simply incapable of conforming to the norms of society as established by its criminal law. By conceding the validity of recidivist statutes generally, Rummel himself concedes that the State of Texas, or any other State, has a valid interest in so dealing with that class of persons. . . . Rummel attempts to ground his proportionality attack on an alleged "nationwide" trend away from mandatory life sentences and toward "lighter, discretionary sentences." According to Rummel, "No jurisdiction in the United States or the Free World punishes habitual offenders as harshly as Texas." In support of this proposition, Rummel offers detailed charts and tables documenting the history of recidivist statutes in the United States since 1776. . . .

In comparing . . . recidivist programs . . . *Rummel* creates a complex hierarchy of statutes and places Texas' recidivist scheme alone on the top rung. This isolation is not entirely convincing. Both West Virginia and Washington, for example, impose mandatory life sentences upon the commission of a third felony. . . . A number of States impose a mandatory life sentence upon conviction of four felonies rather than three. Other States require one or more of the felonies to be "violent" to sup-

port a life sentence. Still other States leave the imposition of a life sentence after three felonies within the discretion of a judge or jury. . . .

Nor do Rummel's extensive charts even begin to reflect the complexity of the comparison he asks this Court to make. Texas, we are told, has a relatively liberal policy of granting "good time" credits to its prisoners, a policy that historically has allowed a prisoner serving a life sentence to become eligible for parole in as little as 12 years. We agree with Rummel that his inability to enforce any "right" to parole precludes us from treating his life sentence as if it were equivalent to a sentence of 12 years. Nevertheless, because parole is "an established variation on imprisonment of convicted criminals," a proper assessment of Texas' treatment of Rummel could hardly ignore the possibility that he will not actually be imprisoned for the rest of his life. If nothing else, the possibility of parole, however slim, serves to distinguish Rummel from a person sentenced under a recidivist statute like Mississippi's, which provides for a sentence of life without parole upon conviction of three felonies including at least one violent felony. . . .

The most casual review of the various criminal justice systems now in force in the 50 States of the Union shows that the line dividing felony theft from petty larceny, a line usually based on the value of the property taken, varies markedly from one State to another. We believe that Texas is entitled to make its own judgment as to where such lines lie, subject only to those strictures of the Eighth Amendment that can be informed by objective factors. Moreover, given Rummel's record, Texas was not required to treat him in the same manner as it might treat him were this his first "petty property offense." Having twice imprisoned him for felonies, Texas was entitled to place upon Rummel the onus of one who is simply unable to bring his conduct within the social norms prescribed by the criminal law of the State.

The purpose of a recidivist statute such as that involved here is not to simplify the task of prosecutors, judges, or juries. Its primary goals are to deter repeat offenders and, at some point in the life of one who repeatedly commits criminal offenses serious enough to be punished as felonies, to segregate that person from the rest of society for an extended period of time. This segregation and its duration are based not merely on that person's most recent offense but also on the propensities he has demonstrated over a period of time during which he has been convicted of and sentenced for other crimes. Like the line dividing felony theft from petty larceny, the point at which a recidivist will be deemed to have demonstrated the necessary propensities and the amount of time that the recidivist will be isolated from society are matters largely within the discretion of the punishing jurisdiction.

We therefore hold that the mandatory life sentence imposed upon this petitioner does not constitute cruel and unusual punishment under the Eighth and Fourteenth Amendments. The judgment of the Court of Appeals will be

Affirmed.

MR. JUSTICE STEWART, concurring: [omitted]
MR. JUSTICE POWELL, with whom MR. JUSTICE BRENNAN, MR. JUSTICE MARSHALL, and MR. JUSTICE STEVENS join, dissenting:. . . .

This Court today affirms the Fifth Circuit's decision. I dissent because I believe that (i) the penalty for a noncapital offense may be unconstitutionally disproportionate, (ii) the possibility of parole should not be considered in assessing the nature of the punishment, (iii) a mandatory life sentence is grossly disproportionate as applied to petitioner, and (iv) the conclusion that this petitioner has suffered a violation of his Eighth Amendment rights is compatible with principles of judicial restraint and federalism. . . .

The scope of the Cruel and Unusual Punishments Clause extends not only to barbarous methods of punishment, but also to punishments that are grossly disproportionate. Disproportionality analysis measures the relationship between the nature and number of offenses committed and the severity of the punishment inflicted upon the offender. The inquiry focuses on whether a person deserves such punishment, not simply on whether punishment would serve a utilitarian goal. A statute that levied a mandatory life sentence for overtime parking might well deter vehicular lawlessness, but it would offend our felt sense of justice. The Court concedes today that the principle of disproportionality plays a role in the review of sentences imposing the death penalty, but suggests that the principle may be less applicable when a noncapital sentence is challenged. Such a limitation finds no support in the history of Eighth Amendment jurisprudence. . . .

. . . [A] few basic principles emerge from the history of the Eighth Amendment. Both barbarous forms of punishment and grossly excessive punishments are cruel and unusual. A sentence may be excessive if it serves no acceptable social purpose, or is grossly disproportionate to the seriousness of the crime. The principle of disproportionality has been acknowledged to apply to both capital and noncapital sentences. . . .

Each of the crimes that underlies the petitioner's conviction as an habitual offender involves the use of fraud to obtain small sums of money ranging from $28.36 to $120.75. In total, the three crimes involved slightly more than $230. None of the crimes involved injury to one's person, threat of injury to one's person, violence, the threat of violence, or the use of a weapon. Nor does the commission of any such crimes ordinarily involve a threat of violent action against another person or his property. It is difficult to imagine felonies that pose less danger to the peace and good order of a civilized society than the three crimes committed by the petitioner. Indeed, the state legislature's recodification of its criminal law supports this conclusion. Since the petitioner was convicted as an habitual offender; the State has reclassified his third offense, theft by false pretext, as a misdemeanor. . . .

More than three-quarters of American jurisdictions have never adopted an habitual offender statute that would commit the petitioner to mandatory life imprisonment. The jurisdictions that currently employ habitual offender statutes either (i) require the commission of more than three offenses, (ii) require the commission of at least one violent crime, (iii) limit a mandatory penalty to less than life, or (iv) grant discretion to the sentencing authority. In none of the jurisdictions could the petitioner have received a mandatory life sentence merely upon the showing that he committed three nonviolent property-related offenses. . . .

Finally, it is necessary to examine the punishment that Texas provides for other criminals. First and second offenders who commit more serious crimes than the petitioner may receive markedly less severe sentences. The only first-time offender subject to a mandatory life sentence is a person convicted of capital murder. A person who commits a first-degree felony, including murder, aggravated kidnapping or aggravated rape, may be imprisoned from 5–99 years. Persons who commit a second-degree felony, including voluntary manslaughter, rape, or robbery, may be punished with a sentence of between two and 20 years. A person who commits a second felony is punished as if he had committed a felony of the next higher degree. Thus, a person who rapes twice may receive a five-year sentence. He also may, but need not, receive a sentence functionally equivalent to life imprisonment.

The State argues that these comparisons are not illuminating because a three-time recidivist may be sentenced more harshly than a first-time offender. Of course, the State may mandate extra punishment for a recidivist. In Texas a person convicted twice of the unauthorized use of a vehicle receives a greater sentence than a person once convicted for that crime, but he does not receive a sentence as great as a person who rapes twice. Such a statutory scheme demonstrates that the state legislature has attempted to choose a punishment in proportion to the nature and number of offenses committed.

Texas recognizes when it sentences two-time offenders that the amount of punishment should vary with the severity of the offenses committed. But all three-time felons receive the same sentence. In my view, imposition of the same punishment upon persons who have committed completely different types of crimes raises serious doubts about the proportionality of the sentence applied to the least harmful offender. . . .

We are construing a living Constitution. The sentence imposed upon the petitioner would be viewed as grossly unjust by virtually every layman and lawyer. In my view, objective criteria clearly establish that a mandatory life sentence for defrauding persons of about $230 crosses any rationally drawn line separating punishment that lawfully may be imposed from that which is proscribed by the Eighth Amendment. I would reverse the decision of the Court of Appeals.

SOLEM v. HELM,
463 U.S. 277 (1983)

Jerry Buckley Helm was no stranger to the South Dakota courts. In 1964, 1966, and 1969 Helm was convicted of third-degree burglary (breaking and entering). In 1972 he was convicted of obtaining money under false pretenses. In 1973 he was convicted of grand larceny followed two years later with a conviction of a third offense of driving while intoxicated. All of these nonviolent crimes are felonies under South Dakota law. In each of these crimes committed by Helm, alcohol was a contributing factor. He clearly had a drinking problem. Then, in 1979, Helm was charged with writing a check for $100 from a bank in which he had no account. Helm testified at his trial that he was drinking that day and did not remember what happened. Ordinarily the maximum punishment for that crime would have been five years' imprisonment and a $5000 fine. Helm, however, was sentenced to life imprisonment without possibility of parole under South Dakota's recidivist statute because of his six prior felony convictions. The South Dakota Supreme Court affirmed the sentence, and Helm's appeal to the Governor for commutation of the sentence was denied. Helm then sought habeas corpus

relief in federal district court contending that his sentence constituted cruel and unusual punishment in violation of the Eighth and Fourteenth Amendments. The district court denied relief but the Court of Appeals reversed. The petition for the writ of habeas corpus named Herman Solem, the warden.

Majority votes: 5
Dissenting votes: 4

JUSTICE POWELL delivered the opinion of the Court:. . . .

When sentences are reviewed under the Eighth Amendment, courts should be guided by objective factors that our cases have recognized . . . including (i) the gravity of the offense and the harshness of the penalty; (ii) the sentences imposed on other criminals in the same jurisdiction; and (iii) the sentences imposed for commission of the same crime in other jurisdictions.

Application of these factors assumes that courts are competent to judge the gravity of an offense, at least on a relative scale. In a broad sense this assumption is justified, and courts traditionally have made these judgments—just as legislatures must make them in the first instance. Comparisons can be made in light of the harm caused or threatened to the victim or society, and the culpability of the offender. . . . Indeed, there are widely shared views as to the relative seriousness of crimes. . . . For example, as the criminal laws make clear, nonviolent crimes are less serious than crimes marked by violence or the threat of violence. . . .

. . . It remains to apply the analytical framework established by our prior decisions to the case before us. We first consider the relevant criteria, viewing Helm's sentence as life imprisonment without possibility of parole. We then consider the State's argument that the possibility of commutation is sufficient to save an otherwise unconstitutional sentence.

Helm's crime was "one of the most passive felonies a person could commit." It involved neither violence nor threat of violence to any person. The $100 face value of Helm's "no account" check was not trivial, but neither was it a large amount. One hundred dollars was less than half the amount South Dakota required for a felonious theft. It is easy to see why such a crime is viewed by society as among the less serious offenses.

Helm, of course, was not charged simply with uttering a "no account" check, but also with being an habitual offender. And a State is justified in punishing a recidivist more severely than it punishes a first offender. Helm's status, however, cannot be considered in the abstract. His prior offenses, although classified as felonies, were all relatively minor. All were nonviolent and none was a crime against a person. Indeed, there was no minimum amount in either the burglary or the false pretenses statutes and the minimum amount covered by the grand larceny statute was fairly small.

Helm's present sentence is life imprisonment without possibility of parole. Barring executive clemency, Helm will spend the rest of his life in the state penitentiary. This sentence is far more severe than the life sentence we considered in *Rummel* v. *Estelle*. Rummel was likely to have been eligible for parole within 12 years of his initial confinement, a fact on which the Court relied heavily. Helm's sentence is the most severe punishment that the State could have imposed on any criminal for any crime. Only capital punishment, a penalty not authorized in South Dakota when Helm was sentenced, exceeds it.

We next consider the sentences that could be imposed on other criminals in the same jurisdiction. . . . [T]here were a handful of crimes that were necessarily punished by life imprisonment: murder, and, on a second or third offense, treason, first degree manslaughter, first degree arson, and kidnapping. There was a larger group for which life imprisonment was authorized in the discretion of the sentencing judge, including: treason, first degree manslaughter, first degree arson, and kidnapping; attempted murder, placing an explosive device on an aircraft, and first degree rape on a second or third offense; and any felony after three prior offenses. Finally, there was a large group of very serious offenses for which life imprisonment was not authorized, including a third offense of heroin dealing or aggravated assault.

Criminals committing any of these offenses ordinarily would be thought more deserving of punishment than one uttering a "no account" check—even when the bad-check writer had already committed six minor felonies. Moreover, there is no indication in the record that any habitual offender other than Helm has ever been given the maximum sentence on the basis of comparable crimes. . . . Helm has been treated in the same manner as, or more severely than, criminals who have committed far more serious crimes.

Finally, we compare the sentences imposed for commission of the same crime in other jurisdictions. . . . It appears that Helm was treated more severely than he would have been in any other State.

The State argues that the present case is essentially the same as *Rummel* v. *Estelle*, for the possibility of parole in that case is matched by the possibility of executive clemency here. The State reasons that the Governor could commute Helm's sentence to a term of years. We conclude, however, that the South Dakota commutation system is fundamentally different from the parole system that was before us in *Rummel*.

As a matter of law, parole and commutation are different concepts, despite some surface similarities. Parole is a regular part of the rehabilitative process. Assuming good behavior, it is the normal expectation in the vast majority of cases. . . . [I]t is possible to predict, at least to some extent, when parole might be granted. Commutation, on the other hand, is an *ad hoc* exercise of executive clemency. A Governor may commute a sentence at any time for any reason without reference to any standards. . . . In South Dakota commutation is more difficult to obtain than parole. . . . In fact, no life sentence has been commuted in over eight years, while parole—where authorized—has been granted regularly during that period. . . .

The Constitution requires us to examine Helm's sentence to determine if it is proportionate to his crime. Applying objective criteria, we find that Helm has received the penultimate sentence for relatively minor criminal conduct. He has been treated more harshly than other criminals in the State who have committed more serious crimes. He has been treated more harshly than he would have been in any other jurisdiction, with the possible exception of a single State. We conclude that his sentence is significantly disproportionate to his crime, and is therefore prohibited by the Eighth Amendment. The judgment of the Court of Appeals is accordingly

Affirmed.

CHIEF JUSTICE BURGER, with whom JUSTICE WHITE, JUSTICE REHNQUIST, and JUSTICE O'CONNOR join, dissenting:

The controlling law governing this case is crystal clear, but today the Court blithely discards any concept of *stare decisis*, trespasses gravely on the authority of the States, and distorts the concept of proportionality of punishment by tearing it from its moorings in capital cases. Only three Terms ago, we held in *Rummel* v. *Estelle*, (1980), that a life sentence imposed after only a *third* nonviolent felony conviction did not constitute cruel and unusual punishment under the Eighth Amendment. Today, the Court ignores its recent precedent and holds that a life sentence imposed after a *seventh* felony conviction constitutes cruel and unusual punishment under the Eighth Amendment. Moreover, I reject the fiction that all Helm's crimes were innocuous or nonviolent. Among his felonies were three burglaries and a third conviction for drunk driving. By comparison Rummel was a relatively "model citizen." Although today's holding cannot rationally be reconciled with *Rummel*, the Court does not purport to overrule *Rummel*. I therefore dissent. . . .

. . . *Rummel* held that the length of a sentence of imprisonment is a matter of legislative discretion; this is so particularly for recidivist statutes. I simply cannot understand how the Court can square *Rummel* with its holding that "a criminal sentence must be proportionate to the crime for which the defendant has been convicted." . . .

By asserting the power to review sentences of imprisonment for excessiveness the Court launches into uncharted and unchartable waters. Today it holds that a sentence of life imprisonment, without the possibility of parole, is excessive punishment for a seventh allegedly "nonviolent" felony. How about the eighth "nonviolent" felony? The ninth? The twelfth? Suppose one offense was a simple assault? Or selling liquor to a minor? Or statutory rape? Or price-fixing? The permutations are endless and the Court's opinion is bankrupt of realistic guiding principles. Instead, it casually lists several allegedly "objective" factors and arbitrarily asserts that they show respondent's sentence to be "significantly disproportionate" to his crimes. Must all these factors be present in order to hold a sentence excessive under the Eighth Amendment? How are they to be weighed against each other? Suppose several States punish severely a crime that the Court views as trivial or petty? I can see no limiting principle in the Court's holding.

There is a real risk that this holding will flood the appellate courts with cases in which equally arbitrary lines must be drawn. . . .

U.S. v. SALERNO,
481 U.S. 739 (1987)

Congress enacted the Bail Reform Act of 1984, which provided for pretrial detention, sometimes referred to as preventive detention, whereby those accused of having committed serious felonies and thought to be dangerous are not freed on bail but are held in jail until the charges are adjudicated. The act provides for a detention hearing during which various procedural rights are provided. The act was challenged in this litigation by Anthony Salerno and Vincent Cafaro, who were arrested and charged with numerous acts of racketeering activity including fraud, extortion, and conspiracy to

commit murder. At arraignment federal prosecutors sought to have Salerno and Cafaro preventively detained and they offered evidence showing that Salerno was the "boss" of the Genovese crime family of La Cosa Nostra and that Cafaro was a "captain" in the family. The federal district court ordered the detention of Salerno and Cafaro. The Court of Appeals for the Second Circuit reversed and ruled that pretrial detention on the ground of future dangerousness is unconstitutional. The government took the case to the Supreme Court.

Majority votes: 6
Dissenting votes: 3

CHIEF JUSTICE REHNQUIST delivered the opinion of the Court:

The Bail Reform Act of 1984 allows a federal court to detain an arrestee pending trial if the government demonstrates by clear and convincing evidence after an adversary hearing that no release conditions "will reasonably assure . . . the safety of any other person and the community." The United States Court of Appeals for the Second Circuit struck down this provision of the Act as facially unconstitutional, because, in that court's words, this type of pretrial detention violates "substantive due process." We granted certiorari because of a conflict among the Courts of Appeals regarding the validity of the Act. We hold that, as against the facial attack mounted by these respondents, the Act fully comports with constitutional requirements. We therefore reverse. . . .

The Due Process Clause of the Fifth Amendment provides that "No person shall . . . be deprived of life, liberty, or property, without due process of law. . . ." This Court has held that the Due Process Clause protects individuals against two types of government action. So-called "substantive due process" prevents the government from engaging in conduct that "shocks the conscience" . . . or interferes with rights "implicit in the concept of ordered liberty." When government action depriving a person of life, liberty, or property survives substantive due process scrutiny, it must still be implemented in a fair manner. This requirement has traditionally been referred to as "procedural" due process.

Respondents first argue that the Act violates substantive due process because the pretrial detention it authorizes constitutes impermissible punishment before trial. . . .

As an initial matter, the mere fact that a person is detained does not inexorably lead to the conclusion that the government has imposed punishment. To determine whether a restriction on liberty constitutes impermissible punishment or permissible regulation, we first look to legislative intent. . . .

We conclude that the detention imposed by the Act falls on the regulatory side of the dichotomy. The legislative history of the Bail Reform Act clearly indicates that Congress did not formulate the pretrial detention provisions as punishment for dangerous individuals. Congress instead perceived pretrial detention as a potential solution to a pressing societal problem. There is no doubt that preventing danger to the community is a legitimate regulatory goal.

Nor are the incidents of pretrial detention excessive in relation to the regulatory goal Congress sought to achieve. The Bail Reform Act carefully limits the circumstances under which detention may be sought to the most serious of crimes. . . . The arrestee is entitled to a prompt detention hearing, and the maximum length of pretrial detention is limited by the stringent time limitations of the Speedy Trial Act. . . . We conclude, therefore, that the pretrial detention contemplated by the Bail Reform Act is regulatory in nature, and does not constitute punishment before trial in violation of the Due Process Clause.

The Court of Appeals nevertheless concluded that "the Due Process Clause prohibits pretrial detention on the ground of danger to the community as a regulatory measure, without regard to the duration of the detention." Respondents characterize the Due Process Clause as erecting an impenetrable "wall" in this area that "no governmental interest—rational, important, compelling or otherwise—may surmount."

We do not think the Clause lays down any such categorical imperative. We have repeatedly held that the government's regulatory interest in community safety can, in appropriate circumstances, outweigh an individual's liberty interest. For example, . . . we have found that sufficiently compelling governmental interests can justify detention of dangerous persons. Thus, we have found no absolute constitutional barrier to detention of potentially dangerous resident aliens pending deportation proceedings. *Carlson* v. *Landon,* 342 U.S. 524, 537–542, (1952); *Wong Wing* v. *United States,* 163 U.S. 228 (1896). We have also held that the government may detain mentally unstable individuals who present a danger to the public, *Addington* v. *Texas,* 441 U.S. 418 (1979), and dangerous defendants who become incompetent to stand trial, *Jackson* v. *Indiana,* 406 U.S. 715, 731–739 (1972); *Greenwood* v. *United States,* 350 U.S. 366 (1956). We have approved of postarrest regulatory detention of juveniles when they present a continuing danger to the community. *Schall* v. *Martin.* . . . Finally, respon-

dents concede and the Court of Appeals noted that an arrestee may be incarcerated until trial if he presents a risk of flight or a danger to witnesses.

Respondents characterize all of these cases as exceptions to the "general rule" of substantive due process that the government may not detain a person prior to a judgment of guilt in a criminal trial. Such a "general rule" may freely be conceded, but we think that these cases show a sufficient number of exceptions to the rule that the congressional action challenged here can hardly be characterized as totally novel. Given the well-established authority of the government, in special circumstances, to restrain individuals' liberty prior to or even without criminal trial and conviction, we think that the present statute providing for pretrial detention on the basis of dangerousness must be evaluated in precisely the same manner that we evaluated the laws in the cases discussed above.

The government's interest in preventing crime by arrestees is both legitimate and compelling. . . . The Bail Reform Act . . . narrowly focuses on a particularly acute problem in which the government interests are overwhelming. The Act operates only on individuals who have been arrested for a specific category of extremely serious offenses. Congress specifically found that these individuals are far more likely to be responsible for dangerous acts in the community after arrest. Nor is the Act by any means a scattershot attempt to incapacitate those who are merely suspected of these serious crimes. The government must first of all demonstrate probable cause to believe that the charged crime has been committed by the arrestee, but that is not enough. In a full-blown adversary hearing, the government must convince a neutral decisionmaker by clear and convincing evidence that no conditions of release can reasonably assure the safety of the community or any person. While the government's general interest in preventing crime is compelling, even this interest is heightened when the government musters convincing proof that the arrestee, already indicted or held to answer for a serious crime, presents a demonstrable danger to the community. Under these narrow circumstances, society's interest in crime prevention is at its greatest.

On the other side of the scale, of course, is the individual's strong interest in liberty. We do not minimize the importance and fundamental nature of this right. But, as our cases hold, this right may, in circumstances where the government's interest is sufficiently weighty, be subordinated to the greater needs of society. . . .

Finally, we may dispose briefly of respondents' facial challenge to the procedures of the Bail Reform Act. . . .

Under the Bail Reform Act, the procedures by which a judicial officer evaluates the likelihood of future dangerousness are specifically designed to further the accuracy of that determination. Detainees have a right to counsel at the detention hearing. They may testify in their own behalf, present information by proffer or otherwise, and cross-examine witnesses who appear at the hearing. The judicial officer charged with the responsibility of determining the appropriateness of detention is guided by statutorily enumerated factors, which include the nature and the circumstances of the charges, the weight of the evidence, the history and characteristics of the putative offender, and the danger to the community. The government must prove its case by clear and convincing evidence. Finally, the judicial officer must include written findings of fact and a written statement of reasons for a decision to detain. The Act's review provisions provide for immediate appellate review of the detention decision.

We think these extensive safeguards suffice to repel a facial challenge. . . . Given the legitimate and compelling regulatory purpose of the Act and the procedural protections it offers, we conclude that the Act is not facially invalid under the Due Process Clause of the Fifth Amendment.

Respondents also contend that the Bail Reform Act violates the Excessive Bail Clause of the Eighth Amendment. . . .

The Eighth Amendment addresses pretrial release by providing merely that "Excessive bail shall not be required." This Clause, of course, says nothing about whether bail shall be available at all. Respondents nevertheless contend that this Clause grants them a right to bail calculated solely upon considerations of flight. . . .

While we agree that a primary function of bail is to safeguard the courts' role in adjudicating the guilt or innocence of defendants, we reject the proposition that the Eighth Amendment categorically prohibits the government from pursuing other admittedly compelling interests through regulation of pretrial release. . . . Nothing in the text of the Bail Clause limits permissible government considerations solely to questions of flight. The only arguable substantive limitation of the Bail Clause is that the government's proposed conditions of release or detention not be "excessive" in light of the perceived evil. Of course, to determine whether the government's response is excessive, we must compare that response against the interest the government seeks to protect by means of that response. Thus, when the government has admitted that its only interest is in preventing flight, bail must be set by a court at a sum designed to ensure that goal,

and no more. We believe that when Congress has mandated detention on the basis of a compelling interest other than prevention of flight, as it has here, the Eighth Amendment does not require release on bail. . . .

The judgment of the Court of Appeals is therefore

Reversed.

JUSTICE MARSHALL, with whom JUSTICE BRENNAM joins, dissenting:

This case brings before the Court for the first time a statute in which Congress declares that a person innocent of any crime may be jailed indefinitely, pending the trial of allegations which are legally presumed to be untrue, if the Government shows to the satisfaction of a judge that the accused is likely to commit crimes, unrelated to the pending charges, at any time in the future. Such statutes, consistent with the usages of tyranny and the excesses of what bitter experience teaches us to call the police state, have long been throught incompatible with the fundamental human rights protected by our Constitution. Today a majority of this Court holds otherwise. Its decision disregards basic principles of justice established centuries ago and enshrined beyond the reach of governmental interference in the Bill of Rights. . . .

The Government . . . invites the Court to address the facial constitutionality of the pretrial detention statute in a case involving two respondents, one of whom has been sentenced to a century of jail time in another case and released pending appeal with the Government's consent, while the other was released on bail *in this case,* with the Government's consent, because he had become an informant. These facts raise, at the very least, a substantial question as to the Court's jurisdiction, for it is far from clear that there is now an actual controversy between these parties. . . .

The majority approaches respondents' challenge to the Act by dividing the discussion into two sections, one concerned with the substantive guarantees implicit in the Due Process Clause, and the other concerned with the protection afforded by the Excessive Bail Clause of the Eighth Amendment. This is a sterile formalism, which divides a unitary argument into two independent parts and then professes to demonstrate that the parts are individually inadequate. . . .

The logic of the majority's Eighth Amendment analysis is . . . unsatisfactory. The Eighth Amendment, as the majority notes, states that "[e]xcessive bail shall not be required." The majority then declares, as if it were undeniable, that: "[t]his Clause, of course, says nothing about whether bail shall be available at all." If excessive bail is imposed the defendant stays in jail. The same result is achieved if bail is denied altogether. Whether the magistrate sets bail at $1 billion or refuses to set bail at all, the consequences are indistinguishable. It would be mere sophistry to suggest that the Eighth Amendment protects against the former decision, and not the latter. Indeed, such a result would lead to the conclusion that there was no need for Congress to pass a preventive detention measure of any kind; every federal magistrate and district judge could simply refuse, despite the absence of any evidence of risk of flight or danger to the community, to set bail. This would be entirely constitutional, since, according to the majority, the Eighth Amendment "says nothing about whether bail shall be available at all."

But perhaps, the majority says, this manifest absurdity can be avoided. Perhaps the Bail Clause is addressed only to the judiciary. . . . The text of the Amendment, which provides simply that "[e]xcessive bail shall not be required, nor excessive fines imposed, nor cruel and unusual punishments inflicted," provides absolutely no support for the majority's speculation that both courts and Congress are forbidden to inflict cruel and unusual punishments, while only the courts are forbidden to require excessive bail. . . .

The essence of this case may be found, ironically enough, in a provision of the Act to which the majority does not refer. Title 18 U.S.C. § 3142(j) (1982 ed., Suppl. III) provides that "[n]othing in this section shall be construed as modifying or limiting the presumption of innocence." But the very pith and purpose of this statute is an abhorrent limitation of the presumption of innocence. The majority's untenable conclusion that the present Act is constitutional arises from a specious denial of the role of the Bail Clause and the Due Process Clause in protecting the invaluable guarantee afforded by the presumption of innocence. . . .

There is a connection between the peculiar facts of this case and the evident constitutional defects in the statute which the Court upholds today. Respondent Cafaro was originally incarcerated for an indeterminate period at the request of the Government, which believed (or professed to believe) that his release imminently threatened the safety of the community. That threat apparently vanished, from the Government's point of view, when Cafaro agreed to act as a covert agent of the Government. There could be no more eloquent demonstration of the coercive power of authority to imprison upon prediction, or of the dangers which the almost inevitable abuses pose to the cherished liberties of a free society. . . .

Honoring the presumption of innocence is often difficult; sometimes we must pay substantial social costs as a result of our commitment to the values we espouse. But at the end of the day the presumption of innocence protects the innocent; the shortcuts we take with those whom we believe to be guilty injure only those wrongfully accused and, ultimately, ourselves.

Throughout the world today there are men, women, and children interned indefinitely, awaiting trials which may never come or which may be a mockery of the word, because their governments believe them to be "dangerous." Our Constitution, whose construction began two centuries ago, can shelter us forever from the evils of such unchecked power. Over two hundred years it has slowly, through our efforts, grown more durable, more expansive, and more just. But it cannot protect us if we lack the courage, and the self-restraint, to protect ourselves. Today a majority of the Court applies itself to an ominous exercise in demolition. Theirs is truly a decision which will go forth without authority, and come back without respect.

I dissent.

JUSTICE STEVENS, dissenting: [omitted]

A Note on Civil Liberties

There are a variety of rights other than those discussed in the previous chapters and distinct from the equality rights discussed in the subsequent three chapters. This note briefly examines five such rights, but, of course, students should be well aware that this far from exhausts the catalogue of already recognized rights or those that are potentially recognizable by the courts under various provisions of the Constitution.

First, it should be recognized that there are procedural due process rights in the civil law realm. In an important decision by the Burger Court with major implications for the rights of those who receive benefits from government, the Court ruled in *Goldberg* v. *Kelly,* 397 U.S. 254 (1970), that public assistance payments to welfare recipients may not be discontinued without first affording recipients a hearing. The hearing, said the Court, should permit recipients to appear personally, with or without counsel, before the official who finally determines continued eligibility, to present written or oral evidence before that official, and to confront or cross-examine adverse witnesses.

There are a variety of other circumstances which require procedural due process; for example, civil servants, said the Court in *Cleveland Board of Education* v. *Loudermill,* 470 U.S. 532 (1985), are entitled to a pretermination hearing to respond to charges that threaten their employment. Even with state laws authorizing repossession of goods, at some point, said the Burger Court in *Fuentes* v. *Shevin,* 407 U.S. 67 (1972), and *Mitchell* v. *W. T. Grant Company,* 416 U.S. 600 (1974), there must be an opportunity for a hearing and a judicial determination. Public school students, according to *Goss* v. *Lopez,* 419 U.S. 565 (1975), also have procedural due process rights not to be suspended from school without first being afforded notice and a hearing. However, the Burger Court also decided in *Ingraham* v. *Wright,* 430 U.S. 651 (1977), that public school students were not entitled to notice and a hearing prior to the imposition of corporal punishment (in this case paddling on the buttocks).

There are procedural due process rights to protect against involuntary confinement of a nondangerous mentally ill person if that person can live safely in freedom (see *O'Connor* v. *Donaldson,* 422 U.S. 563 [1975]). The Court also ruled in *Addington* v. *Texas,* 441 U.S. 418 (1979), that for indefinite commitment to a mental institution, the due process clause requires that the state provide proof that the mental illness necessitates institutional confinement to avoid danger to the patient or to others and the standard of proof to be used must be more strict than the "preponderance of the evidence" measure ordinarily used in civil law, but less strict than the "beyond a reasonable doubt" required in criminal law. More recently, the Court suggested that procedural due process for involuntary admission to a state mental hospital should be followed when the person who "voluntarily" signs forms requesting admission is under medication and is disoriented (*Zinerman* v. *Burch,* 110 S.Ct. 975 [1990]). But there is no due process right to a judicial hearing before a state may treat an unwilling mentally ill prisoner with anti-psychotic drugs if the prisoner is a danger to self or others or if the treatment is in the prisoner's medical interest (*Washington* v. *Harper,* 110 S.Ct. 1028 [1990]).

A second right is the right of access to the civil courts regardless of ability to pay. The Burger Court in 1971 ruled in *Boddie* v. *Connecticut,* 401 U.S. 371, that due process of law prohibits a state from denying, solely because of inability to pay court fees and costs, access to its courts to those seeking a divorce. But the Burger Court did not find a due process violation by a court requiring indigents to pay the ordinary filing fee as a condition to a discharge in voluntary bankruptcy. In *United States* v. *Kras,* 409 U.S. 434 (1973), the Court found no constitutional right to obtain a discharge of one's debt in bankruptcy. The Court in *Lassiter* v. *Department of Social Services of Durham County,* 452 U.S. 18 (1981), emphasized that poor people do not automatically have the right to court-appointed counsel except where their personal liberty is at stake. Thus, any

other circumstances, even the loss of parental custody of a child, does not necessarily add up to a due process right to free legal counsel.

A third right is the right to sue governmental officials for damages for violating rights established under the federal Constitution or federal law. One ruling, *Butz* v. *Economou,* 438 U.S. 478 (1978), permits suits against federal officials who were or should have been aware that they were violating constitutional rights except when it is demonstrated that absolute immunity is essential for conducting the public business. The President of the United States has absolute immunity from damages liability predicated on his official acts, as we saw in **Nixon** v. **Fitzgerald** (chap. 7). So do judges (*Pierson* v. *Ray,* 386 U.S. 547 [1967] except when accused of civil rights violations under section 1983, see *Forrester* v. *White,* 484 U.S. 219 [1988]) and prosecutors (*Imbler* v. *Pachtman,* 424 U.S. 409 [1976]) but *not* public defenders (*Tower* v. *Glover,* 467 U.S. 914 [1984]), prison officials (*Cleavinger* v. *Saxner,* 474 U.S. 193 [1986]), or law enforcement officers for Fourth Amendment violations (*Malley* v. *Briggs,* 475 U.S. 335 [1986]). FBI agents have a qualified immunity against Fourth Amendment suits. That is, FBI agents may not be subject to civil damages if they can establish as a matter of law that a reasonable officer could have believed that the warrantless search of a person's home did not violate the Fourth Amendment even though it actually did (*Anderson* v. *Creighton,* 483 U.S. 635 [1987]). A county may be sued for damages for Fourth Amendment violations (*Pembaur* v. *City of Cincinnati,* 475 U.S. 469 [1986]). The Court in *Monell* v. *New York City Dept. of Social Services,* 436 U.S. 658 (1978) also made local government subject to damage suits for civil rights violations and in *Owen* v. *City of Independence, Missouri,* 445 U.S. 622 (1980), ruled that a municipality may not assert the good faith of its officials as a defense. A municipality may also be held liable for constitutional violations resulting from its failure to train its employees (*City of Canton, Ohio* v. *Harris,* 109 S.Ct. 1197 [1989]). If a constitutional violation is found, a city may be held accountable for compensatory damages for the loss actually suffered but not for punitive damages (*City of Newport* v. *Fact Concerts, Inc.,* 453 U.S. 247 [1981]). Private citizens are entitled to sue their own states, under the Civil Rights Act of 1871, whenever state policy allegedly violates *any* federal law (*Maine* v. *Thiboutot,* 488 U.S. 1 [1980]). And they may sue in state courts, not just in the federal courts (*Howlett By and Through Howlett* v. *Rose,* 110 S.Ct. 2430 [1990]).

Similarly, state officials do not have absolute immunity from state tort-law liability for their conduct if it exceeds the outer perimeter of their official duties and discretion (*Westfall* v. *Erwin,* 484 U.S. 292 [1988]). But the Rehnquist Court has been very sympathetic to state and local officials. For example, in *DeShaney* v. *Winnebago County DDS,* 109 S. Ct. 998 (1989), the Court rejected a suit against social workers and local officials who had received complaints that a child was being abused by his father but did nothing to remove him from his father's custody until the boy was beaten so severely that he suffered permanent brain damage. The majority ruled that the state had no constitutional duty to protect the child from his father after receiving reports of possible abuse.

A fourth right is the right to travel. In 1941 the Supreme Court in **Edwards** v. **California** (chap. 10) struck down a California law aimed at keeping nonresident indigents out of the state. In **Shapiro** v. **Thompson** (chap. 20) the Warren Court struck down a one-year residency requirement for welfare assistance eligibility as interfering with the right to travel interstate. The Burger Court in *Dunn* v. *Blumstein,* 405 U.S. 330 (1972), ruled that a durational residency requirement for voting, that is, the amount of time the person has lived within the jurisdiction in which he or she wishes to vote, must be only for the minimum

time necessary for the jurisdiction to establish accurate voting lists. This decision struck down a residency law that required one year of in-state and three months of county residency. The Court found not only a burden on the right to vote but a fundamental infringement on the right to travel. So, too, was the right to travel invoked by the Burger Court when it struck down in *Memorial Hospital* v. *Maricopa County,* 415 U.S. 250 (1974), a one-year residency requirement as a condition to receiving nonemergency hospitalization or medical care at county expense. The right to travel abroad, subject only to minimal reasonable area restrictions, has also been recognized by the Court (see *Aptheker* v. *Secretary of State,* 378 U.S. 500 [1964]; *Zemel* v. *Rusk,* 381 U.S. 1 [1965]), but the Burger Court in *Regan* v. *Wald,* 468 U.S. 222 (1984), upheld President Reagan's restrictions on tourist travel to Cuba as a reasonable exercise of presidential power under statutory law.

The fifth and final right to be discussed here is the right to personal privacy that includes those rights that inhere in our personhood.[1] The right to be secure in the privacy of our own homes, as integral to our personhood, is, of course, explicitly recognized in the Constitution in both the Third and Fourth Amendments. The Third Amendment is a guarantee that government cannot summarily, without our consent, invade our homes for the purpose of sheltering one or more members of the armed forces. The Fourth Amendment, as we have seen earlier in chapter 16, guarantees our right to be secure in our persons, houses, papers, and effects against unreasonable searches and seizures. The Thirteenth Amendment goes to the heart of personhood and privacy by abolishing slavery. Involuntary servitude is also prohibited except as a legally imposed punishment for someone con-

---

[1] For a formulation of rights of personhood that define a fundamental privacy right, see Laurence H. Tribe, *American Constitutional Law* (Mineola, N.Y.: The Foundation Press, 1978), chap. 15.

victed of a crime. But the right to personal privacy has, in recent years, been interpreted to encompass some of the most personal decisions an individual can make, decisions concerning sexual reproduction.

It was the Warren Court that inaugurated this broader view of the right to personal privacy with the landmark decision of **Griswold** v. **Connecticut,** as we discussed in chapter 6. In that case, it will be recalled, the Court found that various guarantees in the Bill of Rights "have penumbras formed by emanations from those guarantees that help give them life and substance." The specific guarantees of the First, Third, Fourth, Fifth (self-incrimination clause), and Ninth Amendments create zones of privacy. The right to use contraceptives goes to the heart of the intimate decisions made within a marital relationship, suggested the Court, and this is a constitutionally protected manifestation of privacy. The Burger Court went even further, as we saw in chapter 6, culminating in **Roe** v. **Wade.** The key point of that decision is that it is the woman's *right,* as long as the fetus cannot live outside the mother, to determine for herself whether or not to bear a child. A more private right involving the essentials of personhood is hard to imagine. Yet, the fact that a decision to have an abortion means the taking of an innocent life or a potential life makes this decision all the more poignant and troublesome. But the Court recognized that such a personal decision must remain with the woman and not legislative majorities, the only exception being that a *viable* fetus may be protected by the state and such abortions may be prohibited. The Rehnquist Court, however, has since undermined *Roe* v. *Wade* and has been accepting most state restrictions on abortion (see the discussion in chap. 19).

The right to personal privacy covers a variety of other concerns as well, some of which have been recognized by the Supreme Court and some of which have not. For example, while adult consensual heterosexual sexual activity appears for the most part to be protected by the Court's privacy decisions, adult consensual homosexual sexual activity does not. The Court made that clear in the 1986 ruling in **Bowers** v. **Hardwick** (chap. 6). No right to adult sexual preference has been recognized by the Court.[2] To give a different example, outside the sex-related sphere, the Court rejected the privacy argument that had been used to challenge a New York state law under which prescriptions for certain drugs, along with the names and addresses of the patients, were required to be reported to the state and were then to be kept in computer banks for five years. That case was *Whalen* v. *Roe,* 429 U.S. 389 (1977). To give a positive example, the Court found in *Winston* v. *Lee,* 470 U.S. 753 (1985), that a forced surgical operation on a suspect to remove a bullet that would be used as evidence violated the expectation of personal privacy under the Fourth Amendment. At times the right to privacy is in direct confrontation with other rights. The Rehnquist Court upheld a right to residential privacy when it upheld a municipal ordinance prohibiting picketing before or about a residence or dwelling of any individual (*Frisby* v. *Schultz,* 487 U.S. 474 [1988]). The dissenters would have found the ordinance a violation of the First Amendment. Another example was the decision in *U.S. Dept. of Justice* v. *Reporters Committee,* 109 S.Ct. 1468 (1989) in which the Court ruled that disclosure of an FBI rap sheet to a third party including the press fell under the exemptions provided by the Freedom of Information Act because it reasonably could be expected to constitute an invasion of personal privacy. The Justice Department, said a unanimous Court, was correct in refusing to release the rap sheet. In this case, privacy interests outweighed the public's right to know. Clearly the privacy con-

[2]Ibid., pp. 941–948. Also see John Brigham, *Civil Liberties and American Democracy* (Washington, D.C.: C.Q. Press, 1984), pp. 144–146.

cept is a crucial civil libertarian concern and can be expected to continue to be deeply involved in the evolving jurisprudence of rights.

One final point that must be emphasized is that concepts of civil liberties evolve and change. The current constitutional concept of the right to personal privacy is very different from privacy notions of a half century ago. The right of women to make decisions concerning the use of their bodies was not seriously discussed as a potential constitutional right as recently as thirty years ago. In the equality sphere, as we shall see in the following chapters, the concept of racial equality has evolved over the past half century, as has the concept of sexual equality over the past two decades. There are new concepts of rights that are beginning to emerge as society evolves and becomes sensitized to issues long hidden from view, such as rights of spouses to be free from spousal abuse and children from child abuse. The concept of the right to die is another of these issues and was considered by the Rehnquist Court in **Cruzan** v. **Director, Missouri Dept. of Health** (reprinted at the end of this book). There is an emerging concept of a right to a lifestyle including adult sexual preference. It is not inconceivable that at some point in the future the right to breathe clean air, drink pure water, and enjoy the unspoiled wilderness will assume constitutionally protected status. The courts of tomorrow will be grappling with new views of civil liberties, and government officials will be taking actions and refraining from actions that, in turn, will determine the extent to which we as Americans enjoy our old as well as newly recognized rights.

PART
FOUR

EQUAL PROTECTION OF
THE LAWS

Chapter

18

Racial Equality

DECISIONAL TRENDS

The struggle of black people to achieve racial equality in the United States has been a long, hard, and continuing one. Of all minority and ethnic groups in the United States, only blacks were subjected to slavery, an institution present at the founding of the country. Although slavery obviously raises the most fundamental issue of human rights, the framers of the Constitution were divided between the view of slaves as property and the idea that slavery was morally wrong. Being pragmatists, the framers wrote the Constitution so that it neither approved nor disapproved of slavery. There were, however, oblique but unmistakable references to that hideous institution in the provisions for the counting of the population for census and for other governmental purposes (direct taxes and representation in the House of Representatives), an end to the foreign slave trade by 1808, and the return of runaway slaves. The Marshall Court in a variety of contexts dealt with slavery issues, but on the whole the justices, both northern-

ers and southerners, like their fellow Americans showed a lack of sensitivity to this enormous human tragedy. For example, in an 1810 case, *Scott* v. *Negro Ben,* 6 Cranch 3 (1810), the Court ruled that a Maryland law prohibiting the importation of slaves into the state could not be used to take away the "property" of a man who claimed to have owned the slave for the previous three years. In an 1812 case, *Mima Queen and Child, Petitioners for Freedom* v. *Hepburn,* 7 Cranch 290 (1812), Chief Justice Marshall, for the majority, ruled that hearsay evidence that tended to establish the freedom of two slaves must be excluded, thus dooming the mother and daughter to lifetimes of slavery.

Justice Story, in contrast to John Marshall, thought slavery to be a great evil and ruled in a circuit court decision in 1822 that the slave trade was "repugnant to the great principles of Christian duty, the dictates of natural religion, the obligations of good faith and morality, and the eternal maxims of social justice." However, when a case raising a similar issue (the legality of the international slave trade according to international law) was decided by the Court, Story bowed to the contrary views of his colleagues and did not dissent. That case, *The Antelope,* 10 Wheaton 66 (1825), arose when an American ship off the coast of Florida captured a ship with a cargo of 250 slaves. The question of what happens to these slaves—should they be set free or returned to their Spanish and Portuguese owners—was before the Court and the decision depended on the answer to the difficult question of whether the maritime slave trade violated international law (an act of Congress in 1807 had already banned the foreign slave trade). The Court ruled that the international slave trade did *not* violate international law and that the slaves should be returned to their foreign owners.

Until the horrendous decision in **Dred Scott v. Sandford** (chap. 6), the Taney Court sometimes cleverly and sometimes crudely avoided dealing with most of the legal issues of slavery. Three early Taney Court decisions deserve brief mention. *Groves* v. *Slaughter,* 15 Peters 449 (1841), was concerned with the validity of a Mississippi constitutional provision that prohibited the importation of slaves into the state. This provision had been placed in the state's constitution in order to stem the drain of capital away from the state, as well as to protect the state's notorious "slave-breeding" industry. The case seemed to raise the question of the status of slaves. If slaves were articles of commerce, then Mississippi would be impinging on Congress' commerce powers. If slaves were persons, then that raised the touchy question of whether they had any rights at all under the United States Constitution. The Court begged off answering these questions by simply noting that Mississippi had not enacted any legislation implementing the disputed state constitutional provision; thus, a promissory note for the payment of slaves imported into the state was legal under Mississippi law.

In another case decided in 1841, *United*

States v. *Schooner Amistad,* 15 Peters 518, the Court had to determine the fate of black Africans who were enslaved by Spanish slave traders and were being brought illegally to the United States. What had happened was that the Africans managed to overpower and in the process kill the ship's officers. A United States war vessel rescued the slaves, but their Spanish owners claimed them. Justice Story, himself personally opposed to slavery, wrote the opinion of the Court freeing the Africans and ruling that they should be sent home to Africa. The following year Justice Story wrote the opinion of the Court in *Prigg* v. *Pennsylvania,* 16 Peters 539, a decision that had the effect intended by its author (but not the southerners on the Court)—that of hampering the recapture of runaway slaves (although the decision pleased neither North nor South). In later cases the Court upheld the provisions of the national fugitive slave law. (See, e.g., *Jones* v. *Van Zandt,* 5 Howard 215 [1847], and *Norris* v. *Crocker,* 13 Howard 429 [1851].) In 1852, in *Moore* v. *Illinois,* 14 Howard 13, the Court, in effect, overturned the *Prigg* decision by ruling that a state can, under its police powers, act to aid in the capture of runaway slaves.

The Civil War did not bring an end to slavery issues coming to the Supreme Court. As one might expect from a Republican-dominated Court, the Court decided against slave traders in the *Slavers* case, 2 Wallace 366 (1865), but upheld the validity of a contract for the payment of the purchase price of a slave sold before the Civil War in *Osborn* v. *Nicholson,* 13 Wallace 654 (1872). In the latter case, only Chief Justice Chase dissented, insisting that the Thirteenth Amendment prohibiting slavery made such contracts contrary to public policy and therefore unenforceable.

The Fourteenth Amendment became part of the Constitution in 1868 and is the most complex, longest, and in some ways the most ambiguous of the Civil War amendments. The first section of the amendment permits states to set their own standards of rights but requires them to apply them equally (the equal protection clause) as well as to provide minimal procedural standards (the due process clause) along with minimal substantive rights (the privileges and immunities clause). Citizenship was defined in the first sentence of Section 1, which directly overturned the *Dred Scott* ruling's assertion that black people were not citizens of the United States. The opening words of Section 1 are ''All persons born or naturalized in the United States, and subject to the jurisdiction thereof, are citizens of the United States and of the State wherein they reside.'' Black people are incontrovertibly black *Americans* with full rights of citizenship—or so the Fourteenth Amendment promised. (Ironically, the Court was to rule in *Elk* v. *Wilkins,* 112 U.S. 94 [1884], that American Indians or Native Americans were noncitizens and therefore not entitled to the constitutionally protected rights of American citizens.)

It is true that the framers and ratifiers had no consensus as to what ''privileges or immunities'' were protected by Section 1 although some framers of the Fourteenth Amendment thought in expansive terms of the new amendment encompassing the basic rights contained in the Bill of Rights. It should also be pointed out that the due process and equal protection rights were guarantees to ''persons'' and not just citizens. This meant that aliens and blacks who had not been born in the United States (typically those brought over during the slave trade before 1808) were to be given these procedural and equality rights. Section 5 of the amendment gave Congress enforcement powers. This meant that Congress could assume authority over the internal affairs of any state in order to enforce the guarantees of the first section if a state did not voluntarily comply with its mandates.

The record of the Waite and Fuller Courts on the rights of black Americans under the Fourteenth Amendment was a dismal one. **The Slaughterhouse Cases** (chap. 6), although

not involving blacks, nevertheless severely contracted any potential civil rights protection through the privileges and immunities clause. In subsequent decisions the Court dealt directly with legislation affecting the rights of blacks, and the Court in most instances came down firmly on the anti-black side, striking down anti-racist federal legislation and upholding racist state statutes. Some of the highlights of this trend of decisions include:

- An 1876 decision, *United States* v. *Cruikshank,* 92 U.S. 542, invalidating convictions of racist white hoodlums who used violence to break up a political meeting of Louisiana blacks. By overturning the convictions, which had been obtained under the federal Enforcement Act of 1870, the Court severely limited the scope of the act.
- Another 1876 decision, *United States* v. *Reese,* 92 U.S. 214, in which the Court struck down portions of the Enforcement Act of 1870 that provided for federal supervision of the electoral process in the states to assure black Americans that they could actually vote and providing federal penalties for those individuals found impairing the right to vote. The Court ruled that the regulation of suffrage is a state concern and that the Fifteenth Amendment means only that states may not enact laws that prohibit black Americans from voting. If private individuals interfere with black people attempting to exercise their right to vote, that is solely a matter of concern to the state, not Congress.
- A decision of the Court in 1878 in *Hall* v. *Decuir,* 95 U.S. 485, that struck down a state law forbidding public carriers to racially discriminate because the Court found such a law to be a burden on interstate commerce.
- An 1883 decision, *United States* v. *Harris,* 106 U.S. 629, whereby the Court invalidated major provisions of the federal Third Enforcement Act that was also known as the Ku Klux Klan Act and was aimed at that violently racist group.

- The **Civil Rights Cases of 1883,** whereby the Court struck down the public accommodations provisions of the Civil Rights Act of 1875, arguing that the equal protection clause of the Fourteenth Amendment applied only to the explicit actions of the state authorities, as in state legislation.
- Another 1883 decision, *Pace* v. *Alabama,* 106 U.S. 583, in which the Court ruled that Alabama's antimiscegenation statute prohibiting blacks and whites to marry did *not* violate the equal protection clause since it applied equally to *both* blacks and whites.
- The infamous racial segregation decision of 1896, **Plessy** v. **Ferguson,** which legitimized state mandated racial separation in public facilities and services under the guise that as long as the facilities were separate but equal, then the equality guarantee of the Fourteenth Amendment was satisfied. With the *Plessy* decision, the Court gave its constitutional blessing to what was known as "Jim Crow" laws, laws requiring racial apartheid and treating violations of those laws as *criminal* offenses.

There were what seemed to be a few bright spots in this racist decisional trend. The Court *did* rule that a state law excluding nonwhites from serving as jurors violated the Fourteenth Amendment in *Strauder* v. *West Virginia,* 100 U.S. 303 (1880), but this proved to be a Pyrrhic victory with the concurrent decision of *Virginia* v. *Rives,* 100 U.S. 313 (1880), which robbed the *Strauder* decision of its impact. The Court in the latter case ruled that the lack of blacks on a jury cannot be taken to imply unlawful racial discrimination per se, in the absence of a state law prohibiting blacks from serving.

Although the White and Taft Courts and the Court during the first seven years of the chief justiceship of Charles Evans Hughes did not disturb the racist doctrine of *Plessy* v. *Ferguson,* the Court in several modest ways began to move away from the massive indifference if not hostility to black rights displayed by earlier Courts. For example, in *McCabe* v. *Atchison, Topeka & Santa Fe Railroad,* 235 U.S. 151 (1914), the Court struck down as violating equal protection a state law authorizing intrastate railroads to provide white passengers but not black passengers with sleeping and dining cars. In the criminal procedural area, the Court furthered civil liberties in certain cases that involved black defendants in the South. **Powell** v. **Alabama** (chap. 17) served to further the rights of black Americans in particular, as well as to establish general principles applicable to all. However, before the 1940s the Court did not challenge the social and political bases (to say nothing of the legal bases) of racial segregation. For example, in *Grovey* v. *Townsend,* 295 U.S. 45 (1935), the Court ruled that black Americans could be excluded from voting in the Democratic party primaries, since no state action was involved; hence there was no violation of the Fourteenth Amendment. This, of course, legitimized and perpetuated the "white primary" whereby white southerners maintained their political monopoly.

In the post-1937 Roosevelt Court era, the rights of black Americans were extended. In *Missouri ex rel Gaines* v. *Canada,* 305 U.S. 337 (1938), the Court emphasized the "equal" in the separate-but-equal formula that provided the constitutional underpinnings of segregation. Equality of treatment in the selection of grand jurors was emphasized by the Court in two decisions: *Pierre* v. *Louisiana,* 306 U.S. 354 (1939), and *Smith* v. *Texas,* 311 U.S. 128 (1940). Black criminal defendants in the South had their convictions overturned as a result of coercive interrogation that yielded "confessions" in such cases as *Chambers* v. *Florida,* 309 U.S. 227 (1940), and *Ward* v. *Texas,* 316 U.S. 547 (1942). In the important case of *Smith* v. *Allwright,* 321 U.S. 649 (1944), the Court ruled that the Fifteenth Amendment prohibits a party primary from being restricted to white persons. The southern Democratic party, whose primaries were, in 1944 and years afterward, the functional equivalent of the general election, thus could no longer disenfranchise black Democrats. Also on the civil rights front, the Court in *Railway Mail Association* v. *Corsi,* 326 U.S. 88 (1945), ruled that a labor union may not racially discriminate in admitting persons to the union when this violates a state civil rights law. The Court in *Morgan* v. *Virginia,* 328 U.S. 373 (1946), struck down a Virginia law that required the racial segregation of interstate passengers. The state law was considered to be an unwarranted regulation of and a burden on interstate commerce.

Racial equality is one area of civil liberties that since 1938 and until recently has had a straightforward progression expanding individual rights and liberties. It is true that the later Hughes and Stone Courts took small steps rather than giant leaps, but their direction was unmistakable. The same was true of the Vinson Court. In the case of *Shelley* v. *Kraemer,* 334 U.S. 1 (1948), the Vinson Court ruled that state courts cannot enforce antiblack restrictive covenants. Although private individuals are free to contract among themselves not to sell their houses to blacks, they cannot enforce their agreements in a court of law, for that would be state action in violation of the Fourteenth Amendment. In the companion case of *Hurd* v. *Hodge,* 334 U.S. 24 (1948), the Court ruled that restrictive covenants in the District of Columbia could not be enforced in the federal courts because *that* would violate Section 1 of the Civil Rights Act of 1866 that guarantees to all citizens the right to purchase, lease, sell, hold, and convey real and personal property. However, the question soon arose whether someone who violated a restrictive covenant could be sued for damages by the aggrieved participants in the breached agreement. The Court answered that question in the negative in *Barrows* v. *Jackson,* 346 U.S. 249 (1953).

The Vinson Court led the way in Court rulings undermining the principle of "separate but equal" in higher education. In *Sipuel* v. *Board of Regents of the University of Oklahoma,* 332 U.S. 631 (1948), the Court, reaffirming *Missouri ex rel Gaines* v. *Canada,* ordered Ms. Sipuel admitted to the University of Oklahoma law school because there was no separate-but-equal law school for blacks. In *McLaurin* v. *Oklahoma State Regents,* 339 U.S. 637 (1950), the Court confronted a bizarre arrangement concocted by the Oklahoma legislature and the University of Oklahoma graduate school whereby blacks could take courses unavailable elsewhere but only on "a segregated basis." In the classroom, McLaurin, a black Ph.D. candidate in education, was required to sit apart from his fellow students. In the library, he was told to study on a separate floor apart from white students and not to use the desks in the reading room. He was obliged to eat in the school cafeteria at a separate table from the white students. This, said the Court, did not meet the Fourteenth Amendment equal protection requirement. Decided the same day as *McLaurin* was **Sweatt** v. **Painter,** which strongly suggested that separate professional schools for blacks were inherently unequal.

It was the Warren Court, of course, in **Brown** v. **Board of Education,** that directly confronted the separate-but-equal doctrine of *Plessy* v. *Ferguson* and explicitly overturned it. Separate public schools for black youngsters were inherently unequal and a violation of equal protection. The *Brown* decision began the long course of litigation, continuing through the present, to root out the vestiges of racially discriminatory public school systems. The decision also gave encouragement to civil rights groups to challenge racial discrimination in other sectors of American life. In the education sphere, the Court followed through with *Cooper* v. *Aaron,* 358 U.S. 1 (1958), affirming the desegregation decision of the appeals court and the actions of the Eisenhower Administration enforcing it in Little Rock, Arkansas. By 1964 the Warren Court was losing patience with southern evasion, delay, and subterfuge and announced, for example, in *Griffin* v. *Prince Edward School Board,* 377 U.S. 218, that "there has been entirely too much deliberation and not enough speed." By 1968 the Court in *Green* v. *School Board of New Kent County,* 391 U.S. 430, announced that "delays are no longer tolerable." It remained for the Burger Court in *Alexander* v. *Holmes County Board of Education,* 396 U.S. 19 (1969), to announce the constitutional demise of the "all deliberate speed" formula. The Court noted that "all deliberate speed for desegregation is no longer constitutionally permissible. . . . [E]very school district is to terminate dual school systems at once. . . ."

The end of "separate but equal" racial segregation in public accommodations and facilities was given an important push in two cases decided by the Vinson Court. *Bob-Lo Excursion Co.* v. *Michigan,* 333 U.S. 28 (1948), involved the application of the Michigan Civil Rights Act against an amusement park company that operated a Detroit River steamboat that went from Detroit to Bois Blanc Island, Canada, some 15 miles upstream from the city. The company refused the patronage of blacks, arguing that the state law was inapplicable because the boat sailed to Canada. The Court disagreed, ruling that the state proceeding against the steamboat company did not conflict with Congress' commerce powers, because the commerce was sufficiently local and Congress had not sought to regulate such essentially local enterprises. In the 1950 case of *Henderson* v. *United States,* 339 U.S. 816 (1950), the Vinson Court struck down the practice of racial segregation on the Southern Railway's dining cars (whereby only one table was reserved for blacks and ten tables for whites). The black table was cordoned off by a curtain. The Court, without considering the separate-but-equal formula, simply ruled that the railroad's policy inhibited equal access of passengers to interstate train travel in violation of the Interstate Commerce Act.

It was the Warren Court, however, that, after the *Brown* decision, began striking down on constitutional grounds state supported racial segregation in such public facilities as public swimming pools and bathing beaches, municipal golf courses, city buses, publicly owned athletic facilities and stadiums, and state and municipal courthouses and courtrooms. Even a private restaurant operating in a municipally owned building was subject to the Court's desegregation order. But it was Congress, by enacting Title 2 of the Civil Rights Act of 1964, that provided for the end of racial discrimination in public accommodations. The Court quickly upheld the constitutionality of the Act in the test case of **Heart of Atlanta Motel** v. **United States** (chap. 8). The Court also ruled in *Hamm* v. *City of Rock Hill,* 379 U.S. 306 (1964), that by passing Title 2, Congress abated any and all state criminal trespass prosecutions (these concerned the sit-ins aimed at desegregating public accommodations). But the Court had trouble with civil rights demonstrations on public property. For example, in the closely decided *Adderley* v. *Florida* case, 385 U.S. 39 (1966), the Court upheld the trespass convictions of civil rights protestors demonstrating outside the county jail in Tallahassee, Florida. Yet in other cases a shifting majority overturned the 1965 conviction of Dr. Martin Luther King, Jr., and others for parading without a permit in Birmingham, Alabama, in 1963. That case was *Shuttlesworth* v. *Birmingham,* 394 U.S. 147 (1969).

Racial discrimination in housing and voting was also dealt with by the Warren Court. For example, in one noted housing case, *Jones* v. *Mayer Co.,* 392 U.S. 409 (1968), the Court ruled that an 1866 federal civil rights statute prohibits all discrimination against blacks in matters of property by private owners as well as by public authorities; consequently, a discriminated-against black home-buyer could sue the offending real estate agency. The area of voting rights for blacks also occupied the attention of the Court. The Vinson Court decided *Terry* v. *Adams,* 345 U.S. 461 (1953), which invalidated, on Fifteenth Amendment grounds, a Texas whites-only preprimary election—a device hit upon to evade the Court's earlier rulings outlawing the white primary. *Gomillion* v. *Lightfoot,* 364 U.S. 339 (1960), saw the Warren Court invalidate racially motivated gerrymandering in Tuskegee, Alabama. The Voting Rights Act of 1965 was upheld by the Court in **South Carolina** v. **Katzenbach** (chap. 10) and *Katzenbach* v. *Morgan,* 384 U.S. 641 (1966). The Court also struck down the use of the poll tax for state elections in *Harper* v. *Virginia State Board of Elections,* 383 U.S. 663 (1966).

All forms of state-required or -sponsored racial discrimination were struck down by the Warren Court, including antimiscegenation laws that made interracial marriage a criminal offense. In *Loving* v. *Virginia,* 388 U.S. 1 (1967), the Court invalidated one such law of the state of Virginia. The equal protection clause of the Fourteenth Amendment was the constitutional basis for the decision.

By the time of the Burger Court, a number of complex and controversial issues had arisen concerning the role of government, including the courts, in not only eradicating racial discrimination but in devising the appropriate remedies for the harm inflicted on black people. Some of the questions faced by the Court included:

- What *are* the appropriate remedies for correcting the racial discrimination of the past and for alleviating its effects? In education, does this mean that the use of busing to achieve a racial mix in each school proportional to that of the general student population is an appropriate constitutional remedy? In employment, does it mean that racial quotas for the purpose of increasing the proportion of black employees can constitutionally be used? Or should there be "affirmative action" in that racial goals are set (but not necessarily quotas), including an aggressive search for qualified blacks and preference in hiring them? Should colleges and universities set aside a certain number of places in entering classes for qualified minorities who although qualified may not be *as* qualified as some white applicants who are denied admission?

- What are the ultimate goals of racial equality—equality of opportunity—which may mean shutting one's eyes to the racial discrimination of the past and its disabling effects on many of those in the group discriminated against—or equality of results—which may mean that minority individuals who themselves may not have been victims of discrimination are given preference over white Americans who themselves may be innocent of any discriminatory wrongdoing. Is equality of results a reasonable and constitutional criterion by which to determine that racial discrimination is no longer practiced?

The Burger and Rehnquist Courts have confronted these issues of racial equality in a variety of cases, particularly in the realms of education and employment. These issues in a somewhat different form were also raised in the area of the electoral process. We take a brief look at the work of the Burger Court in these matters.

The Burger Court at first continued the Warren Court tradition of unanimity in school desegregation cases. In the controversial busing case of **Swann** v. **Charlotte-Mecklenburg Board of Education,** the Court gave its approval to court-ordered busing of schoolchildren as one of several possible means of dismantling a dual school system. But one year after the Swann decision, unanimity ended as four justices dissented in *Wright* v. *Council of the City of Emporia,* 407 U.S. 451 (1972), in which the narrow majority ruled that a city can be enjoined by a federal court from withdrawing from an existing county school district when that would have the effect of impeding the dismantling of the county's dual school system. In **Keyes** v. **School District No.**

1, Denver, the Court faced up to the problem of racial discrimination in the North. The *Keyes* decision made it clear that racial discrimination *on the part of the school authorities or other public officials* that resulted in the separation of the races in the public schools would be treated in the same way that de jure segregation in the South was treated by the Court. The busing of schoolchildren, said the Court, is an appropriate remedy in such situations. But in its 5–4 decision in the Detroit school busing case, **Milliken** v. **Bradley,** the Court reversed the federal district court's metropolitan areawide busing program, ruling that the Detroit school system was the only one where actions of the school authorities had been shown to have kept the races apart. Therefore, the busing remedy must be confined to Detroit alone.

In *Pasadena City Board of Education* v. *Spangler,* 427 U.S. 424 (1976), the Court took the position that once a school board adopts and implements a desegregation program, subsequent demographic changes do not require the board to make continual adjustments of the racial composition of student bodies. But lest the foes of school desegregation take heart, the Court in *Columbus Board of Education* v. *Penick,* 443 U.S. 449 (1979), and *Dayton Board of Education* v. *Brinkman,* 443 U.S. 526 (1979), took the firm position that a record of past deliberate racial segregation of a major portion of a school district justifies the presumption of a causal connection to current segregation and thus legitimizes the imposition of a broad remedy including a substantial program of busing. The burden is clearly on the school authorities to demonstrate that the current segregation in their schools is unrelated to past intentional separation of the races. The Rehnquist Court even went further and ruled in **Missouri** v. **Jenkins** (reprinted at the end of this book) that federal judges have the authority to order local officials to raise property taxes to pay for public school desegregation and to do so even when that would

violate state law limiting tax increases. But the Court was careful to note that while the judge can order local officials to raise taxes, the judge cannot personally impose the tax.

Another major school desegregation decision was that in *Runyon* v. *McCrary,* 427 U.S. 160 (1976), in which the Court ruled that private, commercially operated, nonsectarian schools may not racially discriminate in their admissions practices. This decision was based on a reading of the Civil Rights Act of 1866 giving "all persons . . . the same right in every State . . . to make and enforce contracts . . . as is enjoyed by white citizens." By refusing to admit (that is, to contract with) black students, the private schools practiced racial discrimination in the making and enforcing of private contracts that was forbidden by law. (But the Court in the 1989 decision of *Patterson* v. *McLean Credit Union,* 109 S. Ct. 2363, refused to apply the 1866 law to permit a suit over racial harassment in the workplace.) Also of note was the decision in *Bob Jones University* v. *United States,* 461 U.S. 574 (1983), in which the Court upheld the Internal Revenue Service's determination that under federal law Bob Jones University was not entitled to tax-exempt status because of its racially discriminatory admissions policy. The university had claimed that its racially discriminatory admissions standards were based on religious doctrine, but the Court rejected this claim and found that such discrimination makes the nonprofit private school not qualified under the Internal Revenue Code for tax-deductible contributions.

Affirmative action programs in education and industry, instituted in order to redress past societal racial discrimination and the attendant inequalities, came before the Court. The first major decision involving affirmative action by a professional school was **Regents of the University of California** v. **Bakke** but the Court was badly split, giving Justice Powell the opportunity to cast the decisive vote and fashion a compromise policy. The following year a less divided Court in **United Steelworkers** v. **Weber** gave its blessing to a voluntarily instituted affirmative action program in industry, and the year after also approved the 10 percent of certain government contracts set aside for minority-owned businesses in **Fullilove** v. **Klutznick** (chap. 9).

In the realm of employment, the Court made a major antidiscrimination ruling in *Griggs* v. *Duke Power Company,* 401 U.S. 424 (1971), when it declared job tests to be violative of Title VII of the Civil Rights Act of 1964 when they were not performance-related and had the effect of screening out blacks from employment. But in *Washington* v. *Davis,* 426 U.S. 229 (1976), the Court found that an employment test which resulted in few blacks qualifying for employment could not be declared invalid under the Fourteenth Amendment unless there is proof of a racially discriminatory intent in the construction and use of the exam. Yet subjective or discretionary employment practices may be analyzed under the disparate impact approach (*Watson* v. *Fort Worth Bank and Trust,* 487 U.S. 977 [1988]). However, in *Wards Cove Packing Co., Inc.* v. *Antonio,* 109 S.Ct. 2115 (1989), the Court rejected part of the *Griggs* decision that had offered criteria for determining disparate impact that placed the burden on the employer. Now the burden of proof is on the challenger and not the employer, making it more difficult to prove racial discrimination. It should be pointed out that the Court ruled in *McDonald* v. *Santa Fe Trail Transportation Company,* 427 U.S. 273 (1976), that both the Civil Rights Acts of 1870 and 1964 prohibit racial discrimination in private employment against white persons as well as against nonwhites. The Court emphasized in *American Tobacco Company* v. *Patterson,* 456 U.S. 63 (1982), and in *Pullman-Standard* v. *Swint,* 456 U.S. 273 (1982), that seniority systems that were not adopted for discriminatory purposes do not violate the law even though they may have a discriminatory effect on blacks or other groups. But when it can be shown that individual blacks were denied jobs because of their race, they are then entitled to the seniority they would have achieved had they been hired initially, and they therefore must be placed ahead of whites hired when the discrimination occurred (*Franks* v. *Bowman Transportation Co.,* 424 U.S. 747 [1976]).

The Reagan administration, unlike previous recent administrations, actively sought the end of affirmative action programs that use numerical goals and quotas designed to remedy the racism and sexism of the past and to assure equal employment opportunities. The Administration specifically asked federal courts to modify affirmative action plans imposed by the courts on state and local governmental units so as to remove goals and quotas. These same plans had been devised by or were accepted by previous administrations. The Reagan Administration made it clear that its goal was the end of all affirmative action programs whether voluntary or court-ordered. The Court rebuffed the administration in **United States** v. **Paradise,** which upheld hiring and promotion quotas to remedy past racial discrimination. But the Court later ruled in **Martin** v. **Wilks** that white workers can challenge long-settled affirmative action consent decrees concerning employment practices.

In the 1984 decision in *Firefighters Local Union No. 1784* v. *Stotts,* 467 U.S. 561, the Court ruled that courts could not interfere with seniority systems in order to protect blacks from job layoffs. This case involved the Memphis Fire Department, which had hired blacks under a court-ordered affirmative action program. But the black employees, being the most recently hired, were subject to being laid off first. Civil rights groups believed that affirmative action programs could be severely undermined and gains for black workers eroded if they did not receive some protection from job layoffs. But the Court seemed to draw the line here, ruling that seniority rights take precedence over minority rights. The

Reagan Administration then took the position that the Court's decision meant that all preferential treatment of blacks, other minorities, and women must end and that no longer should group-based remedies be imposed to correct past discrimination. The Reagan Administration insisted that only when individuals can prove that they personally were victims of discrimination should they be entitled to remedies. This extreme position was rejected in 1986 by the Court in *Wygant* v. *Jackson Board of Education,* 476 U.S. 267, and by its decisions in *Local 93* v. *Cleveland,* 478 U.S. 501, and *Local 28 of Sheet Metal Workers* v. *EEOC,* 478 U.S. 421. The *Wygant* decision itself reinforced the *Firefighters* ruling forbidding interference with seniority for purposes of layoffs. But the Court drew a distinction between *hiring* and *layoffs.* At the hiring stage, employers *can* utilize (or be ordered by a court to utilize) the group-based remedy of affirmative action to correct past racism in which blacks or other minority racial groups were the victims. In *Local 93* v. *Cleveland,* the Court upheld a consent decree agreed to by Cleveland officials of a job discrimination suit that had charged that black and Hispanic firefighters had been discriminated against in hiring and particularly in promotions. The consent decree provided for temporary preferential treatment of blacks and Hispanics by promoting them over whites with more seniority and higher test scores. Such consent decrees concerning hiring or promotions do not violate federal law, said the Court. In *Local 28 of Sheet Metal Workers,* the Court approved a federal district court-ordered affirmative action plan for New York Local 28. The Local had long-established racial discrimination excluding blacks from the union and the apprenticeship program for entry into the union. After years of proceedings without results, the federal district court held Local 28 in contempt, imposed a $150,000 fine, and ordered the Local to meet a 29 percent nonwhite membership goal. In upholding these orders, the

Court emphasized that when racial discrimination has been established, affirmative action hiring of minority members who are not themselves the actual victims of discrimination is a constitutional remedy. Layoffs on the basis of race, however, are a different matter. The Court in its 5–4 ruling in *Wygant* held that preferential treatment against layoffs to some minority employees on the basis of race, even though part of a collective bargaining agreement, violates the equal protection guarantee of the Fourteenth Amendment. In other words, the white employees who were adversely affected because of their race by preferential treatment given black employees had their equal protection rights violated.

The right of black Americans to participate in the electoral process without racial discrimination is another area of racial equality that was addressed by the Court. Involved here is not only the equal protection clause of the Fourteenth Amendment but also the Fifteenth Amendment, which explicitly protects the right to vote free from racial discrimination. One equal protection decision relating to voting was *Hunter* v. *Underwood,* 471 U.S. 222 (1985), in which the Court heard a challenge to a provision in the Alabama Constitution disenfranchising persons convicted of crimes involving moral turpitude. The Court found that the original enactment was motivated by a desire to discriminate against blacks on account of race and was thus a violation of equal protection.

The use of multimember legislative districts has been challenged as diluting the voting strength of the black electorate. In *Whitcomb* v. *Chavis,* 403 U.S. 124 (1971), the Court rejected the claim of black voters in Indiana that multimember districts denied them effective representation in the state legislature. As long as the electoral scheme was not racially motivated, and this had *not* been charged, there was no constitutional violation. In *City of Mobile, Alabama* v. *Bolden,* 466 U.S. 55 (1980), a similar issue as related to city government met with a similar negative decision. However, where racial discrimination was proved to be the basis for an at-large election system, the Court struck it down as it did in *Rogers* v. *Lodge,* 458 U.S. 613 (1982).

The Voting Rights Act of 1965 was a significant piece of congressional legislation that made the federal government responsible for ending bars to voting on account of race anywhere in the nation. Most qualifications for voting were suspended for five years, federal voting examiners could be sent to suspect counties to add to the voting lists those eligible to vote (previously illegally refused registration by local officials), federal observers could be assigned to the polling places, and any changes in the voting laws of the states and counties subject to the act had to be approved by the Attorney General or by the United States District Court for the District of Columbia (this was known as "preclearance"). The Voting Rights Act was extended in 1970, 1975, and 1982. The Warren Court, as we have seen, upheld the constitutionality of the Voting Rights Act. The Burger Court also made it clear in *City of Rome* v. *United States,* 446 U.S. 156 (1980), that a city found to have a past record of racial discrimination in the electoral process cannot weasel out of its responsibilities under the Voting Rights Act, which the Burger Court emphasized was within Congress' power to enact in order to enforce the Fifteenth Amendment.

One important aspect of the Voting Rights Act extension in 1982 was that it liberalized the *City of Mobile, Alabama* v. *Bolden* ruling. That case had accepted the proposition that as long as an electoral scheme provided black voters equal access to the ballot there is no requirement that it must provide for equality of results. Only if it could be proven in a court of law that the intent of the electoral scheme was to adversely affect the ability of blacks to win electoral office could that electoral scheme be struck down. The 1982 Voting Rights Act extension contained the provision

that private individuals may challenge an electoral scheme by showing that it consistently results in racially biased or skewed outcomes. However, the provision directed that courts examine the totality of circumstances in considering whether a violation of the Voting Rights Act has occurred.

There are other decisions of the Court bearing upon the rights of black Americans. Some of these decisions have furthered the value of racial equality while others have not. Among the positive decisions must be counted *Hills* v. *Gantreaux,* 425 U.S. 284 (1976), in which the Court ruled permissible a program for desegregation of public housing in the Chicago metropolitan area that was intended to remedy proven racial discrimination in connection with selecting sites for public housing in the city of Chicago. Another positive decision was that in *Palmore* v. *Sidoti,* 466 U.S. 429 (1984), in which the Court prohibited consideration of race in child custody determinations. In this case the Court reversed a state court which divested a white natural mother of the custody of her child because of her remarriage to a black man. Still another example of positive doctrine was *Rose* v. *Mitchell,* 443 U.S. 76 (1979), in which the Court ruled that a claim of racial discrimination practiced by a state in the selection of a grand jury was a valid basis for a state prisoner to bring a habeas corpus petition into federal district court. Because the trend of the Court was to narrow the avenue of habeas corpus petitions by state prisoners, this decision seemed to emphasize the value of racial equality over the value of contracting the business of the federal courts. But the Court later ruled in *Hobby* v. *United States,* 468 U.S. 339 (1984), that there was no violation of the due process clause of the Fifth Amendment even though during the preceding seven years there had never been a black or a woman who had served as foreman of federal grand juries in the eastern federal judicial district of North Carolina. But the Court insisted in *Vasquez* v. *Hillery,* 474 U.S. 254 (1986), that intentional discrimination in the selection of grand jurors is a violation of the equal protection clause. The Court went even further and ruled that the equal protection clause forbids the use of peremptory challenges by prosecutors to remove potential jurors solely on account of race. This decision, **Batson** v. **Kentucky,** relieved the criminal defendant of the difficult burden of demonstrating a consistent pattern of past practice of removal of blacks from serving on juries. Instead, the Court established that once the defendant shows that he or she is a member of a cognizable racial group, what then needs to be demonstrated is that the prosecutor exercised peremptory challenges to remove members of the defendant's race at *the defendant's trial*. The burden is then on the prosecutor to show that race was not the reason for the exercise of the peremptory challenges. The Court later ruled that this decision is not to be retroactively applied to cases that became final before *Batson* was decided (*Teague* v. *Lane,* 109 S.Ct. 1060 [1989]). However, *Batson* could be retroactively applied to all cases pending on direct review or not yet final when *Batson* was decided (*Griffith* v. *Kentucky,* 479 U.S. 314 [1987]).

The Court interpreted federal civil rights statutes as covering racial discrimination against Jewish Americans (*Shaare Tefila Congregation* v. *Cobb,* 481 U.S. 615 [1987]) and Arab Americans (*Saint Francis College* v. *Al-Khazraji,* 481 U.S. 604 [1987]).

Burger and Rehnquist Court decisions unfavorable to racial equality claims aside from those already mentioned include: *Palmer* v. *Thompson,* 403 U.S. 217 (1971), in which the Court found that the decision of Mississippi authorities to close public swimming pools rather than to integrate them did not violate the Constitution; *Moose Lodge No. 107* v. *Irvis,* 407 U.S. 163 (1972), in which the Court refused to expand the concept of state action to invalidate the racially discriminatory practices of a private club that operated a dining room with a liquor license issued by the public authorities; *Jett* v. *Dallas Independent School District,* 109 S.Ct. 2702 (1989), in which the Court ruled that a municipality may not be held liable for its employees' violation of section 1981 of civil rights law; and **City of Richmond** v. **Croson Co.,** in which the Court struck down the City of Richmond's minority set-aside program for city contracts patterned after the federal program approved in *Fullilove* v. *Klutznick* (chap. 9).

In 1989 the Court produced six major decisions weakening civil rights law (*City of Richmond, Wards Cove, Martin, Patterson, Jett,* and *Lorance* v. *AT&T Technologies, Inc.,* 109 S.Ct. 2261 [discussed in the following chapter]). But the Court may have gone too far. The Civil Rights Act of 1990 was introduced to correct what its backers claim was Supreme Court misinterpretation of civil rights law. Among its other provisions the Act reverses the Court's interpretation of the Civil Rights Act of 1964 in *Wards Cove* and restores the standards previously established in *Griggs* v. *Duke Power Company*. Once again the burden is placed on employers to justify their hiring and promotion practices that have the effect of racially discriminating.

Significantly, the Court in 1990 seemed to backtrack from the *City of Richmond* v. *Croson Co.* decision. In **Metro Broadcasting, Inc.** v. **FCC** (reprinted at the end of this book) a 5–4 majority upheld federal minority preferences in award of broadcast licenses by the FCC. However, the departure of Justice Brennan and the uncertainty of his replacement's views on affirmative action means that this area of law may be in flux.

THE IMPACT OF THE COURT'S DECISIONS

Table 18.1 summarizes the impact of selected Court decisions concerning racial equality. The reprinted cases follow.

Table 18.1 THE IMPACT OF SELECTED COURT DECISIONS, RACIAL EQUALITY

Case	Year	Impact on Parties	Short-Run Impact	Long-Run Impact
Civil Rights Cases of 1883	1883	Original black plaintiffs lose their basic civil rights.	White press in North and South favorable to decision. Encouraged movement in South to enact Jim Crow laws.	By stripping federal government of authority to end racial discrimination in public accommodations, Court further emasculated the civil rights content of the Fourteenth Amendment.
Plessy v. Ferguson	1896	Homer A. Plessy prosecuted and convicted of violating Louisiana's 1890 statute.	Jim Crow laws legitimized, became more widespread in the South and border states.	Legalized apartheid in the South and border states. Solidified and institutionalized racism.
Sweatt v. Painter	1950	Herman Sweatt entered the University of Texas Law School but dropped out after one year.	More than 1,000 blacks admitted to formerly all-white professional and graduate schools.	Landmark civil rights decision that pointed the way to *Brown v. Board of Education.*
Brown v. Board of Education	1954	Only in Delaware and District of Columbia did black plaintiffs attend desegregated schools. Obstruction and delay occurred in South Carolina, Virginia, and Kansas.	Massive resistance to school desegregation occurred in the South. Border states and northern and western states with permissive segregation statutes began compliance at least in dismantling the dual school system and beginning desegregation. *Brown* decision stimulated much litigation to desegregate public schools and other public facilities.	Decision marked the end of apartheid, the beginning of the modern civil rights movement, and the start of the process of reintegrating the states of the old Confederacy into the national political culture. Perhaps most important Warren Court decision. Remains firm precedent and is cornerstone of modern law of race relations.

Case	Year			
Swann v. Charlotte-Mecklenburg Board of Education	1971	James Swann and other plaintiffs successful. Desegregation plan went into effect.	Decision was seen as a rebuff to Nixon Administration's antibusing stance. The use of school busing as a tool to desegregate school systems increased.	By approving busing, decision helped to implement the desegregation of school systems. Improved race relations in Charlotte-Mecklenburg area.
Keyes v. School District No. 1, Denver	1973	Wilfred Keyes and other parents successful. Desegregation plan soon implemented.	The North was put on notice that de facto segregated school systems were to be closely scrutinized as to segregative intent and subject to desegregation remedies including busing.	Distinction between de facto and de jure segregation blurred. Desegregation becomes controversial political issue in the North.
Milliken v. Bradley	1974	The Detroit branch of the NAACP along with Ronald and Richard Bradley and others lose. Black children forced to continue their education in the predominantly black Detroit public schools.	Suburban school systems told they need not fear being part of any plan to desegregate central city school systems. Court perceived as turning its back on realities of white flight to the suburbs and the extensiveness of racial discrimination.	Problems of predominantly black central city school systems persist.
Regents of the University of California v. Bakke	1978	Allan Bakke admitted to medical school.	Little impact apparent on college and university affirmative action programs.	Uncertain.
United Steelworkers v. Weber	1979	Brian Weber loses. Labor-management's affirmative action program upheld.	Voluntary affirmative action plans in industry encouraged. Decision praised by civil rights groups and liberal newspapers.	Uncertain.

CIVIL RIGHTS CASES OF 1883,
109 U.S. 3 (1883)

If the Fourteenth Amendment was meant to accomplish anything, it was to extend basic civil rights to black Americans. After the amendment was adopted, Congress enacted legislation to implement the "equal protection" guarantee. One of the major pieces of legislation was the Civil Rights Act of 1875, which prohibited racial discrimination in "public accommodations." That is, it became a misdemeanor for operators of hotels, restaurants, theaters and other places of amusement, and means of transportation, to deny patronage to blacks on account of their race, or to separate patrons by race. These businesses, although privately owned and operated, were traditionally thought of as public-type businesses subject to the regulation of the state. They usually had been subsidized by the state in land or funds from the public treasury, or given other advantages, and all were licensed by the state. In addition, the act required equality in jury service—but this provision was not involved in the Civil Rights Cases. *Congress' reasoning behind the public accommodations provision was that the states were not permitted to allow private persons operating public businesses to discriminate racially. To permit this would be to deny blacks the equal protection of the laws—the laws of the state granting full rights to all citizens black and white—from being discriminated against by government-regulated private business. Congress had acted on the assumption that Section 5 of the Fourteenth Amendment gave Congress the power to enforce the guarantees of the first section to prevent the state from committing racially discriminatory acts or permitting others to discriminate racially. Furthermore, such racial discrimination was considered a carryover from slavery; thus another justification for the legislation was to enforce the Thirteenth Amendment. The five cases that constitute the* Civil Rights Cases of 1883 *came not only from the South, but from San Francisco, New York City, Topeka (Kansas), and Jefferson City (Missouri). Two cases involved denial to black Americans of restaurant and hotel accommodations, one case involved the refusal to seat a black American in a San Francisco theater, another case involved racial discrimination by New York City's Grand Opera House. The fifth case concerned racial discrimination by a southern railroad.*

Majority votes: 8
Dissenting votes: 1

MR. JUSTICE BRADLEY delivered the opinion of the Court:. . . .

The first section of the Fourteen Amendment (which is the one relied on), after declaring who shall be citizens of the United States, and of the several States, is prohibitory in its character, and prohibitory upon the States. . . .

It is State action of a particular character that is prohibited. Individual invasion of individual rights is not the subject-matter of the amendment. It has a deeper and broader scope. It nullifies and makes void all State legislation, and State action of every kind, which impairs the privileges and immunities of citizens of the United States, or which injures them in life, liberty or property without due process of law, or which denies to any of them the equal protection of the laws. It not only does this, but in the last section of the amendment invests Congress with power to enforce it by appropriate legislation. To enforce what? To enforce the prohibition. To adopt appropriate legislation for correcting the effects of such prohibited State laws and State acts, and thus to render them effectually null, void, and innocuous. This is the legislative power conferred upon Congress, and this is the whole of it. It does not invest Congress with power to legislate upon subjects which are within the domain of State legislation; but to provide modes of relief against State legislation, or State action, of the kind referred to. It does not authorize Congress to create a code of municipal law for the regulation of private rights; but to provide modes of redress against the operation of State laws, and the action of State officers executive or judicial, when these are subversive of the fundamental rights specified in the amendment. Positive rights and privileges are undoubtedly secured by the Fourteenth Amendment; but they are secured by way of prohibition against State laws and State proceedings affecting those rights and privileges, and by power given to Congress to legislate for the purpose of carrying such prohibition into effect: and such legislation must necessarily be predicated upon such supposed State laws or State proceedings, and be directed to the correction of their operation and effect. . . .

[I]n the present case, until some State law has been passed, or some State action through its officers or agents has been taken, adverse to the rights of citizens sought to be protected by the Fourteenth Amendment, no legislation of the United States under said amendment, nor any proceeding under such legislation, can be called into activity: for the prohibitions of the amendment are against State laws and acts done under State authority. Of course, legislation may, and should be, provided in advance to meet the exigency when it arises; but it should be adapted to the mischief and wrong which the amendment was intended to provide against;

and that is, State laws, or State action of some kind, adverse to the rights of the citizen secured by the amendment. Such legislation cannot properly cover the whole domain of rights appertaining to life, liberty and property, defining them and providing for their vindication. That would be to establish a code of municipal law regulative of all private rights between man and man in society. It would be to make Congress take the place of the State legislatures and to supersede them. . . . In fine, the legislation which Congress is authorized to adopt in this behalf is not general legislation upon the rights of the citizen, but corrective legislation, that is, such as may be necessary and proper for counteracting such laws as the States may adopt or enforce, and which, by the amendment, they are prohibited from making or enforcing, or such acts and proceedings as the States may commit or take, and which, by the amendment, they are prohibited from committing or taking. It is not necessary for us to state, if we could, what legislation would be proper for Congress to adopt. It is sufficient for us to examine whether the law in question is of that character.

An inspection of the law shows that it makes no reference whatever to any supposed or apprehended violation of the Fourteenth Amendment on the part of the State. It is not predicated on any such view. It proceeds *ex directo* to declare that certain acts committed by individuals shall be deemed offences, and shall be prosecuted and punished by proceedings in the courts of the United States. It does not profess to be corrective of any constitutional wrong committed by the States; it does not make its operation to depend upon any such wrong committed. It applies equally to cases arising in States which have the justest laws respecting the personal rights of citizens, and whose authorities are ever ready to enforce such laws, as to those which arise in States that may have violated the prohibition of the amendment. In other words, it steps into the domain of local jurisprudence, and lays down rules for the conduct of individuals in society towards each other, and imposes sanctions for the enforcement of those rules without referring in any manner to any supposed action of the State or its authorities.

If this legislation is appropriate for enforcing the prohibitions of the amendment, it is difficult to see where it is to stop. Why may not Congress with equal show of authority enact a code of laws for the enforcement and vindication of all rights of life, liberty, and property? If it is supposable that the States may deprive persons of life, liberty, and property without due process of law (and the amendment itself does suppose this), why should not Congress proceed at once to prescribe due pro-

cess of law for the protection of every one of these fundamental rights, in every possible case, as well as to prescribe equal privileges in inns, public conveyances, and theatres? The truth is, that the implication of a power to legislate in this manner is based upon the assumption that if the States are forbidden to legislate or act in a particular way on a particular subject, and power is conferred upon Congress to enforce the prohibition, this gives Congress power to legislate generally upon that subject, and not merely power to provide modes of redress against such State legislation or action. The assumption is certainly unsound. It is repugnant to the Tenth Amendment of the Constitution, which declares that powers not delegated to the United States by the Constitution, nor prohibited by it to the States, are reserved to the States respectively or to the people. . . .

If the principles of interpretation which we have laid down are correct, as we deem them to be . . . it is clear that the law in question cannot be sustained by any grant of legislative power made to Congress by the Fourteenth Amendment. . . . The law in question, without any reference to adverse State legislation on the subject, declares that all persons shall be entitled to equal accommodations and privileges of inns, public conveyances, and places of public amusement, and imposes a penalty upon any individual who shall deny to any citizen such equal accommodations and privileges. This is not corrective legislation; it is primary and direct; it takes immediate and absolute possession of the subject of the right of admission to inns, public conveyances, and places of amusement. It supersedes and displaces State legislation on the same subject, or only allows it permissive force. It ignores such legislation, and assumes that the matter is one that belongs to the domain of national regulation. Whether it would not have been a more effective protection of the rights of citizens to have clothed Congress with plenary power over the whole subject, is not now the question. What we have to decide is, whether such plenary power has been conferred upon Congress by the Fourteenth Amendment; and, in our judgment, it has not. . . .

But the power of Congress to adopt direct and primary, as distinguished from corrective legislation, on the subject in hand, is sought, in the second place, from the Thirteenth Amendment, which abolishes slavery. . . .

. . . The only question is whether the refusal to any persons of the accommodations of an inn, or a public conveyance, or a place of public amusement, by an individual, and without any sanction or support from any State law or regulation, does inflict upon such persons any manner of servitude, or form of slavery, as those terms are understood in this country? . . . Can the act of a mere individual, the owner of the inn, the public conveyance or place of amusement, refusing the accommodation, be justly regarded as imposing any badge of slavery or servitude upon the applicant, or only as inflicting an ordinary civil injury, properly cognizable by the laws of the State, and presumably subject to redress by those laws until the contrary appears?

After giving to these questions all the consideration which their importance demands, we are forced to the conclusion that such an act of refusal has nothing to do with slavery or involuntary servitude. . . . It would be running the slavery argument into the ground to make it apply to every act of discrimination which a person may see fit to make as to the guests he will entertain, or as to the people he will take into his coach or cab or car, or admit to his concert or theatre, or deal with in other matters of intercourse or business. Innkeepers and public carriers, by the laws of all the States, so far as we are aware, are bound, to the extent of their facilities, to furnish proper accommodation to all unobjectionable persons who in good faith apply for them. If the laws themselves make any unjust discrimination, amenable to the prohibitions of the Fourteenth Amendment, Congress has full power to afford a remedy under that amendment and in accordance with it.

When a man has emerged from slavery, and by the aid of beneficent legislation has shaken off the inseparable concomitants of that state, there must be some stage in the progress of his elevation when he takes the rank of a mere citizen, and ceases to be the special favorite of the laws, and when his rights as a citizen, or a man, are to be protected in the ordinary modes by which other men's rights are protected. There were thousands of free colored people in this country before the abolition of slavery, enjoying all the essential rights of life, liberty, and property the same as white citizens; yet no one, at that time, thought that it was any invasion of his personal status as a freeman because he was not admitted to all the privileges enjoyed by white citizens, or because he was subjected to discriminations in the enjoyment of accommodations in inns, public conveyances and places of amusement. Mere discriminations on account of race or color were not regarded as badges of slavery. . . .

On the whole we are of opinion, that no countenance of authority for the passage of the law in question can be found in either the Thirteenth or Fourteenth Amendment of the Constitution; and no other ground of authority for its passage being suggested, it must necessarily be declared void, at least so far as its operation in the several States is concerned. . . .

And it is so ordered

MR. JUSTICE HARLAN, dissenting:

The opinion in these cases proceeds, it seems to me, upon grounds entirely too narrow and artificial. I cannot resist the conclusion that the substance and spirit of the recent amendments of the Constitution have been sacrificed by a subtle and ingenious verbal criticism. . . .

[Justice Harlan examines the nature of public accommodations, public conveyances, and inns and places of public amusement and finds that they are public or quasi-public businesses.] I am of the opinion that such discrimination practiced by corporations and individuals in the exercise of their public or quasi-public functions is a badge of servitude the imposition of which Congress may prevent under its power, by appropriate legislation, to enforce the Thirteenth Amendment; and, consequently, without reference to its enlarged power under the Fourteenth Amendment, the act of March 1, 1875, is not, in my judgment, repugnant to the Constitution.

It remains now to consider these cases with reference to the power Congress has possessed since the adoption of the Fourteenth Amendment. . . .

The opinion of the court . . . proceeds upon the ground that the power of Congress to legislate for the protection of the rights and privileges secured by the Fourteenth Amendment cannot be brought into activity except with the view, and as it may become necessary, to correct and annul State laws and State proceedings in hostility to such rights and privileges. . . . If the grant to colored citizens of the United States of citizenship in their respective States, imports exemption from race discrimination, in their States, in respect of such civil rights as belong to citizenship, then, to hold that the amendment remits that right to the States for their protection, primarily, and stays the hands of the nation, until it is assailed by State laws or State proceedings, is to adjudge that the amendment, so far from enlarging the powers of Congress—as we have heretofore said it did—not only curtails them, but reverses the policy which the general government has pursued from its very organization. Such an interpretation of the amendment is a denial to Congress of the power, by appropriate legislation, to enforce one of its provisions. . . .

It is said that any interpretation of the Fourteenth Amendment different from that adopted by the majority of the court, would imply that Congress had authority to enact a municipal code for all the States, covering every matter affecting the life, liberty, and property of the citizens of the several States. Not so. Prior to the adoption of that amendment the constitutions of the several States, without perhaps an exception, secured all *persons* against deprivation of life, liberty, or property, otherwise than by due process of law, and, in some form, recognized the right of all *persons* to the equal protection of the laws. Those rights, therefore, existed before that amendment was proposed or adopted, and were not created by it. If, by reason of that fact, it be assumed that protection in these rights of persons still rests primarily with the States, and that Congress may not interfere except to enforce, by means of corrective legislation, the prohibitions upon State laws, or State proceedings inconsistent with those rights, it does not at all follow, that privileges which have been *granted by the nation,* may not be protected by primary legislation upon the part of Congress. The personal rights and immunities recognized in the prohibitive clauses of the amendment were prior to its adoption, under the protection, primarily, of the States, while rights, created by or derived from the United States, have always been, and, in the nature of things, should always be, primarily, under the protection of the general government. Exemption from race discrimination in respect of the civil rights which are fundamental in *citizenship* in a republican government, is, as we have seen, a new right, created by the nation, with express power in Congress, by legislation, to enforce the constitutional provision from which it is derived. If, in some sense, such race discrimination is, within the letter of the last clause of the first section, a denial of that equal protection of the laws which is secured against State denial to all persons, whether citizens or not, it cannot be possible that a mere prohibition upon such State denial, or a prohibition upon State laws abridging the privileges and immunities of citizens of the United States, takes from the nation the power which it has uniformly exercised of protecting, by direct primary legislation, those privileges and immunities which existed under the Constitution before the adoption of the Fourteenth Amendment, or have been created by that amendment in behalf of those thereby made *citizens* of their respective States. . . .

In every material sense applicable to the practical enforcement of the Fourteenth Amendment, railroad corporations, keepers of inns, and managers of places of public amusement are agents or instrumentalities of the State, because they are charged with duties to the public, and are amenable, in respect of their duties and functions, to governmental regulation. . . . A denial, by these instrumentalities of the State, to the citizen, because of his race, of that equality of civil rights secured to him by law, is a denial by the State, within the meaning of the Fourteenth Amendment. If it be not, then that race is left, in respect of the civil rights in question, practically at the mercy of corporations and individuals wielding power under the State. . . .

My brethren say, that when a man has emerged from slavery, and by the aid of beneficent legislation has shaken off the inseparable concomitants of that state, there must be some stage in the progress of his elevation when he takes the rank of a mere citizen, and ceases to be the special favorite of the laws, and when his rights as a citizen, or a man, are to be protected in the ordinary modes by which other men's rights are protected. It is, I submit, scarcely just to say that the colored race has been the special favorite of the laws. The statute of 1875, now adjudged to be unconstitutional, is for the benefit of citizens of every race and color. What the nation, through Congress, has sought to accomplish in reference to that race is—what had already been done in every State of the Union for the white race—to secure and protect rights belonging to them as freemen and citizens; nothing more. . . . The one underlying purpose of congressional legislation has been to enable the black race to take the rank of mere citizens. The difficulty has been to compel a recognition of the legal right of the black race to take the rank of citizens, and to secure the enjoyment of privileges belonging, under the law, to them as a component part of the people for whose welfare and happiness government is ordained. At every step, in this direction, the nation has been confronted with class tyranny. . . . To-day, it is the colored race which is denied, by corporations and individuals wielding public authority, rights fundamental in their freedom and citizenship. At some future time, it may be that some other race will fall under the ban of race discrimination. If the constitutional amendments be enforced, according to the intent with which, as I conceive, they were adopted, there cannot be, in this republic, any class of human beings in practical subjection to another class, with power in the latter to dole out to the former just such privileges as they may choose to grant. The supreme law of the land has decreed that no authority shall be exercised in this country upon the basis of discrimination, in respect of civil rights, against freemen and citizens because of their race, color, or previous condition of servitude. To that decree—for the due enforcement of which, by appropriate legislation, Congress has been invested with express power—every one must bow, whatever may have been, or whatever now are, his individual views as to the wisdom or policy, either of the recent changes in the fundamental law, or of the legislation which has been enacted to give them effect. . . .

PLESSY v. FERGUSON,
163 U.S. 537 (1896)

After the Civil Rights Cases of 1883 *narrowed the scope of the equal protection clause by ruling that it applied only to direct discriminatory action by the state, the southern and border states began to enact racial apartheid laws that legally required the separation of the races in public accommodations and all public facilities. The laws, however, usually mandated "separate but equal" accommodations and facilities so as to demonstrate compliance with the federal equal protection guarantee. The constitutionality of one such law came before the Court in the* Plessy *case. Louisiana, in 1890, had enacted a law requiring separate but equal railroad accommodations for the white and the black races. Plessy, who claimed to be one-eighth black, and was therefore ineligible to sit in the white parlor car of a train going from New Orleans to Covington, Louisiana, nevertheless announced his intention to sit in that car. He refused to move when told to and was arrested. Plessy was working with the opponents of apartheid to test the legality of these "laws." The majority opinion in the* Plessy *case provided the coup de grace to the equal protection clause as the one remaining constitutional provision that potentially could have protected the civil rights and liberties of black Americans.*

Majority votes: 7
Dissenting votes: 1

MR. JUSTICE BROWN delivered the opinion of the Court:

This case turns upon the constitutionality of an act of the General Assembly of the State of Louisiana, passed in 1890, providing for separate railway carriages for the white and colored races. . . .

The constitutionality of this act is attacked upon the ground that it conflicts both with the Thirteenth Amendment of the Constitution, abolishing slavery, and the Fourteenth Amendment, which prohibits certain restrictive legislation on the part of the States.

That it does not conflict with the Thirteenth Amendment, which abolished slavery and involuntary servitude, except as a punishment for a crime, is too clear for argument. . . .

The object of the Fourteenth Amendment was undoubtedly to enforce the absolute equality of the two races before the law, but in the nature of things it could not have been intended to abolish distinctions based upon color, or to enforce social, as distinguished from political equality, or a commingling of the two races upon terms unsatisfactory to either. Laws permitting, and even requiring, their separation in places where they are liable to be brought into contact do not necessarily imply the inferiority of either race to the other, and have been generally, if not universally, recognized as within the competency of the state legislatures in the exercise of their police power. The most common instance of this is connected with the establishment of separate schools for white and colored children, which has been held to be a valid exercise of the legislative power even by courts of States where the political rights of the colored race have been longest and most earnestly enforced.

One of the earliest of these cases is that of *Roberts* v. *City of Boston*, 5 Cush. 198, in which the Supreme Judicial Court of Massachusetts held that the general school committee of Boston had power to make provision for the instruction of colored children in separate schools established exclusively for them, and to prohibit their attendance upon the other schools. . . . It was held that the powers of the committee extended to the establishment of separate schools for children of different ages, sexes and colors, and that they might also establish special schools for poor and neglected children, who have become too old to attend the primary school, and yet have not acquired the rudiments of learning, to enable them to enter the ordinary schools. Similar laws have been enacted by Congress under its general power of legislation over the District of Columbia, as well as by the legislatures of many of the States, and have been generally, if not uniformly, sustained by the courts. . . .

Laws forbidding the intermarriage of the two races may be said in a technical sense to interfere with the freedom of contract, and yet have been universally recognized as within the police power of the State. . . .

. . . [I]t is suggested by the learned counsel for the plaintiff in error that the same argument that will justify the state legislature in requiring railways to provide separate accommodations for the two races will also authorize them to require separate cars to be provided for people whose hair is of a certain color, or who are aliens, or who belong to certain nationalities, or to enact laws requiring colored people to walk upon one side of the street, and white people upon the other, or requiring white men's houses to be painted white, and colored men's black, or their vehicles or business signs to be of different colors, upon the theory that one side of the street is as good as the other, or that a house or vehicle of one color is as good as one of another color. The reply to all this is that every exercise of the police power must be reasonable, and extend only to such laws as are enacted in good faith for the promotion for the public good, and not for the annoyance or oppression of a particular class. . . .

So far, then, as a conflict with the Fourteenth Amendment is concerned, the case reduces itself to the question whether the statute of Louisiana is a reasonable regulation and with respect to this there must necessarily be a large discretion on the part of the legislature. In determining the question of reasonableness it is at liberty to act with reference to the established usages, customs and traditions of the people, and with a view to the promotion of their comfort, and the preservation of the public peace and good order. Gauged by this standard, we cannot say that a law which authorizes or even requires the separation of the two races in public conveyances is unreasonable, or more obnoxious to the Fourteenth Amendment than the acts of Congress requiring separate schools for colored children in the District of Columbia, the constitutionality of which does not seem to have been questioned, or the corresponding acts of state legislatures.

We consider the underlying fallacy of the plaintiff's argument to consist in the assumption that the enforced separation of the two races stamps the colored race with a badge of inferiority. If this be so, it is not by reason of anything found in the act, but solely because the colored race chooses to put that construction upon it. The argument necessarily assumes that if, as has been more than once the case, and is not unlikely to be so again, the colored race should become the dominant power in the state legislature, and should enact a law in precisely similar terms, it would thereby relegate the white race to an inferior position. We imagine that the white race, at least, would not acquiesce in this assumption. The argument also assumes that social prejudices may be overcome by legislation, and that equal rights cannot be secured to the negro except by an enforced commingling of the two races. We cannot accept this proposition. If the two races are to meet upon terms of social equality, it must be the result of natural affinities, a mutual appreciation of each other's merits and a voluntary consent of individuals. . . . Legislation is powerless to eradicate racial instincts or to abolish distinctions based upon physical differences, and the attempt to do so can only result in accentuating the difficulties of the present situation. If the civil and political rights of both races be equal one cannot be inferior to the other civilly or politically. If one race be inferior to the other socially, the Constitution of the United States cannot put them upon the same plane. . . .

The judgment of the court below is, therefore,

Affirmed.

MR. JUSTICE HARLAN, dissenting:. . . .

It was said in argument that the statute of Louisiana does not discriminate against either race, but prescribes a rule applicable alike to white and colored citizens. But this argument does not meet the difficulty. Every one knows that the statute in question had its origin in the purpose, not so much to exclude white persons from railroad cars occupied by blacks, as to exclude colored people from coaches occupied by or assigned to white persons. Railroad corporations of Louisiana did not make discrimination among whites in the matter of accommodation for travellers. The thing to accomplish was, under the guise of giving equal accommodation for whites and blacks, to compel the latter to keep to themselves while travelling in railroad passenger coaches. No one would be so wanting in candor as to assert the contrary. The fundamental objection, therefore, to the statute is that it interferes with the personal freedom of citizens. . . .

The white race deems itself to be the dominant race in this country. And so it is, in prestige, in achievements, in education, in wealth and in power. So, I doubt not, it will continue to be for all time, if it remains true to its great heritage and holds fast to the principles of constitutional liberty. But in view of the Constitution, in the eye of the law, there is in this country no superior, dominant, ruling class of citizens. There is no caste here. Our Constitution is colorblind, and neither knows nor tolerates classes among citizens. In respect of civil rights, all citizens are equal before the law. The humblest is the peer of the most powerful. The law regards man as man, and takes no account of his surroundings or of his color when his civil rights as guaranteed by the supreme law of the land are involved. It is, therefore, to be regretted that this high tribunal, the final expositor of the fundamental law of the land, has reached the conclusion that it is competent for a State to regulate the enjoyment by citizens of their civil rights solely upon the basis of race.

In my opinion, the judgment this day rendered will, in time, prove to be quite as pernicious as the decision made by this tribunal in the *Dred Scott case*. . . . It seems that we have yet, in some of the States, a dominant race—a superior class of citizens, which assumes to regulate the enjoyment of civil rights, common to all citizens, upon the basis of race. The present decision, it may well be apprehended, will not only stimulate aggressions, more or less brutal and irritating, upon the admitted rights of colored citizens, but will encourage the belief that it is possible, by means of state enactments, to defeat the beneficent purposes which the people of the United States had in view when they adopted the recent amendments of the Constitution, by one of which the blacks of this country were made citizens of the United States and of the States in which they respectively reside, and whose privileges and immunities, as citizens the States are forbidden to abridge. Sixty millions of whites are in no danger from the presence here of eight millions of blacks. The destinies of the two races, in this country, are indissolubly linked together, and the interests of both require that the common government of all shall not permit the seeds of race hate to be planted under the sanction of law. What can more certainly arouse race hate, what more certainly create and perpetuate a feeling of distrust between these races, than state enactments, which, in fact, proceed on the ground that colored citizens are so inferior and degraded that they cannot be allowed to sit in public coaches occupied by white citizens? That, as all will admit, is the real meaning of such legislation as was enacted in Louisiana.

. . . State enactments, regulating the enjoyment of civil rights, upon the basis of race, and cunningly devised to defeat legitimate results of the [Civil] war, under the pretense of recognizing equality of rights, can have no other result than to render permanent peace impossible, and to keep alive a conflict of races, the continuance of which must do harm to all concerned. This question is not met by the suggestion that social equality cannot exist between the white and black races in this country. That argument, if it can be properly regarded as one, is scarcely worthy of consideration; for social equality no more exists between two races when travelling in a passenger coach or a public highway than when members of the same races sit by each other in a street car or in a jury box, or stand or sit with each other in a political assembly, or when they use in common the streets of a city or town, or when they are in the same room for the purpose of having their names placed on the registry of voters, or when they approach the ballot-box in order to exercise the high privilege of voting. . . .

I do not deem it necessary to review the decisions of state courts to which reference was made in argument. Some, and the most important, of them are wholly inapplicable, because rendered

prior to adoption of the last amendments of the Constitution, when colored people had very few rights which the dominant race felt obliged to respect. Others were made at a time when public opinion, in many localities, was dominated by the institution of slavery; when it would not have been safe to do justice to the black man; and when, so far as the rights of blacks were concerned, race prejudice was, practically, the supreme law of the land. Those decisions cannot be guides in the era introduced by the recent amendments of the supreme law, which established universal civil freedom, gave citizenship to all born or naturalized in the United States and residing here, obliterated the race line from our systems of governments, National and State, and placed our free institutions upon the broad and sure foundation of the equality of all men before the law.

I am of opinion that the statute of Louisiana is inconsistent with the personal liberty of citizens, white and black, in that State, and hostile to both the spirit and letter of the Constitution of the United States. If laws of like character should be enacted in the several States of the Union, the effect would be in the highest degree mischievous. Slavery, as an institution tolerated by law would, it is true, have disappeared from our country, but there would remain a power in the States, by sinister legislation, to interfere with the full enjoyment of the blessings of freedom; to regulate civil rights, common to all citizens, upon the basis of race; and to place in a condition of legal inferiority a large body of American citizens, now constituting a part of the political community called the People of the United States, for whom, and by whom through representatives, our government is administered. . . .

MR. JUSTICE BREWER did not hear the argument or participate in the decision of this case.

SWEATT v. PAINTER,
339 U.S. 629 (1950)

Herman Marion Sweatt, a black postal clerk in Texas, applied to the University of Texas Law School. He was automatically denied consideration because of his race (state law restricted the university to whites). Sweatt then sued the university and asked the state court to order his admission. What followed is recounted in the opinion of the Court by Chief Justice Vinson as reprinted below.

Votes: Unanimous

MR. CHIEF JUSTICE VINSON delivered the opinion of the Court:

This case and *McLaurin* v. *Oklahoma State Regents* present different aspects of this general question: To what extent does the Equal Protection Clause of the Fourteenth Amendment limit the power of a state to distinguish between students of different races in professional and graduate education in a state university? Broader issues have been urged for our consideration, but we adhere to the principle of deciding constitutional questions only in the context of the particular case before the Court. . . .

In the instant case, petitioner filed an application for admission to the University of Texas Law School for the February, 1946 term. His application was rejected solely because he is a Negro. Petitioner thereupon brought this suit for mandamus against the appropriate school officials, respondents here, to compel his admission. At that time, there was no law school in Texas which admitted Negroes.

The state trial court recognized that the action of the State in denying petitioner the opportunity to gain a legal education while granting it to others deprived him of the equal protection of the laws guaranteed by the Fourteenth Amendment. The court did not grant the relief requested, however, but continued the case for six months to allow the State to supply substantially equal facilities. At the expiration of the six months, in December, 1946, the court denied the writ on the showing that the authorized university officials had adopted an order calling for the opening of a law school for Negroes the following February. While petitioner's appeal was pending, such a school was made available, but petitioner refused to register therein. The Texas Court of Civil Appeals set aside the trial court's judgment and ordered the cause "remanded generally to the trial court for further proceedings without prejudice to the rights of any party to this suit."

On remand, a hearing was held on the issue of the equality of the educational facilities at the newly established school as compared with the University of Texas Law School. Finding that the new school offered petitioner "privileges, advantages, and opportunities for the study of law substantially equivalent to those offered by the State to white students at the University of Texas," the trial court denied mandamus. The Court of Civil Appeals affirmed. Petitioner's application for a writ of error was denied by the Texas Supreme Court. We granted certiorari because of the manifest importance of the constitutional issues involved.

The University of Texas Law School, from which petitioner was excluded, was staffed by a faculty of sixteen full-time and three part-time professors, some of whom are nationally recognized authorities in their field. Its student body numbered 850. The library contained over 65,000 volumes. Among the other facilities available to the students were a law review, moot court facilities, scholarship funds, and Order of the Coif affiliation. The school's alumni occupy the most distinguished positions in the private practice of the law and in the public life of the State. It may properly be considered one of the nation's ranking law schools.

The law school for Negroes which was to have opened in February, 1947, would have had no independent faculty or library. The teaching was to be carried on by four members of the University of Texas Law School faculty, who were to maintain their offices at the University of Texas while teaching at both institutions. Few of the 10,000 volumes ordered for the library had arrived; nor was there any full-time librarian. The school lacked accreditation.

Since the trial of this case, respondents report the opening of a law school at the Texas State University for Negroes. It is apparently on the road to full accreditation. It has a faculty of five full-time professors; a student body of 23; a library of some 16,500 volumes serviced by a full-time staff; a practice court and legal aid association; and one alumnus who has become a member of the Texas Bar.

Whether the University of Texas Law School is compared with the original or the new law school for Negroes, we cannot find substantial equality in the educational opportunities offered white and Negro law students by the State. In terms of number of the faculty, variety of courses and opportunity for specialization, size of the student body, scope of the library, availability of law review and similar activities, the University of Texas Law School is superior. What is more important, the University of Texas Law School possesses to a far greater degree those qualities which are incapable of objective measurement but which make for greatness in a law school. Such qualities, to name but a few, include reputation of the faculty, experience of the administration, position and influence of the alumni, standing in the community, traditions and prestige. It is difficult to believe that one who had a free choice between these law schools would consider the question close.

Moreover, although the law is a highly learned profession, we are well aware that it is an intensely practical one. The law school, the proving ground for legal learning and practice, cannot be effective in isolation from the individuals and institutions with which the law interacts. Few students and no one who has practiced law would choose to study in an academic vacuum, removed from the interplay of ideas and the exchange of views with which the law is concerned. The law school to which Texas is willing to admit petitioner excludes from its student body members of the racial groups which number 85% of the population of the State and include most of the lawyers, witnesses, jurors, judges and other officials with whom petitioner will inevitably be dealing when he becomes a member of the Texas Bar. With such a substantial, and significant segment of society excluded, we cannot conclude that the education offered petitioner is substantially equal to that which he would receive if admitted to the University of Texas Law School. . . . We cannot, therefore, agree with respondents that the doctrine of *Plessy* v. *Ferguson*, 163 U.S. 537 (1896), requires affirmance of the judgment below. Nor need we reach petitioner's contention that *Plessy* v. *Ferguson* should be reexamined in the light of contemporary knowledge respecting the purposes of the Fourteenth Amendment and the effects of racial segregation.

We hold that the Equal Protection Clause of the Fourteenth Amendment requires that petitioner be admitted to the University of Texas Law School. The judgment is reversed and the cause is remanded for proceedings not inconsistent with this opinion.

Reversed.

BROWN v. BOARD OF EDUCATION,
347 U.S. 483 (1954)

With this classic decision, the Supreme Court unanimously threw to the dustheap the constitutional doctrine that had provided the legal foundation for apartheid for over half a century. By discarding the separate-but-equal doctrine and ruling that separate can never be equal in the sense required by the equal protection clause, the Court at once revolutionized the law of race relations in the United States. The case itself was a consolidation of four suits, each involving state or local government requiring separation of the races in public school education. The fifth case, Bolling v. Sharpe, *involved legally required racial segregation in the public schools of the District of Columbia. The lead case involved a suit by Oliver Brown to force the Topeka, Kansas, Board of Education to admit his eight-year-old daughter Linda to a white school only five blocks from her home so that she would not have to continue traveling 21 blocks to the all-black school. The South Carolina case involved the suit of Harry Briggs, Jr., and 66 other black children challenging the dual school system that condemned the black youngsters to markedly inferior*
schools. *The case from Virginia concerned Dorothy Davis and other black high school students who objected to the inferior school facilities for blacks. A case from Delaware involved the suit by Ethel Belton and seven other black parents who protested the grossly unequal facilities in the high school their youngsters were forced to attend. In the District of Columbia case, Spottswood Thomas Bolling, Jr., and other black youngsters asserted that the segregated school system violated their constitutional rights.*

Votes: Unanimous

MR. CHIEF JUSTICE WARREN delivered the opinion of the Court:

These cases come to us from the States of Kansas, South Carolina, Virginia, and Delaware. They are premised on different facts and different local conditions, but a common legal question justifies their consideration together in this consolidated opinion.

In each of the cases, minors of the Negro race, through their legal representatives, seek the aid of the courts in obtaining admission to the public schools of their community on a nonsegregated basis. In each instance, they had been denied admission to schools attended by white children under laws requiring or permitting segregation according to race. This segregation was alleged to deprive the plaintiffs of the equal protection of the laws under the Fourteenth Amendment. In each of the cases other than the Delaware case, a three-judge federal district court denied relief to the plaintiffs on the so-called "separate but equal" doctrine announced by this Court in *Plessy* v. *Ferguson,* 163 U.S. 537. Under that doctrine, equality of treatment is accorded when the races are provided substantially equal facilities, even though these facilities be separate. In the Delaware case, the Supreme Court of Delaware adhered to that doctrine, but ordered that the plaintiffs be admitted to the white schools because of their superiority to the Negro schools.

The plaintiffs contend that segregated public schools are not "equal" and cannot be made "equal," and that hence they are deprived of the equal protection of the laws. Because of the obvious importance of the question presented, the Court took jurisdiction. Argument was heard in the 1952 Term, and reargument was heard this Term on certain questions propounded by the Court.

Reargument was largely devoted to the circumstances surrounding the adoption of the Fourteenth Amendment in 1868. It covered exhaustively consideration of the Amendment in Congress, ratification by the states, then existing practices in racial segregation, and the views of proponents and opponents of the Amendment. This discussion and our own investigation convince us that, although these sources cast some light, it is not enough to resolve the problem with which we are faced. At best, they are inconclusive. The most avid proponents of the post-War Amendments undoubtedly intended them to remove all legal distinctions among "all persons born or naturalized in the United States." Their opponents, just as certainly were antagonistic to both the letter and the spirit of the Amendments and wished them to have the most limited effect. What others in Congress and the state legislatures had in mind cannot be determined with any degree of certainty.

An additional reason for the inconclusive nature of the Amendment's history, with respect to segregated schools, is the status of public education at that time. In the South, the movement toward free common schools, supported by general taxation, had not yet taken hold. Education of white children was largely in the hands of private groups. Education of Negroes was almost nonexistent, and practically all of the race were illiterate. In fact, any education of Negroes was forbidden by law in some states. Today, in contrast, many Negroes have achieved outstanding success in the arts and sciences as well as in the business and professional world. It is true that public education had already advanced further in the North, but the effect of the Amendment on Northern States was generally ignored in the congressional debates. Even in the North, the conditions of public education did not approximate those existing today. The curriculum was usually rudimentary; ungraded schools were common in rural areas; the school term was but three months a year in many states; and compulsory school attendance was virtually unknown. As a consequence, it is not surprising that there should be so little in the history of the Fourteenth Amendment relating to its intended effect on public education.

In the first cases in this Court construing the Fourteenth Amendment, decided shortly after its adoption, the Court interpreted it as proscribing all state-imposed discriminations against the Negro race. The doctrine of "separate but equal" did not make its appearance in this Court until 1896 in the case of *Plessy* v. *Ferguson, supra,* involving not education but transportation. American courts have since labored with the doctrine for over half a century. In this Court, there have been six cases involving the "separate but equal" doctrine in the field of public education. In *Cumming* v. *County Board of Education,* 175 U.S. 528, and *Gong Lum*

v. *Rice,* 275 U.S. 78, the validity of the doctrine itself was not challenged. In more recent cases, all on the graduate school level, inequality was found in that specific benefits enjoyed by white students were denied to Negro students of the same educational qualifications. *Missouri ex rel. Gaines* v. *Canada,* 305 U.S. 337; *Sipuel* v. *Oklahoma,* 332 U.S. 631; *Sweatt* v. *Painter,* 339 U.S. 629; *McLaurin* v. *Oklahoma State Regents,* 339 U.S. 637. In none of these cases was it necessary to reexamine the doctrine to grant relief to the Negro plaintiff. And in *Sweatt* v. *Painter, supra,* the Court expressly reserved decision on the question whether *Plessy* v. *Ferguson* should be held inapplicable to public education.

In the instant cases, that question is directly presented. Here, unlike *Sweatt* v. *Painter,* there are findings below that the Negro and white schools involved have been equalized, or are being equalized, with respect to buildings, curricula, qualifications and salaries of teachers, and other "tangible" factors. Our decision, therefore, cannot turn on merely a comparison of these tangible factors in the Negro and white schools involved in each of the cases. We must look instead to the effect of segregation itself on public education.

In approaching this problem, we cannot turn the clock back to 1868 when the Amendment was adopted, or even to 1896 when *Plessy* v. *Ferguson* was written. We must consider public education in the light of its full development and its present place in American life throughout the Nation. Only in this way can it be determined if segregation in public schools deprives these plaintiffs of the equal protection of the laws.

Today, education is perhaps the most important function of state and local governments. Compulsory school attendance laws and the great expenditures for education both demonstrate our recognition of the importance of education to our democratic society. It is required in the performance of our most basic public responsibilities, even service in the armed forces. It is the very foundation of good citizenship. Today it is a principal instrument in awakening the child to cultural values, in preparing him for later professional training, and in helping him to adjust normally to his environment. In these days, it is doubtful that any child may reasonably be expected to succeed in life if he is denied the opportunity of an education. Such an opportunity, where the state has undertaken to provide it, is a right which must be made available to all on equal terms.

We come then to the question presented: Does segregation of children in public schools solely on the basis of race, even though the physical facilities and other "tangible" factors may be equal, deprive the children of the minority group of equal educational opportunities? We believe that it does.

In *Sweatt* v. *Painter, supra,* in finding that a segregated law school for Negroes could not provide them equal educational opportunities, this Court relied in large part on "those qualities which are incapable of objective measurement but which make for greatness in a law school." In *McLaurin* v. *Oklahoma State Regents, supra,* the Court, in requiring that a Negro admitted to a white graduate school be treated like all other students, again resorted to intangible considerations: ". . . his ability to study, to engage in discussions and exchange views with other students, and, in general, to learn his profession." Such considerations apply with added force to children in grade and high schools. To separate them from others of similar age and qualifications solely because of their race generates a feeling of inferiority as to their status in the community that may affect their hearts and minds in a way unlikely ever to be undone. The effect of this separation on their educational opportunities was well stated by a finding in the Kansas case by a court which nevertheless felt compelled to rule against the Negro plaintiffs:

> "Segregation of white and colored children in public schools has a detrimental effect upon the colored children. The impact is greater when it has the sanction of the law; for the policy of separating the races is usually interpreted as denoting the inferiority of the Negro group. A sense of inferiority affects the motivation of a child to learn. Segregation with the sanction of law, therefore, has a tendency to retard the educational and mental development of Negro children and to deprive them of some of the benefits they would receive in a racially integrated school system."

Whatever may have been the extent of psychological knowledge at the time of *Plessy* v. *Ferguson,* this finding is amply supported by modern authority. Any language in *Plessy* v. *Ferguson* contrary to this finding is rejected.

We conclude that in the field of public education the doctrine of "separate but equal" has no place. Separate educational facilities are inherently unequal. Therefore, we hold that the plaintiffs and others similarly situated for whom the actions have been brought are, by reason of the segregation complained of, deprived of the equal protection of the laws guaranteed by the Fourteenth Amendment.

This disposition makes unnecessary any discussion whether such segregation also violates the Due Process Clause of the Fourteenth Amendment.

Because these are class actions, because of the wide applicability of this decision, and because of the great variety of local conditions, the formulation of decrees in these cases presents problems of considerable complexity. On reargument, the consideration of appropriate relief was necessarily subordinated to the primary question—the constitutionality of segregation in public education. We have now announced that such segregation is a denial of the equal protection of the laws. In order that we may have the full assistance of the parties in formulating decrees, the cases will be restored to the docket, and the parties are requested to present further argument. . . .

It is so ordered.

BOLLING v. SHARPE,
347 U.S. 497 (1954)

MR. CHIEF JUSTICE WARREN delivered the opinion of the Court:

This case challenges the validity of segregation in the public schools of the District of Columbia. The petitioners, minors of the Negro race, allege that such segregation deprives them of due process of law under the Fifth Amendment. They were refused admission to a public school attended by white children solely because of their race. They sought the aid of the District Court for the District of Columbia in obtaining admission. That court dismissed their complaint. We granted a writ of certiorari before judgment in the Court of Appeals because of the importance of the constitutional question presented.

We have this day held that the Equal Protection Clause of the Fourteenth Amendment prohibits the states from maintaining racially segregated public schools. The legal problem in the District of Columbia is somewhat different, however. The Fifth Amendment, which is applicable in the District of Columbia, does not contain an equal protection clause as does the Fourteenth Amendment which applies only to the states. But the concepts of equal protection and due process, both stemming from our American idea of fairness, are not mutually exclusive. The "equal protection of the laws" is a more explicit safeguard of prohibited unfairness than "due process of law," and, therefore, we do not imply that the two are always interchangeable phrases. But, as this Court has recognized, discrimination may be so unjustifiable as to be violative of due process.

Classifications based solely upon race must be scrutinized with particular care, since they are contrary to our traditions and hence constitutionally suspect. As long ago as 1896, this Court declared the principle "that the Constitution of the United States, in its present form, forbids, so far as civil and political rights are concerned, discrimination by the General Government, or by the States, against any citizen because of his race." And in *Buchanan* v. *Warley,* 245 U.S. 60, the Court held that a statute which limited the right of a property owner to convey his property to a person of another race was, as an unreasonable discrimination, a denial of due process of law.

Although the Court has not assumed to define "liberty" with any great precision, that term is not confined to mere freedom from bodily restraint. Liberty under law extends to the full range of conduct which the individual is free to pursue, and it cannot be restricted except for a proper governmental objective. Segregation in public education is not reasonably related to any proper governmental objective, and thus it imposes on Negro children of the District of Columbia a burden that constitutes an arbitrary deprivation of their liberty in violation of the Due Process Clause.

In view of our decision that the Constitution prohibits the states from maintaining racially segregated public schools, it would be unthinkable that the same Constitution would impose a lesser duty on the Federal Government. We hold that racial segregation in the public schools of the District of Columbia is a denial of the due process of law guaranteed by the Fifth Amendment to the Constitution. . . .

It is so ordered.

BROWN v. BOARD OF EDUCATION, 349 U.S. 294 (1955)

MR. CHIEF JUSTICE WARREN delivered the opinion of the Court:

These cases were decided on May 17, 1954. The opinions of that date, declaring the fundamental principle that racial discrimination in public education is unconstitutional, are incorporated herein by reference. All provisions of federal, state, or local law requiring or permitting such discrimination must yield to this principle. There remains for consideration the manner in which relief is to be accorded.

Because these cases arose under different local conditions and their disposition will involve a variety of local problems, we requested further argument on the question of relief. In view of the nation-wide importance of the decision, we invited the Attorney General of the United States and the Attorneys General of all states requiring or permitting racial discrimination in public education to present their views on that question. The parties, the United States, and the States of Florida, North Carolina, Arkansas, Oklahoma, Maryland, and Texas filed briefs and participated in the oral argument.

These presentations were informative and helpful to the Court in its consideration of the complexities arising from the transition to a system of public education freed of racial discrimination. The presentations also demonstrated that substantial steps to eliminate racial discrimination in public schools have already been taken, not only in some of the communities in which these cases arose but in some of the states appearing as *amici curiae,* and in other states as well. Substantial progress has been made in the District of Columbia and in the communities in Kansas and Delaware involved in this litigation. The defendants in the cases coming to us from South Carolina and Virginia are awaiting the decision of this Court concerning relief.

Full implementation of these constitutional principles may require solution of varied local school problems. School authorities have the primary responsibility for elucidating, assessing, and solving these problems; courts will have to consider whether the action of school authorities constitutes good faith implementation of the governing constitutional principles. Because of their proximity to local conditions and the possible need for further hearings, the courts which originally heard these cases can best perform this judicial appraisal. Accordingly, we believe it appropriate to remand the cases to those courts.

In fashioning and effectuating the decrees, the courts will be guided by equitable principles. Traditionally, equity has been characterized by a practical flexibility in shaping its remedies and by a facility for adjusting and reconciling public and private needs. These cases call for the exercise of these traditional attributes of equity power. At stake is the personal interest of the plaintiffs in admission to public schools as soon as practicable on a nondiscriminatory basis. To effectuate this interest may call for elimination of a variety of obstacles in making the transition to school systems operated in accordance with the constitutional principles set forth in our May 17, 1954, decision. Courts of equity may properly take into account the public interest in the elimination of such obstacles in a systematic and effective manner. But it should go without saying that the vitality of these constitutional principles cannot be allowed to yield simply because of disagreement with them.

While giving weight to these public and private considerations, the courts will require that the defendants make a prompt and reasonable start toward full compliance with our May 17, 1954, ruling. Once such a start has been made, the courts may find that additional time is necessary to carry out the ruling in an effective manner. The burden rests upon the defendants to establish that such time is necessary in the public interest and is consistent with good faith compliance at the earliest practicable date. To that end, the courts may consider problems related to administration, arising from the physical condition of the school plant, the school transportation system, personnel, revision of school districts and attendance areas into compact units to achieve a system of determining admission to the public schools on a nonracial basis, and revision of local laws and regulations which may be necessary in solving the foregoing problems. They will also consider the adequacy of any plans the defendants may propose to meet these problems and to effectuate a transition to a racially nondiscriminatory school system. During this period of transition, the courts will retain jurisdiction of these cases.

The judgments below, except that in the Delaware case, are accordingly reversed and the cases are remanded to the District Courts to take such proceedings and enter such orders and decrees consistent with this opinion as are necessary and proper to admit to public schools on a racially nondiscriminatory basis with all deliberate speed the parties to these cases. The judgment in the Delaware case—ordering the immediate admission of the plaintiffs to schools previously attended only by white children—is affirmed on the basis of the principles stated in our May 17, 1954, opinion, but the case is remanded to the Supreme Court of Delaware for such further proceedings as that Court may deem necessary in light of this opinion.

It is so ordered.

SWANN v. CHARLOTTE-MECKLENBURG BOARD OF EDUCATION, 402 U.S. 1 (1971)

School desegregation as mandated by Brown v. Board of Education *has presented a continuing problem of enforcement. Ultimately, the federal courts themselves stepped in and fashioned administrative remedies to achieve the desegregation of public school systems. One device that achieved prominence and generated great controversy was using busing of schoolchildren for the purpose of desegregation. It was somewhat ironic for white southerners now to complain about busing as busing had been a principal tool for maintaining separate school systems. And, of course, busing has been widespread for the simple purpose of transporting children to school. But, in this case, the constitutionality of a school desegregation plan that depended heavily upon the busing of schoolchildren was before the Court. The plan was ordered by federal District Court Judge James B. McMillan after the Board of Education for Charlotte-Mecklenburg had repeatedly failed to produce a satisfactory elementary school desegregation plan. The Supreme Court, as had been its custom with school desegregation cases since* Brown v. Board of Education, *spoke with one voice and, although that voice showed signs of cracking, the Court here upheld the use of court-ordered busing for the purpose of dismantling a dual (segregated) school system.*

Votes: Unanimous

MR. CHIEF JUSTICE BURGER delivered the opinion of the Court:. . . .

. . . These cases present us with the problem of defining in more precise terms than heretofore the scope of the duty of school authorities and district courts in implementing Brown v. *Board of Education* and the mandate to eliminate dual systems and establish unitary systems at once. . . . Once a right and a violation have been shown, the scope of a district court's equitable powers to remedy past wrongs is broad, for breadth and flexibility are inherent in equitable remedies. . . . The task is to correct, by a balancing of the individual and collective interests, the condition that offends the Constitution.

In seeking to define even in broad and general terms how far this remedial power extends it is important to remember that judicial powers may be exercised only on the basis of a constitutional violation. Remedial judicial authority does not put judges automatically in the shoes of school authorities whose powers are plenary. Judicial authority enters only when local authority defaults. . . .

We turn now to the problem of defining with more particularity the responsibilities of school authorities in desegregating a state-enforced dual school system in light of the Equal Protection Clause. . . .

The construction of new schools and the closing of old ones are two of the most important functions of local school authorities and also two of the most complex. They must decide questions of location and capacity in light of population growth, finances, and land values, site availability, through an almost endless list of factors to be considered. The result of this will be a decision which, when combined with one technique or another of student assignment, will determine the racial composition of the student body in each school in the system. Over the long run, the consequences of the choices will be far reaching. People gravitate toward school facilities, just as schools are located in response to the needs of people. The location of schools may thus influence the patterns of residential development of a metropolitan area and have important impact on composition of inner city neighborhoods.

In the past, choices in this respect have been used as a potent weapon for creating or maintaining a state-segregated school system. In addition to the classic pattern of building schools specifically intended for Negro or white students, school authorities have sometimes, since *Brown,* closed schools which appeared likely to become racially mixed through changes in neighborhood residential patterns. This was sometimes accompanied by building new schools in the areas of white suburban expansion farthest from Negro population centers in order to maintain the separation of the races with a minimum departure from the formal principles of "neighborhood zoning." Such a policy does more than simply influence the short-run composition of the student body of a new school. It may well promote segregated residential patterns which, when combined with "neighborhood zoning," further lock the school system into the mold of separation of the races. Upon a proper showing a district court may consider this in fashioning a remedy.

In ascertaining the existence of legally imposed school segregation, the existence of a pattern of school construction and abandonment is thus a factor of great weight. In devising remedies where legally imposed segregation has been established, it is the responsibility of local authorities and district courts to see to it that future school construction and abandonment are not used and do not serve to perpetuate or re-establish the dual system. When necessary, district courts should retain jurisdiction to assure that these responsibilities are carried out. . . .

The central issue in this case is that of student assignment, and there are essentially four problem areas:

(1) to what extent racial balance or racial quotas may be used as an implement in a remedial order to correct a previously segregated system;

(2) whether every all-Negro and all-white school must be eliminated as an indispensable part of a remedial process of desegregation;

(3) what the limits are, if any, on the rearrangement of school districts and attendance zones, as a remedial measure; and

(4) what the limits are, if any, on the use of transportation facilities to correct state-enforced racial school segregation.

(1) RACIAL BALANCES OR RACIAL QUOTAS. . . .

We are concerned in these cases with the elimination of the discrimination inherent in the dual school systems, not with myriad factors of human existence which can cause discrimination in a multitude of ways on racial, religious, or ethnic grounds. . . .

In this case it is urged that the District Court has imposed a racial balance requirement of 71%–29% on individual schools. . . . The District Judge . . . acknowledge[d] that variation "from that norm may be unavoidable." This contains intimations that the "norm" is a fixed mathematical racial balance reflecting the pupil constituency of the system. If we were to read the holding of the District Court to require, as a matter of substantive constitutional right, any particular degree of racial balance or mixing, that approach would be disapproved and we would be obliged to reverse. The constitutional command to desegregate schools does not mean that every school in every community must always reflect the racial composition of the school system as a whole.

As the voluminous record in this case shows, the predicate for the District Court's use of the 71%-29% ratio was twofold: first, its express finding, approved by the Court of Appeals and not challenged here, that a dual school system had been maintained by the school authorities at least until 1969; second, its finding, also approved by the Court of Appeals, that the school board had totally defaulted in its acknowledged duty to come forward with an acceptable plan of its own, notwithstanding the patient efforts of the District Judge who, on at least three occasions, urged the board to submit plans. As the statement of facts shows, these findings are abundantly supported by the record. It was because of this total failure of the school board that the District Court was obliged to turn to other qualified sources. . . .

We see therefore that the use made of mathematical ratios was no more than a starting point in the process of shaping a remedy, rather than an inflexible requirement. . . .

(2) ONE-RACE SCHOOLS

The record in this case reveals the familiar phenomenon that in metropolitan areas minority groups are often found concentrated in one part of the city. In some circumstances certain schools may remain all or largely of one race until new schools can be provided or neighborhood patterns change. Schools all or predominantly of one race in a district of mixed population will require close scrutiny to determine that school assignments are not part of state-enforced segregation.

In light of the above, it should be clear that the existence of some small number of one-race, or virtually one-race, schools within a district is not in and of itself the mark of a system which still practices segregation by law. The district judge or school authorities should make every effort to achieve the greatest possible degree of actual desegregation and will thus necessarily be concerned with the elimination of one-race schools. . . . Where the school authority's proposed plan for conversion from a dual to a unitary system contemplates the continued existence of some schools that are all or predominantly of one race, they have the burden of showing that such school assignments are genuinely nondiscriminatory. The court should scrutinize such schools, and the burden upon the school authorities will be to satisfy the court that their racial composition is not the result of present or past discriminatory action on their part. . . .

(3) REMEDIAL ALTERING OF ATTENDANCE ZONES

The maps submitted in these cases graphically demonstrate that one of the principal tools employed by school planners and by courts to break up the dual school system has been a frank—and sometimes drastic—gerrymandering of school districts and attendance zones. An additional step was pairing, "clustering," or "grouping" of schools with attendance assignments made deliberately to accomplish the transfer of Negro students out of formerly segregated Negro schools and transfer of white students to formerly all-Negro schools. More often than not, these zones are neither compact nor contiguous; indeed they may be on opposite ends of the city. As an interim corrective measure, this cannot be said to be beyond the broad remedial powers of a court. . . .

We hold that the pairing and grouping of non-contiguous school zones is a permissible tool and such action is to be considered in light of the objectives sought. . . . Maps do not tell the whole story since non-contiguous school zones may be more accessible to each other in terms of the critical travel time, because of traffic patterns and good highways, than schools geographically closer together. Conditions in different localities will vary so widely that no rigid rules can be laid down to govern all situations.

(4) TRANSPORTATION OF STUDENTS

The scope of permissible transportation of students as an implement of a remedial decree has never been defined by this Court and by the very nature of the problem it cannot be defined with precision. No right guidelines as to student transportation can be given for application to the infinite variety of problems presented in thousands of situations. Bus transportation has been an integral part of the public education system for years, and was perhaps the single most important factor in the transition from the one-room schoolhouse to the consolidated school. Eighteen million of the Nation's public school children, approximately 39% were transported to their schools by bus in 1969–1970 in all parts of the country.

The importance of bus transportation as a normal and accepted tool of educational policy is readily discernible in this and the companion case. The Charlotte school authorities did not purport to assign students on the basis of geographically drawn zones until 1965 and then they allowed almost unlimited transfer privileges. The District Court's conclusion that assignment of children to the school nearest their home serving their grade would not produce an effective dismantling of the dual system is supported by the record.

Thus the remedial techniques used in the District Court's order were within that Court's power to provide equitable relief; implementation of the decree is well within the capacity of the school authority.

The decree provided that the buses used to implement the plan would operate on direct routes. Students would be picked up at schools near their homes and transported to the schools they were to attend. The trips for elementary school pupils average about seven miles and the District Court found that they would take "not over 35 minutes at the most." This system compares favorably with the transportation plan previously operated in Charlotte under which each day 23,600 students on all grade levels were transported an average of 15 miles one way for an average trip requiring over an hour. In these circumstances, we find no basis for holding that the local school authorities may not be required to employ bus transportation as one tool of school desegregation. Desegregation plans cannot be limited to the walk-in school.

An objection to transportation of students may have validity when the time or distance of travel is so great as to either risk the health of the children or significantly impinge on the educational process. District courts must weigh the soundness of any transportation plan in light of what [we] said. . . . It hardly needs stating that the limits on time of travel will vary with many factors, but probably with none more than the age of the students. The reconciliation of competing values in a desegregation case is, of course, a difficult task with many sensitive facets but fundamentally no more so than remedial measures courts of equity have traditionally employed.

. . . On the facts of this case, we are unable to conclude that the order of the District Court is not reasonable, feasible and workable. However, in seeking to define the scope of remedial power or the limits on remedial power of courts in an area as sensitive as we deal with here, words are poor instruments to convey the sense of basic fairness inherent in equity. Substance, not semantics, must govern, and we have sought to suggest the nature of limitations without frustrating the appropriate scope of equity.

At some point, these school authorities and others like them should have achieved full compliance with this Court's decision in *Brown I*. The systems would then be "unitary" in the sense required by our decisions. . . .

It does not follow that the communities served by such systems will remain demographically stable, for in a growing, mobile society, few will do so. Neither school authorities nor district courts are constitutionally required to make year-by-year adjustments of the racial composition of student bodies once the affirmative duty to desegregate has been accomplished and racial discrimination through official action is eliminated from the system. This does not mean that federal courts are without power to deal with future problems; but in the absence of a showing that either the school authorities or some other agency of the State has deliberately attempted to fix or alter demographic patterns to affect the racial composition of the schools, further intervention by a district court should not be necessary.

For the reasons herein set forth, the judgment of the Court of Appeals is affirmed as to those parts in which it affirmed the judgment of the District Court. The order of the District Court is also affirmed. It is so ordered.

Judgment of Court of Appeals affirmed in part; order of District Court affirmed.

KEYES v. SCHOOL DISTRICT NO. 1, DENVER, 413 U.S. 189 (1973)

The Keyes *decision was immensely important because the Court for the first time recognized a constitutional problem with racial discrimination by a school system in the North. The Denver school board, through its practices and policies, had maintained and perpetuated the separation of the races in certain of its public schools and, in so doing, violated the equal protection clause of the Fourteenth Amendment. It made little difference that Denver had no law requiring the separation of the races. As long as the public school authorities took actions that had the same effect, Fourteenth Amendment remedies, including the busing of schoolchildren, were appropriate.*

Majority votes: 6 + 1 (in part)
Dissenting votes: 1

MR. JUSTICE BRENNAN delivered the opinion of the Court:

This school desegregation case concerns the Denver, Colorado, school system. . . . Petitioners proved that for almost a decade after 1960 respondent School Board had engaged in an unconstitutional policy of deliberate racial segregation in the Park Hill schools. Indeed, the District Court found . . . respondent School Board . . . guilty of following a deliberate segregation policy at schools attended, in 1969, by 37.69% of Denver's total Negro school population, including one-fourth of the Negro elementary pupils, over two-thirds of the Negro junior high pupils, and over two-fifths of the Negro high school pupils. In addition, there was uncontroverted evidence that teachers and staff had for years been assigned on a minority teacher-to-minority school basis throughout the school system. Respondent argues, however, that a finding of state-imposed segregation as to a substantial portion of the school system can be viewed in isolation from the rest of the district, and that even if state-imposed segregation does exist in a substantial part of the Denver school system, it does not follow that the District Court could predicate on that fact a finding that the entire school system is a dual system. We do not agree. . . .

This is not a case, however, where a statutory

dual system has ever existed. Nevertheless, where plaintiffs prove that the school authorities have carried out a systematic program of segregation affecting a substantial portion of the students, schools, teachers and facilities within the school system, it is only common sense to conclude that there exists a predicate for a finding of the existence of a dual school system. Several considerations support this conclusion. First, it is obvious that a practice of concentrating Negroes in certain schools by structuring attendance zones or designating "feeder" schools on the basis of race has the reciprocal effect of keeping other nearby schools predominantly white. Similarly, the practice of building a school— such as the Barrett Elementary School in this case—to a certain size and in a certain location, "with conscious knowledge that it would be a segregated school," has a substantial reciprocal effect on the racial composition of other nearby schools. So also, the use of mobile classrooms, the drafting of student transfer policies, the transportation of students, and the assignment of faculty and staff, on racially identifiable bases, have the clear effect of earmarking schools according to their racial composition, and this, in turn, together with the elements of student assignment and school construction, may have a profound reciprocal effect on the racial composition of residential neighborhoods within a metropolitan area, thereby causing further racial concentration within the schools. . . .

On remand, therefore, the District Court should decide in the first instance whether respondent School Board's deliberate racial segregation policy with respect to the Park Hill schools constitutes the entire Denver school system a dual school system. We observe that on the record now before us there is indication that Denver is not a school district which might be divided into separate, identifiable and unrelated units. . . .

On the question of segregative intent, petitioners presented evidence tending to show that the Board, through its actions over a period of years, intentionally created and maintained the segregated character of the core city schools. Respondents countered this evidence by arguing that the segregation in these schools is the result of a racially neutral "neighborhood school policy" and that the acts of which petitioners complain are explicable within the bounds of that policy. Accepting the School Board's explanation, the District Court and the Court of Appeals agreed that a finding of de jure segregation as to the core city schools was not permissible since petitioners had failed to prove "(1) a racially discriminatory purpose and (2) a causal relationship between the acts complained of and the

racial imbalance admittedly existing in those schools." 445 F.2d at 1006. This assessment of petitioners' proof was clearly incorrect.

Although petitioners had already proved the existence of intentional school segregation in the Park Hill schools, this crucial finding was totally ignored when attention turned to the core city schools. Plainly, a finding of intentional segregation as to a portion of a school system is not devoid of probative value in assessing the school authorities' intent with respect to other parts of the same school system. On the contrary where, as here, the case involves one school board, a finding of intentional segregation on its part in one portion of a school system is highly relevant to the issue of the board's intent with respect to the other segregated schools in the system. . . .

Applying these principles in the special context of school desegregation cases, we hold that a finding of intentionally segregative school board actions in a meaningful portion of a school system, as in this case, creates a presumption that other segregated schooling within the system is not adventitious. It establishes, in other words, a prima facie case of unlawful segregative design on the part of school authorities, and shifts to those authorities the burden of proving that other segregated schools within the system are not also the result of intentionally segregative actions. This is true even if it is determined that different areas of the school district should be viewed independently of each other because, even in that situation, there is high probability that where school authorities have effectuated an intentionally segregative policy in a meaningful portion of the school system, similar impermissible considerations have motivated their actions in other areas of the system. We emphasize that the differentiating factor between *de jure* segregation and so-called *de facto* segregation . . . is *purpose* or *intent* to segregate. Where school authorities have been found to have practiced purposeful segregation in part of a school system, they may be expected to oppose systemwide desegregation, as did the respondents in this case, on the ground that their purposefully segregative actions were isolated and individual events, thus leaving plaintiffs with the burden of proving otherwise. But at that point where an intentionally segregative policy is practiced in a meaningful or significant segment of a school system, as in this case, the school authorities cannot be heard to argue that plaintiffs have proved only "isolated and individual" unlawfully segregative actions. In that circumstance, it is both fair and reasonable to require that the school authorities bear the burden of showing that their actions as to other segregated schools within the system were not also motivated by segregative intent. . . .

In summary, the District Court on remand, *first*, will afford respondent School Board the opportunity to prove its contention that the Park Hill area is a separate, identifiable and unrelated section of the school district that should be treated as isolated from the rest of the district. If respondent School Board fails to prove that contention, the District Court, *second,* will determine whether respondent School Board's conduct over almost a decade after 1960 in carrying out a policy of deliberate racial segregation in the Park Hill schools constitutes the entire school system a dual school system. If the District Court determines that the Denver school system is a dual school system, respondent School Board has the affirmative duty to desegregate the entire system "root and branch." If the District Court determines, however, that the Denver school system is not a dual school system by reason of the Board's actions in Park Hill, the court, *third,* will afford respondent School Board the opportunity to rebut petitioners' prima facie case of intentional segregation in the core city schools raised by the finding of intentional segregation in the Park Hill schools. There, the Board's burden is to show that its policies and practices with respect to school site location, school size, school renovations and additions, student attendance zones, student assignment and transfer options, mobile classroom units, transportation of students, assignment of faculty and staff, etc., considered together and premised on the Board's so-called "neighborhood school" concept, either were not taken in effectuation of a policy to create or maintain segregation in the core city schools, or, if unsuccessful in that effort, were not factors in causing the existing condition of segregation in these schools. Considerations of "fairness" and "policy" demand no less in light of the Board's intentionally segregative actions. If respondent Board fails to rebut petitioners' prima facie case, the District Court must, as in the case of Park Hill, decree all-out desegregation of the core city schools.

The judgment of the Court of Appeals is modified to vacate instead of reverse the parts of the Final Decree that concern the core city schools, and the case is remanded to the District Court for further proceedings consistent with this opinion.

Modified and remanded.

It is so ordered.

MR. CHIEF JUSTICE BURGER concurs in the result. MR. JUSTICE WHITE took no part in the decision of this case.

MR. JUSTICE DOUGLAS, concurring: [omitted]
MR. JUSTICE REHNQUIST, dissenting:

The Court notes at the outset of its opinion the differences between the claims made by the plaintiffs in this case and the classical "de jure" type of claims made by plaintiffs in cases such as *Brown* v. *Board of Education,* 347 U.S. 483 (1954), and its progeny. I think the similarities and differences, not only in the claims, but in the nature of the constitutional violation, deserve somewhat more attention than the Court gives them. . . .

. . . To require that a genuinely "dual" system be disestablished, in the sense that the assignment to a child of a particular school is not made to depend on his race is one thing. To require that school boards affirmatively undertake to achieve racial mixing in schools where such mixing is not achieved in sufficient degree by neutrally drawn boundary lines is quite obviously something else. . . .

The Court has taken a long leap in this area of constitutional law in equating the district-wide consequences of gerrymandering individual attendance zones in a district where separation of the races was never required by law with statutes or ordinances in other jurisdictions which did so require. It then adds to this potpourri a confusing enunciation of evidentiary rules in order to make it more likely that the trial court will on remand reach the result which the Court apparently wants it to reach. Since I believe neither of these steps is justified by prior decisions of this Court, I dissent.

MR. JUSTICE POWELL concurring in part and dissenting in part:. . . .

This is the first school desegregation case to reach this Court which involves a major city outside the South. . . .

The situation in Denver is generally comparable to that in other large cities across the country in which there is a substantial minority population and where desegregation has not been ordered by the federal courts. There is segregation in the schools of many of these cities fully as pervasive as that in southern cities prior to the desegregation decrees of the past decade and a half. The focus of the school desegregation problem has now shifted from the South to the country as a whole. Unwilling and footdragging as the process was in most places, substantial progress toward achieving integration has been made in Southern States. No comparable progress has been made in many nonsouthern cities with large minority populations primarily because of the *de facto/de jure* distinction nurtured by the courts and accepted complacently by many of the same voices which denounced the evils of segregated schools in the South. But if our national concern is for those who attend such schools, rather than for perpetuating a legalism rooted in history rather than present reality, we must recognize that the evil of operating separate schools is no less in Denver than in Atlanta.

In my view we should abandon a distinction which long since has outlived its time, and formulate constitutional principles of national rather than merely regional application. . . .

. . . [W]e should acknowledge that whenever public school segregation exists to a substantial degree there is prima facie evidence of a constitutional violation by the responsible school board. . . . The burden then shifts to the school authorities to demonstrate that they have in fact operated an integrated system as this term is defined. If there is a failure successfully to rebut the prima facie case, the question then becomes what reasonable affirmative desegregative steps district courts may require to place the school system in compliance with the constitutional standard. . . .

It is well to remember that the course we are running is a long one and the goal sought in the end—so often overlooked—is the best possible educational opportunity for all children. Communities deserve the freedom and the incentive to turn their attention and energies to this goal of quality education, free from protracted and debilitating battles over court-ordered student transportation. The single most disruptive element in education today is the widespread use of compulsory transportation, especially at elementary grade levels. This has risked distracting and diverting attention from basic educational ends, dividing and embittering communities, and exacerbating, rather than ameliorating, interracial friction and misunderstanding. It is time to return to a more balanced evaluation of the recognized interests of our society in achieving desegregation with other educational and societal interests a community may legitimately assert. . . .

MILLIKEN v. BRADLEY,
418 U.S. 717 (1974)

In a class action suit brought on behalf of Ronald Bradley, a student in the public schools of Detroit, Michigan, and all others similarly situated, against various state and local officials (including Governor Milliken), the National Association for the Advancement of Colored People (NAACP) alleged that Detroit's school system was racially segregated as a result of official policies and actions of the Detroit school authorities as well as of various other local and state officials. The NAACP asked for a metropolitan areawide desegregation plan that would include the "white" suburbs. In the federal trial, the NAACP presented evidence demonstrating the pervasiveness of racially discriminatory practices in the metropolitan area—from the actions of banks and real estate agencies who perpetrated racial discrimination in housing by not approving mortgage applications submitted by black people or by not showing them houses in certain areas, to the actions of state and local officials who did not enforce the state's antidiscrimination laws. The Detroit school board was found to have drawn attendance zones, chosen locations for new schools, and to have committed other acts that had the "natural, probable, foreseeable and actual effect" of fostering segregation. The judge concluded that because of the racial composition of the Detroit school population, the remedy could not be limited to Detroit because to do so would worsen the situation (i.e., result in more busing at greater expense than if a metropolitan-wide plan were adopted). The suburbs, of course, had been able to maintain their racial homogeneity precisely because of the widespread discriminatory practices demonstrated before the trial court. The court-ordered desegregation plan involved Detroit and 53 suburban school districts. The Court of Appeals for the Sixth Circuit affirmed the district court and the case came before the Supreme Court.

Majority votes: 5
Dissenting votes: 4

MR. CHIEF JUSTICE BURGER delivered the opinion of the Court:. . . .

. . . [W]e first note that in the District Court the complainants sought a remedy aimed at the *condition* alleged to offend the Constitution—the segregation within the Detroit City School District. . . .

Viewing the record as a whole, it seems clear that the District Court and the Court of Appeals shifted the primary focus from a Detroit remedy to the metropolitan area only because of their conclusion that total desegregation of Detroit would not produce the racial balance which they perceived as desirable. Both courts proceeded on an assumption that the Detroit schools could not be truly desegregated—in their view of what constituted desegregation—unless the racial composition of the student body of each school substantially reflected the racial composition of the population of the metropolitan area as a whole. The metropolitan area was then defined as Detroit plus 53 of the outlying school districts. . . .

Here the District Court's approach to what constituted "actual desegregation" raises the fundamental question, not presented in *Swann,* as to the circumstances in which a federal court may order desegregation relief that embraces more than a single school district. The court's analytical starting point was its conclusion that school district lines are no more than arbitrary lines on a map "drawn for political convenience." Boundary lines may be bridged where there has been a constitutional violation calling for inter-district relief, but the notion that school district lines may be casually ignored or treated as a mere administrative convenience is contrary to the history of public education in our country. No single tradition in public education is more deeply rooted than local control over the operation of schools; local autonomy has long been thought essential both to the maintenance of community concern and support for public schools and to quality of the educational process. . . .

The Michigan educational structure involved in this case, in common with most States, provides for a large measure of local control and a review of the scope and character of these local powers indicates the extent to which the inter-district remedy approved by the two courts could disrupt and alter the structure of public education in Michigan. The metropolitan remedy would require, in effect, consolidation of 54 independent school districts historically administered as separate units into a vast new super school district. Entirely apart from the logistical and other serious problems attending large-scale transportation of students, the consolidation would give rise to an array of other problems in financing and operating this new school system. Some of the more obvious questions would be: What would be the status and authority of the present popularly elected school boards? Would the children of Detroit be within the jurisdiction and operating control of a school board elected by the parents and residents of other districts? What board or boards would levy taxes for school operations in these 54 districts constituting the consolidated metropolitan area? What provisions could be made for assuring substantial equality in tax levies among the 54 districts, if this were deemed requisite? What provisions would be made for financing? Would the validity of long-term bonds be jeopardized unless approved by all of the component districts as well as the State? What body would determine that portion of the curricula now left to the discretion of local school boards? Who would establish attendance zones, purchase school equipment, locate and construct new schools, and indeed attend to all the myriad day-to-day decisions that are necessary to school operations affecting potentially more than three-quarters of a million pupils?

It may be suggested that all of these vital operational problems are yet to be resolved by the District Court, and that this is the purpose of the Court of Appeals' proposed remand. But it is obvious from the scope of the inter-district remedy itself that absent a complete restructuring of the laws of Michigan relating to school districts the District Court will become first, a *de facto* "legislative authority" to resolve these complex questions, and then the "school superintendent" for the entire area. This is a task which few, if any, judges are qualified to perform and one which would deprive the people of control of schools through their elected representatives.

Of course, no state law is above the Constitution. School district lines and the present laws with respect to local control are not sacrosanct and if they conflict with the Fourteenth Amendment federal courts have a duty to prescribe appropriate remedies. But our prior holdings have been confined to violations and remedies within a single school district. We therefore turn to address, for the first time, the validity of a remedy mandating cross-district or inter-district consolidation to remedy a condition of segregation found to exist in only one district.

The controlling principle consistently expounded in our holdings is that the scope of the remedy is determined by the nature and extent of the constitutional violation. Before the boundaries of separate and autonomous school districts may be set aside by consolidating the separate units for remedial purposes or by imposing a cross-district remedy, it must first be shown that there has been a constitutional violation within one district that produces a significant segregative effect in another district. Specifically it must be shown that racially discriminatory acts of the state or local school districts, or of a single school district have been a substantial cause of inter-district segregation. Thus an inter-district remedy might be in order where the racially discriminatory acts of one or more school districts caused racial segregation in an adjacent district, or where district lines have been deliberately drawn on the basis of race. In such circumstances an inter-district remedy would be appropriate to eliminate the inter-district segregation directly caused by the constitutional violation. Conversely, without an inter-district violation and inter-district effect, there is no constitutional wrong calling for an inter-district remedy.

The record before us, voluminous as it is, contains evidence of *de jure* segregated conditions only in the Detroit schools; indeed, that was the theory on which the litigation was initially based and on which the District Court took evidence. With no showing of significant violation by the 53 outlying school districts and no evidence of any inter-district violation or effect, the court went beyond the original theory of the case as framed by the pleadings and mandated a metropolitan area remedy. To approve the remedy ordered by the court would impose on the outlying districts, not shown to have committed any constitutional violation, a wholly impermissible remedy based on a standard not hinted at in *Brown I* and *II* or any holding of this Court.

In dissent, Mr. Justice White and Mr. Justice Marshall undertake to demonstrate that agencies having statewide authority participated in maintaining the dual school system found to exist in Detroit. They are apparently of the view that once such participation is shown, the District Court should have a relatively free hand to reconstruct school districts outside of Detroit in fashioning relief. Our assumption, *arguendo,* that state agencies did participate in the maintenance of the Detroit system, should make it clear that it is not on this point that we part company. The difference between us arises instead from established doctrine laid down by our cases [that] . . . addressed the issue of constitutional wrong in terms of an established geographic and administrative school system populated by both Negro and White children. In such a context, terms such as "unitary" and "dual" systems, and "racially identifiable schools," have meaning, and the necessary federal authority to remedy the constitutional wrong is firmly established. But the remedy is necessarily designed, as all remedies are, to restore the victims of discriminatory conduct to the position they would have occupied in the absence of such conduct. Disparate treatment of White and Negro students occurred within the Detroit school system, and not elsewhere, and on this record the remedy must be limited to that system.

The constitutional right of the Negro respondents residing in Detroit is to attend a unitary school system in that district. Unless petitioners drew the district lines in a discriminatory fashion, or arranged for White students residing in the Detroit district to attend schools in Oakland and Macomb Counties, they were under no constitutional duty to make provisions for Negro students to do so. The view of the dissenters, that the existence of a dual system in Detroit can be made the basis for a decree requiring cross-district transportation of pupils, cannot be supported on the grounds that it represents merely the devising of a suitably flexible remedy for the violation of rights already established by our prior decisions. It can be supported only by drastic expansion of the constitutional right itself, an expansion without any support in either constitutional principle or precedent. . . .

We conclude that the relief ordered by the District Court and affirmed by the Court of Appeals was based upon an erroneous standard and was unsupported by record evidence that acts of the outlying districts affected the discrimination found to exist in the schools of Detroit. Accordingly, the judgment of the Court of Appeals is reversed and the case is remanded for further proceedings consistent with this opinion leading to prompt formulation of a decree directed to eliminating the segregation found to exist in Detroit city schools, a remedy which has been delayed since 1970.

Reversed and remanded.

MR. JUSTICE STEWART, concurring: [omitted]
MR. JUSTICE DOUGLAS, dissenting: [omitted]
MR. JUSTICE WHITE, with whom MR. JUSTICE DOUGLAS, MR. JUSTICE BRENNAN, and MR. JUSTICE MARSHALL join, dissenting:. . . .

Regretfully, and for several reasons, I can join neither the Court's judgment nor its opinion. The core of my disagreement is that deliberate acts of segregation and their consequences will go unremedied, not because a remedy would be infeasible or unreasonable in terms of the usual criteria governing school desegregation cases, but because an effective remedy would cause what the Court considers to be undue administrative inconvenience to the State. The result is that the State of Michigan, the entity at which the Fourteenth Amendment is directed, has successfully insulated itself from its duty to provide effective desegregation remedies by vesting sufficient power over its public schools in its local school districts. If this is the case in Michigan, it will be the case in most States. . . .

I am surprised that the Court, sitting at this distance from the State of Michigan, claims better insight than the Court of Appeals and the District Court as to whether an inter-district remedy for equal protection violations practiced by the State of Michigan would involve undue difficulties for the State in the management of its public schools. . . .

I am even more mystified how the Court can ignore the legal reality that the constitutional violations, even if occurring locally, were committed by governmental entities for which the State is responsible and that it is the State that must respond to the command of the Fourteenth Amendment. An inter-district remedy for the infringements that occurred in this case is well within the confines and powers of the State, which is the governmental entity ultimately responsible for desegregating its schools. . . .

MR. JUSTICE MARSHALL, with whom MR. JUSTICE DOUGLAS, MR. JUSTICE BRENNAN, and MR. JUSTICE WHITE join, dissenting:

In *Brown* v. *Board of Education* this Court recognized . . . that remedying decades of segregation in public education would not be an easy task. Subsequent events, unfortunately, have seen that prediction bear bitter fruit. . . .

After 20 years of small, often difficult steps toward that great end, the Court today takes a giant step backwards. Notwithstanding a record showing widespread and pervasive racial segregation in the educational system provided by the State of Michigan for children in Detroit, this Court holds that the District Court was powerless to require the State to remedy its constitutional violation in any meaningful fashion. Ironically purporting to base its result on the principle that the scope of the remedy in a desegregation case should be determined by the nature and the extent of the constitutional violation, the Court's answer is to provide no remedy at all for the violation proved in this case, thereby guaranteeing that Negro children in Detroit will receive the same separate and inherently unequal education in the future as they have been unconstitutionally afforded in the past.

I cannot subscribe to this emasculation of our constitutional guarantee of equal protection of the laws and must respectfully dissent. Our precedents, in my view, firmly establish that where, as here, state-imposed segregation has been demonstrated, it becomes the duty of the State to eliminate root and branch all vestiges of racial discrimination and to achieve the greatest possible degree of actual desegregation. I agree with both the District Court and the Court of Appeals that, under the facts of this case, this duty cannot be fulfilled unless the State of Michigan involves outlying metropolitan area school districts in its desegregation remedy. Furthermore, I perceive no basis either in law or in the practicalities of the situation justifying the State's interposition of school district boundaries as absolute barriers to the implementation of an effective desegregation remedy. Under established and frequently used Michigan procedures, school district lines are both flexible and permeable for a wide variety of purposes, and there is no reason why they must now stand in the way of meaningful desegregation relief.

The rights at issue in this case are too fundamental to be abridged on grounds as superficial as those relied on by the majority today. We deal here with the right of all of our children, whatever their race, to an equal start in life and to an equal opportunity to reach their full potential as citizens. Those children who have been denied that right in the past deserve better than to see fences thrown up to deny them that right in the future. Our Nation, I fear, will be ill-served with the Court's refusal to remedy separate and unequal education, for unless our children begin to learn together, there is little hope that our people will ever learn to live together.

The great irony of the Court's opinion and, in my view, its most serious analytical flaw may be gleaned from its concluding sentence, in which the Court remands for "prompt formulation of a decree directed to eliminating the segregation found to exist in Detroit city schools, a remedy which has been delayed since 1970." The majority, however, seems to have forgotten the District Court's explicit finding that a Detroit-only decree, the only remedy permitted under today's decision, "would not accomplish desegregation."

Nowhere in the Court's opinion does the majority confront, let alone respond to, the District Court's conclusion that a remedy limited to the city of Detroit would not effectively desegregate the Detroit city schools. . . .

Having found a *de jure* segregated public school system in operation in the city of Detroit, the District Court . . . concluded that responsibility for the segregation in the Detroit city schools rested not only with the Detroit Board of Education, but belonged to the State of Michigan itself and the state defendants in this case—that is, the Governor of Michigan, the Attorney General, the State Board of Education, and the State Superintendent of Public Instruction. . . . [T]his conclusion . . . was based on three considerations. First, the evidence at trial showed that the State itself had taken actions contributing to the segregation within the Detroit schools. Second, since the Detroit Board of Education was an agency of the State of Michigan, its acts of racial discrimination were acts of the State for purposes of the Fourteenth Amendment. Finally, the District Court found that under Michigan law and practice, the system of education was in fact a *state* school system, characterized by relatively little local control and a large degree of centralized state regulation, with respect to both educational policy and the structure and operation of school districts.

Having concluded, then, that the school system in the city of Detroit was a *de jure* segregated system and that the State of Michigan had the affirmative duty to remedy that condition of segregation, the District Court then turned to the difficult task of devising an effective remedy. It bears repeating that the District Court's focus at this stage of the litigation remained what it had been at the beginning—the condition of segregation within the Detroit city schools. . . .

. . . The essential foundation of inter-district relief in this case was not to correct conditions within outlying districts who themselves engaged in purposeful segregation. Instead, inter-district relief was seen as a necessary part of any meaningful effort by the State of Michigan to remedy the state-caused segregation within the city of Detroit. . . .

Desegregation is not and was never expected to be an easy task. Racial attitudes ingrained in our Nation's childhood and adolescence are not quickly thrown aside in its middle years. But just as the inconvenience of some cannot be allowed to stand in the way of the rights of others, so public opposition, no matter how strident, cannot be permitted to divert this Court from the enforcement of the constitutional principles at issue in this case. Today's holding, I fear, is more a reflection of a perceived public mood that we have gone far enough in enforcing the Constitution's guarantee of equal justice than it is the product of neutral principles of law. In the short run, it may seem to be the easier course to allow our great metropolitan areas to be divided up each into two cities—one white, the other black—but it is a course, I predict, our people will ultimately regret. I dissent.

REGENTS OF THE UNIVERSITY OF CALIFORNIA v. BAKKE, 438 U.S. 265 (1978)

Allan Bakke, a white male and engineer by profession, was 32 years of age when he decided to apply to medical school. His medical board examination scores were high (his science, verbal, and quantitative scores were in the 97th, 96th, and 94th percentiles, respectively). His undergraduate record was excellent (he had a 3.5 overall grade point average on a 4-point scale). He also had the necessary course prerequisites. He applied to the University of California Medical School at Davis in 1973, late in the academic year. The Davis Medical School admitted 100 new students each year. Of these 100 places, 16 were set aside for its affirmative action program designed to recruit and train racial minorities. One of the purposes of the program was to provide doctors to service the minority communities in California. The program was also considered a modest step toward rectifying long-standing societal racial discrimination, although the Davis Medical School itself, having opened in 1968, had never practiced racial discrimination in its admissions or hiring policies. By the time
Bakke's 1973 application was processed, the only places left in the entering class were those under the affirmative action program for which Bakke was ineligible. Bakke wrote a strongly worded protest letter to the Chairman of the Admissions Committee. Early in the following academic year, Bakke again applied to the Medical School. His faculty interviewer was the Chairman of the Admissions Committee, and he gave Bakke a low rating. Again Bakke's application was rejected. Bakke then sued the Medical School, claiming that by refusing to consider him on racial grounds for the places designated for affirmative action, he was denied his constitutional right to equal protection of the laws. The fact was that students admitted under the affirmative action program had lower test scores and grade point averages than Bakke. It was also true that the average scores of the regular admittees were also lower than Bakke's, but this fact was not given much prominence by the courts. The California Supreme Court ruled in favor of Bakke, struck down the Davis affirmative action program, and ruled that any consideration of an applicant's race violated the equal protection guarantee. The Medical School took the case to the United States Supreme Court.

Majority votes: 5
Dissenting votes: 4

MR. JUSTICE POWELL announced the judgment of the Court:. . . .

For the reasons stated in the following opinion, I believe that so much of the judgment of the California court as holds petitioner's special admissions program unlawful and directs that respondent be admitted to the Medical School must be affirmed. For the reasons expressed in a separate opinion, my Brothers the Chief Justice, Mr. Justice Stewart, Mr. Justice Rehnquist and Mr. Justice Stevens concur in this judgment.

I also conclude for the reasons stated in the following opinion that the portion of the court's judgment enjoining petitioner from according any consideration to race in its admissions process must be reversed. For reasons expressed in separate opinions, my Brothers Mr. Justice Brennan, Mr. Justice White, Mr. Justice Marshall, and Mr. Justice Blackmun concur in this judgment.

Affirmed in part and reversed in part.

MR. JUSTICE BRENNAN, MR. JUSTICE WHITE, MR. JUSTICE MARSHALL, and MR. JUSTICE BLACKMUN join parts I and V-C of this opinion.

MR. JUSTICE WHITE also joins Part III-A of this opinion.

I. . . .

[The facts of the case and the history of the litigation are presented here.]

II. . . .

[The legislative intent of Title VI of the Civil Rights Act of 1964 is discussed.]

III

A

Petitioner does not deny that decisions based on race or ethnic origin by faculties and administrations of state universities are reviewable under the Fourteenth Amendment. For his part, respondent does not argue that all racial or ethnic classifications are per se invalid. The parties do disagree as to the level of judicial scrutiny to be applied to the special admissions program. Petitioner argues that the court below erred in applying strict scrutiny, as this inexact term has been applied in our cases. That level of review, petitioner asserts, should be reserved for classifications that disadvantage "discrete and insular minorities." . . .

. . . [P]etitioner argues that the court below erred in applying strict scrutiny to the special admissions program because white males, such as respondent, are not a "discrete and insular minority" requiring extraordinary protection from the majoritarian political process. This rationale, however, has never been invoked in our decisions as a prerequisite to subjecting racial or ethnic distinctions to strict scrutiny. Nor has this Court held that discreteness and insularity constitute necessary preconditions to a holding that a particular classification is invidious. . . . Racial and ethnic distinctions of any sort are inherently suspect and thus call for the most exacting judicial examination.

B. . . .

Although many of the Framers of the Fourteenth Amendment conceived of its primary function as bridging the vast distance between members of the Negro race and the white "majority," the Amendment itself was framed in universal terms, without reference to color, ethnic origin, or condition of prior servitude. . . . Indeed, it is not unlikely that among the Framers were many who would have applauded a reading of the Equal Protection Clause which states a principle of universal application and is responsive to the racial, ethnic and cultural diversity of the Nation. . . .

Petitioner urges us to adopt for the first time a more restrictive view of the Equal Protection Clause and hold that discrimination against members of the white "majority" cannot be suspect if its purpose can be characterized as "benign." It is far too late to argue that the guarantee of equal protection to all persons permits the recognition of special wards entitled to a degree of protection greater than that accorded others. . . . The white "majority" itself is composed of various minority groups, most of which can lay claim to a history of prior discrimination at the hands of the State and private individuals. Not all of these groups can receive preferential treatment and corresponding judicial tolerance of distinctions drawn in terms of race and nationality, for then the only "majority" left would be a new minority of White Anglo-Saxon Protestants. There is no principled basis for deciding which groups would merit "heightened judicial solicitude" and which would not. Courts would be asked to evaluate the extent of the prejudice and consequent harm suffered by various minority groups. Those whose societal injury is thought to exceed some arbitrary level of tolerability then would be entitled to preferential classifications at the expense of individuals belonging to other groups. Those classifications would be free from exacting judicial scrutiny. As these preferences began to have their desired effect, and the consequences of past discrimination were undone, new judicial rankings would be necessary. The kind of variable sociological and political analysis necessary to produce such rankings simply does not lie within the judicial competence—even if they otherwise were politically feasible and socially desirable.

Moreover, there are serious problems of justice connected with the idea of preference itself. . . . There is a measure of inequity in forcing innocent persons in respondent's position to bear the burdens of redressing grievances not of their making. . . .

IV. . . .

We have never approved a classification that aids persons perceived as members of relatively victimized groups at the expense of other innocent individuals in the absence of judicial, legislative, or administrative findings of constitutional or statutory violations. After such findings have been made, the governmental interest in preferring members of the injured groups at the expense of others is substantial, since the legal rights of the victims must be vindicated. In such a case, the extent of the injury and the consequent remedy will have been judicially, legislatively, or administratively defined. Also, the remedial action usually remains subject to continuing oversight to assure that it will work the least harm possible to other innocent persons competing for the benefit. Without such findings of constitutional or statutory violations, it cannot be said that the government has any greater interest in helping one individual than in refraining from harming another. Thus, the government has no compelling justification for inflicting such harm. . . .

. . . [T]he purpose of helping certain groups whom the faculty of the Davis Medical School perceived as victims of "societal discrimination" does not justify a classification that imposes disadvantages upon persons like respondent, who bear no responsibility for whatever harm the beneficiaries of the special admissions program are thought to have suffered. To hold otherwise would be to convert a remedy heretofore reserved for violations of legal rights into a privilege that all institutions throughout the Nation could grant at their pleasure to whatever groups are perceived as victims of societal discrimination. That is a step we have never approved.

Petitioner identifies, as another purpose of its program, improving the delivery of health care services to communities currently underserved. It may be assumed that in some situations a State's interest in facilitating the health care of its citizens is sufficiently compelling to support the use of a suspect classification. But there is virtually no evidence in the record indicating that petitioner's special admissions program is either needed or geared to promote that goal. . . .

The fourth goal asserted by petitioner is the attainment of a diverse student body. This clearly is a constitutionally permissible goal for an institution of higher education. Academic freedom though not a specifically enumerated constitutional right, long has been viewed as a special concern of the First Amendment. The freedom of a university to make its own judgments as to education includes the selection of its student body. . . . The atmosphere of "speculation, experiment and creation"—so essential to the quality of higher education—is widely believed to be promoted by a diverse student body. . . . It is not too much to say that the "nation's future depends upon leaders trained through wide exposure" to the ideas and mores of students as diverse as this Nation of many peoples.

Thus, in arguing that its universities must be accorded the right to select those students who will contribute the most to the "robust exchange of ideas," petitioner invokes a countervailing constitutional interest, that of the First Amendment. In this light, petitioner must be viewed as seeking to achieve a goal that is of paramount importance in the fulfillment of its mission.

It may be argued that there is greater force to these views at the undergraduate level than in a medical school where the training is centered primarily on professional competency. But even at the graduate level, our tradition and experience lend support to the view that the contribution of diversity is substantial. . . . Physicians serve a heterogeneous population. An otherwise qualified medical student with a particular background—whether it be ethnic, geographic, culturally advantaged or disadvantaged—may bring to a professional school of medicine experiences, outlooks and ideas that enrich the training of its student body and better equip its graduates to render with understanding their vital service to humanity.

Ethnic diversity, however, is only one element in a range of factors a university properly may consider in attaining the goal of a heterogeneous student body. Although a university must have wide discretion in making the sensitive judgments as to who should be admitted, constitutional limitations protecting individual rights may not be disregarded. Respondent urges—and the courts below have held—that petitioner's dual admissions program is a racial classification that impermissibly infringes his rights under the Fourteenth Amendment. As the interest of diversity is compelling in the context of a university's admissions program, the question remains whether the program's racial classification is necessary to promote this interest.

V
A

It may be assumed that the reservation of a specified number of seats in each class for individuals from the preferred ethnic groups would contribute to the attainment of considerable ethnic diversity in the student body. But petitioner's argument that this is the only effective means of serving the interest of diversity is seriously flawed. In a most fundamental sense the argument misconceives the nature of the state interest that would justify consideration of race or ethnic background. It is not an interest in simple ethnic diversity, in which a specified percentage of the student body is in effect guaranteed to be members of selected ethnic groups, with the remaining percentage an undifferentiated aggregation of students. The diversity that furthers a compelling state interest encompasses a far broader array of qualifications and characteristics of which racial or ethnic origin is but a single though important element. Petitioner's special admissions program, focused solely on ethnic diversity, would hinder rather than further attainment of genuine diversity. . . .

The experience of other university admissions

programs, which take race into account in achieving the educational diversity valued by the First Amendment, demonstrates that the assignment of a fixed number of places to a minority group is not a necessary means toward that end. An illuminating example is found in the Harvard College program. . . .

This kind of program treats each applicant as an individual in the admissions process. The applicant who loses out on the last available seat to another candidate receiving a ''plus'' on the basis of ethnic background will not have been foreclosed from all consideration for that seat simply because he was not the right color or had the wrong surname. It would mean only that his combined qualifications, which may have included similar nonobjective factors, did not outweigh those of the other applicant. His qualifications would have been weighed fairly and competitively, and he would have no basis to complain of unequal treatment under the Fourteenth Amendment. . . .

B. . . .

The fatal flaw in petitioner's preferential program is its disregard of individual rights as guaranteed by the Fourteenth Amendment. Such rights are not absolute. But when a State's distribution of benefits or imposition of burdens hinges on ancestry or the color of a person's skin, that individual is entitled to a demonstration that the challenged classification is necessary to promote a substantial state interest. Petitioner has failed to carry this burden. For this reason, that portion of the California court's judgment holding petitioner's special admissions program invalid under the Fourteenth Amendment must be affirmed.

C

In enjoining petitioner from ever considering the race of any applicant, however, the courts below failed to recognize that the State has a substantial interest that legitimately may be served by a properly devised admissions program involving the competitive consideration of race and ethnic origin. For this reason, so much of the California court's judgment as enjoins petitioner from any consideration of the race of any applicant must be reversed.

VI

With respect to respondent's entitlement to an injunction directing his admission to the Medical School, petitioner has conceded that it could not carry its burden of proving that, but for the existence of its unlawful special admissions program, respondent still would not have been admitted. Hence, respondent is entitled to the injunction, and

that portion of the judgment must be affirmed.

Opinion of MR. JUSTICE BRENNAN, MR. JUSTICE WHITE, MR. JUSTICE MARSHALL and MR. JUSTICE BLACKMUN, concurring in the judgment in part and dissenting:. . . .

Respondent argues that racial classifications are always suspect and, consequently, that this Court should weigh the importance of the objectives served by Davis' special admissions program to see if they are compelling. In addition, he asserts that this Court must inquire whether, in its judgment, there are alternatives to racial classifications which would suit Davis' purposes. Petitioner, on the other hand, states that our proper role is simply to accept petitioner's determination that the racial classifications used by its program are reasonably related to what it tells us are its benign purposes. We reject petitioner's view, but, because our prior cases are in many respects inapposite to that before us now, we find it necessary to define with precision the meaning of that inexact term, ''strict scrutiny.''

Unquestionably we have held that a government practice or statute which restricts ''fundamental rights'' or which contains ''suspect classifications'' is to be subjected to ''strict scrutiny'' and can be justified only if it furthers a compelling government purpose and, even then, only if no less restrictive alternative is available. But no fundamental right is involved here. Nor do whites as a class have any of the ''traditional indicia of suspectness: the class is not saddled with such disabilities, or subjected to such a history of purposeful unequal treatment, or relegated to such a position of political powerlessness as to command extraordinary protection from the majoritarian political process.''

Moreover, if the University's representations are credited, this is not a case where racial classifications are ''irrelevant and therefore prohibited.'' Nor has anyone suggested that the University's purposes contravene the cardinal principle that racial classifications that stigmatize—because they are drawn on the presumption that one race is inferior to another or because they put the weight of government behind racial hatred and separatism— are invalid without more.

On the other hand, the fact that this case does not fit neatly into our prior analytic framework for race cases does not mean that it should be analyzed by applying the very loose rational-basis standard of review that is the very least that is always applied in equal protection cases. '' [T]he mere recitation of a benign, compensatory purpose is not an automatic shield which protects against any inquiry into the actual purposes underlying a statutory scheme.' '' Instead, a number of considerations—

developed in gender-discrimination cases but which carry even more force when applied to racial classifications—lead us to conclude that racial classifications designed to further remedial purposes " 'must serve important governmental objectives and must be substantially related to achievement of those objectives.' "

First, race, like, "gender-based classifications too often [has] been inexcusably utilized to stereotype and stigmatize politically powerless segments of society." While a carefully tailored statute designed to remedy past discrimination could avoid these vices, we nonetheless have recognized that the line between honest and thoughtful appraisal of the effects of past discrimination and paternalistic stereotyping is not so clear and that a statute based on the latter is patently capable of stigmatizing all women with a badge of inferiority. State programs designed ostensibly to ameliorate the effects of past racial discrimination obviously create the same hazard of stigma, since they may promote racial separatism and reinforce the views of those who believe that members of racial minorities are inherently incapable of succeeding on their own.

Second, race, like gender and illegitimacy, is an immutable characteristic which its possessors are powerless to escape or set aside. While a classification is not *per se* invalid because it divides classes on the basis of an immutable characteristic, it is nevertheless true that such divisions are contrary to our deep belief that "legal burdens should bear some relationship to individual responsibility or wrongdoing," and that advancement sanctioned, sponsored, or approved by the State should ideally be based on individual merit or achievement, or at the least on factors within the control of an individual. . . .

In sum, because of the significant risk that racial classifications established for ostensibly benign purposes can be misused, causing effects not unlike those created by invidious classifications, it is inappropriate to inquire only whether there is any conceivable basis that might sustain such a classification. Instead, to justify such a classification an important and articulated purpose for its use must be shown. In addition, any statute must be stricken that stigmatizes any group or that singles out those least well represented in the political process to bear the brunt of a benign program. Thus, our review under the Fourteenth Amendment should be strict—not, " 'strict' in theory and fatal in fact," because it is stigma that causes fatality—but strict and searching nonetheless.

Davis's articulated purpose of remedying the effects of past societal discrimination is, under our

cases, sufficiently important to justify the use of race-conscious admissions programs where there is a sound basis for concluding that minority underrepresentation is substantial and chronic, and that the handicap of past discrimination is impeding access of minorities to the medical school. . . .

. . . [O]ur cases under Title VII of the Civil Rights Act have held that, in order to achieve minority participation in previously segregated areas of public life, Congress may require or authorize preferential treatment for those likely disadvantaged by societal racial discrimination. Such legislation has been sustained even without a requirement of findings of intentional racial discrimination by those required or authorized to accord preferential treatment, or a case-by-case determination that those to be benefited suffered from racial discrimination. These decisions compel the conclusion that States also may adopt race-conscious programs designed to overcome substantial, chronic minority underrepresentation where there is reason to believe that the evil addressed is a product of past racial discrimination. . . .

We therefore conclude that Davis' goal of admitting minority students disadvantaged by the effects of past discrimination is sufficiently important to justify use of race-conscious admissions criteria.

Properly construed, therefore, our prior cases unequivocally show that a state government may adopt race-conscious programs if the purpose of such programs is to remove the disparate racial impact its actions might otherwise have and if there is reason to believe that the disparate impact is itself the product of past discrimination, whether its own or that of society at large. There is no question that Davis' program is valid under this test.

Certainly, on the basis of the undisputed factual submissions before this Court, Davis had a sound basis for believing that the problem of underrepresentation of minorities was substantial and chronic and that the problem was attributable to handicaps imposed on minority applicants by past and present racial discrimination. Until at least 1973, the practice of medicine in this country was, in fact, if not in law, largely the prerogative of whites. In 1950, for example, while Negroes comprised 10% of the total population, Negro physicians constituted only 2.2% of the total number of physicians. The overwhelming majority of these, moreover, were educated in two predominantly Negro medical schools, Howard and Meharry. By 1970, the gap between the proportion of Negroes in medicine and their proportion in the population had widened: The number of Negroes employed in medicine remained frozen at 2.2% while the Negro population had increased to 11.1%. The number of Negro admittees to predominantly white medical schools, moreover, had declined in absolute numbers during the years 1955 to 1964. . . .

It is not even claimed that Davis' program in any way operates to stigmatize or single out any discrete and insular, or even any identifiable, nonminority group. Nor will harm comparable to that imposed upon racial minorities by exclusion or separation on grounds of race be the likely result of the program. It does not, for example, establish an exclusive preserve for minority students apart from and exclusive of whites. Rather, its purpose is to overcome the effects of segregation by bringing the races together. True, whites are excluded from participation in the special admissions program, but this fact only operates to reduce the number of whites to be admitted in the regular admissions program in order to permit admission of a reasonable percentage—less than their proportion of the California population—of otherwise underrepresented qualified minority applicants.

Nor was Bakke in any sense stamped as inferior by the Medical School's rejection of him. . . . Unlike discrimination against racial minorities, the use of racial preferences for remedial purposes does not inflict a pervasive injury upon individual whites in the sense that wherever they go or whatever they do there is a significant likelihood that they will be treated as second-class citizens because of their color. This distinction does not mean that the exclusion of a white resulting from the preferential use of race is not sufficiently serious to require justification; but it does mean that the injury inflicted by such a policy is not distinguishable from disadvantages caused by a wide range of government actions, none of which has ever been thought impermissible for that reason alone.

In addition, there is simply no evidence that the Davis program discriminates intentionally or unintentionally against any minority group which it purports to benefit. The program does not establish a quota in the invidious sense of a ceiling on the number of minority applicants to be admitted. Nor can the program reasonably be regarded as stigmatizing the program's beneficiaries or their race as inferior. The Davis program does not simply advance less qualified applicants; rather, it compensates applicants, whom it is uncontested are fully qualified to study medicine, for educational disadvantage which it was reasonable to conclude was a product of state-fostered discrimination. Once admitted, these students must satisfy the same degree requirements as regularly admitted students; they are taught by the same faculty in the same classes; and

their performance is evaluated by the same standards by which regularly admitted students are judged. Under these circumstances, their performance and degrees must be regarded equally with the regularly admitted students with whom they compete for standing. Since minority graduates cannot justifiably be regarded as less well qualified than nonminority graduates by virtue of the special admissions program, there is no reasonable basis to conclude that minority graduates at schools using such programs would be stigmatized as inferior by the existence of such programs. . . .

Accordingly, we would reverse the judgment of the Supreme Court of California holding the Medical School's special admissions program unconstitutional and directing respondent's admission, as well as that portion of the judgment enjoining the Medical School from according any consideration to race in the admissions process.

Separate opinion of MR. JUSTICE WHITE: [omitted]
MR. JUSTICE MARSHALL:

I do not agree that petitioner's admissions program violates the Constitution. For it must be remembered that, during most of the past 200 years, the Constitution as interpreted by this Court did not prohibit the most ingenious and pervasive forms of discrimination against the Negro. Now, when a State acts to remedy the effects of that legacy of discrimination, I cannot believe that this same Constitution stands as a barrier.

Three hundred and fifty years ago, the Negro was dragged to this country in chains to be sold into slavery. Uprooted from his homeland and thrust into bondage for forced labor, the slave was deprived of all legal rights. It was unlawful to teach him to read; he could be sold away from his family and friends at the whim of his master; and killing or maiming him was not a crime. The system of slavery brutalized and dehumanized both master and slave. . . .

The status of the Negro as property was officially erased by his emancipation at the end of the Civil War. But the long awaited emancipation, while freeing the Negro from slavery, did not bring him citizenship or equality in any meaningful way. Slavery was replaced by a system of "laws which imposed upon the colored race onerous disabilities and burdens, and curtailed their rights in the pursuit of life, liberty, and property to such an extent that their freedom was of little value." Despite the passage of the Thirteenth, Fourteenth, and Fifteenth Amendments, the Negro was systematically denied the rights those amendments were supposed to secure. The combined actions and inactions of the State and Federal Government maintained Negroes in a position of legal inferiority for another century after the Civil War. . . .

[T]he laws restricting the rights of Negroes were not limited solely to the Southern States. In many of the Northern States, the Negro was denied the right to vote, prevented from serving on juries and excluded from theaters, restaurants, hotels, and inns. Under President Wilson, the Federal Government began to require segregation in Government buildings; desks of Negro employees were curtained off; separate bathrooms and separate tables in the cafeterias were provided; and even the galleries of the Congress were segregated. . . .

The enforced segregation of the races continued into the middle of the 20th century. In both World Wars, Negroes were for the most part confined to separate military units; it was not until 1948 that an end to segregation in the military was ordered by President Truman. And the history of the exclusion of Negro children from white public schools is too well known and recent to require repeating here. That Negroes were deliberately excluded from public graduate and professional schools—and thereby denied the opportunity to become doctors, lawyers, engineers, and the like—is also well established. It is of course true that some of the Jim Crow laws (which the decisions of this Court had helped to foster) were struck down by this Court in a series of decisions leading up to *Brown* v. *Board of Education of Topeka*. Those decisions, however, did not automatically end segregation, nor did they move Negroes from a position of legal inferiority to one of equality. The legacy of years of slavery and of years of second-class citizenship in the wake of emancipation could not be so easily eliminated.

The position of the Negro today in America is the tragic but inevitable consequence of centuries of unequal treatment. Measured by any benchmark of comfort or achievement, meaningful equality remains a distant dream for the Negro.

A Negro child today has a life expectancy which is shorter by more than five years than that of a white child. The Negro child's mother is over three times more likely to die of complications in childbirth, and the infant mortality rate for Negroes is nearly twice that for whites. The median income of the Negro family is only 60% that of the median of a white family, and the percentage of Negroes who live in families with incomes below the poverty line is nearly four times greater than that of whites.

When the Negro child reaches working age, he finds that America offers him significantly less than it offers his white counterpart. For Negro adults, the unemployment rate is twice that of whites, and the unemployment rate for Negro teenagers is nearly three times that of white teenagers. A Negro male who completes four years of college can expect a median annual income of merely $110 more than a white male who has only a high school diploma. Although Negroes represent 11.5% of the population, they are only 1.2% of the lawyers, and judges, 2% of the physicians, 2.3% of the dentists, 1.1% of the engineers and 2.6% of the college and university professors.

The relationship between those figures and the history of unequal treatment afforded to the Negro cannot be denied. At every point from birth to death the impact of the past is reflected in the still disfavored position of the Negro.

In light of the sorry history of discrimination and its devastating impact on the lives of Negroes, bringing the Negro into the mainstream of American life should be a state interest of the highest order. To fail to do so is to ensure that America will forever remain a divided society.

I do not believe that the Fourteenth Amendment requires us to accept that fate. Neither its history nor our past cases lend any support to the conclusion that a university may not remedy the cumulative effects of society's discrimination by giving consideration to race in an effort to increase the number and percentage of Negro doctors. . . .

While I applaud the judgment of the Court that a university may consider race in its admissions process, it is more than a little ironic that, after several hundred years of class-based discrimination against Negroes, the Court is unwilling to hold that a class-based remedy for that discrimination is permissible. In declining to so hold, today's judgment ignores the fact that for several hundred years Negroes have been discriminated against, not as individuals, but rather solely because of the color of their skins. It is unnecessary in 20th century America to have individual Negroes demonstrate that they have been victims of racial discrimination; the racism of our society has been so pervasive that none, regardless of wealth or position, has managed to escape its impact. The experience of Negroes in America has been different in kind, not just in degree, from that of other ethnic groups. It is not merely the history of slavery alone but also that a whole people were marked as inferior by the law. And that mark has endured. The dream of America as the great melting pot has not been realized for the Negro; because of his skin color he never even made it into the pot.

These differences in the experience of the Negro make it difficult for me to accept that Negroes cannot be afforded greater protection under the Fourteenth Amendment where it is necessary to remedy the effects of past discrimination. . . .

MR. JUSTICE BLACKMUN: [omitted]

MR. JUSTICE STEVENS, with whom CHIEF JUSTICE BURGER, MR. JUSTICE STEWART, and MR. JUSTICE REHNQUIST join, concurring in the judgment in part and dissenting in part:

It is always important at the outset to focus precisely on the controversy before the Court. It is particularly important to do so in this case because correct identification of the issues will determine whether it is necessary or appropriate to express any opinion about the legal status of any admissions program other than petitioner's.

This is not a class action. The controversy is between two specific litigants. Allan Bakke challenged petitioner's special admissions program, claiming that it denied him a place in medical school because of his race in violation of the Federal and California Constitutions and of Title VI of the Civil Rights Act of 1964, 42 U.S.C. § 2000d et seq. The California Supreme Court upheld his challenge and ordered him admitted. If the state court was correct in its view that the University's special program was illegal, and that Bakke was therefore unlawfully excluded from the medical school because of his race, we should affirm its judgment, regardless of our views about the legality of admissions programs that are not now before the Court. . . .

The California Supreme Court, in a holding that is not challenged, ruled that the trial court incorrectly placed the burden on Bakke of showing that he would have been admitted in the absence of discrimination. The University then conceded "that it [could] not meet the burden of proving that the special admissions program did not result in Bakke's exclusion." Accordingly, the California Supreme Court directed the trial court to enter judgment ordering Bakke's admission. Whether the judgment of the state court is affirmed or reversed, in whole or in part, there is no outstanding injunction forbidding any consideration of racial criteria in processing applications.

It is therefore perfectly clear that the question whether race can ever be used as a factor in an admissions decision is not an issue in this case, and that discussion of that issue is inappropriate.

Both petitioner and respondent have asked us to determine the legality of the University's special admissions program by reference to the Constitution. Our settled practice, however, is to avoid the decision of a constitutional issue if a case can be fairly decided on a statutory ground. The more im-

portant the issue, the more force there is to this doctrine. In this case, we are presented with a constitutional question of undoubted and unusual importance. Since, however, a dispositive statutory claim was raised at the very inception of this case, and squarely decided in the portion of the trial court judgment affirmed by the California Supreme Court, it is our plain duty to confront it. Only if petitioner should prevail on the statutory issue would it be necessary to decide whether the University's admissions program violated the Equal Protection Clause of the Fourteenth Amendment.

Section 601 of the Civil Rights Act of 1964 provides:

> "No person in the United States shall, on the ground of race, color, or national origin, be excluded from participation in, be denied the benefits of, or be subjected to discrimination under any program or activity receiving Federal financial assistance."

The University, through its special admissions policy, excluded Bakke from participation in its program of medical education because of his race. The University also acknowledges that it was, and still is, receiving federal financial assistance. The plain language of the statute therefore requires affirmance of the judgment below. A different result cannot be justified unless that language misstates the actual intent of the Congress that enacted the statute or the statute is not enforceable in a private action. Neither conclusion is warranted. . . .

Petitioner contends . . . that exclusion of applicants on the basis of race does not violate Title VI if the exclusion carries with it no racial stigma. No such qualification or limitation of § 601's categorical prohibition of "exclusion" is justified by the statute or its history. The language of the entire section is perfectly clear; the words that follow "excluded from" do not modify or qualify the explicit outlawing of any exclusion on the stated grounds.

The legislative history reinforces this reading. The only suggestion that § 601 would allow exclusion of nonminority applicants came from opponents of the legislation and then only by way of a discussion of the meaning of the word "discrimination." The opponents feared that the term "discrimination" would be read as mandating racial quotas and "racially balanced" colleges and universities, and they pressed for a specific definition of the term in order to avoid this possibility. In response, the proponents of the legislation gave repeated assurances that the Act would be "color-blind" in its application. . . .

In short, nothing in the legislative history justifies the conclusion that the broad language of § 601 should not be given its natural meaning. We are dealing with a distinct statutory prohibition, enacted at a particular time with particular concerns in mind; neither its language nor any prior interpretation suggests that its place in the Civil Rights Act, won after long debate, is simply that of a constitutional appendage. In unmistakable terms the Act prohibits the exclusion of individuals from federally funded programs because of their race. As succinctly phrased during the Senate debate, under Title VI it is not "permissible to say 'yes' to one person, but to say 'no' to another person, only because of the color of his skin.". . .

The University's special admissions program violated Title VI of the Civil Rights Act of 1964 by excluding Bakke from the medical school because of his race. It is therefore our duty to affirm the judgment ordering Bakke admitted to the University.

Accordingly, I concur in the Court's judgment insofar as it affirms the judgment of the Supreme Court of California. To the extent that it purports to do anything else, I respectfully dissent.

UNITED STEELWORKERS v. WEBER,
443 U.S. 193 (1979)

In 1974, the national steelworkers union (the United Steelworkers of America) and Kaiser Aluminum and Chemical Corporation entered into a collective bargaining agreement covering terms and conditions of employment at 15 Kaiser plants. An affirmative action plan was part of the agreement and was designed to reduce the dramatic racial imbalance among the craft workers whose ranks were almost exclusively white. Under the plan, 50 percent of the openings in in-plant craft-training programs were to be reserved for black employees until the percentage of black craft workers in a plant would approximate the proportion of blacks in the local labor force. This case began when a white production worker, Brian Weber, who was refused admission to the craft-training program, instituted a class action in the United States District Court for the Eastern District of Louisiana. Weber worked at the Kaiser plant in Gramercy, Louisiana. Less than 2 percent of the skilled craft workers there were black, although the work force in the Gramercy area was about 39 percent black. Under the terms of the affirmative action program, Kaiser established a training program; selection to *the program was made on the basis of seniority by race, with blacks constituting half the new trainees. Black workers with less seniority than Brian Weber were selected for the program. Weber claimed this was discrimination in violation of Title VII of the Civil Rights Act of 1964. The United States District Court ruled in favor of Weber and granted a permanent injunction prohibiting Kaiser and the union from denying Weber and other whites with more seniority than the most junior black craft trainee access to the on-the-job training programs on the basis of race. A divided Court of Appeals for the Fifth Circuit affirmed and the United States Supreme Court took the case. Although affirmative action raises constitutional issues, this case was decided on statutory grounds.*

Majority votes: 5
Dissenting votes: 2

MR. JUSTICE BRENNAN delivered the opinion of the Court:. . . .

The question for decision is whether Congress, in Title VII of the Civil Rights Act of 1964 as amended, 42 U.S.C. § 2000e, left employers and unions in the private sector free to take such race-conscious steps to eliminate manifest racial imbalances in traditionally segregated job categories. . . .

We emphasize at the outset the narrowness of our inquiry. Since the Kaiser-USWA plan does not involve state action, this case does not present an alleged violation of the Equal Protection Clause of the Constitution. Further, since the Kaiser-USWA plan was adopted voluntarily, we are not concerned with what Title VII requires or with what a court might order to remedy a past proven violation of the Act. The only question before us is the narrow statutory issue of whether Title VII *forbids* private employers and unions from voluntarily agreeing upon bona fide affirmative action plans that accord racial preferences in the manner and for the purpose provided in the Kaiser-USWA [United Steelworkers of America] plan. . . .

Respondent argues that Congress intended in Title VII to prohibit all race-conscious affirmative action plans. Respondent's argument rests upon a literal interpretation of § 703(a) and (d) of the Act. Those sections make it unlawful to "discriminate . . . because of . . . race" in hiring and in the selection of apprentices for training programs. Since, the argument runs, Title VII forbids discrimination against whites as well as blacks, and since the Kaiser-USWA affirmative action plan operates to discriminate against white employees solely because they are white, it follows that the Kaiser-USWA plan violates Title VII.

Respondent's argument is not without force. But it overlooks the significance of the fact that the Kaiser-USWA plan is an affirmative action plan voluntarily adopted by private parties to eliminate traditional patterns of racial segregation. . . . The prohibition against racial discrimination in § 703(a) and (d) of Title VII must be read against the background of the legislative history of Title VII and the historical context from which the Act arose. Examination of those sources makes clear that an interpretation of the sections that forbade all race-conscious affirmative action would "bring about an end completely at variance with the purpose of the statute" and must be rejected. . . .

Given [the] . . . legislative history, we cannot agree with respondent that Congress intended to prohibit the private sector from taking effective steps to accomplish the goal that Congress designed Title VII to achieve. The very statutory words intended as a spur or catalyst to cause "employers and unions to self-examine and to self-evaluate their employment practices and to endeavor to eliminate, so far as possible, the last vestiges of an unfortunate and ignominious page in this country's history," *Albemarle* v. *Moody,* 422 U.S. 405, 418 (1975), cannot be interpreted as an absolute prohibition against all private, voluntary, race-conscious affirmative action efforts to hasten the elimination of such vestiges. It would be ironic indeed if a law triggered by a Nation's concern over centuries of racial injustice and intended to improve the lot of those who had "been excluded from the American dream for so long," 110 Cong. Rec., at 6552 (remarks of Sen. Humphrey), constituted the first legislative prohibition of all voluntary, private race-conscious efforts to abolish traditional patterns of racial segregation and hierarchy. . . .

We therefore hold that Title VII's prohibition in § 703 (a) and (d) against racial discrimination does not condemn all private, voluntary, race-conscious affirmative action plans.

We need not today define in detail the line of demarcation between permissible and impermissible affirmative action plans. It suffices to hold that the challenged Kaiser-USWA affirmative action plan falls on the permissible side of the line. The purposes of the plan mirror those of the statute. Both were designed to break down old patterns of racial segregation and hierarchy. Both were structured to "open employment opportunities for Negroes in occupations which have been traditionally closed to them." 110 Cong. Rec. 6548 (remarks of Sen. Humphrey).

At the same time the plan does not unnecessarily trammel the interests of the white employees. The plan does not require the discharge of white workers and their replacement with new black hires. Nor does the plan create an absolute bar to the advancement of white employees; half of those trained in the program will be white. Moreover, the plan is a temporary measure; it is not intended to maintain racial balance, but simply to eliminate a manifest racial imbalance. Preferential selection of craft trainees at the Gramercy plant will end as soon as the percentage of black skilled craft workers in the Gramercy plant approximates the percentage of blacks in the local labor force.

We conclude, therefore, that the adoption of the Kaiser-USWA plan for the Gramercy plant falls within the area of discretion left by Title VII to the private sector voluntarily to adopt affirmative action plans designed to eliminate conspicuous racial imbalance in traditionally segregated job categories. Accordingly, the judgment of the Court of Appeals for the Fifth Circuit is

Reversed.

MR. JUSTICE POWELL and MR. JUSTICE STEVENS took no part in the consideration or decision of this case.

MR. JUSTICE BLACKMUN, concurring: [omitted]

MR. CHIEF JUSTICE BURGER, dissenting: [omitted]

MR. JUSTICE REHNQUIST, with whom THE CHIEF JUSTICE joins, dissenting:

In a very real sense, the Court's opinion is ahead of its time: it could more appropriately have been handed down five years from now, in 1984, a year coinciding with the title of a book from which the Court's opinion borrows, perhaps subconsciously, at least one idea. . . .

The operative sections of Title VII prohibit racial discrimination in employment *simpliciter.* Taken in its normal meaning and as understood by all Members of Congress who spoke to the issue during the legislative debates, this language prohibits a covered employer from considering race when making an employment decision, whether the race be black or white. Several years ago, however, a United States District Court held that "the dismissal of white employees charged with misappropriating company property while not dismissing a similarly charged Negro employee does not raise a claim upon which Title VII relief may be granted." *McDonald* v. *Santa Fe Trail Transp. Co.,* 427 U.S. 273, 278 (1976). This Court unanimously reversed, concluding from the "uncontradicted legislative history" that "[T]itle VII prohibits racial discrimination against the white petitioners in this case upon the same standards as would be applicable were they Negroes. . . ." 427 U.S., at 280.

We have never wavered in our understanding that Title VII "prohibits *all* racial discrimination in employment, without exception for any particular employees." *Id.*, at 283 (emphasis in original). In *Griggs* v. *Duke Power Co.*, 401 U.S. 424, 431 (1971), our first occasion to interpret Title VII, a unanimous Court observed that "[d]iscriminatory preference, for any group, minority or majority, is precisely and only what Congress has proscribed." And in our most recent discussion of the issue, we uttered words seemingly dispositive of this case: "It is clear beyond cavil that the obligation imposed by Title VII is to provide an equal opportunity for *each* applicant regardless of race, without regard to whether members of the applicant's race are already proportionately represented in the work force." *Furnco Construction Corp.* v. *Waters,* 438 U.S. 567, 579 (1978) (emphasis in original).

Today, however, the Court behaves much like the Orwellian speaker earlier described, as if it had been handed a note indicating that Title VII would lead to a result unacceptable to the Court if interpreted here as it was in our prior decisions. Accordingly, without even a break in syntax, the Court rejects "a literal construction of § 703(a)" in favor of newly discovered "legislative history," which leads it to a conclusion directly contrary to that compelled by the "uncontradicted legislative history" unearthed in *McDonald* and our other prior decisions. Now we are told that the legislative history of Title VII shows that employers are free to discriminate on the basis of race: an employer may, in the Court's words, "trammel the interests of white employees" in favor of black employees in order to eliminate "racial imbalance." . . .

Thus, by a *tour de force* reminiscent not of jurists such as Hale, Holmes, and Hughes, but of escape artists such as Houdini, the Court eludes clear statutory language, "uncontradicted" legislative history and uniform precedent in concluding that employers are, after all, permitted to consider race in making employment decisions. . . .

BATSON v. KENTUCKY,
476 U.S. 79 (1986)

The facts of this case are recounted in Justice Powell's opinion of the Court. This decision is as important for its implications for the conduct of criminal trials as for its implications for the value of racial equality.

Majority votes: 7
Dissenting votes: 2

JUSTICE POWELL delivered the opinion of the Court:

This case requires us to reexamine that portion of *Swain* v. *Alabama,* 380 U.S. 202 (1965), concerning the evidentiary burden placed on a criminal defendant who claims that he has been denied equal protection through the State's use of peremptory challenges to exclude members of his race from the petit jury.

Petitioner, a black man, was indicted in Kentucky on charges of second-degree burglary and receipt of stolen goods. On the first day of trial in Jefferson Circuit Court, the judge conducted *voir dire* examination of the venire, excused certain jurors for cause, and permitted the parties to exercise peremptory challenges. The prosecutor used his peremptory challenges to strike all four black persons on the venire, and a jury composed only of white persons was selected. Defense counsel moved to discharge the jury before it was sworn on the ground that the prosecutor's removal of the black veniremen violated petitioner's rights under the Sixth and Fourteenth Amendments to a jury drawn from a cross-section of the community, and under the Fourteenth Amendment to equal protection of the laws. Counsel requested a hearing on his motion. Without expressly ruling on the request for a hearing, the trial judge observed that the parties were entitled to use their peremptory challenges to "strike anybody they want to." The judge then denied petitioner's motion, reasoning that the cross-section requirement applies only to selection of the venire and not to selection of the petit jury itself.

The jury convicted petitioner on both counts. . . .

The Supreme Court of Kentucky affirmed. . . . We granted certiorari, and now reverse.

In *Swain* v. *Alabama,* this Court recognized that a "State's purposeful or deliberate denial to Negroes on account of race of participation as jurors in the administration of justice violates the Equal Protection Clause." 380 U.S., at 203–204. This principle has been "consistently and repeatedly" reaffirmed, in numerous decisions of this Court both preceding and following *Swain.* We reaffirm the principle today.

More than a century ago, the Court decided that the State denies a black defendant equal protection of the laws when it puts him on trial before a jury from which members of his race have been purposefully excluded. *Strauder* v. *West Virginia,* 100 U.S. 303 (1880). That decision laid the foundation for the Court's unceasing efforts to eradicate racial discrimination in the procedures used to select the venire from which individual jurors are drawn. In *Strauder,* the Court explained that the central concern of the recently ratified Fourteenth Amendment was to put an end to governmental discrimination on account of race. Exclusion of black citizens from service as jurors constitutes a primary example of the evil the Fourteenth Amendment was designed to cure.

In holding that racial discrimination in jury selection offends the Equal Protection Clause, the Court in *Strauder* recognized, however, that a defendant has no right to a "petit jury composed in whole or in part of persons of his own race." . . . But the defendant does have the right to be tried by a jury whose members are selected pursuant to nondiscriminatory criteria. The Equal Protection Clause guarantees the defendant that the State will not exclude members of his race from the jury venire on account of race, or on the false assumption that members of his race as a group are not qualified to serve as jurors, see *Norris* v. *Alabama,* 294 U.S. 587, 599 (1935).

Purposeful racial discrimination in selection of the venire violates a defendant's right to equal protection because it denies him the protection that a trial by jury is intended to secure. "The very idea of a jury is a body . . . composed of the peers or equals of the person whose rights it is selected or summoned to determine; that is, of his neighbors, fellows, associates, persons having the same legal status in society as that which he holds." *Strauder, supra,* 100 U.S., at 308. The petit jury has occupied a central position in our system of justice by safeguarding a person accused of crime against the arbitrary exercise of power by prosecutor or judge. Those on the venire must be "indifferently chosen," to secure the defendant's right under the Fourteenth Amendment to "protection of life and liberty against race or color prejudice." *Strauder, supra,* 100 U.S., at 309.

Racial discrimination in selection of jurors harms not only the accused whose life or liberty they are summoned to try. Competence to serve as a juror ultimately depends on an assessment of individual qualifications and ability impartially to consider evidence presented at a trial. A person's race simply "is unrelated to his fitness as a juror." As long ago as *Strauder,* therefore, the Court recognized that by denying a person participation in jury service on account of his race, the State unconstitutionally discriminated against the excluded juror.

The harm from discriminatory jury selection extends beyond that inflicted on the defendant and the excluded juror to touch the entire community. Selection procedures that purposefully exclude black persons from juries undermines public confidence in the fairness of our system of justice. Discrimination within the judicial system is most pernicious because it is "a stimulant to that race prejudice which is an impediment to securing to [black citizens] that equal justice which the law aims to secure to all others." *Strauder, supra,* 100 U.S., at 308. . . .

Accordingly, the component of the jury selection process at issue here, the State's privilege to strike individual jurors through peremptory challenges, is subject to the commands of the Equal Protection Clause. Although a prosecutor ordinarily is entitled to exercise permitted peremptory challenges "for any reason at all, as long as that reason is related to his view concerning the outcome" of the case to be tried, the Equal Protection Clause forbids the prosecutor to challenge potential jurors solely on account of their race or on the assumption that black jurors as a group will be unable impartially to consider the State's case against a black defendant.

The principles announced in *Strauder* never have been questioned in any subsequent decision of this Court. Rather, the Court has been called upon repeatedly to review the application of those principles to particular facts. A recurring question in these cases, as in any case alleging a violation of the Equal Protection Clause, was whether the defendant had met his burden of proving purposeful discrimination on the part of the State. That question also was at the heart of the portion of *Swain* v. *Alabama* we reexamine today. . . .

To preserve the peremptory nature of the prosecutor's challenge, the Court in *Swain* declined to scrutinize his actions in a particular case by relying on a presumption that he properly exercised the State's challenges.

The Court went on to observe, however, that a state may not exercise its challenges in contravention of the Equal Protection Clause. It was impermissible for a prosecutor to use his challenges to exclude blacks from the jury "for reasons wholly unrelated to the outcome of the particular case on trial" or to deny to blacks "the same right and opportunity to participate in the administration of justice enjoyed by the white population." Accordingly, a black defendant could make out a prima facie case of purposeful discrimination on proof that the peremptory challenge system was "being perverted" in that manner. For example, an inference of purposeful discrimination would be raised on evidence that a prosecutor, "in case after case, whatever the circumstances, whatever the crime and whoever the defendant or the victim may be, is responsible for the removal of Negroes who have been selected as qualified jurors by the jury commissioners and who have survived challenges for cause, with the result that no Negroes ever serve on petit juries.'' Evidence offered by the defendant in *Swain* did not meet that standard. . . . For reasons that follow, we reject this evidentiary formulation as inconsistent with standards that have been developed since *Swain* for assessing a prima facie case under the Equal Protection Clause.

[S]ince *Swain,* we have recognized that a black defendant alleging that members of his race have been impermissibly excluded from the venire may make out a prima facie case of purposeful discrimination by showing that the totality of the relevant facts gives rise to an inference of discriminatory purpose. . . .

Thus, since the decision in *Swain,* this Court has recognized that a defendant may make a prima facie showing of purposeful racial discrimination in selection of the venire by relying solely on the facts concerning its selection *in his case.* These decisions are in accordance with the proposition, articulated in *Arlington Heights* v. *Metropolitan Housing Corp.,* that ''a consistent pattern of official racial discrimination'' is not ''a necessary predicate to a violation of the Equal Protection Clause. A single invidiously discriminatory governmental act'' is not ''immunized by the absence of such discrimination in the making of other comparable decisions.'' 429 U.S., at 266, n.14. For evidentiary requirements to dictate that ''several must suffer discrimination'' before one could object, would be inconsistent with the promise of equal protection to all.

The standards for assessing a prima facie case in the context of discriminatory selection of the venire have been fully articulated since *Swain.* These principles support our conclusion that a defendant may establish a prima facie case of purposeful discrimination in selection of the petit jury solely on evidence concerning the prosecutor's exercise of peremptory challenges at the defendant's trial. To establish such a case, the defendant first must show that he is a member of a cognizable racial group and that the prosecutor has exercised peremptory challenges to remove from the venire members of the defendant's race. Second, the defendant is entitled to rely on the fact, as to which there can be no dispute, that peremptory challenges constitute a jury selection practice that permits ''those to discriminate who are of a mind to discriminate.'' Finally, the defendant must show that these facts and any other relevant circumstances raise an inference

that the prosecutor used that practice to exclude the veniremen from the petit jury on account of their race. This combination of factors in the empanelling of the petit jury, as in the selection of the venire, raises the necessary inference of purposeful discrimination.

In deciding whether the defendant has made the requisite showing, the trial court should consider all relevant circumstances. For example, a ''pattern'' of strikes against black jurors included in the particular venire might give rise to an inference of discrimination. Similarly, the prosecutor's questions and statements during *voir dire* examination and in exercising his challenges may support or refute an inference of discriminatory purpose. These examples are merely illustrative. We have confidence that trial judges, experienced in supervising *voir dire,* will be able to decide if the circumstances concerning the prosecutor's use of peremptory challenges creates a prima facie case of discrimination against black jurors.

Once the defendant makes a prima facie showing, the burden shifts to the State to come forward with a neutral explanation for challenging black jurors. Though this requirement imposes a limitation in some cases on the full peremptory character of the historic challenge, we emphasize that the prosecutor's explanation need not rise to the level justifying exercise of a challenge for cause. But the prosecutor may not rebut the defendant's prima facie case of discrimination by stating merely that he challenged jurors of the defendant's race on the assumption—or his intuitive judgment—that they would be partial to the defendant because of their shared race. Cf. *Norris* v. *Alabama,* 294 U.S., at 598–599. Just as the Equal Protection Clause forbids the States to exclude black persons from the venire on the assumption that blacks as a group are unqualified to serve as jurors, so it forbids the States to strike black veniremen on the assumption that they will be biased in a particular case simply because the defendant is black. The core guarantee of equal protection, ensuring citizens that their State will not discriminate on account of race, would be meaningless were we to approve the exclusion of jurors on the basis of such assumptions, which arise solely from the jurors' race. Nor may the prosecutor rebut the defendant's case merely by denying that he had a discriminatory motive or ''affirming his good faith in individual selections.'' If these general assertions were accepted as rebutting a defendant's prima facie case, the Equal Protection Clause ''would be but a vain and illusory requirement.'' The prosecutor therefore must articulate a neutral explanation related to the particular case to be tried. The trial court then will have the duty to determine if the defendant has established purposeful discrimination. . . .

In this case, petitioner made a timely objection to the prosecutor's removal of all black persons on the venire. Because the trial court flatly rejected the objection without requiring the prosecutor to give an explanation for his action, we remand this case for further proceedings. If the trial court decides that the facts establish, prima facie, purposeful discrimination and the prosecutor does not come forward with a neutral explanation for his action, our precedents require that petitioner's conviction be reversed.

It is so ordered.

JUSTICE WHITE, concurring: [omitted]
JUSTICE MARSHALL, concurring: [omitted]
JUSTICE STEVENS, with whom JUSTICE BRENNAN joins, concurring: [omitted]
JUSTICE O'CONNOR, concurring: [omitted]
CHIEF JUSTICE BURGER, joined by JUSTICE REHNQUIST, dissenting:

We granted certiorari to decide whether petitioner was tried "in violation of constitutional provisions guaranteeing the defendant an impartial jury and a jury composed of persons representing a fair cross section of the community." . . . What makes today's holding truly extraordinary is that it is based on a constitutional argument that the petitioner has *expressly* declined to raise, both in this Court and in the Supreme Court of Kentucky. . . .

Instead of even considering the history or function of the peremptory challenge, the bulk of the Court's opinion is spent recounting the well-established principle that intentional exclusion of racial groups from jury venires is a violation of the Equal Protection Clause. I too reaffirm that principle, which has been a part of our constitutional tradition since at least *Strauder* v. *West Virginia.* But if today's decision is nothing more than mere "application" of the "principles announced in *Strauder*," as the Court maintains, some will consider it curious that the application went unrecognized for over a century. The Court in *Swain* had no difficulty in unanimously concluding that cases such as *Strauder* did not require inquiry into the basis for a peremptory challenge. More recently we held that "[d]efendants are not entitled to a jury of any particular composition. . . ." *Taylor* v. *Louisiana*, 419 U.S., at 538. . . .

JUSTICE REHNQUIST, with whom CHIEF JUSTICE BURGER joins, dissenting:

. . . I cannot subscribe to the Court's unprece-dented use of the Equal Protection Clause to restrict the historic scope of the peremptory challenge, which has been described as "a necessary part of trial by jury." *Swain,* 380 U.S., at 219. In my view, there is simply nothing "unequal" about the State using its peremptory challenges to strike blacks from the jury in cases involving black defendants, so long as such challenges are also used to exclude whites in cases involving white defendants, Hispanics in cases involving Hispanic defendants, Asians in cases involving Asian defendants, and so on. This case-specific use of peremptory challenges by the State does not single out blacks, or members of any other race for that matter, for discriminatory treatment. Such use of peremptories is at best based upon seat-of-the-pants instincts, which are undoubtedly crudely stereotypical and may in many cases be hopelessly mistaken. But as long as they are applied across the board to jurors of all races and nationalities, I do not see—and the Court most certainly has not explained—how their use violates the Equal Protection Clause. . . .

UNITED STATES v. PARADISE,
480 U.S. 149 (1987)

The course of this litigation was long and complicated and will not be reviewed here in great detail. The case began in 1972 as a suit brought by the NAACP challenging the Alabama Department of Public Safety's long-standing practice of excluding blacks from becoming state troopers. The federal district court found in favor of the black plaintiffs and blacks were hired. But over the years black troopers were not promoted and this litigation continued. Eventually the federal district court imposed a requirement that at least half of those promoted to corporal and other upper ranks must be black provided that qualified black candidates were available. Subsequently the department promoted eight blacks and eight whites under the court's order and submitted promotional procedures for corporal and sergeant that were found acceptable to the judge, who then suspended the 50 percent requirement for those ranks. The Justice Department, consistent with the Reagan Administration's policy, opposed affirmative action and intervened in this matter, appealing the district court's order on the ground that it violated the equal protection guarantee of the Fourteenth Amendment. Defending the order was Phillip Paradise, Jr., on behalf of the black troopers. The Court of Appeals for the Eleventh Circuit affirmed the district court and the federal government took the case to the Supreme Court.

Majority votes: 5
Dissenting votes: 4

JUSTICE BRENNAN announced the judgment of the Court and delivered an opinion in which Justice MARSHALL, JUSTICE BLACKMUN, and JUSTICE POWELL join:

The question we must decide is whether relief awarded in this case, in the form of a one-black-for-one-white promotion requirement to be applied as an interim measure to state trooper promotions in the Alabama Department of Public Safety (Department), is permissible under the Equal Protection guarantee of the Fourteenth Amendment.

In 1972 the United States District Court for the Middle District of Alabama held that the Department had systematically excluded blacks from employment in violation of the Fourteenth Amendment. Some 11 years later, confronted with the Department's failure to develop promotion procedures that did not have an adverse impact on blacks, the District Court ordered the promotion of one black trooper for each white trooper elevated in rank, as long as qualified black candidates were available, until the Department implemented an acceptable promotion procedure. . . .

The United States maintains that the race-conscious relief ordered in this case violates the Equal Protection Clause of the Fourteenth Amendment to the Constitution of the United States.

It is now well established that government bodies, including courts, may constitutionally employ racial classifications essential to remedy unlawful treatment of racial or ethnic groups subject to discrimination. . . . But although this Court has consistently held that some elevated level of scrutiny is required when a racial or ethnic distinction is made for remedial purposes, it has yet to reach consensus on the appropriate constitutional analysis. We need not do so in this case, however, because we conclude that the relief ordered survives even strict scrutiny analysis: it is "narrowly tailored" to serve a "compelling governmental purpose."

The government unquestionably has a compelling interest in remedying past and present discrimination by a state actor. . . . In 1972 the District Court found, and the Court of Appeals affirmed, that for almost four decades the Department had excluded blacks from all positions, including jobs in the upper ranks. Such egregious discriminatory conduct was "unquestionably a violation of the Fourteenth Amendment." As the United States concedes, the pervasive, systematic, and obstinate discriminatory conduct of the Department created a profound need and a firm justification for the race-conscious relief ordered by the District Court.

The Department and the intervenors, however, maintain that the Department was found guilty only of discrimination in hiring, and not in its promotional practices. They argue that no remedial relief is justified in the promotion context because the intentional discrimination in hiring was without effect in the upper ranks, and because the Department's promotional procedure was not discriminatory. There is no merit in either premise.

Discrimination at the entry-level necessarily precluded blacks from competing for promotions, and resulted in a departmental hierarchy dominated exclusively by nonminorities. The lower courts determined that this situation was explicable only by reference to the Department's past discriminatory conduct. In 1972 the Department was "not just found guilty of discriminating against blacks in hiring to entry-level positions. The Court found that in thirty-seven years there had never been a black trooper at any rank." In 1979 the District Judge stated that one continuing effect of the Department's historical discrimination was that, "as of November 1, 1978, out of 232 state troopers at the rank of corporal or above, *there is still not one black*." The court explained that the *hiring* quota it had fashioned was intended to provide "an impetus to promote blacks into those positions" and that "[t]o focus only on the entry-level positions would be to ignore that past discrimination by the Department was pervasive, that its effects persist, and that they are manifest." The District Court crafted the relief it did due to "the department's failure after almost twelve years to eradicate the continuing effects of its own discrimination." It is too late for the Department to attempt to segregate the results achieved by its hiring practices and those achieved by its promotional practices. . . .

While conceding that the District Court's order serves a compelling interest, the Government insists that it was not narrowly tailored to accomplish its purposes—to remedy past discrimination and eliminate its lingering effects, to enforce compliance with the 1979 and 1981 Decrees by bringing about the speedy implementation of a promotion procedure that would not have an adverse impact on blacks, and to eradicate the ill effects of the Department's delay in producing such a procedure. We cannot agree. . . .

By 1984 the District Court was plainly justified in imposing the remedy chosen. Any order allowing further delay by the Department was entirely unacceptable. . . . Not only was the immediate promotion of blacks to the rank of corporal essential, but, if the need for continuing judicial oversight was to end, it was also essential that the Department be required to develop a procedure without adverse impact on blacks, and that the effect of past delays be eliminated.

We conclude that in 1983, when the District Judge entered his order, "it is doubtful, given [the Department's] history in this litigation, that the District Court had available to it any other effective remedy." . . .

The features of the one-for-one requirement and its actual operation indicate that it is flexible in application at all ranks. The requirement may be waived if no qualified black candidates are available. . . . Further, it applies only when the Department needs to make promotions. Thus, if external forces, such as budget cuts, necessitate a promotion freeze, the Department will not be required to make gratuitous promotions to remain in compliance with the court's order.

Most significantly, the one-for-one requirement is ephemeral; the term of its application is contingent upon the Department's own conduct. . . .

The one-for-one requirement did not impose an unacceptable burden on innocent third parties. . . . [T]he temporary and extremely limited nature of the requirement substantially limits any potential burden on white applicants for promotion. It was used only once at the rank of corporal and may not be utilized at all in the upper ranks. Nor has the court imposed an "absolute bar" to white advancement. In the one instance in which the quota was employed, 50% of those elevated were white.

The one-for-one requirement does not require the layoff and discharge of white employees and therefore does not impose burdens of the sort that concerned the plurality in *Wygant*. . . .

Finally, the basic limitation, that black troopers promoted must be qualified, remains. Qualified white candidates simply have to compete with qualified black candidates. To be sure, should the District Court's promotion requirement be applied, black applicants would receive some advantage. But this situation is only temporary, and is subject to amelioration by the action of the Department itself.

Accordingly, the one-for-one promotion requirement imposed in this case does not disproportionately harm the interests, or unnecessarily trammel the rights, of innocent individuals.

In determining whether this order was "narrowly tailored," we must acknowledge the respect owed a District Judge's judgment that specified relief is essential to cure a violation of the Fourteenth Amendment. A district court has "not merely the power but the duty to render a decree which will so far as possible eliminate the discriminatory effects of the past as well as bar like discrimination in the future." . . .

Plainly the District Court's discretion in remedying the deeply-rooted Fourteenth Amendment violations here was limited by the rights and interests of the white troopers seeking promotion to corporal. But we conclude that the District Judge properly balanced the individual and collective interests at stake, including the interests of the white troopers eligible for promotion, in shaping this remedy. . . .

The remedy imposed here is an effective, temporary and flexible measure. It applies only if qualified blacks are available, only if the Department has an objective need to make promotions, and only if the Department fails to implement a promotion procedure that does not have an adverse impact on blacks. The one-for-one requirement is the product of the considered judgment of the District Court which, with its knowledge of the parties and their resources, properly determined that strong measures were required in light of the Department's long and shameful record of delay and resistance.

The race-conscious relief imposed here was amply justified, and narrowly tailored to serve the legitimate and laudable purposes of the District Court. The judgment of the Court of Appeals, upholding the order of the District Court, is

Affirmed.

JUSTICE POWELL, concurring: [omitted]
JUSTICE STEVENS, concurring in the judgment: . . .

The District Court, like the school authority in *North Carolina State Board of Education* v. *Swann,* may, and in some instances must, resort to race-conscious remedies to vindicate federal constitutional guarantees. Because the instant employment discrimination case "does not differ fundamentally from other cases involving the framing of equitable remedies to repair the denial of a constitutional right," and because there has been no showing that the District Judge abused his discretion in shaping a remedy, I concur in the Court's judgment.

JUSTICE WHITE, dissenting:

Agreeing with much of what JUSTICE O'CONNOR has written in this case, I find it evident that the District Court exceeded its equitable powers in devising a remedy in this case. I therefore dissent from the judgment of affirmance.

JUSTICE O'CONNOR, with whom THE CHIEF

JUSTICE and JUSTICE SCALIA join, dissenting: . . .

One cannot read the record in this case without concluding that the Alabama Department of Public Safety had undertaken a course of action that amounted to "pervasive, systematic, and obstinate discriminatory conduct." Because the Federal Government has a compelling interest in remedying past and present discrimination by the Department, the District Court unquestionably had the authority to fashion a remedy designed to end the Department's egregious history of discrimination. In doing so, however, the District Court was obligated to fashion a remedy that was narrowly tailored to accomplish this purpose. The Court today purports to apply strict scrutiny, and concludes that the order in this case was narrowly tailored for its remedial purpose. Because the Court adopts a standardless view of "narrowly tailored" far less stringent than that required by strict scrutiny, I dissent. . . .

In my view, whether characterized as a goal or a quota, the District Court's order was not "manifestly necessary" to achieve compliance with that court's previous orders. The order at issue in this case clearly had one purpose, and one purpose only—to compel the Department to develop a promotion procedure that would not have an adverse impact on blacks. Although the Court and the courts below suggest that the order also had the purpose of "eradicat[ing] the ill effects of the Department's delay in producing" such a promotion procedure, the District Court's subsequent implementation of the order makes clear that the order cannot be defended on the basis of such a purpose. . . .

Moreover, even if the one-for-one quota had the purpose of eradicating the effects of the Department's delay, this purpose would not justify the quota imposed in this case. . . . The one-for-one promotion quota used in this case far exceeded the percentage of blacks in the trooper force, and there is no evidence in the record that such an extreme quota was necessary to eradicate the effects of the Department's delay. . . . [P]rotection of the rights of nonminority workers demands that a racial goal not substantially exceed the percentage of minority group members in the relevant population or work force absent compelling justification. In this case the District Court—and indeed this Court—provide no such compelling justification for the choice of a one-for-one promotion quota rather than a lower quota. . . .

I have no quarrel with the Court's conclusion that the recalcitrance of the Department of Public Safety in complying with the consent decrees was reprehensible. In its understandable frustration over the Department's conduct, however, the District Court imposed a racial quota without first considering the effectiveness of alternatives that would have a lesser effect on the rights of nonminority troopers. Because the District Court did not even consider the available alternatives to a one-for-one promotion quota, and because these alternatives would have successfully compelled the Department to comply with the consent decrees, I must respectfully dissent.

MARTIN v. WILKS,
109 S. Ct. 2180 (1989)

In 1974 black individuals and the NAACP initiated a suit in federal district court against the city of Birmingham, Alabama, and the Jefferson County Personnel Board charging them with racial discrimination in hiring and promotion practices in various public service jobs in violation of Title 7 of the Civil Rights Act of 1964. Consent decrees were eventually entered into and approved by the federal district court that included goals for hiring blacks as firefighters and for promoting them. Years later, Robert K. Wilks and other white firefighters brought a suit against the city and county alleging that because of their race they were being denied promotions in favor of less qualified blacks in violation of Title 7. The city and county argued that they did indeed make race-conscious promotion decisions but did so pursuant to the consent decrees. John W. Martin and other black firefighters were allowed to intervene to defend the decrees. The district court ruled in favor of the black firefighters. The Court of Appeals for the Eleventh Circuit reversed.

Majority votes: 5
Dissenting votes: 4

CHIEF JUSTICE REHNQUIST delivered the opinion of the court:

A group of white firefighters sued the City of Birmingham, Alabama (City) and the Jefferson County Personnel Board (Board) alleging that they were being denied promotions in favor of less qualified black firefighters. They claimed that the City and the Board were making promotion decisions on the basis of race in reliance on certain consent decrees, and that these decisions constituted impermissible racial discrimination in violation of the Constitution and federal statute. The District Court held that the white firefighters were precluded from challenging employment decisions taken pursuant to the decrees, even though these firefighters had not been parties to the proceedings in which the decrees were entered. We think this holding contravenes the general rule that a person cannot be deprived of his legal rights in a proceeding to which he is not a party. . . .

Petitioners argue that, because respondents failed to timely intervene in the initial proceedings, their current challenge to actions taken under the consent decree constitutes an impermissible "collateral attack." They argue that respondents were aware that the underlying suit might affect them and if they chose to pass up an opportunity to intervene, they should not be permitted to later litigate the issues in a new action. The position has sufficient appeal to have commanded the approval of the great majority of the federal courts of appeals, but we agree with the contrary view expressed by the Court of Appeals for the Eleventh Circuit in this case.

We begin with the words of Justice Brandeis in *Chase National Bank* v. *Norwalk,* 291 U.S. 431 (1934):

> "The law does not impose upon any person absolutely entitled to a hearing the burden of voluntary intervention in a suit to which he is a stranger. . . . Unless duly summoned to appear in a legal proceeding, a person not a privy may rest assured that a judgment recovered therein will not affect his legal rights." *Id.* at 441.

While these words were written before the adoption of the Federal Rules of Civil Procedure, we think the Rules incorporate the same principle; a party seeking a judgment binding on another cannot obligate that person to intervene; he must be joined. . . . Against the background of permissive intervention set forth in *Chase National Bank*, the drafters cast Rule 24, governing intervention, in permissive terms. . . . They determined that the concern for finality and completeness of judgments would be "better [served] by mandatory joinder procedures." Accordingly, Rule 19(a) provides for mandatory joinder in circumstances where a judgment rendered in the absence of a person may "leave . . . persons already parties subject to a substantial risk of incurring . . . inconsistent obligations. . . ." Rule 19(b) sets forth the factors to be considered by a court in deciding whether to allow an action to proceed in the absence of an interested party.

Joinder as a party, rather than knowledge of a lawsuit and an apportunity to intervene, is the method by which potential parties are subjected to the jurisdiction of the court and bound by a judgment or decree. The parties to a lawsuit presumably know better than anyone else the nature and scope of relief sought in the action, and at whose expense such relief might be granted. It makes sense, therefore, to place on them a burden of bringing in additional parties where such a step is indicated, rather than placing on potential additional parties a duty to intervene when they acquire knowledge of the lawsuit. The linchpin of the "impermissible collateral attack" doctrine—the attribution of preclusive effect to a failure to intervene—is therefore quite inconsistent with Rule 19 and Rule 24. . . .

Petitioners contend that a different result should be reached because the need to join affected parties will be burdensome and ultimately discouraging to civil rights litigation. Potential adverse claimants may be numerous and difficult to identify; if they are not joined, the possibility for inconsistent judgments exists. Judicial resources will be needlessly consumed in relitigation of the same question.

Even if we were wholly persuaded by these arguments as a matter of policy, acceptance of them would require a rewriting rather than an interpretation of the relevant Rules. But we are not persuaded that their acceptance would lead to a more satisfactory method of handling cases like this one. It must be remembered that the alternatives are a duty to intervene based on knowledge, on the one hand, and some form of joinder, as the Rules presently provide, on the other. No one can seriously contend that an employer might successfully defend against a Title VII claim by one group of employees on the ground that its actions were required by an earlier decree entered in a suit brought against it by another, if the later group did not have adequate notice or knowledge of the earlier suit.

The difficulties petitioners foresee in identifying those who could be adversely affected by a decree granting broad remedial relief are undoubtedly present, but they arise from the nature of the relief sought and not because of any choice between mandatory intervention and joinder. Rule 19's provisions for joining interested parties are designed to accommodate the sort of complexities that may arise from a decree affecting numerous people in various ways. We doubt that a mandatory intervention rule would be any less awkward. As mentioned, plaintiffs who seek the aid of the courts to alter existing employment policies, or the employer who might be subject to conflicting decrees, are best able to bear the burden of designating those who would be adversely affected if plaintiffs prevail; these parties will generally have a better understanding of the scope of likely relief than employees who are not named but might be affected. Petitioners' alternative does not eliminate the need for, or difficulty of, identifying persons who, because of their interests, should be included in a lawsuit. It merely shifts that responsibility to less able shoulders.

Nor do we think that the system of joinder called for by the Rules is likely to produce more relitigation of issues than the converse rule. The breadth of a lawsuit and concomitant relief may be at least partially shaped in advance through Rule 19 to avoid needless clashes with future litigation. And even under a regime of mandatory intervention, parties who did not have adequate knowledge of the suit would relitigate issues. Additional questions about the adequacy and timeliness of knowledge would inevitably crop up. We think that the system of joinder presently contemplated by the Rules best serves the many interests involved in the run of litigated cases, including cases like the present one.

Petitioners also urge that the congressional policy favoring voluntary settlement of employment discrimination claims, referred to in cases such as *Carson* v. *American Brands, Inc.,* 450 U.S. 79 (1981), also supports the "impermissible collateral attack" doctrine. But once again it is essential to note just what is meant by "voluntary settlement." A voluntary settlement in the form of a consent decree between one group of employees and their employer cannot possibly "settle," voluntarily or otherwise, the conflicting claims of another group of employees who do not join in the agreement. . . .

For the foregoing reasons we affirm the decision of the Court of Appeals for the Eleventh Circuit. That court remanded the case for trial of the reverse discrimination claims. Petitioners point to language in the District Court's findings of fact and conclusions of law which suggests that respondents will not prevail on the merits. We agree with the view of the Court of Appeals, however, that the proceedings in the District Court may have been affected by the mistaken view that respondents' claims on the merits were barred to the extent they were inconsistent with the consent decree.

Affirmed.

JUSTICE STEVENS, with whom JUSTICE BRENNAN, JUSTICE MARSHALL, and JUSTICE BLACKMUN join, dissenting:

As a matter of law there is a vast difference between persons who are actual parties to litigation and persons who merely have the kind of interest that may as a practical matter be impaired by the outcome of a case. Persons in the first category have a right to participate in a trial and to appeal from an adverse judgment; depending on whether they win or lose, their legal rights may be enhanced or impaired. Persons in the latter category have a right to intervene in the action in a timely fashion, or they may be joined as parties against their will. But if they remain on the sidelines, they may be harmed as a practical matter even though their legal rights are unaffected. One of the disadvantages of sideline-sitting is that the bystander has no right to appeal from a judgment no matter how harmful it may be.

In this case the Court quite rightly concludes that the white firefighters who brought the second series of Title VII cases could not be deprived of their legal rights in the first series of cases because they had neither intervened nor been joined as parties. The consent decrees obviously could not deprive them of any contractual rights, such as seniority or accrued vacation pay, or of any other legal rights, such as the right to have their employer comply with federal statutes like Title VII. There is no reason, however, why the consent decrees might not produce changes in conditions at the white firefighters' place of employment that, as a practical matter, may have a serious effect on their opportunities for employment or promotion even though they are not bound by the decrees in any legal sense. The fact that one of the effects of a decree is to curtail the job opportunities of nonparties does not mean that the nonparties have been deprived of legal rights or that they have standing to appeal from that decree without becoming parties.

Persons who have no right to appeal from a final judgment—either because the time to appeal has elapsed or because they never became parties to the case—may nevertheless collaterally attack a judgment on certain narrow grounds. If the court had no jurisdiction over the subject matter, or if the judgment is the product of corruption, duress, fraud, collusion, or mistake, under limited circumstances it may be set aside in an appropriate collateral proceeding. This rule not only applies to parties to the original action, but also allows interested third parties collaterally to attack judgments. In both civil and criminal cases, however, the grounds that may be invoked to support a collateral attack are much more limited than those that may be asserted as error on direct appeal. Thus, a person who can foresee that a lawsuit is likely to have a practical impact on his interests may pay a heavy price if he elects to sit on the sidelines instead of intervening and taking the risk that his legal rights will be impaired.

In this case there is no dispute about the fact that the respondents are not parties to the consent decrees. It follows as a matter of course that they are not bound by those decrees. Those judgments could not, and did not, deprive them of any legal rights. The judgments did, however, have a practical impact on respondents' opportunities for advancement in their profession. For that reason, respondents had standing to challenge the validity of the decrees, but the grounds that they may advance in support of a collateral challenge are much more limited than would be allowed if they were parties prosecuting a direct appeal.

The District Court's rulings in this case have been described incorrectly by both the Court of Appeals and this Court. The Court of Appeals repeatedly stated that the District Court had "in effect" held that the white firefighters were "bound" by a decree to which they were not parties. And this Court's opinion seems to assume that the District Court had interpreted its consent decrees in the earlier litigation as holding "that the white firefighters were precluded from challenging employment decisions taken pursuant to the decrees." It is important, therefore, to make clear exactly what the District Court did hold and why its judgment should be affirmed. . . .

[I]t is absolutely clear that the court did not hold that respondents were bound by the decree. Nowhere in the District Court's lengthy findings of fact and conclusions of law is there a single word suggesting that respondents were bound by the consent decree or that the court intended to treat them as though they had been actual parties to that litigation and not merely as persons whose interests, as a practical matter, had been affected. Indeed, respondents, the Court of Appeals, and the majority opinion all fail to draw attention to any point in this case's long history at which the judge may have given the impression that any nonparty was legally bound by the consent decree.

Regardless of whether the white firefighters were parties to the decrees granting relief to their black co-workers, it would be quite wrong to assume that they could never collaterally attack such a decree. If a litigant has standing, he or she can always collaterally attack a judgment for certain narrowly defined defects. . . . On the other hand, a district court is not required to retry a case—or to sit in review of another court's judgment—every time an interested nonparty asserts that *some* error that might have been raised on direct appeal was committed. Such a broad allowance of collateral re-

view would destroy the integrity of litigated judgments, would lead to an abundance of vexatious litigation, and would subvert the interest in comity between courts. Here, respondents have offered no circumstance that might justify reopening the District Court's settled judgment.

The implementation of a consent decree affecting the interests of a multitude of nonparties, and the reliance on that decree as a defense to a charge of discrimination in hiring and promotion decisions, raise a legitimate concern of collusion. No such allegation, however, has been raised. Moreover, there is compelling evidence that the decree was not collusive. In its decision approving the consent decree over the objection of the BFA and individual white firefighters, the District Court observed that there had been "no contention or suggestion" that the decrees were fraudulent or collusive. The record of the fairness hearing was made part of the record of this litigation and this finding was not contradicted. More significantly, the consent decrees were not negotiated until after the 1976 trial and the court's finding that the City had discriminated against black candidates for jobs as police officers and firefighters, and until after the 1979 trial, at which substantial evidence was presented suggesting that the City also discriminated against black candidates for promotion in the fire department. Like the record of the 1981 fairness hearing, the records of both of these prior proceedings were made part of the record in this case. Given this history, the lack of any indication of collusion, and the District Court's finding that "there is more than ample reason for . . . the City of Birmingham to be concerned that [it] would be in time held liable for discrimination against blacks at higher level positions in the police and fire departments," it is evident that the decree was a product of genuine arm's-length negotiations.

Nor can it be maintained that the consent judgment is subject to reopening and further litigation because the relief it afforded was so out of line with settled legal doctrine that it "was transparently invalid or had only a frivolous pretense to validity." To the contrary, the type of race-conscious relief ordered in the consent decree is entirely consistent with this Court's approach to affirmative action. Given a sufficient predicate of racial discrimination, neither the Equal Protection Clause of the Fourteenth Amendment nor Title VII of the Civil Rights Act of 1964 erects a bar to affirmative action plans that benefit non-victims and have some adverse effect on non-wrongdoers. As JUSTICE O'CONNOR observed in *Wygant* v. *Jackson Bd. of Education,* 476 U. S. 267 (1986), "[t]his remedial purpose need not be accompanied by contemporaneous findings of actual discrimination to be accepted as legitimate as long as the public actor has a firm basis for believing that remedial action is required.'' Such a belief was clearly justified in this case. After conducting the 1976 trial and finding against the City and after listening to the five days of testimony in the 1979 trial, the judge was well qualified to conclude that there was a sound basis for believing that the City would likely have been found to have violated Title VII if the action had proceeded to a litigated judgment.

Hence, there is no basis for collaterally attacking the judgment as collusive, fraudulent, or transparently invalid. Moreover, respondents do not claim—nor has there been any showing of—mistake, duress, or lack of jurisdiction. Instead, respondents are left to argue that somewhat different relief would have been more appropriate than the relief that was actually granted. Although this sort of issue may provide the basis for a direct appeal, it cannot, and should not, serve to open the door to relitigation of a settled judgment. . . .

The predecessor to this litigation was brought to change a pattern of hiring and promotion practices that had discriminated against black citizens in Birmingham for decades. The white respondents in this case are not responsible for that history of discrimination, but they are nevertheless beneficiaries of the discriminatory practices that the litigation was designed to correct. Any remedy that seeks to create employment conditions that would have obtained if there had been no violations of law will necessarily have an adverse impact on whites, who must now share their job and promotion opportunities with blacks. Just as white employees in the past were innocent beneficiaries of illegal discriminatory practices, so is it inevitable that some of the same white employees will be innocent victims who must share some of the burdens resulting from the redress of the past wrongs.

There is nothing unusual about the fact that litigation between adverse parties may, as a practical matter, seriously impair the interests of third persons who elect to sit on the sidelines. Indeed, in complex litigation this Court has squarely held that a sideline-sitter may be bound as firmly as an actual party if he had adequate notice and a fair opportunity to intervene and if the judicial interest in finality is sufficiently strong. . . .

There is no need, however, to go that far in order to agree with the District Court's eminently sensible view that compliance with the terms of a valid decree remedying violations of Title VII cannot itself violate that statute or the Equal Protection Clause. The City of Birmingham, in entering into

and complying with this decree, has made a substantial step toward the eradication of the long history of pervasive racial discrimination that has plagued its fire department. The District Court, after conducting a trial and carefully considering respondents' arguments, concluded that this effort is lawful and should go forward. Because respondents have thus already had their day in court and have failed to carry their burden, I would vacate the judgment of the Court of Appeals and remand for further proceedings consistent with this opinion.

CITY OF RICHMOND v. J.A. CROSON CO., 109 S.Ct. 706 (1989)

In 1983 the Richmond, Virginia, City Council adopted a Minority Business Utilization Plan requiring those awarded city construction contracts to subcontract at least 30 percent of the dollar amount of each contract to one or more Minority Business Enterprises defined as a business from anywhere in the country at least 51 percent of which is owned and controlled by black or other specified minority citizens. A waiver of the 30 percent set-aside was possible upon proof that sufficient minority businesses were unavailable or unwilling to participate. J.A. Croson Co., a white-run mechanical plumbing and heating contractor, was the sole bidder on a city contract and applied for and was denied a waiver. It lost its contract and subsequently brought suit charging that the set-aside plan violated the equal protection clause of the Fourteenth Amendment. The federal district court upheld the plan as did the Court of Appeals for the Fourth Circuit. The Supreme Court sent the case back to the appeals court to reconsider its decision in light of Wygant *v.* Jackson Board of Education. *The court of appeals reconsidered and struck down the plan. The city appealed to the Supreme Court.*

Majority votes: 6
Dissenting votes: 3

JUSTICE O'CONNOR delivered the opinion of the Court:

In this case, we confront once again the tension between the Fourteenth Amendment's guarantee of equal treatment to all citizens, and the use of race-based measures to ameliorate the effects of past discrimination on the opportunities enjoyed by members of minority groups in our society. In *Fullilove* v. *Klutznick,* 448 U.S. 448 (1980), we held that a congressional program requiring that 10% of certain federal construction grants be awarded to minority contractors did not violate the equal protection principles embodied in the Due Process Clause of the Fifth Amendment. Relying largely on our decision in *Fullilove,* some lower federal courts have applied a similar standard of review in assessing the constitutionality of state and local minority set-aside provisions under the Equal Protection Clause of the Fourteenth Amendment. Since our decision two Terms ago in *Wygant* v. *Jackson Board of Education,* 476 U.S. 267 (1986), the lower federal courts have attempted to apply its standards in evaluating the constitutionality of state and local programs which allocate a portion of public contracting opportunities exclusively to minority-owned businesses. We noted probable jurisdiction in this case to consider the applicability of our decision in *Wygant* to a minority set-aside program adopted by the city of Richmond, Virginia. . . .

We think it clear that the factual predicate offered in support of the Richmond Plan suffers from the same two defects identified as fatal in *Wygant.* The District Court found the city council's "findings sufficient to ensure that, in adopting the Plan, it was remedying the present effects of past discrimination in the *construction industry.*" Like the "role model" theory employed in *Wygant,* a generalized assertion that there has been past discrimination in an entire industry provides no guidance for a legislative body to determine the precise scope of the injury it seeks to remedy. It "has no logical stopping point." "Relief" for such an ill-defined wrong could extend until the percentage of public contracts awarded to MBEs [minority business enterprise] in Richmond mirrored the percentage of minorities in the population as a whole.

Appellant argues that it is attempting to remedy various forms of past discrimination that are alleged to be responsible for the small number of minority businesses in the local contracting industry. Among these the city cites the exclusion of blacks from skilled construction trade unions and training programs. This past discrimination has prevented them "from following the traditional path from laborer to entrepreneur." The city also lists a host of nonracial factors which would seem to face a member of any racial group attempting to establish a new business enterprise, such as deficiencies in working capital, inability to meet bonding requirements, unfamiliarity with bidding procedures, and disability caused by an inadequate track record.

While there is no doubt that the sorry history of both private and public discrimination in this country has contributed to lack of opportunities for black entrepreneurs, this observation, standing alone, cannot justify a rigid racial quota in the awarding of public contracts in Richmond, Virginia. Like the claim that discrimination in primary and secondary schooling justifies a rigid racial preference in medical school admissions, an amorphous claim that there has been past discrimination in a particular industry cannot justify the use of an unyielding racial quota.

It is sheer speculation how many minority firms there would be in Richmond absent past societal discrimination, just as it was sheer speculation how many minority medical students would have been admitted to the medical school at Davis absent past discrimination in educational opportunities. Defining these sorts of injuries as "identified discrimination" would give local governments license to create a patchwork of racial preferences based on statistical generalizations about any particular field of endeavor.

These defects are readily apparent in this case. The 30% quota cannot in any realistic sense be tied to any injury suffered by anyone. The District Court relied upon five predicate "facts" in reaching its conclusion that there was an adequate basis for the 30% quota: (1) the ordinance declares itself to be remedial; (2) several proponents of the measure stated their views that there had been past discrimination in the construction industry; (3) minority businesses received .67% of prime contracts from the city while minorities constituted 50% of the city's population; (4) there were very few minority contractors in local and state contractors' associations; and (5) in 1977, Congress made a determination that the effects of past discrimination had stifled minority participation in the construction industry nationally.

None of these "findings," singly or together, provide the city of Richmond with a "strong basis in evidence for its conclusion that remedial action was necessary." There is nothing approaching a prima facie case of a constitutional or statutory violation by *anyone* in the Richmond construction industry.

The District Court accorded great weight to the fact that the city council designated the Plan as "remedial." But the mere recitation of a "benign" or legitimate purpose for a racial classification, is entitled to little or no weight. . . .

Racial classifications are suspect, and that means that simple legislative assurances of good intention cannot suffice.

The District Court also relied on the highly conclusionary statement of a proponent of the Plan that there was racial discrimination in the construction industry "in this area, and the State, and around the nation." It also noted that the city manager had related his view that racial discrimination still plagued the construction industry in his home city of Pittsburgh. These statements are of little probative value in establishing identified discrimination in the Richmond construction industry. The fact-finding process of legislative bodies is generally entitled to a presumption of regularity and deferential review by the judiciary. But when a legislative body chooses to employ a suspect classification, it cannot rest upon a generalized assertion as to the classification's relevance to its goals. A governmental actor cannot render race a legitimate proxy for a particular condition merely by declaring that the condition exists. The history of racial classifications in this country suggests that blind judicial deference to legislative or executive pronouncements of necessity has no place in equal protection analysis.

Reliance on the disparity between the number of prime contracts awarded to minority firms and the minority population of the city of Richmond is similarly misplaced. There is no doubt that "[w]here gross statistical disparties can be shown, they alone in a proper case may constitute prima facie proof of a pattern or practice of discrimination" under Title VII. But it is equally clear that "[w]hen special qualifications are required to fill particular jobs, comparisons to the general population (rather than to the smaller group of individuals who possess the necessary qualifications) may have little probative value." . . .

In this case, the city does not even know how many MBEs in the relevant market are qualified to undertake prime or subcontracting work in public construction projects. . . . Nor does the city know what percentage of total city construction dollars minority firms now receive as subcontractors on prime contracts let by the city.

To a large extent, the set-aside of subcontracting dollars seems to rest on the unsupported assumption that white prime contractors simply will not hire minority firms. . . . Indeed, there is evidence in this record that overall minority participation in city contracts in Richmond is seven to eight percent, and that minority contractor participation in Community Block Development Grant *construction* projects is 17% to 22%. Without any information on minority participation in subcontracting, it is quite simply impossible to evaluate overall minority representation in the city's construction expenditures. . . .

Finally, the city and the District Court relied on Congress' finding in connection with the set-aside approved in *Fullilove* that there had been nationwide discrimination in the construction industry. The probative value of these findings for demonstrating the existence of discrimination in Richmond is extremely limited. By its inclusion of a waiver procedure in the national program addressed in *Fullilove,* Congress explicitly recognized that the scope of the problem would vary from market area to market area. . . .

Moreover, as noted above, Congress was exercising its powers under § 5 of the Fourteenth Amendment in making a finding that past discrimination would cause federal funds to be distributed in a manner which reinforced prior patterns of discrimination. While the States and their subdivisions may take remedial action when they possess evidence that their own spending practices are exacerbating a pattern of prior discrimination, they must identify that discrimination, public or private, with some specificity before they may use race-conscious relief. Congress has made national findings that there has been societal discrimination in a host of fields. If all a state or local government need do is find a congressional report on the subject to enact a set-aside program, the constraints of the Equal Protection Clause will, in effect, have been rendered a nullity. . . .

JUSTICE MARSHALL apparently views the requirement that Richmond identify the discrimination it seeks to remedy in its own jurisdiction as a mere administrative headache, an "onerous documentary obligatio[n]." We cannot agree. In this regard, we are in accord with JUSTICE STEVENS' observation in *Fullilove,* that "[b]ecause racial characteristics so seldom provide a relevant basis for disparate treatment, and because classifications based on race are potentially so harmful to the entire body politic, it is especially important that the reasons for any such classification be clearly identified and unquestionably legitimate." The "evidence" relied upon by the dissent, the history of school desegregation in Richmond and numerous congressional reports, does little to define the scope of any injury to minority contractors in Richmond or the necessary remedy. The factors relied upon by the dissent could justify a preference of any size or duration.

Moreover, JUSTICE MARSHALL's suggestion that findings of discrimination may be "shared" from jurisdiction to jurisdiction in the same manner as information concerning zoning and property values is unprecedented. We have never approved the extrapolation of discrimination in one jurisdiction from the experience of another. . . .

In sum, none of the evidence presented by the city points to any identified discrimination in the Richmond construction industry. We, therefore, hold that the city has failed to demonstrate a compelling interest in apportioning public contracting opportunities on the basis of race. To accept Richmond's claim that past societal discrimination alone can serve as the basis for rigid racial preferences would be to open the door to competing claims for "remedial relief" for every disadvantaged group. The dream of a Nation of equal citizens in a society where race is irrelevant to personal opportunity and achievement would be lost in a mosaic of shifting preferences based on inherently unmeasurable claims of past wrongs. . . . We think such a result would be contrary to both the letter and spirit of a constitutional provision whose central command is equality.

The foregoing analysis applies only to the inclusion of blacks within the Richmond set-aside program. There is *absolutely no evidence* of past discrimination against Spanish-speaking, Oriental, Indian, Eskimo, or Aleut persons in any aspect of the Richmond construction industry. The District Court took judicial notice of the fact that the vast majority of "minority" persons in Richmond were black. It may well be that Richmond has never had an Aleut or Eskimo citizen. The random inclusion of racial groups that, as a practical matter, may never have suffered from discrimination in the construction industry in Richmond, suggests that perhaps the city's purpose was not in fact to remedy past discrimination.

If a 30% set-aside was "narrowly tailored" to compensate black contractors for past discrimination, one may legitimately ask why they are forced to share this "remedial relief" with an Aleut citizen who moves to Richmond tomorrow? The gross overinclusiveness of Richmond's racial preference strongly impugns the city's claim of remedial motivation. . . . The 30% quota cannot be said to be narrowly tailored to any goal, except perhaps outright racial balancing. It rests upon the "completely unrealistic" assumption that minorities will choose a particular trade in lockstep proportion to their representation in the local population. . . .

Since the city must already consider bids and waivers on a case-by-case basis, it is difficult to see the need for a rigid numerical quota. As noted above, the congressional scheme upheld in *Fullilove* allowed for a waiver of the set-aside provision where an MBE's higher price was not attributable to the effects of past discrimination. Based upon proper findings, such programs are less problematic from an equal protection standpoint because they treat all candidates individually, rather than making the color of an applicant's skin the sole relevant consideration. Unlike the program upheld in *Fullilove,* the Richmond Plan's waiver system focuses solely on the availability of MBEs; there is no inquiry into whether or not the particular MBE seek-

ing a racial preference has suffered from the effects of past discrimination by the city or prime contractors.

Given the existence of an individualized procedure, the city's only interest in maintaining a quota system rather than investigating the need for remedial action in particular cases would seem to be simple administrative convenience. But the interest in avoiding the bureaucratic effort necessary to tailor remedial relief to those who truly have suffered the effects of prior discrimination cannot justify a rigid line drawn on the basis of a suspect classification. . . . Under Richmond's scheme, a successful black, Hispanic, or Oriental entrepreneur from anywhere in the country enjoys an absolute preference over other citizens based solely on their race. We think it obvious that such a program is not narrowly tailored to remedy the effects of prior discrimination. . . .

Accordingly, the judgment of the Court of Appeals for the Fourth Circuit is

Affirmed.

JUSTICE STEVENS, concurring in part and concurring in the judgment: [omitted]
JUSTICE KENNEDY, concurring in part and concurring in the judgment: [omitted]
JUSTICE SCALIA, concurring in the judgment: [omitted]
JUSTICE MARSHALL, with whom JUSTICE BRENNAN and JUSTICE BLACKMUN join, dissenting:

It is a welcome symbol of racial progress when the former capital of the Confederacy acts forthrightly to confront the effects of racial discrimination in its midst. In my view, nothing in the Constitution can be construed to prevent Richmond, Virginia, from allocating a portion of its contracting dollars for businesses owned or controlled by members of minority groups. Indeed, Richmond's set-aside program is indistinguishable in all meaningful respects from—and in fact was patterned upon—the federal set-aside plan which this Court upheld in *Fullilove* v. *Klutznick.*

A majority of this Court holds today, however, that the Equal Protection Clause of the Fourteenth Amendment blocks Richmond's initiative. The essence of the majority's position is that Richmond has failed to catalogue adequate findings to prove that past discrimination has impeded minorities from joining or participating fully in Richmond's construction contracting industry. I find deep irony in second-guessing Richmond's judgment on this point. As much as any municipality in the United States, Richmond knows what racial discrimination is; a century of decisions by this and other federal courts has richly documented the city's disgraceful history of public and private racial discrimination. In any event, the Richmond City Council *has* supported its determination that minorities have been wrongly excluded from local construction contracting. Its proof includes statistics showing that minority-owned businesses have received virtually no city contracting dollars and rarely if ever belonged to area trade associations; testimony by municipal officials that discrimination has been widespread in the local construction industry; and the same exhaustive and widely publicized federal studies relied on in *Fullilove,* studies which showed that pervasive discrimination in the Nation's tight-knit construction industry had operated to exclude minorities from public contracting. These are precisely the types of statistical and testimonial evidence which, until today, this Court had credited in cases approving of race-conscious measures designed to remedy past discrimination.

More fundamentally, today's decision marks a deliberate and giant step backward in this Court's affirmative action jurisprudence. Cynical of one municipality's attempt to redress the effects of past racial discrimination in a particular industry, the majority launches a grapeshot attack on race-conscious remedies in general. The majority's unnecessary pronouncements will inevitably discourage or prevent governmental entities, particularly States and localities, from acting to rectify the scourge of past discrimination. This is the harsh reality of the majority's decision, but it is not the Constitution's command. . . .

Today, for the first time, a majority of this Court has adopted strict scrutiny as its standard of Equal Protection Clause review of race-conscious remedial measures. This is an unwelcome development. A profound difference separates governmental actions that themselves are racist, and governmental actions that seek to remedy the effects of prior racism or to prevent neutral governmental activity from perpetuating the effects of such racism.

Racial classifications "drawn on the presumption that one race is inferior to another or because they put the weight of government behind racial hatred and separatism" warrant the strictest judicial scrutiny because of the very irrelevance of these rationales. By contrast, racial classifications drawn for the purpose of remedying the effects of discrimination that itself was race-based have a highly pertinent basis: the tragic and indelible fact that discrimination against blacks and other racial minorities in this Nation has pervaded our Nation's history and continues to scar our society. . . .

In concluding that remedial classifications warrant no different standard of review under the Constitution than the most brute and repugnant forms of state-sponsored racism, a majority of this Court signals that it regards racial discrimination as largely a phenomenon of the past, and that government bodies need no longer preoccupy themselves with rectifying racial injustice. I, however, do not believe this Nation is anywhere close to eradicating racial discrimination or its vestiges. In constitutionalizing its wishful thinking, the majority today does a grave disservice not only to those victims of past and present racial discrimination in this Nation whom government has sought to assist, but also to this Court's long tradition of approaching issues of race with the utmost sensitivity. . . .

Today's decision, finally, is particularly noteworthy for the daunting standard it imposes upon States and localities contemplating the use of race-conscious measures to eradicate the present effects of prior discrimination and prevent its perpetuation. The majority restricts the use of such measures to situations in which a State or locality can put forth "a prima facie case of a constitutional or statutory violation." In so doing, the majority calls into question the validity of the business set-asides which dozens of municipalities across this Nation have adopted on the authority of *Fullilove.* . . .

[I]t is too late in the day to assert seriously that the Equal Protection Clause prohibits States—or for that matter, the Federal Government, to whom the equal protection guarantee has largely been applied, see *Bolling* v. *Sharpe* (1954)—from enacting race-conscious remedies. Our cases in the areas of school desegregation, voting rights, and affirmative action have demonstrated time and again that race is constitutionally germane, precisely because race remains dismayingly relevant in American life.

In adopting its prima facie standard for States and localities, the majority closes its eyes to this constitutional history and social reality. . . .

But this Court's remedy-stage school desegregation decisions cannot so conveniently be cordoned off. These decisions (like those involving voting rights and affirmative action) stand for the same broad principles of equal protection which Richmond seeks to vindicate in this case: all persons have equal worth, and it is permissible, given a sufficient factual predicate and appropriate tailoring, for government to take account of race to eradicate the present effects of race-based subjugation denying that basic equality. . . .

The majority today sounds a full-scale retreat from the Court's longstanding solicitude to race-conscious remedial efforts "directed toward deliverance of the century-old promise of equality of economic opportunity.'' The new and restrictive tests it applies scuttle one city's effort to surmount its discriminatory past, and imperil those of dozens more localities. I, however, profoundly disagree with the cramped vision of the Equal Protection Clause which the majority offers today and with its application of that vision to Richmond, Virginia's, laudable set-aside plan. The battle against pernicious racial discrimination or its effects is nowhere near won. I must dissent.

JUSTICE BLACKMUN, with whom JUSTICE BRENNAN joins, dissenting:

I join JUSTICE MARSHALL's perceptive and incisive opinion revealing great sensitivity toward those who have suffered the pains of economic discrimination in the construction trades for so long.

I never thought that I would live to see the day when the city of Richmond, Virginia, the cradle of the Old Confederacy, sought on its own, within a narrow confine, to lessen the stark impact of persistent discrimination. But Richmond, to its great credit, acted. Yet this Court, the supposed bastion of equality, strikes down Richmond's efforts as though discrimination had never existed or was not demonstrated in this particular litigation. JUSTICE MARSHALL convincingly discloses the fallacy and the shallowness of that approach. History is irrefutable, even though one might sympathize with those who—though possibly innocent in themselves—benefit from the wrongs of past decades.

So the Court today regresses. I am confident, however, that, given time, it one day again will do its best to fulfill the great promises of the Constitution's Preamble and of the guarantees embodied in the Bill of Rights—a fulfillment that would make this Nation very special.

Chapter

19

Sexual Equality

DECISIONAL TRENDS

Although women were not subject to slavery (black women were subject to slavery because of their race, not their gender), the legal status of women until well into the twentieth century was that of second-class citizenship. Women during much of the nineteenth century, as Justice Brennan noted in **Frontiero** v. **Richardson,** could not hold public office, were barred from serving on juries, and were not allowed to bring lawsuits in their own names. In marriage they were legally subservient to their husbands, which was symbolized by the woman legally adopting the husband's surname and dropping her own, a practice that has outlived the legal inferiority it once represented. As married women they could not own or convey property or be appointed legal guardian of their own children. The 1873 decision in **Bradwell** v. **Illinois** reflected the deeply entrenched sexist attitudes widespread in America. That women were given no protection under the Fourteenth Amendment came as no surprise in light of **The Slaughterhouse Cases** (chap. 6) and the Court's determination to narrowly in-

terpret that amendment. In *Minor* v. *Happersett*, 21 Wallace 162 (1875), the Court ruled that women did not have the right to vote under the Fourteenth Amendment. Not until the Nineteenth Amendment was adopted in 1920 was the right of women to vote protected constitutionally.

Women were also restricted as to their educational and employment opportunities. Even when women began to make progress in fashioning careers for themselves, sexist practices and traditions resulted in discrimination against them in the professions and workplaces.

All branches of government reflected deep-seated, long-prevailing institutional sexism. This could even be seen in a decision of the liberal Warren Court in **Hoyt** v. **Florida** upholding a sexist jury selection scheme. Not until well into the 1960s was sexism to come under sustained attack by the women's rights movement. However, it should be noted that Congress, in the wake of the civil rights movement, enacted the Equal Pay Act in 1963, which prohibited wage discrimination on the basis of race, color, religion, national origin, or *sex*. Congress also added "sex" to Title VII (concerning hiring and employment practices) of the historic Civil Rights Act of 1964, which had as its main focus the ending of racism. Title VII, in particular, provided the legal basis for a major attack on sexism. In 1967 President Johnson issued an executive order prohibiting sexual discrimination by companies or institutions receiving federal government contracts over $10,000. Also in that year Congress enacted the Age Discrimination Act, protecting workers of both sexes aged 40 to 70 from being discriminated against by employers because of age. This was considered to be of immense importance to older women entering the labor force for the first time.

In 1972, after more than a half century of advocacy by feminists, Congress passed the Equal Rights Amendment (ERA), which stated simply: "Equality of rights under the law shall not be denied or abridged by the United States or by any State on account of sex." By the fall of 1977, 35 states ratified the ERA, three short of the 38 states necessary for ratification. In the face of vigorous opposition by the Reagan Administration, the ERA died on June 30, 1982. However, 16 states have their own equal rights amendments in their state constitutions and numerous state laws forbid sex discrimination.

The area of the rights of women and of sexual equality is the one in which the Burger Court most expanded individual rights. One of the earliest issues of the rights of women to come before the Court was the highly controversial abortion issue, in the form of a challenge to state antiabortion statutes. The Court in **Roe** v. **Wade** (chap. 6), in a landmark decision, ruled that women have a right of privacy (part of the liberty that cannot be denied without due process guaranteed by the Fourteenth Amendment) that protects their choice, during the time when the fetus is not viable, whether or not to have an abortion. Subsequent to the intense political controversy following the abortion decision, the Court backed off somewhat on the periphery of the abortion issue. In

Maher v. **Roe** and companion cases, the Court ruled that neither the federal government nor the states were compelled by the Constitution to pay for the abortions of poor women under medical assistance programs financed by government. *Maher* specifically denied any violation of the equal protection guarantee of the Fourteenth Amendment. In **Harris** v. **McRae** the Court specifically upheld the highly restrictive congressional provision known as the Hyde Amendment (after the sponsoring congressman). However, in *Bellotti* v. *Baird,* 443 U.S. 662 (1979), the Court ruled that the states could not impose certain obstacles on young women below the age of majority to deter them from exercising their right to have an abortion. But the Court did sustain a Utah criminal statute requiring parental notification before an abortion can be performed on a minor who lives with and is dependent upon a parent (*H.L.* v. *Matheson,* 450 U.S. 398 [1981]).

In cases decided in 1983, the Court struck down most but not all restrictions on second-trimester abortions. *City of Akron* v. *Akron Center for Reproductive Health,* 462 U.S. 416, saw the Court invalidate an Akron, Ohio, ordinance requiring all second-trimester abortions to be performed in a hospital as opposed to a clinic and requiring physicians to inform patients about the emotional complications following abortion and exactly what happens to the aborted fetus. The ordinance also had instituted a 24-hour waiting period. In *Planned Parenthood, Kansas City, Missouri* v. *Ashcroft,* 462 U.S. 476, the Court struck down that part of the Missouri abortion statute requiring hospitalization for all second-trimester abortions as unreasonably infringing upon a woman's constitutional right to obtain an abortion, but the Court upheld other provisions of the law including the requirement of a second physician's participation, the issuance of a pathology report, and the consent of the parents or guardians of immature minors before such minors underwent abortions. In **Thornburgh** v. **American College of Obstetri-**

cians, the Court struck down Pennsylvania's Abortion Control Act and reaffirmed *Roe* v. *Wade.* Anti-abortion Missouri law returned to the Court three years later, a Court now with two new Reagan associate justices and William Rehnquist elevated by Reagan to the chief justiceship. The Court in **Webster** v. **Reproductive Health Services,** with a new 5–4 majority, upheld the Missouri regulations and restrictions concerning abortion, clearly undermining *Roe* v. *Wade.* In 1990, the Court upheld restrictive state laws on abortion concerning the abortion rights of unmarried women under the age of eighteen. In **Hodgson** v. **Minnesota** (reprinted at the end of this book) the Court ruled it was constitutional to require that two parents be notified but only if there was a judicial bypass option. One-parent notification was upheld in *Ohio* v. *Akron Center for Reproductive Health,* 110 S.Ct. 2972 (1990).

In 1971 the Court first began questioning the rationality of state statutes that discriminate on the basis of sex in *Reed* v. *Reed,* 404 U.S. 71. In that decision, the Court struck down as unconstitutional an Idaho law that made it mandatory that when persons of both sexes are equally qualified to administer estates, males be preferred to females. The Court found this to be an arbitrary legislative choice that did not bear a rational relationship to a legitimate state objective, thereby violating the equal protection guarantee of the Fourteenth Amendment.

One of the landmark sexual equality decisions of the Supreme Court was that in *Frontiero* v. *Richardson.* The Court by a vote of 8 to 1 ruled that the military's different (and not as liberal) treatment of women members of the armed forces as to dependent's benefits violated the equal protection component of the Fifth Amendment's due process clause. What makes this case of special interest is Justice Brennan's sweeping plurality opinion, which sought to make a dramatic advance in the constitutional adjudication of sexual discrimination claims. Because a majority did not join

the opinion, it did not become Court policy. Brennan nevertheless argued that classifications based on sex should be considered to be "inherently suspect," analogous to classifications based on race, thereby justifying a standard of "strict judicial scrutiny" of the asserted compelling governmental interest that supposedly justifies the classification. Had a majority accepted the use of "strict scrutiny" as the standard for examining sexual classifications, a difficult burden would have been placed on government to provide convincing evidence that there is a compelling governmental need for such classification. Three years later, however, in the subsequent sex discrimination case of **Craig** v. **Boren** a majority did accept an intermediate-level scrutiny somewhere between no scrutiny and strict scrutiny.

The Burger Court rejected numerous statutes that called for sexual discrimination in which women and men were treated differently, placing one sex at an advantage. Included in this category of cases are *Stanton* v. *Stanton,* 421 U.S. 7 (1975), in which the Court majority struck down as a violation of equal protection a Utah statute under which females attained the age of majority at 18 but males did not reach it until 21. In the case of *Taylor* v. *Louisiana,* 419 U.S. 522 (1975), and later in *Duren* v. *Missouri,* 439 U.S. 357 (1979), the Court rejected juror selection schemes that discriminated against women (but these were Sixth Amendment cases rather than equal protection ones). In 1975 the Court also invalidated, in *Weinberger* v. *Wiesenfeld,* 420 U.S. 636, the social security provision that granted special benefits to a widow with minor children but not to a widower also with young children. *Craig* v. *Boren* saw the Court declare as a violation of the equal protection clause an Oklahoma law barring the sale of 3.2 percent beer to males under the age of 21, but only prohibiting its sale to females under the age of 18. The Court, although not utilizing the strict scrutiny test (which is tantamount to a presumption of unconstitutionality), nevertheless found the statistical evidence offered by Oklahoma in defense of its statute unconvincing. Similarly in *Califano* v. *Goldfarb,* 430 U.S. 199 (1977), the Court invalidated the provision of the federal Social Security Act giving survivor's benefits to a widow but not to a widower unless he was dependent upon his wife for at least one-half of his income. It found the federal government's reasons in justification of the law to be inadequate. A similar state scheme under a Missouri workers' compensation program was struck down in *Wengler* v. *Druggists Mutual Insurance Co.,* 446 U.S. 142 (1980).

In *Califano* v. *Westcott,* 443 U.S. 76 (1979), the Court struck down a provision of the Social Security Act which governs the Aid to Families with Dependent Children, Unemployed Father Program. That provision offered benefits to families whose dependent children have been deprived of parental support because of the unemployment of the father but did not offer such benefits when the mother became unemployed. The Court reasoned that the gender classification of the program rested on sexist presumptions about the roles of father and mother that could not support the gender classification. As such it violated the due process clause of the Fifth Amendment. Sexual equality was further promoted in the decision in *Orr* v. *Orr,* 440 U.S. 268 (1979), in which the Court struck down as violating the equal protection guarantee of the Fourteenth Amendment an Alabama statute under which husbands but no wives were subject to pay alimony upon divorce. Alabama's use of gender in its statute was held not to be substantially related to the achievement of an important governmental objective and therefore could not satisfy the demands of the equal protection clause. Mississippi was told in *Mississippi University for Women* v. *Hogan,* 458 U.S. 718 (1982), that denial of admission to a qualified male because of his gender to a state-supported nursing school violated the equal protection guarantee. The Supreme Court told the United States Jaycees

in *Roberts* v. *United States Jaycees,* 468 U.S. 609 (1984), that government may prohibit it from using gender as a criterion for full membership in the organization (only men had been so admitted). This decision was reinforced by the ruling in **Board of Dirs. of Rotary International** v. **Rotary Club** and by *New York State Club Ass'n* v. *City of New York,* 487 U.S. 1 (1988). In **University of Pennsylvania** v. **EEOC** (reprinted at the end of this book), the Court rejected the University's claim that academic freedom would be compromised by the release of confidential peer review materials to the Equal Employment Opportunity Commission (EEOC) for the purpose of investigating a discrimination complaint against a woman professor denied tenure. These decisions placed First Amendment rights against the right of government to use its police power to eliminate discrimination on the basis of gender. Although in a constitutional sense First Amendment issues were treated by the Court, *Board of Dirs. of Rotary International* and *University of Pennsylvania* are included in this chapter because they fundamentally deal with the value of sexual equality.

Not all sexual classifications have been struck down by the Court. For example, in *Kahn* v. *Shevin,* 416 U.S. 351 (1974), the Court upheld a Florida law giving a $500 property tax exemption to widows but not to widowers. This differential treatment of the sexes, the Court found, *was* substantially related to the objective of the state to cushion the financial impact of spousal loss upon the sex for whom that loss imposes a disproportionately heavy burden. Women as a class, argued the Court, have suffered economic disadvantage such as job discrimination, and the Florida tax exemption helps to lessen the adverse economic impact of widowhood. In another case, *Geduldig* v. *Aiello,* 417 U.S. 484 (1974), the Court found that California's disability insurance program, which did not cover disability resulting from normal pregnancy, does *not* constitute invidious discrimination in violation of the equal protection clause. The majority argued that the state is not required to sacrifice the self-supporting nature of the program by adding additional risks of disability to those otherwise provided. In *Personnel Administrator of Massachusetts* v. *Feeney,* 442 U.S. 256 (1979), the Court rejected the sex discrimination claim of a Massachusetts woman challenging the state's veterans' preference program. The Court in **Rostker** v. **Goldberg** approved draft registration for men only. It also approved, in *Michael M.* v. *Superior Court of Sonoma County,* 450 U.S. 464 (1981), California's statutory rape law making it a crime to have sex with women under the age of 18 (unless, of course, married to the woman) but not with men under the same age.

In a significant statutory interpretation decision in 1984, *Grove City College* v. *Bell,* 465 U.S. 555, the Court interpreted Title IX of the 1972 Education Amendments to forbid sexual discrimination only in the program or activity actually receiving federal aid. Programs or activities of the college or university not receiving federal assistance were free to sexually discriminate if no other provision of federal law was violated. Congress subsequently enacted civil rights legislation designed to overturn the *Grove City* decision.

Title VII of the Civil Rights Act of 1964 as amended by subsequent legislation has also provided the basis for numerous sexual discrimination suits. The Court, in interpreting Title VII, has ruled, for example, that employer-based retirement programs may not offer women lower monthly retirement benefits than are offered to men who have made the same contributions to the plan (*Arizona Governing Committee* v. *Norris,* 463 U.S. 1073 [1983]). But this decision was not to be retroactively applied. Other examples include: *Hishon* v. *King & Spaulding,* 467 U.S. 69 (1984), in which the Court interpreted Title VII as forbidding sex-based discrimination in the decision of a law firm whether or not to promote

an associate to a full partnership; and *Meritor Savings Bank* v. *Vinson,* 477 U.S. 57 (1986), in which the Court interpreted Title VII as forbidding sexual harassment in the workplace and held that employers can be held responsible for harassment by a supervisor even if the employer was unaware that this form of sexual discrimination was occurring; **Johnson** v. **Transp. Agency, Santa Clara Cty. Cal.,** in which the Court upheld an affirmative action plan that took gender into account, and thus a woman rather than a man was given a promotion to a position in which women and minorities were traditionally underrepresented; and *Price Waterhouse* v. *Hopkins,* 109 S.Ct. 1775 (1989), concerning a woman who was refused admission as a partner in an accounting firm—the Court ruled that the firm did not prove that it would have made the same decision in the absence of discrimination and the standard of proof that must be used is the preponderance of the evidence. However, not all Title VII claims have met with success. For example, in *Lorance* v. *A.T.& T. Technologies, Inc.,* 109 S.Ct. 2261 (1989), the Court rejected a Title VII suit brought by female employees challenging their company's seniority system as discriminatory. The Court ruled that a claim of discrimination based on a seniority system that on its face was non-discriminatory must be filed within 300 days of the day when the system has gone into effect. Because this suit was filed after 300 days, the claim may not be filed. To give another example, in *Independent Fed. of Flight Attendants* v. *Zipes,* 109 S.Ct. 2732 (1989), the Court made it more difficult for winning plaintiffs in Title VII suits to collect attorney fees from the losing litigant.

THE IMPACT OF THE COURT'S DECISIONS

Table 19.1 summarizes the impact of selected Court decisions concerning sexual equality. The reprinted cases follow.

Table 19.1 THE IMPACT OF SELECTED COURT DECISIONS, SEXUAL EQUALITY CASES

Case	Year	Impact on Parties	Short-Run Impact	Long-Run Impact
Bradwell v. State of Illinois	1873	No impact as qualified women became eligible for admission to the Illinois bar before Court rendered its decision.	After case argued, Illinois enacted antisexist employment legislation. Supreme Court, however, in 1876 refused to admit a woman to practice. In 1879 Congress directed Court to admit qualified women.	A monument to sexism and symptomatic of male chauvinist views that were prevalent on the Court for close to a century afterwards.
Hoyt v. Florida	1961	Ms. Hoyt served her sentence.	Warren Court indicated unwillingness to use equal protection clause to protect rights of women.	Long-run impact limited as Burger Court overturned similar Louisiana law in 1975. See *Taylor v. Louisiana*, 419 U.S. 522.
Maher v. Roe	1977	Impact on needy women who were litigants in these cases unknown.	By Court not ruling that state Medicaid programs must fund elective abortions if they also fund normal deliveries, needy women find it more difficult to obtain abortions.	Uncertain.
Harris v. McRae	1980	Mrs. McRae had her abortion financed by Medicaid funds long before Court decision.	Drop in rate of abortions among Medicaid-eligible women. Decision praised by antiabortion groups and certain religious leaders but condemned by ACLU and Planned Parenthood.	Uncertain. Evidence suggests an increase may have occurred in deaths and serious health problems among poor women.
Frontiero v. Richardson	1973	Sharron Frontiero vindicated and collected dependent's benefit for her husband Joseph including back pay and allowances.	Ruling called into question both federal and state legislation providing different monetary benefits depending on the gender of the claimant. Led to further litigation.	Landmark sexual equality decision. May have lessened the urgency of the arguments favoring the Equal Rights Amendment.
Craig v. Boren	1976	Curtis Craig unaffected as he turned 21 when Court took the appeal. Licensed vendor also a party to suit has position vindicated. Ruling good for business.	Some states raise drinking age for both men and women.	Sexual equality precedent.
Rostker v. Goldberg	1981	Government wins and proceeds with draft registration for men.	Decision seen as setback to efforts to end all forms of sexual discrimination in the military.	Uncertain. May only have impact during wartime.

BRADWELL v. STATE OF ILLINOIS,
16 WALLACE 130 (1873)

Majority votes: 8
Dissenting votes: 1

Shortly after The Slaughterhouse Cases *(see chap. 6) were decided, the Court handed down its decision in the* Bradwell *case. From the standpoint of Mr. Justice Miller, this case was an example of what would follow in abundance had the Court given a broad interpretation to the privileges or immunities, due process, and equal protection clauses of the Fourteenth Amendment. For here, a woman, Myra Bradwell, editor of the* Chicago Legal News *(a respected legal periodical) and in all other respects (except her sex) "qualified" to be a lawyer under Illinois law, claimed that she had a constitutional right to practice law in the state of Illinois and that the Illinois Supreme Court could not refuse her a license to practice. The Illinois Supreme Court in 1869, in noting the state law, said: "That God designed the sexes to occupy different spheres of action, and that it belonged to men to make, apply, and execute the laws, was regarded as an almost axiomatic truth. In view of these facts, we are certainly warranted in saying that when the legislature gave to this court the power of granting licenses to practice law it was with not the slightest expectation, that this privilege would be extended to women." The appeal to the United States Supreme Court was argued on January 18, 1872. On March 22, 1872, the Illinois legislature enacted a law "that no person shall be precluded or debarred from any occupation, profession or employment (except military) on account of sex." The only other exception was elective office. Under the terms of the Illinois statute Myra Bradwell could receive a license from the state. But she did not apply for one and the Court took no judicial notice (the justices may have been unaware) of the new Illinois law. The case was placed on the Court's back burner for over a year so that the Court could first consider* The Slaughterhouse Cases. *The* Bradwell *decision was announced on April 15, 1873. Although the case presented the Court with a women's rights question, Justice Miller simply repeated the narrow view of privileges or immunities elaborated in* The Slaughterhouse Cases *decision. However, three of the* Slaughterhouse *dissenters concurred here in an opinion by Justice Bradley that contains the male chauvinist credo: "The paramount destiny and mission of women are to fulfill the noble and benign offices of wife and mother. This is the law of the Creator." Only the Chief Justice dissented, and he did so without an opinion.*

MR. JUSTICE MILLER delivered the opinion of the Court:. . . .

In regard to . . . [the Fourteenth] amendment, counsel for the plaintiff in this court truly says that there are certain privileges and immunities which belong to a citizen of the United States as such; otherwise it would be nonsense for the fourteenth amendment to prohibit a State from abridging them, and he proceeds to argue that admission to the bar of a State of a person who possesses the requisite learning and character is one of those which a State may not deny.

In this latter proposition we are not able to concur with counsel. We agree with him that there are privileges and immunities belonging to citizens of the United States, in that relation and character, and that it is these and these alone which a State is forbidden to abridge. But the right to admission to practice in the courts of a State is not one of them. This right in no sense depends on citizenship of the United States. It has not, as far as we know, ever been made in any State, or in any case, to depend on citizenship at all. Certainly many prominent and distinguished lawyers have been admitted to practice, both in the State and Federal courts, who were not citizens of the United States or of any State. But, on whatever basis this right may be placed, so far as it can have any relation to citizenship at all, it would seem that, as to the courts of a State, it would relate to citizenship of the State, and as to Federal courts, it would relate to citizenship of the United States.

The opinion just delivered in the *Slaughterhouse Cases* renders elaborate argument in the present case unnecessary; for, unless we are wholly and radically mistaken in the principles on which these cases are decided, the right to control and regulate the granting of [a] license to practice law in the courts of a State is one of those powers which are not transferred for its protection to the Federal government, and its exercise is in no manner governed or controlled by citizenship of the United States in the party seeking such license.

It is unnecessary to repeat the argument on which the judgment in those cases is founded. It is sufficient to say they are conclusive of the present case.

Judgment affirmed.

Mr. Justice Bradley [concurring]:

I concur in the judgment of the court in this case, by which the judgment of the Supreme Court of Illinois is affirmed, but not for the reasons specified in the opinion just read. . . .

. . . [T]he civil law, as well as nature herself, has always recognized a wide difference in the respective spheres and destinies of man and woman. Man is, or should be, woman's protector and defender. The natural and proper timidity and delicacy which belongs to the female sex evidently unfits it for many of the occupations of civil life. The constitution of the family organization, which is founded in the divine ordinance, as well as in the nature of things, indicates the domestic sphere as that which properly belongs to the domain and functions of womanhood. The harmony, not to say identity, of interests and views which belong, or should belong, to the family institution is repugnant to the idea of a woman adopting a distinct and independent career from that of her husband. So firmly fixed was this sentiment in the founders of the common law that it became a maxim of that system of jurisprudence that a woman had no legal existence separate from her husband, who was regarded as her head and representative in the social state; and, notwithstanding some recent modifications of this civil status, many of the special rules of law flowing from and dependent upon this cardinal principle still exist in full force in most States. One of these is, that a married woman is incapable, without her husband's consent, of making contracts which shall be binding on her or him. This very incapacity was one circumstance which the Supreme Court of Illinois deemed important in rendering a married woman incompetent fully to perform the duties and trusts that belong to the office of an attorney and counsellor.

It is true that many women are unmarried and not affected by any of the duties, complications, and incapacities arising out of the married state, but these are exceptions to the general rule. The paramount destiny and mission of woman are to fulfil the noble and benign offices of wife and mother. This is the law of the Creator. And the rules of civil society must be adapted to the general constitution of things, and cannot be based upon exceptional cases.

The humane movements of modern society, which have for their object the multiplication of avenues for woman's advancement, and of occupations adapted to her condition and sex, have my heartiest concurrence. But I am not prepared to say that it is one of her fundamental rights and privileges to be admitted into every office and position, including those which require highly special qualifications and demanding special responsibilities. In the nature of things it is not every citizen of every age, sex, and condition that is qualified for every calling and position. It is the prerogative of the legislator to prescribe regulations founded on nature, reason, and experience for the due admission of qualified persons to professions and callings demanding special skill and confidence. This fairly belongs to the police power of the State; and, in my opinion, in view of the peculiar characteristics, destiny, and mission of woman, it is within the province of the legislature to ordain what offices, positions, and callings shall be filled and discharged by men, and shall receive the benefit of those energies and responsibilities, and that decision and firmness which are presumed to predominate in the sterner sex.

For these reasons I think that the laws of Illinois now complained of are not obnoxious to the charge of abridging any of the privileges and immunities of citizens of the United States.

Mr. Justice Swayne and Mr. Justice Field concurred in the foregoing opinion of Mr. Justice Bradley.

Mr. Chief Justice Chase dissented from the judgment of the court, and from all the opinions.

HOYT v. FLORIDA,
368 U.S. 57 (1961)

The equal protection clause of the Fourteenth Amendment was not used by the Warren Court to protect women from sexual discrimination. Hoyt v. Florida concerned a Florida statute automatically excluding women from jury lists and granting them an absolute exemption from jury duty. Under the law, a woman could volunteer and be registered for jury duty. This law was challenged in the context of an appeal from a criminal conviction. Mrs. Hoyt was convicted of second-degree murder of her husband. Her trial was before an all-male jury. She claimed that the Florida statute granting women absolute exemption from jury duty prevented her from having a fair trial and that the statute was a violation of equal protection of the law. The Florida courts rejected this argument. Appeal was taken from the Florida Supreme Court.

Votes: Unanimous

Mr. Justice Harlan delivered the opinion of the Court: . . . .

At the core of appellant's argument is the claim that the nature of the crime of which she was convicted peculiarly demanded the inclusion of persons of her own sex on the jury. She was charged with killing her husband by assaulting him with a baseball bat. . . . It is claimed, in substance, that women jurors would have been more understanding or compassionate than men in assessing the quality of appellant's act and her defense of "temporary insanity." . . .

I. . . .

In the selection of jurors Florida has differentiated between men and women in two respects. It has given women an absolute exemption from jury duty based solely on their sex, no similar exemption obtaining as to men. And it has provided for its effectuation in a manner less onerous than that governing exemptions exercisable by men: women are not to be put on the jury list unless they have voluntarily registered for such service; men, on the other hand, even if entitled to an exemption, are to be included on the list unless they have filed a written claim of exemption as provided by law.

In neither respect can we conclude that Florida's statute is not "based on some reasonable classification," and that it is thus infected with unconstitutionality. Despite the enlightened emancipation of women from the restrictions and protections of bygone years, and their entry into many parts of community life formerly considered to be reserved to men, woman is still regarded as the center of home and family life. We cannot say that it is constitutionally impermissible for a State, acting in pursuit of the general welfare, to conclude that a woman should be relieved from the civic duty of jury service unless she herself determines that such service is consistent with her own special responsibilities. . . .

We cannot hold this statute as written offensive to the Fourteenth Amendment.

II. . . .

This case in no way resembles those involving race or color in which the circumstances shown were found by this Court to compel a conclusion of purposeful discriminatory exclusions from jury service. . . . There is present here neither the unfortunate atmosphere of ethnic or racial prejudices which underlay the situations depicted in those cases, nor the long course of discriminatory administrative practice which the statistical showing in each of them evinced.

In the circumstances here depicted, it indeed "taxes our credulity" to attribute to these adminis-

trative officials a deliberate design to exclude the very class whose eligibility for jury service the state legislature, after many years of contrary policy, had declared only a few years before. It is sufficiently evident from the record that the presence on the jury list of no more than ten or twelve women in the earlier years, and the failure to add in 1957 more women to those already on the list, are attributable not to any discriminatory motive, but to a purpose to put on the list only those women who might be expected to be qualified for service if actually called. Nor is there the slightest suggestion that the list was the product of any plan to place on it only women of a particular economic or other community or organizational group. . . .

Finally, the disproportion of women to men on the list independently carries no constitutional significance. In the administration of the jury laws proportional class representation is not a constitutionally required factor. . . .

Finding no substantial evidence whatever in this record that Florida has arbitrarily undertaken to exclude women from jury service, a showing which it was incumbent on appellant to make, we must sustain the judgment of the Supreme Court of Florida.

Affirmed.

CHIEF JUSTICE WARREN, MR. JUSTICE BLACK, and MR. JUSTICE DOUGLAS, concurring:

We cannot say from this record that Florida is not making a good faith effort to have women perform jury duty without discrimination on the ground of sex. Hence we concur in the result, for the reasons set forth in Part II of the Court's opinion.

BEAL v. DOE,
432 U.S. 438 (1977)
MAHER v. ROE,
432 U.S. 464 (1977)
POELKER v. DOE,
432 U.S. 519 (1977)

The decision in Roe v. Wade *produced considerable controversy. The opponents of the Court's abortion policy initially sought a constitutional amendment to overturn the decision, but when they realized the difficulty of achieving that objective they turned to other efforts to contain the practice of abortion. A major effort was made at the state and local level to prevent public funds from being used to pay for abortions sought by poor women. Pressure was also exerted to prevent public-supported hospitals from permitting abortions to be performed on their premises. The three cases that follow involve challenges to such state and local antiabortion policies.* Maher v. Roe *concerned a regulation of the Connecticut Welfare Department that limits state Medicaid benefits for first-trimester abortions to those that are "medically necessary" as certified by a physician. Susan Roe (not her real name), an indigent woman, sued Edward Maher, the Commissioner of Social Services of Connecticut, challenging the Connecticut regulation on both statutory and constitutional grounds. A three-judge federal district court invalidated the Connecticut regulation as a violation of the equal protection clause.* Beal v. Doe *concerned Pennsylvania regulations that also limited eligibility for Medicaid assistance for abortions to those indigent women for whom physicians would certify that abortions were medically necessary. The district court ruled that the regulations did not conflict with the federal statute that established the federally financed Medicaid program, but that they did violate the equal protection clause. The United States Court of Appeals reversed on the statutory issue and did not consider the constitutional ruling. The third case,* Poelker v. Doe, *involved a suit against the St. Louis Mayor, John Poelker, challenging the city's policy of prohibiting abortions in the two city-owned public hospitals. The federal district court ruled against Jane Doe, but the appeals court reversed, accepting her constitutional arguments. All three cases came to the Supreme Court and were decided at the same time.*

Majority votes: 6
Dissenting votes: 3

BEAL v. DOE

MR. JUSTICE POWELL delivered the opinion of the Court:

The issue in this case is whether Title XIX of the Social Security Act, 42 U.S.C. § 1396 *et seq.*, requires States that participate in the Medical Assistance Program (Medicaid) to fund the cost of nontherapeutic abortions. . . .

Title XIX makes no reference to abortions, or, for that matter, to any other particular medical procedure. Instead, the statute is cast in terms that require participating States to provide financial assistance with respect to five broad categories of medical treatment. But nothing in the statute suggests that participating States are required to fund every medical procedure that falls within the delineated categories of medical care. . . .

The thrust of respondents' argument is that the exclusion of nontherapeutic abortions from medicaid coverage is unreasonable on both economic and health grounds. The economic argument is grounded on the view that abortion is generally a less expensive medical procedure than childbirth. Since a pregnant woman normally will either have an abortion or carry her child full term, a State that elects not to fund nontherapeutic abortions will eventually be confronted with the greater expenses associated with childbirth. The corresponding health argument is based on the view that an early abortion poses less of a risk to the women's health than childbirth. Consequently, respondents argue, the economic and health considerations that ordinarily support the reasonableness of state limitations on financing of unnecessary medical services are not applicable to pregnancy.

Accepting respondents' assumptions as accurate, we do not agree that the exclusion of nontherapeutic abortions from medicaid coverage is unreasonable under Title XIX. As we acknowledged in *Roe* v. *Wade*, 410 U.S. 113 (1973), the State has a valid and important interest in encouraging childbirth. We expressly recognized in *Roe* the "important and legitimate interest [of the State] in protecting the potentiality of human life." That interest alone does not, at least until approximately the third trimester, become sufficiently compelling to justify unduly burdensome state interference with the woman's constitutionally protected privacy interest. But it is a significant state interest existing throughout the course of the woman's pregnancy. Respondents point to nothing in either the language or the legislative history of Title XIX that suggests that it is unreasonable for a participating State to further this unquestionably strong and legitimate interest in encouraging normal childbirth. Absent such a showing, we will not presume that Congress intended to condition a State's participation in the Medicaid Program on its willingness to undercut this important interest by subsidizing the costs of nontherapeutic abortions.

Our interpretation of the statute is reinforced by two other relevant considerations. First, when Congress passed Title XIX in 1965, nontherapeutic abortions were unlawful in most States. In view of the then prevailing state law, the contention that Congress intended to require—rather than permit—participating States to fund nontherapeutic abortions requires far more convincing proof than respondents have offered. Second, the Department of Health, Education, and Welfare, the agency charged with the administration of this complicated statute, takes the position that Title XIX allows—but does not mandate—funding for such abortions. . . .

We therefore hold that Pennsylvania's refusal to extend medicaid coverage to nontherapeutic abortions is not inconsistent with Title XIX. We make clear, however, that the federal statute leaves a State free to provide such coverage if it so desires. . . .

It is so ordered.

MR. JUSTICE BRENNAN, with whom MR. JUSTICE MARSHALL and MR. JUSTICE BLACKMUN join, dissenting: [omitted]

MR. JUSTICE MARSHALL, dissenting:

It is all too obvious that the governmental actions in these cases, ostensibly taken to "encourage" women to carry pregnancies to term, are in reality intended to impose a moral viewpoint that no State may constitutionally enforce. *Roe* v. *Wade,* 410 U.S. 113 (1973); *Doe* v. *Bolton,* 410 U.S. 179 (1973). Since efforts to overturn those decisions have been unsuccessful, the opponents of abortion have attempted every imaginable means to circumvent the commands of the Constitution and impose their moral choices upon the rest of society. The present cases involve the most vicious attacks yet devised. The impact of the regulations here falls tragically upon those among us least able to help or defend themselves. As the Court well knows, these regulations inevitably will have the practical effect of preventing nearly all poor women from obtaining safe and legal abortions.

The enactments challenged here brutally coerce poor women to bear children whom society will scorn for every day of their lives. Many thousands of unwanted minority and mixed race children now spend blighted lives in foster homes, orphanages, and "reform" schools. Many children of the poor will sadly attend second-rate segregated schools. And opposition remains strong against increasing AFDC benefits for impoverished mothers and children, so that there is little chance for the children to grow up in a decent environment. I am appalled at the ethical bankruptcy of those who preach a "right to life" that means, under present social policies, a bare existence in utter misery for so many poor women and their children.

The Court's insensitivity to the human dimension of these decisions is particularly obvious in its cursory discussion of respondents' equal protection claims in *Maher* v. *Roe.* That case points up once again the need for this Court to repudiate its outdated and intellectually disingenuous "two-tier"

equal protection analysis. As I have suggested before, this "model's two fixed modes of analysis, strict scrutiny and mere rationality, simply do not describe the inquiry the Court has undertaken—or should undertake—in equal protection cases." In the present case, in its evident desire to avoid strict scrutiny—or indeed any meaningful scrutiny—of the challenged legislation, which would almost surely result in its invalidation, the Court pulls from thin air a distinction between laws that absolutely prevent exercise of the fundamental right to abortion and those that "merely" make its exercise difficult for some people. . . .

MR. JUSTICE BLACKMUN, with whom MR. JUSTICE BRENNAN and MR. JUSTICE MARSHALL join, dissenting:

The Court today, by its decisions in these cases, allows the States, and such municipalities as choose to do so, to accomplish indirectly what the Court in *Roe* v. *Wade,* 410 U.S. 113 (1973), and *Doe* v. *Bolton,* 410 U.S. 179 (1973)—by a substantial majority and with some emphasis, I had thought—said they could not do directly. The Court concedes the existence of a constitutional right but denies the realization and enjoyment of that right on the ground that existence and realization are separate and distinct. For the individual woman concerned, indigent and financially helpless, as the Court's opinions in the three cases concede her to be, the result is punitive and tragic. Implicit in the Court's holdings in the condescension that she may go elsewhere for her abortion. I find that disingenuous and alarming, almost reminiscent of "let them eat cake." . . .

MAHER V. ROE

MR. JUSTICE POWELL delivered the opinion of the Court:

In *Beal* v. *Doe,* we hold today that Title XIX of the Social Security Act does not require the funding of nontherapeutic abortions as a condition of participation in the joint federal-state medicaid program established by that statute. In this case, as a result of our decision in *Beal,* we must decide whether the Constitution requires a participating State to pay for nontherapeutic abortions when it pays for childbirth. . . .

The Constitution imposes no obligation on the States to pay the pregnancy-related medical expenses of indigent women, or indeed to pay any of the medical expenses of indigents. But when a State decides to alleviate some of the hardships of poverty by providing medical care, the manner in which it dispenses benefits is subject to constitutional limitations. Appellees' claim is that Connecticut must accord equal treatment to both abortion and childbirth, and may not evidence a policy preference by funding only the medical expenses incident to childbirth. This challenge to the classifications established by the Connecticut regulation presents a question arising under the Equal Protection Clause of the Fourteenth Amendment. . . .

This case involves no discrimination against a suspect class. An indigent woman desiring an abortion does not come within the limited category of disadvantaged classes so recognized by our cases. Nor does the fact that the impact of the regulation falls upon those who cannot pay lead to a different conclusion. In a sense, every denial of welfare to an indigent creates a wealth classification as compared to nonindigents who are able to pay for the desired goods or services. But this Court has never held that financial need alone identifies a suspect class for purposes of equal protection analysis. Accordingly, the central question in this case is whether the regulation "impinges upon a fundamental right explicitly or implicitly protected by the Constitution." The District Court read our decisions in *Roe* v. *Wade,* and the subsequent cases applying it, as establishing a fundamental right to abortion and therefore concluded that nothing less than a compelling state interest would justify Connecticut's different treatment of abortion and childbirth. We think the District Court misconceived the nature and scope of the fundamental right recognized in *Roe.* . . .

The Connecticut regulation before us is different in kind from the laws invalidated in our previous abortion decisions. The Connecticut regulation places no obstacles—absolute or otherwise—in the pregnant woman's path to an abortion. An indigent woman who desires an abortion suffers no disadvantage as a consequence of Connecticut's decision to fund childbirth; she continues as before to be dependent on private sources for the service she desires. The State may have made childbirth a more attractive alternative, thereby influencing the woman's decision, but it has imposed no restriction on access to abortions that was not already there. The indigency that may make it difficult—and in some cases, perhaps, impossible—for some women to have abortions is neither created nor in any way affected by the Connecticut regulation. We conclude that the Connecticut regulation does not impinge upon the fundamental right recognized in *Roe.*

Our conclusion signals no retreat from *Roe* or the cases applying it. There is a basic difference between direct state interference with a protected activity and state encouragement of an alternative activity consonant with legislative policy. Constitutional concerns are greatest when the State attempts to impose its will by force of law; the State's power to encourage actions deemed to be in the public interest is necessarily far broader. . . .

The question remains whether Connecticut's regulation can be sustained under the less demanding test of rationality that applies in the absence of a suspect classification or the impingement of a fundamental right. This test requires that the distinction drawn between childbirth and nontherapeutic abortion by the regulation be "rationally related" to a "constitutionally permissible" purpose. We hold that the Connecticut funding scheme satisfies this standard.

Roe itself explicitly acknowledged the State's strong interest in protecting the potential life of the fetus. . . . The State unquestionably has a "strong and legitimate interest in encouraging normal childbirth," an interest honored over the centuries. . . . The subsidizing of costs incident to childbirth is a rational means of encouraging childbirth.

We certainly are not unsympathetic to the plight of an indigent woman who desires an abortion, but "the Constitution does not provide judicial remedies for every social and economic ill." Our cases uniformly have accorded the States a wider latitude in choosing among competing demands for limited public funds. . . .

In conclusion, we emphasize that our decision today does not proscribe government funding of nontherapeutic abortions. It is open to Congress to require provision of medicaid benefits for such abortions as a condition of state participation in the medicaid program. Also, under Title XIX as construed in *Beal* v. *Doe,* Connecticut is free—through normal democratic processes—to decide that such benefits should be provided. We hold only that the Constitution does not require a judicially imposed resolution of these difficult issues. . . .

The judgment of the District Court is reversed, and the case is remanded for further proceedings consistent with this opinion.

MR. CHIEF JUSTICE BURGER, concurring: [omitted]

MR. JUSTICE BRENNAN, with whom MR. JUSTICE MARSHALL and MR. JUSTICE BLACKMUN join, dissenting:. . . .

Until today, I had not thought the nature of the fundamental right established in *Roe* was open to question, let alone susceptible to the interpretation advanced by the Court. The fact that the Connecticut scheme may not operate as an absolute bar preventing all indigent women from having abortions is not critical. What is critical is that the State has inhibited their fundamental right to make that choice free from state interference. . . .

POELKER v. DOE
PER CURIAM . . .

We agree that the constitutional question presented here is identical in principle with that presented by a State's refusal to provide medicaid benefits for abortions while providing them for childbirth. This was the issue before us in *Maher* v. *Roe.* For the reasons set forth in our opinion in that case, we find no constitutional violation by the city of St. Louis in electing, as a policy choice, to provide publicly financed hospital services for childbirth without providing corresponding services for nontherapeutic abortions. We merely hold, for the reasons stated in *Maher,* that the Constitution does not forbid a State or city, pursuant to democratic processes, from expressing a preference for normal childbirth as St. Louis has done.

The judgment of the Court of Appeals for the Eighth Circuit is reversed, and the case is remanded for further proceedings consistent with this opinion.

MR. JUSTICE BRENNAN, with whom MR. JUSTICE MARSHALL and MR. JUSTICE BLACKMUN join, dissenting:

. . . . Here the fundamental right of a woman freely to choose to terminate her pregnancy has been infringed by the city of St. Louis through a deliberate policy based on opposition to elective abortions on moral grounds by city officials. . . . The importance of today's decision is greatly magnified by the fact that during 1975 and the first quarter of 1976 only about 18% of all public hospitals in the country provided abortion services, and in 10 States there were no public hospitals providing such services. . . .

The Court's holding will . . . pose difficulties in small communities where the public hospital is the only nearby health care facility. If such a public hospital is closed to abortions, any woman—rich or poor—will be seriously inconvenienced; and for some women—particularly poor women—the unavailability of abortions in the public hospital will be an insuperable obstacle. . . .

Because the city policy constitutes "coercion [of women] to bear children they do not wish to bear," *Roe* v. *Wade* and the cases following it require that the city show a compelling state interest that justifies this infringement upon the fundamen-

tal right to choose to have an abortion. "[E]xpressing a preference for normal childbirth," does not satisfy that standard. . . . St. Louis' policy . . . "unduly burdens the right to seek an abortion," *Bellotti* v. *Baird,* 428 U.S. 132, 147 (1976).

I would affirm the Court of Appeals.

HARRIS v. McRAE,
448 U.S. 297 (1980)

Representative Henry J. Hyde sponsored an amendment to Title XIX of the Social Security Act to limit severely the use of any federal funds to reimburse the cost of abortions under the Medicaid program. Under the version applicable for fiscal 1980, federal funds are to be used only when the life of the mother would be endangered if the fetus were carried to term or if the woman was the victim of rape or incest that "has been reported promptly to a law enforcement agency or public health service." When the Hyde Amendment was first enacted in 1976, Medicaid recipient Cora McRae, a 24-year-old Brooklyn woman in her first trimester, was refused an abortion although she suffered from various health problems and claimed that pregnancy was detrimental to her health. Mrs. McRae and the New York City Health and Hospitals Corporation went to court to enjoin the enforcement of the funding restriction on abortion. Three weeks later federal District Judge John F. Dooling, Jr., entered a preliminary injunction prohibiting the Secretary of Health, Education, and Welfare from enforcing the Hyde Amendment and requiring the continuation of federal reimbursements for abortions. Judge Dooling also certified the case as a class action. (Mrs. McRae then had her abortion, paid for by Medicaid.) The Secretary appealed the injunction, but the Supreme Court remanded the case in light of its rulings in Beal *and in* Maher. *Judge Dooling subsequently heard from dozens of witnesses. Finally, on January 15, 1980, he struck down all versions of the Hyde Amendment on constitutional grounds in an opinion whose length was 622 pages. Appeal was taken to the Supreme Court.*

Majority votes: 5
Dissenting votes: 4

MR. JUSTICE STEWART delivered the opinion of the Court: . . . .

Although the liberty protected by the Due Process Clause affords protection against unwarranted governmental interference with freedom of choice in the context of certain personal decisions, it does not confer an entitlement to such funds as may be necessary to realize all the advantages of that freedom. To hold otherwise would mark a drastic change in our understanding of the Constitution. It cannot be that because government may not prohibit the use of contraceptives, *Griswold* v. *Connecticut,* 381 U.S. 479, or prevent parents from sending their child to a private school, *Pierce* v. *Society of Sisters,* 268 U.S. 510, government, therefore, has an affirmative constitutional obligation to ensure that all persons have the financial resources to obtain contraceptives or send their children to private schools. To translate the limitation on governmental power implicit in the Due Process Clause into an affirmative obligation would require Congress to subsidize the medically necessary abortion of an indigent woman even if Congress had not enacted a Medicaid program to subsidize other medically necessary services. Nothing in the Due Process Clause supports such an extraordinary result. . . . Accordingly, we conclude that the Hyde Amendment does not impinge on the due process liberty recognized in [*Roe* v.] *Wade.* . . .

It remains to be determined whether the Hyde Amendment violates the equal protection component of the Fifth Amendment. This challenge is premised on the fact that, although federal reimbursement is available under Medicaid for medically necessary services generally, the Hyde Amendment does not permit federal reimbursement of all medically necessary abortions. The District Court held, and the appellees argue here, that this selective subsidization violates the constitutional guarantee of equal protection.

The guarantee of equal protection under the Fifth Amendment is not a source of substantive rights or liberties, but rather a right to be free from invidious discrimination in statutory classifications and other governmental activity. It is well-settled that where a statutory classification does not itself impinge on a right or liberty protected by the Constitution, the validity of classification must be sustained unless "the classification rests on grounds wholly irrelevant to the achievement of [any legitimate governmental] objective." This presumption of constitutional validity, however, disappears if a statutory classification is predicated on criteria that are, in a constitutional sense, "suspect," the principal example of which is a classification based on race, e.g., *Brown* v. *Board of Education,* 347 U.S. 483.

For the reasons stated above, we have already concluded that the Hyde Amendment violates no constitutionally protected substantive rights. We now conclude as well that it is not predicated on a constitutionally suspect classification. In reaching this conclusion, we again draw guidance from the Court's decision in *Maher* v. *Roe.* . . . It is our view that the present case is indistinguishable from *Maher* in this respect. Here, as in *Maher,* the principal impact of the Hyde Amendment falls on the indigent. But that fact does not itself render the funding restriction constitutionally invalid, for this Court has held repeatedly that poverty, standing alone, is not a suspect classification. That *Maher* involved the refusal to fund nontherapeutic abortions, whereas the present case involves the refusal to fund medically necessary abortions, has no bearing on the factors that render a classification "suspect" within the meaning of the constitutional guarantee of equal protection.

The remaining question then is whether the Hyde Amendment is rationally related to a legitimate governmental objective. It is the Government's position that the Hyde Amendment bears a rational relationship to its legitimate interest in protecting the potential life of the fetus. We agree. . . . By subsidizing the medical expenses of indigent women who carry their pregnancies to term while not subsidizing the comparable expenses of women who undergo abortions (except those whose lives are threatened), Congress has established incentives that make childbirth a more attractive alternative than abortion for persons eligible for Medicaid. These incentives bear a direct relationship to the legitimate congressional interest in protecting potential life. Nor is it irrational that Congress has authorized federal reimbursement for medically necessary services generally, but not for certain medically necessary abortions. Abortion is inherently different from other medical procedures, because no other procedure involves the purposeful termination of a potential life. . . .

Where, as here, the Congress has neither invaded a substantive constitutional right or freedom, nor enacted legislation that purposefully operates to the detriment of a suspect class, the only requirement of equal protection is that congressional action be rationally related to a legitimate governmental interest. The Hyde Amendment satisfies that standard. It is not the mission of this Court or any other to decide whether the balance of competing interests reflected in the Hyde Amendment is wise social policy. If that were our mission, not every Justice who has subscribed to the judgment of the Court today could have done so. But we cannot, in the name of the Constitution, overturn duly enacted statutes simply "because they may be unwise, improvident, or out of harmony with a particular school of thought." Rather, "when an issue involves policy choices as sensitive as those implicated [here] . . ., the appropriate forum for their resolution in a democracy is the legislature," *Maher* v. *Roe,* at 479. . . . Accordingly, the judgment of the District Court is reversed, and the case is remanded to that court for further proceedings consistent with this opinion.

It is so ordered.

MR. JUSTICE WHITE, concurring: [omitted]

MR. JUSTICE BRENNAN, with whom MR. JUSTICE MARSHALL and MR. JUSTICE BLACKMUN join, dissenting:

I agree entirely with my Brother Stevens that the State's interest in protecting the potential life of the fetus cannot justify the exclusion of financially and medically needy women from the benefits to which they would otherwise be entitled solely because the treatment that a doctor has concluded is medically necessary involves an abortion. I write separately to express my continuing disagreement with the Court's mischaracterization of the nature of the fundamental right recognized in *Roe* v. *Wade,* and its misconception of the manner in which that right is infringed by federal and state legislation withdrawing all funding for medically necessary abortions. . . . The proposition for which these cases [*Roe* v. *Wade*] stand . . . is not that the State is under an affirmative obligation to ensure access to abortions for all who may desire them; it is that the State must refrain from wielding its enormous power and influence in a manner that might burden the pregnant woman's freedom to choose whether to have an abortion. . . .

MR. JUSTICE MARSHALL, dissenting: . . . .

The Court's opinion studiously avoids recognizing the undeniable fact that for women eligible for Medicaid—poor women—denial of a Medicaid-funded abortion is equivalent to denial of legal abortion altogether. By definition, these women do not have the money to pay for an abortion themselves. If abortion is medically necessary and a funded abortion is unavailable, they must resort to back-alley butchers, attempt to induce an abortion themselves by crude and dangerous methods, or suffer the serious medical consequences of attempting to carry the fetus to term. . . .

MR. JUSTICE BLACKMUN, dissenting: [omitted]

MR. JUSTICE STEVENS, dissenting: [omitted]

THORNBURGH v. AMERICAN COLLEGE OF OBSTETRICIANS, 476 U.S. 747 (1986)

At issue in this case was the Pennsylvania Abortion Control Act of 1982, which contained numerous restrictions on the performing of abortions. The act was challenged as unconstitutional by the Pennsylvania section of the American College of Obstetricians and Gynecologists. There were other plaintiffs as well, including individual physicians, members of the clergy, and Pennsylvania abortion counselors and providers. They sought a preliminary injunction to prevent state officials from enforcing the act and a declaratory judgment that the Pennsylvania law violated the Constitution. Governor Richard Thornburgh (later to be Attorney General in the Reagan and Bush Administrations) and other officials were named in the suit. The federal district court denied the motion for a preliminary injunction except as to one provision of the act, the 24-hour waiting period, which it held was invalid. The plaintiffs appealed to the United States Court of Appeals for the Third Circuit from the denial of the preliminary injunction, and the state officials cross-appealed with respect to the one provision that the district court struck down. The appeals court granted the preliminary injunction and eventually ruled unconstitutional various provisions of the act. The Supreme Court in deciding this case took the opportunity to reaffirm Roe v. Wade *but only by a 5–4 vote.*

Majority votes: 5
Dissenting votes: 4

JUSTICE BLACKMUN delivered the opinion of the Court: . . . .

This case, as it comes to us, concerns the constitutionality of six provisions of the Pennsylvania [Abortion Control] Act that the Court of Appeals struck down as facially invalid: §3205 ("informed consent"); §3208 ("printed information"); §3214(a) and (h) (reporting requirements); §3211(a) (determination of viability); §3210(b) (degree of care required in postviability abortions); and §3210(c) (second-physician requirement). . . .

Less than three years ago, this Court, in *Akron, Ashcroft,* and *Simopoulos,* reviewed challenges to state and municipal legislation regulating the performance of abortions. In *Akron,* the Court specifically reaffirmed *Roe* v. *Wade,* 410 U.S. 113 (1973). Again today, we reaffirm the general principles laid down in *Roe* and in *Akron.*

In the years since this Court's decision in *Roe,* States and municipalities have adopted a number of measures seemingly designed to prevent a woman, with the advice of her physician, from exercising her freedom of choice. *Akron* is but one example. But the constitutional principles that led this Court to its decisions in 1973 still provide the compelling reason for recognizing the constitutional dimensions of a woman's right to decide whether to end her pregnancy. . . . The States are not free, under the guise of protecting maternal health or potential life, to intimidate women into continuing pregnancies. Appellants claim that the statutory provisions before us today further legitimate compelling interests of the Commonwealth. Close analysis of those provisions, however, shows that they wholly subordinate constitutional privacy interests and concerns with maternal health in an effort to deter a woman from making a decision that, with her physician, is hers to make.

We turn to the challenged statutes:

1. Section 3205 ("informed consent") and §3208 ("printed information"). Section 3205(a) requires that the woman give her "voluntary and informed consent" to an abortion. Failure to observe the provisions of §3205 subjects the physician to suspension or revocation of his license, and subjects any other person obligated to provide information relating to informed consent to criminal penalties. §3205(c). A requirement that the woman give what is truly a voluntary and informed consent, as a general proposition, is, of course, proper and is surely not unconstitutional. But the State may not require the delivery of information designed "to influence the woman's informed choice between abortion or childbirth." *Akron,* 462 U.S., at 443–444. . . .

We conclude that, like Akron's ordinance, §§3205 and 3208 fail the *Akron* measurement. The two sections prescribe in detail the method for securing "informed consent." Seven explicit kinds of information must be delivered to the woman at least 24 hours before her consent is given, and five of these must be presented by the woman's physician. The five are: (a) the name of the physician who will perform the abortion, (b) the "fact that there may be detrimental physical and psychological effects which are not accurately foreseeable," (c) the "particular medical risks associated with the particular abortion procedure to be employed," (d) the probable gestational age, and (e) the "medical risks associated with carrying her child to term." The remaining two categories are (f) the "fact that medical assistance benefits may be available for prenatal care, childbirth and neonatal care," and (g) the "fact that the father is liable to assist" in the child's support, "even in instances where the father has offered to pay for the abortion." §§3205(a)(1) and (2). The woman also must be informed that materials printed and supplied by the Commonwealth that describe the fetus and that list agencies offering alternatives to abortion are available for her review. If she chooses to review the materials but is unable

to read, the materials "shall be read to her," and any answer she seeks must be "provided her in her own language." She must certify in writing, prior to the abortion, that all this has been done. . . .

. . . The printed materials required by §§3205 and 3208 seem to us to be nothing less than an outright attempt to wedge the Commonwealth's message discouraging abortion into the privacy of the informed-consent dialogue between the woman and her physician. The mandated description of fetal characteristics at 2-week intervals, no matter how objective, is plainly overinclusive. This is not medical information that is always relevant to the woman's decision, and it may serve only to confuse and punish her and to heighten her anxiety, contrary to accepted medical practice. . . . Forcing the physician or counselor to present the materials and the list to the woman makes him or her in effect an agent of the State in treating the woman and places his or her imprimatur upon both the materials and the list. All this is, or comes close to being, state medicine imposed upon the woman, not the professional medical guidance she seeks, and it officially structures—as it obviously was intended to do—the dialogue between the woman and her physician.

The requirements of §3205(a)(2)(i) and (ii) that the woman be advised that medical assistance benefits may be available and that the father is responsible for financial assistance in the support of the child similarly are poorly disguised elements of discouragement for the abortion decision. Much of this would be nonmedical information beyond the physician's area of expertise and, for many patients, would be irrelevant and inappropriate. For a patient with a life-threatening pregnancy, the "information" in its very rendition may be cruel as well as destructive of the physician-patient relationship. As any experienced social worker or other counsellor knows, theoretical financial responsibility often does not equate with fulfillment. And a victim of rape should not have to hear gratuitous advice that an unidentified perpetrator is liable for support if she continues the pregnancy to term. Under the guise of informed consent, the Act requires the dissemination of information that is not relevant to such consent, and, thus, it advances no legitimate state interest.

The requirements of §3205(a)(1)(ii) and (iii) that the woman be informed by the physician of "detrimental physical and psychological effects" and of all "particular medical risks" compound the problem of medical attendance, increase the patient's anxiety, and intrude upon the physician's exercise of proper professional judgment. This type of compelled information is the antithesis of informed consent. That the Commonwealth does not, and surely would not, compel similar disclosure of every possible peril of necessary surgery or of simple vaccination, reveals the anti-abortion character of the statute and its real purpose. . . .

2. Section 3211(a) requires the physician to report the basis for his determination "that a child is not viable." It applies only after the first trimester. The report required by §3214(a) and (h) is detailed and must include, among other things, identification of the performing and referring physicians and of the facility or agency; information as to the woman's political subdivision and State of residence, age, race, marital status, and number of prior pregnancies; the date of her last menstrual period and the probable gestational age; the basis for any judgment that a medical emergency existed; the basis for any determination of nonviability; and the method of payment for the abortion. The report is to be signed by the attending physician.

Despite the fact that §3214(e)(2) provides that such reports "shall not be deemed public records," within the meaning of the Commonwealth's "Right-to-Know Law," each report "shall be made available for public inspection and copying within 15 days of receipt in a form which will not lead to the disclosure of the identity of any person filing a report." . . .

The scope of the information required and its availability to the public belie any assertions by the Commonwealth that it is advancing any legitimate interest. . . .

. . . The decision to terminate a pregnancy is an intensely private one that must be protected in a way that assures anonymity. A woman and her physician will necessarily be more reluctant to choose an abortion if there exists a possibility that her decision and her identity will become known publicly. Although the statute does not specifically require the reporting of the woman's name, the amount of information about her and the circumstances under which she had an abortion are so detailed that identification is likely. Identification is the obvious purpose of these extreme reporting requirements. . . . Pennsylvania's reporting requirements raise the spectre of public exposure and harassment of women who choose to exercise their personal, intensely private, right, with their physician, to end a pregnancy. Thus, they pose an unacceptable danger of deterring the exercise of that right, and must be invalidated. . . .

Constitutional rights do not always have easily ascertainable boundaries, and controversy over the meaning of our Nation's most majestic guarantees frequently has been turbulent. As judges, however, we are sworn to uphold the law even when its content gives rise to bitter dispute. We recognized at the very beginning of our opinion in *Roe* that abortion raises moral and spiritual questions over which honorable persons can disagree sincerely and profoundly. But those disagreements did not then and do not now relieve us of our duty to apply the Constitution faithfully.

Our cases long have recognized that the Constitution embodies a promise that a certain private sphere of individual liberty will be kept largely beyond the reach of government. . . . That promise extends to women as well as to men. Few decisions are more personal and intimate, more properly private, or more basic to individual dignity and autonomy, than a woman's decision—with the guidance of her physician and within the limits specified in *Roe*—whether to end her pregnancy. A woman's right to make that choice freely is fundamental. Any other result, in our view, would protect inadequately a central part of the sphere of liberty that our law guarantees equally to all.

The Court of Appeals correctly invalidated the specified provisions of Pennsylvania's 1982 Abortion Control Act. Its judgment is affirmed.

It is so ordered.

JUSTICE STEVENS, concurring:. . . .

. . . [T]he aspect of liberty at stake in this case is the freedom from unwarranted governmental intrusion into individual decisions in matters of childbearing. As JUSTICE WHITE explained in *Griswold,* that aspect of liberty comes to this Court with a momentum for respect that is lacking when appeal is made to liberties which derive merely from shifting economic arrangements.

Like the birth control statutes involved in *Griswold* and *Baird,* the abortion statutes involved in *Roe* v. *Wade,* and in the case before us today apply equally to decisions made by married persons and by unmarried persons. Consistently with his views in those cases, JUSTICE WHITE agrees that "a woman's ability to choose an abortion is a species of 'liberty' that is subject to the general protections of the Due Process Clause." His agreement with that "indisputable" proposition, is not qualified or limited to decisions made by pregnant women who are married and, indeed, it would be a strange form of liberty if it were so limited.

Up to this point in JUSTICE WHITE's analysis, his opinion is fully consistent with the accepted teachings of the Court and with the major premises of *Roe* v. *Wade.* For reasons that are not entirely clear, however, JUSTICE WHITE abruptly announces that the interest in "liberty" that is implicated by a decision not to bear a child that is made a few days after conception is *less* fundamental than a comparable decision made before conception. There may, of course, be a significant difference in the strength of the countervailing state interest, but I fail to see how a decision on childbearing becomes *less* important the day after conception than the day before. Indeed, if one decision is more "fundamental" to the individual's freedom than the other, surely it is the post-conception decision that is the more serious. Thus, it is difficult for me to understand how JUSTICE WHITE reaches the conclusion that restraints upon this aspect of a woman's liberty do not "call into play anything more than the most minimal judicial scrutiny." . . .

CHIEF JUSTICE BURGER, dissenting:. . . .

I based my concurring statements in *Roe* and *Maher* on the principle expressed in the Court's opinion in *Roe* that the right to an abortion "is not unqualified and must be considered against important state interests in regulation." In short, every member of the *Roe* Court rejected the idea of abortion on demand. The Court's opinion today, however, plainly undermines that important principle, and I regretfully conclude that some of the concerns of the dissenting Justices in *Roe,* as well as the concerns I expressed in my separate opinion, have now been realized. . . .

JUSTICE WHITE, with whom JUSTICE REHNQUIST joins, dissenting:

Today the Court carries forward the "difficult and continuing venture in substantive due process," that began with the decision in *Roe* v. *Wade,* and has led the Court further and further afield in the 13 years since that decision was handed down. I was in dissent in *Roe* v. *Wade* and am in dissent today. . . . I submit that even accepting *Roe* v. *Wade,* the concerns underlying that decision by no means command or justify the results reached today. Indeed, in my view, our precedents in this area, applied in a manner consistent with sound principles of constitutional adjudication, require reversal of the Court of Appeals on the ground that the provisions before us are facially constitutional. . . .

Fundamental liberties and interests are most clearly present when the Constitution provides specific textual recognition of their existence and importance. Thus, the Court is on relatively firm ground when it deems certain of the liberties set forth in the Bill of Rights to be fundamental and therefore finds them incorporated in the Fourteenth Amendment's guarantee that no State may deprive any person of liberty without due process of law.

When the Court ventures further and defines as "fundamental" liberties that are nowhere mentioned in the Constitution (or that are present only in the so-called "penumbras" of specifically enumerated rights), it must, of necessity, act with more caution, lest it open itself to the accusation that, in the name of identifying constitutional principles to which the people have consented in framing their Constitution, the Court has done nothing more than impose its own controversial choices of value upon the people.

Attempts to articulate the constraints that must operate upon the Court when it employs the Due Process Clause to protect liberties not specifically enumerated in the text of the Constitution have produced varying definitions of "fundamental liberties." One approach has been to limit the class of fundamental liberties to those interests that are "implicit in the concept of ordered liberty" such that "neither liberty nor justice would exist if [they] were sacrificed." *Palko* v. *Connecticut,* 302 U.S. 319, 325, 326 (1937). Another, broader approach is to define fundamental liberties as those that are "deeply rooted in this Nation's history and tradition." . . . What for me is not subject to debate, however, is that either of the basic definitions of fundamental liberties, taken seriously, indicates the illegitimacy of the Court's decision in *Roe* v. *Wade.* . . .

The Court's opinion in *Roe* itself convincingly refutes the notion that the abortion liberty is deeply rooted in the history or tradition of our people, as does the continuing and deep division of the people themselves over the question of abortion. As for the notion that choice in the matter of abortion is implicit in the concept of ordered liberty, it seems apparent to me that a free, egalitarian, and democratic society does not presuppose any particular rule or set of rules with respect to abortion. And again, the fact that many men and women of good will and high commitment to constitutional government place themselves on both sides of the abortion controversy strengthens my own conviction that the values animating the Constitution do not compel recognition of the abortion liberty as fundamental. In so denominating that liberty, the Court engages not in constitutional interpretation, but in the unrestrained imposition of its own, extraconstitutional value preferences. . . .

The governmental interest at issue is in protecting those who will be citizens if their lives are not ended in the womb. The substantiality of this interest is in no way dependent on the probability that the fetus may be capable of surviving outside the womb at any given point in its development, as the possibility of fetal survival is contingent on the state of medical practice and technology, factors that are in essence morally and constitutionally irrelevant. The State's interest is in the fetus as an entity in itself, and the character of this entity does not change at the point of viability under conventional medical wisdom. Accordingly, the State's interest, if compelling after viability, is equally compelling before viability.

Both the characterization of the abortion liberty as fundamental and the denigration of the State's interest in preserving the lives of nonviable fetuses are essential to the detailed set of constitutional rules devised by the Court to limit the States' power to regulate abortion. If either or both of these facets of *Roe* v. *Wade* were rejected, a broad range of limitations on abortion (including outright prohibition) that are now unavailable to the States would again become constitutional possibilities.

In my view, such a state of affairs would be highly desirable from the standpoint of the Constitution. Abortion is a hotly contested moral and political issue. Such issues, in our society, are to be resolved by the will of the people, either as expressed through legislation or through the general principles they have already incorporated into the Constitution they have adopted. *Roe* v. *Wade* implies that the people have already resolved the debate by weaving into the Constitution the values and principles that answer the issue. As I have argued, I believe it is clear that the people have never—not in 1787, 1791, 1868, or at any time since—done any such thing. I would return the issue to the people by overruling *Roe* v. *Wade*. . . .

The Court begins by striking down statutory provisions designed to ensure that the woman's choice of an abortion is fully informed—that is, that she is aware not only of the reasons for having an abortion, but also of the risks associated with an abortion and the availability of assistance that might make the alternative of normal childbirth more attractive than it might otherwise appear. At first blush, the Court's action seems extraordinary: after all, *Roe* v. *Wade* purports to be about freedom of choice, and statutory provisions requiring that a woman seeking an abortion be afforded information regarding her decision not only do not limit her ability to choose abortion, but would also appear to enhance her freedom of choice by helping to ensure that her decision whether or not to terminate her pregnancy is an informed one. Indeed, maximization of the patient's freedom of choice—not restriction of his or her liberty—is generally perceived to be the principal value justifying the imposition of disclosure requirements upon physicians. . . .

One searches the majority's opinion in vain for a convincing reason why the apparently laudable policy of promoting informed consent becomes unconstitutional when the subject is abortion. . . .

Why, then, is the statute unconstitutional? The majority's argument, while primarily rhetorical, appears to offer three answers. First, the information that must be provided will in some cases be irrelevant to the woman's decision. This is true. Its pertinence to the question of the statute's constitutionality, however, is beyond me. . . .

Second, the majority appears to reason that the informed consent provisions are invalid because the information they require may increase the woman's "anxiety" about the procedure and even "influence" her in her choice. Again, both observations are undoubtedly true; but they by no means cast the constitutionality of the provisions into question. It is in the very nature of informed consent provisions that they may produce some anxiety in the patient and influence her in her choice. This is in fact their reason for existence, and—provided that the information required is accurate and nonmisleading—it is an entirely salutary reason. If information may reasonably affect the patient's choice, the patient should have that information. . . .

Third, the majority concludes that the informed consent provisions . . . constitute "state medicine" that "infringes upon [the physician's] professional responsibilities." This is nonsensical. I can concede that the Constitution extends its protection to certain zones of personal autonomy and privacy, and I can understand, if not share, the notion that that protection may extend to a woman's decision regarding abortion. But I cannot concede the possibility that the Constitution provides more than minimal protection for the manner in which a physician practices his or her profession or for the "dialogues" in which he or she chooses to participate in the course of treating patients. I had thought it clear that regulation of the practice of medicine, like regulation of other professions and of economic affairs generally, was a matter peculiarly within the competence of legislatures, and that such regulation was subject to review only for rationality. See *e.g.,* *Williamson* v. *Lee Optical*, 348 U.S. 483 (1955). . . .

The decision today appears symptomatic of the Court's own insecurity over its handiwork in *Roe* v. *Wade* and the cases following that decision. Aware that in *Roe* it essentially created something out of nothing and that there are many in this country who hold that decision to be basically illegitimate, the Court responds defensively. Perceiving, in a statute implementing the State's legitimate policy of preferring childbirth to abortion, a threat to or criticism of the decision in *Roe* v. *Wade*, the majority indiscriminately strikes down statutory provisions that in no way contravene the right recognized in *Roe*. I do not share the warped point of view of the majority, nor can I follow the tortuous path the majority treads in proceeding to strike down the statute before us. I dissent.

JUSTICE O'CONNOR, with whom JUSTICE REHNQUIST joins, dissenting:

This Court's abortion decisions have already worked a major distortion in the Court's constitutional jurisprudence. Today's decision goes further, and makes it painfully clear that no legal rule or doctrine is safe from ad hoc nullification by this Court when an occasion for its application arises in a case involving state regulation of abortion. . . .

WEBSTER v. REPRODUCTIVE HEALTH SERVICES, 109 S. Ct. 3040 (1989)

There was no decision in 1989 more anticipated than this one. The Reagan Administration had urged the Supreme Court to use this case as the basis for overturning Roe v. Wade. *Prochoice organizations used this case to dramatize the threat to* Roe *and staged a massive rally in Washington on April 9, 1989, that attracted as many as half a million people, probably the largest one ever held to date. The decision, handed down on the last day of the Term, July 3, 1989, although it did not explicitly overturn* Roe, *was enormously controversial. The case itself concerned the constitutionality of a Missouri statute regulating abortion which included a preamble asserting that "life . . . begins at conception." A nonprofit corporation, Reproductive Health Services, which offers family planning and gynecological services to the public, including abortion services, along with Planned Parenthood of Kansas City, and five health professionals employed by Missouri, brought a suit in federal district court. They named Missouri Attorney General William L. Webster and other state officials and asked the Court to declare the law unconstitutional and to issue an injunction preventing its enforcement. The district court struck down the law and enjoined its enforcement. The Court of Appeals for the Eighth Circuit affirmed. Missouri took the case to the Supreme Court.*

Majority votes: 5
Dissenting votes: 4

CHIEF JUSTICE REHNQUIST announced the judgment of the Court and delivered the opinion of the Court with respect to Parts I, II-A, II-B, and II-C, and an opinion with respect to Parts II-D and III, in which JUSTICE WHITE and JUSTICE KENNEDY join:

This appeal concerns the constitutionality of a Missouri statute regulating the performance of abortions. The United States Court of Appeals for the Eighth Circuit struck down several provisions of the statute on the ground that they violated this Court's decision in *Roe* v. *Wade*, 410 U.S. 113 (1973), and cases following it. We noted probable jurisdiction and now reverse. . . .

I. . .

II

Decision of this case requires us to address four sections of the Missouri Act: (a) the preamble; (b) the prohibition on the use of public facilities or employees to perform abortions; (c) the prohibition on public funding of abortion counseling; and (d) the requirement that physicians conduct viability tests prior to performing abortions. We address these *seriatim*.

A

The Act's preamble . . . sets forth "findings" by the Missouri legislature that "[t]he life of each human being begins at conception," and that "[u]nborn children have protectable interests in life, health, and well-being." The Act then mandates that state laws be interpreted to provide unborn children with "all the rights, privileges, and immunities available to other persons, citizens, and residents of this state," subject to the Constitution and this Court's precedents. In invalidating the preamble, the Court of Appeals relied on this Court's dictum that " 'a State may not adopt one theory of when life begins to justify its regulation of abortions.' " . . . It rejected Missouri's claim that the preamble was "abortion-neutral," and "merely determine[d] when life begins in a nonabortion context, a traditional state prerogative." . . . . The court thought that "[t]he only plausible inference" from the fact that "every remaining section of the bill save one regulates the performance of abortions" was that "the state intended its abortion regulations to be understood against the backdrop of its theory of life."

The State contends that the preamble itself is precatory and imposes no substantive restrictions on abortions, and that appellees therefore do not have standing to challenge it. Appellees, on the other hand, insist that the preamble is an operative part of the Act intended to guide the interpretation of other provisions of the Act. They maintain, for example, that the preamble's definition of life may prevent physicians in public hospitals from dispensing certain forms of contraceptives, such as the intrauterine device. . . .

Certainly the preamble does not by its terms regulate abortion or any other aspect of appellees' medical practice. The Court has emphasized that *Roe* v. *Wade* "implies no limitation on the authority of a State to make a value judgment favoring childbirth over abortion." The preamble can be read simply to express that sort of value judgment.

We think the extent to which the preamble's language might be used to interpret other state statutes or regulations is something that only the courts of Missouri can definitively decide. State law has offered protections to unborn children in tort and probate law, and § 1.205.2 can be interpreted to do no more than that. . . . It will be time enough for federal courts to address the meaning of the preamble should it be applied to restrict the activities of appellees in some concrete way. Until then, this Court "is not empowered to decide . . . abstract propositions, or to declare, for the government of future cases, principles or rules of law which cannot affect the result as to the thing in issue in the case before it." We therefore need not pass on the constitutionality of the Act's preamble.

B

Section 188.210 provides that "[i]t shall be unlawful for any public employee within the scope of his employment to perform or assist an abortion, not necessary to save the life of the mother," while § 188.215 makes it "unlawful for any public facility to be used for the purpose of performing or assisting an abortion not necessary to save the life of the mother." The Court of Appeals held that these provisions contravened this Court's abortion decisions. We take the contrary view.

As we said earlier this Term in *DeShaney* v. *Winnebago County Dept. of Social Services,* (1989), "our cases have recognized that the Due Process Clauses generally confer no affirmative right to governmental aid, even where such aid may be necessary to secure life, liberty, or property interests of which the government itself may not deprive the individual." In *Maher* v. *Roe,* the Court upheld a Connecticut welfare regulation under which Medicaid recipients received payments for medical services related to childbirth, but not for nontherapeutic abortions. The Court rejected the claim that this unequal subsidization of childbirth and abortion was impermissible under *Roe* v. *Wade.* . . . Just as Congress' refusal to fund abortions in *McRae* left "an indigent woman with at least the same range of choice in deciding whether to obtain a medically necessary abortion as she would have had if Congress had chosen to subsidize no health care costs at all," Missouri's refusal to allow public employees to perform abortions in public hospitals leaves a pregnant woman with the same choices as if the State had chosen not to operate any public hospitals at all. . . .

Having held that the State's refusal to fund abortions does not violate *Roe* v. *Wade,* it strains logic to reach a contrary result for the use of public facilities and employees. If the State may "make a value judgment favoring childbirth over abortion and . . . implement that judgment by the allocation of public funds," surely it may do so through the allocation of other public resources, such as hospitals and medical staff. . . .

C

The Missouri Act contains three provisions relating to "encouraging or counseling a woman to have an abortion not necessary to save her life." Section 188.205 states that no public funds can be used for this purpose; § 188.210 states that public employees cannot, within the scope of their employment, engage in such speech; and § 188.215 forbids such speech in public facilities. The Court of Appeals did not consider § 188.205 separately from §§ 188.210 and 188.215. It held that all three of these provisions were unconstitutionally vague, and that "the ban on using public funds, employees, and facilities to encourage or counsel a woman to have an abortion is an unacceptable infringement of the woman's fourteenth amendment right to choose an abortion after receiving the medical information necessary to exercise the right knowingly and intelligently."

Missouri has chosen only to appeal the Court of Appeals' invalidation of the public funding provision, § 188.205. . . . the State's claim that § 188.205 "is not directed at the conduct of any physician or health care provider, private or public," but "is directed solely at those persons responsible for expending public funds."

Appellees contend that they are not "adversely" affected under the State's interpretation of § 188.205, and therefore that there is no longer a case or controversy before us on this question. Plaintiffs are masters of their complaints and remain so at the appellate stage of a litigation. A majority of the Court agrees with appellees that the controversy over § 188.205 is now moot, because appellees' argument amounts to a decision to no longer seek a declaratory judgment that § 188.205 is unconstitutional and accompanying declarative relief. . . .

D

Section 188.029 of the Missouri Act provides:

"Before a physician performs an abortion on a woman he has reason to believe is carrying an unborn child of twenty or more weeks gestational age, the physician shall first determine if the unborn child is viable by using and exercising that degree of care, skill, and proficiency commonly exercised by the ordinarily skillful, careful, and prudent physician engaged in similar practice under the same or similar conditions. In making this determination of viability, the physician shall perform or cause to be performed such medical examinations and tests as are necessary to make a finding of the gestational age, weight, and lung maturity of the unborn child and shall enter such findings and determination of viability in the medical record of the mother."

As with the preamble, the parties disagree over the meaning of this statutory provision. The State emphasizes the language of the first sentence, which speaks in terms of the physician's determination of viability being made by the standards of ordinary skill in the medical profession. Appellees stress the language of the second sentence, which prescribes such "tests as are necessary" to make a finding of gestational age, fetal weight, and lung maturity.

The Court of Appeals read § 188.029 as requiring that after 20 weeks "doctors *must* perform tests to find gestational age, fetal weight and lung maturity." The court indicated that the tests needed to determine fetal weight at 20 weeks are "unreliable and inaccurate" and would add $125 to $250 to the cost of an abortion. It also stated that "amniocentesis, the only method available to determine lung maturity, is contrary to accepted medical practice until 28–30 weeks of gestation, expensive, and imposes significant health risks for both the pregnant woman and the fetus."

We must first determine the meaning of § 188.029 under Missouri law. Our usual practice is to defer to the lower court's construction of a state statute, but we believe the Court of Appeals has "fallen into plain error" in this case. . . .

We think the viability-testing provision makes sense only if the second sentence is read to require only those tests that are useful to making subsidiary findings as to viability. If we construe this provision to require a physician to perform those tests needed to make the three specified findings *in all circumstances,* including when the physician's reasonable professional judgment indicates that the tests would be irrelevant to determining viability or even dangerous to the mother and the fetus, the second sentence of § 188.029 would conflict with the first sentence's *requirement* that a physician apply his reasonable professional skill and judgment. It would also be incongruous to read this provision,

especially the word "necessary," to require the performance of tests irrelevant to the expressed statutory purpose of determining viability. . . .

The viability-testing provision of the Missouri Act is concerned with promoting the State's interest in potential human life rather than in maternal health. Section 188.029 creates what is essentially a presumption of viability at 20 weeks, which the physician must rebut with tests indicating that the fetus is not viable prior to performing an abortion. It also directs the physician's determination as to viability by specifying consideration, if feasible, of gestational age, fetal weight, and lung capacity. The District Court found that "the medical evidence is uncontradicted that a 20-week fetus is *not* viable," and that "23½ to 24 weeks gestation is the earliest point in pregnancy where a reasonable possibility of viability exists." But it also found that there may be a 4-week error in estimating gestational age, which supports testing at 20 weeks.

In *Roe* v. *Wade*, the Court recognized that the State has " important and legitimate" interests in protecting maternal health and in the potentiality of human life. During the second trimester, the State "may, if it chooses, regulate the abortion procedure in ways that are reasonably related to maternal health." After viability, when the State's interest in potential human life was held to become compelling, the State "may, if it chooses, regulate, and even proscribe, abortion except where it is necessary, in appropriate medical judgment, for the preservation of the life or health of the mother."

In *Colautti* v. *Franklin*, upon which appellees rely, the Court held that a Pennsylvania statute regulating the standard of care to be used by a physician performing an abortion of a possibly viable fetus was void for vagueness. But in the course of reaching that conclusion, the Court reaffirmed its earlier statement in *Planned Parenthood of Central Missouri* v. *Danforth*, 428 U.S. 52, 64 (1976), that " 'the determination of whether a particular fetus is viable is, and must be, a matter for the judgement of the responsible attending physician.' ". . .

To the extent that § 188.029 regulates the method for determining viability, it undoubtedly does superimpose state regulation on the medical determination of whether a particular fetus is viable. The Court of Appeals and the District Court thought it unconstitutional for this reason. To the extent that the viability tests increase the cost of what are in fact second-trimester abortions, their validity may also be questioned under *Akron*, where the Court held that a requirement that second trimester abortions must be performed in hospitals was invalid because it substantially increased the expense of those procedures.

We think that the doubt cast upon the Missouri statute by these cases is not so much a flaw in the statute as it is a reflection of the fact that the rigid trimester analysis of the course of a pregnancy enunciated in *Roe* has resulted in subsequent cases like *Colautti* and *Akron* making constitutional law in this area a virtual Procrustean bed. . . .

Stare decisis is a cornerstone of our legal system, but it has less power in constitutional cases, where, save for constitutional amendments, this Court is the only body able to make needed changes. We have not refrained from reconsideration of a prior construction of the Constitution that has proved "unsound in principle and unworkable in practice." . . . We think the *Roe* trimester framework falls into that category.

In first place, the rigid *Roe* framework is hardly consistent with the notion of a Constitution cast in general terms, as ours is, and usually speaking in general principles, as ours does. The key elements of the *Roe* framework—trimesters and viability— are not found in the text of the constitution or in any place else one would expect to find a constitutional principle. Since the bounds of the inquiry are essentially indeterminate, the result has been a web of legal rules that have become increasingly intricate, resembling a code of regulations rather than a body of constitutional doctrine. As JUSTICE WHITE has put it, the trimester framework has left this Court to serve as the country's "*ex officio* medical board with powers to approve or disapprove medical and operative practices and standards throughout the United States."

In the second place, we do not see why the State's interest in protecting potential human life should come into existence only at the point of viability, and that there should therefore be a rigid line allowing state regulation after viability but prohibiting it before viability. . . .

The tests that § 188.029 requires the physician to perform are designed to determine viability. The State here has chosen viability as the point at which its interest in potential human life must be safeguarded.

It is true that the tests in question increase the expense of abortion, and regulate the discretion of the physician in determining the viability of the fetus. Since the tests will undoubtedly show in many cases that the fetus is not viable, the tests will have been performed for what were in fact second-trimester abortions. But we are satisfied that the requirement of these tests permissibly furthers the State's interest in protecting potential human life, and we therefore believe § 188.029 to be constitutional.

The dissent takes us to task for our failure to join in a "great issues" debate as to whether the Constitution includes an "unenumerated" general right to privacy as recognized in cases such as *Griswold* v. *Connecticut*, and *Roe*. But *Griswold* v. *Connecticut*, unlike *Roe*, did not purport to adopt a whole framework, complete with detailed rules and distinctions, to govern the cases in which the asserted liberty interest would apply. . . .

The dissent also accuses us of cowardice and illegitimacy in dealing with "the most politically divisive domestic legal issue of our time." There is no doubt that our holding today will allow some governmental regulation of abortion that would have been prohibited under the language of cases such as *Colautti* v. *Franklin,* and *Akron* v. *Akron Center for Reproductive Health, Inc.* But the goal of constitutional adjudication is surely not to remove inexorably "politically divisive" issues from the ambit of the legislative process, whereby the people through their elected representatives deal with matters of concern to them. The goal of constitutional adjudication is to hold true the balance between that which the Constitution puts beyond the reach of the democratic process and that which it does not. We think we have done that today. The dissent's suggestion that legislative bodies, in a Nation where more than half of our population is women, will treat our decision today as an invitation to enact abortion regulation reminiscent of the dark ages not only misreads our views but does scant justice to those who serve in such bodies and the people who elect them.

III

Both appellants and the United States as *Amicus Curiae* have urged that we overrule our decision in *Roe* v. *Wade*.

The facts of the present case, however, differ from those at issue in *Roe*. Here, Missouri has determined that viability is the point at which its interest in potential human life must be safeguarded. In *Roe*, on the other hand, the Texas statute criminalized the performance of *all* abortions, except when the mother's life was at stake. This case therefore affords us no occasion to revisit the holding of *Roe*, which was that the Texas statute unconstitutionally infringed the right to an abortion derived from the Due Process Clause, and we leave it undisturbed. To the extent indicated in our opinion, we would modify and narrow *Roe* and succeeding cases.

Because none of the challenged provisions of the Missouri Act properly before us conflict with the Constitution, the judgment of the Court of Appeals is

Reversed.

JUSTICE O'CONNOR, concurring in part and concurring in the judgment:. . .

In its interpretation of Missouri's "determination of viability" provision, Mo. Rev. Stat. § 188.029 (1986), the plurality has proceeded in a manner unneccessary to deciding the question at hand. I agree with the plurality that it was plain error for the Court of Appeals to interpret the second sentence of Mo. Rev. Stat. § 188.029 as meaning that "doctors *must* perform tests to find gestational age, fetal weight and lung maturity." . . .

Unlike the plurality, I do not understand these viability testing requirements to conflict with any of the Court's past decisions concerning state regulation of abortion. Therefore, there is no necessity to accept the State's invitation to reexamine the constitutional validity of *Roe* v. *Wade*. Where there is no need to decide a constitutional question, it is a venerable principle of this Court's adjudicatory processes not to do so for "[t]he Court will not 'anticipate a question of constitutional law in advance of the necessity of deciding it.' " . . . Neither will it generally "formulate a rule of constitutional law broader than is required by the precise facts to which it is to be applied." Quite simply, "[i]t is not the habit of the court to decide questions of a constitutional nature unless absolutely necessary to a decision of the case." . . . The Court today has accepted the State's every interpretation of its abortion statute and has upheld, under our existing precedents, every provision of that statute which is properly before us. Precisely for this reason reconsideration of *Roe* falls not into any "good-cause exception" to this "fundamental rule of judicial restraint. . . ." When the constitutional invalidity of a State's abortion statute actually turns on the constitutional validity of *Roe* v. *Wade,* there will be time enough to reexamine *Roe.* And to do so carefully. . . .

I do not think the second sentence of § 188.029, as interpreted by the Court, imposes a degree of state regulation on the medical determination of viability that in any way conflicts with prior decisions of this Court. As the plurality recognizes, the requirement that, where not imprudent, physicians perform examinations and tests useful to making subsidiary findings to determine viability "promot[es] the State's interest in potential human life rather than in maternal health." No decision of this Court has held that the State may not directly promote its interest in potential life when viability is possible. . . .

I dissented from the Court's opinion in *Akron* because it was my view that, even apart from *Roe's* trimester framework which I continue to consider problematic, the *Akron* majority had distorted and misapplied its own standard for evaluating state regulation of abortion which the Court had applied with fair consistency in the past: that, previability, "a regulation imposed on a lawful abortion is not unconstitutional unless it unduly burdens the right to seek an abortion."

It is clear to me that requiring the performance of examinations and tests useful to determining whether a fetus is viable, when viability is possible, and when it would not be medically imprudent to do so, does not impose an undue burden on a woman's abortion decision. On this ground alone I would reject the suggestion that § 188.029 as interpreted is unconstitutional. . . . I see no conflict between § 188.029 and the Court's opinion in *Akron.* The second-trimester hospitalization requirement struck down in *Akron* imposed, in the majority's view, "a heavy, and unnecessary, burden," more than doubling the cost of "women's access to a relatively inexpensive, otherwise accessible, and safe abortion procedure." By contrast, the cost of examinations and tests that could usefully and prudently be performed when a woman is 20–24 weeks pregnant to determine whether the fetus is viable would only marginally, if at all, increase the cost of an abortion. . . .

In sum, I concur in Parts I, II-A, II-B, and II-C of the Court's opinion and concur in the judgment of Part II-D.

JUSTICE SCALIA, concurring in part and concurring in the judgment:

I join Parts I, II-A, II-B, and II-C of the opinion of THE CHIEF JUSTICE. As to Part II-D, I share JUSTICE BLACKMUN's view, that it effectively would overrule *Roe* v. *Wade.* I think that should be done, but would do it more explicitly. Since today we contrive to avoid doing it, and indeed to avoid almost any decision of national import, I need not set forth my reasons, some of which have been well recited in dissents of my colleagues in other cases. . . .

JUSTICE O'CONNOR's assertion, that a " 'fundamental rule of judicial restraint' " requires us to avoid reconsidering *Roe,* cannot be taken seriously. By finessing *Roe* we do not, as she suggests, adhere to the strict and venerable rule that we should avoid " 'decid[ing] questions of a constitutional nature.' " We have not disposed of this case on some statutory or procedural ground, but have decided, and could not avoid deciding, whether the Missouri statute meets the requirements of the United States Constitution. The only choice available is whether, in deciding that constitutional question, we should use *Roe* v. *Wade* as the benchmark, or something else. What is involved, therefore, is not the rule of avoiding constitutional issues where possible, but the quite separate principle that we will not " 'formulate a rule of constitutional law broader than is required by the precise facts to which it is to be applied.' " The latter is a sound general principle, but one often departed from when good reason exists. . . .

The real question, then, is whether there are valid reasons to go beyond the most stingy possible holding today. It seems to me there are not only valid but compelling ones. Ordinarily, speaking no more broadly than is absolutely required avoids throwing settled law into confusion; doing so today preserves a chaos that is evident to anyone who can read and count. Alone sufficient to justify a broad holding is the fact that our retaining control, through *Roe,* of what I believe to be, and many of our citizens recognize to be, a political issue, continuously distorts the public perception of the role of this Court. We can now look forward to at least another Term with carts full of mail from the public, and streets full of demonstrators, urging us—their unelected and life-tenured judges who have been awarded those extraordinary, undemocratic characteristics precisely in order that we might follow the law despite the popular will—to follow the popular will. Indeed, I expect we can look forward to even more of that than before, given our indecisive decision today. . . .

The result of our vote today is that we will not reconsider [Roe] even if most of the Justices think it is wrong, unless we have before us a statute that in fact contradicts it—and even then (under our newly discovered "no-broader-than-necessary" requirement) only minor problematical aspects of *Roe* will be reconsidered, unless one expects State legislatures to adopt provisions whose compliance with *Roe* cannot even be argued with a straight face. It thus appears that the mansion of constitutionalized abortion-law, constructed overnight in *Roe* v. *Wade,* must be disassembled door-jamb by door-jamb, and never entirely brought down, no matter how wrong it may be. . . .

JUSTICE BLACKMUN, with whom JUSTICE BRENNAN and JUSTICE MARSHALL join, concurring in part and dissenting in part:

Today, *Roe* v. *Wade* and the fundamental constitutional right of women to decide whether to terminate a pregnancy, survive but are not secure. . . . Although today, no less than yesterday, the Constitution and the decisions of this Court prohibit a State from enacting laws that inhibit women from the meaningful exercise of that right, a plurality of this Court implicitly invites every state legislature to enact more and more restrictive abortion regulations in order to provoke more

and more test cases, in the hope that sometime down the line the Court will return the law of procreative freedom to the severe limitations that generally prevailed in this country before January 22, 1973. Never in my memory has a plurality announced a judgment of this Court that so foments disregard for the law and for our standing decisions.

Nor in my memory has a plurality gone about its business in such a deceptive fashion. At every level of its review, from its effort to read the real meaning out of the Missouri statute, to its intended evisceration of precedents and its deafening silence about the constitutional protections that it would jettison, the plurality obscures the portent of its analysis. With feigned restraint, the plurality announces that its analysis leaves *Roe* "undisturbed," albeit "modif[ied] and narrow[ed]." But this disclaimer is totally meaningless. The plurality opinion is filled with winks, and nods, and knowing glances to those who would do away with *Roe* explicitly, but turns a stone face to anyone in search of what the plurality conceives as the scope of a woman's right under the Due Process Clause to terminate a pregnancy free from the coercive and brooding influence of the State. The simple truth is that *Roe* would not survive the plurality's analysis, and that the plurality provides no substitute for *Roe's* protective umbrella.

I fear for the future. I fear for the liberty and equality of the millions of women who have lived and come of age in the 16 years since *Roe* was decided. I fear for the integrity of, and public esteem for, this Court.

I dissent. . . .

At the outset, I note that in its haste to limit abortion rights, the plurality compounds the errors of its analysis by needlessly reaching out to address constitutional questions that are not actually presented. The conflict between § 188.029 and *Roe's* trimester framework, which purportedly drives the plurality to reconsider our past decisions, is a contrived conflict: the product of an aggressive misreading of the viability-testing requirement and a needlessly wooden application of the *Roe* framework. . . .

Had the plurality read the statute as written, it would have had no cause to reconsider the *Roe* framework. As properly construed, the viability-testing provision does not pass constitutional muster under even a rational-basis standard, the least restrictive level of review applied by this Court. By mandating tests to determine fetal weight and lung maturity for every fetus thought to be more than 20 weeks gestational age, the statute requires physicians to undertake procedures, such as amniocentesis, that, in the situation presented, have no medical justification, impose significant additional health risks on both the pregnant woman and the fetus, and bear no rational relation to the State's interest in protecting fetal life. As written, § 188.029 is an arbitrary imposition of discomfort, risk, and expense, furthering no discernible interest except to make the procurement of an abortion as arduous and difficult as possible. Thus, were it not for the plurality's tortured effort to avoid the plain import of §188.029, it could have struck down the testing provision as patently irrational irrespective of the *Roe* framework.

The plurality eschews this straightforward resolution, in the hope of precipitating a constitutional crisis. Far from avoiding constitutional difficulty, the plurality attempts to engineer a dramatic retrenchment in our jurisprudence by exaggerating the conflict between its untenable construction of § 188.029 and the *Roe* trimester framework.

No one contests that under the *Roe* framework the State, in order to promote its interest in potential human life, may regulate and even proscribe non-therapeutic abortions once the fetus becomes viable. If, as the plurality appears to hold, the testing provision simply requires a physician to use appropriate and medically sound tests to determine whether the fetus is actually viable when the estimated gestational age is greater than 20 weeks (and therefore within what the District Court found to be the margin of error for viability), then I see little or no conflict with *Roe*. Nothing in *Roe*, or any of its progeny, holds that a State may not effectuate its compelling interest in the potential life of a viable fetus by seeking to ensure that no viable fetus is mistakenly aborted because of the inherent lack of precision in estimates of gestational age. A requirement that a physician make a finding of viability, one way or the other, for every fetus that falls within the range of possible viability does no more than preserve the State's recognized authority. Although, as the plurality correctly points out, such a testing requirement would have the effect of imposing additional costs on second-trimester abortions where the tests indicated that the fetus was not viable, these costs would be merely incidental to, and a necessary accommodation of, the State's unquestioned right to prohibit non-therapeutic abortions after the point of viability. In short, the testing provision, as construed by the plurality is consistent with the *Roe* framework and could be upheld effortlessly under current doctrine.

How ironic it is, then, and disingenuous, that the plurality scolds the Court of Appeals for adopting a construction of the statute that fails to avoid constitutional difficulties. By distorting the statute, the plurality manages to avoid invalidating the testing provision on what should have been noncontroversial constitutional grounds; having done so, however, the plurality rushes headlong into a much deeper constitutional thicket, burshing past an obvious basis for upholding § 188.029 in search of a pretext for scuttling the trimester framework. Evidently, from the plurality's perspective, the real problem with the Court of Appeals' construction of § 188.029 is not that it raised a constitutional difficulty, but that it raised the wrong constitutional difficulty—one not implicating *Roe*. The plurality has remedied that, traditional canons of construction and judicial forbearance notwithstanding.

Having set up the conflict between §188.029 and the *Roe* trimester framework, the plurality summarily discards *Roe's* analytic core as " 'unsound in principle and unworkable in practice.' " This is so, the plurality claims, because the key elements of the framework do not appear in the text of the Constitution, because the framework more closely resembles a regulatory code than a body of constitutional doctrine, and because under the framework the State's interest in potential human life is considered compelling only after viability, when, in fact, that interest is equally compelling throughout pregnancy. The plurality does not bother to explain these alleged flaws in *Roe*. Bald assertion masquerades as reasoning. The object, quite clearly, is not to persuade, but to prevail.

The plurality opinion is far more remarkable for the arguments that it does not advance than for those that it does. The plurality does not even mention, much less join, the true jurisprudential debate underlying this case: whether the Constitution includes an "unenumerated" general right to privacy as recognized in many of our decisions, most notably *Griswold* v. *Connecticut* and *Roe*, and, more specifically, whether and to what extent such a right to privacy extends to matters of childbearing and family life, including abortion. . . . These are questions of unsurpassed significance in this Court's interpretation of the Constitution, and mark the battleground upon which this case was fought, by the parties, by the Solicitor General as *amicus* on behalf of petitioners, and by an unprecedented number of *amici*. On these grounds, abandoned by the plurality, the Court should decide this case.

But rather than arguing that the text of the Constitution makes no mention of the right to privacy, the plurality complains that the critical elements of the *Roe* framework—trimesters and viability—do not appear in the Constitution and are, therefore, somehow inconsistent with a Constitution cast in general terms. Were this a true concern, we would have to abandon most of our constitutional jurisprudence. As the plurality well knows, or should know, the "critical elements" of countless constitutional doctrines nowhere appear in the Constitution's text. The Constitution makes no mention, for example, of the First Amendment's "actual malice" standard for proving certain libels, see *New York Times* v. *Sullivan,* 376 U.S. 254 (1964), or of the standard for determining when speech is obscene. See *Miller* v. *California,* 413 U.S. 15 (1973). Similarly, the Constitution makes no mention of the rational-basis test, or the specific verbal formulations of intermediate and strict scrutiny by which this Court evaluates claims under the Equal Protection Clause. The reason is simple. Like the *Roe* framework, these tests or standards are not, and do not purport to be, rights protected by the Constitution. Rather, they are judge-made methods for evaluating and measuring the strength and scope of constitutional rights or for balancing the constitutional rights of individuals against the competing interests of government.

With respect to the *Roe* framework, the general constitutional principle, indeed the fundamental constitutional right, for which it was developed is the right to privacy, see, *e.g., Griswold* v. *Connecticut,* a species of "liberty" protected by the Due Process Clause, which under our past decisions safeguards the right of women to exercise some control over their own role in procreation. As we recently reaffirmed in *Thornburgh* v. *American College of Obstetricians and Gynecologists,* (1986), few decisions are "more basic to individual dignity and autonomy" or more appropriate to that "certain private sphere of individual liberty" that the Constitution reserves from the intrusive reach of government than the right to make the uniquely personal, intimate, and self-defining decision whether to end a pregnancy. It is this general principle, the " 'moral fact that a person belongs to himself and not others nor to society as a whole,' " that is found in the Constitution. The trimester framework simply defines and limits that right to privacy in the abortion context to accommodate, not destroy, a State's legitimate interest in protecting the health of pregnant women and in preserving potential human life. Fashioning such accommodations between individual rights and the legitimate interests of government, establishing benchmarks and standards with which to evaluate the competing claims of individuals and government, lies at the very heart of constitutional adjudication. To the ex-

tent that the trimester framework is useful in this enterprise, it is not only consistent with constitutional interpretation, but necessary to the wise and just exercise of this Court's paramount authority to define the scope of constitutional rights.

The plurality next alleges that the result of the trimester framework has "been a web of legal rules that have become increasingly intricate, resembling a code of regulations rather than a body of constitutional doctrine." Again, if this were a true and genuine concern, we would have to abandon vast areas of our constitutional jurisprudence. . . .

That numerous constitutional doctrines result in narrow differentiations between similar circumstances does not mean that this Court has abandoned adjudication in favor of regulation. Rather, these careful distinctions reflect the process of constitutional adjudication itself, which is often highly fact-specific, requiring such determinations as whether state laws are "unduly burdensome" or "reasonable" or bear a "rational" or "necessary" relation to asserted state interests. . . .

Finally, the plurality asserts that the trimester framework cannot stand because the State's interest in potential life is compelling throughout pregnancy, not merely after viability. The opinion contains not one word of rationale for its view of the State's interest. This "it-is-so-because-we-say-so" jurisprudence constitutes nothing other than an attempted exercise of brute force; reason, much less persuasion, has no place. . . .

For my own part, I remain convinced, as six other Members of this Court 16 years ago were convinced, that the *Roe* framework, and the viability standard in particular, fairly, sensibly, and effectively functions to safeguard the constitutional liberties of pregnant women while recognizing and accommodating the State's interest in potential human life. The viability line reflects the biological facts and truths of fetal development; it marks that threshold moment prior to which a fetus cannot survive separate from the woman and cannot reasonably and objectively be regarded as a subject of rights or interests distinct from, or paramount to, those of the pregnant woman. At the same time, the viability standard takes account of the undeniable fact that as the fetus evolves into its postnatal form, and as it loses its dependence on the uterine environment, the State's interest in the fetus' potential human life, and in fostering a regard for human life in general, becomes compelling. . . .

Having contrived an opportunity to reconsider the *Roe* framework, and then having discarded that framework, the plurality finds the testing provision unobjectionable because it "permissibly furthers the State's interest in protecting potential human life." This newly minted standard is circular and totally meaningless. Whether a challenged abortion regulation "permissibly furthers" a legitimate state interest is the *question* that courts must answer in abortion cases, not the standard for courts to apply. In keeping with the rest of its opinion, the plurality makes no attempt to explain or to justify its new standard, either in the abstract or as applied in this case. Nor could it. The "permissibly furthers" standard has no independent meaning, and consists of nothing other than what a majority of this Court may believe at any given moment in any given case. The plurality's novel test appears to be nothing more than a dressed-up version of rational-basis review, this Court's most lenient level of scrutiny. One thing is clear, however: were the plurality's "permissibly furthers" standard adopted by the Court, for all practical purposes, *Roe* would be overruled. . . .

Thus, "not with a bang, but a whimper," the plurality discards a landmark case of the last generation, and casts into darkness the hopes and visions of every woman in this country who had come to believe that the Constitution guaranteed her the right to exercise some control over her unique ability to bear children. The plurality does so either oblivious or insensitive to the fact that millions of women, and their families, have ordered their lives around the right to reproductive choice, and that this right has become vital to the full participation of women in the economic and political walks of American life. The plurality would clear the way once again for government to force upon women the physical labor and specific and direct medical and psychological harms that may accompany carrying a fetus to term. The plurality would clear the way again for the State to conscript a woman's body and to force upon her a "distressful life and future."

The result, as we know from experience, would be that every year hundreds of thousands of women, in desperation, would defy the law, and place their health and safety in the unclean and unsympathetic hands of back-alley abortionists, or they would attempt to perform abortions upon themselves, with disastrous results. Every year, many women, especially poor and minority women, would die or suffer debilitating physical trauma, all in the name of enforced morality or religious dictates or lack of compassion, as it may be.

Of the aspirations and settled understandings of American women, of the inevitable and brutal consequences of what it is doing, the tough-approach plurality utters not a word. This silence is callous. It is also profoundly destructive of this Court as an institution. To overturn a constitutional decision is a rare and grave undertaking. To overturn a constitutional decision that secured a fundamental personal liberty to millions of persons would be unprecedented in our 200 years of constitutional history. Although the doctrine of *stare decisis* applies with somewhat diminished force in constitutional cases generally, even in ordinary constitutional cases "any departure from *stare decisis* demands special justification." . . . This requirement of justification applies with unique force where, as here, the Court's abrogation of precedent would destroy people's firm belief, based on past decisions of this Court, that they possess an unabridgeable right to undertake certain conduct. . . .

Today's decision involves the most politically divisive domestic legal issue of our time. By refusing to explain or to justify its proposed revolutionary revision in the law of abortion, and by refusing to abide not only by our precedents, but also by our canons for reconsidering those precedents, the plurality invites charges of cowardice and illegitimacy to our door. I cannot say that these would be undeserved.

For today, at least, the law of abortion stands undisturbed. For today, the women of this Nation still retain the liberty to control their destinies. But the signs are evident and very ominous, and a chill wind blows.

I dissent.

JUSTICE STEVENS, concurring in part and dissenting in part: . . .

I am persuaded that the absence of any secular purpose for the legislative declarations that life begins at conception and that conception occurs at fertilization makes the relevant portion of the preamble invalid under the Establishment Clause of the First Amendment to the Federal Constitution. This conclusion . . . rests on the fact that the preamble, an unequivocal endorsement of a religious tenet of some but by no means all Christian faiths, serves no identifiable secular purpose. . . .

The preamble to the Missouri statute endorses the theological position that there is the same . . . interest in preserving the life of a fetus during the first 40 or 80 days of pregnancy as there is after viability—indeed, after the time when the fetus has become a "person" with legal rights protected by the Constitution. To sustain that position as a matter of law, I believe Missouri has the burden of identifying the secular interests that differentiate the first 40 days of pregnancy from the period immediately before or after fertilization when, as *Griswold* and related cases establish, the Constitution allows the use of contraceptive procedures to prevent potential life from developing into full personhood. Focusing our attention on the first several weeks of pregnancy is especially appropriate because that is the period when the vast majority of abortions are actually performed.

As a secular matter, there is an obvious difference btween the state interest in protecting the freshly fertilized egg and the state interest in protecting a 9-month-gestated, fully sentient fetus on the eve of birth. There can be no interest in protecting the newly fertilized egg from physical pain or mental anguish, because the capacity for such suffering does not yet exist; respecting a developed fetus, however, that interest is valid. In fact, if one prescinds the theological concept of ensoulment—or one accepts St. Thomas Aquinas' view that ensoulment does not occur for at least 40 days, a State has no greater secular interest in protecting the potential life of an embryo that is still "seed" than in protecting the potential life of a sperm or an unfertilized ovum. . . .

Bolstering my conclusion that the preamble violates the First Amendment is the fact that the intensely divisive character of much of the national debate over the abortion issue reflects the deeply held religious convictions of many participants in the debate. The Missouri Legislature may not inject its endorsement of a particular religious tradition into this debate, for "[t]he Establishment Clause does not allow public bodies to foment such disagreement." . . .

In my opinion the preamble to the Missouri statute is unconstitutional for two reasons. To the extent that it has substantive impact on the freedom to use contraceptive procedures, it is inconsistent with the central holding in *Griswold*. To the extent that it merely makes "legislative findings without operative effect," as the State argues, it violates the Establishment Clause of the First Amendment. Contrary to the theological "finding" of the Missouri Legislature, a woman's constitutionally protected liberty encompasses the right to act on her own belief that—to paraphrase St. Thomas Aquinas—until a seed has acquired the powers of sensation and movement, the life of a human being has not yet begun.

FRONTIERO v. RICHARDSON,
411 U.S. 677 (1973)

Under federal law, wives of members of the military automatically became dependents for purposes of housing allowances, medical and dental coverage, and other benefits. But husbands of female members of the military are not automatically considered dependents unless they are dependent on their spouses for over one-half of their support. Sharron Frontiero, an Air Force Lieutenant, sought a dependent's allowance for her husband, a full-time college student, who was, however, receiving veteran's benefits. She was turned down because she did not demonstrate that her husband was dependent on her for more than half of his support. Lieutenant Frontiero then sued the federal government, arguing that the statute unreasonably discriminated against women members of the military and thereby violated the due process clause of the Fifth Amendment. A three-judge district court denied relief, and Frontiero appealed to the United States Supreme Court.

Majority votes: 8
Dissenting votes: 1

MR. JUSTICE BRENNAN announced the judgment of the Court in an opinion in which MR. JUSTICE DOUGLAS, MR. JUSTICE WHITE, and MR. JUSTICE MARSHALL join:. . . .

At the outset, appellants contend that classification based upon sex, like classifications based upon race, alienage, and national origin, are inherently suspect and must therefore be subjected to close judicial scrutiny. We agree and, indeed, find at least implicit support for such an approach in our unanimous decision only last Term in *Reed* v. *Reed*, 404 U.S. 71 (1971). . . .

There can be no doubt that our Nation has had a long and unfortunate history of sex discrimination. Traditionally, such discrimination was rationalized by an attitude of "romantic paternalism" which, in practical effect, put women, not on a pedestal, but in a cage. . . .

As a result of notions such as these, our statute books gradually became laden with gross, stereotyped distinctions between the sexes and, indeed, throughout much of the 19th century the position of women in our society was, in many respects, comparable to that of blacks under the pre-Civil War slave codes. Neither slaves nor women could hold office, serve on juries, or bring suit in their own names, and married women traditionally were denied the legal capacity to hold or convey property or to serve as legal guardians of their own children. . . . And although blacks were guaranteed the right to vote in 1870, women were denied even that right—which is itself "preservative of other basic civil and political rights"—until adoption of the Nineteenth Amendment half a century later.

It is true, of course, that the position of women in America has improved markedly in recent decades. Nevertheless, it can hardly be doubted that, in part because of the high visibility of the sex characteristic, women still face pervasive, although at times more subtle, discrimination in our educational institutions, in the job market and, perhaps most conspicuously, in the political arena. . . .

Moreover, since sex, like race and national origin, is an immutable characteristic determined solely by the accident of birth, the imposition of special disabilities upon the members of a particular sex because of their sex would seem to violate "the basic concept of our system that legal burdens should bear some relationship to individual responsibility. . . ." *Weber* v. *Aetna Casualty & Surety Co.*, 406 U.S. 164, 175 (1972). And what differentiates sex from such nonsuspect statuses as intelligence or physical disability, and aligns it with the recognized suspect criteria, is that the sex characteristic frequently bears no relation to ability to perform or contribute to society. As a result, statutory distinctions between the sexes often have the effect of invidiously relegating the entire class of females to inferior legal status without regard to the actual capabilities of its individual members.

We might also note that, over the past decade, Congress has itself manifested an increasing sensitivity to sex-based classifications. In Title VII of the Civil Rights Acts of 1964, for example, Congress expressly declared that no employer, labor union, or other organization subject to the provisions of the Act shall discriminate against any individual on the basis of "race, color, religion, *sex,* or national origin." Similarly, the Equal Pay Act of 1963 provides that no employer covered by the Act "shall discriminate . . . between employees on the basis of sex." And § 1 of the Equal Rights Amendment, passed by Congress on March 22, 1972, and submitted to the legislatures of the States for ratification, declares that "[e]quality of rights under the law shall not be denied or abridged by the United States or by any State on account of Sex." Thus, Congress itself has concluded that classifications based upon sex are inherently invidious, and this conclusion of a coequal branch of Government is not without significance to the question presently under consideration.

With these considerations in mind, we can only conclude that classifications based upon sex, like classifications based upon race, alienage, or national origin, are inherently suspect, and must therefore be subjected to strict judicial scrutiny. Applying the analysis mandated by that stricter standard of review, it is clear that the statutory scheme now before us is constitutionally invalid.

The sole basis of the classification established in the challenged statutes is the sex of the individuals involved. Thus, under 37 U.S.C. § 401, 403, and 10 U.S.C. § 2072, 2076, a female member of the uniformed services seeking to obtain housing and medical benefits for her spouse must prove his dependency in fact, whereas no such burden is imposed upon male members. In addition, the statutes operate so as to deny benefits to a female member, such as appellant Sharron Frontiero, who provides less than one-half of her spouse's support, while at the same time granting such benefits to a male member who likewise provides less than one-half of his spouse's support. Thus, to this extent at least, it may fairly be said that these statutes command "dissimilar treatment for men and women who are . . . similarly situated." *Reed* v. *Reed*, 404 U.S., at 77.

Moreover, the Government concedes that the differential treatment accorded men and women under these statutes serves no purpose other than mere "administrative convenience." In essence, the Government maintains that, as an empirical matter, wives in our society frequently are dependent upon their husbands, while husbands rarely are dependent upon their wives. Thus, the Government argues that Congress might reasonably have concluded that it would be both cheaper and easier simply conclusively to presume that wives of male members are financially dependent upon their husbands, while burdening female members with the task of establishing dependency in fact.

The Government offers no concrete evidence, however, tending to support its view that such differential treatment in fact saves the Government any money. In order to satisfy the demands of strict judicial scrutiny, the Government must demonstrate, for example, that it is actually cheaper to grant increased benefits with respect to all male members, than it is to determine which male members are in fact entitled to such benefits and to grant increased benefits only to those members whose wives actually meet the dependency requirement. Here, however, there is substantial evidence that, if put to the test, many of the wives of male members would fail to qualify for benefits. And in light of the fact that the dependency determination with respect to the husbands of female members is presently made solely on the basis of affidavits rather than through the more costly hearing process, the Government's explanation of the statutory scheme is, to say the least, questionable.

In any case, our prior decisions make clear that, although efficacious administration of governmental programs is not without some importance, "the Constitution recognizes higher values than speed and efficiency." And when we enter the realm of "strict judicial scrutiny," there can be no doubt that "administrative convenience" is not a shibboleth, the mere recitation of which dictates constitutionality. On the contrary, any statutory scheme which draws a sharp line between the sexes, solely for the purpose of achieving administrative convenience, necessarily commands "dissimilar treatment for men and women who are . . . similarly situated," and therefore involves the "very kind of arbitrary legislative choice forbidden by the Constitution. . . ." We therefore conclude that, by according differential treatment to male and female members of the uniformed services for the sole purpose of achieving administrative convenience, the challenged statutes violate the Due Process Clause of the Fifth Amendment insofar as they require a female member to prove the dependency of her husband.

Reversed.

MR. JUSTICE STEWART concurs in the judgment, agreeing that the statutes before us work an invidious discrimination in violation of the Constitution. *Reed* v. *Reed,* 404 U.S. 71.

MR. JUSTICE REHNQUIST dissents for the reasons stated by Judge Rives in his opinion for the District Court, *Frontiero* v. *Laird,* 341 F.Supp. 201 (1972).

MR. JUSTICE POWELL, with whom CHIEF JUSTICE BURGER and MR. JUSTICE BLACKMUN join, concurring in the judgment:

I agree that the challenged statutes constitute an unconstitutional discrimination against servicewomen in violation of the Due Process Clause of the Fifth Amendment, but I cannot join the opinion of Mr. Justice Brennan, which would hold that all classifications based upon sex, "like classifications based upon race, alienage, and national origin," are "inherently suspect and must therefore be subjected to close judicial scrutiny." It is unnecessary for the Court in this case to characterize sex as a suspect classification, with all of the far-reaching implications of such a holding. *Reed* v. *Reed,* 404 U.S. 71 (1971), which abundantly supports our decision today, did not add sex to the narrowly limited group of classifications which are inherently suspect. In my view, we can and should decide this case on the authority of *Reed* and reserve for the future any expansion of its rationale.

There is another, and I find compelling, reason for deferring a general categorizing of sex classifications as invoking the strictest test of judicial scrutiny. The Equal Rights Amendment, which if adopted will resolve the substance of this precise question, has been approved by the Congress and submitted for ratification by the States. If this Amendment is duly adopted, it will represent the will of the people accomplished in the manner prescribed by the Constitution. By acting prematurely and unnecessarily, as I view it, the Court has assumed a decisional responsibility at the very time when state legislatures, functioning within the traditional democratic process, are debating the proposed Amendment. It seems to me that this reaching out to pre-empt by judicial action a major political decision which is currently in process of resolution does not reflect appropriate respect for duly prescribed legislative processes.

There are times when this Court, under our system, cannot avoid a constitutional decision on issues which normally should be resolved by the elected representatives of the people. But democratic institutions are weakened, and confidence in the restraint of the Court is impaired, when we appear unnecessarily to decide sensitive issues of broad social and political importance at the very time they are under consideration within the prescribed constitutional processes.

CRAIG v. BOREN,
429 U.S. 190 (1976)

An Oklahoma statute forbade the sale of 3.2 percent beer to males under 21 and to females under 18 years of age. That statute was challenged in this case as violating the equal protection of the laws guarantee of the Fourteenth Amendment by unjustly discriminating against males 18 to 20 years old. Curtis Craig, a young male under the age of 21 at the time of the suit, and Ms. Whitener, a licensed vendor of 3.2 percent beer, brought this legal action to the federal district court. The statute was upheld and appeal was then taken to the Supreme Court.

Majority votes: 7
Dissenting votes: 2

MR. JUSTICE BRENNAN delivered the opinion of the Court:. . . .

We first address a preliminary question of standing. Appellant Craig attained the age of 21 after we noted probable jurisdiction. Therefore, since only declaratory and injunctive relief against enforcement of the gender-based differential is sought, the controversy has been rendered moot as to Craig. The question thus arises whether appellant Whitener, the licensed vendor of 3.2% beer, who has a live controversy against enforcement of the statute, may rely upon the equal protection objections of males 18–20 years of age to establish her claim of unconstitutionality of the age-sex differential. We conclude that she may. . . .

The operation of [37 Okla. Stat.] §§ 241 and 245 plainly has inflicted "injury in fact" upon appellant sufficient to guarantee her "concrete adverseness," and to satisfy the constitutional-based standing requirements imposed by Art. III. The legal duties created by the statutory sections under challenge are addressed directly to vendors such as appellant. She is obliged either to heed the statutory discrimination, thereby incurring a direct economic injury through the constriction of her buyer's market, or to disobey the statutory command and suffer, in the words of Oklahoma's Assistant Attorney General, "sanctions and perhaps loss of license." This Court repeatedly has recognized that such injuries establish the threshold requirements of a "case or controversy" mandated by Art. III. . . . Vendors and those in like positions have been uniformly permitted to resist efforts at restricting their operations by acting as advocates for the rights of third parties who seek access to their market or function. . . .

Analysis may appropriately begin with the reminder that *Reed* v. *Reed* emphasized that statutory classifications that distinguish between males and females are "subject to scrutiny under the Equal Protection Clause." 404 U.S., at 75. To withstand constitutional challenge, previous cases establish that classifications by gender must serve important governmental objectives and must be substantially related to achievement of those objectives. . . .

We accept for purposes of discussion the District Court's identification of the objective underlying §§ 241 and 245 as the enhancement of traffic safety. Clearly, the protection of public health and safety represents an important function of state and local governments. However, appellees' statistics in our view cannot support the conclusion that the gender-based distinction closely serves to achieve that objective and therefore the distinction cannot under *Reed* withstand equal protection challenge. . . .

Even were the statistical evidence accepted as accurate, it nevertheless offers only a weak answer to the equal protection question presented here. The most focused and relevant of the statistical surveys, arrests of 18–20-year-olds for alcohol-related driving offenses, exemplifies the ultimate unpersuasiveness of this evidentiary record. Viewed in terms of the correlation between sex and the actual activity that Oklahoma seeks to regulate—driving

while under the influence of alcohol—the statistics broadly establish that .18% of females and 2% of males in that age group were arrested for that offense. While such a disparity is not trivial in a statistical sense, it hardly can form the basis for employment of a gender line as a classifying device. Certainly if maleness is to serve as a proxy for drinking and driving, a correlation of 2% must be considered an unduly tenuous "fit." Indeed, prior cases have consistently rejected the use of sex as a decisionmaking factor even though the statutes in question certainly rested on far more predictive empirical relationships than this.

Moreover, the statistics exhibit a variety of other shortcomings that seriously impugn their value to equal protection analysis. Setting aside the obvious methodological problems, the surveys do not adequately justify the salient features of Oklahoma's gender-based traffic-safety law. None purports to measure the use and dangerousness of 3.2% beer as opposed to alcohol generally, a detail that is of particular importance since, in light of its low alcohol level, Oklahoma apparently considers the 3.2% beverage to be "non-intoxicating." 37 Okla. Stat. § 163.1 (1971). Moreover, many of the studies, while graphically documenting the unfortunate increase in driving while under the influence of alcohol, make no effort to relate their findings to age-sex differentials as involved here. . . .

There is no reason to belabor this line of analysis. It is unrealistic to expect either members of the judiciary or state officials to be well versed in the rigors of experimental or statistical technique. But this merely illustrates that proving broad sociological propositions by statistics is a dubious business, and one that inevitably is in tension with the normative philosophy that underlies the Equal Protection Clause. Suffice to say that the showing offered by the appellees does not satisfy us that sex represents a legitimate, accurate proxy for the regulation of drinking and driving. In fact, when it is further recognized that Oklahoma's statute prohibits only the selling of 3.2% beer to young males and not their drinking the beverage once acquired (even after purchase by their 18–20-year-old female companions), the relationship between gender and traffic safety becomes far too tenuous to satisfy *Reed*'s requirement that the gender-based difference be substantially related to achievement of the statutory objective.

We hold, therefore, that under *Reed,* Oklahoma's 3.2% beer statute invidiously discriminates against males 18–20 years of age.

Appellees argue, however, that §§ 241 and 245 enforce state policies concerning the sale and distri-

Chapter

20

Political and Other Equality Claims

SUBSTANTIVE EQUAL PROTECTION

The Court, in treating the equal protection claims of blacks and women, as we saw in chapters 18 and 19, was and is being asked to put substantive meaning into the equal protection clause and to strike down the challenged legislation as inherently incompatible with equal protection. When the Court does this, it is engaging in substantive equal protection in much the same way as it once utilized substantive due process. The Court takes the equal protection clause, and particularly with questions of race, scrutinizes strictly the challenged legislation to see what compelling reasons were given for the legislation and the nature of the evidence offered in support of it. The burden is on government to show why the classification should be upheld. Even with a less severe standard of scrutiny, if the Court fails to find a substantial relationship of, for example, the gender classification and the presumably valid legislative purpose, the Court

will strike down the legislation as a violation of the equal protection clause. Substantive equal protection questions before the Burger and Rehnquist Courts raised issues not only of race and sex but also, among others, issues concerning political equality (including voting equality) and the rights of the poor.

POLITICAL EQUALITY

Among the many other claims of equality, political equality, or the right to have one's vote count the same as another's in elections at the local, state, and federal levels, has had special appeal. In part, the problem of political inequality has been linked to racial discrimination. Political inequality was also linked to discrimination against women on account of their gender until the ratification of the Nineteenth Amendment in 1920. But there has been an even broader issue of political equality stemming from malapportionment of electoral districts.

The concept of one-person-one-vote has a pleasing egalitarian ring to it although at the federal level the Constitution explicitly rejects that principle for voting for the U.S. Senate (each state, no matter its population, elects two senators) and in the provisions of the electoral college mechanism of our presidential elections. The Constitution leaves the drawing of congressional district as well as state legislative boundaries up to the state legislatures. As a result, particularly in the first half of the twentieth century, in which major population shifts from the rural to the urban areas occurred, malapportionment of state legislative and congressional districts increased. At first, the Court avoided deciding the issue in *Colegrove* v. *Green*, 328 U.S. 549 (1946), with a bloc of justices taking the position that the issue raised in this case, a challenge to congressional districting in Illinois, was a political question unsuitable for judicial resolution. Not until 1962, in the landmark case of **Baker** v. **Carr** (chap. 6), did the Court reverse itself, declaring that legislative malapportionment raises a Fourteenth Amendment equal protection issue that is indeed justiciable. That decision concerned Tennessee, in which some 37 percent of the voters elected over 60 percent of the state senate and 40 percent of the voters elected 64 percent of the state house of representatives.

After the *Baker* decision, the Warren Court followed through with several important rulings. In *Gray* v. *Sanders*, 372 U.S. 368 (1963), the Court invalidated the scheme used in Georgia primaries for nominating statewide officers, known as the county-unit system, in which the winner of the most counties (not the most votes) won the nomination. In so doing, the Court suggested that the equal protection clause of the Fourteenth Amendment requires the one-person-one-vote standard. In *Wesberry* v. *Sanders*, 376 U.S. 1 (1964), that standard was applied to elections to the U.S. House of Representatives, although the Court based its decision on Article 1 of the Constitu-

tion (mandating that representatives be chosen "by the People of the several States") rather than the Fourteenth Amendment. It was in **Reynolds** v. **Sims** that the Court firmly based the one-person-one-vote standard on the equal protection clause, provided an elaborate justification for this policy, and applied it to elections to both houses of state legislatures. The Court rejected a federal analogy to the United States Senate and reached the conclusion that *both* houses of a state legislature must be apportioned on a population basis. The Court emphasized that the creation of the United States Senate was a unique political compromise necessary for the founding fathers to create a new Constitution. The Warren Court later extended the one-person-one-vote policy to countywide elections in *Avery* v. *Midland County*, 390 U.S. 474 (1968). In several decisions, the Warren Court made it clear that it held the states to a strict standard of equality in legislative districting.

While the Court under the chief justiceship of Earl Warren insisted that districts be as mathematically equal as possible, the Burger Court was less sympathetic to malapportionment claims particularly as they concerned state legislative districts. The decision in *Mahan* v. *Howell*, 410 U.S. 315 (1973), signaled an approach that was elaborated upon in *Gaffney* v. *Cummings*, 412 U.S. 735 (1973), *White* v. *Regester*, 412 U.S. 755 (1973), and *White* v. *Weiser*, 412 U.S. 783 (1973). The culmination of this line of decisions insofar as state legislative districts were concerned was **Brown** v. **Thomson**. Congressional districting proved more troublesome in **Karcher** v. **Daggett**, and a different coalition of judges invalidated New Jersey's congressional districting plan with a population difference of under 1 percent as departing without adequate justification from the one-person-one-vote policy. Complicating matters in this case was the fact that political gerrymandering had been involved in that the political party in control of the legislature drew congressional district boundaries so that not only would they be almost equal in population but they would also maximize the party's ability to win the most seats. In 1986 the Court in **Davis** v. **Bandemer** tackled head-on the issue of purely partisan gerrymandering of election districts and gave its approval as long as the one-person-one-vote standard is maintained and the electoral scheme does not "consistently degrade a voter's or a group of voters' influence on the political process as a whole." But this qualification may turn out to be a stimulus for new litigation that would press the Court into clarifying what criteria would satisfy the "consistently degrade" standard that would move the Court to strike down partisan gerrymandering.

In the 1981 decision of *Ball* v. *James*, 451 U.S. 355, the Court refused to apply the one-person-one-vote standard to electing directors of a public water and power district, thereby upholding an Arizona law allowing only the district's landowners the right to vote. On the other hand, the Court unanimously ruled that the one-person-one-vote standard applies to the New York City Board of Estimate (*Board of Estimate of City of New York* v. *Morris*, 109 S.Ct. 1433 [1989]). The Court also struck down on equal protection grounds the requirement that only landowners can serve on the St. Louis-St. Louis County Board of Freeholders, a body that recommends reorganization of local government (*Quinn* v. *Millsap*, 109 S.Ct. 2324 [1989]). In the voting rights case of *Dunn* v. *Blumstein*, 405 U.S. 330 (1972) the Court strictly scrutinized the durational residency requirements for voter registration imposed by Tennessee and found them to be violations of equal protection. Not so, however, were state statutes disenfranchising ex-felons. In *Richardson* v. *Ramirez*, 418 U.S. 24 (1974), the Court ruled that such statutes did not deny equal protection, particularly since Section 2 of the Fourteenth Amendment seemed to approve of disenfranchising convicted criminals.

RIGHTS OF THE POOR: ECONOMIC EQUALITY

Equality claims of poor people have met with a more mixed reception from the Supreme Court than political equality claims. State residency requirements to be eligible for welfare benefits were found by the Warren Court in **Shapiro** v. **Thompson** to violate equal protection. But the Burger Court, in a major equal protection ruling with broader implications for the poor, ruled in **San Antonio School District** v. **Rodriguez** that financing public schools through local property taxation, even though it meant the poorer school districts had less money to spend on education, did not violate the Fourteenth Amendment. The majority justices frankly were concerned that were they to find a constitutional violation, "then it [local taxation] might be an equally impermissible means of providing other necessary services . . . including local police and fire protection, public health and hospitals, and public utility facilities of various kinds." By implication, the state would then have to assume responsibility not simply for a minimum standard of living for the poor but a standard *equal* to that of the nonpoor.

The majority in the *Rodriguez* case rejected the substantive equal protection claims, as did another Court majority in *Arlington Heights* v. *Metropolitan Housing Development Corporation*, 429 U.S. 252 (1977). The Court in *Arlington Heights* saw no denial of equal protection by the suburb of Arlington Heights in its refusal to rezone land in order to permit the construction of a low-income, racially integrated housing project. The Court also found no violation of equal protection by the North Dakota statute permitting some school districts to charge a user fee for school bus transportation, which meant that poor children who could not afford the fee could not use the bus (*Kadrmas* v. *Dickinson Public Schools*, 487 U.S. 450 [1988]). On the other hand, poor people met equal protection success in the case of *United States Department of Agriculture* v. *Moreno*, 413 U.S. 528 (1973), in which a 1971 amendment to the Food Stamp Act that excluded any household containing unrelated individuals from participation in the food stamp program was ruled unconstitutional. The Court ruled that the legislative classification was clearly irrelevant to the purposes of the program and did not rationally further any other legitimate governmental interest. It therefore violated the equal protection component of the Fifth Amendment's due process clause. However, in *Lyng* v. *Castillo*, 477 U.S. 635 (1986), the Court upheld as not violating equal protection subsequent food stamp legislation that defined "household," for eligibility and benefit-level purposes, in a way that resulted in less advantageous treatment of close relatives than of groups of unrelated persons who live together.

Fourteenth Amendment equal protection was found to have been violated in *Memorial Hospital* v. *Maricopa County*, 415 U.S. 250 (1974). In this case, the Court struck down a residency requirement of one year in Maricopa County as a condition for receiving nonemergency hospitalization or medical care at county expense. The durational residence requirement was seen by the Court as creating an invidious classification that penalized indigents for exercising their constitutional right of interstate migration. No compelling state interest was found by the Court to justify the residence requirement. However, the residence requirement for tuition-free admission to Texas public school districts was upheld in **Martinez** v. **Bynum**.

Other decisions concerning the rights of the poor, such as a free lawyer for a poor person accused of a serious crime, are based on parts of the Constitution other than the equal protection clause. The poor have been recognized as having certain rights concerning their use of and treatment by the courts. But the fundamental economic disparities that exist within American society have remained virtually untouched by constitutional law.

OTHER EQUALITY CLAIMS

It is possible to cite a variety of other constitutional claims for equal treatment that have been or are being made, some of which have been the subject of federal or state legislation or court rulings. These include the claim not to be discriminated against on the basis of age, alienage, illegitimacy, being handicapped, or sexual preference. Some Court decisions involving constitutional as opposed to statutory law claims include *Cabell* v. *Chavez-Salido*, 454 U.S. 432 (1982), in which the Court upheld a California statute requiring peace officers to be United States citizens. Here, because a political function of government was involved, strict judicial scrutiny was out of place, so the Court found no Fourteenth Amendment constitutional violation. In contrast, no political function was involved in *Bernal* v. *Fainter*, 467 U.S. 216 (1984), in which the Court struck down as a violation of equal protection a Texas statute requiring a notary public to be a United States citizen.

A Tennessee statute imposing a two-year-limitation period on paternity and child support actions on behalf of certain illegitimate children was found by the Court in *Pickett* v. *Brown*, 462 U.S. 1 (1983), to deny those children equal protection. A similar Pennsylvania six-year statute of limitations was also struck down in **Clark** v. **Jeter**. So, too, was the denial of an illegitimate daughter's claim of a share in the estate of her natural father, who died intestate (*Reed* v. *Campbell*, 476 U.S. 852 [1986]). But the claim of an unwed father that he has an absolute right to notice and an opportunity to be heard before his child may be adopted was rejected by the Court as not violating either due process or equal protection (*Lehr* v. *Robertson*, 463 U.S. 248 [1983]).

Substantive equal protection was alive and well in 1985 in three decisions. In *City of Cleburne, Texas* v. *Cleburne Living Center*, 473 U.S. 432 (1985), the proposed operator of a group home for the mentally retarded brought suit challenging the validity of a zoning ordinance that was used to deny a special use permit for the home. The Court decided that mental retardation was not a quasi-suspect classification; however, requiring a special use permit for the proposed group home for the mentally retarded violated equal protection in the absence of any rational basis in the record for believing that the group home would pose any special threat to the city's legitimate interests. In *Williams* v. *Vermont*, 472 U.S. 14 (1985), the Court struck down a Vermont credit on the use tax given automobile registrants if they were Vermont residents at the time the tax was paid. Those buying automobiles outside of Vermont before becoming residents of Vermont were denied a similar credit. The Court found that there was no rational relationship to a legitimate state policy and that the residency distinction was therefore a denial of equal protection. In *Hooper* v. *Bernalillo County Assessor*, 472 U.S. 612 (1985), a New Mexico Statute was challenged which exempted from the state's property tax $2000 of the taxable value of the property of Vietnam War veterans who were New Mexico residents before May 8, 1976. The Court found this to violate equal protection because it did not bear a rational relationship to the state's asserted objective of encouraging Vietnam veterans to move to New Mexico. In 1986 the Court followed up on this latter ruling in *Attorney General of New York* v. *Soto-Lopez*, 476 U.S. 898. Here, the Court invalidated a New York State law that added bonus points to the civil service examination scores of veterans who had served during wartime and were New York State residents at the time of their entry into military service. The law, said

the Court, was a violation of the equal protection rights of veterans who did not live in New York when they joined the military. They may not be discriminated against solely on the basis of the date of their arrival in the state, such discrimination being an inherent violation of the equal protection clause. In 1989, in *Allegheny Pittsburgh Coal Co.* v. *County Comm'n*, 109 S.Ct. 633, a unanimous Court struck down as an equal protection violation an assessment on real property by a West Virginia county. There were gross disparities in assessments because the county had done no overall reevaluation.

Clearly, the equal protection clause of the Fourteenth Amendment can be seen as having raised the sensitivity of various groupings in society as to the availability of this constitutional provision to advance their claims to equal treatment. Certainly, from the standpoint of the courts, unequal treatment must, at the very least, bear some rational relationship to a legitimate governmental objective. The decisions of the courts over recent years expanding the concept and scope of equal protection no doubt gave a glimmer of hope to those who believed that they were singled out for unequal treatment. Whether the Rehnquist Court and a lower federal court judiciary with a majority of conservative Republican appointees will continue to offer some hope remains to be seen. But don't bet tuition on it.

THE IMPACT OF THE COURT'S DECISIONS

Table 20.1 summarizes the impact of selected Court decisions concerning political and other equality claims. The reprinted cases follow.

Table 20.1   THE IMPACT OF SELECTED COURT DECISIONS, POLITICAL AND OTHER EQUALITY CLAIMS

Case	Year	Impact on Parties	Short-Run Impact	Long-Run Impact
Reynolds v. Sims	1964	Alabama state legislature reapportioned.	This and related decisions led to ill-fated attempt to pass constitutional amendment overturning one-person-one-vote ruling. Stimulated more litigation.	Subtle but distinct changes in state legislatures and U.S. House of Representatives. Urban and suburban issues receive more attention. Breakup of rural fiefdoms, changes in power relationships. Aided disintegration of some local party structures. More blacks and other ethnic minorities elected to state legislatures and Congress.
Brown v. Thomson	1983	Wyoming reapportionment upheld.	Court permits state legislative districts to deviate from equal population subject to the Court's approval.	Uncertain.
Karcher v. Daggett	1983	New Jersey reapportionment of congressional districts struck down.	Court evades issue of political gerrymandering but issue remained and led to *Davis v. Bandemer* (1986).	Congressional districting remains subject to strict equal population basis.
Shapiro v. Thompson	1969	Welfare applicants received welfare benefits.	Some states including New York resisted compliance and enacted residency requirements that were subsequently struck down. Other states complied, adding thousands to those receiving aid. Stimulated further litigation concerning rights of poor people.	Stands as precedent for protecting rights of poor people under equal protection clause. Major poverty law landmark.

(continued)

Table 20.1 *(continued)*

Case	Year	Impact on Parties	Short-Run Impact	Long-Run Impact
San Antonio School District v. Rodriguez	1973	Mexican-American parents of schoolchildren lose suit.	Disparities continue in financial resources available to school districts throughout the nation. Continuation of reliance on property taxes to finance public education.	Equal protection clause of the Fourteenth Amendment unavailable for an attack on the problems arising from the inequality of wealth in the United States. However, on October 2, 1989, the Texas Supreme Court unanimously struck down the state's system for financing public schools as violating the Texas Constitution.
Martinez v. Bynum	1983	Oralia Martinez loses suit.	Residence requirements for free attendance at public schools continues, safeguarding the wealthier school districts from an unwanted influx of poor children.	Disparities in public education available to the more well-to-do as compared to the less affluent remain unchanged throughout the nation.

REYNOLDS v. SIMS,
377 U.S. 533 (1964)

Once the Court determined, in Baker *v.* Carr, *that legislative malapportionment was an issue suitable for the courts to consider, it remained for the Court to establish appropriate constitutional guidelines. Although it had been implied in* Baker, *the one-person-one-vote doctrine was developed at some length in* Reynolds v. Sims. *Furthermore, the Court ruled that both houses of a state legislature must be apportioned according to the one-person-one-vote principle. The case itself involved Sims and other voters who sued a variety of Alabama officials including Probate Judge Reynolds, challenging the apportionment of the Alabama legislature that had been based on the 1900 federal census. While the case was pending, the Alabama legislature enacted two plans for apportionment, neither of which was based on an equal population principle.*

Majority votes: 8
Dissenting votes: 1

MR. CHIEF JUSTICE WARREN delivered the opinion of the Court:. . . .

A predominant consideration in determining whether a State's legislative apportionment scheme constitutes an invidious discrimination violative of rights asserted under the Equal Protection Clause is that the rights allegedly impaired are individual and personal in nature. . . . Undoubtedly, the right of suffrage is a fundamental matter in a free and democratic society. Especially since the right to exercise the franchise in a free and unimpaired manner is preservative of other basic civil and political rights, any alleged infringement of the right of citizens to vote must be carefully and meticulously scrutinized. . . .

Legislators represent people, not trees or acres. Legislators are elected by voters, not farms or cities or economic interests. As long as ours is a representative form of government, and our legislatures are those instruments of government elected directly by and directly representative of the people, the right to elect legislators in a free and unimpaired fashion is a bedrock of our political system. It could hardly be gainsaid that a constitutional claim had been asserted by an allegation that certain otherwise qualified voters had been entirely prohibited from voting for members of their state legislature. And, if a State should provide that the votes of citizens in one part of the State should be given two times, or five times, or 10 times the weight of votes of citizens in another part of the

State, it could hardly be contended that the right to vote of those residing in the disfavored areas had not been effectively diluted. It would appear extraordinary to suggest that a State could be constitutionally permitted to enact a law providing that certain of the State's voters could vote two, five, or 10 times for their legislative representatives, while voters living elsewhere could vote only once. And it is inconceivable that a state law to the effect that, in counting votes for legislators, the votes of citizens in one part of the State would be multiplied by two, five, or 10, while the votes of persons in another area would be counted only at face value, could be constitutionally sustainable. Of course, the effect of state legislative districting schemes which give the same number of representatives to unequal numbers of constituents is identical. Overweighting and overvaluation of the votes of those living here has the certain effect of dilution and undervaluation of the votes of those living there. The resulting discrimination against those individual voters living in disfavored areas is easily demonstrable mathematically. Their right to vote is simply not the same right to vote as that of those living in a favored part of the State. Two, five, or 10 of them must vote before the effect of their voting is equivalent to that of their favored neighbor. Weighting the votes of citizens differently, by any method or means, merely because of where they happen to reside, hardly seems justifiable. . . .

Logically, in a society ostensibly grounded on representative government, it would seem reasonable that a majority of people of a State could elect a majority of that State's legislators. To conclude differently, and to sanction minority control of state legislative bodies, would appear to deny majority rights in a way that far surpasses any possible denial of minority rights that might otherwise be thought to result. Since legislatures are responsible for enacting laws by which all citizens are to be governed, they should be bodies which are collectively responsive to the popular will. And the concept of equal protection has been traditionally viewed as requiring the uniform treatment of persons standing in the same relation to the governmental action questioned or challenged. With respect to the allocation of legislative representation, all voters, as citizens of a State, stand in the same relation regardless of where they live. Any suggested criteria for the differentiation of citizens are insufficient to justify any discrimination, as to the weight of their votes, unless relevant to the permissible purposes of legislative apportionment. Since the achieving of fair and effective representation for all citizens is concededly the basic aim of legislative apportionment, we conclude that the Equal Protection Clause guarantees the opportunity for equal participation by all voters in the election of state legislators. Diluting the weight of votes because of place of residence impairs basic constitutional rights under the Fourteenth Amendment just as much as invidious discrimination based upon factors such as race. Our constitutional system amply provides for the protection of minorities by means other than giving them majority control of state legislatures. And the democratic ideals of equality and majority rule, which have served this Nation so well in the past, are hardly of any less significance for the present and the future.

We are told that the matter of apportioning representation in a state legislature is a complex and many-faceted one. We are advised that States can rationally consider factors other than population in apportioning legislative representation. We are admonished not to restrict the power of the States to impose differing views as to political philosophy on their citizens. We are cautioned about the dangers of entering into political thickets and mathematical quagmires. Our answer is this: a denial of constitutionally protected rights demands judicial protection; our oath and our office require no less of us. . . . To the extent that a citizen's right to vote is debased, he is that much less a citizen. The fact that an individual lives here or there is not a legitimate reason for overweighting or diluting the efficacy of his vote. The complexions of societies and civilizations change, often with amazing rapidity. A nation once primarily rural in character becomes predominantly urban. Representation schemes once fair and equitable become archaic and outdated. But the basic principle of representative government remains, and must remain, unchanged—the weight of a citizen's vote cannot be made to depend on where he lives. Population is, of necessity, the starting point for consideration and the controlling criterion for judgment in legislative apportionment controversies. A citizen, a qualified voter, is no more nor no less so because he lives in the city or on the farm. This is the clear and strong command of our Constitution's Equal Protection Clause. This is an essential part of the concept of a government of laws and not men. This is at the heart of Lincoln's vision of "government of the people, by the people, and for the people." The Equal Protection Clause demands no less than substantially equal state legislative representation for all citizens, of all places as well as of all races.

We hold that, as a basic constitutional standard, the Equal Protection Clause requires that the seats in both houses of a bicameral state legislature must be apportioned on a population basis. Simply stated, an individual's right to vote for state legislators is unconstitutionally impaired when its weight is in a substantial fashion diluted when compared with votes of citizens living in other parts of the State. Since, under neither the existing apportionment provisions nor either of the proposed plans was either of the houses of the Alabama Legislature apportioned on a population basis, the District Court correctly held that all three of these schemes were constitutionally invalid. . . .

Legislative apportionment in Alabama is signally illustrative and symptomatic of the seriousness of this problem in a number of the States. At the time this litigation was commenced, there had been no reapportionment of seats in the Alabama Legislature for over 60 years. Legislative inaction, coupled with the unavailability of any political or judicial remedy, had resulted, with the passage of years, in the perpetuated scheme becoming little more than an irrational anachronism. Consistent failure by the Alabama Legislature to comply with state constitutional requirements as to the frequency of reapportionment and the bases of legislative representation resulted in a minority stranglehold on the State Legislature. Inequality of representation in one house added to the inequality in the other. . . .

Much has been written since our decision in *Baker* v. *Carr* about the applicability of the so-called federal analogy to state legislative apportionment arrangements. After considering the matter, the court below concluded that no conceivable analogy could be drawn between the federal scheme and the apportionment of seats in the Alabama Legislature under the proposed constitutional amendment. We agree with the District Court, and find the federal analogy inapposite and irrelevant to state legislative districting schemes. Attempted reliance on the federal analogy appears often to be little more than an after-the-fact rationalization offered in defense of maladjusted state apportionment arrangements. The original constitutions of 36 of our States provided that representation in both houses of the state legislatures would be based completely, or predominantly, on population. And the Founding Fathers clearly had no intention of establishing a pattern or model for the apportionment of seats in state legislatures when the system of representation in the Federal Congress was adopted. Demonstrative of this is the fact that the Northwest Ordinance, adopted in the same year, 1787, as the Federal Constitution, provided for the apportionment of seats in territorial legislatures solely on the basis of population.

The system of representation in the two Houses of the Federal Congress is one ingrained in our Constitution, as part of the law of the land. It is one conceived out of compromise and concession indispensable to the establishment of our federal republic. Arising from unique historical circumstances, it is based on the consideration that in establishing our type of federalism a group of formerly independent States bound themselves together under the national government. Admittedly, the original 13 States surrendered some of their sovereignty in agreeing to join together "to form a more perfect Union." But at the heart of our constitutional system remains the concept of separate and distinct governmental entities which have delegated some, but not all, of their formerly held powers to the single national government. The fact that almost three-fourths of our present States were never in fact independently sovereign does not detract from our view that the so-called federal analogy is inapplicable as a sustaining precedent for state legislative apportionments. The developing history and growth of our republic cannot cloud the fact that, at the time of the inception of the system of representation in the Federal Congress, a compromise between the larger and smaller States on this matter averted a deadlock in the Constitutional Convention which had threatened to abort the birth of our Nation. . . .

Political subdivisions of States—counties, cities, or whatever—never were and never have been considered as sovereign entities. Rather, they have been traditionally regarded as subordinate governmental instrumentalities created by the State to assist in the carrying out of state governmental functions. . . .

Since we find the so-called federal analogy inapposite to a consideration of the constitutional validity of state legislative apportionment schemes, we necessarily hold that the Equal Protection Clause requires both houses of a state legislature to be apportioned on a population basis. The right of a citizen to equal representation and to have his vote weighted equally with those of all other citizens in the election of members of one house of a bicameral state legislature would amount to little if States could effectively submerge the equal-population principle in the apportionment of seats in the other house. . . .

By holding that as a federal constitutional requisite both houses of a state legislature must be apportioned on a population basis, we mean that the Equal Protection Clause requires that a State make an honest and good faith effort to construct districts, in both houses of its legislature, as nearly of equal population as is practicable. We realize that it is a practical impossibility to arrange legislative districts so that each one has an identical number of residents, or citizens, or voters. Mathematical exactness or precision is hardly a workable constitutional requirement. . . .

A State may legitimately desire to maintain the integrity of various political subdivisions, insofar as possible, and provide for compact districts of contiguous territory in designing a legislative apportionment scheme. Valid considerations may underlie such aims. Indiscriminate districting without any regard for political subdivision or natural or historical boundary lines, may be little more than an open invitation to partisan gerrymandering. Single-member districts may be the rule in one State, while another State might desire to achieve some flexibility by creating multimember or floterial districts. Whatever the means of accomplishment, the overriding objective must be substantial equality of population among the various districts, so that the vote of any citizen is approximately equal in weight to that of any other citizen in the State. . . .

It is so ordered.

MR. JUSTICE CLARK concurring in the affirmance: [omitted]
MR. JUSTICE STEWART [concurring]: [omitted]
MR. JUSTICE HARLAN, dissenting:. . . .

With these cases the Court approaches the end of the third round set in motion by the complaint filed in *Baker* v. *Carr*. What is done today deepens my conviction that judicial entry into this realm is profoundly ill-advised and constitutionally impermissible. . . . I believe that the vitality of our political system, on which in the last analysis all else depends, is weakened by reliance on the judiciary for political reform; in time a complacent body politic may result.

These decisions also cut deeply into the fabric of our federalism. What must follow from them may eventually appear to be the product of State Legislatures. Nevertheless no thinking person can fail to recognize that the aftermath of these cases, however desirable it may be thought in itself, will have been achieved at the cost of a radical alteration in the relationship between the States and the Federal Government, more particularly the Federal Judiciary. Only one who has an overbearing impatience with the federal system and its political processes will believe that that cost was not too high or was inevitable.

Finally, these decisions give support to a current mistaken view of the Constitution and the constitutional function of this Court. This view, in a nut-shell, is that every major social ill in this country can find its cure in some constitutional "principle," and that this Court should "take the lead" in promoting reform when other branches of government fail to act. The Constitution is not a panacea for every blot upon the public welfare, nor should this Court, ordained as a judicial body, be thought of as a general haven for reform movements. . . . [W]hen, in the name of constitutional interpretation, the Court adds something to the Constitution that was deliberately excluded from it, the Court in reality substitutes its view of what should be so for the amending process. . . .

BROWN v. THOMSON,
462 U.S. 835 (1983)

The Wyoming Constitution provides that each of the state's 23 counties shall constitute a senatorial and representative district and shall have at least one senator and one representative, but that the remainder of the senatorial and representative districts shall be apportioned among the counties on a population basis. After the 1980 census, a Wyoming statute reapportioned the House of Representatives but the reapportionment resulted in an average deviation from population equality of 16 percent and a maximum deviation of 89 percent. Niobrara County, the state's least populous county, was given one representative, even though its population was only 2924, the legislature having provided that a county would have a representative even if the statutory formula rounded the county's population to zero. Members of the League of Women Voters and residents of seven counties in which the population per representative is greater than the state average filed an action in federal district court, alleging that granting Niobrara County a representative diluted the voting privileges of appellants and other voters similarly situated in violation of the Fourteenth Amendment. They sought declaratory and injunctive relief. The district court upheld the constitutionality of the reapportionment statute, and the case came before the Supreme Court.

Majority votes: 5
Dissenting votes: 4

JUSTICE POWELL delivered the opinion of the Court:

The issue is whether the State of Wyoming violated the Equal Protection Clause by allocating one of the 64 seats in its House of Representatives to a county the population of which is considerably lower than the average population per state representative. . . .

In *Reynolds* v. *Sims,* 377 U.S. 533, 568 (1964), the Court held that "the Equal Protection Clause requires that the seats in both houses of a bicameral state legislature must be apportioned on a population basis." This holding requires only "that a State make an honest and good faith effort to construct districts . . . as nearly of equal population as is practicable," for "it is a practical impossibility to arrange legislative districts so that each one has an identical number of residents, or citizens, or voters." . . .

We have recognized that some deviations from population equality may be necessary to permit the States to pursue other legitimate objectives such as "maintain[ing] the integrity of various political subdivisions" and "provid[ing] for compact districts of contiguous territory." *Reynolds, supra,* 377 U.S., at 578.

In view of these considerations, we have held that "minor deviations from mathematical equality among state legislative districts are insufficient to make out a prima facie case of invidious discrimination under the Fourteenth Amendment so as to require justification by the State." Our decisions have established, as a general matter, that an apportionment plan with a maximum population deviation under 10% falls within this category of minor deviations. . . . A plan with larger disparities in population, however, creates a prima facie case of discrimination and therefore must be justified by the State. . . . The ultimate inquiry, therefore, is whether the legislature's plan "may reasonably be said to advance [a] rational state policy" and, if so, "whether the population disparities among the districts that have resulted from the pursuit of this plan exceed constitutional limits." *Mahan* v. *Howell,* 410 U.S. 315, 328 (1973).

In this case there is no question that Niobrara County's deviation from population equality—60% below the mean—is more than minor. There also can be no question that Wyoming's constitutional policy—followed since statehood—of using counties as representative districts and ensuring that each county has one representative is supported by substantial and legitimate state concerns. In *Abate* v. *Mundt,* 403 U.S. 182, 185 the Court held that "a desire to preserve the integrity of political subdivisions may justify an apportionment plan which departs from numerical equality." Indeed, the Court in *Reynolds* v. *Sims* singled out preservation of political subdivisions as a clearly legitimate policy. . . .

Moreover, it is undisputed that Wyoming has

applied this factor in a manner "free from any taint of arbitrariness or discrimination." *Roman* v. *Sincock,* 377 U.S. 695, 710 (1964). The State's policy of preserving county boundaries is based on the state Constitution, has been followed for decades, and has been applied consistently throughout the State. As the District Court found, this policy has particular force given the peculiar size and population of the State and the nature of its governmental structure. In addition, population equality is the sole other criterion used, and the State's apportionment formula ensures that population deviations are no greater than necessary to preserve counties as representative districts. . . . Finally, there is no evidence of "a built-in bias tending to favor particular political interests or geographic areas." . . .

In short, this case presents an unusually strong example of an apportionment plan the population variations of which are entirely the result of the consistent and nondiscriminatory application of a legitimate state policy. This does not mean that population deviations of any magnitude necessarily are acceptable. Even a neutral and consistently applied criterion such as use of counties as representative districts can frustrate *Reynolds'* mandate of fair and effective representation if the population disparities are excessively high. "[A] State's policy urged in justification of disparity in district population, however rational, cannot constitutionally be permitted to emasculate the goal of substantial equality." *Mahan* v. *Howell,* 410 U.S., at 326. It remains true, however, as the Court in *Reynolds* noted, that consideration must be given "to the character as well as the degree of deviations from a strict population basis." The consistency of application and the neutrality of effect of the nonpopulation criteria must be considered along with the size of the population disparities in determining whether a state legislative apportionment plan contravenes the Equal Protection Clause.

Here we are not required to decide whether Wyoming's nondiscriminatory adherence to county boundaries justifies the population deviations that exist throughout Wyoming's representative districts. Appellants deliberately have limited their challenge to the alleged dilution of their voting power resulting from the one representative given to Niobrara County. The issue therefore is not whether a 16% average deviation and an 89% maximum deviation, considering the state apportionment plan as a whole, are constitutionally permissible. Rather, the issue is whether Wyoming's policy of preserving county boundaries justifies the additional deviations from population equality resulting from the provision of representation to Niobrara

County. . . . [C]onsiderable population variations will remain even if Niobrara County's representative is eliminated. Under the 63-member plan, the average deviation per representative would be 13% and the maximum deviation would be 66%. These statistics make clear that the grant of a representative to Niobrara County is not a significant cause of the population deviations that exist in Wyoming. . . .

In these circumstances, we are not persuaded that Wyoming has violated the Fourteenth Amendment by permitting Niobrara County to have its own representative.

The judgment of the District Court is

Affirmed.

JUSTICE O'CONNOR, with whom JUSTICE STEVENS joins, concurring: [omitted]

JUSTICE BRENNAN, with whom JUSTICE WHITE, JUSTICE MARSHALL, and JUSTICE BLACKMUN join, dissenting: . . .

Although I disagree with today's holding, it is worth stressing how extraordinarily narrow it is, and how empty of likely precedential value. The Court goes out of its way to make clear that because appellants have chosen to attack only one small feature of Wyoming's reapportionment scheme, the Court weighs only the *marginal* unequalizing effect of that one feature, and not the overall constitutionality of the entire scheme. Hence, although in my view the Court reaches the wrong result in the case at hand, it is unlikely that any future plaintiffs challenging a state reapportionment scheme as unconstitutional will be so unwise as to limit their challenge to the scheme's single most objectionable feature. Whether this will be a good thing for the speed and cost of constitutional litigation remains to be seen. But at least plaintiffs henceforth will know better than to exercise moderation or restraint in mounting constitutional attacks on state apportionment statutes, lest they forfeit their small claim by omitting to assert a bit one. . . .

As the Court implicitly acknowledges, Niobrara County's overrepresentation—60% compared to the ideal district size—cannot be considered "the kind of 'minor' variatio[n] which *Reynolds* v. *Sims* indicated might be justified by local policies counseling the maintenance of established political subdivisions in apportionment plans." . . . Niobrara County voters are given more than two and a half times the voting strength of the average Wyoming voter, and more than triple the voting strength of voters in some counties. . . .

If the rest of the State is considered as well, the

picture becomes even worse. The scheme's treatment of Niobrara County is not a single, isolated abuse, but merely the worst of many objectionable features. Of Wyoming's 23 counties, only nine are within as much as 10% of population proportionality. . . . It is not surprising, then, that the Court makes no effort to uphold the plan as a whole. . . .

Wyoming's error in granting Niobrara County voters a vote worth double or triple the votes of other Wyoming voters is compounded by the impermissibly large disparities in voting power existing in the rest of the apportionment plan. Yet, astonishingly, the Court manages to turn that damning fact to the State's *favor:*

". . . Here, . . . considerable population variations will remain even if Niobrara County's representative is eliminated. . . . These statistics make clear that the grant of a representative to Niobrara County is not a significant cause of the population deviations that exist in Wyoming."

Under this reasoning, the further Wyoming's apportionment plan departs from substantial equality, the more likely it is to withstand constitutional attack. It is senseless to create a rule whereby a single instance of gross inequality is unconstitutional if it occurs in a plan otherwise letter-perfect, but constitutional if it occurs in a plan that, even without that feature, flagrantly violates the Constitution. That, however, is precisely what the Court does today.

JUSTICE O'CONNOR, joined by JUSTICE STEVENS, states that she has "the gravest doubts that a statewide legislative plan with an 89% maximum deviation could survive constitutional scrutiny. . . ." But the Court today holds that just such a plan does survive constitutional scrutiny. I dissent.

KARCHER v. DAGGETT,
462 U.S. 725 (1983)

New Jersey Democrats, in control of the New Jersey legislature, enacted a congressional redistricting plan, based on the 1980 federal census. That plan was signed into law by the outgoing Democratic governor on January 19, 1982, the day before he left office. His successor was a Republican. The Democrats' reapportionment plan provided for 14 congressional districts with an average population per district of 526,059 persons. The largest district had a population of 527,472 and the smallest a population of 523,798; thus the difference between them was under 1 percent. The New

Jersey plan had been introduced by New Jersey State Senator Feldman and is referred to in the decision as the Feldman Plan. The plan gave every advantage to the Democrats and was a classic instance of political gerrymandering. The districts were virtually equal in population but their shapes were contorted and distorted so as to maximize Democratic voting strength. Republicans were outraged and a group of individuals including George T. Daggett challenged the Feldman Plan's validity. Named in the suit before a three-judge federal district court were the Democratic legislative leaders including Alan J. Karcher, the Speaker of the New Jersey Assembly. What followed is recounted in Justice Brennan's Opinion.

Majority votes: 5
Dissenting votes: 4

JUSTICE BRENNAN delivered the opinion of the Court:

The question presented by this appeal is whether an apportionment plan for congressional districts satisfies Art. I, §2 without need for further justification if the population of the largest district is less than one percent greater than the population of the smallest district. A three-judge District Court declared New Jersey's 1982 reapportionment plan unconstitutional on the authority of *Kirkpatrick* v. *Preisler*, 394 U.S. 526 and *White* v. *Weiser*, 412 U.S. 783 (1973), because the population deviations among districts, although small, were not the result of a good-faith effort to achieve population equality. We affirm. . . .

Article I, §2 establishes a "high standard of justice and common sense" for the apportionment of congressional districts: "equal representation for equal numbers of people." *Wesberry* v. *Sanders*, 376 U.S. 1, 18 (1964). Precise mathematical equality, however, may be impossible to achieve in an imperfect world; therefore the "equal representation" standard is enforced only to the extent of requiring that districts be apportioned to achieve population equality "as nearly as is practicable." . . . Article I, §2, therefore, "permits only the limited population variances which are unavoidable despite a good-faith effort to achieve absolute equality, or for which justification is shown." . . .

Thus two basic questions shape litigation over population deviation, in state legislation apportioning congressional districts. First, the court must consider whether the population differences among districts could have been reduced or eliminated altogether by a good-faith effort to draw districts of equal population. Parties challenging apportionment legislation must bear the burden of proof on this issue, and if they fail to show that the differences could have been avoided the apportionment scheme must be upheld. If, however, the plaintiffs can establish that the population differences were not the result of a good-faith effort to achieve equality, the State must bear the burden of proving that each significant variance between districts was necessary to achieve some legitimate goal. . . .

Appellants' principal argument in this case is addressed to the first question described above. They contend that the [New Jersey] Plan should be regarded *per se* as the product of a good-faith effort to achieve population equality because the maximum population deviation among districts is smaller than the predictable undercount in available census data.

Kirkpatrick squarely rejected a nearly identical argument. . . . Adopting any standard other than population equality, using the best census data available, would subtly erode the Constitution's ideal of equal representation. If state legislators knew that a certain *de minimis* level of population differences were acceptable, they would doubtless strive to achieve that level rather than equality. Furthermore, choosing a different standard would import a high degree of arbitrariness into the process of reviewing apportionment plans. In this case, appellants argue that a maximum deviation of approximately 0.7% should be considered *de minimis*. If we accept that argument, how are we to regard deviations of 0.8%, 0.95%, 1%, or 1.1%?

Any standard, including absolute equality, involves a certain artificiality. As appellants point out, even the census data are not perfect, and the well-known restlessness of the American people means that population counts for particular localities are outdated long before they are completed. Yet problems with the data at hand apply equally to any population-based standard we could choose. As between two standards—equality or something less than equality—only the former reflects the aspirations of Art. I, §2.

To accept the legitimacy of unjustified, though small population deviations in this case would mean to reject the basic premise of *Kirkpatrick* and *Wesberry*. We decline appellants invitation to go that far. The unusual rigor of their standard has been noted several times. Because of that rigor, we have required that absolute population equality be the paramount objective of apportionment only in the case of congressional districts, for which the command of Art. I, §2 as regards the national legislature outweighs the local interests that a State may deem relevant in apportioning districts for representa-

tives to state and local legislatures, but we have not questioned the population equality standard for congressional districts. . . . The principle of population equality for congressional districts has not proved unjust or socially or economically harmful in experience. . . . If anything, this standard should cause less difficulty now for state legislatures than it did when we adopted it in *Wesberry*. The rapid advances in computer technology and education during the last two decades make it relatively simple to draw contiguous districts of equal population and at the same time to further whatever secondary goals the State has. Finally, to abandon unnecessarily a clear and oft-confirmed constitutional interpretation would impair our authority in other cases, . . . would implicitly open the door to a plethora of requests that we reexamine other rules that some may consider burdensome, and would prejudice those who have relied upon the rule of law in seeking an equipopulous congressional apportionment in New Jersey. We thus reaffirm that there are no *de minimis* population variations, which could practically be avoided, but which nonetheless meet the standard of Art. I, §2 without justification. . . .

Given that the census-based population deviations in the Feldman [New Jersey] Plan reflect real differences among the districts, it is clear that they could have been avoided or significantly reduced with a good-faith effort to achieve population equality. For that reason alone, it would be inappropriate to accept the Feldman Plan as "functionally equivalent" to a plan with districts of equal population.

The District Court found that several other plans introduced in the 200th Legislature had smaller maximum deviations than the Feldman Plan. . . . Appellants object that the alternative plans considered by the District Court were not comparable to the Feldman Plan because their political characters differed profoundly. . . . We have never denied that apportionment is a political process, or that state legislatures could pursue legitimate secondary objectives as long as those objectives were consistent with a good-faith effort to achieve population equality at the same time. Nevertheless, the claim that political considerations require population differences among congressional districts belongs more properly to the second level of judicial inquiry in these cases, in which the State bears the burden of justifying the differences with particularity. . . .

. . . Any number of consistently applied legislative policies might justify some variance, including, for instance, making districts compact, respecting municipal boundaries, preserving the cores of prior districts, and avoiding contests between incumbent Representatives. As long as the criteria are nondiscriminatory, these are all legitimate objectives that on a proper showing could justify minor population deviations. . . . The State must, however, show with some specificity that a particular objective required the specific deviations in its plan, rather than simply relying on general assertions. The showing required to justify population deviations is flexible, depending on the size of the deviations, the importance of the State's interests, the consistency with which the plan as a whole reflects those interests, and the availability of alternatives that might substantially vindicate those interests yet approximate population equality more closely. By necessity, whether deviations are justified requires case-by-case attention to these factors. . . .

The District Court properly found that appellants did not justify the population deviations in this case. At argument before the District Court and on appeal in this Court, appellants emphasized only one justification for the Feldman Plan's population deviations—preserving the voting strength of racial minority groups. They submitted affidavits from Mayors Kenneth Gibson of Newark and Thomas Cooke of East Orange, discussing the importance of having a large majority of black voters in Newark's Tenth District. . . . The District Court found, however,

"[Appellants] have not attempted to demonstate, nor can they demonstrate, any causal relationship between the goal of preserving minority voting strength in the Tenth District and the population variances in the other districts. . . . We find that the goal of preserving minority voting strength in the Tenth District is not related in any way to the population deviations in the Fourth and Sixth Districts.". . .

The District Court properly applied the two-part test of *Kirkpatrick* v. *Preisler* to New Jersey's 1982 apportionment of districts for the United States House of Representatives. It correctly held that the population deviations in the plan were not functionally equal as a matter of law, and it found that the plan was not a good-faith effort to achieve population equality using the best available census data. It also correctly rejected appellants' attempt to justify the population deviations as not supported by the evidence. The judgment of the District Court, therefore, is

Affirmed.

JUSTICE STEVENS, concurring:
As an alternate ground for affirmance, the appellees contended at oral argument that the bizarre configuration of New Jersey's congressional districts is sufficient to demonstrate that the plan was not adopted in "good faith." This argument, as I understand it, is a claim that the district boundaries are unconstitutional because they are the product of political gerrymandering. Since my vote is decisive in this case, it seems appropriate to explain how this argument influences my analysis of the question that divides the Court. As I have previously pointed out, political gerrymandering is one species of "vote dilution" that is proscribed by the Equal Protection Clause. . . .

The Equal Protection Clause requires every State to govern impartially. When a State adopts rules governing its election machinery or defining electoral boundaries, those rules must serve the interests of the entire community. . . . If they serve no purpose other than to favor one segment—whether racial, ethnic, religious, economic, or political—that may occupy a position of strength at a particular point in time, or to disadvantage a politically weak segment of the community, they violate the constitutional guarantee of equal protection. . . .

A glance at the map, shows district configurations well deserving the kind of descriptive adjectives—"uncouth" and "bizarre"—that have traditionally been used to describe acknowledged gerrymanders. . . .

Such a map prompts an inquiry into the process that led to its adoption. The plan was sponsored by the leadership in the Democratic party, which controlled both houses of the State Legislature as well as the Governor's office, and was signed into law the day before the inauguration of a Republican Governor. The legislators never formally explained the guidelines used in formulating their plan or in selecting it over other available plans. . . .

In sum, the record indicates that the decision-making process leading to adoption of the challenged plan was far from neutral. It was designed to increase the number of Democrats, and to decrease the number of Republicans, that New Jersey's voters would send to Congress in future years. Finally, the record does not show any legitimate justifications for the irregularities in the New Jersey plan. . . .

JUSTICE WHITE, with whom CHIEF JUSTICE BURGER, JUSTICE POWELL, and JUSTICE REHNQUIST join, dissenting:. . . .

I respectfully dissent from the Court's unreasonable insistence on an unattainable perfection in the equalizing of congressional districts. The Court's decision today is not compelled by *Kirkpatrick* v. *Preisler,* and *White* v. *Weiser,* and if the Court is convinced that our cases demand the result reached today, the time has arrived to reconsider these precedents. . . .

There can be little question but that the variances in the New Jersey plan are "statistically insignificant." . . .

. . . [B]ecause Congressional districts are generally much larger than state legislative districts, each percentage point of variation represents a commensurately greater number of people. But these are differences of degree. They suggest that the level at which courts should entertain challenges to districting plans, absent unusual circumstances, should be lower in the congressional cases, but not altogether non-existent. Although I am not wedded to a precise figure, in light of the current range of population deviations, a 5% cutoff appears reasonable. I would not entertain judicial challenges, absent extraordinary circumstances, where the maximum deviation is less than 5%. Somewhat greater deviations, if rationally related to an important state interest, may also be permissible. Certainly, the maintaining of compact, contiguous districts, the respecting of political subdivisions, and efforts to assure political fairness, . . . constitute such interests.

I would not hold up New Jersey's plan as a model reflection of such interests. Nevertheless, the deviation involved here is *de minimis*, and, regardless of what other infirmities the plan may have, constitutional or otherwise, there is no violation of Art. I, §2—the sole issue before us. It would, of course, be a different matter if appellees could demonstrate that New Jersey's plan invidiously discriminated against a racial or political group. . . .

JUSTICE POWELL, dissenting: . . .

In this case, one cannot rationally believe that the New Jersey Legislature considered factors other than the most partisan political goals and population equality. It hardly could be suggested, for example, that the contorted districts 3, 5, and 7 reflect any attempt to follow natural, historical, or local political boundaries. Nor do these district lines reflect any consideration of the likely effect on the quality of representation when the boundaries are so artificial that they are likely to confound the congressmen themselves. . . .

[There is] . . . powerful and persuasive support for a conclusion that the New Jersey Legislature's redistricting plan is an unconstitutional gerrymander. Because this precise issue was not addressed by the District Court, however, it need not be reached here. As to the issue of population equality, I dissent for the reasons set forth . . . in JUSTICE WHITE's dissenting opinion.

DAVIS v. BANDEMER,
478 U.S. 109 (1986)

The issue of political gerrymandering of electoral districts was faced by the Court in this case. The facts concerned the 1981 reapportionment of state legislative districts in Indiana that was made after the 1980 census. Republicans were in the majority in both the Indiana House and Senate. Their reapportionment plan was in conformity with the one-person-one-vote standard but was designed to maximize Republican electoral strength to ensure continued Republican control of the state legislature in the 1980s. The results of the 1982 elections under this plan lived up to the Republican's expectations. Democratic candidates for the House received 51.9 percent of the votes cast statewide but only 43 percent of the seats. Only half the Senate seats were up for election and Democratic candidates received 53.1 percent of the votes cast statewide and 52 percent of the seats. The adverse effects on the Democrats were most clearly felt with the House results. In 1982, before the elections, Indiana Democrats filed suit in federal district court against state officials, alleging that the Republican reapportionment plan violated their rights as Democrats to equal protection as guaranteed by the Fourteenth Amendment. By the time the case went to trial, the 1982 elections already had been held and the Democrats used the results as proof of unconstitutionally discriminatory vote dilution. The district court found for the Democrats, invalidated the 1981 reapportionment plan, enjoined state officials from holding elections under the plan, and ordered the legislature to prepare a new plan. Appeal was taken directly to the Supreme Court, which first had to decide the threshold question as to whether political gerrymandering of districts with equal population was justiciable, and, if so, was the political gerrymandering contained within the Republicans' 1981 reapportionment plan a violation of equal protection. Note that the Court was badly split on these two issues.

Majority votes on jurisdiction: 6
Dissenting votes on jurisdiction: 3
Majority votes to reverse: 7
Dissenting votes: 2

JUSTICE WHITE announced the judgment of the Court and delivered the opinion of the Court as to Part II and an opinion in which JUSTICE BRENNAN, JUSTICE MARSHALL, and JUSTICE BLACKMUN joined as to Parts I, III, and IV:

In this case, we review a judgment from a three-judge District Court, which sustained an equal protection challenge to Indiana's 1981 state apportionment on the basis that the law unconstitutionally diluted the votes of Indiana Democrats. 603 F.Supp. 1479 (1984). Although we find such political gerrymandering to be justiciable, we conclude that the District Court applied an insufficiently demanding standard in finding unconstitutional vote dilution. Consequently, we reverse.

I [THE FACTS OF THE CASE]
. . . .
II . . .

The outlines of the political question doctrine were described and to a large extent defined in *Baker* v. *Carr*. . . . Th[e] analysis [in *Baker*] applies equally to the question now before us. Disposition of this question does not involve us in a matter more properly decided by a coequal branch of our Government. There is no risk of foreign or domestic disturbance, and in light of our cases since *Baker* we are not persuaded that there are no judicially discernible and manageable standards by which political gerrymander cases are to be decided.

It is true that the type of claim that was presented in *Baker* v. *Carr* was subsequently resolved in this Court by the formulation of the "one person, one vote" rule. See, *e.g., Reynolds* v. *Sims,* 377 U.S., at 557–561. The mere fact, however, that we may not now similarly perceive a likely arithmetic presumption in the instant context does not compel a conclusion that the claims presented here are nonjusticiable. The one person, one vote principle had not yet been developed when *Baker* was decided. At that time, the Court did not rely on the potential for such a rule in finding justiciability. Instead, . . . the Court contemplated simply that legislative linedrawing in the districting context would be susceptible of adjudication under the applicable constitutional criteria.

Furthermore, in formulating the one-person, one-vote formula, the Court characterized the question posed by election districts of disparate size as an issue of fair representation. In such cases, it is not that anyone is deprived of a vote or that any person's vote is not counted. Rather, it is that one electoral district elects a single representative and another district of the same size elects two or more—the elector's vote in the former district having less weight in the sense that he may vote for and his district be represented by only one legislator, while his neighbor in the adjoining district votes for and is represented by two or more. . . .

The issue here is of course different from that adjudicated in *Reynolds*. It does not concern dis-

tricts of unequal size. Not only does everyone have the right to vote and to have his vote counted, but each elector may vote for and be represented by the same number of lawmakers. Rather, the claim is that each political group in a State should have the same chance to elect representatives of its choice as any other political group. Nevertheless, the issue is one of representation, and we decline to hold that such claims are never justiciable.

Our racial gerrymander cases such as *White* v. *Regester* and *Whitcomb* v. *Chavis* indicate as much. In those cases, there was no population variation among the districts, and no one was precluded from voting. The claim instead was that an identifiable racial or ethnic group had an insufficient chance to elect a representative of its choice and that district lines should be redrawn to remedy this alleged defect. In both cases, we adjudicated the merits of such claims, rejecting the claim in *Whitcomb* and sustaining it in *Regester*. Just as clearly, in *Gaffney* v. *Cummings,* where the districts also passed muster under the *Reynolds* formula, the claim was that the legislature had manipulated district lines to afford political groups in various districts an enhanced opportunity to elect legislators of their choice. Although advising caution, we said that "we *must* . . . respond to [the] claims . . . that even if acceptable populationwise, the . . . plan was invidiously discriminatory because a 'political fairness principle' was followed. . . ." 412 U.S., at 751–752 (emphasis added). We went on to hold that the statute at issue did not violate the Equal Protection Clause.

These decisions support a conclusion that this case is justiciable. . . .

In fact, JUSTICE O'CONNOR's attempt to distinguish this political gerrymandering claim from the racial gerrymandering claims that we have consistently adjudicated demonstrates the futility of such an effort. Her conclusion that the claim in this case is not justiciable seems to rest on a dual concern that no judicially manageable standards exist and that adjudication of such claims requires an initial policy decision that the judiciary should not make. Yet she does not point out how the standards that we set forth here for adjudicating this political gerrymandering claim are less manageable than the standards that have been developed for racial gerrymandering claims. Nor does she demonstrate what initial policy decision—regarding, for example, the desirability of fair group representation—we have made here that we have not made in the race cases. She merely asserts that because race has historically been a suspect classification individual minority voters' rights are more immediately related to a racial minority group's voting strength. This, in combination with "the greater warrant the Equal Protection Clause gives the federal courts to intervene for protection against racial discrimination, suffice to render racial gerrymandering claims justiciable."

Reliance on these assertions to determine justiciability would transform the narrow categories of "political questions" that *Baker* v. *Carr* carefully defined into an ad hoc litmus test of this Court's reactions to the desirability of and need for judicial application of constitutional or statutory standards to a given type of claim. JUSTICE O'CONNOR's own discussion seems to reflect such an approach: She concludes that because political gerrymandering may be a "self-limiting enterprise" there is no need for judicial intervention. She also expresses concern that our decision today will lead to "political instability and judicial malaise," because nothing will prevent members of other identifiable groups from bringing similar claims. To begin with, JUSTICE O'CONNOR's factual assumptions are by no means obviously correct: It is not clear that political gerrymandering *is* a self-limiting enterprise or that other groups will have any great incentive to bring gerrymandering claims, given the requirement of a showing of discriminatory intent. At a more fundamental level, however, JUSTICE O'CONNOR's analysis is flawed because it focuses on the perceived need for judicial review and on the potential practical problems with allowing such review. Validation of the consideration of such amorphous and wide-ranging factors in assessing justiciability would alter substantially the analysis the Court enunciated in *Baker* v. *Carr,* and we decline JUSTICE O'CONNOR's implicit invitation to rethink that approach.

III

Having determined that the political gerrymandering claim in this case is justiciable, we turn to the question whether the District Court erred in holding that appellees had alleged and proved a violation of the Equal Protection Clause. . . .

[T]he question is whether a particular group has been unconstitutionally denied its chance to effectively influence the political process. In a challenge to an individual district, this inquiry focuses on the opportunity of members of the group to participate in party deliberations in the slating and nomination of candidates, their opportunity to register and vote, and hence their chance to directly influence the election returns and to secure the attention of the winning candidate. Statewide, however, the inquiry centers on the voters' direct or indirect influence on the elections of the state legislature as a whole. And, as in individual district cases, an equal protection violation may be found only where the electoral system substantially disadvantages certain voters in their opportunity to influence the political process effectively. In this context such a finding of unconstitutionality must be supported by evidence of continued frustration of the will of a majority of the voters or effective denial to a minority of voters of a fair chance to influence the political process.

Based on these views, we would reject the District Court's apparent holding that *any* interference with an opportunity to elect a representative of one's choice would be sufficient to allege or make out an equal protection violation, unless justified by some acceptable state interest that the State would be required to demonstrate. In addition to being contrary to the above-described conception of an unconstitutional political gerrymander such a low threshold for legal action would invite attack on all or almost all reapportionment statutes. District-based elections hardly ever produce a perfect fit between votes and representation. The one-person, one-vote imperative often mandates departure from this result as does the no-retrogression rule required by §5 of the Voting Rights Act. Inviting attack on minor departures from some supposed norm would too much embroil the judiciary in second-guessing what has consistently been referred to as a political task for the legislature, a task that should not be monitored too closely unless the express or tacit goal is to effect its removal from legislative halls. We decline to take a major step toward that end, which would be so much at odds with our history and experience.

The view that a prima facie case of illegal discrimination in reapportionment requires a showing of more than a *de minimis* effect is not unprecedented. Reapportionment cases involving the one-person, one-vote principle such as *Gaffney* v. *Cummings* and *White* v. *Regester* provide support for such a requirement. In the present, considerably more complex context, it is also appropriate to require allegations and proof that the challenged legislative plan has had or will have effects that are sufficiently serious to require intervention by the federal courts in state reapportionment decisions.

The District Court's findings do not satisfy this threshold condition to stating and proving a cause of action. . . .

Relying on a single election to prove unconstitutional discrimination is unsatisfactory. . . . Nor was there any finding that the 1981 reapportionment would consign the Democrats to a minority status in the Assembly throughout the 1980's or that the Democrats would have no hope of doing any better in the reapportionment that would occur after the 1990 census. Without findings of this nature, the District Court erred in concluding that the 1981 Act violated the Equal Protection Clause. . . .

In response to our approach, JUSTICE POWELL suggests an alternative method for evaluating equal protection claims of political gerrymandering. . . .

In rejecting JUSTICE POWELL's approach, we do not mean to intimate that the factors he considers are entirely irrelevant. The election results obviously are relevant to a showing of the effects required to prove a political gerrymandering claim under our view. And the district configurations may be combined with vote projections to predict future election results, which are also relevant to the effects showing. The other factors, even if not relevant to the effects issue, might well be relevant to an equal protection claim. The equal protection argument would proceed along the following lines: If there were a discriminatory effect and a discriminatory intent, then the legislation would be examined for valid underpinnings. Thus, evidence of exclusive legislative process and deliberate drawing of district lines in accordance with accepted gerrymandering principles would be relevant to intent, and evidence of valid and invalid configuration would be relevant to whether the districting plan met legitimate state interests.

This course is consistent with our equal protection cases generally and is the course we follow here: We assumed that there was discriminatory intent, found that there was insufficient discriminatory effect to constitute an equal protection violation, and therefore did not reach the question of the state interests (legitimate or otherwise) served by the particular districts as they were created by the legislature. Consequently, the valid or invalid configuration of the districts was an issue we did not need to consider.

It seems inappropriate, however, to view these separate components of an equal protection analysis as "factors" to be considered together without regard for their separate functions or meaning. This undifferentiated consideration of the various factors confuses the import of each factor and disguises the essential conclusion of JUSTICE POWELL's opinion: that disproportionate election results alone are a sufficient effect to support a finding of a constitutional violation.

In sum, we decline to adopt the approach enunciated by JUSTICE POWELL. In our view, that approach departs from our past cases and invites judi-

cial interference in legislative districting whenever a political party suffers at the polls. We recognize that our own view may be difficult of application. Determining when an electoral system has been "arranged in a manner that will consistently degrade a voter's or a group of voters' influence on the political process as a whole," is of necessity a difficult inquiry. Nevertheless, we believe that it recognizes the delicacy of intruding on this most political of legislative functions and is at the same time consistent with our prior cases regarding individual multi-member districts, which have formulated a parallel standard.

IV

In sum, we hold that political gerrymandering cases are properly justiciable under the Equal Protection Clause. We also conclude, however, that a threshold showing of discriminatory vote dilution is required for a prima facie case of an equal protection violation. In this case, the findings made by the District Court of an adverse effect on the appellees do not surmount the threshold requirement. Consequently, the judgment of the District Court is

Reversed.

CHIEF JUSTICE BURGER, concurring in the judgment: [omitted]

JUSTICE O'CONNOR, with whom CHIEF JUSTICE BURGER and JUSTICE REHNQUIST join, concurring in the judgment:

Today the Court holds that claims of political gerrymandering lodged by members of one of the political parties that make up our two-party system are justiciable under the Equal Protection Clause of the Fourteenth Amendment. Nothing in our precedents compels us to take this step, and there is every reason not to do so. I would hold that the partisan gerrymandering claims of major political parties raise a nonjusticiable political question that the judiciary should leave to the legislative branch as the Framers of the Constitution unquestionably intended. Accordingly, I would reverse the District Court's judgment on the grounds that appellees' claim is nonjusticiable.

There can be little doubt that the emergence of a strong and stable two-party system in this country has contributed enormously to sound and effective government. The preservation and health of our political institutions, state and federal, depends to no small extent on the continued vitality of our two-party system, which permits both stability and measured change. The opportunity to control the drawing of electoral boundaries through the legislative process of apportionment is a critical and traditional part of politics in the United States, and one that plays no small role in fostering active participation in the political parties at every level. Thus, the legislative business of apportionment is fundamentally a political affair, and challenges to the manner in which an apportionment has been carried out— by the very parties that are responsible for this process—present a political question in the truest sense of the term.

To turn these matters over to the federal judiciary is to inject the courts into the most heated partisan issues. It is predictable that the courts will respond by moving away from the nebulous standard a plurality of the Court fashions today and toward some form of rough proportional representation for all political groups. The consequences of this shift will be as immense as they are unfortunate. I do not believe, and the Court offers not a shred of evidence to suggest, that the Framers of the Constitution intended the judicial power to encompass the making of such fundamental choices about how this Nation is to governed. Nor do I believe that the proportional representation towards which the Court's expansion of equal protection doctrine will lead is consistent with our history, our traditions, or our political institutions.

The Court pays little heed to these considerations, which should inform any sensible jurisprudence of Article III and of the Equal Protection Clause. . . .

The step taken today is a momentous one, which if followed in the future can only lead to political instability and judicial malaise. If members of the major political parties are protected by the Equal Protection Clause from dilution of their voting strength, then members of every identifiable group that possesses distinctive interests and tends to vote on the basis of those interests should be able to bring similar claims. Federal courts will have no alternative but to attempt to recreate the complex process of legislative apportionment in the context of adversary litigation in order to reconcile the competing claims of political, religious, ethnic, racial, occupational, and socioeconomic groups. Even if there were some way of limiting such claims to organized political parties, the fact remains that the losing party or the losing group of legislators in every reapportionment will now be invited to fight the battle anew in federal court. Apportionment is so important to legislators and political parties that the burden of proof the plurality places on political gerrymandering plaintiffs is unlikely to deter the routine lodging of such complaints. Notwithstanding the plurality's threshold requirement of discrim-

inatory effects, the Court's holding that political gerrymandering claims are justiciable has opened the door to pervasive and unwarranted judicial superintendence of the legislative task of apportionment. There is simply no clear stopping point to prevent the gradual evolution of a requirement of roughly proportional representation for every cohesive political group. . . .

. . . [T]here is good reason to think that political gerrymandering is a self-limiting enterprise. In order to gerrymander, the legislative majority must weaken some of its safe seats, thus exposing its own incumbents to greater risks of defeat—risks they may refuse to accept past a certain point. Similarly, an overambitious gerrymander can lead to disaster for the legislative majority: because it has created more seats in which it hopes to win relatively narrow victories, the same swing in overall voting strength will tend to cost the legislative majority more and more seats as the gerrymander becomes more ambitious. More generally, each major party presumably has ample weapons at its disposal to conduct the partisan struggle that often leads to a partisan apportionment, but also often leads to a bipartisan one. There is no proof before us that political gerrymandering is an evil that cannot be checked or cured by the people or by the parties themselves. Absent such proof, I see no basis for concluding that there is a need, let alone a constitutional basis, for judicial intervention. . . .

JUSTICE POWELL, with whom JUSTICE STEVENS joins, concurring in Part II [of JUSTICE WHITE's opinion] and dissenting: . . .

. . . The plurality acknowledges that the record in this case supports a finding that the challenged redistricting plan was adopted for the purpose of discriminating against Democratic voters. The plurality argues, however, that appellees failed to establish that their voting strength was diluted statewide despite uncontradicted proof that certain key districts were grotesquely gerrymandered to enhance the election prospects of Republican candidates. This argument appears to rest solely on the ground that the legislature accomplished its gerrymander consistent with "one person, one vote," in the sense that the legislature designed voting districts of approximately equal population and erected no direct barriers to Democratic voters' exercise of the franchise. Since the essence of a gerrymandering claim is that the members of a political party as a group have been denied their right to "fair and effective representation," I believe that the claim cannot be tested solely by reference to "one person, one vote." Rather, a number of other relevant neutral factors must be considered. Because the plurality ignores such factors and fails to enunciate standards by which to determine whether a legislature has enacted an unconstitutional gerrymander, I dissent. . . .

In this case, appellees offered convincing proof of the ease with which mapmakers, consistent with the "one person, one vote" standard, may design a districting plan that purposefully discriminates against political opponents as well as racial minorities. Computer technology now enables gerrymanderers to achieve their purpose while adhering perfectly to the requirement that districts be of equal population. Relying on the factors correctly described by JUSTICE STEVENS in *Karcher* v. *Daggett*, the District Court carefully reviewed appellees' evidence and found that the redistricting law was intended to and did unconstitutionally discriminate against Democrats as a group. We have held that a district court's ultimate determination that a redistricting plan was "being maintained for discriminatory purposes," as well as its "subsidiary findings of fact," may not be set aside by a reviewing court unless they are clearly erroneous. The plurality ignores these precedents. The plurality also disregards the various factors discussed by the District Court as adequate indicia of unconstitutional gerrymandering.

A court should look first to the legislative process by which the challenged plan was adopted. Here, the District Court found that the procedures used in redistricting Indiana were carefully designed to exclude Democrats from participating in the legislative process. . . .

Next, the District Court found that the maps "conspicuously ignore[d] traditional political subdivisions, with no concern for any adherence to principles of community interest." The court carefully described how the mapmakers carved up counties, cities, and even townships in their effort to draw lines beneficial to the majority party. Many districts meander through several counties, picking up a number of townships from each. The District Court explained why this failure to honor county boundaries could be expected to have a detrimental impact on citizens' exercise of their vote. In Indiana, the county government is the seat of local affairs. The redistricting dissects counties into strange shapes lacking in common interests, on one occasion even placing the seat of one county in a voting district composed of townships from other counties. Under these conditions, the District Court expressly found that "the potential for voter disillusion and nonparticipation is great," as voters are forced to focus their political activities in artificial electoral units. Intelligent voters, regardless of

party affiliation, resent this sort of political manipulation of the electorate for no public purpose. . . .

In addition to the foregoing findings that apply to both the House and Senate plans, the District Court also noted the substantial evidence that appellants were motivated solely by partisan considerations. . . . In short, the record unequivocally demonstrates that in 1981 the Republican-dominated General Assembly deliberately sought to design a redistricting plan under which members of the Democratic party would be deprived of a fair opportunity to win control of the General Assembly at least until 1991, the date of the next redistricting. . . .

The District Court found, and I agree, that appellants failed to justify the discriminatory impact of the plan by showing that the plan had a rational basis in permissible neutral criteria. Appellants' primary justification was that the plan comports with the principle of "one person, one vote." Their plan did adhere to that objective, with population deviations between House districts of 1.05 percent and between Senate districts of 1.15 percent. But reliance on "one person, one vote" does not sufficiently explain or justify the discrimination the plan inflicted on Democratic voters as a group. The District Court expressly found that the irregular district shapes could not be justified on the basis of population distribution. Nor does adherence to "one person, one vote" excuse the mapmakers' failure to honor establish political or community boundaries. It does not excuse the irrational use of multimember districts, with their devastating impact on the voting strength of Democrats. . . .

SHAPIRO v. THOMPSON,
394 U.S. 618 (1969)

This decision considered three separate appeals, all involving the denial of welfare benefits to poor people because of failure to meet a one-year residency requirement. In the lead case, Vivian Marie Thompson, a 19-year-old unwed mother of one child pregnant with another, moved from Boston to Hartford to be with her mother. Ms. Thompson applied for and was denied assistance under the program for Aid to Families with Dependent Children on the ground that she failed to meet the Connecticut statutory requirement of living in the state for one year before filing an application. She subsequently sued Bernard Shapiro, the Commissioner of Welfare for the State of Connecticut, in the federal District Court for the District of Connecticut. A three-judge court ruled the Connecticut provision to be unconstitutional, infringing the right to travel and also violating the equal protection clause of the Fourteenth Amendment. A similar set of events transpired with other litigants in an appeal from Pennsylvania. Here, too, a three-judge federal district court struck down the state residency requirement. The third appeal was from the District of Columbia; a three-judge district court ruled that Washington, D.C.'s residency requirement for welfare recipients violated the due process clause of the Fifth Amendment.

Majority votes: 6
Dissenting votes: 3

MR. JUSTICE BRENNAN delivered the opinion of the Court:. . . .

There is no dispute that the effect of the waiting-period requirement in each case is to create two classes of needy resident families indistinguishable from each other except that one is composed of residents who have resided a year or more, and the second of residents who have resided less than a year in the jurisdiction. On the basis of this sole difference the first class is granted and the second class is denied welfare aid upon which may depend the ability of the families to obtain the very means to subsist—food, shelter, and other necessities of life. In each case, the District Court found that appellees met the test for residence in their jurisdictions, as well as all other eligibility requirements except the requirement of residence for a full year prior to their applications. On reargument, appellees' central contention is that the statutory prohibition of benefits to residents of less than a year creates a classification which constitutes an invidious discrimination denying them equal protection of the laws. We agree. The interests which appellants assert are promoted by the classification either may not constitutionally be promoted by government or are not compelling governmental interests.

Primarily, appellants justify the waiting-period requirement as a protective device to preserve the fiscal integrity of state public assistance programs. It is asserted that people who require welfare assistance during their first year of residence in a State are likely to become continuing burdens on state welfare programs. Therefore, the argument runs, if such people can be deterred from entering the jurisdiction by denying them welfare benefits during the first year, state programs to assist long-time residents will not be impaired by a substantial influx of indigent newcomers.

There is weighty evidence that exclusion from the jurisdiction of the poor who need or may need

relief was the specific objective of these provisions. In the Congress, sponsors of federal legislation to eliminate all residence requirements have been consistently opposed by representatives of state and local welfare agencies who have stressed the fears of the States that elimination of the requirements would result in a heavy influx of individuals into States providing the most generous benefits. . . .

We do not doubt that the one-year waiting period device is well suited to discourage the influx of poor families in need of assistance. An indigent who desires to migrate, resettle, find a new job, and start a new life will doubtless hesitate if he knows that he must risk making the move without the possibility of falling back on state welfare assistance during his first year of residence, when his need may be most acute. But the purpose of inhibiting migration by needy persons into the State is constitutionally impermissible.

This Court long ago recognized that the nature of our Federal Union and our constitutional concepts of personal liberty unite to require that all citizens be free to travel throughout the length and breadth of our land uninhibited by statutes, rules, or regulations which unreasonably burden or restrict this movement. . . .

Alternatively, appellants argue that even if it is impermissible for a State to attempt to deter the entry of all indigents, the challenged classification may be justified as a permissible state attempt to discourage those indigents who would enter the State solely to obtain larger benefits. We observe first that none of the statutes before us is tailored to serve that objective. Rather, the class of barred newcomers is all-inclusive, lumping the great majority who come to the State for other purposes with those who come for the sole purpose of collecting higher benefits. In actual operation, therefore, the three statutes enact what in effect are non-rebuttable presumptions that every applicant for assistance in his first year of residence came to the jurisdiction solely to obtain higher benefits. Nothing whatever in any of these records supplies any basis in fact for such a presumption.

More fundamentally, a State may no more try to fence out those indigents who seek higher welfare benefits than it may try to fence out indigents generally. Implicit in any such distinction is the notion that indigents who enter a State with the hope of securing higher welfare benefits are somehow less deserving than indigents who do not take this consideration into account. But we do not perceive why a mother who is seeking to make a new life for herself and her children should be regarded as less deserving because she considers, among other factors, the level of a State's public assistance. Surely such a mother is no less deserving than a mother who moves into a particular State in order to take advantage of its better educational facilities. . . .

We recognize that a State has a valid interest in preserving the fiscal integrity of its programs. It may legitimately attempt to limit its expenditures, whether for public assistance, public education, or any other program. But a State may not accomplish such a purpose by invidious distinctions between classes of its citizens. It could not, for example, reduce expenditures for education by barring indigent children from its schools. Similarly, in the cases before us, appellants must do more than show that denying welfare benefits to new residents saves money. The saving of welfare costs cannot justify an otherwise invidious classification.

In sum, neither deterrence of indigents from migrating to the State nor limitation of welfare benefits to those regarded as contributing to the State is a constitutionally permissible state objective.

Appellants next advance as justification certain administrative and related governmental objectives allegedly served by the waiting-period requirement. They argue that the requirement (1) facilitates the planning of the welfare budget; (2) provides an objective test of residency; (3) minimizes the opportunity for recipients fraudulently to receive payments from more than one jurisdiction; and (4) encourages early entry of new residents into the labor force.

At the outset, we reject appellants' argument that a mere showing of a rational relationship between the waiting period and these four admittedly permissible state objectives will suffice to justify the classification. . . .

The argument that the waiting-period requirement facilitates budget predictability is wholly unfounded. The records in all three cases are utterly devoid of evidence that either State or the District of Columbia in fact uses the one-year requirement as a means to predict the number of people who will require assistance in the budget year. . . .

Similarly, there is no need for a State to use the one-year waiting period as a safeguard against fraudulent receipt of benefits; for less drastic means are available, and are employed, to minimize that hazard. . . .

We conclude therefore that appellants in these cases do not use and have no need to use the one-year requirement for the governmental purposes suggested. Thus, even under traditional equal protection tests a classification of welfare applicants according to whether they have lived in the State for one year would seem irrational and unconstitutional. But, of course, the traditional criteria do not

apply in these cases. Since the classification here touches on the fundamental right of interstate movement, its constitutionality must be judged by the stricter standard of whether it promotes a *compelling* state interest. Under this standard, the waiting-period requirement clearly violates the Equal Protection Clause. . . .

The waiting-period requirement in the District of Columbia Code . . . is also unconstitutional even though it was adopted by Congress as an exercise of federal power. In terms of federal power, the discrimination created by the one-year requirement violates the Due Process Clause of the Fifth Amendment . . . . For the reasons we have stated in invalidating the Pennsylvania and Connecticut provisions, the District of Columbia provision is also invalid—the Due Process Clause of the Fifth Amendment prohibits Congress from denying public assistance to poor persons otherwise eligible solely on the ground that they have not been residents of the District of Columbia for one year at the time their applications are filed.

Accordingly, the judgments are

Affirmed.

MR. JUSTICE STEWART, concurring: [omitted]
MR. CHIEF JUSTICE WARREN, with whom MR. JUSTICE BLACK joins, dissenting:

In my opinion the issue before us can be simply stated: May Congress, acting under one of its enumerated powers, impose minimal nationwide residence requirements or authorize the States to do so? Since I believe that Congress does have this power and has constitutionally exercised it in these cases, I must dissent. . . .

Congress has imposed a residence requirement in the District of Columbia and authorized the States to impose similar requirements. The issue before us must therefore be framed in terms of whether Congress may create minimal residence requirements, not whether the States, acting alone, may do so. Appellees insist that a congressionally mandated residence requirement would violate their right to travel. The import of their contention is that Congress, even under its "plenary" power to control interstate commerce, is constitutionally prohibited from imposing residence requirements. I reach a contrary conclusion for I am convinced that the extent of the burden on interstate travel when compared with the justification for its imposition requires the Court to uphold this exertion of federal power.

Congress, pursuant to its commerce power, has enacted a variety of restrictions upon interstate travel. It has taxed air and rail fares and the gasoline needed to power cars and trucks which move interstate. Many of the federal safety regulations of common carriers which cross state lines burden the right to travel. And Congress has prohibited by criminal statute interstate travel for certain purposes. . . . Although these restrictions operate as a limitation upon free interstate movement of persons, their constitutionality appears well settled. . . .

Appellees suggest . . . that Congress was not motivated by rational considerations. Residence requirements are imposed, they insist, for the illegitimate purpose of keeping poor people from migrating. Not only does the legislative history point to an opposite conclusion, but it also must be noted that "[i]nto the motives which induced members of Congress to [act] this Court may not inquire." We do not attribute an impermissible purpose to Congress if the result would be to strike down an otherwise valid statute. Since the congressional decision is rational and the restriction on travel insubstantial, I conclude that residence requirements can be imposed by Congress as an exercise of its power to control interstate commerce consistent with the constitutionally guaranteed right to travel. . . .

The Court's decision reveals only the top of the iceberg. Lurking beneath are the multitude of situations in which States have imposed residence requirements including eligibility to vote, to engage in certain professions or occupations or to attend a state-supported university. Although the Court takes pains to avoid acknowledging the ramifications of its decision, its implications cannot be ignored. I dissent.

MR. JUSTICE HARLAN, dissenting: . . . .

In upholding the equal protection argument, the Court has applied an equal protection doctrine of relatively recent vintage: the rule that statutory classifications which either are based upon certain "suspect" criteria or affect "fundamental rights" will be held to deny equal protection unless justified by a "compelling" governmental interest. . . .

I think that . . . the "compelling interest" doctrine is sound when applied to racial classifications, for historically the Equal Protection Clause was largely a product of the desire to eradicate legal distinctions founded upon race. However, I believe that the more recent extensions have been unwise. . . . For it has been held that a statutory classification is subject to the "compelling interest" test if the result of the classification may be to affect a "fundamental right," regardless of the basis of the classification. . . .

I think this branch of the "compelling interest"

doctrine particularly unfortunate and unnecessary. It is unfortunate because it creates an exception which threatens to swallow the standard equal protection rule. Virtually every state statute affects important rights. This Court has repeatedly held, for example, that the traditional equal protection standard is applicable to statutory classifications affecting such fundamental matters as the right to pursue a particular occupation, the right to receive greater or smaller wages or to work more or less hours, and the right to inherit property. Rights such as these are in principle indistinguishable from those involved here, and to extend the "compelling interest" rule to all cases in which such rights are affected would go far toward making this Court a "super-legislature." This branch of the doctrine is also unnecessary. When the right affected is one assured by the Federal Constitution, any infringement can be dealt with under the Due Process Clause. But when a statute affects only matters not mentioned in the Federal Constitution and is not arbitrary or irrational, I must reiterate that I know of nothing which entitles this Court to pick out particular human activities, characterize them as "fundamental," and give them added protection under an unusually stringent equal protection test. . . .

SAN ANTONIO SCHOOL DISTRICT v. RODRIGUEZ, 411 U.S. 1 (1973)

This case raised the issue of the constitutionality of the traditional method of financing local public schools through the local property tax. In practice, this has meant that the more well-to-do communities have more money to spend on public education than the poorer communities, which has led some to charge that children in less affluent communities necessarily receive an inferior education because those communities have fewer resources upon which to draw. The Rodriguez family argued through their attorneys that the Texas system of financing public schools through local property taxation denied them equal protection of the laws in violation of the Fourteenth Amendment.

Majority votes: 5
Dissenting votes: 4

MR. JUSTICE POWELL delivered the opinion of the Court: . . . .

. . . The District Court held that the Texas system [of financing public education] discriminates on the basis of wealth in the manner in which education is provided for its people. Finding that wealth is a "suspect" classification and that education is a "fundamental" interest, the District Court held that the Texas system could be sustained only if the State could show that it was premised upon some compelling state interest. On this issue the court concluded that "[n]ot only are defendants unable to demonstrate compelling state interests . . . they fail even to establish a reasonable basis for these classifications." . . .

Texas virtually concedes that its historically rooted dual system of financing education could not withstand the strict judicial scrutiny that this Court has found appropriate in reviewing legislative judgments that interfere with fundamental constitutional rights or that involve suspect classifications. If, as previous decisions have indicated, strict scrutiny means that the State's system is not entitled to the usual presumption of validity, that the State rather than the complainants must carry a "heavy burden of justification," that the State must demonstrate that its educational system has been structured with "precision," and is "tailored" narrowly to serve legitimate objectives and that it has selected the "less drastic means" for effectuating its objectives, the Texas financing system and its counterpart in virtually every other State will not pass muster. . . . [T]he State defends the system's rationality with vigor and disputes the District Court's finding that it lacks a "reasonable basis."

This, then, establishes the framework for our analysis. We must decide, first, whether the Texas system of financing public education operates to the disadvantage of some suspect class or impinges upon a fundamental right explicitly or implicitly protected by the Constitution, thereby requiring strict judicial scrutiny. If so, the judgment of the District Court should be affirmed. If not, the Texas scheme must still be examined to determine whether it rationally furthers some legitimate, articulated state purpose and therefore does not constitute an invidious discrimination in violation of the Equal Protection Clause of the Fourteenth Amendment.

The District Court's opinion does not reflect the novelty and complexity of the constitutional questions posed by appellees' challenge to Texas' system of school financing. In concluding that strict judicial scrutiny was required, that court relied on decisions dealing with the rights of indigents to equal treatment in the criminal trial and appellate processes, and on cases disapproving wealth restrictions on the right to vote. Those cases, the District Court concluded, established wealth as a suspect classification. Finding that the local property tax system discriminated on the basis of wealth, it regarded those precedents as controlling. It then

reasoned, based on decisions of this Court affirming the undeniable importance of education, that there is a fundamental right to education and that, absent some compelling state justification, the Texas system could not stand.

We are unable to agree that this case, which in significant aspects is *sui generis*, may be so neatly fitted into the conventional mosaic of constitutional analysis under the Equal Protection Clause. Indeed, for the several reasons that follow, we find neither the suspect-classification nor the fundamental-interest analysis persuasive.

The wealth discrimination discovered by the District Court in this case, and by several other courts that have recently struck down school-financing laws in other States, is quite unlike any of the forms of wealth discrimination heretofore reviewed by this Court. Rather than focusing on the unique features of the alleged discrimination, the courts in these cases have virtually assumed their findings of a suspect classification through a simplistic process of analysis: since, under the traditional systems of financing public schools, some poorer people receive less expensive educations than other more affluent people, these systems discriminate on the basis of wealth. This approach largely ignores the hard threshold questions, including whether it makes a difference for purposes of consideration under the Constitution that the class of disadvantaged "poor" cannot be identified or defined in customary equal protection terms, and whether the relative—rather than absolute—nature of the asserted deprivation is of significant consequence. Before a State's laws and the justifications for the classifications they create are subjected to strict judicial scrutiny, we think these threshold considerations must be analyzed more closely than they were in the court below. . . .

. . . First, in support of their charge that the system discriminates against the "poor," appellees have made no effort to demonstrate that it operates to the peculiar disadvantage of any class fairly definable as indigent, or as composed of persons whose incomes are beneath any designated poverty level. Indeed, there is reason to believe that the poorest families are not necessarily clustered in the poorest property districts. . . .

Second, neither appellees nor the District Court addressed the fact that . . . lack of personal resources has not occasioned an absolute deprivation of the desired benefit. The argument here is not that the children in districts having relatively low assessable property values are receiving no public education; rather, it is that they are receiving a poorer quality education than that available to children in districts having more assessable wealth. Apart from the unsettled and disputed question whether the quality of education may be determined by the amount of money expended for it, a sufficient answer to appellees' argument is that, at least where wealth is involved, the Equal Protection Clause does not require absolute equality or precisely equal advantages. . . .

For these two reasons . . . the disadvantaged class is not susceptible of identification in traditional terms. . . .

. . . [I]t is clear that appellees' suit asks this Court to extend its most exacting scrutiny to review a system that allegedly discriminates against a large, diverse, and amorphous class, unified only by the common factor of residence in districts that happen to have less taxable wealth than other districts. The system of alleged discrimination and the class it defines have none of the traditional indicia of suspectness: the class is not saddled with such disabilities, or subjected to such a history of purposeful unequal treatment, or relegated to such a position of political powerlessness as to command extraordinary protection from the majoritarian political process.

We thus conclude that the Texas system does not operate to the peculiar disadvantage of any suspect class. . . .

Nothing this Court holds today in any way detracts from our historic dedication to public education. We are in complete agreement with the conclusion of the three-judge panel below that "the grave significance of education both to the individual and to our society" cannot be doubted. But the importance of a service performed by the State does not determine whether it must be regarded as fundamental for purposes of examination under the Equal Protection Clause. . . . It is not the province of this Court to create substantive constitutional rights in the name of guaranteeing equal protection of the laws. . . .

Education, of course, is not among the rights afforded explicit protection under our Federal Constitution. Nor do we find any basis for saying it is implicitly so protected. . . .

Even if it were conceded that some identifiable quantum of education is a constitutionally protected prerequisite to the meaningful exercise of . . . [both the First Amendment rights and the right to vote] we have no indication that the present levels of educational expenditures in Texas provide an education that falls short. Whatever merit appellees' argument might have if a State's financing system occasioned an absolute denial of educational opportunities to any of its children, that argument provides no basis for finding any interference with fundamental rights where only relative differences in spending levels are involved and where—as is true in the present case—no charge fairly could be made that the system fails to provide each child with an opportunity to acquire the basic minimal skills necessary for the enjoyment of the rights of speech and of full participation in the political process. . . .

Appellees . . . urge that the Texas system is unconstitutionally arbitrary because it allows the availability of local taxable resources to turn on "happenstance." . . . But any scheme of local taxation—indeed the very existence of identifiable local government units—requires the establishment of jurisdictional boundaries that are inevitably arbitrary. It is equally inevitable that some localities are going to be blessed with more taxable assets than others. Nor is local wealth a static quantity. Changes in the level of taxable wealth within any district may result from any number of events, some of which local residents can and do influence. For instance, commercial and industrial enterprises may be encouraged to locate within a district by various actions—public and private.

Moreover, if local taxation for local expenditures were an unconstitutional method of providing for education then it might be an equally impermissible means of providing other necessary services customarily financed largely from local property taxes, including local police and fire protection, public health and hospitals, and public utility facilities of various kinds. We perceive no justification for such a severe denigration of local property taxation and control as would follow from appellees' contentions. It has simply never been within the constitutional prerogative of this Court to nullify statewide measures for financing public services merely because the burdens or benefits thereof fall unevenly depending upon the relative wealth of the political subdivisions in which citizens live.

In sum, to the extent that the Texas system of school financing results in unequal expenditures between children who happen to reside in different districts, we cannot say that such disparities are the product of a system that is so irrational as to be invidiously discriminatory. . . . We are unwilling to assume for ourselves a level of wisdom superior to that of legislators, scholars, and educational authorities in 50 States, especially where the alternatives proposed are only recently conceived and nowhere yet tested. The constitutional standard under the Equal Protection Clause is whether the challenged state action rationally furthers a legitimate state purpose or interest. We hold that the Texas plan abundantly satisfies this standard.

We hardly need add that this Court's action today is not to be viewed as placing its judicial imprimatur on the status quo. The need is apparent for reform in tax systems which may well have relied too long and too heavily on the local property tax. And certainly innovative thinking as to public education, its methods, and its funding is necessary to assure both a higher level of quality and greater uniformity of opportunity. These matters merit the continued attention of the scholars who already have contributed much by their challenges. But the ultimate solutions must come from the law makers and from the democratic pressures of those who elect them.

Reversed.

MR. JUSTICE STEWART, concurring: [omitted]
MR. JUSTICE BRENNAN, dissenting: [omitted]
MR. JUSTICE WHITE, with whom MR. JUSTICE DOUGLAS and Mr. JUSTICE BRENNAN join, dissenting:. . . .

If the State aims at maximizing local initiative and local choice, by permitting school districts to resort to the real property tax if they choose to do so, it utterly fails in achieving its purpose in districts with property tax bases so low that there is little if any opportunity for interested parents, rich or poor, to augment school district revenues. Requiring the State to establish only that unequal treatment is in furtherance of a permissible goal, without also requiring the State to show that the means chosen to effectuate that goal are rationally related to its achievement, makes equal protection analysis no more than an empty gesture. In my view, the parents and children in Edgewood, and in like districts, suffer from an invidious discrimination violative of the Equal Protection Clause. . . .

There is no difficulty in identifying the class that is subject to the alleged discrimination and that is entitled to the benefits of the Equal Protection Clause. I need go no further than the parents and children in the Edgewood district, who are plaintiffs here and who assert that they are entitled to the same choice as Alamo Heights to augment local expenditures for schools but are denied that choice by state law. This group constitutes a class sufficiently definite to invoke the protection of the Constitution. They are as entitled to the protection of the Equal Protection Clause as were the voters in allegedly underrepresented counties in the reapportionment cases. . . .

MR. JUSTICE MARSHALL, with whom MR. JUSTICE DOUGLAS concurs, dissenting:

The Court today decides, in effect, that a State may constitutionally vary the quality of education which it offers its children in accordance with the amount of taxable wealth located in the school districts within which they reside. The majority's decision represents an abrupt departure from the mainstream of recent state and federal court decisions concerning the unconstitutionality of state educational financing schemes dependent upon taxable local wealth. More unfortunately, though, the majority's holding can only be seen as a retreat from our historic commitment to equality of educational opportunity and as unsupportable acquiescence in a system which deprives children in their earliest years of the chance to reach their full potential as citizens. The Court does this despite the absence of any substantial justification for a scheme which arbitrarily channels educational resources in accordance with the fortuity of the amount of taxable wealth within each district.

In my judgment, the right of every American to an equal start in life, so far as the provision of a state service as important as education is concerned, is far too vital to permit state discrimination on grounds as tenuous as those presented by this record. Nor can I accept the notion that it is sufficient to remit these appellees to the vagaries of the political process which, contrary to the majority's suggestion, has proved singularly unsuited to the task of providing a remedy for this discrimination. I, for one, am unsatisfied with the hope of an ultimate "political" solution sometime in the indefinite future while, in the meantime, countless children unjustifiably receive inferior education that "may affect their hearts and minds in a way unlikely ever to be undone." I must therefore respectfully dissent. . . .

Education directly affects the ability of a child to exercise his First Amendment rights, both as a source and as a receiver of information and ideas, whatever interests he may pursue in life. . . . [S]uch an opportunity may enhance the individual's enjoyment of those rights, not only during but also following school attendance. Thus, in the final analysis, "the pivotal position of education to success in American society and its essential role in opening up to the individual the central experiences of our culture lend it an importance that is undeniable."

Of particular importance is the relationship between education and the political process. . . .

The only justification offered by appellants to sustain the discrimination in educational opportunity caused by the Texas financing scheme is local educational control. Presented with this justification, the District Court concluded that "[n]ot only are defendants unable to demonstrate compelling state interests for their classifications based upon wealth, they fail even to establish a reasonable basis for these classifications." I must agree with this conclusion. . . .

In Texas, statewide laws regulate in fact the most minute details of local public education. For example, the State prescribes required courses. All textbooks must be submitted for state approval, and only approved textbooks may be used. The State has established the qualifications necessary for teaching in Texas public schools and the procedures for obtaining certification. The State has even legislated on the length of the school day. . . .

Moreover, even if we accept Texas' general dedication to local control in educational matters, it is difficult to find any evidence of such dedication with respect to fiscal matters. It ignores reality to suggest—as the Court does, that the local property tax element of the Texas financing scheme reflects a conscious legislative effort to provide school districts with local fiscal control. . . . In fact, [under] the Texas scheme . . . [l]ocal school districts cannot choose to have the best education in the State by imposing the highest tax rate. Instead, the quality of the educational opportunity offered by any particular district is largely determined by the amount of taxable property located in the district—a factor over which local voters can exercise no control. . . .

In my judgment, any substantial degree of scrutiny of the operation of the Texas financing scheme reveals that the State has selected means wholly inappropriate to secure its purported interest in assuring its school districts local fiscal control. . . .

MARTINEZ v. BYNUM,
461 U.S. 321 (1983)

Oralia Martinez's brother, Roberto Morales, left his parents' home in Mexico to live with his sister in McAllen, Texas, for the primary purpose of attending school there. The school district, following Texas law, denied her brother's application for tuition-free admission, and a suit was brought challenging the law as unconstitutional on its face. The law permitted a school district to deny free admission to its public schools to a minor who lives apart from a parent or guardian if the presence in the district "is for the primary purpose of attending the public free schools." The district court upheld the statute holding that it was justified by the state's legitimate interests in protecting and preserving the quality of its educational system and the right of its bona fide residents to attend state schools without cost. The Court of Appeals for the Fifth Circuit affirmed, and certiorari was granted by the Supreme Court.

Majority votes: 8
Dissenting votes: 1

JUSTICE POWELL delivered the opinion of the Court: . . . .

This Court frequently has considered constitutional challenges to residence requirements. On several occasions the Court has invalidated requirements that condition receipt of a benefit on a minimum period of residence within a jurisdiction, but it alway has been careful to distinguish such durational residence requirements from bona fide residence requirements. In *Shapiro* v. *Thompson,* 394 U.S. 618 (1969), for example, the Court invalidated one-year durational residence requirements that applicants for public assistance benefits were required to satisfy despite the fact that they otherwise had "met the test for residence in their jurisdictions." JUSTICE BRENNAN, writing for the Court, stressed that "[t]he residence requirement and the one-year waiting-period requirement are distinct and independent prerequisites for assistance," and carefully "impl[ied] no view of the validity of waiting-period *or* residence requirements determining eligibility to vote, eligibility for tuition-free education, to obtain a license to practice a profession, to hunt or fish, and so forth." . . .

We specifically have approved bona fide residence requirements in the field of public education. The Connecticut statute before us in *Vlandis* v. *Kline,* 412 U.S. 441 (1973), for example, was unconstitutional because it created an irrebuttable presumption of nonresidency for state university students whose legal addresses were outside of the State before they applied for admission. The statute violated the Due Process Clause because it in effect classified some bona fide state residents as nonresidents for tuition purposes. But we "fully recognize[d] that a State has a legitimate interest in protecting and preserving . . . the right of its own bona fide residents to attend [its colleges and universities] on a preferential tuition basis." This "legitimate interest" permits a "State [to] establish such reasonable criteria for in-state status as to make virtually certain that students who are not, in fact, bona fide residents of the State, but who have come there solely for educational purposes, cannot take advantage of the in-state rates.'' Last term, in *Plyer v. Doe*, we reviewed an aspect of Tex. Educ. Code Ann. §21.031—the statute at issue in this case. Although we invalidated the portion of the statute that excludes undocumented alien children from the public free schools, we recognized the school districts' right ''to apply . . . established criteria for determining residence.'' . . .

A bona fide residence requirement, appropriately defined and uniformly applied, furthers the substantial state interest in assuring that services provided for its residents are enjoyed only by residents. Such a requirement with respect to attendance in public free schools does not violate the Equal Protection Clause of the Fourteenth Amendment. It does not burden or penalize the constitutional right of interstate travel, for any person is free to move to a State and to establish residence there. A bona fide residence requirement simply requires that the person *does* establish residence before demanding the services that are restricted to residents. . . .

The central question we must decide here is whether §21.031(d) is a bona fide residence requirement. Although the meaning may vary according to context, ''residence'' generally requires both physical presence and an intention to remain. . . .

Section 21.031 is far more generous than this traditional standard. . . . The statute goes further and extends . . . benefits to many children even if they (or their families) do not intentd to remain in the district indefinitely. As long as the child is not living in the district for the sole purpose of attending school he satisfies the statutory test. For example, if a person comes to Texas to work for a year, his children will be eligible for tuition-free admission to the public schools. Or if a child comes to Texas for six months for health reasons, he would qualify for tuition-free education. In short, §21.031 grants the benefits of residency to everyone who satisfies the traditional residence definition and to some who legitimately could be classified as nonresidents. Since there is no indication that this extension of the traditional definition has any impermissible basis, we certainly cannot say that §21.031(d) violates the Constitution.

The Constitution permits a State to restrict eligibility for tuition-free education to its bona fide residents. We hold that §21.031 is a bona fide residence requirement that satisfies constitutional standards. The judgment of the Court of Appeals accordingly is

Affirmed.

JUSTICE BRENNAN, concurring:

I join the Court's opinion. I write separately, however, to stress that this case involves only a facial challenge to the constitutionality of the Texas statute. In upholding the statute, the Court does not pass on its validity as applied to children in a range of specific factual contexts. In particular, the Court does not decide whether the statute is constitutional as applied to Roberto Morales, a United States citizen whose parents are non-resident aliens. If this question were before the Court, I believe that a different set of considerations would be implicated which might affect significantly an analysis of the statute's constitutionality.

JUSTICE MARSHALL, dissenting:. . . .

The majority's approach reflects a misinterpretation of the Texas statute, a misunderstanding of the concept of residence, and a misapplication of this Court's past decisions concerning the constitutionality of residence requirements. In my view, the statutory classification, which deprives some children of an education because of their motive for residing in Texas, is not adequately justified by the asserted state interests. Because I would hold the statute unconstitutional on its face under the Equal Protection Clause, I respectfully dissent. . . .

The majority reasons that because §21.031 imposes a bona fide residence requirement in a uniform fashion, it is *ipso facto* constitutional. . . . [But] §21.031 is neither a bone fide residence requirement nor one which is uniformly applied to all school-aged children living in Texas. Quite the contrary, §21.031 denies free public education to some persons who satisfy the traditional tests not only of residence but also of domicile. In my view §21.031 should be subjected to careful judicial scrutiny.

The interest adversely affected by §21.031, a child's education, is one which I continue to regard as fundamental. . . . The fundamental importance of education is reflected in ''the unique status accorded public education by our society, and by the close relationship between education and some of our most basic constitutional values.'' . . . Therefore, simply on the ground that §21.031 significantly impedes access to education, I would subject the statutory classification to careful scrutiny.

The Texas statute is not narrowly tailored to achieve a substantial state interest. The State of Texas does not attempt to justify the classification by reference to its interest in the safety and well-being of children within its boundaries. The State instead contends that the principal purpose of the classification is to preserve educational and financial resources for those most closely connected to the State. The classification of children according to their motive for residing in the State cannot be justified as a narrowly tailored means of limiting public education to children "closely connected" with the State. Under the Texas scheme, some children who are "residents" of the State in every sense of that word are nevertheless denied an education. Other children whose only connection with the State is their physical presence are entitled to free public education as long as their presence is not motivated by a desire to obtain a free education. A child residing in the State for *any other reason*, no matter how ephemeral, will receive a free education even if he plans to leave before the end of the school year. Whatever interest a State may have in preserving its educational resources for those who have a sufficiently close connection with the State, that interest does not justify a crude statutory classification which grants and withholds public education on a basis which is related only in a haphazard way to the extent of that child's connection with the State.

For similar reasons, the statute is not carefully designed to reserve State resources only for those who will have the most enduring connection with the State. As a general matter, the State concededly enrolls "school age children [who intend] to remain only six months" in Texas. . . . Yet the State excludes from its schools a child who enters the district at the age of seven with the intent to remain for at least ten more years in order to complete his education.

The State also seeks to justify §21.031(d) as a means of preventing undesirable fluctuations in the student population from year to year. The classification of students based on their motive for residing in the State cannot be justified on this basis. To begin with, Texas may not rely on a vague, unsubstantiated fear that, in the absence of a barrier to migration, children throughout the State and from outside the State will leave their parents and relocate within Texas solely to attend the school of a particular district, and that they will do so in numbers that are wholly unpredictable. There is no evidence whatsoever that the migration of school-age children in unpredictable numbers has caused administrative problems, and the mere conjecture that such problems would arise in the absence of §21.031 (d) cannot be the basis for upholding a classification that singles out some children who reside in the State and denies them a public education. . . .

CLARK v. JETER,
486 U.S. 456 (1988)

Tiffany Clark was born out of wedlock on June 11, 1973. Ten years later, Tiffany's mother, Cherlyn Clark, named Gene Jeter as Tiffany's father in a child support complaint filed in the Allegheny Court of Common Pleas. The court ordered blood tests, which showed a 99.3% probability that Jeter is Tiffany's father. Jeter asked the court to dismiss the complaint on the ground that it was barred by Pennsylvania's six-year statute of limitations for paternity actions. Clark argued in turn that the law violated the equal protection guarantee of the Fourteenth Amendment. The court ruled against Clark, as did the Superior Court of Pennsylvania. The Pennsylvania Supreme Court denied her petition for allowance of appeal. The United States Supreme Court granted certiorari.

Votes: Unanimous

JUSTICE O'CONNOR delivered the opinion of the Court:

Under Pennsylvania law, an illegitimate child must prove paternity before seeking support from his or her father, and a suit to establish paternity ordinarily must be brought within six years of an illegitimate child's birth. By contrast, a legitimate child may seek support from his or her parents at any time. We granted certiorari to consider the constitutionality of this legislative scheme. . . .

In considering whether state legislation violates the Equal Protection Clause of the Fourteenth Amendment, we apply different levels of scrutiny to different types of classifications. At a minimum, a statutory classification must be rationally related to a legitimate governmental purpose. Classifications based on race or national origin, and classifications affecting fundamental rights, are given the most exacting scrutiny. Between these extremes of rational basis review and strict scrutiny lies a level of intermediate scrutiny, which generally has been applied to discriminatory classifications based on sex or illegitimacy.

To withstand intermediate scrutiny, a statutory classification must be substantially related to an important governmental objective. Consequently we have invalidated classifications that burden illegitimate children for the sake of punishing the illicit relations of their parents, because "visiting this condemnation on the head of an infant is illogical and unjust." *Weber* v. *Aetna Casualty & Surety Co.*, 406 U.S. 164, 175, (1972). Yet, in the seminal case concerning the child's right to support, this Court acknowledged that it might be appropriate to treat illegitimate children differently in the support context because of "lurking problems with respect to proof of paternity." *Gomez* v. *Perez*, 409 U.S. 535, 538 (1973).

This Court has developed a particular framework for evaluating equal protection challenges to statutes of limitations that apply to suits to establish paternity, and thereby limit the ability of illegitimate children to obtain support.

"First, the period for obtaining support . . . must be sufficiently long in duration to present a reasonable opportunity for those with an interest in such children to assert claims on their behalf. Second, any time limitation placed on that opportunity must be substantially related to the State's interest in avoiding the litigation of stale or fraudulent claims." *Mills* v. *Habluetzel*, 456 U.S. 91, 99–100 (1982).

In *Mills*, we held that Texas' 1-year statute of limitations failed both steps of the analysis. We explained that paternity suits typically will be brought by the child's mother, who might not act swiftly amidst the emotional and financial complications of the child's first year. And, it is unlikely that the lapse of a mere 12 months will result in the loss of evidence or appreciably increase the likelihood of fraudulent claims. A concurring opinion in *Mills* explained why statutes of limitations longer than one year also may be unconstitutional. First, the State has a countervailing interest in ensuring that genuine claims for child support are satisfied. Second, the fact that Texas tolled most other causes of action during a child's minority suggested that proof problems do not become overwhelming during this period. Finally, the practical obstacles to filing a claim for support are likely to continue after the first year of the child's life.

In *Pickett* v. *Brown*, 462 U.S. 1 (1983), the Court unanimously struck down Tennessee's 2-year statute of limitations for paternity and child support actions brought on behalf of certain illegitimate children. . . . [T]he Court concluded that the 2-year period was too short in light of the persisting financial and emotional problems that are likely to afflict the child's mother. Proceeding to the second step of the analysis, the Court decided that the 2-year statute of limitations was not substantially related to Tennessee's asserted interest in preventing stale and fraudulent claims. The period during which suit could be brought was only a year longer than the period considered in *Mills,* and this incremental difference would not create substantially greater proof and fraud problems. . . .

In light of this authority, we conclude that Pennsylvania's 6-year statute of limitations violates the Equal Protection Clause. Even six years does not necessarily provide a reasonable opportunity to as-

sert a claim on behalf of an illegitimate child. . . . A mother might realize only belatedly "a loss of income attributable to the need to care for the child." Furthermore, financial difficulties are likely to increase as the child matures and incurs expenses for clothing, school, and medical care. Thus it is questionable whether a State acts reasonably when it requires most paternity and support actions to be brought within six years of an illegitimate child's birth.

We do not rest our decision on this ground, however, for it is not entirely evident that six years would necessarily be an unreasonable limitations period for child support actions involving illegitimate children. We are, however, confident that the 6-year statute of limitations is not substantially related to Pennsylvania's interest in avoiding the litigation of stale or fraudulent claims. In a number of circumstances, Pennsylvania permits the issue of paternity to be litigated more than six years after the birth of an illegitimate child. The statute itself permits a suit to be brought more than six years after the child's birth if it is brought within two years of a support payment made by the father. And in other types of suits, Pennsylvania places no limits on when the issue of paternity may be litigated. For example, the intestacy statute permits a child born out of wedlock to establish paternity as long as "there is clear and convincing evidence that the man was the father of the child." Likewise, no statute of limitations applies to a father's action to establish paternity. Recently, the Pennsylvania Legislature enacted a statute that tolls most other civil actions during a child's minority. In *Pickett* and *Mills,* similar tolling statutes cast doubt on the State's purported interest in avoiding the litigation of stale or fraudulent claims. Pennsylvania's tolling statute has the same implications here.

A more recent indication that Pennsylvania does not consider proof problems insurmountable is the enactment by the Pennsylvania Legislature in 1985 of an 18-year statute of limitations for paternity and support actions. To be sure the legislature did not act spontaneously, but rather under the threat of losing some federal funds. Nevertheless, the new statute is a tacit concession that proof problems are not overwhelming. The legislative history of the federal Child Support Enforcement Amendments explains why Congress thought such statutes of limitations are reasonable. Congress adverted to the problem of stale and fraudulent claims, but recognized that increasingly sophisticated tests for genetic markers permit the exclusion of over 99% of those who might be accused of paternity, regardless of the age of the child. This scientific evidence is available throughout the child's minority, and it is an additional reason to doubt that Pennsylvania had a substantial reason for limiting the time within which paternity and support actions could be brought.

We conclude that the Pennsylvania statute does not withstand heightened scrutiny under the Equal Protection Clause. . . . The judgment of the Superior Court is reversed and the case is remanded for further proceedings not inconsistent with this opinion.

It is so ordered.

Additional Cases 1990

FIRST AMENDMENT RIGHTS

AUSTIN v. MICHIGAN CHAMBER OF COMMERCE 110 S.Ct. 1391 (1990)

Under the provisions of Michigan's Campaign Finance Act, corporations (with the exception of print and broadcast media corporations) are prohibited from using general treasury funds for independent expenditures in state candidate election campaigns. Corporations, however, are permitted to set up political action committees with funds collected and used solely for political purposes. The Michigan State Chamber of Commerce, a nonprofit corporation, wished to use general treasury funds to place a local newspaper advertisement supporting a specific candidate for the Michigan House of Representatives. However, to do so would be committing a felony under the law. To avoid such a dire consequence and to challenge the law, the Chamber brought suit in federal district court against Michigan Secretary of State Richard Austin and State Attorney General Frank Kelley asking the court to enjoin them from enforcing an unconstitutional statute. The federal district court upheld the statute but the U.S. Court of Appeals for the Sixth Circuit reversed and found that the statute as applied to the Chamber violated the First Amendment.

Majority votes: 6
Dissenting votes: 3

JUSTICE MARSHALL delivered the opinion of the Court:

In this appeal, we must determine whether § 54(1) of the Michigan Campaign Finance Act violates either the First or the Fourteenth Amendment to the Constitution. Section 54(1) prohibits corporations from using corporate treasury funds for independent expenditures in support of or in opposition to any candidate in elections for state office. Corporations are allowed, however, to make such expenditures from segregated funds used solely for political purposes. In response to a challenge brought by the Michigan State Chamber of Commerce, the Sixth Circuit held that § 54(1) could not be applied to the Chamber, a Michigan nonprofit corporation, without violating the First Amendment. Although we agree that expressive rights are implicated in this case, we hold that application of § 54(1) to the Chamber is constitutional because the provision is narrowly tailored to serve a compelling state interest. Accordingly, we reverse the judgment of the Court of Appeals.

. . . .

The State contends that the unique legal and economic characteristics of corporations necessitate some regulation of their political expenditures to avoid corruption or the appearance of corruption. State law grants corporations special advantages—such as limited liability, perpetual life, and favorable treatment of the accumulation and distribution of assets—that enhance their ability to attract capital and to deploy their resources in ways that maximize the return on their shareholders' investments. These state-created advantages not only allow corporations to play a dominant role in the nation's economy, but also permit them to use "resources amassed in the economic marketplace" to obtain "an unfair advantage in the political marketplace." As the Court explained in *FEC* v. *Massachusetts Citizens for Life*, 479 U.S. 238 (1986) (MCFL), the political advantage of corporations is unfair because

> "[t]he resources in the treasury of a business corporation . . . are not an indication of popular support for the corporation's political ideas. They reflect instead the economically motivated decisions of investors and customers. The availability of these resources may make a corporation a formidable political presence, even though the power of the corporation may be no reflection of the power of its ideas."

We therefore have recognized that "the compelling governmental interest in preventing corruption support[s] the restriction of the influence of political war chests funneled through the corporate form.''

The Chamber argues that this concern about corporate domination of the political process is insufficient to justify restrictions on independent expenditures. Although this Court has distinguished these expenditures from direct contributions in the context of federal laws regulating individual donors, it has also recognized that a legislature might demonstrate a danger of real or apparent corruption posed by such expenditures when made by corporations to influence candidate elections. Regardless of whether this danger of "financial *quid pro quo*" corruption may be sufficient to justify a restriction on independent expenditures, Michigan's regulation aims at a different type of corruption in the political arena: the corrosive and distorting effects of immense aggregations of wealth that are accumulated with the help of the corporate form and that have little or no correlation to the public's support for the corporation's political ideas. The Act does not attempt "to equalize the relative influence of speakers on elections''; rather, it ensures that expenditures reflect actual public support for the political ideas espoused by corporations. We emphasize that the mere fact that corporations may accumulate large amounts of wealth is not the justification for § 54; rather, the unique state-conferred corporate structure that facilitates the amassing of large treasuries warrants the limit on independent expenditures. Corporate wealth can unfairly influence elections when it is deployed in the form of independent expenditures, just as it can when it assumes the guise of political contributions. We therefore hold that the State has articulated a sufficiently compelling rationale to support its restriction on independent expenditures by corporations.

We next turn to the question whether the Act is sufficiently narrowly tailored to achieve its goal. We find that the Act is precisely targeted to eliminate the distortion caused by corporate spending while also allowing corporations to express their political views. Contrary to the dissents' critical assumptions, the Act does not impose an *absolute* ban on all forms of corporate political spending but permits corporations to make independent political expenditures through separate segregated funds. Because persons contributing to such funds understand that their money will be used solely for political purposes, the speech generated accurately reflects contributors' support for the corporation's political views. . . .

The Chamber contends that even if the Campaign Finance Act is constitutional with respect to for-profit corporations, it nonetheless cannot be applied to a nonprofit ideological corporation like a chamber of commerce. In *MCFL,* we held that the nonprofit organization there had "features more akin to voluntary political associations than business firms, and therefore should not have to bear burdens on independent spending solely because of [its] incorporated status.'' In reaching that conclusion, we enumerated three characteristics of the corporation that were "essential'' to our holding. Because the Chamber does not share these crucial features, the Constitution does not require that it be exempted from the generally applicable provisions of § 54(1).

The first characteristic of Massachusetts Citizens for Life, Inc., that distinguished it from ordinary business corporations was that the organization "was formed for the express purpose of promoting political ideas, and cannot engage in business activities.'' . . .

In contrast, the Chamber's bylaws set forth more varied purposes, several of which are not inherently political. For instance, the Chamber compiles and disseminates information relating to social, civic, and economic conditions, trains and educates its members, and promotes ethical business practices. Unlike MCFL's, the Chamber's educational activities are not expressly tied to political goals; many of its seminars, conventions, and publications are politically neutral and focus on business and economic issues. . . . The Chamber's nonpolitical activities therefore suffice to distinguish it from MCFL in the context of this characteristic.

We described the second feature of MCFL as the absence of "shareholders or other persons affiliated so as to have a claim on its assets or earnings. This ensures that persons connected with the organization will have no economic disincentive for disassociating with it if they disagree with its political activity.'' Although the Chamber also lacks shareholders, many of its members may be similarly reluctant to withdraw as members even if they disagree with the Chamber's political expression, because they wish to benefit from the Chamber's nonpolitical programs and to establish contacts with other members of the business community. The Chamber's political agenda is sufficiently distinct from its educational and outreach programs that members who disagree with the former may continue to pay dues to participate in the latter. JUSTICE KENNEDY ignores these disincentives for withdrawing as a member of the Chamber, stating only that "[o]ne need not become a member . . . to earn a living.'' Certainly, members would be disinclined to terminate their involvement with the organization on the basis of less extreme disincentives than the loss of employment. Thus, we are persuaded that the Chamber's members are more similar to shareholders of a business corporation than to the members of MCFL in this respect.

The final characteristic upon which we relied in *MCFL* was the organization's independence from the influence of business corporations. On this score, the Chamber differs most greatly from the Massachusetts organization. MCFL was not established by, and had a policy of not accepting contributions from, business corporations. Thus it could not "serv[e] as [a] condui[t] for the type of direct spending that creates a threat to the political marketplace." In striking contrast, more than three-quarters of the Chamber's members are business corporations, whose political contributions and expenditures can constitutionally be regulated by the State. As we read the Act, a corporation's payments into the Chamber's general treasury would not be considered payments to influence an election, so they would not be "contributions" or "expenditures," and would not be subject to the Act's limitations. Business corporations therefore could circumvent the Act's restrictions by funneling money through the Chamber's general treasury. Because the Chamber accepts money from for-profit corporations, it could, absent application of § 54(1), serve as a conduit for corporate political spending. In sum, the Chamber does not possess the features that would compel the State to exempt it from restrictions on independent political expenditures.

The Chamber also attacks § 54(1) as under-inclusive because it does not regulate the independent expenditures of unincorporated labor unions. Whereas unincorporated unions, and indeed individuals, may be able to amass large treasuries, they do so without the significant state-conferred advantages of the corporate structure; corporations are "by far the most prominent example of entities that enjoy legal advantages enhancing their ability to accumulate wealth." The desire to counterbalance those advantages unique to the corporate form is the State's compelling interest in this case; thus, excluding from the statute's coverage unincorporated entities that also have the capacity to accumulate wealth "does not undermine its justification for regulating corporations." . . .

Michigan identified as a serious danger the significant possibility that corporate political expenditures will undermine the integrity of the political process, and it has implemented a narrowly tailored solution to that problem. By requiring corporations to make all independent political expenditures through a separate fund made up of money solicited expressly for political purposes, the Michigan Campaign Finance Act reduces the threat that huge corporate treasuries amassed with the aid of favorable state laws will be used to influence unfairly the outcome of elections. The Michigan Chamber of Commerce does not exhibit the characteristics identified in *MCFL* that would require the State to exempt it from generally applicable restrictions on independent corporate expenditures. We therefore reverse the decision of the Court of Appeals.

It is so ordered.

JUSTICE BRENNAN, concurring: [omitted]
JUSTICE STEVENS, concurring: [omitted]
JUSTICE SCALIA, dissenting: [omitted]
JUSTICE KENNEDY, with whom JUSTICE O'CONNOR and JUSTICE SCALIA join, dissenting:

The majority opinion validates not one censorship of speech but two. One is Michigan's content-based law which decrees it a crime for a nonprofit corporate speaker to endorse or oppose candidates for Michigan public office. By permitting the statute to stand, the Court upholds a direct restriction on the independent expenditure of funds for political speech for the first time in its history.

The other censorship scheme, I most regret to say, is of our own creation. It is value-laden, content-based speech suppression that permits some nonprofit corporate groups but not others to engage in political speech. After failing to disguise its animosity and distrust for the particular kind of political speech here at issue—the qualifications of a candidate to understand economic matters—the Court adopts a rule that allows Michigan to stifle the voices of some of the most respected groups in public life, on subjects central to the integrity of our democratic system. Each of these schemes is repugnant to the First Amendment and contradicts its central guarantee, the freedom to speak in the electoral process. I dissent.

To understand the force of the Michigan statutory censorship scheme, one need not go beyond the facts of the case before us. The Michigan Chamber of Commerce is a nonprofit corporation with an interest in candidates and public policy issues throughout the State of Michigan. The Chamber sought, on its own initiative and without communication with the candidate, to place a newspaper advertisement in support of one Richard Bandstra, a candidate for the House of Representatives in Michigan. The advertisement discussed the local economy and unemployment and explained why the candidate supported by the Chamber would understand and improve local economic conditions.

This communication is banned by the law here in question, the Michigan Campaign Finance Act (Act). . . .

The State has conceded that among those communications prohibited by its statute are the publication by a nonprofit corporation of its own assessment of a candidate's voting record. With the imprimatur of this Court, it is now a felony in Michigan for the Sierra Club, or the American Civil Liberties Union, or the Michigan State Chamber of Commerce, to advise the public how a candidate voted on issues of urgent concern to their members. In both practice and theory, the prohibition aims at the heart of political debate. . . .

Far more than the interest of the Chamber is at stake. We confront here society's interest in free and informed discussion on political issues, a discourse vital to the capacity for self-government. "In the realm of protected speech, the legislature is constitutionally disqualified from dictating the subjects about which persons may speak and the speakers who may address a public issue."

By using distinctions based upon both the speech and the speaker, the Act engages in the rawest form of censorship: the State censors what a particular segment of the political community might say with regard to candidates who stand for election. The Court's holding cannot be reconciled with the principle that " 'legislative restrictions on advocacy of the election or defeat of political candidates are wholly at odds with the guarantees of the First Amendment.' ". . . .

The Act does not meet our standards for laws that burden fundamental rights. The State cannot demonstrate that a compelling interest supports its speech restriction, nor can it show that its law is narrowly tailored to the purported statutory end. . . .

The key to the majority's reasoning appears to be that because some corporate speakers are well-supported and can buy press space or broadcast time to express their ideas, government may ban all corporate speech to ensure that it will not dominate political debate. The argument is flawed in at least two respects. First, the statute is overinclusive because it covers all groups which use the corporate form, including all nonprofit corporations. Second, it assumes that the government has a legitimate interest in equalizing the relative influence of speakers.

With regard to nonprofit corporations in particular, there is no reason to assume that the corporate form has an intrinsic flaw that makes it corrupt, or that all corporations possess great wealth, or that all corporations can buy more media coverage for their views than can individuals or other groups. There is no reason to conclude that independent speech by a corporation is any more likely to dominate the political arena than speech by the wealthy individual, protected in *Buckley* v. *Valeo,* or by the well-funded PAC, protected in *FEC* v. *NCPAC,* (protecting speech rights of PAC's against expenditure limitations). In *NCPAC,* we discredited the argument that because PAC's spend larger amounts than individuals, the potential for corruption is greater. We distinguished between the campaign contribution at issue in *FEC* v. *National Right to Work Committee,* and independent expenditures, by noting that while "the compelling governmental interest in preventing corruption supported the restriction of the influence of political war chests funneled through the corporate form" with regard to candidate campaign contributions, a similar finding could not be supported for independent expenditures.

In addition, the notion that the government has a legitimate interest in restricting the quantity of speech to equalize the relative influence of speakers on elections, is antithetical to the First Amendment. . . .

That those who can afford to publicize their views may succeed in the political arena as a result does not detract from the fact that they are exercising a First Amendment right. . . .

The suggestion that the government has an interest in shaping the political debate by insulating the electorate from too much exposure to certain views is incompatible with the First Amendment. . . .

The Act, as the State itself says, prevents a nonprofit corporate speaker from using its own funds to inform the voting public that a particular candidate has a good or bad voting record on issues of interest to the association's adherents. Though our era may not be alone in deploring the lack of mechanisms for holding candidates accountable for the votes they cast, that lack of accountability is one of the major concerns of our time. The speech suppressed in this case was directed to political qualifications. The fact that it was spoken by the Michigan Chamber of Commerce, and not a man or woman standing on a soapbox, detracts not a scintilla from its validity, its persuasiveness, or its contribution to the political dialogue.

The Court purports to distinguish *MCFL,* on the ground that the nonprofit corporation permitted to speak in that case received no funds from profit-making corporations. It is undisputed that the Michigan Chamber of Commerce is itself a nonprofit corporation. The crucial difference, it is said, is that the Chamber receives corporate contributions. But this distinction rests on the fallacy that the source of the speaker's funds is somehow relevant to the speaker's right of expression or society's interest in hearing what the speaker has to say. There is no reason that the free speech rights of an individual or of an association of individuals should turn on the circumstance that funds used to engage in the speech come from a corporation. Many persons can trace their funds to corporations, if not in the form of donations, then in the form of dividends, interest, or salary. That does not provide a basis to deprive such individuals or associations of their First Amendment freedoms. The more narrow alternative of recordkeeping and funding disclosure is available. . . .

That the censorship applies to the nonprofit corporate speaker itself and not to a PAC that it has organized, far from being a saving feature of the regulation, further condemns it. The argument that the availability of a PAC as an alternate means can save a restriction on independent corporate expenditures was rejected by the Court in *MCFL* as a costly and burdensome disincentive to speech. The record in this case tended to show that between 25 and 50 percent of a PAC's funds are required to establish and administer the PAC. While the corporation can direct the PAC to make expenditures on behalf of candidates, the PAC can be funded only by contributions from shareholders, directors, officers, and managerial employees, and cannot receive corporate treasury funds. That the avenue left open is more burdensome than the one foreclosed is "sufficient to characterize [a statute] as an infringement on First Amendment activities." . . .

The secondhand endorsement structure required by the Michigan state law debases the value of the voice of nonprofit corporate speakers. The public is not interested in what a PAC says; it does care what the group itself says, so that the group itself can be given credit or blame for the candidates it has endorsed or opposed. PAC's suffer from a poor public image. An advertisement for which a nonprofit group takes direct responsibility, in all likelihood, will have more credibility and generate less distrust than one funded by a PAC. PAC's are interim, ad hoc organizations with little continuity or responsibility. The respected organizations affected by this case have a continuity, a stability and an influence that makes it critical for their members and the public at large to evaluate their official policies to determine whether the organization has earned credibility over a period of time. If a particular organization supports a candidate who injures its cause or offends its ideals, the organization itself, not some intermediary committee, ought to take the blame. It is a sad irony that the group before us wishes to assume that responsibility but the

action of the State, endorsed by this Court, does not allow it to do so.

The diffusion of the corporate message produced by the PAC requirement also ensures a lack of fit between the statute's ends and its means. If the concern is that nonprofit corporate speech distorts the political process, it would seem that injecting the confusion of a PAC as an intermediary, albeit one controlled and directed by the corporation, further diffuses responsibility. Even if there were any possibility of corruption by allowing the Michigan Chamber of Commerce to finance the proposed advertisement supporting a candidate, it makes no sense to argue that such a possibility would be eliminated by requiring the disclaimer at the bottom to read "Paid for by the Michigan Chamber of Commerce PAC" rather than "Paid for by the Michigan Chamber of Commerce." . . .

The Court takes refuge in the argument that some members or contributors to non-profit corporations may find their own views distorted by the organization. . . . One need not become a member of the Michigan Chamber of Commerce or the Sierra Club in order to earn a living. To the extent that members disagree with a nonprofit corporation's policies, they can seek change from within, withhold financial support, cease to associate with the group, or form a rival group of their own. Allowing government to use the excuse of protecting shareholder rights to stifle the speech of private, voluntary organizations undermines the First Amendment.

To create second-class speakers that can be stifled on the subject of candidate qualifications is to silence some of the most significant participants in the American public dialogue, as evidenced by the *amici* briefs filed on behalf of the Chamber of Commerce by the American Civil Liberties Union, the Center for Public Interest Law, the American Medical Association, the National Association of Realtors, the American Insurance Association, the National Organization for Women, Greenpeace Action, the National Abortion Rights Action League, the National Right to Work Committee, the Planned Parenthood Federation of America, the Fund for the Feminist Majority, the Washington Legal Foundation, and the Allied Educational Foundation. I reject any argument based on the idea that these groups and their views are not of importance and value to the self-fulfillment and self-expression of their members, and to the rich public dialogue that must be the mark of any free society. To suggest otherwise is contrary to the American political experience and our own judicial knowledge. . . .

By constructing a rationale for the jurisprudence

of this Court that prevents distinguished organizations in public affairs from announcing that a candidate is qualified or not qualified for public office, the Court imposes its own model of speech, one far removed from economic and political reality. It is an unhappy paradox that this Court, which has the role of protecting speech and of barring censorship from all aspects of political life, now becomes itself the censor. In the course of doing so, the Court reveals a lack of concern for speech rights that have the full protection of the First Amendment. I would affirm the judgment.

UNITED STATES v. EICHMAN
110 S.Ct. 2404 (1990)

After the Supreme Court decided Texas *v.* Johnson *in 1989, striking down a state statute criminalizing flag burning, Congress considered overturning the decision by way of a constitutional amendment. Wary of amending the Bill of Rights, Congress instead enacted the Flag Protection Act of 1989 that its backers claimed was sufficiently different from the Texas statute and would be upheld by the Supreme Court. The backers were wrong as this decision demonstrates. What happened was that after Congress enacted the new law Shawn D. Eichman and others burned United States flags in the context of a political demonstration on the steps of the United States Capitol. Mark John Haggerty and others burned American flags in another demonstration in Seattle. Both sets of demonstrators were arrested and charged with violating the Act. They in turn moved to dismiss the charges on the ground that the Act violates the First Amendment. The federal district courts citing* Texas *v.* Johnson *agreed and dismissed the cases. The United States appealed.*

Majority votes: 5
Dissenting votes: 4

JUSTICE BRENNAN delivered the opinion of the Court:. . . .

Last Term in *Texas* v. *Johnson,* we held that a Texas statute criminalizing the desecration of venerated objects, including the United States flag, was unconstitutional as applied to an individual who had set such a flag on fire during a political demonstration. . . .

After our decision in *Johnson,* Congress passed the Flag Protection Act of 1989. The Act provides in relevant part:

"(a)(1) Whoever knowingly mutilates, defaces, physically defiles, burns, maintains on the floor or ground, or tramples upon any flag of the United States shall be fined under this title or imprisoned for not more than one year, or both.

"(2) This subsection does not prohibit any conduct consisting of the disposal of a flag when it has become worn or soiled.

"(b) As used in this section, the term 'flag of the United States' means any flag of the United States, or any part thereof, made of any substance, of any size, in a form that is commonly displayed."

The Government concedes in this case, as it must, that appellees' flag burning constituted expressive conduct but invites us to reconsider our rejection in *Johnson* of the claim that flag burning as a mode of expression, like obscenity or "fighting words," does not enjoy the full protection of the First Amendment. This we decline to do. The only remaining question is whether the Flag Protection Act is sufficiently distinct from the Texas statute that it may constitutionally be applied to proscribe appellees' expressive conduct.

The Government contends that the Flag Protection Act is constitutional because, unlike the statute addressed in *Johnson,* the Act does not target expressive conduct on the basis of the content of its message. The Government asserts an interest in "protect[ing] the physical integrity of the flag under all circumstances" in order to safeguard the flag's identity " 'as the unique and unalloyed symbol of the Nation.' " The Act proscribes conduct (other than disposal) that damages or mistreats a flag, without regard to the actor's motive, his intended message, or the likely effects of his conduct on onlookers. By contrast, the Texas statute expressly prohibited only those acts of physical flag desecration "that the actor knows will seriously offend" onlookers, and the former federal statute prohibited only those acts of desecration that "cas[t] contempt upon" the flag.

Although the Flag Protection Act contains no explicit content-based limitation on the scope of prohibited conduct, it is nevertheless clear that the Government's asserted *interest* is "related 'to the suppression of free expression,' " and concerned with the content of such expression. The Government's interest in protecting the "physical integrity" of a privately owned flag rests upon a perceived need to preserve the flag's status as a symbol of our Nation and certain national ideals. But the mere destruction or disfigurement of a particular physical manifestation of the symbol, without more, does not diminish or otherwise affect the symbol itself in any way. For example, the secret destruction of a flag in one's own basement would not threaten the flag's recognized meaning. Rather, the Government's desire to preserve the flag as a symbol for certain national ideals is implicated "only when a person's treatment of the flag communicates [a] message" to others that is inconsistent with those ideals.

Moreover, the precise language of the Act's prohibitions confirms Congress' interest in the communicative impact of flag destruction. The Act criminalizes the conduct of anyone who "knowingly mutilates, defaces, physically defiles, burns, maintains on the floor or ground, or tramples upon any flag." Each of the specified terms—with the possible exception of "burns"—unmistakably connotes disrespectful treatment of the flag and suggests a focus on those acts likely to damage the flag's symbolic value. And the explicit exemption in § 700(a)(2) for disposal of "worn or soiled" flags protects certain acts traditionally associated with patriotic respect for the flag. . . . Although Congress cast the Flag Protection Act in somewhat broader terms than the Texas statute at issue in *Johnson,* the Act still suffers from the same fundamental flaw: it suppresses expression out of concern for its likely communicative impact. Despite the Act's wider scope, its restriction on expression cannot be " 'justified without reference to the content of the regulated speech.' " . . . The Act therefore must be subjected to "the most exacting scrutiny," and for the reasons stated in *Johnson* the Government's interest cannot justify its infringement on First Amendment rights. We decline the Government's invitation to reassess this conclusion in light of Congress' recent recognition of a purported "national consensus" favoring a prohibition on flag burning. Even assuming such a consensus exists, any suggestion that the Government's interest in suppressing speech becomes more weighty as popular opposition to that speech grows is foreign to the First Amendment. . . .

We are aware that desecration of the flag is deeply offensive to many. But the same might be said, for example, of virulent ethnic and religious epithets, see *Terminiello* v. *Chicago,* 337 U. S. 1 (1949), vulgar repudiations of the draft, see *Cohen* v. *California,* 403 U. S. 15 (1971), and scurrilous caricatures, see *Hustler Magazine, Inc.* v. *Falwell,* 485 U. S. 46 (1988). "If there is a bedrock principle underlying the First Amendment, it is that the Government may not prohibit the expression of an idea simply because society finds the idea itself offensive or disagreeable." Punishing desecration of the flag dilutes the very freedom that makes this emblem so revered, and worth revering. The judgments are

Affirmed.

JUSTICE STEVENS, with whom THE CHIEF JUSTICE, JUSTICE WHITE and JUSTICE O'CONNOR join, dissenting:

The Court's opinion ends where proper analysis of the issue should begin. Of course "the Government may not prohibit the expression of an idea simply because society finds the idea itself offensive or disagreeable." None of us disagrees with that proposition. But it is equally well settled that certain methods of expression may be prohibited if (a) the prohibition is supported by a legitimate societal interest that is unrelated to suppression of the ideas the speaker desires to express; (b) the prohibition does not entail any interference with the speaker's freedom to express those ideas by other means; and (c) the interest in allowing the speaker complete freedom of choice among alternative methods of expression is less important than the societal interest supporting the prohibition.

Contrary to the position taken by counsel for the flag burners in *Texas* v. *Johnson,* it is now conceded that the Federal Government has a legitimate interest in protecting the symbolic value of the American flag. Obviously that value cannot be measured, or even described, with any precision. It has at least these two components: in times of national crisis, it inspires and motivates the average citizen to make personal sacrifices in order to achieve societal goals of overriding importance; at all times, it serves as a reminder of the paramount importance of pursuing the ideals that characterize our society.

The first question the Court should consider is whether the interest in preserving the value of that symbol is unrelated to suppression of the ideas that flag burners are trying to express. In my judgment the answer depends, at least in part, on what those ideas are. A flag burner might intend various messages. The flag burner may wish simply to convey hatred, contempt, or sheer opposition directed at the United States. This might be the case if the flag were burned by an enemy during time of war. A flag burner may also, or instead, seek to convey the depth of his personal conviction about some issue, by willingly provoking the use of force against himself. In so doing, he says that "my disagreement with certain policies is so strong that I am prepared to risk physical harm (and perhaps imprisonment) in order to call attention to my views." This second possibility apparently describes the expressive conduct of the flag burners in these cases. Like the protesters who dramatized their opposition to our engagement in Vietnam by publicly burning their draft cards—and who were punished for doing so—their expressive conduct is consistent with affection for this country and respect for the ideals that the flag symbolizes. There is at least one further possibility: a flag burner may intend to make an accusation against the integrity of the American people who disagree with him. By burning the embodiment of America's collective commitment to freedom and equality, the flag burner charges that the majority has forsaken that commitment—that continued respect for the flag is nothing more than hypocrisy. Such a charge may be made even if the flag burner loves the country and zealously pursues the ideals that the country claims to honor.

The idea expressed by a particular act of flag burning is necessarily dependent on the temporal and political context in which it occurs. In the 1960's it may have expressed opposition to the country's Vietnam policies, or at least to the compulsory draft. In *Texas* v. *Johnson*, it apparently expressed opposition to the platform of the Republican party. In these cases, the respondents have explained that it expressed their opposition to racial discrimination, to the failure to care for the homeless, and of course to statutory prohibitions of flag burning. In any of these examples, the protestors may wish both to say that their own position is the only one faithful to liberty and equality, and to accuse their fellow citizens of hypocritical indifference to—or even of a selfish departure from—the ideals which the flag is supposed to symbolize. The ideas expressed by flag burners are thus various and often ambiguous.

The Government's legitimate interest in preserving the symbolic value of the flag is, however, essentially the same regardless of which of many different ideas may have motivated a particular act of flag burning. As I explained in my dissent in *Johnson*, the flag uniquely symbolizes the ideas of liberty, equality, and tolerance—ideas that Americans have passionately defended and debated throughout our history. The flag embodies the spirit of our national commitment to those ideals. The message thereby transmitted does not take a stand upon our disagreements, except to say that those disagreements are best regarded as competing interpretations of shared ideals. It does not judge particular policies, except to say that they command respect when they are enlightened by the spirit of liberty and equality. To the world, the flag is our promise that we will continue to strive for these ideals. To us, the flag is a reminder both that the struggle for liberty and equality is unceasing, and that our obligation of tolerance and respect for all our fellow citizens encompasses those who disagree with us—

indeed, even those whose ideas are disagreeable or offensive.

Thus, the Government may—indeed, it should—protect the symbolic value of the flag without regard to the specific content of the flag burners' speech. The prosecution in this case does not depend upon the object of the defendants' protest. It is, moreover, equally clear that the prohibition does not entail any interference with the speaker's freedom to express his or her ideas by other means. It may well be true that other means of expression may be less effective in drawing attention to those ideas, but that is not itself a sufficient reason for immunizing flag burning. Presumably a gigantic fireworks display or a parade of nude models in a public park might draw even more attention to a controversial message, but such methods of expression are nevertheless subject to regulation.

This case therefore comes down to a question of judgment. Does the admittedly important interest in allowing every speaker to choose the method of expressing his or her ideas that he or she deems most effective and appropriate outweigh the societal interest in preserving the symbolic value of the flag? This question, in turn, involves three different judgments: (1) the importance of the individual interest in selecting the preferred means of communication; (2) the importance of the national symbol; and (3) the question whether tolerance of flag burning will enhance or tarnish that value. The opinions in *Texas* v. *Johnson* demonstrate that reasonable judges may differ with respect to each of these judgments. . . .

Burning a flag is not . . . equivalent to burning a public building. Assuming that the protester is burning his own flag, it causes no physical harm to other persons or to their property. The impact is purely symbolic, and it is apparent that some thoughtful persons believe that impact, far from depreciating the value of the symbol, will actually enhance its meaning. I most respectfully disagree. Indeed, what makes this case particularly difficult for me is what I regard as the damage to the symbol that has already occurred as a result of this Court's decision to place its stamp of approval on the act of flag burning. A formerly dramatic expression of protest is now rather commonplace. In today's marketplace of ideas, the public burning of a Vietnam draft card is probably less provocative than lighting a cigarette. Tomorrow flag burning may produce a similar reaction. There is surely a direct relationship between the communicative value of the act of flag burning and the symbolic value of the object being burned.

The symbolic value of the American flag is not

the same today as it was yesterday. Events during the last three decades have altered the country's image in the eyes of numerous Americans, and some now have difficulty understanding the message that the flag conveyed to their parents and grandparents—whether born abroad and naturalized or native born. Moreover, the integrity of the symbol has been compromised by those leaders who seem to advocate compulsory worship of the flag even by individuals whom it offends, or who seem to manipulate the symbol of national purpose into a pretext for partisan disputes about meaner ends. And, as I have suggested, the residual value of the symbol after this Court's decision in *Texas v. Johnson* is surely not the same as it was a year ago.

Given all these considerations, plus the fact that the Court today is really doing nothing more than reconfirming what it has already decided, it might be appropriate to defer to the judgment of the majority and merely apply the doctrine of *stare decisis* to the case at hand. That action, however, would not honestly reflect my considered judgment concerning the relative importance of the conflicting interests that are at stake. I remain persuaded that the considerations identified in my opinion in *Texas v. Johnson* are of controlling importance in this case as well.

Accordingly, I respectfully dissent.

RUTAN v. REPUBLICAN PARTY OF ILLINOIS 110 S.Ct. 2729 (1990)

Illinois Governor James Thompson on November 12, 1980, issued an executive order instituting a hiring freeze prohibiting state officials from hiring new employees, promoting or transferring state employees, and recalling employees after layoffs without the approval of the Governor's Office of Personnel. In making such decisions the Office has looked at whether the particular applicant has contributed money or other support to the Republican party and its candidates, has promised to work for the party in the future, and has the support of state or local party officials. This patronage system was challenged by Cynthia B. Rutan, a state rehabilitation counselor, who claimed that she was repeatedly denied promotions to supervisory positions for which she was qualified because she had not worked for or supported the Republican party. Another challenger maintained that he was denied a transfer to an office closer to his home because of local party leader opposition. A third claimed he was denied a state job as a prison guard because he did not have party support. Two others alleged

that they were not recalled after layoffs because they lacked Republican credentials. The federal district court dismissed the complaints. The U.S. Court of Appeals for the Seventh Circuit affirmed in part and reversed in part ruling that only patronage practices that are the substantial equivalent of a dismissal are prohibited by the First Amendment.

Majority votes: 5
Dissenting votes: 4

JUSTICE BRENNAN delivered the opinion of the Court:

To the victor belong only those spoils that may be constitutionally obtained. *Elrod* v. *Burns,* 427 U.S. 347 (1976), and *Branti* v. *Finkel,* 445 U.S. 507 (1980), decided that the First Amendment forbids government officials to discharge or threaten to discharge public employees solely for not being supporters of the political party in power, unless party affiliation is an appropriate requirement for the position involved. Today we are asked to decide the constitutionality of several related political patronage practices—whether promotion, transfer, recall, and hiring decisions involving low-level public employees may be constitutionally based on party affiliation and support. We hold that they may not. . . .

We first address the claims of the four current or former employees. Respondents urge us to view *Elrod* and *Branti* as inapplicable because the patronage dismissals at issue in those cases are different in kind from failure to promote, failure to transfer, and failure to recall after layoff. Respondents initially contend that the employee petitioners' First Amendment rights have not been infringed because they have no entitlement to promotion, transfer, or rehire. We rejected just such an argument in *Elrod,* and *Branti,* as both cases involved state workers who were employees at will with no legal entitlement to continued employment. In *Perry* v. *Sindermann,* 408 U.S., at 596–598, we held explicitly that the plaintiff teacher's lack of a contractual or tenure right to reemployment was immaterial to his First Amendment claim. We explained the viability of his First Amendment claim as follows:

"For at least a quarter-century, this Court has made clear that even though a person has no 'right' to a valuable governmental benefit and even though the government may deny him the benefit for any number of reasons, *there are some reasons upon which the government may not rely. It may not deny a benefit to a person on a basis that infringes his constitutionally pro-*

tected interests—especially, his interest in freedom of speech. For if the government could deny a benefit to a person because of his constitutionally protected speech or associations, his exercise of those freedoms would in effect be penalized and inhibited. This would allow the government to 'produce a result which [it] could not command directly.' *Speiser* v. *Randall,* 357 U.S. 513, 526 [1958]. Such interference with constitutional rights is impermissible.'' *Perry, id.,* at 597 (emphasis added).

Likewise, we find assertion here that the employee petitioners had no legal entitlement to promotion, transfer, or recall beside the point.

Respondents next argue that the employment decisions at issue here do not violate the First Amendment because the decisions are not punitive, do not in any way adversely affect the terms of employment, and therefore do not chill the exercise of protected belief and association by public employees. This is not credible. Employees who find themselves in dead-end positions due to their political backgrounds *are* adversely affected. They will feel a significant obligation to support political positions held by their superiors, and to refrain from acting on the political views they actually hold, in order to progress up the career ladder. Employees denied transfers to workplaces reasonably close to their homes until they join and work for the Republican party will feel a daily pressure from their long commutes to do so. And employees who have been laid off may well feel compelled to engage in whatever political activity is necessary to regain regular paychecks and positions corresponding to their skill and experience.

The same First Amendment concerns that underlay our decisions in *Elrod, supra,* and *Branti, supra,* are implicated here. Employees who do not compromise their beliefs stand to lose the considerable increases in pay and job satisfaction attendant to promotions, the hours and maintenance expenses that are consumed by long daily commutes, and even their jobs if they are not rehired after a "temporary" layoff. These are significant penalties and are imposed for the exercise of rights guaranteed by the First Amendment. Unless these patronage practices are narrowly tailored to further vital government interests, we must conclude that they impermissibly encroach on First Amendment freedoms.

We find, however, that our conclusions in *Elrod, supra,* and *Branti, supra,* are equally applicable to the patronage practices at issue here. A government's interest in securing effective employees can be met by discharging, demoting or transferring staffmembers whose work is deficient. A government's interest in securing employees who will loyally implement its policies can be adequately served by choosing or dismissing certain high-level employees on the basis of their political views. Likewise, the "preservation of the democratic process" is no more furthered by the patronage promotions, transfers, and rehires at issue here than it is by patronage dismissals. First, "political parties are nurtured by other, less intrusive and equally effective methods." . . . Second, patronage decidedly impairs the elective process by discouraging free political expression by public employees. Respondents, who include the Governor of Illinois and other state officials, do not suggest any other overriding government interest in favoring Republican party supporters for promotion, transfer, and rehire.

We therefore determine that promotions, transfers, and recalls after layoffs based on political affiliation or support are an impermissible infringement on the First Amendment rights of public employees. In doing so, we reject the Seventh Circuit's view of the appropriate constitutional standard by which to measure alleged patronage practices in government employment. The Seventh Circuit proposed that only those employment decisions that are the "substantial equivalent of a dismissal" violate a public employee's rights under the First Amendment. We find this test unduly restrictive because it fails to recognize that there are deprivations less harsh than dismissal that nevertheless press state employees and applicants to conform their beliefs and associations to some state-selected orthodoxy. The First Amendment is not a tenure provision, protecting public employees from actual or constructive discharge. The First Amendment prevents the government, except in the most compelling circumstances, from wielding its power to interfere with its employees' freedom to believe and associate, or to not believe and not associate.

Whether the four employees were in fact denied promotions, transfers, or rehire for failure to affiliate with and support the Republican Party is for the District Court to decide in the first instance. What we decide today is that such denials are irreconcilable with the Constitution and that the allegations of the four employees state claims under 42 U.S.C. § 1983 (1982 ed.) for violations of the First and Fourteenth Amendments. Therefore, although we affirm the Seventh Circuit's judgment to reverse the District Court's dismissal of these claims and remand them for further proceedings, we do not adopt the Seventh Circuit's reasoning.

Petitioner James W. Moore presents the closely related question whether patronage hiring violates the First Amendment. Patronage hiring places burdens on free speech and association similar to those imposed by the patronage practices discussed above. A state job is valuable. Like most employment, it provides regular paychecks, health insurance, and other benefits. In addition, there may be openings with the State when business in the private sector is slow. There are also occupations for which the government is a major (or the only) source of employment, such as social workers, elementary school teachers, and prison guards. Thus, denial of a state job is a serious privation. . . .

Almost half a century ago, this Court made clear that the government "may not enact a regulation providing that no Republican . . . shall be appointed to federal office." *Public Workers* v. *Mitchell,* 330 U.S. 75, 100 (1947). What the First Amendment precludes the government from commanding directly, it also precludes the government from accomplishing indirectly. Under our sustained precedent, conditioning hiring decisions on political belief and association plainly constitutes an unconstitutional condition, unless the government has a vital interest in doing so. We find no such government interest here, for the same reasons that we found the government lacks justification for patronage promotions, transfers or recalls. . . .

If Moore's employment application was set aside because he chose not to support the Republican Party, as he asserts, then Moore's First Amendment rights have been violated. Therefore, we find that Moore's complaint was improperly dismissed.

We hold that the rule of *Elrod* and *Branti* extends to promotion, transfer, recall, and hiring decisions based on party affiliation and support and that all of the petitioners and cross-respondents have stated claims upon which relief may be granted. We affirm the Seventh Circuit insofar as it remanded Rutan's, Taylor's, Standefer's, and O'Brien's claims. However, we reverse the Circuit Court's decision to uphold the dismissal of Moore's claim. All five claims are remanded for proceedings consistent with this opinion.

It is so ordered.

JUSTICE STEVENS, concurring: [omitted]
JUSTICE SCALIA, with whom THE CHIEF JUSTICE and JUSTICE KENNEDY join, and with whom JUSTICE O'CONNOR joins as to Parts II and III, dissenting:
Today the Court establishes the constitutional principle that party membership is not a permissible factor in the dispensation of government jobs, except those jobs for the performance of which party affiliation is an "appropriate requirement." It is hard to say precisely (or even generally) what that exception means, but if there is any category of jobs for whose performance party affiliation is not an appropriate requirement, it is the job of being a judge, where partisanship is not only unneeded but positively undesirable. It is, however, rare that a federal administration of one party will appoint a judge from another party. And it has always been rare. Thus, the new principle that the Court today announces will be enforced by a corps of judges (the Members of this Court included) who overwhelmingly owe their office to its violation. Something must be wrong here, and I suggest it is the Court.

The merit principle for government employment is probably the most favored in modern America, having been widely adopted by civil-service legislation at both the state and federal levels. But there is another point of view, described in characteristically Jacksonian fashion by an eminent practitioner of the patronage system, George Washington Plunkitt of Tammany Hall:

"I ain't up on syllygisms, but I can give you some arguments that nobody can answer.

"First, this great and glorious country was built up by political parties; second, parties can't hold together if their workers don't get offices when they win; third, if the parties go to pieces, the government they built up must go to pieces, too; fourth, then there'll be hell to pay." W. Riordon, Plunkitt of Tammany Hall 13 (1963).

It may well be that the Good Government Leagues of America were right, and that Plunkitt, James Michael Curley and their ilk were wrong; but that is not entirely certain. As the merit principle has been extended and its effects increasingly felt; as the Boss Tweeds, the Tammany Halls, the Pendergast Machines, the Byrd Machines and the Daley Machines have faded into history; we find that political leaders at all levels increasingly complain of the helplessness of elected government, unprotected by "party discipline," before the demands of small and cohesive interest-groups.

The choice between patronage and the merit principle—or, to be more realistic about it, the choice between the desirable mix of merit and patronage principles in widely varying federal, state, and local political contexts—is not so clear that I would be prepared, as an original matter, to chisel a single, inflexible prescription into the Constitution. Fourteen years ago, in *Elrod* v. *Burns,* 427 U.S. 347 (1976), the Court did that. *Elrod* was limited however, as was the later decision of *Branti* v. *Finkel,* 445 U.S. 507 (1980), to patronage firings, leaving it to state and federal legislatures to determine when and where political affiliation could be taken into account in hirings and promotions. Today the Court makes its constitutional civil-service reform absolute, extending to all decisions regarding government employment. Because the First Amendment has never been thought to require this disposition, which may well have disastrous consequences for our political system, I dissent.

I

. . . The provisions of the Bill of Rights were designed to restrain transient majorities from impairing long-recognized personal liberties. They did not create by implication novel individual rights overturning accepted political norms. Thus, when a practice not expressly prohibited by the text of the Bill of Rights bears the endorsement of a long tradition of open, widespread, and unchallenged use that dates back to the beginning of the Republic, we have no proper basis for striking it down. Such a venerable and accepted tradition is not to be laid on the examining table and scrutinized for its conformity to some abstract principle of First-Amendment adjudication devised by this Court. To the contrary, such traditions are themselves the stuff out of which the Court's principles are to be formed. They are, in these uncertain areas, the very points of reference by which the legitimacy or illegitimacy of *other* practices are to be figured out. When it appears that the latest "rule," or "three-part test," or "balancing test" devised by the Court has placed us on a collision course with such a landmark practice, it is the former that must be recalculated by us, and not the latter that must be abandoned by our citizens. I know of no other way to formulate a constitutional jurisprudence that reflects, as it should, the principles adhered to, over time, by the American people, rather than those favored by the personal (and necessarily shifting) philosophical dispositions of a majority of this Court.

I will not describe at length the claim of patronage to landmark status as one of our accepted political traditions. Justice Powell discussed it in his dissenting opinions in *Elrod* and *Branti.* . . . Suffice it to say that patronage was, without any thought that it could be unconstitutional, a basis for government employment from the earliest days of the Republic until *Elrod*—and has continued unabated *since El-*

rod, to the extent still permitted by that unfortunate decision. . . . Given that unbroken tradition regarding the application of an ambiguous constitutional text, there was in my view no basis for holding that patronage-based dismissals violated the First Amendment—much less for holding, as the Court does today, that even patronage hiring does so.

II

Even accepting the Court's own mode of analysis, however, and engaging in "balancing" a tradition that ought to be part of the scales, *Elrod, Branti,* and today's extension of them seem to me wrong.

The Court limits patronage on the ground that the individual's interest in uncoerced belief and expression outweighs the systemic interests invoked to justify the practice. The opinion indicates that the government may prevail only if it proves that the practice is "narrowly tailored to further vital government interests."

That strict-scrutiny standard finds no support in our cases. Although our decisions establish that government employees do not lose all constitutional rights, we have consistently applied a lower level of scrutiny when "the governmental function operating . . . [is] not the power to regulate or license, as lawmaker, an entire trade or profession, or to control an entire branch of private business, but, rather, as proprietor, to manage [its] internal operatio[ns]. . . ." *Cafeteria & Restaurant Workers* v. *McElroy,* 367 U. S. 886, 896 (1961). When dealing with its own employees, the government may not act in a manner that is "patently arbitrary or discriminatory," but its regulations are valid if they bear a "rational connection" to the governmental end sought to be served.

In particular, restrictions on speech by public employees are not judged by the test applicable to similar restrictions on speech by nonemployees. . . . Because the restriction on speech is more attenuated when the government conditions employment than when it imposes criminal penalties, and because "government offices could not function if every employment decision became a constitutional matter," we have held that government employment decisions taken on the basis of an employee's speech do not "abridg[e] the freedom of speech" merely because they fail the narrow-tailoring and compelling-interest tests applicable to direct regulation of speech. We have not subjected such decisions to strict scrutiny, but have accorded "a wide degree of deference to the employer's judgment" that an employee's speech will interfere with close working relationships.

When the government takes adverse action

against an employee on the basis of his political affiliation (an interest whose constitutional protection is derived from the interest in speech), the same analysis applies. . . .

While it is clear from the above cases that the normal "strict scrutiny" that we accord to government regulation of speech is not applicable in this field, the precise test that replaces it is not so clear; we have used various formulations. The one that appears in the case dealing with an employment practice closest in its effects to patronage is whether the practice could be "reasonably deemed" by the enacting legislature to further a legitimate goal. For purposes of my ensuing discussion, however, I will apply a less permissive standard that seems more in accord with our general "balancing" test: can the governmental advantages of this employment practice reasonably be deemed to outweigh its "coercive" effects?

Preliminarily, I may observe that the Court today not only declines, in this area replete with constitutional ambiguities, to give the clear and continuing tradition of our people the *dispositive* effect I think it deserves, but even declines to give it substantial weight in the balancing. That is contrary to what the Court has done in many other contexts. . . .

But even laying tradition entirely aside, it seems to me our balancing test is amply met. I assume, as the Court's opinion assumes, that the balancing is to be done on a generalized basis, and not case-by-case. The Court holds that the governmental benefits of patronage cannot reasonably be thought to outweigh its "coercive" effects (even the lesser "coercive" effects of patronage hiring as opposed to patronage firing) not merely in 1990 in the State of Illinois, but at any time in any of the numerous political subdivisions of this vast country. It seems to me that that categorical pronouncement reflects a naive vision of politics and an inadequate appreciation of the systemic effects of patronage in promoting political stability and facilitating the social and political integration of previously powerless groups.

The whole point of my dissent is that the desirability of patronage is a policy question to be decided by the people's representatives; I do not mean, therefore, to endorse that system. But in order to demonstrate that a legislature could reasonably determine that its benefits outweigh its "coercive" effects, I must describe those benefits as the proponents of patronage see them: As Justice Powell discussed at length in his *Elrod* dissent, patronage stabilizes political parties and prevents excessive political fragmentation—both of which are results in which States have a strong governmental

interest. Party strength requires the efforts of the rank-and-file, especially in "the dull periods between elections," to perform such tasks as organizing precincts, registering new voters, and providing constituent services. Even the most enthusiastic supporter of a party's program will shrink before such drudgery, and it is folly to think that ideological conviction alone will motivate sufficient numbers to keep the party going through the off-years. . . .

The Court simply refuses to acknowledge the link between patronage and party discipline, and between that and party success. . . . It is unpersuasive to claim, as the Court does, that party workers are obsolete because campaigns are now conducted through media and other money-intensive means. Those techniques have supplemented but not supplanted personal contacts. Certainly they have not made personal contacts unnecessary in campaigns for the lower-level offices that are the foundations of party strength, nor have they replaced the myriad functions performed by party regulars not directly related to campaigning. And to the extent such techniques have replaced older methods of campaigning (partly in response to the limitations the Court has placed on patronage), the political system is not clearly better off. Increased reliance on money-intensive campaign techniques tends to entrench those in power much more effectively than patronage—but without the attendant benefit of strengthening the party system. A challenger can more easily obtain the support of party-workers (who can expect to be rewarded even if the candidate loses—if not this year, then the next) than the financial support of political action committees (which will generally support incumbents, who are likely to prevail).

It is self-evident that eliminating patronage will significantly undermine party discipline; and that as party discipline wanes, so will the strength of the two-party system. But, says the Court, "[p]olitical parties have already survived the substantial decline in patronage employment practices in this century." This is almost verbatim what was said in *Elrod*, see 427 U. S., at 369. Fourteen years later it seems much less convincing. Indeed, now that we have witnessed, in 18 of the last 22 years, an Exccutive Branch of the Federal Government under the control of one party while the Congress is entirely or (for two years) partially within the control of the other party; now that we have undergone the most recent federal election, in which 98% of the incumbents, of whatever party, were returned to office; and now that we have seen elected officials changing their political affiliation with unprecedented readiness, the statement that "political parties have already survived" has a positively whistling-in-the-graveyard character to it. Parties have assuredly survived—but as what? As the forges upon which many of the essential compromises of American political life are hammered out? Or merely as convenient vehicles for the conducting of national presidential elections?

The patronage system does not, of course, merely foster political parties in general; it fosters the two-party system in particular. When getting a job, as opposed to effectuating a particular substantive policy, is an available incentive for party-workers, those attracted by that incentive are likely to work for the party that has the best chance of displacing the "ins," rather than for some splinter group that has a more attractive political philosophy but little hope of success. Not only is a two-party system more likely to emerge, but the differences between those parties are more likely to be moderated, as each has a relatively greater interest in appealing to a majority of the electorate and a relatively lesser interest in furthering philosophies or programs that are far from the mainstream. The stabilizing effects of such a system are obvious.

. . .

Equally apparent is the relatively destabilizing nature of a system in which candidates cannot rely upon patronage–based party loyalty for their campaign support, but must attract workers and raise funds by appealing to various interest-groups. There is little doubt that our decisions in *Elrod* and *Branti*, by contributing to the decline of party strength, have also contributed to the growth of interest-group politics in the last decade. Our decision today will greatly accelerate the trend. It is not only campaigns that are affected, of course, but the subsequent behavior of politicians once they are in power. The replacement of a system firmly based in party discipline with one in which each office-holder comes to his own accommodation with competing interest groups produces "a dispersion of political influence that may inhibit a political party from enacting its programs into law."

Patronage, moreover, has been a powerful means of achieving the social and political integration of excluded groups. . . .

While the patronage system has the benefits argued for above, it also has undoubted disadvantages. It facilitates financial corruption, such as salary kickbacks and partisan political activity on government-paid time. It reduces the efficiency of government, because it creates incentives to hire more and less-qualified workers and because highly qualified workers are reluctant to accept jobs that may only last until the next election. And, of course, it applies some greater or lesser inducement for individuals to join and work for the party in power. . . .

Elrod and *Branti* should be overruled, rather than merely not extended. Even in the field of constitutional adjudication, where the pull of *stare decisis* is at its weakest, one is reluctant to depart from precedent. But when that precedent is not only wrong, not only recent, not only contradicted by a long prior tradition, but also has proved unworkable in practice, then all reluctance ought to disappear. In my view that is the situation here. Though unwilling to leave it to the political process to draw the line between desirable and undesirable patronage, the Court has neither been prepared to rule that no such line exists (*i.e*, that *all* patronage is unconstitutional) nor able to design the line itself in a manner that judges, lawyers, and public employees can understand. *Elrod* allowed patronage dismissals of persons in "policymaking" or "confidential" positions. *Branti* retreated from that formulation, asking instead "whether the hiring authority can demonstrate that party affiliation is an appropriate requirement for the effective performance of the public office involved." What that means is anybody's guess. The Courts of Appeals have devised various tests for determining when "affiliation is an appropriate requirement." These interpretations of *Branti* are not only significantly at variance with each other; they are still so general that for most positions it is impossible to know whether party affiliation is a permissible requirement until a court renders its decision.

A few examples will illustrate the shambles *Branti* has produced. A city cannot fire a deputy sheriff because of his political affiliation, but then again perhaps it can, especially if he is called the "police captain." A county cannot fire on that basis its attorney for the department of social services, nor its assistant attorney for family court, but a city can fire its solicitor and his assistants, or its assistant city attorney, or its assistant state's attorney, or its corporation counsel. A city cannot discharge its deputy court clerk for his political affiliation, but it can fire its legal assistant to the clerk on that basis. Firing a juvenile court bailiff seems impermissible, but it may be permissible if he is assigned permanently to a single judge. A city cannot fire on partisan grounds its director of roads, but it can fire the second in command of the water department. A government cannot discharge for political reasons the senior vice president of its development bank, but it can discharge the regional director of its rural housing administration.

The examples could be multiplied, but this summary should make obvious that the "tests" devised to implement *Branti* have produced inconsistent and unpredictable results. . . .

III

Even were I not convinced that *Elrod* and *Branti* were wrongly decided, I would hold that they should not be extended beyond their facts, viz., actual discharge of employees for their political affiliation. Those cases invalidated patronage firing in order to prevent the "restraint it places on freedoms of belief and association." The loss of one's current livelihood is an appreciably greater constraint than such other disappointments as the failure to obtain a promotion or selection for an uncongenial transfer. . . . We have drawn a line between firing and other employment decisions in other contexts and should do so here as well. . . .

OSBORNE v. OHIO
110 S.Ct. 1691 (1990)

Police obtained a search warrant and searched Clyde Osborne's home. They found explicit photographs of a nude sexually aroused male adolescent. Osborne was subsequently convicted of violating the Ohio law making it a state crime to possess child pornography. Osborne's conviction was upheld by the Ohio courts which rejected his First Amendment challenge to the law. The Ohio statute was clearly in conflict with the Warren Court precedent of Stanley v. Georgia.

Majority votes: 6
Dissenting votes: 3

JUSTICE WHITE delivered the opinion of the Court:
In order to combat child pornography, Ohio enacted Rev. Code Ann. § 2907.323(A)(3) (Supp. 1989), which provides in pertinent part:

"(A) No person shall do any of the following:
. . .

"(3) Possess or view any material or performance that shows a minor who is not the person's child or ward in a state of nudity, unless one of the following applies:
"(a) The material or performance is sold, disseminated, displayed, possessed, controlled, brought or caused to be brought into this state,

or presented for a bona fide artistic, medical, scientific, educational, religious, governmental, judicial, or other proper purpose, by or to a physician, psychologist, sociologist, scientist, teacher, person pursuing bona fide studies or research, librarian, clergyman, prosecutor, judge, or other person having a proper interest in the material or performance.

"(b) The person knows that the parents, guardian, or custodian has consented in writing to the photographing or use of the minor in a state of nudity and to the manner in which the material or performance is used or transferred."

Petitioner, Clyde Osborne, was convicted of violating this statute and sentenced to six months in prison, after the Columbus, Ohio, police, pursuant to a valid search, found four photographs in Osborne's home. Each photograph depicts a nude male adolescent posed in a sexually explicit position.

The Ohio Supreme Court affirmed Osborne's conviction, after an intermediate appellate court did the same. . . .

The threshold question in this case is whether Ohio may constitutionally proscribe the possession and viewing of child pornography or whether, as Osborne argues, our decision in *Stanley* v. *Georgia,* 394 U.S. 557 (1969), compels the contrary result. In *Stanley,* we struck down a Georgia law outlawing the private possession of obscene material. We recognized that the statute impinged upon Stanley's right to receive information in the privacy of his home, and we found Georgia's justifications for its law inadequate.

Stanley should not be read too broadly. . . . [A]ssuming, for the sake of argument, that Osborne has a First Amendment interest in viewing and possessing child pornography, we nonetheless find this case distinct from *Stanley* because the interests underlying child pornography prohibitions far exceed the interests justifying the Georgia law at issue in *Stanley.* Every court to address the issue has so concluded. . . .

In *Stanley,* Georgia primarily sought to proscribe the private possession of obscenity because it was concerned that obscenity would poison the minds of its viewers. We responded that "[w]hatever the power of the state to control public dissemination of ideas inimical to the public morality, it cannot constitutionally premise legislation on the desirability of controlling a person's private thoughts." The difference here is obvious: the State does not rely on a paternalistic interest in regulating Osborne's mind. Rather, Ohio has enacted § 2907.323(A)(3) in order to protect the victims of child pornography; it hopes to destroy a market for the exploitative use of children. . . .

It is also surely reasonable for the State to conclude that it will decrease the production of child pornography if it penalizes those who possess and view the product, thereby decreasing demand. In *New York* v. *Ferber,* where we upheld a New York statute outlawing the distribution of child pornography, we found a similar argument persuasive. . . .

Osborne contends that the State should use other measures, besides penalizing possession, to dry up the child pornography market. Osborne points out that in *Stanley* we rejected Georgia's argument that its prohibition on obscenity possession was a necessary incident to its proscription on obscenity distribution. This holding, however, must be viewed in light of the weak interests asserted by the State in that case. . . .

Given the importance of the State's interest in protecting the victims of child pornography, we cannot fault Ohio for attempting to stamp out this vice at all levels in the distribution chain. According to the State, since the time of our decision in *Ferber,* much of the child pornography market has been driven underground; as a result, it is now difficult, if not impossible, to solve the child pornography problem by only attacking production and distribution. Indeed, 19 States have found it necessary to proscribe the possession of this material.

Other interests also support the Ohio law. First, as *Ferber* recognized, the materials produced by child pornographers permanently record the victim's abuse. The pornography's continued existence causes the child victims continuing harm by haunting the children in years to come. The State's ban on possession and viewing encourages the possessors of these materials to destroy them. Second, encouraging the destruction of these materials is also desirable because evidence suggests that pedophiles use child pornography to seduce other children into sexual activity.

Given the gravity of the State's interests in this context, we find that Ohio may constitutionally proscribe the possession and viewing of child pornography. . . .

Having rejected Obsorne's *Stanley* and overbreadth arguments, we now reach Osborne's final objection to his conviction: his contention that he was denied due process because it is unclear that his conviction was based on a finding that each of the elements of § 2907.323(A)(3) was present. According to the Ohio Supreme Court, in order to secure a con-

viction under § 2907.323(A)(3), the State must prove both scienter [knows it is wrong] and that the defendant possessed material depicting a lewd exhibition or a graphic focus on genitals. The jury in this case was not instructed that it could convict Osborne only for conduct that satisfied these requirements.

The State concedes the omissions in the jury instructions, but argues that Osborne waived his right to assert this due process challenge because he failed to object when the instructions were given at his trial. The Ohio Supreme Court so held, citing Ohio law. The question before us now, therefore, is whether we are precluded from reaching Osborne's due process challenge because counsel's failure to comply with the procedural rule constitutes an independent state law ground adequate to support the result below. We have no difficulty agreeing with the State that Osborne's counsel's failure to urge that the court instruct the jury on scienter constitutes an independent and adequate state law ground preventing us from reaching Osborne's due process contention on that point. Ohio law states that proof of scienter is required in instances, like the present one, where a criminal statute does not specify the applicable mental state. The state procedural rule, moreover, serves the State's important interest in ensuring that counsel do their part in preventing trial courts from providing juries with erroneous instructions.

With respect to the trial court's failure to instruct on lewdness, however, we reach a different conclusion: based upon our review of the record, we believe that counsel's failure to object on this point does not prevent us from considering Osborne's constitutional claim. Osborne's trial was brief: the State called only the two arresting officers to the stand; the defense summoned only Osborne himself. Right before trial, Osborne's counsel moved to dismiss the case, contending that § 2907.323(A)(3) is unconstitutionally overbroad. . . .

[W]e believe that we may reach Osborne's due process claim because we are convinced that Osborne's attorney pressed the issue of the State's failure of proof on lewdness before the trial court and, under the circumstances, nothing would be gained by requiring Osborne's lawyer to object a second time, specifically to the jury instructions. The trial judge, in no uncertain terms, rejected counsel's argument that the statute as written was overbroad. The State contends that counsel should then have insisted that the court instruct the jury on lewdness because, absent a finding that this element existed, a conviction would be unconstitutional. Were we to accept this position, we would "'force resort to an arid ritual of meaningless form,' . . . and would further no perceivable state interest." . . .

To conclude, although we find Osborne's First Amendment arguments unpersuasive, we reverse his conviction and remand for a new trial in order to ensure that Osborne's conviction stemmed from a finding that the State had proved each of the elements of § 2907.323(A)(3).

So Ordered.

JUSTICE BLACKMUN, concurring: [omitted]
JUSTICE BRENNAN, with whom JUSTICE MARSHALL and JUSTICE STEVENS join, dissenting:

I agree with the Court that appellant's conviction must be reversed. I do not agree, however, that Ohio is free on remand to retry him under Ohio Rev. Code Ann. §2907.323(A)(3) (Supp. 1989) as it currently exists. In my view, the state law, even as construed authoritatively by the Ohio Supreme Court, is still fatally overbroad, and our decision in *Stanley* v. *Georgia,* 394 U.S. 557 (1969), prevents the State from criminalizing appellant's possession of the photographs at issue in this case. I therefore respectfully dissent. . . .

Even if the statute was not overbroad, our decision in *Stanley* v. *Georgia* forbids the criminalization of appellant's private possession in his home of the materials at issue. "If the First Amendment means anything, it means that the State has no business telling a man, sitting alone in his own house, what books he may read or what films he may watch." Appellant was convicted for possessing four photographs of nude minors, seized from a desk drawer in the bedroom of his house during a search executed pursuant to a warrant. Appellant testified that he had been given the pictures in his home by a friend. There was no evidence that the photographs had been produced commercially or distributed. All were kept in an album that appellant had assembled for his personal use and had possessed privately for several years.

In these circumstances, the Court's focus on *Ferber* rather than *Stanley* is misplaced. *Ferber* held only that child pornography is "a category of material the *production* and *distribution* of which is not entitled to First Amendment protection;" our decision did not extend to private *possession.* The authority of a State to regulate the production and distribution of such materials is not dispositive of its power to penalize possession. Indeed, in *Stanley* we assumed that the films at issue were obscene and their production, sale, and distribution thus could have been prohibited under our decisions. Nevertheless, we reasoned that although the States

"retain broad power to regulate obscenity"—and child pornography as well—"that power simply does not extend to mere possession by the individual in the privacy of his own home." *Ferber* did nothing more than place child pornography on the same level of First Amendment protection as *obscene* adult pornography, meaning that its production and distribution could be proscribed. The distinction established in *Stanley* between *what* materials may be regulated and *how* they may be regulated still stands. . . .

The Court today finds *Stanley* inapposite on the ground that "the interests underlying child pornography prohibitions far exceed the interests justifying the Georgia law at issue in *Stanley*." The majority's analysis does not withstand scrutiny. While the sexual exploitation of children is undoubtedly a serious problem, Ohio may employ other weapons to combat it. Indeed, the State already has enacted a panoply of laws prohibiting the creation, sale, and distribution of child pornography and obscenity involving minors. Ohio has not demonstrated why these laws are inadequate and why the State must forbid mere possession as well.

The Court today speculates that Ohio "will decrease the production of child pornography if it penalizes those who possess and view the product, thereby decreasing demand." Criminalizing possession is thought necessary because "since the time of our decision in *Ferber,* much of the child pornography market has been driven underground; as a result, it is now difficult, if not impossible, to solve the child pornography problem by only attacking production and distribution." As support, the Court notes that 19 States have "found it necessary" to prohibit simple possession. Even were I to accept the Court's empirical assumptions, I would find the Court's approach foreclosed by *Stanley,* which rejected precisely the same contention Ohio makes today. . . .

At bottom, the Court today is so disquieted by the possible exploitation of children in the *production* of the pornography that it is willing to tolerate the imposition of criminal penalties for simple *possession.* While I share the majority's concerns, I do not believe that it has struck the proper balance between the First Amendment and the State's interests, especially in light of the other means available to Ohio to protect children from exploitation and the State's failure to demonstrate a causal link between a ban on possession of child pornography and a decrease in its production. "The existence of the State's power to prevent the distribution of obscene matter"—and of child pornography—"does not mean that there can be no constitutional barrier to any form of practical exercise of that power." . . .

When speech is eloquent and the ideas expressed lofty, it is easy to find restrictions on them invalid. But were the First Amendment limited to such discourse, our freedom would be sterile indeed. Mr. Osborne's pictures may be distasteful, but the Constitution guarantees both his right to possess them privately and his right to avoid punishment under an overbroad law. I respectfully dissent.

EMPLOYMENT DIVISION, OREGON DEPARTMENT OF HUMAN RESOURCES v. SMITH
110 S. Ct. 1595 (1990)

Alfred Smith and Galen Black, members of the Native American Church, were employed by a private drug rehabilitation clinic located in Oregon. They were fired when their employer discovered that they ingested the drug peyote for sacramental purposes as part of their church's religious service. They applied for unemployment compensation but the Employment Division of the Oregon Department of Human Resources denied the claims under a state law disqualifying employees discharged for work-related "misconduct." The State Court of Appeals and the Oregon Supreme Court both found that the denials violated Smith and Black's right to free exercise of religion as guaranteed by the First Amendment. In 1988, the U.S. Supreme Court vacated the judgment and sent the case back to the Oregon Supreme Court for it to determine whether sacramental peyote use is prohibited by Oregon's controlled substance law which makes it a felony to knowingly or intentionally possess the drug. On remand the Oregon Supreme Court ruled that Oregon law provided no exceptions for sacramental use and that such prohibition violated the free exercise of religion guarantee. The court thus reaffirmed its previous ruling that Oregon could not deny unemployment benefits to Smith and Black for having engaged in constitutionally protected activity. Once again, Oregon came to the U.S. Supreme Court and this time the Court squarely faced the issue.

Majority votes: 6
Dissenting votes: 3

JUSTICE SCALIA delivered the opinion of the Court:

This case requires us to decide whether the Free Exercise Clause of the First Amendment permits the State of Oregon to include religiously inspired peyote use within the reach of its general criminal prohibition on use of that drug, and thus permits the State to deny unemployment benefits to persons dismissed from their jobs because of such religiously inspired use. . . .

The Free Exercise Clause of the First Amendment, which has been made applicable to the States by incorporation into the Fourteenth Amendment, see *Cantwell* v. *Connecticut,* 310 U.S. 296, 303 (1940) . . . means, first and foremost, the right to believe and profess whatever religious doctrine one desires. . . .

But the "exercise of religion" often involves not only belief and profession but the performance of (or abstention from) physical acts: assembling with others for a worship service, participating in sacramental use of bread and wine, proselytizing, abstaining from certain foods or certain modes of transportation. . . .

Respondents in the present case, however, seek to carry the meaning of "prohibiting the free exercise [of religion]" one large step further. They contend that their religious motivation for using peyote places them beyond the reach of a criminal law that is not specifically directed at their religious practice, and that is concededly constitutional as applied to those who use the drug for other reasons. They assert, in other words, that "prohibiting the free exercise [of religion]" includes requiring any individual to observe a generally applicable law that requires (or forbids) the performance of an act that his religious belief forbids (or requires). As a textual matter, we do not think the words must be given that meaning. It is no more necessary to regard the collection of a general tax, for example, as "prohibiting the free exercise [of religion]" by those citizens who believe support of organized government to be sinful, than it is to regard the same tax as "abridging the freedom . . . of the press" of those publishing companies that must pay the tax as a condition of staying in business. It is a permissible reading of the text, in the one case as in the other, to say that if prohibiting the exercise of religion (or burdening the activity of printing) is not the object of the tax but merely the incidental effect of a generally applicable and otherwise valid provision, the First Amendment has not been offended. . . .

Our decisions reveal that the latter reading is the correct one. We have never held that an individual's religious beliefs excuse him from compliance with an otherwise valid law prohibiting conduct that the State is free to regulate. On the contrary, the record of more than a century of our free exercise jurisprudence contradicts that proposition. . . . We first had occasion to assert that principle in *Reynolds* v. *United States,* 98 U.S. 145 (1879), where we rejected the claim that criminal laws against polygamy could not be constitutionally applied to those whose religion commanded the practice. "Laws," we said, "are made for the government of actions, and while they cannot interfere with mere religious belief and opinions, they may with practices. . . . Can a man excuse his practices to the contrary because of his religious belief? To permit this would be to make the professed doctrines of religious belief superior to the law of the land, and in effect to permit every citizen to become a law unto himself." *Id.,* at 166–167.

Subsequent decisions have consistently held that the right of free exercise does not relieve an individual of the obligation to comply with a "valid and neutral law of general applicability on the ground that the law proscribes (or prescribes) conduct that his religion prescribes (or proscribes)." . . .

Respondents urge us to hold, quite simply, that when otherwise prohibitable conduct is accompanied by religious convictions, not only the convictions but the conduct itself must be free from governmental regulation. We have never held that, and decline to do so now. There being no contention that Oregon's drug law represents an attempt to regulate religious beliefs, the communication of religious beliefs, or the raising of one's children in those beliefs, the rule to which we have adhered ever since *Reynolds* plainly controls. . . .

Respondents argue that even though exemption from generally applicable criminal laws need not automatically be extended to religiously motivated actors, at least the claim for a religious exemption must be evaluated under the balancing test set forth in *Sherbert* v. *Verner,* 374 U.S. 398 (1963). Under the *Sherbert* test, governmental actions that substantially burden a religious practice must be justified by a compelling governmental interest. Applying that test we have, on three occasions, invalidated state unemployment compensation rules that conditioned the availability of benefits upon an applicant's willingness to work under conditions forbidden by his religion. . . . We have never invalidated any governmental action on the basis of the *Sherbert* test except the denial of unemployment compensation. . . .

Even if we were inclined to breathe into *Sherbert* some life beyond the unemployment compensation field, we would not apply it to require exemptions from a generally applicable criminal law. . . .

We conclude today that the sounder approach, and the approach in accord with the vast majority of our precedents, is to hold the test inapplicable to such challenges. The government's ability to enforce generally applicable prohibitions of socially harmful conduct, like its ability to carry out other aspects of public policy, "cannot depend on measuring the effects of a governmental action on a religious objector's spiritual development." To make an individual's obligation to obey such a law contingent upon the law's coincidence with his religious beliefs, except where the State's interest is "compelling"—permitting him, by virtue of his beliefs, "to become a law unto himself"—contradicts both constitutional tradition and common sense.

The "compelling government interest" requirement seems benign, because it is familiar from other fields. But using it as the standard that must be met before the government may accord different treatment on the basis of race or before the government may regulate the content of speech is not remotely comparable to using it for the purpose asserted here. What it produces in those other fields—equality of treatment, and an unrestricted flow of contending speech—are constitutional norms; what it would produce here—a private right to ignore generally applicable laws—is a constitutional anomaly.

Nor is it possible to limit the impact of respondents' proposal by requiring a "compelling state interest" only when the conduct prohibited is "central" to the individual's religion. It is no more appropriate for judges to determine the "centrality" of religious beliefs before applying a "compelling interest" test in the free exercise field, than it would be for them to determine the "importance" of ideas before applying the "compelling interest" test in the free speech field. What principle of law or logic can be brought to bear to contradict a believer's assertion that a particular act is "central" to his personal faith? Judging the centrality of different religious practices is akin to the unacceptable "business of evaluating the relative merits of differing religious claims." . . .

If the "compelling interest" test is to be applied at all, then, it must be applied across the board, to all actions thought to be religiously commanded. Moreover, if "compelling interest" really means what it says (and watering it down here would subvert its rigor in the other fields where it is applied), many laws will not meet the test. Any society adopting such a system would be courting anarchy, but that danger increases in direct proportion to the society's diversity of religious beliefs, and its determination to coerce or suppress none of them. Precisely because "we are a cosmopolitan nation made up of people of almost every conceivable religious preference," and precisely because we value and protect that religious divergence, we cannot afford the luxury of deeming *presumptively invalid,* as applied to the religious objector, every regulation of conduct that does not protect an interest of the highest order. The rule respondents favor would open the prospect of constitutionally required religious exemptions from civic obligations of almost every conceivable kind—ranging from compulsory military service to the payment of taxes, to health and safety regulation such as manslaughter and child neglect laws . . . compulsory vaccination laws . . . drug laws . . . and traffic laws, . . . to social welfare legislation such as minimum wage laws . . . child labor laws . . . animal cruelty laws . . . environmental protection laws . . . and laws providing for equality of opportunity for the races. . . . The First Amendment's protection of religious liberty does not require this. . . .

Because respondents' ingestion of peyote was prohibited under Oregon law, and because that prohibition is constitutional, Oregon may, consistent with the Free Exercise Clause, deny respondents unemployment compensation when their dismissal results from use of the drug. The decision of the Oregon Supreme Court is accordingly reversed.

It is so ordered.

JUSTICE O'CONNOR, with whom JUSTICE BRENNAN, JUSTICE MARSHALL, and JUSTICE BLACKMUN join as to Parts I and II, concurring in the judgment:*

Although I agree with the result the Court reaches in this case, I cannot join its opinion. In my view, today's holding dramatically departs from well-settled First Amendment jurisprudence, appears unnecessary to resolve the question presented, and is incompatible with our Nation's fundamental commitment to individual religious liberty.

I. . . . [omitted; description of case and issues]

II. . . .

The Free Exercise Clause of the First Amendment . . . does not distinguish between religious belief and religious conduct, [therefore] conduct motivated by sincere religious belief, like the belief itself, must . . . be at least presumptively protected by the Free Exercise Clause.

The Court today, however, interprets the Clause to permit the government to prohibit, without justification, conduct mandated by an individual's religious beliefs, so long as that prohibition is generally

*Although JUSTICE BRENNAN, JUSTICE MARSHALL, and JUSTICE BLACKMUN join Parts I and II of this opinion, they do not concur in the judgment.

applicable. But a law that prohibits certain conduct—conduct that happens to be an act of worship for someone—manifestly does prohibit that person's free exercise of his religion. A person who is barred from engaging in religiously motivated conduct is barred from freely exercising his religion. Moreover, that person is barred from freely exercising his religion regardless of whether the law prohibits the conduct only when engaged in for religious reasons, only by members of that religion, or by all persons. It is difficult to deny that a law that prohibits religiously motivated conduct, even if the law is generally applicable, does not at least implicate First Amendment concerns.

The Court responds that generally applicable laws are "one large step" removed from laws aimed at specific religious practices. The First Amendment, however, does not distinguish between laws that are generally applicable and laws that target particular religious practices. Indeed, few States would be so naive as to enact a law directly prohibiting or burdening a religious practice as such. Our free exercise cases have all concerned generally applicable laws that had the effect of significantly burdening a religious practice. If the First Amendment is to have any vitality, it ought not be construed to cover only the extreme and hypothetical situation in which a State directly targets a religious practice. . . . To say that a person's right to free exercise has been burdened, of course, does not mean that he has an absolute right to engage in the conduct. Under our established First Amendment jurisprudence, we have recognized that the freedom to act, unlike the freedom to believe, cannot be absolute. Instead, we have respected both the First Amendment's express textual mandate and the governmental interest in regulation of conduct by requiring the Government to justify any substantial burden on religiously motivated conduct by a compelling state interest and by means narrowly tailored to achieve that interest. . . . The compelling interest test effectuates the First Amendment's command that religious liberty is an independent liberty, that it occupies a preferred position, and that the Court will not permit encroachments upon this liberty, whether direct or indirect, unless required by clear and compelling governmental interests "of the highest order." "Only an especially important governmental interest pursued by narrowly tailored means can justify exacting a sacrifice of First Amendment freedoms as the price for an equal share of the rights, benefits, and privileges enjoyed by other citizens."

The Court attempts to support its narrow reading of the Clause by claiming that "[w]e have never held that an individual's religious beliefs excuse him from compliance with an otherwise valid law prohibiting conduct that the State is free to regulate." But as the Court later notes, as it must, in cases such as *Cantwell* and *Wisconsin* v. *Yoder* we have in fact interpreted the Free Exercise Clause to forbid application of a generally applicable prohibition to religiously motivated conduct. Indeed, in *Yoder* we expressly rejected the interpretation the Court now adopts:

"[O]ur decisions have rejected the idea that religiously grounded conduct is always outside the protection of the Free Exercise Clause. It is true that activities of individuals, even when religiously based, are often subject to regulation by the States in the exercise of their undoubted power to promote the health, safety, and general welfare, or the Federal Government in the exercise of its delegated powers. But to agree that religiously grounded conduct must often be subject to the broad police power of the State is not to deny that there are areas of conduct protected by the Free Exercise Clause of the First Amendment and thus beyond the power of the State to control, *even under regulations of general applicability*. . . .

". . . A regulation neutral on its face may, in its application, nonetheless offend the constitutional requirement for government neutrality if it unduly burdens the free exercise of religion." 406 U.S., at 219–220 (emphasis added; citations omitted).

The Court endeavors to escape from our decisions in *Cantwell* and *Yoder* by labeling them "hybrid" decisions, but there is no denying that both cases expressly relied on the Free Exercise Clause and that we have consistently regarded those cases as part of the mainstream of our free exercise jurisprudence. Moreover, in each of the other cases cited by the Court to support its categorical rule, we rejected the particular constitutional claims before us only after carefully weighing the competing interests. See *Prince* v. *Massachusetts*, 321 U.S. 158, 168–170 (1944) (state interest in regulating children's activities justifies denial of religious exemption from child labor laws); *Braunfield* v. *Brown*, 366 U.S. 599, 608–609 (1961) (plurality opinion) (state interest in uniform day of rest justifies denial of religious exemption from Sunday closing law) . . . That we rejected the free exercise claims in those cases hardly calls into question the applicability of First Amendment doctrine in the first place. Indeed, it is surely unusual to judge the vitality of a constitutional doctrine by looking to the win-loss record of the plaintiffs who happen to come before us.

Respondents, of course, do not contend that their conduct is automatically immune from all governmental regulation simply because it is motivated by their sincere religious beliefs. The Court's rejection of that argument might therefore be regarded as merely harmless dictum. Rather, respondents invoke our traditional compelling interest test to argue that the Free Exercise Clause requires the State to grant them a limited exemption from its general criminal prohibition against the possession of peyote. The Court today, however, denies them even the opportunity to make that argument, concluding that "the sounder approach, and the approach in accord with the vast majority of our precedents, is to hold the [compelling interest] test inapplicable to" challenges to general criminal prohibitions.

In my view, however, the essence of a free exercise claim is relief from a burden imposed by government on religious practices or beliefs, whether the burden is imposed directly through laws that prohibit or compel specific religious practices, or indirectly through laws that, in effect, make abandonment of one's own religion or conformity to the religious beliefs of others the price of an equal place in the civil community. . . . A State that makes criminal an individual's religiously motivated conduct burdens that individual's free exercise of religion in the severest manner possible, for it "results in the choice to the individual of either abandoning his religious principle or facing criminal prosecution." I would have thought it beyond argument that such laws implicate free exercise concerns. . . .

. . . Once it has been shown that a government regulation or criminal prohibition burdens the free exercise of religion, we have consistently asked the Government to demonstrate that unbending application of its regulation to the religious objector "is essential to accomplish an overriding governmental interest," or represents "the least restrictive means of achieving some compelling state interest." . . . To me, the sounder approach—the approach more consistent with our role as judges to decide each case on its individual merits—is to apply this test in each case to determine whether the burden on the specific plaintiffs before us is constitutionally significant and whether the particular criminal interest asserted by the State before us is compelling. Even if, as an empirical matter, a government's criminal laws might usually serve a compelling interest in health, safety, or public order, the First Amendment at least requires a case-by-case determination of the question, sensitive to the facts of each particular claim. . . . Given the range of conduct that a State might legitimately make criminal, we cannot assume, merely because a law carries criminal sanctions and is generally applicable, that the First Amendment *never* requires the State to grant a limited exemption for religiously motivated conduct.

Moreover, we have not "rejected" or "declined to apply" the compelling interest test in our recent cases. . . . Recent cases have instead affirmed that test as a fundamental part of our First Amendment doctrine. . . . The cases cited by the Court signal no retreat from our consistent adherence to the compelling interest test. . . .

III

The Court's holding today not only misreads settled First Amendment precedent; it appears to be unnecessary to this case. I would reach the same result applying our established free exercise jurisprudence.

There is no dispute that Oregon's criminal prohibition of peyote places a severe burden on the ability of respondents to freely exercise their religion. . . .

There is also no dispute that Oregon has a significant interest in enforcing laws that control the possession and use of controlled substances by its citizens. . . . As we recently noted, drug abuse is "one of the greatest problems affecting the health and welfare of our population" and thus "one of the most serious problems confronting our society today." *Treasury Employees* v. *Von Raab* (1989). Indeed, under federal law (incorporated by Oregon law in relevant part), peyote is specifically regulated as a Schedule I controlled substance, which means that Congress has found that it has a high potential for abuse, that there is no currently accepted medical use, and that there is a lack of accepted safety for use of the drug under medical supervision. In light of our recent decisions holding that the governmental interests in the collection of income tax, a comprehensive social security system, and military conscription are compelling, respondents do not seriously dispute that Oregon has a compelling interest in prohibiting the possession of peyote by its citizens.

Thus, the critical question in this case is whether exempting respondents from the State's general criminal prohibition "will unduly interfere with fulfillment of the governmental interest." . . . Although the question is close, I would conclude that uniform application of Oregon's criminal prohibition is "essential to accomplish" its overriding interest in preventing the physical harm caused by the use of a Schedule I controlled substance. Oregon's criminal prohibition represents that State's judgment that the possession and use of controlled substances, even by only one person, is inherently

harmful and dangerous. Because the health effects caused by the use of controlled substances exist regardless of the motivation of the user, the use of such substances, even for religious purposes, violates the very purpose of the laws that prohibit them. . . . Moreover, in view of the societal interest in preventing trafficking in controlled substances, uniform application of the criminal prohibition at issue is essential to the effectiveness of Oregon's stated interest in preventing any possession of peyote. . . .

. . . Accordingly, I concur in the judgment of the Court.

JUSTICE BLACKMUN, with whom JUSTICE BRENNAN and JUSTICE MARSHALL join, dissenting:. . . .

I agree with JUSTICE O'CONNOR'S analysis of the applicable free exercise doctrine, and I join parts I and II of her opinion. As she points out, "the critical question in this case is whether exempting respondents from the State's general criminal prohibition 'will unduly interfere with fulfillment of the governmental interest.' " I do disagree, however, with her specific answer to that question.

In weighing respondents' clear interest in the free exercise of their religion against Oregon's asserted interest in enforcing its drug laws, it is important to articulate in precise terms the state interest involved. It is not the State's broad interest in fighting the critical "war on drugs" that must be weighed against respondents' claim, but the State's narrow interest in refusing to make an exception for the religious, ceremonial use of peyote. . . .

The State's interest in enforcing its prohibition, in order to be sufficiently compelling to outweigh a free exercise claim, cannot be merely abstract or symbolic. The State cannot plausibly assert that unbending application of a criminal prohibition is essential to fulfill any compelling interest, if it does not, in fact, attempt to enforce that prohibition. In this case, the State actually has not evinced any concrete interest in enforcing its drug laws against religious users of peyote. Oregon has never sought to prosecute respondents, and does not claim that it has made significant enforcement efforts against other religious users of peyote. The State's asserted interest thus amounts only to the symbolic preservation of an unenforced prohibition. But a government interest in "symbolism, even symbolism for so worthy a cause as the abolition of unlawful drugs," cannot suffice to abrogate the constitutional rights of individuals.

Similarly, this Court's prior decisions have not allowed a government to rely on mere speculation about potential harms, but have demanded evidentiary support for a refusal to allow a religious exception. . . . In this case, the State's justification for refusing to recognize an exception to its criminal laws for religious peyote use is entirely speculative.

The State proclaims an interest in protecting the health and safety of its citizens from the dangers of unlawful drugs. It offers, however, no evidence that the religious use of peyote has ever harmed anyone. The factual findings of other courts cast doubt on the State's assumption that religious use of peyote is harmful. . . .

The fact that peyote is classified as a Schedule I controlled substance does not, by itself, show that any and all uses of peyote, in any circumstance, are inherently harmful and dangerous. The Federal Government, which created the classifications of unlawful drugs from which Oregon's drug laws are derived, apparently does not find peyote so dangerous as to preclude an exemption for religious use. Moreover, other Schedule I drugs have lawful uses. . . .

The carefully circumscribed ritual context in which respondents used peyote is far removed from the irresponsible and unrestricted recreational use of unlawful drugs. The Native American Church's internal restrictions on, and supervision of, its members' use of peyote substantially obviate the State's health and safety concerns. . . .

Moreover, just as in *Yoder,* the values and interests of those seeking a religious exemption in this case are congruent, to a great degree, with those the State seeks to promote through its drug laws. . . . Not only does the Church's doctrine forbid nonreligious use of peyote; it also generally advocates self-reliance, familial responsibility, and abstinence from alcohol. . . . There is considerable evidence that the spiritual and social support provided by the Church has been effective in combatting the tragic effects of alcoholism on the Native American population. Two noted experts on peyotism, Dr. Omer C. Stewart and Dr. Robert Bergman, testified by affidavit to this effect on behalf of respondent Smith before the Employment Appeal Board. . . . Far from promoting the lawless and irresponsible use of drugs, Native American Church members' spiritual code exemplifies values that Oregon's drug laws are presumably intended to foster.

The State also seeks to support its refusal to make an exception for religious use of peyote by invoking its interest in abolishing drug trafficking. There is, however, practically no illegal traffic in peyote. . . . Peyote simply is not a popular drug; its distribution for use in religious rituals has nothing to do with the vast and violent traffic in illegal narcotics that plagues this country.

Finally, the State argues that granting an exception for religious peyote use would erode its interest in the uniform, fair, and certain enforcement of its drug laws. The State fears that, if it grants an exemption for religious peyote use, a flood of other claims to religious exemptions will follow. . . .

The State's apprehension of a flood of other religious claims is purely speculative. Almost half the States, and the Federal Government, have maintained an exemption for religious peyote use for many years, and apparently have not found themselves overwhelmed by claims to other religious exemptions. Allowing an exemption for religious peyote use would not necessarily oblige the State to grant a similar exemption to other religious groups. The unusual circumstances that make the religious use of peyote compatible with the State's interests in health and safety and in preventing drug trafficking would not apply to other religious claims. Some religions, for example, might not restrict drug use to a limited ceremonial context, as does the Native American Church. Some religious claims involve drugs such as marijuana and heroin, in which there is significant illegal traffic, with its attendant greed and violence, so that it would be difficult to grant a religious exemption without seriously compromising law enforcement efforts. That the State might grant an exemption for religious peyote use, but deny other religious claims arising in different circumstances, would not violate the Establishment Clause. Though the State must treat all religions equally, and not favor one over another, this obligation is fulfilled by the uniform application of the "compelling interest" *test* to all free exercise claims, not by reaching uniform *results* as to all claims. A showing that religious peyote use does not unduly interfere with the State's interests is "one that probably few other religious groups or sects could make;" this does not mean that an exemption limited to peyote use is tantamount to an establishment of religion. . . .

Respondents believe, and their sincerity has *never* been at issue, that the peyote plant embodies their deity, and eating it is an act of worship and communion. Without peyote, they could not enact the essential ritual of their religion. . . .

If Oregon can constitutionally prosecute them for this act of worship, they, like the Amish, may be "forced to migrate to some other and more tolerant region." This potentially devastating impact must be viewed in light of the federal policy—reached in reaction to many years of religious persecution and intolerance—of protecting the religious freedom of Native Americans. See American Indian Religious Freedom Act, 92 Stat. 469, 42 U.S.C. § 1996 ("it shall be the policy of the United States to protect and preserve for American Indians their inherent right of freedom to believe, express, and exercise the traditional religions . . ., including but not limited to access to sites, use and possession of sacred objects, and the freedom to worship through ceremonials and traditional rites''). Congress recognized that certain substances, such as peyote, ''have religious significance because they are sacred, they have power, they heal, they are necessary to the exercise of the rites of the religion, they are necessary to the cultural integrity of the tribe, and, therefore, religious survival.''

The American Indian Religious Freedom Act, in itself, may not create rights enforceable against government action restricting religious freedom, but this Court must scrupulously apply its free exercise analysis to the religious claims of Native Americans, however unorthodox they may be. Otherwise, both the First Amendment and the stated policy of Congress will offer to Native Americans merely an unfulfilled and hollow promise.

For these reasons, I conclude that Oregon's interest in enforcing its drug laws against religious use of peyote is not sufficiently compelling to outweigh respondents' right to the free exercise of their religion. Since the State could not constitutionally enforce its criminal prohibition against respondents, the interests underlying the State's drug laws cannot justify its denial of unemployment benefits. Absent such justification, the State's regulatory interest in denying benefits for religiously motivated ''misconduct'' is indistinguishable from the state interests this Court has rejected in *Frazee, Hobbie, Thomas,* and *Sherbert.* The State of Oregon cannot, consistently with the Free Exercise Clause, deny respondents unemployment benefits.

I dissent.

RIGHTS OF THE ACCUSED

MICHIGAN v. SITZ
110 S.Ct. 2481 (1990)

The toll that drunk driving takes in the United States today is enormous—thousands of lives lost, tens of thousands of serious injuries, many millions of dollars in property damage. The Michigan State Police Department established a sobriety checkpoint (roadblock) pilot program in early 1986 in an attempt to catch drunk drivers before they caused trouble. The State Police established guidelines governing the selection of the roadblock sites and publicity of the program. The first site was announced for Saginaw County. On the day before the operation of that checkpoint, Rick Sitz and

other licensed Michigan drivers filed a complaint in a county court seeking declaratory and injunctive relief from potentially being subjected to the checkpoints. The checkpoint operated for only one night because the following day during pretrial proceedings Michigan agreed to delay further implementation of the checkpoint program pending the outcome of this litigation. After a trial, the court ruled that Michigan's program violated the Fourth Amendment. The Michigan Court of Appeals affirmed and state officials took the case to the United States Supreme Court.

Majority votes: 6
Dissenting votes: 3

CHIEF JUSTICE REHNQUIST delivered the opinion of the Court:. . . .

It is important to recognize what our inquiry is *not* about. No allegations are before us of unreasonable treatment of any person after an actual detention at a particular checkpoint. . . . As pursued in the lower courts, the instant action challenges only the use of sobriety checkpoints generally. We address only the initial stop of each motorist passing through a checkpoint and the associated preliminary questioning and observation by checkpoint officers. Detention of particular motorists for more extensive field sobriety testing may require satisfaction of an individualized suspicion standard.

No one can seriously dispute the magnitude of the drunken driving problem or the States' interest in eradicating it. Media reports of alcohol-related death and mutilation on the Nation's roads are legion. The anecdotal is confirmed by the statistical. ''Drunk drivers cause an annual death toll of over 25,000 and in the same time span cause nearly one million personal injuries and more than five billion dollars in property damage.'' 4 W. LaFave, Search and Seizure: A Treatise on the Fourth Amendment § 10.8(d), p. 71 (2d ed. 1987). For decades, this Court has ''repeatedly lamented the tragedy.'' . . .

Conversely, the weight bearing on the other scale—the measure of the intrusion on motorists stopped briefly at sobriety checkpoints—is slight. We reached a similar conclusion as to the intrusion on motorists subjected to a brief stop at a highway checkpoint for detecting illegal aliens. See *United States* v. *Martinez-Fuerte,* 428 U.S. 543 (1976). We see virtually no difference between the levels of intrusion on law-abiding motorists from the brief stops necessary to the effectuation of these two types of checkpoints, which to the average motorist would seem identical save for the nature of the questions the checkpoint officers might ask. The trial court and the Court of Appeals, thus, accurately gauged the "objective" intrusion, measured by the duration of the seizure and the intensity of the investigation, as minimal.

With respect to what it perceived to be the "subjective" intrusion on motorists, however, the Court of Appeals found such intrusion substantial. The court first affirmed the trial court's finding that the guidelines governing checkpoint operation minimize the discretion of the officers on the scene. But the court also agreed with the trial court's conclusion that the checkpoints have the potential to generate fear and surprise in motorists. This was so because the record failed to demonstrate that approaching motorists would be aware of their option to make U-turns or turnoffs to avoid the checkpoints. On that basis, the court deemed the subjective intrusion from the checkpoints unreasonable.

We believe the Michigan courts misread our cases concerning the degree of "subjective intrusion" and the potential for generating fear and surprise. The "fear and surprise" to be considered are not the natural fear of one who has been drinking over the prospect of being stopped at a sobriety checkpoint but, rather, the fear and surprise engendered in law abiding motorists by the nature of the stop. This was made clear in *Martinez-Fuerte*. . . . Here, checkpoints are selected pursuant to the guidelines, and uniformed police officers stop every approaching vehicle. The intrusion resulting from the brief stop at the sobriety checkpoint is for constitutional purposes indistinguishable from the checkpoint stops we upheld in *Martinez-Fuerte*. . . .

In *Delaware* v. *Prouse,* 440 U.S. 648 (1979), we disapproved random stops made by Delaware Highway Patrol officers in an effort to apprehend unlicensed drivers and unsafe vehicles. We observed that *no* empirical evidence indicated that such stops would be an effective means of promoting roadway safety and said that "[i]t seems common sense that the percentage of all drivers on the road who are driving without a license is very small and that the number of licensed drivers who will be stopped in order to find one unlicensed operator will be large indeed." 440 U.S., at 659–660. We observed that the random stops involved the "kind of standardless and unconstrained discretion [which] is the evil the Court has discerned when in previous cases it has insisted that the discretion of the official in the field be circumscribed, at least to some extent." *Id.,* at 661. We went on to state that our holding did not "cast doubt on the permissibility of roadside truck weigh-stations and inspection checkpoints, at which some vehicles may be sub-

ject to further detention for safety and regulatory inspection than are others." *Id.,* at 663, n. 26.

Unlike *Prouse,* this case involves neither a complete absence of empirical data nor a challenge to random highway stops. During the operation of the Saginaw County checkpoint, the detention of each of the 126 vehicles that entered the checkpoint resulted in the arrest of two drunken drivers. Stated as a percentage, approximately 1.5 percent of the drivers passing through the checkpoint were arrested for alcohol impairment. In addition, an expert witness testified at the trial that experience in other States demonstrated that, on the whole, sobriety checkpoints resulted in drunken driving arrests of around 1 percent of all motorists stopped. By way of comparison, the record from one of the consolidated cases in *Martinez-Fuerte,* showed that in the associated checkpoint, illegal aliens were found in only 0.12 percent of the vehicles passing through the checkpoint. The ratio of illegal aliens detected to vehicles stopped (considering that on occasion two or more illegal aliens were found in a single vehicle) was approximately 0.5 percent. We concluded that this "record . . . provides a rather complete picture of the effectiveness of the San Clemente checkpoint", and we sustained its constitutionality. We see no justification for a different conclusion here.

In sum, the balance of the State's interest in preventing drunken driving, the extent to which this system can reasonably be said to advance that interest, and the degree of intrusion upon individual motorists who are briefly stopped, weighs in favor of the state program. We therefore hold that it is consistent with the Fourth Amendment. The judgment of the Michigan Court of Appeals is accordingly reversed, and the cause is remanded for further proceedings not inconsistent with this opinion.

Reversed.

JUSTICE BLACKMUN, Concurring in the judgment: [omitted]
JUSTICE BRENNAN, with whom JUSTICE MARSHALL joins, dissenting: [omitted]
JUSTICE STEVENS, with whom JUSTICE BRENNAN and JUSTICE MARSHALL join as to Parts I and II, dissenting:. . . .

I

There is a critical difference between a seizure that is preceded by fair notice and one that is effected by surprise. That is one reason why a border search, or indeed any search at a permanent and fixed checkpoint, is much less intrusive than a random stop. A motorist with advance notice of the location of a permanent checkpoint has an opportunity to avoid the search entirely, or at least to prepare for, and limit, the intrusion on her privacy.

No such opportunity is available in the case of a random stop or a temporary checkpoint, which both depend for their effectiveness on the element of surprise. A driver who discovers an unexpected checkpoint on a familiar local road will be startled and distressed. She may infer, correctly, that the checkpoint is not simply "business as usual," and may likewise infer, again correctly, that the police have made a discretionary decision to focus their law enforcement efforts upon her and others who pass the chosen point.

This element of surprise is the most obvious distinction between the sobriety checkpoints permitted by today's majority and the interior border checkpoints approved by this Court in *Martinez-Fuerte*. The distinction casts immediate doubt upon the majority's argument, for *Martinez-Fuerte* is the only case in which we have upheld suspicionless seizures of motorists. But the difference between notice and surprise is only one of the important reasons for distinguishing between permanent and mobile checkpoints. With respect to the former, there is no room for discretion in either the timing or the location of the stop—it is a permanent part of the landscape. In the latter case, however, although the checkpoint is most frequently employed during the hours of darkness on weekends (because that is when drivers with alcohol in their blood are most apt to be found on the road), the police have extremely broad discretion in determining the exact timing and placement of the roadblock.

There is also a significant difference between the kind of discretion that the officer exercises after the stop is made. A check for a driver's license, or for identification papers at an immigration checkpoint, is far more easily standardized than is a search for evidence of intoxication. A Michigan officer who questions a motorist at a sobriety checkpoint has virtually unlimited discretion to detain the driver on the basis of the slightest suspicion. A ruddy complexion, an unbuttoned shirt, bloodshot eyes or a speech impediment may suffice to prolong the detention. Any driver who had just consumed a glass of beer, or even a sip of wine, would almost certainly have the burden of demonstrating to the officer that her driving ability was not impaired.

Finally, it is significant that many of the stops at permanent checkpoints occur during daylight hours, whereas the sobriety checkpoints are almost invariably operated at night. A seizure followed by interrogation and even a cursory search at night is surely more offensive than a daytime stop that is almost as routine as going through a toll gate. . . .

These fears are not, as the Court would have it, solely the lot of the guilty. To be law abiding is not necessarily to be spotless, and even the most virtuous can be unlucky. Unwanted attention from the local police need not be less discomforting simply because one's secrets are not the stuff of criminal prosecutions. Moreover, those who have found—by reason of prejudice or misfortune—that encounters with the police may become adversarial or unpleasant without good cause will have grounds for worrying at any stop designed to elicit signs of suspicious behavior. Being stopped by the police is distressing even when it should not be terrifying, and what begins mildly may by happenstance turn severe.

For all these reasons, I do not believe that this case is analogous to *Martinez-Fuerte*. In my opinion, the sobriety checkpoints are instead similar to—and in some respects more intrusive than—the random investigative stops that the Court held unconstitutional in *Prouse*. . . .

II

The Court, unable to draw any persuasive analogy to *Martinez-Fuerte*, rests its decision today on application of a more general balancing test taken from *Brown* v. *Texas*, 443 U.S. 47 (1979). In that case the appellant, a pedestrian, had been stopped for questioning in an area of El Paso, Texas, that had "a high incidence of drug traffic" because he "looked suspicious." He was then arrested and convicted for refusing to identify himself to police officers. We set aside his conviction because the officers stopped him when they lacked any reasonable suspicion that he was engaged in criminal activity. In our opinion, we stated:

"Consideration of the constitutionality of such seizures involves a weighing of the gravity of the public concerns served by the seizure, the degree to which the seizure advances the public interest, and the severity of the interference with individual liberty." *Id.*, at 50–51.

The gravity of the public concern with highway safety that is implicated by this case is, of course, undisputed. Yet, that same grave concern was implicated in *Delaware* v. *Prouse*. Moreover, I do not understand the Court to have placed any lesser value on the importance of the drug problem implicated in *Brown*, or on the need to control illegal border crossings. . . . A different result in this case must be justified by the other two factors in the *Brown* formulation.

As I have already explained, I believe the Court is quite wrong in blithely asserting that a sobriety checkpoint is no more intrusive than a permanent checkpoint. In my opinion, unannounced investigatory seizures are, particularly when they take place at night, the hallmark of regimes far different from ours; the surprise intrusion upon individual liberty is not minimal. On that issue, my difference with the Court may amount to nothing less than a difference in our respective evaluations of the importance of individual liberty, a serious albeit inevitable source of constitutional disagreement. On the degree to which the sobriety checkpoint seizures advance the public interest, however, the Court's position is wholly indefensible.

The Court's analysis of this issue resembles a business decision that measures profits by counting gross receipts and ignoring expenses. The evidence in this case indicates that sobriety checkpoints result in the arrest of a fraction of one percent of the drivers who are stopped, but there is absolutely no evidence that this figure represents an increase over the number of arrests that would have been made by using the same law enforcement resources in conventional patrols. Thus, although the *gross* number of arrests is more than zero, there is a complete failure of proof on the question whether the wholesale seizures have produced any *net* advance in the public interest in arresting intoxicated drivers.

Indeed, the position adopted today by the Court is not one endorsed by any of the law enforcement authorities to whom the Court purports to defer. The Michigan police do not rely, as the Court does, on the *arrest rate* at sobriety checkpoints to justify the stops made there. Colonel Hough, the commander of the Michigan State Police and a leading proponent of the checkpoints, admitted at trial that the arrest rate at the checkpoints was "very low." Instead, Colonel Hough and the State have maintained that the mere *threat* of such arrests is sufficient to deter drunk driving and so to reduce the accident rate. The Maryland police officer who testified at trial took the same position with respect to his State's program. There is, obviously, nothing wrong with a law enforcement technique that reduces crime by pure deterrence without punishing anybody; on the contrary, such an approach is highly commendable. One cannot, however, prove its efficacy by counting the arrests that were made. One must instead measure the number of crimes that were avoided. Perhaps because the record is wanting, the Court simply ignores this point.

The Court's sparse analysis of this issue differs markedly from Justice Powell's opinion for the Court in *Martinez-Fuerte*. He did not merely count the 17,000 arrests made at the San Clemente checkpoint in 1973; he also carefully explained why those arrests represented a net benefit to the law enforcement interest at stake. Common sense, moreover, suggests that immigration checkpoints are more necessary than sobriety checkpoints: there is no reason why smuggling illegal aliens should impair a motorist's driving ability, but if intoxication did not noticeably affect driving ability it would not be unlawful. Drunk driving, unlike smuggling, may thus be detected absent any checkpoints. A program that produces thousands of otherwise impossible arrests is not a relevant precedent for a program that produces only a handful of arrests which would be more easily obtained without resort to suspicionless seizures of hundreds of innocent citizens.

III. . . .

[M]y objections to random seizures or temporary checkpoints do not apply to a host of other investigatory procedures that do not depend upon surprise and are unquestionably permissible. These procedures have been used to address other threats to human life no less pressing than the threat posed by drunken drivers. It is, for example, common practice to require every prospective airline passenger, or every visitor to a public building, to pass through a metal detector that will reveal the presence of a firearm or an explosive. Permanent, non-discretionary checkpoints could be used to control serious dangers at other publicly operated facilities. Because concealed weapons obviously represent one such substantial threat to public safety, I would suppose that all subway passengers could be required to pass through metal detectors, so long as the detectors were permanent and every passenger was subjected to the same search. Likewise, I would suppose that a State could condition access to its toll roads upon not only paying the toll but also taking a uniformly administered breathalyzer test. That requirement might well keep all drunken drivers off the highways that serve the fastest and most dangerous traffic. This procedure would not be subject to the constitutional objections that control this case: the checkpoints would be permanently fixed, the stopping procedure would apply to all users of the toll road in precisely the same way, and police officers would not be free to make arbitrary choices about which neighborhoods should be targeted or about which individuals should be more thoroughly searched. Random, suspicionless seizures designed to search for evidence of firearms, drugs, or intoxication belong, however, in a fundamentally different category. These seizures play upon the detained individual's reasonable expectations of privacy, injecting a suspicionless search into a context where none would normally occur. The imposition that seems diaphanous today may be intolerable tomorrow. . . .

This is a case that is driven by nothing more than symbolic state action—an insufficient justification for an otherwise unreasonable program of random seizures. Unfortunately, the Court is transfixed by the wrong symbol—the illusory prospect of punishing countless intoxicated motorists—when it should keep its eyes on the road plainly marked by the Constitution.

I respectfully dissent.

JAMES v. ILLINOIS
110 S.Ct. 648 (1990)

On the night of August 30, 1982, eight young boys returning home from a party were confronted by three boys who demanded money. When the eight boys refused, one of the three assailants took out a gun and fired at the eight, killing one and seriously injuring another. The police obtained a description of the muggers and the next evening two detectives took 15-year-old Darryl James into custody as a suspect. James was found at his mother's beauty parlor sitting under a hair dryer and when he emerged his hair was black and curly. After James was in the police car, he was asked about his hair and admitted that the previous day his hair had been reddish-brown, long, and combed straight back, and that he had just dyed and curled it so as to change his appearance. After James was indicted for murder and attempted murder, the trial court ruled favorably on his motion to suppress the statements about his hair as having been illegally obtained. At the trial, five of the victims of the confrontation testified that the murderer had slicked-back, shoulder-length, reddish hair, and that they had seen James weeks earlier with hair that color and style. They identified James as the murderer even though James was wearing his hair black and natural. James did not testify in his defense but a family friend, Jewell Henderson, testified that on the day of the shooting James had black hair. The trial judge then permitted the prosecutor to introduce James' illegally obtained statements to impeach Henderson's testimony. James was convicted of both murder and attempted murder and sentenced to 30 years' imprisonment. On appeal, the Illinois Appellate Court reversed the convictions and ordered a new trial without the illegally

obtained statements. The Illinois Supreme Court, however, ordered the reinstatement of the convictions, reasoning that in order to deter the defendant from engaging in perjury "by proxy," the impeachment exception to the exclusionary rule ought to be expanded to allow the prosecution to introduce illegally obtained evidence to impeach the testimony of defense witnesses other than the defendant himself. The U.S. Supreme Court granted certiorari.

Majority votes: 5
Dissenting votes: 4

JUSTICE BRENNAN delivered the opinion of the Court:

The impeachment exception to the exclusionary rule permits the prosecution in a criminal proceeding to introduce illegally obtained evidence to impeach the defendant's own testimony. The Illinois Supreme Court extended this exception to permit the prosecution to impeach the testimony of *all* defense witnesses with illegally obtained evidence. Finding this extension inconsistent with the balance of values underlying our previous applications of the exclusionary rule, we reverse. . . .

. . . Expanding the class of impeachable witnesses from the defendant alone to all defense witnesses would create different incentives affecting the behavior of both defendants and law enforcement officers. As a result, this expansion would not promote the truthseeking function to the same extent as did creation of the original exception, and yet it would significantly undermine the deterrent effect of the general exclusionary rule. Hence, we believe that this proposed expansion would frustrate rather than further the purposes underlying the exclusionary rule.

The previously recognized exception penalizes defendants for committing perjury by allowing the prosecution to expose their perjury through impeachment using illegally obtained evidence. Thus defendants are discouraged in the first instance from "affirmatively resort[ing] to perjurious testimony." But the exception leaves defendants free to testify truthfully on their own behalf; they can offer probative and exculpatory evidence to the jury without opening the door to impeachment by carefully avoiding any statements that directly contradict the suppressed evidence. The exception thus generally discourages perjured testimony without discouraging truthful testimony.

In contrast, expanding the impeachment exception to encompass the testimony of all defense witnesses would not have the same beneficial effects. First, the mere threat of a subsequent criminal prosecution for perjury is far more likely to deter a witness from intentionally lying on a defendant's behalf than to deter a defendant, already facing conviction for the underlying offense, from lying on his own behalf. Hence the Illinois Supreme Court's underlying premise that a defendant frustrated by our previous impeachment exception can easily find a witness to engage in "perjury by proxy" is suspect.

More significantly, expanding the impeachment exception to encompass the testimony of all defense witnesses likely would chill some defendants from presenting their best defense—and sometimes any defense at all—through the testimony of others. Whenever police obtained evidence illegally, defendants would have to assess prior to trial the likelihood that the evidence would be admitted to impeach the otherwise favorable testimony of any witness they call. Defendants might reasonably fear that one or more of their witnesses, in a position to offer truthful and favorable testimony, would also make some statement in sufficient tension with the tainted evidence to allow the prosecutor to introduce that evidence for impeachment. First, defendants sometimes need to call "reluctant" or "hostile" witnesses to provide reliable and probative exculpatory testimony, and such witnesses likely will not share the defendants' concern for avoiding statements that invite impeachment through contradictory evidence. Moreover, defendants often cannot trust even "friendly" witnesses to testify without subjecting themselves to impeachment, simply due to insufficient care or attentiveness. This concern is magnified in those occasional situations when defendants must call witnesses to testify despite having had only a limited opportunity to consult with or prepare them in advance. For these reasons, we have recognized in a variety of contexts that a party "cannot be absolutely certain that his witnesses will testify as expected." As a result, an expanded impeachment exception likely would chill some defendants from calling witnesses who would otherwise offer probative evidence.

This realization alters the balance of values underlying the current impeachment exception governing defendants' testimony. Our prior cases make clear that defendants ought not be able to "pervert" the exclusion of illegally obtained evidence into a shield for perjury, but it seems no more appropriate for the State to brandish such evidence as a sword with which to dissuade defendants from presenting a meaningful defense through other witnesses. Given the potential chill created by expanding the impeachment exception, the conceded gains to the truthseeking process from discouraging or disclosing perjured testimony would be offset to some extent by the concomitant loss of probative witness testimony. Thus, the truthseeking rationale supporting the impeachment of defendants in *Walder* v. *U.S.* and its progeny does not apply to other witnesses with equal force.

Moreover, the proposed expansion of the current impeachment exception would significantly weaken the exclusionary rule's deterrent effect on police misconduct. This Court has characterized as a mere "speculative possibility" the likelihood that permitting prosecutors to impeach defendants with illegally obtained evidence would encourage police misconduct. Law enforcement officers will think it unlikely that the defendant will first decide to testify at trial and will also open the door inadvertently to admission of any illegally obtained evidence. Hence, the officers' incentive to acquire evidence through illegal means is quite weak.

In contrast, expanding the impeachment exception to *all* defense witnesses would significantly enhance the expected value to the prosecution of illegally obtained evidence. First, this expansion would vastly increase the number of occasions on which such evidence could be used. Defense witnesses easily outnumber testifying defendants, both because many defendants do not testify themselves and because many if not most defendants call multiple witnesses on their behalf. Moreover, due to the chilling effect identified above illegally obtained evidence holds even greater value to the prosecution for each individual witness than for each defendant. The prosecutor's access to impeachment evidence would not just deter perjury; it would also deter defendants from calling witnesses in the first place, thereby keeping from the jury much probative exculpatory evidence. For both of these reasons, police officers and their superiors would recognize that obtaining evidence through illegal means stacks the deck heavily in the prosecution's favor. It is thus far more than a "speculative possibility" that police misconduct will be encouraged by permitting such use of illegally obtained evidence.

The United States argues that this result is constitutionally acceptable because excluding illegally obtained evidence solely from the prosecution's case in chief would still provide a quantum of deterrence sufficient to protect the privacy interests underlying the exclusionary rule. We disagree. Of course, a police officer might in certain situations believe that obtaining particular evidence through illegal means, resulting in its suppression from the case in chief, would prevent the prosecution from establishing a prima facie case to take to a jury. In such situations, the officer likely would be deterred from obtaining the evidence illegally for fear of jeopardizing the entire case. But much if not most of the time, police officers confront opportunities to obtain evidence illegally after they have already legally obtained (or know that they have other means of legally obtaining) sufficient evidence to sustain a prima facie case. In these situations, a rule requiring exclusion of illegally obtained evidence from only the government's case in chief would leave officers with little to lose and much to gain by overstepping constitutional limits on evidence gathering. Narrowing the exclusionary rule in this manner, therefore, would significantly undermine the rule's ability "to compel respect for the constitutional guaranty in the only effectively available way—by removing the incentive to disregard it." So long as we are committed to protecting the people from the disregard of their constitutional rights during the course of criminal investigations, inadmissibility of illegally obtained evidence must remain the rule, not the exception.

The cost to the truthseeking process of evidentiary exclusion invariably is perceived more tangibly in discrete prosecutions than is the protection of privacy values through deterrence of future police misconduct. When defining the precise scope of the exclusionary rule, however, we must focus on systemic effects of proposed exceptions to ensure that individual liberty from arbitrary or oppressive police conduct does not succumb to the inexorable pressure to introduce all incriminating evidence, no matter how obtained, in each and every criminal case. Our previous recognition of an impeachment exception limited to the testimony of defendants reflects a careful weighing of the competing values. Because expanding the exception to encompass the testimony of all defense witnesses would not further the truthseeking value with equal force but would appreciably undermine the deterrent effect of the exclusionary rule, we adhere to the line drawn in our previous cases.

Accordingly, we hold that the Illinois Supreme Court erred in affirming James' convictions despite the prosecutor's use of illegally obtained statements to impeach a defense witness' testimony. The court's judgment is reversed, and the case is remanded for further proceedings not inconsistent with this opinion.

It is so ordered.

JUSTICE STEVENS, concurring: . . .

While I join the opinion of the Court, certain comments in the dissent prompt this postscript. . . .

In "contested criminal trials," the urge to win can unfortunately lead both sides to overstate their case. As the Court properly observes, the ability of the dishonest defendant to procure false testimony is tempered by the availability of the illegally obtained evidence for use in a subsequent perjury prosecution of the defense witness. A witness who is not on trial faces a far different calculus than one whose testimony can mean the difference between acquittal and a prison sentence. He or she will think long and hard before accepting a defendant's invitation to knowingly offer false testimony that is directly contradicted by the State's evidence. The dissent ignores this "hard reality," in presuming that a defense witness will offer false testimony when that testimony is immunized from rebuttal at trial.

While the dissent assumes false testimony or, at least, faulty recollection with respect to defense witnesses, it is unwilling to entertain the same assumption with respect to the prosecution's witnesses. The evidentiary issue in this case involves the testimony of a police officer about a statement that he allegedly heard the defendant make at the time of his arrest. An officer whose testimony provides the foundation for admission of an oral statement or physical evidence may be influenced by his interest in effective law enforcement or may simply have faulty recollection. It is only by giving 100 percent credence to every word of the officer's testimony that the dissent can so categorically state that "the defendant himself revealed the witness' testimony to be false," that "James . . . said his hair was previously red," or that information presented to the jury was "known to be untrue." That assumption is no more warranted in the case of prosecution witnesses than the opposite assumption is warranted in the case of defense witnesses.

In this case, in which the guilty verdict is supported by the testimony of five eyewitnesses, it is highly probable that these characterizations are accurate. . . . Were the officer's testimony not so corroborated, it would surely be improper to presume—as the dissenters do—that the conflict between the testimony of the officer and Henderson should necessarily be resolved in the officer's favor or that exclusion of the evidence would result in a decision by jurors who are "positively misled."

JUSTICE KENNEDY, with whom THE CHIEF JUSTICE, JUSTICE O'CONNOR, and JUSTICE SCALIA join, dissenting:

To deprive the prosecution of probative evidence acquired in violation of the law may be a tolerable and necessary cost of the exclusionary rule. Implementation of the rule requires us to draw certain lines to effect its purpose of deterring unlawful conduct. But the line drawn by today's opinion grants the defense side in a criminal case broad immunity to introduce whatever false testimony it can produce from the mouth of a friendly witness. Unless petitioner's conviction is reversed, we are told, police would flout the Fourth Amendment, and as a result, the accused would be unable to offer any defense. This exaggerated view leads to a drastic remedy: The jury cannot learn that defense testimony is inconsistent with probative evidence of undoubted value. A more cautious course is available, one that retains Fourth Amendment protections and yet safeguards the truth-seeking function of the criminal trial. . . .

I agree with the majority that the resolution of this case depends on a balance of values that informs our exclusionary rule jurisprudence. We weigh the " 'likelihood of . . . deterrence against the costs of withholding reliable information from the truth-seeking process.' " The majority adopts a sweeping rule that the testimony of witnesses other than the defendant may never be rebutted with excludable evidence. I cannot draw the line where the majority does.

The interest in protecting the truth-seeking function of the criminal trial is every bit as strong in this case as in our earlier cases that allowed rebuttal with evidence that was inadmissible as part of the prosecution's case in chief. Here a witness who knew the accused well took the stand to testify about the accused's personal appearance. The testimony could be expected to create real doubt in the mind of jurors concerning the eyewitness identifications by persons who did not know the accused. To deprive the jurors of knowledge that statements of the defendant himself revealed the witness' testimony to be false would result in a decision by triers of fact who were not just kept in the dark as to excluded evidence, but positively misled. The potential for harm to the truth-seeking process resulting from the majority's new rule in fact will be greater than if the defendant himself had testified. It is natural for jurors to be skeptical of self-serving testimony by the defendant. Testimony by a witness said to be independent has the greater potential to deceive. And if a defense witness can present false testimony with impunity, the jurors may find the rest of the prosecution's case suspect, for ineffective and artificial cross-examination will be viewed as a real weakness in the State's case. Jurors will assume that if the prosecution had any proof the statement was false, it would make the proof known. The majority does more than deprive the prosecution of evidence. The State must also suffer the introduction of false testimony and appear to bolster the falsehood by its own silence. . . .

ILLINOIS v. PERKINS
110 S.Ct. 2394 (1990)

John Parisi, an undercover police agent, was placed in a jail cell block with Lloyd Perkins after Donald Charlton told police that Perkins had told him (Charlton) that he (Perkins) had committed a murder. Perkins was incarcerated on charges unrelated to the murder that Parisi was investigating. Parisi, posing as a jail inmate along with Charlton, suggested to Perkins that they break out of jail. The three then met late at night to work out an escape plan. Perkins volunteered that his girlfriend could smuggle in a pistol to which Charlton responded: "Hey, I'm not a murderer, I'm a burglar. That's you guys' profession." Parisi responded to Charlton that he, Parisi, would take responsibility for any murder that occurred. Parisi then turned to Perkins and asked if he had ever "done" anybody. Perkins said that he had and proceeded to describe at length the murder that Parisi was concerned with. Of course, Parisi did not give Perkins any Miranda *warnings before the conversation. Perkins was subsequently charged with murder. The trial court threw out the statements Perkins made to Parisi on the ground that Parisi had not given the required* Miranda *warnings. The Appellate Court of Illinois affirmed the ruling that* Miranda *prohibits all undercover contacts with incarcerated suspects that are reasonably likely to elicit an incriminating response. Illinois asked the United States Supreme Court to review the state court decision.*

Majority votes: 8
Dissenting votes: 1

JUSTICE KENNEDY delivered the opinion of the Court: . . . .

In *Miranda* v. *Arizona* the Court held that the Fifth Amendment privilege against self-incrimination prohibits admitting statements given by a suspect during "custodial interrogation" without a prior warning. Custodial interrogation means "questioning initiated by law enforcement officers after a person has been taken into custody. . . ." The warning mandated by *Miranda* was meant to preserve the privilege during "incommunicado interrogation of individuals in a police-dominated atmosphere." That atmosphere is said to generate "inherently compelling pressures which work to undermine the individual's will to resist and to compel him to speak where he would not otherwise do so freely." "Fidelity to the doctrine announced in *Miranda* requires that it be enforced strictly, but only in those types of situations in which the concerns that powered the decision are implicated." *Berkemer* v. *McCarty,* 468 U. S. 420, 437 (1984).

Conversations between suspects and undercover agents do not implicate the concerns underlying *Miranda*. The essential ingredients of a "police-dominated atmosphere" and compulsion are not present when an incarcerated person speaks freely to someone that he believes to be a fellow inmate. Coercion is determined from the perspective of the suspect. When a suspect considers himself in the company of cellmates and not officers, the coercive atmosphere is lacking. . . . There is no empirical basis for the assumption that a suspect speaking to those whom he assumes are not officers will feel compelled to speak by the fear of reprisal for remaining silent or in the hope of more lenient treatment should he confess.

It is the premise of *Miranda* that the danger of coercion results from the interaction of custody and official interrogation. We reject the argument that *Miranda* warnings are required whenever a suspect is in custody in a technical sense and converses with someone who happens to be a government agent. Questioning by captors, who appear to control the suspect's fate, may create mutually reinforcing pressures that the Court has assumed will weaken the suspect's will, but where a suspect does not know that he is conversing with a government agent, these pressures do not exist. The State Court here mistakenly assumed that because the suspect was in custody, no undercover questioning could take place. When the suspect has no reason to think that the listeners have official power over him, it should not be assumed that his words are motivated by the reaction he expects from his listeners. . . .

Miranda was not meant to protect suspects from boasting about their criminal activities in front of persons whom they believe to be their cellmates. This case is illustrative. Respondent had no reason to feel that undercover agent Parisi had any legal authority to force him to answer questions or that Parisi could affect respondent's future treatment. Respondent viewed the cellmate-agent as an equal and showed no hint of being intimidated by the atmosphere of the jail. In recounting the details of the Stephenson murder, respondent was motivated solely by the desire to impress his fellow inmates. He spoke at his own peril. . . .

Our decision in *Mathis* v. *United States*, 391 U. S. 1 (1968), is distinguishable. In *Mathis*, an inmate in a state prison was interviewed by an Internal Revenue Service agent about possible tax violations. No *Miranda* warning was given before questioning. The Court held that the suspect's incriminating statements were not admissible at his subsequent trial on tax fraud charges. The suspect in *Mathis* was aware that the agent was a government official, investigating the possibility of non-

compliance with the tax laws. The case before us now is different. Where the suspect does not know that he is speaking to a government agent there is no reason to assume the possibility that the suspect might feel coerced. (The bare fact of custody may not in every instance require a warning even when the suspect is aware that he is speaking to an official, but we do not have occasion to explore that issue here.)

This Court's Sixth Amendment decisions in *Massiah* v. *United States*, 377 U. S. 201 (1964), *United States* v. *Henry*, 447 U. S. 264 (1980), and *Maine* v. *Moulton*, 474 U. S. 159 (1985), also do not avail respondent. We held in those cases that the government may not use an undercover agent to circumvent the Sixth Amendment right to counsel once a suspect has been charged with the crime. After charges have been filed, the Sixth Amendment prevents the government from interfering with the accused's right to counsel. In the instant case no charges had been filed on the subject of the interrogation, and our Sixth Amendment precedents are not applicable.

Respondent can seek no help from his argument that a bright-line rule for the application of *Miranda* is desirable. Law enforcement officers will have little difficulty putting into practice our holding that undercover agents need not give *Miranda* warnings to incarcerated suspects. The use of undercover agents is a recognized law enforcement technique, often employed in the prison context to detect violence against correctional officials or inmates, as well as for the purposes served here. The interests protected by *Miranda* are not implicated in these cases, and the warnings are not required to safeguard the constitutional rights of inmates who make voluntary statements to undercover agents.

We hold that an undercover law enforcement officer posing as a fellow inmate need not give *Miranda* warnings to an incarcerated suspect before asking questions that may elicit an incriminating response. The statements at issue in this case were voluntary, and there is no federal obstacle to their admissibility at trial. We now reverse and remand for proceedings not inconsistent with our opinion.

It is so ordered.

JUSTICE BRENNAN, concurring in the judgment:. . . .

Although I do not subscribe to the majority's characterization of *Miranda* in its entirety, I do agree that when a suspect does not know that his questioner is a police agent, such questioning does not amount to "interrogation" in an "inherently coercive" environment so as to require application of *Miranda*. Since the only issue raised at this stage of the litigation is the applicability of *Miranda*, I concur in the judgment of the Court. . . .

JUSTICE MARSHALL, dissenting:. . . .

Custody works to the State's advantage in obtaining incriminating information. The psychological pressures inherent in confinement increase the suspect's anxiety, making him likely to seek relief by talking with others. . . . The inmate is thus more susceptible to efforts by undercover agents to elicit information from him. Similarly, where the suspect is incarcerated, the constant threat of physical danger peculiar to the prison environment may make him demonstrate his toughness to other inmates by recounting or inventing past violent acts. . . . In this case, the police deceptively took advantage of Perkins' psychological vulnerability by including him in a sham escape plot, a situation in which he would feel compelled to demonstrate his willingness to shoot a prison guard by revealing his past involvement in a murder. . . .

Thus, the pressures unique to custody allow the police to use deceptive interrogation tactics to compel a suspect to make an incriminating statement. The compulsion is not eliminated by the suspect's ignorance of his interrogator's true identity. The Court therefore need not inquire past the bare facts of custody and interrogation to determine whether *Miranda* warnings are required.

The Court's adoption of an exception to the *Miranda* doctrine is incompatible with the principle, consistently applied by this Court, that the doctrine should remain simple and clear. . . .

The Court's holding today complicates a previously clear and straightforward doctrine. The Court opines that "[l]aw enforcement officers will have little difficulty putting into practice our holding that undercover agents need not give *Miranda* warnings to incarcerated suspects." Perhaps this prediction is true with respect to fact patterns virtually identical to the one before the Court today. But the outer boundaries of the exception created by the Court are by no means clear. Would *Miranda* be violated, for instance, if an undercover police officer beat a confession out of a suspect, but the suspect thought the officer was another prisoner who wanted the information for his own purposes?

Even if *Miranda*, as interpreted by the Court, would not permit such obviously compelled confessions, the ramifications of today's opinion are still disturbing. The exception carved out of the *Miranda* doctrine today may well result in a proliferation of departmental policies to encourage police officers to conduct interrogations of confined suspects through undercover agents, thereby circumventing the need to administer *Miranda* warnings.

Indeed, if *Miranda* now requires a police officer to issue warnings only in those situations in which the suspect might feel compelled "to speak by the fear of reprisal for remaining silent or in the hope of more lenient treatment should he confess," presumably it allows custodial interrogation by an undercover officer posing as a member of the clergy or a suspect's defense attorney. Although such abhorrent tricks would play on a suspect's need to confide in a trusted adviser, neither would cause the suspect to "think that the listeners have official power over him." The Court's adoption of the "undercover agent" exception to the *Miranda* rule thus is necessarily also the adoption of a substantial loophole in our jurisprudence protecting suspects' Fifth Amendment rights.

I dissent.

MARYLAND v. CRAIG
110 S.Ct. 3157 (1990)

Sandra Ann Craig, the owner and operator of a kindergarten and prekindergarten center, was charged with sexual abuse of a six-year-old child. Before her trial began, the prosecutor asked the judge to apply a Maryland statutory procedure permitting a judge to receive, by one-way closed circuit television, the testimony of the alleged child abuse victim upon determining that the child's courtroom testimony would result in the child suffering serious emotional distress, such that the child could not reasonably communicate. The prosecutor presented expert testimony that the child, along with other children who were allegedly sexually abused by Mrs. Craig, would indeed suffer serious emotional distress and would not be able to reasonably communicate if required to testify in the courtroom. Mrs. Craig objected to the procedure, claiming it would violate her Sixth Amendment right to confront adverse witnesses. The trial court rejected this claim, and under the statutory procedure the child and three other children were permitted to testify using one-way closed circuit television. The children, the prosecutor, and the defense counsel were present in the special television-equipped room where the children were examined and cross-examined. The judge, jury, and Mrs. Craig remained in the courtroom where the children's testimony was viewed. Although the children could not see Mrs. Craig, she remained in electronic communication with her lawyer and her lawyer could make objections on which the judge could rule as if the witnesses were in the courtroom. The jury convicted Mrs. Craig but the highest state court reversed. Maryland took the case to the United States Supreme Court.

Majority votes: 5
Dissenting votes: 4

JUSTICE O'CONNOR delivered the opinion of the Court:

This case requires us to decide whether the Confrontation Clause of the Sixth Amendment categorically prohibits a child witness in a child abuse case from testifying against a defendant at trial, outside the defendant's physical presence, by one-way closed circuit television. . . .

The Confrontation Clause of the Sixth Amendment, made applicable to the States through the Fourteenth Amendment, provides: "In all criminal prosecutions, the accused shall enjoy the right . . . to be confronted with the witnesses against him."

We observed in *Coy* v. *Iowa* that "the Confrontation Clause guarantees the defendant a face-to-face meeting with witnesses appearing before the trier of fact." 487 U.S., at 1016. . . . This interpretation derives not only from the literal text of the Clause, but also from our understanding of its historical roots. . . .

We have never held, however, that the Confrontation Clause guarantees criminal defendants the *absolute* right to a face-to-face meeting with witnesses against them at trial. Indeed, in *Coy* v. *Iowa,* we expressly "le[ft] for another day . . . the question whether any exceptions exist" to the "irreducible literal meaning of the Clause: 'a right to *meet face to face* all those who appear and give evidence *at trial*.'" The procedure challenged in *Coy* involved the placement of a screen that prevented two child witnesses in a child abuse case from seeing the defendant as they testified against him at trial. In holding that the use of this procedure violated the defendant's right to confront witnesses against him, we suggested that any exception to the right "would surely be allowed only when necessary to further an important public policy"—*i.e.*, only upon a showing of something more than the generalized, "legislatively imposed presumption of trauma" underlying the statute at issue in that case. We concluded that "[s]ince there ha[d] been no individualized findings that these particular witnesses needed special protection, the judgment [in the case before us] could not be sustained by any conceivable exception." Because the trial court in this case made individualized findings that each of the child witnesses needed special protection, this case requires us to decide the question reserved in *Coy*.

The central concern of the Confrontation Clause is to ensure the reliability of the evidence against a criminal defendant by subjecting it to rigorous testing in the context of an adversary proceeding before the trier of fact. The word "confront," after all, also means a clashing of forces or ideas, thus carrying with it the notion of adversariness. . . . [T]he right guaranteed by the Confrontation Clause includes not only a "personal examination," but also "(1) insures that the witness will give his statements under oath—thus impressing him with the seriousness of the matter and guarding against the lie by the possibility of a penalty for perjury; (2) forces the witness to submit to cross-examination, the 'greatest legal engine ever invented for the discovery of truth'; [and] (3) permits the jury that is to decide the defendant's fate to observe the demeanor of the witness in making his statement, thus aiding the jury in assessing his credibility."

The combined effect of these elements of confrontation—physical presence, oath, cross-examination, and observation of demeanor by the trier of fact—serves the purposes of the Confrontation Clause by ensuring that evidence admitted against an accused is reliable and subject to the rigorous adversarial testing that is the norm of Anglo-American criminal proceedings. . . .

We have recognized, for example, that face-to-face confrontation enhances the accuracy of fact-finding by reducing the risk that a witness will wrongfully implicate an innocent person. . . . We have also noted the strong symbolic purpose served by requiring adverse witnesses at trial to testify in the accused's presence. . . .

Although face-to-face confrontation forms "the core of the values furthered by the Confrontation Clause," we have nevertheless recognized that it is not the *sine qua non* of the confrontation right. . . . ("[T]he Confrontation Clause is generally satisfied when the defense is given a full and fair opportunity to probe and expose [testimonial] infirmities [such as forgetfulness, confusion, or evasion] through cross-examination, thereby calling to the attention of the factfinder the reasons for giving scant weight to the witness' testimony"). . . .

For this reason, we have never insisted on an actual face-to-face encounter at trial in *every* instance in which testimony is admitted against a defendant. Instead, we have repeatedly held that the Clause permits, where necessary, the admission of certain hearsay statements against a defendant despite the defendant's inability to confront the declarant at trial. . . . In *Mattox* v. *United States,* 156 U.S. 237 (1895), for example, we held that the testimony of a government witness at a former trial against the defendant, where the witness was fully cross-examined but had died after the first trial, was admissible in evidence against the defendant at his second trial. We explained:

"To say that a criminal, after having once been

convicted by the testimony of a certain witness, should go scot free simply because death has closed the mouth of that witness, would be carrying his constitutional protection to an unwarrantable extent. The law in its wisdom declares that the rights of the public shall not be wholly sacrificed in order that an incidental benefit may be preserved to the accused." *Id.*, at 243.

We have accordingly stated that a literal reading of the Confrontation Clause would "abrogate virtually every hearsay exception, a result long rejected as unintended and too extreme." Thus, in certain narrow circumstances, "competing interests, if 'closely examined,' may warrant dispensing with confrontation at trial." . . .

In sum, our precedents establish that "the Confrontation Clause reflects a *preference* for face-to-face confrontation at trial," a preference that "must occasionally give way to considerations of public policy and the necessities of the case," *Mattox, supra,* at 243. . . . We have accordingly interpreted the Confrontation Clause in a manner sensitive to its purposes and sensitive to the necessities of trial and the adversary process. . . . Thus, though we reaffirm the importance of face-to-face confrontation with witnesses appearing at trial, we cannot say that such confrontation is an indispensable element of the Sixth Amendment's guarantee of the right to confront one's accusers. . . .

That the face-to-face confrontation requirement is not absolute does not, of course, mean that it may easily be dispensed with. As we suggested in *Coy,* our precedents confirm that a defendant's right to confront accusatory witnesses may be satisfied absent a physical, face-to-face confrontation at trial only where denial of such confrontation is necessary to further an important public policy and only where the reliability of the testimony is otherwise assured. . . .

Maryland's statutory procedure, when invoked, prevents a child witness from seeing the defendant as he or she testifies against the defendant at trial. We find it significant, however, that Maryland's procedure preserves all of the other elements of the confrontation right: the child witness must be competent to testify and must testify under oath; the defendant retains full opportunity for contemporaneous cross-examination; and the judge, jury, and defendant are able to view (albeit by video monitor) the demeanor (and body) of the witness as he or she testifies. Although we are mindful of the many subtle effects face-to-face confrontation may have on an adversary criminal proceeding, the presence of these other elements of confrontation—oath,

cross-examination, and observation of the witness' demeanor—adequately ensures that the testimony is both reliable and subject to rigorous adversarial testing in a manner functionally equivalent to that accorded live, in-person testimony. These safeguards of reliability and adversariness render the use of such a procedure a far cry from the undisputed prohibition of the Confrontation Clause: trial by *ex parte* affidavit or inquisition. . . . Rather, we think these elements of effective confrontation not only permit a defendant to "confound and undo the false accuser, or reveal the child coached by a malevolent adult," *Coy,* 487 U.S., at 1020, but may well aid a defendant in eliciting favorable testimony from the child witness. Indeed, to the extent the child witness' testimony may be said to be technically given out-of-court (though we do not so hold), these assurances of reliability and adversariness are far greater than those required for admission of hearsay testimony under the Confrontation Clause. We are therefore confident that use of the one-way closed-circuit television procedure, where necessary to further an important state interest, does not impinge upon the truth-seeking or symbolic purposes of the Confrontation Clause.

The critical inquiry in this case, therefore, is whether use of the procedure is necessary to further an important state interest. The State contends that it has a substantial interest in protecting children who are allegedly victims of child abuse from the trauma of testifying against the alleged perpetrator and that its statutory procedure for receiving testimony from such witnesses is necessary to further that interest. . . .

We . . . conclude today that a State's interest in the physical and psychological well-being of child abuse victims may be sufficiently important to outweigh, at least in some cases, a defendant's right to face his or her accusers in court. That a significant majority of States has enacted statutes to protect child witnesses from the trauma of giving testimony in child abuse cases attests to the widespread belief in the importance of such a public policy. . . . Thirty-seven States, for example, permit the use of videotaped testimony of sexually abused children; 24 States have authorized the use of one-way closed circuit television testimony in child abuse cases; and 8 States authorize the use of a two-way system in which the child-witness is permitted to see the courtroom and the defendant on a video monitor and in which the jury and judge is permitted to view the child during the testimony.

The statute at issue in this case, for example, was specifically intended "to safeguard the physical and psychological well-being of child victims by avoiding, or at least minimizing, the emotional trauma produced by testifying.''. . . Accordingly, we hold that, if the State makes an adequate showing of necessity, the state interest in protecting child witnesses from the trauma of testifying in a child abuse case is sufficiently important to justify the use of a special procedure that permits a child witness in such cases to testify at trial against a defendant in the absence of face-to-face confrontation with the defendant.

The requisite finding of necessity must of course be a case-specific one: the trial court must hear evidence and determine whether use of the one-way closed circuit television procedure is necessary to protect the welfare of the particular child witness who seeks to testify. . . . The trial court must also find that the child witness would be traumatized, not by the courtroom generally, but by the presence of the defendant. . . . Denial of face-to-face confrontation is not needed to further the state interest in protecting the child witness from trauma unless it is the presence of the defendant that causes the trauma. In other words, if the state interest were merely the interest in protecting child witnesses from courtroom trauma generally, denial of face-to-face confrontation would be unnecessary because the child could be permitted to testify in less intimidating surroundings, albeit with the defendant present. Finally, the trial court must find that the emotional distress suffered by the child witness in the presence of the defendant is more than *de minimis, i.e.,* more than ''mere nervousness or excitement or some reluctance to testify.'' We need not decide the minimum showing of emotional trauma required for use of the special procedure, however, because the Maryland statute, which requires a determination that the child witness will suffer ''serious emotional distress such that the child cannot reasonably communicate,'' § 9–102(a)(1)(ii), clearly suffices to meet constitutional standards. . . .

In sum, we conclude that where necessary to protect a child witness from trauma that would be caused by testifying in the physical presence of the defendant, at least where such trauma would impair the child's ability to communicate, the Confrontation Clause does not prohibit use of a procedure that, despite the absence of face-to-face confrontation, ensures the reliability of the evidence by subjecting it to rigorous adversarial testing and thereby preserves the essence of effective confrontation. Because there is no dispute that the child witnesses in this case testified under oath, were subject to full cross-examination, and were able to be observed by the judge, jury, and defendant as they testified, we conclude that, to the extent that a proper finding

of necessity has been made, the admission of such testimony would be consonant with the Confrontation Clause. . . .

. . . We vacate the judgment of the Court of Appeals of Maryland and remand the case for further proceedings not inconsistent with this opinion.

It is so ordered.

JUSTICE SCALIA, with whom JUSTICE BRENNAN, JUSTICE MARSHALL, and JUSTICE STEVENS join, dissenting:

Seldom has this Court failed so conspicuously to sustain a categorical guarantee of the Constitution against the tide of prevailing current opinion. The Sixth Amendment provides, with unmistakable clarity, that ''[i]n all criminal prosecutions, the accused shall enjoy the right . . . to be confronted with the witnesses against him.'' The purpose of enshrining this protection in the Constitution was to assure that none of the many policy interests from time to time pursued by statutory law could overcome a defendant's right to face his or her accusers in court. . . .

Because the text of the Sixth Amendment is clear, and because the Constitution is meant to protect against, rather than conform to, current ''widespread belief,'' I respectfully dissent.

According to the Court, ''we cannot say that [face-to-face] confrontation [with witnesses appearing at trial] is an indispensable element of the Sixth Amendment's guarantee of the right to confront one's accusers.'' That is rather like saying ''we cannot say that being tried before a jury is an indispensable element of the Sixth Amendment's guarantee of the right to jury trial.'' The Court makes the impossible plausible by recharacterizing the Confrontation Clause, so that confrontation (redesignated ''face-to-face confrontation'') becomes only one of many ''elements of confrontation.'' The reasoning is as follows: The Confrontation Clause guarantees not only what it explicitly provides for—''face-to-face'' confrontation—but also implied and collateral rights such as cross-examination, oath, and observation of demeanor (TRUE); the purpose of this entire cluster of rights is to ensure the reliability of evidence (TRUE); the Maryland procedure preserves the implied and collateral rights (TRUE), which adequately ensure the reliability of evidence (perhaps TRUE); therefore the Confrontation Clause is not violated by denying what it explicitly provides for—''face-to-face'' confrontation (unquestionably FALSE). This reasoning abstracts from the right to its purposes, and then eliminates the right. It is wrong because the Confrontation Clause does not guarantee reliable evidence; it guarantees specific trial procedures that were thought to *assure* reliable evidence, undeniably among which was "face-to-face" confrontation. Whatever else it may mean in addition, the defendant's constitutional right "to be confronted with the witnesses against him" means, always and everywhere, at least what it explicitly says: the " 'right to meet face to face all those who appear and give evidence at trial.' "

The Court supports its antitextual conclusion by cobbling together scraps of dicta from various cases that have no bearing here. . . . [T]hat the defendant should be confronted by the witnesses who appear at trial is not a preference "reflected" by the Confrontation Clause; it is a constitutional right unqualifiedly guaranteed. . . .

The Court characterizes the States's interest which "outweigh[s]" the explicit text of the Constitution as an "interest in the physical and psychological well-being of child abuse victims," an "interest in protecting" such victims "from the emotional trauma of testifying." That is not so. A child who meets the Maryland statute's requirement of suffering such "serious emotional distress" from confrontation that he "cannot reasonably communicate" would seem entirely safe. Why would a prosecutor want to call a witness who cannot reasonably communicate? And if he did, it would be the State's own fault. Protection of the child's interest—as far as the Confrontation Clause is concerned—is entirely within Maryland's control. The State's interest here is in fact no more and no less than what the State's interest always is when it seeks to get a class of evidence admitted in criminal proceedings: more convictions of guilty defendants. That is not an unworthy interest, but it should not be dressed up as a humanitarian one.

And the interest on the other side is also what it usually is when the State seeks to get a new class of evidence admitted: fewer convictions of innocent defendants—specifically, in the present context, innocent defendants accused of particularly heinous crimes. The "special" reasons that exist for suspending one of the usual guarantees of reliability in the case of children's testimony are perhaps matched by "special" reasons for being particularly insistent upon it in the case of children's testimony. Some studies show that children are substantially more vulnerable to suggestion than adults, and often unable to separate recollected fantasy (or suggestion) from reality. . . . The injustice their erroneous testimony can produce is evidenced by the tragic Scott County investigations of 1983–

1984, which disrupted the lives of many (as far as we know) innocent people in the small town of Jordan, Minnesota. At one stage those investigations were pursuing allegations by at least eight children of multiple murders, but the prosecutions actually initiated charged only sexual abuse. Specifically, 24 adults were charged with molesting 37 children. In the course of the investigations, 25 children were placed in foster homes. Of the 24 indicted defendants, one pleaded guilty, two were acquitted at trial, and the charges against the remaining 21 were voluntarily dismissed. There is no doubt that some sexual abuse took place in Jordan; but there is no reason to believe it was as widespread as charged. A report by the Minnesota Attorney General's office, based on inquiries conducted by the Minnesota Bureau of Criminal Apprehension and the Federal Bureau of Investigation, concluded that there was an "absence of credible testimony and [a] lack of significant corroboration" to support reinstitution of sex-abuse charges, and "no credible evidence of murders." The report describes an investigation full of well-intentioned techniques employed by the prosecution team, police, child protection workers, and foster parents, that distorted and in some cases even coerced the children's recollection. Children were interrogated repeatedly, in some cases as many as 50 times; answers were suggested by telling the children what other witnesses had said; and children (even some who did not at first complain of abuse) were separated from their parents for months. . . . The value of the confrontation right in guarding against a child's distorted or coerced recollections is dramatically evident with respect to one of the misguided investigative techniques the report cited: some children were told by their foster parents that reunion with their real parents would be hastened by "admission" of their parents' abuse. Is it difficult to imagine how unconvincing such a testimonial admission might be to a jury that witnessed the child's delight at seeing his parents in the courtroom? Or how devastating it might be if, pursuant to a psychiatric evaluation that "trauma would impair the child's ability to communicate" in front of his parents, the child were permitted to tell his story to the jury on closed-circuit television?

In the last analysis, however, this debate is not an appropriate one. I have no need to defend the value of confrontation, because the Court has no authority to question it. . . . For good or bad, the Sixth Amendment requires confrontation, and we are not at liberty to ignore it. To quote the document one last time (for it plainly says all that need be said): "In *all* criminal prosecutions, the accused shall enjoy the right . . . to be confronted with the witnesses against him'' (emphasis added). . . .

We are not free to conduct a cost-benefit analysis of clear and explicit constitutional guarantees, and then to adjust their meaning to comport with our findings. The Court has convincingly proved that the Maryland procedure serves a valid interest, and gives the defendant virtually everything the Confrontation Clause guarantees (everything, that is, except confrontation). I am persuaded, therefore, that the Maryland procedure is virtually constitutional. Since it is not, however, actually constitutional I would affirm the judgment of the Maryland Court of Appeals reversing the judgment of conviction.

PRIVACY

CRUZAN v. DIRECTOR, MISSOURI DEPT. OF HEALTH
110 S.Ct. 2841 (1990)

Nancy Beth Cruzan lost control of her car as she traveled down Elm Road in Jasper County, Missouri, on the night of January 11, 1983. Her car overturned and she was soon found not breathing and with no heartbeat. Paramedics at the scene were able to revive her and she was taken unconscious to a hospital. She suffered significant lack of oxygen that caused permanent brain damage. Ms. Cruzan was 26 years old at the time of her accident. She remained in a coma for three weeks and then progressed to an unconscious state in which she remains today in a Missouri state hospital. She is in a persistent vegetative state in which she exhibits motor reflexes but no real cognitive functions. She is a spastic quadraplegic and her arms and legs are contracted with irreversible muscular and tendon damage. She is unable to swallow food or drink water on her own. Medical experts testified that attached to tubes providing food and water, Nancy Cruzan could live another 30 years. Once it became apparent that she had no chance of regaining her mental ability, her parents asked the hospital to remove the tubes and permit her to die. Hospital employees refused to honor this request without a court order. A state trial court heard testimony that the year before the accident Ms. Cruzan told a former housemate that she would not wish to continue her life if sick or injured unless she could live at least halfway normally. The trial court judge ruled that a person in Ms. Cruzan's condition has a fundamental constitutional right to direct or refuse the withdrawal of death-prolonging procedures and
that Ms. Cruzan's previous statements suggested that she would not wish to continue on with the feeding tubes. The judge therefore ordered removal of the tubes. The Missouri Supreme Court, however, reversed, refusing to recognize a broad right to privacy that would support an unrestricted right to refuse treatment. Any such right, said the court, is limited by Missouri law to the formalities of Missouri's Living Will statute or clear and convincing evidence of the patient's wishes. The court determined that Ms. Cruzan's statements to her former housemate were unreliable for the purpose of determining Ms. Cruzan's intent. Nancy Beth Cruzan's parents then went to the United States Supreme Court.

Majority votes: 5
Dissenting votes: 4

CHIEF JUSTICE REHNQUIST delivered the opinion of the Court:. . . .

At common law, even the touching of one person by another without consent and without legal justification was a battery. Before the turn of the century, this Court observed that "[n]o right is held more sacred, or is more carefully guarded, by the common law, than the right of every individual to the possession and control of his own person, free from all restraint or interference of others, unless by clear and unquestionable authority of law." *Union Pacific R. Co.* v. *Botsford*, 141 U.S. 250, 251 (1891). This notion of bodily integrity has been embodied in the requirement that informed consent is generally required for medical treatment. . . . The informed consent doctrine has become firmly entrenched in American tort law. . . .

The logical corollary of the doctrine of informed consent is that the patient generally possesses the right not to consent, that is, to refuse treatment. . . . Until about 15 years ago and the seminal decision in *In re Quinlan*, 70 N.J. 10, 355 A. 2d 647, cert. denied *sub nom.*, *Garger* v. *New Jersey*, 429 U.S. 922 (1976), the number of right-to-refuse-treatment decisions were relatively few. Most of the earlier cases involved patients who refused medical treatment forbidden by their religious beliefs, thus implicating First Amendment rights as well as common law rights of self-determination. More recently, however, with the advance of medical technology capable of sustaining life well past the point where natural forces would have brought certain death in earlier times, cases involving the right to refuse life-sustaining treatment have burgeoned. . . .

In the *Quinlan* case, young Karen Quinlan suffered severe brain damage as the result of anoxia, and entered a persistent vegetative state. Karen's father sought judicial approval to disconnect his daughter's respirator. The New Jersey Supreme Court granted the relief, holding that Karen had a right of privacy grounded in the Federal Constitution to terminate treatment. . . .

After *Quinlan,* however, most courts have based a right to refuse treatment either solely on the common law right to informed consent or on both the common law right and a constitutional privacy right. . . .

[JUSTICE REHNQUIST reviews state court decisions dealing with these issues]

As these cases demonstrate, the common-law doctrine of informed consent is viewed as generally encompassing the right of a competent individual to refuse medical treatment. Beyond that, these decisions demonstrate both similarity and diversity in their approach to decision of what all agree is a perplexing question with unusually strong moral and ethical overtones. State courts have available to them for decision a number of sources—state constitutions, statutes, and common law—which are not available to us. In this Court, the question is simply and starkly whether the United States Constitution prohibits Missouri from choosing the rule of decision which it did. This is the first case in which we have been squarely presented with the issue of whether the United States Constitution grants what is in common parlance referred to as a "right to die." . . .

The Fourteenth Amendment provides that no State shall "deprive any person of life, liberty, or property, without due process of law." The principle that a competent person has a constitutionally protected liberty interest in refusing unwanted medical treatment may be inferred from our prior decisions. . . .

But determining that a person has a "liberty interest" under the Due Process Clause does not end the inquiry; "whether respondent's constitutional rights have been violated must be determined by balancing his liberty interests against the relevant state interests." . . .

Petitioners insist that under the general holdings of our cases, the forced administration of life-sustaining medical treatment, and even of artificially-delivered food and water essential to life, would implicate a competent person's liberty interest. Although we think the logic of the cases discussed above would embrace such a liberty interest, the dramatic consequences involved in refusal of such treatment would inform the inquiry as to whether the deprivation of that interest is constitutionally permissible. But for purposes of this case, we assume that the United States Constitution would grant a competent person a constitutionally protected right to refuse lifesaving hydration and nutrition.

Petitioners go on to assert that an incompetent person should possess the same right in this respect as is possessed by a competent person. . . .

The difficulty with petitioners' claim is that in a sense it begs the question: an incompetent person is not able to make an informed and voluntary choice to exercise a hypothetical right to refuse treatment or any other right. Such a "right" must be exercised for her, if at all, by some sort of surrogate. Here, Missouri has in effect recognized that under certain circumstances a surrogate may act for the patient in electing to have hydration and nutrition withdrawn in such a way as to cause death, but it has established a procedural safeguard to assure that the action of the surrogate conforms as best it may to the wishes expressed by the patient while competent. Missouri requires that evidence of the incompetent's wishes as to the withdrawal of treatment be proved by clear and convincing evidence. The question, then, is whether the United States Constitution forbids the establishment of this procedural requirement by the State. We hold that it does not.

Whether or not Missouri's clear and convincing evidence requirement comports with the United States Constitution depends in part on what interests the State may properly seek to protect in this situation. Missouri relies on its interest in the protection and preservation of human life, and there can be no gainsaying this interest. As a general matter, the States—indeed, all civilized nations—demonstrate their commitment to life by treating homicide as serious crime. Moreover, the majority of States in this country have laws imposing criminal penalties on one who assists another to commit suicide. We do not think a State is required to remain neutral in the face of an informed and voluntary decision by a physically-able adult to starve to death.

But in the context presented here, a State has more particular interests at stake. The choice between life and death is a deeply personal decision of obvious and overwhelming finality. We believe Missouri may legitimately seek to safeguard the personal element of this choice through the imposition of heightened evidentiary requirements. It cannot be disputed that the Due Process Clause protects an interest in life as well as an interest in refusing life-sustaining medical treatment. Not all incompetent patients will have loved ones available to serve as surrogate decisionmakers. And even where family members are present, "[t]here will, of course, be some unfortunate situations in which family members will not act to protect a patient." A State is entitled to guard against potential abuses in such situations. Similarly, a State is entitled to consider that a judicial proceeding to make a determination regarding an incompetent's wishes may very well not be an adversarial one, with the added guarantee of accurate factfinding that the adversary process brings with it. Finally, we think a State may properly decline to make judgments about the "quality" of life that a particular individual may enjoy, and simply assert an unqualified interest in the preservation of human life to be weighed against the constitutionally protected interests of the individual.

In our view, Missouri has permissibly sought to advance these interests through the adoption of a "clear and convincing" standard of proof to govern such proceedings. . . .

The Supreme Court of Missouri held that in this case the testimony adduced at trial did not amount to clear and convincing proof of the patient's desire to have hydration and nutrition withdrawn. In so doing, it reversed a decision of the Missouri trial court which had found that the evidence "suggest[ed]" Nancy Cruzan would not have desired to continue such measures but which had not adopted the standard of "clear and convincing evidence" enunciated by the Supreme Court. The testimony adduced at trial consisted primarily of Nancy Cruzan's statements made to a housemate about a year before her accident that she would not want to live should she face life as a "vegetable," and other observations to the same effect. The observations did not deal in terms with withdrawal of medical treatment or of hydration and nutrition. We cannot say that the Supreme Court of Missouri committed constitutional error in reaching the conclusion that it did.

Petitioners alternatively contend that Missouri must accept the "substituted judgment" of close family members even in the absence of substantial proof that their views reflect the views of the patient. . . .

No doubt is engendered by anything in this record but that Nancy Cruzan's mother and father are loving and caring parents. If the State were required by the United States Constitution to repose a right of "substituted judgment" with anyone, the Cruzans would surely qualify. But we do not think the Due Process Clause requires the State to repose judgment on these matters with anyone but the patient herself. Close family members may have a strong feeling—a feeling not at all ignoble or unwor-thy, but not entirely disinterested, either—that they do not wish to witness the continuation of the life of a loved one which they regard as hopeless, meaningless, and even degrading. But there is no automatic assurance that the view of close family members will necessarily be the same as the patient's would have been had she been confronted with the prospect of her situation while competent. All of the reasons previously discussed for allowing Missouri to require clear and convincing evidence of the patient's wishes lead us to conclude that the State may choose to defer only to those wishes, rather than confide the decision to close family members.

The judgment of the Supreme Court of Missouri is

Affirmed.

JUSTICE O'CONNOR, concurring: [omitted]
JUSTICE SCALIA, concurring:

The various opinions in this case portray quite clearly the difficult, indeed agonizing, questions that are presented by the constantly increasing power of science to keep the human body alive for longer than any reasonable person would want to inhabit it. The States have begun to grapple with these problems through legislation. I am concerned, from the tenor of today's opinions, that we are poised to confuse that enterprise as successfully as we have confused the enterprise of legislating concerning abortion—requiring it to be conducted against a background of federal constitutional imperatives that are unknown because they are being newly crafted from Term to Term. That would be a great misfortune.

While I agree with the Court's analysis today, and therefore join in its opinion, I would have preferred that we announce, clearly and promptly, that the federal courts have no business in this field; that American law has always accorded the State the power to prevent, by force if necessary, suicide—including suicide by refusing to take appropriate measures necessary to preserve one's life; that the point at which life becomes "worthless," and the point at which the means necessary to preserve it become "extraordinary" or "inappropriate," are neither set forth in the Constitution nor known to the nine Justices of this Court any better than they are known to nine people picked at random from the Kansas City telephone directory; and hence, that even when it *is* demonstrated by clear and convincing evidence that a patient no longer wishes certain measures to be taken to preserve her life, it is up to the citizens of Missouri to decide, through their elected representatives, whether that wish will be honored. It is quite impossible (because the Constitution says nothing about the matter) that those citizens will decide upon a line less lawful than the one we would choose; and it is unlikely (because we know no more about "life-and-death" than they do) that they will decide upon a line less reasonable. . . .

. . . I assert . . . that the Constitution has nothing to say about the subject. To raise up a constitutional right here we would have to create out of nothing (for it exists neither in text nor tradition) some constitutional principle whereby, although the State may insist that an individual come in out of the cold and eat food, it may not insist that he take medicine; and although it may pump his stomach empty of poison he has ingested, it may not fill his stomach with food he has failed to ingest. Are there, then, no reasonable and humane limits that ought not to be exceeded in requiring an individual to preserve his own life? There obviously are, but they are not set forth in the Due Process Clause. What assures us that those limits will not be exceeded is the same constitutional guarantee that is the source of most of our protection—what protects us, for example, from being assessed a tax of 100% of our income above the subsistence level, from being forbidden to drive cars, or from being required to send our children to school for 10 hours a day, none of which horribles is categorically prohibited by the Constitution. Our salvation is the Equal Protection Clause, which requires the democratic majority to accept for themselves and their loved ones what they impose on you and me. This Court need not, and has no authority to, inject itself into every field of human activity where irrationality and oppression may theoretically occur, and if it tries to do so it will destroy itself.

JUSTICE BRENNAN, with whom JUSTICE MARSHALL and JUSTICE BLACKMUN join, dissenting: . . .

Today the Court, while tentatively accepting that there is some degree of constitutionally protected liberty interest in avoiding unwanted medical treatment, including life-sustaining medical treatment such as artificial nutrition and hydration, affirms the decision of the Missouri Supreme Court. The majority opinion, as I read it, would affirm that decision on the ground that a State may require "clear and convincing" evidence of Nancy Cruzan's prior decision to forgo life-sustaining treatment under circumstances such as hers in order to ensure that her actual wishes are honored. Because I believe that Nancy Cruzan has a fundamental right to be free of unwanted artificial nutrition and hydration, which right is not outweighed by any in-

terests of the State, and because I find that the improperly biased procedural obstacles imposed by the Missouri Supreme Court impermissibly burden that right, I respectfully dissent. Nancy Cruzan is entitled to choose to die with dignity. . . .

The right to be free from medical attention without consent, to determine what shall be done with one's own body, *is* deeply rooted in this Nation's traditions, as the majority acknowledges. This right has long been "firmly entrenched in American tort law" and is securely grounded in the earliest common law. . . .

Although the right to be free of unwanted medical intervention, like other constitutionally protected interests, may not be absolute, no State interest could outweigh the rights of an individual in Nancy Cruzan's position. Whatever a State's possible interests in mandating life-support treatment under other circumstances, there is no good to be obtained here by Missouri's insistence that Nancy Cruzan remain on life-support systems if it is indeed her wish not to do so. Missouri does not claim, nor could it, that society as a whole will be benefited by Nancy's receiving medical treatment. No third party's situation will be improved and no harm to others will be averted.

The only state interest asserted here is a general interest in the preservation of life. But the State has no legitimate general interest in someone's life, completely abstracted from the interest of the person living that life, that could outweigh the person's choice to avoid medical treatment. . . . Thus, the State's general interest in life must accede to Nancy Cruzan's particularized and intense interest in self-determination in her choice of medical treatment. There is simply nothing legitimately within the State's purview to be gained by superseding her decision. . . .

This is not to say that the State has no legitimate interests to assert here. As the majority recognizes, Missouri has a *parens patriae* interest in providing Nancy Cruzan, now incompetent, with as accurate as possible a determination of how she would exercise her rights under these circumstances. Second, if and when it is determined that Nancy Cruzan would want to continue treatment, the State may legitimately assert an interest in providing that treatment. But *until* Nancy's wishes have been determined, the only state interest that may be asserted is an interest in safeguarding the accuracy of that determination.

Accuracy, therefore, must be our touchstone. Missouri may constitutionally impose only those procedural requirements that serve to enhance the accuracy of a determination of Nancy Cruzan's wishes or are at least consistent with an accurate determination. The Missouri ''safeguard'' that the Court upholds today does not meet that standard. The determination needed in this context is whether the incompetent person would choose to live in a persistent vegetative state on life-support or to avoid this medical treatment. Missouri's rule of decision imposes a markedly asymmetrical evidentiary burden. Only evidence of specific statements of treatment choice made by the patient when competent is admissible to support a finding that the patient, now in a persistent vegetative state, would wish to avoid further medical treatment. Moreover, this evidence must be clear and convincing. No proof is required to support a finding that the incompetent person would wish to continue treatment. . . .

The majority offers several justifications for Missouri's heightened evidentiary standard. First, the majority explains that the State may constitutionally adopt this rule to govern determinations of an incompetent's wishes in order to advance the State's substantive interests, including its unqualified interest in the preservation of human life. Missouri's evidentiary standard, however, cannot rest on the State's own interest in a particular substantive result. To be sure, courts have long erected clear and convincing evidence standards to place the greater risk of erroneous decisions on those bringing disfavored claims. In such cases, however, the choice to discourage certain claims was a legitimate, constitutional policy choice. In contrast, Missouri has no such power to disfavor a choice by Nancy Cruzan to avoid medical treatment, because Missouri has no legitimate interest in providing Nancy with treatment until it is established that this represents her choice. Just as a State may not override Nancy's choice directly, it may not do so indirectly through the imposition of a procedural rule.

Second, the majority offers two explanations for why Missouri's clear and convincing evidence standard is a means of enhancing accuracy, but neither is persuasive. The majority initially argues that a clear and convincing evidence standard is necessary to compensate for the possibility that such proceedings will lack the ''guarantee of accurate factfinding that the adversary process brings with it.'' . . .

An adversarial proceeding is of particular importance when one side has a strong personal interest which needs to be counterbalanced to assure the court that the questions will be fully explored. . . . Barring venal motives, which a trial court has the means of ferreting out, the decision to come forward to request a judicial order to stop treatment represents a slowly and carefully considered reso-

lution by at least one adult and more frequently several adults that discontinuation of treatment is the patient's wish. . . .

. . . Missouri's heightened evidentiary standard attempts to achieve balance by discounting evidence; the guardian ad litem technique achieves balance by probing for additional evidence. Where, as here, the family members, friends, doctors and guardian ad litem agree, it is not because the process has failed, as the majority suggests. It is because there is no genuine dispute as to Nancy's preference. . . .

The majority claims that the allocation of the risk of error is justified because it is more important not to terminate life-support for someone who would wish it continued than to honor the wishes of someone who would not. An erroneous decision to terminate life-support is irrevocable, says the majority, while an erroneous decision not to terminate ''results in a maintenance of the status quo.'' But, from the point of view of the patient, an erroneous decision in either direction is irrevocable. An erroneous decision to terminate artificial nutrition and hydration, to be sure, will lead to failure of that last remnant of physiological life, the brain stem, and result in complete brain death. An erroneous decision not to terminate life-support, however, robs a patient of the very qualities protected by the right to avoid unwanted medical treatment. His own degraded existence is perpetuated; his family's suffering is protracted; the memory he leaves behind becomes more and more distorted.

Even a later decision to grant him his wish cannot undo the intervening harm. But a later decision is unlikely in any event. ''[T]he discovery of new evidence,'' to which the majority refers, is more hypothetical than plausible. The majority also misconceives the relevance of the possibility of ''advancements in medical science,'' by treating it as a reason to force someone to continue medical treatment against his will. The possibility of a medical miracle is indeed part of the calculus, but it is a part of the *patient's* calculus. If current research suggests that some hope for cure or even moderate improvement is possible within the life-span projected, this is a factor that should be and would be accorded significant weight in assessing what the patient himself would choose. . . .

The Missouri court's disdain for Nancy's statements in serious conversations not long before her accident, for the opinions of Nancy's family and friends as to her values, beliefs and certain choice, and even for the opinion of an outside objective factfinder appointed by the State evinces a disdain for Nancy Cruzan's own right to choose. The rules by which an incompetent person's wishes are determined must represent every effort to determine those wishes. The rule that the Missouri court adopted and that this Court upholds, however, skews the result away from a determination that as accurately as possible reflects the individual's own preferences and beliefs. It is a rule that transforms human beings into passive subjects of medical technology. . . .

. . . A State's legitimate interest in safeguarding a patient's choice cannot be furthered by simply appropriating it.

The majority justifies its position by arguing that, while close family members may have a strong feeling about the question, "there is no automatic assurance that the view of close family members will necessarily be the same as the patient's would have been had she been confronted with the prospect of her situation while competent." I cannot quarrel with this observation. But it leads only to another question: Is there any reason to suppose that a State is *more* likely to make the choice that the patient would have made than someone who knew the patient intimately? To ask this is to answer it. . . .

A State's inability to discern an incompetent patient's choice still need not mean that a State is rendered powerless to protect that choice. But I would find that the Due Process Clause prohibits a State from doing more than that. A State may ensure that the person who makes the decision on the patient's behalf is the one whom the patient himself would have selected to make that choice for him. And a State may exclude from consideration anyone having improper motives. But a State generally must either repose the choice with the person whom the patient himself would most likely have chosen as proxy or leave the decision to the patient's family.

. . . Missouri and this Court have displaced Nancy's own assessment of the processes associated with dying. They have discarded evidence of her will, ignored her values, and deprived her of the right to a decision as closely approximating her own choice as humanly possible. They have done so disingenuously in her name, and openly in Missouri's own. That Missouri and this Court may truly be motivated only by concern for incompetent patients makes no matter. As one of our most prominent jurists warned us decades ago: "Experience should teach us to be most on our guard to protect liberty when the government's purposes are beneficent. . . . The greatest dangers to liberty lurk in insidious encroachment by men of zeal, well meaning but without understanding." *Olmstead* v. *United States,* 277 U.S. 438, 479 (1928) (Brandeis, J., dissenting).

I respectfully dissent.

JUSTICE STEVENS, dissenting:. . . .

. . . Because Nancy Beth Cruzan did not have the foresight to preserve her constitutional right in a living will, or some comparable "clear and convincing" alternative, her right is gone forever and her fate is in the hands of the state legislature instead of in those of her family, her independent neutral guardian ad litem, and an impartial judge—all of whom agree on the course of action that is in her best interests. The Court's willingness to find a waiver of this constitutional right reveals a distressing misunderstanding of the importance of individual liberty. . . .

The more precise constitutional significance of death is difficult to describe; not much may be said with confidence about death unless it is said from faith, and that alone is reason enough to protect the freedom to conform choices about death to individual conscience. . . .

These considerations cast into stark relief the injustice, and unconstitutionality, of Missouri's treatment of Nancy Beth Cruzan. Nancy Cruzan's death, when it comes, cannot be an historic act of heroism; it will inevitably be the consequence of her tragic accident. But Nancy Cruzan's interest in life, no less than that of any other person, includes an interest in how she will be thought of after her death by those whose opinions mattered to her. There can be no doubt that her life made her dear to her family, and to others. How she dies will affect how that life is remembered. The trial court's order authorizing Nancy's parents to cease their daughter's treatment would have permitted the family that cares for Nancy to bring to a close her tragedy and her death. Missouri's objection to that order subordinates Nancy's body, her family, and the lasting significance of her life to the State's own interests. The decision we review thereby interferes with constitutional interests of the highest order. . . .

My disagreement with the Court is . . . unrelated to its endorsement of the clear and convincing standard of proof for cases of this kind. Indeed, I agree that the controlling facts must be established with unmistakable clarity. The critical question, however, is not how to prove the controlling facts but rather what proven facts should be controlling. In my view, the constitutional answer is clear: the best interests of the individual, especially when buttressed by the interests of all related third parties, must prevail over any general state policy that simply ignores those interests. Indeed, the only apparent *secular* basis for the State's interest in life is the policy's persuasive impact upon people other than Nancy and her family. . . . The failure of Missouri's policy to heed the interests of a dying individual with respect to matters so private is ample evidence of the policy's illegitimacy. . . .

. . . However commendable may be the State's interest in human life, it cannot pursue that interest by appropriating Nancy Cruzan's life as a symbol for its own purposes. Lives do not exist in abstraction from persons, and to pretend otherwise is not to honor but to desecrate the State's responsibility for protecting life. A State that seeks to demonstrate its commitment to life may do so by aiding those who are actively struggling for life and health. In this endeavor, unfortunately, no State can lack for opportunities: there can be no need to make an example of tragic cases like that of Nancy Cruzan.

I respectfully dissent.

HODGSON v. MINNESOTA
110 S.Ct. 2926 (1990)

Subdivision 2 of Minnesota statute, section 144.343, provides that no abortion shall be performed on a woman under 18 years of age until at least 48 hours after both of her parents have been notified. The two-parent notice requirement is mandatory unless an immediate abortion is necessary to save her life, or both parents have already consented in writing, or the woman declares that she is a victim of parental abuse or neglect and so notifies the proper authorities. Subdivision 6 provides for a judicial bypass, that is, if a court enjoins the enforcement of Subdivision 2, the same two-parent notice requirement must be observed unless a court finds that the minor is mature and capable of giving informed consent or that an abortion without notice to both parents is in the woman's best interest. The statute makes no exceptions as to parents; thus it applies to a divorced parent, a noncustodial parent, or a biological parent who never married or lived with the woman's mother. Two days before the statute was to go into effect, Dr. Jane Hodgson, along with another physician, four clinics providing abortion services in Minnesota, six pregnant minors representing a class of pregnant minors, and the mother of a pregnant minor, filed suit in federal district court. The plaintiffs alleged that the statute violated the due process and equal protection clauses of the Fourteenth Amendment. The district court found for the plaintiffs and struck down the entire statute as unconstitutional. The United States Court of Appeals for the Eighth Circuit reversed, ruling that while Subdivision 2 was invalid, the judicial bypass procedure of Subdivision 6 was constitutional, thus saving the statute as a whole.

Dr. Hodgson et al. brought the case to the United States Supreme Court, which took this case along with one from Ohio that concerned an Ohio law requiring one-parent notification and that provided for a judicial bypass (Ohio v. Akron Center for Reproductive Health). As is clear in the opinions that follow, the Supreme Court was badly split. Five justices (Stevens, Blackmun, Brennan, Marshall, and O'Connor) struck down Subdivision 2 while another configuration of five justices (O'Connor joining with Kennedy, Rehnquist, Scalia, and White) upheld Subdivision 6. There was a different breakdown in the companion Akron decision (not reprinted here).

Majority votes: 5
Dissenting votes: 4

JUSTICE STEVENS announced the judgment of the Court and delivered the opinion of the Court with respect to Parts I, II, IV, and VII, an opinion with respect to Part III in which JUSTICE BRENNAN joins, an opinion with respect to Parts V and VI in which JUSTICE O'CONNOR joins, and a dissenting opinion with respect to Part VIII:. . . .

I. . . .

[Description of the statute]

II. . . .

[Description of the litigation history of the case]

III

There is a natural difference between men and women: only women have the capacity to bear children. A woman's decision to beget or to bear a child is a component of her liberty that is protected by the Due Process Clause of the Fourteenth Amendment to the Constitution. . . . That Clause, as interpreted in those cases, protects the woman's right to make such decisions independently and privately free of unwarranted governmental intrusion. . . .

. . . As we stated in *Planned Parenthood of Central Missouri* v. *Danforth*, 428 U.S. 52, 74 (1976), the right to make this decision "do[es] not mature and come into being magically only when one attains the state-defined age of majority." Thus, the constitutional protection against unjustified state intrusion into the process of deciding whether or not to bear a child extends to pregnant minors as well as adult women.

In cases involving abortion, as in cases involving the right to travel or the right to marry, the identification of the constitutionally protected interest is merely the beginning of the analysis. State regulation of travel and of marriage is obviously permissible even though a State may not categorically exclude nonresidents from its borders, *Shapiro* v. *Thompson,* 394 U.S. 618, 631 (1969), or deny prisoners the right to marry, *Turner* v. *Safley,* 482 U.S. 78, 94–99 (1987). But the regulation of constitutionally protected decisions, such as where a person shall reside or whom he or she shall marry, must be predicated on legitimate state concerns other than disagreement with the choice the individual has made. In the abortion area, a State may have no obligation to spend its own money, or use its own facilities, to subsidize nontherapeutic abortions for minors or adults. See, *e.g., Maher* v. *Roe,* 432 U.S. 464 (1977). A State's value judgment favoring childbirth over abortion may provide adequate support for decisions involving such allocation of public funds, but not for simply substituting a state decision for an individual decision that a woman has a right to make for herself. Otherwise, the interest in liberty protected by the Due Process Clause would be a nullity. A state policy favoring childbirth over abortion is not in itself a sufficient justification for overriding the woman's decision or for placing "obstacles—absolute or otherwise—in the pregnant woman's path to an abortion."

In these cases the State of Minnesota does not rest its defense of this statute on any such value judgment. Indeed, it affirmatively disavows that state interest as a basis for upholding this law. Moreover, it is clear that the state judges who have interpreted the statute in over 3,000 decisions implementing its bypass procedures have found no legislative intent to disfavor the decision to terminate a pregnancy. On the contrary, in all but a handful of cases they have approved such decisions. Because the Minnesota statute unquestionably places obstacles in the pregnant minor's path to an abortion, the State has the burden of establishing its constitutionality. Under any analysis, the Minnesota statute cannot be sustained if the obstacles it imposes are not reasonably related to legitimate state interests. . . .

IV

The Court has considered the constitutionality of statutes providing for parental consent or parental notification in six abortion cases decided during the last 14 years. Although the Massachusetts statute reviewed in *Bellotti* v. *Baird,* 428 U.S. 132 (1976)

(Bellotti I,) and *Bellotti II* required the consent of both parents, and the Utah statute reviewed in *H. L.* v. *Matheson,* 450 U.S. 398 (1981), required notice to "the parents," none of the opinions in any of those cases focused on the possible significance of making the consent or the notice requirement applicable to both parents instead of just one. In contrast, the arguments in these cases, as well as the extensive findings of the District Court, are directed primarily at that distinction. . . .

The District Court found—on the basis of extensive testimony at trial—that the two-parent notification requirement had particularly harmful effects on both the minor and the custodial parent when the parents were divorced or separated. Relations between the minor and absent parent were not reestablished as a result of the forced notification thereby often producing disappointment in the minor "when an anticipated reestablishment of her relationship with the absent parent d[id] not occur." Moreover, "[t]he reaction of the custodial parent to the requirement of forced notification is often one of anger, resentment and frustration at the intrusion of the absent parent," and fear that notification will threaten the custody rights of the parent or otherwise promote intrafamily violence. Tragically, those fears were often realized. . . .

The District Court also found that the two-parent notification requirement had adverse effects in families in which the minor lives with both parents. These effects were particularly pronounced in the distressingly large number of cases in which family violence is a serious problem. . . .

The great majority of bypass petitions are filed in the three metropolitan counties in Minnesota, where courts schedule bypass hearings on a regular basis and have in place procedures for hearing emergency petitions. Courts in the nonmetropolitan areas are acquainted with the statute and, for the most part, apply it conscientiously, but a number of counties are served by judges who are unwilling to hear bypass petitions. . . .

During the period between August 1, 1981, and March 1, 1986, 3,573 judicial bypass petitions were filed in Minnesota courts. All but 15 were granted. The judges who adjudicated over 90% of these petitions testified; none of them identified any positive effects of the law. The court experience produced fear, tension, anxiety, and shame among minors, causing some who were mature, and some whose best interests would have been served by an abortion, to "forgo the bypass option and either notify their parents or carry to term." Among parents who supported their daughters in the bypass proceedings, the court experience evoked similar reactions. . . .

V

Three separate but related interests—the interest in the welfare of the pregnant minor, the interest of the parents, and the interest of the family unit—are relevant to our consideration of the constitutionality of the 48-hour waiting period and the two-parent notification requirement.

The State has a strong and legitimate interest in the welfare of its young citizens, whose immaturity, inexperience, and lack of judgment may sometimes impair their ability to exercise their rights wisely. That interest, which justifies state-imposed requirements that a minor obtain his or her parent's consent before undergoing an operation, marrying, or entering military service, extends also to the minor's decision to terminate her pregnancy. Although the Court has held that parents may not exercise "an absolute, and possibly arbitrary, veto" over that decision, it has never challenged a State's reasonable judgment that the decision should be made after notification to and consultation with a parent. . . . The fact of biological parentage generally offers a person only "an opportunity . . . to develop a relationship with his offspring." But the demonstration of commitment to the child through the assumption of personal, financial, or custodial responsibility may give the natural parent a stake in the relationship with the child rising to the level of a liberty interest. . . .

While the State has a legitimate interest in the creation and dissolution of the marriage contract, the family has a privacy interest in the upbringing and education of children and the intimacies of the marital relationship which is protected by the Constitution against undue state interference. . . . We have long held that there exists a "private realm of family life which the state cannot enter." Thus, when the government intrudes on choices concerning the arrangement of the household, this Court has carefully examined the "governmental interests advanced and the extent to which they are served by the challenged regulation."

A natural parent who has demonstrated sufficient commitment to his or her children is thereafter entitled to raise the children free from undue state interference. . . .

VI

We think it is clear that a requirement that a minor wait 48 hours after notifying a single parent of her intention to get an abortion would reasonably further the legitimate state interest in ensuring that the minor's decision is knowing and intelligent. We

have held that when a parent or another person has assumed "primary responsibility" for a minor's well-being, the State may properly enact "laws designed to aid discharge of that responsibility." To the extent that subdivision 2 of the Minnesota statute requires notification of only one parent, it does just that. The brief waiting period provides the parent the opportunity to consult with his or her spouse and a family physician, and it permits the parent to inquire into the competency of the doctor performing the abortion, discuss the religious or moral implications of the abortion decision, and provide the daughter needed guidance and counsel in evaluating the impact of the decision on her future.

The 48-hour delay imposes only a minimal burden on the right of the minor to decide whether or not to terminate her pregnancy. Although the District Court found that scheduling factors, weather, and the minor's school and work commitments may combine, in many cases, to create a delay of a week or longer between the initiation of notification and the abortion, there is no evidence that the 48-hour period itself is unreasonable or longer than appropriate for adequate consultation between parent and child. The statute does not impose any period of delay once the parents or a court, acting *in loco parentis,* express their agreement that the minor is mature or that the procedure would be in her best interest. Indeed, as the Court of Appeals noted and the record reveals, the 48-hour waiting period may run concurrently with the time necessary to make an appointment for the procedure, thus resulting in little or no delay.

VII

It is equally clear that the requirement that *both* parents be notified, whether or not both wish to be notified or have assumed responsibility for the upbringing of the child, does not reasonably further any legitimate state interest. The usual justification for a parental consent or notification provision is that it supports the authority of a parent who is presumed to act in the minor's best interest and thereby assures that the minor's decision to terminate her pregnancy is knowing, intelligent, and deliberate. To the extent that such an interest is legitimate, it would be fully served by a requirement that the minor notify one parent who can then seek the counsel of his or her mate or any other party, when such advice and support is deemed necessary to help the child make a difficult decision. In the ideal family setting, of course, notice to either parent would normally constitute notice to both. A statute requiring two-parent notification would not further any state interest in those instances. In many families, however, the parent notified by the child would not notify the other parent. In those cases the State has no legitimate interest in questioning one parent's judgment that notice to the other parent would not assist the minor or in presuming that the parent who has assumed parental duties is incompetent to make decisions regarding the health and welfare of the child.

Not only does two-parent notification fail to serve any state interest with respect to functioning families, it disserves the state interest in protecting and assisting the minor with respect to dysfunctional families. . . .

The State does not rely primarily on the best interests of the minor in defending this statute. Rather, it argues that, in the ideal family, the minor should make her decision only after consultation with both parents who should naturally be concerned with the child's welfare and that the State has an interest in protecting the independent right of the parents "to determine and strive for what they believe to be best for their children." Neither of these reasons can justify the two-parent notification requirement. The second parent may well have an interest in the minor's abortion decision, making full communication among all members of a family desirable in some cases, but such communication may not be decreed by the State. The State has no more interest in requiring all family members to talk with one another than it has in requiring certain of them to live together. In *Moore* v. *East Cleveland,* 431 U.S. 494 (1977), we invalidated a zoning ordinance which "slic[ed] deeply into the family itself," permitting the city to "standardiz[e] its children—and its adults—by forcing all to live in certain narrowly defined family patterns." Although the ordinance was supported by state interests other than the state interest in substituting its conception of family life for the family's own view, the ordinance's relation to those state interests was too "tenuous" to satisfy constitutional standards. By implication, a state interest in standardizing its children and adults, making the "private realm of family life" conform to some state-designed ideal, is not a legitimate state interest at all. . . .

Unsurprisingly, the Minnesota two-parent notification requirement is an oddity among state and federal consent provisions governing the health, welfare, and education of children. A minor desiring to enlist in the armed services or the Reserve Officers' Training Corps (ROTC) need only obtain the consent of "his parent or guardian." The consent of "*a* parent or guardian" is also sufficient to obtain a passport for foreign travel from the United States Department of State and to participate as a subject in most forms of medical research. In virtually every State, the consent of one parent is enough to obtain a driver's license or operator's permit. The same may be said with respect to the decision to submit to any medical or surgical procedure other than an abortion. Indeed, the only other Minnesota statute that the State has identified which requires two-parent consent is that authorizing the minor to change his name. These statutes provide testimony to the unreasonableness of the Minnesota two-parent notification requirement and to the ease with which the State can adopt less burdensome means to protect the minor's welfare. We therefore hold that this requirement violates the Constitution.

VII

The Court holds that the constitutional objection to the two-parent notice requirement is removed by the judicial bypass option provided in subdivision 6 of the Minnesota statute. I respectfully dissent from that holding. . . .

For reasons already set forth at length, a rule requiring consent or notification of both parents is not reasonably related to the state interest in giving the pregnant minor the benefit of parental advice. The State has not called our attention to, nor am I aware of, any other medical situation in Minnesota or elsewhere in which the provision of treatment for a child has been conditioned on notice to, or consent by, both parents rather than just one. Indeed, the fact that one-parent consent is the virtually uniform rule for any other activity which affects the minor's health, safety or welfare emphasizes the aberrant quality of the two-parent notice requirement.

A judicial bypass that is designed to handle exceptions from a reasonable general rule, and thereby preserve the constitutionality of that rule, is quite different from a requirement that a minor— or a minor and one of her parents—must apply to a court for permission to avoid the application of a rule that is not reasonably related to legitimate state goals. A requirement that a minor acting with the consent of *both* parents apply to a court for permission to effectuate her decision clearly would constitute an unjustified official interference with the privacy of the minor and her family. The requirement that the bypass procedure must be invoked when the minor and one parent agree that the other parent should not be notified represents an equally unjustified governmental intrusion into the family's decisional process. . . . As the Court of Appeals panel originally concluded, the "minor and custodial parent, . . . by virtue of their major interest and superior position, should alone have the opportunity to decide to whom, if anyone, notice of the minor's abortion decision should be given." I agree with that conclusion.

The judgment of the Court of Appeals in its entirety is affirmed.

It is so ordered.

JUSTICE O'CONNOR, concurring in part and concurring in the judgment in part:

I join all but Parts III and VIII of JUSTICE STEVENS' opinion. While I agree with some of the central points made in Part III, I cannot join the broader discussion. I agree that the Court has characterized "[a] woman's decision to beget or to bear a child [as] a component of her liberty that is protected by the Due Process Clause of the Fourteenth Amendment to the Constitution." This Court extended that liberty interest to minors in *Bellotti* v. *Baird,* 443 U.S 622, 642 (1979) *(Bellotti II),* and *Planned Parenthood of Central Missourl* v. *Danforth,* 428 U.S. 52, 74 (1976), albeit with some important limitations: "[P]arental notice and consent are qualifications that typically may be imposed by the State on a minor's right to make important decisions. As immature minors often lack the ability to make fully informed choices that take account of both immediate and long-range consequences, a State reasonably may determine that parental consultation often is desirable and in the best interest of the minor." *Bellotti II, supra,* at 640–641. . . .

It has been my understanding in this area that "[i]f the particular regulation does not 'unduly burde[n]' the fundamental right, . . . then our evaluation of that regulation is limited to our determination that the regulation rationally relates to a legitimate state purpose." *Akron* v. *Akron Center for Reproductive Health, Inc.,* 462 U.S. 416, 453 (1983) (O'CONNOR, J., dissenting). . . . It is with that understanding that I agree with JUSTICE STEVENS' statement that the "statute cannot be sustained if the obstacles it imposes are not reasonably related to legitimate state interests.

I agree with JUSTICE STEVENS that Minnesota has offered no sufficient justification for its interference with the family's decisionmaking processes created by subdivision 2—two parent notification. Subdivision 2 is the most stringent notification statute in the country. . . .

Minnesota's two-parent notice requirement is all the more unreasonable when one considers that only half of the minors in the State of Minnesota reside with both biological parents. A third live with only one parent. Given its broad sweep and its failure to serve the purposes asserted by the State in too many cases, I join the Court's striking of subdivision 2.

Subdivision 6 passes constitutional muster because the interference with the internal operation of the family required by subdivision 2 simply does not exist where the minor can avoid notifying one or both parents by use of the bypass procedure.

JUSTICE MARSHALL, with whom JUSTICE BRENNAN and JUSTICE BLACKMUN join, concurring in part, concurring in the judgment in part, and dissenting in part:

I concur in Parts I, II, IV, and VII of JUSTICE STEVENS' opinion for the Court. Although I do not believe that the Constitution permits a State to require a minor to notify or consult with a parent before obtaining an abortion, I am in substantial agreement with the remainder of the reasoning in Part V of the Court's opinion. For the reasons stated by JUSTICE STEVENS, Minnesota's two-parent notification requirement is not even reasonably related to a legitimate state interest. Therefore, that requirement surely would not pass the strict scrutiny applicable to restrictions on a woman's fundamental right to have an abortion.

I dissent from the judgment of the Court, however, that the judicial bypass option renders the parental notification and 48-hour delay requirements constitutional. The bypass procedure cannot save those requirements because the bypass itself is unconstitutional both on its face and as applied. At the very least, this scheme substantially burdens a woman's right to privacy without advancing a compelling state interest. More significantly, in some instances it usurps a young woman's control over her own body by giving either a parent or a court the power effectively to veto her decision to have an abortion. . . .

Roe v. *Wade* remains the law of the land. Indeed, today's decision reaffirms the vitality of *Roe,* as five Justices have voted to strike down a state law restricting a woman's right to have an abortion. . . .

I strongly disagree with the Court's conclusion that the State may constitutionally force a minor woman either to notify both parents (or in some cases only one parent) and then wait 48 hours before proceeding with an abortion, or disclose her intimate affairs to a judge and ask that he grant her permission to have an abortion. . . . First, the parental notification and delay requirements significantly restrict a young woman's right to reproductive choice. I base my conclusion not on my intuition about the needs and attitudes of young women, but on a sizable and impressive collection of empirical data documenting the effects of parental notification statutes and of delaying an abortion. Second, the burdensome restrictions are not narrowly tailored to serve any compelling state interest. Finally, the judicial bypass procedure does not save the notice and delay requirements.

I continue to believe . . . that a judicial bypass procedure . . . is itself unconstitutional because it effectively gives a judge "an absolute veto over the decision of the physician and his patient." No person may veto *any* minor's decision, made in consultation with her physician, to terminate her pregnancy. An "immature" minor has no less right to make decisions regarding her own body than a mature adult.

Minnesota's bypass provision allows a judge to authorize an abortion if he determines either that a woman is sufficiently mature to make the decision on her own or, if she is not sufficiently mature, that an abortion without parental notification would serve her best interests. Of course, if a judge refuses to authorize an abortion, a young woman can then reevaluate whether she wants to notify a parent. But many women will carry the fetus to term rather than notify a parent. Other women may decide to inform a parent but then confront parental pressure or abuse so severe as to obstruct the abortion. For these women, the judge's refusal to authorize an abortion effectively constitutes an absolute veto.

The constitutional defects in any provision allowing someone to veto a woman's abortion decision are exacerbated by the vagueness of the standards contained in this statute. The statute gives no guidance on how a judge is to determine whether a minor is sufficiently "mature" and "capable" to make the decision on her own. . . . The statute similarly is silent as to how a judge is to determine whether an abortion without parental notification would serve an immature minor's "best interests." . . . Is the judge expected to know more about the woman's medical needs or psychological makeup than her doctor? Should he consider the woman's financial and emotional status to determine the quality of life the woman and her future child would enjoy in this world? Neither the record nor the Court answers such questions. . . . It is difficult to conceive of any reason, aside from a judge's personal opposition to abortion, that would justify a finding that an immature woman's best interests would be served by forcing her to endure pregnancy and childbirth against her will.

Even if I did not believe that a judicial bypass

procedure was facially unconstitutional, the experience of Minnesota's procedure in operation demonstrates that the bypass provision before us cannot save the parental notification and delay requirements. . . .

The District Court found that the bypass procedure imposed significant burdens on minors. First, "scheduling practices in Minnesota courts typically require minors to wait two or three days between their first contact with the court and the hearing on their petitions. This delay may combine with other factors to result in a delay of a week or more." 648 F. Supp., at 763. A delay of only a few days can significantly increase the health risks to the minor; a week-long delay inevitably does. Furthermore, in several counties in Minnesota, no judge is willing to hear bypass petitions, forcing women in those areas to travel long distances to obtain a hearing. . . . The burden of such travel, often requiring an overnight stay in a distant city, is particularly heavy for poor women from rural areas. Furthermore, a young woman's absence from home, school, or work during the time required for such travel and for the hearing itself can jeopardize the woman's confidentiality.

The District Court also found that the bypass procedure can be extremely traumatic for young women. . . .

Yet, despite the substantial burdens imposed by these proceedings, the bypass is, in effect, a "rubber stamp," . . . only an extremely small number of petitions are denied. . . . ("Although they represent substantial intrusion on minors' privacy and take up significant amounts of court time, there is no evidence that they promote more reasoned decision making or screen out adolescents who may be particularly immature or vulnerable. . . . The hearings typically last less than 15 minutes. . . . Despite the complex issues involved (maturity and the best interests of the minor), experts are rarely if ever called to testify"). The judges who have adjudicated over 90% of the bypass petitions between 1981 and 1986 could not identify any positive effects of the bypass procedure. The large number of women who undergo the bypass process do not receive any sort of counseling from the court—which is not surprising, given the court's limited role and lack of expertise in that area. The bypass process itself thus cannot serve the state interest of promoting informed decisionmaking by all minors. If the State truly were concerned about ensuring that all minors consult with a knowledgeable and caring adult, it would provide for some form of counseling rather than for a judicial procedure in which a judge merely gives or withholds his consent.

Thus, regardless of one's view of the facial validity of a bypass procedure, Minnesota's procedure in practice imposes an excessive burden on young women's right to choose an abortion. . . . The Court's holding that the burdensome bypass procedure saves the State's burdensome notification and delay requirements thus strikes me as the equivalent of saying that two wrongs make a right. I cannot accept such a novel judicial calculus.

A majority of the Court today strikes down an unreasonable and vastly overbroad requirement that a pregnant minor notify both her parents of her decision to obtain an abortion. With that decision I agree. At the same time, though, a different majority holds that a State may require a young woman to notify one or even both parents and then wait 48 hours before having an abortion, as long as the State provides a judicial bypass procedure. From that decision I vehemently dissent. This scheme forces a young woman in an already dire situation to choose between two fundamentally unacceptable alternatives: notifying a possibly dictatorial or even abusive parent and justifying her profoundly personal decision in an intimidating judicial proceeding to a black-robed stranger. For such a woman, this dilemma is more likely to result in trauma and pain than in an informed and voluntary decision.

JUSTICE SCALIA, concurring in the judgment in part and dissenting in part:

As I understand the various opinions today: One Justice holds that two-parent notification is unconstitutional (at least in the present circumstances) without judicial bypass, but constitutional with bypass (O'CONNOR, J., concurring in part and concurring in judgment); four Justices would hold that two-parent notification is constitutional with or without bypass (KENNEDY, J., concurring in judgment in part and dissenting in part); four Justices would hold that two-parent notification is unconstitutional with or without bypass, though the four apply two different standards (opinion of STEVENS, J.) [and] (MARSHALL, J., concurring in part and dissenting in part); six Justices hold that one-parent notification with bypass is constitutional, though for two different sets of reasons, *Ohio* v. *Akron Center for Reproductive Health* (STEVENS, J., concurring in judgment); and three Justices would hold that one-parent notification with bypass is unconstitutional (BLACKMUN, J., dissenting). One will search in vain the document we are supposed to be construing for text that provides the basis for the argument over these distinctions; and will find in our society's tradition regarding abortion no hint that the distinctions are constitutionally relevant, much less any indication how a constitutional argument about them ought to be resolved. The random and unpredictable results of our consequently un-

channeled individual views make it increasingly evident, Term after Term, that the tools for this job are not to be found in the lawyer's—and hence not in the judge's—workbox. I continue to dissent from this enterprise of devising an Abortion Code, and from the illusion that we have authority to do so.

JUSTICE KENNEDY, with whom THE CHIEF JUSTICE, JUSTICE WHITE, and JUSTICE SCALIA join, concurring in the judgment in part and dissenting in part: . . . .

The State identifies two interests served by the law. The first is the State's interest in the welfare of pregnant minors. The second is the State's interest in acknowledging and promoting the role of parents in the care and upbringing of their children. JUSTICE STEVENS, writing for two Members of the Court, acknowledges the legitimacy of the first interest, but decides that the second interest is somehow illegitimate, at least as to whichever parent a minor chooses not to notify. I cannot agree that the Constitution prevents a State from keeping both parents informed of the medical condition or medical treatment of their child under the terms and conditions of this statute. . . .

A State pursues a legitimate end under the Constitution when it attempts to foster and preserve the parent-child relation by giving all parents the opportunity to participate in the care and nurture of their children. We have held that parents have a liberty interest, protected by the Constitution, in having a reasonable opportunity to develop close relations with their children. We have recognized, of course, that there are limits to the constitutional right of parents to have custody of or to participate in decisions affecting their children. If a parent has relinquished the opportunity to develop a relation with the child, and his or her only link to the child is biological, the Constitution does not require a State to allow parental participation. But the fact that the Constitution does not protect the parent-child relationship in all circumstances does not mean that the State cannot attempt to foster parental participation where the Constitution does not demand that it do so. A State may seek to protect and facilitate the parent-child bond on the assumption that parents will act in their child's best interests. Indeed, we have held that a State cannot terminate parental rights based upon a presumption that a class of parents is unfit without affording individual parents an opportunity to rebut the presumption. If a State cannot legislate on the broad assumption that classes of parents are unfit and undeserving of parental rights without affording an opportunity to rebut the assumption, it is at least permissible for a State to legislate on the premise that parents, as a general rule, are interested in their children's welfare and will act in accord with it.

The Court's descriptions of the State's interests in this case are caricatures, both of the law and of our most revered institutions. The Court labels these interests as ones in "standardizing its children and adults," and in ensuring that each family, to the extent possible, "conform to some state-designed ideal." . . . Minnesota asserts no such purpose, by explicit statement or by any permissible inference. All that Minnesota asserts is an interest in seeing that parents know about a vital decision facing their child. That interest is a valid one without regard to whether the child is living with either one or both parents, or to the attachment between the minor's parents. How the family unit responds to such notice is, for the most part, beyond the State's control. The State would no doubt prefer that all parents, after being notified under the statute, would contact their daughters and assist them in making their decisions with the child's best interests at heart; but it has not, contrary to the Court's intimation, "decreed" communication, nor could it. What the State can do is make the communication possible by at least informing parents of their daughter's intentions.

Minnesota has done no more than act upon the commonsense proposition that, in assisting their daughter in deciding whether to have an abortion, parents can best fulfill their roles if they have the same information about their own child's medical condition and medical choices as the child's doctor does; and that to deny parents this knowledge is to risk, or perpetuate, estrangement or alienation from the child when she is in the greatest need of parental guidance and support. The Court does the State, and our constitutional tradition, sad disservice by impugning the legitimacy of these elemental objectives. . . .

At least two Members of the Court concede, as they must, that a State has a legitimate interest in the welfare of the pregnant minor and that, in furtherance of this interest, the State may require the minor to notify, and consult with, one of her parents. The Court nonetheless holds the Minnesota statute unconstitutional because it requires the minor to notify not one parent, but both parents, a requirement that the Court says bears no reasonable relation to the minor's welfare. The Court also concludes that Minnesota does not have a legitimate interest in facilitating the participation of both parents in the care and upbringing of their children. Given the substantial protection that minors have under Minnesota law generally, and under the statute in question, the judicial bypass provisions of the law are not necessary to its validity. The two-parent notification law enacted by Minnesota is, in my view, valid without the judicial bypass provision of subdivision 6.

We have been over much of this ground before. It is beyond dispute that in many families, whether the parents are living together or apart, notice to both parents serves the interests of the parents and the minor, and that the State can legislate with this fact in mind. In *H. L.* v. *Matheson,* 450 U.S. 398 (1981), we considered the constitutionality of a statute which required a physician, before performing an abortion on a minor, to " '[n]otify, if possible, the [minor's] *parents* or guardian.' " (emphasis added). We held that the statute, as applied to unmarried, dependent, and immature minors, "plainly serves important state interests, is narrowly drawn to protect only those interests, and does not violate any guarantees of the Constitution." 450 U.S., at 413. Our holding was made with knowledge of the contentions, supported by citations to medical and sociological literature, that are proffered again today for the proposition that notification imposes burdens on minors. We nonetheless rejected arguments that a requirement of parental notification was the equivalent of a requirement of parental consent; that the statute was unconstitutional because it required notification only as to abortions, and not as to other medical procedures; and that the statute was unconstitutional because it might deter some minors from seeking abortions.

Our decision was based upon the well-accepted premise that we must defer to a reasonable judgment by the state legislature when it determines what is sound public policy. JUSTICE STEVENS'S opinion concurring in the Court's judgment relied upon an explicit statement of this principle. Concluding that the Utah statute requiring notification of both parents was valid as to all unmarried minors, both mature and immature, JUSTICE STEVENS reasoned that the State's interest in ensuring that a young woman considering an abortion receive appropriate consultation was "plainly sufficient to support a state legislature's determination that such appropriate consultation should include parental advice." *Id.,* at 423. The Court today departs from this rule. It now suggests that a general requirement that both parents be notified is unconstitutional because of its own conclusion that the law is unnecessary when notice produces favorable results, and irrational in all of the instances when it produces unfavorable results. In *Matheson,* JUSTICE STEVENS rejected these same arguments as insufficient to establish that the Utah statute was unconstitutional. . . .

In applying the standards established in our prior decisions to the case at hand, "we must keep in mind that when we are concerned with extremely sensitive issues, such as the one involved here, the appropriate forum for their resolution in a democracy is the legislature. We should not forget that "legislatures are ultimate guardians of the liberties and welfare of the people in quite as great a degree as the courts." . . . The Minnesota Legislature, like the legislatures of many States, has found it necessary to address the issue of parental notice in its statutory laws. In my view it has acted in a permissible manner. . . .

The difference between notice and consent was apparent to us before, and is apparent now. Unlike parental consent laws, a law requiring parental notice does not give any third party the legal right to make the minor's decision for her, or to prevent her from obtaining an abortion should she choose to have one performed. We have acknowledged this distinction as "fundamental," and as one "substantially modify[ing]" the federal constitutional challenge." *Bellotti* v. *Baird (Bellotti I), 428* U.S. *132,* 145, 148 (1976); see also *Matheson, supra,* at 411, n. 17. The law before us does not place an absolute obstacle before any minor seeking to obtain an abortion, and it represents a considered weighing of the competing interests of minors and their parents. . . .

. . . Like all laws of general application, the Minnesota statute cannot produce perfect results in every situation to which it applies; but the State is under no obligation to enact perfect laws. The statute before us, including the 48-hour waiting period, which is necessary to enable notified parents to consult with their daughter or their daughter's physician, if they so wish, and results in little or no delay, represents a permissible, reasoned attempt to preserve the parent's role in a minor's decision to have an abortion without placing any absolute obstacles before a minor who is determined to elect an abortion for her own interest as she sees it. Section 144.343, without the judicial bypass provision of subdivision 6, is constitutional. I would reverse the contrary judgment of the Court of Appeals. . . .

Because a majority of the Court holds that the two-parent notice requirement contained in subdivision 2 is unconstitutional, it is necessary for the Court to consider whether the same notice requirement is constitutional if the minor has the option of obtaining a court order permitting the abortion to proceed in lieu of the required notice. Assuming, as I am bound to do for this part of the analysis, that the notice provisions standing alone are invalid, I conclude that the two-parent notice requirement

with the judicial bypass alternative is constitutional. . . .

In this case, the Court rejects a legislature's judgment that parents should at least be aware of their daughter's intention to seek an abortion, even if the State does not empower the parents to control the child's decision. That judgment is rejected although it rests upon a tradition of a parental role in the care and upbringing of children that is as old as civilization itself. Our precedents do not permit this result.

It is true that for all too many young women the prospect of two parents, perhaps even one parent, sustaining her with support that is compassionate and committed is an illusion. Statistics on drug and alcohol abuse by parents and documentations of child neglect and mistreatment are but fragments of the evidence showing the tragic reality that becomes day-to-day life for thousands of minors. But the Court errs in serious degree when it commands its own solution to the cruel consequences of individual misconduct, parental failure, and social ills. The legislative authority is entitled to attempt to meet these wrongs by taking reasonable measures to recognize and promote the primacy of the family tie, a concept which this Court now seems intent on declaring a constitutional irrelevance.

RACIAL EQUALITY

MISSOURI v. JENKINS
110 S.Ct. 1651 (1990)

This case concerning the Kansas City, Missouri, School District (KCMSD) began as a school desegregation suit in 1977. The controversy went through numerous lower court proceedings and many complications. The basic facts, however, are that a federal district court found that the KCMSD and the State of Missouri had operated a segregated school system in Kansas City. Kansas City schools had been segregated by law, and once the dual school system was dismantled, white flight to the suburbs resulted in the KCMSD becoming heavily black. Unlike metropolitan Detroit in Milliken v. Bradley, *the surrounding suburbs also had been segregated by law. But rather than seek massive busing involving the suburbs, the student plaintiffs and the cooperating Kansas City school board sought to raise the quality of the public schools so that they would attract more white students. A major hitch to achieving this goal was that the KCMSD was limited by state law in its ability to raise taxes. The KCMSD proposed and federal district judge Rus-*

sell G. Clark adopted an extensive "magnet school" plan requiring the expenditure of hundreds of millions of dollars. The state was ordered to pay 75 percent of the cost and the KCMSD 25 percent. After Judge Clark determined that the KCMSD had been unable to raise the necessary money, having exhausted all available means of raising additional revenue, he ordered an increase in the local property tax (approximately a doubling of the rate) through the 1991–1992 fiscal year. On appeal, the U.S. Court of Appeals for the Eighth Circuit affirmed all of Judge Clark's actions taken until then but said that in the future the judge should not set the tax rate himself but should order the KCMSD to raise the money necessary to fund the desegregation remedy. Furthermore the appeals court said that the district judge should enjoin the operation of state tax laws that prevent the KCMSD from raising the funds. The U.S. Supreme Court granted certiorari limited to the question of the legitimacy of the property tax increase.

Judgment of Court: Unanimous

Other Issues: **Majority votes: 5**
                     Dissenting votes: 4

JUSTICE WHITE delivered the opinion of the Court:

The United States District Court for the Western District of Missouri imposed an increase in the property taxes levied by the Kansas City, Missouri, School District (KCMSD) to ensure funding for the desegregation of KCMSD's public schools. We granted certiorari to consider the State of Missouri's argument that the District Court lacked the power to raise local property taxes. For the reasons given below, we hold that the District Court abused its discretion in imposing the tax increase. We also hold, however, that the modifications of the District Court's order made by the Court of Appeals do satisfy equitable and constitutional principles governing the District Court's power. . . .

. . . The State urges us to hold that the tax increase violated Article III, the Tenth Amendment, and principles of federal/state comity. We find it unnecessary to reach the difficult constitutional issues, for we agree with the State that the tax increase contravened the principles of comity that must govern the exercise of the District Court's equitable discretion in this area.

It is accepted by all the parties, as it was by the courts below, that the imposition of a tax increase by a federal court was an extraordinary event. In assuming for itself the fundamental and delicate power of taxation the District Court not only intruded on local authority but circumvented it altogether. Before taking such a drastic step the District Court was obliged to assure itself that no permissible alternative would have accomplished the required task. We have emphasized that although the "remedial powers of an equity court must be adequate to the task, . . . they are not unlimited," *Whitcomb* v. *Chavis,* 403 U.S. 124, 161 (1971), and one of the most important considerations governing the exercise of equitable power is a proper respect for the integrity and function of local government institutions. Especially is this true where, as here, those institutions are ready, willing, and—but for the operation of state law curtailing their powers—able to remedy the deprivation of constitutional rights themselves.

The District Court believed that it had no alternative to imposing a tax increase. But there was an alternative, the very one outlined by the Court of Appeals: it could have authorized or required KCMSD to levy property taxes at a rate adequate to fund the desegregation remedy and could have enjoined the operation of state laws that would have prevented KCMSD from exercising this power. The difference between the two approaches is far more than a matter of form. Authorizing and directing local government institutions to devise and implement remedies not only protects the function of those institutions but, to the extent possible, also places the responsibility for solutions to the problems of segregation upon those who have themselves created the problems.

As *Brown* v. *Board of Education* (1955), observed, local authorities have the "primary responsibility for elucidating, assessing, and solving" the problems of desegregation. This is true as well of the problems of financing desegregation, for no matter has been more consistently placed upon the shoulders of local government than that of financing public schools. As was said in another context, "[t]he very complexity of the problems of financing and managing a . . . public school system suggests that 'there will be more than one constitutionally permissible method of solving them,' and that . . . 'the legislature's efforts to tackle the problems' should be entitled to respect." By no means should a district court grant local government *carte blanche,* but local officials should at least have the opportunity to devise their own solutions to these problems.

The District Court therefore abused its discretion in imposing the tax itself. The Court of Appeals should not have allowed the tax increase to stand and should have reversed the District Court in this respect.

We stand on different ground when we review the modifications to the District Court's order made by the Court of Appeals. [T]he Court of Appeals held that the District Court in the future should authorize KCMSD to submit a levy to the state tax collection authorities adequate to fund its budget and should enjoin the operation of state laws that would limit or reduce the levy below that amount.

The State argues that the funding ordered by the District Court violates principles of equity and comity because the remedial order itself was excessive. As the State puts it, "[t]he only reason that the court below needed to consider an unprecedented tax increase was the equally unprecedented cost of its remedial programs." We think this argument aims at the scope of the remedy rather than the manner in which the remedy is to be funded and thus falls outside our limited grant of certiorari in this case. . . . We accept, without approving or disapproving, the Court of Appeals' conclusion that the District Court's remedy was proper.

The State has argued here that the District Court, having found the State and KCMSD jointly and severally liable, should have allowed any monetary obligations that KCMSD could not meet to fall on the State rather than interfere with state law to permit KCMSD to meet them. Under the circumstances of this case, we cannot say it was an abuse of discretion for the District Court to rule that KCMSD should be responsible for funding its share of the remedy. The State strenuously opposed efforts by respondents to make it responsible for the cost of implementing the order and had secured a reversal of the District Court's earlier decision placing on it all of the cost of substantial portions of the order. The District Court declined to require the State to pay for KCMSD's obligations because it believed that the Court of Appeals had ordered it to allocate the costs between the two governmental entities. Furthermore, if the District Court had chosen the route now suggested by the State, implementation of the remedial order might have been delayed if the State resisted efforts by KCMSD to obtain contribution. . . .

We turn to the constitutional issues. The modifications ordered by the Court of Appeals cannot be assailed as invalid under the Tenth Amendment. "The Tenth Amendment's reservation of nondelegated powers to the States is not implicated by a federal-court judgment enforcing the express prohibitions of unlawful state conduct enacted by the Fourteenth Amendment." "The Fourteenth Amendment . . . was avowedly directed against the power of the States," *Pennsylvania* v. *Union Gas Co.*, (1989) (SCALIA, J., concurring in part and dissenting in part), and so permits a federal court to disestablish local government institutions that interfere with its commands.

Finally, the State argues that an order to increase taxes cannot be sustained under the judicial power of Article III. Whatever the merits of this argument when applied to the District Court's own order increasing taxes, a point we have not reached, a court order directing a local government body to levy its own taxes is plainly a judicial act within the power of a federal court. We held as much in *Griffin* v. *Prince Edward County School Bd.*, where we stated that a District Court, faced with a county's attempt to avoid desegregation of the public schools by refusing to operate those schools, could "require the [County] Supervisors to exercise the power that is theirs to levy taxes to raise funds adequate to reopen, operate, and maintain without racial discrimination a public school system. . . ." *Griffin* followed a long and venerable line of cases in which this Court held that federal courts could issue the writ of mandamus to compel local governmental bodies to levy taxes adequate to satisfy their debt obligations. . . .

The State maintains, however, that even under these cases, the federal judicial power can go no further than to require local governments to levy taxes *as authorized under state law*. In other words, the State argues that federal courts cannot set aside state-imposed limitations on local taxing authority because to do so is to do more than to require the local government "to exercise the power *that is theirs*." We disagree. This argument was rejected as early as *Von Hoffman* v. *City of Quincy*, 4 Wall. 535 (1867). There the holder of bonds issued by the City sought a writ of mandamus against the City requiring it to levy taxes sufficient to pay interest coupons then due. The City defended based on a state statute that limited its power of taxation, and the Circuit Court refused to mandamus the City. This Court reversed, observing that the statute relied on by the City was passed after the bonds were issued and holding that because the City had ample authority to levy taxes to pay its bonds when they were issued, the statute impaired the contractual entitlements of the bondholders, contrary to Art. I, § 10, cl. 1 of the Constitution, under which a State may not pass any law impairing the obligation of contracts. The statutory limitation, therefore, could be disregarded and the

City ordered to levy the necessary taxes to pay its bonds.

It is therefore clear that a local government with taxing authority may be ordered to levy taxes in excess of the limit set by state statute where there is reason based in the Constitution for not observing the statutory limitation. In *Von Hoffman,* the limitation was disregarded because of the Contract Clause. Here the KCMSD may be ordered to levy taxes despite the statutory limitations on its authority in order to compel the discharge of an obligation imposed on KCMSD by the Fourteenth Amendment. To hold otherwise would fail to take account of the obligations of local governments, under the Supremacy Clause, to fulfill the requirements that the Constitution imposes on them. However wide the discretion of local authorities in fashioning desegregation remedies may be, "if a state-imposed limitation on a school authority's discretion operates to inhibit or obstruct the operation of a unitary school system or impede the disestablishing of a dual school system, it must fall; state policy must give way when it operates to hinder vindication of federal constitutional guarantees." *North Carolina State Bd. of Education* v. *Swann,* 402 U.S. 43, 45 (1971). Even though a particular remedy may not be required in every case to vindicate constitutional guarantees, where (as here) it has been found that a particular remedy is required, the State cannot hinder the process by preventing a local government from implementing that remedy.

Accordingly, the judgment of the Court of Appeals is affirmed insofar as it required the District Court to modify its funding order and reversed insofar as it allowed the tax increase imposed by the District Court to stand. The case is remanded for further proceedings consistent with this opinion.

It is so ordered.

JUSTICE KENNEDY, with whom THE CHIEF JUSTICE, JUSTICE O'CONNOR, and JUSTICE SCALIA join, concurring in part and concurring in the judgment:. . . .

The Court is unanimous in its holding, that the Court of Appeals' judgment affirming "the actions that the [district] court has taken to this point," must be reversed. This is consistent with our precedents and the basic principles defining judicial power.

In my view, however, the Court transgresses these same principles when it goes further, much further, to embrace by broad dictum an expansion of power in the federal judiciary beyond all precedent. Today's casual embrace of taxation imposed by the unelected, life-tenured federal judiciary disregards fundamental precepts for the democratic control of public institutions. I cannot acquiesce in the majority's statements on this point, and should there arise an actual dispute over the collection of taxes as here contemplated in a case that is not, like this one, premature, we should not confirm the outcome of premises adopted with so little constitutional justification. The Court's statements, in my view, cannot be seen as necessary for its judgment, or as precedent for the future. . . .

Some essential litigation history is necessary for a full understanding of what is at stake here and what will be wrought if the implications of all the Court's statements are followed to the full extent. The District Court's remedial plan was proposed for the most part by the Kansas City, Missouri, School District (KCMSD) itself, which is in name a defendant in the suit. Defendants, and above all defendants that are public entities, act in the highest and best tradition of our legal system when they acknowledge fault and cooperate to suggest remedies. But in the context of this dispute, it is of vital importance to note the KCMSD demonstrated little concern for the fiscal consequences of the remedy that it helped design.

As the District Court acknowledged, the plaintiffs and the KCMSD pursued a "friendly adversary" relationship. Throughout the remedial phase of the litigation, the KCMSD proposed ever more expensive capital improvements with the agreement of the plaintiffs, and the State objected. Some of these improvements involved basic repairs to deteriorating facilities within the school system. The KCMSD, however, devised a broader concept for district-wide improvement, and the District Court approved it. The plan involved a variation of the magnet school concept. Magnet schools, as the majority opinion notes, offer special programs, often used to encourage voluntary movement of students within the district in a pattern that aids desegregation.

Although we have approved desegregation plans involving magnet schools of this conventional definition . . . the District Court found this insufficient. Instead, the court and the KCMSD decided to make a magnet of the district as a whole. The hope was to draw new nonminority students from outside the district. . . .

It comes as no surprise that the cost of this approach to the remedy far exceeded KCMSD's budget, or for that matter, its authority to tax. . . .

By the time of the order at issue here, the District Court's remedies included some "$260 million in capital improvements and a magnet-school plan costing over $200 million." And the remedial orders grew more expensive as shortfalls in revenue became severe. As the Eighth Circuit judges dissenting from denial of rehearing in banc put it: "The remedies ordered go far beyond anything previously seen in a school desegregation case. The sheer immensity of the programs encompassed by the district court's order—the large number of magnet schools and the quantity of capital renovations and new construction—are concededly without parallel in any other school district in the country."

The judicial taxation approved by the Eighth Circuit is also without parallel. . . . The case before us represents the first in which a lower federal court has in fact upheld taxation to fund a remedial decree.

For reasons explained below, I agree with the Court that the Eighth Circuit's judgment affirming the District Court's direct levy of a property tax must be reversed. I cannot agree, however, that we "stand on different ground when we review the modifications to the District Court's order made by the Court of Appeals." . . .

The premise of the Court's analysis, I submit, is infirm. Any purported distinction between direct imposition of a tax by the federal court and an order commanding the school district to impose the tax is but a convenient formalism where the court's action is predicated on elimination of state law limitations on the school district's taxing authority. . . .

The power of taxation is one that the federal judiciary does not possess. In our system "the legislative department alone has access to the pockets of the people," The Federalist No. 48, for it is the legislature that is accountable to them and represents their will. The authority that would levy the tax at issue here shares none of these qualities. Our federal judiciary, by design, is not representative or responsible to the people in a political sense; it is independent. Federal judges do not depend on the popular will for their office. They may not even share the burden of taxes they attempt to impose, for they may live outside the jurisdiction their orders affect. And federal judges have no fear that the competition for scarce public resources could result in a diminution of their salaries. It is not surprising that imposition of taxes by an authority so insulated from public communication or control can lead to deep feelings of frustration, powerlessness, and anger on the part of taxpaying citizens. . . .

The Court relies on dicta from *Griffin* v. *School Bd. of Prince Edward County*, 377 U.S. 218 (1964) to support its statements on judicial taxation. In *Griffin*, the Court faced an unrepentant and recalcitrant school board that attempted to provide finan-

cial support for white schools while refusing to operate schools for black schoolchildren. We stated that the district court could "require the Supervisors to exercise the power *that is theirs* to levy taxes to raise funds adequate to reopen, operate, and maintain without racial discrimination a public school system." *Id.*, at 233 (emphasis added). There is no occasion in this case to discuss the full implications of *Griffin's* observation, for it has no application here. *Griffin* endorsed the power of a federal court to order the local authority to exercise *existing* authority to tax.

This case does not involve an order to a local government with plenary taxing power to impose a tax, or an order directed at one whose taxing power has been limited by a state law enacted in order to thwart a federal court order. An order of this type would find support in the *Griffin* dicta, and present a closer question than the one before us. Yet that order might implicate as well the "perversion of the normal legislative process" that we have found troubling in other contexts. A legislative vote taken under judicial compulsion blurs lines of accountability by making it appear that a decision was reached by elected representatives when the reality is otherwise. For this reason, it is difficult to see the difference between an order to tax and direct judicial imposition of a tax. . . .

The Court cites a single case, *Von Hoffman* v. *City of Quincy*, for the proposition that a federal court may set aside state taxation limits that interfere with the remedy sought by the district court. But the Court does not heed *Von Hoffman's* holding. There a municipality had authorized a tax levy in support of a specific bond obligation, but later limited the taxation authority in a way that impaired the bond obligation. The Court held the subsequent limitation itself unconstitutional, a violation of the Contracts Clause. Once the limitation was held invalid, the original specific grant of authority remained. There is no allegation here, nor could there be, that the neutral tax limitations imposed by the people of Missouri are unconstitutional. . . . The majority appears to concede that the Missouri tax law does not violate a specific provision of the Constitution, stating instead that state laws may be disregarded on the basis of a vague "reason based in the Constitution." But this broad suggestion does not follow from the holding in *Von Hoffman*. . . .

At bottom, today's discussion seems motivated by the fear that failure to endorse judicial taxation power might in some extreme circumstance leave a court unable to remedy a constitutional violation. . . . I do not think this possibility is in reality a significant one. More important, this possibility is nothing more or less than the necessary consequence of *any* limit on judicial power. If, however, judicial discretion is to provide the sole limit on judicial remedies, that discretion must counsel restraint. Ill-considered entry into the volatile field of taxation is a step that may place at risk the legitimacy that justifies judicial independence.

One of the most troubling aspects of the Court's opinion is that discussion of the important constitutional issues of judicial authority to tax need never have been undertaken to decide this case. Even were I willing to accept the Court's proposition that a federal court might in some extreme case authorize taxation, this case is not the one. The suggestion that failure to approve judicial taxation here would leave constitutional rights unvindicated rests on a presumption that the District Court's remedy is the *only* possible cure for the constitutional violations it found. Neither our precedents nor the record support this view. In fact, the taxation power is sought here on behalf of a remedial order unlike any before seen.

It cannot be contended that interdistrict comparability, which was the ultimate goal of the District Court's orders, is itself a constitutional command. We have long since determined that "unequal expenditures between children who happen to reside in different districts" do not violate the Equal Protection Clause. *San Antonio Independent School Dist.* v. *Rodriguez,* 411 U.S. 1, 54–55 (1973). The District Court in this case found, and the Court of Appeals affirmed, that there was no interdistrict constitutional violation that would support mandatory interdistrict relief. Instead, the District Court's conclusion that desegregation might be easier if more nonminority students could be attracted into the KCMSD was used as the hook on which to hang numerous policy choices about improving the quality of education in general within the KCMSD. The State's complaint that this suit represents the attempt of a school district that could not obtain public support for increased spending to enlist the District Court to finance its educational policy cannot be dismissed out of hand. The plaintiffs and KCMSD might well be seen as parties that have "joined forces apparently for the purpose of extracting funds from the state treasury."

This Court has never approved a remedy of the type adopted by the District Court. There are strong arguments against the validity of such a plan. A remedy that uses the quality of education as a lure to attract nonminority students will place the District Court at the center of controversies over educational philosophy that by tradition are left to this Nation's communities. Such a plan as a practical matter raises many of the concerns involved in interdistrict desegregation remedies. District Courts can and must take needed steps to eliminate racial discrimination and ensure the operation of unitary school systems. But it is discrimination, not the ineptitude of educators or the indifference of the public, that is the evil to be remedied. An initial finding of discrimination cannot be used as the basis for a wholesale shift of authority over day-to-day school operations from parents, teachers, and elected officials to an unaccountable district judge whose province is law, not education.

Perhaps it is good educational policy to provide a school district with the items included in the KCMSD capital improvement plan, for example: high schools in which every classroom will have air conditioning, an alarm system, and 15 microcomputers; a 2,000-square-foot planetarium; greenhouses and vivariums; a 25-acre farm with an air-conditioned meeting room for 104 people; a Model United Nations wired for language translation; broadcast capable radio and television studios with an editing and animation lab; a temperature controlled art gallery; movie editing and screening rooms; a 3,500-square-foot dust-free diesel mechanics room; 1,875-square-foot elementary school animal rooms for use in a Zoo Project; swimming pools; and numerous other facilities. But these items are a part of legitimate political debate over educational policy and spending priorities, not the Constitution's command of racial equality. Indeed, it may be that a mere 12-acre petting farm, or other corresponding reductions in court-ordered spending, might satisfy constitutional requirements, while preserving scarce public funds for legislative allocation to other public needs, such as paving streets, feeding the poor, building prisons, or housing the homeless. Perhaps the KCMSD's Classical Greek theme schools emphasizing forensics and self-government will provide exemplary training in participatory democracy. But if today's dicta become law, such lessons will be of little use to students who grow up to become taxpayers in the KCMSD. . . .

Any argument that the remedy chosen by the District Court was the only one possible is in fact unsupportable in light of our previous cases. We have approved desegregation orders using assignment changes and some ancillary education programs to ensure the operation of a unitary school system for the district's children. To suggest that a constitutional violation will go unremedied if a district does not, through capital improvements or other means, turn every school into a magnet school, and the entire district into a magnet district, is to suggest that the remedies approved in our past cases should have been disapproved as insufficient to deal with the violations. The truth of the matter is that the remedies in those cases were permissible choices among the many that might be adopted by a district court. . . .

. . . [A]s a prerequisite to considering a taxation order, I would require a finding that any remedy less costly than the one at issue would so plainly leave the violation unremedied that its implementation would itself be an abuse of discretion. There is no showing in this record that, faced with the revenue shortfall, the District Court gave due consideration to the possibility that another remedy among the "wide range of possibilities" would have addressed the constitutional violations without giving rise to a funding crisis. . . .

This case is a stark illustration of the ever-present question whether ends justify means. Few ends are more important than enforcing the guarantee of equal educational opportunity for our Nation's children. But rules of taxation that override state political structures not themselves subject to any constitutional infirmity raise serious questions of federal authority, questions compounded by the odd posture of a case in which the Court assumes the validity of a novel conception of desegregation remedies we never before have approved. The historical record of voluntary compliance with the decree of *Brown* v. *Board of Education* is not a proud chapter in our constitutional history, and the judges of the District Courts and Courts of Appeals have been courageous and skillful in implementing its mandate. But courage and skill must be exercised with due regard for the proper and historic role of the courts.

I do not acknowledge the troubling departures in today's majority opinion as either necessary or appropriate to ensure full compliance with the Equal Protection Clause and its mandate to eliminate the cause and effects of racial discrimination in the schools. Indeed, while this case happens to arise in the compelling context of school desegregation, the principles involved are not limited to that context. There is no obvious limit to today's discussion that would prevent judicial taxation in cases involving prisons, hospitals, or other public institutions, or indeed to pay a large damages award levied against a municipality under 42 U.S.C. § 1983. This assertion of judicial power in one of the most sensitive of policy areas, that involving taxation, begins a process that over time could threaten fundamental alteration of the form of government our Constitution embodies. . . .

METRO BROADCASTING, INC. v. FCC
110 S.Ct. 2997 (1990)

This decision involved two cases that considered the constitutionality of two minority preference policies adopted by the Federal Communications Commission (FCC). Under the first policy, a minority applicant for a broadcast license to operate a new radio or television station is given a special edge in the license competition if all other relevant factors are roughly equal. Under the second policy, a radio or television station in danger of losing its license may be sold to a minority broadcaster that meets certain requirements and this may be done before the FCC resolves the matter. This is called the FCC's "distress sale" policy. These policies were adopted by the FCC in an attempt to satisfy its obligation under the Communications Act of 1934 to promote diversification of programming. The FCC determined that past efforts to encourage minority participation in the broadcast industry were unsuccessful and that there was insufficient broadcast diversity. In the lead case, Metro Broadcasting, Inc., challenged the FCC's award of a new television license to Rainbow Broadcasting to construct and operate a new UHF television station in the Orlando, Florida, metropolitan area. Rainbow was 90 percent Hispanic-owned whereas Metro had only one minority partner who owned 19.8 percent of the corporation. The U.S. Court of Appeals for the District of Columbia first sent the case back to the FCC to reconsider the validity of its policies. But Congress, in the fiscal 1988 appropriations for the FCC, prohibited the FCC from spending any appropriated funds to examine or change its minority policies. Consequently, the FCC reaffirmed its grant of the license to Rainbow and the Court of Appeals affirmed.

In the second case, Shurberg Broadcasting of Hartford, Inc., challenged the FCC's minority distress sale policy as violating equal protection. What had happened was that Faith Center, Inc., owner of a Hartford, Connecticut, television station, sought and received the FCC's approval for a distress sale to minority-owned Astroline Communications Company. Shurberg Broadcasting opposed the sale and asked for a hearing to examine Shurberg's application for a permit to build a television station in Hartford. The FCC rejected Shurberg's equal protection challenge. The U.S. Court of Appeals for the District of Columbia Circuit struck down the distress sale policy ruling that it deprived Shurberg, a nonminority license applicant, of its right to equal protection under the F___

Amendment. Metro Broadcasting, Inc., and Astro-line Communications Company took their cases to the U.S. Supreme Court.

Majority votes: 5
Dissenting votes: 4

JUSTICE BRENNAN delivered the opinion of the Court:

The issue in these cases, consolidated for decision today, is whether certain minority preference policies of the Federal Communications Commission violate the equal protection component of the Fifth Amendment. The policies in question are (1) a program awarding an enhancement for minority ownership in comparative proceedings for new licenses, and (2) the minority "distress sale" program, which permits a limited category of existing radio and television broadcast stations to be transferred only to minority-controlled firms. We hold that these policies do not violate equal protection principles. . . .

It is of overriding significance in these cases that the FCC's minority ownership programs have been specifically approved—indeed, mandated—by Congress. In *Fullilove* v. *Klutznick,* 448 U.S. 448 (1980), Chief Justice Burger, writing for himself and two other Justices, observed that although "[a] program that employs racial or ethnic criteria . . . calls for close examination," when a program employing a benign racial classification is adopted by an administrative agency at the explicit direction of Congress, we are "bound to approach our task with appropriate deference to the Congress, a co-equal branch charged by the Constitution with the power to 'provide for the . . . general Welfare of the United States' and 'to enforce, by appropriate legislation,' the equal protection guarantees of the Fourteenth Amendment." We explained that deference was appropriate in light of Congress' institutional competence as the national legislature as well as Congress' powers under the Commerce Clause, the Spending Clause and the Civil War Amendments.

A majority of the Court in *Fullilove* did not apply strict scrutiny to the race-based classification at issue. Three Members inquired "whether the *objectives* of th[e] legislation are within the power of Congress" and "whether the limited use of racial and ethnic criteria . . . is a constitutionally permissible *means* for achieving the congressional objectives." *Id.,* at 473 (opinion of Burger, C. J.) (emphasis in original). Three other Members would have upheld benign racial classifications that "serve important governmental objectives and are substantially related to achievement of those objectives." *Id.,* at 519 (MARSHALL, J., concurring in judgment). We apply that standard today. We hold that benign race-conscious measures mandated by Congress—even if those measures are not "remedial" in the sense of being designed to compensate victims of past governmental or societal discrimination—are constitutionally permissible to the extent that they serve important governmental objectives within the power of Congress and are substantially related to achievement of those objectives.

Our decision last Term in *Richmond* v. *J. A. Croson Co.,* 488 U.S. 469 (1989), concerning a minority set-aside program adopted by a municipality, does not prescribe the level of scrutiny to be applied to a benign racial classification employed by Congress. As JUSTICE KENNEDY noted, the question of congressional action was not before the Court, *id.,* at 518 (opinion concurring in part and concurring in judgment), and so *Croson* cannot be read to undermine our decision in *Fullilove.* In fact, much of the language and reasoning in *Croson* reaffirmed the lesson of *Fullilove* that race-conscious classifications adopted by Congress to address racial and ethnic discrimination are subject to a different standard than such classifications prescribed by state and local governments. For example, JUSTICE O'CONNOR, joined by two other Members of this Court, noted that "Congress may identify and redress the effects of society-wide discrimination," 488 U.S., at 490, and that Congress "need not make specific findings of discrimination to engage in race-conscious relief." *Id.,* at 489. Echoing *Fullilove's* emphasis on Congress as a national legislature that stands above factional politics, JUSTICE SCALIA argued that as a matter of "social reality and governmental theory," the Federal Government is unlikely to be captured by minority racial or ethnic groups and used as an instrument of discrimination. 488 U.S., at 522 (opinion concurring in judgment). JUSTICE SCALIA explained that "[t]he struggle for racial justice has historically been a struggle by the national society against oppression in the individual States," because of the "heightened danger of oppression from political factions in small, rather than large, political units." *Id.,* at 522, 523.

We hold that the FCC minority ownership policies pass muster under the test we announce today. First, we find that they serve the important governmental objective of broadcast diversity. Second, we conclude that they are substantially related to the achievement of that objective. . . .

. . . Although we do not " 'defer' to the judgment of the Congress and the Commission on a constitutional question," and would not "hesitate to invoke the Constitution should we determine that the Commission has not fulfilled its task with appropriate sensitivity" to equal protection principles, *Columbia Broadcasting System, Inc.* v. *Democratic National Committee,* 412 U.S. 94 (1973) at 103, we must pay close attention to the expertise of the Commission and the factfinding of Congress when analyzing the nexus between minority ownership and programming diversity. With respect to this "complex" empirical question, *ibid.,* we are required to give "great weight to the decisions of Congress and the experience of the Commission." . . .

Congress also has made clear its view that the minority ownership policies advance the goal of diverse programming. In recent years, Congress has specifically required the Commission, through appropriations legislation, to maintain the minority ownership policies without alteration. We would be remiss, however, if we ignored the long history of congressional support for those policies prior to the passage of the appropriations acts because, for the past two decades, Congress has consistently recognized the barriers encountered by minorities in entering the broadcast industry and has expressed emphatic support for the Commission's attempts to promote programming diversity by increasing minority ownership. Limiting our analysis to the immediate legislative history of the appropriations acts in question "would erect an artificial barrier to [a] full understanding of the legislative process." *Fullilove* v. *Klutznick,* 488 U.S., at 502 (Powell, J., concurring). The "special attribute [of Congress] as a legislative body lies in its broader mission to investigate and consider all facts and opinions that may be relevant to the resolution of an issue. One appropriate source is the information and expertise that Congress acquires in the consideration and enactment of earlier legislation. After Congress has legislated repeatedly in an area of national concern, its Members gain experience that may reduce the need for fresh hearings or prolonged debate when Congress again considers action in that area." *Id.,* at 502–503; see also *id.,* at 478 (opinion of Burger, C. J.) ("Congress, of course, may legislate without compiling the kind of 'record' appropriate with respect to judicial or administrative proceedings").

Congress's experience began in 1969, when it considered a bill that would have eliminated the comparative hearing in license renewal proceedings, in order to avoid "the filing of a multiplicity of competing applications, often from groups unknown" and to restore order and predictability to the renewal process to "give the current license holder the benefit of the doubt warranted by his previous investment and experience." Congress heard testimony that, because the most valuable broadcast licenses were assigned many years ago, comparative hearings at the renewal stage afford an important opportunity for excluded groups, particularly minorities, to gain entry into the industry. Opponents warned that the bill would "exclude minority groups from station ownership in important markets" by "fr[eezing]" the distribution of existing licenses. Congress rejected the bill.

Congress confronted the issue again in 1973 and 1974, when congressional committees held extensive hearings on proposals to extend the broadcast license period from three to five years and to modify the comparative hearing process for license renewals. Witnesses reiterated that renewals provided a valuable opportunity for minorities to obtain a foothold in the industry. The proposals were never enacted, and the renewal process was left intact.

During 1978, both the FCC and the Office of Telecommunications Policy presented their views to Congress as it considered a bill to deregulate the broadcast industry. The proposed Communications Act of 1978 would have, among other things, replaced comparative hearings with a lottery and created a fund for minorities who sought to purchase stations. As described by Representative Markey, the measure was intended to increase "the opportunities for blacks and women and other minorities in this country to get into the communications systems in this country so that their point of view and their interests can be represented." . . . The bill's sponsor, Representative Van Deerlin, stated, "It was the hope, and with some reason the expectation of the framers of the bill, that the most effective way to reach the inadequacies of the broadcast industry in employment and programming would be by doing something at the top, that is, increasing minority ownership and management and control in broadcast stations." . . .

Although no lottery legislation was enacted that year, Congress continued to explore the idea, and when in 1981 it ultimately authorized a lottery procedure, Congress established a concomitant system of minority preferences. . . .

Congress chose to employ its appropriations power to keep the FCC's minority ownership policies in place for fiscal year 1988. . . . Congress has twice extended the prohibition on the use of appropriated funds to modify or repeal minority ownership policies and has continued to focus upon the issue. . . .

As revealed by the historical evolution of current federal policy, both Congress and the Commission have concluded that the minority ownership programs are critical means of promoting broadcast diversity. We must give great weight to their joint determination.

The judgment that there is a link between expanded minority ownership and broadcast diversity does not rest on impermissible stereotyping. Congressional policy does not assume that in every case minority ownership and management will lead to more minority-oriented programming or to the expression of a discrete "minority viewpoint" on the airwaves. Neither does it pretend that all programming that appeals to minority audiences can be labeled "minority programming" or that programming that might be described as "minority" does not appeal to nonminorities. Rather, both Congress and the FCC maintain simply that expanded minority ownership of broadcast outlets will, in the aggregate, result in greater broadcast diversity. A broadcasting industry with representative minority participation will produce more variation and diversity than will one whose ownership is drawn from a single racially and ethnically homogeneous group. The predictive judgment about the overall result of minority entry into broadcasting is not a rigid assumption about how minority owners will behave in every case but rather is akin to Justice Powell's conclusion in *Bakke* that greater admission of minorities would contribute, on average, "to the 'robust exchange of ideas.' " To be sure, there is no ironclad guarantee that each minority owner will contribute to diversity. But neither was there an assurance in *Bakke* that minority students would interact with nonminority students or that the particular minority students admitted would have typical or distinct "minority" viewpoints. . . .

Although all station owners are guided to some extent by market demand in their programming decisions, Congress and the Commission have determined that there may be important differences between the broadcasting practices of minority owners and those of their nonminority counterparts. This judgment—and the conclusion that there is a nexus between minority ownership and broadcasting diversity—is corroborated by a host of empirical evidence. Evidence suggests that an owner's minority status influences the selection of topics for news coverage and the presentation of editorial viewpoint, especially on matters of particular concern to minorities. "[M]inority ownership does appear to have specific impact on the presentation of minority images in local news, inasmuch as minority-owned stations tend to devote more news time to topics of minority interest and to

avoid racial and ethnic stereotypes in portraying minorities. In addition, studies show that a minority owner is more likely to employ minorities in managerial and other important roles where they can have an impact on station policies. If the FCC's equal employment policies "ensure that . . . licensees' programming fairly reflects the tastes and viewpoints of minority groups," it is difficult to deny that minority-owned stations that follow such employment policies on their own will also contribute to diversity. While we are under no illusion that members of a particular minority group share some cohesive, collective viewpoint, we believe it a legitimate inference for Congress and the Commission to draw that as more minorities gain ownership and policymaking roles in the media, varying perspectives will be more fairly represented on the airwaves. The policies are thus a product of " 'analysis' " rather than a " 'stereotyped reaction' " based on " '[h]abit.' " . . .

Finally, we do not believe that the minority ownership policies at issue impose impermissible burdens on nonminorities. Although the nonminority challengers in these cases concede that they have not suffered the loss of an already-awarded broadcast license, they claim that they have been handicapped in their ability to obtain one in the first instance. But just as we have determined that "[a]s part of this Nation's dedication to eradicating racial discrimination, innocent persons may be called upon to bear some of the burden of the remedy," we similarly find that a congressionally mandated benign race-conscious program that is substantially related to the achievement of an important governmental interest is consistent with equal protection principles so long as it does not impose *undue* burdens on nonminorities. . . .

In the context of broadcasting licenses, the burden on nonminorities is slight. The FCC's responsibility is to grant licenses in the "public interest, convenience, or necessity," and the limited number of frequencies on the electromagnetic spectrum means that "[n]o one has a First Amendment right to a license." Applicants have no settled expectation that their applications will be granted without consideration of public interest factors such as minority ownership. Award of a preference in a comparative hearing or transfer of a station in a distress sale thus contravenes "no legitimate firmly rooted expectation[s]" of competing applicants.

Respondent Shurberg insists that because the minority distress sale policy operates to exclude nonminority firms completely from consideration in the transfer of certain stations, it is a greater burden than the comparative hearing preference for minori-

level of scrutiny of a racial classification. First, it too casually extends the justifications that might support racial classifications, beyond that of remedying past discrimination. We have recognized that racial classifications are so harmful that "[u]nless they are strictly reserved for remedial settings, they may in fact promote notions of racial inferiority and lead to a politics of racial hostility." *Croson, supra,* at 493. . . . Second, it has initiated this departure by endorsing an insubstantial interest, one that is certainly insufficiently weighty to justify tolerance of the Government's distinctions among citizens based on race and ethnicity. This endorsement trivializes the constitutional command to guard against such discrimination and has loosed a potentially far-reaching principle disturbingly at odds with our traditional equal protection doctrine. . . .

[T]he FCC's programs cannot survive even intermediate scrutiny because race-neutral and untried means of directly accomplishing the governmental interest are readily available. The FCC could directly advance its interest by requiring licensees to provide programming that the FCC believes would add to diversity. The interest the FCC asserts is in programming diversity, yet in adopting the challenged policies, the FCC expressly disclaimed having attempted *any* direct efforts to achieve its asserted goal. The Court suggests that administrative convenience excuses this failure, yet intermediate scrutiny bars the Government from relying upon that excuse to avoid measures that directly further the asserted interest. The FCC and the Court suggest that First Amendment interests in some manner should exempt the FCC from employing this direct, race-neutral means to achieve its asserted interest. They essentially argue that we may bend our equal protection principles to avoid more readily apparent harm to our First Amendment values. But the FCC cannot have it both ways: either the First Amendment bars the FCC from seeking to accomplish indirectly what it may not accomplish directly; or the FCC may pursue the goal, but must do so in a manner that comports with equal protection principles. And if the FCC can direct programming in any fashion, it must employ that direct means before resorting to indirect race-conscious means.

Other race-neutral means also exist, and all are at least as direct as the FCC's racial classifications. The FCC could evaluate applicants upon their ability to provide and commitment to offer whatever programming the FCC believes would reflect underrepresented viewpoints. If the FCC truly seeks diverse programming rather than allocation of goods to persons of particular racial backgrounds, it has little excuse to look to racial background rather than programming to further the programming interest. Additionally, if the FCC believes that certain persons by virtue of their unique experiences will contribute as owners to more diverse broadcasting, the FCC could simply favor applicants whose particular background indicates that they will add to the diversity of programming, rather than rely solely upon suspect classifications. Also, race-neutral means exist to allow access to the broadcasting industry for those persons excluded for financial and related reasons. The Court reasons that various minority preferences, including those reflected in the distress sale, overcome barriers of information, experience, and financing that inhibit minority ownership. Race-neutral financial and informational measures most directly reduce financial and informational barriers. . . .

Finally, the Government cannot employ race classifications that unduly burden individuals who are not members of the favored racial and ethnic groups. The challenged policies fail this independent requirement, as well as the other constitutional requirements. The comparative licensing and distress sale programs provide the eventual licensee with an exceptionally valuable property and with a rare and unique opportunity to serve the local community. The distress sale imposes a particularly significant burden. The FCC has at base created a specialized market research exclusively for minority controlled applicants. There is no more rigid quota than a 100% set-aside. This fact is not altered by the observation that the FCC and seller have some discretion over whether stations may be sold through the distress program. For the would-be purchaser or person who seeks to compete for the station, that opportunity depends entirely upon race or ethnicity. The Court's argument that the distress sale allocates only a small percentage of all license sales also misses the mark. This argument readily supports complete preferences and avoids scrutiny of particular programs: it is no response to a person denied admission at one school, or discharged from one job, solely on the basis of race, that other schools or employers do not discriminate.

The comparative licensing program, too, imposes a significant burden. The Court's emphasis on the multifactor process should not be confused with the claim that the preference is in some sense a minor one. It is not. The basic nonrace criteria are not difficult to meet, and, given the sums at stake, applicants have every incentive to structure their ownership arrangement to prevail in the comparative process. Applicants cannot alter their race, of

ties, which is simply a "plus" factor considered together with other characteristics of the applicants. We disagree that the distress sale policy imposes an undue burden on nonminorities. By its terms, the policy may be invoked at the Commission's discretion only with respect to a small fraction of broadcast licenses—those designated for revocation or renewal hearings to examine basic qualification issues—and only when the licensee chooses to sell out at a distress price rather than to go through with the hearing. The distress sale policy is not a quota or fixed quantity set-aside. Indeed, the nonminority firm exercises control over whether a distress sale will ever occur at all, because the policy operates only where the qualifications of an existing licensee to continue broadcasting have been designated for hearing and no other applications for the station in question have been filed with the Commission at the time of the designation. Thus, a nonminority can prevent the distress sale procedures from ever being invoked by filing a competing application in a timely manner.

In practice, distress sales have represented a tiny fraction—less than four tenths of one percent—of all broadcast sales since 1979. There have been only 38 distress sales since the policy was commenced in 1978. . . . Nonminority firms are free to compete for the vast remainder of license opportunities available in a market that contains over 11,000 broadcast properties. Nonminorities can apply for a new station, buy an existing station, file a competing application against a renewal application of an existing station, or seek financial participation in enterprises that qualify for distress sale treatment. The burden on nonminority firms is at least as "relatively light" as that created by the program at issue in *Fullilove,* which set aside for minorities 10 percent of federal funds granted for local public works projects.

The Commission's minority ownership policies bear the imprimatur of longstanding congressional support and direction and are substantially related to the achievement of the important governmental objective of broadcast diversity. The judgment in No. 89–453 [concerning Metro Broadcasting] is affirmed, the judgment in No. 89–700 [concerning Astroline Communications] is reversed, and the cases are remanded for proceedings consistent with this opinion.

It is so ordered.

JUSTICE STEVENS, concurring:
Today the Court squarely rejects the proposition that a governmental decision that rests on a racial classification is never permissible except as a remedy for a past wrong. I endorse this focus on the future benefit, rather than the remedial justification, of such decisions.

I remain convinced, of course, that racial or ethnic characteristics provide a relevant basis for disparate treatment only in extremely rare situations and that it is therefore "especially important that the reasons for any such classification be clearly identified and unquestionably legitimate." *Fullilove* v. *Klutznick,* 448 U.S. 448, 534–535 (1980) (dissenting opinion). The Court's opinion explains how both elements of that standard are satisfied. Specifically, the reason for the classification—the recognized interest in broadcast diversity—is clearly identified and does not imply any judgment concerning the abilities of owners of different races or the merits of different kinds of programming. Neither the favored nor the disfavored class is stigmatized in any way. In addition, the Court demonstrates that this case falls within the extremely narrow category of governmental decisions for which racial or ethnic heritage may provide a rational basis for differential treatment. The public interest in broadcast diversity—like the interest in an integrated police force, diversity in the composition of a public school faculty or diversity in the student body of a professional school—is in my view unquestionably legitimate.

Therefore, I join both the opinion and the judgment of the Court.

JUSTICE O'CONNOR, with whom THE CHIEF JUSTICE, JUSTICE SCALIA, and JUSTICE KENNEDY join, dissenting:
At the heart of the Constitution's guarantee of equal protection lies the simple command that the Government must treat citizens "as *individuals,* not 'as simply components of a racial, religious, sexual or national class.'" *Arizona Governing Committee* v. *Norris,* 463 U.S. 1073, 1083 (1983). Social scientists may debate how peoples' thoughts and behavior reflect their background, but the Constitution provides that the Government may not allocate benefits and burdens among individuals based on the the assumption that race or ethnicity determines how they act or think. To uphold the challenged programs, the Court departs from these fundamental principles and from our traditional requirement that racial classifications are permissible only if necessary and narrowly tailored to achieve a compelling interest. This departure marks a renewed toleration of racial classifications and a repudiation of our recent affirmation that the Constitution's equal protection guarantees extend equally to all citizens. The Court's application of a lessened equal protection standard to congressional actions

finds no support in our cases or in the Constitution. I respectfully dissent. . . .

As we recognized last Term, the Constitution requires that the Court apply a strict standard of scrutiny to evaluate racial classifications such as those contained in the challenged FCC distress sale and comparative licensing policies. See *Richmond* v. *J. A. Croson Co.*, 488 U.S. 469 (1989); see also *Bolling* v. *Sharpe*, 347 U.S. 497 (1954). "Strict scrutiny" requires that, to be upheld, racial classifications must be determined to be necessary and narrowly tailored to achieve a compelling state interest. The Court abandons this traditional safeguard against discrimination for a lower standard of review, and in practice applies a standard like that applicable to routine legislation. Yet the Government's different treatment of citizens according to race is no routine concern. This Court's precedents in no way justify the Court's marked departure from our traditional treatment of race classifications and its conclusion that different equal protection principles apply to these federal actions.

In both the challenged policies, the FCC provides benefits to some members of our society and denies benefits to others based on race or ethnicity. Except in the narrowest of circumstances, the Constitution bars such racial classifications as a denial to particular individuals, of any race or ethnicity, of "the equal protection of the laws." The dangers of such classifications are clear. They endorse race-based reasoning and the conception of a Nation divided into racial blocs, thus contributing to an escalation of racial hostility and conflict. . . . Such policies may embody stereotypes that treat individuals as the product of their race, evaluating their thoughts and efforts—their very worth as citizens—according to a criterion barred to the Government by history and the Constitution. . . .

The Court asserts that *Fullilove* supports its novel application of intermediate scrutiny to "benign" race conscious measures adopted by Congress. Three reasons defeat this claim. First, *Fullilove* concerned an exercise of Congress' powers under § 5 of the Fourteenth Amendment. In *Fullilove*, the Court reviewed an act of Congress that had required States to set aside a percentage of federal construction funds for certain minority-owned businesses to remedy past discrimination in the award of construction contracts. Although the various opinions in *Fullilove* referred to several sources of congressional authority, the opinions make clear that it was § 5 that led the Court to apply a different form of review to the challenged program. . . . Last Term, *Croson* resolved any doubt that might remain regarding this point. In *Croson*, we invali-

dated a local set-aside for minority contractors. We distinguished *Fullilove*, in which we upheld a similar set-aside enacted by Congress, on the ground that in *Fullilove* "Congress was exercising its powers under § 5 of the Fourteenth Amendment." . . .

Second, *Fullilove* applies at most only to congressional measures that seek to remedy identified past discrimination. The Court upheld the challenged measures in *Fullilove* only because Congress had identified discrimination that had particularly affected the construction industry and had carefully constructed corresponding remedial measures. . . .

Finally, even if *Fullilove* applied outside a remedial exercise of Congress' § 5 power, it would not support today's adoption of the intermediate standard of review. . . . *Fullilove* preceded our determination in *Croson* that strict scrutiny applies to preferences that favor members of minority groups, including challenges considered under the Fourteenth Amendment. . . .

The Court's reliance on "benign racial classifications," is particularly troubling. " 'Benign' racial classification" is a contradiction in terms. Governmental distinctions among citizens based on race or ethnicity, even in the rare circumstances permitted by our cases, exact costs and carry with them substantial dangers. To the person denied an opportunity or right based on race, the classification is hardly benign. . . .

This dispute regarding the appropriate standard of review may strike some as a lawyers' quibble over words, but it is not. The standard of review establishes whether and when the Court and Constitution allow the Government to employ racial classifications. A lower standard signals that the Government may resort to racial distinctions more readily. The Court's departure from our cases is disturbing enough, but more disturbing still is the renewed toleration of racial classifications that its new standard of review embodies. . . .

Under the appropriate standard, strict scrutiny, only a compelling interest may support the Government's use of racial classifications. Modern equal protection doctrine has recognized only one such interest: remedying the effects of racial discrimination. The interest in increasing the diversity of broadcast viewpoints is clearly not a compelling interest. It is simply too amorphous, too insubstantial, and too unrelated to any legitimate basis for employing racial classifications. The Court does not claim otherwise. Rather, it employs its novel standard and claims that this asserted interest need only be, and is, "important." This conclusion twice compounds the Court's initial error of reducing its

Vallandigham, Ex parte, 1 Wallace 243 (1864), 29, 411

Valley Forge Christian College v. Americans United for Separation of Church and State, 454 U.S. 464 (1982), 163

Vasquez v. Hillery, 474 U.S. 254 (1986), 696

Village of Schaumburg v. Citizens for a Better Environment, 444 U.S. 620 (1980), 418, 527

Virginia State Board of Pharmacy v. Virginia Citizens Consumer Council, Inc., 425 U.S. 748 (1976), 466, 527

Virginia v. Rives, 100 U.S. 313 (1880), 689

Vlandis v. Kline 412 U.S. 441 (1973), 815

Von Hoffman v. City of Quincy, 4 Wallace 535 (1867), 873, 874, 875

Wabash, St. Louis and Pacific Railway Co. v. Illinois (The Wabash Case), 118 U.S. 557 (1886), 33, 89, 264

Wainwright v. Greenfield, 474 U.S. 284 (1986), 580

Wainwright v. Sykes, 433 U.S. 72 (1977), 578

Walder v. United States, 347 U.S. 62 (1954), 626, 627, 848

Wallace v. Jaffree, 472 U.S. 38 (1985), 58, 515, 517, 520, **547–550,** 561

Walters v. National Association of Radiation Survivors, 473 U.S. 305 (1985), 637

Walz v. Tax Commission of the City of New York, 397 U.S. 664 (1970), 515, 555, 565

Wardair Canada, Inc. v. Florida Dept. of Revenue, 477 U.S. 1 (1986), 271

Wards Cove Packing Co., Inc. v. Antonio, 109 S.Ct. 2115 (1989), 694, 697

Ward v. Maryland, 12 Wallace 418 (1871), 355

Ward v. Rock Against Racism, 109 S.Ct. 2746 (1989), 420

Ward v. Texas, 316 U.S. 547 (1942), 577, 689

Ware v. Hylton, 3 Dallas 199 (1796), 320

Washington v. Chrisman, 455 U.S. 1 (1982), 573

Washington v. Davis, 426 U.S. 229 (1976), 694

Washington v. Harper, 110 S.Ct. 1028 (1990), 681

Washington v. Texas, 388 U.S. 14 (1967), 634

Watkins v. United States, 354 U.S. 178 (1957), 415, 416

Watson v. Fort Worth Bank and Trust, 487 U.S. 977 (1988), 694

Wayte v. United States, 470 U.S. 598 (1985), 420

Weber v. Aetna Casualty & Surity Co., 406 U.S. 164 (1972), 777, 784, 785, 817

Webster v. Doe, 486 U.S. 592 (1988), 165

Webster v. Reproductive Health Services, 109 S.Ct. 3040 (1989), 58, 142, 156, 164, 750, **767–776**

Weeks v. United States, 232 U.S. 383 (1914), 570, 571, 582, 588, 589, 590, 591, 627

Weeks v. United States, 245 U.S. 618 (1918), 297

Weinberger v. Wiesenfeld, 420 U.S. 636 (1975), 750

Welch v. State Dept. of Highways and Public Transp., 483 U.S. 468 (1987), 321

Welsh v. Wisconsin, 466 U.S. 740 (1984), 572

Wengler v. Druggists Mutual Insurance Company, 446 U.S. 142 (1980), 751, 783

Wesberry v. Sanders, 376 U.S. 1 (1964), 789, 800, 801

West Coast Hotel v. Parrish, 300 U.S. 379 (1937), 43, 295, 383, 386, **402–404**

Westfall v. Erwin, 484 U.S. 292 (1988), 682

West River Bridge Co. v. Dix, 6 Howard 507 (1848), 358

West Virginia State Board of Education v. Barnette, 319 U.S. 624 (1943), 46, 213, 413, 513, 519, **522–526,** 602, 606

Westinghouse v. Tully, 466 U.S. 388 (1984), 270

Whalen v. Roe, 429 U.S. 389 (1977), 683

Whitcomb v. Chavis, 403 U.S. 124 (1971), 695, 804, 872

White v. Mass. Council of Construction Employers, 460 U.S 204 (1983), 270

White v. Regester, 412 U.S. 755 (1973), 789, 804, 805

White v. Weiser, 412 U.S. 783 (1973), 789, 800, 802

Whitley v. Albers, 475 U.S. 312 (1986), 641

Whitney v. California, 274 U.S. 357 (1927), 39, 50, 412, 415, 421, **428–430,** 441

Wickard v. Filburn, 317 U.S. 111 (1942), 44, 118, 268, 273, **291–293**

Widmar v. Vincent, 454 U.S. 263 (1981), 551

Wieman v. Updegraff, 344 U.S. 183 (1952), 414

Williamson v. Lee Optical Co., 348 U.S. 483 (1955), 383, 386, **404–405,** 766

Williams v. Florida, 399 U.S. 78 (1970), 637

Williams v. Standard Oil, Co., 278 U.S. 235 (1929), 383

Williams v. Vermont, 472 U.S. 14 (1985), 792

Willson v. Blackbird Creek Marsh Company, 2 Peters 245 (1829), 25, 263, 322, 324, **340,** 341

Wilson v. New, 243 U.S. 332 (1917), 37, 266, 339

Winston v. Lee, 470 U.S. 753 (1985), 574, 683

Wisconsin v. Yoder, 406 U.S. 205 (1972), 211, 514, 519, **524–526** 533, 534, 535, 536, 840, 842